Lecture Notes in Computer Science 12955

More information about this subseries at http://www.springer.com/series/7407

Osvaldo Gervasi · Beniamino Murgante ·
Sanjay Misra · Chiara Garau ·
Ivan Blečić · David Taniar ·
Bernady O. Apduhan · Ana Maria A. C. Rocha ·
Eufemia Tarantino · Carmelo Maria Torre (Eds.)

Computational Science and Its Applications – ICCSA 2021

21st International Conference
Cagliari, Italy, September 13–16, 2021
Proceedings, Part VII

Springer

Editors
Osvaldo Gervasi ⓘ
University of Perugia
Perugia, Italy

Sanjay Misra ⓘ
Covenant University
Ota, Nigeria

Ivan Blečić ⓘ
University of Cagliari
Cagliari, Italy

Bernady O. Apduhan
Kyushu Sangyo University
Fukuoka, Japan

Eufemia Tarantino ⓘ
Polytechnic University of Bari
Bari, Italy

Beniamino Murgante ⓘ
University of Basilicata
Potenza, Potenza, Italy

Chiara Garau ⓘ
University of Cagliari
Cagliari, Italy

David Taniar ⓘ
Monash University
Clayton, VIC, Australia

Ana Maria A. C. Rocha ⓘ
University of Minho
Braga, Portugal

Carmelo Maria Torre ⓘ
Polytechnic University of Bari
Bari, Italy

ISSN 0302-9743   ISSN 1611-3349 (electronic)
Lecture Notes in Computer Science
ISBN 978-3-030-87006-5   ISBN 978-3-030-87007-2 (eBook)
https://doi.org/10.1007/978-3-030-87007-2

LNCS Sublibrary: SL1 – Theoretical Computer Science and General Issues

This Springer imprint is published by the registered company Springer Nature Switzerland AG
The registered company address is: Gewerbestrasse 11, 6330 Cham, Switzerland

Preface

These 10 volumes (LNCS volumes 12949–12958) consist of the peer-reviewed papers from the 21st International Conference on Computational Science and Its Applications (ICCSA 2021) which took place during September 13–16, 2021. By virtue of the vaccination campaign conducted in various countries around the world, we decided to try a hybrid conference, with some of the delegates attending in person at the University of Cagliari and others attending in virtual mode, reproducing the infrastructure established last year.

This year's edition was a successful continuation of the ICCSA conference series, which was also held as a virtual event in 2020, and previously held in Saint Petersburg, Russia (2019), Melbourne, Australia (2018), Trieste, Italy (2017), Beijing. China (2016), Banff, Canada (2015), Guimaraes, Portugal (2014), Ho Chi Minh City, Vietnam (2013), Salvador, Brazil (2012), Santander, Spain (2011), Fukuoka, Japan (2010), Suwon, South Korea (2009), Perugia, Italy (2008), Kuala Lumpur, Malaysia (2007), Glasgow, UK (2006), Singapore (2005), Assisi, Italy (2004), Montreal, Canada (2003), and (as ICCS) Amsterdam, The Netherlands (2002) and San Francisco, USA (2001).

Computational science is the main pillar of most of the present research on understanding and solving complex problems. It plays a unique role in exploiting innovative ICT technologies and in the development of industrial and commercial applications. The ICCSA conference series provides a venue for researchers and industry practitioners to discuss new ideas, to share complex problems and their solutions, and to shape new trends in computational science.

Apart from the six main conference tracks, ICCSA 2021 also included 52 workshops in various areas of computational sciences, ranging from computational science technologies to specific areas of computational sciences, such as software engineering, security, machine learning and artificial intelligence, blockchain technologies, and applications in many fields. In total, we accepted 494 papers, giving an acceptance rate of 30%, of which 18 papers were short papers and 6 were published open access. We would like to express our appreciation for the workshop chairs and co-chairs for their hard work and dedication.

The success of the ICCSA conference series in general, and of ICCSA 2021 in particular, vitally depends on the support of many people: authors, presenters, participants, keynote speakers, workshop chairs, session chairs, organizing committee members, student volunteers, Program Committee members, advisory committee members, international liaison chairs, reviewers, and others in various roles. We take this opportunity to wholehartedly thank them all.

We also wish to thank Springer for publishing the proceedings, for sponsoring some of the best paper awards, and for their kind assistance and cooperation during the editing process.

We cordially invite you to visit the ICCSA website https://iccsa.org where you can find all the relevant information about this interesting and exciting event.

September 2021

Osvaldo Gervasi
Beniamino Murgante
Sanjay Misra

Welcome Message from the Organizers

COVID-19 has continued to alter our plans for organizing the ICCSA 2021 conference, so although vaccination plans are progressing worldwide, the spread of virus variants still forces us into a period of profound uncertainty. Only a very limited number of participants were able to enjoy the beauty of Sardinia and Cagliari in particular, rediscovering the immense pleasure of meeting again, albeit safely spaced out. The social events, in which we rediscovered the ancient values that abound on this wonderful island and in this city, gave us even more strength and hope for the future. For the management of the virtual part of the conference, we consolidated the methods, organization, and infrastructure of ICCSA 2020.

The technological infrastructure was based on open source software, with the addition of the streaming channels on YouTube. In particular, we used Jitsi (jitsi.org) for videoconferencing, Riot (riot.im) together with Matrix (matrix.org) for chat and ansynchronous communication, and Jibri (github.com/jitsi/jibri) for streaming live sessions to YouTube.

Seven Jitsi servers were set up, one for each parallel session. The participants of the sessions were helped and assisted by eight student volunteers (from the universities of Cagliari, Florence, Perugia, and Bari), who provided technical support and ensured smooth running of the conference proceedings.

The implementation of the software infrastructure and the technical coordination of the volunteers were carried out by Damiano Perri and Marco Simonetti.

Our warmest thanks go to all the student volunteers, to the technical coordinators, and to the development communities of Jitsi, Jibri, Riot, and Matrix, who made their terrific platforms available as open source software.

A big thank you goes to all of the 450 speakers, many of whom showed an enormous collaborative spirit, sometimes participating and presenting at almost prohibitive times of the day, given that the participants of this year's conference came from 58 countries scattered over many time zones of the globe.

Finally, we would like to thank Google for letting us stream all the live events via YouTube. In addition to lightening the load of our Jitsi servers, this allowed us to record the event and to be able to review the most exciting moments of the conference.

Ivan Blečić
Chiara Garau

Organization

ICCSA 2021 was organized by the University of Cagliari (Italy), the University of Perugia (Italy), the University of Basilicata (Italy), Monash University (Australia), Kyushu Sangyo University (Japan), and the University of Minho (Portugal).

Honorary General Chairs

Norio Shiratori	Chuo University, Japan
Kenneth C. J. Tan	Sardina Systems, UK
Corrado Zoppi	University of Cagliari, Italy

General Chairs

Osvaldo Gervasi	University of Perugia, Italy
Ivan Blečić	University of Cagliari, Italy
David Taniar	Monash University, Australia

Program Committee Chairs

Beniamino Murgante	University of Basilicata, Italy
Bernady O. Apduhan	Kyushu Sangyo University, Japan
Chiara Garau	University of Cagliari, Italy
Ana Maria A. C. Rocha	University of Minho, Portugal

International Advisory Committee

Jemal Abawajy	Deakin University, Australia
Dharma P. Agarwal	University of Cincinnati, USA
Rajkumar Buyya	University of Melbourne, Australia
Claudia Bauzer Medeiros	University of Campinas, Brazil
Manfred M. Fisher	Vienna University of Economics and Business, Austria
Marina L. Gavrilova	University of Calgary, Canada
Yee Leung	Chinese University of Hong Kong, China

International Liaison Chairs

Giuseppe Borruso	University of Trieste, Italy
Elise De Donker	Western Michigan University, USA
Maria Irene Falcão	University of Minho, Portugal
Robert C. H. Hsu	Chung Hua University, Taiwan
Tai-Hoon Kim	Beijing Jaotong University, China

Vladimir Korkhov	St. Petersburg University, Russia
Sanjay Misra	Covenant University, Nigeria
Takashi Naka	Kyushu Sangyo University, Japan
Rafael D. C. Santos	National Institute for Space Research, Brazil
Maribel Yasmina Santos	University of Minho, Portugal
Elena Stankova	St. Petersburg University, Russia

Workshop and Session Chairs

Beniamino Murgante	University of Basilicata, Italy
Sanjay Misra	Covenant University, Nigeria
Jorge Gustavo Rocha	University of Minho, Portugal

Awards Chair

Wenny Rahayu	La Trobe University, Australia

Publicity Committee Chairs

Elmer Dadios	De La Salle University, Philippines
Nataliia Kulabukhova	St. Petersburg University, Russia
Daisuke Takahashi	Tsukuba University, Japan
Shangwang Wang	Beijing University of Posts and Telecommunications, China

Technology Chairs

Damiano Perri	University of Florence, Italy
Marco Simonetti	University of Florence, Italy

Local Arrangement Chairs

Ivan Blečić	University of Cagliari, Italy
Chiara Garau	University of Cagliari, Italy
Alfonso Annunziata	University of Cagliari, Italy
Ginevra Balletto	University of Cagliari, Italy
Giuseppe Borruso	University of Trieste, Italy
Alessandro Buccini	University of Cagliari, Italy
Michele Campagna	University of Cagliari, Italy
Mauro Coni	University of Cagliari, Italy
Anna Maria Colavitti	University of Cagliari, Italy
Giulia Desogus	University of Cagliari, Italy
Caterina Fenu	University of Cagliari, Italy
Sabrina Lai	University of Cagliari, Italy
Francesca Maltinti	University of Cagliari, Italy
Pasquale Mistretta	University of Cagliari, Italy

Augusto Montisci	University of Cagliari, Italy
Francesco Pinna	University of Cagliari, Italy
Davide Spano	University of Cagliari, Italy
Giuseppe A. Trunfio	University of Sassari, Italy
Corrado Zoppi	University of Cagliari, Italy

Program Committee

Vera Afreixo	University of Aveiro, Portugal
Filipe Alvelos	University of Minho, Portugal
Hartmut Asche	University of Potsdam, Germany
Ginevra Balletto	University of Cagliari, Italy
Michela Bertolotto	University College Dublin, Ireland
Sandro Bimonte	INRAE-TSCF, France
Rod Blais	University of Calgary, Canada
Ivan Blečić	University of Sassari, Italy
Giuseppe Borruso	University of Trieste, Italy
Ana Cristina Braga	University of Minho, Portugal
Massimo Cafaro	University of Salento, Italy
Yves Caniou	University of Lyon, France
José A. Cardoso e Cunha	Universidade Nova de Lisboa, Portugal
Rui Cardoso	University of Beira Interior, Portugal
Leocadio G. Casado	University of Almeria, Spain
Carlo Cattani	University of Salerno, Italy
Mete Celik	Erciyes University, Turkey
Maria Cerreta	University of Naples "Federico II", Italy
Hyunseung Choo	Sungkyunkwan University, South Korea
Chien-Sing Lee	Sunway University, Malaysia
Min Young Chung	Sungkyunkwan University, South Korea
Florbela Maria da Cruz Domingues Correia	Polytechnic Institute of Viana do Castelo, Portugal
Gilberto Corso Pereira	Federal University of Bahia, Brazil
Fernanda Costa	University of Minho, Portugal
Alessandro Costantini	INFN, Italy
Carla Dal Sasso Freitas	Universidade Federal do Rio Grande do Sul, Brazil
Pradesh Debba	The Council for Scientific and Industrial Research (CSIR), South Africa
Hendrik Decker	Instituto Tecnológico de Informática, Spain
Robertas Damaševičius	Kausan University of Technology, Lithuania
Frank Devai	London South Bank University, UK
Rodolphe Devillers	Memorial University of Newfoundland, Canada
Joana Matos Dias	University of Coimbra, Portugal
Paolino Di Felice	University of L'Aquila, Italy
Prabu Dorairaj	NetApp, India/USA
Noelia Faginas Lago	University of Perugia, Italy
M. Irene Falcao	University of Minho, Portugal

Cherry Liu Fang	Ames Laboratory, USA
Florbela P. Fernandes	Polytechnic Institute of Bragança, Portugal
Jose-Jesus Fernandez	National Centre for Biotechnology, Spain
Paula Odete Fernandes	Polytechnic Institute of Bragança, Portugal
Adelaide de Fátima Baptista Valente Freitas	University of Aveiro, Portugal
Manuel Carlos Figueiredo	University of Minho, Portugal
Maria Celia Furtado Rocha	Universidade Federal da Bahia, Brazil
Chiara Garau	University of Cagliari, Italy
Paulino Jose Garcia Nieto	University of Oviedo, Spain
Jerome Gensel	LSR-IMAG, France
Maria Giaoutzi	National Technical University of Athens, Greece
Arminda Manuela Andrade Pereira Gonçalves	University of Minho, Portugal
Andrzej M. Goscinski	Deakin University, Australia
Eduardo Guerra	Free University of Bozen-Bolzano, Italy
Sevin Gümgüm	Izmir University of Economics, Turkey
Alex Hagen-Zanker	University of Cambridge, UK
Shanmugasundaram Hariharan	B.S. Abdur Rahman University, India
Eligius M. T. Hendrix	University of Malaga, Spain/Wageningen University, The Netherlands
Hisamoto Hiyoshi	Gunma University, Japan
Mustafa Inceoglu	EGE University, Turkey
Peter Jimack	University of Leeds, UK
Qun Jin	Waseda University, Japan
Yeliz Karaca	University of Massachusetts Medical School, USA
Farid Karimipour	Vienna University of Technology, Austria
Baris Kazar	Oracle Corp., USA
Maulana Adhinugraha Kiki	Telkom University, Indonesia
DongSeong Kim	University of Canterbury, New Zealand
Taihoon Kim	Hannam University, South Korea
Ivana Kolingerova	University of West Bohemia, Czech Republic
Nataliia Kulabukhova	St. Petersburg University, Russia
Vladimir Korkhov	St. Petersburg University, Russia
Rosa Lasaponara	National Research Council, Italy
Maurizio Lazzari	National Research Council, Italy
Cheng Siong Lee	Monash University, Australia
Sangyoun Lee	Yonsei University, South Korea
Jongchan Lee	Kunsan National University, South Korea
Chendong Li	University of Connecticut, USA
Gang Li	Deakin University, Australia
Fang Liu	Ames Laboratory, USA
Xin Liu	University of Calgary, Canada
Andrea Lombardi	University of Perugia, Italy
Savino Longo	University of Bari, Italy

Tinghuai Ma	Nanjing University of Information Science and Technology, China
Ernesto Marcheggiani	Katholieke Universiteit Leuven, Belgium
Antonino Marvuglia	Research Centre Henri Tudor, Luxembourg
Nicola Masini	National Research Council, Italy
Ilaria Matteucci	National Research Council, Italy
Eric Medvet	University of Trieste, Italy
Nirvana Meratnia	University of Twente, The Netherlands
Giuseppe Modica	University of Reggio Calabria, Italy
Josè Luis Montaña	University of Cantabria, Spain
Maria Filipa Mourão	Instituto Politécnico de Viana do Castelo, Portugal
Louiza de Macedo Mourelle	State University of Rio de Janeiro, Brazil
Nadia Nedjah	State University of Rio de Janeiro, Brazil
Laszlo Neumann	University of Girona, Spain
Kok-Leong Ong	Deakin University, Australia
Belen Palop	Universidad de Valladolid, Spain
Marcin Paprzycki	Polish Academy of Sciences, Poland
Eric Pardede	La Trobe University, Australia
Kwangjin Park	Wonkwang University, South Korea
Ana Isabel Pereira	Polytechnic Institute of Bragança, Portugal
Massimiliano Petri	University of Pisa, Italy
Telmo Pinto	University of Coimbra, Portugal
Maurizio Pollino	Italian National Agency for New Technologies, Energy and Sustainable Economic Development, Italy
Alenka Poplin	University of Hamburg, Germany
Vidyasagar Potdar	Curtin University of Technology, Australia
David C. Prosperi	Florida Atlantic University, USA
Wenny Rahayu	La Trobe University, Australia
Jerzy Respondek	Silesian University of Technology Poland
Humberto Rocha	INESC-Coimbra, Portugal
Jon Rokne	University of Calgary, Canada
Octavio Roncero	CSIC, Spain
Maytham Safar	Kuwait University, Kuwait
Francesco Santini	University of Perugia, Italy
Chiara Saracino	A.O. Ospedale Niguarda Ca' Granda, Italy
Haiduke Sarafian	Pennsylvania State University, USA
Marco Paulo Seabra dos Reis	University of Coimbra, Portugal
Jie Shen	University of Michigan, USA
Qi Shi	Liverpool John Moores University, UK
Dale Shires	U.S. Army Research Laboratory, USA
Inês Soares	University of Coimbra, Portugal
Elena Stankova	St. Petersburg University, Russia
Takuo Suganuma	Tohoku University, Japan
Eufemia Tarantino	Polytechnic University of Bari, Italy
Sergio Tasso	University of Perugia, Italy

Ana Paula Teixeira	University of Trás-os-Montes and Alto Douro, Portugal
Senhorinha Teixeira	University of Minho, Portugal
M. Filomena Teodoro	Portuguese Naval Academy/University of Lisbon, Portugal
Parimala Thulasiraman	University of Manitoba, Canada
Carmelo Torre	Polytechnic University of Bari, Italy
Javier Martinez Torres	Centro Universitario de la Defensa Zaragoza, Spain
Giuseppe A. Trunfio	University of Sassari, Italy
Pablo Vanegas	University of Cuenca, Equador
Marco Vizzari	University of Perugia, Italy
Varun Vohra	Merck Inc., USA
Koichi Wada	University of Tsukuba, Japan
Krzysztof Walkowiak	Wroclaw University of Technology, Poland
Zequn Wang	Intelligent Automation Inc, USA
Robert Weibel	University of Zurich, Switzerland
Frank Westad	Norwegian University of Science and Technology, Norway
Roland Wismüller	Universität Siegen, Germany
Mudasser Wyne	National University, USA
Chung-Huang Yang	National Kaohsiung Normal University, Taiwan
Xin-She Yang	National Physical Laboratory, UK
Salim Zabir	National Institute of Technology, Tsuruoka, Japan
Haifeng Zhao	University of California, Davis, USA
Fabiana Zollo	University of Venice "Cà Foscari", Italy
Albert Y. Zomaya	University of Sydney, Australia

Workshop Organizers

Advanced Transport Tools and Methods (A2TM 2021)

| Massimiliano Petri | University of Pisa, Italy |
| Antonio Pratelli | University of Pisa, Italy |

Advances in Artificial Intelligence Learning Technologies: Blended Learning, STEM, Computational Thinking and Coding (AAILT 2021)

Alfredo Milani	University of Perugia, Italy
Giulio Biondi	University of Florence, Italy
Sergio Tasso	University of Perugia, Italy

Workshop on Advancements in Applied Machine Learning and Data Analytics (AAMDA 2021)

Alessandro Costantini	INFN, Italy
Davide Salomoni	INFN, Italy
Doina Cristina Duma	INFN, Italy
Daniele Cesini	INFN, Italy

Automatic Landform Classification: Spatial Methods and Applications (ALCSMA 2021)

Maria Danese	ISPC, National Research Council, Italy
Dario Gioia	ISPC, National Research Council, Italy

Application of Numerical Analysis to Imaging Science (ANAIS 2021)

Caterina Fenu	University of Cagliari, Italy
Alessandro Buccini	University of Cagliari, Italy

Advances in Information Systems and Technologies for Emergency Management, Risk Assessment and Mitigation Based on the Resilience Concepts (ASTER 2021)

Maurizio Pollino	ENEA, Italy
Marco Vona	University of Basilicata, Italy
Amedeo Flora	University of Basilicata, Italy
Chiara Iacovino	University of Basilicata, Italy
Beniamino Murgante	University of Basilicata, Italy

Advances in Web Based Learning (AWBL 2021)

Birol Ciloglugil	Ege University, Turkey
Mustafa Murat Inceoglu	Ege University, Turkey

Blockchain and Distributed Ledgers: Technologies and Applications (BDLTA 2021)

Vladimir Korkhov	St. Petersburg University, Russia
Elena Stankova	St. Petersburg University, Russia
Nataliia Kulabukhova	St. Petersburg University, Russia

Bio and Neuro Inspired Computing and Applications (BIONCA 2021)

Nadia Nedjah	State University of Rio de Janeiro, Brazil
Luiza De Macedo Mourelle	State University of Rio de Janeiro, Brazil

Computational and Applied Mathematics (CAM 2021)

Maria Irene Falcão	University of Minho, Portugal
Fernando Miranda	University of Minho, Portugal

Computational and Applied Statistics (CAS 2021)

Ana Cristina Braga	University of Minho, Portugal

Computerized Evaluation of Economic Activities: Urban Spaces (CEEA 2021)

Diego Altafini	Università di Pisa, Italy
Valerio Cutini	Università di Pisa, Italy

Computational Geometry and Applications (CGA 2021)

Marina Gavrilova   University of Calgary, Canada

Collaborative Intelligence in Multimodal Applications (CIMA 2021)

Robertas Damasevicius   Kaunas University of Technology, Lithuania
Rytis Maskeliunas   Kaunas University of Technology, Lithuania

Computational Optimization and Applications (COA 2021)

Ana Rocha   University of Minho, Portugal
Humberto Rocha   University of Coimbra, Portugal

Computational Astrochemistry (CompAstro 2021)

Marzio Rosi   University of Perugia, Italy
Cecilia Ceccarelli   University of Grenoble, France
Stefano Falcinelli   University of Perugia, Italy
Dimitrios Skouteris   Master-Up, Italy

Computational Science and HPC (CSHPC 2021)

Elise de Doncker   Western Michigan University, USA
Fukuko Yuasa   High Energy Accelerator Research Organization
                                    (KEK), Japan
Hideo Matsufuru   High Energy Accelerator Research Organization
                                    (KEK), Japan

Cities, Technologies and Planning (CTP 2021)

Malgorzata Hanzl   University of Łódź, Poland
Beniamino Murgante   University of Basilicata, Italy
Ljiljana Zivkovic   Ministry of Construction, Transport and
                                    Infrastructure/Institute of Architecture and Urban
                                    and Spatial Planning of Serbia, Serbia
Anastasia Stratigea   National Technical University of Athens, Greece
Giuseppe Borruso   University of Trieste, Italy
Ginevra Balletto   University of Cagliari, Italy

Advanced Modeling E-Mobility in Urban Spaces (DEMOS 2021)

Tiziana Campisi   Kore University of Enna, Italy
Socrates Basbas   Aristotle University of Thessaloniki, Greece
Ioannis Politis   Aristotle University of Thessaloniki, Greece
Florin Nemtanu   Polytechnic University of Bucharest, Romania
Giovanna Acampa   Kore University of Enna, Italy
Wolfgang Schulz   Zeppelin University, Germany

Digital Transformation and Smart City (DIGISMART 2021)

Mauro Mazzei   National Research Council, Italy

Econometric and Multidimensional Evaluation in Urban Environment (EMEUE 2021)

Carmelo Maria Torre   Polytechnic University of Bari, Italy
Maria Cerreta   University "Federico II" of Naples, Italy
Pierluigi Morano   Polytechnic University of Bari, Italy
Simona Panaro   University of Portsmouth, UK
Francesco Tajani   Sapienza University of Rome, Italy
Marco Locurcio   Polytechnic University of Bari, Italy

The 11th International Workshop on Future Computing System Technologies and Applications (FiSTA 2021)

Bernady Apduhan   Kyushu Sangyo University, Japan
Rafael Santos   Brazilian National Institute for Space Research, Brazil

Transformational Urban Mobility: Challenges and Opportunities During and Post COVID Era (FURTHER 2021)

Tiziana Campisi   Kore University of Enna, Italy
Socrates Basbas   Aristotle University of Thessaloniki, Greece
Dilum Dissanayake   Newcastle University, UK
Kh Md Nahiduzzaman   University of British Columbia, Canada
Nurten Akgün Tanbay   Bursa Technical University, Turkey
Khaled J. Assi   King Fahd University of Petroleum and Minerals,
                             Saudi Arabia
Giovanni Tesoriere   Kore University of Enna, Italy
Motasem Darwish   Middle East University, Jordan

Geodesign in Decision Making: Meta Planning and Collaborative Design for Sustainable and Inclusive Development (GDM 2021)

Francesco Scorza   University of Basilicata, Italy
Michele Campagna   University of Cagliari, Italy
Ana Clara Mourao Moura   Federal University of Minas Gerais, Brazil

Geomatics in Forestry and Agriculture: New Advances and Perspectives (GeoForAgr 2021)

Maurizio Pollino   ENEA, Italy
Giuseppe Modica   University of Reggio Calabria, Italy
Marco Vizzari   University of Perugia, Italy

Geographical Analysis, Urban Modeling, Spatial Statistics (GEOG-AND-MOD 2021)

Beniamino Murgante	University of Basilicata, Italy
Giuseppe Borruso	University of Trieste, Italy
Hartmut Asche	University of Potsdam, Germany

Geomatics for Resource Monitoring and Management (GRMM 2021)

Eufemia Tarantino	Polytechnic University of Bari, Italy
Enrico Borgogno Mondino	University of Turin, Italy
Alessandra Capolupo	Polytechnic University of Bari, Italy
Mirko Saponaro	Polytechnic University of Bari, Italy

12th International Symposium on Software Quality (ISSQ 2021)

Sanjay Misra	Covenant University, Nigeria

10th International Workshop on Collective, Massive and Evolutionary Systems (IWCES 2021)

Alfredo Milani	University of Perugia, Italy
Rajdeep Niyogi	Indian Institute of Technology, Roorkee, India

Land Use Monitoring for Sustainability (LUMS 2021)

Carmelo Maria Torre	Polytechnic University of Bari, Italy
Maria Cerreta	University "Federico II" of Naples, Italy
Massimiliano Bencardino	University of Salerno, Italy
Alessandro Bonifazi	Polytechnic University of Bari, Italy
Pasquale Balena	Polytechnic University of Bari, Italy
Giuliano Poli	University "Federico II" of Naples, Italy

Machine Learning for Space and Earth Observation Data (MALSEOD 2021)

Rafael Santos	Instituto Nacional de Pesquisas Espaciais, Brazil
Karine Ferreira	Instituto Nacional de Pesquisas Espaciais, Brazil

Building Multi-dimensional Models for Assessing Complex Environmental Systems (MES 2021)

Marta Dell'Ovo	Polytechnic University of Milan, Italy
Vanessa Assumma	Polytechnic University of Turin, Italy
Caterina Caprioli	Polytechnic University of Turin, Italy
Giulia Datola	Polytechnic University of Turin, Italy
Federico dell'Anna	Polytechnic University of Turin, Italy

Ecosystem Services: Nature's Contribution to People in Practice. Assessment Frameworks, Models, Mapping, and Implications (NC2P 2021)

Francesco Scorza   University of Basilicata, Italy
Sabrina Lai   University of Cagliari, Italy
Ana Clara Mourao Moura   Federal University of Minas Gerais, Brazil
Corrado Zoppi   University of Cagliari, Italy
Dani Broitman   Technion, Israel Institute of Technology, Israel

Privacy in the Cloud/Edge/IoT World (PCEIoT 2021)

Michele Mastroianni   University of Campania Luigi Vanvitelli, Italy
Lelio Campanile   University of Campania Luigi Vanvitelli, Italy
Mauro Iacono   University of Campania Luigi Vanvitelli, Italy

Processes, Methods and Tools Towards RESilient Cities and Cultural Heritage Prone to SOD and ROD Disasters (RES 2021)

Elena Cantatore   Polytechnic University of Bari, Italy
Alberico Sonnessa   Polytechnic University of Bari, Italy
Dario Esposito   Polytechnic University of Bari, Italy

Risk, Resilience and Sustainability in the Efficient Management of Water Resources: Approaches, Tools, Methodologies and Multidisciplinary Integrated Applications (RRS 2021)

Maria Macchiaroli   University of Salerno, Italy
Chiara D'Alpaos   Università degli Studi di Padova, Italy
Mirka Mobilia   Università degli Studi di Salerno, Italy
Antonia Longobardi   Università degli Studi di Salerno, Italy
Grazia Fattoruso   ENEA Research Center, Italy
Vincenzo Pellecchia   Ente Idrico Campano, Italy

Scientific Computing Infrastructure (SCI 2021)

Elena Stankova   St. Petersburg University, Russia
Vladimir Korkhov   St. Petersburg University, Russia
Natalia Kulabukhova   St. Petersburg University, Russia

Smart Cities and User Data Management (SCIDAM 2021)

Chiara Garau   University of Cagliari, Italy
Luigi Mundula   University of Cagliari, Italy
Gianni Fenu   University of Cagliari, Italy
Paolo Nesi   University of Florence, Italy
Paola Zamperlin   University of Pisa, Italy

13th International Symposium on Software Engineering Processes and Applications (SEPA 2021)

Sanjay Misra   Covenant University, Nigeria

Ports of the Future - Smartness and Sustainability (SmartPorts 2021)

Patrizia Serra   University of Cagliari, Italy
Gianfranco Fancello   University of Cagliari, Italy
Ginevra Balletto   University of Cagliari, Italy
Luigi Mundula   University of Cagliari, Italy
Marco Mazzarino   University of Venice, Italy
Giuseppe Borruso   University of Trieste, Italy
Maria del Mar Munoz   Universidad de Cádiz, Spain
  Leonisio

Smart Tourism (SmartTourism 2021)

Giuseppe Borruso   University of Trieste, Italy
Silvia Battino   University of Sassari, Italy
Ginevra Balletto   University of Cagliari, Italy
Maria del Mar Munoz   Universidad de Cádiz, Spain
  Leonisio
Ainhoa Amaro Garcia   Universidad de Alcalà/Universidad de Las Palmas,
                                         Spain
Francesca Krasna   University of Trieste, Italy

Sustainability Performance Assessment: Models, Approaches and Applications toward Interdisciplinary and Integrated Solutions (SPA 2021)

Francesco Scorza   University of Basilicata, Italy
Sabrina Lai   University of Cagliari, Italy
Jolanta Dvarioniene   Kaunas University of Technology, Lithuania
Valentin Grecu   Lucian Blaga University, Romania
Corrado Zoppi   University of Cagliari, Italy
Iole Cerminara   University of Basilicata, Italy

Smart and Sustainable Island Communities (SSIC 2021)

Chiara Garau   University of Cagliari, Italy
Anastasia Stratigea   National Technical University of Athens, Greece
Paola Zamperlin   University of Pisa, Italy
Francesco Scorza   University of Basilicata, Italy

Science, Technologies and Policies to Innovate Spatial Planning (STP4P 2021)

Chiara Garau   University of Cagliari, Italy
Daniele La Rosa   University of Catania, Italy
Francesco Scorza   University of Basilicata, Italy

Anna Maria Colavitti   University of Cagliari, Italy
Beniamino Murgante   University of Basilicata, Italy
Paolo La Greca   University of Catania, Italy

Sustainable Urban Energy Systems (SURENSYS 2021)

Luigi Mundula   University of Cagliari, Italy
Emilio Ghiani   University of Cagliari, Italy

Space Syntax for Cities in Theory and Practice (Syntax_City 2021)

Claudia Yamu   University of Groningen, The Netherlands
Akkelies van Nes   Western Norway University of Applied Sciences,
                                  Norway
Chiara Garau   University of Cagliari, Italy

Theoretical and Computational Chemistry and Its Applications (TCCMA 2021)

Noelia Faginas-Lago   University of Perugia, Italy

13th International Workshop on Tools and Techniques in Software Development Process (TTSDP 2021)

Sanjay Misra   Covenant University, Nigeria

Urban Form Studies (UForm 2021)

Malgorzata Hanzl   Łódź University of Technology, Poland
Beniamino Murgante   University of Basilicata, Italy
Eufemia Tarantino   Polytechnic University of Bari, Italy
Irena Itova   University of Westminster, UK

Urban Space Accessibility and Safety (USAS 2021)

Chiara Garau   University of Cagliari, Italy
Francesco Pinna   University of Cagliari, Italy
Claudia Yamu   University of Groningen, The Netherlands
Vincenza Torrisi   University of Catania, Italy
Matteo Ignaccolo   University of Catania, Italy
Michela Tiboni   University of Brescia, Italy
Silvia Rossetti   University of Parma, Italy

Virtual and Augmented Reality and Applications (VRA 2021)

Osvaldo Gervasi   University of Perugia, Italy
Damiano Perri   University of Perugia, Italy
Marco Simonetti   University of Perugia, Italy
Sergio Tasso   University of Perugia, Italy

Workshop on Advanced and Computational Methods for Earth Science Applications (WACM4ES 2021)

Luca Piroddi	University of Cagliari, Italy
Laura Foddis	University of Cagliari, Italy
Augusto Montisci	University of Cagliari, Italy
Sergio Vincenzo Calcina	University of Cagliari, Italy
Sebastiano D'Amico	University of Malta, Malta
Giovanni Martinelli	Istituto Nazionale di Geofisica e Vulcanologia, Italy/Chinese Academy of Sciences, China

Sponsoring Organizations

ICCSA 2021 would not have been possible without the tremendous support of many organizations and institutions, for which all organizers and participants of ICCSA 2021 express their sincere gratitude:

Springer International Publishing AG, Germany
(https://www.springer.com)

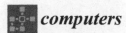

Computers Open Access Journal
(https://www.mdpi.com/journal/computers)

IEEE Italy Section, Italy
(https://italy.ieeer8.org/)

Centre-North Italy Chapter IEEE GRSS, Italy
(https://cispio.diet.uniroma1.it/marzano/ieee-grs/index.html)

Italy Section of the Computer Society, Italy
(https://site.ieee.org/italy-cs/)

University of Perugia, Italy
(https://www.unipg.it)

University of Cagliari, Italy
(https://unica.it/)

University of Basilicata, Italy
(http://www.unibas.it)

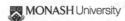
Monash University, Australia
(https://www.monash.edu/)

Kyushu Sangyo University, Japan
(https://www.kyusan-u.ac.jp/)

University of Minho, Portugal
(https://www.uminho.pt/)

Scientific Association Transport Infrastructures,
Italy
(https://www.stradeeautostrade.it/associazioni-e-
organizzazioni/asit-associazione-scientifica-
infrastrutture-trasporto/)

Regione Sardegna, Italy
(https://regione.sardegna.it/)

Comune di Cagliari, Italy
(https://www.comune.cagliari.it/)

Città Metropolitana di Cagliari

Cagliari Accessibility Lab (CAL)
(https://www.unica.it/unica/it/cagliari_
accessibility_lab.page/)

Referees

Nicodemo Abate	IMAA, National Research Council, Italy
Andre Ricardo Abed Grégio	Federal University of Paraná State, Brazil
Nasser Abu Zeid	Università di Ferrara, Italy
Lidia Aceto	Università del Piemonte Orientale, Italy
Nurten Akgün Tanbay	Bursa Technical University, Turkey
Filipe Alvelos	Universidade do Minho, Portugal
Paula Amaral	Universidade Nova de Lisboa, Portugal
Federico Amato	University of Lausanne, Switzerland
Marina Alexandra Pedro Andrade	ISCTE-IUL, Portugal
Debora Anelli	Sapienza University of Rome, Italy
Alfonso Annunziata	University of Cagliari, Italy
Fahim Anzum	University of Calgary, Canada
Tatsumi Aoyama	High Energy Accelerator Research Organization, Japan
Bernady Apduhan	Kyushu Sangyo University, Japan
Jonathan Apeh	Covenant University, Nigeria
Vasilike Argyropoulos	University of West Attica, Greece
Giuseppe Aronica	Università di Messina, Italy
Daniela Ascenzi	Università degli Studi di Trento, Italy
Vanessa Assumma	Politecnico di Torino, Italy
Muhammad Attique Khan	HITEC University Taxila, Pakistan
Vecdi Aytaç	Ege University, Turkey
Alina Elena Baia	University of Perugia, Italy
Ginevra Balletto	University of Cagliari, Italy
Marialaura Bancheri	ISAFOM, National Research Council, Italy
Benedetto Barabino	University of Brescia, Italy
Simona Barbaro	Università degli Studi di Palermo, Italy
Enrico Barbierato	Università Cattolica del Sacro Cuore di Milano, Italy
Jeniffer Barreto	Istituto Superior Técnico, Lisboa, Portugal
Michele Bartalini	TAGES, Italy
Socrates Basbas	Aristotle University of Thessaloniki, Greece
Silvia Battino	University of Sassari, Italy
Marcelo Becerra Rozas	Pontificia Universidad Católica de Valparaíso, Chile
Ranjan Kumar Behera	National Institute of Technology, Rourkela, India
Emanuele Bellini	University of Campania Luigi Vanvitelli, Italy
Massimo Bilancia	University of Bari Aldo Moro, Italy
Giulio Biondi	University of Firenze, Italy
Adriano Bisello	Eurac Research, Italy
Ignacio Blanquer	Universitat Politècnica de València, Spain
Semen Bochkov	Ulyanovsk State Technical University, Russia
Alexander Bogdanov	St. Petersburg University, Russia
Silvia Bonettini	University of Modena and Reggio Emilia, Italy
Enrico Borgogno Mondino	Università di Torino, Italy
Giuseppe Borruso	University of Trieste, Italy

Michele Bottazzi	University of Trento, Italy
Rahma Bouaziz	Taibah University, Saudi Arabia
Ouafik Boulariah	University of Salerno, Italy
Tulin Boyar	Yildiz Technical University, Turkey
Ana Cristina Braga	University of Minho, Portugal
Paolo Bragolusi	University of Padova, Italy
Luca Braidotti	University of Trieste, Italy
Alessandro Buccini	University of Cagliari, Italy
Jorge Buele	Universidad Tecnológica Indoamérica, Ecuador
Andrea Buffoni	TAGES, Italy
Sergio Vincenzo Calcina	University of Cagliari, Italy
Michele Campagna	University of Cagliari, Italy
Lelio Campanile	Università degli Studi della Campania Luigi Vanvitelli, Italy
Tiziana Campisi	Kore University of Enna, Italy
Antonino Canale	Kore University of Enna, Italy
Elena Cantatore	DICATECh, Polytechnic University of Bari, Italy
Pasquale Cantiello	Istituto Nazionale di Geofisica e Vulcanologia, Italy
Alessandra Capolupo	Polytechnic University of Bari, Italy
David Michele Cappelletti	University of Perugia, Italy
Caterina Caprioli	Politecnico di Torino, Italy
Sara Carcangiu	University of Cagliari, Italy
Pedro Carrasqueira	INESC Coimbra, Portugal
Arcangelo Castiglione	University of Salerno, Italy
Giulio Cavana	Politecnico di Torino, Italy
Davide Cerati	Politecnico di Milano, Italy
Maria Cerreta	University of Naples Federico II, Italy
Daniele Cesini	INFN-CNAF, Italy
Jabed Chowdhury	La Trobe University, Australia
Gennaro Ciccarelli	Iuav University of Venice, Italy
Birol Ciloglugil	Ege University, Turkey
Elena Cocuzza	Univesity of Catania, Italy
Anna Maria Colavitt	University of Cagliari, Italy
Cecilia Coletti	Università "G. d'Annunzio" di Chieti-Pescara, Italy
Alberto Collu	Independent Researcher, Italy
Anna Concas	University of Basilicata, Italy
Mauro Coni	University of Cagliari, Italy
Melchiorre Contino	Università di Palermo, Italy
Antonella Cornelio	Università degli Studi di Brescia, Italy
Aldina Correia	Politécnico do Porto, Portugal
Elisete Correia	Universidade de Trás-os-Montes e Alto Douro, Portugal
Florbela Correia	Polytechnic Institute of Viana do Castelo, Portugal
Stefano Corsi	Università degli Studi di Milano, Italy
Alberto Cortez	Polytechnic of University Coimbra, Portugal
Lino Costa	Universidade do Minho, Portugal

Alessandro Costantini	INFN, Italy
Marilena Cozzolino	Università del Molise, Italy
Giulia Crespi	Politecnico di Torino, Italy
Maurizio Crispino	Politecnico di Milano, Italy
Chiara D'Alpaos	University of Padova, Italy
Roberta D'Ambrosio	Università di Salerno, Italy
Sebastiano D'Amico	University of Malta, Malta
Hiroshi Daisaka	Hitotsubashi University, Japan
Gaia Daldanise	Italian National Research Council, Italy
Robertas Damasevicius	Silesian University of Technology, Poland
Maria Danese	ISPC, National Research Council, Italy
Bartoli Daniele	University of Perugia, Italy
Motasem Darwish	Middle East University, Jordan
Giulia Datola	Politecnico di Torino, Italy
Regina de Almeida	UTAD, Portugal
Elise de Doncker	Western Michigan University, USA
Mariella De Fino	Politecnico di Bari, Italy
Giandomenico De Luca	Mediterranean University of Reggio Calabria, Italy
Luiza de Macedo Mourelle	State University of Rio de Janeiro, Brazil
Gianluigi De Mare	University of Salerno, Italy
Itamir de Morais Barroca Filho	Federal University of Rio Grande do Norte, Brazil
Samuele De Petris	Università di Torino, Italy
Marcilio de Souto	LIFO, University of Orléans, France
Alexander Degtyarev	St. Petersburg University, Russia
Federico Dell'Anna	Politecnico di Torino, Italy
Marta Dell'Ovo	Politecnico di Milano, Italy
Fernanda Della Mura	University of Naples "Federico II", Italy
Ahu Dereli Dursun	Istanbul Commerce University, Turkey
Bashir Derradji	University of Sfax, Tunisia
Giulia Desogus	Università degli Studi di Cagliari, Italy
Marco Dettori	Università degli Studi di Sassari, Italy
Frank Devai	London South Bank University, UK
Felicia Di Liddo	Polytechnic University of Bari, Italy
Valerio Di Pinto	University of Naples "Federico II", Italy
Joana Dias	University of Coimbra, Portugal
Luis Dias	University of Minho, Portugal
Patricia Diaz de Alba	Gran Sasso Science Institute, Italy
Isabel Dimas	University of Coimbra, Portugal
Aleksandra Djordjevic	University of Belgrade, Serbia
Luigi Dolores	Università degli Studi di Salerno, Italy
Marco Donatelli	University of Insubria, Italy
Doina Cristina Duma	INFN-CNAF, Italy
Fabio Durastante	University of Pisa, Italy
Aziz Dursun	Virginia Tech University, USA
Juan Enrique-Romero	Université Grenoble Alpes, France

Annunziata Esposito Amideo	University College Dublin, Ireland
Dario Esposito	Polytechnic University of Bari, Italy
Claudio Estatico	University of Genova, Italy
Noelia Faginas-Lago	Università di Perugia, Italy
Maria Irene Falcão	University of Minho, Portugal
Stefano Falcinelli	University of Perugia, Italy
Alessandro Farina	University of Pisa, Italy
Grazia Fattoruso	ENEA, Italy
Caterina Fenu	University of Cagliari, Italy
Luisa Fermo	University of Cagliari, Italy
Florbela Fernandes	Instituto Politecnico de Braganca, Portugal
Rosário Fernandes	University of Minho, Portugal
Luis Fernandez-Sanz	University of Alcala, Spain
Alessia Ferrari	Università di Parma, Italy
Luís Ferrás	University of Minho, Portugal
Ângela Ferreira	Instituto Politécnico de Bragança, Portugal
Flora Ferreira	University of Minho, Portugal
Manuel Carlos Figueiredo	University of Minho, Portugal
Ugo Fiore	University of Naples "Parthenope", Italy
Amedeo Flora	University of Basilicata, Italy
Hector Florez	Universidad Distrital Francisco Jose de Caldas, Colombia
Maria Laura Foddis	University of Cagliari, Italy
Valentina Franzoni	Perugia University, Italy
Adelaide Freitas	University of Aveiro, Portugal
Samuel Frimpong	Durban University of Technology, South Africa
Ioannis Fyrogenis	Aristotle University of Thessaloniki, Greece
Marika Gaballo	Politecnico di Torino, Italy
Laura Gabrielli	Iuav University of Venice, Italy
Ivan Gankevich	St. Petersburg University, Russia
Chiara Garau	University of Cagliari, Italy
Ernesto Garcia Para	Universidad del País Vasco, Spain,
Fernando Garrido	Universidad Técnica del Norte, Ecuador
Marina Gavrilova	University of Calgary, Canada
Silvia Gazzola	University of Bath, UK
Georgios Georgiadis	Aristotle University of Thessaloniki, Greece
Osvaldo Gervasi	University of Perugia, Italy
Andrea Gioia	Polytechnic University of Bari, Italy
Dario Gioia	ISPC-CNT, Italy
Raffaele Giordano	IRSS, National Research Council, Italy
Giacomo Giorgi	University of Perugia, Italy
Eleonora Giovene di Girasole	IRISS, National Research Council, Italy
Salvatore Giuffrida	Università di Catania, Italy
Marco Gola	Politecnico di Milano, Italy

A. Manuela Gonçalves	University of Minho, Portugal
Yuriy Gorbachev	Coddan Technologies LLC, Russia
Angela Gorgoglione	Universidad de la República, Uruguay
Yusuke Gotoh	Okayama University, Japan
Anestis Gourgiotis	University of Thessaly, Greece
Valery Grishkin	St. Petersburg University, Russia
Alessandro Grottesi	CINECA, Italy
Eduardo Guerra	Free University of Bozen-Bolzano, Italy
Ayse Giz Gulnerman	Ankara HBV University, Turkey
Sevin Gümgüm	Izmir University of Economics, Turkey
Himanshu Gupta	BITS Pilani, Hyderabad, India
Sandra Haddad	Arab Academy for Science, Egypt
Malgorzata Hanzl	Lodz University of Technology, Poland
Shoji Hashimoto	KEK, Japan
Peter Hegedus	University of Szeged, Hungary
Eligius M. T. Hendrix	Universidad de Málaga, Spain
Edmond Ho	Northumbria University, UK
Guan Yue Hong	Western Michigan University, USA
Vito Iacobellis	Polytechnic University of Bari, Italy
Mauro Iacono	Università degli Studi della Campania, Italy
Chiara Iacovino	University of Basilicata, Italy
Antonino Iannuzzo	ETH Zurich, Switzerland
Ali Idri	University Mohammed V, Morocco
Oana-Ramona Ilovan	Babeş-Bolyai University, Romania
Mustafa Inceoglu	Ege University, Turkey
Tadashi Ishikawa	KEK, Japan
Federica Isola	University of Cagliari, Italy
Irena Itova	University of Westminster, UK
Edgar David de Izeppi	VTTI, USA
Marija Jankovic	CERTH, Greece
Adrian Jaramillo	Universidad Tecnológica Metropolitana, Chile
Monalisa Jena	Fakir Mohan University, India
Dorota Kamrowska-Załuska	Gdansk University of Technology, Poland
Issaku Kanamori	RIKEN Center for Computational Science, Japan
Korhan Karabulut	Yasar University, Turkey
Yeliz Karaca	University of Massachusetts Medical School, USA
Vicky Katsoni	University of West Attica, Greece
Dimitris Kavroudakis	University of the Aegean, Greece
Shuhei Kimura	Okayama University, Japan
Joanna Kolozej	Cracow University of Technology, Poland
Vladimir Korkhov	St. Petersburg University, Russia
Thales Körting	INPE, Brazil
Tomonori Kouya	Shizuoka Institute of Science and Technology, Japan
Sylwia Krzysztofik	Lodz University of Technology, Poland
Nataliia Kulabukhova	St. Petersburg University, Russia
Shrinivas B. Kulkarni	SDM College of Engineering and Technology, India

Pavan Kumar	University of Calgary, Canada
Anisha Kumari	National Institute of Technology, Rourkela, India
Ludovica La Rocca	University of Naples "Federico II", Italy
Daniele La Rosa	University of Catania, Italy
Sabrina Lai	University of Cagliari, Italy
Giuseppe Francesco Cesare Lama	University of Naples "Federico II", Italy
Mariusz Lamprecht	University of Lodz, Poland
Vincenzo Laporta	National Research Council, Italy
Chien-Sing Lee	Sunway University, Malaysia
José Isaac Lemus Romani	Pontifical Catholic University of Valparaíso, Chile
Federica Leone	University of Cagliari, Italy
Alexander H. Levis	George Mason University, USA
Carola Lingua	Polytechnic University of Turin, Italy
Marco Locurcio	Polytechnic University of Bari, Italy
Andrea Lombardi	University of Perugia, Italy
Savino Longo	University of Bari, Italy
Fernando Lopez Gayarre	University of Oviedo, Spain
Yan Lu	Western Michigan University, USA
Maria Macchiaroli	University of Salerno, Italy
Helmuth Malonek	University of Aveiro, Portugal
Francesca Maltinti	University of Cagliari, Italy
Luca Mancini	University of Perugia, Italy
Marcos Mandado	University of Vigo, Spain
Ernesto Marcheggiani	Università Politecnica delle Marche, Italy
Krassimir Markov	University of Telecommunications and Post, Bulgaria
Giovanni Martinelli	INGV, Italy
Alessandro Marucci	University of L'Aquila, Italy
Fiammetta Marulli	University of Campania Luigi Vanvitelli, Italy
Gabriella Maselli	University of Salerno, Italy
Rytis Maskeliunas	Kaunas University of Technology, Lithuania
Michele Mastroianni	University of Campania Luigi Vanvitelli, Italy
Cristian Mateos	Universidad Nacional del Centro de la Provincia de Buenos Aires, Argentina
Hideo Matsufuru	High Energy Accelerator Research Organization (KEK), Japan
D'Apuzzo Mauro	University of Cassino and Southern Lazio, Italy
Chiara Mazzarella	University Federico II, Italy
Marco Mazzarino	University of Venice, Italy
Giovanni Mei	University of Cagliari, Italy
Mário Melo	Federal Institute of Rio Grande do Norte, Brazil
Francesco Mercaldo	University of Molise, Italy
Alfredo Milani	University of Perugia, Italy
Alessandra Milesi	University of Cagliari, Italy
Antonio Minervino	ISPC, National Research Council, Italy
Fernando Miranda	Universidade do Minho, Portugal

B. Mishra	University of Szeged, Hungary
Sanjay Misra	Covenant University, Nigeria
Mirka Mobilia	University of Salerno, Italy
Giuseppe Modica	Università degli Studi di Reggio Calabria, Italy
Mohammadsadegh Mohagheghi	Vali-e-Asr University of Rafsanjan, Iran
Mohamad Molaei Qelichi	University of Tehran, Iran
Mario Molinara	University of Cassino and Southern Lazio, Italy
Augusto Montisci	Università degli Studi di Cagliari, Italy
Pierluigi Morano	Polytechnic University of Bari, Italy
Ricardo Moura	Universidade Nova de Lisboa, Portugal
Ana Clara Mourao Moura	Federal University of Minas Gerais, Brazil
Maria Mourao	Polytechnic Institute of Viana do Castelo, Portugal
Daichi Mukunoki	RIKEN Center for Computational Science, Japan
Beniamino Murgante	University of Basilicata, Italy
Naohito Nakasato	University of Aizu, Japan
Grazia Napoli	Università degli Studi di Palermo, Italy
Isabel Cristina Natário	Universidade Nova de Lisboa, Portugal
Nadia Nedjah	State University of Rio de Janeiro, Brazil
Antonio Nesticò	University of Salerno, Italy
Andreas Nikiforiadis	Aristotle University of Thessaloniki, Greece
Keigo Nitadori	RIKEN Center for Computational Science, Japan
Silvio Nocera	Iuav University of Venice, Italy
Giuseppina Oliva	University of Salerno, Italy
Arogundade Oluwasefunmi	Academy of Mathematics and System Science, China
Ken-ichi Oohara	University of Tokyo, Japan
Tommaso Orusa	University of Turin, Italy
M. Fernanda P. Costa	University of Minho, Portugal
Roberta Padulano	Centro Euro-Mediterraneo sui Cambiamenti Climatici, Italy
Maria Panagiotopoulou	National Technical University of Athens, Greece
Jay Pancham	Durban University of Technology, South Africa
Gianni Pantaleo	University of Florence, Italy
Dimos Pantazis	University of West Attica, Greece
Michela Paolucci	University of Florence, Italy
Eric Pardede	La Trobe University, Australia
Olivier Parisot	Luxembourg Institute of Science and Technology, Luxembourg
Vincenzo Pellecchia	Ente Idrico Campano, Italy
Anna Pelosi	University of Salerno, Italy
Edit Pengő	University of Szeged, Hungary
Marco Pepe	University of Salerno, Italy
Paola Perchinunno	University of Cagliari, Italy
Ana Pereira	Polytechnic Institute of Bragança, Portugal
Mariano Pernetti	University of Campania, Italy
Damiano Perri	University of Perugia, Italy

Federica Pes	University of Cagliari, Italy
Marco Petrelli	Roma Tre University, Italy
Massimiliano Petri	University of Pisa, Italy
Khiem Phan	Duy Tan University, Vietnam
Alberto Ferruccio Piccinni	Polytechnic of Bari, Italy
Angela Pilogallo	University of Basilicata, Italy
Francesco Pinna	University of Cagliari, Italy
Telmo Pinto	University of Coimbra, Portugal
Luca Piroddi	University of Cagliari, Italy
Darius Plonis	Vilnius Gediminas Technical University, Lithuania
Giuliano Poli	University of Naples "Federico II", Italy
Maria João Polidoro	Polytecnic Institute of Porto, Portugal
Ioannis Politis	Aristotle University of Thessaloniki, Greece
Maurizio Pollino	ENEA, Italy
Antonio Pratelli	University of Pisa, Italy
Salvatore Praticò	Mediterranean University of Reggio Calabria, Italy
Marco Prato	University of Modena and Reggio Emilia, Italy
Carlotta Quagliolo	Polytechnic University of Turin, Italy
Emanuela Quaquero	Univesity of Cagliari, Italy
Garrisi Raffaele	Polizia postale e delle Comunicazioni, Italy
Nicoletta Rassu	University of Cagliari, Italy
Hafiz Tayyab Rauf	University of Bradford, UK
Michela Ravanelli	Sapienza University of Rome, Italy
Roberta Ravanelli	Sapienza University of Rome, Italy
Alfredo Reder	Centro Euro-Mediterraneo sui Cambiamenti Climatici, Italy
Stefania Regalbuto	University of Naples "Federico II", Italy
Rommel Regis	Saint Joseph's University, USA
Lothar Reichel	Kent State University, USA
Marco Reis	University of Coimbra, Portugal
Maria Reitano	University of Naples "Federico II", Italy
Jerzy Respondek	Silesian University of Technology, Poland
Elisa Riccietti	École Normale Supérieure de Lyon, France
Albert Rimola	Universitat Autònoma de Barcelona, Spain
Angela Rizzo	University of Bari, Italy
Ana Maria A. C. Rocha	University of Minho, Portugal
Fabio Rocha	Institute of Technology and Research, Brazil
Humberto Rocha	University of Coimbra, Portugal
Maria Clara Rocha	Polytechnic Institute of Coimbra, Portugal
Miguel Rocha	University of Minho, Portugal
Giuseppe Rodriguez	University of Cagliari, Italy
Guillermo Rodriguez	UNICEN, Argentina
Elisabetta Ronchieri	INFN, Italy
Marzio Rosi	University of Perugia, Italy
Silvia Rossetti	University of Parma, Italy
Marco Rossitti	Polytechnic University of Milan, Italy

Francesco Rotondo   Marche Polytechnic University, Italy
Irene Rubino   Polytechnic University of Turin, Italy
Agustín Salas   Pontifical Catholic University of Valparaíso, Chile
Juan Pablo Sandoval   Universidad Católica Boliviana "San Pablo", Bolivia
  Alcocer
Luigi Santopietro   University of Basilicata, Italy
Rafael Santos   National Institute for Space Research, Brazil
Valentino Santucci   Università per Stranieri di Perugia, Italy
Mirko Saponaro   Polytechnic University of Bari, Italy
Filippo Sarvia   University of Turin, Italy
Marco Scaioni   Polytechnic University of Milan, Italy
Rafal Scherer   Częstochowa University of Technology, Poland
Francesco Scorza   University of Basilicata, Italy
Ester Scotto di Perta   University of Napoli "Federico II", Italy
Monica Sebillo   University of Salerno, Italy
Patrizia Serra   University of Cagliari, Italy
Ricardo Severino   University of Minho, Portugal
Jie Shen   University of Michigan, USA
Huahao Shou   Zhejiang University of Technology, China
Miltiadis Siavvas   Centre for Research and Technology Hellas, Greece
Brandon Sieu   University of Calgary, Canada
Ângela Silva   Instituto Politécnico de Viana do Castelo, Portugal
Carina Silva   Polytechic Institute of Lisbon, Portugal
Joao Carlos Silva   Polytechnic Institute of Cavado and Ave, Portugal
Fabio Silveira   Federal University of Sao Paulo, Brazil
Marco Simonetti   University of Florence, Italy
Ana Jacinta Soares   University of Minho, Portugal
Maria Joana Soares   University of Minho, Portugal
Michel Soares   Federal University of Sergipe, Brazil
George Somarakis   Foundation for Research and Technology Hellas,
                             Greece
Maria Somma   University of Naples "Federico II", Italy
Alberico Sonnessa   Polytechnic University of Bari, Italy
Elena Stankova   St. Petersburg University, Russia
Flavio Stochino   University of Cagliari, Italy
Anastasia Stratigea   National Technical University of Athens, Greece
Yasuaki Sumida   Kyushu Sangyo University, Japan
Yue Sun   European X-Ray Free-Electron Laser Facility,
                             Germany
Kirill Sviatov   Ulyanovsk State Technical University, Russia
Daisuke Takahashi   University of Tsukuba, Japan
Aladics Tamás   University of Szeged, Hungary
David Taniar   Monash University, Australia
Rodrigo Tapia McClung   Centro de Investigación en Ciencias de Información
                             Geoespacial, Mexico
Eufemia Tarantino   Polytechnic University of Bari, Italy

Sergio Tasso	University of Perugia, Italy
Ana Paula Teixeira	Universidade de Trás-os-Montes e Alto Douro, Portugal
Senhorinha Teixeira	University of Minho, Portugal
Tengku Adil Tengku Izhar	Universiti Teknologi MARA, Malaysia
Maria Filomena Teodoro	University of Lisbon/Portuguese Naval Academy, Portugal
Giovanni Tesoriere	Kore University of Enna, Italy
Yiota Theodora	National Technical Univeristy of Athens, Greece
Graça Tomaz	Polytechnic Institute of Guarda, Portugal
Carmelo Maria Torre	Polytechnic University of Bari, Italy
Francesca Torrieri	University of Naples "Federico II", Italy
Vincenza Torrisi	University of Catania, Italy
Vincenzo Totaro	Polytechnic University of Bari, Italy
Pham Trung	Ho Chi Minh City University of Technology, Vietnam
Dimitrios Tsoukalas	Centre of Research and Technology Hellas (CERTH), Greece
Sanjida Tumpa	University of Calgary, Canada
Iñaki Tuñon	Universidad de Valencia, Spain
Takahiro Ueda	Seikei University, Japan
Piero Ugliengo	University of Turin, Italy
Abdi Usman	Haramaya University, Ethiopia
Ettore Valente	University of Naples "Federico II", Italy
Jordi Vallverdu	Universitat Autònoma de Barcelona, Spain
Cornelis Van Der Mee	University of Cagliari, Italy
José Varela-Aldás	Universidad Tecnológica Indoamérica, Ecuador
Fanny Vazart	University of Grenoble Alpes, France
Franco Vecchiocattivi	University of Perugia, Italy
Laura Verde	University of Campania Luigi Vanvitelli, Italy
Giulia Vergerio	Polytechnic University of Turin, Italy
Jos Vermaseren	Nikhef, The Netherlands
Giacomo Viccione	University of Salerno, Italy
Marco Vizzari	University of Perugia, Italy
Corrado Vizzarri	Polytechnic University of Bari, Italy
Alexander Vodyaho	St. Petersburg State Electrotechnical University "LETI", Russia
Nikolay N. Voit	Ulyanovsk State Technical University, Russia
Marco Vona	University of Basilicata, Italy
Agustinus Borgy Waluyo	Monash University, Australia
Fernando Wanderley	Catholic University of Pernambuco, Brazil
Chao Wang	University of Science and Technology of China, China
Marcin Wozniak	Silesian University of Technology, Poland
Tiang Xian	Nathong University, China
Rekha Yadav	KL University, India
Claudia Yamu	University of Groningen, The Netherlands
Fenghui Yao	Tennessee State University, USA

Fukuko Yuasa   KEK, Japan
Moayid Ali Zaidi   Ostfold University College Norway, Norway
Paola Zamperlin   University of Pisa, Italy
Peter Zeile   Karlsruhe Institute of Technology, Germany
Milliam Maxime Zekeng   University of Dschang, Cameroon
  Ndadji
Nataly Zhukova   ITMO University, Russia
Ljiljana Zivkovic   Ministry of Construction, Transport and
                                       Infrastructure/Institute of Architecture and Urban
                                       and Spatial Planning of Serbia, Serbia

Contents – Part VII

International Workshop on Geomatics in Agriculture and Forestry: New Advances and Perspectives (Geo-for-Agr 2021)

12th International Symposium on Software Quality (SQ 2021)

International Workshop on Building Multi-dimensional Models for Assessing Complex Environmental Systems (MES 2021)

International Workshop on Ecosystem Services: Nature's Contribution to People in Practice. Assessment Frameworks, Models, Mapping, and Implications (NC2P 2021)

International Workshop on Geomatics for Resource Monitoring and Management (GRMM 2021)

Landslide Dam Failure Analysis Using Imaging and Ranging Sensors

Keivan Tavakoli[1], Ehsan Zadehali[1], Arsalan Malekian[1], Sara Darsi[1], Laura Longoni[2], and Marco Scaioni[3](✉) (iD)

[1] Politecnico di Milano, Lecco Campus, via G. Previati 1/c, 23900 Lecco, Italy
{keivan.tavakoli,ehsan.zadehali,arsalan.malekian,
sara.darsi}@mail.polimi.it

[2] Department of Civil and Environmental Engineering, Politecnico di Milano,
piazza L. da Vinci 32, 20133 Milano, Italy
laura.longoni@polimi.it

[3] Department of Architecture, Built Environment and Construction Engineering,
Politecnico di Milano, via Ponzio 31, 20133 Milano, Italy
marco.scaioni@polimi.it

Abstract. Landslide dam failure may be triggered by heavy rainfall or earthquake and may fail due to seepage or piping because of the asymmetric compaction. Hence, they have the potential to result in serious natural hazards. Rapid assessment of this phenomenon requires the application of investigation and monitoring techniques providing information on the ongoing failure process. To this aim, a downscaled model of a natural dam landslide was reconstructed in a simulation facility (the 'Landslide Simulator') located in the Lecco Campus of Politecnico di Milano university, Italy. The failure of the dam was induced by artificial rainfall. A sensor network was setup to record observations during the simulation experiment, including geotechnical, geophysical, and imaging/ranging sensors. This paper focuses on the analysis of deformation measurement and other changes over time, which were observed in the recorded image sequences and 3D point clouds to analyze and predict the failure of the dam. Results showed that water seepage may play a dominant role in the dam failure process, which is anticipated by a sharp increase of strain in the dam body. Furthermore, image processing techniques may help scientists to calibrate numerical models to improve their quality and reliability.

Keywords: Digital image correlation · Landslide dam failure · Monitoring · Sensor network · Terrestrial laser scanning

1 Introduction

Climate factors and/or geological processes may generate natural dams, including landslide dams, glacier dams, moraine dams as classified by Costa and Schuster [4].

Among these, landslide dams may be generated by earthquakes or heavy rainfall events [21]. Because the accumulated material that creates a landslide dam comes mainly

© Springer Nature Switzerland AG 2021
O. Gervasi et al. (Eds.): ICCSA 2021, LNCS 12955, pp. 3–17, 2021.
https://doi.org/10.1007/978-3-030-87007-2_1

from the surrounding mountain and is not artificially stabilized, it is much looser, less compact, and has lower cohesive strength than earth artificial dams. This condition makes landslide dams more susceptible to burst failure, potentially leading to catastrophic flooding in the downstream region.

A landslide dam in its natural state is made up of a heterogeneous mass of poorly consolidated earth material and has no channelized spillway or other protected outlets. Due to these reasons, landslide dams commonly fail by overtopping, followed by breaching from erosion by the overflowing stream, as reported in an exhaustive study by Costa and Schuster [4], who analyzed the failure of 73 landslide dams known up to-date (see Fig. 1). In most cases, the breach is the result of the fluvial erosion of the landslide material by head cutting generating at the toe of the dam and progressively moving upstream towards the basin. When the head cut reaches the lake, breaching occurs [18]. Smaller lakes may remain after dam failure because the breach commonly does not erode down to the original river level. In some situations, the landslide dam will not fail during first filling and overtopping. Subsequent failure may occur by surface erosion accompanying unusually large runoff periods. This was the case in the failure of the landslide dams at Lower Gros Ventre, Wyoming, and Val Pola [1–29].

Because landslide dams have not undergone systematic compaction, they may be porous, and seepage through the dams potentially could also lead to collapse by internal erosion (piping). On the downstream slope of many landslide dams, seeps have been noted. Examples is the Cerro Condor-Seneca landslide dam in Peru, which failed in 1945, probably because of "violent" seepage and piping [30].

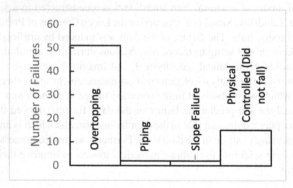

Fig. 1. Graph showing modes of failure of natural landslide dams, based on 55 failures from the literature and the authors' experience [4].

The most critical consequence of the landslide dam failure is flooding, which may result in devastating effects on the population, the urban, industrial and rural settlements, the infrastructures and the social/economic activity in the downstream area of the dam due to the discharge of water and sediments. Flooding may develop in both upstream (backwater) direction as the impoundment fills, and downstream direction because of the failure of the dam. Schuster [28] also reports some mitigation measures to reduce the risk related to flooding. These measures aim at controlling the water flow using different strategies [22].

On the other hand, especially the downstream flooding depends upon the stability of the landslide dam. An accurate monitoring of its geotechnical conditions may help understand and predict a potential collapse. Several techniques have been developed and tested for monitoring the safety condition of man-made dams, including the use of geotechnical and in-situ deformation sensors for investigating the inner part of the structure, as well as geodetic and remote sensing methods for detection of surface displacements [27]. In the case of landslide dams that have a casual nature and an unorganized structure, the establishment of permanent sensor networks may be more involved. On one side, because it would require some time before a monitoring network might become operational. On the other hand, because landslide dams may present a complex topographic surface and are not generally provided with infrastructures to access them with easy.

The use of remote sensing techniques from satellite (i.e., Differential Interferometric Synthetic Aperture Radar – DInSAR – [20], unmanned aerial vehicles (drone photogrammetry [11], and the ground surface (terrestrial laser scanning, Ground-based InSAR [13–15] platforms represent a valid solution to collect data for monitoring the safety conditions of the landslide-dam body and the basin, especially in the immediate post-disaster time. To this purpose, imaging and ranging sensors may be rapidly applied to predict possible failures and warn everyone to suffer less damage [34].

The limited availability of documented events makes quite difficult to understand the dynamics of landslide-dam failure processes in order to model them for prediction [7]. An alternative approach for investigating this problem may be found in laboratory simulations on downscaled models, which have been already exploited in landslide research [9–26]. Xu [33] showed that the development of the discharge channel and the failure of a landslide dam may be simulated in laboratory and monitored by digital cameras. Experimental results revealed that the upstream inflow and the dam size are the main factors that impact the dam break process. The peak flow may be reduced by an excavated discharge channel with trapezoidal section. The depth of the discharge channel may significantly influence the dam-break process.

In recent years, some experimental research activities have been undertaken at Lecco Campus of Politecnico di Milano (Italy) to investigate the relationship of earth slope stability and water infiltration due to rainfall [31]. This process has been physically simulated at smaller scale in a 'Landslide Simulator,' see Sect. 2.1. This facility is used in both research projects and teaching activities of the MSc course on Civil Engineering for Risk Management [25].

In this research, a landslide dam has been reproduced and infiltrated by water located in a basin in the upstream surface. Some geotechnical, geophysical and imaging/ranging sensors have been used to collect data useful to predict the failure sequence of the landslide dam. This paper is focused in particular on the analysis of imaging and ranging data.

2 Experimental Setup

2.1 The 'Landslide Simulator'

A 'Landslide Simulator' consists of a flume where a downscaled earth slope may be reconstructed and a landslide physically simulated. Within a such facility, rainfall may be induced as triggering factor, while the slope inclination may be controlled to analyze how it may influence the slope stability. The main goal of the 'Landslide Simulator' built up at Lecco Campus of Politecnico di Milano is to investigate the modes of collapse of earth slopes and the factors which may control this kind of processes: rainfall intensity, material property, discharge flow, initial moisture content, as well as gradient of the inclined topographic surface and geometrical properties of the slope [23]. The 'Landslide Simulator' is composed of two adjustable metallic surfaces, as shown in Fig. 2a. The upper part of the flume has dimensions 2 m × 0.8 m and could be lifted up to an inclination of 45°. During the experiment presented in this paper, it was lifted up to an inclination of 20°. Geogrid is supplied at the bottom to maintain friction between soil and structure, whilst the lateral sides of the flume are made of transparent plexiglass to allow the visual evaluation of the inner slope. A water distribution system is located in the upper side of the flume, from where artificial rainfall can be poured down.

The 'Landslide Simulator' has been equipped with different types of sensors, including geotechnical, geophysical and some digital cameras in different positions, while a total station (TS) and a terrestrial laser scanner (TLS) are used in front of it (see Fig. 2b). The TS is adopted for georeferencing different data sets into a common topographic reference system, while TLS is applied to collect point clouds to record the surface of the downscaled model at different times during the simulation experiment.

2.2 The Downscaled Model of a Natural Landslide Dam

In the experiment described in this paper a natural landslide dam has been simulated. The adopted material is made of medium-size sand with 26.2 kN/m³ specific weight, zero cohesion and internal friction of 35°. The dam has dimensions of 30 cm high at the crest and 110 cm in length. The downstream slope is 1/2 and the upstream slope is 3/4, which gives a steep slope at the side where failure may occur (see Fig. 2a).

2.3 The Sensor Network

Progressively, by adding water in the basin behind the dam, water infiltration has developed and led to the collapse of the embankment. During this process, a sensor network has been used to record data for monitoring purpose. Adopted sensors can be split in three groups: (1) geotechnical sensors; (2) geophysical sensors; and (3) imaging and ranging sensors. Environmental parameters have not been recorded, since they did not significantly influence the experiment. Each sensor technology is provided with its own data logger device. Some outputs may be displayed in real time during the experiment, but the main purpose is to record all observations and to process them offline.

Geotechnical sensors (1) consist of two tensiometers for measuring pore-water pressure, which have been installed in the upstream and downstream slopes (Fig. 2c).

Geophysical sensors (2) are employed for resistivity measurements. A system based on two 24-channel mini-cables assembled in-house and terminated with 48 stainless-steel 2 cm-long mini-electrodes has been tentatively installed [2]. A practical problem of cable failure resulted in the positioning of 41 cables only. These are consistent with the commercial IRIS Syscal Pro instrument (www.iris-instruments.com). The electrode configuration used in both profiles has been a Wenner array. In this way, 24 electrodes with interdistance 3 cm have been installed in Profile A (downslope), while 17 electrodes with 4.5 cm spacing in Profile B.

Group (3) of sensors consisted of two different technologies. A TLS FARO Focus 3D X330 has been used during the landslide simulation experiment to collect 3D point clouds of the dam surface. Due to its very-high scanning speed, the acquisition of a point cloud covering the full downscaled model could be accomplished in approx. 1 min. The point density of the point cloud was quite high, with an average point spacing of 2 mm. The FARO Focus 3D X330 is equipped with an internal levelling sensor able to define the z-axis of the intrinsic reference system of the adopted point cloud along the local plumb line [32]. A TS has been also adopted for georeferencing data into the topographic reference frame (Fig. 2b). Figure 3 shows that due to the presence of tensiometers and mini-cables for geoelectrical resistivity measurements, TLS data were affected by some occlusions.

A couple of digital cameras YiCameras by XiaoYi (16 Mpixels sensor, 155° view angle) have been installed for image acquisition from the top of the landslide dam. The installation of low-cost grade cameras has been motivated by the critical condition inside the flume, which may lead to damaging the imaging sensors. As visible in Fig. 2d, a grid has been painted on one side of the downscaled dam model to measure the inner deformation field by using images collected by a single-lens-reflex (SLR) camera Nikon D700 equipped with a 28 mm lens. An additional mirror-less camera Nikon V1 has been placed in front of the 'Landslide Simulator' to record time-lapse images for documenting the whole experiment. Since multiple monitoring sensors have been deployed in the downscaled dam, such as resistivity measurement electrodes and tensiometers, attention has been paid not to limit the field-of-view of the imaging sensors. Despite of this, some mini-cables for georesistivity measurement have resulted in some occlusions in the images, as shown in Fig. 3.

All adopted cameras have been used to record image sequences for documentation purpose. One of the action cameras hang in upper position and the lateral SLR camera have been used for digital image correlation (DIC) analysis, as described in next section. In this experiment, no 3D photogrammetric reconstruction has been accomplished due to the concurrent use of TLS to provide accurate 3D point clouds [23].

3 Methods

3.1 Digital Image Correlation

The evaluation of surface displacements from image sequences has been retained suitable for the prediction of slope failures [24], while the volumetric changes have been evaluated using TLS data. In particular, the image sequences obtained from time-lapse acquisition have been processed using 2D digital image correlation (2D DIC) [8]. The concept of DIC is to track surface displacements by selecting a grid of correlation windows, whose size and spacing may be selected case-by-case.

The DIC analysis has been carried out by multiple commercial and open-source software packages with the aim of comparing their results with each other. The first group comprehended VIC-2D® ver. 6 (www.correlatedsolutions.com) and GOM Correlate® (www.gom.com), which are offered in 30-days free trial-demo version that may be used

Fig. 2. (a) The landslide 'Landslide Simulator' and the sensor network with two adjustable metallic surfaces and natural landslide dam model made up of homogeneous sand; (b) different kind of sensors, cameras, and monitoring devices (in particular terrestrial laser scanning – TLS and total station – TS); (c) sensor network deployment: cameras installed over the model (top red circle), tensiometer installed in the downstream slope (down red circle), and mini-cables for resistivity measurement (red arrow); (d) grid painted on the model's side and lateral single-lens-reflex (SLR) camera (Color figure online).

by students to accomplish their experiments during classes. VIC-2D® is an innovative system implementing the DIC technique to provide strain measurements through 2D contour maps for planar surface specimens. GOM Correlate® is a software package that can be used for 2D/3D (in this research we just used GOM-3D) DIC and motion analysis in material and component testing. The open-source MATLAB® code for 2D DIC by Eberl [6] has been also applied.

After choosing the area of interest to be analyzed, the position of correlation windows is compared at different times (Fig. 4a and b). The rate of image acquisition has been setup to record one image every 30 s.

DIC outputs consisted of displacements and strains that can be visualized at different time. AutoCAD (Student Edition-2019) Autodesk® software has been used to display the final deformation fields obtained from DIC.

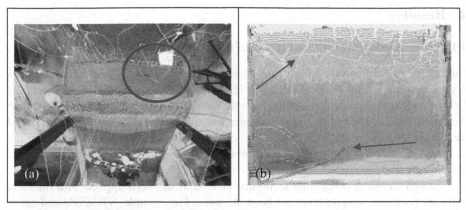

Fig. 3. (a) Data gaps due to the copresence of multiple sensors: (a) effect of the of wires in the results from 2D-DIC (digital image correlation) analysis (red circle); (b) effects of the wires (top arrow) and tensiometer (down arrow) in the point cloud obtained from TLS measurements.

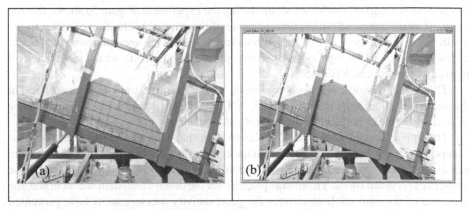

Fig. 4. Selected area of interest for DIC. Red dots show the initial positions of correlation window in the case of MATLAB code (a) and VIC-2D® (b)

3.2 Point Cloud Processing

The open-source CloudCompare software in its latest stable version (ver. 2.11.3 'Anoia') has been used for processing point clouds collected by TLS (www.cloudcompare.org). This popular software allows to directly import scans recorded by FARO Focus 3D X330, to apply pre-processing tasks (data cleaning, subsampling, filtering), to co-register/georeferencing multiple scans, and to compute changes between pairs of aligned scans [19]. About the last operation, CloudCompare offers several methods to compute distances between two point clouds (see Sect. 4.2) or volumes between them (see Sect. 4.3).

4   Results

4.1   Image Processing for Calibration of the Numerical Model

One of the most important application of image processing in laboratory experiments is to record data useful for the calibration of numerical models [8]. In this research, 2D DIC provided experimental information on the dam's deformation and the strain field on the downstream slope and the right hydrographic side of the landslide dam. The lateral image sequence from the SLR Nikon 700 camera was used for visually detecting the variation of the water level in the basin and correlate it with the water infiltration in the body of the landslide dam.

Though the same processing technique (DIC-2D) has been applied with different software packages, outputs have not been the same. For example, VIC-2D® and open-source 2D DIC code by Eberl [6] have been successfully used to process a sequence of 71 images recorded by the side SLR camera. This data set spans from the beginning of the experiment up until the appearance of first crack observed by the side SLR camera.

The application of 2D-DIC in the sequence of 71 images from the lateral camera has provided a map of Von Mises strain during the experiment. Figure 5a shows that the value of strain increased within time because of the gradual infiltration of water in the upstream side (see the area 'A1' in the red circle). Before the appearance of first crack, a new area ('A2') with high value of strain appears (see Fig. 5a), which may be useful to predict the first crack (Fig. 5b).

This visual outcome has been confirmed by the average strain values measured at the same time, which are reported in Fig. 6. This plot shows that before the appearance of first crack, the average strain has sharply skyrocketed.

The application of GOM-3D Correlate® with the same data set has not provided acceptable results, probably due to the image configuration and the distance of dam from cameras and the presence of some wires resulting in occlusions. Indeed, as far as those sequences recorded by the YiCameras placed over the downscaled dam is concerned, the presence of the mini-cable electrodes for georesistivity measurements have prevented the successful application of GOM-3D Correlate® (Fig. 7).

4.2   Point-Cloud Analysis

In this subsection, the evaluation of surface changes of the dam body obtained from the comparison of point clouds collected by TLS are illustrated. The open-source software CloudCompare has been used to this purpose. A set of three point clouds (see Fig. 8) have been considered, whose acquisition was accomplished before the experiment (Point cloud 'a'), after the opening of the first crack on the dam downstream face (Point cloud 'b'), and after the dam failure (Point cloud 'c').

First of all, point clouds have been registered together in the same reference system. This task has been carried out by cascading two methods: (1) matching bounding-box centers for the approximate alignment of two point clouds; and (2) Iterative Closest Point (ICP) registration algorithm to refine the alignment [3].

CloudCompare software implements different methods to compare point clouds in a pairwise manner [5]:

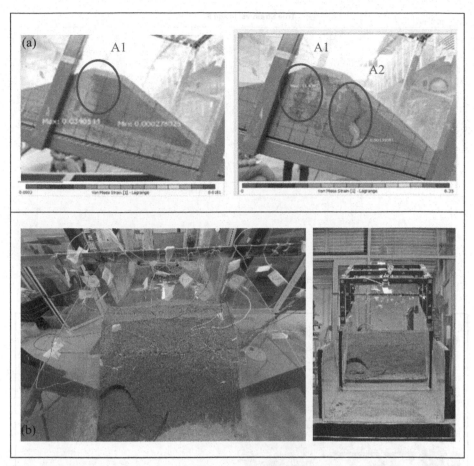

Fig. 5. Comparing the place of first crack and the position of area with high strain (a). The result of VIC-2D at time = 16:15 (left figure) and at time = 16:36, one minute before the first crack (right figure). (b) Top and front image which show the first crack at time 16:37.

- 'Cloud-to-Cloud' (C2C): distances between points from both 'reference' and 'compared' point clouds are considered;
- 'Cloud-to-Mesh' (C2M): distances between points from the 'compared' point cloud and a triangular (TIN – Triangulated Irregular Network) mesh interpolating the 'reference' point cloud are considered;
- 'Mesh-to-Mesh' (M2M): distances between triangular meshes derived from both 'reference' and 'compared' point clouds are considered; and
- 'Multiscale Model-to-Model Cloud Comparison' [17]: this algorithm computes local normals in the 'reference' point cloud and detect those points from the 'compared' point cloud that fall inside a cylinder parallel to the normal. Planes (or other regular surfaces) are estimated from both selected point sets, and the distance between these surfaces considered for measuring the distance between point clouds in that location.

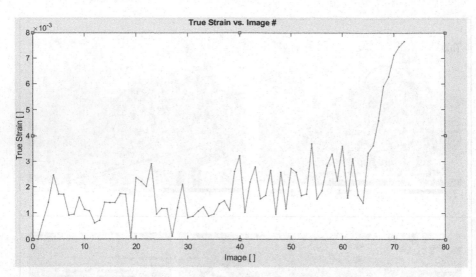

Fig. 6. Average value of measured strains obtained from DIC during the experiment.

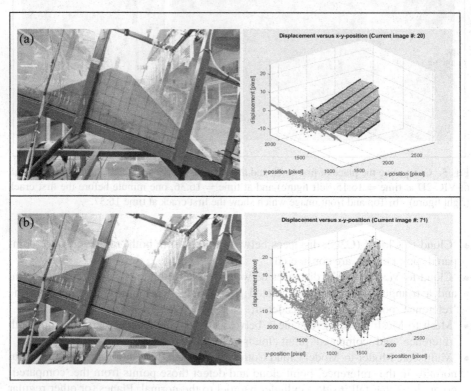

Fig. 7. (a) Displacement from Image 20 (b) Displacement from Image 71.

M3C2 algorithm also estimates the local noise and (optionally) may be input the registration error to detect a significant Level-of-Detection (LoD) for changes [10].

The selection of one method depends on the surface geometry of the object, the point resolution and noise, the direction of expected displacements (e.g., preferably in the normal or tangential directions with respect to the 'reference' point cloud), and the presence of subregions with displacements in different orientations. In addition, the 'C2C' method cannot provide signed distances since points cannot define a positive direction, such as surfaces may do.

Point clouds 'b' and 'c' have been compared to point cloud 'a' used as 'reference'. Considering the expected homogeneous direction of the surface displacements, the 'C2C' method has been applied. Results are visually mapped in Fig. 9.

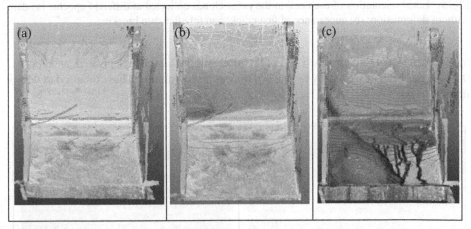

Fig. 8. Visualization of point clouds collected by using TLS at different phases of the experiment: (a) landslide dam without deformation at the beginning of the experiment; (b) appearance of first crack; and (c) after dam failure.

4.3 Computing Volume Change

After registration and comparison between point cloud surfaces, volumetric change has been analyzed to understand how much sediment has been lost during the different stages of the dam failure process. Indeed, the dam breaching resulted in the generation of a rapid mud flow able to transport a huge amount of sediment.

A function implemented in CloudCompare has been applied to compute volume between point clouds, requiring the selection of a reference surface. In this case, the bottom surface of the flume has been chosen to this purpose.

This analysis has highlighted that between situations (a) and (b) reported in Fig. 10, which corresponded to the initial undeformed condition, and the post-breaching, 5.3% of total volume has been removed from the body of the landslide dam in the meanwhile between both epochs. By comparing the sediment volume in the downstream region, it

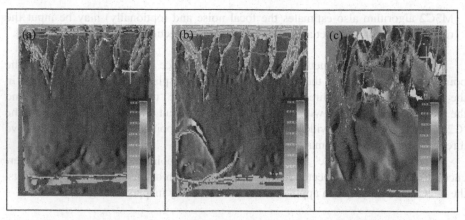

Fig. 9. Local orientation of each cell in the point clouds collected at different epochs: (a) dam without deformation; (b) appearance of first crack; and (c) after dam breaking.

has been detected that approx. 1.1% of the total volume has been deposited, and approx. 0.042% has been moved away by water. This amount of sediment has collapsed as debris flow.

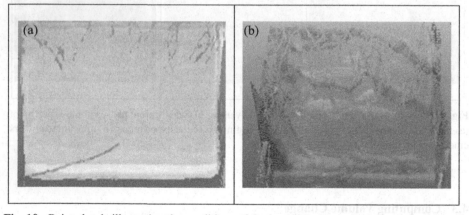

Fig. 10. Point clouds illustrating the conditions of the landslide dam at both epochs considered for computing volume change: (a) before deformation start; (b) after dam breaking.

5   Conclusion

In this paper the problem of landslide dam failure has been studied by reproducing a downscaled model in a laboratory facility ('Landslide Simulator') established on the Lecco Campus of Politecnico di Milano university, Italy. The process has been observed and monitored by adopting a sensor network including geotechnical and geophysical in-situ sensors, integrated by some imaging and ranging sensors. In particular, in this paper this last category of observations has been focused.

Imaging sensors consisted of a couple of action-grade cameras installed above the downscaled model to investigate surface displacements by means of 2D Digital Image Correlation (DIC). An additional single-lens-reflex camera has been placed to collect an image sequence of the lateral side of the landslide dam body through a transparent panel. In this way, the 2D-DIC on the inner layers of the dam in contact with the lateral glass could be investigated to detect the water seepage process, to be correlated to the level of water in the upstream basin. The results show that by using 2D-DIC, strain and displacements could be measured and the sudden acceleration of these two parameters could be useful for predicting the failure of the landslide dam. Furthermore, a relationship has been found between the quantity of water infiltrated on the upstream body of the dam and surface displacements.

A phase-shift terrestrial laser scanner for medium range data acquisition has been used for collecting 3D point clouds at significant epochs of the experiment run. By a point cloud management and processing software (CloudCompare), surface changes and volumes have been computed. By considering volume changing before and after dam failure, the volume of sediment that has flown away corresponded to approx. 28% of the whole sand volume in the landslide dam body. This sediment flow might be main reason of direct damage in a real-world failure.

Acknowledgements. The authors would like to acknowledge companies that provided free trial-demo version of software packages VIC-2D® and GOM Correlate® to allow students to accomplish their experiments. They would like also to acknowledge Eberl [6] for the open-source Matlab® code for 2D DIC and the authors of CloudCompare open-source software. Eventually, acknowledgements go to the Lecco Campus of Politecnico di Milano and to Prof. Monica Papini for the availability of the 'Landslide Simulator'.

References

1. Alden, W.C.: Landslide and flood at Gros Ventre, Wyoming. In: Tank, R. (ed.) Focus on Environmental Geology (1928)
2. Hojat, A., et al.: Quantifying seasonal 3D effects for a permanent electrical resistivity tomography monitoring system along the embankment of an irrigation canal. Near Surf. Geophys. **18**, 427–443 (2020). https://doi.org/10.1002/nsg.12110
3. Besl, P.J., McKay, N.D.: Method for registration of 3-d shapes. In: Sensor Fusion IV: Control Paradigms and Data Structures, pp. 586–560. International Society for Optics and Photonics. https://doi.org/10.1109/34.121791 (1992)
4. Costa, J.E., Schuster, R.L.: The formation and failure of natural dams. USGS Open-File, Report 87-392, https://doi.org/10.3133/ofr87392 (1987)
5. DiFrancesco, Paul-Mark., Bonneau, D., Hutchinson, D.J.: The implications of M3C2 projection diameter on 3D semi-automated Rockfall extraction from sequential terrestrial laser scanning point clouds. Remote Sens. **12**(11), 1885 (2020). https://doi.org/10.3390/rs1211 1885
6. Eberl, C.: MATLAB Central File Exchange. Digital Image Correlation and Tracking. https://www.mathworks.com/matlabcentral/fileexchange/12413-digital-image-correlation-and-tracking (2021)

7. Ermini, L., Casagli, N.: Prediction of the behaviour of landslide dams using a geomorphological dimensionless index. Earth Surf. Proc. Land. **28**, 31–47 (2003). https://doi.org/10.1002/esp.424

8. Fedele, R., Scaioni, M., Barazzetti, L., Rosati, G., Biolzi, L., Condoleo, P.: Delamination tests on CFRP-reinforced masonry pillars: optical monitoring and mechanical modelling. Cement Concr. Compos. **45**, 243–254 (2014). https://doi.org/10.1016/j.cemconcomp.2013.10.006

9. Feng, T., et al.: Measurement of surface changes in a scaled-down landslide model using high-speed stereo image sequences. Photogrammetr. Eng. Remote Sens. **82**(7), 547–557 (2016). https://doi.org/10.14358/PERS.82.7.547

10. Fey, C., Wichmann, V.: Long-range terrestrial laser scanning for geomorphological change detection in alpine terrain – handling uncertainties. Earth Surf. Proc. Land. **42**, 789–802 (2017). https://doi.org/10.1002/esp.4022

11. Giordan, D., Manconi, A., Remondino, F., Nex, F.: Use of unmanned aerial vehicles in monitoring application and management of natural hazards. Geomat. Nat. Haz. Risk **8**, 1–4 (2017). https://doi.org/10.1080/19475705.2017.1315619

12. Glazyrin, G.Y., Reyzvikh, V.N.: Computation of the flow hydrograph for the breach of landslide lakes. Soviet Hydrol. **5**, 492–496 (1968)

13. Gonzalez-Aguilera, D., Gomez-Lahoz, J., Sanchez, J.: A new approach for structural monitoring of large dams with a three-dimensional laser scanner. Sensors **8**, 5866–5883 (2008). https://doi.org/10.3390/s8095866

14. Hänsel, P., Schindewolf, M., Eltner, A., Kaiser, A., Schmidt, J.: Feasibility of high-resolution soil erosion measurements by means of rainfall simulations and SfM photogrammetry. Hydrology **3**(4), 38 (2016). https://doi.org/10.3390/hydrology3040038

15. Huang, Q., Luzi, G., Monserrat, O., Crosetto, M.: Ground-based synthetic aperture radar interferometry for deformation monitoring: a case study at Geheyan Dam, China. J. Appl. Remote Sens. **11**(3), 1 (2017). https://doi.org/10.1117/1.JRS.11.036030

16. Hungr, O., Leroueil, S., Picarelli, L.: The Varnes classification of landslide types, an update. J. Appl. Remote Sens. **11**, 167–194 (2014). https://doi.org/10.1117/1.JRS.11.036030

17. Lague, D., Brodu, N., Leroux, J.: Accurate 3D comparison of complex topography with terrestrial laser scanner: application to the Rangitikei canyon (N-Z). ISPRS J. Photogramm. Remote. Sens. **82**, 10–26 (2013). https://doi.org/10.1016/j.isprsjprs.2013.04.009

18. Lee, K.L., Duncan, J.M.: Landslide of April 25, 1974 on the Mantaro River, Peru. National Academy of Sciences, Washington, DC (1975)

19. Lindenbergh, R., Pietrzyk, P.: Change detection and deformation analysis using static and mobile laser scanning. Appl. Geomatics **7**(2), 65–74 (2015). https://doi.org/10.1007/s12518-014-0151-y

20. Osmanoğlu, B., Sunar, F., Wdowinski, S., Cabral-Cano, E.: Time series analysis of InSAR data: methods and trends. ISPRS J. Photogramm. Remote Sens. **115**, 90–102 (2016). https://doi.org/10.1016/j.isprsjprs.2015.10.003

21. Awal, R., Nakagawa, H., Baba, Y., Sharma, R.H., Ito, N.: Study on landslide dam failure by sliding. Annuals of Disas. Prev. Res. Inst, Kyoto Univ., No. 50 B (2007)

22. Sattar, A., Konagai, K.: Recent Landslide Damming Events and Their Hazard Mitigation Strategies. In: Moustafa, A. (ed.) Advances in Geotechnical Earthquake Engineering – Soil Liquefaction and Seismic Safety of Dams and Monuments. InTech (2012). https://doi.org/10.5772/28044

23. Scaioni, M., Crippa, J., Longoni, L., Papini, M., Zanzi, L.: Image-based reconstruction and analysis of dynamic scenes in a landslide simulation facility. ISPRS Annals of the Photogrammetry, Remote Sensing and Spatial Information Sciences **IV-5/W1**, 63–70 (2017). https://doi.org/10.5194/isprs-annals-IV-5-W1-63-2017

24. Scaioni, M., et al.: Some applications of 2-D and 3-D photogrammetry during laboratory experiments for hydrogeological risk assessment. Geomat. Nat. Haz. Risk 6(5–7), 473–496 (2015). https://doi.org/10.1080/19475705.2014.885090
25. Scaioni, M., Longoni, L., Zanzi, L., Ivanov, V., Papini, M.: Teaching geomatics for geohazard mitigation and management in the COVID-19 time. The International Archives of the Photogrammetry, Remote Sensing and Spatial Information Sciences **XLIV-3/W1-2020**, 131–138 (2020). https://doi.org/10.5194/isprs-archives-XLIV-3-W1-2020-131-2020
26. Scaioni, M., et al.: Analysis of spatial sensor network observations during landslide simulation experiments. Eur. J. Environ. Civ. Eng. **17**(9), 802–825 (2013). https://doi.org/10.1080/196 48189.2013.822427
27. Scaioni, M., Marsella, M., Crosetto, M., Tornatore, V., Wang, J.: Geodetic and remote-sensing sensors for dam deformation monitoring. Sensors **18**(11), 3682 (2018). https://doi.org/10. 3390/s18113682
28. Schuster, R.L.: Interaction of dams and landslides: case studies and mitigation. US Geol. Surv. (2006). https://doi.org/10.3133/PP1723
29. Schuster, R.L.: Risk-reduction measures for landslide dams. Ital. J. Eng. Geol. Environ. (2006). https://doi.org/10.4408/IJEGE.2006-01.S-01
30. Snow, D.: Landslide of Cerro Condor-Sencca, Department of Ayacucho, Peru. In: Kiersch, G.A. (ed.) Engineering Geology Case Histories Number 5, pp. 1–6. Geological Society of America, New York (1964). https://doi.org/10.1130/Eng-Case-5.1
31. Ivanov, I.V., et al.: Investigation on the role of water for the stability of shallow landslides—insights from experimental tests. Water **12**, 1203 (2020). https://doi.org/10.3390/w12041203
32. Vosselman, G., Maas, H.G.: Airborne and Terrestrial Laser Scanning. Taylor and Francis Group, Boca Raton, FL, USA (2010)
33. Fu-gang, X., Yang, Xing-guo, Zhou, Jia-wen, Hao, Ming-hui: Experimental research on the dam-break mechanisms of the Jiadanwan landslide dam triggered by the Wenchuan earthquake in China. Sci. World J. **2013**, 1–13 (2013). https://doi.org/10.1155/2013/272363
34. Doa, X.K., Kimb, M., Nguyenc, T., Jungd, K.: Analysis of landslide dam failure caused by overtopping. Procedia Eng. **154**, 990–994 (2016). https://doi.org/10.1016/j.proeng.2016. 07.587

Daily Rainfall-Runoff Modeling at Watershed Scale: A Comparison Between Physically-Based and Data-Driven Models

Federico Vilaseca[✉] [iD], Alberto Castro[iD], Christian Chreties[iD], and Angela Gorgoglione[iD]

Universidad de la República, 11300 Montevideo, Uruguay
fvilaseca@fing.edu.uy

Abstract. In the last decades, data-driven (DD) machine-learning models have been rapidly developed and widely applied to solve hydrologic problems. To explore DD approaches' capability in rainfall-runoff modeling compared to knowledge-driven models, we conducted a thorough comparison between Soil & Water Assessment Tool (SWAT) and Random Forest (RF) models. They were implemented to simulate the daily surface runoff at Santa Lucía Chico watershed in Uruguay. Aiming at making a fair comparison, the same input time series for RF and SWAT models were considered. Both approaches are able to represent the daily surface runoff adequately. The RF model shows a higher accuracy for calibration/training, while the SWAT model yields better results for validation/testing, indicating that the latter has a better generalization capacity. Furthermore, RF outperforms SWAT in terms of computational time needed for a proper calibration/training. Strategies to improve RF performance and interpretability should include feature selection, feature engineering and a more sophisticated sensitivity analysis technique.

Keywords: Hydrology · SWAT · Random Forest · Machine learning

1 Introduction

Due to heavy rainfall events, floods are among the most catastrophic natural hazards in terms of losses of lives and economic damages [1]. Therefore, to reduce natural disasters, it is of paramount importance to have accurate and reliable predictions of daily runoff discharges [2]. With the aim of dealing with pragmatic needs, such as warning alerts, a substantial amount of research effort has been invested in developing and implementing reliable hydrologic models as tools for better understanding and characterizing the complex and non-linear rainfall-runoff process at watershed scale [3–5]. Its multifaceted nature is due to the high temporal and spatial variability and its dependence on different factors: climatic conditions, land use/land cover, soil type, and physical watershed characteristics [6].

© Springer Nature Switzerland AG 2021
O. Gervasi et al. (Eds.): ICCSA 2021, LNCS 12955, pp. 18–33, 2021.
https://doi.org/10.1007/978-3-030-87007-2_2

Numerous methods have been adopted to simulate and/or predict the rainfall-runoff process. Overall, such methods can be divided into physically-based (PB) and data-driven (DD) models. The former approach, also called knowledge-driven models, simplifies the system under study and represents its inner processes by solving mathematical equations assessed from physics. In river hydraulics, these are the 1D- and 2D-hydrodynamic models, and in hydrology, these are the conceptual and distributed models [7]. The DD approach, or empirical models, involves mathematical equations evaluated not from the physical process in the catchment but from the analysis of simultaneous input and output time series [8].

During the last decades, among the PB models, the ones based in geographical information systems (GIS) couple the descriptions of hydrologic features on a spatial scale with the simulation and predictive power of models [7]. The Soil & Water Assessment Tool (SWAT) is one of these models, widely used worldwide [9–11]. It is a process-based model that embeds most hydrologic processes using the water-balance principle [9]. Its versatility ensures its multiple uses in hydrologic matters. In recent years, it has been used to assess the impact and variation of different runoff-induced processes such as erosion [12], suspended-sediment transport [13], and nutrient contribution to water bodies from non-point sources [14] at a watershed scale. Its spatially distributed scheme gives the possibility to simulate different land-use and water-management scenarios and assess their impact on water quantity and quality [15–17].

However, several researchers have stated that the PB modeling approach deals with the need of numerous input data and a higher computational time to reach a reasonable accuracy and reliability [1, 18, 19]. For this reason, recently, DD models have received significant attention from environmental engineers and researchers. Among several techniques, Random Forest (RF) is one of the most adopted since it has the advantage of being a white box method and provides feature importance based on out of the bag sampling, which allows a better understanding of the learning process [20].

Many successful applications of RF to hydrologic rainfall-runoff modeling have been reported in recent years [20–23]. However, there still exist challenges about improving the modeling performance with daily (and sub-daily) time-step, particularly in complex watersheds with highly non-linear behavior [24]. The proper selection of input variables (*feature engineering*), and their influence on model accuracy, is another point currently under discussion [25, 26].

It is clear that a rigorous analysis and comprehensive discussion are needed to understand which are the capabilities and drawbacks of both modeling approaches when applied to the same case study. In particular, it is important to extend the body of knowledge with crucial insights into the application of machine-learning techniques for modeling physical-water-related processes at watershed scale.

Based on these considerations, the main objective of this study is to provide an in-depth comparison between a PB distributed model, SWAT, and a DD model, RF, in simulating the daily rainfall-runoff process at watershed scale. In particular, the comparison will tackle the following aspects: *(i)* accuracy in simulating the physical rainfall-runoff process, *(ii)* computational cost in terms of hardware resource requirements and computational time, and *(iii)* model sensitivity (most influencing parameters).

2   Materials

2.1   Study Area

The study area selected for this work is Santa Lucía Chico watershed, with the outlet located at the closure point of Paso Severino dam (Fig. 1). It is positioned in the south-central region of Uruguay, covering an area equal to 2478 km^2. Its main urban center is Florida city (Fig. 1), and the major land covers are grassland (82.4% of total area) and agriculture (9.4%). The climate is temperate with a total annual precipitation that ranges between 1000 mm and 1500 mm and an air temperature that varies between 3 °C and 30 °C [27].

It is a watershed of national importance due to the intense agricultural activity that takes place in its territory and because it is one of the primary sources of drinking water for the country. Paso Severino dam, in activity since the '80s, was created as a reservoir to support the water treatment plant of Aguas Corrientes during dry periods.

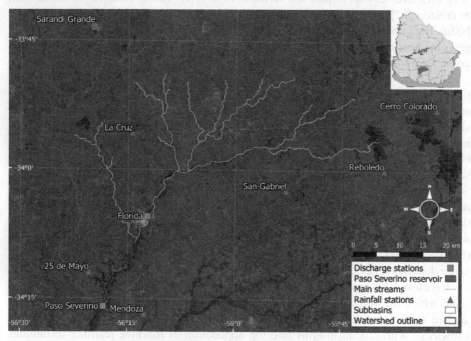

Fig. 1. Santa Lucía Chico watershed and location of the discharge stations (orange squares) and rainfall stations (green triangles). The box in the top right corner shows the location of the watershed (dark green) in Uruguay. Grid's coordinates are Latitude and Longitude in degrees. (Color figure online)

2.2 Data Description

Time Series: Mean daily streamflow was recorded at the station located in Florida city, which is owned and managed by the Uruguay National Water Board (DINAGUA). Data were available from 1/1/1980 to 6/30/2020. In addition, the mean daily discharge of Paso Severino dam was available, covering the period from 1/1/1990 to 12/31/2015. The data was provided by the State Sanitary Infrastructures (OSE), which is the state company in charge of the distribution of drinking water and dam management.

Accumulated daily rainfall records were obtained for eight pluviometric stations located around the watershed at Cerro Colorado, Florida, La Cruz, Mendoza, Reboledo, San Gabriel, Sarandí Grande, and 25 de Mayo (Fig. 1). Most of them have records from 1/1/1980 to 6/30/2020, except for Florida, the only meteorological station, where records start from 5/1/1989. The information was provided by the National Institute of Meteorology (INUMET), the Uruguayan state agency in charge of the meteorological forecasting.

Other climatic variables were also considered to compute evapotranspiration: relative humidity (RH), solar radiation (SR), maximum and minimum daily temperatures (T_{max} and T_{min}), and wind speed (WS). The time series of such variables, covering the period from 1/1/1980 to 6/30/2020 were obtained from the database of the National Institute of Agricultural Research (INIA). Records from Las Brujas meteorological station were used (Lat: -34.67, Lon: -56.34), as it was the closest to the study area.

Spatial Information: Spatial information used for this study includes land use/land cover, soil types, and topography. The three digital maps were obtained in raster format, with cell size 30 m $\times$ 30 m from the Ministry of Livestock, Agriculture, and Fisheries (MGAP) (Fig. 2).

The current national land use/land cover map corresponds to the year 2018 and has a scale of 1:50,000 [28]. The main land use, covering 82.4% of the total area, is grassland, which is mostly used for extensive livestock farming. The second important land use in terms of surface is agriculture, which occupies 9.4% of the area. Crops include oats, soy, wheat, and corn. The remaining is occupied by forestry (4.9%), dairy farming (1.2%), urban areas (0.9%), water bodies (0.7%) and wetlands (0.5%) (Fig. 2(a)).

The soil map adopted for this study uses soil classification according to a national productivity index (CONEAT) [29]. Nineteen different soil types are present, mainly loamy soils belonging to hydrological groups B and C (Fig. 2(b)).

The digital terrain model comes from a national topographical map with scale 1:50000 [30]. Watershed slopes are low, with less than 5% for 77% of the area and more than 10% for only 2% (Fig. 2(c)).

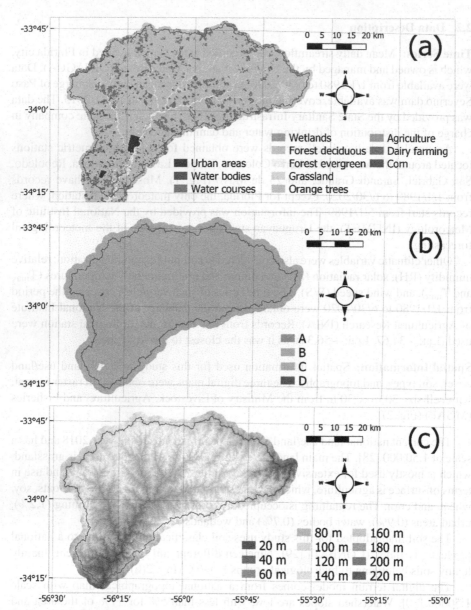

Fig. 2. (a) Land use/land cover map; (b) map of hydrological group of soils; (c) digital terrain model of Santa Lucía Chico watershed. Grid's coordinates are Latitude and Longitude in degrees. (Color figure online)

2.3 Software and Computational Equipment

To build the PB SWAT model, the QGIS based tool QSWAT was used. It consists in a graphical interphase which allows to easily generate the model input files from spatial data shapefiles. The calibration and validation process were carried out using the SWAT-CUP software [31], which is designed specifically for SWAT calibration and uncertainty analysis, enabling the use of several optimization functions. SWAT computations ran in a 3 GHz Intel i5 processor with 8 GB of memory.

The RF algorithm [32] was coded in Python 3.8 and ran on a 2 GHz Intel i3 PC with 8 GB of memory. The library *scikit-learn* [33] was used for this implementation.

3 Methods

3.1 Physically-Based Model Setup

The SWAT hydrologic model was chosen for the PB implementation. It is widely used for rainfall-runoff simulation at watershed scale and has been proven to yield accurate results for both monthly and daily time steps. Its capabilities exceed rainfall-runoff modelling, as it incorporates models for sediment and nutrient generation and transport [34].

Calculations are made in a spatially distributed scheme, considering the physical characteristics of the watershed. Its surface is divided into two scales: *i)* subbasins, which are determined based on the distribution of the channel network, and *ii)* hydrological response units (HRUs), which are a sub-division of the subbasin. HRUs are determined by the intersection of land use, soil type, and slope maps. Runoff calculations are made for each HRU, and the result is then aggregated for each subbasin and for the entire watershed. For this implementation 20 subbasins (Fig. 1) and 317 HRUs were delineated. HRUs were determined by setting a filter threshold of 5% for land use, soil type, and elevation maps.

SWAT includes different methods to perform the calculations of the hydrological processes. In this case, daily surface-runoff computation was based in the Soil Conservation Service (SCS) Curve Number (CN) method. For evapotranspiration, the Penman-Monteith option was chosen, and the Variable Storage method was selected to simulate transport from the subbasins to the watershed's outlet.

Information on land-use management was obtained from a previous SWAT model setup in the same basin [35]. Climatic input for the model includes rainfall at the eight stations with available data (Fig. 1), and relative humidity, solar radiation, maximum and minimum daily temperatures, and wind speed from INIA Las Brujas station. Paso Severino reservoir, located downstream, close to the watershed outlet, was included in the model as an uncontrolled reservoir with an average annual release rate. In this way, its output is not fixed, allowing to calibrate the model including reservoir parameters in the iteration.

The initial model setup, previous to the calibration and validation process, was carried out covering the period between 1/1/1990 and 12/31/2015 (26 years), where all the required information is available, leaving the first three years for model warmup.

3.2 Data-Driven Model Setup

The chosen algorithm for the DD model was RF. It consists in an ensemble of several classification and regression trees (CART) [32]. Each CART is trained from a random subset of features and variables taken with replacement from the full training dataset (bootstrap). After the RF is trained, the value of the output variable corresponding to a new observation is calculated for all the trees. Then the final output of the RF is the average of the output of each individual tree (RF regressor). It is proven that this approach yields models able to represent non-linear behaviors without overfitting to the training data [24].

It is regarded as a "white-box" machine-learning algorithm since information about the training process can be easily extracted. It also has the advantage of being able to provide a sensitivity score for each variable, based on the error calculated from out-of-the-bag samples during the training process [22].

To provide a fair comparison between PB and DD models, for the latter, we considered the same input variables adopted by SWAT: rainfall, relative humidity, solar radiation, maximum and minimum daily temperatures, and wind speed. The streamflow time series of Florida was also included among the inputs, and discharge at Paso Severino was defined as the model output. To provide the model with time awareness, past values of all the selected input variables for the three previous days (lagged variables) were also included. Finally, date information was incorporated through categorical input variables (year, month, week, day, day of the week, and boolean variables indicating if it is the start or the end day of the month), and elapsed date (continuous variable). Table 1 shows a summary of the input variables for the RF model.

Table 1. Summary of input variables for the RF model.

Variable	Stations	Type	Lag
Runoff	Florida	Continuous	$t-1, t-2, t-3$
Rainfall	Cerro Colorado, Florida, La Cruz, Mendoza, Reboledo, San Gabriel, Sarandí Grande y Villa 25 de Mayo	Continuous	$t-1, t-2, t-3$
Relative humidity	Las Brujas	Continuous	$t-1, t-2, t-3$
Solar radiation	Las Brujas	Continuous	$t-1, t-2, t-3$
Max. temperature	Las Brujas	Continuous	$t-1, t-2, t-3$
Min. temperature	Las Brujas	Continuous	$t-1, t-2, t-3$
Wind speed	Las Brujas	Continuous	$t-1, t-2, t-3$
Year		Categorical	
Month		Categorical	
Week		Categorical	
Day		Categorical	

(*continued*)

Table 1. (*continued*)

Variable	Stations	Type	Lag
Day of week		Categorical	
Is month end		Categorical	
Is month start		Categorical	
Elapsed date		Continuous	

3.3 Calibration, Validation and Sensitivity Analysis of the Physically-Based Model

For SWAT calibration/validation, SWAT-CUP [31] was adopted, by exploiting the SUFI-2 algorithm [36] for model optimization. A set of 17 parameters was selected based on literature recommendations [34, 36, 37] and consideration of the main physical processes that influence watershed hydrology. The optimization considered the output at both Paso Severino and Florida, using Nash-Sutcliffe efficiency (NSE) as the objective function. The process involved over seven sets of 100 model-runs each. The calibration period considered was from 1/1/1993 to 12/31/2006. After calibration, the model was validated by making one run with the best parameter ranges resulting from calibration, for the period 1/1/2010 to 12/31/2015. The period between 1/1/2007 and 12/31/2009 was not used for calibration or validation due to the high amount of missing data in the Florida runoff time series.

Model performance was evaluated using coefficient of determination (R^2), Kling-Gupta Efficiency (KGE), and root mean squared error (RMSE).

Calibration in SWAT-CUP with SUFI-2 algorithm yields a sensitivity analysis for calibration parameters. This tool was used for the first 100 iterations to identify the parameters and physical processes that have a major influence on watershed hydrology. Sensitivity is characterized by p-value and t-stat resulting from a t-test over model iterations [34]. Lower values of p-value and higher absolute values of t-stat indicate a higher sensitivity.

3.4 Training, Testing and Sensitivity Analysis of the Data-Driven Model

For the DD model, the training/validation process consisted of fitting several RFs to the data varying the hyperparameters of the algorithm to find the ones that determine the most accurate model. To this end, several instances of 5-fold cross-validation were run, combining the hyperparameter values shown in Table 2. The best model was chosen based on the resulting NSE.

Table 2. Value of hyperparameters tested during 5-fold cross-validation.

Hyperparameter	Values
min_samples_leaf	1, 5, 10
max_features	$n^{0.5}$, n
max_samples	$0.5 \times m$, $0.75 \times m$, m
n_estimators	1×10^3, 1×10^4

For a better comparison, the data period considered is the same as in the calibration of the SWAT model (from 1/1/1993 to 12/31/2006). Once the best hyperparameters for the model were determined, it was fit to the data of the calibration period and then used to predict the output for a testing period, which matched the one chosen to validate the PB model (from 1/1/2010 to 12/31/2015). The same metrics (R^2, KGE and RMSE) were used for performance evaluation.

The RF out-of-the-bag feature-importance score was used to assess the model's output sensitivity to input variables. It takes values between 0 and 1, with bigger values indicating higher sensitivity. In the Discussion section, results were interpreted from a physical point of view and compared with the resulting parameter sensitivity from the PB SWAT model.

4 Results

4.1 Simulation Accuracy

Table 3 shows comparative model performance at Paso Severino, based on the selected goodness-of-fit indicators, while Fig. 3 displays comparative time series plots of both models results and measured streamflow at Paso Severino. Two-year periods with varying hydrological conditions were chosen for the calibration and validation comparison.

Table 3. Comparison of performance measures for both models.

Model	Instance	NSE	R^2	KGE	RMSE
SWAT	Calibration	0.61	0.62	0.66	60.8
SWAT	Validation	0.47	0.56	0.67	64.0
Random Forest	Training	0.90	0.91	0.75	31.5
Random Forest	Testing	0.43	0.47	0.57	67.5

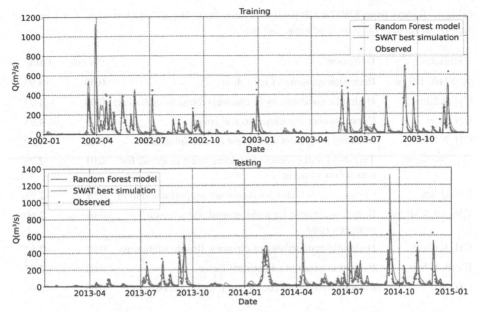

Fig. 3. Comparison of observed flow rate (green dots) with the simulations of RF (blue line) and SWAT model (orange line) at Paso Severino. Selected two-year windows for training/calibration (2002–2004) and testing/validation (2013–2015). (Color figure online)

4.2 Computational Cost

In terms of computational time, running 17 years of the SWAT model takes 70 s with the used equipment. Taking into account that over 700 runs were required for a full calibration process, the overall time is around 817 min (nearly 14 h) to obtain a working version of the model. The training process of the RF model needed 88 s to run. The hyperparameter search through cross-validation required 36 training instances correspondent to the different hyperparameter value combinations, so, in total it took 53 min to obtain the model.

4.3 Sensitivity Analysis

Parameter sensitivity of SWAT model, and feature importance from RF model are shown respectively in Table 4 and Table 5.

Table 4. Results from SWAT-CUP parameter sensitivity. Bigger absolute values of t-stat and smaller values of p-value indicate higher sensitivity.

Parameter	Definition	P-value	T-stat
ALPHA_BF.gw	Recession constant of base flow	0.00	13.95
CH_K2.rte	Hydraulic conductivity of channels (outside subbasins)	0.00	−4.77
CN2.mgt	Curve number associated to soil cover	0.00	4.75
CH_N1.sub	Manning roughness coefficient (inside subbasins)	0.00	−4.59
GWQMN.gw	Threshold water content in underground reservoir for return flow to occur	0.01	2.75
ESCO.hru	Compensation factor for soil water evapotranspiration	0.01	−2.71
GW_REVAP.gw	Return coefficient for underground water to soil saturated zone	0.01	2.60
CH_K1.sub	Hydraulic conductivity of channels (inside subbasins)	0.01	−2.52
EVRCH.bsn	Evapotranspiration adjustment factor	0.02	−2.47
CH_N2	Manning roughness coefficient (outside subbasins)	0.05	−2.01

Table 5. Feature importance resulting from Random Forest out of the bag scoring.

Variable	Location	Lag	Feature importance
Runoff	Florida		0.593
Runoff	Florida	t − 1	0.124
Runoff	Florida	t − 2	0.018
Elapsed date			0.015
Runoff	Florida	t − 3	0.014
Rainfall	La Cruz		0.009
Rainfall	Cerro Colorado		0.008
Rainfall	Sarandí Grande		0.007
Rainfall	25 de Mayo	t − 1	0.007
Wind speed	Las Brujas		0.007
Rainfall	Cerro Colorado	t − 1	0.007

5 Discussion

The DD model has a better performance for the training/calibration set than the PB, while for the testing/validation set the opposite is observed. This indicates a tendency to overfit by RF model, which is a common issue in DD modeling, while the SWAT model shows a better generalization capacity. This result illustrates the ongoing discussion between both types of models. While DD models usually show better accuracy, they lack the level of generalization usually achieved by PB models, which reduces their reliability to simulate fictitious scenarios. In this case, the RF model's accuracy is below expected for the testing set. This could be due to the complexity of the watershed, which has an irregular shape and a large reservoir near its output. Another reason could be the lack of a proper analysis for input variable selection. In this case, they were chosen with a comparative criterion, but the inclusion of excess information could have led to the introduction of noise in the training process.

According to the guidelines set by Moriasi et al. [38], a threshold value of 0.5 for NS should be considered to rate a hydrological model as satisfactory. With this reference, both presented models achieve satisfactory performance for calibration/training (NS = 0.61 for PB model and NS = 0.90 for DD model) but are unsatisfactory for validation/testing (NS = 0.47 for PB model and NS = 0.43 for DD model).

A review of the performance of other recently developed watershed-scale rainfall runoff models, taken from the cited works of this paper, shows that NS values of SWAT models range between 0.36 and 0.99, being 0.78 the average value, while R^2 varies between 0.59 and 0.99, with an average value of 0.82 [9–15]. For DD models, NS is in the range of 0.36 to 0.99, with an average of 0.79, and R^2 varies between 0.50 and 0.93, averaging 0.72 [22, 23, 25, 26]. In comparison with these results, the PB model falls below average regarding performance metrics, while the DD model has an above-average performance for calibration, but not for validation, indicating, as stated before, that there might be overfitting issues.

Another important reference to be taken into account for comparison is the work of Narbondo et al. [3], who implemented a PB lumped model in the same watershed, using the GR4J model, and obtained calibration values of 0.68 and 0.83 for NS and R^2 respectively. This implementation shows a better performance for calibration than the SWAT model, while being also below average in comparison with the other results for PB models taken from the state-of-the-art. That may indicate that the performance of PB hydrological models is limited for the case study, due to the physical characteristics of the watershed, the high temporal and spatial variability that characterizes the hydro-meteorological variables of the country, and the quality issues in the input available data. However, there is still room for improvement of the performance of both models.

The time series plots show that both models are able to adequately represent the main physical processes such as base flow and hydrogram increment and descent. This is expected from the PB model, which has such processes considered in its parametrization, but not from the DD model in which they are learned from the data themselves. In both cases, an underestimation of peak flows is observed for major floods. This behavior is a common issue in SWAT but is not reported as such for RF models.

Sensitivity analysis for the SWAT model yields that ALPHA_BF.gw is the most sensitive parameter. It takes part in the process of the contribution of groundwater to base flow, indicating the relevance of this component in the total outflow of the watershed. CH_K2.rte and CH_N1.sub are also among the most sensitive parameters, and they intervene in the concentrated transport process. Then, CN2.mgt is the SCS runoff curve number, which has relevance in initial abstraction and flow concentration speed during rainfall events.

RF feature importance shows that runoff in Florida, for the actual and previous days, has major relevance in the output at Paso Severino. This is to be expected, due to the high correlation between both variables, and highlights the importance of including past values of relevant variables as inputs, to provide the algorithm with insight on the temporality of hydrological processes. The following variables in importance are rainfall measurements at Cerro Colorado, Sarandí Grande, and 25 de Mayo. It is interesting that they surpass in importance those that are located closer to the watershed's geometrical center. Wind speed, representative of the evapotranspiration process, shows similar importance to rainfall. The extracted feature importance does not show a high potential for physical interpretation, as it resumes correlation in a single value. In that sense, maybe other more complex machine-learning sensitivity analysis techniques, such as SHAP value analysis [39] could be implemented to enrich model interpretation.

In terms of computational time, the RF model clearly outperformed the SWAT model during the training/calibration stage, even when it ran in less powerful processing hardware. This highlights a strong point of DD modeling. However, it should be noted that the overall working time to develop an adequate model is more even, from a qualitative perspective. While the calibration/training process is faster for DD models, it is compensated with the selection of input features and feature engineering, which is often case-specific and necessary to develop the best possible model. This stage is not needed for PB modelling, where input variables are determined by the selected model. In this case, the RF model was developed considerably faster than the SWAT model, because input variables were chosen to be the same in both cases. It is also worth mentioning that GIS-based distributed models such as SWAT take a considerable amount of time for model setup, due to the complexity of their parametrization. This is not the case for DD models or simpler (lumped) PB models.

6 Conclusions

A PB model, SWAT, and a DD model, RF, were successfully implemented and compared for the Santa Lucía Chico watershed in Uruguay. The comparison was carried out in terms of simulation accuracy, computational cost, and model sensitivity.

RF model showed a better performance for calibration/training, while the SWAT model outperformed RF in validation/testing, considering the selected goodness-of-fit indicators. This indicated a tendency to overfit by the RF model and a better generalization capacity for the SWAT model.

Sensitivity analysis showed that the most relevant parameters for SWAT are linked to the processes of groundwater that contribute to base flow, concentrated transport, and flow concentration during rainfall events. For the RF model, feature importance shows the relevance of present and past values of runoff at Florida, located upstream, for prediction of discharge at the watershed's outlet.

The RF model outperformed the SWAT model in terms of computational calculation time. However, this difference in required modeling time is reduced if input feature selection and engineering are taken into account.

The comparison with other similar watershed-scale rainfall-runoff models, showed that both SWAT and RF models have room for improvement. Performance and interpretability of the RF model could be improved through feature engineering on input variables and the incorporation of more complex sensitivity analysis techniques respectively. These aspects will be taken into account in our future works.

References

1. Pappenberger, F., et al.: Cascading model uncertainty from medium range weather forecasts (10 days) through a rainfall-runoff model to flood inundation predictions within the European Flood Forecasting System (EFFS). Hydrol. Earth Syst. Sci. **9**(4), 381–393 (2005)
2. Young, C.C., Liu, W.-C., Wu, M.-C.: A physically based and machine learning hybrid approach for accurate rainfall-runoff modeling during extreme typhoon events. Appl. Soft Comput. **53**, 205–216 (2017)
3. Narbondo, S., Gorgoglione, A., Crisci, M., Chreties, C.: Enhancing physical similarity approach to predict runoff in ungauged watersheds in sub-tropical regions. Water **12**, 528 (2020)
4. Gorgoglione, A., Crisci, M., Kayser, R.H., Chreties, C., Collischonn, W.: A new scenario-based framework for conflict resolution in water allocation in transboundary watersheds. Water **11**, 1174 (2019)
5. Chang, W., Chen, X.: Monthly rainfall-runoff modeling at watershed scale: a comparative study of data-driven and theory-driven approaches. Water **10**, 1116 (2018)
6. Wang, W., Ding, J.: Wavelet network model and its application to the prediction of hydrology. Nat. Sci. **1**(1), 67–71 (2003)
7. Solomatine, D., Ostfeld, A.: Data-driven modelling: some past experiences and new approaches. J. Hydroinform. **10**(1), 3–22 (2008). https://doi.org/10.2166/hydro.2008.015
8. Wu, C.L., Chau, K.L.: Rainfall-runoff modelling using artificial neural network coupled with singular spectrum analysis. J. Hydrol. **399**(3–4), 394–409 (2003)
9. Apostel, A., et al.: Simulating internal watershed processes using multiple SWAT models. Sci. Total Environ. **759**, 143920 (2021). https://doi.org/10.1016/j.scitotenv.2020.143920
10. Chen, H., Luo, Y., Potter, C., Moran, P.J., Grieneisen, M., Zhang, M.: Modeling pesticide diuron loading from the San Joaquin watershed into the Sacramento-San Joaquin Delta using SWAT. Water Res. **121**, 374–385 (2017)
11. Pang, S., Wang, X., Melching, C., Feger, Karl-Heinz.: Development and testing of a modified SWAT model based on slope condition and precipitation intensity. J. Hydrol. **588**, 125098 (2020). https://doi.org/10.1016/j.jhydrol.2020.125098
12. Zhu, X., Wang, X., Zeng, S., Zhou, W.: Simulation of runoff and sediment yield in Zhuxi watershed in Changting county of China based on SWAT model. In: IEEE International Geoscience and Remote Sensing Symposium (IGARSS), Fort Worth, Texas (2017)
13. Hallouz, F., Meddi, M., Mahé, G., Alirahmani, S., Keddar, A.: Modeling of discharge and sediment transport through the SWAT model in the basin of Harazza (Northwest of Algeria). Water Sci. **32**(1), 79–88 (2018)
14. Cheng, J., et al.: Modeling the sources and retention of phosphorus nutrient in a coastal river system in China using SWAT. J. Environ. Manag. **278**, 111556 (2021). https://doi.org/10.1016/j.jenvman.2020.111556
15. Busico, G., Colombani, N., Fronzi, D., Pellegrini, M., Tazioli, A., Mastrocicco, M.: Evaluating SWAT model performance, considering different soils data input, to quantify actual and future runoff susceptibility in a highly urbanized basin. J. Environ. Manag. **266**, 110625 (2020). https://doi.org/10.1016/j.jenvman.2020.110625

16. Marin, M., et al.: Assessing the vulnerability of water resources in the context of climate changes in a small forested watershed using SWAT: a review. Environ. Res. **184**, 109330 (2020). https://doi.org/10.1016/j.envres.2020.109330

17. Zhang, H., Wang, B., Liu, De Li., Zhang, M., Leslie, L., Qiang, Y.: Using an improved SWAT model to simulate hydrological responses to land use change: a case study of a catchment in tropical Australia. J. Hydrol. **585**, 124822 (2020). https://doi.org/10.1016/j.jhydrol.2020.124822

18. Rezaeianzadeh, M., et al.: Assessment of a conceptual hydrological model and artificial neural networks for daily outflows forecasting. Int. J. Environ. Sci. Technol. **10**(6), 1181–1192 (2013). https://doi.org/10.1007/s13762-013-0209-0

19. Ahmadi, M., Moeini, A., Ahmadi, H., Motamedvaziri, B., Zehtabijan, G.R.: Comparison of the performance of SWAT, IHACRES and artificial neural networks models in rainfall-runoff simulation (case study: Kan watershed, Iran). Phys. Chem. Earth A/B/C **111**, 65–77 (2019)

20. Li, M., Zhang, Y., Wallace, J., Campbell, E.: Estimating annual runoff in response to forest change: a statistical method based on random forest. J. Hydrol. **589**, 125168 (2020). https://doi.org/10.1016/j.jhydrol.2020.125168

21. Desai, S., Ouarda, T.: Regional hydrological frequency analysis at ungauged sites with random forest regression. J. Hydrol. **594**, 125861 (2021). https://doi.org/10.1016/j.jhydrol.2020.125861

22. Muñoz, P., Orellana-Alvear, J., Willems, P., Célleri, R.: Flash-flood forecasting in an Andean Mountain catchment—development of a step-wise methodology based on the random forest algorithm. Water **10**(11), 1519 (2018). https://doi.org/10.3390/w10111519

23. Pini, M., Scalvini, A., Liaqat, M.U., Ranzi, R., Serina, I., Mehmood, T.: Evaluation of machine learning techniques for inflow prediction in Lake Como, Italy. Procedia Comput. Sci. **176**, 918–927 (2020)

24. Schoppa, L., Disse, M., Bachmair, S.: Evaluating the performance of random forest for large-scale flood discharge simulation. J. Hydrol. **590**, 125531 (2020). https://doi.org/10.1016/j.jhydrol.2020.125531

25. Abbasi, M., Farokhnia, A., Bahreinimotlagh, M., Roozbahani, R.: A hybrid of random forest and deep auto-encoder with support vector regression methods for accuracy improvement and uncertainty reduction of long-term streamflow prediction. J. Hydrol. (2020). https://doi.org/10.1016/j.jhydrol.2020.125717

26. Adnan, R.M., Petroselli, A., Heddam, S., Guimarães, C.A., Kisi, O.: Comparison of different methodologies for rainfall-runoff modelling: machine learning vs conceptual approach. Nat. Hazards **105**, 2987–3011 (2021)

27. Gorgoglione, A., Gregorio, J., Ríos, A., Alonso, J., Chreties, C., Fossati, M.: Influence of land use/land cover on surface-water quality of Santa Lucía River, Uruguay. Sustainability **12**(11), 4692 (2020)

28. MGAP: Uruguayan Integrated Land Use/Land Cover Map. Available online: https://www.gub.uy/ministerio-ganaderia-agricultura-pesca/comunicacion/publicaciones/mapa-integrado-coberturauso-del-suelo-del-uruguay-ano-2018 (2018). Accessed 22 March 2021

29. MGAP: Soil classification with CONEAT productivity index for Uruguayan soils. Available: https://www.gub.uy/ministerio-ganaderia-agricultura-pesca/tramites-y-servicios/servicios/consulta-coneat. Accessed 24 March 2021

30. MGAP: Digital terrain map of Uruguay. Available: https://www.gub.uy/ministerio-ganaderia-agricultura-pesca/tramites-y-servicios/servicios/modelo-digital-terreno. Accessed 24 March 2021

31. Abbaspour, K., et al.: Modelling hydrology and water quality in the pre-alpine/alpine Thur watershed using SWAT. J. Hydrol. **333**(2–4), 413–430 (2007). https://doi.org/10.1016/j.jhydrol.2006.09.014

32. Brieman, L.: Random forests. Mach. Learn. **45**, 5–32 (2001)
33. Pedregosa, F., et al.: Scikit-learn: machine learning in Python. J. Mach. Learn. Res. **12**(85), 2825–2830 (2011)
34. Abbaspour, K., Vaghefi, S., Srinivasan, R.: A guideline for successful calibration and uncertainty analysis for soil and water assessment: a review of papers from the 2016 International SWAT Conference. Water **10**(1), 6 (2017). https://doi.org/10.3390/w10010006
35. Mer, F., et al.: SWAT Subcuenca Santa Lucia. https://doi.org/10.17605/OSF.IO/UQB5J (2020, October 11)
36. Abbaspour, K.C., Johnson, C.A., van Genuchten, M.: Estimating uncertain flow and transport parameters using a sequential uncertainty fitting procedure. Vadose Zone J. **3**(4), 1340–1352 (2004). https://doi.org/10.2136/vzj2004.1340
37. Abbaspour, K.C., Rouholahnejad, E., Vaghefi, S., Srinivasan, R., Yang, H., Kløve, B.: A continental-scale hydrology and water quality model for Europe: calibration and uncertainty of a high-resolution large-scale SWAT model. J. Hydrol. **524**, 733–752 (2015). https://doi.org/10.1016/j.jhydrol.2015.03.027
38. Moriasi, D.N., Arnold, J.G., Van Liew, M.W., Bingner, R.L., Harmel, R.D., Veith, T.L.: Model evaluation guidelines for systematic quantification and accuracy in watershed simulations. Trans. ASABE **50**(3), 885–900 (2007)
39. Lundberg, S.M., Lee, S.: A unified approach to interpreting model predictions. In: 31st Conference on Neural Information Processing Systems (NIPS), Long Beach, California, USA. arXiv:1705.07874 (2017)

Improving the Performance of an Operational Flood Early Warning System with the Assimilation of Satellite-Soil-Moisture Data

Santiago Narbondo⬡, Angela Gorgoglione⬡, and Christian Chreties(✉)

Universidad de la República, Julio Herrera y Reissig 565, Montevideo, Uruguay
chreties@fing.edu.uy

Abstract. Soil Moisture (SM) plays a vital role in the hydrologic cycle at watershed scale by influencing the partitioning of precipitation into infiltration, runoff, and evapotranspiration. Therefore, SM assimilation into rainfall-runoff models is considered a way to enhance their performance. Knowing if a storm event is occurring in dry or wet soil conditions means understanding if it may trigger or not a potentially hazardous flood event. Considering the scarcity of *in situ* SM records, satellite SM observations represent a reliable input for improving hydrologic model predictions. In this study, we assess whether the assimilation of satellite SM observations can enhance the water level simulations of an operational early warning system implemented in Uruguay for Durazno city. In particular, the possible improvement is evaluated taking into account the assimilation of SM retrievals from the Advanced SCATterometer (ASCAT). According to the results, an improvement higher than 100% was registered for peak level, and an enhancement higher than 30% was obtained for peak time.

Keywords: Soil Moisture · Flood prediction · Early Warning System · Remote sensing · ASCAT · Uruguay

1 Introduction

Worldwide, river floods represent one of the most frequent and most hazardous natural menaces [1]. Overall, non-structural measures, such as Early Warning Systems and land use planning policies aimed to prevent these catastrophic events, prevail over structural measures, designed, instead, to reduce the consequences of such calamity [1].

Among the non-structural measures, hydrologic and hydrodynamic modeling play a key role. In particular, in hydrologic modeling, a reasonable determination of soil moisture (SM) is essential for a good representation of the hydrologic cycle. SM represents the amount of water that is stored in the pores generated among the unsaturated soil particles. The capability to determine the spatial and temporal distribution of SM is fundamental to explain an integrated system from the hydrologic point of view. In other words, for hydrological, biological, and chemical processes, the knowledge of SM is

O. Gervasi et al. (Eds.): ICCSA 2021, LNCS 12955, pp. 34–46, 2021.
https://doi.org/10.1007/978-3-030-87007-2_3

essential for the exchange of water and energy between the surface and the atmosphere through plant evapotranspiration [2]. Furthermore, SM influences the partitioning of precipitation into infiltration, runoff, and evapotranspiration; therefore, it is a critical factor to define the flood event magnitude [3]. A storm event occurring in dry or wet soil conditions exhibits significant differences in terms of hydrologic response by triggering or not a potentially hazardous flood event [4].

Different techniques for measuring soil moisture can be classified into two main groups: *in situ* (contact-based) and remote sensing (contact-free) [5]. For *in situ* measurements, the main disadvantage is their spatial distribution. In other words, even though they allow accurate measurement of SM near the surface and at different ground depths, they are not capable of representing large-scale spatial distributions [6], e.g., watershed scale. Furthermore, *in situ* measurements are seldom assimilated in hydrologic models due to their scarcity in many parts of the world. For this reason, recently, the number of studies considering coarser SM satellite data is growing tremendously, despite its limitation of surface estimation [7].

Since the 1980s, research results about the estimation of SM from microwave sensors have been published [8,9]. In the last 25 years, the advance of remote sensing with microwaves made it possible to successfully estimate the dielectric properties of the soil surface based on its emissivity and, consequently, estimate humidity [10]. Moreover, in the last 15 years, with the launch of specific missions dedicated to measuring these parameters, the determination of satellite SM has become an increasingly used input in hydrologic modeling. In particular, missions that use low-frequency band sensors (C, X, and L bands) are capable of estimating SM. There are two types of sensors that manage to capture radiation for these uses, active and passive sensors. For the former, the synthetic aperture radars and scatterometers stand out. Among the active sensors, the Advanced Scatterometer (ASCAT) onboard MetOp (Meteorological Operational Satellite) is an instrument that measures the C band operated at a frequency of 5.255 GHz. The central objective of the ASCAT installation is to monitor speed and wind direction over the oceans, and it also has become a good option for SM measurement.

Some experiences have been developed in the assimilation of SM satellite information into hydrologic modeling. For example, in Brocca et al. [11], significant improvements were found when assimilating the daily ASCAT product of 25 km to the "Modello Idrologico SemiDistribuito in continuo" (MISDc) model in the Niccone river basin (140 km^2) in Italy. With the same satellite SM product, in Matgen et al. [12], enhancements in the implementation of the BibModel were found in an experimental basin of 10 km^2 in Luxembourg, where differences in the improvements were determined depending on the season of the year, dividing into dry, humid, and transition periods. Massari et al. [13] used the product of "Satellite Application Facility on Support to Operational Hydrology and Water Management" (H-SAF) derived from ASCAT to apply in five sub-basins of the Tibber River with areas from 140 to 2000 km^2 in Italy, improving flow prediction when assimilating surface and root-zone-SM data in the MISDc model. Patil and Ramsankaran [14] used the ASCAT product to assimilate it to the Soil and Water Assessment Tool (SWAT) hydrologic model in two watersheds of India of 1600 (Wyara river) and 5000 km^2 (Varada river), obtaining moderate improvements in flow simulation.

Uruguay is a country affected by catastrophic flood events that occur with an average frequency of two years. According to the local authorities responsible for emergency management, Durazno is the second-largest city regularly affected by floods, causing significant socio-economic damage [15]. In this context, since 2011, an early warning system (SATI) has been operating to predict extreme events and prevent socio-economical and human-life loss. Although the overall performance of the Durazno warning system is satisfactory, many situations continue to be identified where the rainfall-runoff relationship is not correctly modeled, generating in some cases an underestimation of the peak level up to two meters [16]. This is due to the fact that the humidity condition preceding the event is indirectly represented, based on the precipitation of the five days prior to the event, regardless of the soil type and use in each area of the catchment. This point is highly sensitive in the extreme-event-hydrologic model.

Based on these considerations, the main objective of this study is to assess whether the assimilation of ASCAT SM observations can enhance the water level simulation of the operational early warning system at Durazno city, Uruguay. In particular, the possible improvement will be evaluated taking into account peak level and peak time, the two most critical variables in flood event simulations.

2   Materials and Methods

2.1   Methodology

As shown in Fig. 1, the present work is based on two main blocks. The first block (in green) corresponds to the original SATI operating in Durazno city. It starts with the data acquisition process and continues with the classical hydrological SATI model coupled with the hydrodynamic model. The second block (in red) includes the acquisition of satellite-SM data and the assimilation of such data into the hydrological modeling proposed for the SATI taking into account different formulations. Finally, a comparison of the performance of the different models was carried out.

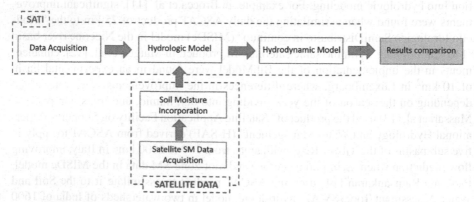

Fig. 1. Flowchart describing the methodological approach (Color figure online).

2.2 Study Area

The area considered in this study is the Yí river basin, located in the central part of Uruguay (South America). Since the city of Durazno is the most affected one by flood events, we focused our study on such a city. Therefore, we considered the Yí watershed with the outlet located at its mouth in the Negro river, including Durazno in the study area (Fig. 2). This watershed has a surface equal to 8,850 km^2 and an average slope of 4.2%. The average available water is equal to 99 mm, and the concentration time is 54 h. The primary land use of the catchment is natural pasture (grassland) used for extensive livestock (82%). Agricultural and forestry land uses also cover a significant surface of the watershed, 9% and 8% respectively.

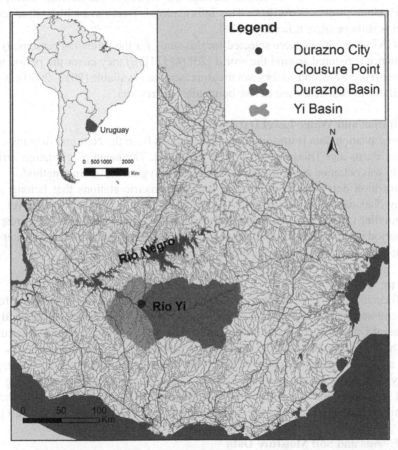

Fig. 2. The Yí river basin and location of Durazno city.

2.3 Data Collection

Satellite Data

For this work, ASCAT SM product was adopted. These observations are available from 2006 to the present. ASCAT uses an active microwave at a frequency of 5.3 GHz (C band) to determine SM content [17]. ASCAT SM provided is related to the SM content of the wettest (field capacity) and driest (wilting point) SM conditions registered [18]. For this product, the cell size is 25 km and estimates the SM for the first 5 cm. It measures the degree of saturation and the values are presented between 0 and 1. The SM is a daily ASCAT product with a few missing values. In particular, for the product used in this work, the level 3 product data were downloaded, provided by National Commission for Space Activities (CONAE) from Argentina, through the viewer of the Satellite Information for Agriculture project (ISAGRO). This information is freely available online and the mission is still operative nowadays. [19].

ASCAT observations were selected for this study for the following reasons: *i)* good performance registered around the world [20] [4] [21]; *ii)* they cover the period where flood events occurred, and water level measurements are available (2013–2020); *iii)* they are available in near-real-time (a few hours after the revisit).

Precipitation and Water-Level Data

Daily precipitation data from four telemetric stations from the National Administration of Power Plants and Transmission (UTE) were used. The mean precipitation series in the basin was obtained according to the Thiessen polygons weighting method.

Water-level data were registered at four hydrometric stations that belong to the Uruguay National Water Board (DINAGUA) and UTE (Fig. 3). The water-level series corresponding to each station has an hourly frequency in 2013–2020, which corresponds to the period in which SM-satellite data are available. Both precipitation and water-level data are freely available online for these stations [22].

Soil Type

The information of the soil type was obtained from the National Commission for the Agro-economic of the Land (CONEAT) soil map, with a scale of 1:40,000, obtained from the General Directorate of Natural Resources of the Ministry of Livestock, Agriculture, and Fisheries (RENARE-MGAP) freely available online [23]. This map provides information about the soil composition based on the percentage of organic matter, silt, sand, and clay [24]. Furthermore, the soil hydrological groups are determined according to the Natural Resources and soil Conservation Service (NRCS) classification with the Soil Recognition map of Uruguay, scale 1:1,000,000 [25] freely available on the web [26].

Flood Events and Soil Moisture Data

The most severe flood events that occurred in the study area were identified, and we selected the ones for which satellite data were available (period 2013–2020) (Table 1). It is worth noting that such events occurred throughout the entire year (during summer and winter), showing the non-stationarity of flood events. This is of particular interest because Uruguay is characterized by high hydro-climatic variability, particularly for precipitation and streamflow [27].

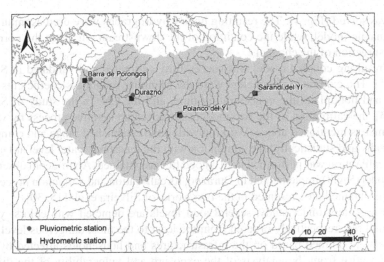

Fig. 3. Telemetric (precipitation) and hydrometric (water level) stations.

Table 1. Selected flood events.

Event name	Start-end (dd/mm/yyyy)	Peak level (m)
Sep-13	09/09/2013–21/09/2013	9.59
Feb-14	25/01/2014–06/02/2014	10.69
Apr-14	05/04/2014–17/04/2014	8.45
Jul-14	27/06/2014–09/07/2014	9.46
Sep-14	18/09/2014–20/09/2014	12.21
Nov-14	01/11/2014–07/11/2014	8.45
Dec-14	22/11/2014–28/11/2014	8.80
Dec-16	20/12/2016–01/01/2016	7.05
Aug-17	25/08/2017–15/09/2017	9.84
Dec-18	18/12/2018–20/12 /2018	8.20
Jan-19	08/01/2019–14/01/2019	11.09
Jun-19	16/06/2019–24/06/2019	12.82
Oct-19	05/10/2019–19/10/2019	10.00
Jun-20	25/06/2014–29/06/2020	9.27

2.4 Rainfall-Runoff and Hydrodynamic Model

For the SATI Durazno, the adopted model consisted of coupling the Curve Number (CN) hydrologic model [28] to the hydrodynamic model implemented in HEC-RAS [29], which solves the flow dynamics equations along the channel and the floodplain in one dimension. The Yi watershed was divided into 16 sub-basins where the hydrologic model was solved (Fig. 4). The resulting hourly hydrographs were used as input of the hydrodynamic model, while the condition of the downstream edge was the normal tie of the last section of the channel.

The resulting coupled model was successfully calibrated and validated in Silveira et al. [15]. The calibrated parameters were the Manning roughness coefficients in the channel and floodplain, the concentration time, and the CN. In the study of Silveira et al. [15], the calibration of the two models employed an iterative process by varying the parameters mentioned above. Working within the established range and comparing (numerically and statistically) the simulation with the measured water level at Durazno city, the calibration was performed until a good fit was obtained. An in-depth description of the model (SATI) implemented in Durazno, its calibration and validation process and the results obtained are presented in the two works of Silveira et al. [15, 30].

For the system under study, several alert levels are depicted with colors: yellow, orange, and red, respectively ordered from the least to the most dangerous level. Such alert levels are defined based on the infrastructures and households affected by flood events and arise from the analysis of the exposure and vulnerability of the different components of the corresponding spatial system in Durazno city. For this work, the red security alert, corresponding to 8.5 m above the local zero, was considered since it is the most dangerous one. Therefore, improving model predictions related to this alert level would lead to a significant reduction in the number of unnecessary expensive precautions taken by the government (false flood alarms). To this aim, we considered not only events that registered a water level higher than 8.5 m, but also events with water lever close to this threshold to take into account possible false alarms.

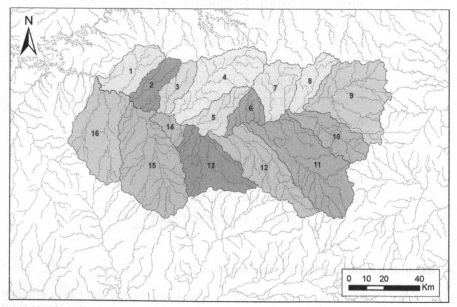

Fig. 4. Sub-basins of the Yí River considered for the coupled hydrologic-hydrodynamic model [30].

From the beginning of SATI Durazno operation, a periodic update of the model performance is carried out for new flood events. This allows us to identify the events where the model showed the best or the worst performance and, therefore, understand the robustness of the SATI Durazno [16].

For the sake of clarification, the expressions "SATI," "SATI Durazno," "current model" refer to the model described in this Section.

Assimilation of Soil Moisture

The assimilation of SM was carried out in the hydrologic model. To this aim, we briefly explain its components related to this process.

The method assumes that the infiltration has two components: one where the infiltration rate is equal to the rainfall intensity, which implies that there is no runoff, and another one where the infiltration rate decreases as a function of time. In this way, the initial abstraction (I_a) and the continued abstraction (F_a) are defined. Thus, the method assumes the relationship between these two variables and precipitation (Eq. 1).

$$\frac{P_e}{S} = \frac{P_e}{P - I_a} \tag{1}$$

P_e represents the effective precipitation [L], and P is the precipitation [L]. Applying the continuity of the event, we have Eq. 2

$$P = P_e + I_a + F_a \tag{2}$$

Defining P_e as Eq. 3.

$$P_e = \frac{(P - I_a)^2}{P - I_a + S} \tag{3}$$

At last, we have Eq. 4 and 5.

$$P_e = 0 \quad \rightarrow \quad \text{if } P \le 0.2S \tag{4}$$

$$P_e = \frac{(P - 0.2S)^2}{P + 0.8S} \quad \rightarrow \quad \text{if } P \ge 0.2S \tag{5}$$

Defining S as the maximum storage of the basin [L], knowing that this depends on the use and type of soil and the antecedent humidity conditions. This relationship can be standardized by defining the CN as expressed in Eq. 6

$$S = 25.4 \left(\frac{1000}{CN} - 10 \right) \tag{6}$$

For the CN model, the possibility of taking the NCII is proposed as an explicit function of the SM content when this measure is obtained. In this way, there is a variable CN that depends on the update of the state of humidity in the basin. This relationship is given by the following formulation (Eq. 7):

$$CN_t = CN(\theta_t) = CN(I) + (CN(III) - CN(I)) \left(\frac{\theta_t - \theta_{pwp}}{\theta_{fc} - \theta_{pwp}} \right) \tag{7}$$

θ_t represents the soil water content [L], θ_{pwp} is the wilting point [L], and θ_{fc} is the field capacity [L]. Thus, for each update of the humidity data, the CN is updated, and the effective precipitation is calculated. In this way, there is a CN dependent on humidity and variable according to the antecedent condition. Thus, from the ASCAT SM data, an SM value per sub-basin is calculated for each day of the event and the value of the CN for that day is corrected.

3 Results and Discussion

The results of the 14 events simulated (period 2013–2020) are presented in Fig. 4 and Table 2. In particular, we are showing the comparison between water-level observations and simulations at the red alert levels that corresponds to 8.5 m (red horizontal line in Fig. 5).

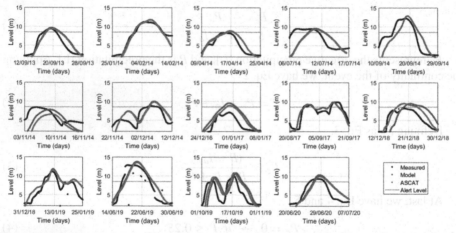

Fig. 5. Comparison between observed (black dots) and simulated limnigraphs obtained with the actual model (SATI) (blue dots) and the actual model + ASCAT (orange dots) for the 14 events (Color figure online).

From the graphs, we can see that the values of the observed peak level are very similar to the simulated ones, with a slight tendency to be closer to the ones obtained with the actual model + ASCAT. If we look at the peak time, the differences between observations and simulations seem to be even smaller. In particular, there is a very similar tendency in their ascending and descending branches, even though the values do not exactly match. This could indicate that although the time and peak level can be improved, the behavior of the measured limnigraph is not fully captured especially in the ascending branch. This can be explained because of the model limitations or by the type of events. On the one hand, the NRCS model indirectly represents the antecedent moisture state, leading to a poor representation of the ascending branch of the hydrograph. On the other hand, the type of event can affect the modeling performance since convective precipitation events can generate more abrupt flood hydrographs that are not correctly captured by the model. In Table 3 and Table 4, the averaged numerical and statistical results of the peak level and peak time comparison (observed *vs*. actual model and observed *vs*. actual model + ASCAT) respectively are shown. For this comparison, the root mean square error (RMSE), the coefficient of determination (R^2), and the absolute difference between observed and simulated values (AbsDif) were adopted.

Table 2. Values of the peak level and difference of peak time to the peak time measure.

Event name	Peak level			Peak time		
	Observations (m)	Current model (m)	Current model + ASCAT (m)	Observations date (dd/mm/yyyy hh:mm)	Current model (days)	Current model + ASCAT (days)
Sep-13	9.59	9.63	9.39	19/09/2013 03:00	−0.42	−0.46
Feb-14	10.69	11.15	11.06	04/02/2014 18:00	−2.08	−2.08
Apr-14	8.45	8.40	8.22	14/04/2014 21:00	−1.92	−2.00
Jul-14	9.46	9.88	9.70	07/07/2014 12:00	−3.33	−3.38
Sep-14	12.21	13.22	13.22	18/09/2014 15:00	−0.58	−0.58
Nov-14	8.45	8.13	7.66	05/11/2014 12:00	−3.25	−3.63
Dec-14	8.80	10.36	10.17	04/12/2014 18:00	−1.29	−1.29
Dec-16	7.05	8.93	8.14	31/12/2016 02:00	0.04	−0.08
Aug-17	9.84	10.15	10.15	17/09/2017 00:00	−0.50	−0.38
Dec-18	8.20	9.83	9.82	19/12/2018 15:00	−5.00	0.04
Jan-19	11.09	12.13	11.42	12/01/2019 00:00	−0.33	−0.38
Jun-19	12.82	14.10	13.32	18/06/2019 03:00	−2.50	−2.54
Oct-19	10.00	11.16	11.15	17/10/2019 21:00	−0.29	−0.29
Jun-20	9.27	10.63	9.68	28/06/2020 06:00	−0.33	−0.46

Table 3. Averaged numerical comparison between simulated and measured peak levels for the 14-rainfall events.

Model	RMSE (m)	R^2 (–)	AbsDif (m)
Current model	1.11	0.91	0.89
Current model + ASCAT	0.75	0.94	0.62

Table 4. Averaged numerical comparison between simulated and measured peak times for the 14-rainfall events.

Model	RMSE (days)	AbsDif (days)
Current model	2.21	1.56
Current model + ASCAT	1.80	1.26

From the average indicators, we can see a noticeable improvement in the model performance when ASCAT SM is assimilated. In particular, for the peak level, RMSE, R^2, and AbsDif respectively improved by 148%, 97%, and 144%; for peak time, 41% and 31% are the improvements registered for RMSE and AbsDif respectively. This is consistent with the results obtained in Brocca et al. [11], where, for continuous modeling, a value for the Nash-Sutcliffe (NS) efficiency improved from 0.76 to 0.86 due to the assimilation of the SM data in the entire root zone. Also, in Matgen et al. [12], improvements of 15% in the efficiency of the BibModel are obtained. In Massari et al. [13], there are improvements in the MISDc model's efficiency used of up to 30%. Furthermore, in Patil and Ramsankaran [14], the performance of the continuous hydrologic model adopted improved with the incorporation of SM from NS = 0.23 to NS = 0.42 in one of the basins considered in their study, and from NS = 0.25 to NS = 0.70 for the remaining basins of their work. Also, in Chreties et al. [16], certain events were identified in which the difference between the measured water level and the simulated water level was up to two meters. According to this work, this occurred mainly in multimodal events, in part due to the poor representation of the antecedent SM state of the basin simulated by the model. This is partially improved by assimilating the SM data, as can be seen in the August 2017 event, where differences in level and peak time are enhanced. Although some of these errors are corrected, the spatial variability of precipitation should also be explored, as well as the application of continuous models to incorporate SM.

4 Summary and Conclusions

In this study, we demonstrated that the assimilation of ASCAT SM observations substantially improved the water level simulations of the Flood Early Warning Systems currently operating in Durazno city, Uruguay.

To this aim, SM measured with the satellite was assimilated to the hydrologic part of the model. For the flood events between 2013 and 2020, it was found that the difference in absolute value between simulated and measured is 0.89 m for the current model. According to the results, the current model with the ASCAT data assimilation shows better performance in terms of both peak level and peak time, the two most critical variables in flood event simulations. In particular, an improvement higher than 100% was registered for peak level, and an enhancement higher than 30% was obtained for peak time. In other words, an average improvement of 0.27 m (AbsDif) in terms of peak level is obtained for assimilating ASCAT SM to the current model.

It is clear that the addition of remotely sensed SM to the existing operational Flood Early Warning System increases its accuracy and, therefore, its reliability. Although the amount of satellite data is still a challenge in operational systems, the potential benefit may lead to a substantial reduction of false flood alerts. This will help governments and water managers in reducing the number of unnecessary precautions and increasing the confidence to act upon these flood alerts.

Based on the current promising results, a further step to be considered to improve the model outcomes is the assimilation of other satellite products and other hydrologic models.

References

1. WMO: Manual on Flood Forecasting and Warning. WMO-No. 1072. ISBN 978-92-63-11072-5 (2011)
2. Liang, S., Wang, J.: Advanced Remote Sensing. Academic Press (2019)
3. Koster, R.D., Mahanama, S.P., Livneh, B., Lettenmaier, D.P., Reichle, R.H.: Skill in stream flow forecasts derived from large-scale estimates of soil moisture and snow. Nat. Geosci. **3**, 613–616 (2010)
4. Massari, C., Camici, S., Ciabatta, L., Brocca, L.: Exploiting satellite-based surface soil moisture for flood forecasting in the Mediterranean area: state update versus rainfall correction. Remote Sens. **10**, 292 (2018)
5. Bittelli, M.: Measuring soil water content: a review. HortTechnology **21**(3), 293–300 (2011). https://doi.org/10.21273/HORTTECH.21.3.293
6. Petropoulos, G.P., Griffiths, H., Dorigo, W., Xaver, A., Gruber, A.: Surface soil moisture estimation: significance, controls and conventional. Meas. Tech. (2013). https://doi.org/10.1201/b15610-4
7. Srivastava, P., Kerr, Y.: Satellite Soil Moisture Retrieval: Techniques and Applications (2016)
8. Wang, J., Schmugge, T.: An empirical model for the complex dielectric permittivity of soils as a function of water content. IEEE Trans. Geosci. Remote Sens. **GE-18**(4), 288–295 (1980). https://doi.org/10.1109/TGRS.1980.350304
9. Ulaby, F.T., Moore, M.K., Fung, A.K.: Microwave Remote Sensing, Active and Passive, vol. 3. Artech House, Norwood, MA (1986)
10. Mohanty, B., Cosh, M., Lakshmi, V., Montzka, C.: Soil moisture remote sensing: state-of-the-science. Vadose Zone J. **16**(1), 1–9 (2017). https://doi.org/10.2136/vzj2016.10.0105
11. Brocca, L., Moramarco, T., Melone, F., Wagner, W., Hasenauer, S., Hahn, S.: Assimilation of surface- and root-zone ASCAT soil moisture products into rainfall–runoff modeling. IEEE Trans. Geosci. Remote Sens. **50**(7), 2542–2555 (2012). https://doi.org/10.1109/TGRS.2011.2177468
12. Matgen, P., et al.: Can ASCAT-derived soil wetness indices reduce predictive uncertainty in well-gauged areas? A comparison with in situ observed soil moisture in an assimilation application. Adv. Water Resour. **44**, 49–65 (2012). https://doi.org/10.1016/j.advwatres.2012.03.022

13. Massari, C., Brocca, L., Tarpanelli, A., Moramarco, T.: Data assimilation of satellite soil moisture into rainfall-runoff modelling: a complex recipe? Remote Sens. 7(9), 11403–11433 (2015). https://doi.org/10.3390/rs70911403
14. Patil, A., Ramsankaran, R.A.A.J.: Improved streamflow simulations by coupling soil moisture analytical relationship in EnKF based hydrological data assimilation framework. Adv. Water Resour. 121, 173–188 (2018). https://doi.org/10.1016/j.advwatres.2018.08.010
15. Silveira, L., Lopez, G., Chreties, C., Crisci, M.: Steps towards an early warning model for flood forecasting in Durazno city in Uruguay. J. Flood Risk Manag. 5, 270–280 (2012)
16. Chreties, C., De Vera, A., Crisci, M., Alonso, J., Silveira, L.: Sistema de Alerta Temprana para la previsión de avenidas en la ciudad de Durazno: Evaluación de su desempeño y extensión a otras ciudades de Uruguay. In: Memorias del XXVII Congreso Latinoamericano de Hidráulica, IAHR LAD, Lima, Perú (2016)
17. Wanders, N., Karssenberg, D., de Roo, A., de Jong, S.M., Bierkens, M.F.P.: The suitability of remotely sensed soil moisture for improving operational flood forecasting. Hydrol. Earth Syst. Sci. 18, 2343–2357 (2014)
18. Wagner, W., Lemoine, G., Rott, H.: A method for estimating soil moisture from ERS scatterometer and soil data. Remote Sens. Environ. 70, 191–207 (1999)
19. ASCAT Soil Moisture product: Available: http://200.16.81.92/geoexplorer/composer/#Humedad_de_Suelo:_ASCAT_Advanced. Last accessed 10 May 2021
20. Brocca, L., et al.: River flow prediction in data scarce regions: soil moisture integrated satellite rainfall products outperform rain gauge observations in West Africa. Sci. Rep. 10, 12517 (2020)
21. Cenci, L., et al.: An evaluation of the potential of Sentinel 1 for improving flash flood predictions via soil moisture–data assimilation. Adv. Geosci. 44, 89–100 (2017). https://doi.org/10.5194/adgeo-44-89-2017
22. Precipitation and water-level data: Available: https://portal.ute.com.uy/precipitaciones-ocurridas-y-prevision-de-niveles. Last accessed 10 May 2021
23. CONEAT soil map: Available: https://www.gub.uy/ministerio-ganaderia-agricultura-pesca/tramites-y-servicios/servicios/consulta-coneat. Last accessed 10 May 2021
24. Molfino, J.H., Califra, A.: Agua Disponible de las Tierras del Uruguay. División de Suelos y Aguas, Ministerio de Ganadería Agricultura y Pesca, Uruguay (2001)
25. MGAP: Carta de Reconocimiento de Suelos del Uruguay, vol. 111. Ministerio de Ganadería, Agricultura y Pesca, Dirección de Suelos y Aguas (1979)
26. Soil recognition map of Uruguay: Available: https://www.gub.uy/ministerio-ganaderia-agricultura-pesca/politicas-y-gestion/carta-reconocimiento-suelos-del-uruguay-escala-110 00000. Last accessed 10 May 2021
27. Narbondo, S., Gorgoglione, A., Crisci, M., Chreties, C.: Enhancing physical similarity approach to predict runoff in ungauged watersheds in sub-tropical regions. Water 12, 528 (2020). https://doi.org/10.3390/w12020528
28. USDA: Part 630 Hydrology -National Engineering Handbook (NEH). Natural Resources Conservation Service, U.S. Department of Agriculture, Washington, DC (2010)
29. US Army Corps of Engineers: HEC-RAS 4.1 Hydraulics Manual. US Army, Washington (2011)
30. Silveira, L., Chreties, C., Crisci, M., Usera, G., Alonso, A.: Sistema de Alerta Temprana Para Previsión de Avenidas En La Ciudad de Durazno. Innotec (10), 56–63. https://doi.org/10.26461/innotec.v0i10 (2015)

Dimensionality Features Extraction Based-on Multi-scale Neighborhood of Multi-samples UAV Point Clouds

Mirko Saponaro[✉] [iD]

Polytechnic University of Bari, Via Orabona 4, 70125 Bari, Italy
mirko.saponaro@poliba.it

Abstract. The growth in quantity and quality of collected point clouds has made inevitable to find methods of algorithmic interpretation of these data for any engineering analysis. To date, the most critical steps are still usually performed manually. The fully automated analysis of point clouds acquired from the most arising technologies, such as those generated by photogrammetry obtained from the increasing use of Unmanned Aerial Vehicles (UAVs), has therefore become a topic of great involvement. In order to describe the local geometry at a given point, the spatial distribution of the others 3D points within a local neighborhood was typically taken into account. From the analysis of the covariance matrix, it was thus possible to extract the geometric characteristics useful for identifying any linear, planar or scattering behaviors of the digital reconstruction. Hence, a suitable scalar dimensionality approach had to be planned to identify all the interpretable geometric behaviors of the points at various research scales. Subsequently, one can opt for a single representative scale or a multi-scale approach that serves the purpose of the work. The proposal of this work was to analyze the behavior of the scalar dimensional approach but varying the average Ground Sample Distance (GSD) values of UAV imagery of the same scenario. Encouraging results were obtained expressing how the scenario reproduces the same dimensional behavior irrespective of the acquisition conditions and an empirical finding between the scale parameter r and just the geometric resolution value.

Keywords: Covariance features · Neighborhood scale · Point-based · UAV

1 Introduction

The development of techniques and technologies to collect huge point clouds has made unavoidable to find methodologies oriented to an automated interpretation of these data for any engineering application. As pointed out by Weidner et al. [1], this presents an interesting challenge as today the most critical managing steps are still usually performed manually. Manual analysis of these enormous masses of points is clearly time-consuming and laborious and could never guarantee explicit and exclusive information, thus highlighting the need for efficiently techniques able to identify objective features [2]. Blomley et al. [3] stated that being able to extract reliable geometric features from these point

© Springer Nature Switzerland AG 2021
O. Gervasi et al. (Eds.): ICCSA 2021, LNCS 12955, pp. 47–62, 2021.
https://doi.org/10.1007/978-3-030-87007-2_4

clouds is crucial to exploit the full potential of these data, e.g., for structural analysis or object detection. Indeed, starting from the characteristics of the points distribution such as smoothness, regularity and vertical dispersion, these encourage the distinction among the points of the surface or object type they represent [4]. The fully automated analysis of point clouds acquired from the most established technologies, such as those recorded by laser scanners (i.e., Terrestrial or Airborne LS) [5, 6], or also obtained by photogrammetry, in particular those taken from the increasing use of Unmanned Aerial Vehicles (UAVs), has therefore become a topic of great involvement [7–9].

In order to describe the local 3D geometry at a given point, the spatial distribution of the others points within a reasonable local neighborhood is typically taken into account. Hence, identifying the best neighborhood for each point was a main issue for a large variety of works in literature: data down-sampling, template fitting, feature detection and computation, interpolation, registration, segmentation, filtering, or modelling purposes [10–13]. Precisely, an optimal neighborhood may be defined as the largest set of spatially close points that belong to the same object, then able to express some 1D, 2D or 3D features [8, 12]. For example, Weinmann et al. [14] considered the optimal neighborhood of each individual 3D point focusing on the extraction of relevant, but no redundant, features able to increase their distinctiveness. But dealing with the complexity of 3D scenes, caused on the one hand by irregular sampling and on the other hand by the heterogeneity of the objects, involves a considerable computational capacity and detects a variety of available geometric features, often also marginal or poorly weighted. Moreover, the parameterization of the neighborhood is still typically selected with respect to the a priori empirical or heuristic knowledge of the study environment. Several works therefore focused their attention on the improvement of automated interpretation methodologies capable of targeting the learning of certain useful features [14].

Building on established image-based techniques, the idea of analyzing invariant moments has been found to be valuable for observing the geometric properties of point clouds. Indeed, from the analysis of the covariance matrix or the structure tensor calculated within the local neighborhood, one proceeds to the extraction of their geometric characteristics [3]. The obtained eigenvalues were understood as neighborhood features providing additional information useful to discriminate planes, edges, corners, lines and volumes. Trivially, these features describe thus the local spatial distribution of 3D points [6]. In addition, the use of such features ensures their feasibility for heterogeneous and unstructured data and at the same time no a-priori knowledge of the scene was required [12].

The local neighborhood for each point can be defined by a spherical or cylindrical neighborhood with a fixed radius r [15]. Alternatively, it could be identified by setting a fixed number $k \in \mathbb{N}$ of neighbors closest to the point of interest. Regardless of the definition mode, both are based on a scaling parameter that is either a radius or k, which is commonly selected to be identical for all points in the cloud but, ideally, it would be optimal to obtain a variable scaling parameter dependent on the local 3D structure as well as the local point density. Calculating these features at multiple scales results in higher accuracy than for only one scale because objects may have differing properties at different scales of analysis [3]. However, multiscale approaches result in larger feature spaces where it will be necessary to use feature selection schemes appropriate for the scope of work and at the same time reduce the computational load. Deriving features at a single scale, on the other hand, means that one scale must be considered to describe some features better than others [7]. Therefore, a suitable scalar dimensionality approach can be used to define a targeted geometric behavior of the points. Understandably, the dimensionality of an object also depends on the spatial scale at which it is examined. An object that appears planar up close (at a smaller spatial scale) may be three-dimensional at a larger spatial scale. For example, in Kim et al. [4] at varying spatial scales, considering a histogrammetric distribution of features, the selection of the most useful features was done by observing in which attributes the mean distance between the averages exceeds the mean standard deviation [4]. The creation of a representative inventory is also a function of the size of the smallest event that can be detected. In particular, Williams et al. [16] suggested that the minimum detectable movement, or Level of Detection (LoD), is a key parameter firstly in delineating model dimensionality and subsequently in calculating erosion or rockfall volumes. This involves masking regions of change that exceed a strict threshold at the LoD.

Lastly, in the geometric analysis of point clouds, each individual observation can only be interpreted on the basis of its relations to other elements and its probability of belonging to a certain class of objects [12]. Each class of objects actually shows a characteristic coherence at different spatial scales, so it is crucial to establish invariable features that can represent structural information that is not observable at other scales. Consequently, a suitable scale may depend on the type of the chosen feature. Blomley et al. [3] therefore deduced that when pursuing a covariance approach, the same homogeneous environment at a smaller scale can define more distinctive features, while the distribution of shapes may be significant at a larger scale.

The proposal of this work was to analyze the behavior of the scalar dimensional approach when varying the geometric resolution of point cloud acquisition from UAVs of the same scenario. Given the above considerations, it was key to verify if the deducible spatial characteristics (1D, 2D and 3D) of the same scenario can be considered comparable when varying the acquisition strategy, considering the other conditions fixed.

In Sect. 2, the properties of the covariance matrix and the potential of the geo-metric characteristics that can be deduced as the neighborhood parameter varies were explained. Given the conceptualization of the approach, the same section then described the operations performed on the point clouds. Finally, the results were extensively discussed in the following Sect. 3, indicating the learned remarks in the Conclusion.

2 Methods

2.1 Focus on the Surveyed Area and Field Activities

A portion of the waterfront of about 400 m located on the southern coast of Bari (Apulia Region, Italy) was selected as the investigation site [17]. The area (Fig. 1) has been explored in previous studies because of the complexity of the hydrogeological phenomena to which it is subject, causing advanced instability [18]. An exhaustive description of the latter is presented in Capolupo et al. [19].

A monthly flight campaign was planned between 2018 and 2019, excluding the summer period due to the zonal limits imposed by national regulations. In this research work, two missions performed on 15 and 16 March 2019 were considered, characterized by two different flight altitudes of 70 m and 100 m Above Ground Level (AGL).

Fig. 1. Study area investigated for the tests in this work (Reference System: RDN2008/UTM zone 33N (NE) (EPSG:6708)). The yellow crosses, with red interiors, represent the distribution of targets measured using GNSS technologies (Color figure online).

The flights were performed with a DJI Inspire 1 v.2 prosumer, equipped with a DJI Zenmuse X3 (focal length 3.61 mm, pixel size 1.56 m, 12.4 MP) on a 3-axis gimbal. The flight plan included for both missions a cruising speed (4.0 m/s) and a front and side overlap of 85% and 75%. The camera was oriented nadirally and the acquisition set in stop-go mode in order to reduce the collection of blurred images due to the settling movements of the vehicle. The position of the UAV was recorded by a low-cost GNSS/INS positioning receiver and saved in the metadata of each image.

Framing the same area but at two different elevations resulted in two Ground Sample Distance (GSD) values of 0.03 m/pix and 0.043 m/pix, respectively. A total of 77 images were collected at 100 m AGL, while 89 images were collected for the flight at 70 m AGL.

The acquisitions described were accompanied by a Global Navigation Satellite System (GNSS) survey campaign of 30 permanent natural targets of appropriate size and color with respect to the characteristics of the images collected (Fig. 1). The measurements were carried out using Leica Viva CS10/GS10 GNSS technology in network Real-Time Kinematic (nRTK) mode based on the Leica SmartNet Italpos network with a final 3D accuracy of 0.02 m. The reference system was RDN2008/UTM zone 33N (NE) (EPSG: 6708).

2.2 Data Processing Planning

The photogrammetric processing of the acquired data was articulated in Agisoft Metashape (v.1.5.2) using an ordinary Intel(R) Core (TM) i7-3970X CPU 3.50GHz hardware, with 16GB of RAM and an NVIDIA GeForce GTX 650 graphics card. The parameterization used in the processes is summarized in Table 1. The entire workflow adopts the technical findings validated in the extensive literature on currently accepted methodologies for consistent photogrammetric modelling [20].

Table 1. Summary sheet of the parameterization used in Agisoft Metashape processing.

AGISOFT METASHAPE PARAMETRIZATION	
REFERENCE SETTINGS	
Coordinate system	RDN2008/UTM zone 33N (NE) (EPSG:6708)
Initial Principal Point Position (xp, yp)	(0, 0)
Camera positioning accuracy	3 m
Camera accuracy, attitude	10 deg
Marker accuracy (object space)	0.02 m
Marker accuracy (image space)	0.5 pixel
GPS/INS offset vector value	$\Delta x = 0.005 \pm 0.005m$ $\Delta y = 0.100 \pm 0.01m$ $\Delta z = 0.250 \pm 0.01m$
PROCESSES PLANNED	
Estimate image quality	100 m [max, min]: 0.919395, 0.808475 70 [max, min]: 0.907735, 0.843747
Set brightness	100 m [Brightness, Contrast]: 80, 140 (%) 70 m [Brightness, Contrast]: 80, 140 (%)
Alignment cameras	Accuracy: High Generic Preselection: Yes Reference Preselection: Yes Key Point Limit: 0 Tie Point Limit: 0 Adaptive Camera Model Fitting: No
Gradual Selection	Reconstruction Uncertainty: 10 Projection Accuracy: 3 Reprojection Error: 0.4
Optimize cameras	K3, K4, P3, P4: No
Build dense cloud	Quality: High Depth Filtering: Aggressive

Given the optimal results achieved in Capolupo et al. [19], the 30 targets in the two datasets were marked, and 14 Ground Control Points (GCPs) were chosen for model georeferencing. The remaining part of the markers were then considered as Check Points (CPs) of the models.

2.3 Neighborhood Recovery and Features Extraction

Most current approaches to finding features of 3D geometries are based on features derived from the local covariance matrix representing the invariant second-order moments within the point positions [3]. In particular, it is possible to extract from the covariance matrix three eigenvalues $(\lambda_1 > \lambda_2 > \lambda_3)$ through the statistical Principal Component Analysis (PCA). These represent the local 3D structure and each one measure the variation of the local point set along the direction of the corresponding eigenvector. Briefly, the PCA defines the principal directions in three orthogonal vectors and the respective point distribution variation magnitude around the center of the defined neighborhood, named centroid, in the eigenvalues [12]. The proportions of variance explained by each eigenvalue are defined as:

$$PCA(1) = \lambda_1/(\lambda_1 + \lambda_2 + \lambda_3) \tag{1}$$

$$PCA(2) = \lambda_2/(\lambda_1 + \lambda_2 + \lambda_3) \tag{2}$$

$$PCA(3) = \lambda_3/(\lambda_1 + \lambda_2 + \lambda_3) \tag{3}$$

As explained in Fig. 3 in Brodu et al. [11], the triangular domain of all possible proportions represents the dimensionality cases of the model as the weight of each eigenvalue varies. Given the constraint:

$$PCA(1) + PCA(2) + PCA(3) = 1 \tag{4}$$

when only a single eigenvalue λ_1 accounts for the total variance in the neighborhood sphere the points are oriented along one dimension. Alternatively, when two eigenvalues were necessary to account for the variance but the third one does not contribute the cloud is locally mostly planar. Conversely, a fully 3D cloud is one where all three eigenvalues have the same magnitude. The proportions of eigenvalues thus define a measure of how much 1D, 2D or 3D the cloud appears locally at a given scale.

Moreover, the combination of these eigenvalues generates some shape descriptors, designed to point out a prevalent linear, planar or scatter behavior of the neighborhood, otherwise other measures such as omnivariance, anisotropy and eigenentropy. These local 3D shape features are called eigen-features.

The feature of linearity is used to investigate whether a set of points can be modeled by a 3D line [21]:

$$L = (\lambda_1 - \lambda_2)/\lambda_1 \tag{5}$$

The planarity feature is used to describe the smoothness of a surface:

$$P = (\lambda_2 - \lambda_3)/\lambda_1 \tag{6}$$

The feature of sphericity investigates the scattering of a neighborhood:

$$S = \lambda_3/\lambda_1 \tag{7}$$

Following, the feature of omnivariance describes how a neighborhood of points spread inhomogeneously across a 3D volume:

$$O = (\lambda_1 * \lambda_2 * \lambda_3)^{\frac{1}{3}} \tag{8}$$

Anisotropy is a measure which is higher if the eigenvectors differ a lot. These measures have the potential to discriminate between orientated and non-orientated objects, as oriented objects have a higher anisotropy [22]:

$$A = (\lambda_1 - \lambda_3)/\lambda_1 \tag{9}$$

Lastly, the feature of eigenentropy provides a measure of the order or disorder of 3D points within the covariance ellipsoid [14]:

$$E_\lambda = -(\lambda_1 * \ln\lambda_1 - \lambda_2 * \ln\lambda_2 + \lambda_3 * \ln\lambda_3) \tag{10}$$

Eigenentropy values tending towards 1 identify disturbances within the ellipsoid, thus highlighting the presence of points with 3D behavior. Vice versa, values up to 0 detect an increasing order, passing from planar to linear dimensionality.

One of the approaches proposed by Weinmann et al. [14] for the identification of a suitable scaling parameter for the dimensional analysis of models analyses the change in curvature by means of the PCA (3) value. The curvature using PCA (3) is then calculated as seen in Eq. (3) from the ratio of the minimum eigenvalue to the sum of the eigenvalues. This ratio approximates the change in curvature in the vicinity of a point. Given the fact that the accreted jumps indicate strong deviations in the normal directions, a suitable scaling parameter value would identify concordant values of PCA (3) and thus be able to describe various consistent levels of curvature.

The most common approach to defining a local neighborhood depends on a user-defined radial distance r or a fixed value k of neighborhood points. In this research work, the radius approach was adopted. The radius defines a spherical or cylindrical volume within which the neighborhood of points is incorporated. The radius must be large enough to incorporate enough points to calculate meaningful statistics, but not so large as to lose spatial detail [4]. The expressible geometric features will therefore be influenced by the search radius, which determines the size of the neighborhood over which these features will be calculated. In addition, autocorrelation and other features might only be observed at some scales less than at others [3]. In many works of literature therefore, authors propose different approaches in order to identify the most suitable research parameter r for different purposes, already mentioned in the Sect. 1. It is the nature of second-order moments that the distance of an element from the mean contributes quadratically and thus elements in the vicinity are less important than those further away [3]. Since principal component analysis is an orthogonal transformation and therefore unitary, the resulting eigenvalues are sensitive to the original scale. It remains to be shown whether this optimal neighborhood dimension for covariance characteristics corresponds to the characteristic scale of any structure. The scale-based dimensional approach finds, for each 3D point, the optimal search radius by computing the neighborhood at different and increasing radii (between a minimum and a maximum value) and selecting the one that minimizes a measure of unpredictability of the set of points.

The dense point clouds obtained in the previous step were then imported in the open-source software CloudCompare. Given the GSD values (m/pix) described in Sect. 2.1, the following features were computed using the Computes Geometries tool:

- 1st, 2nd and 3rd Eigenvalues (λ_1, λ_2, λ_3)
- PCA (1), PCA (2) and PCA (3)
- Anisotropy and Omnivariance
- Linearity, Planarity and Sphericity
- Eigenentropy.

These were computed for ten values of the scale-parameter r of sphere, varying the latter from a minimum equal to the value of the GSD and from time to time multiplying it up to 10. Table 2 summarizes the values of r for the two cases under study. The behaviors of these characteristics were analyzed and finally the most significant dimensionality behaviors were identified by observing the Eigenentropy trends.

Table 2. Summary of the used scale parameters r.

r	[70 m]	[100 m]
GSD * 1	0.030 m	0.043 m
GSD * 2	0.060 m	0.086 m
GSD * 3	0.090 m	0.129 m
GSD * 4	0.120 m	0.172 m
GSD * 5	0.150 m	0.215 m
GSD * 6	0.180 m	0.258 m
GSD * 7	0.210 m	0.301 m
GSD * 8	0.240 m	0.344 m
GSD * 9	0.270 m	0.387 m
GSD * 10	0.300 m	0.43 m

3   Results and Discussion

3.1   Eigenvalues Behaviors

The recorded trends of the eigenvalues as the scale parameter r changes in the two dense point clouds obtained from images acquired at 70 m and 100 m AGL were analyzed below.

Figure 2 shows how, in general, the behaviors recorded for the two cases were completely comparable even if the scale parameter r varies. In fact, the values of the eigenvalues undergone a reproportioning, approximately double, passing from the [70 m] to the [100 m] case. This suggests that the magnitude of the eigenvalues was proportional

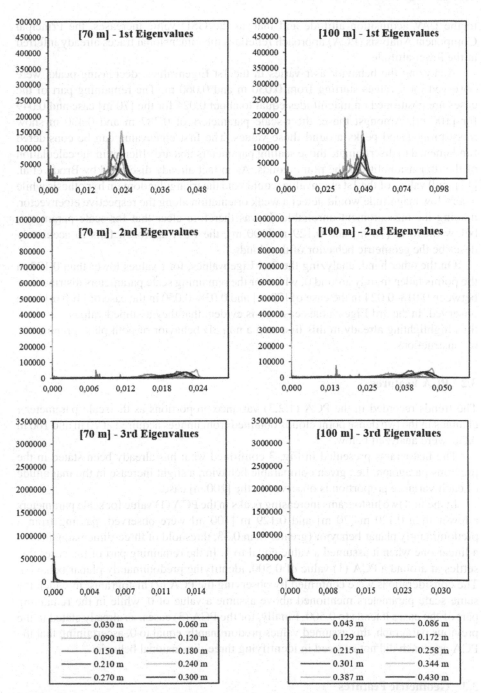

Fig. 2. Histograms of the three eigenvalues as the scale parameter r changes. The abscissae show the values of the eigenvalues, the ordinates the number of points in each class. Below is the legend with the colour scale for each scale parameter r.

to the UAV acquisition altitude and that, as the GSD value increases, the Principal Component Analysis (PCA) approach reiterates the dimensional traces already inferred at the lower altitude.

Analyzing the behavior as r varies in the 1st Eigenvalues, decreasing peaks were observed for r values starting from 0.030 m and 0.060 m. The remaining part of the cases are positioned on magnitudes equal to about 0.024 for the [70 m] case and 0.049 for [100 m]. Amongst these, the r-scale parameters of 0.387 m and 0.430 m show more pronounced peaks around those values. The first eigenvalue can be considered fundamental to discriminate those scaling parameters that are efficient in the calculation of the dimensionality of the point clouds. As in fact already discussed by Brodu et al. [11], null values of the 1st eigenvalue would void the triangular domain hypothesis while a very low magnitude would detect a weak orientation along the respective eigenvector, making the measurement unreliable. It was therefore clear that for scale parameters below 0.090 m [70 m] and 0.129 m [100 m], the PCA approach fails to accurately describe the geometric behavior of the clouds.

On the other hand, analyzing the 2nd Eigenvalues, for r values lower than 0.172 m the points fallen mainly around 0, while for the remaining scale parameters distributions between 0.018–0.024 in the case of [70 m] and 0.038–0.050 in the case of [100 m] were observed. In the 3rd Eigenvalues cases, it is evident that they assumed values around 0, thus highlighting already in this first step a non 3D behavior of both photogrammetric reconstructions.

3.2 PCA Features

The trends recorded in the PCA (1,2,3) variance proportions as the scale parameter r changes in the two dense point clouds obtained from images acquired at 70 m and 100 m AGL were analyzed below.

The histograms presented in Fig. 3 confirmed what has already been stated in the previous paragraph, i.e., given comparable behavior, a slight increase in the magnitude of each variance proportion is observed in the [100 m] case.

In the first two histograms increasing peaks in the PCA (1) value for scale parameters r lower than 0.120 m [70 m] and 0.129 m [100 m] were observed, passing from a predominantly planar behavior (greater than 0.33, threshold of three-dimensionality) to a linear one when it assumed a value equal to 1. In the remaining part of the cases this settles at around a PCA (1) value of 0.500, identifying predominantly planar behavior. The considerations were confirmed by observing the PCA (2) histograms, in which the same scale parameters mentioned above assume a value of 0, while in the remaining part of the cases it tends to 0.500. Finally, for the PCA (3) cases, as already stated in the previous paragraph, this assumed values predominantly equal to 0, ascertaining that the PCA approach did not succeed in identifying three-dimensional behavior.

3.3 Geometric Features

Figure 4 analyzed the trends of the Geometric Features Anisotropy and Omnivariance as the scale parameter r changes in the two dense point clouds obtained from images acquired at 70 m and 100 m AGL.

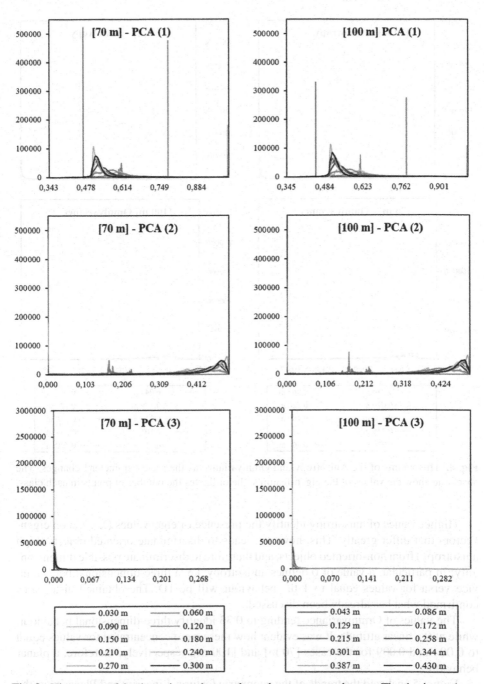

Fig. 3. Histograms of the three eigenvalues as the scale parameter r changes. The abscissae show the values of the eigenvalues, the ordinates the number of points in each class.

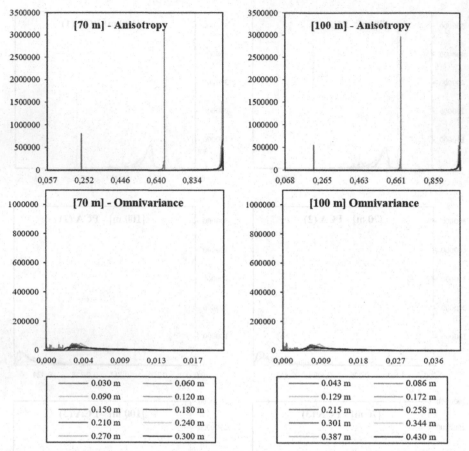

Fig. 4. Histograms of the Anisotropy and Omnivariance as the scale parameter r changes. The abscissae show the values of the eigen-features, the ordinates the number of points in each class.

Higher values of anisotropy identify the presence of eigenvalues (λ_1, λ_3) on eigenvectors that differ greatly. This, however, leads to discriminate oriented objects (high anisotropy) from non-oriented objects, and therefore to discriminate possible dimensionality: in particular, a value of 0 defines an isotropy, i.e. a three-dimensional behaviour, vice versa for values equal to 1 the behaviour will be 1D. The obtained histograms confirmed what has already been discussed.

The values of Ominivariance tending to 0.33 identify three-dimensional behaviour, while at 0 a linear attitude. It was evident how these were concentrated for values equal to 0.004 and 0.009 for the cases [70 m] and [100 m], respectively: therefore, a planar behaviour.

Figure 5 analyzed the trends of the geometric features Linearity and Planarity as the scale parameter r varies in the two dense point clouds obtained from images acquired at 70 m and 100 m AGL. It has been chosen not to propose the histograms concerning

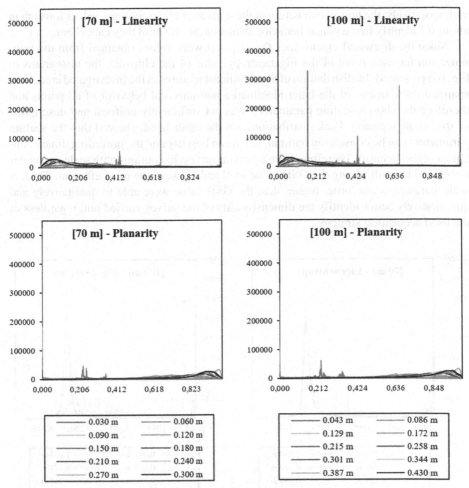

Fig. 5. Histograms of linearity and planarity as the scale parameter r changes. The abscissae show the values of the eigen-features, the ordinates the number of points in each class.

Sphericity as they were not significant by proposing values equal to 0, not demonstrating anything else than what has already been discussed.

The histograms complete the discussion examined so far. Since there were no significant three-dimensional behaviors, the two represented geometric characteristics were almost complementary.

3.4 Eigenentropy Analysis

The entropy function provides for each reconstructed 3D point a measure of the probability of belonging to a part of the scene with a specific geometric behavior. High entropy values, i.e., tending to 1, indicate a disordered geometric behavior of the neighboring point and, most likely, the non-planar nature of these points. On the contrary, values lower than about 0.7 identify first a planar behavior, then a linear one until they cancel out.

Since the discussed eigenvalues (λ_1, λ_2, λ_3) were values obtained from the minimization for each point of the Eigenentropy value of the ellipsoid, the histograms in Fig. 6 represented the distribution of the significant features in the investigated area. Very spanned distributions of the latter identified a non-univocal behavior of all points and therefore the chosen scaling parameter r was not sufficiently uniform and descriptive of the whole scenario. Peak distributions, on the other hand, showed that the scaling parameter r can be considered optimal, i.e., it can best explain the prevailing dimensionalities of the scenario. Therefore, from a general survey, histograms with scale parameter r obtained by multiplying the GSD value by 9 and 10 were the most efficient. Thus, r-scale parameters one order higher than the GSD value were able to qualitatively and quantitatively better identify the dimensionality of the survey carried out, regardless of the used acquisition strategy.

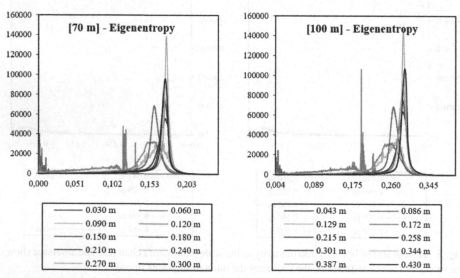

Fig. 6. Histograms of eigenentropy as the scale parameter r changes. The abscissae show the values of the eigen-feature, the ordinates the number of points in each class.

4   Conclusion

The increase of high-density and accurate UAV-based point clouds has made challenging to structure fully automated methods for feature-interpretation of these data for various applications, i.e., segmentation, classification, filtering and dimensional feature learning for cloud-to-cloud analysis. In order to describe the local geometry at a given point, the spatial distribution of the others 3D points within a local neighborhood is typically taken into account. From the covariance matrix it is possible to extract the geometric characteristics useful for identifying any linear, planar or scattering behaviors of the point clouds.

The proposal of this work was to analyze the behavior of the scalar dimensional app-roach but varying the average GSD values of two UAV dataset of the same scenario. The results achieved demonstrate how this field of application can advance new point-based learning methodologies useful for the extraction of valid morphological information. In general, the behaviors recorded for the two different flight height cases were completely comparable even if the scale parameter r varies. In fact, the values of geometric features undergone a reproportioning passing from the [70 m] to the [100 m] case. This suggests that the magnitude of the eigenvalues was proportional to the UAV acquisition altitude and that, as the GSD value increases, the PCA approach reiterates the dimensional traces already inferred at the lower altitude. At last, r-scale parameters one order higher than the GSD value were able to qualitatively and quantitatively better identify the dimension-ality of the survey carried out, regardless of the acquisition strategy used. Considering the findings outlined above, further processing and interpretation can be structured to exploit the dimensionality information provided.

References

1. Weidner, L., Walton, G., Krajnovich, A.: Classifying rock slope materials in photogrammetric point clouds using robust color and geometric features (2021)
2. Jafari, B., Khaloo, A., Lattanzi, D.: Deformation tracking in 3D point clouds via statistical sampling of direct cloud-to-cloud distances. J. Nondestr. Eval. **36**(4), 1 (2017). https://doi.org/10.1007/s10921-017-0444-2
3. Blomley, R., Weinmann, M., Leitloff, J., Jutzi, B.: Shape distribution features for point cloud analysis - a geometric histogram approach on multiple scales. ISPRS Ann. Photogramm. Remote Sens. Spatial Inf. Sci. **II-3**, 9–16 (2014)
4. Kim, A., Olsen, R., Kruse, F.: Methods for LiDAR point cloud classification using local neighborhood statistics. SPIE (2013)
5. Mallet, C., Bretar, F., Roux, M., Soergel, U., Heipke, C.: Relevance assessment of full-waveform lidar data for urban area classification. ISPRS J. Photogramm. Remote. Sens. **66**, S71–S84 (2011)
6. Chehata, N., Guo, L., Mallet, C.: Airborne lidar feature selection for urban classification using random forests. In: Laserscanning (2009)
7. Weinmann, M., Schmidt, A., Mallet, C., Hinz, S., Rottensteiner, F., Jutzi, B.: Contextual classification of point cloud data by exploiting individual 3D neigbourhoods. ISPRS Ann. Photogramm. Remote Sens. Spatial Inf. Sci. **II-3/W4**, 271–278 (2015)
8. Farella, E.M., Torresani, A., Remondino, F.: Quality features for the integration of terrestrial and UAV images. Int. Arch. Photogramm. Remote Sens. Spatial Inf. Sci. **XLII-2/W9**, 339–346 (2019)
9. Karantanellis, E., et al.: Evaluating the quality of photogrammetric point-clouds in challenging geo-environments – a case study in an Alpine Valley. Int. Arch. Photogramm. Remote Sens. Spatial Inf. Sci. **XLIII-B2–2020**, 1099–1105 (2020)
10. Demantké, J., Mallet, C., David, N., Vallet, B.: Dimensionality based scale selection in 3D lidar point clouds. In: Laserscanning (2011)
11. Brodu, N., Lague, D.: 3D terrestrial lidar data classification of complex natural scenes using a multi-scale dimensionality criterion: applications in geomorphology. ISPRS J. Photogramm. Remote. Sens. **68**, 121–134 (2012)
12. Farella, E.M., Torresani, A., Remondino, F.: Sparse point cloud filtering based on covariance features. Int. Arch. Photogramm. Remote Sens. Spatial Inf. Sci. **XLII-2/W15**, 465–472 (2019)

13. Weidner, L., Walton, G., Kromer, R.: Classification methods for point clouds in rock slope monitoring: a novel machine learning approach and comparative analysis. Eng. Geol. **263**, 105326 (2019)
14. Weinmann, M., Jutzi, B., Mallet, C.: Semantic 3D scene interpretation: a framework combining optimal neighborhood size selection with relevant features. ISPRS Ann. Photogramm. Remote Sens. Spatial Inf. Sci. **II-3**, 181–188 (2014)
15. Thomas, H., Goulette, F., Deschaud, J.-E., Marcotegui, B., LeGall, Y.: Semantic classification of 3D point clouds with multiscale spherical neighborhoods. In: 2018 International Conference on 3D Vision (3DV). IEEE, pp. 390–398 (2018)
16. Williams, J.G., Rosser, N.J., Hardy, R.J., Brain, M.J., Afana, A.A.: Optimising 4-D surface change detection: an approach for capturing rockfall magnitude–frequency. Earth Surf. Dynam. **6**, 101–119 (2018)
17. Saponaro, M., Capolupo, A., Tarantino, E., Fratino, U.: Comparative Analysis of Different UAV-Based Photogrammetric Processes to Improve Product Accuracies. In: Misra, S., et al. (eds.) ICCSA 2019. LNCS, vol. 11622, pp. 225–238. Springer, Cham (2019). https://doi.org/10.1007/978-3-030-24305-0_18
18. Saponaro, M., Tarantino, E., Reina, A., Furfaro, G., Fratino, U.: Assessing the impact of the number of GCPS on the accuracy of photogrammetric mapping from UAV imagery. Baltic Surveying 43 (2019)
19. Capolupo, A., Saponaro, M., Borgogno Mondino, E., Tarantino, E.: Combining interior orientation variables to predict the accuracy of Rpas-Sfm 3D models. Remote Sens. **12**, 2674 (2020)
20. Saponaro, M., Turso, A., Tarantino, E.: Parallel Development of Comparable Photogrammetric Workflows Based on UAV Data Inside SW Platforms. In: Gervasi, O., et al. (eds.) ICCSA 2020. LNCS, vol. 12252, pp. 693–708. Springer, Cham (2020). https://doi.org/10.1007/978-3-030-58811-3_50
21. Waldhauser, C., et al.: Automated classification of airborne laser scanning point clouds. In: Solving Computationally Expensive Engineering Problems. Springer, pp. 269–292 (2014)
22. Elberink, S.O., Maas, H.-G.: The use of anisotropic height texture measures for the segmentation of airborne laser scanner data. Int. Archiv. Photogram. Remote Sens. **33**, 678–684 (2000)

MAIA S2 Versus Sentinel 2: Spectral Issues and Their Effects in the Precision Farming Context

Filippo Sarvia(✉) ⓘ, Samuele De Petris ⓘ, Tommaso Orusa ⓘ,
and Enrico Borgogno-Mondino ⓘ

DISAFA, University of Torino, L-go Braccini 2, 10095 Grugliasco, TO, Italy
Filippo.sarvia@unito.it

Abstract. Precision agriculture involves the integration of new technologies including Geographic Information Systems (GIS), Global Navigation Satellites Systems (GNSS) and Remote Sensing (RS) platforms and sensors to allow farmers to maximize the cost-benefit ratio, rather than using the traditional whole-field approach. MAIA S2 is a recent multispectral aerial sensor in strong expansion in the agricultural sector. In this work, MAIA S2 spectral properties were compared with the correspondent Sentinel-2 ones, focusing on possible effects that differences could induce onto agriculture related deductions. The reference dataset was acquired by aerial survey and radiometric and geometric pre-processing achieved to generate the correspondent at-the-ground reflectance multispectral orthomosaic by ordinary workflow as suggested by sensor suppliers. A comparison was achieved at single band level to test spectral consistency of the two data. It showed a low correlation in the red-edge and infrared bands ($r < 0.5$); oppositely, a higher correlation was found for the visible bands ($r > 0.8$). To test the effects of found discrepancies between the two data, the correspondent prescription maps were generated using the same clustering criterion. They were then compared to test consistency of deductions.

Keywords: Precision agriculture · MAIA S2 sensor · Sentinel-2 · Precision farming · Prescription maps · MAIA S2 radiometric accuracy

1 Introduction

1.1 Precision Agriculture Requirements and Expected Applications

Precision agriculture, better defined as technological agriculture, involves the integration of new technologies including Geographic Information Systems (GIS), Global Navigation Satellites Systems (GNSS) and Remote Sensing (RS) platforms and sensors with the aim of making farmers able to better manage within field variability and maximize the cost-benefit ratio. Variable Rate Technology (VRT) available for many machineries, such as fertilizers or pesticide applicators and yield monitors, has evolved rapidly and have fostered the technological agriculture (TA) [1]. RS provides input data for many applications including pre-growth soil fertility and moisture analyses, crop growth and yield

© Springer Nature Switzerland AG 2021
O. Gervasi et al. (Eds.): ICCSA 2021, LNCS 12955, pp. 63–77, 2021.
https://doi.org/10.1007/978-3-030-87007-2_5

forecasting [2]. This information helps the farmer in his decision-making. Nevertheless, in spite of its fame, precision agriculture still suffers from many lacks/weaknesses to be effectively retained as fully operational. With special concerns about RS, some important issues are still to be completely clarified concerning both radiometric and geometric requirements. The unprecedented availability of satellite images guaranteeing proper spatial, spectral and temporal resolutions, has promoted the use of remote sensing in many TA applications [3] like crop monitoring, crop insurance [4–6], irrigation management, tree stability assessment [7, 8], nutrient application, Common Agricultural Policy controls [9], disease and pest management, natural hazards monitoring [10–12], assessment of climate change effects on vegetation [13], wildlife disease assessment [14], and yield prediction [15, 16]. In spite of these applications airborne multispectral sensor were greatly involved in TA. This work focuses on the comparison between Copernicus Sentinel 2 data (hereinafter called S2) and those acquired by the MAIA S2 (hereinafter called MS2, SAL Engineering s.r.l.) during a flight operated by airplane over an agricultural landscape contemporarily to the S2 passage. The comparison was specifically addressed to highlight spectral differences trying to figure out possible consequences in TA related deductions. The main issue concerned the evaluation of the spectral consistency between the two dataset and the eventual operational consequences that differences can generate in intepretating the data.

1.2 Multispectral Sensors in TA

RS solutions used for TA, can be classified in function of: (i) sensor platform and (ii) type of sensor. Sensors are typically mounted on board of satellite, aerial, and ground-based platforms. From the 1970s, satellite technology and products were widely used for TA. Recently, airborne systems including aircraft and RPAS (Remotely Piloted Aerial Vehicle) are also being used in TA. Ground-based platforms adopted in TA can be classified into three classes: (i) hand-held, (ii) free standing in the field, and (iii) mounted on tractor or farm machinery. Ground-based solutions are referred to as proximal RS systems since they are located closer to the target surfaces (terrain or plants). Multispectral sensors seem to play a particular role, given the whole of applications they can be suitable for [17]. RS Sensors differ for spatial, spectral, radiometric, and temporal resolution [18–20]. Aerial platforms generally provide higher spatial resolution (today often lower than 1 m) and a great productivity making them more desirable than satellites when moving the analysis within the single field. Nevertheless, the significantly improved temporal, spatial, and spectral resolution of the European Space Agency (ESA) Copernicus Sentinel-2 A/B twin platform is paving the way to their popularization in TA.

1.3 MAIA S2 Sensor

A wide selection of multispectral imaging sensors are currently offered on the market, most of them designed to be placed on various platform, in particular on airplanes or small drones. MAIA S2 [21] was developed to be preferably used on RPAS, but recent experiences have demonstrated that it could be also used from airplane flying at AGL (Above Ground Level) height higher than 250 m. MS2 can acquire the VIS-NIR spectral range (390–950 nm), running at a frame rate of up 6 Hz per sensor [1]. All sensors (one for each band, Table 1) is equipped with a calibrated bandpass filter. The nine band-pass filters that are installed in the MS2 camera have the identical central wavelength and bandwidth as those implemented by the MSI (Multi Spectral Instrument) of S2 [18].

MS2 sensor [18] was used for all the acquisitions having the following technical features: focal length = 7.5 mm, physical pixel size = 3.75 μm, sensor size = 1280 × 960 pixels.

It is expected that MS2 and S2 data could be efficiently integrated for analysis downscaling in the agricultural field [22].

Table 1. Nominal technical features of MAIA S2 sensor.

MAIA/S2			
Bands (MS2, S2)	Central wavelength (nm)	Bands width (nm)	Spectral region
b1, b1	443	20	Violet
b2, b2	490	65	Blue
b3, b3	560	35	Green
b4, b4	665	30	Red
b5, b5	705	15	Red Edge 1
b6, b6	740	15	Red Edge 2
b7, b7	783	20	NIR 1
b8, b8	842	115	NIR 2
b9, b8a	865	20	NIR 3

In MS2, acquisition settings, such as the exposure time and acquisition frame rate, may be adjusted through the user's interface to suit specific work conditions. Images are recorded on an internal solid state hard disk (SSD), which can store more than 10,000 RAW images. Images were stored in a proprietary RAW format where the radiometric resolution can be configured to 8, 10 or 12 bits. Camera settings can be accessed by user through the proprietary software making possible to (i) configure the parameters, (ii) visualize a live preview during the acquisition and (iii) capture and store the selected images to the internal storage. Several interfaces are available for these purposes: the keyboard control, NTSC/PAL video output, a web panel, and 2 inputs for remote controllers. Remote control can be accessed via a high-speed GigaEthernet connection or WiFi connection to a tablet, personal computer or smartphone, which can be convenient when used in the field. Finally, the MS2 camera can be connected with other sensors:

- a radio transmitter to transmit the images to the user for real-time monitoring;
- a gimbal controlled by the sensor inertial within the camera in order to maintain a constant or adapt the sensor posture during flight;
- a remote controller to modify certain parameters manually during the flight;
- an external GNSS receiver to geo-tag the images;

– other devices that may provide or need a precise synchronization signal at the same moment of image exposure.

The system is completed with the Irradiance Light Sensor (ILS) that was mounted on the upper part of the aerial fuselage. ILS operates with the same CMOS sensor of MS2 and is devoted to measure Sun irradiance in the same bands as MS2.

2   Materials and Methods

2.1   Study Area

An area of interest (AOI) was selected within the province of Vercelli (NW-Italy) having a size of about 166 ha (Fig. 1). AOI is mainly characterized by an agricultural landscape where corn, grassland and wheat represent the most important crops. In particular, to evaluate the effects of inconsistencies on prescription maps obtained from the two sensors, a focus area (FA), covering a corn field (about 7.2 ha), was selected.

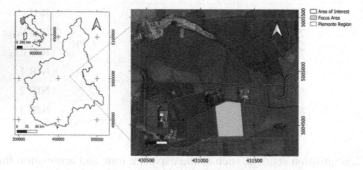

Fig. 1. Study area. Area of interest (red). Focus area covering a corn field (yellow). Reference system is WGS 84 UTM zone 32 N, EPSG: 32632 (Color figure online).

2.2   Available Data

An aerial survey was performed on 6th August 2020 from a Tecnam P92 JS airplane. Forward and side overlap were set equal to 82% and 87% respectively and the aerial survey was performed @ 600 m AGL. MS2 sensor was hosted in the SkyMetry©/SmartBay© platform by Digisky s.r.l. company [23].

Image block was adjusted using 6 ground control points (GCPs, Fig. 2). GCPs were collimated from available high resolution orthoimages (planimetric coordinates) and DTM (height coordinate) in order to reduce costs and speed up the process. The reference true color orthoimage was produced by the TeA Consortium in summer 2015 with a Ground Sampling Distance (GSD) equal to 0.40 m and georeferenced in the WGS84 UTM 32 reference frame. GCP height coordinate was obtained from the Piemonte Region digital terrain model (DTM, Ground Sample Distance = 5 m, height accuracy = 0.33 m).

These data were obtained for free from the regional Geoportal (www.geoportale.piemon te.it). GCPs were selected in correspondence of well recognizable features like road crossings, houses corners, backhoes, plinths, etc.

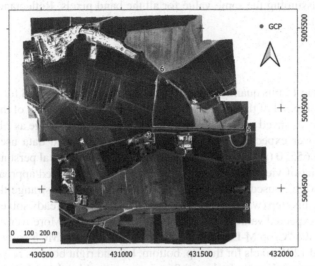

Fig. 2. Number and position of ground control points. Reference system is WGS 84 UTM zone 32 N, EPSG: 32632.

Multispectral satellite data from the Copernicus Sentinel-2 mission [24] were used to test spectral quality of MS2 multispectral acquisitions. A S2 Level-2A image acquired on 7th August 2020 (one day later of MS2 acquisition) was obtained from the official European Space Agency data hub (ESA, https://scihub.copernicus.eu/). It is worth to remind that a S2 tile covers an area of 100×100 km^2 and is supplied projected in the WGS84 UTM reference system. Level 2A imagery is provided calibrated in at-the-ground reflectance (Bottom of the Atmosphere, BOA) [25] making it immediately suitable for terrestrial applications.

2.3 Data Processing

MS2 Data Pre-processing. Acquired raw images were processed by the MAIA pro-prietary software named MultiCam Stitcher Pro v 1.4-Beta 2 (MCS). Initially, images were geometrically corrected to remove/minimize distortions related to sensor lens system and design using the available automatic procedure in MCS. Nominal calibration parameters, different for each band, are recorded within MCS and automatically applied during processing [17]. Successively, a co-registration step aiming at aligning bands (since acquired from different lens systems) was achieved by MCS. A block made of multi-layer images containing 9 co-registered and undistorted bands was therefore generated. Data from MS2 were quantized at 12 bits and saved as integer numbers at 2 bytes (16 bits) determining a range of variation between 0 and 65520. Radiometric calibration, aimed at recovering reflectance from DN, was achieved again using the automatic procedure available in MSC based on the measurement of Sun irradiance as coming from ILS. The calibration approach assumes that the incoming radiation measured by ILS corresponds to the same that lights the scene recorded by MS2. This is, obviously, a significant simplification that does not consider topographic effect during reflectance computation, assuming the same value for all the band pixels. Reflectance is obtained by MCS by (1).

$$\rho_\lambda^i = \frac{1}{ILS_\lambda} DN_\lambda^i \tag{1}$$

where ILS_λ is the 12 bits quantized value of irradiance detected by ILS for the λ spectral band and the i-th pixel of the image; DN_λ^i is the 12 bits quantized DN of the i-th pixel of band λ. Since ρ_λ^i is saved in the output multispectral calibrated image as 2 byte unsigned integer, to recover expected reflectance values from calibrated data user is called to divide them by 65520 (as suggested by SAL Engineering technical personnel). From an operational point of view this appears a weakness of the proposed approach especially when the software is used by unskilled people. It also appears strange that the 65520 value is used at this step (when quantization problem has been already solved by ratio (1)) in place of the expected value of 65535 (16 bits upper bound). Moreover the parameters applied during the "Crop M-Layer Tiff" phase, required by the MCS software, were set: 30; 881; 49 and 1206 pixels for the top, bottom, left and right borders respectively. This approach, following the standard workflow as suggested by the software, moves data from the rigorous conditions required by ordinary photogrammetric processes. In fact, an asymmetric crop of image is expected to shift the fiducial centre of images, making interior orientation parameters potentially wrong. At this point it is not clear the effects of such strategy during image bundle adjustment. We also expect that radiometric radial distortions could be somehow affected [26]. Some further investigations have still to be done.

MS2 Data Bundle Adjustment. The radiometrically calibrated image block was then processed by Agisoft PhotoScan vs 1.2.4 software (AGS) to solve images orientation (bundle adjustment) needed to generate the multispectral orthomosaic (MOM). It is worth to remind that AGS operates according to the Structure-from-Motion (SfM) approach to estimate exterior and, eventually, interior orientation parameters of images and makes possible the generation of a photogrammetric point cloud (PPC) with a proper reference system (WGS84 UTM 32N for this work). During block adjustment 6 GCPs were collimated on reference data. Obtained PPC was therefore filtered to remove outliers and the correspondent Digital Surface Model (DSM) computed by regularization setting a GSD of 1.2 m. A leave-one out (LOO) procedure [27] was adopted to test bundle adjustment accuracy. Altimetric and planimetric RMSE (Root Mean Squared Error) were computed. Finally, MOM having a GSD of 0.3 m was generated using the above mentioned DSM from the calibrated multispectral images. While mosaicking images blending mode was set to "disabled" to not further move native radiometry of calibrated images.

MAIA S2 and S2 Comparison

Band Spectral Correlation. In order to test MS2 and S2 spectral consistency, the temporally closest S2 acquisition was used as reference. It is worth to remind that S2 imagery is provided already calibrated in at-the-ground reflectance by Copernicus SciHub provider and represents a sort of standard to compare other sensors reflectances with. MS2 image was preliminary down-sampled to the same S2 geometric resolution (10 m) adopting the mean method [28]. Subsequently, correspondent bands from MS2 and S2 were compared and relationship modeled by I order polynomial regression. Correspondent gain, offset, Pearson's r and coefficient of determination (R^2) were computed.

Spectral Signature Comparison. Starting from the down-sampled MOM spectral signatures were compared at pixel level. Pearson's *r* and Mean Absolute Error (MAE) [29] were calculated and mapped into separate layers hereafter called *r* map (RM) and MAE map (MM) respectively.

Vegetation Index Comparison. MS2 is extensively adopted for agricultural purposes [18, 30]. The majority of works involving MS2 use spectral vegetation indices (NDVI, Normalized Difference Vegetation Index or NDRE, Normalized Difference Red Edge Index) as predictors to base agronomic deductions on (e.g. prescription map generation). With special focus on NDVI, authors compared resulting maps from MS2 and S2 datasets, hereinafter called $NDVI_{MS2}$ and $NDVI_{S2}$. With reference to the standard deviation of both NDVI maps, a F-test was performed to test the hypothesis that the two NDVI variances were significantly different. Additionally, a I order polynomial regression was calibrated between $NDVI_{MS2}$ and $NDVI_{S2}$ and correspondent gain, offset, Pearson's r and coefficient of determination computed.

Effects of Differences on Precision Farming Products. It is worth to remind that in the precision agriculture context spectral measures inconsistencies can drive to different deductions making probable that wrong agricultural practices are adopted [31]. To test this condition, an assessment about consistency of MS2 and S2 derived prescription maps was performed. To map behavioral zones within a test field (FA) an approach based on the cluster analysis was adopted. Several works propose this approach to generate prescription maps and address focused local treatments [32]. In this work a K-means clustering was performed, asking for 3 clusters, for both $NDVI_{MS2}$ and $NDVI_{S2}$. Results were interpreted as the spatial basis to define prescription maps on. Since in a cluster analysis class meaning is not a-priori known, to recover it, NDVI mean and standard deviation were computed for all clusters for both the maps. After interpretation, a transition matrix was computed to test consistency of results.

3 Results and Discussions

3.1 MAIA S2 Calibration

The image block bundle adjustment accuracy using LOO procedure resulting in $RMSE_{x,y}$ and $RMSE_z$ equal to 0.39 m and 0.03 m respectively (Table 2). These accuracies well fits the TA requirements [33, 34], allowing fine spatially spectral measures of crops.

Table 2. GCP errors. For each GCP, reported values are those obtained during LOO when the considered GCP was excluded from bundle adjustment.

GCP ID	East err. (m)	North err. (m)	Height err. (m)	Total err. (m)	Projections	Error (# pixel)
1	0.248	0.239	−0.034	0.346	2	0.002
2	0.196	0.014	0.005	0.196	7	0.038
3	0.011	−0.443	0.022	0.445	6	0.008
4	−0.383	0.250	0.003	0.458	14	0.010
5	0.108	−0.433	0.044	0.449	3	0.007
6	−0.178	0.374	−0.045	0.416	8	0.018

3.2 Comparing MS2 and S2 Data

Band Correlation. Figure 3 and Table 3 show, for a I order polynomial regression model, the correspondent gain (α), offset (β), Pearson's r and coefficient of determination (R^2) values obtained from the comparison between MS2 and S2 datasets.

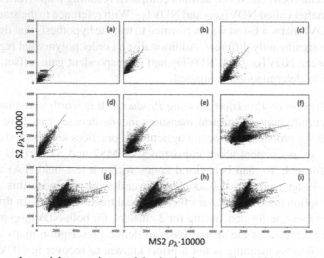

Fig. 3. I order polynomial regression models obtained comparing MS2 and S2 bands. (a) b1, (b) b2, (c) b3, (d) b4, (e) b5, (f) b6, (g) b7, (h) b8, (i) b8a.

Table 3 shows that compared bands provide different values of r and R^2. in particular, high values of r and R^2 were observed for visible bands (b2, b3 and b4), while red-edge and infrared bands (b6, b7 and b8) showed lower value.

3.3 Spectral Signature Assessment

Figure 4 shows RM and MM with the corresponding histograms as related to the spectral signature assessment.

Table 3. Slope (α), offset (β), correlation (r) and determination (R^2) values obtained comparing MS2 and S2 datasets. In red high values of r and R^2, in blue low values.

MAIA S2 and S-2 bands	r	α	β	R^2
b1	0.70	101.8876	0.9504	0.49
b2	0.88	-7.2242	1.6316	0.77
b3	0.79	25.4228	1.3984	0.63
b4	0.91	-27.9461	1.4640	0.83
b5	0.68	207.0060	1.1493	0.46
b6	0.27	1804.1660	0.2102	0.07
b7	0.43	1930.6425	0.3039	0.19
b8	0.55	1448.5376	0.5419	0.31
b8a	0.42	1867.7151	0.4572	0.18

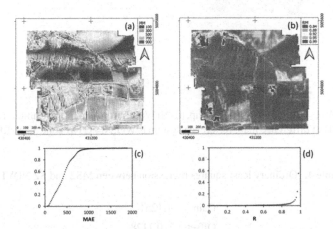

Fig. 4. (a) MM, (b) RM (c) cumulative frequency graph of MAE, (d) cumulative frequency graph of correlation. Reference system is WGS 84 UTM zone 32 N, EPSG: 32632.

In general, correlation between MS2 and S2 spectral signatures was always greater than 0.8, while MAE was lower than 600 in the 80% of the pixels. Nevertheless, some critical errors persist. Unexpectedly, MM and RM show a peculiar distribution over the scene. In particular, r and MAE values were lower in bare soils/built-up areas and where radiometric borders were present.

3.4 Vegetation Index Comparison

NDVI$_{MS2}$ and NDVI$_{S2}$ maps are reported in Fig. 5. The F-test proved that NDVI$_{MS2}$ and NDVI$_{S2}$ were significantly different (F = 1.424, p < 0.001) and NDVI$_{S2}$ variance was greater than NDVI$_{MS2}$ one, supporting the hypothesis that, in spite of the higher resolution, MS2 can detect a lower NDVI variability than S2. Figure 5c reports NDVI difference. It shows that the majority of differences were located in bare soils, roads and built-up areas while, in the vegetated areas, differences were lower than 0.02. According to Borgogno et al. [35] these differences are not significant considering the NDVI uncertainty. To further explore NDVI differences a I order polynomial regression model was calibrated with reference to the scatterplot (Fig. 6) relating NDVI images (parameters are reported in Table 4).

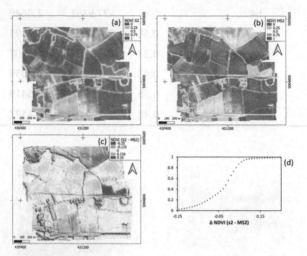

Fig. 5. (a) NDVI$_{S2}$ maps, (b) NDVI$_{MS2}$ map, (c) NDVI difference map, (d) Cumulative frequency histogram of NDVI difference map. Reference system is WGS 84 UTM zone 32 N, EPSG: 32632.

Table 4. Ordinary least squares regression between MS2 and S2 NDVI

Gain	1.1251
Offset	−0.1128
r	0.943
R^2	0.889
t	348.440
p-value	<0.001

Gain and offset values reported in Table 4 (1.125 and −0.11 respectively) suggest that MS2 tends to overestimate NDVI (with respect to S2). Overestimation reduces while NDVI value increases. With reference to the existence range of NDVI [−1.00, + 1.00], it can be noticed that the maximum overestimation value (about +0.24) occurs at NDVI$_{MS2}$ = −1.00. Oppositely, the two measures can be retained as consistent when the difference between S2 NDVI and its estimation from MS2 is greater than 0.74.

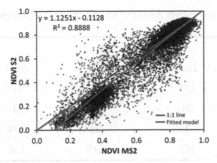

Fig. 6. Scatterplot and calibrated I order polynomial model relating MS2 and S2 NDVI maps.

These results raise some doubts about the consistency between aerial and satellite based remote sensing in precision agriculture and suggests that some questions, concerning their integration, remain open.

3.5 Effects of Datasets Spectral Inconsistencies on Prescription Maps

To test the effects of NDVI spectral inconsistencies a K-means clustering (3 clusters and 100 iterations) was run aimed at deriving the correspondent prescription maps (Fig. 7).

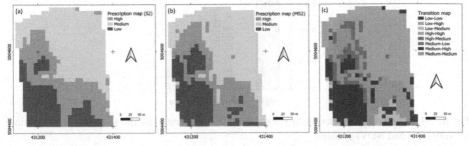

Fig. 7. (a) K-means clustering for $NDVI_{MS2}$, (b) K-means clustering for $NDVI_{S2}$, (c) transition map. Reference system is WGS 84 UTM zone 32 N, EPSG: 32632.

Meaning of classes was recovered considering their NDVI mean and standard deviation values (Fig. 8) assuming that "high", "medium" and "low" vigour classes were assigned with reference to the NDVI class mean values. A transition matrix (Table 5) and related map (Fig. 7c) were also computed by comparing the two obtained prescription maps. Results show that omission and commission errors range between 8 and 29% depending on the class. Higher commission values are related to low and medium vigour classes, i.e. where the most of spectral inconsistencies are placed according to the previously mentioned comparisons. The overall accuracy was found to be equal to 71%. These results suggest that MAIA and S2 sensors could drive to significantly different deductions while working with prescription maps involving vegetation spectral indices, where about 30% of pixels could be possibly assigned to different classes.

Table 5. Transition matrix between S2 and MS2 derived prescription maps.

	(# pixels)	S2			
		Low	*Medium*	*High*	Total
MS2	*Low*	131	36	0	167
	Medium	33	159	31	223
	High	1	24	299	324
	Total	165	219	330	714

(%)	Producer's Accuracy	User's Accuracy	Omission Error	Commission Error
Low	79.4	78.4	20.6	21.6
Medium	72.6	71.3	27.4	28.7
High	90.6	92.3	9.4	7.7
Overall Accuracy		70.8		

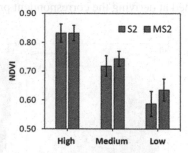

Fig. 8. Mean and standard deviation values of clusters generated by the K-means classification of NDVI$_{MS2}$ and NDVI$_{S2}$ maps.

4 Conclusions

In this work, MS2 and S2 radiometric consistency was assessed having comparable spectral bands. Assessment was aimed at testing if significantly different deductions could come from the adoption of the 2 sensors, with special concern about NDVI computation and its interpretation for prescription maps generation in the agriculture context. MS2 dataset was acquired by aerial survey and the subsequent radiometric and geometric calibration were performed following an ordinary workflow based on the MultiCam Stitcher Pro v 1.4-Beta 2 supplied with MAIA S2 sensor. Some potential weaknesses where preliminarily identified and highlighted concerning the data processing strategy implemented in the above mentioned software. MS2 was preliminarily downsampled from its native GSD down to S2 one (10 m). At the ground reflectance calibrated bands were compared at pixel level and showed a low correlation especially in the red-edge and infrared bands ($r < 0.5$); differently, a high correlation was found for visible bands ($r > 0.8$). Moreover, MAE and r were also computed comparing, at pixel level, the local spectral signature of both multispectral stacks. Correlation resulted poor for bare soils/building areas and over radiometric borders. A further comparison was made focusing on NDVI maps from both the sensors, since it is widely used in precision agriculture. The analysis focused out that MS2 tends to overestimate NDVI values especially when working with values lower than 0.74. The difference increases while moving to lower values up to 0.23 when NDVI $= -1.00$. Results also showed that MS2 derived NDVI map presents a lower contrast if compared with the S2 one; this suggests a general a weakness of MS2 of appreciating NDVI differences. Based on these evidences a further analysis was performed for a focus area corresponding to a corn field to test possible effects in prescription maps as derivable from S2 and MS2 NDVI maps. Comparison highlighted commission/omission errors higher for low and medium vigour classes. This fact is consistent with the overestimation that was measured in the previous step. Finally, some doubts about the consistency between aerial and satellite based remote sensing in precision agriculture still persist, suggesting that some questions, concerning their integration, remain open. With these premises and considering cost related issues of aerial data, it appears to be desirable a further deepening concerning the reliability of spectral measures from airborne low cost sensors. Conversely, it is worth to remind that aerial surveys equipped with MS2 sensor can provide imagery having centimeter geometric resolution and 3D measurement potentialities that can be effectively used to improve crop related deductions.

References

1. Babaeian, E., et al.: others: A new optical remote sensing technique for high-resolution mapping of soil moisture. Front. Big Data **2**, 37 (2019)
2. Sishodia, R.P., Ray, R.L., Singh, S.K.: Applications of remote sensing in precision agriculture: A review. Remote Sens. **12**, 3136 (2020)
3. Monteleone, S., et al.: Exploring the adoption of precision agriculture for irrigation in the context of agriculture 4.0: the key role of internet of things. Sensors. **20**, 7091 (2020)
4. Borgogno-Mondino, E., Sarvia, F., Gomarasca, M.A.: Supporting insurance strategies in agriculture by remote sensing: a possible approach at regional level. In: Misra, Sanjay, Gervasi, Osvaldo, Murgante, Beniamino, Stankova, Elena, Korkhov, Vladimir, Torre, Carmelo, Rocha, Ana Maria A C., Taniar, David, Apduhan, Bernady O., Tarantino, Eufemia (eds.) ICCSA 2019. LNCS, vol. 11622, pp. 186–199. Springer, Cham (2019). https://doi.org/10.1007/978-3-030-24305-0_15
5. Sarvia, F., De Petris, S., Borgogno-Mondino, E.: Remotely sensed data to support insurance strategies in agriculture. In: Remote Sensing for Agriculture, Ecosystems, and Hydrology XXI, p. 111491H. International Society for Optics and Photonics (2019)
6. Sarvia, F., De Petris, S., Borgogno-Mondino, E.: Multi-scale remote sensing to support insurance policies in agriculture: from mid-term to instantaneous deductions. GISci. Remote Sens. **57**, 770–784 (2020). https://doi.org/10.1080/15481603.2020.1798600
7. De Petris, S., Sarvia, F., Borgogno-Mondino, E.: A new index for assessing tree vigour decline based on sentinel-2 multitemporal data. Application to tree failure risk management. Remote Sens. Lett. **12**(1), 58–67 (2020)

8. De Petris, S., Sarvia, F., Borgogno-Mondino, E.: RPAS-based photogrammetry to support tree stability assessment: Longing for precision arboriculture. Urban Forest. Urban Green. **55**, 126862 (2020). https://doi.org/10.1016/j.ufug.2020.126862

9. Sarvia, F., Xausa, E., Petris, S.D., Cantamessa, G., Borgogno-Mondino, E.: A possible role of copernicus sentinel-2 data to support common agricultural policy controls in agriculture. Agronomy **11**, 110 (2021)

10. Sarvia, F., De Petris, S., Borgogno-Mondino, E.: A methodological proposal to support estimation of damages from hailstorms based on copernicus sentinel 2 data times series. In: Gervasi, O., et al. (eds.) ICCSA 2020. LNCS, vol. 12252, pp. 737–751. Springer, Cham (2020). https://doi.org/10.1007/978-3-030-58811-3_53

11. De Petris, S., Sarvia, F., Gullino, M., Tarantino, E., Borgogno-Mondino, E.: Sentinel-1 polarimetry to map apple orchard damage after a storm. Remote Sens. **13**, 1030 (2021). https://doi.org/10.3390/rs13051030

12. De Petris, S., Sarvia, F., Borgogno-Mondino, E.: Multi-temporal mapping of flood damage to crops using sentinel-1 imagery: a case study of the Sesia River (October 2020), (2021)

13. Sarvia, F., De Petris, S., Borgogno-Mondino, E.: Exploring climate change effects on vegetation phenology by MOD13Q1 data: the Piemonte region case study in the period 2001–2019. Agronomy **11**, 555 (2021). https://doi.org/10.3390/agronomy11030555

14. Orusa, T., Orusa, R., Viani, A., Carella, E., Borgogno Mondino, E.: Geomatics and EO data to support wildlife diseases assessment at landscape level: a pilot experience to map infectious Keratoconjunctivitis in Chamois and phenological trends in Aosta Valley (NW Italy). Remote Sens. **12**, 3542 (2020)

15. van Klompenburg, T., Kassahun, A., Catal, C.: Crop yield prediction using machine learning: a systematic literature review. Comput. Electron. Agric. **177**, 105709 (2020)

16. Lessio, A., Fissore, V., Borgogno-Mondino, E.: Preliminary tests and results concerning integration of Sentinel-2 and Landsat-8 OLI for crop monitoring. J. Imaging **3**, 49 (2017)

17. Nocerino, E., Dubbini, M., Menna, F., Remondino, F., Gattelli, M., Covi, D.: Geometric calibration and radiometric correction of the MAIA multispectral camera. Int. Arch. Photogramm. Remote Sens. Spatial Inf. Sci. **42**(3), 149–156 (2017)

18. Marinello, F.: Last generation instrument for agriculture multispectral data collection. Agric. Eng. Int. CIGR J. **19**, 87–93 (2017)

19. Boccardo, P., Mondino, E.B., Tonolo, F.G.: High resolution satellite images position accuracy tests. In: IGARSS 2003. 2003 IEEE International Geoscience and Remote Sensing Symposium. Proceedings (IEEE Cat. No. 03CH37477), pp. 2320–2322. IEEE (2003)

20. Mondino, E.B., Perotti, L., Piras, M.: High resolution satellite images for archeological applications: the Karima case study (Nubia region, Sudan). Eur. J. Remote Sens. **45**, 243–259 (2012)

21. Ryan, C.G., et al.: MAIA mapper: high definition XRF imaging in the lab. J. Instrum. **13**, C03020 (2018)

22. Segarra, J., Buchaillot, M.L., Araus, J.L., Kefauver, S.C.: Remote sensing for precision agriculture: sentinel-2 improved features and applications. Agronomy **10**, 641 (2020)

23. Maggiore, P., Greco, A.: Development of the SmartGimbal Control System for the SmartBay Platform (2019).

24. Gascon, F., Cadau, E., Colin, O., Hoersch, B., Isola, C., Fernández, B.L., Martimort, P.: Copernicus sentinel-2 mission: products, algorithms and Cal/Val. In: Earth Observing Systems XIX, p. 92181E. International Society for Optics and Photonics (2014)

25. Dechoz, C., et al.: Sentinel 2 global reference image. In: Image and Signal Processing for Remote Sensing XXI, p. 96430A. International Society for Optics and Photonics (2015)

26. Borgogno-Mondino, E.: Remote sensing from RPAS in agriculture: an overview of expectations and unanswered questions. In: Ferraresi, C., Quaglia, G. (eds.) RAAD 2017. MMS, vol. 49, pp. 483–492. Springer, Cham (2018). https://doi.org/10.1007/978-3-319-61276-8_51

27. Brovelli, M.A., Crespi, M., Fratarcangeli, F., Giannone, F., Realini, E.: Accuracy assessment of high resolution satellite imagery orientation by leave-one-out method. ISPRS J. Photogramm. Remote. Sens. **63**, 427–440 (2008)
28. Lanaras, C., Bioucas-Dias, J., Galliani, S., Baltsavias, E., Schindler, K.: Super-resolution of Sentinel-2 images: learning a globally applicable deep neural network. ISPRS J. Photogramm. Remote. Sens. **146**, 305–319 (2018)
29. Willmott, C.J., Matsuura, K.: Advantages of the mean absolute error (MAE) over the root mean square error (RMSE) in assessing average model performance. Climate Res. **30**, 79–82 (2005)
30. Chauhan, S., et al.: Wheat lodging assessment using multispectral UAV data. Int. Arch. Photogramm. Remote Sens. Spatial Inf. Sci. **42**, 235–240 (2019)
31. Gómez-Candón, D., López-Granados, F., Caballero-Novella, J.J., Peña-Barragán, J.M., García-Torres, L.: Understanding the errors in input prescription maps based on high spatial resolution remote sensing images. Precision Agric. **13**, 581–593 (2012). https://doi.org/10.1007/s11119-012-9270-9
32. Bates, T., Dresser, J., Eckstrom, R., Badr, G., Betts, T., Taylor, J.: Variable-rate mechanical crop adjustment for crop load balance in "Concord" vineyards. In: Presented at the 2018 IoT Vertical and Topical Summit on Agriculture - Tuscany, IOT Tuscany 2018 (2018). https://doi.org/10.1109/IOT-TUSCANY.2018.8373046
33. Borgogno-Mondino, E., Lessio, A., Tarricone, L., Novello, V., de Palma, L.: A comparison between multispectral aerial and satellite imagery in precision viticulture. Precision Agric. **19**(2), 195–217 (2017). https://doi.org/10.1007/s11119-017-9510-0
34. Rokhmana, C.A.: The potential of UAV-based remote sensing for supporting precision agriculture in Indonesia. Procedia Environ. Sci. **24**, 245–253 (2015)
35. Borgogno-Mondino, E., Lessio, A., Gomarasca, M.A.: A fast operative method for NDVI uncertainty estimation and its role in vegetation analysis. Eur. J. Remote Sens. **49**, 137–156 (2016)

Notes on the Performances of Morphological Descriptors for the Evaluation of Flood Susceptibility in Apulian Ephemeral Streams

Filomena Carbone[1], Gabriella Balacco[2], Vincenzo Totaro[2], and Andrea Gioia[2(✉)]

[1] ASSET – Regional Strategic Agency for the Eco-sustainable Development of the Territory, Regione Puglia, via Gentile 52, 70125 Bari, Italy
f.carbone@asset.regione.puglia.it

[2] DICATECh – Department of Civil, Environmental, Land, Building Engineering and Chemistry, Politecnico Di Bari, via Orabona 4, 70125 Bari, Italy
{gabriella.balacco,vincenzo.totaro,andrea.gioia}@poliba.it

Abstract. Different tools and models are nowadays available for the identification of flood-prone areas. The application of these approaches is strongly influenced by the availability of site-specific hydrological information. As an example, a combined scheme of hydrological and hydraulic models for the definition of flood events is reliable when there are lots of hydrological and hydraulic information, which makes it difficult to be exploited in ungauged catchment. In this context, DTM-based geomorphological methods are able to provide a rapid identification of a flood susceptibility where the availability of data directly observed in situ is limited. In this study we investigated ability and performances of two morphological descriptors in defining flood exposure with respect to accuracy of morphological information in the context of ephemeral streams located in Puglia region (Southern Italy). Results showed an influence of data resolution on descriptors performances, providing an additional contribution to the investigations carried out in similar areas during last years.

Keywords: Morphological descriptors · DTM-based approach · Flood-prone areas

1 Introduction

Floods are one of the most important natural phenomena, which have the potential to cause deaths and widespread damages to the environment. These effects are especially observed where rivers have been cut off from their natural area of inundation and confined to main channels, in order to enable the urban expansion. In the last few years this kind of floods are becoming highly frequent and produce strong damaging consequences with particular reference to high vulnerably territories like shallow karst ephemeral/episodic streams known as *lame*, typical of Puglia region (southern Italy), where the combination of physical characteristics of river basins and intense and irregularly distributed rain can generate flash floods.

© Springer Nature Switzerland AG 2021
O. Gervasi et al. (Eds.): ICCSA 2021, LNCS 12955, pp. 78–88, 2021.
https://doi.org/10.1007/978-3-030-87007-2_6

A high infiltration capacity is ensured by the limestone of the Murgia, with the consequence of the absence of a significant drainage networks for long period, except for several natural incisions; this is the reason why, during extreme rainfall events, lame are typically unprepared to deal with these natural phenomena generating awful effects. This is what happened in lama Balice on days 16th, 17th, 18th of June 2014 [1].

This kind of consequences can be exacerbated by the increased flood risk caused by climate change effects (e.g., [2–4]). In particular, future changes in floods and environmental related risks are expected to be conducted by a combination of potential changes in climate, catchment conditions and vulnerability of the territory and assets (e.g., [5–9]). Interpretation of changes is the focus of the new Panta Rhei decade of the International Association of Hydrological Sciences (IAHS) [10]. On the other hand, the increasing of urbanization and soil sealing has led to the growth of impermeable surfaces (e.g., [11–13]) causing the reduction of soil infiltration capacity and consequently the increasing effects of the short-duration highly intense rainfall. In this context, according to the recent European legislation on flood risk protection (Flood Directive 2007/60/EC), European programs of scientific research (as Horizon 2020) and scientific community are looking for new techniques able to provide a rapid identification of a flood susceptibility.

Different tools and models are nowadays available for the identification of flood-prone areas (e.g., [14–17]). Some of them essentially consists in using a combined scheme of hydrological and hydraulic models [18–20] for the definition of flood events but are not always applicable because they are reliable when there are lots of hydrological and hydraulic information. In addition, in ungauged catchment the use of these methodologies become difficult due to their parameterization (e.g., [21–23]), leading to the need of looking for alternative source of data and insights (e.g., [24, 25]).

This is the reason why, in areas with limited availability of data, is important the preliminary detecting of flood susceptibility, to avoid expensive analyses that could take a significant employment of resources. In the last few decades methodologies for the identification of flood prone areas to monitor the spatio-temporal evolution of terrestrial phenomena have been developed (e.g., [26–28]) thanks to the availability of new technologies for remote surface elevation observation; in particular global positioning system [GPS], synthetic aperture radar [SAR] interferometry, airborne laser altimetry technology LiDAR (e.g., [29]) can provide reliable information on flood susceptibility [30, 31] considering the increasing availability of high resolution topographical maps developed by Digital Terrain Models [DTMs] (e.g., [32]), and their capacity to give lots of information on morphology and earth surface's characteristic.

Although these methodologies are useful for the investigation of prone areas to flood inundation, mono- and two-dimensional hydraulic numerical models approach is necessary in order to calibrate their information to reference flood maps.

In the proposed work, the DTM-based hydrogeomorphic methods application integrated with the use of Remote Sensing techniques for the derivation of high resolution topographical maps were developed on a case study of an ephemeral stream network known as Lama Balice located in the Puglia region (southern Italy), with the purpose of comparing the inundated areas for three design events characterized by return periods (T) of 30, 200 and 500 years in the context of the evaluation of best performing spatial resolution (considering 2 m × 2 m, 8 m × 8 m and 30 m × 30 m grid cells) of DTM topographical maps.

2 Case Study and Data

Lama Balice is an ephemeral stream located in Puglia region (Southern Italy), mainly flowing in the municipal areas of Bitonto and Bari, oriented in a SW-NE direction. According to Iacobellis et al. [1], its catchment originates in the territories of Ruvo di Puglia and Corato and the main channel proceeds its path running down to the Adriatic Sea. Lama Balice represents one of the most significant karst ephemeral streams of metropolitan area of Bari, with a length of the main channel of about 20 km, average slope equal to 4.84% and maximum altitude of 635 m.a.s.l [33].

Lama Balice has always been a place of strategic importance for local population and wildlife, because its role of crossroad between the hinterland and the coast [34]. It provided shelters and water, even in arid conditions, since Neolithic period: different lithium finds were found near cities of Bari Palese, Bari San Paolo and Bitonto, supporting the historical importance of these stream networks. In these areas, there are some evidences about prehistoric villages; in fact, its karst cliffs, easily excavated, allowed a protection from cold winds. This is why is part of a protected area of a Regional Natural Park (see Fig. 1).

Due to the social, archeological and naturalistic importance, in the area of lama Balice a natural park was established since 2007, whose extension is about 500 ha and is characterized by a Mediterranean, thermophilic and xerophilic vegetation. Furthermore, the karstification allowed water to penetrate in some limestones fractures, attack rocks and create caverns and passages, where it is possible to appreciate the so-called stalagmites and stalactites. It is estimated that in the park there are six natural caves at least, two sink holes and a thousand of natural shelter in which stalactites and stalagmites hide [34].

One of the last events occurred in June 2014, with an intensity peak in the afternoon of day 17th when more than 100 mm of cumulative rain were recorded [1]. As a consequence, Lama Balice has reactivated itself causing several problems in terms of the effect of ungovernable and chaotic anthropogenic impact, that, associated with incorrect planning, result in catastrophic events [35].

In the proposed research, the Remote Sensing techniques were used for the derivation of high resolution topographical maps, useful for the application of the DTM-based hydrogeomorphic approaches on a case study of Lama Balice; in particular the DTM map with 2 m × 2 m resolution was obtained using the new technologies for the measurement of surface elevation (i.e. Light Detection And Ranging – LiDAR); instead the 8 m × 8 m and 30 m × 30 m DTM topographical maps were extracted from the official regional technical base map of Puglia region, called CTR.

3 Methodologies

As recalled in the Introduction, methodologies applied into this paper relies on the use of geomorphic descriptors computed at catchment scale, coupled with the method of

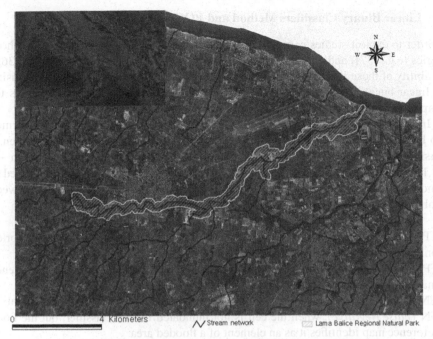

0   4 Kilometers $\wedge\!\!\!\wedge$ Stream network   Lama Balice Regional Natural Park

Fig. 1. Development of the stream network of Lama Balice (in blue) (Color figure online).

linear binary classifiers and the Receiver Operating Characteristics (ROC) curves. In this paragraph these approaches are summarizing and described in their main features.

3.1 Morphological Descriptors of Basin

Following results of studies carried out on similar areas (e.g., [33, 36]), we exploited properties of the following descriptors:

- *elevation to the nearest stream*, H [m]: this index is defined as the elevation difference between a point on the catchment and the hydrologically connected point on the drainage network;
- *Geomorphic Flood Index* (GFI), $\ln(h_r/H)$: this descriptor is evaluated as the natural logarithm of the ratio between h_r and H, where h_r is an intrinsic cell quantity that can be defined as:

$$h_r \cong bA_r^n$$

where A_r is, for the selected cell, the upslope contributing area related to that hydrologically connected on the stream network, while b and n were respectively set equal to 10^{-2} and 0.3.

3.2 Linear Binary Classifiers Method and ROC Curves

In order to exploit studies carried out in the previous decades with the same method-ologies (e.g., [37]) and on similar case studies located in Puglia region (e.g., [33, 36]), the ability of these indices in the evaluation of flood-prone areas has been tested using the linear binary classifiers method. This allowed us to obtain uniform measures for comparing main findings of our study with those reported in literature.

In order to apply this method, reference and descriptors maps have to be transformed into binary ones, where value 1 is devoted to inundated cells and 0 to others. Then, a transformation is performed for geomorphic indices by scaling each map between −1 and 1 and applying a mobile threshold with a step of 0.001. Cell is therefore classified as inundated or not according to the physical meaning of the index. Comparison between so-obtained maps is carried out by identifying each cell as:

- TP (*True Positive*): when the classifier correctly identifies a flooded element reported on the reference map;
- FP (*False Positive*): when the cell is inundated for the classifier, but the flood reference map doesn't identify it as an element of a flooded area;
- TN (*True Negative*): when the classifier correctly identifies a not flooded element;
- FN (*False Negative*): when the cell is not inundated for the classifier, but the flood reference map identifies it as an element of a flooded area.

By this point the *true positive rate* r_{tp} and *false positive rate* r_{fp} are defined:

$$r_{tp} = \frac{TP}{TP + FN}$$

$$r_{fp} = \frac{FP}{FP + TN}$$

and the best performing threshold is measured by minimizing the following objective function:

$$OB = r_{fp} + (1 - r_{tp})$$

Above-mentioned rates can be exploited also for deriving two performance measures, namely the Receiver Operating Characteristics (ROC) curves and the Area Under Curve (AUC), evaluated for each ROC line [37].

4 Results and Discussion

Results of the calibration steps for the case study are illustrated with respect to metrics described in Sect. 3, and summarized accordingly:

- Figure 2 a visual comparison between reference and descriptor maps for a 30-years return period event is shown;

- in Table 1 numerical outputs of linear binary classifiers method are reported, together to AUC values;
- in Fig. 3 ROC curves for H and GFI descriptors evaluated for a 30-year return period event are illustrated.

Table 1. Results of the calibration procedure for morphological descriptors for investigated return periods

Return period	Descriptor	Resolution (m)	τ	r_{fp}	r_{tp}	*min(ob)*	AUC
30 years	H	2	−0.791	0.047	0.975	0.071	0.987
		8	−0.855	0.091	0.907	0.184	0.955
		30	−0.595	0.250	0.900	0.349	0.898
	GFI	2	−0.479	0.058	0.856	0.202	0.949
		8	−0.492	0.092	0.890	0.202	0.946
		30	−0.310	0.266	0.900	0.365	0.876
200 years	H	2	−0.753	0.051	0.975	0.077	0.989
		8	−0.824	0.105	0.909	0.196	0.955
		30	−0.392	0.310	0.947	0.363	0.903
	GFI	2	−0.491	0.057	0.819	0.237	0.933
		8	−0.564	0.133	0.907	0.226	0.946
		30	−0.310	0.258	0.874	0.383	0.882
500 years	H	2	−0.753	0.044	0.967	0.077	0.990
		8	−0.824	0.105	0.892	0.213	0.951
		30	−0.392	0.310	0.942	0.367	0.895
	GFI	2	−0.493	0.053	0.815	0.238	0.931
		8	−0.561	0.131	0.888	0.243	0.941
		30	−0.505	0.334	0.942	0.392	0.874

The visual analysis of the flooded areas obtained by applying the calibration procedure described is illustrated in Fig. 2 for the GFI index for the event with a return time of 30 years. It is possible to appreciate the effects of the related resolution of the digital terrain model on the distribution of the flooded areas, which faithfully follow the reference ones up to the intersection with the railway network, beyond which is less evident the ability of the descriptors in interpreting the phenomenology of the formation of flooded areas.

Results reported in Table 1 show a general tendency of both geomorphological descriptors to increase their performances in passing from a resolution of 30 m × 30 m to one of 2 m × 2 m. Moreover, this behavior does not seem to be affected by the return

2 m x 2 m   8 m x 8 m

30 m x 30 m

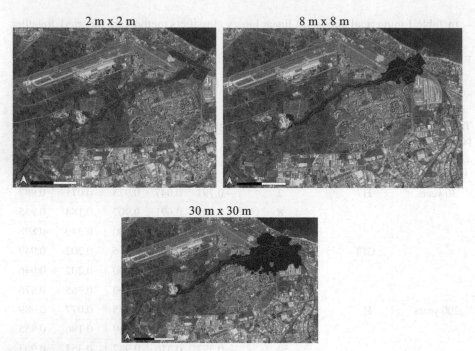

Fig. 2. High hydraulic hazard is represented by using the descriptor GFI for a 30-year return period event. In blue is represented flooded area obtained with the calibration procedure, while red line represents borders of reference map (Color figure online).

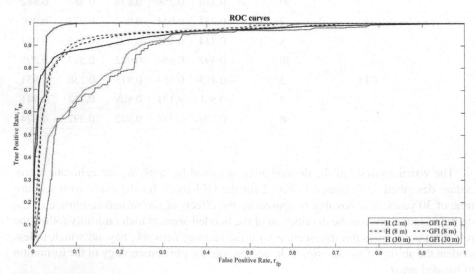

Fig. 3. Comparison of ROC curves for H and GFI descriptors evaluated for a 30-year return period event.

period of the simulated event, in accordance with what already observed by Gioia et al. [33].

The descriptor H is the one that presents the best results. Numerical evidence of this can be found in Table 1. In fact, with reference to the resolution of 2 m × 2 m and the three investigated return periods, it can be noted that the objective function assumes a minimum value of 0.071, with a maximum rate of true positives equal to 0.975. These are excellent performances, which are also reflected in the AUC values, which are close to 0.990. At the other resolutions, on the other hand, a progressive loss of performance is observed, due to the lower accuracy in the reproduction of the real flooded surface.

These results and considerations can also be extended to the GFI, albeit with lower performance over the entire study area. In any case, the results are still good, and reflect, in absolute values, what already emerged in previous studies conducted in similar areas [33, 36].

A visual inspection of these results can be obtained by the analysis of Fig. 3, where ROC curves for H and GFI descriptors evaluated for a 30-year return period event are reported.

The illustrated results confirm good performances of investigated descriptors in interpreting the flood susceptibility of the areas conterminous to those of the Lama Balice. This seems to reflect the effect of the singular morphology of these karst structures. The effect of the resolution of the digital terrain model is confirmed to be an important element for the accuracy of the results, to the detriment, however, of the computational effort. In fact, in passing from the resolution of 2 m × 2 m to the others, the number of cells of the raster greatly decreased, decreasing the time necessary for the completion of the algorithms. This seems to suggest the possibility of adopting an intermediate resolution for a preliminary rough mapping to be carried out on larger areas, reserving more detailed analyzes for particular cases.

5 Conclusions

Taking advantage of the case study of lama Balice, the morphological descriptors of basin and the linear binary classifiers method were applied in order to compare the results for different DTM resolution.

Aim of this study was to provide a further research contribution carried out on karst ephemeral streams conducted in last years, trying to provide technical insights for supporting further analyses in similar areas, characterized by a common nature and hydrological phenomenology. This paper can be considered as a starting point for setting up a hierarchical approach aimed at mapping flood-prone areas in these areas, supporting decision-makers and local authorities in a sustainable management of these territories.

References

1. Iacobellis, V., et al.: Investigation of a Flood Event Occurred on Lama Balice, in the Context of Hazard Map Evaluation in Karstic-Ephemeral Streams. In: Gervasi, O., et al. (eds.) ICCSA 2018. LNCS, vol. 10964, pp. 317–333. Springer, Cham (2018). https://doi.org/10.1007/978-3-319-95174-4_26

2. Morita, M., Yamaguchi, H.: Quantification of increased flood risk caused by global climate change for urban river management planning. In: 7th NOVATECH, Conference on Sustainable Techniques and Strategies for Urban Water Management, Lyon, France (2010)
3. Kazama, S., Sato, A., Kawagoe, S.: Evaluating the cost of flood damage based on changes in extreme rainfall in Japan. Sustain. Sci. **4**(1), 61–69 (2009)
4. Zhou, Q., Mikkelsen, P.S., Halsnæs, K., Arnbjerg-Nielsen, K.: Framework for economic pluvial flood risk assessment considering climate change effects and adaptation benefits. J. Hydrol. **414–415**, 539–549 (2012)
5. Kundzewicz, Z.W., et al.: Flood risk and climate change: global and regional perspectives. Hydrol. Sci. J. **59**(1), 1–28 (2014). https://doi.org/10.1080/02626667.2013.857411
6. Sangiorgio, V., Fiorito, F., Santamouris, M.: Development of a holistic urban heat island evaluation methodology. Sci. Rep. **10**(1), 1–13 (2020). https://doi.org/10.1038/s41598-020-75018-4
7. Sangiorgio, V., Uva, G., Adam, J.M.: Integrated seismic vulnerability assessment of historical masonry churches including architectural and artistic assets based on macro-element approach. Int. J. Arch. Heritage (2020). https://doi.org/10.1080/15583058.2019.1709916
8. Fidelibus, M.D., Balacco, G., Gioia, A., Iacobellis, V., Spilotro, G.: Mass transport triggered by heavy rainfall: the role of endorheic basins and epikarst in a regional karst aquifer. Hydrol. Process. (2017). https://doi.org/10.1002/hyp.11037
9. Balacco, G.: The interrill erosion for a sandy loam soil. Int. J. Sediment Res. (2013). https://doi.org/10.1016/S1001-6279(13)60043-8
10. Montanari, A., et al.: "Panta Rhei—everything flows": change in hydrology and society—the IAHS Scientific Decade 2013–2022. Hydrol. Sci. J. **58**(6), 1256–1275 (2013). https://doi.org/10.1080/02626667.2013.809088
11. Morse, C.C., Huryn, A.D., Cronan, C.: Impervious surface areas as a predictor of the effects of urbanization on stream insect communities in Maine, USA. Environ. Monit. Assess. **89**, 95–127 (2003)
12. Carlson, T.N., Arthur, S.T.: The impact of land use — land cover changes due to urbanization on surface microclimate and hydrology: a satellite perspective. Global Planet. Change **25**(1), 49–65 (2000)
13. Mattia, F., et al.: Time series of COSMO-SkyMed data for landcover classification and surface parameter retrieval over agricultural sites. In: Proceedings of the IEEE 2012 International Geoscience and Remote Sensing Symposium, IGARSS 2012, Munich, Germany, 22–27 July, 2012, IEEE Publications (USA, 2012), pp. 6511–6514, ISBN:978-1-4673-1159-5.
14. Jain, S.K., Singh, R.D., Jain, M.K., Lohani, A.K.: Delineation of flood-prone areas using remote sensing techniques. Water Resour. Manage. **19**, 333 (2005). https://doi.org/10.1007/s11269-005-3281-5
15. De Giorgis, M., Gnecco, G., Gorni, S., Roth, G., Sanguineti, M., Taramasso, A.C.: Classifiers for the detection of flood-prone areas using remote sensed elevation data. J. Hydrol. **470–471**, 302–315 (2012)
16. Manfreda, S., et al.: Flood-prone areas assessment using linear binary classifiers based on flood maps obtained from 1D and 2D hydraulic models. Nat. Hazards **79**(2), 735–754 (2015). https://doi.org/10.1007/s11069-015-1869-5
17. Balenzano, A., et al.: A ground network for sar-derived soil moisture product calibration, validation and exploitation in southern Italy. In: Proceedings of the IEEE 2014 International Geoscience and Remote Sensing Symposium, IGARSS 2014, Quèbec, Canada July 13–18 (2014)
18. Beven, K.: Rainfall-Runoff Modelling The Primer, 2nd edn. Wiley-Blackwell, Chichester, UK (2012)

19. Gioia, A., Manfreda, S., Iacobellis, V., Fiorentino, M.: Performance of a theoretical model for the description of water balance and runoff dynamics in Southern Italy. J. Hydrol. Eng. **19**(6), 1113–1123 (2014). https://doi.org/10.1061/(ASCE)HE.1943-5584.0000879
20. Gioia, A.: Reservoir routing on double-peak design flood. Water **8**, 553 (2016)
21. Johnston, P.R., Pilgrim, D.H.: Parameter optimization for watershed models. Water Resour. Res. **12**(3), 477–486 (1976)
22. Williams, B.J., Yeh, W.W.G.: Parameter estimation in rainfall-runoff models. J. Hydrol. **63**, 373–393 (1983)
23. Jiang, Y., Liu, C., Li, X., Liu, L., Wang, H.: Rainfall-runoff modeling, parameter estimation and sensitivity analysis in a semiarid catchment. Environ. Model. Softw. **67**, 72–88 (2015)
24. Grimaldi, S., Nardi, F., Piscopia, R., Petroselli, A., Apollonio, C.: Continuous hydrologic modelling for design simulation in small and ungauged basins: a step forward and some tests for its practical use. J. Hydrol. 595, 125664 (2021). ISSN 0022-1694, https://doi.org/10.1016/j.jhydrol.2020.125664.
25. Annis, A., et al.: UAV-DEMs for small-scale flood hazard mapping. Water **12**, 1717 (2020). https://doi.org/10.3390/w12061717
26. Manfreda, S., Di Leo, M., Sole, A.: Detection of flood prone areas using digital elevation models. J. Hydrol. Eng. **16**(10), 781–790 (2011). https://doi.org/10.1061/(ASCE)HE.1943-5584.0000367
27. Samela, C., Manfreda, S., Paola, F.D., Giugni, M., Sole, A., Fiorentino, M.: DEM-based approaches for the delineation of flood-prone areas in an ungauged basin in Africa. J. Hydrol. Eng. (2015). https://doi.org/10.1061/(ASCE)HE.1943-5584
28. Samela, C., Troy, T.J., Manfreda, S.: Flood hazard mapping over large regions. Adv. Water Resour. (2017)
29. Slatton, K.C., Carter, W.E., Shrestha, R.L., Dietrich, W.E.: Airborne laser swath mapping: achieving the resolution and accuracy required for geosurficial research. Geophys. Res. Lett. **34**, L23S10 (2007). https://doi.org/10.1029/2007GL031939
30. Dodov, B.A., Foufoula-Georgiou, E.: Floodplain morphometry extraction from a high-resolution digital elevation model: a simple algorithm for regional analysis studies. Geosci. Remote Sens. Lett. IEEE **3**(3), 410–413 (2006). https://doi.org/10.1109/LGRS.2006.874161
31. De Risi, R., Jalayer, F., De Paola, F., Giugni, M.: Probabilistic delineation of flood-prone areas based on a digital elevation model and the extent of historical flooding: the case of Ouagadougou. Boletín Geol. Minero **125**, 329–340 (2014)
32. Nardi, F., Vivoni, E.R., Grimaldi, S.: Investigating a floodplain scaling relation using a hydrogeomorphic delineation method. Water Resour. Res. **42**(9), W09409 (2006)
33. Gioia, A., Totaro, V., Bonelli, R., Esposito, A.A.M.G., Balacco, G., Iacobellis, V.: Flood susceptibility evaluation on ephemeral streams of southern Italy: a case study of Lama Balice. In: Gervasi, O., et al. (eds.) ICCSA 2018. LNCS, vol. 10964, pp. 334–348. Springer, Cham (2018). https://doi.org/10.1007/978-3-319-95174-4_27
34. Natural Park of Lama Balice: https://www.parcolamabalice.it/. Accessed 5 May 2021
35. Mossa, M.: The floods in Bari: what history should have taught. J. Hydraul. Res. **45**(5), 579–594 (2007). https://doi.org/10.1080/00221686.2007.9521795

36. Balacco, G., Totaro, V., Gioia, A., Piccinni, A.F.: Evaluation of geomorphic descriptors thresholds for flood prone areas detection on ephemeral streams in the metropolitan area of Bari (Italy). In: Misra, S., et al. (eds.) ICCSA 2019. LNCS, vol. 11622, pp. 239–254. Springer, Cham (2019). https://doi.org/10.1007/978-3-030-24305-0_19

37. Samela, C., Manfreda, S., Paola, F.D., Giugni, M., Sole, A., Fiorentino, M.: DEM-based approaches for the delineation of flood-prone areas in an ungauged basin in Africa. J. Hydrol. Eng. (2015). https://doi.org/10.1061/(ASCE)HE.1943-5584.0001272

Modeling Land Cover Impact on Albedo Changes in Google Earth Engine Environment

Alessandra Capolupo(✉) ⊙, Cristina Monterisi, Alberico Sonnessa,
Giacomo Caporusso, and Eufemia Tarantino⊙

Department of Civil, Environmental, Land, Construction and Chemistry (DICATECh),
Politecnico di Bari, Via Orabona 4, 70125 Bari, Italy
alessandra.capolupo@poliba.it

Abstract. Over the last decades, Earth's surface has suffered an intense urbanisation process that has impacted Land Use/Land Cover (LULC) and Earth's surface energy balance. Such a rapid and unexpected phenomenon was not carried out in a sustainable way compromising Earth's existence in the long term. Therefore, the United States identified 17 Sustainable Development Goals (SDGs) to meet within 2030. To make the world more resilient and sustainable and combat climate changes, information concerning LULC conversion trends and land surface albedo is essential. Such variables are directly responsible for the increment and decrement of air and surface temperature and, consequently, to the Urban Heat Island (UHI) phenomenon. The present paper explores Google Earth Engine (GEE) platform potentialities in investigating the relationship between LULC transformation and land surface albedo extracted from medium-resolution satellite data. The present analysis was performed on the study area of Berlin for 8 years, from 2011 to 2019. Two radiometrically and atmospherically corrected Landsat images were gathered from Landsat 5 and Landsat 8 missions, respectively. Once clouds have been masked, SwirTirRed (STRed) and Normalized Difference Bareness (version 1) (NDBaI1) indices were implemented to distinguish LULC types. Subsequently, LULC changes were assessed, and land surface albedo was estimated by programming a proper code. Thus, the relationship among those features was investigated in such areas in the considered period. GEE appears as the optimal solution to meet research goals and to extend the analysis at a global scale.

Keywords: Geospatial big data · Sustainable development · Urban Heat Island · Climate change · Landsat satellite images

1 Introduction

Environmental ecosystem degradation and human well-being reduction are mainly due to global warming, which is enhanced by anthropogenic activities [1, 2]. Urbanisation phenomenon, indeed, defaces natural Land Use/Land Cover (LULC) and this directly impacts on Earth's surface energy balance of such area [3–8] and, consequently, on its air and surface temperatures. The wide use of non-evaporating impervious materials in the

© Springer Nature Switzerland AG 2021
O. Gervasi et al. (Eds.): ICCSA 2021, LNCS 12955, pp. 89–101, 2021.
https://doi.org/10.1007/978-3-030-87007-2_7

built environment is one of the main factors causing the Urban Heat Island (UHI) phenomenon [9], which describes the higher air and surface temperatures in built-up areas in comparison to surrounding rural environments [10]. This issue is further intensified by the unchecked, unsustainable urban sprawl that occurred in the last few years.

To face such a situation and to improve cities sustainability and resilience to climate changes, the United States detected 17 Sustainable Development Goals (SDGs) to meet within 2030. Thus, LULC transformation and albedo changes are the main driving forces to be investigated in order to address the SDGs [11, 12]. Well-defined indices to detect such features globally and locally and to explore their relationship are needed. Among the various techniques developed over the years, Remote Sensing is a powerful tool to accurately quantify them in a short time [13, 14]. According to study areas characteristics and variables to analyse, different approaches may be adopted. Each of them requires a different amount of a priori information and a specific processing time, allowing to achieve a given accuracy. Thus, the optimal strategy should be selected as a compromise among resultant map accuracy, processing time and algorithms complexity to be implemented [15]. For instance, LULC classes extraction is commonly carried out using one of the following approaches: Maximum Likelihood (ML) [16], Index-Based approach (IB) [17], Object-Based Image Analysis (OBIA) [17–19], Machine Learning Algorithms (MLA) [20]. Nonetheless, each of them shows some weakness: ML achieves the lowest accuracy [21], IB involves the application of several indices to classify a large area [15], OBIA requires a huge number of a priori information [22], and, lastly, MLA are based on very complex algorithms [20].

The estimation of land surface albedo is still difficult to derive from satellite images. Satellites, cannot measure such parameter directly and, therefore, over the years, several algorithms, consistent with sensor features mounted on the applied platforms, have been proposed. Nevertheless, all of them are based on Top Of the Atmosphere (TOA) corrected images because of the need to remove the atmospheric scattering inferring with the surface albedo [23].

Defining LULC trends and albedo changes over the years is time-consuming since a considerable number of geospatial data covering a large interval should be handled. Just the introduction of cloud-based platforms allowed to meet such emerging needs. Therefore, Google Earth Engine (GEE) environment has appeared as a good solution to process big geospatial data provided by several sources [24]. A proper infrastructure, a storage unit, daily updated with nearly free-available 6000 raw and pre-processed data, and a python/JavaScript-based Application Programming Interface (API) are its main components [25]. Mainly, API makes it more flexible than traditional desktop system because it ensures the opportunity to exploit complex and advanced algorithms already implemented in GEE libraries or to program new ones [24, 25].

Additionally, it allows minimising processing time thanks to many processors working in parallel. Hansen et al. (2013) [26] demonstrated the time needed to track forest cover changes between 2000 and 2012 by processing 654,178 Landsat 7 scenes (707 terabytes) was of 100 h and 1,000,000 h in GEE and desktop system, respectively. Such an experiment confirmed the substantial improvements introduced by GEE platform in the remote sensing world. Nevertheless, a significant effort is still needed to develop good algorithms to produce accurate classification and land surface albedo maps.

The present research is framed in such a context. This study is aimed at developing a proper Javascript code in GEE environment to analyse: i) LULC transformation over 8 years, from 2011 up to 2019; and ii) land surface albedo trends over the same period. Lastly, the relationship between such phenomena was explored too. The municipality of Berlin was selected as a pilot case. Both features were extracted from medium-resolution Landsat satellite images belonging to mission 5 and 8.

2   Material and Methods

2.1   Area of Interest and Selected Data

Berlin city, located in the eastern part of Germany, was selected as the experimental site to investigate the impact of LULC variation on land surface albedo (Fig. 1). Such area was characterised by a significant urban sprawl between 2011 and 2019. This phenomenon was enhanced by the flat topography of such zone as well as economic interests. Indeed, an average inhabits increment equal to 16% per year in the residential zone was detected [27]. Simultaneously, new projections indicate a continuous population growth in the inner area within 2030.

Nonetheless, currently, it is one of the greenest cities in the world, thanks to the presence of large public green spaces and forested areas. Such features cover about the 30% of the whole territory [28]. Because of the above-mentioned properties, it was considered as the optimal site to meet the research purposes.

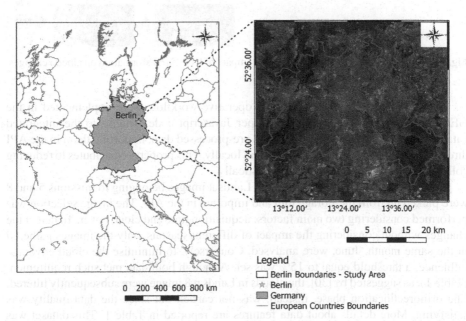

Fig. 1. Overview of the study area. Germany position in the European context on the left and zoom on Berlin city on the right. (Color figure online)

2.2 Operative Workflow and Database Construction

Figure 2 reports the operative workflow adopted to meet the research purposes. Once selecting satellite data and constructing the geo-database, images quality was assessed and improved. Such pre-processed data were used as input of the subsequent processing investigations. Firstly, LULC classification map was extracted through the computation of proper vegetation indices. Simultaneously, the land surface albedo was estimated too. Lastly, before statistically investigating the correlation among the outputs of previous processing steps, the reliability of such findings was investigated. Each phase is detailed in what follows.

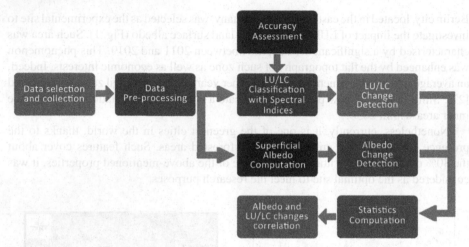

Fig. 2. Operative workflow to investigate the impact of LULC transformation on albedo changes.

All phases of the above-mentioned operative workflow were implemented in the GEE environment by developing a proper Javascript code. Thanks to the integrated catalogue, users can access both raw and pre-processed data, importing them in the API directly without needing to download them locally. This property contributes to reducing collecting and operational time [27] drastically.

Thus, two atmospherically corrected Landsat images belonging to missions 5 and 8 were picked up from the storage unit and imported in the API. The image selection was performed considering two main factors: acquisition time and cloud cover. To detect the changes without considering the impact of different seasons, only the images gathered in the same month, June, were analysed. Conversely, to minimise the cloud coverage influence, a threshold equal to 15% was set. Although both data met such requirement (Table 1), as suggested by [30], the clouds in Landsat 8 image were subsequently filtered. The orthorectification phase, instead, was not carried out since the data quality was satisfying. More details about data features are reported in Table 1. This dataset was further investigated in the subsequent steps.

Table 1. Main features of selected Landsat data. TM: thematic mapper; OLI-TIRS: operational land imager - thermal infrared.

ID	Landsat Mission	Sensor	Landsat Images	Acquisition Date (mm/dd/yyyy)	Acquisition Time	Average Cloud Cover (%)
1	Landsat 5	TM	LT05_L1TP_193023_ 20110602_20161009 _01_T1	06/02/2011	09:52	0
2	Landsat 8	OLI-TIRS	LC08_L1TP_193023_ 20190624_20190704 _01_T1	06/24/2019	10:02	12

2.3 LULC Classification and Change Detection Analysis and Accuracy Assessment

Index-based methods are commonly applied to quickly produce thematic maps of a certain area, albeit each index can automatically get just a few LULC classes. Therefore, the combination of more indices is often required to classify the whole experimental site. This was the case of the present research where the version 1 of the Normalized Difference Bareness Index (NDBaI1) (Eq. 1) [31] and the SwirTirRed (STRed) index (Eq. 2) [32] were integrated.

$$NDBaI1 = \frac{SWIR2 - TIR1}{SWIR2 + TIR1} \tag{1}$$

$$STRed = \frac{SWIR1 + R - TIR1}{SWIR1 + R + TIR1} \tag{2}$$

NDBaI1 allowed detecting bare soil and built-up classes, as well as STRed, by permitting to distinguish water, dense and sparse vegetation. This procedure was separately implemented on both pre-processed images.

The accuracy of the resultant maps was assessed by computing three widely applied statistical metrics: i) the Overall Accuracy (OA), ii) the Producer's Accuracy (PA), and, lastly, iii) the User's Accuracy (UA) [33, 34]. All of them can assume a value comprised between 0 and 1. The highest value, the most accurate the finding is. These indicators were calculated by comparing the obtained thematic maps with a reference set of 40068 testing pixels, generated using the "stratified random sampling polygon" approach [35]. A testing sample number consistent with the classes size was selected. Thus, 5354, 14063, 4302, 4179, and, lastly, 12170 were picked up from water, dense vegetation, sparse vegetation, built-up and bare soil categories, respectively.

2.4 Land Surface Albedo Computation

In 2000, Liang et al. [36] developed various processes to estimate the land surface albedo from different satellite platforms. They handled the most widely spread satellite images at that time, like Landsat, using hundreds of filed measurements as calibration data. Equation 3 reports the formula to compute the albedo (a) from Landsat images:

$$a = 0.356 * \varrho_1 + 0.130 * \varrho_3 + 0.373 * \varrho_4 + 0.085 * \varrho_5 + 0.072 * \varrho_7 - 0.0018 \quad (3)$$

ϱ_i are the Top of Atmosphere (ToA) Landsat bands.

This formula was, subsequently, snormalised by Smith et al. (2000) [37] (Eq. 4).

$$a = \frac{0.356 * \varrho_1 + 0.130 * \varrho_3 + 0.373 * \varrho_4 + 0.085 * \varrho_5 + 0.072 * \varrho_7 - 0.0018}{0.356 + 0.130 + 0.373 + 0.085 + 0.072} \quad (4)$$

Equation 4 was implemented in the GEE environment to compute a from the two Landsat images.

2.5 Change Detection Analysis and Relationship Between LULC and Albedo

A multitemporal analysis over a period of 8 years considering both LULC and a was performed. Although various methods have been developed, the approach based on the comparison of the resultant thematic maps was preferred. Indeed, this time-saving approach allows detecting the altered areas without using a hard computational power [38]. It involves the subtraction of a thematic map from that one produced on the previous date. Equations 5 and 6 report the formula to compute the LULC and a changes, respectively.

$$CD_{LULC} = LULC_2 - LULC_1 \quad (5)$$

where $LULC_2$ and $LULC_1$ are the LULC maps generated from the images collected in 2019 and 2011, respectively.

$$CD_a = a_2 - a_1 \quad (6)$$

where a_2 and a_1 are the albedo charts produced from the Landsat images acquired in 2019 and 2011, respectively.

This approach does not suffer from topographic characteristics influence, and, consequently, it may be applied in all LULC environment [39]. Nevertheless, the accuracy of its outcomes is affected by the random noise [39]. Thus, the variation percentage of both parameters was computed for each LULC class.

Once the change detection analysis was completed, the correlation between the two resultant maps was carried out. This step was essential to analyse the influence of LULC alteration on surface energy balance.

3 Results and Discussion

Figure 3 reports the outcome of the index-based method, separately applied on the input set of data. As previously described, it was generated by computing the STRed and the NDBaI1 indices. The former detected water, sparse and dense vegetation, while the latter distinguished bare soil and built-up zone. Although this method does not allow quantitatively detecting the changes occurring in such a site, it permits a preliminary idea of the transformation process. Thus, a visual inspection of the resultant thematic maps was performed as well as the area covered by each LULC category was computed. These steps provided information regarding the relevant urban sprawl phenomenon that occurred around the city centre and the increment of the green areas in the peri-urban areas. Indeed, the number of red and green pixels is higher in the middle and on the border of the Landsat images acquired on the 24th of June 2019 (Fig. 3D) than the one collected on the 2nd of June 2011.

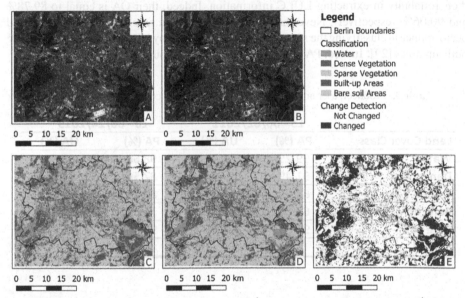

Legend

☐ Berlin Boundaries

Classification
- Water
- Dense Vegetation
- Sparse Vegetation
- Built-up Areas
- Bare soil Areas

Change Detection
- Not Changed
- Changed

Fig. 3. Landsat data acquired by missions five on 2nd of June 2011 (A) and eight on 24th of June 2019 (B); the corresponding LULC classifications in (C) and (D); and LULC changes occurred between 2011 and 2019 (E). (Color figure online)

Nevertheless, considering the whole study area, an urban zone and bare soil extension reduction were identified (Table 2). Conversely, sparse and dense vegetated pixels covered a higher extended area. This analysis was subsequently detailed during the change detection investigation phase.

Table 2. LULC classes extension extracted by handling satellite images acquired by Landsat missions 5 and 8, respectively.

LU/LC Class coverage	L5 - 06/02/2011	L8 - 06/24/2019
Water (%)	3.38	3.58
Dense Vegetation (%)	15.21	15.76
Sparse Vegetation (%)	16.76	17.46
Built-up (%)	5.42	5.25
Bare soil (%)	59.23	57.95

Before proceeding with the change detection phase, STRed and NDBaI1 accuracy was evaluated. Indeed, such indices were selected according to their effectiveness shown in the previous studies [17, 29, 31]. Metrics accuracy, reported in Table 3, confirms their reliability in extracting LULC information. Indeed, their OA is equal to 89.78% and 90.06%, respectively. Nevertheless, the classification result is affected by STRed performance in classifying the sparse vegetation zone and by NDBaI1 ability in detecting built-up areas [29]. Indeed, PA and UA values of such groups are the smallest.

Table 3. Producer, user and overall accuracy of the two collected satellite images

	L5 - 06/02/2011		L8 - 06/24/2019	
Land Cover Class	PA (%)	UA (%)	PA (%)	UA (%)
Water	99.25	99.42	98.66	98.51
Dense Veg.	91.49	97.44	87.56	97.84
Sparse Veg.	83.26	64.18	83.24	36.9
Built-up	67.84	89.66	77.64	99.22
Bare soil	95.89	85.79	95.88	89.44
OA (%)	89.78		90.07	

On the basis of the accuracy results, the generated classification maps were considered reliable, and thus, they were applied in the subsequent investigation phase through the computation of CD_{LULC}. Figure 3E shows CD_{LULC} result: transformed and not transformed areas are described in blue and white, respectively. This analysis confirms the results obtained by the qualitative investigation. Although an urban sprawl phenomenon is visible, a substantial increment of the green areas is reported on the surrounding. Figure 3E allows spatially allocating the transformed zone, while Table 4 gives the conversion percentage. Most of the changes were in the urban and sparse vegetated areas. The former class was drastically reduced in favour of bare soil and sparse vegetation; conversely, the latter was partially converted in dense vegetation and partially in bare soil. The conversion of sparse green areas is mainly linked to the difficulties of STRed index in correctly classifying such group. Probably, the images acquisition period affected the discrimination of such group too. Similarly, the scarce accuracy of NDBaI1 in detecting built-up areas compromised CD$_{LULC}$ results too.

Table 4. LULC conversion over an investigated period of 8 years (2011–2019).

L5 02/06/2011	Water (%)	Dense Veg. (%)	Sparse Veg. (%)	Bare soil Areas (%)	Built-up Areas (%)
			L8 24/06/2019		
Water (%)	98.13	0.64	0.36	0.16	0.71
Dense Veg. (%)	1.25	73.37	20.19	4.85	0.34
Sparse Veg. (%)	0.04	33.74	35.63	28.51	2.09
Bare soil Areas (%)	0.01	0.51	8.78	88.39	2.31
Built-up Areas (%)	0.02	0.10	2.15	24.27	73.46

Figure 4 reports the land surface albedo obtained from the input pre-processed satellite images using the snormalised version of Liang et al. [36] algorithm. Visually comparing the two colour-graduated maps, an increment of the land surface albedo can be detected over the investigated period. Specifically, detected changes are reported in Fig. 4E. Thus, LULC and albedo transformations were correlated to sanalyse the impact of LULC changes on surface energy.

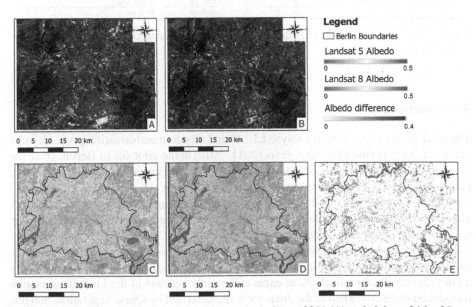

Fig. 4. Landsat data acquired by missions five on 2nd of June 2011 (A) and eight on 24th of June 2019 (B); the corresponding land surface albedo in (C) and (D); and land surface albedo changes occurred between 2011 and 2019 (E).

Both alterations are reported in Fig. 5, which shows the location correspondence between the two outcomes. Additionally, a substantial increment of albedo can be detected in those areas converted from dense to sparse vegetation or to bare soil. A slight increment, instead, is seen in the other cases. Figure 5 shows percentage variation too.

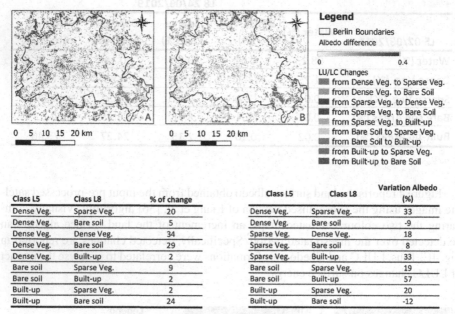

Legend

☐ Berlin Boundaries
Albedo difference

0   0.4

LU/LC Changes
▰ from Dense Veg. to Sparse Veg.
▰ from Dense Veg. to Bare Soil
▰ from Sparse Veg. to Dense Veg.
▰ from Sparse Veg. to Bare Soil
▰ from Sparse Veg. to Built-up
▰ from Bare Soil to Sparse Veg.
▰ from Bare Soil to Built-up
▰ from Built-up to Sparse Veg.
▰ from Built-up to Bare Soil

Class L5	Class L8	% of change
Dense Veg.	Sparse Veg.	20
Dense Veg.	Bare soil	5
Dense Veg.	Dense Veg.	34
Dense Veg.	Bare soil	29
Dense Veg.	Built-up	2
Bare soil	Sparse Veg.	9
Bare soil	Built-up	2
Built-up	Sparse Veg.	2
Built-up	Bare soil	24

Class L5	Class L8	Variation Albedo (%)
Dense Veg.	Sparse Veg.	33
Dense Veg.	Bare soil	-9
Sparse Veg.	Dense Veg.	18
Sparse Veg.	Bare soil	8
Sparse Veg.	Built-up	33
Bare soil	Sparse Veg.	19
Bare soil	Built-up	57
Built-up	Sparse Veg.	20
Built-up	Bare soil	-12

Fig. 5. LULC (A) and albedo (B) changes and the corresponding percentage variation in the tables at the bottom

4   Conclusion

The goal of this paper was to analyse LULC and albedo transformation processes that occurred over a period of about 8 years (2011–2019) in the pilot site of Berlin. Once the detection phase was concluded, the impact of LULC alteration on the surface energy balance was investigated. Berlin was selected as the pilot site of this work because of the urbanisation process that it suffered to address the strong population growth. Indeed, although berlin is still considered one of the greenest cities worldwide, a strong urban sprawl phenomenon can be detected in the urban areas. Conversely, green areas were further intensified in semi-urban zones. Nonetheless, considering the whole study area, the greenery conversion was more relevant than the urbanisation one. This did not imply a land surface albedo reduction, as expected, mainly because of the kind of vegetation introduced in the city. Most of the areas were characterised by sparse vegetation, and it is widely known that its albedo value is pretty like that of built-up areas. Thus, the adopted planning strategies were not suitable for improving the land surface albedo condition and tackling climate change issues.

All the investigation was performed in a GEE environment that appeared as an essential tool to meet the research purposes. Indeed, thanks to its great versatility, mainly due to the possibility to customise the algorithms; it allowed to build a proper Javascript code able to meet all the investigation steps. Additionally, being a cloud environment, it allows reducing the operational time overcoming standard desktop limitations.

Thus, combining the implemented operative workflow and GEE environment allows obtaining promising findings in detecting the impact of LULC transformation on albedo alteration. Thus, in the near future, such developed code will be applied worldwide to produce a thematic map to explore the linkage between such indicators.

Acknowledgements. This research is partially funded under the project "AIM1871082-1" of the AIM (Attraction and International Mobility) Program, financed by the Italian Ministry of Education, University and Research (MIUR).

References

1. Singh, A., Purohit, B.M.: Public health impacts of global warming and climate change. Peace Rev. **26**, 112–120 (2014)
2. Al-Ghussain, L.: Global warming: review on driving forces and mitigation. Environ. Prog. Sustain. Energy **38**, 13–21 (2019)
3. Boccia, L., Capolupo, A., Rigillo, M., Russo, V.: Terrace abandonment hazards in a mediterranean cultural landscape. J. Hazard. Toxic Radioact. Waste **24**(1), 04019034 (2020)
4. Lama, G.F.C., Chirico, G.B.: Effects of reed beds management on the hydrodynamic behaviour of vegetated open channels. In: 2020 IEEE International Workshop on Metrology for Agriculture and Forestry (MetroAgriFor), pp. 149–154. IEEE, November (2020)
5. Capolupo, A., Boccia, L.: Innovative method for linking anthropisation process to vulnerability. World Rev. Sci. Technol. Sustain. Dev. **17**(1), 4–22 (2021)
6. Errico, A., Lama, G.F.C., Francalanci, S., Chirico, G.B., Solari, L., Preti, F.: Flow dynamics and turbulence patterns in a drainage channel colonized by common reed (Phragmites australis) under different scenarios of vegetation management. Ecol. Eng. **133**, 39–52 (2019). https://doi.org/10.1016/j.ecoleng.2019.04.016
7. Apollonio, C., Balacco, G., Novelli, A., Tarantino, E., Piccinni, A.F.: Land use change impact on flooding areas: the case study of Cervaro Basin (Italy). Sustainability **8**(10), 996 (2016)
8. Lama, G.F.C., Crimaldi, M., Pasquino, V., Padulano, R., Chirico, G.B.: Bulk drag predictions of riparian arundo donax stands through UAV-acquired multispectral images. Water **13**(10), 1333 (2021). https://doi.org/10.3390/w13101333
9. Stathopoulou, E., Mihalakakou, G., Santamouris, M., Bagiorgas, H.S.: On the impact of temperature on tropospheric ozone concentration levels in urban environments. J. Earth Syst. Sci. **117**(3), 227–236 (2008)
10. Santamouris, M.: Urban reality – solar design and refurbishment in the built environment. United Kingdom (2001)
11. Voogt, J.A., Oke, T.R.: Thermal remote sensing of urban climates. Remote Sens. Environ. **86**, 370–384 (2003)
12. Souch, C., Grimmond, S.: Applied climatology: urban climate. Prog. Phys. Geogr. **30**, 270–279 (2006)
13. Chen, X.L., Zhao, H.M., Li, P.X., Yin, Z.Y.: Remote sensing image-based analysis of the relationship between urban heat island and land use/cover changes. Remote Sens. Environ. **104**(2), 133–146 (2006)

14. Mirzaei, M., Verrelst, J., Arbabi, M., Shaklabadi, Z., Lotfizadeh, M.: Urban heat island monitoring and impacts on citizen's general health status in Isfahan metropolis: a remote sensing and field survey approach. Remote Sens. **12**(8), 1350 (2020)

15. Patel, N., et al.: Multitemporalsettlement and population mapping from Landsat using Google Earth Engine. Int. J. Appl. Earth Obs. Geoinf. **35**(199–208), 2015 (2015)

16. Susaki, J., Shibasaki, R.: Maximum likelihood method modified in estimating a prior probability and in improving misclassification errors. Int. Arch. Photogramm. Remote Sens. **33**, 1499–1504 (2000)

17. Capolupo, A., Monterisi, C., Caporusso, G., Tarantino, E.: Extracting land cover data using GEE: a review of the classification indices. In: Gervasi, O., Murgante, B., Misra, S., Garau, C., Blečić, I., Taniar, D., Apduhan, B.O., Rocha, A.M.A.C., Tarantino, E., Torre, C.M., Karaca, Y. (eds.) ICCSA 2020. LNCS, vol. 12252, pp. 782–796. Springer, Cham (2020). https://doi.org/10.1007/978-3-030-58811-3_56

18. Crocetto, N., Tarantino, E.: A class-oriented strategy for features extraction from multidate ASTER imagery. Remote Sens. **1**, 1171–1189 (2009)

19. Sarzana, T., Maltese, A., Capolupo, A., Tarantino, E.: Post-processing of pixel and object-based land cover classifications of very high spatial resolution images. In: Gervasi, O., Murgante, B., Misra, S., Garau, C., Blečić, I., Taniar, D., Apduhan, B.O., Ana, M.A., Rocha, C., Tarantino, E., Torre, C.M., Karaca, Y. (eds.) Computational Science and Its Applications – ICCSA 2020: 20th International Conference, Cagliari, Italy, July 1–4, 2020, Proceedings, Part IV, pp. 797–812. Springer International Publishing, Cham (2020). https://doi.org/10.1007/978-3-030-58811-3_57

20. Praticò, S., Solano, F., Di Fazio, S., Modica, G.: Machine learning classification of mediterranean forest habitats in Google earth engine based on seasonal sentinel-2 time-series and input image composition optimisation. Remote Sens. **13**(4), 586 (2021)

21. Chen, J., Gong, P., He, C., Pu, R., Shi, P.: Land-use/land-cover change detection using improved change-vector analysis. Photogramm. Eng. Remote Sens. **69**, 369–380 (2003)

22. Whiteside, T.G., Boggs, G.S., Maier, S.W.: Comparing object-based and pixel-based classifications for mapping savannas. Int. J. Appl. Earth Obs. Geoinf. **136**, 884–893 (2011)

23. Li, Z., Garand, L.: Estimation of surface albedo from space: a parameterization for global application. J. Geophys. Res.: Atmos. **99**(D4), 8335–8350 (1994)

24. Gorelick, N., Hancher, M., Dixon, M., Ilyushchenko, S., Thau, D., Moore, R.: Google Earth Engine: planetary-scale geospatial analysis for everyone. Remote Sens. Environ. **202**, 18–27 (2017)

25. Kumar, L., Mutanga, O.: Google earth engine applications since inception: usage, trends, and potential. Remote Sens. **10**(10), 1509 (2018)

26. Hansen, M., et al.: Observing the forest and the trees: the first high resolution global maps of forest cover change. Science **342**, 850–853 (2013)

27. Amt für Statistik: Berlin-Brandenburg Statistik Berlin-Brandenburg (2019). http://www.statistik-berlin-brandenburg.de/home.asp. Accessed 10 May 2019

28. Senatsverwaltung für Stadtentwicklung und Umwelt Berlin Stadtentwicklungsplan Wohnen 2025, Berlin, p. 119 (2014). http://www.stadtentwicklung.berlin.de/planen/stadtentwicklungsplanung/de/wohnen/download/step_wohnen_2025_bericht.pdf

29. Capolupo, A., Monterisi, C., Saponaro, M., Tarantino, E.: Multi-temporal analysis of land cover changes using Landsat data through Google Earth Engine platform. In: Eighth International Conference on Remote Sensing and Geoinformation of the Environment (RSCy2020), vol. 11524, p. 1152419. International Society for Optics and Photonics, August (2020)

30. Kauth, R.J.; Thomas, G.S.: The tasselled cap—a graphic description of the spectraltemporal development of agricultural crops as seen by landsat. In: Symposium on Machine Processing of Remotely Sensed Data. Purdue University, West Lafayette, Indiana, pp. 41–51 (1976)

31. Li, S., Chen, X.: A new bare-soil index for rapid mapping developing areas using landsat 8 data. Int. Arch. Photogramm. Remote Sens. Spatial Inf. Sci. **40**, 139–144 (2014)
32. Capolupo, A., Monterisi, C., Tarantino, E.: Landsat Images Classification Algorithm (LICA) to automatically extract land cover information in Google earth engine environment. Remote Sens. **12**(7), 1201 (2020)
33. Caprioli, M., Tarantino, E.: Accuracy assessment of per-field classification integrating very fine spatial resolution satellite imagery with topographic data. J. Geospat. Eng. **3**, 127–134 (2001)
34. Caprioli, M., Scognamiglio, A., Strisciuglio, G., Tarantino, E.: Rules and standards for spatial data quality in GIS environments. In: 21st Int. Cartographic Conf. Durban, South Africa, 10–16 August (2003)
35. Pengra, B., Long, J., Dahal, D., Stehman, S.V., Loveland, T.R.: A global reference database from very high resolution commercial satellite data and methodology for application to Landsat derived 30 m continuous field tree cover data. Remote Sens. Environ. **165**, 234–248 (2015)
36. Liang, S.: Narrowband to broadband conversions of land surface albedo I algorithms. Remote Sens. Environ. **76**, 213–238 (2000)
37. Smith, R.B. The heat budget of the earth's surface deduced from space (2010). Available on this site
38. Pindozzi, S., Cervelli, E., Capolupo, A., Okello, C., Boccia, L.: Using historical maps to analyze two hundred years of land cover changes: case study of Sorrento peninsula (south Italy). Cartogr. Geogr. Inf. Sci. **43**(3), 250–265 (2016)
39. Li, Y., Chen, J., Lu, R., Gong P., Yue, T.: Study on land cover change detection method based on NDVI time series batasets: change detection indexes design. In: IGARSS, pp. 2323–2326 (2005)

Using GNSS Observation for Mitigating the Impact of SODs and RODs on the Built Environment – Introducing the New SNIK Continuously Operating Reference Station and Its Applications

Alberico Sonnessa(✉) and Eufemia Tarantino

Department of Civil, Environmental, Land, Construction and Chemistry (DICATECh),
Politecnico di Bari, Via Orabona 4, 70125 Bari, Italy
{alberico.sonnessa,eufemia.tarantino}@poliba.it

Abstract. Continuously Operating Reference Station (CORS), based on GNSS observations, are widely used in many fields, both scientific and professional, related to the need of precise positioning. Several GNSS-based applications deal with the safeguard of the cities and, consequently, their inhabitants, from the effects of Slow-Onset Disasters (SODs), and Rapid Onset Disasters (RODs). With the focus of reducing the impact of these critical events on the built environment, by guaranteeing a more accurate and continuous monitoring, a new CORS, named SNIK, was installed by the research group Applied Geomatics Laboratory (AGlab) at the Polytechnic University of Bari, with the support of Stonex Italy. At the same time, an integrated test field, consisting of four GNSS rover receivers so far, was planned to be implemented on the new Rectorate building, currently under construction. The test field is set up to be upgraded with additional sensors, such as SAR corner reflectors, accelerometers, and weather stations. The availability of a continuous stream of GNSS observations will allow the development of new algorithms and approaches aimed at facing the consequences of potentially catastrophic events over the short and long-term period and implementing strategies aimed at mitigating their impact on the safety and the healthiness of the cities.

Keywords: Geomatics monitoring of structures · Displacement monitoring · Structural health monitoring · CORS · GNSS reference station · RODs · SODs · Tropospheric water content

1 Introduction

Due to heavy anthropogenic pressure suffered by large portions of our countries, natural events such as landslides, subsidence, earthquakes and heavy rainfalls with flooding are having a growing impact on structures and infrastructures, and the built environment in general. In most cases, these occurrences also cause a significant loss of human lives, especially in countries with a large presence of historic towns.

© Springer Nature Switzerland AG 2021
O. Gervasi et al. (Eds.): ICCSA 2021, LNCS 12955, pp. 102–111, 2021.
https://doi.org/10.1007/978-3-030-87007-2_8

Over the long-term period, very slow phenomena, such as the global warming, closely related with the climate of the cities, pollution and rainfall levels, energy requirement and ageing of constructions [1], add their negative effect on the safety of structures and the healthiness of our towns.

For instance, as a direct consequence of the climate change, heavy rainfalls (water-bombs) are becoming increasingly frequent, and, in some cases, may have a devastating effect on the territories, cities and population, as described in [2].

Such critical occurrences, with reference to the catastrophes they can lead to and how fast they can occur, are generally referred to as Slow-Onset Disasters (SODs), and Rapid Onset Disasters (RODs), as stated by United Nation [3].

The mitigation of the impact of SODs and RODs on the safety of territories and cities may be included among the major challenges of the coming years.

In the context of an integrated approach that must encompass multiple disciplines, innovative strategies implemented starting from data acquired by GNSS reference stations can help to develop tools aimed at tackling the effects of these occurrences on the built environment and their users.

To this end, a brand-new CORS is currently about to be installed at the Faculty of Engineering at the Polytechnic University of Bari (PoliBA), Italy.

Under the acronym CORS (Continuously Operating Reference Stations), reference is made to GNSS (Global Navigation Satellite Systems) permanent stations using the satellite systems orbiting the Earth for positioning and navigation purposes.

A continuously operating reference station consists of a high-precision GNSS receiver and antenna, placed on a safe mounting structure.

A CORS should guarantee:

- a full and non-stop operation (24/7);
- the logging and the (possibly redundant) storing of raw data;
- if included in GNSS networks aimed at providing positioning services [4], also the streaming of collected data useful to perform real-time positioning and/or observations for post-processing;
- its stability over a long-term period through an appropriate choice of the installation site.

Since 1990-ies, CORS started to be established around the world to support high-precision positioning applications. At the very beginning, GNSS reference stations have been used mainly in the framing of global geodetic networks, the monitoring of geodetic reference systems/frames [5–8] and crustal deformations [9–12]. In the last three decades, an increasing and extensive usage of GNSS data, both broadcasted in real-time or acquired and stored for post-processing, there has been in applications such as geomatics monitoring of structures [13–15], ground motion control [16–18], precise farming, machine guidance, and seismology [19–21]. In more recent years, GNSS data have also been widely employed in the automotive field for navigation and assisted/autonomous driving [22–25].

A very interesting application of GNSS observations in evaluating the effects of natural occurrences in structures can be recognized in the use of Precise Point Positioning (PPP) technique for assessing the seismic effects on constructions [26]. Focusing on the study of the seismic risk, earthquake effects derive from the combination of local conditions (e.g., seismic micro-zonation) and different level of vulnerability as inherent qualities of buildings. Therefore, the GNSS monitoring process of weak areas (or buildings) naturally exposed to earthquake can help technicians in evaluating post-emergency damages (e.g., horizontal and vertical displacements).

When GNSS is combined with Precipitable Water Vapor (PWV) measurements, retrieved by using the tropospheric delay parameter, it can provide support in the analysis of climatological events. It is the case of flash floods [27, 28], fast meteorological events caused by sudden rainy occurrences, that can increase the total risk for cities and their parts (not only near to basins) when combined with the low drainage capacity of urban surfaces. Here, the effects on the Built Environment can be amplified when buildings are already characterized by a poor state of maintenance or increased by local modification of the natural terrain profile [29, 30]. Thus, if PWV data can help in providing a quick alert system for people and local emergency groups when measurements are linked to a network system (pre-emergency relevance), their combination with GNSS data can help in recognizing the long-term effects on the built environment (i.e., horizontal translations and assessment of post-event damages).

Near such rapid events, GNSS observations can also be applied for the indirect evaluation of slow events related to climate changes [31]. The process of desertification is a direct effect of the modification of the precipitation mode/rate, as in the Mediterranean area. The monitoring process, over the long period, of PWV measurements can support the analysis of a) local variation of such local meteorological features when single stations are considered and b) wide territory when the monitoring is included in a coordinated network of measures.

In the context of the mitigation of the impact of potentially critical occurrences, the precise positioning and tracking of people acting in a built environment constitute a key factor in the improvement of high-resolution spatial models simulating the behaviour of people under certain constraints. For example, modelling approach for social system analysis suited for spatial simulations resulting from the dynamic development of multiple local interactions of heterogeneous human-like actors, such as the Agent-Based Model (ABM), can reproduce in a realistic manner human-scale behaviours, which are usually stochastic in nature, in order to capture complex macrophenomena of real-life systems [32]. ABMs are applied to study many types of collective complex systems, ranging from crowds of people, urban traffic networks, companies' market competition, emergency evacuations, to biological systems [33].

In this powerful model, which is helpful for describing the human behaviour during emergencies, GNSS observations could provide useful data aimed at validating risk analyses based on predictive model estimation of the combined impact of SODs and RODs on people.

The above-mentioned applications show how the availability of reliable GNSS data, provided by CORS networks, constitutes a relevant support in many scientific fields related to geosciences and, at the same time, how this methodology is constantly boosting the development of technologies devoted at monitoring and preserving the territory, its infrastructures, and their users.

2 The SNIK CORS

Following the EUREF permanent GNSS network indications (requiring a four-character abbreviation code for the unique identification of a CORS), the PoliBA Reference Station has been named SNIK.

The SNIK CORS is based on a high-precision Stonex SC2200 GNSS receiver equipped with a SA1500 choke-ring antenna (Fig. 1). Stonex Italy is supporting the AGlab, by supplying its high-end sensor, in developing innovative approaches and algorithms to be applied in the use of GNSS observations.

After the installation phase, PoliBA will start the procedure to include the CORS in the EUREF Permanent Network (EPN), that is the "federation of over 100 self-funding agencies, universities, and research institutions in more than 30 European countries working together to maintain the European Terrestrial Reference System (ETRS89), namely the single Europe-wide standard coordinate reference system adopted by the European Commission" [34].

Due to its capability to permanently get observations from most of the recent satellite constellations designed for positioning purposes, in addition to the "traditionally" available GPS and GLONASS positioning systems, SNIK will be the first institutional reference station in the Apulia Region able to track the European GALILEO and the Chinese BeiDou systems.

As widely demonstrated, [35–37] the opportunity to acquire and process multi-GNSS observations provides relevant benefits to the achievable positioning accuracy and consequently, the quality of the GNSS-based possible applications.

The analysis of GNSS dataset will also take advantage from the presence of rain gauge already installed in close proximity (about 50 m) of the SNIK station, framed in the Apulian Civil Protection weather station network (Bari Campus pluviometer [38]).

The main specifications of the SNIK CORS are summarized in Table 1.

Table 1. The SNIK CORS – Technical specifications

Receiver	Stonex SC2200
Satellite systems tracked	GPS/Glonass/BeiDou/Galileo
Position rate	5 Hz
Precision in positioning – Horizontal	3.0 mm
Precision in positioning – Vertical	3.5 mm
Antenna	Stonex SA1500 Choke Ring with RADOME
Noise	$\leq$2 dB
Waterproof/Dustproof	IP67

The SNIK permanent station will also contribute to develop the ResCUDE (RESilient Cultural Urban context to Disaster Exposure) project, aimed at facing RODs and SODs effects on the urban setting by mean of a holistic methodology that includes geomatics

Fig. 1. Stonex SC2200 GNSS receiver with SA1500 choke-ring antenna

disciplines, resilient urban methodologies, land-use and managing techniques and an agent-based approach, as better detailed in [1].

Focusing on the safety of people and the built environment, the opportunity to take advantage from a comprehensive database of high-precision position data and additional information that can be retrieved from GNSS permanent stations (e.g. precipitable water vapor content in the troposphere [39]) will permit to implement innovative algorithms and strategies useful to improve:

- the geomatics monitoring of building/structures (control of displacements, implementation of early warning alert systems, structural health monitoring - SHM purposes);
- the monitoring of subsidence, both natural and induced by human activities (e.g. excavations, construction works);
- the reconstruction of earthquake waveshapes to retrieve information for the seismic risk;
- the short-term forecast on heavy atmospheric precipitation (waterbombs) by evaluating the tropospheric water content;
- the tracking of pedestrian paths using mobile devices to be used in innovative agent-based models;
- the accuracy in vehicle positioning/tracking in applications related to assisted/autonomous driving;
- more in general, to boost the analysis in the field of the positioning and navigation-related issues.

In this long-term program, the SNIK permanent station will be the core of a test field which includes the installation of four additional GNSS rover receivers on the roof of the new Rectorate Building (currently under construction), and the future integration with different sensors (Table 2). To date, accelerometers, active SAR (Synthetic Aperture Radar) corner reflectors and a weather station are planned to be installed in the next year(s).

Table 2. Sensors planned for the test field

Sensor	Application
GNSS	Displacement and acceleration detection, SHM
SAR corner reflectors	Subsidence, SHM
Accelerometers	SHM
Weather station	Metereological parameters to be related with observations

The scheme of the test field is showed in Fig. 2.

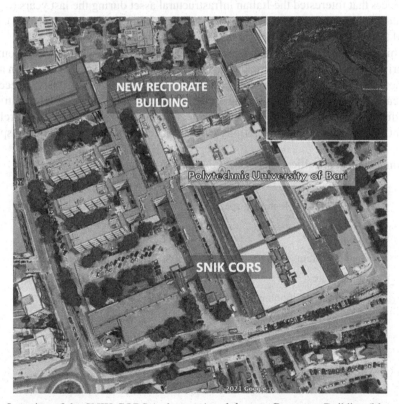

Fig. 2. Location of the SNIK CORS (red square) and the new Rectorate Building (blue square) (Color figure online)

3   A First Application for Structure Monitoring – the Geomatics Monitoring System of the New Rectorate Building at PoliBA

As aforementioned in Sect. 1, four high-precision Stonex SC600A GNSS receivers will be placed on the roof of the new Rectorate building at the PoliBA, currently under construction. The four receivers will act both as rovers (in differential positioning applications with the SNIK station) and single monitoring points.

These sensors constitute the first piece of a multi-sensor test field useful for the assessment of innovative algorithms to be used in the evaluation of SODs (e.g. climate change, slow subsidence, ageing) and RODs (e.g. earthquakes) on a structure. The receivers will be installed on the building as soon as the construction works will end, introducing a good practice aimed at the preventive monitoring during its whole life cycle.

The need of a new paradigm in the control and maintenance of the built environment, which is essential for ensuring its safe fruition and avoiding potentially critical events (i.e. large deformations or, at worst, collapses) arises, especially in light of the destructive occurrences that interested the Italian infrastructural asset during the last years (e.g. the recent collapses of the road bridge between Albiano Magra and Aulla (Tuscany), Italy, in April 2020, of the Morandi bridge in Genoa, Italy, in August 2018.

In this frame, an effective management strategy should include a real-time geomatics monitoring of our cities; this approach can be easily implemented (in particular on newly constructed buildings) and can now rely on a new generation of low-cost GNSS receivers which can be simply architecturally integrated in the structure and remotely controlled.

Additional sensors will be gradually added, giving the opportunity of correlating different information (e.g. accelerations with displacements, rainfall with tropospheric delay).

Main technical specifications of the GNSS receivers are listed in Table 3.

Table 3. Technical specification of the GNSS receivers

Receiver	Stonex SC600A
Satellite systems tracked	GPS/Glonass/BeiuDou/Galileo,
Position rate	10 Hz
Precision in positioning – Horizontal	3.0 mm
Precision in positioning – Vertical	5.0 mm
Antenna	Stonex SA65
Noise	$\leq$2 dB
Waterproof/Dustproof	IP67

4 Conclusive Remarks

The increasing accuracy of high-precision GNSS receivers and their decreasing cost is favouring the establishment of continuously operating reference stations. GNSS observations acquired by CORS (and CORS networks) constitute a consolidated and powerful tool for the understanding of issues related to the need of a precise positioning.

In this frame, the mitigation of the impact of RODs and SODs on the built environment and their users can strongly benefit from the analyses of extensive GNSS dataset, by taking advantage from the opportunity to obtain the position of a receiver (stationary or mobile) with high precision and retrieve additional information on parameters directly related with the climate. The SNIK permanent station will allow to have available a continuous stream of observations and develop new approaches to face the consequences of potentially catastrophic events over the short and long-term period.

Acknowledgements. This research is partially funded under the project "AIM1871082-1" of the AIM (Attraction and International Mobility) Program, financed by the Italian Ministry of Education, University and Research (MIUR). All authors have read and agreed to the published version of the manuscript. We are very grateful to Stonex Italy and Paolo Centanni for making possible, with their unparalleled support, the implementation of the SNIK CORS.

References

1. Sonnessa, A., Cantatore, E., Esposito, D., Fiorito, F.: A Multidisciplinary Approach for Multirisk Analysis and Monitoring of Influence of SODs and RODs on Historic Centres: The ResCUDE Project. In: Gervasi, O., et al. (eds.) ICCSA 2020. LNCS, vol. 12252, pp. 752–766. Springer, Cham (2020). https://doi.org/10.1007/978-3-030-58811-3_54
2. Viswanadhapalli, Y., et al.: A diagnostic study of extreme precipitation over Kerala during August 2018. Atmos. Sci. Lett. **20** (2019), https://doi.org/10.1002/asl.941
3. Assembly, U.N.G.: Report of the open-ended intergovernmental expert working group on indicators and terminology relating to disaster risk reduction (2016)
4. Li, B., Shen, Y., Feng, Y., Gao, W., Yang, L.: GNSS ambiguity resolution with controllable failure rate for long baseline network RTK. J. Geodesy **88**(2), 99–112 (2013). https://doi.org/10.1007/s00190-013-0670-z
5. Metsar, J., Kollo, K., Ellmann, A.: Modernization of the estonian national gnss reference station network. Geod. Cartogr. **44** (2018), https://doi.org/10.3846/gac.2018.2023
6. Nicolini, L., Caporali, A.: Investigation on reference frames and time systems in Multi-GNSS. Remote Sens. **10** (2018), https://doi.org/10.3390/rs10010080
7. Altamimi, Z., Rebischung, P., Métivier, L., Collilieux, X.: ITRF2014: A new release of the International Terrestrial Reference Frame modeling nonlinear station motions. J. Geophys. Res. Solid Earth. **121** (2016), https://doi.org/10.1002/2016JB013098
8. Dow, J.M., Neilan, R.E., Gendt, G.: The International GPS Service: celebrating the 10th anniversary and looking to the next decade. Adv. Space Res. (2005). https://doi.org/10.1016/j.asr.2005.05.125
9. Fadil, A., et al.: Active tectonics of the western Mediterranean: Geodetic evidence for rollback of a delaminated subcontinental lithospheric slab beneath the Rif Mountains, Morocco. Geology **34** (2006), https://doi.org/10.1130/G22291.1

10. Ohta, Y., et al.: Quasi real-time fault model estimation for near-field tsunami forecasting based on RTK-GPS analysis: application to the 2011 Tohoku-Oki earthquake (M w 9.0). J. Geophys. Res. Solid Earth. **117** (2012), https://doi.org/10.1029/2011JB008750
11. Zanutta, A., et al.: Victoria land, Antarctica: an improved geodynamic interpretation based on the strain rate field of the current crustal motion and moho depth model. Remote Sens. **13** (2021), https://doi.org/10.3390/rs13010087
12. Danezis, C., Chatzinikos, M., Kotsakis, C.: Linear and nonlinear deformation effects in the permanent gnss network of cyprus. Sensors (Switzerland) **20** (2020), https://doi.org/10.3390/s20061768
13. Shen, N., et al.: A review of Global Navigation Satellite System (GNSS)-based dynamic monitoring technologies for structural health monitoring (2019), https://doi.org/10.3390/rs11091001
14. Yunus, M.Z.M., Ibrahim, N., Ahmad, F.S.: A review on bridge dynamic displacement monitoring using global positioning system and accelerometer. In: AIP Conference Proceedings (2018), https://doi.org/10.1063/1.5022933
15. Manzini, N., et al.: Performance analysis of low-cost GNSS stations for structural health monitoring of civil engineering structures. Struct. Infrastruct. Eng. (2020). https://doi.org/10.1080/15732479.2020.1849320
16. Grapenthin, R., West, M., Gardine, M., Tape, C., Freymueller, J.: Single-frequency instantaneous GNSS velocities resolve dynamic ground motion of the 2016 Mw 7.1 Iniskin, Alaska, Earthquake. Seismol. Res. Lett. **89** (2018), https://doi.org/10.1785/0220170235
17. Chen, Y., et al.: Long-term ground displacement observations using InSAR and GNSS at Piton de la Fournaise volcano between 2009 and 2014. Remote Sens. Environ. **194** (2017), https://doi.org/10.1016/j.rse.2017.03.038
18. Cenni, N., Fiaschi, S., Fabris, M.: Integrated use of archival aerial photogrammetry, GNSS, and InSAR data for the monitoring of the Patigno landslide (Northern Apennines, Italy). Landslides **18**(6), 2247–2263 (2021). https://doi.org/10.1007/s10346-021-01635-3
19. Colosimo, G., Crespi, M., Mazzoni, A.: Real-time GPS seismology with a stand-alone receiver: a preliminary feasibility demonstration. J. Geophys. Res. Solid Earth. **116** (2011), https://doi.org/10.1029/2010JB007941
20. Ravanelli, M., Occhipinti, G., Savastano, G., Komjathy, A., Shume, E.B., Crespi, M.: GNSS total variometric approach: first demonstration of a tool for real-time tsunami genesis estimation. Sci. Rep. **11** (2021), https://doi.org/10.1038/s41598-021-82532-6
21. Paziewski, J., et al.: Towards Galileo + GPS seismology: validation of high-rate GNSS-based system for seismic events characterisation. Meas. J. Int. Meas. Confed. **166** (2020), https://doi.org/10.1016/j.measurement.2020.108236
22. Vivacqua, R., Vassallo, R., Martins, F.: A low cost sensors approach for accurate vehicle localization and autonomous driving application. Sensors (Switzerland) **17** (2017), https://doi.org/10.3390/s17102359
23. Marinelli, M., Palmisano, G., Astarita, V., Ottomanelli, M., Dell'Orco, M.: A fuzzy set-based method to identify the car position in a road lane at intersections by smartphone GPS data. Transport. Res. Proc. (2017). https://doi.org/10.1016/j.trpro.2017.12.047
24. Chiang, K.W., Tsai, G.J., Li, Y.H., Li, Y., El-Sheimy, N.: Navigation engine design for automated driving using INS/GNSS/3D LiDAR-SLAM and integrity assessment. Remote Sens. **12** (2020), https://doi.org/10.3390/rs12101564
25. de Miguel, M.Á., García, F., Armingol, J.M.: Improved LiDAR probabilistic localization for autonomous vehicles using GNSS. Sensors (Switzerland) **20** (2020), https://doi.org/10.3390/s20113145
26. Gatti, M.: Elastic period of vibration calculated experimentally in buildings hosting permanent GPS stations. Earthq. Eng. Eng. Vib. **17**(3), 607–625 (2018). https://doi.org/10.1007/s11803-018-0466-5

27. Suparta, W., Rahman, R., Singh, M.S.J.: Monitoring the variability of precipitable water vapor over the Klang Valley, Malaysia during flash flood. In: IOP Conference Series: Earth and Environmental Science. IOP Publishing, p. 12057 (2014)
28. Khaniani, A.S., Motieyan, H., Mohammadi, A.: Rainfall forecast based on GPS PWV together with meteorological parameters using neural network models. J. Atmos. Solar-Terrestrial Phys. **214**, 105533 (2021)
29. Garrote, J., Diez-Herrero, A., Escudero, C., García, I.: A framework proposal for regional-scale flood-risk assessment of cultural heritage sites and application to the Castile and León Region (Central Spain). Water **12**, 329 (2020)
30. Tutunaru, I.D., Blindaru, T.V., Pricop, I.C.: The assessment of the cultural heritage's vulnerability to flash floods in Bahlui river basin Iasi County. Eur. J. Sci. Theol. **9**, 233–242 (2013)
31. Seneviratne, S.I., et al.: Changes in climate extremes and their impacts on the natural physical environment. In: Field, C.B., V. Barros, T.F. Stocker, D. Qin, D.J. Dokken, K.L. Ebi, M.D. Mastrandrea, K.J. Mach, G.-K. Plattner, S.K. Allen, M. Tignor, P.M.M. (eds.) Managing the Risks of Extreme Events and Disasters to Advance Climate Change Adaptation. Cambridge University Press, Cambridge, UK, and New York, NY, USA, pp. 109–230 (2012)
32. Esposito, D., Abbattista, I.: Dynamic Network Visualization of Space Use Patterns to Support Agent-based Modelling for Spatial Design. In: Luo, Y. (ed.) CDVE 2020. LNCS, vol. 12341, pp. 260–269. Springer, Cham (2020). https://doi.org/10.1007/978-3-030-60816-3_29
33. Crooks, A., Heppenstall, A., Malleson, N., Manley, E.: Agent-Based Modeling and the City: A Gallery of Applications. In: Shi, W., Goodchild, M.F., Batty, M., Kwan, M.-P., Zhang, A. (eds.) Urban Informatics. TUBS, pp. 885–910. Springer, Singapore (2021). https://doi.org/10.1007/978-981-15-8983-6_46
34. EUREF (Institution/Organization): No Title, https://www.epncb.oma.be/_organisation/about.php. Accessed 4 May 2021
35. Li, X., et al.: Accuracy and reliability of multi-GNSS real-time precise positioning: GPS, GLONASS, BeiDou, and Galileo. J. Geodesy **89**(6), 607–635 (2015). https://doi.org/10.1007/s00190-015-0802-8
36. Kaloop, M.R., Yigit, C.O., El-Mowafy, A., Bezcioglu, M., Dindar, A.A., Hu, J.W.: Evaluation of multi-GNSS high-rate relative positioning for monitoring dynamic structural movements in the urban environment. Geomatics Nat. Hazards Risk. **11** (2020), https://doi.org/10.1080/19475705.2020.1836040
37. Li, X., Zhang, X., Ren, X., Fritsche, M., Wickert, J., Schuh, H.: Precise positioning with current multi-constellation Global Navigation Satellite Systems: GPS, GLONASS, Galileo and BeiDou. Sci. Rep. **5** (2015), https://doi.org/10.1038/srep08328
38. Apulian Civil Protection: PLUVIOMETRO BARI CAMPUS, http://93.57.89.4:8081/temporeale/stazioni/466/anagrafica. Accessed 7 May 2021
39. Campanelli, M., et al.: Precipitable water vapour content from ESR/SKYNET sun-sky radiometers: validation against GNSS/GPS and AERONET over three different sites in Europe. Atmos. Meas. Tech. **11** (2018), https://doi.org/10.5194/amt-11-81-2018

International Workshop on Geomatics in Agriculture and Forestry: New Advances and Perspectives (Geo-for-Agr 2021)

Two-Stage CNN-Based Wood Log Recognition

Georg Wimmer[1](✉)(iD), Rudolf Schraml[1](iD), Heinz Hofbauer[1],
Alexander Petutschnigg[2], and Andreas Uhl[1](iD)

[1] University of Salzburg, Jakob Haringer Street 2, 5020 Salzburg, Austria
{gwimmer,uhl}@cs.sbg.ac.at, rudolf.schraml@sbg.ac.at
[2] University of Applied Sciences Salzburg, Markt 136a, 5431 Kuchl, Austria

Abstract. The proof of origin of logs is becoming increasingly important. In the context of Industry 4.0 and to combat illegal logging there is an increasing motivation to track each individual log. This work presents a two-stage convolutional neural network (CNN) based approach for wood log tracing based on digital log end images. First, the log cross section is segmented from the background by applying a CNN-based segmentation method using the Mask R-CNN framework. In the second step, wood log recognition is applied using CNNs that are trained on the segmented wood log images using the triplet loss function. Our proposed two-stage CNN-based approach achieves Equal Error Rates between 0.6 and 3.4% on the six employed wood log image data sets and clearly outperforms previous approaches for image based wood log recognition.

Keywords: Wood log tracking · Deep learning · Segmentation

1 Introduction

Methods for wood log tracking are an essential component in solving a wide variety of problems and requirements of an ecological, legal and social nature. Currently, this mainly relates to proof the origin of wood products, e.g. by certification companies like the Forest Stewardship Council (FSC). However, efforts towards traceability down to the individual log have been intensified by a variety of stakeholders. The motivation for this is that, on the one hand, illegal logging can be better combated and, on the other hand, the identification of each individual log forms a basis for steps towards forest-based industry 4.0. In the context of Industry 4.0, Radio Frequency Identification (RFID) is the state-of-the-art for object recognition/tracking. However, like a set of other tracking technologies for wood logs (e.g. punching, coloring or barcoding log ends [14]), RFID requires physical marking of each tree which suffers costs. An alternative to physical marking is to use biometric characteristics to recognize each individual log. A short summary on biometric log tracking using various characteristics

This work is partially funded by the Austrian Science Fund (FWF) under Project No. I 3653.

O. Gervasi et al. (Eds.): ICCSA 2021, LNCS 12955, pp. 115–125, 2021.
https://doi.org/10.1007/978-3-030-87007-2_9

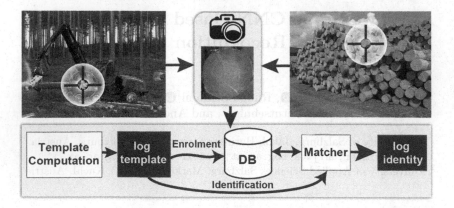

Fig. 1. Exemplary scheme of enrolment and identification for wood log tracking

is presented in [7]. In a series of works between 2014–2016 we investigated wood log tracking based on digital log end images in regard to the distinctiveness and robustness of the annual ring pattern. For a literature review we refer to [6]. Figure 1 presents the scheme of such a log tracking system. Significant for this work is that the utilized approaches were inspired by human fingerprint and iris-recognition methods. Those rely on traditional feature extraction methods (e.g. Gabor filterbanks) and moreover require a sophisticated pre-processing (segmentation, pith estimation, rotational pre-alignment) of each log end image prior to feature extraction. Comparison of the extracted features is also complex. Furthermore, it has to be noted that for our previous works manually segmented log end images and determined pith positions were utilized. Time has passed and deep learning based approaches have become state-of-the-art. Not surprisingly, deep learning-based methods have also been investigated in many application areas in the forestry and timber industry in recent years. Exemplary applications are wood species identification using cross-section (CS) images [5,13], remote sensing-based tree species classification [1] or lumber grading [3] using wood board surface images.

In this work we apply convolutional neural networks (CNNs) for two-stage wood log recognition. CNNs are used for segmentation of the CS in the log end image as well as for feature extraction that offers advantages in many ways. The experimental evaluation is based on a database (DB) which was utilized in [10] and a new DB denoted as 100 logs DB (HLDB). This work significantly contributes to biometric log end recognition by showing that a CNN-based approach does not require to determine the pith position and moreover no rotational pre-alignment is required. Results show that CNN-based segmentation and feature extraction shows a similar performance as the results presented in [10] which are based on groundtruth data and traditional feature extraction methods. The experimental evaluation on the new HLDB, for which no groundtruth data is available, underpins this statement and shows the weaknesses of the traditional methods that are mainly caused by inaccurate segmentation and pith estimation results.

(a) $CSLD_{DB1}$ (b) $CSLD_{DB2}$ (c) $CSLD_{DB3}$

Fig. 2. Example image of each of the three sub-databases of CSLD

Section 2 introduces the DBs and describes the CNN-based segmentation of the CS as well as the CNN-based log recognition and the experimental setup. Section 3 presents the results and Sect. 4 concludes this work.

2 Materials and Methods

2.1 Data Bases

Two different DBs are utilized: (i) the Cross Section Log Database (CSLD) which was already utilized in [9,10] and (ii) a new database referred to as 100 Logs Database (HLDB).

The CSLD is a combination of images from three sub-databases with 50, 120 and 109 different logs, respectively. The images are recorded with a Canon EOS DMark with a 35 mm lens. In total, this database comprises 2270 CS images from 279 different logs. For this database, a manual segmentation of the log cross section is available. For a detailed description of CSLD we refer to [10]. The CSLD is utilized (i) to compare the CNN-based results to previous results which were based on annotated groundtruth data and (ii) to train a segmentation CNN in order to segment the images of HLDB, for which no manual segmentation is available. Figure 2, shows one example image of each of the three sub-databases of the CSLD dataset.

HLDB comprises different datasets which were all taken from the same 100 logs. CS-Images were acquired from both ends of each log. The first two datasets $HLDB_{FH}$ and $HLDB_{FL}$ were taken in the forest (see Fig. 3(a)) using a Lumix camera (Panasonic FZ45 Lumix camera) and a Huawei smartphone (Huawei P8 Lite 2017), respectively. Both datasets consist of 4 images for each log end. After two images the camera was rotated by approximately 45° and two more images were captured. The next dataset, denoted as Sawmill dataset ($HLDB_{SM}$), was captured after cutting off a thin disc from each log end (see Fig. 3(b)). Three images with different rotations for each fresh cross-cut log end were acquired using the Huawei smartphone.

The CS-Images of $HLDB_{FH,FL,SM}$ were taken without tripod which causes different rotations, slightly varying perspectives toward the CS and slightly different positions of the CS in the image. Finally, one side of the 200 discs was acquired using a Canon EOS 70D with a tripod and lighting, once raw ($HLDB_R$)

(a) Forest site - HLDB$_{FH,FL}$

(b) Sawmill yard - HLDB$_{SM}$ - discs were cut for HLDB$_{R,S}$

Fig. 3. 100 Logs Image Database (HLDB): Fig. 3(a) shows log piles close to the forest at which the forest datatsets were acquired. Figure 3(b) shows the data acquisition at the sawmill yard where discs of each log end were cut off.

and once after they were sanded (HLDB$_S$). The captured CSs are mirrored versions of the CSs in the Sawmill dataset. For HLDB$_R$ four and for HLDB$_S$ six CS-Images with different rotations were captured, respectively. Figure 4 shows exemplary images for all HLDB datasets from the bottom end of log labelled #E001. It can be observed that the CS-Images of the two forest datasets HLDB$_{FH,FL}$ look quite similar since the images were taken with the same surrounding, the same log cut pattern and hardly any time shift between the taking of the images of the two datasets. The CS-Images captured at the sawmill yard HLDB$_{SM}$ look completely different because of the fresh cut that results in a totally different saw cut pattern and wood coloration. The disc CS-Images HLDB$_{R,S}$ are captured under idealistic conditions and serve as a reference in the experiments, especially the sanded CS-Images in HLDB$_S$ which show a undisturbed annual ring pattern.

2.2   CS-Segmentation

Prior to any feature extraction, the CS area in the CS-Image needs to be localized and segmented from the background. We apply the Mask R-CNN framework [2] to get a segmentation mask. As net architecture we employ the ResNet-50

(a) HLDB$_{FH}$ (b) HLDB$_{FL}$ (c) HLDB$_{SM}$ (d) HLDB$_R$ (e) HLDB$_S$

Fig. 4. HLDB: Exemplary images for both log ends of log #E001 from all datasets HLDB$_{FH,FL,SM,R,S}$

architecture using a model pretrained on the COCO dataset. The segmentation net is then trained on CSLD for which groundtruth segmentation masks are available. The segmentation net is trained for 30 epochs in order to differentiate the CS from the background. Then, the trained segmentation net is applied to the HLDB datasets to segment the CS from the background. To also get CNN-based segmentation masks for CSLD, we apply a 4-fold cross validation, where one fold consists of a fourth of the 279 logs (the images of one log are all in the same fold). 3 folds are used to train the segmentation net and the trained net is applied to segment the images of the remaining fold.

The obtained segmentation mask of a CS-Image, which consists of probability values between 0 and 1 for each pixel of the image, is binarized. All values of the CNN segmentation mask that are below the threshold value t ($t = 0.5$ for HLDB$_{SM,R,S}$ and CSLD and $t = 0.25$ for HLDB$_{FH,FL}$) are set to zero and the remaining values are set to one. The binarized segmentation mask of the CS is further used to set the background (all image positions with a zero in the segmentation mask) to black. Finally, each CS-Image is reduced to the smallest possible square shaped image section so that the CS (all image positions with a '1' in the segmentation mask) is still completely included in the image together with a five pixel thick black border on each side of the image. A schematic representation of the segmentation including the extraction of the square shaped image patch containing the CS is displayed in Fig. 5. For CSLD we can quantitatively assess the outcome of the segmentation. Averaged over all CS-Images in CSLD, 99.26% of the pixels per image were correctly segmented. In Fig. 6, we present exemplar outcomes of the segmentation and patch extraction process for HLDB$_{FL,FH,SM}$. The segmentation outcomes on HLDB$_{SM,R,S}$ all look perfectly fine based on the authors' visual impression. For the two forest datasets HLDB$_{FH,FL}$, most images were well segmented, but on some images, parts of the log CS were predicted as background which was the reason why we used a smaller threshold ($t = 0.25$ instead of 0.5) to binarize the segmentation masks. This reduced the risk to predict parts of the CS as background (as can be seen in Fig. 6(d)) but also led to the problem that for some images a bit of background surrounding the log CS was predicted as being part of the log CS (see Fig. 6(f)).

The advantage of our proposed segmentation and square image patch extraction approach for log recognition is that the background of a log CS image does not influence the log recognition. For CNN based recognition systems, where the images usually have to be resized to a fixed size before feeding them through

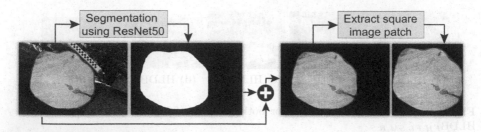

Fig. 5. Segmentation & patch extraction of the CS-Image

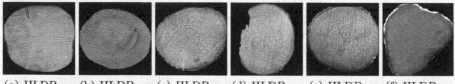

(a) HLDB$_{SM}$ (b) HLDB$_{SM}$ (c) HLDB$_{FH}$ (d) HLDB$_{FH}$ (e) HLDB$_{FL}$ (f) HLDB$_{FL}$

Fig. 6. Exemplary outcomes of the segmentation in combination with square image patch extraction

the network, an additional advantage is the reduced loss of image quality. The segmented square shaped image patches are clearly smaller than the original CS-Image and so less information on the log is lost by reducing the image resolution to fit the required CNN input size.

2.3 Wood Log Recognition Using CNN Triplet Loss

In biometric applications, the problem with common CNN loss functions (e.g. the SoftMax loss) is that CNNs are only able to identify those subjects which have been used for the training of the neural network. If new subjects are added in a biometric application system, then the nets need to be trained again or else a new subject can only be classified as one of the subjects that were used for training (the one that is most similar to the newly added subject with respect to the CNN). This of course renders the practical application of common CNN loss functions impossible for biometric applications.

Contrary to more common loss functions like the Soft-Max loss, the triplet loss [12] does not directly learn the CNN to classify images to their respective classes. The triplet loss requires three input images at once (a so called triplet), where two images belong to the same class (the so called Anchor image and a sample image from the same class, further denoted as Positive) and the third image belongs to a different class (further denoted as Negative). The triplet loss learns the network to minimize the distance between the Anchor and the Positive and maximize the distance between the Anchor and the Negative. The triplet loss using the squared Euclidean distance is defined as follows:

$$L(A, P, N) = \max(||f(A) - f(P)||^2 - ||f(A) - f(N)||^2 + \alpha, 0), \qquad (1)$$

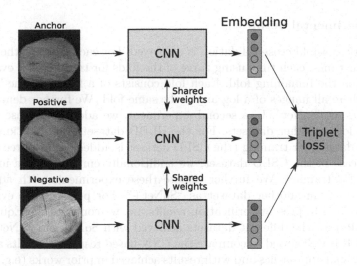

Fig. 7. CNN training using the triplet loss

where A is the Anchor, P the Positive and N the Negative. α is a margin that is enforced between positive and negative pairs and is set to $\alpha = 1$. $f(x)$ is an embedding (the CNN output) of an input image x. Figure 7 shows the scheme of learning a CNN using the triplet loss. A triplet of training images (Anchor, Positive and Negative) is fed through the CNN resulting in an embedding for each of the three images. The embeddings of the three images are then used to compute the triplet loss to update the CNN.

For our application this means that the CNN is trained so that the Euclidean distances between the CNN feature vectors of all log CS-Images of the same class (log) is small, whereas the Euclidean distance between any pairs of CS-Images from different logs is large. We employ hard triplet selection [12] (only those triplets are chosen for training that actively contribute to improving the model) and the Squeeze-Net (SqNet) architecture [4]. SqNet is a small neural networks that is specifically created to have few parameters and only small memory requirements.

The size of the CNN's last layer convolutional filter is adapted so that a 256-dimensional output vector (embedding) is produced. Training is performed on batches of 128 images. To make the CNN more invariant to shifts and rotations and increase the amount of training data, we employ data augmentation for CNN training. The images are randomly rotated in the range of 0–360° and random shifts in horizontal and vertical directions are applied by first resizing the input images to a size of 234×234 and then extracting a patch of size 224×224 (the best working input size using the SqNet for log recognition) at a random position of the resized image (± 10 pixels in each direction). The CNN is trained for 400 epochs, starting with a learning rate of 0.001 that is divided by 10 every 120 epochs.

2.4   Experimental Setup

In this work, a 4-fold cross validation is employed. For each dataset, the CNN is trained four times, each time using three of the folds for training and evaluation is applied on the remaining fold. Each fold consists of a fourth of the logs of a dataset, where all images of a log are in the same fold. We further denote these experiments as "SqNet". In a second experiment, we additionally use training data from logs of other datasets. For the HLDB datasets, we additionally use the CSLD dataset for training (the CSLD dataset is added to the three training folds). In case of the CSLD dataset, we additionally employ all the images of HLDB$_{FH}$ for training. We further denote these experiments with additional training data from another dataset as "SqNet+". For performance evaluation we have decided to present verification results, i.e. we compute the Equal Error Rates (EERs) for the different datasets achieved with SqNet and SqNet+.

The EER is well suited to compare the CNN-based results to results achieved with traditional approaches and with results achieved in prior works (e.g. in [10]). We have to consider that each of the four trained CNNs per dataset (one per fold) has a different mapping of the images to the CNN output feature space. Thus, feature vectors of different folds cannot be compared in the evaluation and the EER has to be computed separately for each fold. We report the mean EER over the four folds.

As already mentioned before, the HLDB datasets consist of images from both log ends which show no obvious visible similarities. To employ the maximum number of images for CNN training, both ends are considered as different classes thus resulting in 200 classes in total. To avoid any bias by assigning different classes to the two sides of a log, we exclude those triplets during training where the Anchor and the Negative are from the same log but different sides. The same is applied for EER computation, where those comparison scores (scores between images from different sides of the same log) are ignored.

Comparison Methods: In order to assess the performance of CNN-based wood log recognition we compute EERs using the fingerprint- and iris-based approaches proposed in [10]. For rotational pre-alignment, the CM (center of mass to pith estimate vector) strategy is applied.

The iris-based results IRIS$_V$ and IRIS$_H$ are computed in the exact same way as described in [10]. Features are computed with the Log Gabor configuration LG (64/08) and for matching the shifting is done in the range of -21 to 21 feature vector positions.

For the fingerprint-based approach we utilize a modified approach, based on a circular grid, as introduced in [8], which does not require to compute feature vectors for rotated versions of the registrated CS-Image. Identical as the template comparison procedure for the iris-based approach, rotation compensation in the matching stage is performed by shifting the feature vectors of each band. This circular grid fingerprint-based approach is referred to as FP$_{CG}$. Contrasting to our previous work, we do not utilize manually extracted groundtruth data and instead use the CNN-based CS-Segmentation results and the pith position determined using the approach described in [11].

3   Results and Discussion

In Table 1, we present the EERs of the CNN-based approaches and the comparison methods for each dataset. The best result for each dataset is marked in bold letters. The main finding in Table 1 is that the CNN-based approaches are clearly superior to the traditional ones. SqNet+ performs slightly better than SqNet. So additional training data improves the results, although the additional data is from another database with different image acquisition conditions and a different camera.

Interestingly, the CNN results are quite similar across the different HLDB datasets, despite the differing image acquisition conditions and cameras. For example, the images of the $HLDB_S$ dataset offer a perfectly visible annual ring pattern (sanded surface) and the scale and viewpoint of the images is constant, whereas the two datasets acquired at the forest ($HLDB_{FH,FL}$) offer a poor visibility of the annual ring pattern due to the saw cut pattern and the images were taken under varying scales and viewpoints. Despite that, the CNN results of the forest datasets are slightly better than those of the $HLDB_S$. So this together with the fact that the CNN results on $HLDB_R$ (raw CS) are slightly better than those on $HLDB_S$ (sanded CS) indicates that the saw cut pattern is an important feature for CNNs that could be even more important for wood log recognition than the annual ring pattern. Varying viewpoints and scales of the recorded images does not seem to be a problem for the CNNs.

Considering the CSLD results, an EER of 0.9% achieved by $IRIS_V$ with manually segmented images was the best result presented in [10]. Using the automated CS-segmentation instead of the manually segmented image data, the results of the comparison approaches deteriorate greatly (3.4–5.8% EER). The results for the CNN-based approaches using segmentation groundtruth data (SqNet = 0.7%, SqNet+ = 0.6%) outperform our previous results and the EERs achieved with the automated CS-Segmentation (SqNet/+ = 1%) are only slightly worse than those with manually segmented image data.

Thus, another main advantage of our proposed approach is that the proposed CS-Segmentation is well suited to be used with the CNN-based recognition. This statement is confirmed by the EERs presented for the HLDB datasets, which are all below 3.4% for our proposed approach. The EERs presented for the comparison approaches are not even close to this performance. By comparing the EERs for the HLDB computed with the traditional approaches, it is obvious that the EERs computed for $HLDB_{S,R}$ are better than those computed for $HLDB_{FL,FH,SM}$. The reason is that for $HLDB_{S,R}$ rotational pre-alignment is more accurate than for the other datasets because of the more accurate CNN segmentation for $HLDB_{S,R}$. However, these observations highlight the main advantage of the CNN-based approaches: They work in combination with a fully automated CNN-based segmentation and do not require any rotational pre-alignment prior to feature extraction.

Table 1. Recognition performance (Mean EER in [%]) on the 6 log CS datasets for the proposed CNN-based method using the two different training strategies, as well as three comparison approaches (Comp.) using classical hand-crafted biometric features. On the CSLD dataset, recognition is applied on the manually segmented images (value before the slash) and the CNN segmented images (value after the slash).

	Methods	CSLD	$HLDB_{FH}$	$HLDB_{FL}$	$HLDB_{SM}$	$HLDB_S$	$HLDB_R$
CNN	SqNet	0.7/1.0	3.2	2.4	3.1	**3.4**	2.8
	SqNet+	**0.6 /1.0**	**2.8**	**1.7**	**2.6**	**3.4**	**2.6**
Comp.	$Iris_H$	2.12 [10] /5.8	26.8	27.3	22.4	10.6	12.5
	$Iris_V$	0.9 [10]/3.4	20.5	21.0	15.1	5.3	6.1
	FP_{CG}	2.1/3.9	16.9	19.5	20.3	8.0	8.3

4   Conclusion

Recently, there has been an increasing interest in methods for tracking round-wood on the basis of each individual log. In prior works we proposed a physical free approach using log end images and methods inspired by fingerprint and iris recognition-based approaches. Results were promising and showed good performances when using groundtruth data for segmentation of the log end in each image. However, in a real world application a fully automated system is required. In order to close this gap, we employ a CNN-based segmentation approach combined with a CNN-based log recognition approach which is compared to results achieved with the traditional log recognition approaches when using automatically segmented images. Results showed, that the CNN-based wood log recognition works well in combination with the CNN-based segmentation. On the contrary, the traditional approaches suffer from the inaccuracies of the CNN-based segmentation which affects the required rotational pre-alignment strategy. It can be concluded that the proposed two-stage CNN-based wood log recognition approach is well suited for individual wood log tracking. What remains is to prove that this two-stage approach also works in a realistic scenario, i.e. if logs can be tracked when using imagery captured at various stages of the log tracking chain.

References

1. Fricker, G.A., Ventura, J.D., Wolf, J.A., North, M.P., Davis, F.W., Franklin, J.: A convolutional neural network classifier identifies tree species in mixed-conifer forest from hyperspectral imagery. Remote Sens. **11**(19), 2326 (2019). https://doi.org/10.3390/rs11192326
2. He, K., Gkioxari, G., Dollar, P., Girshick, R.: Mask r-CNN. In: 2017 IEEE International Conference on Computer Vision (ICCV). IEEE (October 2017). https://doi.org/10.1109/iccv.2017.322
3. Hu, J., Song, W., Zhang, W., Zhao, Y., Yilmaz, A.: Deep learning for use in lumber classification tasks. Wood Sci. Technol. **53**(2), 505–517 (2019). https://doi.org/10.1007/s00226-019-01086-z

4. Iandola, F.N., Moskewicz, M.W., Ashraf, K., Han, S., Dally, W.J., Keutzer, K.: SqueezeNet: Alexnet-level accuracy with 50x fewer parameters and <1 mb model size. CoRR abs/1602.07360 (2016). http://arxiv.org/abs/1602.07360

5. Olschofsky, K., Köhl, M.: Rapid field identification of cites timber species by deep learning. Trees Forest. People **2**, 100016 (2020). https://doi.org/10.1016/j.tfp.2020.100016

6. Schraml, R., Charwat-Pessler, J., Entacher, K., Petutschnigg, A., Uhl, A.: Roundwood tracking using log end biometrics. In: Proceedings of the Annual GIL Meeting, GIL 2016. LNI, pp. 189–192. Gesellschaft für Informatik (2016)

7. Schraml, R., Charwat-Pessler, J., Petutschnigg, A., Uhl, A.: Towards the applicability of biometric wood log traceability using digital log end images. Comput. Electron. Agric. **119**, 112–122 (2015). https://doi.org/10.1016/j.compag.2015.10.003

8. Schraml, R., Entacher, K., Petutschnigg, A., Young, T., Uhl, A.: Matching score models for hyperspectral range analysis to improve wood log traceability by fingerprint methods. Mathematics **8**(7), 10 (2020)

9. Schraml, R., Hofbauer, H., Petutschnigg, A., Uhl, A.: Tree log identification based on digital cross-section images of log ends using fingerprint and iris recognition methods. In: Azzopardi, G., Petkov, N. (eds.) CAIP 2015. LNCS, vol. 9256, pp. 752–765. Springer, Cham (2015). https://doi.org/10.1007/978-3-319-23192-1_63

10. Schraml, R., Hofbauer, H., Petutschnigg, A., Uhl, A.: On rotational pre-alignment for tree log identification using methods inspired by fingerprint and iris recognition. Mach. Vis. Appl. **27**(8), 1289–1298 (2016). https://doi.org/10.1007/s00138-016-0814-2

11. Schraml, R., Uhl, A.: Pith estimation on rough log end images using local Fourier spectrum analysis. In: Proceedings of the 14th Conference on Computer Graphics and Imaging, CGIM 2013. Innsbruck, AUT (February 2013). https://doi.org/10.2316/P.2013.797-012

12. Schroff, F., Kalenichenko, D., Philbin, J.: FaceNet: a unified embedding for face recognition and clustering. In: 2015 IEEE Conference on Computer Vision and Pattern Recognition (CVPR), pp. 815–823 (June 2015). https://doi.org/10.1109/CVPR.2015.7298682

13. Tang, X.J., Tay, Y.H., Siam, N.A., Lim, S.C.: MyWood-ID. In: Proceedings of the 2018 International Conference on Computational Intelligence and Intelligent Systems, CIIS 2018. ACM Press (2018). https://doi.org/10.1145/3293475.3293493

14. Tzoulis, I., Andreopoulou, Z.: Emerging traceability technologies as a tool for quality wood trade. Procedia Technol. **8**, 606–611 (2013)

Unmanned Aerial Vehicle (UAV) Derived Canopy Gaps in the Old-Growth Beech Forest of Mount Pollinello (Italy): Preliminary Results

Francesco Solano[1] ⓘ, Salvatore Praticò[2](✉) ⓘ, Gianluca Piovesan[1] ⓘ, and Giuseppe Modica[2] ⓘ

[1] Department of Agriculture and Forest Sciences (DAFNE), University of Tuscia, Via San Camillo de Lellis, 01100 Viterbo, Italy
[2] Dipartimento di Agraria, Università Degli Studi Mediterranea di Reggio Calabria, Località Feo di Vito, 89122 Reggio Calabria, Italy
`salvatore.pratico@unirc.it`

Abstract. Forest canopy gaps caused by natural disturbances represent the primary driver of forest regeneration dynamics, modifying several ecological factors such as the light environment within an ecosystem. Canopy openings constantly change the shape and structure of forests as well as tree species diversity. The analysis of forest canopy gap spatial patterns in old-growth forests can provide helpful information for their conservation. Moreover, it can be an important reference for outlining sustainable forest management to restore and maintain the original biodiversity and accelerate forest succession towards old-growth characteristics. The main goal of this research was to assess a first forest gap size distribution and analyze their spatial pattern in an old-growth beech (*Fagus sylvatica* L.) forest in the Pollino National Park (Italy) strict reserve, with no human influence in at least the past 70 years due to its remote location. Using an unmanned aerial vehicle (UAV)-based canopy height model (CHM), we detected and classified 196 canopy gaps ranging from 10 to 343 m^2. The gap size-frequency reflected a power-law distribution. Using second-order statistics, following the K and L Ripley's function, we found that the canopy gaps were spatially clustered distributed. These preliminary results show the predominance of small-scale disturbances, confirmed by the spatial structure analyses highlighting the single tree nature of these processes influenced by site-specific conditions.

Keywords: Canopy height model (CHM) · Old-growth beech · Forest regeneration dynamics · Forest canopy gaps · Pollino National Park (Italy)

1 Introduction

Forest structure results from the interactions between different ecological factors that affect regeneration establishment, competition, and mortality dynamics. Past disturbances often drive these dynamics. Tree-fall gaps are the most frequent small-scale

© Springer Nature Switzerland AG 2021
O. Gervasi et al. (Eds.): ICCSA 2021, LNCS 12955, pp. 126–138, 2021.
https://doi.org/10.1007/978-3-030-87007-2_10

natural disturbances in many forest ecosystems [1], playing an important role in maintaining biodiversity [2–5]. Natural disturbances can create small canopy gaps (e.g., single dead trees) or large canopy gaps, allowing different scale patterns and processes. These phenomena play an important role in many forest ecosystems and represent the dominant form of forest regeneration due to the continual reshaping of forest structure after creating canopy openings [6]. The analysis of forest canopy gaps spatial patterns can provide helpful information on these dynamics [7], playing an important role in old-growth forest conservation. It is an essential reference for delineating a sustainable management approach to restore and maintain native biodiversity and accelerate forest succession towards old-growth characteristics within managed forests [8–10]. Understanding natural patterns and processes, including forest canopy gaps, size-frequency distribution, and spatial patterns, better enables forest managers to enhance biodiversity conservation in these forests, providing insight into ecosystem-level successional processes and disturbance patterns [11]. Disturbance-driven canopy gaps need to be quantified and monitored, studying variation and size distribution in different forest types to understand the different gap dynamics and their ecological perspectives.

Remote sensing techniques allow to map entire landscapes and describe changes based on time series [12–14]. However, tiny gaps can not easily be recorded even with the latest medium resolution satellite imagery (i.e., Sentinel-2), but very high-resolution images provided by commercial satellites should be used. For small-scale forest monitoring, there is a need for a new and cost-effective survey methodology.

In recent times, several remote sensing platforms have been used for mapping canopy gaps, including multispectral satellite images [15], unmanned aerial vehicles (UAV) [16], RGB and infrared stereo aerial images [17, 18], airborne laser scanning (ALS) [19, 20] and terrestrial laser scanning data (TLS) [21]. The latter two acquisition systems use a pulsed 3D laser scanner and their reflections to measure the earth's surface. To date, despite the very high costs, ALS data provide more detailed gap characterization compared to the other sensors due to their higher accuracy. Before developing these LiDAR-based approaches, few studies had characterized canopy gaps because of the time-consuming nature of the field-based methods. These limitations can be overcome by UAVs' availability, being able to accurately map all gaps of a small forest stand at very high resolution and precision levels [22]. These UAVs represent a cost-effective solution for usual forest stand sizes because of their easy repeatability and the almost total absence of clouds in the images.

The main aim of this research was to assess a first canopy gap detection and spatial pattern distribution from a UAV-derived canopy height model (CHM) in an old-growth beech (*Fagus sylvatica* L.) forest in the Pollino National Park (southern Italy). This forest, growing on Mount Pollinello and including the upper elevation limit (2000 m a.s.l.) of beech distribution, represents a high conservation priority area and, for its ecosystem integrity, is a candidate to join the UNESCO World Natural Heritage of transboundary "Ancient and Primeval Beech Forests of the Carpathians and Other Regions of Europe" serial sites.

2   Materials and Methods

2.1   Study Area

The study area is represented by an old-growth beech (*Fagus sylvatica* L.) forest, a candidate as UNESCO World Heritage serial site for its ecosystem integrity, located in the Pollino national park, on Mount Pollinello in southern Italy (Fig. 1). The Pollino massif is the southernmost component of this UNESCO network of ancient beech forests. The old-growth forest core extends for 10.5 hectares with a perimeter of 1860 m, at an altitude between 1900–2000 m. a.s.l. The forest is characterized by a very complex structure, with no human influence in at least the past 70 years due to its remote location. It has an uneven-aged structure, and within this area, beech trees up to 620 years old are in close contact with old (800–1200 years) *Pinus heldreichii* trees [23]. It is a characteristic example of the association *Asyneumato-Fagetum sylvaticae*, a high-altitude community endemic in the Southern Apennines.

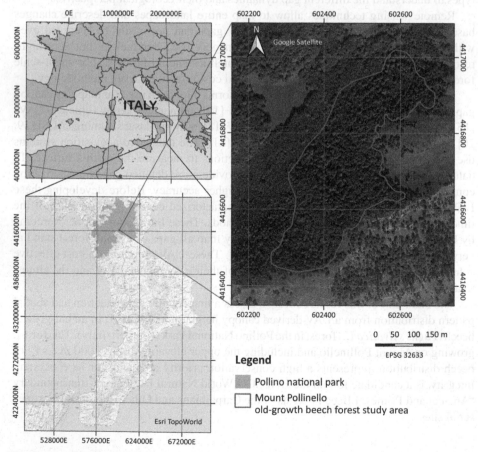

Fig. 1. Localization of the old-growth beech (*Fagus sylvatica* L.) forest of Mount Pollinello study area, within the Pollino national park (southern Italy).

2.2 UAV Data Acquisition and Processing

The UAV survey was conducted using the quadricopter DJI Phantom 4Pro +. This UAV has an integrated RGB sensor with a 20 megapixel 1" CMOS. The field of view (FOV) is 84° (https://www.dji.com/it/phantom-4-pro/info#specs – last access 23/03/2021). To ensure the same mean altitude above ground level for the entire study area, four different flights have been carried on. Each flight was conducted in a semi-automatic mode. The pilot's take-off and landing phases were handled manually, while the photogrammetric flight was carried out under autopilot using the flight planning app Pix4Dcapture (https://www.pix4d.com/product/pix4dcapture - last access: 23/03/2021). Each flight was georeferenced using the GPS mounted on board the vehicle. Once surveyed the aerial images, the entire photogrammetric process to obtain the needed output data of the whole study area was conducted in Pix4Dmapper Pro 4.3 (Pix4D SA, Switzerland). First, a 3D points cloud was reconstructed by a structure from motion (SfM) process as described in Modica et al. [24], and then the orthomosaic (see Fig. 2), digital surface model (DSM), and digital terrain model (DTM) were produced. The final resolution of the orthomosaic reached 3 cm/px.

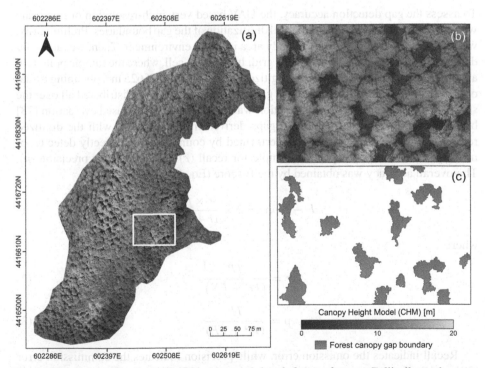

Fig. 2. Canopy gap distribution in the old-growth beech forest of mount Pollinello study area. (a): UAV-derived orthomosaic overview, (b): detail of gap boundaries superimposed on the UAV-derived canopy height model (CHM), (c): canopy gap vector polygons derived from canopy height model (CHM). Coordinates reference system UTM 33N, Datum WGS84 (EPSG 32633).

2.3 Mapping Forest Canopy Gaps

To estimate forest canopy height, the vertical difference between the DSM and DTM was used to obtain the canopy height model (CHM). The CHM raster layer was then resampled at 0.5 m spatial resolution. The R package ForestGapR [25] was used to locate canopy gaps across the CHM and generate metrics on gap extent. The algorithm implemented in the package, developed by Asner et al. [26], defines forest canopy gaps as contiguous areas where the vegetation height is minus or equal to a defined height threshold and between a minimum and maximum gap size (area in m^2) to be detected.

For this study, a value of 5 m was set as the vegetation height threshold [27] and 10 m^2 as the minimum gap size. After identifying the grid cells with height values $\leq$ than the defined threshold and assigning a unique label to them, the algorithm evaluates the 8 neighbors of the grid cells identified. If they are part of the same canopy gap, the same forest canopy gap label is assigned, iterating the process until there are no unlabeled CHM grid cells.

2.4 Data Validation and Accuracy Assessment

To assess the gap detection accuracy, the UAV-based very high-resolution orthomosaic was used as a reference layer for manual digitization of the gap boundaries. Preliminarily, we built a 25 × 25 m grid over the study area in a GIS environment. Then, we randomly distributed 10 sample points within the grid. Inside each cell, where the sample point fell, all gaps present have been manually digitized within this area of 625 m^2, obtaining a total of 58 vector polygons representing the gap boundaries, randomly distributed all over the study area. The accuracy of gap detection was assessed as object-based evaluation [28] by comparing the correctly detected gaps derived from the CHM, with the digitized reference data. The assessment was performed by counting gaps correctly detected or missing, based on an independent sample for recall (r) and another for precision (p). The overall accuracy was obtained by the F-score (Eq. 1):

$$F - score = 2 \times \frac{(r \times p)}{(r + p)} \tag{1}$$

where

$$r = \frac{TP}{(TP + FN)} \tag{2}$$

$$p = \frac{TP}{(TP + FP)} \tag{3}$$

Recall indicates the omission error, while precision indicates the commission error [29], and the *F-score* represents their harmonic mean [30]. These performance indicators were evaluated considering: true positives (TP), representing correctly detected gaps; false positives (FP), which are the erroneously detected gaps; and false negatives (FN), i.e., not detected gaps. The F-score value ranges from 1.0, indicating perfect precision and recall, to 0, if either the precision or the recall is zero.

2.5 Forest Canopy Gap Analysis

Once all boundaries of the forest canopy gaps were extracted and converted as vector polygons, several gap statistics were calculated to define structural gap properties such as i) area of gap (m^2) (gap_area); ii) maximum canopy height (m) (ch_max); iii) minimum canopy height (m) (ch_min); iv) mean canopy height (m) (ch_mean); v) standard deviation of canopy height (m) (ch_sd); vi) Gini coefficient of canopy height (m) (ch_gini); and vii) range of canopy height (m) (ch_range). Moreover, we analyzed the geometrical properties of each gap by exploring the perimeter-area relationship and calculating the gap shape complexity index (GSCI) metric. The GSCI is widely used as a forest gap measure [19] and is a measure of the complexity of gap shape compared to a circular shape of the same size (Eq. 4).

$$\text{GSCI} = \frac{P}{\sqrt{4\pi A}} \tag{4}$$

Where P is the perimeter and A is the area. A value of 1.0 describes a circle while increasing values indicate increasing shape complexity.

The Zeta distribution function was used to quantify the size-frequency distribution of forest canopy gaps as it is a discrete power-law probability density [26]. For the Zeta distribution with parameter λ, the probability that the gap size takes the integer value k is:

$$f(k) = \frac{k^{-\lambda}}{\zeta(\lambda)} \tag{5}$$

where the denominator is the Riemann zeta function, being the sum of all terms $k^{-\lambda}$ for positive integer k, and is undefined for $\lambda = 1$. The function calculates the maximum likelihood estimates of λ by minimizing a negative log-likelihood function [26]. The negative slope of the relationship between gap sizes and their frequency (on a log-log scale) is the exponent (λ). As a result, a log-log plot of gap-size frequency distributions and a vector containing λ and the minimum value of the likelihood were obtained. According to [26, 31], values of λ higher than 2.0 suggest a forest with many small gaps that might indicate high growth-low mortality dynamics. In comparison, values of λ smaller than 2.0 indicate the prevalence of larger canopy gaps that might be associated with considerable canopy mortality or emergent trees.

Through the use of second-order statistics, we finally investigate the spatial pattern of the detected forest gaps, calculating the position of each gap, analyzing whether they are significantly distributed in clusters or uniformly, with the null hypothesis being a random distribution (Poisson process). The output is the resulting Ripley's $K(r)$ function [32], showing the number of gaps located at a distance lower than r, and its $L(r)$ function transformation, which enhances visual interpretation. Results also return the value of the Clark and Evans [33] aggregation index R. Values for $R < 1$ suggest a clustered pattern, while values for $R > 1$ suggest a uniformly ordered pattern [34]. All statistical analyses were performed with the R package ForestGapR [25, 35].

3   Results and Discussions

3.1   CHM Derived Gaps Accuracy

The total number of gaps in the 10 plots, derived from the manual digitization, was 58, while those from the CHM were 56. This was because of the very high resolution of the orthomosaic, thanks to which it was possible to manually digitize 2 gaps that were lower than the pre-established threshold size of $10m^2$. Therefore, these 2 gaps were not considered in the accuracy assessment. Out of the 56 gaps, 50 were correctly extracted, 4 were missing, and 2 were falsely detected. The r (omission error) value resulted in 0.93 while p value (commission error) was 0.96. The F-score, which considers both r and p, was 0.94. The overall detection rate has reached a value of 89%. This result can be explained by assuming that in-between tree crown spaces intercepted by the orthomosaic were actually occupied by vegetation with height above the defined threshold, which can only be deduced through the CHM. Likewise, the four gaps erroneously identified are spaces where the tree branches fall back inside them, causing the increase in vegetation height along the inner gap edge, reducing the minimum gap width considered in the CHM. Considering the study area's imperviousness and the complex forest structure, the results obtained can be regarded as more than satisfactory if compared with other similar studies [12, 16, 22, 36].

3.2   Canopy Gap Detection, Distribution and Structural Property

Within the whole study area, we were able to detect 196 gaps, primarily located in the forest's central and southern parts. The mean canopy gap fraction was 10% of the total forest extension (1.05 ha). Gaps were highly variable in size, ranging from 10 m^2 to a maximum value of 343 m^2 with a mean value of 64 m^2 (Table 1). The data are in line with other Italian old-growth beech forests, as stated by Piovesan et al. [23], and other European old-growth forests [16, 37]. Similar values are also found in tropical rain forests, ranging from tiny size to 500 m^2 [38, 39] and temperate rain forests [40, 41].

Differences in vegetation heights inside canopy gaps, ranging from 1 m up to 4 m, show how the underway renewal processes are due to disturbance events differentiated over time (Table 1). The Gini coefficient's low values (Table 1) indicate that such events have not caused major disturbances in the forest ecosystem's light environment [42].

Table 1. Forest canopy gap statistics. Area of gap (m^2) (gap_area); maximum canopy height (ch_max); minimum canopy height (ch_min); mean canopy height (ch_mean); standard deviation of canopy height (ch_sd); Gini coefficient of canopy height (ch_gini); range of canopy height (ch_range); gap shape complexity index (GSCI); standard deviation (±.).

gap_area (m^2)	ch_max (m)	ch_min (m)	ch_mean (m)	ch_sd (m)	ch_gini	ch_range (m)	GSCI min (mean) max
64 (±52)	4	0.95	2.89	0.95	0.19	3	1.2 (2.1) 4.1

Our results showed that the gap area-perimeter relationship differed markedly from circular reference gaps as the canopy gap size increased, indicating that the gap geometry became more complex with gap size (see Fig. 3). The perimeter-area ratio for all gaps ranged from 0.5 to 2.5, and the mean perimeter-to-area ratio was 1.2 ($\pm$ 0.38 standard deviation). This result is also consistent with the mean GSCI value, meaning that the gap shape reached 110% complexity (Table 1) with a maximum of 310% complexity. This condition points out the vital role of old-growth forests in conserving biodiversity as higher values of GSCI are strictly correlated with species richness [22].

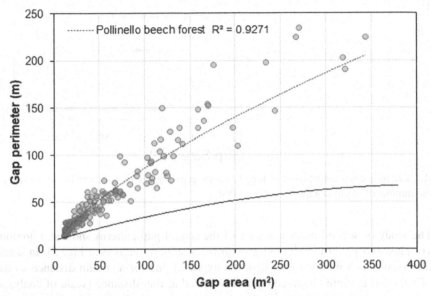

Fig. 3. The gap area–perimeter relationship for the old-growth beech forest of mount Pollinello. The dashed black line indicates the area-perimeter ratio for a circle.

According to results reported in tropical [2] and boreal forests [11], we found that the gap size frequency in a representative Mediterranean forest followed a power-law distribution. The observed gap size distribution (see Fig. 4) has a negative slope. Thanks to its size frequency, plotted on a logarithmic scale, we infer the scaling parameter $\lambda = 1.95$. The obtained value close to 2 means that the forest is dominated by small canopy openings, indicating high growth and low mortality dynamics. In contrast, smaller values of λ indicate an increased frequency of large gap events [43]. Our results are slightly different from those reported in other studies on old-growth forests in different environments [36, 44].

On the one hand, this may be due to the smaller size of the study area, which may produce systematically biased estimates of λ or the gap area fraction [45]. Other factors affecting the frequency distribution of gaps are related to the frequency distribution of tree sizes [46, 47], comprising the tree canopies spatial configuration within and among canopy strata and disturbance regime [48] of different forest environments.

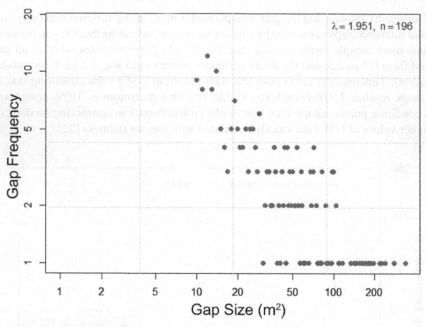

Fig. 4. Size frequency distribution of forest canopy gaps log-log plot. Power-low exponent (λ) and the number of mapped gaps (n) are provided.

The study of second-order statistics of the spatial gap patterns showed a predominantly clustered pattern in the old-growth forest canopy gaps (see Fig. 5). In detail, the observed $K(r)$ value is higher than the expected one for a certain distance so that the distribution is more clustered than randomized at that distance (scale of analysis). Moreover, the spatial clustering for that distance is statistically significant because the observed K value was larger than the upper confidence envelope value. The same pattern was observed considering the K-function modification Ripley's $L(r)$ that showed statistically significant dispersion only for a smaller distance within 15 m.

The value of the Clark and Evans index R of 0.81 (*p-value* < 0.001) confirms a cluster aggregation. However, suggesting a tendency towards randomness. Our results reflect the possibly patchy recruitment on these particular soils and slopes [49]. Gaps clustering at greater distances could be caused by factors related to the site's nature, such as slope or aspect, which may influence the formation of gaps in the study area, as reported in other studies [50]. The clustered distribution of natural canopy gaps differs from other studies dealing with temperate forests in Europe [51] and North America [7]. This could be due to the dynamics that generate the gaps in this forest. The death of single big trees with large crowns appears to be primarily responsible for gap opening phenomena next to the edges of other gaps and a lateral expansion of branches and their following destruction [52].

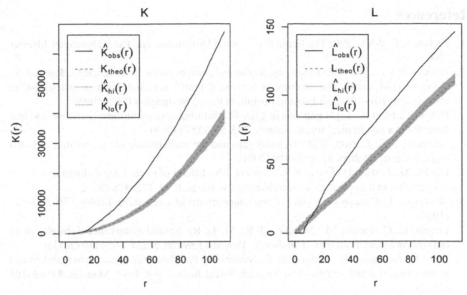

Fig. 5. Spatial pattern analysis for the old-growth forest of mount Pollinello. Ripley's K and L function (black line); theoretical random distribution function (red dashed line); higher and lower confidence interval (grey line) (Color figure online).

4 Conclusions

The analysis of forest canopy gaps, size, and spatial pattern distribution in an old-growth forest are parameters to be considered. They provide helpful information for conservation and sustainability to restore and maintain biodiversity and accelerate forest succession towards old-growth characteristics within managed ones. Using advanced geomatic techniques, as a low-cost effective UAV survey, we were able to derive very high-resolution CHM of the old-growth beech forest of Mount Pollinello in a strict reserve in the Pollino National Park, obtaining consistent results in detecting canopy gaps. First of all, these preliminary results showed the potential reliability of a CHM-based gap automatic extraction procedure. Moreover, it showed the nature of gap opening processes, such as tree mortality and local stand-level disturbance. At the local scale, the prevalence of small-scale processes was confirmed by spatial structure analyses highlighting the absence of major and intermediate disturbances due to the absence of human pressure and its remote location. Further studies will be needed to increase the accuracy of the survey adopted to ensure reliable ground truth to better understand the ongoing ecological processes. Furthermore, establishing a continuous monitoring system of the disturbance dynamics will allow to better reconstruct these ecological processes, also allowing the sharing of data through the creation of dedicated web map tools [53, 54]. Canopy gap disturbance dynamics, coupled with forest complexity metrics, could then be used to evaluate forest ecosystems naturality [55]. Finally, UAV-based CHM extraction could be a helpful tool to derive tree height for carbon stock management, also in other contexts, like urban green [56].

References

1. Pickett, S.T., White, P.S.: The Ecology of Natural Disturbance and Patch Dynamics. Elsevier (2013)
2. Brokaw, N.V.L.: Treefalls: frequency, timing and consequences. In: Leigh, E.G., Rand, A.S., Windsor, D.M. (eds.) The ecology of a tropical forest: seasonal rhythms and long-term changes, pp. 101–108. Smithsonian Institution Press, Washington D.C. (1996)
3. Hubbell, S.P., et al.: Light gap ants in gaps 477 disturbances, recruitment limitation and tree diversity in a neo tropical forest. Science 283, 554–557 (1999)
4. Schnitzer, S.A., Carson, W.P.: Tree-fall gaps and the maintenance of species diversity in a tropical forest. Ecology 82, 913–919 (2001)
5. Patrick, M., Fowler, D., Dunn, R.R., Sanders, J.N.: Effects of treefall gap disturbances on ant assemblages in a tropical mountain cloud forest. Biogr. J. 44, 472–478 (2012)
6. Whitmore, T.: Canopy gaps and the two major groups of forest trees. Ecology 70, 536–538 (1989)
7. Lingua, E., Garbarino, M., Mondino, E.B., Motta, R.: Natural disturbance dynamics in an old-growth forest: from tree to landscape. Procedia Environ. Sci. 7, 365–370 (2011)
8. Fries, C., Johansson, O., Pettersson, B., Simonsson, P.: Silvicultural models to maintain and restore natural stand structures in Swedish boreal forests. For. Ecol. Manage. 94, 89–103 (1997)
9. Seymour, R.S., White, A.S., DeMaynadier, P.G.: Natural disturbance regimes in northeastern North America – evaluating silvicultural systems using natural scales and frequencies. For. Ecol. Manage. 155, 357–367 (2002)
10. Modica, G., Merlino, A., Solano, F., Mercurio, R.: An index for the assessment of degraded Mediterranean forest ecosystems. For. Syst. 24, e037 (2015). https://doi.org/10.5424/fs/201 5243-07855
11. Goodbody, T.R., Tompalski, P., Coops, N.C., White, J.C., Wulder, M.A., Sanelli, M.: Uncovering spatial and ecological variability in gap size frequency distributions in the Canadian boreal forest. Sci. Rep. 10(1), 1–12 (2020)
12. White, J.C., Tompalski, P., Coops, N.C., Wulder, M.A.: Comparison of airborne laser scanning and digital stereo imagery for characterizing forest canopy gaps in coastal temperate rainforests. Remote Sensing of Environment 208, 1–14 (2018), https://doi.org/10.1016/j.rse.2018.02.002
13. Di Fazio, S., Modica, G., Zoccali, P.: Evolution Trends of Land Use/Land Cover in a Mediterranean Forest Landscape in Italy. In: Murgante, B., Gervasi, O., Iglesias, A., Taniar, D., Apduhan, B.O. (eds.) ICCSA 2011. LNCS, vol. 6782, pp. 284–299. Springer, Heidelberg (2011). https://doi.org/10.1007/978-3-642-21928-3_20
14. Modica, G., Praticò, S., Di Fazio, S.: Abandonment of traditional terraced landscape: a change detection approach (a case study in Costa Viola, Calabria, Italy). L. Degrad. Dev. 28, 2608–2622 (2017). https://doi.org/10.1002/ldr.2824
15. Hobi, M.L., Ginzler, C., Commarmot, B., Bugmann, H.: Gap pattern of the largest primeval beech forest of Europe revealed by remote sensing. Ecosphere 6(5), 1–15 (2015), https://doi.org/10.1890/ES14-00390.1.
16. Getzin, S., Nuske, S.R., Wiegand, K.: Using unmanned aerial vehicles (UAV) to quantify spatial gap patterns in forests. Remote Sens. 6(8), 6988–7004 (2014)
17. Brunig, E.: Some further evidence on the amount of damage attributed to lightning and wind-throw in Shorea albida-forest in Sarawak. Commonwealth Forestry Rev. 52(3), 260–265 (1973)
18. Nuske, R.S.: A retrospective study of canopy gap dynamics of a European beech stand. In: Koukal, T., Schneider, W. (Ed.) Proceedings of International Workshop "3D Remote Sensing in Forestry". International Workshop "3D Remote Sensing in Forestry" 14–15 February 2006. Vienna, Austria, pp. 40–44 (2006)

19. Koukoulas, S., Blackburn, G.A.: Quantifying the spatial properties of forest canopy gaps using LiDAR imagery and GIS. Int. J. Remote Sens. **25**(15), 3049–3072 (2004). https://doi.org/10.1080/01431160310001657786
20. Vepakomma, U., St-Onge, B., Kneeshaw, D.: Spatially explicit characterization of boreal forest gap dynamics using multi-temporal lidar data. Remote Sens. Environ. **112**(5), 2326–2340 (2008). https://doi.org/10.1016/j.rse.2007.10.001
21. Seidel, D., Ammer, C., Puettmann, K.: Describing forest canopy gaps efficiently, accurately, and objectively: new prospects through the use of terrestrial laser scanning. Agric. For. Meteorol. **213**, 23–32 (2015). https://doi.org/10.1016/j.agrformet.2015.06.006
22. Getzin, S., Wiegand, K., Schöning, I.: Assessing biodiversity in forests using very high-resolution images and unmanned aerial vehicles: assessing biodiversity in forests. Methods Ecol. Evol. **3**(2), 397–404 (2012). https://doi.org/10.1111/j.2041-210X.2011.00158.x
23. Piovesan, G., et al.: Lessons from the wild: slow but increasing long-term growth allows for maximum longevity in European beech. Ecology **100**(9), e02737 (2019). https://doi.org/10.1002/ecy.2737
24. Modica, G., Messina, G., De Luca, G., Fiozzo, V., Praticò, S.: Monitoring the vegetation vigor in heterogeneous citrus and olive orchards. A multiscale object-based approach to extract trees' crowns from UAV multispectral imagery. Comput. Electron. Agric. **175**, 105500 (2020). https://doi.org/10.1016/j.compag.2020.105500
25. Silva, C.A., et al.: ForestGapR: An r Package for forest gap analysis from canopy height models. Methods Ecol. Evol. **10**(8) 1347–1356 (2019)
26. Asner, G.P., Kellner, J.R., Kennedy-Bowdoin, T., Knapp, D.E., Anderson, C., Martin, R.E.,: Forest canopy gap distributions in the Southern Peruvian Amazon, PLoS ONE (4), e60875 (2013)
27. FRA: Global Forest Resources Assessment 2020: Terms and Definition. Resources Assessment Working Paper 188 (2018)
28. Solano, F., Di Fazio, S., Modica, G.: A methodology based on GEOBIA and WorldView-3 imagery to derive vegetation indices at tree crown detail in olive orchards. Int. J. Appl. Earth Observ. Geoinform. **83**, 101912 (2019). https://doi.org/10.1016/j.jag.2019.101912
29. Li, W., Guo, Q., Jakubowski, M.K., Kelly, M.: A new method for segmenting individual trees from the Lidar point cloud. Photogramm. Eng. Remote Sens. **78**, 75–84 (2012), https://doi.org/10.14358/PERS.78.1.75
30. Praticò, S., Solano, F., Di Fazio, S., Modica, G.: Machine learning classification of mediterranean forest habitats in Google Earth engine based on seasonal Sentinel-2 time-series and input image composition optimisation. Remote Sens. **13**(4), 586 (2021). https://doi.org/10.3390/rs13040586
31. White, E.P., Enquist, B.J., Green, J.L.: On estimating the exponent of power law frequency distributions. Ecology **89**, 905–912 (2008)
32. Ripley, B.D.: Modelling spatial patterns. J. Roy. Stat. Soc. B **39**, 172–212 (1977)
33. Clark, P.J., Evans, F.C.: Distance to nearest neighbor as a measure of spatial relationships in populations. Ecology **35**, 23–30 (1954)
34. Law, R., Illian, J., Burslem, D.F., Gratzer, G., Gunatilleke, C.V., Gunatilleke, I.A.: Ecological information from spatial patterns of plants: Insights from point process theory. J. Ecol. **97**, 616–628 (2009), https://doi.org/10.1111/j.1365-2745.2009.01510.x
35. R Core Team: A Language and Environment for Statistical Computing. R Foundation for Statistical Computing, Vienna, Austria (2021)
36. Kent, R., Lindsell, J.A., Laurin, G.V., Valentini, R., Coomes, D.A.: Airborne LiDAR detects selectively logged tropical forest even in an advanced stage of recovery. Remote Sens. **7**, 8348–8367 (2015). https://doi.org/10.3390/rs70708348
37. Kenderes, K., Mihók, B., Standovar, T.: Thirty years of gap dynamics in a Central European beech forest reserve. Forestry **81**(1), 111–123 (2008)

38. Asner, G.P., Keller, M., Silva, J.N.M.: Spatial and temporal dynamics of forest canopy gaps following selective logging in the eastern Amazon. Glob. Change Biol. **10**, 765–783 (2004)
39. Lloyd, J., Gloor, E.U., Lewis, S.L.: Are the dynamics of tropical forests dominated by large and rare disturbance events? Ecol. Lett. **12**, E19–E21 (2009)
40. Williamson, G.B.: Pattern and seral composition in an old-growth beech-maple forest. Ecology **56**(3), 727–731 (1975)
41. Lertzman, K.P., Sutherland, G.D., Inselberg, A., Saunders, S.C.: Canopy gaps and the landscape mosaic in a coastal temperate rainforest. Ecology **77**, 1254–1270 (1996)
42. Valbuena, R., Maltamo, M., Mehtätalo, L., Packalen, P.: Key structural features of boreal forests may be detected directly using L-moments from airborne lidar data. Remote Sens. Environ. **194**, 437–446 (2017), https://doi.org/10.1016/j.rse.2016.10.024
43. Fisher, J.I., Hurtt, G.C., Thomas, R.Q., Chambers, J.Q.: Clustered disturbances lead to bias in large-scale estimates based on forest sample plots. Ecol. Lett. **11**, 554–563 (2008)
44. Goulamoussène, Y., Bedeau, C., Descroix, L., Linguet, L., Hérault, B.: Environmental control of natural gap size distribution in tropical forests. Biogeosciences **14**(2), 353–364 (2017)
45. Lobo, E., Dalling, J.W.: Spatial scale and sampling resolution affect measures of gap disturbance in a lowland tropical forest: implications for understanding forest regeneration and carbon storage. Proc. Roy. Soc. B: Biol. Sci. **281**(1778), 20133218 (2014)
46. Kellner, J.R., Asner, G.P.: Convergent structural responses of tropical forests to diverse disturbance regimes. Ecol. Lett. **12**, 887–897 (2009)
47. Asner, G.P., Kellner, J.R., Kennedy-Bowdoin, T., Knapp, D.E., Anderson, C., Martin, R.E.: Forest canopy gap distributions in the southern Peruvian Amazon. PLoS ONE 8 (2013)
48. Lieberman, M., Lieberman, D., Peralta, R.: Forest are not just Swiss cheeese: canopy steregeometry of non-gaps in tropical forests. Ecology **70**, 550–552 (1989)
49. Aldrich, P.R., Parker, G.R., Ward, J.S., Michler, C.H.: Spatial dispersion of trees in an old-growth temperate hardwood forest over 60 years of succession. For. Ecol. Manage. **180**(1–3), 475–491 (2003)
50. Moayeri, M.H., Hajivand, A., Shataee Joybari, S., Rahbari Sisakht, S.: Spatial pattern and characteristic of tree-fall gaps to approach ecological forestry in Northern Iran. Environ. Resour. Res. **5**(1), 51–61 (2017)
51. Splechtna, B.E., Gratzer, G.: Natural disturbances in Central European forests: approaches and preliminary results from Rothwald. Austria. For. Snow Landsc. Res. **67**, 57–67 (2005)
52. Torimaru, T., Itaya, A., Yamamoto, S.I.: Quantification of repeated gap formation events and their spatial patterns in three types of old-growth forests: analysis of long-term canopy dynamics using aerial photographs and digital surface models. For. Ecol. Manage. **284**, 1–11 (2012)
53. Pollino, M., Modica, G.: Free Web Mapping Tools to Characterise Landscape Dynamics and to Favour e-Participation. In: Murgante, B., et al. (eds.) ICCSA 2013. LNCS, vol. 7973, pp. 566–581. Springer, Heidelberg (2013). https://doi.org/10.1007/978-3-642-39646-5_41
54. Lanucara, S., Praticò, S., Modica, G.: Harmonization and interoperable sharing of multi-temporal geospatial data of rural landscapes. In: International Symposium on New Metropolitan Perspectives. Springer, Cham, pp. 51–59 (2018). https://doi.org/10.1007/978-3-319-920 99-3_7
55. Di Filippo, A., Biondi, F., Piovesan, G., Ziaco, E.: Tree ring-based metrics for assessing old-growth forest naturalness. J. Appl. Ecol. **54**(3), 737–749 (2017)
56. Choudhury, M.A.M., et al.: Urban tree species identification and carbon stock mapping for urban green planning and management. Forests **11**(11), 1226 (2020). https://doi.org/10.3390/f11111226

Combined Use of Sentinel-1 and Sentinel-2 for Burn Severity Mapping in a Mediterranean Region

Giandomenico De Luca[1] (ID), João M. N. Silva[2] (ID), Duarte Oom[2,3P] (ID),
and Giuseppe Modica[1(✉)] (ID)

[1] Dipartimento Di Agraria, Università Degli Studi Mediterranea Di Reggio Calabria,
Località Feo di Vito, 89122 Reggio Calabria, Italy
{giandomenico.deluca,giuseppe.modica}@unirc.it
[2] Forest Research Centre, School of Agriculture, University of Lisbon, Tapada da Ajuda,
1349-017 Lisboa, Portugal
joaosilva@isa.ulisboa.pt
[3] European Commission, Joint Research Centre, Ispra Site, Ispra, Italy
Duarte.Oom@ec.europa.eu

Abstract. The present study is focused on investigating the capabilities of the combined use of synthetic aperture radar (SAR) Sentinel-1 (S1) and optical Sentinel-2 (S2) for burn severity mapping. For this purpose, a fire that occurred in August 2018 in southern Portugal was analyzed. The composite burn index (CBI) was used to visually classify geo-referenced photographs in the field and create the training data for image classification. A supervised classification was carried out using the machine learning random forests (RF) algorithm, on which the optimization of the parameters setting was carried out through an exhaustive grid search approach. In order to assess the advantages of combining optical and SAR data, and the importance of each band, the approach was tested separately on three data combinations (S1, S2 and S1 + S2) and feature importance was computed to evaluate the contribution of each input layer. The multi-class F-score, used to assess the accuracy of the map, reached a value of 0.844 when both the datasets were combined (S1 + S2), compared with the values 0.514 and 0.805 achieved by only SAR (S1) and only optical (S2), respectively.

Keywords: Composite burn index (CBI) · Random forest (RF) · Exhaustive grid search (GridSearchCV) · Scikit-learn · SNAP-Python (snappy) interface

1 Introduction

Wildfires are one of the most important ecological factors in Mediterranean ecosystems, with different degrees of impact depending on the severity and distribution of burns [1–6]. These effects determine, at different spatial and temporal scales, microclimatic and ecological changes that rearrange the habitats assets, positively (i.e., regeneration, regrowth, vegetation composition enrichment) or negatively (i.e., degradation, desertification, higher exosystemic vulnerability) [1, 4, 7–12]. Burn severity is defined as the

© Springer Nature Switzerland AG 2021
O. Gervasi et al. (Eds.): ICCSA 2021, LNCS 12955, pp. 139–154, 2021.
https://doi.org/10.1007/978-3-030-87007-2_11

degree of environmental change caused by fire, analytically measured as the degree of chemical-physical changes, decomposition and loss of above/belowground organic matter [13, 14]. It influences and determines, at various degrees, the transformation of the organic and mineral components of the soil, the conversion of biomass into inorganic carbon, structural transformation of habitats and, at the most extreme degree, the destruction of the biological communities of an ecosystem [14]. The spatial distribution of the burn severity is a crucial and essential step for assessing and monitoring the impacts of fire on ecosystems and addressing optimal and timely post-fire management operations [2, 7, 10, 15–17]. Key & Benson [14] proposed the composite burn index (CBI) for determining the burn severity, becoming a standard metric in literature. This index is based on the qualitative/quantitative measurement of ecosystem alterations and carried out through visual interpretation in sample field plots, comparing the aboveground biomass and necromass after the fire with their pre-fire conditions. In the CBI protocol, several ecological attributes are measured to estimate the effect of fire in the post-fire environment in five vertical structural layers (strata): litter and duff consumption, canopy cover reduction, branch and wood consumption and plant mortality [13, 14, 18].

Remote sensing techniques and satellite data are effective when retrieving the spatial distribution over large areas of the burn severity information carried out in the field plots, with a high level of correlation [2, 13, 16, 19–21]. Their use was encouraged by the availability of open-source data, acquired from satellite sensors with increasing spatial and temporal resolutions [22, 23], and software that provides advanced process and analysis tools. In this context, the Sentinel constellation (Copernicus mission) launched by the European Space Agency (ESA) provides free high temporal and spatial resolution data acquired by several sensors. The Sentinel-1 (S1) and Sentinel-2 (S2) missions consist, respectively, of a C-band synthetic aperture radar (SAR) and an optical multispectral sensor, both composed of two polar-orbiting satellites (S1A/B and S2A/B) [24].

The high sensitivity in the visible, near-infrared (NIR) and short-wave infrared (SWIR) spectral bands to the effects of fire on ecosystems [25, 26] allowed the rapid development and diffusion of optical-based approaches for this purpose, achieving efficient results [10, 22, 27–30]. In the past decades, numerous authors proposed different methods aimed at estimating and mapping burn severity using remotely sensed data [2–4, 17, 27, 31–33] and effective vegetation indices using optical sensors [2, 34–38]. SAR data have also been explored in recent years for burn severity mapping [39–42]. Tanase et al. [43] and Tanase et al. [44] explored the suitability of different frequency SAR sensors for burn severity purposes in Mediterranean vegetation. Tanase et al. [21] proposed a SAR index to estimate fire severity in temperate forests, based on the ratio between post and pre-fire SAR images. The sensitivity of SAR signal is given by the variation in vegetation and soil structure and moisture content, which affect the dielectric properties of the surface and influence the level of microwave backscatter, in synergy with various environmental factors and/or intrinsic sensors characteristics (e.g., wavelength and polarization) [44, 45]. Therefore, this type of active sensor may be a complementary source for monitoring the fire impacts on ecosystems, considering that it is not sensitive to cloud cover conditions [46–49]. However, few studies focused on integrating the two types of sensors for the estimation of burnt area [48, 50] and, even less, for burn severity [51].

This study aims to contribute to the state of the art by evaluating the capability of the integrated use of S1 and S2 to estimate burn severity using the random forest (RF) machine learning algorithm and the field-based CBI measurements as training data. A series of processing steps anticipated the severity estimation: a) download and preprocessing of optical and SAR time series and subsequent creation of input image layers; b) creation of three dataset combinations: S1, S2 and S1 + S2, in order to evaluate the contribution of each sensor to the final accuracy; c) search and setting of optimal values of RF parameters using an exhaustive grid search approach. The single and multi-class F-score was calculated to assess the accuracy of the maps. The feature importance was extracted to evaluate each input variable's contribution to the final map accuracy. All the processes were carried out using open-source software and libraries executed in python-script language [52].

2   Study Area

The study area is located in the south of Portugal (Algarve, 37° 18′N; 08° 30′W), in the Serra de Monchique mountain range. The site is characterized by typical Mediter-ranean vegetation. The forest areas were composed of coniferous (*Pinus pinea* L., *Pinus pinaster* Aiton.), broad-leaves trees (*Quercus suber* L., *Quercus ilex* L., other secondary Mediterranean native species), and Eucalyptus plantations (*Eucalyptus globulus*, Labill. 1800). A large part of the territory is covered by sclerophyllous shrublands or pastures, interspersed with agricultural and urban landscapes [53]. The fire event occurred in August from the 3rd to the 10th of 2018, covering 268.9 km^2 (Fig. 1).

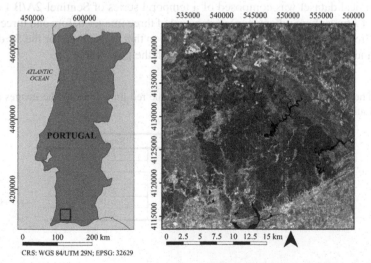

Fig. 1. Location of the study burned area in Portugal (on the left). On the right, overview of the study area (Sentinel-2 image on August 13th, 2018 false-colour composite SWIR-NIR-RED), where the red area represents the burned area.

3 Materials and Methods

3.1 Satellite Datasets

The SAR dataset was composed of a temporal series of Sentinel-1A/B ground range detected (GRD), acquired in interferometric wide (IW) mode, dual-polarized (vertical-vertical VV, and vertical-horizontal VH polarizations). Five images for the pre-fire period (covering around the month before the event starting date) and five images for the post-fire period (covering the period from the end of the event until the end of the same month), including both the ascending and descending orbits (Table 1).

Table 1. The Sentinel-1 dataset used in this study. The red lines separate the images acquired before and after the fire.

Mission	Orbit	Product	Sensing Date
S1A	Ascending		2018/07/07
S1A	Descending		2018/07/08
S1A	Ascending		2018/07/19
S1A	Descending		2018/07/20
S1A	Ascending	IW Level-1 GRDH	2018/07/31
S1A	Ascending		2018/08/12
S1B	Ascending		2018/08/18
S1A	Ascending		2018/08/24
S1A	Descending		2018/08/25
S1B	Ascending		2018/08/30

The optical dataset was composed of a temporal series of Sentinel-2A/B Level 2A (Bottom of Atmosphere reflectance), composed of three images before and three images after the fire (accounting for a similar time frame to that considered for the S1 dataset). Both S1 and S2 images were downloaded through the [54] (Table 2).

Table 2. The Sentinel-2 dataset used in this study. The red lines separate the images acquired before and after the fire.

Mission	Product	Sensing Date
S2A		2018/07/09
S2A		2018/07/19
S2A	Level-2A MS	2018/07/29
S2B		2018/08/13
S2A		2018/08/18
S2B		2018/08/23

3.2 Field Data and ROIs Selection

The field sampling involved capturing post-fire conditions through geo-referenced photographs in different points sampled on the burned surface. Field data were collected in November of the same year of the fire (2018), before the growing season, to avoid confusion between regenerated and unburned vegetation. Fire severity quantification was based on the visual interpretation of the photographs, supported by the Esri ArcGIS World Imagery map [55], providing post-fire medium/high-resolution images and by the field notes taken during the on-field surveys. The protocol used in this study to quantify fire severity was the Composite Burn Index (CBI), consisting of visually estimation of post-fire change in several ecological variables for each of the five vegetation stratum (inert understory substrate and fuel; herbs, low shrubs and <1 m high trees; tall shrubs and <5 m high trees; subcanopy intermediate trees; dominant and codominant cover trees). The level of changed inducted by the fire was ranked between 0 (unburned) and 3 (highest level of severity). The average of all the index values for each variable and stratum represented the severity CBI value of the entire single plot observed. Based on the CBI values obtained, six fire severity categories were created: 1) Unburned soil/rock; 2) Unburned vegetation; 3) Low severity; 4) Moderate severity; 5) Moderate-High severity; 6) High severity. During the field surveying, 200 sampling photographs were taken, from which 185 sampling plots were observed. Each of these points was the centre of a 20 m × 20 m square sampling area (region of interest, ROI), homogeneous in terms of burn severity, matching 2 × 2 pixel areas on Sentinel images (considering resampling of the pixels at 10 m; see Subsect. 3.3). Each ROI was finally labelled with one of the six severity categories.

3.3 Satellite Data Pre-processing and Layers Creation

The data pre-processing was carried out using the Sentinel-1 and Sentinel-2 Toolboxes implemented in the SNAP v.8.0.1 open-source software [56] provided by ESA and executed through Snappy [57], the SNAP-Python interface.

S1. The S1 pre-processing workflow started from the auto-downloaded orbit file application and the thermal noise removal. After the radiometric calibration to beta ($\beta 0$) noughts backscatter standard conventions, the radiometric terrain correction (RTC) process was applied to the dataset, flattening (radiometric terrain flattening) and geometrically correcting (terrain correction) the images using the shuttle radar topography mission (SRTM) digital elevation model (DEM), presenting a spatial-sampling of 1 arc-second. The bilinear interpolation resampling method was used for both DEM and output image resampling. All the S1 images were stacked using the product geolocation as the initial offset method. A multitemporal Lee filter [58, 59], with a 5 × 5 pixel window size, was applied to reduce speckle noise effects. The backscatter time average (BTA) was computed separately for the images before and after the event and for polarization to improve speckle reduction [15, 21, 41]. From the four resulted BTA image layers, three S1-adapted dual-polarimetric SAR indices were computed to have layers expressing the two polarizations' combination [60–62]:

$$RVI_t = 4 \cdot BTA\_VH_t/(BTA\_VV_t + BTA\_VH_t) \tag{1}$$

$$DPSVI_t = (BTA\_VV_t + BTA\_VH_t)/BTA\_VV_t \tag{2}$$

$$RFDI_t = (BTA\_VV_t - BTA\_VH_t)/(BTA\_VV_t + BTA\_VH_t) \tag{3}$$

Where t represents one of the two time periods: before or after the fire.

Moreover, the difference between pre- and post-fire of each respective image layer was computed (Δ = pre-fire – post-fire). In the end, the BTA_VH$_{post-fire}$, ΔBTA_VH, BTA_VV$_{post-fire}$, ΔBTA_VV, RVI$_{post-fire}$, ΔRVI, DPSVI$_{post-fire}$, ΔDPSVI, RFDI$_{post-fire}$, ΔRFDI formed the SAR-based input image layers in the next classification steps.

S2. The S2 pre-processing concerned the pixel resampling to 10 m $\times$ 10 m pixel size. As with the S1 dataset, the time average was computed for the images before and after the fire. All 10 m and 20 m spatial resolution, and their respective pre- and postfire difference (Δ), were used as image input layers in the classification processes: B2 (Blue), ΔB2, B3 (Green), ΔB3, B4 (Red), ΔB4, B5 (RedEdge1), ΔB5, B6 (RedEdge2), ΔB6, B7 (RedEdge3), ΔB7, B8 (NIR), ΔB8, B8A (NarrowNIR), ΔB8A, B11 (SWIR1), ΔB11, B12 (SWIR2), ΔB12.

The two S1 and S2 datasets, clipped on the same area, were stacked together using the S1 dataset as the master extent. The bilinear interpolation was performed to resample the pixels between master and slaves.

3.4 Image Classification

The random forests (RF) algorithm [63, 64] was used to perform a supervised pixel-based classification, using a part (2/3) of the pixels contained and labeled in the ROIs (described in Subsect. 3.2) as training data. Three different dataset combinations were evaluated: only optical (S2); only SAR (S1); optical and SAR (S1+S2). To assess each image layer's contribution to the classification, the feature importance (Gini importance) was computed for each of the three dataset combinations. The classification algorithm was implemented in the scikitlearn library (*RFclassifier* module) [65] and executed via a Python script.

Parameters optimization. The optimal values of the algorithm parameters were determined using an exhaustive grid search approach. The exhaustive grid search is based on testing and cross-validation of each possible combination of the set of values given for each parameter, returning the best combination for a given training input set. The *GridSearchCV* algorithm implemented in scikit-learn was used for this purpose. The combination of parameters tested is reported in Table 3.

3.5 Accuracy Assessment

The remainder of ROIs pixels (1/3) was used to validate the classification accuracy of the three burn severity maps (S2, S1 and S1+S2). The confusion matrix was carried out, from which the *producer's* accuracy (defined as the ratio between the correctly classified pixels in a given class and the number of validation pixels for that class) and the *user's* accuracy (the ratio between the correctly classified pixels in a given class and all the classified objects in that class) were calculated [66]. From these measures, we calculated the single-class F-score ($F\text{-}score_i$) (Eq. 4) [15, 67–71] and the multi-class F-score ($F\text{-}score_M$) (Eq. 5) [73], representing a form of overall accuracy. The F-score is the harmonic mean of *recall* and *precision* measures, which have the same respective

Table 3. Sets of parameters values tested and combined for exhaustive grid search-based optimization. The name and the definition of each parameter are the original ones reported in the *RFclassifier* module user guide.

Parameter name	Values set	Description
n_estimators	100, 650, 1200, 1750, 2300, 2850, 3400, 3950, 4500, 5050, 5600, 6150, 6700, 7250, 7800, 8350, 8900, 9450, 10000	The number of trees in the RF model
max_depth	10, 20, 30, 40, 50, 60, 70, 80, 90, 100, 110, 300, 500, 800, 1000	The maximum depth of the tree
min_samples_split	2, 5, 10	The minimum number of samples required to split an internal node
min_samples_leaf	1, 2, 4	The minimum number of samples required to be at a leaf node
max_features	"auto", "None", "log2"	The number of features to consider when looking for the best split

meaning of *producer's* and *user's* accuracy. Therefore they were replaced in the equations (Eq. 4, 6, 7) [73].

$$F-score_i = 2 \cdot \left(producer's_i \cdot user's_i\right) / \left(producer's_i + user's_i\right) \qquad (4)$$

$$F-score_M = 2 \cdot \left(producer's_M \cdot user's_M\right) / \left(producer's_M + user's_M\right) \qquad (5)$$

Where i is a single class; *producer's_M* and *user's_M* metrics are expressed as follows (Eq. 6, 7):

$$producer's_M = \left(\sum_{i=1} producer's_i\right) / n \qquad (6)$$

$$user's_M = \left(\sum_{i=1} user's_i\right) / n \qquad (7)$$

Where n is the total number of classes.

4 Results

4.1 Classified Burn Severity Map

Table 4 shows the RF classification algorithm's optimal parameters values, set using an exhaustive grid search approach. This was carried out for each of the three data combination (S1, S2 and S1+S2) separately.

Figure 2 shows the three burn severity maps resulted from the classification processes tested: only S1, only S2 and S1+S2, respectively.

In Table 5, the distribution (%) of the area of each burn severity classes is reported.

Table 4. Random forests (RF) parameters values used for each of the three data combinations (S1, S2 and S1 + S2) and set using an exhaustive grid search approach.

Parameter name	Values set		
	S1	S2	S1+S2
n_estimators	650	1200	1200
max_depth	1000	90	110
min_samples_split	2	2	2
min_samples_leaf	1	1	1
max_features	"log2"	"auto"	"auto"

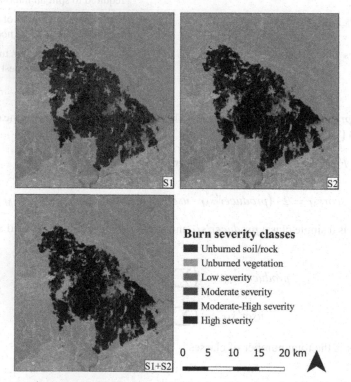

Burn severity classes
- ■ Unburned soil/rock
- ■ Unburned vegetation
- ■ Low severity
- ■ Moderate severity
- ■ Moderate-High severity
- ■ High severity

0   5   10   15   20 km

Fig. 2. Burn severity maps resulted from the classification of the three data combination: Sentinel-1 dataset only (S1); Sentinel-2 dataset only (S2); Sentinel-1 and Sentinel-2 data (S1+S2).

4.2 Feature Importance

Each image layer's influence on the classification of each of the three respective data combinations is expressed by the feature importance, whose results are presented below by dividing them by dataset combination. The dataset S1+S2 is reported in Fig. 3; the other two data combinations show almost the same behavior.

Table 5. Distribution (%) of the area of each burn severity class for each data combination: Sentinel-1 dataset only (S1); Sentinel-2 dataset only (S2); S-1 and S-2 data stack (S1+S2).

Burn severity classes	Distribution (%)		
	S1	S2	S1+S2
Unburned soil/rock	6.55	8.35	8.31
Unburned vegetation	11.92	1.85	2.15
Low severity	6.83	2.90	3.03
Moderate severity	17.67	12.54	13.15
Moderate-High severity	16.29	16.84	16.02
High severity	40.74	57.51	57.34

S1. The $BTA\_VH_{post-fire}$ had the highest value of importance (0.1431), followed by its respective ΔBTA_VH image layer (0.1349) and by the VV bands (0.1125 and 0.0983 for ΔBTA_VV and $BTA\_VV_{post-fire}$, respectively). The Δ of the dual-polarimetric indices presented close values of feature importance (from 0.0924 to 0.0886), while the post-fire dual-polarization indices reached a range of values between 0.0814 and 0.0788.

S2. The two-NIR, RedEdge2/3, $\Delta SWIR2$ and Red bands for post-fire ($B8A_{post-fire}$, $B8_{post-fire}$, $B7_{post-fire}$, $\Delta B12$, $B6_{post-fire}$, $B4_{post-fire}$) reached the highest values of feature importance: 0.0913, 0.0798, 0.0785, 0.0592, 0.0591 and 0.0554, respectively, followed by the Blue and SWIR2 post-fire (0.0481 and 0.0444). The lowest values are achieved mainly by the NIR-based Δ layers and the RedEdge1 bands (0.0384 to 0.0346).

S1+S2. The feature importance values roughly reflect what has already been seen for individual datasets. The $B8A_{post-fire}$, $B8_{post-fire}$, $B7_{post-fire}$, $\Delta B12$, $B6_{post-fire}$, $B4_{post-fire}$ image layers reported highest values: 0.0812, 0.0660, 0.0648, 0.0506, 0.0483, 0.0431, respectively. The $B2_{post-fire}$ (0.0298) preceded the $B12_{post-fire}$ (0.0334). The $BTA\_VH_{post-fire}$ reached the fifteenth value of importance (0.0316); the other SAR based, especially both the BTA_VV layers, returned the lowest values.

4.3 Map Accuracy

The accuracy of each map was evaluated using several accuracy metrics, and the resulted values are reported below. The F-score was calculated both for the single classes (*F-score$_i$*) to have a more comprehensive measure for each of them and for all the classes (*F-score$_M$*), thus expressing the map's overall accuracy. The initial out-of-bag (OOB) error, representing a forecast accuracy performance estimated by the RF model during the training step, was also reported.

S1. Considering the *F-score$_i$* for each class, the values are 0.732 (unburned soil/rock), 0.372 (unburned vegetation), 0.267 (low severity), 0.434 (moderate severity), 0.489 (moderate-high severity), 0.721 (high severity). The overall accuracy expressed by the *F-score$_M$* is 0.513. The OOB error was equal to 0.5101.

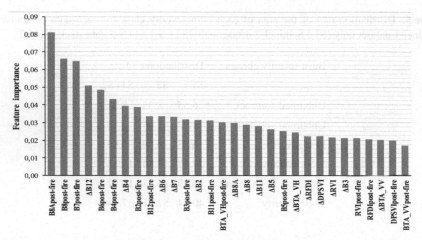

Fig. 3. Feature importance (Gini importance) expressed by each image layer used in the classification process of the Sentinel-1 and Sentinel-2 data stack (S1+S2).

S2. The $F\text{-}score_i$ for each class is 0.933 (unburned soil/rock), 0.879 (unburned vegetation), 0.615 (low severity), 0.683 (moderate severity), 0.773 (moderate-high severity), 0.898 (high severity). The $F\text{-}score_M$ is 0.805. The OOB error was 0.7805.

S1+S2. For each single class, the values of $F\text{-}score_i$ reached are 0.933 (unburned soil/rock), 0.899 (unburned vegetation), 0.696 (low severity), 0.738 (moderate severity), 0.818 (moderate-high severity), 0.916 (high severity). The $F\text{-}score_M$ resulted 0.838. The OOB error was equal to 0.7996.

5 Discussion

This study tested the capability of the integrated use of the two types of SAR (S1) and optical (S2) data in order to map the burn severity in a heterogeneous Mediterranean environment. Few studies have tested and compared the results of the combined use of S1 and S2 for burn mapping and burn severity purposes [48, 50, 51]. The burn severity maps obtained in this study provided a different level of accuracy. Although the optical information could already suffice to map burn severity, thanks to the univocal spectral properties that characterize these effects [25, 26], the use of both types of sensors, with the integration of SAR data, leads to better accuracy values. This confirms what other authors had already observed in their studies, such as Stroppiana et al. [48] for burnt area mapping and Tanase et al. [51] for burn severity mapping, proving the importance of integrated information in burned areas monitoring framework. However, when using only optical data, several factors can be a source of spectral confusion, especially at medium-low severity classes, such as the presence of mixed spectral characteristics within the pixels due, for example, to the mixture of unburned and partially unburned vegetation [33]. Tanase et al. [51] noted that the joint use of optical and SAR data improved the classification of areas unburned or affected with low severity. Other authors also considered the phenological status of vegetation as an element that can lead to errors (e.g., low photosynthetic activity, summer drought stress, leaves fall) [74–77]. Moreover, ash and smoke encrustations on the green leaves surface can alter the optical spectral reflectance [4].

Considering the performance of only SAR data, we achieved the worst result. In other studies using SAR data, such as Addison et al. [39], a level of 60% of overall accuracy is considered high for this type of data. The better performance of VH polarization, compared to VV polarization, in both data configurations (S1 and S1+S2) confirmed what literature reported [21, 41, 45]. We achieved these results using mono-temporal image layers (pre- or post-fire) in order to understand the contribution of each of those to fire severity estimation. However, the bi-temporal spectral indices were more correlated to CBI field measurements [2, 14]. Moreover, the CBI index could present different correlation performances with different vegetation cover types. Studies demonstrate that the CBI is more correlated with forest areas than with shrubs and herbs [14, 18, 28], indicating that the performance of burn severity assessment may vary as vegetation type varies [32]. The contribution of each input layer was explained using the feature importance analysis. The sensitivity of the NIR and SWIR bands was confirmed [26, 32]. However, it is interesting to observe how the RedEdge, Red and Blue bands were also fundamental in achieving the result. Some authors had already hypothesized this aspect. Filipponi et al. [35] proposed a second version of the burn area index (BAI2), built also using the S2 RedEdge (B6, B7) and the narrower bands. Fernández-Manso et al. [34] tested the suitability of RedEdge-based indices for burn severity estimation, achieving good results. Fernández-García et al. [2] used more spectral information than the other NBR type indices, combining Red, Blue, NIR and SWIR bands, considering them very suitable for initial burn severity assessments across different climatic gradients due to their respective sensitivity to atmospheric aerosols, chlorophyll levels, the cellular structure of the leaves and canopy density, and soil and vegetation moisture.

6 Conclusions

This study aims to assess the potential of integrating SAR data to optical datasets to estimate and map burn severity and contribute to the state of the art. The integration improved the accuracy of the results. A more in-depth investigation would be helpful to understand how these data can effectively complete the derived information. In the present work, the various types of vegetation cover were not distinguished. For example, a high severity was attributed without distinction to both pastures, shrubs and forests, as required by the CBI protocol. Future studies could investigate the correlations between severity mapped and vegetation type, an essential key in post-fire monitoring and management of forest regeneration processes and spatial patterns.

Acknowledgments. Giandomenico De Luca was supported by the European Commission through the European Social Fund (ESF) and the Regione Calabria. The authors thank Francisca C. Aguiar (School of Agriculture, University of Lisbon) and Neil E. Pettit (University of Western Australia) for their participation in the fieldwork done in Monchique in the framework of the project RIPONFIRE: Riparian forests: firebreaks or wicks to fire spread?, where the photographs used in this work were taken. RIPONFIRE was funded by the Forest Research Centre,

School of Agriculture, University of Lisbon. The Forest Research Centre is a research unit funded by Fundação para a Ciência e a Tecnologia I.P. (FCT), Portugal (UIDB/00239/2020).

References

1. Chuvieco, E.: Earth Observation of Wildland Fires in Mediterranean Ecosystems. Springer, Berlin Heidelberg (2009), https://doi.org/10.1007/978-3-642-01754-4
2. Fernández-García, V., Santamarta, M., Fernández-Manso, A., Quintano, C., Marcos, E., Calvo, L.: Burn severity metrics in fire-prone pine ecosystems along a climatic gradient using Landsat imagery. Remote Sens. Environ. **206**, 205–217 (2018). https://doi.org/10.1016/j.rse.2017.12.029
3. Lanorte, A., Danese, M., Lasaponara, R., Murgante, B.: Multiscale mapping of burn area and severity using multisensor satellite data and spatial autocorrelation analysis. Int. J. Appl. Earth Obs. Geoinf. **20**, 42–51 (2013). https://doi.org/10.1016/j.jag.2011.09.005
4. Saulino, L., et al.: Detecting burn severity across Mediterranean forest types by coupling medium-spatial resolution satellite imagery and field data. Remote Sens. **12**, 1–21 (2020), https://doi.org/10.3390/rs12040741
5. San-Miguel-Ayanza, J., et al.: Forest fires in Europe, Middle East and North Africa 2018. JRC Technical Report. Publications Office of the European Union (2019), https://doi.org/10.2760/1128
6. Silva, J.M.N., Moreno, M.V., Le Page, Y., Oom, D., Bistinas, I., Pereira, J.M.C.: Spatiotemporal trends of area burnt in the Iberian Peninsula, 1975–2013. Reg. Environ. Change **19**(2), 515–527 (2018). https://doi.org/10.1007/s10113-018-1415-6
7. Mitri, G.H., Gitas, I.Z.: Mapping post-fire forest regeneration and vegetation recovery using a combination of very high spatial resolution and hyperspectral satellite imagery. Int. J. Appl. Earth Obs. Geoinf. **20**, 60–66 (2012). https://doi.org/10.1016/j.jag.2011.09.001
8. Häusler, M., et al.: Assessment of the indirect impact of wildfire (severity) on actual evapotranspiration in eucalyptus forest based on the surface energy balance estimated from remote-sensing techniques. Int. J. Remote Sens. **39**, 6499–6524 (2018). https://doi.org/10.1080/01431161.2018.1460508
9. Modica, G., Merlino, A., Solano, F., Mercurio, R.: An index for the assessment of degraded Mediterranean forest ecosystems. For. Syst. (2015). https://doi.org/10.5424/fs/2015243-07855
10. Morresi, D., Vitali, A., Urbinati, C., Garbarino, M.: Forest spectral recovery and regeneration dynamics in stand-replacing wildfires of central Apennines derived from Landsat time series. Remote Sens. 11 (2019), https://doi.org/10.3390/rs11030308
11. Semeraro, T., Vacchiano, G., Aretano, R., Ascoli, D.: Application of vegetation index time series to value fire effect on primary production in a Southern European rare wetland. Ecol. Eng. **134**, 9–17 (2019). https://doi.org/10.1016/j.ecoleng.2019.04.004
12. Di Fazio, S., Modica, G., Zoccali, P.: Evolution trends of land use/land cover in a mediterranean forest landscape in Italy. In: Murgante, B., et al. (eds.) Computational Science and Its Applications - ICCSA 2011. ICCSA 2011. LNCS, vol. 6782, pp. 284–299. Springer, Berlin, Heidelberg (2011). https://doi.org/10.1007/978-3-642-21928-3_20
13. Keeley, J.E.: Fire intensity, fire severity and burn severity: a brief review and suggested usage. Int. J. Wildl. Fire. **18**, 116–126 (2009). https://doi.org/10.1071/WF07049
14. Key, C.H., Benson, N.C.: Landscape Assessment (LA) sampling and analysis methods. In: FIREMON: Fire Effects Monitoring and Inventory System (2006)

15. De Luca, G., Modica, G., Fattore, C., Lasaponara, R.: Unsupervised Burned Area Mapping in a Protected Natural Site. An Approach Using SAR Sentinel-1 Data and K-mean Algorithm. In: Gervasi, O., et al. (eds.) ICCSA 2020. LNCS, vol. 12253, pp. 63–77. Springer, Cham (2020). https://doi.org/10.1007/978-3-030-58814-4_5

16. Gitas, I., Mitri, G., Veraverbeke, S., Polychronaki, A.: Advances in remote sensing of post-fire vegetation recovery monitoring - a review. Remote Sens. Biomass - Princ. Appl. (2012). https://doi.org/10.5772/20571

17. Meng, R., Wu, J., Zhao, F., Cook, B.D., Hanavan, R.P., Serbin, S.P.: Measuring short-term post-fire forest recovery across a burn severity gradient in a mixed pine-oak forest using multi-sensor remote sensing techniques. Remote Sens. Environ. **210**, 282–296 (2018). https://doi.org/10.1016/j.rse.2018.03.019

18. De Santis, A., Chuvieco, E.: GeoCBI: A modified version of the Composite Burn Index for the initial assessment of the short-term burn severity from remotely sensed data. Remote Sens. Environ. **113**, 554–562 (2009). https://doi.org/10.1016/j.rse.2008.10.011

19. Otón, G., Ramo, R., Lizundia-Loiola, J., Chuvieco, E.: Global detection of long-term (1982–2017) burned area with AVHRR-LTDR data. Remote Sens. **11** (2019), https://doi.org/10.3390/rs11182079

20. De Santis, A., Chuvieco, E.: Burn severity estimation from remotely sensed data: performance of simulation versus empirical models. Remote Sens. Environ. **108**, 422–435 (2007). https://doi.org/10.1016/j.rse.2006.11.022

21. Tanase, M.A., Kennedy, R., Aponte, C.: Radar Burn Ratio for fire severity estimation at canopy level: an example for temperate forests. Remote Sens. Environ. **170**, 14–31 (2015). https://doi.org/10.1016/j.rse.2015.08.025

22. Chuvieco, E., et al.: Historical background and current developments for mapping burned area from satellite Earth observation. Remote Sens. Environ. **225**, 45–64 (2019). https://doi.org/10.1016/j.rse.2019.02.013

23. Praticò, S., Solano, F., Di Fazio, S., Modica, G.: Machine learning classification of Mediterranean forest habitats in google earth engine based on seasonal sentinel-2 time-series and input image composition optimisation. Remote Sens. **13**, 1–28 (2021)

24. ESA Sentinel Homepage (2021): https://sentinels.copernicus.eu/web/sentinel/home. Accessed 11 Mar 2021

25. Silva, J.M.N., Cadima, J.F.C.L., Pereira, J.M.C., Grégoire, J.M.: Assessing the feasibility of a global model for multi-temporal burned area mapping using SPOT-VEGETATION data. Int. J. Remote Sens. (2004)

26. Pereira, J.M.C., Sá, A.C.L., Sousa, A.M.O., Silva, J.M.N., Santos, T.N., Carreiras, J.M.B.: Spectral characterisation and discrimination of burnt areas. Remote Sens. Large Wildfires (1999). https://doi.org/10.1007/978-3-642-60164-4_7

27. Cansler, C.A., McKenzie, D.: How robust are burn severity indices when applied in a new region? Evaluation of alternate field-based and remote-sensing methods. Remote Sens. **4**, 456–483 (2012). https://doi.org/10.3390/rs4020456

28. Epting, J., Verbyla, D., Sorbel, B.: Evaluation of remotely sensed indices for assessing burn severity in interior Alaska using Landsat TM and ETM+. Remote Sens. Environ. (2005). https://doi.org/10.1016/j.rse.2005.03.002

29. Fornacca, D., Ren, G., Xiao, W.: Evaluating the best spectral indices for the detection of burn scars at several post-fire dates in a Mountainous Region of Northwest Yunnan, China. Remote Sens. **10** (2018), https://doi.org/10.3390/rs10081196

30. Mallinis, G., Mitsopoulos, I., Chrysafi, I.: Evaluating and comparing sentinel 2A and landsat-8 operational land imager (OLI) spectral indices for estimating fire severity in a Mediterranean pine ecosystem of Greece. GIScience Remote Sens. (2018)

31. De Santis, A., Chuvieco, E., Vaughan, P.J.: Short-term assessment of burn severity using the inversion of PROSPECT and GeoSail models. Remote Sens. Environ. **113**, 126–136 (2009). https://doi.org/10.1016/j.rse.2008.08.008
32. Schepers, L., et al..: Burned area detection and burn severity assessment of a heathland fire in Belgium using airborne imaging spectroscopy (APEX). Remote Sens. **6**, 1803–1826 (2014)
33. Quintano, C., Fernández-Manso, A., Roberts, D.A.: Multiple endmember spectral mixture analysis (MESMA) to map burn severity levels from Landsat images in Mediterranean countries. Remote Sens. Environ. **136**, 76–88 (2013)
34. Fernández-Manso, A., Fernández-Manso, O., Quintano, C.: SENTINEL-2A red-edge spectral indices suitability for discriminating burn severity. Int. J. Appl. Earth Obs. Geoinf. (2016). https://doi.org/10.1016/j.jag.2016.03.005
35. Filipponi, F.: BAIS2: Burned Area Index for Sentinel-2. 5177 (2018)
36. Miller, J.D., et al.: Calibration and validation of the relative differenced Normalized Burn Ratio (RdNBR) to three measures of fire severity in the Sierra Nevada and Klamath Mountains, California, USA. Remote Sens. Environ. **113**, 645–656 (2009)
37. Parks, S.A., Dillon, G.K., Miller, C.: A new metric for quantifying burn severity: the relativized burn ratio. Remote Sens. **6**, 1827–1844 (2014). https://doi.org/10.3390/rs6031827
38. Zheng, Z., Zeng, Y., Li, S., Huang, W.: A new burn severity index based on land surface temperature and enhanced vegetation index. Int. J. Appl. Earth Obs. Geoinf. (2016). https://doi.org/10.1016/j.jag.2015.11.002
39. Addison, P., Oommen, T.: Utilizing satellite radar remote sensing for burn severity estimation. Int. J. Appl. Earth Obs. Geoinf. (2018)
40. Kurum, M.: C-Band SAR Backscatter Evaluation of 2008 Gallipoli Forest Fire. **12**, 1091–1095 (2015)
41. Lasaponara, R., Tucci, B.: Identification of burned areas and severity. IEEE Geosci. Remote Sens. Lett. **16**, 917–921 (2019). https://doi.org/10.1109/LGRS.2018.2888641
42. Tanase, M.A., Santoro, M., Aponte, C., De La Riva, J.: Polarimetric properties of burned forest areas at C- and L-band. IEEE J. Sel. Top. Appl. Earth Obs. Remote Sens. (2014), https://doi.org/10.1109/JSTARS.2013.2261053
43. Tanase, M.A., Santoro, M., Wegmüller, U., de la Riva, J., Pérez-Cabello, F.: Properties of X-, C- and L-band repeat-pass interferometric SAR coherence in Mediterranean pine forests affected by fires. Remote Sens. Environ. (2010a)
44. Tanase, M.A., Santoro, M., De La Riva, J., Pérez-Cabello, F., Le Toan, T.: Sensitivity of X-, C-, and L-band SAR backscatter to burn severity in Mediterranean pine forests. IEEE Trans. Geosci. Remote Sens. **48**, 3663–3675 (2010)
45. Imperatore, P., Azar, R., Calo, F., Stroppiana, D., Brivio, P.A., Lanari, R., Pepe, A.: Effect of the vegetation fire on backscattering: an investigation based on Sentinel-1 observations. IEEE J. Sel. Top. Appl. Earth Obs. Remote Sens. **10**, 4478–4492 (2017), https://doi.org/10.1109/JSTARS.2017.2717039
46. Lasko, K.: Incorporating Sentinel-1 SAR imagery with the MODIS MCD64A1 burned area product to improve burn date estimates and reduce burn date uncertainty in wildland fire mapping. Geocarto Int. 1–21 (2019), https://doi.org/10.1080/10106049.2019.1608592
47. Lehmann, E.A., et al.: SAR and optical remote sensing: assessment of complementarity and interoperability in the context of a large-scale operational forest monitoring system. Remote Sens. Environ. **156**, 335–348 (2015)
48. Stroppiana, D., et al.: Integration of optical and SAR data for burned area mapping in Mediterranean regions. Remote Sens. **7**, 1320–1345 (2015)
49. De Luca, G., Silva, J.M.N., Modica, G.: A workflow based on Sentinel-1 SAR data and open-source algorithms for unsupervised burned area detection in Mediterranean ecosystems. GIScience Remote Sens. **00**, 1–26 (2021)

50. Verhegghen, A., et al.: The potential of sentinel satellites for burnt area mapping and monitoring in the Congo Basin forests. Remote Sens. **8**, 1–22 (2016)
51. Tanase, M.A., Kennedy, R., Aponte, C.: Fire severity estimation from space: a comparison of active and passive sensors and their synergy for different forest types. Int. J. Wildl. Fire. **24**, 1062–1075 (2015). https://doi.org/10.1071/WF15059
52. The Python Language Reference (2021): https://docs.python.org/3/reference/. Accessed 15 Mar 2021
53. Sistema Nacional de Informação Geográfica (SNIG) (2021): https://snig.dgterritorio.gov.pt/. Accessed 15 Mar 2021
54. Copernicus Open Access Hub (2021): https://scihub.copernicus.eu/. Accessed 15 Mar 2021
55. Esri ArcGIS World Imagery (2021): https://www.arcgis.com/home/item.html?id=10df2279f 9684e4a9f6a7f08febac2a9. Accessed 19 Mar 2021
56. ESA SNAP Homepage (2021): http://step.esa.int/main/toolboxes/snap/. Accessed 11 Mar 2021
57. ESA SNAP Cookbook (2021): https://senbox.atlassian.net/wiki/spaces/SNAP/pages/240 51769/Cookbook
58. Quegan, S., Toan, T.L., Yu, J.J., Ribbes, F., Floury, N.: Multitemporal ERS SAR analysis applied to forest mapping. IEEE Trans. Geosci. Remote Sens. (2000). https://doi.org/10. 1109/36.842003
59. Santoso, A.W., Pebrianti, D., Bayuaji, L., Zain, J.M.: Performance of various speckle reduction filters on Synthetic Aperture Radar image. In: 2015 4th Int. Conf. Softw. Eng. Comput. Syst. ICSECS 2015 Virtuous Softw. Solut. Big Data, pp. 11–14 (2015)
60. Mandal, D., et al.: Remote sensing of environment dual polarimetric radar vegetation index for crop growth monitoring using sentinel-1 SAR data. Remote Sens. Environ. **247**, 111954 (2020). https://doi.org/10.1016/j.rse.2020.111954
61. Nasirzadehdizaji, R., Sanli, F.B., Abdikan, S., Cakir, Z., Sekertekin, A., Ustuner, M.: Sensitivity analysis of multi-temporal Sentinel-1 SAR parameters to crop height and canopy coverage. Appl. Sci. (2019). https://doi.org/10.3390/app9040655
62. Nicolau, A.P., Flores-Anderson, A., Griffin, R., Herndon, K., Meyer, F.J.: Assessing SAR C-band data to effectively distinguish modified land uses in a heavily disturbed Amazon forest. Int. J. Appl. Earth Obs. Geoinf. **94**, 102214 (2021). https://doi.org/10.1016/j.jag.2020.102214
63. Breiman, L.: Random forests. Mach. Learn. **45**, 5–32 (2001)
64. Cutler, D.R., et al.: Random forests for classification in ecology. Ecology **88**, 2783–2792 (2007)
65. Pedregosa, F., et al.: Scikit-learn: machine learning in Python. J. Mach. Learn. Res. **12**, 2825–2830 (2011)
66. Congalton, R.G., Green, K.: Assessing the Accuracy of Remotely Sensed Data. Principles and Practices (2019)
67. Goutte, C., Gaussier, E.: A Probabilistic Interpretation of Precision, Recall and F-Score, with Implication for Evaluation. In: Losada, D.E., Fernández-Luna, J.M. (eds.) ECIR 2005. LNCS, vol. 3408, pp. 345–359. Springer, Heidelberg (2005). https://doi.org/10.1007/978-3-540-31865-1_25
68. Ok, A.O., Senaras, C., Yuksel, B.: Automated detection of arbitrarily shaped buildings in complex environments from monocular VHR optical satellite imagery. IEEE Trans. Geosci. Remote Sens. **51**, 1701–1717 (2013)
69. Shufelt, J.A.: Performance evaluation and analysis of monocular building extraction from aerial imagery. IEEE Trans. Pattern Anal. Mach. Intell. **21**, 311–326 (1999)
70. Sokolova, M., Japkowicz, N., Szpakowicz, S.: Beyond Accuracy, F-Score and ROC: A Family of Discriminant Measures for Performance Evaluation. In: Sattar, A., Kang, B.-h (eds.) AI 2006. LNCS (LNAI), vol. 4304, pp. 1015–1021. Springer, Heidelberg (2006). https://doi.org/ 10.1007/11941439_114

71. Modica, G., Messina, G., De Luca, G., Fiozzo, V., Praticò, S.: Monitoring the vegetation vigor in heterogeneous citrus and olive orchards. A multiscale object-based approach to extract trees' crowns from UAV multispectral imagery. Comput. Electron. Agric. **175**, 105500 (2020)

72. Sokolova, M., Lapalme, G.: A systematic analysis of performance measures for classification tasks. Inf. Process. Manag. **45**, 427–437 (2009)

73. Modica, G., De Luca, G., Messina, G., Praticò, S.: Comparison and assessment of different object-based classifications using machine learning algorithms and UAVs multispectral imagery in the framework of precision agriculture. Eur. J. Remote Sens. **54**, 431–460 (2021). https://doi.org/10.1080/22797254.2021.1951623

74. Gallagher, M.R., et al.: An improved approach for selecting and validating burn severity indices in forested landscapes an improved approach for selecting and validating burn severity indices in feux dans des milieux forestiers. Can. J. Remote Sens. **46**, 100–111 (2020). https://doi.org/10.1080/07038992.2020.1735931

75. Inoue, Y., et al.: Reflectance characteristics of major land surfaces in slash - and - burn ecosystems in Laos. 1161 (2019), https://doi.org/10.1080/01431160701442039

76. Picotte, J.J., Robertson, K.M.: Validation of remote sensing of burn severity in south-eastern US ecosystems. Int. J. Wildl. Fire. (2011). https://doi.org/10.1071/WF10013

77. Verbyla, D.L.V., Kasischke, E.S.K., Hoy, E.E.H.: Seasonal and topographic effects on estimating fire severity from Landsat TM/ETM + data. 527–534 (2008)

A Machine Learning Approach for Mapping Forest Categories: An Application of Google Earth Engine for the Case Study of Monte Sant'Angelo, Central Italy

Mattia Balestra[1], Stefano Chiappini[1]([⊠]), Eva Savina Malinverni[2], Andrea Galli[1], and Ernesto Marcheggiani[1,3]

[1] Dipartimento di Scienze Agrarie, Alimentari e Ambientali (D3A), Università Politecnica delle Marche, Via Brecce Bianche 10, 60131 Ancona, Italy
{m.balestra,s.chiappini}@pm.univpm.it, {a.galli, e.marcheggiani}@univpm.it

[2] Dipartimento d'Ingegneria Civile, Edile e Architettura (DICEA), Università Politecnica delle Marche, Via Brecce Bianche 12, 60131 Ancona, Italy
e.s.malinverni@univpm.it

[3] Department of Earth and Environmental Sciences, KU Leuven, 3001 Leuven, Belgium

Abstract. Remote Sensing plays a critical role in forest tree species identification. Regarding the current debate on earth observation and monitoring, many see this valuable technology useful for a wide range of purposes, including forest conservation and management. This paper focuses on a workflow for mapping forest tree species from satellite images, by statistic algorithms and machine learning. Among the world satellite platforms, the Sentinel-2 program was selected to investigate the mixed forest area of Monte Sant'Angelo in Central Italy. A list of monthly images from 2018 to 2020 have been processed using the Google Earth Engine geospatial processing service. The process includes the computation of vegetation indexes like the Normalized Difference Vegetation Index (NDVI), Transformed Difference Vegetation Index (TDVI), the Enhanced Vegetation Index (EVI) and the Green Normalized Difference Vegetation Index (GNDVI). A forest class time series was generated for each index. The Artificial Intelligence algorithm models (Machine Learning) were trained identifying accurate ground truths. Principal Component Analysis (PCA) was performed to reduce variables redundancy in Random Forest classifications. Four forest categories have been identified: holm oak woodlands, conifer reforestation, Ostryo Carpinion alliance and mixed hardwood forest. Due to the phenological differences among species, the classification global accuracy ranges from 70% to 80%.

Keywords: Google Earth Engine · PCA · Random forest · Sentinel-2 · Time-series · Tree species classification

© Springer Nature Switzerland AG 2021
O. Gervasi et al. (Eds.): ICCSA 2021, LNCS 12955, pp. 155–168, 2021.
https://doi.org/10.1007/978-3-030-87007-2_12

1 Introduction

Vegetation maps are a key tool to represent habitats patterns and their distribution. Monitoring is a critical to an effective conservation of the habitats (92/43/EEC Habitats Directive and the "Natura 2000"), and a timely and constant production of updated coverages maps is required. Traditional techniques for vegetation map production are based on time consuming and expensive field surveys and direct observations [1] or manual comparison of images. The average vegetation canopies (e.g., deciduous shrubs, deciduous trees, grasslands) are complex mixes of interviewed species life cycles marked by different stages of growth and senescence, each one with different leaves colors and photosynthetic activity [2]. Recurring changes in foliage affects the electromagnetic radiation reflectance of surfaces captured by the sensors [3]. The timing recurring reflectance changes of bio-surfaces under a changing environment is known as land surface phenology (LSP) [4].

In this context, our experiment aims at testing a fast time and less expensive method to get to a classification of forest categories using a set of three-year-set Sentinel-2 Images in Google Earth Engine (GEE; https://earthengine.google.com) [5] from 2018 to 2020, in a case study in center Italy. The Earth Engine service can be joined by APIs (Application Programming Interfaces). Client libraries for JavaScript and Python translates complex geospatial analyses into Earth Engine requests, the REST API connects to the Earth Engine servers [6]. Time-series generated for each category allow for identifying the specific class composition verified by ground truths. Principal Component Analysis (PCA) was used to reduce output data redundancy, pruning the variable set composition, before the Random Forest [7] supervised classification.

As shown in Fig. 1, the case study, Forest of Arcevia, is located in central Italy in the Apennines (43°30′36.71″N 12°55′02.98″E, WGS84). With an area of 990 ha at 752 m above sea level, the study area is characterized by four dominant forest categories: Holm oak woods, Conifer reforestation, Mixed hardwood woods, and Orno ostryenion woods.

The area was reforested using *Pinus nigra* J.F. Arnold, an alien species that has been planted for protective purposes in the post-war period. Being an allochthonous species, its natural regeneration suffers from competition. Due to the lack of management or of specific intervention polices, the autochthonous vegetation recolonized most of the area. The abandonment also favored the development of local floras under the forest understory, which currently is composed by a mixture of deciduous broad-leaved species usually present in the area. A monitoring key issue is linked to the spectral signature responses to that peculiar structure characterized by an upper *P. nigra* canopy and the lower deciduous forest understory.

Considering these categories, the classification [8] had been carried out, as described in the following paragraphs.

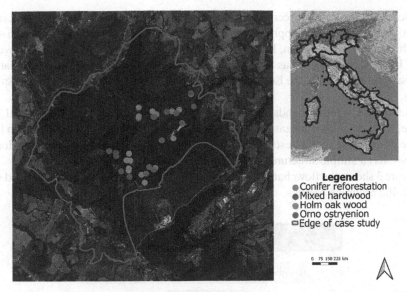

Fig. 1. The location of the study area and the points surveyed on the ground using a GNSS, to collect the Region of Interests as ground truths.

2 Materials and Methods

The Sentinel-2 Images set considered for in this study, is a product of the European Space Agency (ESA) Copernicus Service. The Sentinel-2A and Sentinel-2B platforms are operational since 2015 and 2017 respectively [9]; whose scopes ranges from land management [10], agriculture and forestry [11], up to disaster control, humanitarian relief operations, risk mapping [12] and security. The Sentinel-2 mission is equipped with Multi-Spectral Instrument (MSI), sampling 13 spectral bands, each with its own

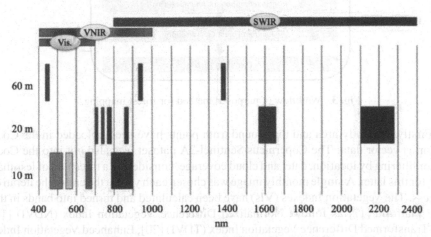

Fig. 2. Sentinel-2 10, 20 and 60 m spatial resolution bands: B1 (443 nm), B2 (490 nm), B3 (560 nm), B4 (665 nm), B5 (705 nm), B6 (740 nm), B7 (783 nm), B8 (842 nm), B9 (940 nm), B10 (1375 nm), B11 (1610 nm) and B12 (2190 nm) [13] (Color figure online)

specific spatial resolution. According to the literature, we opted for a bands composition commonly used in forest mapping, the bands n. 2,3,4 and 8 with a spatial resolution of 10 m on the ground. Blue, Green, Red and Near InfraRed (NIR), respectively, as showed in Fig. 2. Usually, the Copernicus Service offers atmospheric corrected open access data, in our case we could acquire the Level-1C and Level-2A, corrected by Top-Of-Atmosphere (TOA).

The chosen satellite bands have been processed by GEE [14], a geospatial data storage, analysis and visualization service powered by the Google Cloud Platform [15]. In spite of its lower spatial resolution, Sentinel-2 allows reliable forest classifications if the forest has a simple structure, composed by few different species [16].

Figure 3 shows the flowchart up to the final classification map outputs, provided with the specific accuracy metrics.

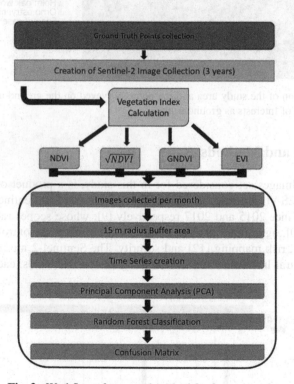

Fig. 3. Workflow of purposed method for forest mapping.

Firstly, the study area and the ground truth points have been uploaded in the Code Editor as vector data. The Copernicus Sentinel-2A dataset was also got into the Code Editor filtering by location, date, and cloud coverage, considering a threshold of less than 50% for this latter. A single monthly image was chosen each year at the end of the iterative process. The Vegetation Indexes (VIs) have been calculated and turned into bands in the GEE platform [17] as follow: Normalized Difference Vegetation Index (NDVI) [18, 19], Transformed Difference Vegetation Index (TDVI) [20], Enhanced Vegetation Index

(EVI) [21] and the Green Normalized Difference Vegetation Index (GNDVI) [22]. The following are the formulas used to calculate the different VIs:

$$NDVI = \frac{NIR - RED}{NIR + RED}$$

$$TDVI = \sqrt{\frac{NIR - RED}{NIR + RED} + 0.5}$$

$$EVI = \frac{NIR - RED}{NIR + C1 \cdot RED - C2 \cdot BLUE + L'}$$

$$GNDVI = \frac{NIR - GREEN}{NIR + GREEN}$$

Considering the images analyzed in these time series, the overcome are showed in Fig. 4, 5 and 6.

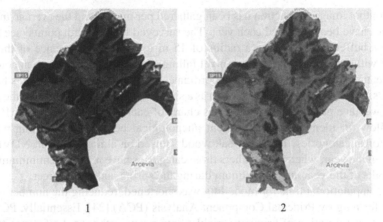

Fig. 4. The output stock images by vegetation indices computed in: 1) January 2018 RGB image; 2) January 2018 mean NDVI..

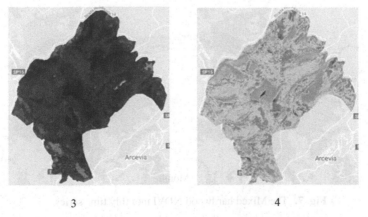

Fig. 5. The output stock images by vegetation indices computed in: 3) January 2018 mean Transformed Difference Vegetation Index (TDVI) and 4) January 2018 mean EVI

Fig. 6. The output stock images computed in January 2018: mean GNDVI.

The output images collection has been gathered per month, and the average monthly VIs values have been recorded each year. The surveyed ground truth points (see Fig. 1) have been buffered considering a radius of 15 m to verify the presence of the same category within the buffer area. Each pixel falling within the buffer has been converted into a "feature", recording the pixel's coordinates (Latitude and Longitude) as features properties. By plot each pixel time pattern as a single random color line during the twelve months, we have produced the time-series charts of each VI (Figs. 7, 8, 9 and 10). The charts allow for identifying the different phenological behaviors [23] along with the various forest categories. The holm oak wood showed an almost constant NDVI value throughout the year, whereas the others three categories have reached a minimum in the first months of the year and a maximum during the spring and the summer.

The computational time for modelling was shortened, reducing the number of variables performing by Principal Component Analysis (PCA) [24]. Essentially, PCA represents a transformation of original variables into a new orthogonal reference system, with fewer variables, where the variable with higher variance is projected on the first axis, the second invariance on the second, and so on.

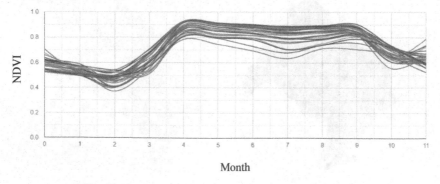

Month

Fig. 7. The Mixed hardwood NDVI monthly time series.

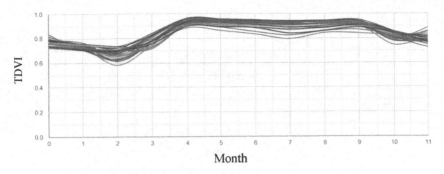

Fig. 8. The Mixed hardwood TDVI monthly time series.

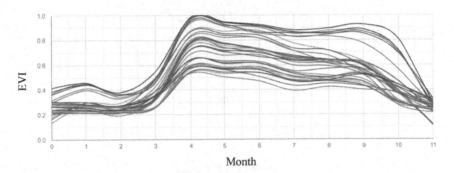

Fig. 9. The Mixed hardwood EVI monthly time series

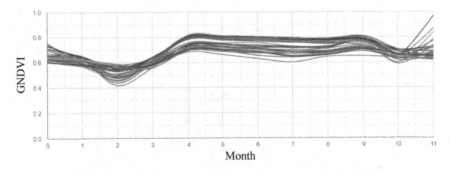

Fig. 10. The Mixed hardwood GNDVI monthly time series

PCA results are called scores and represent the "coordinates" of each point in the new reference system. PC1 and PC2 (the first two principal components) can be used to define the reduced phenological ordination space of ground truth known locations. The plot of PC1 and PC2, called score plot, support the interpretation of a distinct forest plant community phenology [25], showing clusters of samples (plant associations) based on their similarity. Close samples have a similar composition, whereas distant samples

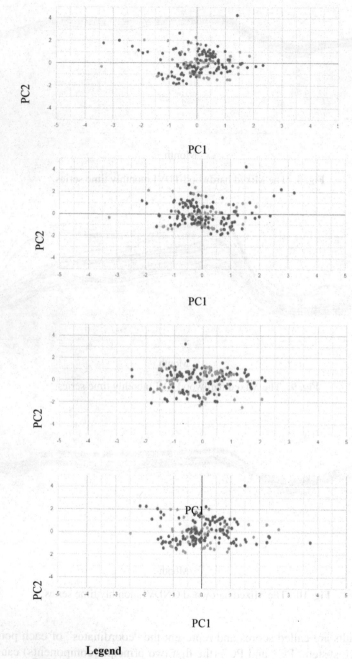

Legend
- Conifer reforestation
- Orno ostryenion
- Mixed hardwood
- Holm oak wood

Fig. 11. The PCA scores show a cluster of plant associations based on following Vis

are much different from each other. To provide a score plot for each plant association, the first two principal component values of pixels belonging to a buffered region have been extracted. As shown in Fig. 11, the EVI shows values gathering along both axes compared with other indexes. On the other hand, these latter ones show a relatively uniform pattern among the different forest categories.

The classification was performed by Random Forest (RF) [7], a supervised learning method. To perform the RF, the number of classification trees has been set to 500 and the number of input variables used at each split node has been set to 2, which are the default setting of this classifier. In this case, the presence of ground truth points "supervises" the process of pixel classification by training the model with data on plant associations, verified in the field by direct observation. Then, the computer algorithm uses values from training areas (or points) to classify the whole image, predicting the same forest category in each pixel. It is necessary to divide the dataset into two parts for the classification model creation: "training-set" to perform the system training and "test-set" to try the algorithm accuracy. The GEE scripts allowed for splitting the dataset along with a specific percentage, with "training points" as 30% of the total and the "validation points" the remaining 70%. Indeed, to assure a "fair" assessment of a classifier's generalization, the training data must be separated from data to assess accuracy [26]. Each forest category has its own class number, in which Class 0 are the Holm oak woods, Class 1 the Conifer, Class 3 the Mixed Hardwood forest and Class 3 the Orno-ostryenion association.

3 Experiment Results and Discussion

This paragraph describes the output confusion matrices based on training data. Moreover, the results of the overall training accuracy are computed. The algorithm accuracy was validated by a test-set, assessing the classification's error through independent data. The error matrix and accuracy are matrices comparing two columns of the validated test-set: one containing the actual values and the other the predicted values. The matrix rows correspond to the actual values, whereas the columns to the predicted values. The obtained accuracies are calculated utilizing the confusion matrices obtained for each VI, as shown in the Table 1 [27].

The maximum classification accuracy is reached using NDVI and GNDVI, the most frequent VIs in literature, thanks to their ability to enhance the reflectance between the Red/Green and the NIR bands. The principle behind the chosen VIs for forest classifications is that the vegetation shows a higher reflectance in the NIR, than other bands. This contrast has been used as a proxy of the vegetation healthy status VIs are indeed biophysical parameters, related to the photosynthetic activities. The analysis of the time-series composed by different images in different periods offers valuable information to monitoring the forest dynamics [28].

The experiment has proven to be effective, as shown by the accuracy threshold of the confusion matrix. NDVI and GNDVI are within the range of 84%, while the TDVI is 81%, and EVI is 78%, as it is possible to observe in Table 1. These results show that Sentinel-2 free images can be safely used to classify different forest categories over a large area, even with limited input sample data collected on the ground.

Table 1. The consumer accuracy values using different Vegetation Indices as Input into Random Forestry. The different tree species are noted as follow: 0 = Holm oak wood, 1 = Conifer reforestation, 2 = Mixed hardwood, 3 = Orno ostryenion

NDVI					
Class	0	1	2	3	User accuracy
0	7	0	0	0	1
1	3	20	0	0	0.87
2	0	0	9	4	0.69
3	0	0	3	17	0.85
Producer Accuracy	0.70	1	0.75	0.81	
Validation overall accuracy: 0.84					

TDVI					
Class	0	1	2	3	User Accuracy
0	7	0	0	0	1
1	3	20	2	0	0.80
2	0	0	7	4	0.64
3	0	0	3	17	0.85
Producer Accuracy	0.70	1	0.58	0.81	
Validation overall accuracy: 0.81					

EVI					
Class	0	1	2	3	User accuracy
0	9	0	0	0	1
1	1	20	5	3	0.69
2	0	0	4	2	0.67
3	0	0	3	16	0.84
Producer Accuracy	0.90	1	0.33	0.76	
Validation overall accuracy: 0.78					

GNDVI					
Class	0	1	2	3	User Accuracy
0	8	0	0	0	1
1	2	20	2	0	0.83
2	0	0	7	3	0.70
3	0	0	3	18	0.86
Producer Accuracy	0.80	1	0.58	0.86	
Validation overall accuracy: 0.84					

The use of PCA allows for a higher classification accuracy of forest areas. According to Xu et al. [29] an overall accuracy of more than 82% was obtained using NDVI to a forest species classification of five classes. Gimire et al. [30] employed RF to mapping the variety of tree species, using time-series of wooded landscapes, obtaining an overall accuracy of 78% for EVI. Praticò et al. [15] created a stack of images of all the Sentinel-2 bands and added the computation of the GNDVI index, obtaining an overall accuracy of 86%.

Noteworthy, there is no literature about similar workflow employing the TDVI index. Therefore, in accordance with these authors, the obtained results are in line with those achieved by their research team.

Moreover, looking at the classification results for each different vegetation index shown in Fig. 12, it is possible to observe that all the classified maps have a similar pattern but the case n. 3, shows a limited holm oak wood area and a large conifers' reforestation area if compared with the other outputs. This result, in our study, indicates a lesser effectiveness of EVI to clearly represent the phenological behaviour of the 4 forest categories.

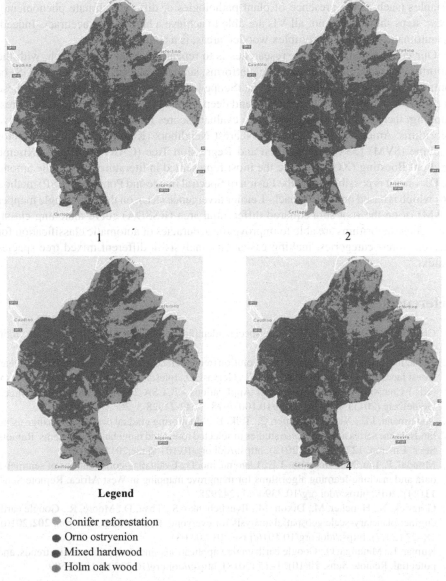

Legend

- Conifer reforestation
- Orno ostryenion
- Mixed hardwood
- Holm oak wood

Fig. 12. Image classification by Random Forest algorithm: 1) NDVI; 2) TDVI; 3) EVI; 4) GNDVI.

4 Conclusion

The increasing availability of earth observation data and satellite missions with a wide range of spectral sets at different spatial resolutions offers the opportunity to map large forest areas in less time-consuming ways. Researchers are constantly looking at improved and ground-breaking workflows and methods. The aim is to obtain accurate and reliable representations and classification of the forest categories analyzed in a certain area. This study examined different vegetation indexes through a time-series composed by Sentinel-2 images stack over 4 years on GEE platform. The methodology described in this paper reduce the seasonal variability of the vegetation data, lowering the effect of external variables (such as the presence of plant pathologies or different climate phenomena). These steps showed that not all VIs are able to achieve a high global accuracy. Indeed, the automatic mapping of complex wooden areas, is a complex activity.

Our commitment for future researches is to repeat this kind of approach, with the opportunity to test other free satellite platforms, such as Landsat-8 (NASA - USGS) or commercial constellations such as PlanetScope [31] Thanks to the integration of these platforms with machine learning (ML) and deep learning (DL) methodologies for forest mapping, there will be the possibility to evaluate scores from traditional or innovative algorithms. Among the ML ones, K-Nearest Neighbors (KNN) [32], Support Vector Machine (SVM) [33], Classification and Regression Tree (CART) [34] and eXtreme Gradient Boosting (XGBoost) are the most represented in literature [35], while among the DL ones it is possible to use the Fusion of Spectral image and Point data (FSP) method [36] which is based on the Kullback–Leibler divergence (KL), on the curve angle mapper (CAM) or on the root sum squared differential area (RSSDA) curve matching classifiers. These algorithms are able to improve the accuracies of automatic classification for different forest categories, making easier this analysis in different mixed tree species context.

References

1. Choudhury, A.M., et al.: Urban tree species identification. Forest **11**, 22 (2020). https://doi.org/10.3390/f11111226
2. Di Fazio, S., Modica, G., Zoccali, P.: Evolution trends of land use/land cover in a mediterranean forest landscape in Italy. In: Murgante, B., Gervasi, O., Iglesias, A., Taniar, D., Apduhan, B.O. (eds.) Computational Science and Its Applications - ICCSA 2011, pp. 284–299. Springer, Heidelberg (2011). https://doi.org/10.1007/978-3-642-21928-3_20
3. Vogelmann, J.E., Xian, G., Homer, C., Tolk, B.: Monitoring gradual ecosystem change using landsat time series analyses: case studies in selected forest and rangeland ecosystems. Remote Sens. Environ. **122**, 92–105 (2012). https://doi.org/10.1016/j.rse.2011.06.027
4. Mondal, P., Liu, X., Fatoyinbo, T.E., Lagomasino, D.: Evaluating combinations of sentinel-2 data and machine-learning algorithms for mangrove mapping in West Africa. Remote Sens. **11**(24), 2019. https://doi.org/10.3390/rs11242928
5. Gorelick, N., Hancher, M., Dixon, M., Ilyushchenko, S., Thau, D., Moore, R.: Google earth engine: planetary-scale geospatial analysis for everyone. Remote Sens. Environ. **202**(2016), 18–27 (2017). https://doi.org/10.1016/j.rse.2017.06.031
6. Kumar, L., Mutanga, O.: Google earth engine applications since inception: usage, trends, and potential. Remote Sens. **10**(10), 1–15 (2018). https://doi.org/10.3390/rs10101509

7. Breiman, L.: Random forests. Mach. Learn. 1–28 (2001). https://doi.org/10.1201/978042946 9275-8.
8. Modica, G., Merlino, A., Solano, F., Mercurio, R.: An index for the assessment of degraded mediterranean forest ecosystems. For. Syst. 24(3) (2015). https://doi.org/10.5424/fs/2015243-07855.
9. Copernicus, E.: The European Space Agency - Sentinel. https://sentinel.esa.int/web/sentinel/missions/sentinel-2.
10. Gulinck, H., et al.: The fourth regime of open space. Sustain. 10(7), 1–15 (2018). https://doi.org/10.3390/su10072143
11. Li, J., Wang, L.: Forest type classification with multitemporal sentinel-2 data. In: Proceedings - IEEE Congress on Cybermatics, IEEE International Conferences on Internet of Things, iThings 2020, IEEE green computing and communications, greencom 2020, IEEE cyber, physical and social computing, CPSCom 2020 and IEEE smart data. SmartD 2020, pp. 498–504 (2020). https://doi.org/10.1109/iThings-GreenCom-CPSCom-SmartData-Cybermatics5 0389.2020.00091
12. Solano, F., Colonna, N., Marani, M., Pollino, M.: Geospatial analysis to assess natural park biomass resources for energy uses in the context of the Rome metropolitan area. In: Calabrò, F., Della Spina, L., Bevilacqua, C. (eds.) ISHT 2018. SIST, vol. 100, pp. 173–181. Springer, Cham (2019). https://doi.org/10.1007/978-3-319-92099-3_21
13. Regan, A., Silvestrin, P., Fernandez, D., Gabriele, A., Leveque, N.: Sentinel convoy: synergetic observations with satellites flying in formation with European Operational Missions. In: Proc. 4S Symp. Small Satell. Syst. Serv. January, pp. 1–12 (2010)
14. Chung, L.C.H., Xie, J., Ren, C.: Improved machine-learning mapping of local climate zones in metropolitan areas using composite Earth observation data in Google Earth Engine. Build. Environ. 199(15), 107879 (2021). https://doi.org/10.1016/j.buildenv.2021.107879
15. Praticò, S., Solano, F., Di Fazio, S., Modica, G.: Machine learning classification of mediterranean forest habitats in google earth engine based on seasonal sentinel-2 time-series and input image composition optimisation. Remote Sens. 13(4), 1–28 (2021). https://doi.org/10.3390/rs13040586
16. Wessel, M., Brandmeier, M., Tiede, D.: Evaluation of different machine learning algorithms for scalable classification of tree types and tree species based on Sentinel-2 data. Remote Sens. 10(9), 1419 (2018). https://doi.org/10.3390/rs10091419
17. Tassi, A., Vizzari, M.: Object-oriented lulc classification in google earth engine combining snic, glcm, and machine learning algorithms. Remote Sens. 12(22), 1–17 (2020). https://doi.org/10.3390/rs12223776
18. Hanes, J.M. (ed.): Biophysical Applications of Satellite Remote Sensing. SRS, Springer, Heidelberg (2014). https://doi.org/10.1007/978-3-642-25047-7
19. Choudhury, M.A.M., Marcheggiani, E., Galli, A., Modica, G., Somers, B.: Mapping the urban atmospheric carbon stock by lidar and worldview-3 data. Forests 12(6), 692 (2021). https://doi.org/10.3390/f12060692
20. Tsafack, N., Fattorini, S., Frias, C.B., Xie, Y., Wang, X., Rebaudo, F.: Competing vegetation structure indices for estimating spatial constrains in carabid abundance patterns in chinese grasslands reveal complex scale and habitat patterns. Insects. 11(4), 249 (2020). https://doi.org/10.3390/insects11040249
21. Choubin, B., et al.: Effects of drought on vegetative cover changes: investigating spatiotemporal patterns, Elsevier Inc. 2, 213–222 (2019)
22. Isip, M.F., Alberto, R.T., Biagtan, A.R.: Exploring vegetation indices adequate in detecting twister disease of onion using Sentinel-2 imagery. Spat. Inf. Res. 28(3), 369–375 (2019). https://doi.org/10.1007/s41324-019-00297-7

23. Pesaresi, S., Mancini, A., Quattrini, G., Casavecchia, S.: Mapping mediterranean forest plant associations and habitats with functional principal component analysis using Landsat 8 NDVI time series. Remote Sens. **12**(7), 1132 (2020). https://doi.org/10.3390/rs12071132

24. Macintyre, P., van Niekerk, A., Mucina, L.: Efficacy of multi-season Sentinel-2 imagery for compositional vegetation classification. Int. J. Appl. Earth Obs. Geoinf. **85**, 101980 (2020). https://doi.org/10.1016/j.jag.2019.101980

25. Pesaresi, S., Mancini, A., Casavecchia, S.: Recognition and characterization of forest plant communities through remote-sensing NDVI Time Series divers. **2**(8), 1–192 (2011). https://doi.org/10.3390/d12080313.

26. Goldblatt, R., You, W., Hanson, G., Khandelwal, A.K.: Detecting the boundaries of urban areas in India: a dataset for pixel-based image classification in google earth engine. Remote Sens. **8**(8), 634 (2016). https://doi.org/10.3390/rs8080634

27. Stehman, S.V., Foody, G.M.: Key issues in rigorous accuracy assessment of land cover products. Remote Sens. Environ. **231**, 111199 (2019). https://doi.org/10.1016/j.rse.2019.05.018

28. Xie, Y., Sha, Z., Yu, M.: Remote sensing imagery in vegetation mapping: a review. J. Plant Ecol. **1**(1), 9–23 (2008). https://doi.org/10.1093/jpe/rtm005

29. Xu, K., Tian, Q., Zhang, Z., Yue, J., Te Chang, C.: Tree species (Genera) identification with GF-1 time-series in a forested landscape, Northeast China. Remote Sens. **12**(10), 1–18 (2020). https://doi.org/10.3390/rs12101554

30. Ghimire, B.R., Nagai, M., Tripathi, N.K., Witayangkurn, A., Mishara, B., Sasaki, N.: Mapping of Shorea robusta forest using time series MODIS data. Forest **8**(10), 384 (2017). https://doi.org/10.3390/f8100384

31. Parente, L., Taquary, E., Silva, A.P., Souza, C., Ferreira, L.: Next generation mapping: combining deep learning, cloud computing, and big remote sensing data. Remote Sens. **11**(23), 2881 (2019). https://doi.org/10.3390/rs11232881

32. Zhang, Z.: Introduction to machine learning: K-nearest neighbors. Ann. Transl. Med. **4**(11), 1–7 (2016). https://doi.org/10.21037/atm.2016.03.37

33. Cortes, C., Vapnik, V.N.: Support-vector networks. Mach. Learn. **20**, 273–297 (1995). https://doi.org/10.1023/A:1022627411411

34. Breiman, L., Friedman, J.H., Olshen, R.A., Stone, C.J.: Classification and Regression Trees. Chapman & Hall/CRC (1984)

35. Karasiak, N., Sheeren, D., Fauvel, M., Willm, J., Dejoux, J.F., Monteil, C.: Mapping tree species of forests in southwest France using Sentinel-2 image time series. In: 2017 9th Int. Work. Anal. Multitemporal Remote Sens. Images, MultiTemp 2017, pp. 1–4. Brugge, Belgium (2017). https://doi.org/10.1109/Multi-Temp.2017.8035215.

36. Wan, H., Tang, Y., Jing, L., Li, H., Qiu, F., Wu, W.: Tree species classification of forest stands using multisource remote sensing data. Remote Sens. **13**(1), 1–24 (2021). https://doi.org/10.3390/rs13010144

Monitor Mangrove Forest Dynamics
from Multi-temporal Landsat 8-OLI Images
in the Southern Coast of Sancti Spíritus
Province (Cuba)

Ernesto Marcheggiani[1,2]([⊠]), Andrea Galli[1], Osmany Ceballo Melendres[1],
Ben Somers[2], Julio P. García-Lahera[2], Wanda De Keersmaecker[2],
and MD Abdul Mueed Choudhury[1]([⊠])

[1] Department of Agricultural, Food, and Environmental Sciences, Marche Polytechnic
University, Ancona, Italy
{e.marcheggiani,e.galli}@staff.univpm.it,
m.choudhury@pm.univpm.it
[2] Division of Forest, Nature, and Landscape, Department of Earth and Environmental Sciences,
KU Leuven, 3001 Leuven, Belgium
ben.somers@kuleuven.be

Abstract. In the coastal tropics and subtropical regions, fragile ecosystems such
as deltas, mangrove forests, and swamps are common, whose ecological stability
strictly depends on the quality management of hydrological resources at the basin
level. The National Hydrographic Basin Council in Cuba, protect the hydrographic
basins, considered as the reference unit for the integrated management of water
resources. Moreover, the council aims at preventing negative impacts on of these
vital ecosystems for their key services to the overall social and economic wellbeing. As an example, the Zaza River basin in the of Province of Sancti Spiritus, the
mangrove forest is suffering from significant decay, in particular on the southern
coasts. A significant improvement of the water resources sustainable management
in Cuba, is a more reliable and timely monitoring. Considering the extreme conditions and the limited accessibility of mangroves, remote sensing and others earth
observations techniques represents a suitable tool for monitoring the mangrove
forest in coastal areas. In our study, we used a set of 10 multispectral Landsat – 8
OLI images from November 2014 to December 2015.

By collecting campaigns on mangroves' phenology, we have: 1) studied the
relationships between phenology and spectral behavior of species; and, 2) set up a
classification framework to assess the forests composition remotely, with special
attention to mangroves. The methodology here implemented could be effectively
applied in all coastal natural ecosystems of this island to improve the knowledge
about the critical issues of these very fragile ecosystems.

Keywords: Mangrove forest · Remote sensing · Landsat – 8 OLI images

© Springer Nature Switzerland AG 2021
O. Gervasi et al. (Eds.): ICCSA 2021, LNCS 12955, pp. 169–182, 2021.
https://doi.org/10.1007/978-3-030-87007-2_13

1 Introduction

Hydrographic basins in Cuba are considered the functional reference unit for programming and planning the social, economic and ecological integrate management of natural resources. Among the natural resources, water is a key resource for human wellbeing and productivity. Basin and watersheds are noteworthy for the overall water cycle and *"constitutes the area of land from which all surface run-off flows through a sequence of streams, rivers and, possibly, lakes into the sea at a single river mouth, estuary or delta"* [1]. In the Caribbean islands (i.e. Cuba, Grenada, Antigua-Barbuda), a freshwater shortage is critical since supply depends mainly on rainwater. Integrated Water Resources Management (IWRM) at river basin scale is a key management strategy to preserve water resources and their long-term social, economic, and environmental exploitation [2]. As defined by the Global Water Partnership [3], the IWRM is *"a process that promotes the coordinated development and the management of water, land and related resources, to maximise the resultant economic and social welfare equitably without compromising the sustainability of vital ecosystems"*. Unfortunately, a sectoral approach is still prevailing worldwide. For instance water management policies does not comply with the fundamental IWRM principles in Cuba. The Hydrographic Council and territorial councils at national and provincial level respectively, adopt manage water distribution looking only at the agriculture and urban water supply without considering the ecological needs of natural ecosystems, like coastal mangrove forests. Temperature, salinity, sediment, and energy conditions, mostly depend on the ways water is managed, impact on the ecological balance of the ecosystems. Any alteration in mangrove forest composition, distribution, and extension, could get problems in specific aspects of water management. According to Feller and Sitnik [4], mangroves are a mix of tropical trees and shrubs growing in the inter sea zone. The mix composition can be up to 16 families and 40 to 50 species approximately. Cuban mangroves, in general, settles in the biogenetic and accumulative coast estuaries, where the tides and freshwater determine their spatial pattern. Mangrove forest constitutes a precious backup, representing 26% of forest surface in Cuba [5]. Monodominant or mixed mangroves can establish a great variety of communities or ecological types. *Rhizophora mangrove* (red mangrove) generally occupies the first shoreline forming practically a monospecific fringe. It also located in the borderlines of rivers, canals, estuaries, and coastal lagoons. For this reason, a special focus should be dedicated to the dynamics of red mangroves along the coasts as one of the most interesting potential indicators of water management issues at the basin level. To this end, an efficient management of the mangrove ecosystems, requires effective monitoring and decision support frameworks. Because of the extension of the studied area and the difficulty of manned survey operations in mangrove forests [24] and their rich biodiversity [25] earth observation, remote sensing and GIS have widely proven to be essential tools [6–23]. Conventional spaceborne multispectral data (e.g. Landsat and SPOT series, IRS, ASTER) play pivotal role in earth observation. In fact, medium spatial resolution (several meters) imageries are effective for extensive areas [26]. Furthermore, the availability of temporal data series, three decades at least, and the detail of yearly acquired data (same Path and Row) allow users to perform Change Detection [27].

The significant spectral mix of mangrove canopies [28] is the reason why alternative high-resolution optical data processing are adopted in addition to the usual pixel-based methods, including neural network [28] and linear spectral unmixing [29].

We have applied the Multiple Endmember Spectral Mixture Analysis (MESMA), by Somers & Asner [30], to improve the classification accuracy and quality mapping. In our experiment, Hyperion satellite rainforests spectral images, for different periods of the growing season, have been coupled with the specific phenological phases of mangroves. Three main characteristics of the spectral response (foliage, soil, and water) interactions of seasonal and daily tides [6, 17], and cloudiness are considered. The method consists also of aerial photo detection [15] and human interpretation [31, 32]. In particular a multitemporal set of Landsat – 8 OLI multispectral images have been processed by MESMA to improve the spectral separability of high of classified pixels to better identify the different land covers, with special attention to the possibility of distinguish among mangrove species in the coastal southern Sancti Spíritus. The outcome are as follow: 1) we could evaluate the relationship between phenology of mangrove forest species and their reflectance on images within a specific climatic period (December 2014-July 2015); 2) we could get improved results using the MESMA methodology.

The general objective is to set up a significant approachable to be applied in any region with the presence of forests of mangroves in tropical and subtropical countries.

In our beliefs, the present work can contribute to the general objective to set up an effective monitoring standard, replicable in others tropical and subtropical regions of the world with significant forests of mangroves. Secondly to contribute to the debate for improved water management policy in Cuba.

2   Study Area

The study area (Fig. 1) is of 1608.17 square km located in the Southern coast of the Sancti Spíritus province in Cuba (upper left East vertex 591094.32 m, Nord vertex 2380724.03 m; low right East vertex 706320.94 m, Nord vertex 2414462.33 m as UTM zone 17N WGS84 projection). The political-administrative boundaries are represented by Cabagán river which borders with Cienfuegos province (West side), and the port of Palo Alto (Est side) close to the borders of Ciego de Ávila province. Within this area are located Trinidad, on the coast, Sancti Spíritus and La Sierpe municipalities in the central inner region. The geology of this area is characterised by the presence of rocks and structures from the Cuban Neoautocton period, which originated after the consolidation of the plicated substratum in Superior Eocene. The Southern plains are characterised by red ferallitic soils occupying the abrasive terraces. The yellow leached ferallitic and quartz soils occupy the intermediate terraces in the marine plains. Besides, we find dark plastic vertisoils with high content of montmorillonite clay, determining an insufficient drainage, linked to hydromorphic soils of swamps. The littoral swamps with accumulative delta and plain are characterised by hydromorphic soils made by peat-silt and muddy clay.

Cuban rivers are sourced by only natural rain, this reflects their irregular hydric regime with floods and draught periods depending on climate conditions. The climatology of the Cuban archipelago is characterised by two climatic periods with very clean-cut differences: the rainy season (from May to October) and the dry season (from November to April). The yearly average temperature is 25.8 °C, the lower average temperature is 21.9 °C and higher average temperature is 30.7 °C, according to 1981–2010 historical series. The highest temperatures occur in July and August while the lowest temperatures occur in January. In the study area, the yearly rainfall is 1106.88 mm, but during the dry period the average rainfall is 224.80 mm (21%) while in the rainy period the average rainfall is 882.08 mm (79%).

Fig. 1. The study area at the Southern coast of Sancti Spíritus province in Cuba.

3   Materials and Data

3.1   Satellite Data

We used a time series of 10 multispectral Landsat – 8 OLI (path: 14 / Row: 45) images with 30 m resolution on the ground, from the Geological Service of the United States (USGS) (http://earthexplorer.usgs.gov/). The cloudiness thresholded was set to 10%. As shown in Table.1. November and December was chosen for 2014 and January, February, March, April, May, July, October, and December for 2015, including images from the rainy season, the most interesting for spectral discrimination among different species of mangroves [28].

Table 1. Market share [%] of the main three container shipping alliances along the East-West routes. Year 2018. (% TEUs of capacity).

Date	Sensor	Path	Row	Projection	Lat./Long.
November, 11-2014	Landsat 8 - OLI	14	45	UTM-17N/WGS-84	21.6753 -79.9260
December, 13-2014	Landsat 8 - OLI	14	45	UTM-17N/WGS-84	21.6753 -79.9260
January, 14 -2015	Landsat 8 - OLI	14	45	UTM-17N/WGS-84	21.6753 -79.9260
February, 19-2015	Landsat 8 - OLI	14	45	UTM-17N/WGS-84	21.6753 -79.9260
March, 19-2015	Landsat 8 - OLI	14	45	UTM-17N/WGS-84	21.6753 -79.9260
April, 20 -2015	Landsat 8 - OLI	14	45	UTM-17N/WGS-84	21.6753 -79.9260
May, 03-2015	Landsat 8 - OLI	14	45	UTM-17N/WGS-84	21.6753 -79.9260
July, 25-2015	Landsat 8 - OLI	14	45	UTM-17N/WGS-84	21.6753, -79.9260
October, 29 /2015	Landsat 8 - OLI	14	45	UTM-17N/WGS-84	21.6753, -79.9260
December, 16-2015	**Landsat 8 - OLI**	**14**	**45**	**UTM-17N/WGS-84**	**21.6753, -79.9260**

From every multispectral Landsat 8-OLI image, we selected the most suitable bands to investigate the spectral behavior of wetland vegetation [11, 19, 20]. In particular: the bands are as follw: B2 (0.452 – 0.512 μ), B3 (0.533 – 0.590 μ) and B4 (0.636 – 0,673 μ) in the visible (VIS) region; B5(0.851 – 0.879 μ) in the near infrared (NIR) region; B6 (1.566 – 1.651 μ) and B7 (2.107 – 2.294 μ) in the short wavelength infrared (SWIR) region. Rough data were pre-processed to perform a radiometric conversion (from radiance to reflectance) and a geometric correction (georeferencing in WGS84, UTM Projection, Zone 17 N).

3.2 Ground Reference Data

The ground truth collection is a critical step of supervised classification for processing the imagery and validate the results. Often a key issue is the limited accessibility to that characterises these ecosystems. In particular, ground truths are essential in studying the spectral behavior of mangrove canopies, which include a great number of species not so different for what concerns phenology and physiology which usually grow in a very complex habitat. The collection of ground reference data was carried out on August and September 2015 in the following deltaic zones of the Southern coast of Sancti Spiritus province: Jatibonico del Sur river, Agabama river, Zaza river. Globally, this surveys interested 61 plots with a surface of 10 m x 10 m (100 m2) each one, in the field work was adopted the Cuban "Protocol for monitoring the mangrove ecosystems" [33–35]. The geographic location of plots was determined by using Global Position System (GPS) tools to define the centroid coordinates of each plot. Monospecific and mixed canopies of species shaping the local mangrove ecosystems (Rhizophora mangrove, Avicennia germinans, Laguncularia racemosa, Conocarpus erectus) were surveyed. In each plot, some structural and phenological parameters were determined: flora species in the centroid, dominant flora, height (m), water flood (permanent, temporal, seasonal), total ground coverage (%), red mangrove (Rhizophora mangrove) coverage (%), black mangrove (Avicennia germinans) coverage, patabán (Laguncularia racemose) coverage (%), yana (Conocarpus erectus) coverage (%), abundance of fruits, abundance of flowers, adult trees coverage (%), young trees coverage (%) and the number of individuals died. An additional set of plots was surveyed in order to collect reference data for the others typologies of coverages of interest in the study area like not vegetated soils, deep water, lagoon water, other vegetation, not photosynthetic vegetation alias dead vegetation (NPV).

Finally, by integrating "on field" information with the specific bibliography concerning the mangrove's phenology, it has been possible outlining the main phenological stages for the four species of mangroves considered in our study. In Fig. 2 examples for Red and Black Mangrove are shown.

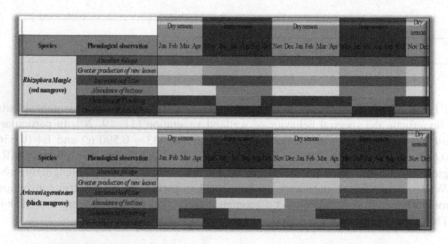

Fig. 2. Main characteristics of the Red and Black mangrove phenology.

In the reporting area, the four most representing species of tree composition in the mangroves forest (R. mangle, A. germinans, L. racemosa, C. erectus) shown abundant foliage during the whole year, boosting their condition of evergreen species. The leaves falling occurs all year long and the new leaves appear during the main rainy period (May-October) but the most significance falling of leaves also occurs in the same time as general tendency. The most abundant flowering of Red mangroves (*Rhizophora mangle*) occurs during the dry period, conversely the flowering of Black mangroves (*Avicennia germinans*) extends also in the rainy period, as well as *Laguncularia racemosa* and *Conocarpus erectus* (White mangroves) usually do. All phenological phases of the four mangrove species may present small displacements within each year, by adapting to climatic condition, and the differences among years, on the other hand, are very limited. Finally, all four mangrove species show the rainy period as the period of maximum production of fruits, since this stability is related to natural regeneration needs according to the survival strategies of these species in own habitat.

4 Methodology

The main steps of the method used for processing monotemporal and multitemporal Landsat 8-OLI imagery are shown in the Fig. 3. Before applying the unmixing processing, a study to analyse the spectral behavior of mangrove species has been carried out. The goal of this analysis was to improve the knowledge on spectral discriminability among the three species of mangroves considered in our study, an information not yet frequent in the Cuban literature on mangroves.

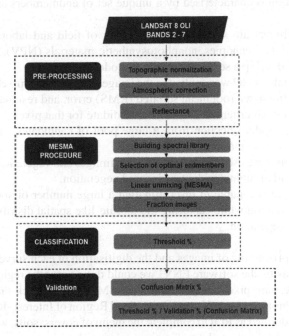

Fig. 3. Main steps of Landsat 8-OLI processing.

The Multiple Endmember Spectral Mixture Analysis (MESMA) method, although not previously applied in Cuba, is widely used. This modeling allows to transform original satellite images into new images with full physical meaning which, in our case, could facilitate the study of mangroves in the Southern coastal zone of the province of Sancti Spíritus by improving the extremely complicated and time consuming field work did in these regions.

The analysis of spectral mixture by MESMA was successfully applied to the phenological effects on spectral behavior of species in the Californian chaparral. Other Authors [36] evaluated the seasonal leaf-level spectral separability in the Panamanian dry forests and Somers & Asner [30] have shown the benefits obtained by integrating time series of Hyperion images in the data set for endmembers definition in a MESMA application. In mapping, invasive species located in the Hawaiian jungle, they have successfully observed a significant increase in invasive species identification when they have incorporated in MESMA some spectral information related to different stages of growth of such species, thanks to the multi-temporality of the data set.

The Methodology MESMA, implements the process of inversion to estimate the abundances making use of a set variable of endmembers. Using the following procedure to do the crossbred process, according to [37]:

i.   It is a technique enabling spectral analysis as a linear combinations of pure signatures, called endmembers, while allowing the types and number of endmembers to vary on a per pixel basis.

ii.   The vegetation is characterised by a unique set of endmembers as well as by the fractions.

iii.   The endmembers are selected from a library of field and laboratory measured spectra of leaves, canopies, nonphotosynthetic materials (NPV), water and soils and used to develop a series of candidate models.

iv.   Each candidate model was applied to the image, then, on a per pixel basis, assessed in terms of fractions, root mean squared (RMS) error, and residuals.

v.   If a model met all criteria, is listed as a candidate for that pixel.

vi.   To facilitate model selection from a large pool of candidates, an optimal set is selected to provide maximal areal coverage.

vii.   These models were used to generate fraction images and vegetation maps showing evergreen and drought deciduous senesced vegetation.

viii. The technique is capable of discriminating a large number of spectrally distinct types of vegetation while capturing the mosaic-like spatial distribution typical of a particular vegetation.

After the pre-processing of images and the digitisation of each surveyed plot during the field campaigns by the software ENVI we could define specific regions of the forest canopy. These are pure pixel composition of Red Mangrove, Black mangrove, White Mangrove, Non-Photosynthetic Vegetation, defined Region of Interest -ROI. In addition, other classes was defined as ROI to complete the menu of covers: soils, water, vegetation and water in lagoons are created.

To describe spectral behaviors of mangrove species the average response (at 95% of confidence) of pure pixels for each species and all Landsat selected bands (VIS, NIR and SWIR) were computed.

4.1   Analysis of Spectral Behavior of Mangrove Species

We obtained multitemporal plots (Fig. 4) showing the relationships between the phenology [34] and the specific spectral response the mangrove forest in the study area (Rhizophora mangrove, Avicennia germinans, Laguncularia racemosa, Conocarpus erectus). This has allowed shed light on the spectral phenology of each mangrove species.

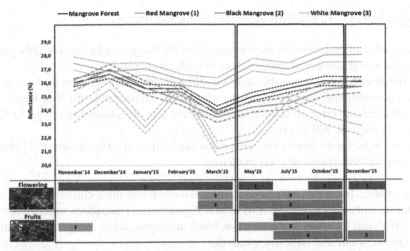

Fig. 4. Relationship between the spectral response in visible blue (reflectance (%)) and the phenology of the mangrove forest and its species (red mangrove (Rhizophora Mangle), black mangrove (Avicennia germinans), white (Laguncularia racemosa and Conocarpus erectus)), in the climatic period (November 2014 - December 2015). (Color figure online)

In the VIS spectral region there are no differences among the species. On the other hand, Red Mangroves and White Mangrove show significant differences from each others in the NIR and SWIR regions. It was also possible to link the spectral behavior of mangroves to the different climatic seasons and phenological stages. In the dry season (e.g. February) all species show higer reflectance in VIS region, while reflectance decrease during the rainy period (e.g. July). An opposite situation can be observed in the NIR region, mainly for Red Mangrove, whose reflectance become higher in the rainy period when flowering, fructification and new leaves production are particularly active.

4.2 MESMA Application

In our experiment we have computed MESMA to Landsat - 8 OLI multispectral images using a stand-alone open Software VIPER [38]. MESMA was applied to a Landsat image in February 2015 representing the dry season, and an image of July 2015 for the rainy season. Moreover a multitemporal image composition for the 2015 (February, March, May and July) was processed. According to the methodology, this allowed for generating a series of fraction images related to monotemporal images or multitemporal images. The fraction images were used firstly in a qualitative way, assembling several RGB compositions to visualise the spatial distribution of each fraction (class). Secondly, a segmentation (density slice) was applied to each fraction image (mono and multitemporal, classes number ranging from 4 to 8) for computing the Confusion Matrix accuracy at different level of spectral pureness (or mixing) of different mangrove species. This allowed to improve spectral separability among the species.

According to [39], MESMA algorithm is characerised by:

- The number of endmembers used to unmixing the image can be considerably greater than the actual number of endmembers of each single pixel.
- On the other hand, it is possible to use a different set of endmembers for each pixel.
- The computational complexity of the algorithm is remarkable for it is based on a iterative test and error procedure, using different sets of endmembers, to get to the as lower as possible RMSE error.
- The key issue for an quality outcome is the availability of adequate spectral libraries, to optimize the process of pixel unmixing.

The maps of each fraction have been computed considering three classification types: 4 (vegetation, soils, water, Non-Photosynthetic Vegetation), 5 (mangrove, vegetation, soils, water, NPV) and 8 classes (red mangrove, black mangrove, white mangrove, vegetation, soils, lagoon, water and NPV), respectively.

These monotemporal and multitemporal supervised classifications have been classified considering ground thrust (Classes-ROI) from 61 surveyed plots during survey campaigns in the southern coastal mangrove forest in the province. From them we could get to a set of endmembers computed in VIPER to define the higher and lower admissible thresholds of the fraction (2) and (3) the higher admissible mean square error (RMSE) to get the image of fraction [37].

$$P'_{i\lambda} = \sum_{k=1}^{N} f_{ki} * P_{k\lambda} + \varepsilon_{i\lambda} \ and \ \sum_{k=1}^{N} f_{ki} = 1 \tag{1}$$

$$RMS = \left(\sum_{k=1}^{\lambda} (\varepsilon_{i\lambda})^2 / N \right)^{1/2} \tag{2}$$

The fraction images obtained from monotemporal images of February and July 2015, for 4 and 8 classes and multitemporal images of the months (February, March, May, July) of 2015, for 4, 5 and 8 Classes was validated by confusion matrix in ENVI.

5   Results and Discussion

The main result from the application of MESMA concerns the good separation obtained for Red Mangrove with respect to other coverages. An accuracy of more than 80% for fraction of pixels of Red Mangrove with a good level of purity has resulted from the Confusion Matrix performed on the multitemporal image classified in 8 classes. Furthermore, interesting results were obtained for turbid water or water with suspended sediments. MESMA methodology seems to be able to put in evidence the distribution of sediments in the marine areas of deltas, this phenomena being related to rain seasons and water resource management model in all the hydrographic basin.

According to Menéndez et al., [34], the phenological patterns of the main Cuban mangrove arboreal species have the following characteristics:

- The four main arboreal species which form the woods of mangroves in Cuba: *Rhizophora Mangle, Avicennia germinans, Laguncularia racemosa* y *Conocarpus erectu*; they have abundant foliage during the whole year, corroborating their condition as evergreen
- The leaves falling occurs all year long and new leaves appear during the biggest rainfall (May–October), when as a general tendency the greater leaves falling occurs.
- The phase of flowering of *Rhizophora mangrove* occurs during the months of less rainfall though they keep flowering during the whole year.
- The species of *Avicennia germinans, Laguncularia racemosa* and *Conocarpus erectus* present defined periods of time during their flowering and fructification phases.
- The fenophases of the four species *Rhizophora mangle, Avicennia germinans, Laguncularia racemosa* and *Conocarpus erectus* present displacement of the phases within years with small differences between the years.
- *Rhizophora Mangle, Avicennia germinans, Laguncularia racemosa* and *Conocarpus erectus* show periods of maximum fructification coinciding to the period of the greater rainfall, evidencing a stationary of this main phenological phase for the natural regeneration according to the regenerative strategies of every species.

6 Conclusion

Mangroves are special environments. The species characterizing the mangroves show morphological and functional specialisations typical of pioneering species, to survive at the extreme conditions in aquatic and saline mixed environments and in muddy unstable grounds. By special devices of breathing and support, the metabolism is adapted to high concentrations of salt, viviparity and long germinative power [40, 41]. The survival of these important ecotonal habitats is of paramount importance, and a cornerstone is the possibility of monitoring their evolution in time. Our research allowed to get to a remarkable result in mangrove forest detection for developing countries. Using open source Landsat 8-OLI images we could classifying and mapping the mangrove forest in the southern coast of Cuba. Moreover, the application of MESMA has given an improved result with higher accuracy. In particular, the analysis of the spectral behavior of three species leaded to the important result to separate the Red Mangrove from others mangroves. This is very important, since Red Mangrove represents the most fragile component of mangrove forests, the first barrier against natural and human impacts. Future development of the research will challenge are in progress. In particular we aim at performing further survey campaigns to collect more ground truth samples to better validate the supervised classification process. Moreover will be important to improve the communication with the government and the water management bodies to impulse the creation of a permanent observatory of mangroves in Cuba.

References

1. E.C.: Directive 2000/60/EC: European parliament and of the European union (2000)
2. Gain, A.K., Rouillard, J.J., Benson, D.: can integrated water resources management increase adaptive capacity to climate change adaptation? a critical review. J. Water Resour. Prot. **5**, 11–20 (2013)

3. GWP.: Integrated Water Resources Management. TAC background paper No. 4, GWP, Stockholm, Sweden (2000)
4. Feller, I.C., Sitnik, M. (eds.).: Mangrove Ecology Workshop Manual. Smithsonian Institution, Washington, DC, USA (1996)
5. Menéndez, L,. Priego, A.: Los manglares de Cuba: Ecología. En El ecosistema de manglar en América Latina y la Cuenca del Caribe: su manejo y conservación (D. Suman, ed.), Rosenstiel School of Marine and Atmospheric Science & The Tinker Foundation, pp. 64–75 (1994)
6. Blasco, F., Gauquelin, T., Rasolofoharinoro, M., Denis, J., Aizpuru, M., Caldairou, V.: Recent advances in mangrove studies using remote sensing data. Mar. Freshwater Res. **49**, 287–296 (1998)
7. Kovacs, J.M., Wang, J., Blanco-Correa, M.: Mapping disturbances in a mangrove forest using multi-data Landsat TM imagery. Environ. Manag. **27**(5), 763–776 (2001)
8. Modica, G., Solano, F., Merlino, A., Di Fazio, S., Barreca, F., Laudari, L., Fichera, C.R.: Using Landsat 8 imagery in detecting cork oak (Quercus suber L.) woodlands: a case study in Calabria Italy. J. Agric. Eng. **47**(4), 205–215 (2016). https://doi.org/10.4081/jae.2016.571
9. Melaas, E.K., et al.: Multisite analysis of land surface phenology in North American temperate and boreal deciduous forests from Landsat. Remote Sens. Environ. **186**, 452–464 (2016)
10. Krause, G., Bock, M., Weiers, S., Braun, G.: mapping land-cover and mangrove structures with remote sensing techniques: a contribution to a synoptic gis in support of coastal management in North Brazil. Environ. Manag. **34**(3), 429–440 (2004)
11. Vaiphasa, C., Omsongwang, S., Vaiphasa, T., Skidmore, A.K.: tropical mangrove species discrimination using hyperspectral data: a laboratory study. Estuar. Coast. Shelf Sci. **65**, 371–379 (2006)
12. Vogelmann, J.E., Xian, G., Homer, C., Tolk, B.: monitoring gradual ecosystem change using landsat time series analyses: case studies in selected forest and rangeland ecosystems. Remote Sens. Environ. **122**, 92–105 (2012)
13. Kovacs, J.M., Zhang, C., Flores-Verdugo, F.J.: mapping the condition of mangroves of the Mexican pacific using c-band ENVISAT ASAR and landsat optical data. Cienc. Mar. **34**(4), 407–418 (2008)
14. Berlanga-Robles, Ruiz-Luna, A.: Análisis de las tendencias de cambio del bosque de mangle del sistema lagunar Teacapán-Agua brava, México. Una aproximación con el uso de imágenes de satélite Landsat. Publicaciones UCiencia. **23**(1), 29–46 (2007)
15. Adam, E., Mutanga, O., Rugege, D.: Multispectral and hyperspectral remote sensing for identification and mapping of wetland vegetation: a review. Wetlands Ecol. Manage. **18**, 281–296 (2010)
16. Kasawani, I., Norsaliza, U., Mohd, H.I.: analysis of spectral vegetation indices related to soil-line for mapping mangrove forest using satellite imagery. Appl. Remote Sens. J. **1**(1), 25–31 (2010)
17. Kuenzer, C., Bluemel, A., Gebhardt, S., Vo, Q.T., Dech, S.: remote sensing of mangrove ecosystems: a review. Remote Sens. **3**, 878–928 (2011)
18. Giri, C., Pengra, B., Zhu, Z., Singh, A., Tiszen, L.L.: monitoring mangrove forest dynamics of the sundarsban in bangladesh nd india using multi-temporal satellite data from 1973 to 2000. Estuar. Coast. Shelf Sci. **73**, 91–100 (2007)
19. Alatorre, L.C., Sanchez-Andres, R., Cirujano, S., Begueria, S., Sanchez-Carrillo, S.: identification of mangrove areas by remote sensing: the roc curve technique applied to northwestern Mexico Coastal zone using landsat imagery. Remote Sens. **3**, 1568–1583 (2011)
20. Chen, B., et al.: a mangrove forest map of china in 2015: analysis of time series landsat 7/8 and sentinel-1a imagery in google earth engine cloud computing platform. ISPRS J. Photogramm. Remote Sens. **131**, 104–120 (2017)

21. Somers, B., Verbesselt, J., Ampe, E.M., Sims, N., Verstraeten, W.W., Coppin, P.: spectral mixture analysis to monitor defoliation in mixed-aged Eucalyptus globulus Labill plantations in southern Australia using landsat 5-TM and EO-1 hyperion data. Int. J. Appl. Earth Obs. Geoinf. **12**(4), 270–277 (2010)

22. Praticò, S., Solano, F., Di Fazio, S., Modica, G.: machine learning classification of mediterranean forest habitats in google earth engine based on seasonal sentinel-2 time-series and input image composition optimisation. Remote Sens. **13**, 586 (2021). https://doi.org/10.3390/rs13040586

23. Modica, G., Merlino, A., Solano, F., Mercurio, R.: an index for the assessment of degraded Mediterranean forest ecosystems. For. Syst. **24**, 5 (2015). https://doi.org/10.5424/fs/2015243-07855

24. FAO.: The world's mangroves 1980–2005. FAO FORESTRY PAPER 153, Rome. ISBN 978–92–5–105856–5 (2007)

25. Tomlinson, P.B.: The botany of mangroves. Cambridge University Press, Cambridge, United Kingdom (1986)

26. Choudhury, M.A.M., et al.: urban tree species identification and carbon stock mapping for urban green planning and management. Forests **11**, 1226 (2020). https://doi.org/10.3390/f11111226

27. Giri, C., et al.: status and distribution of mangrove forests of the world using earth observation satellite data. Glob. Ecol. Biogeogr. **20**, 154–159 (2011)

28. Wang, L., Silván-Cárdenas, L., Sousa, W.P.: neural network classification of mangrove species from multi-seasonal Ikonos imagery. Photogram. Eng. Remote Sens. **2008**(74), 921–927 (2008)

29. Kanniah, K.D., Wai, N.S., Shin, A.L., Rasib, A.W.: per pixel and sub-pixel classifications of high-resolution satellite data for mangrove species mapping. Appl. GIS **3**, 1–22 (2007)

30. Somers, B., Asner, G.P.: multi-temporal hyperspectral mixture analysis and feature selection for invasive species mapping in rainforest. Remote Sens. Environ. **136**, 14–27 (2013)

31. Howland, W.G.: multispectral aerial photography for wetland vegetation mapping. Photogram. Eng. Remote Sens. **46**, 87–99 (1980)

32. Verheyeden, A., Dahdouh-Guebas, F., Thomaes, K., De Genst, W., Hettiarachch, S., Koedam, N.: High-resolution vegetation dat for mangrove research as obtained from aerial photography. Environ. Dev. Sustain. **4**, 113–133 (2002)

33. Menéndez, L., Guzmán, J.M., Capote, R.T., Rodríguez, L.F., González, A.V.: Situación Ambiental de los Manglares del Archipiélago Cubano. Casos de estudios: archipiélago Sabana Camagüey, franja sur de la Habana y costa norte de Ciudad Habana. En Memorias IV Convención Internacional sobre medio ambiente y desarrollo, 2 al 6 de junio de 2003, La Habana, pp. 435–451 (2003)

34. Menéndez, L., Guzmán, J.M.: Los manglares del archipiélago cubano: aspectos generales. In: L. Menéndez, J.M. Guzmán (eds.) Ecosistema de Manglar en el Archipiélago Cubano. UNESCO, Ciudad de la Habana, pp. 329 (2006)

35. Menéndez, J.M.G., Menéndez Carrera, L.: Protocolo para el monitoreo del ecosistema de manglar. Proyecto GEF/PNUD, Application de un enfoque regional al manejo de las àreas marino-costeras protegida en la Regiòn Archipiélagos del Sur de Cuba, La Habana (2013). ISBN: 978-959-287-042-0

36. Hesketh, M., Sanchez-Azofeifa, G.A.: the effect of seasonal spectral variation on species classification in the Panamanian Tropical Forest. Remote Sens. Environ. **118**, 73–82 (2012)

37. Roberts, D.A., Gardner, M., Church, R., Ustin, S., Scheer, G., Green, R.O.: mapping chaparral in the Santa Monica Mountains using multiple endmember spectral mixture models. Remote Sens. Environ. **65**, 267–279 (1998)

38. Roberts, D.A., Halligan, K., Dennison, P.: VIPER Tools User Manual Version 1.5 (2007)

39. Plaza, A.: Proposición, validación y prueba de una metodología para el análisis de datos hiperespectrales que integra información espacial y espectral. Tesis doctoral (2002)

40. Menéndez, L., et al.: *Informe de proyecto de investigación: Bases ecológicas para la restauración de manglares en áreas seleccionadas del Archipiélago cubano y su relación con los cambios globales.* Informe final del proyecto. Programa Nacional de Cambios Globales y Evolución del Medio Ambiente Cubano. IES. CITMA, pp 153 (2000)

41. Meza Diaz, B., Blackburn, G.A.: remote sensing of mangrove biophysical properties: evidence from a laboratory simulation of the possible effects of background variation on spectral vegetation indices. Int. J. Remote Sens. **24**, 53–73 (2003)

12th International Symposium on Software Quality (SQ 2021)

Examining the Bug Prediction Capabilities of Primitive Obsession Metrics

Edit Pengő[(⊠)] [iD]

University of Szeged, Dugonics square 13, Szeged 6720, Hungary
pengoe@inf.u-szeged.hu

Abstract. Bug prediction is an approach that helps make bug detection more automated during software development. Based on a bug dataset a prediction model is built to locate future bugs. Bug datasets contain information about previous defects in the code, process metrics, or source code metrics, etc. As code smells can indicate potential flaws in the source code, they can be used for bug prediction as well.

In our previous work, we introduced several source code metrics to detect and describe the occurrence of Primitive Obsession in Java. This paper is a further study on three of the Primitive Obsession metrics. We integrated them into an existing, source code metrics-based bug dataset, and studied the effectiveness of the prediction built upon it. We performed a 10 fold cross-validation on the whole dataset and a cross-project validation as well. We compared the new models with the results of the original dataset. While the cross-validation showed no significant change, in the case of the cross-project validation, we have found that the amount of improvement exceeded the amount of deterioration by 5%. Furthermore, the variance added to the dataset was confirmed by correlation and PCA calculations.

Keywords: Bug prediction · Code smells · Primitive obsession · Static analysis · Refactoring

1 Introduction

Finding and fixing bugs is a very important task during software development to ensure the quality of the product. Software defects are very costly. The later

This work was partially supported by grant 2018-1.2.1-NKP-2018-00004 Security Enhancing Technologies for the IoT" funded by the Hungarian National Research, Development and Innovation Office. It was also supported by the European Union, co-financed by the European Social Fund (EFOP-3.6.3-VEKOP-16-2017-00002). The research was supported by the Ministry of Innovation and Technology NRDI Office within the framework of the Artificial Intelligence National Laboratory Program (MILAB).

O. Gervasi et al. (Eds.): ICCSA 2021, LNCS 12955, pp. 185–200, 2021.
https://doi.org/10.1007/978-3-030-87007-2_14

they are discovered, the more expensive they are [3], therefore, there is considerable research interest in making the bug detection process more automated and efficient. Software fault prediction or, in other words, bug prediction is a possible approach to this effort. Considering this, it is no surprise, that there is a huge amount of literature on refining bug prediction [33,34,38]. In this paper, we also aim to find improvements with the help of our previously introduced Primitive Obsession metrics [25].

Primitve Obsession is a previously little-studied code smell [37]. As a code smell it can be a useful indicator for coding flaws [12], therefore, we introduced six metrics for its detection in our previous work [25]. The current paper examines the bug prediction ability of three of these metrics. We expanded an existing, source code metrics-based bug dataset [6] and studied the impact of the alteration. We performed a 10 fold cross-validation on the whole dataset and a cross-project validation as well. We compared the new models with the results of the original dataset and analyzed the results. In addition, a Principal Component Analysis (PCA) [28] was performed to examine the dimensionality of the new metrics.

The paper is organised as follows. Section 2 provides the background and the related work for our paper. Section 3 is an overview of the Primitive Obsession metrics on which we based our research. The three research questions and their answers are presented in Sect. 4. Section 5 describes the threats to validity. We conclude our work in Sect. 6.

2   Background

The following subsections introduce the major domains of our research, such as bug prediction and Primitive Obsession.

2.1   Bug Prediction and Bug Datasets

Bug prediction is a method that supports the quality assurance during software development. It is a cost-effective approach compared to software testing and reviews. Menzies et al. report in their study [21] that the probability of detecting a bug by fault prediction may be higher than detecting it by the review process currently used in industrial environments.

Bug prediction can be used to estimate the number of remaining bugs in the codebase or to identify the bug-prone parts of the code. Historic data can help to build models to predict the severity of bug reports [30] or to estimate the reliability of a system [2,29]. Another possible use is to mine software defect associations [26]. What we call a defect association for example is if a type A and type B defect occur in the code, then type C is likely to occur as well. Our research examines the type of bug prediction that helps identify potentially buggy code parts.

Bug prediction can be based on statistical, expert-driven, or machine learning models [4]. This paper focuses on machine learning-based bug prediction.

We used a unified bug dataset, which was introduced by Ferenc et al. [6]. Bug datasets contain historical data, such as previous defects, process metrics, or source code metrics [14], on which the prediction data is built. The dataset of Ferenc contains data from five publicly available bug datasets in a unified format: the PROMISE dataset [17], the Eclipse Bug Dataset [39], the Bug Prediction Dataset [5], the Bugcatchers Bug Dataset [15], and the GitHub Bug Dataset [32]. They contain class and/or file level source code metrics and information about the previous defects. We only utilized the PROMISE, the GitHub, and the Bug Prediction datasets, as only these contain class-level metrics. There are 66 projects in the three datasets, the smallest only contains 6 classes while the largest contains 5908. To reduce noise, we decided to exclude those systems that contain less than 100 classes. Thus, a total of 58 systems remained containing a total of 45519 classes.

2.2 Code Smells

Code smells that were introduced in Fowler's 1999 book [7], demonstrate the violation of fundamental design principles, therefore, their presence can indicate underlying flaws in the source code. There are numerous studies about the impact of code smells on code quality. Moonen and Yamashita demonstrated in an empirical study [22] that some of the code smell definitions are useful to evaluate the maintainability of a project. In another study [35] they investigated how the interactions of multiple smells affect maintainability. With the help of co-located smells they identified several artefacts that need to be prioritized during refactoring. Khomh et al. [19] found a relation between code smells and class change-proneness, which can support quality assurance and focus testing activities. In contrast to these studies, Sjøberg et al. investigated the connection between code smells and maintenance effort [31], and found that the work of changing code with smells was not significantly higher than the work of changing code without smells. The 12 examined smells have limited impact on maintenance effort in contrast to code size and the number of changes.

The results of these studies suggest that although code smells are not silver bullets for defect prediction, they can still provide valuable insights into some important maintainability factors, especially when more of them are combined. Palomba et al. [24] built a bug prediction model using code smell information as well. They combined the severity of the code smells involved (God Class, Data Class, Brain Method, Shotgun Surgery, Dispersed Coupling, Message Chains) with existing bug prediction models. They found that the accuracy of the models increases by adding the code smell information as a predictor.

2.3 PCA and Correlation

Principal Component Analysis (PCA) is a widely used data reduction technique [28]. Since this is one of the best-known dimension reduction methods, we selected it to examine the dimensionality of PO metrics. PCA reduces the dimensions of a large data set – in which the variables are interrelated – while retaining the variance of the data as much as possible. An orthogonal transformation is used to calculate the so-called principal components, which are a set of linearly uncorrelated variables calculated from the possibly correlated variables of the data. The first principal component holds the greatest possible variance, each subsequent component will have the greatest variance remaining. PCA can be used for dimensionality reduction in large datasets, and it can uncover patterns in the data as well [1].

In this research, we used PCA to examine the variance represented by the new metrics. We also calculated the correlation of the metrics to study the magnitude and direction of their linear relationships [11].

2.4 Defining Primitive Obsession

The following description of Primitive Obsession is taken from our previous work [25] for clarity. In most programming languages, there are two categories of data types: primitive and complex. Primitive types are the most basic data types that a language provides, e.g. *boolean, integer, char*, etc. Complex types like *classes* and *structs* are made up of other existing data types e.g. primitive types and complex types. The advantage of complex types is that semantic knowledge can be connected to the data with them. For example, three integers alone do not mean anything, but if we include them in a class called 3DPoint, it is immediately clear what they represent. This is a more readable and maintainable solution that also supports encapsulation, which is one of the main principles of object-oriented programming.

Primitive Obsession can be categorized as a bloater-type code smell [20]. It means that the code relies too much on the use of primitive data types. Its occurrence is a symptom of chaotic, overgrown code parts. The programmer does not create small classes e.g. value objects to perform small tasks, therefore, the data is scattered among primitive types.

Figure 1 shows several occurrences of Primitive Obsession. There are two class constants at Lines 3 and 4. ENGINEER and SALESMAN can be considered as type codes. Type codes are a set of integer or string variables that usually have an understandable name, and they are employed to simulate types. In this case, they symbolize the different types of employees. Although type codes are preferred in projects, they are considered Primitive Obsession. Not only do they violate the object oriented paradigm, but they can cause *hidden dependencies* [36] as well. A refactoring option is if developers employ *State* or *Strategy* pattern [10].

The next Primitive Obsession example is shown in Line 6. Consider the parameter list of the work function. The first three of its parameters are integers, whilst the fourth is a string. Parameter lists like this can be considered a kind of Primitive Obsession, especially if they appear repeatedly in the code. It is worth noting here that, strictly speaking, a string does not qualify as a primitive type, but logically it is practical to include them in the definition. The parameter list of the work function can be refactored by introducing a parameter object. Lines 8 and 9 also show the symptoms of Primitive Obsession. Such value checks

```
1  class Employee
2  {
3    static const int ENGINEER = 1;
4    static const int SALESMAN = 2;
5
6    public void work(int from, int to, int numberOfBreaks,
          String task)
7    {
8      if(task == null
9          || task.length() == 0) {
10     /* ... */
11     }
12   }
13 }
```

Fig. 1. Sample code containing three primitive obsessions

should usually be encapsulated. More Primitive Obsession examples are available in Steven A. Lowe's GitHub project[1]. It shows step-by-step how to refactor a project heavily infected by Primitive Obsession.

2.5 Study of Primitive Obsession

Primitive Obsession is a code smell that has received little research attention in previous years. Only a few studies paid attention to this type of smell. Zhang et al. performed a systematic literature review about code smells [37]. They examined 309 articles between 2000 and 2009, 39 of which were analyzed in detail. They studied which were the most frequently researched code smells. The results showed that Primitive Obsession was among the unpopular smells. They only found 5 corresponding papers, although these papers examined all 22 of Fowler's bad smells. The more recent systematic literature review [13] of Gupta et al. came to a similar conclusion. They investigated 60 research papers between 1999 and 2016, and found that four of Fowler's bad smells – including Primitive Obsession – had no detection method in any of the papers.

The example in the previous section highlighted that it is hard to define Primitive Obsession with one exact formula. It has various aspects. The challenging definition can be the reason for the lack of articles and detection methods. We only found one thesis [27] that proposed an automated tool, JSmell, for detecting Primitive Obsession based on the number of primitive data types declared in a class. Sadly, no comparison or in-depth study was possible as we were unable to get hold of JSmell.

Driven by the lack of literature about Primitive Obsession we decided to study it. We introduced several metrics in our previous work [25] to describe the aspects of Primitive Obsession. These metrics are described in Sect. 3.

---

[1] https://github.com/stevenalowe/kata-2-tinytypes.

3   Primitive Obsession Metrics

This section describes the Primitive Obsession metrics on which we based the research of this paper. There were 6 metrics introduced in our previous papers[9, 25]. In this paper, we used only three of them: the MPC, the SFP, and the $SFP - SCU$ metrics. Their definitions are taken from the previous article[25], so that this article can be understood on its own. These metrics were originally defined as class-level metrics. Collectively, we will refer to these metrics as PO metrics.

3.1   Method Parameter Clones

First, we present the Method Parameter Clones (MPC) metric which is a class-level metric. If a class is infected by Primitive Obsession, several method parameters will appear repetitively in the parameter lists of multiple methods. These parameters have the same type and the same name because logically they correspond to the same data. These are the parameters that could be extracted to a value object instead of being used separately. The MPC metric highlights this aspect. The following steps are performed for each class in a project:

1. Initially, the MPC value for a class is set to zero.
2. For each method parameter in the class, create a $(type, name)$ pair.
3. Select only those pairs where the type is in the $PrimitiveTypes$ set.
4. Increment MPC value by one for every $(type, name)$ pair that appears at least three times.

The reason that only three or more repetitions are counted is *The Rule of Three* [7]. This means that two instances of similar code do not require refactoring, but when similar code is used three times, it needs to be corrected.

3.2   Static Final Primitives

Another class-level metric is the Static Final Primitives (SFP) metric. It captures one more essential aspect of the Primitive Obsession bad smell. The SFP metric quantifies the usage of type codes. To check whether a variable can be a candidate for type code the Static Final Primitive function is used which is described in Formula 1.

$$
\begin{aligned}
SFP(V) \; := \; & isClassLevel(V) \\
& \wedge \, isStatic(V) \\
& \wedge \, isFinal(V) \\
& \wedge \, isUpperCase(V) \\
& \wedge \, typeOf(V) \in PrimitiveTypes
\end{aligned}
\tag{1}
$$

The SFP function marks a variable (V) if it has all the following properties, thus it might serve as a type code:

- V is a class-level variable,
- V is static (e.g. has a `static` modifier in Java)
- V can be assigned only once (e.g. has a `final` modifier in Java),
- the name of V contains only upper case characters, numbers, and underscores,
- and the type of V is included in the previously defined *PrimitiveTypes* set (i.e. primitive).

Other than that, SFP returns false for the investigated variable. With this function, it is possible to filter out static final primitive variable usages in methods.

Formula 2 defines the Static Final Variable Usage (SFPU) function. There are three parameters: M_c and V denote the function and variable under investigation, respectively, while F is a filter function. In the formula, U_V denotes one usage of variable V. The $U_V \in M_c$ relation means that the U_V variable usage (access or modification) is performed in the M_c method. By applying the F filter function it is possible to select a subset of the U_V variable usages. The $SFPU$ function gathers every access and modification statement for variable V in the M_c method, for which both the SFP function and the F filter function return true.

$$
SFPU(M_c, V, F) := \{U_V \mid \\
U_V \in M_c \wedge SFP(V) \wedge F(U_V)\} \tag{2}
$$

In the following paragraph, we present a specific application of the $SFPU$ function. Type code usages will most possibly appear in branching structures, particularly in `switch-case` statements. To capture this aspect, let us supply an F filter function to count the number of static final primitive variables that are used as case labels in `switch` statements. The F filter function will determine for a given U_V variable usage if it is a case label. By using the $SFPU$ and this F filter function we constructed a class-level metric named Static Final Primitive - Switch Case Usage (SFP-SCU). The calculation is done for each class to see how many times its SFP variables appear as case labels globally in the project.

4   Evaluation

We formulated three research questions to examine the effect on bug prediction and the dimensionality of the PO metrics. In this section, we enumerate and answer these questions.

4.1   RQ1: How Does Adding the PO Metrics Affect the Prediction Capability of the Original Dataset?

Our first attempt was to merge the PO metrics into the original dataset. We calculated the previously introduced class-level PO metrics for the 58 Java systems. The measurements were performed by extending the OpenStaticAnalyser (OSA) [23], which is an open source static analyser tool developed by the University of Szeged. Only those classes were kept in the dataset that were present

in the original dataset as well, i.e. the classes that have bug information. We
performed a 10-fold cross-validation training with Weka [8] using the J48 algorithm on the original and on the extended dataset. Although many classifiers
were applied for bug prediction [16,18], Ferenc [6] used the J48 algorithm for
the evaluation of the original dataset, therefore, we decided to utilize the same
algorithm with its default parameters as well.

The results of the two datasets are compared in Table 1. The first column
shows the values of the original dataset, while the second column shows the values
of the extended dataset. In the rows, we see the most important attributes that
characterize the performance of the J48 classifier: the precision[2], the recall[3], the
F-measure[4], and the AUC[5]. It can be seen that the numbers show stagnation or
a slight decrease. These changes are not significant. It causes changes of similar
magnitude if the random seed is changed in the 10 fold cross-validation.

Table 1. The comparison of the results of the original and extended data set for J48
classifier

	Original	Extended
Precision for the not bugged class	0.876	0.876
Precision for the bugged class	0.537	0.537
Recall for the not bugged class	0.919	0.919
Recall for the bugged class	0.421	0.419
F-measure of the not bugged class	0.897	0.897
F-measure of the bugged class	0.472	0.470

We concluded that adding the PO metrics to the original dataset does not
improve the overall prediction ability. Seeing this result, we decided to examine
whether there is an improvement in cross-project validation. We analyse this in
the next RQ.

4.2   RQ2: Does Including PO Metrics Increase the Cross-Project Bug Prediction Capability of the Metric Set?

With this RQ, we wanted to examine if there is a project on which a better
model could be built using PO metrics. A project-wise evaluation was performed

---

[2] The precision can be calculated as the number of true positive elements divided by
the sum of the true and false positive elements. It describes what portion of the
identifications was actually correct.

[3] It describes what portion of the actual relevant elements was identified correctly.

[4] F-measure is the harmonic mean of precision and recall.

[5] The ROC curve displays the performance of a classification model at all classification
threshold. The Area under the ROC curve (AUC) means the area under this curve.
It is an aggregated measure of the performance across every classification thresholds.

meaning that we trained a model on each project and evaluated it on every other project. Out of the projects that were included in the database more than once, we used the ones with the highest version number. We found that the results for the different versions of the same systems are quite similar, therefore, they would have too much weight in the cross-project validation. A total of 29 systems were used for the cross-project validation.

The F-measure difference between the evaluations performed on the original and the expanded dataset is shown in Table 2. Here, we used the Weighted Average F-measure[6] to compactly present the change of the F-measure values for both classes. The examination was performed with the J48 algorithm as well. The first column on the left shows which system the teaching was done on and the column labels indicate which system the trained model was evaluated on. The second column contains the ID we gave to the system. These IDs are used in the column headers. The third column, called Class, shows how many classes are in the system, while the fourth column indicates the percentage of bugs. A colourmap is applied to these columns: in the third column, large class numbers are highlighted in orange, while in the fourth column orange colour represents a low bug ratio and blue colour represents a high bug ratio. We sorted the systems in such a way that the bug rate increases from top to bottom and from left to right. The green-coloured cells indicate a significant improvement, while values written in green denote slight improvements (less than 0.05). Due to the subsequent rounding, the value of 0.05 may appear in the table with both notations. For cells with a red background and values written in red, the same rule applies but in the negative direction. They indicate a slight or a significant decrease (larger than 0.05 in absolute value) in the F-measures of the expanded dataset.

It can be seen that if there were a disproportionate number of non-bugged classes (MCT, Neo4J) or bugged classes (Log4j 1.2, Xalan 2.7) in a system, then the models will be unusable on other systems. This is the explanation for the empty cells. The models are too fitted to one of the classes, therefore, no items are classified to the other class and the F-measure cannot be calculated. Where there is a 0.00 in the cell, the change in the F-measure is so insignificant that it does not appear in the rounded value. Significant F-measure reductions can be seen in the right half of the table. This can be explained by the fact that the models were built on systems with a low bug count, while in the last few columns the bug count of the systems is high, therefore, the models cannot function well.

Most of the significant improvements were achieved with the Xerces 2.0 model. It has a lower bug ratio than the Xalan 2.7 system, but still has plenty of examples to learn and has 1.8 times more classes for the J48 algorithm. The model of the mcMMO project has also been significantly improved, at least for

---

[6] Weka calculates the Weighted Avg. F-Measure with the following formula for an n and y class: $Weighted\ Avg.\ F - measure = \frac{F-measure(n)\cdot NumOfInstances(x)+F-measure(y)\cdot NumOfInstances(y)}{NumOfInstances(n)+NumOfInstances(y)}$, where $NumOf$ $Instances(n), NumOfInstances(y)$ correspond to the number of instances in the given class.

projects with similarly low bug ratios. Out of the 841 cells containing F-measure changes, 350 cells hold zero value and there are 126 blank ones (including the diagonal elements). The F-measure is reduced in 170 cases and improved in 195 cases. There are 45 significant F-measure increases in contrast to the 24 significant F-measure decreases.

Overall, the addition of PO metrics brings more improvement than deterioration in the case of cross-project validation, but it is important to choose the right system to build the model on. Further research is needed for the Xerces 2.0 and the mcMMO systems.

4.3   RQ3: Do the Three PO Metrics Add Valuable Information to the Dataset?

We calculated the correlation matrix[7] of the metrics and used Principal Component Analysis (PCA) to show the dimensionality of the PO metrics.

Table 3 only shows those parts of the correlation matrix which are relevant for the PO metrics. For better readability, the table is divided into two parts. We used a colourmap to help better understand the correlations between metrics. The greater the positive correlation between two metrics the greener the cell is. Values close to 1 are labeled with pure green colour. A negative correlation would be marked in red, but there are no values close to −1 in the tables. If the value is zero or close to zero (meaning that the correlation is insignificant) the cells have a white background. It can be seen in the tables that there is no significant correlation, neither within the PO metrics, nor between the PO metrics and the other metrics.

In the following paragraphs, the results of the PCA will be discussed. The bug information was omitted for the calculations, but the other attributes were retained. Figure 2 depicts the cumulative variability for the principal components. It can be seen that the curve is gradual, i.e., a high number of principal components are required to maintain much of the variance. To cover 99% of the variance in the dataset, 33 principal components are required, which is more than half of the original attributes. Even 95% requires 20 factors.

To further investigate the significance of PO metrics we computed the so-called factor loadings. A loading represents how much each original attribute contributes to the corresponding principal component. Table 4 shows the loadings for the first 20 principal components. Cells with an absolute value of 0.7 or greater were coloured with dark green. The absolute value of the bright green fields is between 0.5 and 0.7. Since there were very few outstanding values, only the rows where they occurred are shown in the table. To illustrate how small the loading values in the table are, we took the absolute value of the table and calculated the average and the median values. The average is 0,086, while the median is 0,06. It is clear that the 20 factors are made up of many metrics, and only a few of them have a prominent role in the composition of a factor. The PO

---

[7] Correlation shows the degree to which a pair of variables are linearly related. We used Pearson correlation for our experiment.

Table 2. Change in weighted average F-measure values for the cross project validation

Name	ID	Class	Bug	1	2	3	4	5	6	7	8	9	10	11	12	13	14	15	16	17	18	19	20	21	22	23	24	25	26	27	28	29
mct	1	1887	0.5			0.00	0.00	0.00				0.00	0.00	0.00	0.00		0.00	0.00	0.00	0.00	0.00	0.00	0.00	0.00	0.00			0.00	0.00		0.00	0.00
neo4j	2	5899	1.0																													
jedit4.3	3	439	2.5	0.00	0.00			0.00		0.00	0.00	0.00	0.00		0.00	0.00	0.00	0.00	0.00	0.00	0.00		0.00									
ceylon	4	1619	4.2	0.00	0.00	0.00		0.00	0.00	0.00	0.00	0.00	0.00	0.00	0.00	0.00	0.00	0.00	0.00	0.00	0.00	0.00	0.00	0.00	0.00	0.00	0.00	0.00	0.00	0.00	0.00	0.00
antlr	5	479	4.4	-0.01	0.00	0.01	0.00		0.00	-0.01	0.00	0.00	0.01		0.00	0.00	0.00	0.00	0.00	0.00	-0.01	-0.01	0.00		-0.07				-0.05	0.07	-0.04	-0.11
junit	6	731	4.8	0.01	0.00	-0.03	0.00	-0.01		0.00	0.00	0.00	0.00	0.00	0.00		0.01	0.00	-0.01	-0.02	0.09	0.00	0.00	0.05		-0.05	-0.06		-0.09	-0.09	-0.04	-0.24
titan	7	1466	6.5	0.00	0.00	0.00	0.00	0.00	0.00		0.00	0.00	0.00	0.00	0.00		0.00	0.00	0.00	0.00	0.00	0.00	0.00	0.00	0.00	0.00	0.00	0.00	0.00	0.00	0.00	0.00
hazelcast	8	3412	11.0	0.00	0.01	0.00	-0.02	0.01	-0.01	0.00		0.00	-0.02	0.00		0.01	-0.01	0.00		-0.03	-0.03	0.00	-0.02	-0.02		-0.01	0.01	-0.02		-0.04	0.00	0.18
elasticsearch	9	5908	11.5	0.00	0.00	-0.02	0.01	0.00	0.00	0.00				0.01	0.00	0.00	-0.01	-0.02	0.00		-0.01		-0.01		-0.03	-0.01	-0.02	
mapdb	10	331	12.1	0.00	0.01	0.00	0.00	0.01	0.00	0.00	0.01	0.01			0.00		0.01	0.01	0.00	-0.01		0.01	0.00	-0.01	-0.02	-0.01	-0.02	-0.11	-0.07	0.01	0.01
ivy2.0	11	294	12.6	0.00	0.00	0.00	-0.04	0.00	0.00		0.00	0.00	0.00		0.00	0.00		0.00		0.00	0.01	0.01	-0.01	0.01			0.01	0.04	0.00
oryx	12	533	13.9	0.00	0.00	0.00	0.00	0.00	0.00	0.00	0.00			0.00	0.00	0.00	0.00	0.00	0.00	0.00	0.00	0.00	0.00	0.00	0.00	0.00	0.00	0.00	0.00	0.00
pdeui	13	1491	14.0	-0.01	0.00	-0.01	0.00	-0.01	0.00	0.00	-0.01	-0.01	0.00	-0.01		-0.01	0.00		-0.02	0.00	0.00	0.00		0.00	0.00	0.00	0.01			-0.01	
mylly	14	1405	14.9	0.00	-0.01	0.00	-0.01	-0.01	-0.01	0.00	0.00	-0.01	-0.02	-0.03	0.00	-0.01		-0.01	0.00	0.00	-0.01	-0.01	-0.01	-0.04	0.00	0.00	0.01	-0.02	0.00	-0.05	0.01	-0.02
orientdb	15	1847	15.2	0.00	0.00	0.00	0.00	0.00	0.00	0.00	0.00	0.00	0.01	0.00	0.00	0.00		0.00	-0.01	-0.01	0.00	0.00	-0.03		-0.02	0.00	-0.02	0.00		0.01	0.00	-0.03
broadleaf	16	1593	18.3	0.00	0.00	0.00	0.00	0.00	0.00		0.00	-0.02	-0.01	-0.01	0.01	0.00	-0.01		-0.01		0.00	0.00	0.00	-0.04	-0.05		-0.02	-0.07
mcMMO	17	301	18.9			0.06	0.05		0.01			0.05	0.05			0.07				0.06			0.09		-0.04	0.00	-0.07		-0.13	-0.11	-0.18
Eclipse JDT	18	997	20.7	-0.01	0.01	-0.01	0.01				0.00	0.00	0.00						0.00					-0.01	0.01	-0.01	-0.01				
camell.6	19	795	21.4	0.00	0.00	-0.03	0.00		-0.01	0.01	0.00	0.01		-0.02	0.00	0.01	0.00		-0.03	-0.03	0.00		0.00	-0.04		0.00	0.00		0.08		0.04	0.15
netty	20	1143	23.7	0.00	0.00	-0.01	0.00	0.00		-0.01		0.00	0.00	-0.02	0.00	-0.01		0.00	0.00	0.00	-0.01			-0.06	0.00	-0.01	-0.01	-0.02	-0.01	-0.02	0.01
antl.7	21	681	24.2	0.01	0.00	0.01	0.01	0.00	0.00	0.00		0.01	0.01	-0.02	-0.01	-0.01	0.00		0.00	-0.02	-0.01	0.00	0.00		-0.02	-0.04	-0.02	-0.02	-0.02	0.00	0.00
velocity1.6	22	188	35.1	0.00	0.00		0.00	0.00	0.00	0.00	0.00	0.00	0.00	0.00	-0.03	0.00		0.01	0.00	-0.04	-0.03		0.01		0.01			0.00			0.08
synapse1.2	23	228	36.8	-0.01	-0.01	-0.03	-0.02	-0.01	0.00	-0.02	-0.01	0.00	-0.05	-0.01	-0.01	0.00	-0.01	-0.02	0.00	0.00	-0.05	-0.01	-0.03	-0.01	-0.01		-0.05		-0.07	0.00	-0.02
equinox	24	319	39.5	0.00	0.00	0.00	0.00	0.00	0.00	0.00	0.00	0.00	0.00	0.00	0.00	0.00	0.00	0.00	0.00	0.00	0.00	0.00	0.00	0.00		0.00	0.00	0.00	0.00	0.00	0.00
lucene2.4	25	320	60.3		0.00			-0.01		0.00	0.00	-0.02		-0.03	0.00	-0.04	0.00	-0.01		0.00		-0.02		0.00	0.00		0.07			0.00	
poi3.0	26	414	66.7	0.01	0.01	0.00	0.00			0.00	0.00			0.00	0.00	0.01	0.01			-0.01	0.01	0.00	0.00	0.00	0.00	0.00			0.01	0.00	0.00
xerces2.0	27	342	88.6	0.25	0.26	0.21	0.34	0.29	0.26	0.39	0.22	0.16	0.34	0.18	0.40	0.24	0.28	0.16	0.12	0.28	0.12	0.09	0.17	0.13	0.14	0.07	0.09		-0.16		-0.10	-0.01
log4j1.2	28	191	91.6																													
xalan2.7	29	848	98.7		0.00				0.00	0.00	0.00													0.00				0.00		0.00	

Table 3. Correlation between the metrics containing only the columns that are relevant for the PO metrics

	MPC	SFP-SCU	SFP		MPC	SFP-SCU	SFP
MPC	1.00	0.09	0.29	NLM	0.48	0.10	0.35
SFP-SCU	0.09	1.00	0.23	TNPM	0.18	0.01	0.16
SFP	0.29	0.23	1.00	NG	0.14	0.01	0.13
CLOC	0.40	0.17	0.45	NLG	0.32	0.05	0.23
NOD	0.02	0.03	0.01	TNLA	0.11	0.11	0.35
TNPA	0.04	0.04	0.17	NOA	0.02	-0.01	0.02
NLPM	0.43	0.04	0.27	TNM	0.18	0.06	0.19
TNLPA	0.02	0.05	0.25	TCD	0.07	0.03	0.07
NLPA	0.01	0.05	0.24	AD	0.10	0.04	0.11
TNOS	0.41	0.14	0.44	PUA	0.23	0.00	0.14
TLLOC	0.47	0.15	0.51	LDC	0.22	0.04	0.26
LLOC	0.48	0.15	0.52	NL	0.23	0.09	0.27
CLC	0.01	0.00	0.03	CBO	0.25	0.07	0.31
WMC	0.44	0.14	0.42	NS	0.09	0.01	0.07
CCL	0.17	0.06	0.24	NOP	0.03	-0.01	0.02
CC	0.02	0.00	0.04	CLLC	0.02	0.00	0.04
TNA	0.08	0.07	0.21	LOC	0.49	0.17	0.55
NOC	0.02	0.01	0.00	DIT	-0.01	-0.01	0.01
PDA	0.38	0.05	0.24	NPM	0.19	0.01	0.15
TLOC	0.48	0.17	0.55	TNLM	0.45	0.11	0.35
CCO	0.13	0.07	0.19	NOI	0.33	0.07	0.35
TNS	0.10	0.02	0.10	LCOM5	0.18	0.01	0.07
NA	0.07	0.07	0.20	TNLPM	0.41	0.04	0.28
NLA	0.10	0.11	0.34	NM	0.21	0.05	0.19
DLOC	0.40	0.15	0.31	CD	0.07	0.03	0.07
NPA	0.03	0.04	0.16	NOS	0.42	0.14	0.44
NII	0.23	0.10	0.11	TNLG	0.30	0.06	0.23
NLS	0.18	0.03	0.11	CBOI	0.17	0.06	0.09
LLDC	0.22	0.04	0.27	RFC	0.45	0.10	0.40
TNLS	0.18	0.03	0.12	TNG	0.13	0.03	0.14
CI	0.15	0.05	0.21	NLE	0.24	0.08	0.26
TCLOC	0.40	0.17	0.45	bugs	0.12	0.04	0.18

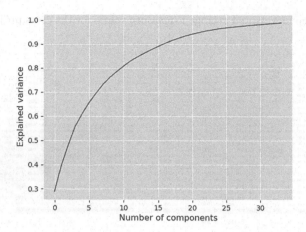

Fig. 2. Variability of the principal components

metrics contribute significantly to components 13, 18, 19. That is, using PCA analysis, we concluded that PO metrics contributed notably to the variance of the dataset.

Table 4. Factor loadings of the first 20 factors showing only the significant values

	0	1	2	3	4	5	6	7	8	9	10	11	12	13	14	15	16	17	18	19
MPC	0.12	0.04	-0.04	-0.07	0.03	-0.02	-0.07	-0.06	0	0.16	0.04	0.12	0.03	0	-0.09	-0.09	0.53	-0.13	0.73	-0.11
SFP-SCU	0.03	0.03	0.03	-0.03	-0.02	-0.01	-0.02	-0.03	0.08	0.01	0.12	0.29	0.06	0.82	0.1	-0.18	-0.21	0.11	0.02	-0.31
SFP	0.12	0.07	0.08	-0.03	0	-0.01	0	-0.11	0.14	0.04	0.08	0.16	0.09	0.24	0.2	0.06	0.14	-0.26	-0.09	0.79
NII	0.08	-0.01	-0.03	-0.14	0.07	0	-0.21	0.33	0.08	0	0.03	0.05	-0.01	0.13	-0.55	0.05	-0.03	0.02	-0.03	0.15
TNLG	0.14	-0.09	-0.08	-0.11	0.14	0.09	0.07	0.01	-0.07	-0.02	0.07	-0.03	0.51	-0.09	0.06	-0.06	-0.17	0.03	0.08	0

5   Threats to Validity

The results are based on only one learning algorithm. Further studies with other classifiers are needed for the full picture. It is possible that for different learning algorithms, such as Random Forest or KNN, the extended dataset would yield different results.

The bug prediction database we used is widely known and accepted, however, it is relatively old and does not have a system newer than Java 8. Although we discarded projects that did not have a sufficient number of classes, there were still some systems in which the bug ratio was too low or too high to build a usable model. For real applications, a bug rate above 90% is unlikely. Our results also confirmed the idea that these systems are not effective for bug prediction. Additional databases should be tested for comparison.

The calculation of the PO metrics is currently only implemented for one programming language, Java. In order to fully evaluate their usefulness, it is necessary to adapt them to other languages as well, e.g. C ++, JavaScript. However, in addition to the implementation tasks, building a bug database for these languages would also be a challenge.

6 Conclusion and Future Work

In this paper, three Primitive Obsession metrics were investigated: the Method Parameter Clones (MPC), the Static Final Primitives (SFP), and the Static Final Primitive - Switch Case Usage $(SFP - SCU)$ metric. We examined the usefulness of these new metrics by integrating them into an existing bug prediction dataset and checking how they change the bug prediction ability of the dataset. RQ1 showed that adding them to the entire dataset did not result in an improvement, however, in the case of cross-project bug prediction they significantly contributed to the improvement of multiple prediction models. Even though they also caused a decrease in the predictive ability of some models, the number of improvements is larger than the number of declines by an extent of 25. That is, the PO metrics bring improvement in 28,5% of the cases, while the amount of deterioration is 23%. For the Xerces 2.0 system, the improvement was remarkably high on systems that have a low bug count. Adding PO metrics brings improvement in 90% of cases and a decrease in only 7% of cases.

With RQ3 we found that the PO metrics indeed contribute to the variance of the dataset. They did not correlate with the previous source code metrics. It can be seen that PO metrics are a new, useful approach for describing and measuring the source code.

In the future, we would like to expand the study with other learning algorithms and datasets. We want to take a closer look at the case of different versions of the same system. We want to study what systems can be used well for model building to stably improve bug prediction capability using PO metrics.

References

1. Becker, B., Mooney, C.: Categorizing compiler error messages with principal component analysis. In: Proceedings of the 12th China-Europe International Symposium on Software Engineering Education (CEISEE 2016), pp. 1–8 (2016). https://researchrepository.ucd.ie/handle/10197/7889
2. Behera, R.K., Rath, S.K., Misra, S., Leon, M., Adewumi, A.: Machine learning approach for reliability assessment of open source software. In: Misra, S., et al. (eds.) ICCSA 2019. LNCS, vol. 11622, pp. 472–482. Springer, Cham (2019). https://doi.org/10.1007/978-3-030-24305-0_35
3. Boehm, B., Basili, V.R.: Software defect reduction top 10 list. Computer **34**(1), 135–137 (2001). https://doi.org/10.1109/2.962984
4. Catal, C., Diri, B.: A systematic review of software fault prediction studies. Expert Syst. Appl. **36**(4), 7346–7354 (2009). https://doi.org/10.1016/j.eswa.2008.10.027. http://www.sciencedirect.com/science/article/pii/S0957417408007215
5. D'Ambros, M., Lanza, M., Robbes, R.: An extensive comparison of bug prediction approaches. In: 2010 7th IEEE Working Conference on Mining Software Repositories (MSR 2010), pp. 31–41 (2010). https://doi.org/10.1109/MSR.2010.5463279

6. Ferenc, R., Tóth, Z., Ladányi, G., Siket, I., Gyimóthy, T.: A public unified bug dataset for java and its assessment regarding metrics and bug prediction. Softw. Qual. J. (2020). https://doi.org/10.1007/s11219-020-09515-0
7. Fowler, M.: Refactoring: Improving the Design of Existing Code. Addison-Wesley, Boston (1999)
8. Frank, E., Hall, M.A., Witten, I.H.: Online Appendix for Data Mining: Practical Machine Learning Tools and Techniques, Fourth Edition. Morgan Kaufmann (2016)
9. Gál, P., Pengő, E.: Primitive enthusiasm: a road to primitive obsession. In: The 11th Conference of PhD Students in Computer Science, pp. 134–137. University of Szeged (2018)
10. Gamma, E., Helm, R., Johnson, R., Vlissides, J.: Design Patterns: Elements of Reusable Object-Oriented Software. Addison-Wesley Longman Publishing Co. Inc., USA (1995)
11. Godfrey, K.: Correlation methods. In: IFAC Proceedings, vol. 12, pp. 527–534 (1979). https://doi.org/10.1016/S1474-6670(17)53974-9. Tutorials presented at the 5th IFAC Symposium on Identification and System Parameter Estimation, Darmstadt, Germany, September
12. Gupta, A., Suri, B., Kumar, V., Misra, S., Blazauskas, T., Damasevicius, R.: Software code smell prediction model using shannon, rényi and tsallis entropies. Entropy 20, 372 (2018). https://doi.org/10.3390/e20050372
13. Gupta, A., Suri, B., Misra, S.: A systematic literature review: code bad smells in java source code. In: Gervasi, O., et al. (eds.) ICCSA 2017. LNCS, vol. 10408, pp. 665–682. Springer, Cham (2017). https://doi.org/10.1007/978-3-319-62404-4_49
14. Gyimóthy, T., Ferenc, R., Siket, I.: Empirical validation of object-oriented metrics on open source software for fault prediction. IEEE Trans. Softw. Eng. 31(10), 897–910 (2005). https://doi.org/10.1109/TSE.2005.112
15. Hall, T., Zhang, M., Bowes, D., Sun, Y.: Some code smells have a significant but small effect on faults. ACM Trans. Softw. Eng. Methodol. 23(4) (2014). https://doi.org/10.1145/2629648
16. Jiang, Y., Cukic, B., Ma, Y.: Techniques for evaluating fault prediction models. Empirical Softw. Engg. 13(5), 561–595 (2008). https://doi.org/10.1007/s10664-008-9079-3
17. Jureczko, M., Madeyski, L.: Towards identifying software project clusters with regard to defect prediction. In: Proceedings of the 6th International Conference on Predictive Models in Software Engineering. PROMISE 2010. ACM (2010). https://doi.org/10.1145/1868328.1868342
18. Kaur, A., Kaur, I.: An empirical evaluation of classification algorithms for fault prediction in open source projects. J. King Saud Univ. Comput. Inf. Sci. 30 (2016). https://doi.org/10.1016/j.jksuci.2016.04.002
19. Khomh, F., Di Penta, M., Gueheneuc, Y.: An exploratory study of the impact of code smells on software change-proneness. In: 2009 16th Working Conference on Reverse Engineering, pp. 75–84 (2009). https://doi.org/10.1109/WCRE.2009.28
20. Mäntylä, M.V., Vanhanen, J., Lassenius, C.: A taxonomy and an initial empirical study of bad smells in code. In: Proceedings of the International Conference on Software Maintenance. ICSM, pp. 381–384. IEEE (2003). https://doi.org/10.1109/ICSM.2003.1235447
21. Menzies, T., Milton, Z., Turhan, B., Cukic, B., Jiang, Y., Bener, A.: Defect prediction from static code features: current results, limitations, new approaches. Autom. Softw. Eng. 17, 375–407 (2010). https://doi.org/10.1007/s10515-010-0069-5

22. Moonen, L., Yamashita, A.: Do code smells reflect important maintainability aspects? In: Proceedings of the 2012 IEEE International Conference on Software Maintenance. ICSM, pp. 306–315. IEEE (2012). https://doi.org/10.1109/ICSM. 2012.6405287
23. Open Static Analyser GitHub Page: https://github.com/sed-inf-u-szeged/ OpenStaticAnalyzer
24. Palomba, F., Zanoni, M., Fontana, F.A., De Lucia, A., Oliveto, R.: Toward a smell-aware bug prediction model. IEEE Trans. Softw. Eng. 45(2), 194–218 (2019). https://doi.org/10.1109/TSE.2017.2770122
25. Pengő, E., Gál, P.: Grasping primitive enthusiasm - approaching primitive obsession in steps. In: Proceedings of the 13th International Conference on Software Technologies. ICSOFT, pp. 389–396. INSTICC, SciTePress (2018). https://doi. org/10.5220/0006918804230430
26. Song, Q., Shepperd, M., Cartwright, M., Mair, C.: Software defect association mining and defect correction effort prediction. IEEE Trans. Softw. Eng. 32(2), 69–82 (2006). https://doi.org/10.1109/TSE.2006.1599417
27. Roperia, N.: JSmell: a bad smell detection tool for java systems. Master's thesis, Maharishi Dayanand University (2009)
28. Shlens, J.: A tutorial on principal component analysis (2014)
29. Shukla, S., Behera, R.K., Misra, S., Rath, S.K.: Software reliability assessment using deep learning technique. In: Chakraverty, S., Goel, A., Misra, S. (eds.) Towards Extensible and Adaptable Methods in Computing, pp. 57–68. Springer, Singapore (2018). https://doi.org/10.1007/978-981-13-2348-5_5
30. Singh, V., Misra, S., Sharma, M.: Bug severity assessment in cross project context and identifying training candidates. J. Inf. Knowl. Manage. 16, 1750005 (2017). https://doi.org/10.1142/S0219649217500058
31. Sjøberg, D.I.K., Yamashita, A., Anda, B.C.D., Mockus, A., Dybå, T.: Quantifying the effect of code smells on maintenance effort. IEEE Trans. Softw. Eng. 39(8), 1144–1156 (2013). https://doi.org/10.1109/TSE.2012.89
32. Tóth, Z., Gyimesi, P., Ferenc, R.: A public bug database of github projects and its application in bug prediction. In: Gervasi, O., et al. (eds.) ICCSA 2016. LNCS, vol. 9789, pp. 625–638. Springer, Cham (2016). https://doi.org/10.1007/978-3-319-42089-9_44
33. Wahono, R.S.: A systematic literature review of software defect prediction: research trends, datasets, methods and frameworks. J. Softw. Eng. 1, 1–16 (2015). https:// doi.org/10.3923/JSE.2007.1.12
34. Weyuker, E., Ostrand, T., Bell, R.: Comparing the effectiveness of several modeling methods for fault prediction. Empirical Softw. Eng. 15, 277–295 (2010). https:// doi.org/10.1007/s10664-009-9111-2
35. Yamashita, A., Moonen, L.: Exploring the impact of inter-smell relations on software maintainability: an empirical study. In: 2013 35th International Conference on Software Engineering (ICSE), pp. 682–691 (2013). https://doi.org/10.1109/ICSE. 2013.6606614
36. Yu, Z., Rajlich, V.: Hidden dependencies in program comprehension and change propagation. In: Proceedings 9th International Workshop on Program Comprehension. IWPC 2001, pp. 293–299 (2001). https://doi.org/10.1109/WPC.2001.921739
37. Zhang, M., Hall, T., Baddoo, N.: Code bad smells: a review of current knowledge. J. Softw. Maintenance Evol. 23(3), 179–202 (2011). https://doi.org/10.1002/smr. 521

38. Zimmermann, T., Nagappan, N., Gall, H., Giger, E., Murphy, B.: Cross-project defect prediction: a large scale experiment on data vs. domain vs. process. In: Proceedings of the 7th Joint Meeting of the European Software Engineering Conference and the ACM SIGSOFT Symposium on The Foundations of Software Engineering, pp. 91–100. ESEC/FSE 2009, Association for Computing Machinery, New York (2009). https://doi.org/10.1145/1595696.1595713
39. Zimmermann, T., Premraj, R., Zeller, A.: Predicting defects for eclipse. In: Proceedings of the Third International Workshop on Predictor Models in Software Engineering, p. 9. PROMISE 2007, IEEE (2007). https://doi.org/10.1109/PROMISE.2007.10

A Novel Approach to Test Case Prioritization for Software Regression Tests

Tulin Boyar[1(✉)], Mert Oz[1], Ekin Oncu[2], and Mehmet S. Aktas[1]

[1] Yildiz Technical University, Istanbul, Turkey
{tulin.boyar,mert.oz}@std.yildiz.edu.tr,
aktas@yildiz.edu.tr
[2] Research and Development Center, Testinium, Istanbul, Turkey
ekin.oncu@testinium.com

Abstract. Regression testing of a comprehensive software system is very costly and time-consuming. Test prioritization techniques are used to reduce the time and cost spent in regression tests. Data such as various software quality metrics and past test run results are used when prioritizing test cases in the literature. In this study, a new test prioritization method is proposed based on the number and speed of detected errors. Applying the proposed technique aims to see the errors in the system as soon as possible. In our method, historical test data is analyzed to prioritize test cases. The extent to which the analysis focuses on the recent and distant past is controlled by the parameter. For each test case; prioritization is made based on the number of detected errors and the speed of error detection. We observe its effectiveness by applying our method on regression testing for a developer performance portal software. The experimental study shows that the proposed method is valid, and the results are promising. Our approach improves the error detection rate of test sets. This improvement can be applied even in the most complex situations. With the advancement in the error detection rate, the cost and effort spent on regression tests are also reduced.

Keywords: Test cases prioritization · Regression tests · Test prioritization techniques · Test cases · Average percentage of fault detected (APFD) metric

1 Introduction

Large-scale software constantly evolves to adapt to changing business requirements. A software development process of such software projects includes an endless loop of deleting, updating, or adding new elements. To ensure the robustness of the software systems, engineers should test them in every single change. Since testing complex software forms a considerable expense and time-consuming process via traditional methods, the importance of regression testing becomes

© Springer Nature Switzerland AG 2021
O. Gervasi et al. (Eds.): ICCSA 2021, LNCS 12955, pp. 201–216, 2021.
https://doi.org/10.1007/978-3-030-87007-2_15

evident at this point. Regression testing aims to detect maximum errors in software systems with minimum time and effort. Literature introduces several great works for this purpose [6–13]. The regression testing for prioritizing test cases is used to determine the best order that saves money and time when they are run with their best order [30]. Software systems using regression tests are tested on all codes and modules again, even if a tiny change occurs in the codebase [1].

Regression testing of an extensive and comprehensive software system is also quite large. Regression test continues to grow as a result of all the studies and improvements made in the software. Regression tests are costly and time-consuming. In addition, in cases where there are limited resources, evaluating all test cases of the regression test may not be suitable.

There exits studies that take into account software metrics in order to improve the quality of software systems [28,29,34]. With the help of software quality metrics, some studies investigate the human factor in software system quality [35,36]. There are some studies that take into account collective behaviour of testers/users to be able to test the software systems [31,32]. There are also testing approaches that conduct testing based on the model-based approaches [33]. Different from these studies, this manuscript focuses on software regression tests and test case prioritization.

Approaches used to reduce the cost of regression testing: 1) Retest All: One technique to perform regression testing is to retest all test cases; it takes much time to run all test cases in an existing test suite. 2) Regression Test Selection: It selects certain test cases to carry out the regression testing. Ignoring some scenarios is the disadvantage of the Regression Test Selection technique. 3) Test Case Prioritization: It prioritizes tests in regression tests with too many test scenarios. Testing all available tests is carried out, but it brings a certain ranking according to the determined criteria. 4) Hybrid Approach: The Regression Test Selection and Test Case Prioritization techniques are used together. [1,6]

Motivation: One of the essential parts of a software system is software testing. One of the most critical points in comprehensive and extensive software is regression tests. Regression tests are crucial to software system reliability. In regression testing, prioritizing test cases and detecting errors in the minimum time provides excellent benefits to reducing effort and reducing costs. Furthermore, developing different methods in regression test prioritization techniques will contribute to software engineering. For these reasons, we study a test prioritization within the scope of this research.

Research Questions: In this research, we focus on the problem of prioritizing test cases by using metrics (working time, number of errors, past test results). In this study, we propose a method to prioritize test cases. The primary purpose of our research is to identify the errors as soon as possible by prioritizing the regression test cases. For this reason, the main research questions we focus on are as follows. 1) How should one evaluate error situations in test scenarios, which have an essential effect on ordering test cases? 2) How should the running times and fault detection times of test scenarios be evaluated? 3) How should previous test effectiveness be used in deciding on the new test sequences? 4) How should the efficiency of the ordering of test cases be measured? 5) How does the prioritization of test cases affect resource utilization?

Contributions: In this paper, we propose a method based on past test case results for prioritizing test cases. The purpose of the method is to list the test cases to detect errors as soon as possible. Based on the test analysis made in the past, the amount of error detected by each test case and the error detection speed effectively take role in ordering test cases. When compared with other studies in the literature, this study has two main contributions.

- To prioritize test scenarios, a methodology is proposed by using data on the number of errors detected, the number of errors controlled, and error detection time.
- By performing case analysis on an industrial system, the method's success is evaluated, and the effects of different parameter values are analyzed.

Organization: Section 2 presents a literature review on test case prioritization studies for regression test cases. Section 3 explains the essential parts of the method we propose. Section 4 details the prototype application of our proposed method. Section 5 evaluates the study results and explains future studies.

2   Literature Review

In a software development process, a lot of effort is spent on the testing process. For this reason, researchers are working to make test processes more efficient, and effective [14–16]. Prioritization of test cases is a technique used in a software development process to find the best order that gives maximum benefits. In many studies, the prioritization technique and algorithm of various test cases have been proposed and used [12, 20–26].

Software TCP Survey, one of the pioneers of Rothermel et al., is an approach that recommends and comprehensively evaluates TCP. For prioritization, it examines the effectiveness of different prioritization techniques with seven programs written in C languages containing 1000–5500 test scenarios by defining a few technical definitions such as random approaches, context-based approaches. A significant performance difference was observed in the study, where they suggested applying the inclusion-based technique. To prioritize the test cases, the properties of the examined systems, the abstraction level of the developed techniques (source code line level, architectural component level, function level, etc.) were also evaluated [27].

S. Raju and G.V. Uma [10] has introduced a test case prioritization technique based on clustering. In this study, test cases are clustered according to dynamic runtime behavior. The researchers presented a test scenario prioritization approach that prioritizes system-level testing requirements by reducing the number of pairwise comparisons required. In this approach, the pre-qualification of test cases is based on four factors: speed of fault detection, variability of requirements, fault impact, and implementation complexity. The researchers evaluated

Table 1. Literature review summary

Reference	Finding
Aljawabrah, et al. (2021)	A study in which test cases are created automatically and prioritized based on software risk
Misra, S., et al. (2017)	A class complexity metric has been proposed in object-oriented programming
S. Singhal, et al. (2017)	A study in which the hybrid approach, in which the Genetic algorithm and Colony optimization are used together, is examined according to the time constraint
Jatana, N. et al. (2016)	A research on the applicability of PSO in test data generation with mutation testing
Sozer and Kurt (2014)	A based on history approach using defect detection rates to prioritize test cases
S. Raju and G.V. Uma (2012)	A test case prioritization technique based on clustering
Rothermel et al. (2001)	Examining different test prioritization approaches

the efficiency of test case prioritization techniques by performing loss-gain analysis for different abstraction levels. To prioritize test cases, many techniques and methods have been proposed, experimentally evaluated, and compared with each other [2,3]. Sozer and Kurt [5] presented a based on history method in their study. Test cases are prioritized according to the amount of error detection obtained from the analysis of past tests. In the study, how much to focus on the recent or distant past is controlled by a parameter.

Aljawabrah et al. Developed a method to automatically generate test cases based on software risk in prioritizing test cases. He confirmed the technique he developed by many software experts [15]. Jatana, N. et al. proposed an approach to generate optimized test data based on Particle Swarm Optimization combined with mutation testing [17]. S. Singhal et al. examined the results of the hybrid method (MHBG_TCS tool) that uses the Genetic algorithm and Colony optimization together in the Regression Test Selection method against the changing time constraint [18].

When the studies in the literature are examined, various metrics such as APFD, APFDc, f-measure, Relative Position, APSC have been used to measure the effectiveness of the proposed test prioritization technique. Among these metrics, the most used APFD metric [2,5,19,23,27] (Table 1).

3   Methodology

Several workflow steps need to be performed to validate the proposed study. Our research aims to detect the errors in the software with a regression test as soon as possible. For this purpose, the first step is to provide a regression test data set applied to a software system. It should contain test cases that include test scenarios grouped within the regression test and control the whole system.

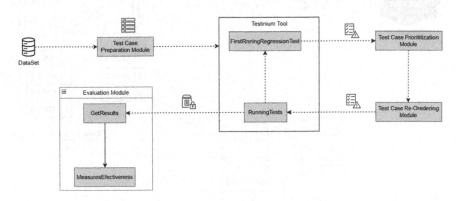

Fig. 1. The proposed system architecture

Within the regression test data set applied for an existing software system, initial data to be used to prioritize test cases are created. The regression test is then run without any prioritization work. Priority score is found for each test scenario by making test prioritization calculations from the data obtained through test runs. Test scenarios are ranked according to the test prioritization score. The test senates in the regression test are sorted according to the prioritization account and run again.

The method suggested in our study is also effective in test case prioritization. For this reason, the efficiency of the method will increase in successive test runs. Once the test results are obtained, efficiency is measured using the APFD metric for each new ranking. Figure 1 shows the workflow.

3.1   Test Case Preparation

Regression tests include test sets grouped by related test scenarios. There are one or more test scenarios in each test set. Each test case checks at least one error condition. Multiple sub-conditions are also checked according to the process steps in the test scenario. In our study, the number of situations controlled by each test scenario is considered the scenario's size. In the first step of our research, as shown in Figure 2, the error condition that it controls for each test scenario is determined first.

The number of cases checked by the test scenario and the number of errors detected are used to prioritize test cases. Suppose in a regression test shown in

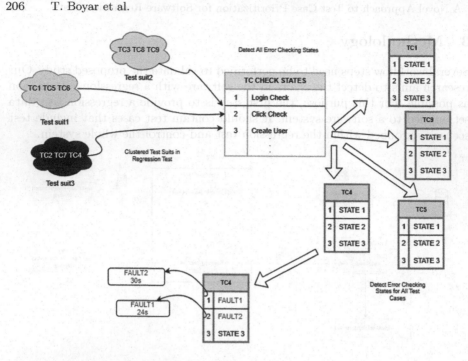

Fig. 2. Data processing

Table 2, 10 error conditions of 5 test scenarios are checked. Each test case can detect many errors, and various test cases can catch the same error. In our study, the number of matched cases will be referred to as the size of the test scenario.

Table 2. Test cases and states example

TC1	TC2	TC3	TC4	TC5
State1	State1	State1	State1	State1
State2	State3	State6	State2	State2
State3	State5		State4	State9
State4			State7	State10
			State8	
4	3	2	5	4

3.2 Test Case Re-ordering Module

First, the regression test consisting of randomly ordered test cases is run on its original form without prioritizing test cases. Second, data from test run results are recorded. Third, for each test scenario, the run time, the error detection time,

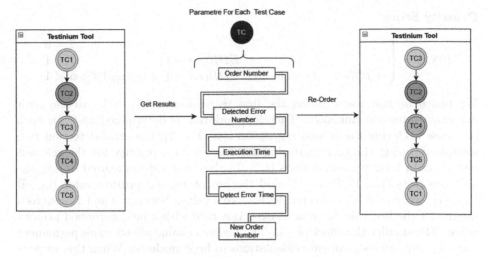

Fig. 3. Running regresion tests and getting data

the size of the scenario, the number of errors detected is used in the prioritization score calculation.

The test cases included in the regression tests prioritize the amount of error they have detected in the past and the speed of error detection.

As shown in Fig. 3, the result data to be used in the prioritization calculation is analyzed, and the new order of the regression test is obtained.

In our study, the regression test was run over Testinium Tool [4]. We took prioritization parameters through the tool.

3.3 Test Case Prioritization Calculation Module

Error Detection Rate. In the method we propose, error rates detected in the past are evaluated to prioritize the test scenarios. Our study focuses on the calculation of error detection rates, and a unique method is recommended. Error detection rate is calculated as follows.

i = Tested scenario

t = Time to be tested

EDC: Error detection capacity

EDS: Error detection speed

EDR: Error detection rate

$$EDC(i,t) = \frac{number\ of\ errors\ caught\ by\ scenario\ i\ at\ time\ t}{size\ of\ scenario\ i} \tag{1}$$

$$EDS(i,t) = 1 - \frac{time\ to\ catch\ the\ error\ at\ time\ t\ of\ scenario\ i}{time\ to\ complete\ scenario\ i} \tag{2}$$

$$EDR(i,t) = EDC(i,t) + EDS(i,t) \tag{3}$$

While calculating the error detection rate, it was aimed to further refine the EDR score by taking into account the error detection rate of test cases.

Priority Score

$$R(i,t) = \begin{cases} 0 & t = 0 \\ EDR(i, t-1) & t = 1 \\ \alpha\, xR(i, t-1) + (1-\alpha)xEDR(i, t-1) & t > 2 \text{ and } 0 < \alpha < 1 \end{cases}$$

We tested no test cases during the first regression test $(t = 1)$, so the error detection rates are unknown. Therefore, priority is determined as 0 for each test case i. During the second regression test $(t = 2)$, the error detection rate measured during the first regression tests is set as a priority for the relevant test case. In later regression tests $(t > 2)$, the error rate measured during the previous tests (i.e., EDR(i, t−1) and the predetermined priority value (i.e., R (i, t−1)) where the α parameter, which takes values between 0 and 1, assigns a weight for the last calculated fault detection rate with a predetermined priority value. The smaller the effect of −n. The higher α value allows more permanent memory of previous error rate calculations to be considered. When this value is 0, the priority of a test case is always equal to the error detection rate calculated in previous tests. At higher α values, the last and previously calculated error detection rates affect the priority calculation.

4　Evaluation

We conducted an experimental study on the OObeya software regression test data set, which we have obtained from Testinium, the method we propose within the scope of this study. Below, we explain the data set we use, the metric we use to evaluate the effectiveness of our research, and the results of the experimental study.

4.1　Dataset

For our study, the OObeya software regression test, which is under development, was used as a data set. The regression test consists of 14 test teams and 73 test scenarios within the test sets. A total of 90 error conditions are checked (Tables 3 and 4).

　　A regression test takes an hour or a few hours to run. The data set consists of the regression test results, which are performed consecutively over the weekend, lasting 60 days in total. The data about each test scenario, the number of errors it controls, the error time it detects, the test run time, and the moment of error detection are kept. In addition, we recorded error detection rate (EDR) and regression test score (t) data for each scenario obtained with test run results.

4.2　Effectiveness Measure

We need to use a measurement technique to evaluate the prioritization study effectiveness in our research questions. Our study used the APFD metric, which calculates the weighted average of the error percentage, to measure how quickly a

Table 3. Example of data set for test cases

Test cases	The number of errors it checks	The number of errors detected	Time to catch errors(s)	Execution time(s)
T1	5	2	20	50
T2	7	3	25	43
T3	4	1	10	52
T4	3	2	15	22
T5	2	1	12	30

Table 4. Example of data for running tests

Running the test	Date	Time	Total execution time(m)	Number of detected errors
Random order	05.04.2021	20:00	125	14
Order-1	10.04.2021	15:13	107	14
Order-2	15.04.2021	18:36	112	13
Order-3	20.04.2021	17:25	88	13
Order-4	25.04.2021	19:16	93	12
Order-5	30.04.2021	11:30	95	13

prioritized test package detects errors. [1] The weight value assigned to a test case increases in direct proportion to the rate of errors detected before this test case. APFD value is between 0 and 100; higher values indicate a high error detection rate. Below is an example calculated with the APFD metric. Suppose there are 10 errors in a software system, and there are only 5 test cases in the test set, and test cases can detect all errors together. The test cases are named TC1-TC2-TC3-TC4-TC5. The error-test case matrix generated is shown in Table 5.

Table 5. Test cases with detected faults

TESTS		FAULTS									
		1	2	3	4	5	6	7	8	9	10
TC1	Create a new dash-board	X					X				
TC2	Update dash-board	X					X	X		X	
TC3	Delete the test dashboard	X	X		X	X	X	X			X
TC4	Add jira widget					X					
TC5	Add sonar widget			X						X	X

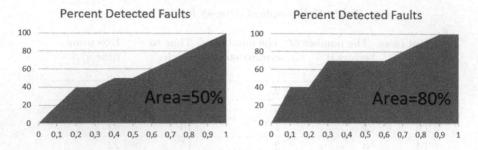

Fig. 4. Test case orders and APFD values

TC1 test case detects 1st and 7th errors, while TC2 test case detects 1st, 6th, 7th and 9th the errors. TC3 test case detects 7 errors at once. TC4 test case detects only 5th error, TC5 test case detects 3 errors. We created the ordering of test cases in 2 different ways, and APFD values were calculated. The x-axis shows the number of cases tested, the y-axis the ratio of the number of detected errors to the total number of errors. The area under the curve shows the weighted percentage of errors detected for all test cases. (APFD)

In Fig. 4, the APFD value calculated for TC1-TC2-TC3-TC4-TC5 is 50%. It is desired to reach the optimum APFD value by ordering the test cases in different ways. For the test cases ordered as TC3-TC5-TC2-TC1-TC4, the APFD value is seen as 80%. The fewer test cases are tested to detect all errors, and the APFD value will increase inversely. For this purpose, the best order in which a test can detect all errors by testing fewer test cases should be from the test case that detected the most error to the test case that caught the least.

4.3   Experimental Study Results

We used a selenium Gauge-based test automation system to run OObeya regression tests automatically. This system acts as a user in the web browser and compares the results obtained with reference images. Inconsistencies detected in the comparison are reported as errors. Test automation is run on the Testinium Tool.

The automatically tested test set contains hundreds of test steps. The test cases we used for case analysis were grouped under 14 groups and included 73 different scenarios. ($1 <= i <= 73$) It takes an average of one hour to perform the tests. Without applying the technique, we ran the regression test in the order of the original. ($t = 1$) The test completion time is 64 min and 21 s. The number of detected errors is 15. The calculated APFD value is 0.39. The ratio of the number of errors detected in Fig. 5 to the total number of errors on the y axis; error detection time is shown on the x-axis. We performed three consecutive tests using the prioritization technique we suggested in the regression tests. In the prioritization of the test scenarios, we used the error detection rates obtained from the test results data ($t = 1$) run in the original order. Data of TC1 and TC2 test cases are sampled in Table 6. In data processing, we obtained information

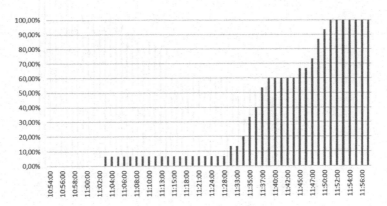

Fig. 5. Original order test results

about how many error conditions each test case controls. At the time $t = 1$, TC1 test case detected 1 out of 2 error conditions it controls as an error. The run time for TC1 is 46 s. The time to catch 1 error it detects is 21 s.

Table 6. EDR calculation example

Test cases	Number of states	Number of detected faults	Fault detecting time(s)	Execution time(s)	EDR
TC1	2	1	21	46	1,043478
TC2	2	1	40	46	0,630431

Calculation for test case TC1:

$$EDR = \frac{1}{2} + (1 - \frac{21}{46}) \tag{4}$$

Calculation for test case TC2:

$$EDR = \frac{1}{2} + (1 - \frac{40}{46}) \tag{5}$$

All test cases are reordered according to the EDR scores sampled in Table 6. We reran the regression test with the new order. The total run time of the test is 58 min, and the number of errors detected is 19. The APFD value for the test run with the new order is 0.56 ($t = 2$).

All test cases are reordered according to the EDR scores sampled in Table 6. We reran the regression test with the new order. The total run time of the test is 58 min, and the number of errors detected is 19. The APFD value for the test

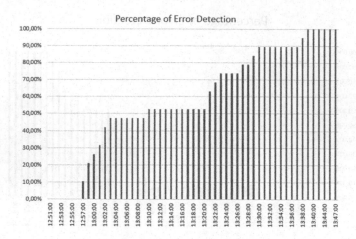

Fig. 6. Test results for t = 2

run with the new order is 0.56 ($t = 2$). According to the results obtained, the
scores for each test scenario were calculated again. We created a new ordering
for the regression test. The test run according to this order is 45 min and 23 s
to complete. The number of errors detected is 13, and its APFD value is 0.64
($t = 3$).

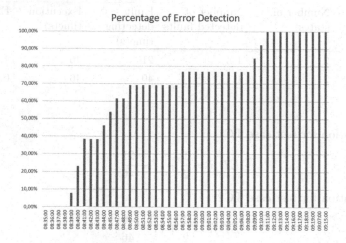

Fig. 7. Test results for t = 3

According to the last ordering results, the regression test completion time
is 49 min and 30 s. The number of errors detected was 17, and the test APFD
value was 0.74 ($t = 4$).

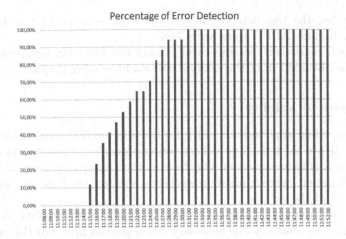

Fig. 8. Test results for t = 4

4.4   Discussion

This study aims to prioritize the test cases with the error detection rate obtained from the historical regression tests and detect the system's errors as soon as possible. It has been worked on OObeya software, where a real-time regression test is applied. The regression test cases are ordered with the method of prioritizing the test cases we recommend. We measured the results obtained with the APFD metric. When the regression test is tested with its original order (t = 1), as seen in Fig. 5, all test cases should be tested to detect all errors. APFD value calculated at time $t = 1$ is 39%. The regression test $(t = 2)$ run with the first sequencing study in Fig. 6 lasted 59 min. 70% of the errors are detected at the 32nd minute of the test. At $t = 2$, it is close to the test period to detect all errors in the order in which our method is first applied. The exceptional situation encountered is that six more errors that were not in the system at $t = 1$ were detected. The fact that a few of these errors were at the bottom of the ordering extended this time. Increasing errors in the system reduce the effectiveness of the method. The method's efficiency increases when the number of errors is the same in the system or when the number of errors decreases. When looking at the results against this unfavorable situation, the APFD value calculated at $t = 2$ time is 56%. APFD value is increased compared to time $t = 1$.

When the results obtained with the second ordering in Fig. 7 are examined, it takes about 50 min to test all test cases $(t = 3)$. While the test detected 17 errors at time $t = 2$, the test detected 13 errors at time $t = 3$. 80% of the errors were detected in the 12th min of the test, and the test detected all the errors in the 35th minute. APFD value calculated at time $t = 3$ is 64%. APFD value has increased compared to previous tests. The results of the test run with the third-ordering are shown in Fig. 8 $(t = 4)$. The test detected all errors at the 22nd minute of the total test period that lasted 49 min. In less than half of the total test time, the test detected all errors in the system. At $t = 4$, the test reached the highest APFD value with 74%.

Since each regression test run result affects the following test sequence, the APFD value obtained from the study draws an increasing graph.

4.5 Threats to Validity

In this study, while applying our test prioritization method, consecutive running is necessary to see the technique's effectiveness, as each test result data will affect the following test sequence order. Our tests on the Oobeya software, which is still under development, were applied on weekends and nights. This way, we ensured the reliability of the results.

Not all cases in our test case set are independent. In other words, to run some test scenarios, we must run the necessary test scenarios first. For this reason, we checked whether there exits any prerequisites within the test sequences, at the beginning of each regression test. In case of the deterioration of the prerequisite status, we changed the ordering of the test cases regardless of the prioritization score. Since we applied this situation in every test sequence, it did not affect the test results.

5 Conclusion and Future Works

In this study, we propose a viable method for prioritizing test cases and empirically examine how quickly we can detect errors. Our approach improves the error detection rate of test sets. This improvement can be applied even in the most complex situations. With the advancement in the error detection rate, the cost and effort spent on regression tests are also reduced.

We used our proposed method to prioritize software development regression tests. When we applied the regression test ordered according to our method, we saw that the error detection rate was increased. Without using any test case prioritization, the APFD value was 39%. We were able to increase the APFD value to 74% by applying our test prioritization method.

Our results indicate that regression tests that run without any test case prioritization use resources inefficiently. We should note that there may not be enough resources to evaluate all test cases. Therefore, it is essential to use resources efficiently and detect errors as soon as possible. We plan on taking into account various other features/metrics of the software systems, such as code coverage, in the future work.

Acknowledgment. We thank Saha Bilgi Teknolojileri Egitim Danismanlık San. Tic. A.S. R&D Center for providing the computational facilities that made this study possible.

References

1. Patel, K.M., et al.: A study of regression testing for trade me website. In: CS & IT Conference Proceedings. CS & IT Conference Proceedings (2021)
2. Rothermel, G., et al.: Test case prioritization: an empirical study. In: Proceedings IEEE International Conference on Software Maintenance-1999 (ICSM 1999). Software Maintenance for Business Change (Cat. No. 99CB36360), pp. 179–188. IEEE (1999)
3. Elbaum, S., Malishevsky, A.G., Rothermel, G.: Test case prioritization: a family of empirical studies. IEEE Trans. Softw. Eng. **28**(2), 159–182 (2002)
4. Testinium Homepage. http://www.testinium.com. Accessed 17 May 2021
5. Kurt, D., Sözer, H.: Geçmişe dönük hata tespit oranlarının zamanla değişen etkisine göre regresyon testlerinin önceliklendirilmesi. In: CEUR Workshop Proceedings. CEUR-WS (2014)
6. Ansari, A., et al.: Optimized regression test using test case prioritization. Procedia Comput. Sci. **79**, 152–160 (2016)
7. Alazzam, I., Nahar, K.M.O.: Combined source code approach for test case prioritization. In: Proceedings of the 2018 International Conference on Information Science and System, pp. 12–15 (2018)
8. Muthusamy, T., Seetharaman, K.: Effectiveness of test case prioritization techniques based on regression testing. Int. J. Softw. Eng. Appl. **5**(6), 113 (2014)
9. Staats, M., Loyola, P., Rothermel, G.: Oracle-centric test case prioritization. In: IEEE 23rd International Symposium on Software Reliability Engineering, vol. 2012, pp. 311–320. IEEE (2012)
10. Raju, S., Uma, G.V.: An efficient method to achieve effective test case prioritization in regression testing using prioritization factors. Asian J. Inf. Technol. **11**(5), 169–180 (2012)
11. Shahid, M., Ibrahim, S.: A new code based test case prioritization technique. Int. J. Softw. Eng. Appl. **8**(6), 31–38 (2014)
12. Zhang, L., et al.: Bridging the gap between the total and additional test-case prioritization strategies. In: 2013 35th International Conference on Software Engineering (ICSE), pp. 192–201. IEEE (2013)
13. Yoon, M., et al.: A test case prioritization through correlation of requirement and risk. J. Softw. Eng. Appl. **5**(10), 823 (2012)
14. Misra, S., Adewumi, A., Maskeliūnas, R., Damaševičius, R., Cafer, F.: Unit testing in global software development environment. In: Panda, B., Sharma, S., Roy, N.R. (eds.) REDSET 2017. CCIS, vol. 799, pp. 309–317. Springer, Singapore (2018). https://doi.org/10.1007/978-981-10-8527-7_25
15. Aljawabrah, N., et al.: Automated recovery and visualization of test-to-code traceability (TCT) links: an evaluation. IEEE Access **9**, 40111–40123 (2021)
16. Jonathan, O., Omoregbe, N., Misra, S.: Empirical comparison of cross-validation and test data on internet traffic classification methods. In: Journal of Physics: Conference Series, p. 012044. IOP Publishing (2019)
17. Jatana, N., Suri, B., Misra, S., Kumar, P., Choudhury, A.R.: Particle swarm based evolution and generation of test data using mutation testing. In: Gervasi, O., et al. (eds.) ICCSA 2016. LNCS, vol. 9790, pp. 585–594. Springer, Cham (2016). https://doi.org/10.1007/978-3-319-42092-9_44
18. Singhal, S., Suri, B., Misra, S.: An empirical study of regression test suite reduction using MHBG_TCS tool. In: Proceedings International Conference Computation Network Information (ICCNI), pp. 1–5 (2017)

19. Nawar, M.N., Ragheb, M.M.: Multi-heuristic based algorithm for test case prioritization. In: Murgante, B., et al. (eds.) ICCSA 2014. LNCS, vol. 8583, pp. 449–460. Springer, Cham (2014). https://doi.org/10.1007/978-3-319-09156-3_32

20. Lin, X., et al.: Test case minimization for regression testing of composite service based on modification impact analysis. In: Wang, G., Lin, X., Hendler, J., Song, W., Xu, Z., Liu, G. (eds.) WISA 2020. LNCS, vol. 12432, pp. 15–26. Springer, Cham (2020). https://doi.org/10.1007/978-3-030-60029-7_2

21. Arora, P.K., Bhatia, R.: A systematic review of agent-based test case generation for regression testing. Arabian J. Sci. Eng. **43**(2), 447–470 (2018)

22. Onoma, A.K., et al.: Regression testing in an industrial environment. Commun. ACM **41**(5), 81–86 (1998)

23. Malishevsky, A.G., et al.: Cost-cognizant test case prioritization. Technical Report TR-UNL-CSE-2006-0004, University of Nebraska-Lincoln (2006)

24. Hao, D., et al.: A unified test case prioritization approach. ACM Trans. Softw. Eng. Methodol. (TOSEM) **24**(2), 1–31 (2014)

25. Jeffrey, D., Gupta, N.: Test case prioritization using relevant slices. In: 30th Annual International Computer Software and Applications Conference (COMPSAC 2006), pp. 411–420. IEEE (2006)

26. Jiang, B., et al.: Adaptive random test case prioritization. In: 2009 IEEE/ACM International Conference on Automated Software Engineering, pp. 233–244. IEEE (2009)

27. Rothermel, G., et al.: Prioritizing test cases for regression testing. IEEE Trans. Softw. Eng. **27**(10), 929–948 (2001)

28. Aktas, M.S., Kapdan, M.: Structural code clone detection methodology using software metrics. Int. J. Softw. Eng. Knowl. Eng. **26**(2), 307–332 (2016)

29. Aktas, M.S., Kapdan, M.: Implementation of analytical hierarchy process in detecting structural code clones. In: The 17th International Conference on Computational Science and its Applications (ICCSA 2017) (2017)

30. Ozturk, S., et al.: Test case prioritization related to code quality. In: The 2013 International Conference on Software Engineering Research and Practice (SERP-13) (2013)

31. Uygun, Y., et al.: On the large-scale graph data processing for user interface testing in big data science projects. In: 2020 IEEE Big Data, 6th International Workshop to Improve Big Data Science Project Team Processes (2020)

32. Tekin, C., et al.: Opinion mining on usability testing data. In: IEEE SIU Conference, Gaziantep, Turkey (2020)

33. Akpinar, P., et al.: Web application testing with model based testing method: case study. In: 2nd International Conference on Electrical, Communication and Computer Engineering, Turkey (2020)

34. Kapdan, M., Aktas, M., Yigit, M.: On the structural code clone detection problem: a survey and software metric based approach. In: ICCSA 2014: Computational Science and its Applications - ICCSA 2014, pp. 492–507 (2014)

35. Guveyi, E., Aktas, M., Kalipsiz, O.: Human factor on software quality: a systematic literature review. In: ICCSA 2020: Computational Science and its Applications - ICCSA 2020 (2020)

36. Guveyi, E., Aktas, M., Kalipsiz, O.: Impact of personal factors on software quality. In: UYMS 2020 (2020)

A Novel Approach for the Detection of Web Service Anti-Patterns Using Word Embedding Techniques

Sahithi Tummalapalli[1], Lov Kumar[1(✉)], Lalitha Bhanu Murthy Neti[1],
Vipul Kocher[2], and Srinivas Padmanabhuni[2]

[1] BITS Pilani Hyderabad, Hyderabad, India
{P20170433,lovkumar,bhanu}@hyderabad.bitspilani.ac.in
[2] Testaing.Com, Bengaluru, India
{vipulkocher,srinivas}@testAing.com

Abstract. An anti-pattern is defined as a standard but ineffective solution to solve a problem. Anti-patterns in software design make it hard for software maintenance and development by making source code very complicated for understanding. Various studies revealed that the presence of anti-patterns in web services leads to maintenance and evolution-related problems. Identification of anti-patterns at the design level helps in reducing efforts, resources, and costs. This makes the identification of anti-patterns an exciting issue for researchers. This work introduces a novel approach for detecting anti-patterns using text metrics extracted from the Web Service Description Language (WSDL) file. The framework used in this paper builds on the presumption that text metrics extracted at the web service level have been considered as a predictor for anti-patterns. This paper empirically investigates the effectiveness of three feature selection techniques and the original features, three data sampling techniques, the original data, four word embedding techniques, and nine classifier techniques in detecting web service anti-patterns. Data Sampling techniques are employed to counter the class imbalance problem suffered by the data set. The results confirm the predictive ability of text metrics obtained by different word embedding techniques in predicting anti-patterns.

Keywords: Web service · Word embedding techniques · Machine learning · Classifier techniques · Class imbalance · Anti-pattern · Text metrics

1 Introduction

Service-Oriented Architecture (SOA) is defined as: "a style of multi-tier computing that helps organizations share logic and data among multiple applications and usage modes [6]". *SOA* is an architecture used to create systems based

© Springer Nature Switzerland AG 2021
O. Gervasi et al. (Eds.): ICCSA 2021, LNCS 12955, pp. 217–230, 2021.
https://doi.org/10.1007/978-3-030-87007-2_16

on autonomous coarse-grained and loosely coupled interactions between components called services. Each service bears behavior and processes through contracts, including messages sent to recognizable addresses (called endpoints). The software industry has considered SOA as a structure to improve the ordering between the IT industry and the business models to adapt more flexibly to the businesses' ever-changing requirements, increasing the business agility. The ever-changing requirement of the business makes many modules introduced into the initial software design, evolving it over time and making it very complicated to maintain and understand. The evolution of software design to fit user and business demands degrades the software's quality. It leads to an ineffective solution to a frequently occurring problem, called *Anti-Pattern*. In this work, We considered the following four web service anti-patterns, namely: AP1: GOWS(God Object Web Service), AP2:FGWS(Fine-Grained Web Service), AWS: Ambiguous Web Service, AP4: CWS(Chatty Web Service). Various studies revealed that the presence of anti-patterns in web services leads to maintenance and evolution-related problems. Identification of anti-patterns at the design level helps in reducing efforts, resources, and costs. This makes the identification of anti-patterns an interesting problem for the researchers.

Segev et al. [7] in their work analyzed two methods, namely: Term Frequency/Inverse Document Frequency (Tf-IDF) and context analysis for processing text. The authors have explored WSDL files and free textual descriptors publicly available in service repositories for analyzing the services. By analyzing the WSDL and free text descriptions, authors proved by their approach that web service usage can be broadened by exploiting the data present in the web for building rich context for client queries rather than burdening users to marginalize their services with formal concepts and explanations. This work motivated us to utilize the TF/IDF approach and three other word embedding techniques to generate text metrics from the WSDL description files, which are further used as input for building autonomous models to detect anti-patterns in web services. In our previous work [8–10], We have build web service anti-pattern detection techniques using the object-oriented metrics and the WSDL metrics that are generated from the web service description language (WSDL) files as input. This paper empirically investigates the effectiveness of three feature selection techniques and the original features, three data sampling techniques, the original data, four word embedding techniques, and nine classifier techniques in detecting web service anti-patterns. Data Sampling techniques are employed to counter the class imbalance problem suffered by the data set.

2   Literature Survey

Pietrzak and Walter [5] defined and analyzed various relationships among the smells and provided hints on how they could be exploited to reduce anti-patterns detection. Authors performed experiments in the Jakarta Tomcat code to prove that knowledge about identified smells improves detecting other smells existing in the code. Jaafar et al. [3] argued in his paper that classes taking part in anti-pattern and patterns of software designs have dependencies with other classes, i.e., unvarying and mutating dependencies, that may spread issues to different classes. In this paper, the authors have empirically investigated the consequences of dependencies in the object-oriented system by focusing and analyzing the relationship between co-change and static dependencies and change proness, fault proness, and fault types classes are exhibiting. The hypothesis is validated on six design anti-patterns and ten anti-patterns in 39 releases of XercesJ, JFreeChart, and ArgoUML. Experimental results showed that the classes with anti-patterns are more prone to fault proness when compared to other classes. The limitations of this work are 1. Authors have conducted their experiments on a limited set of anti-patterns and design patterns. 2. The metrics used in the study are also limited. Velioglu and Selcuk [11] developed a Y-CSD tool that detects and reduces anti-patterns and code smells in the software project. The proposed tool is used to detect two anti-patterns, namely Brain Method and Data Class. Y-CSD uses structural analysis for the detection of code smells and anti-patterns. Kumar and Sureka [4] proposed an approach for the automatic detection of anti-patterns by static analysis of the source code. In this paper, the author proposed that the aggregate values of the source code metrics computed at the web-service level can be used as predictors for anti-pattern detection. In this paper, the author has empirically investigated the application of eight machine learning algorithms, i.e., Bagging, Multilayer Perceptron, Random Forest, Naive Bayes, Decision Tree, Logistic Boost, AdaBoost, Logistic regression, four data sampling techniques, namely: Downsampling, Random Sampling, and Synthetic Minority oversampling Technique (SMOTE) and four feature selection techniques, i.e., Information Gain, Symmetric Uncertainty, Gain Ratio and OneR in the prediction of anti-patterns. Borovits et al. [2] proposed technique for the detection of linguistic anti-patterns in infrastructure as code (Iac) scripts. The authors employed deep learning and word embedding techniques for the proposed approach. Further, the authors build the abstract syntax tree of Iac code units to create their code embedments. Authors validated their approach on the dataset extracted from open source repositories, and experimental results showed an accuracy ranging from 0.78–0.91 in detecting linguistic anti-patterns in Iac.

3   Proposed Framework and Research Background

In this work, experiments were carried on a downloaded dataset from GitHub repository[1]. Figure 1 shows the quantity of web services in which each of the anti-patterns exist (%AP) and does not exist (%NAP) in the dataset.

	GOWS	FGWS	DWS	CWS
# AP	21	13	14	21
% AP	9.29	5.75	6.19	9.29

Fig. 1. Percentages(%AP) and number(#AP) of anti-patterns in dataset

[1] https://github.com/ouniali/WSantipatterns.

Figure 2 shows the proposed framework for the experimental work. The experimental dataset has WSDL description files collected from various domains like weather, education, finance, etc. The first step comprises generating text metrics from the WSDL file by applying four word embedding techniques, namely: Term frequency-inverse Document Frequency (Tf-IDF), Continuous Bag Of Words (CBOW), Global Vectors for Word Representation (GloVe), and SKip Gram (SKG). Each of these techniques is producing around 450–1200 features for each of the WSDL files. There is a chance that some of these features are irrelevant in the detection of anti-patterns. To remove such features, we used three feature selection techniques to select the significant features in the next step. As we have discussed in Sect. 3, the dataset considered for the experiment is suffering from the class imbalance problem. Therefore, we used three data sampling techniques, namely: Synthetic Minority Oversampling Technique (SMOTE), BSMOTE (Borderline SMOTE), and ADASYN (Adaptive Synthetic), to overcome the class imbalance problem. Further, We used nine different classifier techniques to generate models for the prediction of web service anti-patterns. Finally, we did the comparative analysis of various models developed to predict web service anti-patterns using performance measures such as Accuracy, Area under Curve (AUC), and F-measure.

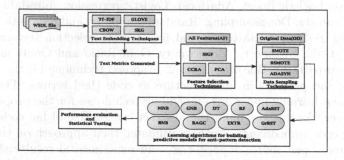

Fig. 2. Proposed framework

3.1 Word Embedding Techniques for the Generation of Text Metrics

In this work, we use four different word embedding techniques to generate text metrics that are later used as input for generating the models for detecting web service anti-patterns. As discussed in Sect. 3, the considered dataset has a collection of WSDL description files. All the word embedding techniques are applied on each of the WSDL files in which each line of code is considered text to generate the text metrics. A brief of each of the word embedding technique used in this work are given below:

– **Term frequency- Inverse Document Frequency (Tf-IDF):** is a numerical approach that shows the importance of a word in a file. Tf-IDF value increases in proportion with the number of times a word surfaces in a file and is balanced by the number of files in the corpus that has the word.

$$Tf(w) = \frac{\text{(no. of times w surfaces in a file)}}{\text{(total no. of words in the file)}}$$

$$IDF(w) = \log_e\left(\frac{\text{total no. of files}}{\text{no.of files with w in it}}\right) \tag{1}$$

- **Continuous Bag Of Words(CBOW):** CBOW model predicts the center words based on the context of the surrounding words. CBOW predicts the center word based on the context-window words.
- **SKip Gram(SKG):** Skip-gram model computes the probability of the center word appearing with the context words by computing the similarity with the dot product, then it converts the similarity into probability by passing it through the soft-max functions.
- **Global Vectors for Word Representation(GLOVE):** Glove uses matrix factorization techniques on the word-context matrix. In this technique, we construct a matrix of co-occurrence information, in which we count each word shown in rows and the frequency of occurrence of the word in a particular context shown in the column. For each word, we search for the context terms within a specified range defined by the window size before the word and a window size post the word.

3.2 Feature Selection Techniques

As discussed in Subsect. 3.1, we applied four different word embedding techniques individually on each of the WSDL description files for generating text metrics as features. Each of the techniques produced around 450–1200 features for every WSDL file. All the features generated may not be significant in the detection of anti-patterns. Hence, it is vital to remove all the irrelevant and insignificant features from the data before generating the models. Firstly, we applied a set of feature selection and ranking techniques used in previous work [9] to select the significant features (SIGF). Then we applied two other techniques, Compactness Centroid based Average($CC_r a$) [1], Principal Component Analysis(PCA) for selecting the relevant and significant features. We use the features selected by different feature selection techniques and the original features as input for building the models to detect web service anti-patterns.

3.3 Data Sampling Techniques

As discussed in Sect. 3.1, the dataset considered for experiments is suffering from the class imbalance problem. To counter this problem, We used three different sampling techniques in this work, namely: Synthetic Minority Oversampling Technique (SMOTE), BSMOTE (Borderline SMOTE), and ADASYN (Adaptive Synthetic). We developed the models to detect anti-patterns using the data after applying different sampling techniques and the original data.

3.4   Classifier Techniques

We apply various classifiers such as Naive Bayes classifier with different kernels, i.e., Multinomial (MNB), Bernoulli (BNB) and Gaussian (GNB), Decision Tree (DT), Bagging classifier (BAGC), Random Forest (RF), Extra Randomized Tree classifier (EXTR), AdaBoost (AdaBST) and Gradient Boost (GRBST) for training the models for the detection of various anti-patterns considered in this study. Furthermore, while training the models, we split the data in the ratio of 80:20 for training and testing.

4   Experimental Results

This paper empirically investigates the effectiveness of three feature selection techniques and the original features, three data sampling techniques, the original data, four word embedding techniques, and nine classifier techniques in detecting web service anti-patterns. The total number of predictive models built to detect web service anti-patterns using text metrics as input are $4 \times 4 \times 4 \times 9 \times 4 = 2304$. Performance metrics such as accuracy, Area Under Curve (AUC) are used for evaluating the predictive ability of the models generated for the detection of web service anti-patterns. Table 1 shows the accuracy values for all the models generated to detect GOWS anti-pattern. From Table 1, we observed that the:

- We observed that the models trained on data after applying sampling techniques show good performance compared to the models trained on the original data.
- It is observed that the model developed by data after applying the data sampling technique SMOTE shows better performance.
- We observed that the anti-pattern prediction model developed using the features generated by applying the word embedding technique Tf-IDF shows the best performance with the mean accuracy value of 91.93.
- It is also observed that the mean accuracy value of the model developed using the features selected as significant features(SIGF) as input is higher than the models developed using the features selected by $CC_r a$, and PCA as input.
- We observed that the model trained using ensemble technique Extra Trees classifier with a mean accuracy of 95.35 is higher when compared to the models trained using other classifier techniques.

5   Comparative Analysis

This section compares the models' performance using various word embedding techniques, data sampling techniques, feature selection techniques, and classifier techniques to detect multiple anti-patterns using box-plots, descriptive statistics, and statistical hypothesis testing.

Table 1. AUC Value of GOWS anti-pattern

Feature selection	Data sampling technique	Word embedding technique	MNB	BNB	GNB	DT	BAGC	RF	EXTR	AdaBST	GrBST
AF	OD	tf-idf	0.55	0.91	0.89	0.89	0.91	0.91	0.91	0.90	0.86
AF	OD	cbow	0.62	0.87	0.66	0.88	0.91	0.90	0.91	0.85	0.88
AF	OD	skg	0.62	0.86	0.64	0.88	0.91	0.91	0.93	0.90	0.86
AF	OD	Glove	0.76	0.84	0.65	0.84	0.92	0.92	0.91	0.88	0.84
AF	SMOTE	tf-idf	0.98	0.99	0.98	0.92	0.95	0.97	0.99	0.95	0.90
AF	SMOTE	cbow	0.77	0.53	0.82	0.92	0.81	0.90	0.92	0.90	0.88
AF	SMOTE	skg	0.76	0.52	0.81	0.90	0.83	0.94	0.95	0.93	0.93
AF	SMOTE	Glove	0.77	0.52	0.80	0.91	0.81	0.93	0.96	0.93	0.90
AF	BSMOTE	tf-idf	0.98	0.99	0.97	0.94	0.96	0.98	0.99	0.93	0.91
AF	BSMOTE	cbow	0.79	0.53	0.85	0.95	0.84	0.96	0.94	0.93	0.93
AF	BSMOTE	skg	0.80	0.52	0.84	0.94	0.86	0.96	0.96	0.94	0.95
AF	BSMOTE	Glove	0.80	0.52	0.83	0.88	0.83	0.96	0.96	0.92	0.93
AF	ADASYN	tf-idf	0.98	1.00	0.98	0.92	0.92	0.99	0.99	0.95	0.86
AF	ADASYN	cbow	0.73	0.53	0.76	0.82	0.74	0.85	0.85	0.86	0.86
AF	ADASYN	skg	0.71	0.53	0.78	0.88	0.79	0.88	0.87	0.87	0.87
AF	ADASYN	Glove	0.72	0.52	0.74	0.83	0.73	0.89	0.93	0.82	0.82
SIGF	OD	tf-idf	0.93	0.99	0.72	0.92	0.91	0.91	0.91	0.91	0.89
SIGF	OD	cbow	0.62	0.87	0.64	0.89	0.91	0.90	0.89	0.90	0.88
SIGF	OD	skg	0.63	0.86	0.62	0.87	0.91	0.91	0.92	0.89	0.85
SIGF	OD	Glove	0.77	0.85	0.65	0.87	0.92	0.92	0.91	0.86	0.82
SIGF	SMOTE	tf-idf	0.99	0.99	0.96	0.92	0.96	0.97	0.99	0.96	0.91
SIGF	SMOTE	cbow	0.77	0.52	0.82	0.92	0.82	0.94	0.93	0.90	0.88
SIGF	SMOTE	skg	0.76	0.52	0.81	0.90	0.84	0.94	0.95	0.92	0.91
SIGF	SMOTE	Glove	0.77	0.52	0.80	0.91	0.82	0.93	0.94	0.89	0.92
SIGF	BSMOTE	tf-idf	0.99	0.99	0.96	0.93	0.98	0.97	0.98	0.92	0.92
SIGF	BSMOTE	cbow	0.79	0.52	0.85	0.96	0.84	0.96	0.96	0.93	0.93
SIGF	BSMOTE	skg	0.80	0.52	0.84	0.94	0.86	0.96	0.96	0.94	0.94
SIGF	BSMOTE	Glove	0.80	0.52	0.83	0.90	0.84	0.96	0.96	0.91	0.90
SIGF	ADASYN	tf-idf	0.99	0.99	0.96	0.91	0.89	0.97	0.99	0.90	0.87
SIGF	ADASYN	cbow	0.73	0.53	0.75	0.84	0.76	0.83	0.85	0.86	0.84
SIGF	ADASYN	skg	0.71	0.53	0.78	0.89	0.80	0.87	0.89	0.87	0.87
SIGF	ADASYN	Glove	0.72	0.52	0.75	0.84	0.75	0.91	0.91	0.84	0.74
CCRA	OD	tf-idf	0.95	0.97	0.90	0.90	0.91	0.91	0.91	0.92	0.92
CCRA	OD	cbow	0.91	0.89	0.65	0.87	0.91	0.89	0.91	0.88	0.86
CCRA	OD	skg	0.91	0.88	0.63	0.88	0.91	0.90	0.92	0.90	0.89
CCRA	OD	Glove	0.91	0.87	0.66	0.87	0.91	0.91	0.92	0.88	0.87
CCRA	SMOTE	tf-idf	0.97	0.98	0.96	0.93	0.96	0.96	0.99	0.89	0.90
CCRA	SMOTE	cbow	0.76	0.11	0.81	0.87	0.82	0.89	0.89	0.84	0.86
CCRA	SMOTE	skg	0.77	0.13	0.81	0.90	0.85	0.94	0.93	0.90	0.91
CCRA	SMOTE	Glove	0.77	0.52	0.80	0.93	0.81	0.94	0.95	0.90	0.90
CCRA	BSMOTE	tf-idf	0.97	0.98	0.96	0.93	0.98	0.98	0.99	0.93	0.92
CCRA	BSMOTE	cbow	0.79	0.12	0.86	0.93	0.83	0.94	0.93	0.89	0.88
CCRA	BSMOTE	skg	0.80	0.12	0.84	0.94	0.85	0.96	0.97	0.94	0.93
CCRA	BSMOTE	Glove	0.81	0.52	0.83	0.93	0.85	0.94	0.96	0.90	0.90
CCRA	ADASYN	tf-idf	0.96	0.97	0.97	0.89	0.90	0.96	0.98	0.89	0.80
CCRA	ADASYN	cbow	0.72	0.11	0.76	0.78	0.73	0.78	0.84	0.71	0.76
CCRA	ADASYN	skg	0.71	0.13	0.78	0.84	0.80	0.90	0.87	0.83	0.82
CCRA	ADASYN	Glove	0.72	0.52	0.76	0.78	0.78	0.86	0.90	0.88	0.78
PCA	OD	tf-idf	0.91	0.91	0.85	0.85	0.91	0.91	0.89	0.90	0.89
PCA	OD	cbow	0.91	0.90	0.81	0.84	0.91	0.90	0.92	0.92	0.89
PCA	OD	skg	0.91	0.91	0.75	0.85	0.91	0.92	0.89	0.89	0.90
PCA	OD	Glove	0.91	0.91	0.79	0.83	0.91	0.90	0.91	0.87	0.89
PCA	SMOTE	tf-idf	0.67	0.10	0.78	0.87	0.84	0.88	0.90	0.79	0.81
PCA	SMOTE	cbow	0.36	0.11	0.84	0.88	0.84	0.88	0.91	0.79	0.81
PCA	SMOTE	skg	0.38	0.11	0.82	0.90	0.85	0.93	0.94	0.91	0.90
PCA	SMOTE	Glove	0.29	0.11	0.79	0.86	0.84	0.90	0.94	0.81	0.85
PCA	BSMOTE	tf-idf	0.71	0.09	0.83	0.90	0.88	0.91	0.93	0.86	0.88
PCA	BSMOTE	cbow	0.41	0.10	0.87	0.92	0.86	0.93	0.94	0.86	0.87
PCA	BSMOTE	skg	0.53	0.10	0.86	0.93	0.85	0.94	0.94	0.91	0.90
PCA	BSMOTE	Glove	0.31	0.10	0.82	0.89	0.88	0.93	0.95	0.86	0.88
PCA	ADASYN	tf-idf	0.53	0.11	0.73	0.82	0.77	0.85	0.84	0.78	0.76
PCA	ADASYN	cbow	0.36	0.11	0.77	0.81	0.77	0.80	0.86	0.70	0.73
PCA	ADASYN	skg	0.39	0.12	0.77	0.80	0.80	0.84	0.89	0.77	0.82
PCA	ADASYN	Glove	0.28	0.10	0.71	0.83	0.76	0.83	0.86	0.78	0.72

5.1   Word Embedding Techniques

Figure 3 shows the performance values, i.e., Accuracy and AUC of the models developed using text metrics generated by applying different word embedding techniques as input using Box-plot diagrams. Table 2 shows the descriptive statistics for different word embedding techniques used in this work. From Fig. 3 and Table 2, we infer that the performance of the model developed using the text metrics generated by applying the Tf-IDF technique as input is showing better performance, with 91.93 mean, 96.44 median, 91.45 Q1, and 98.07 Q3 accuracy values. On the other hand, the model developed with the CBOW technique's metrics shows the worst performance with a mean accuracy value of 83.21. Further, We used Wilcoxon signed-rank test for statistically comparing the performance of the various web service anti-pattern prediction models developed using text metrics generated by applying different word embedding techniques as input and the original metrics. The null hypothesis considered in this paper is: "The web service anti-pattern prediction model trained using text metrics generated by applying different word embedding techniques as input are not significantly different". The considered null hypothesis is accepted if calculated p-values as ≥ 0.05. Table 3 shows the p-value obtained for the models developed using metrics generated by applying various word embedding techniques. A closer look at Table 3 showed that most of the comparison points have the p-value as '0', i.e., the considered hypothesis is rejected. Hence, we conclude a significant difference between the models' performance developed using the text metrics generated by applying different word embedding techniques as input.

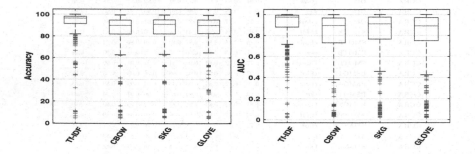

Fig. 3. Box-plot for word embedding techniques

Table 2. Descriptive statistics: word embedding technique

	Min	Max	Mean	Median	Q1	Q3
tf-idf	4.79	100.00	91.93	96.44	91.45	98.07
cbow	4.79	99.47	83.21	89.90	81.82	94.72
skg	5.05	99.46	83.73	90.88	82.07	94.95
Glove	4.52	99.20	84.26	89.90	82.27	94.81

Table 3. Statistical hypothesis: word embedding technique

	tf-idf	cbow	skg	Glove
tf-idf	1	0	0	0
cbow	0	1	0	1
skg	0	0	1	0
Glove	0	1	0	1

5.2 Data Sampling Techniques

Figure 4 shows the performance values, i.e., Accuracy and AUC of the models developed using the data after applying the data sampling techniques along with the original data using Box-plot diagrams. Table 4 shows the descriptive statistics of various data sampling techniques used in this study. From Fig. 4 and Table 4, we conclude that the performance of the models developed after applying data sampling techniques is better when compared to the performance of the models developed using the original data. We also observed that the model developed using SMOTE shows the best performance value with the mean accuracy value of 85.95. On the other hand, the model developed using actual data (OD) delivers the worst performance with the mean accuracy value of 79.71. Further, We used Wilcoxon signed-rank test to statistically compare the performance of the web service anti-pattern prediction models developed using the data after applying various data sampling techniques and the original data. The null hypothesis considered in this paper is: "The web service anti-pattern prediction model trained using the data after applying various data sampling techniques are not significantly different". The considered null hypothesis is accepted if calculated p-values as ≥ 0.05. Table 5 shows the p-value obtained for the models developed using data after applying various data sampling techniques. From Table 5, We observed that most of the comparison points have the p-value of '0'. Therefore, we conclude that the null hypothesis is rejected and that there is a significant difference between the performance of the models developed using the data after applying various data sampling techniques.

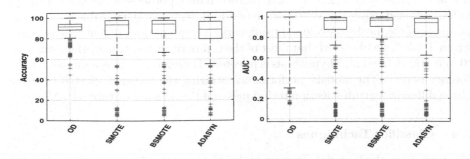

Fig. 4. Box-plots for data sampling techniques

Table 4. Descriptive statistics: data sampling techniques

	Min	Max	Mean	Median	Q1	Q3
OD	44.44	100.00	79.71	88.41	78.38	93.94
SMOTE	4.52	99.73	85.95	94.01	84.96	97.41
BSMOTE	4.79	99.73	85.80	93.88	84.81	97.33
ADASYN	4.80	100.00	82.52	88.66	79.59	96.34

Table 5. Statistical hypothesis: data sampling techniques

	OD	SMOTE	BSMOTE	ADASYN
OD	1	0	0	0
SMOTE	0	1	1	0
BSMOTE	0	1	1	0
ADASYN	0	0	0	1

5.3   Feature Selection Techniques

Figure 5 depicts the performance values, i.e., Accuracy and AUC of the models developed using the features selected by different feature selection techniques as input using Box-plot diagrams. Table 6 shows the descriptive statistics for the various feature selection techniques used in this study. Table 6 show that the mean accuracy value of the model developed using the features selected as significant features (SIGF) using various feature selection and ranking techniques as input is higher than the models developed using the features selected by $CC_r a$, and PCA as input. Furthermore, Fig. 5 shows that the inter-quartile range for the AUC value for the model generated using PCA is comparatively tall compared to the other models. This indicates that the performance parameters obtained using multiple executions in PCA are exhibiting more variation when compared to other models. Next, we compare the models' performance using the features selected by different feature selection techniques by using the Wilcoxon signed-rank test. The null hypothesis considered here is: "The performance of the anti-pattern prediction models developed using features selected by different feature selection techniques are not significantly different". The defined null-hypothesis is accepted if the p-value obtained using the Wilcoxon signed-rank test is ≥ 0.05. Table 7 shows the p-values of the models developed using various combinations of features as input. From Table 7, we observed that most of the comparison points have the p-value as '0,' i.e., the defined null-hypothesis is rejected. Therefore, there is a significant difference between the models' performance utilizing the features selected by using three different feature selection techniques and the original feature set (AF).

5.4   Classifier Techniques

Figure 6 shows the box-plot diagram of the AUC and the Accuracy of the classifier techniques. Table 8 shows the descriptive statistics for the models trained using

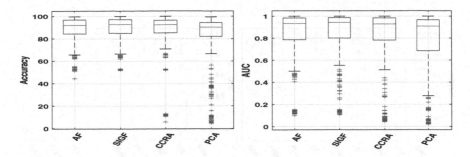

Fig. 5. Box-plots for feature selection techniques

Table 6. Descriptive statistics: feature selection techniques

	Min	Max	Mean	Median	Q1	Q3
AF	44.44	99.73	87.93	92.12	84.38	96.97
SIGF	51.80	100.00	88.72	92.85	84.93	97.22
CCRA	5.85	100.00	86.89	92.42	85.22	96.46
PCA	4.52	99.47	79.60	90.40	82.08	94.44

Table 7. Statistical hypothesis: feature selection techniques

	AF	SIGF	CCRA	PCA
AF	1	0	1	0
SIGF	0	1	0	0
CCRA	1	0	1	0
PCA	0	0	0	1

classifier techniques along with the ensemble techniques. From Table 8 and Fig. 6, we observed that the performance of the model trained using the Extra Trees classifier (EXTR) is higher when compared to the models trained using other classifier techniques. The model trained using the Extra Trees classifier (EXTR) shows good performance with a mean accuracy of 95.35, median accuracy of 96.06, Q1 93.09, and Q3 of 98.36. For Wilcoxon signed rank-sum test, we considered the hypothesis as: "The performance of the anti-pattern prediction models trained using various classifier techniques is not significantly different". The defined null-hypothesis is accepted if the p-value obtained using the Wilcoxon signed-rank test is ≥ 0.05 and is rejected if the p-value is '0'. Table 9 shows the p-values of the models trained using various classifier techniques. From Table 9, we observed that most of the comparison points have the p-value as '0', i.e., the defined null-hypothesis is rejected. Hence we conclude that there is a significant difference between the performance of the models trained using various classifier techniques.

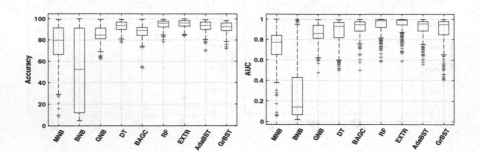

Fig. 6. Box-plots for classifier techniques

Table 8. Descriptive statistics: classifier techniques

	Min	Max	Mean	Median	Q1	Q3
MNB	8.24	99.20	74.47	79.72	66.49	91.41
BNB	4.52	100.00	56.48	52.55	11.99	91.16
GNB	62.12	99.45	85.37	84.57	81.22	91.15
DT	77.78	99.46	92.99	93.65	90.03	96.81
BAGC	53.72	99.73	87.93	89.10	84.41	91.93
RF	78.33	99.73	94.72	95.91	92.42	97.85
EXTR	83.70	100.00	95.35	96.06	93.09	98.36
AdaBST	69.72	99.19	93.00	93.94	90.18	96.97
GrBST	71.75	98.39	91.75	92.50	88.89	96.14

Table 9. Statistical hypothesis: classifier techniques

	MNB	BNB	GNB	DT	BAGC	RF	EXTR	AdaBST	GrBST
MNB	1	0	0	0	0	0	0	0	0
BNB	0	1	0	0	0	0	0	0	0
GNB	0	0	1	0	0	0	0	0	0
DT	0	0	0	1	0	0	0	0	0
BAGC	0	0	0	0	1	0	0	1	0
RF	0	0	0	0	0	1	0	0	0
EXTR	0	0	0	0	0	0	1	0	0
AdaBST	0	0	0	0	1	0	0	1	0
GrBST	0	0	0	0	0	0	0	0	1

6   Conclusion

In this work, we empirically investigated the correlation between the occurrence of anti-patterns and the text metrics. We also investigated the effectiveness of applying four word embedding techniques, three feature selection techniques, three data sampling techniques, and nine classifier techniques to detect web service anti-patterns. Our main findings in this study are:

- Our analysis proved the relationship between anti-patterns in WSDL files and the text metrics generated from the WSDL file.
- We observed that the models trained on data after applying sampling techniques show good performance compared to the models trained on the original data.
- It is also observed that the mean accuracy value of the model developed using the features selected as significant features(SIGF) using various feature selection and ranking techniques as input is higher than the models developed using the features selected by CC_ra, and PCA as input.
- It is observed that the model developed by data after applying the data sampling technique SMOTE shows better performance.
- We observed that the anti-pattern prediction model developed using the features generated by applying the word embedding technique Tf-IDF shows the best performance.
- We observed that the model trained using the ensemble technique Extra Trees classifier is better than the models trained using other classifier techniques.

References

1. Alakuş, C.: Neighborhood construction-based multi-objective evolutionary clustering algorithm with feature selection. Master's thesis (2018)
2. Borovits, N., et al.: Deepiac: deep learning-based linguistic anti-pattern detection in IAC. In: Proceedings of the 4th ACM SIGSOFT International Workshop on Machine-Learning Techniques for Software-Quality Evaluation, pp. 7–12 (2020)
3. Jaafar, F., Guéhéneuc, Y.-G., Hamel, S., Khomh, F., Zulkernine, M.: Evaluating the impact of design pattern and anti-pattern dependencies on changes and faults. Empirical Softw. Eng. **21**(3), 896–931 (2015). https://doi.org/10.1007/s10664-015-9361-0
4. Kumar, L., Sureka, A.: An empirical analysis on web service anti-pattern detection using a machine learning framework. In: 2018 IEEE 42nd Annual Computer Software and Applications Conference (COMPSAC), vol. 1, pp. 2–11. IEEE (2018)
5. Pietrzak, B., Walter, B.: Leveraging code smell detection with inter-smell relations. In: Abrahamsson, P., Marchesi, M., Succi, G. (eds.) XP 2006. LNCS, vol. 4044, pp. 75–84. Springer, Heidelberg (2006). https://doi.org/10.1007/11774129_8
6. Schulte, R.W., Natis, Y.V.: Service oriented architectures, part 1. Gartner, SSA Research Note SPA-401-068 (1996)
7. Segev, A., Toch, E.: Context-based matching and ranking of web services for composition. IEEE Trans. Serv. Comput. **2**(3), 210–222 (2009)

8. Tummalapalli, S., Kumar, L., Bhanu Murthy, N.L.: Detection of web service anti-patterns using machine learning framework. In: Singh, J., Bilgaiyan, S., Mishra, B.S.P., Dehuri, S. (eds.) A Journey Towards Bio-inspired Techniques in Software Engineering. ISRL, vol. 185, pp. 189–210. Springer, Cham (2020). https://doi.org/10.1007/978-3-030-40928-9_10

9. Tummalapalli, S., Kumar, L., Neti, L.B.M.: An empirical framework for web service anti-pattern prediction using machine learning techniques. In: 2019 9th Annual Information Technology, Electromechanical Engineering and Microelectronics Conference (IEMECON), pp. 137–143. IEEE (2019)

10. Tummalapalli, S., Kumar, L., Murthy, N.L.B., Krishna, A.: Detection of web service anti-patterns using neural networks with multiple layers. In: Yang, H., Pasupa, K., Leung, A.C.-S., Kwok, J.T., Chan, J.H., King, I. (eds.) ICONIP 2020. CCIS, vol. 1333, pp. 571–579. Springer, Cham (2020). https://doi.org/10.1007/978-3-030-63823-8_65

11. Velioğlu, S., Selçuk, Y.E.: An automated code smell and anti-pattern detection approach. In: 2017 IEEE 15th International Conference on Software Engineering Research, Management and Applications (SERA), pp. 271–275. IEEE (2017)

A Cost Estimating Method for Agile Software Development

Shariq Aziz Butt[1](✉), Sanjay Misra[2], Gabriel Piñeres-Espitia[3], Paola Ariza-Colpas[3], and Mayank Mohan Sharma[4]

[1] The University of Lahore, Lahore, Pakistan
[2] Covenant University, Ota, Nigeria
sanjay.misra@covenantuniversity.edu.ng
[3] Universidad de la Costa, CUC, Barranquilla, Colombia
{gpineres1,pariza1}@cuc.edu.co
[4] Zillow Inc, San Francisco, USA
mayankmohans@zillowgroup.com

Abstract. In every software development project, the software effort estimating procedure is an important process in software engineering and always critical. The consistency of effort and timeline estimation, along with several factors, determines whether a project succeeds or fails. Both academics and professionals worked on the estimation approaches in software engineering. But, all these approaches have many problems that need to be addressed. One of the most difficult aspects of software engineering is estimating effort in agile development. This study aims to provide an effort estimation method for agile software development projects. Because in software engineering, the agile method is widely used for the development of software applications. The development and usage of the agile method are described in depth in this study. The framework is configured with empirical data gathered by projects from the software industry. The test findings reveal that the estimation method has great estimation accuracy in respect of mean magnitude of relative error (MMRE) and Prediction of Error PRED (n). The suggested approach achieves more accuracy for effort estimation as compare to others.

Keywords: Software effort estimate · Agile development · User stories · Metrics and measurement · Maintainability

1 Introduction

Since the 1940s, when the software era began, estimating software costs has been a critical but challenging task. Because the scale and significance of software applications have increased, so has the accuracy of software cost estimation. Software development professionals and academics are now working on developing techniques to measure development costs and schedules throughout the early 1950s. In the last 3 decades, software effort estimation techniques have been reported in the existing research. On the other hand, the domain of software effort estimation is still in its infancy [1, 2].

© Springer Nature Switzerland AG 2021
O. Gervasi et al. (Eds.): ICCSA 2021, LNCS 12955, pp. 231–245, 2021.
https://doi.org/10.1007/978-3-030-87007-2_17

Despite the introduction of various software cost estimation approaches that are successfully used in conventional software development, the complexity of modern software development techniques has resulted in a circumstance in which the usefulness of current effort prediction techniques tends to be limited [3]. One major challenge is agile software development. This approach is focused on a completely different definition of application development which can be measured using the FP analysis approach, nor can traditional effort estimation approaches that were designed primarily for sequential application development methods be used. As a modern software engineering approach, that is, agile development has received a lot of attention. It emphasizes good developer communication, fast product delivery, and change on request as the core components of agile development. For industrial applications, agile development practices are becoming more prevalent. The usage of effort estimation techniques in these types of projects is a challenging but essential process. Traditional estimation techniques necessarily require well-defined specifications. Agile methodologies do not support this activity. Changing demands, on the other hand, is viewed as a significant problem. Both of these factors are rendering estimation difficult in agile development. This paper provides an overall view of the current estimation methods and explains how to estimate agile development projects in depth [4, 5]. We are also proposing an estimation technique in this paper and used it for a case study. We also use a case study in this study and explain the outcomes in detail.

The paper contains 5 sections. Next, Sects. 2 and 3 summarize the works on cost estimation techniques and agile methodologies—Sects. 4, 5, and 6 present the proposed work, experimentations and conclusion, and future work.

2   Cost Estimation Techniques

To measure project costs, cost estimation methods, also known as model-dependent estimation methods that integrate statistics from previous projects with mathematical equations. As an input, these methods include the size of the system. COCOMO, SLIM, RCA PRICE-S, EER-SEM, and ESTIMACS are the most popular model-based techniques. Regression-based models, learning-oriented models, expert-based approaches, and composite Bayesian methods are some of the current effort estimation techniques. The regression methodology is used in the majority of software estimation models. Regression models are typically built using previously collected data from completed projects and the development of regression equations that describe the relationships between various variables. The mathematical method is based on the new project scope. To make predictions, this model is assessed using regression data. In such methods, the effort for efficient software development is merely a dependent variable for regression equations involving some expected variables such as size, effort adaptation factor, scale factor, and so on [6]. In certain cases, therefore, regression models require the fulfillment of specific requirements. Boehm and Sullivan (1999) addressed these conditions, which are focused on their experience with regression-based methods. These standard conditions contain the availability of a considerable dataset, with the absence of missing data objects, the absence of outliers, and the absence of correlation between the predictor factors. Ordinary least-squares regression (OLS), classification and regression trees (CART), step-wise examination of variance for inconsistent data sets (stepwise ANOVA), configuration of CART with OLS regression and comparison, multiple linear regression, and stepwise regression are all examples of regression models [7].

Other kinds of models, known as Learning-oriented methods, are focused on prior estimation knowledge and learning. These approaches aim to automate the estimating process through training themselves to create automated models based on existing experiences. These methods are able to incremental learning and refinement as new data is presented with time. Artificial intelligence methods, artificial neural networks, particular scenario analysis, machine learning techniques, decision-tree learning, fuzzy logic approaches, content knowledge, and linear regression are all examples of learning-oriented modeling techniques. COCOMO, SLIM, RCA PRICE-S, SEER-SEM, and ESTIMACS are the most popular model-based approaches. Depending on criteria like the size and required functionality of the application, these calculation approaches provide an estimated cost, effort, or time of a project. "Comparative analysis with previous related projects depending on individual memory" was discovered to be an effective expertise-based method. Where neither quantified quantitative evidence is available, expertise-based methods are beneficial [8].

They offer a simple, low-cost, and extremely productive method. Analogy-based estimation is another estimation method of estimating software effort. The method looks at previous projects and is using the details obtained as a rough approximation for the current project. The Checkpoint approach is a representation of a software estimation technique dependent on analogy. Heuristics are extracted from real project data or a formalization of expert analysis in this method. Some type of project data and details is being used to extracting these heuristics. The performance of these heuristics can then be used to estimating efficiency, quality, and scale. Expert opinion estimation is another common estimation method within software effort estimate and it is focused on the collective expertise of teams of expertise to generate project estimates. Where the estimation method is largely focused on "non-explicit, non-recoverable reasoning mechanisms," such as observation and experience, this method has been used.

Experts have chastised expert judgment methods regarding their dependency on human memory and the absence of replicability of these memory-based methods. Still, studies reveal that it is the most popular method for application development and estimation. Expert decision methods include the Delphi method and job breakdown structure (WBS), top-down and bottom-up estimation, and thumb rule [9].

The advantages of expertise-dependent estimation approaches are merged to implement a new semiformal estimating approach known as the Bayesian approach. The bayesian analysis considers that almost all estimation methods require datathat is either of limited quality or incomplete. This approach incorporates expert judgment to manage missing data and enables a better rigorous estimation method. The COCOMO II model was developed using Bayesian analysis, which is used in multiple scientific fields. A hybrid estimation method is Cost Estimation, Benchmarking, and Risk Analysis (COBRA) [10].

3 Agile Software Development

Agile software development is a set of iterative and gradual application development approaches in which specifications and ideas emerge from collaboration within self-organizing, cross-functional teams. Evolutionary planning, evolutionary growth and execution, a time-boxed iterative strategy, and fast and scalable responsiveness to change are encouraged. It has a theoretical model that encourages foreseen experiences during the creation process. In 2001, the Agile Manifesto invented the term. Scrum, Crystal Clear, Extreme Programming, Adaptive Software Development, Features Oriented Development, and Dynamic Systems Development Process are examples of earlier lightweight approaches. Following the publication of the Agile Manifesto in 2001, these are now commonly pointed to as agile methodologies. Methods vary from adaptive to predictive. In this continuum, agile strategies are on the adaptive side. Adaptive approaches concentrate on rapidly adjusting to changing circumstances. When a project's requirements change, an agile team must respond as well. Predictive strategies, on the other hand, concentrate on meticulously planning the future. For the duration of the development phase, a predictive team may disclose precisely what functionality and activities are expected. Predictive teams have a hard time modifying functionality [10].

Agile Software Processes Features
Modularity: it is a significant aspect of the agile software development process since it enables a process to be split down into modules called activities.

Iterative: Agile software systems are iterative, based on short intervals. A specific collection of tasks is performed during each loop.

Time-Bound: Each iteration and scheduling has a time limit. Sprint is the name given to this period.

Parsimony: is a key component of agile software development. That is, they only need a limited number of activities to reduce risks and accomplish their objectives.

Adaptive: The agile process adapts to new threats that are discovered through any iteration. Likewise, agile processes can handle any new operation or changes to existing ones [11].

Incremental: Agile processes are incremental, rather than trying to construct the whole system at once. Instead, it divides the complex structure into increments that can be worked on in sequence, at various times, and at different speeds.

Convergent: The central tenet of agile development is to get the structure closer to reality. This aim is attained by using all available strategies to achieve performance as quickly as possible [12].

People-Oriented: Agile methods emphasize people over processes and technologies. They change organically as a result of adaptation. Motivated developers increase their efficiency and performance. After all, they are the most skilled people in the industry to create these improvements.

Collaborative: Agile methods enable team members to interact with one another. Any software development project needs effective communication. Collaboration is needed to quickly integrate a large project, although increments are now being created in parallel.

3.1 Effort Estimation in Agile Modeling

In waterfall, the manager calculates a team member's productivity potential by calculating how long those activities may take and then assigning work depending on the team member's maximum time available. In regard to evaluating a team member's ability, agile methodology provides a specific method. To begin with, it assigned work to an overall team rather than a single person. This stresses the importance of group effort from a theoretical perspective. Second, it declines to calculate work in terms of effort due to doing so would adversely affect the self-organization necessary for the methodology's effectiveness. This is a substantial departure from the waterfall: rather than a boss, calculating time on behalf of others and setting priorities based on conjecture, Scrum team members determine their own tasks based on commitment and degree of complexity [13].

There is no only method for teams to quantify their work in Agile Methodology. It recommends that teams cannot calculate effort in terms of time but rather use a much more obfuscated measure. Numeric scaling, t-shirt size, the Fibonacci series are all common estimation approaches. The most significant thing is that the team has shared knowledge of the scale it employs. Therefore each team member is familiar with the scale's values.

The team gathers for the Sprint Planning Session to quantify their commitment to the user stories in the backlog. The product client requires these forecasts in order for him or her to efficiently priority products in the backlog and, as a response, predict delivery depending on the team's velocity. This necessitates an accurate evaluation of the work's complexity by the Product Owner. To avoid forcing a team to decrease its commitment evaluation and bring on new work, it is suggested that the Product Owner does not follow the estimations. And when a team determines itself, measures must be taken to decrease the cost of influencing those results. As a result, it is suggested that all team members reveal their predictions at the same time. This method parallels a game of poker in that everyone "shows their hands" at the same time [14].

And when teams have a common interpretation of their size, they cannot help but make various estimates. It also takes several rounds of calculation to conclude in a single effort estimate which represents the entire team's perception of a story's complexity. Experienced teams, on the other hand, should be able to reach an agreement after merely a few sessions of planning poker. Usually, effort calculation occurs throughout Release Preparation at the start of the new iteration. The figure depicts a part of the XP-Project [15].

Research Problem
The majority of current effort estimation methods were designed to help conventional sequential application development methodologies, while Agile Software Development is an iterative process. If conventional methods are used to estimate the commitment of agile software projects, the findings would almost certainly be unreliable. The existing practice of effort estimation for agile development projects, on the other hand, is focused on a complete iteration. As a result, an effort estimation method is required to estimate the development effort for agile software projects depending on Agile Software Development features [13].

4 Proposed Model

The majority of Software Effort Estimating Models estimate a project's budget, length, and resources. In the case of Agile Development, however, this will not be the case. There are some main distinctions within the agile and conventional approaches to team organization.

4.1 Agile Teams Are Whole Teams

The whole team is an Extreme Programming (XP) activity that suggests getting enough expertise inside the team to complete the mission. The idea is that the software team possesses the necessary testing, databases, user interface, and other expertise and does not depend on external experts or specialists' teams.

4.2 Agile Teams Are Formed (Mostly) of Generalized Specialists

A generalizing professional, also known as a craftsperson, is someone who has one or even more technological skill sets to which they can directly contribute to the team has had at least a basic understanding of the software development and the application domain wherein they operate, and most significantly consistently tries to learn new expertise in both their current professions and other fields. Evidently, new IT specialists and experienced IT professionals will have to work for this objective because they have often experienced just one field. The sweet spot among the two extremes of expertise is generalizing with experts.

4.3 Agile Teams Are Stable

Agilests realize that shifting team composition can be counterproductive to a project's progress.

A performance we work hard to maintain our team as stable as possible, which is much simpler to do when people are generalizing experts.

Since there is no requirement to measure the project's manpower needs, the suggested approach is designed to measure the Agile Software 'project's delivery time and expense.

Agile professionals, particularly Scrum professionals, have suggested a range of scales for measuring project expected effort, such as:

- On a level of one to three, we rate the effort, with one being the minimum and three being the maximum.
- The Fibonacci series [1, 2, 3, 5, 8.... ... so on] is used. So, for example, a Story rated as eight is one that is too big to measure accurately and must be graded as an epic and broken down into shorter stories.

Other approaches exist, but these are two widely prominent. In both cases, the calculations are not formulated in terms of time modules; instead, they are simply measures of Relative Effort, that is, a reasonable yardstick for comparison. Both of these approaches are successful and commonly used, but they ignore the fundamental factors that influence effort and uncertainty. As a result, we created a new model which we think is very successful. This method is also consistent with how to build Plot, defect, and risk rankings [16].

4.4 Determining the Effort

A number of factors influence our potential to calculate effort precisely. To produce reliable and efficient estimates, precise prediction requires a multivariate model. The problem is deciding which dimensions to calculate. Suppose we use a SWOT analysis to category the scenarios based on internal vs. external factors. In that case, we can exclude several possibilities by concentrating our focus on the factors we can control and paying little consideration to the factors we cannot. We restrict the vectors to two to make the method as easy as practicable so that we use it and do not try to avoid it because 'it's too complicated. The use of two vectors is also consistent with the rest of the technique.

4.5 Story Size

The project size is a rough approximation of the work's relative size in terms of real development time. Table 1 displays 5 elements that have been allocated to various types of user stories based on their scale. The team has the potential to adjust the wording of the Guideline summary and redefine the requirements.

Table 1. Scaling of stories.

Value	Rules
5	• An incredibly long story • Moreover broad to estimation correctly • Almost definitely could be divided into a series of minor stories • Could be separated into a new project
4	• A huge size of story • Needs a developer's concentrated effort over a prolonged period of time (think and over a week of task) • Try splitting it up into a series of shorter stories
3	• Abstemiously huge stories • Consider working for two to five days
2	• Plan on putting in a day or two of effort
1	• A very short tale with a very low effort amount • Imagine working for just a few hours

4.6 Complexity

This is the level of difficulty in one or both the Story's specifications and its technical complexity. The estimate's uncertainty causes concern; the higher the difficulty, the greater the uncertainty. Table 2 displays the five meanings that have been allocated to user stories based on their existence. These rules, such as the Story Length table, are not set in stone. It can be tweaked through the team, but we have classified them to account for all aspects of agile software development [17].

Table 2. Scaling of user stories as per difficulty.

Value	Guidelines
5	• Exceptionally difficult • There are several needs on other stories, processes, and subcomponents • Signifies a valuable set of skills or expertise that's also missing from the team • It's complicated to define how difficult it is to say a story • Many unknowns • Important refactoring is required • Substantial research is needed • It necessitates making tough decisions • Relative to the story, the story's consequences have a huge influence
4	• Huge Difficult • There are several dependency on other stories, processes, or subcomponents • Signifies a valuable set of skills or expertise that's not well-represented on the team • The product owner may find it challenging to accurately explain the story • A considerable amount of refactoring is needed • Completion necessitates specialized programming skills • It necessitates some tough decisions
3	• Interconnections on other stories, structures, or subsystems are medium • Signifies a relatively good skill set or expertise within the team • The owner finds it challenging to correctly interpret the tale • Completion necessitates intermediate technical skills • The story's implications have a minor influence outside of the story
2	• Technical and business specifications that are easy to comprehend • To finish, you'll need basic to moderate tech skills • The Story's impact are mostly entirely contained inside the Story
1	• There are very few, if any, unknown factors in this situation • There are no ambiguities in the technological and business specifications • The Story's impact are entirely contained inside the Story

The effort of a specific User Story is estimated with these two parameters by the following basic equation as shown in Eq. 1:

$$Effort\ of\ Suer\ Story = ES = Complexity \times Size \tag{1}$$

The overall project effort will become the amount of all actual customer story efforts as per Eq. 2.

$$E_f = \sum_{x=1}^{n} (ES)_x \tag{2}$$

The cumulative project commitment would be equal to the number of all client story efforts.

4.7 Defining Agile Velocity:

The length is measured in the unit of effort, and the time (numerator) is the duration of the sprint. As a result, the velocity is measured as follows in Eq. 3:

$$V = \frac{User\ Stories\ Completed}{Sprint\ Time} \tag{3}$$

In a standard sprint, the Measured Velocity is literally the number of user stories of effort your team achieves. Velocity is classified as the amount of product backlog effort the team may manage in one module of time in Agile.

4.8 Velocity Configuration

Before you start calibration, you must finish the optimization method. Therefore, in our calibration, there are focused on two aspects.

i.   The Friction or Persistent Factors that minimize Project Velocity also are a persistent drag on performance.
ii. The Variable or Dynamic Factors which trigger the Project Velocity to be abnormal by decelerating the project or members of the team.

Prior to calibration, optimize both of these variables to increase the accuracy of the velocity measurement. It is necessary to get a reliable Velocity because it's the base for several Agile and Scrum parameters.

Numerous powers can impact the team's velocity in software development. It is your responsibility as a team leader, project manager, or manager to reduce external factors that negatively affect the team's speed.

- Staff placement is the team made up of the right required skills?
- Improvements to the procedures, such as agile techniques, build, deliver, testing, and so on.
- Interruptions, noise, insufficient ventilation, low lighting, awkward seating and chairs, insufficient hardware or software, and so on are all examples of environmental causes.
- Team dynamics certain team members could not get along with others.

The environment influences majority of friction forces. Their consequences are long-lasting. They are often usually the easiest to deal with. Friction forces are typically weak forces on their own. They can have a substantial effect when added together. They must be removed or minimized to achieve maximum Team Velocity. The sum of all four fraction factors is used to measure friction, as presented in Eq. 4.

$$FR = \sum_{x=1}^{4} (FF)_x \tag{4}$$

4.9 Variable or Dynamic Forces:

Forces that are complex or dynamic are often volatile and unpredictable. They slow down the project and will its velocity. Their effects may be dramatic at times; however, they are typically temporary. For our objectives, we are looking at the cost (in terms of productivity) to members of the team and the team as a whole. If you cannot completely eradicate a force that decreases velocity, render it as stable and accurate as possible (minimal and infrequent deceleration). Your velocity would be more consistent and reliable if the force is stable and predictive [18].

- Team changes: new members, changes, and shifts in duties and responsibilities.
- New software: Discovering new programming tools, database systems, languages, and so on necessitates a reduction in velocity until they are mastered.
- Outside-of-project tasks: Team members carry on additional duties outside of the project. Switching projects can have a considerable impact on efficiency.
- Stakeholders: Stakeholders can be slow to respond to requests for information from developers or testers, causing delays. They may well have unrealistic expectations from the teams as well.
- Changing project requirements: New project requirements can necessitate expertise that the team lacks or is lacking. Obtaining the expertise, whether by introducing new team members or acquiring the skill set of a current team member, would affect productivity.

Table 3 shows the force factors that are variable or adaptive. Again, the same comparison is used to assign a value as it can be for size.

Table 3. Friction factors

Variable factor	Moderate	High	Very high
Changes in the Team to Be Required	1	0.87	0.86
New Tools are Introduced	1	0.88	0.74
Activities of members of the team beyond of the project	1	0.86	0.98
Stakeholder responses is supposed to take longer than expected	1	0.98	0.77
Inconsistency in the details is to be anticipated	1	0.85	0.87
Changes in the environment that are anticipated	1	0.88	0.84

The product among all six predictor factors is used to measure Dynamic Force (DF), as mentioned in the Eq. 5.

$$DF = \sum_{x=1}^{9}(VF)_x \tag{5}$$

The frequency of negative velocity eventually became known as deceleration. Deceleration is the result of friction and Dynamic Forces acting on the velocity in our scenario. It's estimated as follows Eq. 6:

$$D = FR \times DF \tag{6}$$

We quantify Final Velocity in addition to adapting velocity towards a more predictable range in Eq. 7:

$$V = (Vx)^D \tag{7}$$

4.10 Completion Time

The time required to complete the project time of completion as per Eq. 8:

$$T = \frac{E}{V} \ days$$
$$= \frac{\sum_{x=1}^{n}(ES)_x}{(Vx)^D} days \tag{8}$$

In this computation, as mentioned in Eq. 9, the unit of T is days that may be transformed to months by dividing by the number of working days per month. Here the *WD* is describing the working days.

$$T = \frac{\sum_{x=1}^{n}(ES)_x}{(Vx)^D} \times \frac{1}{WD} \ days \tag{9}$$

4.11 Cost of Development

While there is no specific attribute in the method to estimate cost, some of the Agile Software Development team is also present. We performed a survey of 14 software industries at CMMI level 3 to determine monthly spending per project using Project Team Salary as the component. Because some industries have multiple teams working on multiple projects at the same time, all costs have been estimated for one project per month. Table 4, the average monthly costs, as well as their ratios to Team Salary, are discussed.

The Development Cost are computed using the Net Ratio of the Table 5 is as follows:

$$Cost = 2.933 \times TS \times T \tag{10}$$

Here T is the computed time in months, and TS is the monthly Team Salary mentioned in Eq. 10.

Table 4. monthly average costs, their ratios to Team Salary.

Costs	Amount	Ratio as per 'Team's Salary
Team salary	457897	0.787
Non IT members salary	147895	0.558
Tools	25436	0.444
Softwares	7845	0.478
Rent	12456	0.245
Traveling	32456	0.024
Repair and maintenance	7854	0.255
Changes accommodation	2547	0.142

4.12   Uncertainty of Calculation

The estimated time is only likely predicted when you are not assured with estimates. For example, when you are 100 percent assured in your estimate, the estimated time would also be the highest possible time; however, if you are not assured with your estimation method, the estimated time will only be unlikely predicted. Based on the level of assurance, the times vary in this situation. This variation is known as the span of uncertainty. Optimism Point is the lower limit of this range, and Pessimistic Point is the upper bound. We present a new variable with Confidence Level (CL) that will be used to estimate optimistic and Pessimistic Time in calculating the esteem impact on time as stated in Eq. 11.

$$Time_{prob} = T$$

$$Time_{prob} = \frac{1 - (100 - CL)}{100} \times T \qquad (11)$$

Summary of the Model

- Number of User Stories
- Work Days per Month (WD)
- Monthly Staff Pay
- Number of Days inside a Sprint (Sprint Time)
- Units of Effort Done by the Team in a Sprint
- Estimator's Estimation Confidence (CL).
- Metric for Story Size (Table 1)
- Metric for Story Complexity (Table 2)
- Metric for Friction Factor (Table 3)
- Metric for Variable Factors (Table 4)

5   Evaluation

Completion time (T) is estimated as:

$$T = \frac{\sum_{x=1}^{n}(ES)_x}{(Vx)^D} \times \frac{1}{WD}\ days$$

5.1   Case Study

The total number of user stories is 54.
Sprint Size = 14 Days Team Velocity = 52.
No of Working days per Month = 20.
Monthly Team Salary = 450000.
85 percent assurance level in estimates.

5.2   Outcomes

EFFORT = 320 SP.
INITIL VELOCITY = 4.7

Table 5. Development Cost are computed using the Net Ratio.

P.No	Effort	Vi	D	V	Size of sprint	Working days	Team's Salary	Act: Time	Est time	Real Cost	Calculated cost	Time MRE	Cost MRE
1	145	3.1	.576	2.6	10	22	240000	54	67	1300000	1134105.13	6.84	13.84
2	211	4.5	.612	3.4	10	21	250000	80	92	1500000	1571554.8	12.84	4.13
3	154	5	.787	2.2	10	22	240000	67	43	1100000	781058.42	6.23	1.88
4	212	3.4	.775	2.7	10	22	200000	75	78	2200000	3013676.1	1.25	5.54
5	135	3.8	.814	3.1	10	22	400000	29	38	640000	565172.21	8.257	8.73
6	248	5.2	.814	4.5	10	22	300000	72	84	3100000	278400.74	3.28	8.43
7	98	3.1	.848	2.3	10	22	160000	46	28	500000	451022.75	18.13	8.97
8	146	2.7	.724	4	10	22	270000	82	93	2700000	1523187.3	8.56	10.23
9	75	4.8	.857	2.3	10	22	290000	45	48	600000	416175.47	3.78	2.15
10	123	4.7	.847	2.1	10	22	150000	73	45	2100000	1356288.4	5.36	4.48
11	254	5.7	.747	4.0	10	22	340000	36	39	700000	678821.11	7.67	1.76
12	143	4.8	.754	3.8	10	22	220000	28	29	540000	486251.52	6.32	7.24
13	112	4.8	.864	2.7	10	22	210000	41	46	500000	547583.57	9.264	11.16
14	85	2.7	.882	1.5	10	22	100000	41	35	300000	383636.54	14.12	2.45
15	73	3.6	.854	1.8	10	22	100000	35	33	240000	321452.12	5.67	4.46
16	278	6	.921	3.7	10	22	230000	12	12	3000000	1782574.3	9.12	1.52
17	201	5	.751	2.7	10	22	280000	48	51	700000	881740.21	3.45	3.56
18	152	7	.651	2.6	10	22	240000	43	42	2000000	852765.53	3.73	4.70
19	124	3	.701	1.5	10	22	120000	71	65	1400000	1544111.18	4	2.42

(*continued*)

Table 5. (*continued*)

P.No	Effort	Vi	D	V	Size of sprint	Working days	Team's Salary	Act: Time	Est time	Real Cost	Calculated cost	Time MRE	Cost MRE
20	245	2.4	.607	3.8	10	22	320000	65	42	700000	763438.54	7.81	5.68

FRICTION FACTOR (FR) = 0.612413.
DYNAMIC FORCES = 0.87658.
DECELRATION = 0.531456.
VELOCITY = 2.4
TIME = 5.2 MONTHS.
COST = 5152552.18.
$Time_{Prob}$ = 5.1 MONTHS.
$Time_{Optim}$ = 5.4 MONTHS.
$Time_{Pessi}$ = 6.8 MONTHS.
$Cost_{Prob}$ = 5132782.18.
$Cost_{Optim}$ = 4628615.25.
$Cost_{Pessi}$ = 5674727.31.

6   Conclusion

A software effort estimation modeling for Agile Software projects is discussed in this work. The model's prediction is based on User Stories. The concept is designed to meet most of the features of agile methodology, particularly updated versions and iteration, with the aim to address the major issues faced by agilests. We have designed this method for the accurate estimation based on 'developer's expertise and experience of working and skills to predict the accurate estimation of the effort to done a user story. We have revealed that the estimation of the user stories are almost accurate as per the method suggested in this paper. Due to the biased nature of the developers and different levels of expertise, the estimation needs a significant method.

References

1. Popli, R., Chauhan, N.: Sprint-point based estimation in scrum In: Proceedings of IEEE Conference, GLA University, Mathura, 9–10 March 2013
2. Bhalereo, S., Ingle, M.: Incorporating vital factors in agile estimation through algorithmic methods Int. J. Comput. Sci. Appl. Technomath. Res. Foundat. **6**(1) 85–97 (2009)
3. Misra, S., Omorodion, F.M., Damasevicius, R.: Metrics for measuring progress and productivity in agile software development. In: Abraham, A., Sasaki, H., Rios, R., Gandhi, N., Singh, U., Ma, K. (eds.) IBICA 2020. AISC, vol. 1372, pp. 469–478. Springer, Cham (2021). https://doi.org/10.1007/978-3-030-73603-3_44
4. Attarzadeh, I., Hock Ow, S.: Software development effort estimation based on a new fuzzy logic model. Int. J. Comput. Theory Eng. **1**, 1793–8201 (2009)
5. Butt, S.A., Misra, S., Anjum, M.W., Hassan, S.A.: Agile project development issues during COVID-19. In: International Conference on Lean and Agile Software Development, pp. 59–70. Springer, Cham (2021). https://doi.org/10.1007/978-3-030-67084-9_4

6. Misra, S.: Pair programming: an empirical investigation in an agile software development environment. In: Przybyłek, A., Miler, J., Poth, A., Riel, A. (eds.) LASD 2021. LNBIP, vol. 408, pp. 195–199. Springer, Cham (2021). https://doi.org/10.1007/978-3-030-67084-9_13

7. Abioye, T.E., Arogundade, O.T., Misra, S., Akinwale, A.T., Adeniran, O.J.: Toward ontology-based risk management framework for software projects: an empirical study. J. Softw. Evol. Process 32(12), e2269 (2020)

8. Rimal, Y., Pandit, P., Gocchait, S., Butt, S.A., Obaid, A.J.: Hyperparameter determines the best learning curve on single, multi-layer and deep neural network of student grade prediction of Pokhara University Nepal. J. Phys. Conf. Ser. 1804(1), 012054 (2021). IOP Publishing

9. Butt, S.A., Abbas, S.A., Ahsan, M.: Software development life cycle & software quality measuring types. Asian J. Math. Comput. Res 11(2), 112–122 (2016)

10. Przybyłek, A., Kowalski, W.: Utilizing online collaborative games to facilitate agile software development. In: 2018 Federated Conference on Computer Science and Information Systems (FedCSIS), pp. 811–815. IEEE, September 2018

11. Butt, S.A., Gochhait, S., Andleeb, S., Adeel, M.: Games features for health disciplines for patient learning as entertainment. In: Digital Entertainment, pp. 65–86. Palgrave Macmillan, Singapore (2021).

12. Przybyłek, A., Kotecka, D.: Making agile retrospectives more awesome. In: 2017 Federated Conference on Computer Science and Information Systems (FedCSIS), pp. 1211–1216. IEEE, September 2017

13. Behera, R.K., Jena, M., Rath, S.K., Misra, S.: Co-LSTM: Convolutional LSTM model for sentiment analysis in social big data. Inf. Process. Manage. 58(1), 102435 (2021)

14. Kumari, A., Behera, R.K., Sahoo, K.S., Nayyar, A., Kumar Luhach, A., Prakash Sahoo, S.: Supervised link prediction using structured-based feature extraction in social network. Concurrency Comput. Pract. Exp. e5839 (2020)

15. Anusuya, V., Gomathi, V.: An efficient technique for disease prediction by using enhanced machine learning algorithms for categorical medical dataset. Inf. Technol. Control 50(1), 102–122 (2021)

16. Behera, R.K., Shukla, S., Rath, S.K., Misra, S.: Software reliability assessment using machine learning technique. In: International Conference on Computational Science and Its Applications, pp. 403–411. Springer, Cham (2018). https://doi.org/10.1007/978-3-319-95174-4_32

17. Arogundade, O.T., Atasie, C. Misra, S., Sakpere, A.B., Abayomi-Alli, O.O., Adesemowo K.A.: Improved predictive system for soil test fertility performance using fuzzy rule approach. In: Soft Computing and Its Engineering Applications: Second International Conference, IcSoftComp 2020, Changa, Anand, India, 11–12 December 2020, Proceedings, vol. 1374, p. 249. Springer, Cham (2021). https://doi.org/10.1007/978-981-16-0708-0_21

18. Butt, S.A.: Study of agile methodology with the cloud. Pacific Sci. Rev. B Human. Soc. Sci. 2(1), 22–28 (2016)

Bug Prediction Capability of Primitive Enthusiasm Metrics

Péter Gál(✉) 🄳

Department of Software Engineering, University of Szeged,
Dugonics ter 13, Szeged 6720, Hungary
galpeter@inf.u-szeged.hu

Abstract. Bugs in software development life cycle are unavoidable. Manually finding these bugs is not always the most effective way. To aid this, various bug prediction approaches which are using code metrics are developed and are also still in active development.

In a previous work, the Primitive Enthusiasm code metrics were introduced to add detection capabilities for Primitive Obsession code smells. This paper explores the usability of the Primitive Enthusiasm metrics in a bug prediction scenario. To evaluate the new metrics, an existing source code bug data set was used. The correlation between existing metrics and the new PE metrics was investigated. Furthermore the effectiveness of bug prediction is investigated by building training models with and without the new metrics. Using a cross-project and a project version-based evaluation the results show that adding PE metrics can be beneficial for bug prediction.

Keywords: Bug prediction · Code metrics · Primitive obsession · Primitive enthusiasm · Static analysis

1 Introduction

Bugs during software development are bound to be introduced unwillingly. Each bug can have a different effect, one can cripple the whole system or it will just provide a minor annoyance, for example the layout or colouring is incorrect. Finding various bugs in applications could take from several minutes to hours or even more. As a project development continues, finding and fixing a bug costs more and more [1], therefore, researchers are also working on creating and improving various automated tools that can help a developer to quickly find a bug or even just provide hints on where the bug could be in the system. In pursuit of automated tools to provide bug predictions there are already several papers present [10,18]. Some of these tools use various source-level metrics to train and build models which will be used for bug predictions.

In this paper, we discuss the addition of Primitive Obsession-related metrics to improve bug prediction capabilities. To do this, an existing bug dataset [3] was extended with the Primitive Enthusiasm source-level metrics [15] and the impact of the new metrics was investigated.

© Springer Nature Switzerland AG 2021
O. Gervasi et al. (Eds.): ICCSA 2021, LNCS 12955, pp. 246–262, 2021.
https://doi.org/10.1007/978-3-030-87007-2_18

The rest of the paper is organised as follows. In Sect. 2, the background and related works are discussed. Section 3 is an overview of the Primitive Enthusiasm metrics. Evaluation of the newly added metrics for bug prediction is presented in Sect. 4. In Sect. 5, the threats to validity are described. Finally, the paper is concluded in Sect. 6.

2 Background

Before investigating bug prediction capabilities we need to have a bit of background on related datasets and other bug prediction research. In addition, we need to discuss the Primitive Obsession code smell and related problems. This section provides an insight into these topics.

2.1 Bug Prediction and Datasets

Using a bug predictor tool could help developers to quickly triage an issue in a given system in a cost-effective manner. In one research [8] the authors used source code metrics in conjunction with machine learning methods to provide fault predictions. They observed that on the Mozilla suite there are source code metrics that can help to predict fault-prone classes. A different study [13] concluded that defect predictors that learned from source code metrics was useful and easy to use, in addition they are widely-used. Another conclusion of the paper that the goal of the learning should be used to select a preferred machine learning algorithm.

In order to evaluate a method that provides bug prediction capabilities, a dataset is required. Such dataset should provide additional data, such as various source code metrics and a correct classification of classes or methods that have bugs in them. In addition, it is favourable to have real-world software in a dataset, as ultimately a bug prediction tool should be used on real applications not on small benchmarks. To achieve this, a unified Java dataset was used in this paper, which was introduced by Ferenc et al. [3] This dataset is a collection of five publicly available bug datasets in a unified format. These are the following: the PROMISE dataset [11], the Eclipse bug dataset [22], the Bug Prediction dataset [2], the Bugcatchers dataset [9], and the GitHub bug dataset [17]. These datasets contain class and/or file level code metrics including information on defects. From these bug datasets the PROMISE, GitHub, and the Bug Prediction datasets were used in this paper, as these provide class-level metrics. In total, there are 66 systems in these three datasets and they range from small applications with few classes to large systems with thousands of classes.

2.2 Definition of Primitive Obsession

Usually data types can be categorized into two groups: primitive and complex. Primitive types are simple data types provided by a language, e.g. *char*, *integer*, etc. Complex types are constructed from these primitive types or by using other complex types, and are usually named *class* or *struct*. Additionally, such complex types can encapsulate operations on their data, providing semantic knowledge on how the data can or should be used. For example, it would be convenient to place a *string* and two *integers* that represent a task name, a start, and end time into a class instead of using them separately. By doing such data coupling and providing a name for the class will allow the developers to understand the connections between the data. However, it is also common to neglect such small, but useful code compositions. Similarly adding additional method parameters to an already long parameter list seems to be a quick solution to achieve a programming goal, but in the long run, this will make the relation between data harder to understand and will also decrease the maintainability of the source code. Excessive usage of primitive data types instead of creating small objects is the core of Primitive Obsession. Mäntylä et al. classify Primitive Obsession as a type of *bloater* smell [12], in addition it is symptom of the existence of overgrown, chaotic code parts. A simple example for Primitive Obsession is depicted in Fig. 1. The NORMAL and URGENT class constants on Lines 2 and 3, can be considered type codes. Such type codes are usually integers or strings that have a name, and are used to simulate types. In this case these are used to indicate task priorities. Type codes are widely used in various projects, and they can be considered a version of Primitive Obsession. They break the object-orient paradigm and can cause hidden dependencies [20]. There are various ways to remove such type codes from a project, for example, with a *Strategy* or *State* pattern [6].

```
1  class Task {
2      static const int NORMAL = 1;
3      static const int URGENT = 2;
4
5      public void work(int from, int to, int breakCount, String
           worker) {
6          if(worker == null || worker.length() == 0) {
7              /* ... */
8          }
9      }
10 }
```

Fig. 1. Sample code containing primitive obsessions

At Line 5, the work method is presented. This method has three integer parameters and a single string argument. As all of these arguments are primitive types, the method can be considered having the Primitive Obsession code smell. Even more if these arguments are repetitively used throughout the project's codebase. Please note, that in Java string are classes, thus they are not really primitive types, but logically it makes sense to categorize it as a kind of primitive type. Line 6 is also a good target for refactoring, because the checks present in this line should be encapsulated into a class. Especially, if these checks are used multiple places. For more that contains Primitive Obsession examples, Steven A. Lowe's GitHub project[1] is a good start. This project provides a set of steps on how to clean up this kind of code smell.

2.3 Challenges Using Primitive Obsession

Previously, the Primitive Obsession was not in the main focus of researchers. A team of researchers conducted a literature overview on code smells [21]. During the review, they gathered 319 papers from year 2000 till 2009. From these they examined 39 in more detail. One of the investigation point was to determine which code smells attracted the most attention from researchers. The most discussed topic was the Duplicated Code smell – from 39 papers 21 elaborated on this –, at the same time other code bad smells received very little attention. Among the unpopular smells was the Primitive Obsession that was only present in 5 papers. However, these papers also discussed Fowler's other code bad smells.

Another literature overview [7] by Gupta et al. collected 60 papers from 1999 to 2016, and concluded that four code bad smells did not have any detection method, including Primitive Obsession. An investigation on five tools that could detect code smells reported that none of them were able to find the Primitive Obsession code smells.

In a thesis, Roperia introduced JSmell for Java applications that could detect Primitive Obsession smells [16]. The detection technique for this smell was based on the number of primitive data types declared in a class. JSmell reports Primitive obsession when the number of primitively typed data is above than the average of a project, and the class was not instantiated. As the tool was not accessible, a comparison was not done between the JSmell's approach and the Primitive Enthusiasm metrics solution.

Other papers elaborated on the usefulness of code smells for maintenance indicators [14,19]. However, these cannot be considered as an all-in-one solution for defect predictions, but they still give insights into important maintainability aspects for a project, even more if they are combined.

3   Primitive Enthusiasm

The Primitive Enthusiasm (PE) metrics were previously introduced in various papers [5,15]. However, for the sake of completeness and to make the paper self-contained the metrics are shortly described here.

The base of the metrics iss the Formula 1 which describes how the primitive-typed parameters are collected for a given M_i method.

$$Primitives(M_i) := \langle P_{M_i,j} | 1 \le j \le |P_{M_i}| \wedge P_{M_i,j} \in PrimitiveTypes \rangle \qquad (1)$$

For this formula the definitions of the parameters are the following:

---

[1] https://github.com/stevenalowe/kata-2-tinytypes.

- **PrimitiveTypes** is the set of types that are handled as primitive ones. For Java this contains the following types: `boolean`, `byte`, `short`, `int`, `long`, `char`, `float`, `double`, and `String`.
- N represents the number of methods in the current class.
- M_i denotes the ith method of the current class.
- M_c denotes the current method under investigation in the current class.
- P_{M_i} denotes the list of types used for parameters in the M_i method.
- $P_{M_i,j}$ defines the type of the jth parameter in the M_i method.

Then, using this *Primitives* function three metrics were constructed. These are the LPE, GPE, and HPE metrics. These metrics are calculated for methods that have at least a single parameter.

Local Primitive Enthusiasm. Formula 2 depicts the calculation of the LPE metric.

$$LPE(M_c) := \frac{\sum_{i=1}^{N} |Primitives(M_i)|}{\sum_{i=1}^{N} |P_{M_i}|} < \frac{|Primitives(M_c)|}{|P_{M_c}|} \qquad (2)$$

The left-hand side of the inequality calculates the percentage of how many parameters of the current class are of primitive types. While the right-hand side denotes how many parameters of the M_c method are of primitive types. This can be considered as the method's primitiveness ratio. If the right-hand side is greater than the left-hand side, that is, there are more primitive types in the M_c method's parameter list than in the given class on average, then the method is considered to be an LPE true method.

The formula is calculated method-by-method in a given class context, therefore, it is considered as a local value.

Global Primitive Enthusiasm. GPE is shown in Formula 3. In this formula, the G is the list of methods in the analysed system, and G_i is the ith method in this list. The main difference from LPE is that the left-hand side now describes the average number of primitive-typed arguments in the whole system and this is compared to the right-hand, side which is the current method's primitiveness ratio.

$$GPE(M_c) := \frac{\sum_{i=1}^{|G|} |Primitives(G_i)|}{\sum_{i=1}^{|G|} |P_{G_i}|} < \frac{|Primitives(M_c)|}{|P_{M_c}|} \qquad (3)$$

The idea behind GPE was that this compares the current method to the methods in the whole project, which in turn can highlight methods that are above the system's average.

Hot Primitive Enthusiasm. By combining the LPE and GPE formulae Formula 4 was constructed. The purpose of this combination is to direct the attention of the developer to more suspicious code parts.

$$HPE(M_c) := LPE(M_c) \land GPE(M_c) \tag{4}$$

If a method is HPE true then it indicates that in terms of primitive method arguments it is an outstanding method in both a given class and in the whole system.

4 Evaluation

To investigate the Bug prediction capabilities of the PE metrics, an already existing Java-based bug dataset was used [3]. There are 66 systems in this bug data set. For each system, 63 commonly used source code metrics are already calculated and in addition, classes with bugs are marked. This data set was extended with the previously mentioned PE metrics and were calculated by the OpenStaticAnalyzer[2] (OSA), which is an open-source, multi-language, static code analyser framework developed at the Department of Software Engineering, University of Szeged.

In this section, we will describe the evaluation process: how the metrics were calculated, how the systems were selected from the bug data set, the correlation between metrics, a cross-project validation for bug prediction, and a project version-based bug prediction.

4.1 Calculating the Metrics

The selected bug data already contains mainly class-based metrics, and for each of the classes in this dataset, the PE metrics were calculated. However, the PE metrics are inherently method-based metrics. To resolve this minor incompatibility, the PE metrics were aggregated by class. That is, for a given class the number of LPE, GPE, and HPE true functions are counted and these values are used as class-level metrics. This aggregation inherently connects the PE metrics with the number of methods in a class. If there are more methods in a class, the class has a higher probability to have more PE true methods. After the aggregation, the class level PE metric value could have a value between 0 and the number of methods in that class.

In the following sections, the PE metrics will refer to this kind of aggregated value, if not mentioned otherwise.

Information on Selected Systems. In the used bug dataset, there are multiple versions present for some projects. To make the tables smaller in the paper, we have only selected the latest version of each project if there were multiple variants. Based on this criteria, 33 systems were selected from the original dataset.

---

[2] https://github.com/sed-inf-u-szeged/OpenStaticAnalyzer.

Table 1. Class count, bug count, and PE metric count information on selected systems

	Class	Bugs	Bugs/Class %	LPE	GPE	HPE
Equinox	319	126	39.5	78	114	74
Lucene	670	63	9.4	115	175	85
Myly	1405	209	14.9	240	421	206
Eclipse PDE UI	1491	208	14.0	357	510	321
Android U. I. L.	73	20	27.4	7	23	7
ANTLR	479	21	4.4	60	119	56
Broadleaf	1593	292	18.3	173	271	164
Eclipse p. for Ceylon	1610	68	4.2	187	284	176
Elasticsearch	5908	678	11.5	560	1063	480
Hazelcast	3412	377	11.0	204	391	185
JUnit	731	35	4.8	17	29	12
MapDB	331	40	12.1	64	89	62
mcMMO	301	57	18.9	41	35	26
MCT	1887	9	0.5	146	219	106
Neo4j	5899	58	1.0	582	1025	498
Netty	1143	271	23.7	128	191	122
OrientDB	1847	280	15.2	288	402	253
Oryx	533	74	13.9	36	97	32
Titan	1468	96	6.5	135	263	126
Ant 1.7	681	165	24.2	100	190	84
Camel 1.6	795	170	21.4	88	173	87
Ckjm 1.8	8	5	62.5	1	1	1
Forrest 0.8	31	2	6.5	7	14	7
Ivy 2.0	294	37	12.6	81	97	68
JEdit 4.3	439	11	2.5	150	162	119
Log4J 1.2	191	175	91.6	30	71	29
Lucene 2.4	320	193	60.3	65	92	46
Pbeans 2	37	8	21.6	13	18	12
Poi 3.0	414	276	66.7	62	274	50
Synapse 1.2	228	84	36.8	47	83	46
Velocity 1.6	188	66	35.1	51	76	46
Xalan 2.7	848	837	98.7	191	208	147
Xerces 2.0	342	303	88.6	78	102	64

For these systems, we first checked how many classes there are and how many bugs were reported. In addition the aggregated PE metric values were calculated for each system. These values can be seen in Table 1.

The first column, Class describes the number of classes in the given system. The second, "Bugs" column represents the number of classes which have at least a single reported bugs in them, and the third "Bugs/Class" column gives a view on how many of the system classes have a bug in them. The LPE, GPE, and HPE columns show how many classes have at least a single LPE, GPE, or HPE method. There are various-sized projects ranging from a small 8 class system to a more than 5500 class system. What is interesting to see is that there are usually more GPE true classes than LPE true ones. For example, in the case of the Elasticsearch system, there are 503 more GPE true classes than LPE ones. In addition, the HPE value is usually lower than LPE value. This indicates that the combination of the LPE and GPE metrics can help focus the developers' attention.

There are two very small projects on this list: the Ckjm 1.8 and Forrest 0.8. For these two, as there are already a small number of classes present, the PE metric values are also small. These two systems will be interesting in Sect. 4.3.

4.2   Correlation Between Metrics

As there are various metrics already present in the bug dataset it is worthwhile to consider how the PE metrics are behaving compared to other metrics. The main question is this: Are there any metrics that have strong connections with these new PE metrics?

To answer this question, a correlation matrix was calculated using Pearson's correlation for each metric, merging all of the selected systems into a single input dataset. This matrix is shown in Table 2. A colour map was applied to help show the correlation values between the metrics. The greater the correlation between the metrics the darker the cell color.

Based on the correlation matrix, the LPE, GPE, and HPE metrics have a strong correlation. The LPE and GPE metrics have a 0.86 correlation value which is caused by the fact that there is only a minor difference between the calculation of these two metrics. In addition, the fact that the HPE has a high correlation with both LPE and GPE is not a surprise as the HPE metric by definition is calculated from these two metrics.

The highest correlation between the PE metrics and traditional metrics can be found for the NLM and LPE metrics that have the value of 0.58. All other correlation values are less than this value. By investigating some of the higher correlation values we could have an insight into the connection between the metrics.

Table 2. Correlation between PE and other metrics.

	LPE	GPE	HPE		LPE	GPE	HPE
LPE	1.00	0.86	0.96	NM	0.28	0.27	0.26
GPE	0.86	1.00	0.91	NOA	0.03	0.01	0.03
HPE	0.96	0.91	1.00	NOC	0.04	0.04	0.03
AD	0.10	0.09	0.08	NOD	0.04	0.03	0.03
CBO	0.31	0.24	0.27	NOI	0.39	0.33	0.36
CBOI	0.19	0.20	0.19	NOP	0.06	0.04	0.05
CC	0.00	-0.01	0.00	NOS	0.40	0.35	0.38
CCL	0.11	0.09	0.10	NPA	0.02	0.02	0.02
CCO	0.09	0.08	0.09	NPM	0.26	0.27	0.25
CD	0.08	0.08	0.07	NS	0.11	0.12	0.11
CI	0.08	0.07	0.08	PDA	0.37	0.34	0.36
CLC	-0.01	-0.02	-0.01	PUA	0.36	0.41	0.36
CLLC	0.00	-0.01	0.00	RFC	0.53	0.49	0.50
CLOC	0.41	0.35	0.39	TCD	0.07	0.08	0.07
DIT	0.01	0.00	0.01	TCLOC	0.41	0.35	0.39
DLOC	0.38	0.33	0.36	TLLOC	0.49	0.44	0.47
LCOM5	0.26	0.28	0.24	TLOC	0.51	0.45	0.49
LDC	0.15	0.13	0.15	TNA	0.11	0.10	0.11
LLDC	0.16	0.14	0.16	TNG	0.17	0.15	0.17
LLOC	0.49	0.44	0.46	TNLA	0.13	0.12	0.13
LOC	0.51	0.45	0.48	TNLG	0.35	0.33	0.34
NA	0.09	0.07	0.08	TNLM	0.54	0.52	0.51
NG	0.18	0.17	0.18	TNLPA	0.02	0.02	0.02
NII	0.26	0.28	0.26	TNLPM	0.48	0.49	0.46
NL	0.28	0.25	0.26	TNLS	0.20	0.22	0.21
NLA	0.10	0.09	0.10	TNM	0.23	0.21	0.22
NLE	0.30	0.27	0.28	TNOS	0.42	0.36	0.39
NLG	0.36	0.34	0.35	TNPA	0.03	0.02	0.03
NLM	0.58	0.57	0.55	TNPM	0.23	0.22	0.22
NLPA	0.01	0.01	0.01	TNS	0.13	0.12	0.13
NLPM	0.50	0.52	0.49	WMC	0.51	0.45	0.49
NLS	0.20	0.22	0.20	bugs	0.15	0.14	0.14

The PE metrics have greater correlations with metrics that are calculated from the number of methods. These metrics are the NLM[3], TNLM[4], NLPM[5], TNLPM[6], RFC[7], and WMC[8] and their highest correlation values for PE metrics are 0.58, 0.54, 0.52, 0.48, 0.53, and 0.51 in the same order. These correlations are understandable, as the PE metrics have connections to the number of methods since the aggregation was done by class (as was described in Sect. 4.1). If there are more methods there is a higher chance to have a PE true method(s). In addition, the PE metrics are calculated from method argument lists, thus, if there are more

---

[3] NLM: Number of Local Methods.
[4] TNLM: Total Number of Local Methods.
[5] NLPM: Number of Local Public Methods.
[6] TNLPM: Total Number of Local Public Methods.
[7] RFC: Response set For Class.
[8] WMC: Weighted Methods per Class.

methods there are usually more arguments. Another interesting insight can be given if the correlation between these common metrics is investigated. Table 3 elaborates on the correlation between these commonly used metrics.

Table 3. Correlation between a selected set of method count related metrics.

	NLM	NLPM	RFC	TNLM	TNLPM	WMC
NLM	1	0.92	0.84	0.91	0.86	0.75
NLPM	0.92	1	0.75	0.82	0.89	0.55
RFC	0.84	0.75	1	0.79	0.72	0.68
TNLM	0.91	0.82	0.79	1	0.94	0.69
TNLPM	0.86	0.89	0.72	0.94	1	0.53
WMC	0.75	0.55	0.68	0.69	0.53	1

A strong correlation can be seen in most cases between these method-based metrics, and these values are not a surprise as the metrics are also calculated mainly or partially from the number of methods in a class. As shown in Table 2 and Table 3, the PE metrics have less correlation than these method-related metrics have between each other. This shows that the PE metrics can give an extra dimension – aside from the already existing method related metrics – as they are not tightly coupled even if there is a connection between PE and traditional method-based metrics.

The other set of interesting correlations with PE metrics are the ones related to lines of code: LOC[9], LLOC[10], CLOC[11], DLOC[12], TLOC[13], TLLOC[14], TCLOC[15], TNOS[16], NOS[17], The connection between these and the PE metrics can be attributed to the fact that if there are more lines of code then there are usually more methods in an application. Just like previously it is also worth checking the correlations between these common metrics. This matrix is depicted in Table 4.

As shown in Table 4, most of these metrics have high correlation values between each other. Just like before, these values are understandable since all of them are size-related metrics and calculated from various types of code lines.

Based on these data, it can be concluded that although the PE metrics have some kind of connection between already existing metrics they can still give extra information for a developer.

---

[9] LOC: Lines of Code.
[10] LLOC: Logical Lines of Code.
[11] CLOC: Comment Lines of Code.
[12] DLOC: Documentation Lines of Code.
[13] TLOC: Total Lines of Code.
[14] TLLOC: Total Logical Lines of Code.
[15] TCLOC: Total Comment Lines of Code.
[16] TNOS: Total Number of Statements.
[17] NOS: Number of Statements.

Table 4. Correlation between a selected set of line count related metrics.

	CLOC	DLOC	LLOC	LOC	NOS	TCLOC	TLLOC	TLOC	TNOS
CLOC	1.00	0.95	0.53	0.69	0.46	0.99	0.53	0.68	0.48
DLOC	0.95	1.00	0.39	0.56	0.32	0.94	0.40	0.56	0.34
LLOC	0.53	0.39	1.00	0.97	0.97	0.52	0.97	0.95	0.96
LOC	0.69	0.56	0.97	1.00	0.93	0.68	0.95	0.97	0.92
NOS	0.46	0.32	0.97	0.93	1.00	0.46	0.93	0.90	0.98
TCLOC	0.99	0.94	0.52	0.68	0.46	1.00	0.54	0.69	0.48
TLLOC	0.53	0.40	0.97	0.95	0.93	0.54	1.00	0.98	0.97
TLOC	0.68	0.56	0.95	0.97	0.90	0.69	0.98	1.00	0.93
TNOS	0.48	0.34	0.96	0.92	0.98	0.48	0.97	0.93	1.00

4.3 Cross-Project Bug Prediction

To evaluate the bug prediction capabilities of the PE metrics, a cross-project validation was performed. The cross-project validation was chosen as a method to see how the newly added metric changes the bug prediction, and classification.

To do this prediction, the Weka [4] tool was used with the default Random Forest classificator. The classification label was the bug presence for a given class. For each project, a model was trained and all other projects were used as test data. This process was done for the original metrics in the dataset and for the PE extended metrics giving us two sets of classification results. After this, the weighted average F-measure[18] difference was calculated for each train-test system pair. This difference can show us how the classification results changed after adding the new metrics to the dataset. These differences can be examined in Table 5.

The first and second column describes the project on which the training was done. The IDs of the projects are used as column labels to reduce the size of the table a bit. The columns after these are the project IDs on which the trained model was evaluated.

In pursuit to improve understandability, a colour-coding was applied to the values in the table. To indicate improvement, cells that have a value of 0.05 or higher are coloured green and values less or equal to -0.05 are coloured red to indicate a decrease in weighted F-measure values. Due to rounding, it is possible that a value that is equal to one of these thresholds is not coloured. There are also cells that do not have any value, aside from the matrix main diagonal. In these cases, the classificator was unable to calculate the weighted F-measure, that usually means that there were only bugged or non-bugged classes reported by the classificator resulting in an invalid weighted F-measure value.

The highest decrease in F-measure value was in the case of the Xerces 2.0 system. Based on Table 1, most of the classes in the system have a bugged class. Due to this, an over-fitting can be observed by the classificator marking

---

[18] Weighted average F-measure is calculated with the following formula: $\frac{Fmeasure(a)*InstanceCount(a)+Fmeasure(b)*InstanceCount(b)}{InstanceCount(a)+InstanceCount(b)}$ Where a and b are the two classes for classification.

Table 5. Weighted fmeasure changes in case of cross-project validation

ID	Name	1	2	3	4	5	6	7	8	9	10	11	12	13	14	15	16	17	18	19	20	21	22	23	24	25	26	27	28	29	30	31	32	33
1	Equinox		-0.00	-0.02	-0.03	0.06	0.01	0.00	-0.01	-0.01	0.01	0.02	0.03	-0.03	0.01	-0.00	0.04	0.00	0.00	0.01	-0.05	-0.03	0.26	0.25	-0.01	-0.02	0.00	0.04	0.00	-0.11	0.00	0.04	0.01	0.08
2	Lucene	-0.04		-0.00	0.01	-0.04	0.01	0.01	-0.01	0.01	-0.00	-0.00	-0.02	0.03	-0.00	-0.00	-0.00	0.01	-0.02	0.00	0.03	0.03	0.26		0.01	0.01	-0.02	0.01	0.01	0.03	-0.00	0.07	-0.03	-0.03
3	Mylyn	0.01	0.03		0.01	-0.05	-0.01	-0.03			0.06	0.01	0.04	-0.07	-0.00	-0.00	-0.01	0.01	0.00	-0.01	-0.03	0.01	0.28	0.02	0.04	0.03	0.04	0.01	0.03	-0.02	0.09	-0.04	0.03	0.03
4	Eclipse PDE UI	-0.02	0.00	-0.00		0.09	-0.02	-0.03	0.01	-0.02	0.02	-0.01	-0.03	-0.00	-0.00	-0.00	-0.02	-0.01	-0.01	0.01	0.02	0.02	0.46	-0.09	-0.04	0.04	0.02	0.02	0.03	0.04	-0.07	-0.03	-0.08	0.00
5	Android U. I. L.	0.02	0.00	0.02	-0.04		-0.03	-0.07	-0.04	-0.02	-0.02	-0.12	-0.01	-0.04	-0.02	-0.04	-0.06	0.03	-0.01	-0.03	0.10	-0.04	0.12	-0.06	-0.10	0.05	-0.02	0.03	0.08	-0.10	-0.04	0.04	-0.05	-0.04
6	ANTLR	0.03	0.00	0.01	0.00	0.03		-0.03	-0.02	-0.01	-0.00	-0.00	-0.02	-0.01	0.01	0.00	0.02	0.00	0.02	0.01	-0.03	-0.02	-0.05	-0.05	0.00	-0.02	0.00	0.10	-0.02	-0.02	0.03	0.04	-0.01	-0.10
7	Broadleaf	-0.04	0.00	0.01	-0.00	-0.07	-0.03		-0.01	0.01	-0.00	-0.00	-0.03	-0.04	0.00	-0.01	0.01	0.00	-0.01	0.01	0.03	-0.02	0.28	0.02	-0.04	-0.01	0.00	0.05	0.02	-0.00	-0.09	-0.05	0.04	0.03
8	Ceylon	-0.04	-0.00	0.02	-0.01		0.01			-0.01	-0.01	-0.00	-0.03	0.02	0.00	0.01	0.03	-0.01	0.01	0.01	-0.00	0.00		0.02	-0.04	-0.02	-0.07	0.05	-0.02	-0.02	0.02	0.02	0.01	-0.04
9	Elasticsearch	-0.02	-0.01	-0.02	-0.01	0.03	-0.01	0.02		-0.00	0.02	-0.01	-0.03	-0.01	0.00	0.01	-0.01	-0.00	-0.02	0.01	-0.01	0.00	-0.09	-0.07	0.01	-0.02	-0.03	0.01	-0.02	-0.02	-0.01	-0.05	0.04	-0.12
10	Hazelcast	0.02	0.00	0.00	0.00	0.03	-0.01	-0.03		0.01		-0.00	-0.03	0.03	-0.00	-0.00	0.02	0.00	-0.02	0.01	-0.01	-0.00	-0.07	0.11	0.01	-0.02	-0.07	0.01	-0.14	-0.06	-0.06	-0.05	0.12	-0.02
11	JUnit	0.00	-0.02	0.00	-0.04	-0.02	0.01	0.05		-0.01	0.02		0.00	0.03	-0.01	-0.00	0.02	0.0c	0.05	0.00	0.03	0.04	0.25	0.07	-0.02	-0.09	0.07	0.06	0.13	0.11	0.03	0.02	0.01	0.24
12	MapDB	-0.02	-0.01	0.01	0.02	0.04	0.01	-0.03			-0.01	-0.02		0.05	0.00	-0.01	0.01	-0.01	-0.02	-0.01	-0.02	-0.01		0.04	0.03	0.00	-0.02	-0.03	-0.02	-0.09	-0.07	0.13	-0.12	-0.06
13	mcMMO	0.05	0.03	-0.01	0.02	0.01	0.04	0.02		-0.01	-0.05	0.01	0.00		-0.02	-0.03	-0.03	-0.01	-0.03	0.00	0.06	0.03	0.07	0.07	0.01	0.02	0.08	0.05	-0.13	-0.09	0.02	0.02	-0.13	-0.10
14	MCT	-0.01	0.01	0.00	0.00	0.01	-0.02	0.00	-0.01	0.00	-0.00	0.00	0.02	-0.00		-0.00	-0.02	0.00	-0.01	0.00	-0.01	-0.00	0.28	-0.01	-0.01	-0.01	0.00	0.01	0.13	-0.01	-0.00	-0.05	-0.03	-0.07
15	Neo4j	0.02	-0.00	0.00	0.01	-0.02	0.00	-0.01	0.00	-0.01	-0.01	0.00	0.00	0.02	-0.00		-0.00	0.00	0.00	-0.00	-0.00	-0.01	0.35	0.05	-0.01	-0.01	0.00	0.02	-0.02	-0.01	-0.01	0.04	0.02	0.01
16	Netty	-0.00	-0.02	-0.00	0.03	-0.05	-0.02	0.01	0.01	-0.02	0.02	0.00	0.00	-0.01	-0.02	-0.00		-0.04	0.04	0.02	-0.05	-0.04		-0.03	-0.02	0.00	-0.05	-0.01	-0.04	-0.01	0.08	0.01	0.04	0.08
17	OrientDB	0.00	0.03	-0.01	0.01	-0.02	-0.02	-0.03	0.02	-0.01	-0.02	-0.01	-0.06	0.01	0.00	0.02	0.02		0.01	0.00	0.01	0.02		0.03	-0.01	-0.00	-0.00	-0.01	-0.05	0.03	0.02	-0.04	0.08	-0.10
18	Oryx	-0.06	-0.02	0.01	0.01	0.08	0.01	-0.00	-0.01	-0.02	-0.01	0.01	-0.02	-0.05	-0.02	0.01	-0.03	-0.01		0.01	0.03	-0.02	0.28	-0.01	0.05	0.01	-0.01	-0.01	0.08	-0.05	0.05	-0.06	-0.06	-0.08
19	Titan	-0.03	0.02	-0.01	-0.01	-0.01	0.05	-0.00	-0.00	-0.00	-0.01	0.00	0.07	0.02	-0.00	-0.01	-0.00	0.01	-0.02		-0.02	-0.00		0.05	-0.01	0.02	0.04	-0.05	0.00	-0.02	-0.02	0.07	0.04	0.02
20	Ant 1.7	0.08	-0.00	-0.01	-0.02	0.01	0.03	0.03	0.09	0.07	0.06	0.15	0.07	0.01			0.06	0.01	-0.04	0.06		-0.01	0.35	-0.05	-0.01	-0.01	-0.00	-0.05	0.06	0.09	-0.05	-0.16	0.05	0.00
21	Camel 1.6	0.01	0.02	0.00	-0.00	-0.01	0.04	-0.02	-0.00	-0.01	0.00	0.00	-0.00	-0.05	-0.02	-0.02	0.02	-0.00	-0.04	0.01	-0.05		-0.04	-0.07	-0.03	-0.04	0.04	-0.00	0.07	-0.09	0.17	-0.01	0.05	0.14
22	Ckjm 1.8	-0.00	0.09	0.00	0.08	-0.04	0.04	0.05	0.03	0.00	0.12	0.08	0.05	-0.05	0.11	0.09	0.03	0.07	-0.01	0.02	0.12	-0.04		-0.04	0.01	0.04	-0.09	-0.03	0.02	-0.09	0.17	-0.01	-0.03	-0.07
23	Forrest 0.8	-0.02	0.06	-0.01	0.04	-0.03	0.05		0.01	0.00	0.05	0.03	0.04	0.04	0.05	0.04	-0.02	0.01	0.00	0.05	0.05	-0.02	-0.15	-0.05	0.01	0.04	-0.00	-0.01	0.02	-0.04	-0.05	-0.06	0.08	0.05
24	Ivy 2.0	-0.02	-0.02	0.01	0.02		0.02		0.00	-0.00	-0.00	-0.00	0.03	-0.01	0.00	0.00	-0.01	-0.01	-0.01	0.00	0.04	0.01	0.00	-0.05	-0.00	0.05	-0.09	0.01	-0.08	0.02	-0.00	0.00	0.04	0.02
25	JEdit 4.3	-0.01	-0.00	-0.00	0.00	0.00	0.01	-0.00	-0.00	0.01	0.03	0.01	0.03	0.01	-0.01	-0.00	-0.01	-0.01		0.00	0.01	0.01	0.13	-0.04	-0.00		0.02	0.00	0.00	0.06	0.01	0.00	0.03	0.03
26	Log4J 1.2	-0.06	0.03	0.01	0.04	0.04	0.19	-0.01	-0.01	0.08	-0.04	0.05	0.03	0.08	0.07	0.03	0.04	-0.03	-0.01	0.01	0.05	0.07		0.05	0.06	0.11	0.06	0.00	0.10	0.05	-0.02	0.04	-0.01	-0.07
27	Lucene 2.4	-0.08	0.00	0.04	-0.00	-0.05	-0.02	-0.04	-0.03	0.01	-0.01	-0.05	-0.04	-0.00	-0.02	-0.02	-0.02	-0.01	0.00	-0.03	-0.00	-0.03	0.00	-0.05	-0.08	-0.05	0.06	-0.05	-0.12	0.02	0.02	0.05	0.05	0.11
28	Phoenix 2	-0.06	-0.03	0.04	-0.02	0.05	0.04	0.01	0.01	-0.00	0.03	0.01	-0.01	0.01	0.01	-0.02	0.00	0.00	0.04	0.01	0.03	0.00	0.13	-0.04	0.03	-0.09	0.12	0.06	0.01	-0.05	-0.04	-0.03	0.12	0.05
29	Poi 3.0	0.08	0.01	-0.03	0.01	0.04	-0.06	0.07	0.01	0.03	0.05	0.08	0.07	0.15	0.03	0.03	0.04	0.04	-0.01	0.05	0.01	-0.06	-0.16	-0.12	0.03	0.01	-0.02	-0.01	0.01		0.00	0.00	0.02	0.07
30	Synapse 1.2	0.12	-0.03	0.05	0.03	-0.06	0.03	0.04	0.04	0.02	0.00	0.08	0.04	0.05	0.02	0.02	0.06	0.01	0.05	0.01	0.01	-0.06	0.00	0.01	-0.00	-0.03	0.04	-0.02	0.12	0.03		0.02	0.02	-0.09
31	Velocity 1.6	-0.03	0.03	0.05	0.00	-0.01	0.03	0.01	-0.02	-0.02	0.02	-0.01	-0.05	-0.03	0.03	0.02	0.00	-0.04	0.04	0.01	0.04	-0.00	0.13	-0.05	0.04	-0.03	0.04	-0.02	0.10	-0.13	0.04		0.01	0.12
32	Xalan 2.7	-0.05	-0.04	0.02	-0.02	0.02	-0.02	0.01	0.03	-0.00	-0.01	-0.05	0.01	0.02	0.03	0.00	0.03	0.03	-0.02	-0.01	0.01	0.04	0.00	-0.06	-0.01	0.01	-0.02	0.01	0.01	0.01	0.01	-0.02		0.00
33	Xerces 2.0	-0.11	-0.06	-0.02	-0.10	-0.06	0.04	-0.05	-0.08	-0.06	-0.08	-0.13	-0.08	0.08	-0.11	-0.10	-0.10	-0.09	0.01	-0.16	-0.04	-0.04	0.00	-0.06	-0.08	0.03	-0.04	0.02	-0.17	-0.01	0.07	0.04	-0.00	

more classes as bugged. A similar over-fitting can be observed in the case of the Xalan 2.7 project. However, the F-measure change cannot be observed in Table 5, and this is due to the fact that in most cases by using the original dataset for classification the calculated weighted F-measure was already low as it was unable to correctly predict if the class is bugged or not.

Most of the increase can be seen when the classifier was trained on the JUnit, Ant 1.7, Ckjm 1.8, Log4J 1.2, or Poi 3.0 projects. For these systems, there are multiple instances where the F-measure change is greater or equal to 0.05 and there are a only few instances where a decrease can be observed.

The two small systems, Ckjm 1.8 and Forrest 0.8, have an overall improvement. Additionally, using these systems as test data could make the classificator over-fit in some cases as shown by the empty cells in the row ID 22 and 23. However, in other cases there are quite big improvements when using bigger systems for training and these two as test data. For example, in the case of the equinox training data the F-measure improvements were 0.26 and 0.25.

Overall, there are 123 instances where the weighted F-measure changes are greater than or equal to 0.05. In 107 cases the changes of F-measure are less than -0.05. These cases clearly indicate that adding the PE metrics can be beneficial for bug prediction. Furthermore, the increase of the weighted F-measure is greater than the decrease present in the change matrix. Based on these data, adding the PE metrics for further bug prediction classifications can be worthwhile.

4.4   Bug Prediction Across Versions

Training and testing the bug prediction across projects is good and can be useful. However, during a software development process usually a single application is developed from which multiple releases are created. As the system, evolves an earlier version of the project could be used to predict bugs. In this case, an earlier version can be used to train a bug prediction model and used on later versions. Fortunately, the selected bug data set contains multiple versions for some systems. These systems are the Ant, Camel, Ivy, JEdit, Log4J, Lucene, Pbeans, Poi, Synapse, Velocity, Xalan, and xerces. Due to size constraints, only a small subset of these projects will be presented here for this bug prediction evaluation across versions.

In the case of the Xerces 2.0 system in Table 5 the weighted F-measure values were usually in the negative. That is, the model trained with Xerces 2.0 was unable to improve the prediction for other projects. In this case, it is worth investigating what would happen if the various Xerces versions were compared by weighted F-measure changes between the original data set and the PE extended data set. This comparison can be observed in Table 6.

Same as before, the first column describes the systems on which the training was performed and the other columns are the systems where the evaluation was performed. This table describes that using an older Xerces version for training data set with the added PE metrics can improve the bug prediction capabilities for future Xerces versions. The most notable change is when Xerces 1.3 was used as a train data set and the 2.0 version was used to evaluate the predictions.

Table 6. Weighted f-measure changes in case of the Xerces project across versions

	Xerces 1.2	Xerces 1.3	Xerces 2.0
Xerces 1.2		0.02	-0.00
Xerces 1.3	0.02		0.06
Xerces 2.0	-0.01	-0.01	

During the comparison of the other projects with multiple versions, the most negative changes can be observed in case of the Ant system and all other projects have better values. The Ant system's comparison is depicted in Table 7.

Table 7. Weighted f-measure changes in the case of the ant project across versions

	Ant 1.3	Ant 1.4	Ant 1.5	Ant 1.6	Ant 1.7
Ant 1.3		-0.01	0.01	-0.07	-0.01
Ant 1.4	-0.01		0.05	-0.02	-0.02
Ant 1.5	-0.05	-0.03		0.02	0.01
Ant 1.6	-0.08	-0.01	0.03		-0.02
Ant 1.7	0.00	-0.02	-0.02	0.03	

In this case, there are a bit more than 10 cases where the addition of the PE metrics resulted in slightly negative values. Still, most of the changes are less than 0.05 indicating that in most cases the change is very small and can be ignored.

The Velocity project gave one of the best results when the PE metrics were added. The improvement in the weighted F-measure value can be observed in Table 8.

Table 8. Weighted f-measure changes in the case of the Velocity project across versions

	Velocity 1.4	Velocity 1.5	Velocity 1.6
Velocity 1.4		0.03	0.09
Velocity 1.5	0.13		-0.00
Velocity 1.6	0.03	0.03	

In almost every version combination, the addition of PE metrics improved the F-measure value. If the 1.4 version was used as the training data, the evaluation of the bug prediction improved on newer versions of the project.

Overall, the investigation of the bug prediction capabilities across multiple versions can be concluded as a viable option with the PE metrics.

5   Threats to Validity

The results shown in this paper are only using a small selected set of bug datasets. Although these datasets are widely known and used, they are relatively old, and there is no system among them that would be using a newer version than Java 8. Additional databases should be included in further research.

Calculations of the PE metrics were aggregated into class-level metrics, which could also skew results a bit. In addition, the metric calculation is currently only available for the Java language, but in order to fully evaluate their usefulness it would be good to adapt the metrics for other languages, e.g. C++.

The machine learning results are based only on a single algorithm. In further studies other classifiers should be investigated to see how the metrics perform.

6   Conclusion

In this paper, the Primitive Enthusiasm metrics were investigated to see how they perform in the case of bug prediction. The three PE metrics are the Local Primitive Enthusiasm, the Global Primitive Enthusiasm, and the Hot Primitive Enthusiasm metrics which capture the usages of primitively typed arguments in methods. The correlation between already existing metrics and the PE metrics is presented. Based on this correlation data the PE metrics did provide additional aspects. Although they have a bit of a connection with other metrics, the PE metrics still have a clear differentiation from traditional metrics.

In a cross-project validation, the bug prediction capabilities of the PE metrics were tested. Although there were cases where the trained models performed less adequately overall, there were improvements in classification of bugged classes.

Investigation of the project version-based bug prediction lead to a result where the PE metrics were able to add improvements in terms of weighted F-measure.

Based on these information, the addition of PE metrics for already existing metrics data sets can indeed improve bug prediction capabilities. In the future, we would like to continue to investigate the PE metric capabilities with other machine learning algorithms to see how they perform. Additionally, we would like to add other bug datasets into this research.

Acknowledgements. This research was supported by the EU-supported Hungarian national grant GINOP-2.3.2-15-2016-00037 and by grant NKFIH-1279-2/2020 of the Ministry for Innovation and Technology, Hungary.

References

1. Boehm, B., Basili, V.R.: Software defect reduction top 10 list. Computer **34**(1), 135–137 (2001). https://doi.org/10.1109/2.962984
2. D'Ambros, M., Lanza, M., Robbes, R.: An extensive comparison of bug prediction approaches. In: 2010 7th IEEE Working Conference on Mining Software Repositories (MSR 2010), pp. 31–41 (2010). https://doi.org/10.1109/MSR.2010.5463279
3. Ferenc, R., Tóth, Z., Ladányi, G., Siket, I., Gyimóthy, T.: A public unified bug dataset for java and its assessment regarding metrics and bug prediction. Softw. Q. J. 1–60 (2020). https://doi.org/10.1007/s11219-020-09515-0
4. Frank, E., Hall, M.A., Witten, I.H.: Online Appendix for Data Mining: Practical Machine Learning Tools and Techniques. Fourth Edition, Morgan Kaufmann, Burlington (2016)
5. Gál, P., Pengő, E.: Primitive enthusiasm: a road to primitive obsession. In: The 11h Conference of PhD Students in Computer Science, pp. 134–137. University of Szeged (2018)
6. Gamma, E., Helm, R., Johnson, R., Vlissides, J.: Design Patterns: Elements of Reusable Object-Oriented Software. Addison-Wesley Longman Publishing Co. Inc, USA (1995)
7. Gupta, A., Suri, B., Misra, S.: A systematic literature review: code bad smells in java source code. In: Gervasi, O., et al. (eds.) ICCSA 2017. LNCS, vol. 10408, pp. 665–682. Springer, Cham (2017). https://doi.org/10.1007/978-3-319-62404-4_49
8. Gyimóthy, T., Ferenc, R., Siket, I.: Empirical validation of object-oriented metrics on open source software for fault prediction. IEEE Trans. Softw. Eng. **31**(10), 897–910 (2005). https://doi.org/10.1109/TSE.2005.112
9. Hall, T., Zhang, M., Bowes, D., Sun, Y.: Some code smells have a significant but small effect on faults. ACM Trans. Softw. Eng. Method. **23**(4) (2014). https://doi.org/10.1145/2629648
10. Jayanthi, R., Florence, L.: Software defect prediction techniques using metrics based on neural network classifier. Cluster Comput. **22**(1), 77–88 (2018). https://doi.org/10.1007/s10586-018-1730-1
11. Jureczko, M., Madeyski, L.: Towards identifying software project clusters with regard to defect prediction. In: Proceedings of the 6th International Conference on Predictive Models in Software Engineering, PROMISE 2010, ACM (2010). https://doi.org/10.1145/1868328.1868342
12. Mäntylä, M.V., Vanhanen, J., Lassenius, C.: A taxonomy and an initial empirical study of bad smells in code. In: Proceedings of the International Conference on Software Maintenance. ICSM. pp. 381–384. IEEE (2003). https://doi.org/10.1109/ICSM.2003.1235447
13. Menzies, T., Milton, Z., Turhan, B., Cukic, B., Jiang, Y., Bener, A.: Defect prediction from static code features: current results, limitations, new approaches. Autom. Softw. Eng. **17**, 375–407 (2010). https://doi.org/10.1007/s10515-010-0069-5
14. Moonen, L., Yamashita, A.: Do code smells reflect important maintainability aspects? In: Proceedings of the 2012 IEEE International Conference on Software Maintenance. ICSM, pp. 306–315. IEEE (2012). https://doi.org/10.1109/ICSM.2012.6405287
15. Pengő, E., Gál, P.: Grasping primitive enthusiasm - approaching primitive obsession in steps. In: Proceedings of the 13th International Conference on Software Technologies, ICSOFT, pp. 389–396. INSTICC, SciTePress (2018). https://doi.org/10.5220/0006918804230430

16. Roperia, N.: JSmell: A Bad Smell detection tool for Java systems. Master's thesis, Maharishi Dayanand University (2009)
17. Tóth, Z., Gyimesi, P., Ferenc, R.: A public bug database of Github projects and its application in bug prediction. In: Gervasi, O., et al. (eds.) ICCSA 2016. LNCS, vol. 9789, pp. 625–638. Springer, Cham (2016). https://doi.org/10.1007/978-3-319-42089-9_44
18. Wahono, R.S.: A systematic literature review of software defect prediction: research trends, datasets, methods and frameworks. J. Softw. Eng. **1**, 1–16 (2015)
19. Yamashita, A., Moonen, L.: To what extent can maintenance problems be predicted by code smell detection? - an empirical study. Inf. Softw. Technol. **55**(12), 2223–2242 (2013). https://doi.org/10.1016/j.infsof.2013.08.002
20. Yu, Z., Rajlich, V.: Hidden dependencies in program comprehension and change propagation. In: Proceedings 9th International Workshop on Program Comprehension, IWPC 2001, pp. 293–299 (2001). https://doi.org/10.1109/WPC.2001.921739
21. Zhang, M., Hall, T., Baddoo, N.: Code bad smells: a review of current knowledge. J. Softw. Maintenance Evol. **23**(3), 179–202 (2011). https://doi.org/10.1002/smr.521
22. Zimmermann, T., Premraj, R., Zeller, A.: Predicting defects for eclipse. In: Proceedings of the Third International Workshop on Predictor Models in Software Engineering, PROMISE 2007, p. 9. IEEE (2007). https://doi.org/10.1109/PROMISE.2007.10

An Empirical Analysis on the Prediction of Web Service Anti-patterns Using Source Code Metrics and Ensemble Techniques

Sahithi Tummalapalli[1]($\boxtimes$), Juhi Mittal[1], Lov Kumar[1],
Lalitha Bhanu Murthy Neti[1], and Santanu Kumar Rath[2]

[1] BITS Pilani Hyderabad, Hyderabad, India
{P20170433,f20160298,lovkumar,bhanu}@hyderabad.bitspilani.ac.in
[2] NIT, Rourkela, India
skrath@nitrkl.ac.in

Abstract. Today's software program enterprise uses web services to construct distributed software systems based on the Service Oriented Architecture (SOA) paradigm. The web service description is posted by a web service provider, which may be observed and invoked by a distributed application. Service-Based Systems (SBS) need to conform themselves through years to fit within the new user necessities. These may result in the deterioration of the quality and design of the software systems and might reason the materialization of insufficient solutions called Anti-patterns. Anti-pattern detection using object-oriented source code metrics may be used as part of the software program improvement life cycle to lessen the maintenance of the software system and enhance the quality of the software. The work is motivated by developing an automatic predictive model for predicting web services anti-patterns using static evaluations of the source code metrics. The center ideology of this work is to empirically investigate the effectiveness of different variants of data sampling technique, Synthetic Minority Over Sampling TEchnique (SMOTE), and the ensemble learning techniques in the prediction of web service anti-patterns.

Keywords: Anti-pattern · WSDL · Ensemble techniques · Code quality

1 Introduction

Service-Oriented Architecture (SOA) is a tiered structure that assists corporations in sharing information and logic between different applications and usage modes. An excellent SOA solution leads to loosely coupled devices that empower the readiness expected to align IT and the enterprise team. A wide variety of technologies, particularly OSGi, SCA, and web services, are used for imposing

© Springer Nature Switzerland AG 2021
O. Gervasi et al. (Eds.): ICCSA 2021, LNCS 12955, pp. 263–276, 2021.
https://doi.org/10.1007/978-3-030-87007-2_19

the SOA structure. Various service-based systems (SBS), starting from business frameworks to cloud-based frameworks, are built using SOA architectures. The developing requirement of the customers forces the SBS's to conform to fit the new needs of the users. This evolving may additionally cause the deterioration of the design and quality of the software-based systems, ensuing in a systematic strategy to a repeating hassle, referred to as Anti-patterns [4]. Anti-patterns are the structures in the design that suggests infringement of critical design concepts and contrarily sway design quality [4]. These are not accidental but rather normal slip-ups and are nearly consistently accompanied with sincere intentions. Anti-patterns makes it challenging for the advancement and maintenance of the software program systems; however, they likewise will assist in figuring out troubles within the design, the code, and the management of software program initiatives. In this paper, we have developed models for the detection of four unique anti-patterns, namely: AP1: Chatty Web Service(CWS); AP2: Fine-Grained Web Service (FGWS); AP3: Data Web Service (DWS); AP4: God Web Service (GWS).

The vital motivation of the work added in this paper is to investigate the utilization of ensemble learning techniques in the detection of web-service anti-patterns. This work is roused by the need to fabricate procedures and tools to detect anti-patterns in web services automatically.

2   Related Work

Moha et al. [6] introduced a novel framework for specification and detection of anti-patterns in Service-based systems to detect new patterns like Tiny Service and Multiservice and achieved a precision of more than 0.9. Ouni et al. [8] introduced innovative genetic programming to detect web services anti-pattern by generating detection rules based on threshold values and a combination of different metrics. The validation of the above approach is done on 310 Web services to detect the five anti-patterns. Dimitrios et al. [12] used the Protege platform, a web-based environment, to facilitate collaborative ontology editing allowing multiple users to edit and enrich the anti-pattern ontology simultaneously. Palma et al. [9] used a rule-based search to detect and identify BP anti-patterns in the Business Process Execution Language (BPEL) processes generated via orchestrating web services. Coscia et al. [7] proposed a statistical correlation analysis on the WSDL-level service metrics and the number of traditional OO metrics and found a correlation between them. SODA-W, an extension of the SOFA framework, detects the SOAP and REST anti-patterns using the pre-established DSL. Upadhyaya et al. [15] proposed an approach to detect 9 SOA patterns. It is observed from the literature reviewed here that the research on SOA anti-pattern detection still needs to be explored thoroughly. Dimitrios et al. [13] have proposed a novel OWL ontology-based knowledge system, SPARSE, that helps in detecting anti-patterns. The ontology provides documentation for the anti-patterns, describing their relationship with other anti-patterns through their causes, symptoms, and consequences. Jaffar et al. [3] argued in his paper that classes taking part in anti-pattern and patterns of software designs have dependencies with other classes i.e., unvarying and mutating dependencies, that may spread issues to other classes. In this paper, authors have empirically investigated the consequences of dependencies in object-oriented system by focusing and analysing the relationship between the presence of co-change and static dependencies and change proness, fault proness and fault types that the classes are exhibiting. Kumar et al. [5] proposed an approach for the automatic detection of anti-patterns by static analysis of the source code. In this paper, author proposed that the aggregate values of the source code metrics computed at the web-service level can be used as predictors for anti-pattern detection. Saluja et al. [11] proposed a new optimized algorithm that uses dynamic metrics for execution in addition to the static metrics. The results obtained are further optimized using genetic algorithms. The proposed results achieved better results than the existing methods and had a recall rate of approximately 0.9

3   Dataset

The data set with 226 publicly available web services that are shared by Ouni et al. on GitHub[1] are used for experiments in this paper. Figure 1 shows the distribution of the web services in which the anti-patterns exists (#AP) and does not exist (#NAP).

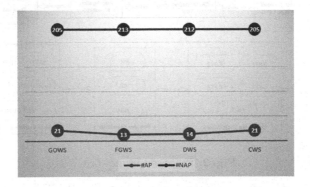

Fig. 1. Distribution of anti-patterns in web services

4   Proposed Solution Framework

Figure 2 shows the detailed overview of the proposed framework. Figure 2 depicts that the proposed framework is a multi−step procedure consisting of computing CK metrics from the WSDL file, applying aggregation metrics for computing

---

[1] https://github.com/ouniali/WSantipatterns.

metrics at file level, handling class imbalance problem using different variants of SMOTE discussed in Sect. 4.2, removal of irrelevant features using techniques such as PCA and RSA discussed in Sect. 4.3, and lastly the development of anti-pattern prediction models using five different ensemble learning techniques. First, the java files are extracted from each of the WSDL file, for which the CK metrics discussed in Table 3 are computed using CKJM tool. To convert the metrics computed at file level to system level, aggregation measures which are discussed in Table 3 are applied. This forms the dataset using which the anti-pattern prediction models are developed. Next, we used different variants of SMOTE technique for handling the class imbalance problem. Further, we compare the models trained using balanced data with the models developed using original data. After this, we use features selected using three different feature selection techniques namely, significant features using rank−sum test, Rough Set Analysis (RSA), and Principal Component Analysis (PCA). Finally, five ensemble learning techniques namely: Bagging Classifier (EST1), Random Forest Classifier (EST2), Extra Trees Classifier (EST3), AdaBoost Classifier (EST4), Gradient Boosting Classifier (EST5) are used to generate models for the prediction of web service anti-patterns. We use performance measures such as: AUC, F-measure, and accuracy for computing and comparing the performance of the models generated for the prediction of web service anti-patterns.

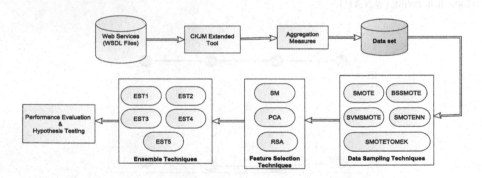

Fig. 2. Proposed framework

4.1   Preprocessing of the Dataset

Preprocessing of the dataset involves the extraction of java files from the WSDL files (raw data) from which the source code metrics are computed. The dataset considered has a collection of 226 WSDL files. In this paper, A step-wise procedure for preprocessing of data is detailed here.

Step-1: Source code metrics computation:
We used WSDL2Java tool in this work to extract java files from each of the WSDL file, and the Chidamber and Kemerer metrics (CK metrics) along

with other java metrics are computed for each of the java file using CKJM extended tool[2]. The list of various CK metrics used in this paper are listed in Fig. 3. The definition of each of the CK metric along with their computation formula are documented in [2].

Step-2: Aggregation measures on the source code metrics:

In this study, our objective is to develop one model for predicting an anti-pattern present in the WSDL file. Here, we have used CK metrics to measure each java file and the metrics computed here are at the file level. Further a total of sixteen aggregation measures are applied to the metrics computed at the file level to obtain the metrics at the system level. The list of aggregation measures used in this paper are given in Fig. 3.

CKJM Metrics	Measure of Aggregation(MOA), Number of Public Methods(NPM), Number of Children in Tree(NOC), Coupling Between Objects(CBO), Depth of Inheritance(DIT), Weighted Methods per Class(WMC), Efferent Coupling(Ce), Measure of Functional Abstraction(MFA), Average Method Complexity(AMC), Afferent Coupling(Ca), Data Access Metric(DAM), Response for Class (RFC), Inheritance Coupling(IC) Lack of Cohesion in Methods(LCOM), Lines of Code(LOC), Cohesion Among Methods of Class(CAM), LCOM3, Coupling Between Methods(CBM)
Aggregation Measures	Quartile 1, Mean, Quartile 3,Hoover Index, Minimum, Skewness, Shannon Entropy, Maximum, Theil Index, Gini Index, Atkinson Index, Generalized Entropy, Standard deviation, Variance, Median, Kurtosis

Fig. 3. List of CKJM metrics and aggregation measures

4.2 Data Sampling Techniques

The selection of an appropriate sampling technique plays a critical role in the research study, as it significantly impacts the quality of our results and findings. As discussed in Sect. 3, the dataset considered is having a class imbalance problem, and we are choosing the data sampling technique SMOTE and its variants to solve this problem [1]. In this paper, we are considering the five different data sampling techniques namely SMOTE, Borderline Smote (BSMOTE), SVM-SMOTE (SVMSMOTE), SMOTE- Edited Nearest Neighbour (SMOTEENN), and SMOTETOMEK along with the original dataset (OD) to generate the predictive models.

4.3 Effectiveness of Metrics

A total of three models are considered in this study where the occurrence of an anti-pattern is considered as the dependent variable, and the source code metrics computed are taken as an independent variable for developing the relation.

Subset of Features Selected as Significant Features (SIGF): In our previous work, We applied a set of feature selection techniques on original source code metrics to obtain the significant source code metrics(SM). This

---

[2] http://gromit.iiar.pwr.wroc.pl/pinf/ckjm/.

Table 1. Source code metrics selected using RSA: all anti-patterns

Anti-pattern	Reduced set of metrics
GOWS	Hoover index (WMC), Min (DIT), Mean (DIT), Max (RFC), skewness (LCOM), skewness (Ca), Q1 (DAM), Gini index (DAM), Gini index (IC)
FGWS	Median (CBO), Gini index (LCOM), skewness (Ca), Mean (LCOM3), Std (LCOM3), Gini index (CAM), Hoover index (CAM)
DWS	Q1 (WMC), Var (NOC), Gini index (CBO), skewness (LCOM), Median (MOA)
CWS	Mean (DIT), Q1 (CBO), Generalized entropy (CBO), Mean (RFC), skewness (Ca), Generalized entropy (MOA), skewness (AMC)

features are used as input to develop the predictive models for various anti-patterns prediction [14].

$$Anti\text{-}pattern \text{ predictability} = f(\text{Significant features}) \tag{1}$$

Subset of Features Selected Using RSA: In order to reduce the complexity of the model developed, it is important to remove irrelevant features. For this purpose, we use a feature reduction technique known as **"Rough Set Analysis (RSA)"** to obtain a reduced set of features. Here the anti-pattern predictability is defined as a function of a reduced set of metrics.

$$Anti\text{-}pattern \text{ predictability} = f(\text{Reduced set of features}) \tag{2}$$

RSA enables the developer to find the subset of the original source code metrics that are most illuminating removing all the irrelevant attributes with minimal information loss [10]. Table 1 shows the reduced significant feature set for all the anti-patterns considered in this study. For example, Hoover index (WMC), Min (DIT), Mean (DIT), Max (RFC), skewness (LCOM), skewness (Ca), Q1 (DAM), Gini index (DAM), Gini index (IC) are selected features using RSA analysis for GOWS anti-pattern.

Subset of Features Selected Using PCA: A feature extraction technique known as **"Principle Component Analysis(PCA)"** is used to develop a model with less complexity using reduced set of features. PCA reduces the dimensionality of the data. It helps in reducing the computational complexity of the model. The primary idea of PCA is to diminish the dimensionality of a dataset comprising of numerous features correlated with one another, either vigorously or softly, while holding the variation present in the dataset, up to the greatest degree. Table 2a illustrates the eigenvalue, % variance, % cumulative for principal component (PC) domain metrics selected for GOWS anti-pattern. Similarly, 22, 21, and 21 PCs are selected for the FGWS, DWS, and CWS anti-patterns, respectively.

$$Anti\text{-}pattern \text{ predictability } = f(\text{Extracted set of features}) \qquad (3)$$

The same is done by transforming the features into a new set of features, which are known as the principal components or simply, the pc's.

4.4 Classifier Techniques

In this paper, we applied five ensemble techniques for training the predictive models for the detection of web service anti-patterns. The ensemble techniques we have used in this paper are: Bagging classifier (EST1), Random Forest classifier (EST2), Extra Trees classifier (EST3), AdaBoost classifier (EST4) and Gradient Boosting classifier (EST5).

Table 2. Subset of features selected using PCA for anti-patterns

(a) GOWS

	Eigen value	Variance (%)	Cumulative (%)
pc-1	32.87	20.81	20.81
pc-2	24.39	15.43	36.24
pc-3	20.40	12.91	49.15
pc-4	13.19	8.35	57.50
pc-5	10.22	6.47	63.97
pc-6	9.12	5.77	69.74
pc-7	8.23	5.21	74.95
pc-8	5.50	3.48	78.43
pc-9	3.27	2.07	80.50
pc-10	3.02	1.91	82.41
pc-11	2.89	1.83	84.24
pc-12	2.88	1.82	86.06
pc-13	2.60	1.64	87.70
pc-14	2.43	1.54	89.24
pc-15	2.32	1.47	90.71
pc-16	2.02	1.28	91.99
pc-17	1.84	1.17	93.15
pc-18	1.62	1.03	94.18

(b) FGWS

	Eigen value	Variance(%)	Cumulative(%)
pc-1	30.37	20.38	20.38
pc-2	24.28	16.30	36.68
pc-3	19.59	13.15	49.83
pc-4	11.98	8.04	57.87
pc-5	10.98	7.37	65.24
pc-6	7.96	5.35	70.59
pc-7	5.07	3.40	73.99
pc-8	4.31	2.89	76.88
pc-9	3.47	2.33	79.21
pc-10	2.99	2.00	81.21
pc-11	2.44	1.64	82.85
pc-12	2.41	1.62	84.47
pc-13	2.38	1.60	86.07
pc-14	2.30	1.55	87.61
pc-15	2.03	1.36	88.97
pc-16	1.92	1.29	90.26
pc-17	1.87	1.25	91.51
pc-18	1.62	1.09	92.60
pc-19	1.23	0.83	93.43
pc-20	1.19	0.80	94.23
pc-21	1.07	0.72	94.94
pc-22	1.04	0.70	95.64

5 Experimental Results

In this work, five sampling techniques besides the original data set (OD), features selected by three different feature selection techniques and five ensemble

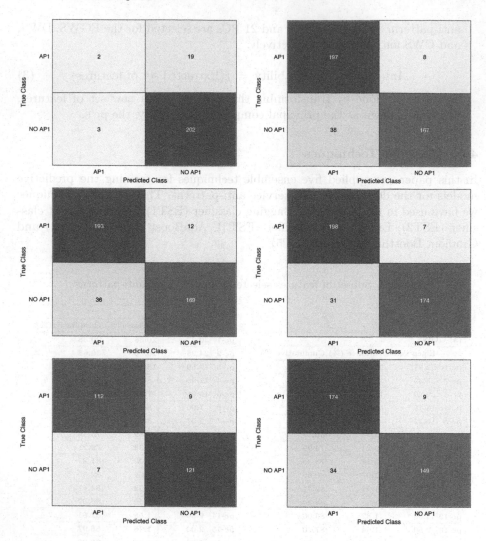

Fig. 4. Confusion matrix of EST1

techniques are applied for generating the models for the detection of four web service anti-patterns. A total of $6 \times 3 \times 5 \times 4 = 240$ predictive models are built for anti-pattern detection in this study. The predictive ability of these models are evaluated using Accuracy, and AUC performance values. Table 3 shows the Accuracy values for all the models generated. Figure 4 shows the confusion matrix obtained for the ensemble technique EST1 i.e. Bagging classifier. From Table 3 and Fig. 4, we observed that the:

- The performance values of the models trained on data after applying sampling techniques is better than models trained on the original data.

Table 3. Accuracy of all models

Data Sampling Techniques	Feature Selection Techniques	Antipatterns	EST-1	EST-2	EST-3	EST-4	EST-5	DataSampling Techniques	Feature Selection Techniques	Antipatterns	EST-1	EST-2	EST-3	EST-4	EST-5
ORG	SM	AP1	90.27	92.04	91.59	92.48	91.15	SVMSMOTE	SM	AP1	90.73	94.39	95.37	90.98	91.95
ORG	SM	AP2	94.25	95.13	95.13	93.81	91.59	SVMSMOTE	SM	AP2	86.61	95.83	96.13	92.26	93.75
ORG	SM	AP3	96.46	96.02	97.79	97.35	97.35	SVMSMOTE	SM	AP3	93.13	93.90	99.70	98.81	98.81
ORG	SM	AP4	95.13	94.69	96.02	93.81	93.36	SVMSMOTE	SM	AP4	90.83	96.33	96.64	92.97	94.80
ORG	PCA	AP1	90.71	89.82	92.48	91.59	90.71	SVMSMOTE	PCA	AP1	91.46	94.39	95.85	90.49	90.98
ORG	PCA	AP2	94.25	95.13	95.58	93.36	92.48	SVMSMOTE	PCA	AP2	84.82	94.64	96.73	88.69	86.31
ORG	PCA	AP3	94.69	93.81	94.69	94.69	88.94	SVMSMOTE	PCA	AP3	97.41	99.06	98.82	97.64	96.46
ORG	PCA	AP4	91.15	93.36	92.92	93.36	87.17	SVMSMOTE	PCA	AP4	89.51	95.61	96.10	89.02	91.71
ORG	RSA	AP1	91.15	90.71	92.92	90.71	90.71	SVMSMOTE	RSA	AP1	93.17	94.39	96.10	93.90	91.71
ORG	RSA	AP2	94.25	94.25	95.58	94.69	94.25	SVMSMOTE	RSA	AP2	89.88	94.94	97.32	88.69	88.99
ORG	RSA	AP3	94.69	97.79	98.23	96.90	90.71	SVMSMOTE	RSA	AP3	98.11	99.29	100.00	97.88	97.88
ORG	RSA	AP4	91.59	96.02	95.58	95.13	93.81	SVMSMOTE	RSA	AP4	91.74	96.02	96.64	95.41	94.80
SMOTE	SM	AP1	88.78	93.41	96.10	91.46	90.24	SMOTEENN	SM	AP1	93.57	99.60	99.20	98.30	97.59
SMOTE	SM	AP2	86.15	95.77	98.36	91.08	94.13	SMOTEENN	SM	AP2	88.52	94.43	97.05	94.43	88.52
SMOTE	SM	AP3	94.10	90.53	99.76	90.53	98.82	SMOTEENN	SM	AP3	93.89	99.40	99.40	99.70	98.50
SMOTE	SM	AP4	87.32	97.32	98.05	95.61	94.63	SMOTEENN	SM	AP4	87.40	98.09	98.47	95.04	96.18
SMOTE	PCA	AP1	89.02	94.15	95.85	91.22	89.76	SMOTEENN	PCA	AP1	93.31	96.94	98.33	90.53	93.59
SMOTE	PCA	AP2	84.98	95.77	97.18	90.14	89.20	SMOTEENN	PCA	AP2	90.60	95.04	97.39	90.60	92.43
SMOTE	PCA	AP3	95.99	99.29	99.53	98.82	97.88	SMOTEENN	PCA	AP3	97.54	99.26	99.26	99.51	97.04
SMOTE	PCA	AP4	88.29	95.61	95.37	91.22	91.95	SMOTEENN	PCA	AP4	94.54	97.27	98.36	91.26	92.90
SMOTE	RSA	AP1	90.24	93.66	95.61	90.00	89.02	SMOTEENN	RSA	AP1	98.58	98.58	98.94	98.23	97.87
SMOTE	RSA	AP2	90.85	95.07	97.18	88.03	89.44	SMOTEENN	RSA	AP2	91.62	96.22	97.57	90.27	91.08
SMOTE	RSA	AP3	97.88	99.29	99.76	98.58	98.11	SMOTEENN	RSA	AP3	98.28	98.53	98.53	99.26	99.75
SMOTE	RSA	AP4	91.46	95.37	96.83	95.12	93.41	SMOTEENN	RSA	AP4	94.13	97.21	99.72	99.77	94.97
BSMOTE	SM	AP1	88.29	92.93	95.37	91.95	89.76	SMOTETOMEK	SM	AP1	88.25	93.44	95.36	94.81	92.62
BSMOTE	SM	AP2	84.51	96.01	97.89	92.96	91.55	SMOTETOMEK	SM	AP2	87.43	96.34	97.64	91.88	90.84
BSMOTE	SM	AP3	94.58	96.29	100.00	99.29	98.35	SMOTETOMEK	SM	AP3	94.06	99.50	100.00	99.26	98.27
BSMOTE	SM	AP4	90.24	96.83	97.80	95.12	96.34	SMOTETOMEK	SM	AP4	87.77	97.87	97.61	95.48	96.54
BSMOTE	PCA	AP1	90.98	95.85	96.34	93.41	91.71	SMOTETOMEK	PCA	AP1	90.49	94.15	95.85	91.22	89.76
BSMOTE	PCA	AP2	84.51	95.54	97.18	90.14	89.20	SMOTETOMEK	PCA	AP2	88.03	97.42	97.18	90.14	89.20
BSMOTE	PCA	AP3	96.93	100.00	99.53	98.82	97.17	SMOTETOMEK	PCA	AP3	95.75	99.29	99.53	98.82	97.88
BSMOTE	PCA	AP4	88.05	94.39	96.10	90.73	91.46	SMOTETOMEK	PCA	AP4	85.61	96.83	95.37	91.22	91.95
BSMOTE	RSA	AP1	88.29	90.73	94.88	89.76	90.00	SMOTETOMEK	RSA	AP1	92.27	94.33	95.36	89.18	90.98
BSMOTE	RSA	AP2	88.26	95.77	97.18	88.97	88.97	SMOTETOMEK	RSA	AP2	89.20	94.84	97.18	88.03	89.44
BSMOTE	RSA	AP3	99.06	98.82	100.00	98.35	98.11	SMOTETOMEK	RSA	AP3	99.05	98.58	99.05	98.82	98.58
BSMOTE	RSA	AP4	92.44	96.59	97.80	94.88	96.10	SMOTETOMEK	RSA	AP4	93.25	96.75	97.75	95.75	93.25

- SMOTEENN is showing the best performance, while the model developed using the original data (ORG) is showing the worst performance.
- The model trained using features selected by PCA as input have better performance.
- The performance of the model trained using EST3 i.e. Extra Trees classifier with a mean accuracy of 97.13 is higher when compared to the models trained using other ensemble techniques.

6 Competitive Analysis

In this section, we compare the performance of the various models generated using Box-plots, Descriptive statistics and Wilcoxon ranksum test.

6.1 Data Sampling Techniques

Figure 5 depicts the performance values, i.e., Accuracy, AUC, and F-measure of the models developed using different variants of SMOTE using Box-plot diagrams. Table 4 shows the descriptive statistics for the different SMOTE techniques used in this study. From Fig. 5 and Table 4, we infer that the technique SMOTEENN is showing the best performance, with 0.989 mean, 1.000 max, 0.986 Q1 and 0.999 Q3 AUC values. The model developed using the original data(ORG) is showing the worst performance with the AUC value of 0.823. It is also observed that the model developed with the dataset after applying the data sampling technique(any) is showing better performance when compared to the model developed using the original data, as the sampling technique deals with the class imbalance problem.

Table 4. Descriptive statistics of data sampling techniques

	Accuracy					
	Max	Min	Median	Mean	Q3	Q1
ORG	98.23	87.17	93.81	93.60	95.13	91.59
SMOTE	99.76	84.98	95.10	94.11	97.60	90.54
BSMOTE	100.00	84.51	95.24	94.20	97.49	90.73
SVMSMOTE	100.00	84.82	94.80	94.20	96.68	91.59
SMOTEENN	99.75	87.40	97.33	96.00	98.53	93.64
SMOTETOMEK	100.00	85.61	95.36	94.37	97.70	91.10

Table 5. P-value: data sampling techniques

	ORG	SMOTE	BSMOTE	SVMSMOTE	SMOTEENN	SMOTETOMEK
ORG	1	0	0	0	0	0
SMOTE	0	1	1	0	0	1
BSMOTE	0	1	1	0	0	1
SVMSMOTE	0	0	0	1	0	0
SMOTEENN	0	0	0	0	1	0
SMOTETOMEK	0	1	1	0	0	1

Wilcoxon signed-rank test is used in this study for statistically comparing the performance of the various web service anti-pattern prediction models developed using different variants of smote sampled data and the original data. The main

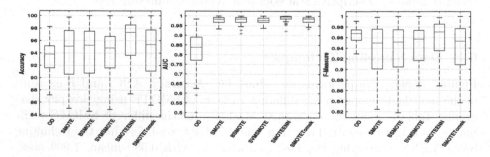

Fig. 5. Box-plot: data sampling techniques

motivation of the wilcoxon signed-rank test is to find whether there is a significant difference between the performance of the various models developed using different Smote sampled data or not. The null hypothesis considered for this paper is: "The web service anti-pattern prediction model trained using different variants of smote sampled data are not significantly different". The considered null hypothesis is accepted, if the p-value obtained using the wilcoxon signed-rank test is '1'. Table 5 shows the p-values obtained for the models developed using all the data sampling techniques along with the original dataset. A close inspection of Table shows that most of the comparison points are having p-values as '0', i.e., the considered hypothesis is rejected. Hence we conclude that there is a significant difference between the performance of the models generated using different variants of smote sampled data and the original data.

6.2   Feature Selection Techniques

Figure 6 depicts the performance values, i.e., Accuracy, AUC, and F-measure of the models developed using the features selected by different feature selection techniques as input using Box-plot diagrams. Table 6 shows the descriptive statistics for the various feature selection techniques used in this study. Table 6 show that the mean value of the model developed using the features selected by PCA as input is higher than the models developed using the features selected by rank-sum test, and RSA as input. From Fig. 6, we observe that the inter-quartile range for AUC value for the model generated using PCA is compa ratively small when compared to the other models. This indicates that the performance parameters obtained using multiple executions in PCA are showing less variation when compared to other models.

The null-hypothesis considered in this section is: "The performance of the anti-pattern prediction models developed using features selected by different feature selection techniques are significantly different." The defined null-hypothesis is accepted, if the p-value obtained using the wilcoxon signed rank test is '1'. Table 7 shows the p-values of the models developed using various combination of features as input. From Table 7, we observed that most of the comparison points have p-value as '1' i.e. the defined null-hypothesis is accepted. Therefore, there is

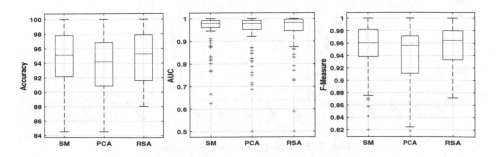

Fig. 6. Box-plot: feature selection techniques

Table 6. Descriptive statistics of feature selection techniques

	Accuracy					
	Max	Min	Median	Mean	Q3	Q1
SM	100.00	84.51	95.13	94.71	97.80	92.15
PCA	100.00	84.51	94.20	93.72	96.83	90.85
RSA	100.00	88.03	95.25	94.84	97.88	91.61

no significant difference between the performance of the models builds utilizing the features selected by using three different feature selection techniques.

Table 7. P-value: feature selection

	SM	PCA	RSA
SM	1	0	
PCA	0	1	0
RSA	1	0	1

6.3   Classifier Techniques

Figure 7 shows the box-plot diagram of the AUC, Accuracy and F-measure of the classifier techniques. Table 8 shows the descriptive statistics for the models trained using distinct ensemble techniques. From Table 8 and Fig. 7, we observed that the performance of the model trained using EST3 i.e. Extra Trees classifier is higher when compared to the models trained using other ensemble techniques. The model trained using EST3 is showing good performance with a mean accuracy of 97.13, median accuracy 97.18 and min accuracy of 91.59.

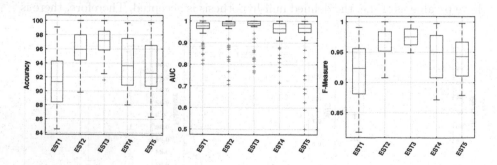

Fig. 7. Box-plot: classifier techniques

Table 8. Statistical description for ensemble techniques

	Accuracy					
	Max	Min	Median	Mean	Q3	Q1
EST1	99.06	84.51	91.31	91.67	94.25	88.41
EST2	100.00	89.82	95.93	96.11	97.98	94.41
EST3	100.00	91.59	97.18	97.13	98.50	95.85
EST4	99.70	88.03	93.61	93.88	97.49	90.85
EST5	99.75	86.31	92.55	93.27	96.50	90.71

The null-hypothesis considered in this work is: "The performance of the anti-pattern prediction models trained using various ensemble techniques are significantly different. " The defined null-hypothesis is accepted, if the p-value obtained using the wilcoxon signed rank test is '1' and is rejected if the p-value is '0'. Table 9 shows the p-values of the models trained using different ensemble techniques. From Table 9, we observed that most of the comparison points have p-value as '0' i.e. the defined null-hypothesis is rejected. Hence we conclude that there is a significant difference between the performance of the models trained using various ensemble techniques.

Table 9. P-value: ensemble techniques

	EST1	EST2	EST3	EST4	EST5
EST1	1	0	0	0	0
EST2	0	1	0	0	0
EST3	0	0	1	0	0
EST4	0	0	0	1	1
EST5	0	0	0	1	1

7 Conclusion

We present the empirical analysis on anti-pattern prediction models developed using data sampling, feature selection and ensemble techniques. Five-fold cross validation is used for validating the performance of the models built. We used three performance parameters i.e. Accuracy, F-measure and AUC to compare the performance of the models built. We observed that the performance values of the models trained on data after applying sampling techniques is better than models trained on the original data. Wilcoxon sign rank test suggested that model trained using balanced data have significant improvement in predicting anti-patterns. It is observed that the performance of the model trained using features selected by PCA as input have better performance. Wilcoxon sign rank test suggested that there is no significant difference between the performance of the models builds utilizing the features selected by using three different feature selection techniques. We also observe that the model trained using EST3 i.e. Extra Trees classifier is showing good performance with a mean accuracy of 97.13.

References

1. Batista, G.E., Prati, R.C., Monard, M.C.: A study of the behavior of several methods for balancing machine learning training data. ACM SIGKDD Explor. Newsl. **6**(1), 20–29 (2004)
2. Chidamber, S.R., Kemerer, C.F.: A metrics suite for object oriented design. IEEE Trans. Softw. Eng. **20**(6), 476–493 (1994)
3. Jaafar, F., Guéhéneuc, Y.-G., Hamel, S., Khomh, F., Zulkernine, M.: Evaluating the impact of design pattern and anti-pattern dependencies on changes and faults. Empir. Softw. Eng. **21**(3), 896–931 (2015). https://doi.org/10.1007/s10664-015-9361-0
4. Král, J., Zemlicka, M.: Crucial service-oriented antipatterns, vol. 2, pp. 160–171. International Academy, Research and Industry Association (IARIA) (2008)
5. Kumar, L., Sureka, A.: An empirical analysis on web service anti-pattern detection using a machine learning framework. In: 2018 IEEE 42nd Annual Computer Software and Applications Conference (COMPSAC), vol. 1, pp. 2–11. IEEE (2018)
6. Moha, N., et al.: Specification and detection of SOA antipatterns. In: Service-Oriented Computing, pp. 1–16 (2012)
7. Ordiales Coscia, J.L., Mateos, C., Crasso, M., Zunino, A.: Anti-pattern free code-first web services for state-of-the-art Java WSDL generation tools. Int. J. Web Grid Serv. **9**(2), 107–126 (2013)
8. Ouni, A., Kula, R.G., Kessentini, M., Inoue, K.: Web service antipatterns detection using genetic programming. In: Proceedings of the 2015 Annual Conference on Genetic and Evolutionary Computation, pp. 1351–1358. ACM (2015)
9. Palma, F., Nayrolles, M., Moha, N., Guéhéneuc, Y.G., Baudry, B., Jézéquel, J.M.: SOA antipatterns: an approach for their specification and detection. Int. J. Coop. Inf. Syst. **22**(04), 1341004 (2013)
10. Pawlak, Z.: Rough Sets: Theoretical Aspects of Reasoning About Data, vol. 9. Springer Science and Business Media (2012). https://doi.org/10.1007/978-94-011-3534-4
11. Saluja, S., Batra, U.: Optimized approach for antipattern detection in service computing architecture. J. Inf. Optim. Sci. **40**(5), 1069–1080 (2019)
12. Settas, D., Cerone, A., Fenz, S.: Enhancing ontology-based antipattern detection using Bayesian networks. Expert Syst. Appl. **39**(10), 9041–9053 (2012)
13. Settas, D.L., Meditskos, G., Stamelos, I.G., Bassiliades, N.: SPARSE: a symptom-based antipattern retrieval knowledge-based system using semantic web technologies. Expert Syst. Appl. **38**(6), 7633–7646 (2011)
14. Tummalapalli, S., Kumar, L., Neti, L.B.M.: An empirical framework for web service anti-pattern prediction using machine learning techniques. In: 2019 9th Annual Information Technology, Electromechanical Engineering and Microelectronics Conference (IEMECON), pp. 137–143. IEEE (2019)
15. Upadhyaya, B., Tang, R., Zou, Y.: An approach for mining service composition patterns from execution logs. J. Softw. Evol. Process **25**(8), 841–870 (2013)

Evaluation of Integrated Frameworks for Optimizing QoS in Serverless Computing

Anisha Kumari[1], Bibhudatta Sahoo[1], Ranjan Kumar Behera[2(✉)],
Sanjay Misra[3], and Mayank Mohan Sharma[4]

[1] Department of CSE, National Institute of Technology, Rourkela, India
bdsahu@nitrkl.ac.in
[2] School of Computer Science and Engineering, XIM University, Bhubaneswar, India
ranjanbehera@xim.edu.in
[3] Department of Electrical and Information Engineering, Covenant University,
Ota1023, Nigeria
sanjay.misra@covenantuniversity.edu.ng
[4] Zillow Inc., San Francisco, USA
mayankmohans@zillowgroup.com

Abstract. Serverless computing is an emerging cloud deployment model
where developers can concentrate on developing application logic without
worrying about the underlying architecture. It is similar to the platform
as a service (PaaS) but at the functional level. Applications are usually
deployed in the form of a set of functions independently and each function may be executed at separate servers thus also named as function as
a service (FaaS). Serverless at the edge can handle thousands of concurrent functions invocations to process various kinds of events generated
from resources like database, system logs, and other storage units, etc.
A number of serverless frameworks like Openfaas, Openwhisk, Microsoft
Azure, Amazon AWS allow dynamic scaling to handle the parallel request
of stateless functions from the client-side. A separate container manager
may be provisioned to handle distributed load for data processing. In this
paper, we have evaluated the performance of serverless frameworks for
parallel loads in terms of response time and throughput. In this paper,
we have shown that the serverless framework is suitable for handling
dynamic applications that can be executed on a number of stateless functions. An extensive comparison of the performance of serverless frameworks in handling concurrent invocations in terms of response time and
throughput is also presented. It has been observed that Openwhisk is
found to be the better serverless framework in terms of elasticity and
scalability.

Keywords: Serverless computing · Function-as-a-service ·
Orchestration · OpenWhisk · Openfaas

1 Introduction

Serverless computing has attracted a lot of attention to small and medium
scale industries for fulfill customer demands. Unlike traditional computing,

© Springer Nature Switzerland AG 2021
O. Gervasi et al. (Eds.): ICCSA 2021, LNCS 12955, pp. 277–288, 2021.
https://doi.org/10.1007/978-3-030-87007-2_20

where users are required to maintain on-premises infrastructure, cloud computing abstains from these requirements as well as provides services as per user's demands. There is no need to purchase and maintain hardware, storage, and processing units etc. by the users. The data are accessed and stored over the Internet so that at any time from anywhere cloud users could able to access their stored data. Generally, cloud systems deliver three types of deployment models such as Infrastructure as a Service (IaaS) [1], Platform as a Service (PaaS) [2] and Software as a Service (SaaS). The environment of cloud computing is scalable and flexible which provides the users for leasing or releasing services as per the requirement. Users may rent the services with short-term dynamic plans or long-term preservation plans. Several cloud service providers facilitate the same type of services like network services, storage and computing. These services are approximating to non-functional Quality of Service (QoS) parameters for instance energy consumption, time, availability, cost, etc. Meanwhile, several cloud service providers, like Google Cloud Platform (GCP) [3], Amazon Web Services (AWS), Microsoft Azure, and IBM Bluemix showed up offering various cloud infrastructures and services in the cloud computing marketplace. Function-as-a-service (FaaS) leverages the best functionalities of Infrastructure as a Service (IaaS) and Container as a Service (CaaS), where services are delivered in the form of bundles known as containers. The basic architecture for FaaS also include service oriented and event driven features, which allow the users to develop Service oriented applications. Several cloud providers having started their FaaS platforms such as Azure Functions, AWS Lambda, IBM Openwhisk, and Google Cloud Functions, which are based upon container-orchestration systems such as Kubernetes. Over the evolution of FaaS platforms as well as the advancement of the cloud computing archetype, the serverless computing framework, whereupon the application is abstracted as a combined form of functions hosted on FaaS platforms orchestrated in a workflow has emerged [12].

Serverless computing has a number of advantages over the traditional cloud computating models by abstracting the management of underlying infrastructure. In serverless computing, FaaS platforms taking over entire operational and computational responsibilities for resource management, scaling, function deployment, and monitoring [16]. Developers can primarily concentrate on the business logic of functions, rather than expediting the application development. The execution model for serverless computing is shown in Fig. 1. The serverless computing models are found to be more effective due to its reduced cost model which is more flexible and the bill is based on exact usages of resources. Even though serverless architecture eases resource management and cost-effectiveness, some challenges are hindering its use by potential users due to its tradeoff between performance and cost [6]. Cost modeling, performance and optimization are non-trivial as well as the necessary measures, which needs to be taken care in SLA of computation model in serverless platform [4].

As shown in Fig. 1, there is no single traditional back end for serverless execution model. The application's front end communicates straightaway with the database, compute functions, or services through an API gateway. However, several services are hidden backside compute service functions, in which additional security steps and validation could take place.

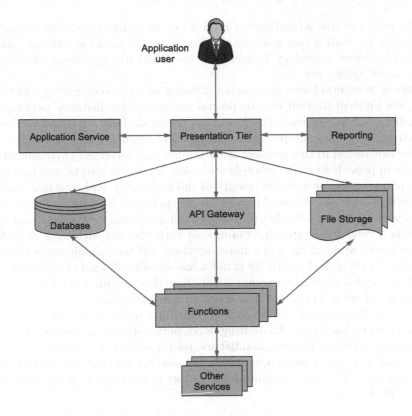

Fig. 1. Execution model for serverless computing

Serverless frameworks may help with the problem of layering and having to upgrade too much ground. There is room for developers to minimize or remove layering by breaching the system as a group of functions, also authorizing the front end to communicate with services securely and even the database directly, as illustrated in Fig. 1. All these things might be done in a structured manner to prevent complex implementations as well as dependency nightmares by defining service boundaries clearly, which allow functions to be autonomous, and planning how services and functions will interact.

The rest of this paper is organized as follows: Sect. 2 describes the motivation toward the work. In Sect. 3, some of the related work in this area have been discussed. Section 4 focuses on various aspect of the serverless computing framework. Section 5 describes the evaluation of various serverless frameworks and Sect. 6 conclude the paper.

2 Motivation

The motivation towards the research work may be described as these folds:

- The most suitable advantages of serverless computing are aligning computational costs with actual business requirements and reducing costs in general, but also more secondary benefits are identified like diminished lead time, enhanced agility, etc.
- Currently, several businesses are not utilizing serverless computing techniques or are underutilization due to several unknowns for instance performance challenges, complex cost structures, and uncertain facts regarding the implementation of this concept towards the current application architecture.
- The motivation in this research work is such as a serverless environment has more to provide to software application developers, architects, and providers, despite that, because of the novelty of the technology and economic and the relatively high architectural impact, its acceptance is inadequate behind or at the very least, is not highly utilized. Switching towards a serverless framework needs a considerable switch, comparable with the one architects as well as developers could make when micro-services will be suitable for a common architectural style. It certainly is not a one-size-fits-all kind of approach. The adoption of successful serverless computing depends on several factors and also needs many important non-arbitrary considerations.
- We hope this research will be able to contribute to the successful adoption of serverless technology by facilitating developers, software architects, and cloud providers with the insights, handlebars, references, etc. for making prior decisions of their particular applications and also for maximizing the potentials of this interesting new computing technology towards software deployment in the cloud.

3   Literature Survey

The serverless computing model focuses on revolutionizing the archetype and advancement of modern scalable applications, where developers can run event-driven code without managing or provisioning servers. This new technique experiments with an industry momentum around the cloud event abstraction. Very few research publications are there for the practical implementation of theoretical serverless concepts.

One of the reason behind the popularity of serverless computing is that it allows more responsiveness towards both providers and users, using market based schemes incorporation for resource allocation and pricing. Vipul et al. [19] have carried out a work, in which their approach brings about dynamic pricing strategy obtained as a result of optimization problem with dual form. They further developed mechanism of feedback which allows the cloud provider to achieve the optimal resource allocation, also when the utilities of users are unidentified. As a result of their simulation, it is shown that their approach can trail market-demand.

Maissen et al. [10] introduced a user-space application FaaSdom that facilitating benchmark tests over different types of serverless archetypes. It can be used to evaluate the serverless computing platform. An open-source standard suite FaaSdom is easily deployed and facilitating significant perceptions over several metrics as well as serverless providers. They envisioned extending FaaSdom towards the following directions. Firstly, they have expanded the runtime environment and category of supported languages, as well as integrating the supports from the freely accessible orchestration tools. Secondly, they have planed to preserve an online, publicly accessible, and continuous deployment of the FaaSdom, to frame a large dataset of factual measurements which would be quite helpful for the researchers.

Another work has been carried out by Mistry et al. [13] in which authors proposed to investigate unikernel, an alternative to containers to build serverless platform at the edge, having security concerns and addressing in particular performance. They have presented UniFaaS, a prototype edge-serverless platform that leverages unikernels – tiny library single-address-space operating systems only containing the parts of the OS required to run a given application – for executing functions. The result is a serverless platform with less CPU footprints and extremely low memory, along with excellent performance. UniFaaS has been designed and deployed on low-powered single-board computer systems, like Arduino or Raspberry Pi, without compromising on performance.

In the public cloud, machine learning applications deployment considering prediction problems having a key challenge such as integrating the framework as well as the heterogeneity of resources towards optimizing the constraints [5]. Gunasekaran et al. [7] have proposed a model to frame a machine learning prediction model, which is self-managed and could optimize the various needs of the application, to have relied on peculiarities of the heterogeneous resource offered by the public cloud. In doing so, the authors discussed the compromises for intermixed resources such as functions besides Virtual Machines in serverless, also identified the fundamental issue closely related to the configuration of the resources. They proposed several resource management key policies making; (i) multi-dimensional SLO awareness, (ii) fluctuated request load awareness and (iii) latency awareness. These measures could be collectively utilized for cost-efficient prediction serving to have uncompromising accuracy as well as latency.

In a research paper by Sreekanti et al. [18] the authors argued about a well-suited dataflow API is preferable to the latency-sensitive task, also manageable for optimization even with faultless black-box machine learning frameworks. They presented the Cloudflow design, an archetype providing auto-scaling serverless an API, and realized it on the backend. The Cloudflow implements competitive execution and performance-critical optimizations transparently comprising operator fusion. Their analysis results that on synthetic workloads Cloudflow's optimizations having significantly improved performance, also on real-world prediction pipelines Cloudflow outperforms state-of-the-art prediction serving systems by as much as two times, achieving latency goals of trending applications such as real-time video analysis.

An event-driven Extract, Transform, and Load (ETL) pipeline serverless architecture was presented in a paper by Pogiatzis and Samakovitis [14], which provides an evaluation of its performance over a range of dataflow tasks of changing velocity, payload size and frequency. They have designed an experiment utilizing the generated tabular data throughout varying event frequencies, processing power and data volumes in order to measure: (i) reliability on data delivery; (ii) the consistency of pipeline executions; (iii) economic scalability (cost of chargeable tasks); and, (iv) maximum payload size per pipeline.

Wen and Liu [20] have presented the first empiric survey on characterization and comparison of existing serverless workflow services, i.e., Azure Durable Functions, AWS Step Functions, Google Cloud Composer, and Alibaba Serverless Workflow. They firstly compare the characteristics from six dimensions, e.g., parallelism support, orchestration way, data payload limit, etc. After that they have measured the performance of these serverless workflow services beneath various experimental settings (i.e. data-flow complexity, function complexity, and different levels of activity complexity). On the basis of the results, some interesting findings, e.g., only under high data-flow complexity conditions, the performance of serverless workflow have a certain impact, can be useful and helpful for the developers and the cloud providers. Finally, they reported a series of findings and implications to further facilitate the current practice of serverless workflow.

4   Serverless Computing Framework

In this section, a brief introduction to FaaS, serverless workflow and integrated tools for serverless platform has been discussed.

4.1   Function as a Service (FaaS)

Serverless computing can also be called Function as a Service or FaaS. Clients upload their business logics and providers maintain the traffic routing, scaling, etc. as well as mainly focus on deployment. From a client's viewpoint, the serverless technique can facilitate the approach of deploying business logic into production. Capacity planning, maintaining the virtual machines (VM's), and Scaling are hidden from the developer. Additionally, the billing mechanism relies on the actual amount of resources consumed by an application.

Abstraction is one of the core feature in FaaS model, where set of instructions known as functions abstracts the implementation part of the business logic in an application. The unit of execution are the functions in serverless computing, which are similar to the methods in object oriented programming model or the functions in functional programming. The major task of function is to handle stateless job required by an application. Containers are used to bundle the source codes along with their dependencies. However, each of the function are executed separately with independent manner with the help of lightweight virtualization approaches such as Uni-kernels [17], Docker containers [11], or even processes. The sequence diagram for execute a function in response to a event is shown in Fig. 2.

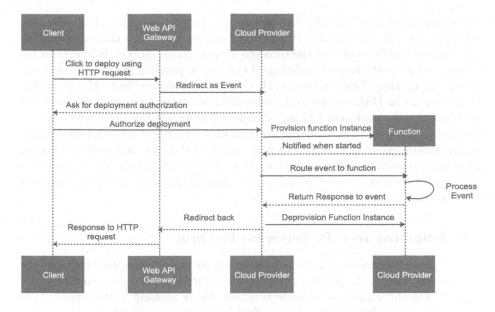

Fig. 2. Sequence diagram for execution of FaaS

The first FaaS model was lunch by AWS known as Lambda in 2014 which can deploy, store bundles of function and provide functions as services through event triggers. It also facilitates monitoring of resource utilization and auto scaling features. Some of the other platforms also provides the same functionalities by open-source communities and public cloud service providers such as Microsoft azure Google functions etc. In FaaS, developers have very little control over resources and the infrastructure. They are only responsible for deploying their applications along with the triggered events [9]. For example; in AWS Lambda during execution, the concurrency level and the amount of allocated memory are the only options for tuning the performances of functions. By provisioning and reserving additional instances to the host functions making high concurrency level and warm instance unavailable so that delay in container initialization provisioning has also referred to as cold starts which decreases the performance of framework as well as the number of throttles with extremely heavy requests of workloads.

4.2 Serverless Execution Model

Generally, the serverless framework is the function orchestration for implementing the complete programming instructions to run a serverless application. Several existing platforms such as AWS, IBM, Microsoft, etc. give an idea about, how a serverless framework considers as a process of grouping individual functions and coordination among those functions. The examples for deploying a serverless application are existing in various environments and it is shown that the serverless framework is having four types of structure, which include cycle, self-loop, branch, and parallel. It is proved in prior researches that a framework appropriate to Petri net and the directed acyclic graph (DAG), is beneficial for cost as well as performance modeling of systems in parallel, distributed and scientific, computing. Despite that, each of them is unfavorable to the serverless archetype, as in DAGs loops and cycles are restrictive because they cause the problem of state explosion lacking efficient solutions for the Petri nets. Also in cloud computing, Petri nets are having their limited support and high complexity of non-functional requirements which are considered as the major shortcomings. Therefore, cost modeling and performance of serverless applications require a brief concept about a serverless archetype, that adapts to new characteristics of the serverless framework.

4.3   Integrated Tools for Serverless Platform

Though FaaS frameworks are beneficial for simple stateless applications likewise web-serving and ETL, several complex distributed applications could not be expressed in the context of a single function. Many existing FaaS orchestration tools offer clients for composing manifold functions to facilitate more complex application semantics.

Since 2014 Amazon Lambda's appearance, large-scale industries providing cloud services, have accepted FaaS framework to develop serverless applications using various tools. In this research work, serverless framework like IBM apache Openwhisk [15], Openfaas [8], AWS and Microsoft Azure have been considered for the implementation. Apache Openwhisk is a distributed serverless model which executes functions in response to a triggered event in a scalable manner. It inherently manages infrastructure, scalable servers with the help of a docker container which allows the users to develop applications seamlessly without worrying about the underlying infrastructure. It also supports multiple languages like Go, Java, Python, NodeJs, Ruby, Swift, etc. It is event-driven which allows the serverless execution of functional code known as actions that may be triggered from external sources like web or mobile-based applications, chat-bots, scheduled alarm, etc.

5   Evaluation of the Execution Model

In this paper we, have evaluated the serverless computing environment by deploying functions concurrently for various applications. The performance has been evaluated in term of throughput and response time. Each of the performance parameters are measured using concurrent function invocations. Response time corresponding to various frameworks are measured with respect to number of users.

5.1   Experimental Setup

Several functions from Openwhisk, Openfaas, Azure Functions were deployed having similar configuration. Each of the function are stateless and allocated with one CPU and 1.0 GB of memory for execution with respect to an event. All the events are triggered by HTTP request. Apart from the HTTP Trigger other triggers like database trigger and object storage trigger have also been used in some framework for generating event. Apache benchmark (ab) tool3 have been used to generate HTTP request to invoke the functions deployed on server.

5.2   Results and Observations

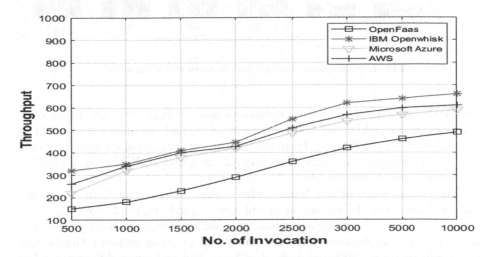

Fig. 3. Comparative analysis in term of throughput

The frameworks that are considered in this paper are evaluated based on the function throughput as it is one of the metric used to identify the quality of concurrent process. It deals with how many functions instances are supplied at the time of extensive request. It is important to note that maximum allowable concurrent function invocations varies from framework to framework. The resources for function invocations are also different for frameworks. For example, AWS use S3 object storage or DynamoDB database for parallel function invocations, OpenWhisk use couchDB database as the resource for function invocations. Figure 3 shows the change of throughput per second over the number of function invocations. It can be observed that IBM Openwhisk framework offers better throughput as compared to other frameworks. It attains maximum throughput at 3000 invocations. The average throughput is found to be 500 per second, which is highest as compared to other serverless frameworks. The throughput of Openfaas is very less as at all the invocations. Microsoft Azure

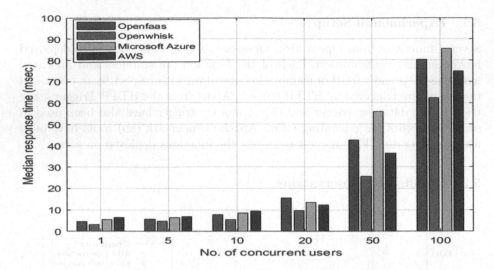

Fig. 4. Performance comparison in term of response time

and AWS functions shows similar bahaviour in attaining maximum throughput. The average throughput for AWS, microsoft Azure and Openfaas are found to be 465, 440 and 322 respectively. From the experimental analysis, it can be observed that the performance in term of throughput is better in IBM's Openwhisk as compared to other frameworks.

The performance of the frameworks is also evaluated in term of median response time over the no. of concurrent user request. Figure 4 shows the comparative analysis of various serverless frameworks in term of median response time. The median response has been calculated by using response time across all 10000 iterations. 10000 requests has been deployed using different level of concurrency users (1, 5, 10, 20 and 50). It can be observed from Fig. 4 that the fastest response is obtained by Openwhisk in all the scenario. The response time for microsoft Azure and AWS is almost same for request by 5 concurrent users. Microsoft Azure has median response time about 55 msec for 50 concurrent users which is highest among all the frameworks. The clear difference in mean response time is reflected at 50 number of concurrent users where Openwhisk is better as compared to others.

6   Conclusion

Serverless framework in cloud computing offers a number of advantages which include cost-efficiency, scalability, low latency, better responsiveness while deploying applications in servers. Developers need not to worry about the underlying architecture and the cost of service is based on pay as you go basis. Applications are deployed in the form of independent stateless functions which can be invoke to process the event triggered by user. Several framework have been emerging to provide services in serverless platform. In this paper, we have demonstrated four open source serverless frameworks such as Openfaas, Openwhisk, AWS and Microsoft Azure to prove service in low cost and scalability manner. Their performance has been compared based on the response time and throughput on concurrent request from the client side. Each of the request may be in the form of triggers which leads to execution of functions at the server side. It has been concluded that Openwhish is found to be better severeness framework in term of median response time and throughput.

In future, parameters other than throughput and response time may be taken into consideration for evaluating the performance of serverless tools.

References

1. Al Nuaimi, K., Mohamed, N., Al Nuaimi, M., Al-Jaroodi, J.: A survey of load balancing in cloud computing: challenges and algorithms. In: 2012 2nd Symposium on Network Cloud Computing and Applications, pp. 137–142. IEEE (2012)
2. Al-Roomi, M., Al-Ebrahim, S., Buqrais, S., Ahmad, I.: Cloud computing pricing models: a survey. Int. J. Grid Distrib. Comput. 6(5), 93–106 (2013)
3. Arteaga, D., Cabrera, J., Xu, J., Sundararaman, S., Zhao, M. CloudCache: on-demand flash cache management for cloud computing. In: 14th USENIX Conference on File and Storage Technologies, FAST 2016, pp. 355–369 (2016)
4. Baldini, I., et al.: Serverless computing: current trends and open problems. In: Chaudhary, S., Somani, G., Buyya, R. (eds.) Research Advances in Cloud Computing, pp. 1–20. Springer, Singapore (2017). https://doi.org/10.1007/978-981-10-5026-8_1
5. Behera, R.K., Jena, M., Rath, S.K., Misra, S.: Co-LSTM: convolutional LSTM model for sentiment analysis in social big data. Inf. Process. Manage. 58(1), 102435 (2021)
6. Behera, R.K., Shukla, S., Rath, S.K., Misra, S.: Software reliability assessment using machine learning technique. In: Gervasi, O., et al. (eds.) ICCSA 2018. LNCS, vol. 10964, pp. 403–411. Springer, Cham (2018). https://doi.org/10.1007/978-3-319-95174-4_32
7. Gunasekaran, J.R., Mishra, C.S., Thinakaran, P., Kandemir, M.T., Das, C.R.: Implications of public cloud resource heterogeneity for inference serving. In: Proceedings of the 2020 6th International Workshop on Serverless Computing, pp. 7–12 (2020)
8. Kaewkasi, C.: Docker for Serverless Applications: Containerize and orchestrate functions using OpenFaas, OpenWhisk, and Fn. Packt Publishing Ltd. (2018)
9. Kumari, A., Behera, R.K., Sahoo, K.S., Nayyar, A., Kumar Luhach, A., Prakash Sahoo, S.: Supervised link prediction using structured-based feature extraction in social network. Concurrency Comput. Pract. Exp., e5839 (2020). https://doi.org/10.1002/cpe.5839
10. Maissen, P., Felber, P., Kropf, P., Schiavoni, V.: FaaSdom: a benchmark suite for serverless computing. In: Proceedings of the 14th ACM International Conference on Distributed and Event-Based Systems, pp. 73–84 (2020)
11. Merkel, D.: Docker: lightweight Linux containers for consistent development and deployment. Linux J. 2014(239), 2 (2014)

12. Misra, S.: A step by step guide for choosing project topics and writing research papers in ICT related disciplines (2021). https://doi.org/10.1007/978-3-030-69143-1_55
13. Mistry, C., Stelea, B., Kumar, V., Pasquier, T.: Demonstrating the practicality of unikernels to build a serverless platform at the edge (2020)
14. Pogiatzis, A., Samakovitis, G.: An event-driven serverless ETL pipeline on AWS. Appl. Sci. **11**(1), 191 (2021)
15. Quevedo, S., Merchán, F., Rivadeneira, R., Dominguez, F.X.: Evaluating apache OpenWhisk-FaaS. In: 2019 IEEE 4th Ecuador Technical Chapters Meeting (ETCM), pp. 1–5. IEEE (2019)
16. Rodríguez, G., Mateos, C., Misra, S.: Exploring Web service QoS estimation for web service composition. In: Lopata, A., Butkienė, R., Gudonienė, D., Sukackė, V. (eds.) ICIST 2020. CCIS, vol. 1283, pp. 171–184. Springer, Cham (2020). https://doi.org/10.1007/978-3-030-59506-7_15
17. Scherb, C., Marxer, C., Tschudin, C.: Execution plans for serverless computing in information centric networking. In: Proceedings of the 1st ACM CoNEXT Workshop on Emerging in Network Computing Paradigms, pp. 34–40 (2019)
18. Sreekanti, V., Subbaraj, H., Wu, C., Gonzalez, J.E., Hellerstein, J.M.: Optimizing prediction serving on low-latency serverless dataflow. arXiv preprint arXiv:2007.05832 (2020)
19. Van Eyk, E., Toader, L., Talluri, S., Versluis, L., Uă, A., Iosup, A.: Serverless is more: from PaaS to present cloud computing. IEEE Internet Comput. **22**(5), 8–17 (2018)
20. Wen, J., Liu, Y.: An empirical study on serverless workflow service. arXiv preprint arXiv:2101.03513 (2021)

A Self-adaptive Approach for Assessing the Criticality of Security-Related Static Analysis Alerts

Miltiadis Siavvas[✉], Ilias Kalouptsoglou, Dimitrios Tsoukalas, and Dionysios Kehagias

Centre for Research and Technology Hellas, Thessaloniki, Greece
{siavvasm,iliaskaloup,tsoukj,diok}@iti.gr

Abstract. Despite the acknowledged ability of automated static analysis to detect software vulnerabilities, its adoption in practice is limited, mainly due to the large number of false alerts (i.e., false positives) that it generates. Although several machine learning-based techniques for assessing the actionability of the produced alerts and for filtering out false positives have been proposed, none of them have demonstrated sufficient results, whereas limited attempts focus on assessing the criticality of the alerts from a security viewpoint. To this end, in the present paper we propose an approach for assessing the criticality of security-related static analysis alerts. In particular, we develop a machine learning-based technique for prioritizing and classifying security-related static analysis alerts based on their criticality, by considering information retrieved from the alerts themselves, vulnerability prediction models, and user feedback. The concept of retraining is also adopted to enable the model to correct itself and adapt to previously unknown software products. The technique has been evaluated through a case study, which revealed its capacity to effectively assess the criticality of alerts of previously unknown projects, as well as its ability to dynamically adapt to the characteristics of the new project and provide more accurate assessments through retraining.

Keywords: Software quality · Software security · Automated static analysis · Self-adaptive systems · Vulnerability prediction

1 Introduction

Security is an important aspect for modern software products, especially for those that are accessible through the Internet and handle sensitive information. The exploitation of a single vulnerability may lead to far reaching consequences both for the users and for the owning enterprises, ranging from information exposure to reputation damages and financial losses [1]. As a result, the software industry has recently shifted its focus towards building software that is highly secure from the ground up [2,3]. For this purpose, several mechanisms have been proposed for adding security during the overall software development lifecycle

© Springer Nature Switzerland AG 2021
O. Gervasi et al. (Eds.): ICCSA 2021, LNCS 12955, pp. 289–305, 2021.
https://doi.org/10.1007/978-3-030-87007-2_21

(SDLC) [2,3]. Among them, automated static analysis (ASA) has been proven effective in uncovering software vulnerabilities, and therefore adding security, during the coding phase of the SDLC [4–6], whereas several well-established secure SDLCs (e.g., Microsoft's SDL [7]), as well as leading technological firms like Google, Microsoft, and Intel (according to the BSIMM[1] initiative) highlight its importance in improving software security.

Despite its effectiveness in detecting vulnerabilities, static analysis has been observed to be underused in practice [8,9]. The main reason for its limited adoption is that it tends to produce a large number of false alerts (i.e., false positives), that is, alerts that do not correspond to actual issues. This leads to the generation of large reports of alerts that developers and reviewers have to manually inspect in order to detect those that are actionable (i.e., that correspond to actual issues, which require immediate fix). This process, called triaging [8], is very time-consuming and effort demanding, discouraging developers from using ASA in practice. Several attempts have been made in the literature to reduce the number of the produced false positives. Since the construction of an ASA tool able to detect all existing issues while maintaining satisfactory performance is an undecidable problem [10], the majority of the research endeavors focus on proposing techniques that post-process the produced alerts, to detect those that are actionable, known as actionable alerts identification techniques (AAITs).

Despite the large number of AAITs that have been proposed until today, none of them have demonstrated very sufficient results [10–12]. In fact, their accuracy is observed to drop significantly when applied to software products that have not been used during their training. In addition to this, almost no contributions have been made with respect to extending these techniques towards the security realm, i.e., for assessing the criticality of security-related static analysis alerts (i.e., potential vulnerabilities). This would be beneficial for the production of secure software, as it would allow developers better prioritize their refactoring activities by focusing on fixing issues that are more likely to correspond to actual vulnerabilities. An extension is necessary, as vulnerabilities are considered special types of bugs that exhibit unique characteristics [13].

To this end, in the present paper, we propose a technique for assessing the criticality of security-related static analysis alerts. In particular, we propose a technique for prioritizing (and classifying) security-related static analysis alerts based on their criticality, by taking into account information retrieved from (i) the alerts themselves, (ii) vulnerability prediction models, and (iii) user feedback. The proposed technique is based on machine learning models, with emphasis on neural networks, which were built based on data retrieved from static analysis reports of real-world software applications. It is grounded on the generation of a general model based on real world data and on the regular application of retraining (based on user feedback) so that the model could provide more accurate results for the project on which it is applied. The proposed technique is operationalized in the form of web services that can be used in practice,

---

[1] https://www.bsimm.com/.

whereas an intuitive web-based interface is also provided. Finally, the approach is demonstrated through a case study on a real-world commercial software product.

2 Related Work

A large number of techniques have been proposed with the purpose to report alerts that are actionable and eliminate false positives produced by ASA. These techniques, which are known as actionable alerts identification techniques (AAITs), typically utilize machine learning to discriminate between actionable and non-actionable alerts [10,11,14,15]. They are normally classified into two categories [10,14]: (i) classification AAITs, and (ii) prioritization AAITs.

Classification AAITs (e.g., [16]) classify alerts into two groups, particularly alerts that are likely to be actionable (i.e. actual issues identified by static code analyzers that require fix) and alerts that are likely to be unactionable (i.e. false positives or less critical issues that are reported by static code analyzers and do no require immediate correction), and they prune those that are marked as unactionable. For instance, a static analysis alert that corresponds to a bug that can lead to a system crash (e.g., memory leak) is an actionable alert, whereas a wrong naming convention issue (e.g., a variable name that is very long) can be considered unactionable. The main advantage of the classification AAITs is that, due to alert pruning, they lead to a significant reduction in the number of the alerts that are reported to the developers. However, these techniques may lead to the introduction of false negatives, as they may mistakenly prune alerts that are in fact actionable due to the model's error [10,11,14]. Prioritization AAITs (e.g., [17,18]) rank the alerts based on their "actionability", i.e., their likelihood to be actionable, without eliminating any of the reported alerts. This allows the developers to better prioritize their fortification activities, by starting their refactoring from alerts that are more likely to be actionable. Since no pruning is applied, no false negatives are introduced, but the volume of the alerts is not reduced as well, which may be still overwhelming.

None of these techniques has been widely-adopted in practice, mainly due to their inaccuracies, especially when applied to projects that were not used during their training [14,19,20]. In fact, the predictive performance of these models significantly drops, when applied to assess alerts from previously unknown projects, hindering, in that way, their practicality. For instance, Heckman et al. [17,21] observed that updating the models adaptively may lead to more accurate rankings in future versions of a project. However, further work is needed [14].

AAITs focus on assessing the "actionability" of static analysis alerts in general. Security-related static analysis alerts are considered good indicators of software vulnerabilities [5,6]. However, AAITs cannot be applied directly for assessing the criticality of security-related static analysis alerts, since software vulnerabilities are considered special types of software bugs, with unique characteristics [13]. In particular, the accessibility of a security bug from the attack surface determines its criticality, something that does not hold for common bugs [4,22]. In fact, the criticality of a vulnerability, apart from its type, also depends on project-specific parameters, like its location in the source code, its reachability from the attack surface, the system configuration, etc. [4,22,23]. Therefore, these parameters (i.e., code semantics) need to be considered for assessing the criticality of a security issue, normally through code analysis and user feedback.

Hence, AAITs need to be extended towards the security realm. Very limited contributions exist toward this direction. The most representative contribution was made by Baca [4], who used context-sensitive data flow analysis in order to detect locations of code that are tainted, and marked all the alerts that belonged to these lines as potentially critical from a security viewpoint. However, no model was built, whereas emphasis was given only on the reachability, neglecting other information that may provide inference about the actual criticality of the alerts.

From the above analysis, it is clear that none of the existing AAITs has managed to sufficiently address the problem and therefore to be broadly adopted in practice. The main reason for this is that the accuracy drops when they are applied to previously unknown projects. Another open issue is that little work has been conducted with respect to the criticality of security-related static analysis alerts, which are alerts that are characterized by unique characteristics. To this end, in the present paper we focus on security-related static analysis alerts, and we propose an ML-based approach for assessing their criticality, leveraging the concept of retraining based on user feedback. The approach supports both the classification and prioritization concepts. Another novelty is that it considers information from vulnerability prediction, which has not been studied before.

3 Methodology

3.1 Overview of the Methodology

In Fig. 1, a high-level overview of the proposed approach, as well as of the methodology that was adopted for constructing the required model is illustrated. The left part of Fig. 1 (termed as "Model Construction") demonstrates the process that was followed for building the ML model that is used as the basis of our proposed approach based on real-world data. More specifically, as can be seen by Fig. 1, we split the open-source projects that constitute our dataset into a list of software classes and then these classes were analysed both by a static code analyzer and by a vulnerability prediction model (VPM), to collect the required features of the dataset. Subsequently, a process for assigning labels in the dataset was followed, and, after the pre-processing, the final dataset was produced. The extracted features of the classes of the final dataset (i.e., static analysis alerts and vulnerability prediction results) along with their corresponding labels composed the input to our supervised learning model during its training. The right part of Fig. 1 (termed as "Model Execution") illustrates how the produced model is used in practice for assessing the criticality of security-related static analysis alerts. In brief, as can be seen by the figure, the produced model receives as input a new static analysis alert and classifies it as critical or non-critical. As will be discussed later, it also reports the likelihood of the alert to be critical from a security viewpoint, allowing the developers to prioritize the reported alerts based on their criticality. Finally, the users are allowed to express their disagreement with respect to the model decisions by providing feedback. This feedback is stored in order to be used for the future retraining (see Sect. 3.4).

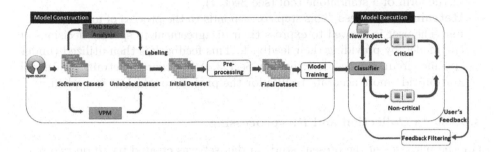

Fig. 1. High-level overview of the proposed approach

The overall approach that is depicted in Fig. 1, can be summarized in the following seven steps:

1. **Data Definition.** The first step of the study is to define the input variables that will be used for the construction of the ML models, as well as the class attribute of the model. Regarding the input variables, we decided to use information retrieved from the static analysis alerts themselves (e.g., vulnerability type, severity, etc.), along with information retrieved from vulnerability prediction models (see Sect. 4). The model's output is actually a binary prediction, indicating whether the analyzed alert is critical (from a security viewpoint). It also reports a continuous value, indicating the alert's "criticality", i.e., its likelihood to correspond to a critical security issue.

2. **Data Collection.** In this step, we applied a popular automated static analysis tool that was properly configured in order to report only security-related issues, on two real-world software projects, in order to retrieve the alerts that exist in source code. Text mining-based vulnerability prediction models were also used to get information about the vulnerability hot spots on source code (see Sect. 4). Regarding the labeling of these alerts as critical or non-critical, a manual code review method was followed (see Sect. 3.2).

3. **Data Pre-processing.** Pre-processing is responsible for bringing the dataset in a form suitable for ML model training. More specifically, the categorical features were encoded in 1-hot vector representation. No sampling techniques were performed since the dataset is quite balanced.

4. **Classification Techniques Selection.** In this step, the most suitable classification techniques are selected. A comparison of these techniques is also performed. Our selection is based on classification evaluation metrics.

5. **Model Training.** This step is responsible for building the model selected at the previous step, based on a carefully selected set of hyper-parameters.

6. **Model Execution.** This step corresponds to the actual execution of the produced model in practice. The pre-trained model is used in order to assess the criticality of previously unknown security-related static analysis alerts. To facilitate the adoption of the approach in practice, it has been operationalized in the form of a standalone tool (see Sect. 4).
7. **Retraining Process.** This step corresponds to the process of model retraining. The user is allowed to express their disagreement to specific decisions of the model, by providing their feedback. This feedback is then utilized (under specific circumstances described in Sect. 3.4) in order to retrain the model and provide more accurate results for the project to which it is applied.

3.2 Data Collection and Pre-processing

For the purposes of the present study, a dataset was created based on two real-world software products developed by colleagues in CERTH as part of ongoing and past EU Projects. The reasoning behind the decision to use in-house software products for the construction of our dataset is threefold. Firstly, we have complete access to the source code of these products, allowing us to verify the correctness of the retrieved data. Secondly, we have direct communication with their developers, allowing us to request their assistance with respect to the manual labeling of the produced alerts. Finally, it also allows us to request a sufficient number of instances, leading to the construction of reliable ML models.

The selected software projects are mid-size projects written in Java programming language with an approximate lifetime of three years. The first project is a cloud-based platform for analyzing software products written in Java and C/C++ with respect to their quality. The platform is implemented as a collection of RESTfull microservices that are interconnected. The second project is a crawler that crawls projects from online Git-based repositories (e.g., GitHub, Bitbucket, etc.) with the purpose to find software projects that have dependencies on third-party software that contain known vulnerabilities. The tool is accessible through command line and it is actually based on the OWASP Dependency Check[2] tool. For privacy reasons, the names of the projects are not disclosed, since they are not open-source projects.

For the construction of the dataset, a static code analyzer, which was properly configured for detecting security issues through the utilization of a novel Security Assessment Model [2,24] (see Sect. 4), was applied on these software projects. The SAM is able to detect important security-related issues, including Null Pointer, Resource Handling, Exception Handling, Synchronization, and Logging issues [24]. The produced static analysis alerts were presented to the actual developers of the associated projects, who labelled them as critical and non critical. Since the developers were not security experts, in order to prevent instances of mislabelling, the labelling was inspected by the authors of the paper. Several instances of potential mislabelling were spotted and discussed with the developers. Based on the discussion outcomes the final labelling was decided.

---

[2] https://owasp.org/www-project-dependency-check/.

Apart from alert-specific information, we decided to integrate security-related information retrieved from the software project itself. In particular, we applied text mining-based deep learning vulnerability prediction models [25–27] (see Sect. 4), in order to spot the security hot-spots of the software products, i.e., software classes that are likely to contain vulnerabilities. By highlighting the security hot-spots, we expect our approach to consider as more critical those static analysis alerts that belong to the identified hot-spots. We included this information in the produced dataset, to empirically examine this assumption through the construction of ML models.

In brief, the features that we focused on and we used for model's training are the rule name, ruleset name, priority, and vulnerability score. It should be noted that the first three features are alert specific, whereas the last one is project specific. Since the approach is based on a binary classifier, the outcome of the model is a binary value (which is termed *crtiticality flag*), i.e., 0 or 1, where 0 denotes that the analyzed alert is not critical and 1 that the analyzed alert is critical. The model also reports a *criticality score*, i.e., a continuous value in the [0,1] interval that indicates the likelihood of the analyzed alert to be critical from a security viewpoint. A description of the selected features is provided below:

- The **rule name** is the name of the rule of the static code analyzer that is violated. It indicates the type of the issue that is reported by the alert.
- The **rule set** is a grouping of code analysis rules that can be detected by the selected static code analyzer. It actually indicates the broader category that the issue that is reported by the alert belongs to.
- **Priority** is the severity score provided by the vendor and it represents the importance of each alert based on static analysis. It usually gets discrete values between one (more severe) and five (less severe). It should be noted that the vendor-specific priority cannot be used solely as a reliable measure of the criticality of security related alerts, as it is highly subjective and it neglects the important code semantics that may affect the criticality of security issues [8,13,22]. It needs to be used in conjunction with other features.
- **Vulnerability score** is the score produced by a vulnerability prediction model. Actually, it is the probability of a software component to be vulnerable, and therefore it receives a continuous value in the [0,1] interval.

The final dataset comprises 1200 alerts produced by the aforementioned process. From these 1200 alerts, 650 are marked as non-critical, whereas the rest 550 are defined as critical. Hence, the final dataset is rather balanced, which is important for the construction of the ML models that are described in the following sections, as it reduces the probability of overfitting. From a preprocessing viewpoint, since the "rule name" and "rule set" features are categorical variables, and considering that ML models understand numerical values, 1-hot vector representation was used.

3.3   Model Selection

After constructing the final dataset, the next step was to build a set of ML models and select the one that demonstrates the best predictive performance as the basis of our approach. For this purpose, different ML algorithms are trained in order to discriminate static analysis alerts, which point to code lines in the classes, between critical and non-critical. We investigate various ML algorithms, including Support Vector Machines (SVM), Random Forest, Decision Tree and the Naïve Bayes method. We also examine the ability of deep learning, specifically the Multi-Layer Perceptron (MLP), to provide reliable predictions in our dataset. The evaluation is performed using 10-fold cross-validation. As performance indicators we use accuracy, precision and recall. The results of the evaluation process are presented in Table 1.

Table 1. Comparison of main machine learning classification algorithms

Classifier	Accuracy	Precision	Recall
Decision Tree	76.36	78.08	75.48
Naïve Bayes	56.06	53.50	88.33
Support Vector Machines	78.44	80.38	75.24
MLP	**86.33**	**90.52**	**83.33**
Random Forest	79.52	80.19	77.14

From Table 1, it is clear that the MLP is the best performing model. In fact, MLP is the only model that outperforms all the others with respect to all the three selected performance metrics, except the recall which is higher in the case of Naive Bayes. However, Naive Bayes accuracy and precision are observed to be the lowest (i.e., 53.5% and 56.06%) indicating that it generates an excessive number of false positives.

For the construction of these models, hyper-parameter tuning was employed to find the parameters that produce the optimal predictive performance for each model. More specifically, we performed the commonly used Grid-search method. The selected properties of the best performing model (i.e., the MLP model) are presented in Table 2. As can be seen in the Table 2, specific techniques were employed in order to avoid overfitting (e.g., dropout layer, regularizer, etc.) and make the produced model as generic as possible. As explained later, even if minor bias exists in the parameters of the original model, they are expected to be corrected through the applied retraining.

Table 2. The selected hyperparameters of the Multi-layer Perceptrons (MLPs)

Hyperparameter name	Value
Number of layers	4
Number of hidden layers	3
Number of hidden units (per hidden layer)	1000/500/50
Weight initialization technique	Glorot Xavier
Learning rate	0.01
Gradient descent optimizer	Adagrad
Batch size	128
Activation function	relu
Regularizer	Max norm (3)
Output activation function	sigmoid
Loss function	Binnary cross-entropy
Over-fitting prevention	Dropout = 0.15 (after last hidden layer)

3.4 Retraining Process

The best performing model that was selected in Sect. 3.3, can be then used in practice in order to assess the criticality of previously unknown static analysis alerts. In brief, after executing the model, the predictions (i.e., *criticality flags* and *criticality scores*) of the analyzed alerts are returned to the user and he/she can agree or disagree with the proposed criticalities. The users are equipped with the capacity to correct the model and improve its predictive performance, by sending their feedback to the model and retraining it. Developers can change the criticality of any alert they believe the model has classified wrongfully. They are able to submit to the system a non-critical alert as critical and vice versa, depending on which alerts they consider to be critical or not, for their own code.

As already stated, this is an important feature as the accuracy of AAITs normally drop when they are applied to previously unknown software projects [10,11,14]. This behavior is expected due to the fact that (i) there are types of alerts that were not part of the dataset used for the training of the models, and (ii) some types of alerts may be more (or less) important for specific types of software. For instance, an SQL Injection issue may not be critical for an offline application, but highly important for a cloud-based software. Hence, retraining, enables the developers to start with an original model and frequently update it in order to adapt to the specific needs of the project to which it is applied.

As can be seen in Fig. 1, after the initial predictions, a user can give his/her feedback to the classifier and choose whether to retrain the model (i.e., retraining is an on-demand feature). The retraining process that is adopted by our approach is relatively simple, and it is summarized in the following steps:

1. Initially, the system collects the user feedback that has been retrieved through the several iterations of alerts inspection. This feedback consists of alerts with which the user disagreed with the criticality assigned by the model.
2. Subsequently, the system checks the user's changes, which are the user's corrections on the initial decisions of the model, in order to determine the subset of the alerts that can be used for retraining. In fact, the user feedback (i.e.,

user's changes) are passed through two filters to verify that (i) sufficient information has been provided by the user, and (ii) the user feedback is not contradictory. Those filters are described in detail later in this section.

3. The alerts that pass these filters are included in the training set that will be used for the retraining process, whereas those that do not pass, remain in the memory in order to be used in future retraining attempts.

4. Finally, the original dataset is updated by including the user-labeled alerts that passed the previous filtering process, and then the model is retrained.

As stated above, an important step of the retraining process is the filtering mechanism that is applied in order to choose the subset of the user-labeled alerts that could lead to the reliable retraining of the model. This process is based on two filters (i.e., criteria) that are applied to the user-labeled alerts:

- The user changes that are related to a specific alert type (i.e., rule name) have to be more than N in number.
- If there are contradictory samples (i.e., alerts), the proportion of the alerts that belong to the minority group, has to be less than $M\%$ of the overall feedback alerts of the same rule name (alert type). Two samples are contradictory if they have exactly the same values to their features, but the user assigned different criticalities to each other.

Hence, the model is retrained based on the user-labeled alerts that satisfied the above criteria. As can be seen the filters (i.e., criteria) are highly configurable. The values of N and M can be defined by the user, depending on how loose or strict they would like the retraining process to be. For instance, by assigning a large value in N and a small value in M, the retraining process is enforced to be feasible only when a large number of non-contradictory feedback is collected. In that way, the retraining process is less frequent, but the retrained model is expected to be more reliable, as it was built based on a lot of user feedback. The effectiveness of the retraining mechanism to improve the predictive performance of the original model when applied to a previously unknown software is examined in Sect. 5 through a case study.

4 Implementation

As a proof of concept, the proposed approach has been implemented in the form of a tool. This would enable its adoption by developers in practice, and, in turn, its further quantitative and qualitative evaluation by the community. The high-level overview of the tool is presented in Fig. 2.

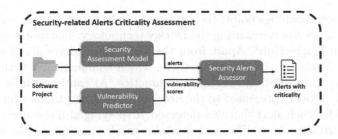

Fig. 2. High-level overview of the Security-related Alerts Criticality Assessment tool

As can be seen by Fig. 2, the proposed tool, i.e., the Security Alert Assessor (SAA), depends on the outputs of two other components, namely the Security Assessment Model (SAM) and the Vulnerability Predictor (VP). The former is responsible for providing the security-related static analysis alerts that need to be assessed by the SAA, whereas the VP provides the vulnerability scores of the classes of the analyzed software, which is a feature that is considered by SAA during the assessment of the alerts' criticality.

The Security Assessment Model (SAM) [24] is a novel hierarchical model that quantifies the internal security level of software products that are written in Java based exclusively on static analysis. In brief, it employs static analysis in order to detect security-related static analysis alerts that reside in the source code and aggregates these alerts in a sophisticated way [28] in order to produce a single score (i.e., the Security Index) that reflects the internal security of the analyzed software. SAM is based on the PMD[3] static code analyzer, which is a popular open-source ASA tool. SAM is able to detect seven vulnerability categories based on their relevance, namely *Null Pointer, Logging, Exception Handling, Resource Handling, Misused Functionality, Assignment* and *Synchronization*.

The Vulnerability Predictor (VP) is based on machine learning models that are able to detect security hot spots that reside in the source code of a software product. More specifically, these models, which are based on deep neural networks, utilize text mining and software metrics in order to assess the likelihood of a software class to contain a vulnerability. The selected models are the outcome of previous research endeavors [25, 26, 29].

Hence, as can be seen by Fig. 2, initially the given software product is analyzed using SAM and VP, to produce the security-related static analysis alerts that need to be assessed, and the vulnerability scores of its classes. This information is passed to the SAA, which combines them in order to assess the criticality of the reported alerts, by assigning a *criticality flag* and computing a *criticality score* for each alert (see Sect. 3.2). The tool also equips the users with the ability to express their disagreement with specific choices of the model, and retrain the model based on this feedback (see Sect. 3.4).

---

[3] https://pmd.github.io/.

From a technical viewpoint, the back-end of the tool has been implemented in the form of microservices using the Docker technology. The tool is available for download on DockerHub[4]. Apart from the back-end we have also implemented an intuitive front-end (i.e., user interface), which communicates with the back-end, in order to facilitate its adoption in practice. As can be seen by Fig. 3, the results of the tool are presented to the user in the form of a table, which provides information for each alert that was detected, displaying also the alerts *criticality flag* and *criticality score*. The user can also mark those alerts for which they disagree with the criticality assigned by the model through dedicated checkboxes and retrain the model based on their feedback. Useful guidelines on how to install and use the tool, can be found on the tool's wiki page[5].

5   Case Study

In this section, a case study on a real-world commercial software product is presented in order to demonstrate the proposed approach and evaluate its correctness. For the purposes of the case study, we used a software application developed by a company that is working in the automotive industry. It is an Android application, written in Java programming language, consisting of 87 classes and 382 methods, comprising approximately 15,409 lines of code. It runs on Augmented Reality (AR) glasses and its main purpose is to connect a technician in the field with an engineer in a support center, in order to appropriately guide him/her to successfully complete a manual task.

Initially, the selected software application was analyzed with the Security Assessment Model (SAM) [24], in order to produce a report with the security-related static analysis alerts that it contains. Then its source code was parsed by our Vulnerability Prediction Models [25, 26, 29], in order to compute the vulnerability scores of the 87 classes of the software, which is a required input for the proposed approach for assessing the criticality of the observed alerts. Then the Security Alerts Assessor (SAA) analyzed the produced alerts and assigned a *criticality flag* and a *criticality score* to each one of them (see Fig. 2).

The above mentioned process resulted in a list of 133 security alerts. These alerts were presented to developers with security expertise, who manually inspected them and expressed their agreement or disagreement with the criticalities assigned by the model. The criticalities assigned by the model were compared to the criticalities assigned by the manual inspection in order to evaluate the accuracy of the model when applied to a new (i.e., previously unseen) software. The results of the evaluation are presented in Table 3. As can be seen by Table 3, the overall accuracy of the model was approximately 82%, which is 4% lower than the model's descriptive accuracy, and the recall was found to be approximately 73%, which is 10% lower than the descriptive recall (see Table 1).

---

[4] https://hub.docker.com/repository/registry-1.docker.io/iliakalo/evit-image/.
[5] https://gitlab.com/iliaskalou/aait/-/wikis/Exploitable-Vulnerability-Identification-Wiki.

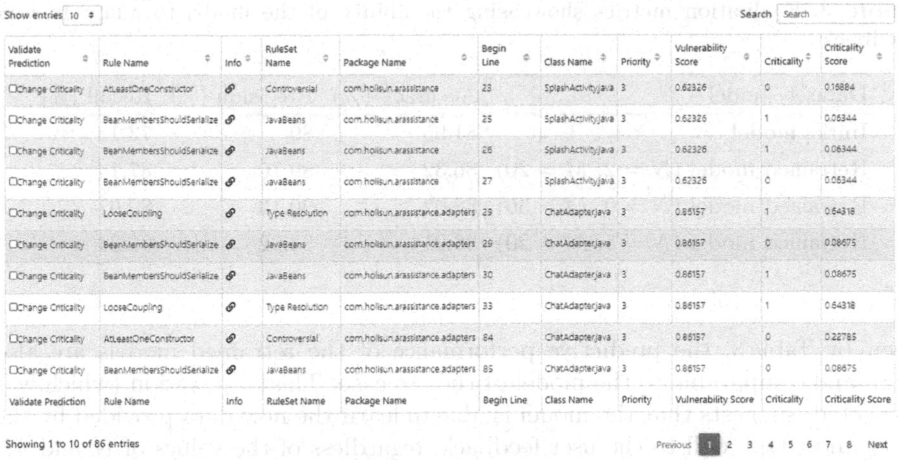

Show entries 10 Search Search

Validate Prediction	Rule Name	Info	RuleSet Name	Package Name	Begin Line	Class Name	Priority	Vulnerability Score	Criticality	Criticality Score
☐Change Criticality	AtLeastOneConstructor		Controversial	com.holisun.arassistance	23	SplashActivity.java	3	0.62326	0	0.15884
☐Change Criticality	BeanMembersShouldSerialize		JavaBeans	com.holisun.arassistance	25	SplashActivity.java	3	0.62326	1	0.06344
☐Change Criticality	BeanMembersShouldSerialize		JavaBeans	com.holisun.arassistance	26	SplashActivity.java	3	0.62326	1	0.06344
☐Change Criticality	BeanMembersShouldSerialize		JavaBeans	com.holisun.arassistance	27	SplashActivity.java	3	0.62326	0	0.06344
☐Change Criticality	LooseCoupling		Type Resolution	com.holisun.arassistance.adapters	29	ChatAdapter.java	3	0.86157	1	0.64318
☐Change Criticality	BeanMembersShouldSerialize		JavaBeans	com.holisun.arassistance.adapters	29	ChatAdapter.java	3	0.86157	0	0.08675
☐Change Criticality	BeanMembersShouldSerialize		JavaBeans	com.holisun.arassistance.adapters	30	ChatAdapter.java	3	0.86157	1	0.08675
☐Change Criticality	LooseCoupling		Type Resolution	com.holisun.arassistance.adapters	33	ChatAdapter.java	3	0.86157	1	0.64318
☐Change Criticality	AtLeastOneConstructor		Controversial	com.holisun.arassistance.adapters	84	ChatAdapter.java	3	0.86157	0	0.22785
☐Change Criticality	BeanMembersShouldSerialize		JavaBeans	com.holisun.arassistance.adapters	85	ChatAdapter.java	3	0.86157	0	0.08675
Validate Prediction	Rule Name	Info	RuleSet Name	Package Name	Begin Line	Class Name	Priority	Vulnerability Score	Criticality	Criticality Score

Showing 1 to 10 of 86 entries Previous 1 2 3 4 5 6 7 8 Next

Fig. 3. A snapshot of the front-end data table of the Security Alerts Criticality Assessor

From this experiment, it is obvious that there is a drop in the predictive performance of the model. This drop was expected since it is applied to a previously unknown software product, which may exhibit alerts of specific types that were not present during the training of the model, whereas some of the already trained alert types may be more (or less) critical for the specific type of software. However, at least for the given example, this drop is not observed to be significant. This provides confidence that sufficient prediction performance can be achieved when the model is applied to a project that was not used during its training, indicating that some general trends in the criticality of alerts are horizontal across different project types.

Subsequently, we retrained the model based on the feedback that was provided by the developers through the aforementioned manual inspection, and we evaluated its predictive performance. In fact, part of the user feedback was selected randomly and excluded from the model retraining to be used for the model evaluation. We considered the case of $N = 2$ and $M = 20$, as it was the most representative for the given dataset. The performance metrics of the retrained model are also presented in Table 3. As can be seen by Table 3, there is a significant increase in all the performance metrics, all of them being higher than 85%. This suggests that the retraining process leads to a significant increase in the predictive performance of the model, and, thus, that it is able to capture the user feedback.

For reasons of completeness, in Table 3, the evaluation results of the retrained model for two additional cases of N and M values are provided. In particular, we consider a more loose model ($N = 0$, $M = 50$), i.e., a model that accepts the user feedback without much filtering, and a more conservative model ($N = 5$, $M = 20$), i.e., a model that requires more data to be collected by the user in order to consider their input reliable to be used for retraining. As can be

Table 3. Evaluation metrics showcasing the ability of the model to adapt to user feedback

Dataset/model	Accuracy (%)	Precision (%)	Recall (%)
Initial model	81.95	89	73.13
Retrained model ($N = 2$, $M = 20$)	86.32	89.70	87.14
Retrained model ($N = 0$, $M = 50$)	88.02	90.13	89.67
Retrained model ($N = 5$, $M = 20$)	86.21	84.92	96.34

seen by Table 3, the predictive performance of the retrained models are also high and comparable to the model of the use case. This observation (which was expected) suggests that the model is able to learn the new data provided by the user and adapt well to the user feedback, regardless of the values of N and M. As mentioned in Sect. 3.4, the purpose of N and M are to allow the developer define how loose or strict the retraining process should be. In fact, the more conservative the model, the more non-contradictory data should be collected by the user, making the retraining process less frequent, but the produced model more reliable.

To sum up, the above analysis, although preliminary, led to some interesting observations. The results of the analysis highlight that when applying the original model to previously unknown alerts, the accuracy does not drop massively. This indicates that our approach can provide a relatively accurate assessment even on a dataset with alerts of different defined criticality. We can also notice that the model retraining process based on user feedback, leads to a substantial increase in the accuracy of the model. This fact suggests that the model, retrained based on feedback provided by the user, is capable of adapting to dynamically changing behaviors and it can actually improve its accuracy. Hence, frequent application of retraining would allow the model to adapt to the characteristics of the specific project to which it is applied.

At this point, it should be noted that a comparison with similar approaches and models was not feasible. Although a large number of AAITs have been proposed in the literature, very few contributions have been made with respect to security. In addition to this, the existing contributions (e.g., [4]), are not operationalized and have become obsolete, whereas no sufficient information and data are available that would enable their replication.

A note with respect to the validity threats of the present work is considered necessary. First of all, the model was based on information retrieved exclusively from Java projects, potentially affecting its generalizability to other programming languages. However, the adopted techniques are language agnostic enabling the developers to apply them in other programming languages. In addition, the selection of the model hyperparameters could be biased to the specific dataset that has been used for its training. However, techniques for avoiding over-fitting were employed (see Sect. 3.3), whereas the applied retraining process is expected to adjust the parameters to the project to which it is applied, neutralizing the potential bias of the parameters of the initial model.

6 Conclusions and Future Work

The purpose of the present paper was to develop a mechanism for assessing the criticality of security-related static analysis alerts. To this end, we developed a technique for prioritizing and classifying security-related static analysis alerts based on their criticality, by taking into account information retrieved from the alerts themselves, vulnerability prediction models, and user feedback.

To achieve this, a manually curated dataset of security-related static analysis alerts was constructed, by statically analyzing two real-world Java software products that were developed by CERTH as part of past and ongoing EU Projects. Based on this dataset, several machine learning models were built, for predicting alerts' criticality. Among the studied models, the Multi-layer Perceptron (MLP) demonstrated the best results, and thus it was chosen as the basis of our approach. The proposed approach was evaluated through a simple case study on a real-world commercial Java application provided by the automotive industry. The results of the case study revealed that the proposed model can be used as a good basis for assessing the criticality of the alerts of a new project, and that, through regular retraining, it can easily adapt to the characteristics of the model to which it is applied, providing more accurate assessments with time. The proposed technique has been operationalized in the form of web-services, providing also a web interface, to facilitate its adoption in practice. To the best of our knowledge, this is the first technique that focuses exclusively on security-related static analysis alerts, and adopts the concept of retraining. It is also the first approach that combines information retrieved from: (i) the alerts themselves, (ii) vulnerability prediction models, and (iii) user feedback.

Future work includes the investigation of the generalizability of the produced results by replicating our method using software products that are written in other programming languages (e.g., C/C++, Python, JavaScript, etc.), as well as by using different VPMs and static code analyzers. We are also planning to investigate how legacy systems could benefit from the proposed approach, such as those implemented in outdated languages like COBOL [30,31].

Acknowledgements. This work is partially funded by the European Union's Horizon 2020 Research and Innovation Programme through IoTAC project under Grant Agreement No. 952684.

References

1. Luszcz, J.: Apache struts 2: how technical and development gaps caused the equifax breach. Netw. Secur. **2018**(1), 5–8 (2018)

2. Siavvas, M., Gelenbe, E., Kehagias, D., Tzovaras, D.: Static analysis-based approaches for secure software development. In: Gelenbe, E., et al. (eds.) Euro-CYBERSEC 2018. CCIS, vol. 821, pp. 142–157. Springer, Cham (2018). https://doi.org/10.1007/978-3-319-95189-8_13

3. Mohammed, N.M., Niazi, M., Alshayeb, M., Mahmood, S.: Exploring software security approaches in software development lifecycle: a systematic mapping study. Comp. Stand. Interf. **50**, 107–115 (2016)

4. Baca, D.: Identifying security relevant warnings from static code analysis tools through code tainting. In: 2010 International Conference on Availability, Reliability and Security, pp. 386–390. IEEE (2010)

5. Yang, J., Ryu, D., Baik, J.: Improving vulnerability prediction accuracy with secure coding standard violation measures. In: 2016 International Conference on Big Data and Smart Computing (BigComp), pp. 115–122. IEEE (2016)

6. McGraw, G.: Software security. Datenschutz und Datensicherheit - DuD (2012)

7. Howard, M., Lipner, S.: The Security Development Lifecycle: SDL: A Process for Developing Demonstrably More Secure Software. Microsoft Press (2006)

8. Johnson, B., Song, Y., Murphy-Hill, E., Bowdidge, R.: Why don't software developers use static analysis tools to find bugs? In: 2013 35th International Conference on Software Engineering (ICSE), pp. 672–681. IEEE (2013)

9. Vassallo, C., Panichella, S., Palomba, F., Proksch, S., Gall, H.C., Zaidman, A.: How developers engage with static analysis tools in different contexts. Empirical Softw. Eng. **25**(2), 1419–1457 (2019). https://doi.org/10.1007/s10664-019-09750-5

10. Muske, T., Serebrenik, A.: Survey of approaches for handling static analysis alarms. In: 2016 IEEE 16th International Working Conference on Source Code Analysis and Manipulation (SCAM). pp. 157–166. IEEE (2016)

11. Heckman, S., Williams, L.: A systematic literature review of actionable alert identification techniques for automated static code analysis. Inf. and Soft, Tech (2011)

12. Yang, X., Chen, J., Yedida, R., Yu, Z., Menzies, T.: Learning to recognize actionable static code warnings. Empirical Softw. Eng. **26**, 56 (2021). https://doi.org/10.1007/s10664-021-09948-6

13. Munaiah, N., Camilo, F., Wigham, W., Meneely, A., Nagappan, M.: Do bugs foreshadow vulnerabilities? An in-depth study of the chromium project. Empirical Softw. Eng. **22**(3), 1305–1347 (2017)

14. Heckman, S., Williams, L.: A comparative evaluation of static analysis actionable alert identification techniques. In: Proceedings of the 9th International Conference on Predictive Models in Software Engineering, pp. 1–10 (2013)

15. Misra, S.: A step by step guide for choosing project topics and writing research papers in ICT related disciplines. In: ICTA 2020. CCIS, vol. 1350, pp. 727–744. Springer, Cham (2021). https://doi.org/10.1007/978-3-030-69143-1_55

16. Heckman, S., Williams, L.: A model building process for identifying actionable static analysis alerts. In: 2009 International Conference on Software Testing Verification and Validation, pp. 161–170 (2009)

17. Heckman, S.S.: Adaptively ranking alerts generated from automated static analysis. XRDS: Crossroads. ACM Mag. Stud. **14**(1), 1–11 (2007)

18. Ruthruff, J.R., Penix, J., Morgenthaler, J.D., Elbaum, S., Rothermel, G.: Predicting accurate and actionable static analysis warnings: an experimental approach. In: Proceedings of the 30th International Conference on Software Engineering. ICSE 2008. Association for Computing Machinery, New York, pp. 341–350 (2008)

19. Kremenek, T., Ashcraft, K., Yang, J., Engler, D.: Correlation exploitation in error ranking. In: Proceedings of the 12th ACM SIGSOFT Twelfth International Symposium on Foundations of Software Engineering. SIGSOFT 2004/FSE-12. Association for Computing Machinery, New York, pp. 83–93 (2004)
20. Tripp, O., Guarnieri, S., Pistoia, M., Aravkin, A.: ALETHEIA: improving the usability of static security analysis. In: Proceedings of the 2014 ACM SIGSAC Conference on Computer and Communications Security (2014)
21. Heckman, S., Williams, L.: On establishing a benchmark for evaluating static analysis alert prioritization and classification techniques. In: 2nd International Symposium on Empirical Software Engineering and Measurement (2008)
22. Younis, A.A., Malaiya, Y.K., Ray, I.: Using attack surface entry points and reachability analysis to assess the risk of software vulnerability exploitability. In: 15th International Symposium on High-Assurance Systems Engineering (2014)
23. Younis, A.A., Malaiya, Y.K.: Using software structure to predict vulnerability exploitation potential. In: 8th International Conference on Software Security and Reliability-Companion, pp. 13–18 (2014)
24. Siavvas, M., Kehagias, D., Tzovaras, D., Gelenbe, E.: A hierarchical model for quantifying software security based on static analysis alerts and software metrics. Softw. Qual. J. 29(2), 431–507 (2021). https://doi.org/10.1007/s11219-021-09555-0
25. Kalouptsoglou, I., Siavvas, M., Tsoukalas, D., Kehagias, D.: Cross-project vulnerability prediction based on software metrics and deep learning. In: Gervasi, O., et al. (eds.) ICCSA 2020. LNCS, vol. 12252, pp. 877–893. Springer, Cham (2020). https://doi.org/10.1007/978-3-030-58811-3_62
26. Filus, K., Siavvas, M., Domańska, J., Gelenbe, E.: The random neural network as a bonding model for software vulnerability prediction. In: Modelling, Analysis, and Simulation of Computer and Telecommunication Systems (2021)
27. Filus, K., Boryszko, P., Domańska, J., Siavvas, M., Gelenbe, E.: Efficient feature selection for static analysis vulnerability prediction. Sensors 21(4), 1133 (2021)
28. Siavvas, M.G., Chatzidimitriou, K.C., Symeonidis, A.L.: QATCH-an adaptive framework for software product quality assessment. Expert Syst. Appl. 86, 350–366 (2017)
29. Siavvas, M., Kehagias, D., Tzovaras, D.: A preliminary study on the relationship among software metrics and specific vulnerability types. In: 2017 International Conference on Computational Science and Computational Intelligence (2017)
30. Mateos, C., Zunino, A., Misra, S., Anabalon, D., Flores, A.: Migration from COBOL to SOA: measuring the impact on web services interfaces complexity. In: Damaševičius, R., Mikašytė, V. (eds.) ICIST 2017. CCIS, vol. 756, pp. 266–279. Springer, Cham (2017). https://doi.org/10.1007/978-3-319-67642-5_22
31. Mateos, C., Zunino, A., Flores, A., Misra, S.: Cobol systems migration to SOA: assessing antipatterns and complexity. Inf. Technol. Control 48, 71–89 (2019)

Technical Debt Forecasting Based on Deep Learning Techniques

Maria Mathioudaki, Dimitrios Tsoukalas[✉], Miltiadis Siavvas, and Dionysios Kehagias

Centre for Research and Technology Hellas, Thessaloniki, Greece
{mariamathi,tsoukj,siavvasm,diok}@iti.gr

Abstract. Technical debt (TD) is a metaphor commonly used to reflect the consequences of quality compromises that can derive short-term benefits but may result in quality decay of software products in the long run. While a broad variety of methods and tools have been proposed over the years for the identification and quantification of TD during the software development cycle, it is not until recently that researchers have turned their interest towards methods aiming to forecast the future TD evolution of a software project. Predicting the future value of TD could facilitate decision-making tasks regarding software maintenance and assist developers and project managers in taking proactive actions regarding TD repayment. In previous relevant studies, time series analysis and Machine Learning techniques have been employed in order to generate meaningful TD forecasts. While these approaches have been proven capable of producing reliable TD predictions, their predictive performance has been observed to decrease significantly for long-term predictions. To this end, in the present paper we investigate whether the adoption of Deep Learning may lead to more accurate long-term TD prediction. For this purpose, Deep Learning models are constructed, evaluated, and compared based on a dataset of five popular real-world software applications. The results of our analysis indicate that the adoption of Deep Learning results in TD forecasting models with sufficient predictive performance up to 150 steps ahead into the future.

Keywords: Software quality · Technical debt · Forecasting · Deep learning

1 Introduction

The Technical Debt (TD) term was first introduced by Ward Cunningham [1] to outline the issue of additional software maintenance effort caused by technical shortcuts taken usually in favor of shorter time-to-market. Since then, it is widely used in practice to facilitate the discussion among technical and non-technical stakeholders, due to its ability to convey the consequences of deliberate or inadvertent quality compromises in monetary terms. While initially associated with the software implementation phase, the TD metaphor was later broadened to

© Springer Nature Switzerland AG 2021
O. Gervasi et al. (Eds.): ICCSA 2021, LNCS 12955, pp. 306–322, 2021.
https://doi.org/10.1007/978-3-030-87007-2_22

other phases of the software development lifecycle (SDLC) [2], such as design and architecture. Similarly to financial debt, TD that is accumulated due to problematic design and implementation choices needs to be repaid early enough in the SDLC, mainly by performing refactoring operations. If not done so, then it can generate interest payments in the form of increased future costs that would be difficult to be paid off and in extreme situations may lead to an unmaintainable software product and thus, to technical bankruptcy [3].

Managing TD across the entire SDLC is a challenging task and therefore, a multitude of methods and tools have been proposed by researchers and adopted by practitioners [4] towards this direction. Most of these approaches however focus on the TD value (in terms of money or effort) of a software project in its current state and often tend to overlook the potential utility that a future approximation of this value would introduce in the TD Management process [5]. More specifically, being able to predict the future TD evolution of a software project could allow project managers and developers to timely react to the accumulation of TD and, thus, employ suitable repayment activities promptly [5] to preserve a software application to a satisfactory quality level. Although to date numerous research endeavours have dealt with predicting the evolution of various aspects directly or indirectly related to TD, such as software maintainability [6,7], fault-proneness [8–11], change-proneness [12,13] and code smells [14], the contributions that exist in the literature regarding the forecasting of TD itself are limited.

In our previous work towards this direction [15–17], we have contributed to the TD forecasting challenge by investigating the performance of a multitude of different forecasting methods ranging from simple statistical time series models to more sophisticated approaches, such as causal and Machine Learning (ML) models. The outcome of our work indicated that these methods are indeed capable of providing accurate and useful results. However, despite the fact that these approaches were proven able to produce reliable TD predictions for relatively short forecasting horizons, their predictive performance dropped significantly for longer forecasting horizons (i.e., long-term predictions). More specifically, the performance of statistical time series models was found to be satisfactory for forecasts up to 8 commits ahead, while the causal and ML models were able to provide reliable results up to 40 commits ahead. This obviously affects the practicality of the produced models, as they cannot be applied to cases where a software company requires a long-term TD management plan.

To this end, in the present paper we investigate whether the adoption of Deep Learning models may lead to accurate and practical TD forecasts, giving particular emphasis on the long-term predictions that have been the most important limitation of our previous relevant studies [15,16]. For this purpose, we utilize TD measurements throughout the different commits of five open-source Java projects obtained from the Technical Debt Dataset [18]. Subsequently, based on this dataset, a Multi-layer Perceptron (MLP) model is constructed and experiments are performed for each of the five projects for 5 to 150 commits ahead.

In each one of these cases, the produced models are evaluated with respect to their accuracy and practicality based on a set of performance metrics.

The rest of the paper is organised as follows: Sect. 2 explores the related work in the field of TD forecasting. Section 3 discusses details regarding the methodology that we followed throughout this work, while Sect. 4 presents the results of the analysis and a discussion on the findings. Finally, Sect. 5 concludes the paper and proposes directions for future work.

2   Related Work

A groundbreaking study on the laws of software evolution by Lehman [19] states that while any software system needs to be continually evolving and adapting to the environment, doing so will increase its complexity and decrease its quality unless maintained properly. Thereby, analyzing, understanding, and predicting the evolution of a software system can provide estimates and insight on the evolution of its quality as well. In a relevant study, Mens [20] raises the awareness on the need for accurate models able to track software evolution and thus estimate the quality and predict the future maintenance cost of a software system. Towards this direction, numerous research endeavors have addressed the topic of predicting the evolution of various quality aspects directly or indirectly related to the TD of a software project, such as software maintainability [6,7], fault-proneness [8,9,11], change-proneness [12,13] and code smells [14].

As regards the software maintainability prediction, in a study by Chug and Malhotra [6], the authors employ 17 ML techniques using object-oriented metrics as predictors and conclude that the best performance is achieved by genetically adaptive learning models. In a similar study, Elish and Elish [7] compare various ML techniques and conclude that the TreeNet model is the best-performing model for predicting software maintainability. Regarding fault-proneness prediction, a study by Arisholm et al. [8] proposes a multivariate model that uses historical fault and change data of various open-source systems as predictors. The authors report that a satisfactory level of accuracy can be achieved using their model. In another study, Nagappan et al. [9] accurately predict future fault-proneness using regression models trained on code metrics, while in a similar study, Gondra et al. [11] employ and train an Artificial Neural Network having software metrics as input and conclude that their model outperforms those of similar studies on fault-proneness prediction. Regarding change-proneness prediction, in a study by Pritam et al. [12], the authors investigate various ML techniques using code smells as predictors and conclude that code smells are indeed a good predictor of class change proneness. In another study by Abbas et al. [13], the authors apply 10 ML techniques to investigate the effectiveness of object-oriented metrics in predicting software change-prone modules. They report that Random Forest is the best-performing model. Finally, regarding code smells prediction, Fontana et al. [14] employ 16 ML techniques on 74 software projects and conclude that J48 and Random Forest demonstrate the highest performance among the investigated models.

The large number of relevant studies trying to contribute towards predicting the evolution of various software quality aspects unveils the importance of this challenge in the software engineering community [21]. However, since TD is considered as an indicator of software quality, predicting its future value can be deemed equally significant. A careful search in the relevant literature reveals that while several existing research works deal with the evolution of TD and its implications for the software development process [22], it is not until recently that researchers have turned their interest towards investigating efficient methods aiming to forecast the future TD evolution of a software project.

The potential impact of developing forecasting models for accurate prediction of TD evolution has been discussed in a related study [5], in which the authors point out that it would be interesting to investigate if the adoption of such models in practice would result in higher-quality software products. In a first attempt towards modelling and forecasting the TD evolution of long-lived, open-source software projects, a study by Tsoukalas et al. [15] proposes the use of time series analysis techniques and more specifically, an autoregressive integrated moving average (ARIMA) model. While concluding that a single ARIMA model can generate accurate short-term TD forecasts for each one of the five investigated open-source projects, the authors notice that the performance of this model decreases significantly for forecasting horizons longer than eight commits ahead. In an attempt to extend their previous work and present a more holistic view on the TD forecasting concept, the same authors [16] conduct a follow-up study, where they investigate the ability of a large set of ML methods to predict the TD evolution of 15 open-source projects. By examining various forecasting horizons, they conclude that the non-linear Random Forest regression is able to achieve a sufficient level of accuracy for forecasts up to 40 commits ahead.

Existing TD forecasting methods have not demonstrated satisfactory results in long-term TD forecasts. Under those circumstances, we aim to examine whether taking advantage of deep learning approaches could be the key for overcoming this challenge. Such a contribution would enable software companies to plan accurate TD management strategies on time and thus, avoid unforeseen situations long-term.

3   Methodology and Experiment Setup

In this section, detailed information is provided on the overall methodology that was adopted in the present paper. More specifically, this section describes the dataset that was used for the purposes of this study, the data pre-processing that took place before the experiments, the model construction process and model performance metrics that were used, and last but not least, the strategy that was followed for the experimental execution.

3.1   Dataset

The first step of the proposed approach comprises the construction of the dataset. For the purposes of investigating whether the adoption of Deep Learning models may lead to accurate short-, but most importantly, long-term TD forecasts, our dataset needs to consist of multiple software projects along with their past TD evolution, i.e., TD measurements spanning across their commit history. These TD measurements will serve as input to train and evaluate our models.

For the purposes of the present study, we decided to exploit the "Technical Debt dataset"[1], that is, a dataset that was constructed and made publicly available in a study by Lenarduzzi et al. [18] to facilitate TD research. This dataset is based on 33 real-world open-source Java projects obtained from the Apache Software Foundation and contains TD measurements for all available commits of the aforementioned projects. TD measurements were obtained using Sonar-Qube[2], a widely-used open-source static code analysis tool that has been used as proof of concept in multiple research studies [4]. Each one of the 33 projects is provided as a csv file, where the columns contain the software-related metrics (including TD measurements), as extracted from SonarQube, and the rows correspond to the different commits through time. In the context of the present work, we decided to select five projects for constructing and evaluating our TD forecasting models. The selection criteria were based on the commit frequency (at least once per week) and project lifespan (at least 3 years of commit activity). Therefore, our final set consists of the following projects: Ambari, Commons-codec, Commons-io, Httpcomponents-client and Mina-sshd. These projects are presented in Table 1 accompanied by additional information on the total number of analyzed commits and the analysis lifetime.

Table 1. Selected projects of the TD dataset

Project name	Analyzed commits	Analysis lifetime
Ambari	13397	09/11–06/15
Commons-codec	1726	04/03–05/18
Commons-io	2118	01/02–06/18
Httpcomponents-client	2867	12/05–06/18
Mina-sshd	1370	12/08–06/18

For the purposes of the current study, we did not exploit all of the software-related metrics that are available in the Technical Debt dataset. In fact, to construct the TD forecasting models we followed a *univariate* modelling approach, meaning that no indicators other than the TD value itself were taken under consideration during the model training process. The reason behind this choice is that we are interested in investigating whether the MLP models are capable of discovering patterns within the TD evolution itself, setting aside causes and relationships with other software-related metrics that could potentially act as TD indicators (i.e., predictors).

---

[1] https://github.com/clowee/The-Technical-Debt-Dataset.
[2] https://www.sonarqube.org/.

That being said, we set *total technical debt* as our target variable, i.e., the metric that we try to forecast. Similarly to our previous work [16], we define *total technical debt* as the total remediation effort (in minutes) that is required in order to fix all reliability, maintainability and security issues that are detected in the source code of a software project. This metric is therefore calculated as the sum of three metrics taken from the "Technical Debt dataset", namely *reliability remediation effort, security remediation effort*, and *maintainability remediation effort*. As explained in Sect. 3.2, values of *total technical debt* in previous time steps will act as independent variables.

3.2 Data Pre-processing

In this section, we briefly describe the data pre-processing techniques that were applied on the final dataset (described in Sect. 3.1), in order to transform it in a form that is suitable for further analysis. In particular, we first describe the sliding window method, i.e., a commonly used method able to transform time series data into a form that is suitable for ML tasks. Secondly, we describe the data scaling step, which is deemed necessary in order to improve the accuracy and performance of Deep Learning models.

Sliding Window. As mentioned earlier, the dataset that was used in this study consists only of TD values computed throughout the whole evolution of five different software projects. Therefore, we eventually end up with five tables, where each table contains a single column representing the *total technical debt* of a specific commit, throughout different commits in time (rows) of each project, in a form of time series data. As ML (and therefore Deep Learning) models do not at first hand support the idea of evolution over time, time series data need to be reconstructed in a form appropriate for supervised learning problems.

Sliding window is a commonly used method that can be applied to address such problems. In short, this method transforms each initial sample (i.e., row) of a time series dataset by introducing, besides the current information, also past information (e.g., the TD values of multiple prior commits) and future information (e.g., the TD value of a future commit) simultaneously into a single row. By that, all rows of the dataset will be extended to include new columns containing not only information regarding the present, but also information regarding the past and the future. In our case, after applying the sliding window method, TD values of prior commits will be treated as independent variables, while the TD value of the future commit will become the target variable. Obviously, the selection of the future commit depends on the forecasting horizon that we want to make predictions for. The number of new columns (i.e., past time steps) that we want to include into each new row is called the "window size" and in fact denotes the number of independent variables that will be considered as input to our models. Generally speaking, there is no "golden rule" that can point to an ideal window size for a particular dataset or forecasting horizon. Most of the time, repeated tests with a wide range of window sizes need to take place, so that one can empirically decide on the most suitable number based on error minimization criteria. In our case, after examining the performance of the models while testing for different window sizes, we observed that for forecasts generated for 5–40 steps ahead, the window size that provides us with the lowest errors is 5. For predictions concerning larger steps ahead in time (i.e., 60–150) we ended up using a window size of 10. These observations apply to each one of the five different project datasets that are investigated in this study.

Data Scaling. One of the most critical steps before employing any ML or Deep Learning algorithm is data scaling, due to the fact that ML techniques (especially neural networks) produce better results when data are normalized. Therefore, we used *StandardScaler*, which scales the data so that the final distribution centers around 0 with a standard deviation of 1 (Gaussian Distribution). Centering and scaling are two processes that happen independently by calculating the corresponding statistics on the values of the dataset samples. StandardScaler transformation was integrated into the Walk-forward Train-Test validation process (described in Sect. 3.4) where, during each iteration, it was fitted only to the training set (to create realistic conditions) and then, used to transform both the training and test set. For data pre-processing tasks we used Python programming language and more specifically the scikit-learn[3] ML library.

3.3   Model Construction and Performance Metrics

Trying to forecast the future TD evolution of a software project can be considered as a regression problem, as the target variable (i.e., *total technical debt*) is a continuous variable and thus, it should be treated accordingly. Contrary to the previous studies, where statistical time series and ML models were examined, in the present work we chose to employ the Multilayer Perceptron (MLP), a supervised Deep Learning model suitable for regression tasks. In this section, we will describe in detail the model that was employed for this purpose, as well as the performance metrics that were used in order to evaluate its performance.

Model Construction. An MLP is a class of feedforward Artificial Neural Networks (ANNs). It receives as input a set of features and a target variable and it uses a non-linear function for either classification or regression problems in order to "learn" how to predict the values of the target variable. Most of the times, it consists of an input layer that corresponds to a set of neurons representing the input features, one or more hidden layers that transform the values of the previous layer using a weighted linear sum followed by a non-linear activation function, and finally, an output layer that takes the values from the last hidden layer and transforms them into output values.

An MLP model is extremely sensitive to input features and therefore the configuration of its parameters strongly depends on the dataset that will be

---

[3] https://scikit-learn.org/stable/index.html.

used to train it. These parameters include the number of hidden layers, neurons, epochs but also, the different activation and loss functions, the batch size and the optimizer that can be put in practice. Thus, there is a process that needs to take place in order to determine the optimal parameters, called hyperparamater tuning. In the context of this work, we performed hyperparameter tuning using the *GridSearch* method, which is commonly used to find the optimal hyperparameters, by performing an exhaustive search over specified parameter values for an estimator. We chose the Mean Absolute Percentage Error (MAPE) (more details in Sect. 3.3) as the objective function of the estimator.

In Table 2 we present the optimal MLP parameters as calculated during Grid-Search. It should be noted that these parameters are common for each one of the five datasets (i.e., five projects) that are examined in this study.

Table 2. The optimal hyperparameters of the Multi-layer Perceptron (MLP).

Hyperparameter name	Value
Number of layers	4
Number of hidden layers	3
Number of hidden units (per hidden layer)	200/100/50
Gradient descent optimizer	Adam
Batch size	5
Epochs	50
Activation function	Relu
Loss function	Mean squared error

For the implementation of the MLP model we used Python and more specifically the Tensorflow Keras[4] library.

Performance Metrics. As in any ML task, in this study we aim to generate predictions for the target variable (i.e., *total technical debt*) which will be as close as possible to the ground truth values and at the same time avoid overfitting. In a few words, we aim to maximise the accuracy of our models towards forecasting the future TD evolution of a software project. For evaluating the models predictive power, we decided to use the *Mean Absolute Percentage Error* (MAPE). MAPE is a commonly used measure for the evaluation of forecasting models that uses absolute values to calculate the error in percentage terms. The equation describing MAPE is offered below:

$$MAPE = \frac{100}{n} \sum_{i=1}^{n} \frac{|y_i - \widehat{y_i}|}{y_i} \qquad (1)$$

where n is the number of observations, y_i the real and $\widehat{y_i}$ the predicted values.

---

[4] https://www.tensorflow.org/guide/keras/sequential_model.

To complement the evaluation of our results and at the same time remain inline with our previous studies [15,16], we also calculated the *Mean Absolute Error* (MAE) and the *Root Mean Squared Error* (RMSE), whose presence is usual when it comes to forecasting tasks. MAE calculates the magnitude of the errors coming from a group of forecasts by not taking under consideration their trend. RMSE represents the quantification of the quadratic mean of the differences between the observed and the predicted values. The equations of MAE and RMSE are the following:

$$MAE = \frac{\sum_{i=1}^{n} |y_i - \widehat{y_i}|}{n} \qquad (2)$$

$$RMSE = \sqrt{\frac{1}{n} \sum_{i=1}^{n} (y_i - \widehat{y_i})^2} \qquad (3)$$

again, n is the number of observations, y_i the real and $\widehat{y_i}$ the predicted values.

3.4   Model Training and Execution

Once the data pre-processing and model construction phases are over, we may start the experimental process aiming towards the evaluation of the constructed model. In this section, we provide a brief description of the experiments which were performed towards two different directions so that we can be able to evaluate whether the constructed MLP model can provide meaningful short-term and most importantly long-term forecasts. First, Walk-Forward Train-Test experiments are performed so as to compute and evaluate the performance metrics of the model for different horizons in the future by means of time series validation. Secondly, we present indicative examples where we execute the constructed model in order to visualise the results and hence, gain an extensive perception on the model's ability to capture the potential patterns hidden in the datasets.

Walk-Forward Validation. In ML problems, k-fold cross-validation is a widely used method in order to efficiently evaluate a model's performance. However, the concept of k-fold cross-validation is to randomly split the dataset into k folds, from which k−1 participate in training and the remaining one participates in testing. As a result, it is not the right tool as far as time series data are concerned, since in the case of time series data, samples cannot be randomly split into folds without respecting the temporal order. To overcome this issue, we adopted *Walk-forward Train-Test validation*, a process similar to cross-validation that is suitable for evaluating time series data based on the notion that models are updated when new observations are made available. Shortly, in Walk-forward Train-Test validation, the dataset is split into n equally distanced points, hence, we end up with $n+1$ subsets. Initially, the first subset is used to train a model whose accuracy is tested against the consecutive subsets. Then, the first subset is merged with the second one and a new model is trained and tested against the consecutive remaining subsets. The process is repeated until there is only one subset left to serve as a test set. The results of the n constructed models are then averaged to offer an estimation of the model's accuracy.

In our case, each of the five datasets (i.e., projects) was split at five equally distanced points and Walk-forward Train-Test validation was followed as described above. Experiments were performed for producing forecasts for 5, 10, 20, 40, 60, 80, 100, 120 and 150 steps ahead for each iteration of the process. All of the forecasts that were generated were then compared to the corresponding real values to compute the averaged MAE, RMSE and MAPE errors. In this way, we extract information which step by step illustrate the model's performance.

Model Execution. After evaluating the performance of the produced models through the Walk-forward Train-Test validation, the next step is to execute the produced models and present indicative visualizations of the forecasting results. This process will allow us to visually judge whether the models are able to catch the underlying trends or patterns throughout the evolution of the TD.

Since the structure of the Deep Learning models examined in this study does not directly support more than one outputs, in this type of experiments we decided to use the *Direct* approach, which basically means that for a chosen forecasting horizon, an equal number of independent models will be used to forecast each of the intermediate steps. To make this more clear, let's assume that we want to forecast the TD evolution of a software project for k steps ahead. To achieve this, k models will be executed, where each one of them will be responsible for predicting a specific step (starting from 1 step to k steps), while their forecasted TD values will be aggregated into a common vector, and then plotted as the projected TD evolution.

4   Results and Discussion

In this section, we present the results of our experiments, following the strategy that has been described in Sect. 3.4. Firstly, we present and discuss the results of the Walk-forward Train-Test validation experiments using the constructed MLP model (described in Sect. 3.3) on the selected five projects under investigation. In Table 3, the reader may find the main performance metric used in this study (i.e., MAPE), along with the two complement performance metrics (i.e., MAE and RMSE) across the five different projects that were analysed, for 5 up to 150 versions ahead.

By having a first look at Table 3, we observe that the three performance metrics of the MLP model across the five investigated projects indicate a quite sufficient level of accuracy. This is also depicted in their total averaged values (in bold font) for all investigated forecasting horizons. More specifically, by inspecting the average MAPE values of each project, we observe that they range between 3.04% for the Ambari project and 8.28% for the Mina-sshd project. In addition, while observing the MAPE fluctuation between the various forecasting horizons, we can state that the MLP model has achieved a stable performance for all

Table 3. TD forecasting performance metrics of the MLP on the 5 projects using walk-forward train-test validation

Project	Commits ahead	MAE (min)	RMSE (min)	MAPE (%)
Ambari	5–50 (avg)	1526.332	1873.303	1.252
	60–100 (avg)	3815.803	4451.718	3.503
	110–140 (avg)	6745.792	7584.719	6.121
	150	6864.296	7702.084	6.677
	Total Average	**3341.409**	**3888.185**	**3.037**
Commons-codec	5–50 (avg)	362.476	461.219	3.475
	60–100 (avg)	738.392	900.343	6.630
	110–140 (avg)	858.872	1066.487	7.581
	150	946.965	1131.661	8.420
	Total Average	**580.437**	**722.427**	**5.268**
Commons-io	5–50 (avg)	519.536	621.641	2.684
	60–100 (avg)	980.595	1143.73	4.778
	110–140 (avg)	1099.282	1330.886	5.473
	150	896.301	1050.964	4.223
	Total Average	**737.863**	**878.834**	**3.644**
Httpcomponents-client	5–50 (avg)	1450.848	1974.844	3.468
	60–100 (avg)	2288.026	2836.171	5.377
	110–140 (avg)	3207.025	3868.439	7.614
	150	3294.445	4028.666	7.433
	Total Average	**2031.452**	**2589.210**	**4.763**
Mina-sshd	5–50 (avg)	1647.925	2037.843	4.492
	60–100 (avg)	3792.056	4484.627	10.371
	110–140 (avg)	4877.660	5742.890	12.264
	150	5719.797	6886.471	14.436
	Total Average	**3111.452**	**3726.793**	**8.283**

steps (i.e., commits) ahead. Of course, it is reasonable to expect that while the model's predictive power is higher for shorter forecasting horizons, it decreases as we try to forecast for longer horizons into the future. This is an expected outcome in the field of forecasting, verified also by our previous studies on TD. However, even though longer forecasting horizons have a noticeable impact on the model's performance, the quality of the forecasts remains quite satisfactory. More specifically, the MAPE values of the MLP model for 150 commits-ahead forecasts range between 4.22% for Commons-io and 14.44% for Mina-sshd.

In order to gain a deeper understanding on the results and on their potentially underlying patterns, Fig. 1 shows the evolution of the MAPE values for each project across the various forecasting horizons. By taking a closer look at Fig. 1, we can observe that the lowest MAPE values (ranging from 0.27% to 6.67%) were obtained when the MLP model was trained and tested on the Ambari project (green line), except for the cases of 120 and 150 commits ahead, where the MLP on Commons-io (blue line) demonstrated slightly better results (i.e., MAPE values of 5.47% and 4.22% respectively). On the other hand, the highest MAPE values (ranging from 3.26% to 16.18%) were observed in the case of the Minasshd project (orange line). The MLP model exhibited quite similar performance with respect to Commons-codec (red line) and Httpcomponents-client (purple line) projects.

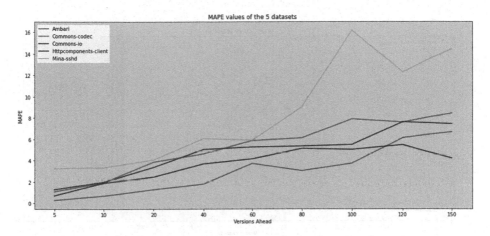

Fig. 1. MAPE values of the MLP on the 5 projects using Walk-forward Train-Test validation for 5 to 150 commits ahead. (Color figure online)

While there is a natural tendency for MAPE values to increase proportionally to the horizon of forecast, there are some exceptions identified throughout our experiments that need to be noted. More specifically, regarding the Mina-sshd (orange line) and Httpcomponents-client (red line) projects, we can observe a spike of the MAPE value at 100 commits-ahead, followed by a drop and then an increase. Similarly, Httpcomponents-client (purple line) and Commons-io (blue line) exhibit a slight decrease of the MAPE value at 150 commits ahead compared to the higher MAPE value observed at 120 commits ahead. As these "abnormalities" do not seem to appear consistently at the same forecasting horizons for every project, we can only assume that they are caused by strong variabilities in the structure of the data itself (i.e., a smooth TD evolution would be much easier to predict compared to a TD evolution with many fluctuations).

As previously stated, in our past studies we have employed a wide range of statistical and ML techniques, which have proven capable of producing reliable short-and mid-term TD predictions, but failed to do so for longer-term forecasts. Specifically, in our study on ML models [16], our best performing model (i.e., Random Forest) demonstrated good performance for forecasts up to 40 commits ahead (average MAPE value 5.94%) whereas, in our study on time series forecasting [15], the ARIMA model's predictions were satisfactory for up to 12 steps ahead (average MAPE value of 1.77%). We believe that the MLP model employed within the context of this study managed to fill this gap by demonstrating promising results even for long-term forecasts. That said, we need to examine and compare the short- mid- and long-term performance of our MLP model with the models used in our previous studies. To do so, we decided to employ both the Random Forest and ARIMA as *baseline models* and directly compare their performance with the MLP so that we may validly assess the contribution that the latter possibly offers.

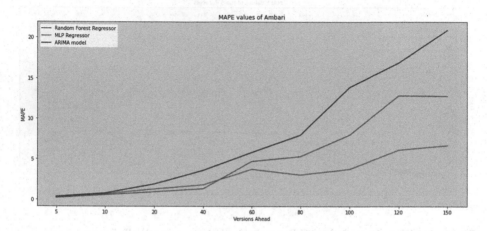

Fig. 2. MAPE values of MLP, Random Forest and the ARIMA model on Ambari project for 5 to 150 commits ahead. (Color figure online)

Figure 2 presents the MAPE values that were obtained when running the Random Forest (green line), the ARIMA (blue line), and the MLP Regressor (red line) on the Ambari project for 5 up to 150 commits-ahead forecasts. As can be seen, for 5 commits ahead the performance of the three models is quite similar. Starting from 10 commits ahead however, the lines are starting to be distinguishable with Random Forest providing slightly lower errors than the MLP, while the ARIMA model's performance starts to drop significantly. This pattern continues for up to 60 commits ahead, where we can clearly notice a shift between MLP and Random Forest. Overall, we conclude that the results are in line with the observations made not only within this paper, but also in our previous works. More specifically, for short-term forecasts (up to 10 commits ahead) the Random Forest, MLP and ARIMA models display equivalent performance. For 20 to 40 commits-ahead predictions, we obtain the lowest MAPE values when Random Forest is employed and the highest when the ARIMA model is used. The scene takes an interesting swift for horizons longer than 60 and up to 150 commits ahead. For these cases, the MLP model clearly outperforms the other two baseline models providing us with a maximum MAPE value of 6.67%.

Following the performance evaluation and comparison between the MLP and the baseline models through the Walk-forward Train-Test validation, the next step is to actually execute the three models on the projects under investigation and visualize the results. As stated in Sect. 3.4, this process will allow us to visually judge whether the MLP model is able to catch the underlying patterns throughout the evolution of the TD (especially for long-term forecasts), in a more accurate way than the other two baseline models do. In Fig. 3, we provide an example of forecasting the TD evolution of Ambari project for 150 steps (commits), using the three models under investigation. The blue line depicts the ground truth, while the red, green and purple lines depict the forecasted values using the MLP, ARIMA, and Random Forest models respectively. It should be noted that the samples covered by the lines that represent forecasts were excluded from the training set.

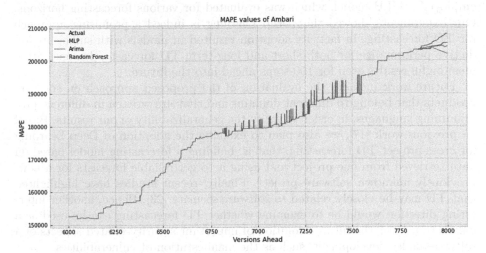

Fig. 3. Ambari TD forecasting for 150 commits ahead using MLP, Random Forest and the ARIMA model.

As can be seen by inspecting Fig. 3, the MLP model outperforms the rest of the models and seems to provide meaningful long-term forecasts for the studied case of Ambari project for up to 150 commits ahead. In fact, the selected model is able to capture the trend of the future TD evolution with a sufficient level of accuracy. For reasons of brevity, illustrations of TD forecasts for the rest of the studied projects are available online[5]. As can be seen, similarly to the case of Ambari, valuable forecasts were also obtained for the rest of the four projects.

To sum up, the novel contribution provided throughout this study is the ability of Deep Learning to accurately predict the future TD evolution of a software project in the long term, an area that was mainly unexplored until now. Furthermore, short and mid-term experiments also demonstrate meaningful

---

[5] https://drive.google.com/drive/folders/14QP6_gw3GGe6_mHSow9sJrfPKRrgd3q8.

results. In order to be able to value the new contribution of the MLP model, we employed two of the models that we widely used throughout our previous studies and thus, we were able to recognize that Deep Learning Neural Networks comprise a new promising path towards the TD Forecasting concept.

5   Conclusion and Future Work

In previous studies we have employed statistical and ML techniques, able to generate accurate short-and mid-term TD forecasts. However, the fact that TD Management activities usually tend to focus on the long term raised the need for more sophisticated forecasting approaches. The purpose of this work was to investigate whether Deep Learning may lead to more accurate long-term TD predictions. We utilized a dataset comprising five open-source Java applications and employed a MLP model, which was evaluated for various forecasting horizons. Our experiments showed that Deep Learning is indeed a promising approach for TD forecasting. In fact, its adoption resulted in models with sufficient predictive performance for both short-and long-term TD forecasts, demonstrating meaningful results even for 150 steps ahead into the future.

Future work includes the evaluation of the proposed approach on software products that belong to different domains and that are written in different programming languages, in order to verify the generalizability of our results. Based on previous work [17], we also plan to examine the adoption of Deep Learning for cross-project TD forecasting, that is, building a forecasting model based on data retrieved from one project and using it to get reliable forecasts for a new, previously unknown software project. Finally, recent studies have highlighted that TD may be closely related to software security [23]. Hence, another interesting direction would be to examine whether TD forecasting can be used as a means to project the future evolution of important security-related aspects of a software under development, such as the manifestation of vulnerabilities.

Acknowledgements. This work is partially funded by the European Union's Horizon 2020 Research and Innovation Programme through EXA2PRO project under Grant Agreement No. 801015.

References

1. Cunningham, W.: The WyCash portfolio management system. ACM SIGPLAN OOPS Mess. 4(2), 29–30 (1993)
2. Brown, N., et al.: Managing technical debt in software-reliant systems. In: Proceedings of the Workshop on Future of Software Engineering Research (FSE/SDP), pp. 47–52. ACM (2010)
3. Suryanarayana, G., Samarthyam, G., Sharma, T.: Refactoring for Software Design Smells: Managing Technical Debt. Morgan Kaufmann (2014)
4. Li, Z., Avgeriou, P., Liang, P.: A systematic mapping study on technical debt and its management. J. Syst. Softw. 101, 193–220 (2015)

5. Tsoukalas, D., Siavvas, M., Jankovic, M., Kehagias, D., Chatzigeorgiou, A., Tzo-varas, D.: Methods and tools for TD estimation and forecasting: a state-of-the-art Survey. In: International Conference on Intelligent Systems (IS 2018) (2018)
6. Chug, A., Malhotra, R.: Benchmarking framework for maintainability prediction of open source software using object oriented metrics. Int. J. Innovat. Comput. Inf. Control **12**(2), 615–634 (2016)
7. Elish, M.O., Elish, K.O.: Application of TreeNet in predicting object-oriented soft-ware maintainability: a comparative study. In: 2009 13th European Conference on Software Maintenance and Reengineering (CSMR), pp. 69–78, March 2009
8. Arisholm, E., Briand, L.C.: Predicting fault-prone components in a java legacy sys-tem. In: Proceedings of the 2006 ACM/IEEE International Symposium on Empir-ical Software Engineering and Measurement (ESEM), pp. 8–17. ACM (2006)
9. Nagappan, N., Ball, T., Zeller, A.: Mining metrics to predict component failures. In: Proceedings of the 28th International Conference on Software Engineering (ICSE), pp. 452–461. ACM (2006)
10. Misra, S.: A step by step guide for choosing project topics and writing research papers in ict related disciplines. In: Information and Communication Technology and Applications: Third International Conference (2021)
11. Gondra, I.: Applying machine learning to software fault-proneness prediction. J. Syst. Softw. **81**(2), 186–195 (2008)
12. Pritam, N., et al.: Assessment of code smell for predicting class change proneness using machine learning. IEEE Access **7**, 37414–37425 (2019)
13. Abbas, R., Albalooshi, F.A., Hammad, M.: Software change proneness prediction using machine learning. In: 2020 International Conference on Innovation and Intel-ligence for Informatics, Computing and Technologies (3ICT), pp. 1–7 (2020)
14. Arcelli Fontana, F., Mäntylä, M.V., Zanoni, M., Marino, A.: Comparing and exper-imenting machine learning techniques for code smell detection. Empirical Softw. Eng. **21**(3), 1143–1191 (2015). https://doi.org/10.1007/s10664-015-9378-4
15. Tsoukalas, D., Jankovic, M., Siavvas, M., Kehagias, D., Chatzigeorgiou, A., Tzo-varas, D.: On the applicability of time series models for technical debt forecasting. In: 15th China-Europe International Symposium on Software Engineering Educa-tion (CEISEE 2019). (2019, in press)
16. Tsoukalas, D., Kehagias, D., Siavvas, M., Chatzigeorgiou, A.: Technical debt fore-casting: an empirical study on open-source repositories. J. Syst. Softw. **170**, 110777 (2020)
17. Tsoukalas, D., Mathioudaki, M., Siavvas, M., Kehagias, D., Chatzigeorgiou, A.: A clustering approach towards cross-project technical debt forecasting. SN Comput. Sci. **2**(1), 1–30 (2021)
18. Lenarduzzi, V., Saarimäki, N., Taibi, D.: The technical debt dataset. In: Pro-ceedings of the Fifteenth International Conference on Predictive Models and Data Analytics in Software Engineering, pp. 2–11 (2019)
19. Lehman, M.M.: Programs, life cycles, and laws of software evolution. Proc. IEEE **68**(9), 1060–1076 (1980)
20. Mens, T.: Introduction and roadmap: history and challenges of software evolution. In: Software Evolution. Springer, Heidelberg (2008). https://doi.org/10.1007/978-3-540-76440-3_1
21. Siavvas, M.G., Chatzidimitriou, K.C., Symeonidis, A.L.: QATCH-an adaptive framework for software product quality assessment. Expert Syst. Appl. **86**, 350–366 (2017)

22. Digkas, G., Lungu, M., Chatzigeorgiou, A., Avgeriou, P.: The evolution of technical debt in the apache ecosystem. In: Lopes, A., de Lemos, R. (eds.) ECSA 2017. LNCS, vol. 10475, pp. 51–66. Springer, Cham (2017). https://doi.org/10.1007/978-3-319-65831-5_4

23. Siavvas, M., Tsoukalas, D., Jankovic, M., Kehagias, D., Tzovaras, D.: Technical debt as an indicator of software security risk: a machine learning approach for software development enterprises. Enterp. Inf. Syst., 1–43 (2020)

How Do Developers Use the Java Stream API?

Joshua Nostas[1] , Juan Pablo Sandoval Alcocer[2]([✉]) , Diego Elias Costa[3] ,
and Alexandre Bergel[4]

[1] Departamento de Ciencias Exactas e Ingenierías,
Universidad Catolica Boliviana "San Pablo", Cochabamba, Bolivia
joshua.nostas@ucb.edu.bo
[2] Department of Computer Science, Pontificia Universidad Católica de Chile,
Santiago, Chile
[3] Department of Computer Science and Software Engineering, Concordia University,
Montreal, Canada
[4] Department of Computer Science (DCC), University of Chile, Santiago, Chile

Abstract. Java 8 marked a shift in the Java development landscape by introducing functional-like concepts in its stream library. Java developers can now rely on stream pipelines to simplify data processing, reduce verbosity, easily enable parallel processing and increase the expressiveness of their code. While streams have seemingly positive effects in Java development, little is known to what extent Java developers have incorporated streams into their programs and the degree of adoption by the Java community of individual stream's features.

This paper presents a replication study on which we analyze the stream usage of 610 Java projects. Our findings show that the Java streams are used mostly by software libraries rather than regular applications. Developers rarely use parallel processing, and when they do so, they only superficially use parallelism features and most of the parallel streams are used on simple *forEach* operations. The most common used pipelines involve *map*, *filter* and *collect* operations. We carefully describe a number of stream idioms we identified, and detail how we addressed the challenges we faced to complete our study. Our findings will help developers at (i) making better decisions about which features to consider when improving the API and (ii) supporting stream-related IDEs features, such as refactoring.

Keywords: Software quality · Software maintenance · Java streams · Empirical study

1 Introduction

While the notion of stream processing has been around for decades [1], the Java 8 released in 2014 officially introduces this paradigm to Java programming with the stream library. The stream library provides a concise API for processing elements

© Springer Nature Switzerland AG 2021
O. Gervasi et al. (Eds.): ICCSA 2021, LNCS 12955, pp. 323–335, 2021.
https://doi.org/10.1007/978-3-030-87007-2_23

(objects and primitives) described as a *pipeline*, made of aggregated operations (*e.g.*, map and filter). Pipelines aim at supporting a declarative programming style: the code focuses on "what" it does as opposed to "how" it is supposed to do it. Through the API proposed by stream, a series of collections operations can be performed with just a few lines of code, increasing code comprehension and allowing developers to safely exploit multi-threaded processing through the use of parallel streams.

Java Stream Library Overview. A *stream* is basically a view on a sequence of elements (objects or primitives), organized by the underlying data structure, a *stream source*. A stream source can be of any data type that implements the interface java.util.Spliterator, collections (including arrays), and I/O channels. Developers process a stream by defining *stream pipelines*, composed by functional *operations*, for which the typically are filter and map, as shown in the example of Listing 1.1.

```
int average = studentsList.stream()
               .filter(Student::hasPassedFinalExam)
               .mapToInt(Student::score)
               .average();
```

Listing 1.1. A stream pipeline that calculates the average score of students that have passed the final exam.

Stream pipelines are designed to be used in a functional style, thus favoring operation composition. Each operation is implemented in a way that the stream source is never modified, and the result of a pipeline is stored on newly created object, making them natural to parallel processing. However, some operations may receive a *behavioral parameter*, a parameter that describes a user-specified behavior. In the example of Listing 1.1, the method Student::hasPassedFinalExam is such a behavioral parameter.

To embrace this newly introduced library, numerous tools have adopted lambdas and the stream library, and researchers have proposed new methods to facilitate the adoption of the benefits of stream processing. Modern Java IDEs, including IntelliJ IDEA, provide an extended support to refactor old Java code to use Java 8 functional features [4], like collapsing for loops to the more expressive stream pipelines. In research, some focus has been put to address the potential performance benefits of parallel streams [11]. Streams have also reported to be a major driver for the increase of Lambda functions in Java programming [16], due to their benefits in expressiveness and convenience.

Despite the extensive support of tools and methods, there is little empirical evidence on how developers have adopted stream processing into their Java programs and what are the most used features in practice. Some studies have investigated the broad scope of adoption of lambdas in Java [16], a critical aspect when using behavioral parameters and therefore streams. However, having an empirical study tailored to the usage of streams will help guide the Java community at better providing effective updates to the Stream API, foment better tools and help the research community at focusing on the pressing issues facing adopters of the stream library.

Partial Replication. In 2020, Khatchadourian *et al.* [12] presented an empirical study on the use of the stream library in 34 Java projects and 719 code patches. To track streams and their attributes Khatchadourian *et al.* use a series of labeled transitions systems, static analysis and type-state analysis. A small set of project make possible to fully analyze stream usage in a reasonable amount of time. However, it may limit the generality of the findings. To address this threat, our paper partially replicate the effort of Khatchadourian *et al.*. In particular, we analyze 610 java project selected from a initial bag of 10,000 open source Java projects hosted on GitHub. The scope of our effort is slight different, as such, we limit our analysis to track stream pipelines fully declared within a method, excluding inter-procedural stream operations. In particular, we focus our analysis on answering the following research questions:

- *RQ1 - What is the trend of the stream library adoption in Java projects?* Getting a picture on how do Java developers are adopting the stream library is crucial to determine the importance of the library within the Java ecosystem.
- *RQ2 - How do Java developers use streams in their projects?* In particular, we are interested in the following questions: *What is the most commonly used stream operations? What are the most commonly used pipelines?*, and, *What are the common operations that developers do using streams?* Understanding how the API is used in practice is key for the stream library maintainers to understand expectations and concern from the Java community, in addition to improve the most used subset of operations and pipelines. Likewise, researchers that have the interest on researching the Streams API, may focus on the more prevalent cases.

Findings. Our study reveals findings related to stream pipelines usage that largely match and complement Khatchadourian *et al.* study:

- Similarly than Khatchadourian *et al.* we found that developers rarely rely on parallel processing, and that most of the parallel streams are used on simple `forEach` operations.
- The most common used non-parallel pipelines involve map, filter and collect operations. These results largely match with Khatchadourian *et al.*, which also shows that developers tend to favor more simplistic (linear) operations rather than more specialized non-scalar reductions.
- Complementary to Khatchadourian *et al.*, we find that most of the project under analysis are libraries or tools for developers, only 10% of the projects correspond to conventional applications.
- The most used Collector operations are `toList`, `toSet`, `joining`, and `toMap`. While the API provides more advanced collector operations, they are not commonly used by developers.

The following sections details the related work, the methodology we adopted, and our results.

2   Related Work

Numerous studies have investigated how developers adopt language and API features. In most of the works we discuss in this section, researchers adopt a similar methodology to ours, from selecting projects based on popularity criteria to mining software repositories to quantitatively assess the level of adoption of language features from developers. Particular effort has been put towards understanding how developers adopt unsafe language features, such as breaking type safety in Go [7], Rust [9] and using the infamous goto command in C [18]. In the context of Java programming, some studies have investigated the usage of Unsafe APIs [15], and dynamic type casting [14]. In both studies [14,15], researchers report that the use of unsafe library features is widespread in the Java ecosystem. Developers often trade compiler checks for better flexibility, putting their programs at a higher risk of runtime errors. Other studies focuses on source code aspects related to memory consumption [3], performance regressions [20–22], or complexity [8,17].

Some works that have investigated how developers use the Java collections API, a framework that is directly related to how developers use streams. Costa *et al.* [6] investigated how developers select Java collections in their projects. While the study showed that developers could benefit from using more specialized data structures for better performance, developers only rarely go beyond the general-purposed collection types. As such, several tools have been proposed to better guide developers in selecting their data structures in Java for better time and memory allocation [2,5], and better energy consumption [19]. This finding that developers only rarely tune their collections has a similar parallel to our set of findings. In our study, we found that only in rare occasions developers make use of more complex stream operations and the parallelism of stream pipelines. Hence, there is the need for tools that can better guide developers at exploring the benefits of stream parallelism.

Similarly to the Streams API, lambdas have been introduced in Java 8, in an effort to enable Java developers to use functional idioms. The work of Mazinanian *et al.* have investigated the usage of lambda functions in Java program, including their usage in stream pipelines [16]. This study reported that streams are frequently used as replacement to for-loops, as they provide a more concise and easy-to-read idiom. However, the profiling of stream features used by developers remained out the paper's scope.

The work that is most related to ours is the work of Khatchadourian *et al.* [12], in which we partially replicate in this study. Khatchadourian *et al.* have investigated the use and misuse of the java stream API over 34 java projects [12]. Similarly to our findings, they have reported that parallelization is seldom used and that developers frequently use ordered streams, which are not optimal for parallelism. Khatchadourian *et al.* also reported that developers favor more straightforward stream pipelines, which corroborated with our findings that the most frequently used pipelines contain map-collect or filter-collect operation chains. Developers use functional-like streams to process data but collect them back to the imperative programming style they are most accustomed to. We complement their work by confirming part of their results with an analysis a the analysis of a large set of 610 projects. Furthermore, we investigate what types of projects use Java streams which help us understand what profile of projects tend to use streams.

3 Experimental Setup

This section highlights some aspects of the methodology we used to answer the two research questions stated above.

3.1 Methodology

To carry out the mining of stream API usage in a large corpus of Java applications, we use the following 3-steps process:

1. *Project selections* – Our very first step is to select GitHub repositories of Java software projects, which we consider relevant for the scope of our study.
2. *Detect* – To detect the stream pipeline usage, we analyze the abstract syntax tree (AST) of each Java file for all selected projects. Stream usage, expressed in term of pipelines, are extracted from the AST. In particular, the source code mining focuses on extracting components of a pipeline: stream factories (`studentsList.stream()` in Listing 1.1), intermediate operations (`filter`, `mapToInt`), and terminal operations (`average`).
3. *Categorize* – We quantitatively and qualitatively analyze stream pipelines and characterize their usage.

The following sections details each one of these steps.

3.2 Challenges of Using Type Inference

We consider a stream API usage as a method call performed on a stream object. As such, determining whether or not an object is a stream is key in our analysis. Since most GitHub repositories contain application source code and rarely contain the result of a compilation process, we need to identify stream API usage by solely inspecting source code. Type inferencers are tools designed to determine the type of each object and the signature of each method call. Using a type inferencer to identify stream usage is therefore appealing. Despite their solid theoretical foundation, using type inferencers in our context suffers from two different aspects:

Project Dependencies. The precision of the type inference heavily depends on the resolution of dependent libraries used by each project. However, many projects in GitHub do not have their dependencies explicitly declared. This fact may limit the accuracy of our study. Previous studies show that automatically download all the dependencies of great portion of the projects is an open problem [13].

Overhead. Infering the type of objects from the source code of a large project is time consuming. Consider the JavaSymbolSolver type inferencer[1]. Computing the type of each variable and the signature of each method call takes hours for any sizeable number of Java source code files. A rough estimation based on an initial estimation indicates that type inferencing 10k projects takes up to 48 d of computation[2].

Because of the aforementioned challenges, we adopted a sequentially staged process to investigate stream usage in a large number of projects. The goal of this style of methodology is to reduce the overhead of running type inference analysis, by removing projects that clearly do not rely on streams. We describe this in more detail in Sect. 3.3.

3.3 Sequential Staged Project Filtering

We start our study with a initial sample of 10,000 most starred Java projects from GitHub. Their stars range from 142 to 44,779 stars. Stars on GitHub are used as a token of appreciation from their users and also indicates how often people tagged projects for later exploration. Hence, stars are considered as a good proxy for project popularity and is commonly used on empirical studies to filter out unpopular projects [6,7].

Initial Project Filtering. To discard toy or small projects, we initially select for further analysis projects that meet following criteria:

– Projects not archived, disabled or forked, as these projects do not have current development activity.
– Projects with 3 or more contributors.
– Projects with more than 50 commits.

After applying the filter, from the initial 10,000 projects, we were left with 5,386 projects for further analysis.

Data Cleaning. To discard educational or example projects, the first three authors (with experience in Java development) manually read the project name and description to categorize each one of these 5,386 projects. We discard projects that were categorized by at least two authors as toy, educational, or example projects. In total, we discard 317 projects. Therefore, after this step our sample is reduced from 5,386 projects to 5,096 projects.

Sequential Staged Filtering. Due to the two challenges described in (Sect. 3.2), we cannot blindly run a type inference on our projects. Instead, we adopt a *sequential staged filtering* of the projects: from the set of 5,096 Java projects, we apply a sequence of filtering and expansion techniques: a sequence of keyword filtering, data cleaning, resolving dependencies, and type inference filtering.

---

[1] https://github.com/javaparser/javasymbolsolver.
[2] It takes 28 h to process 7,700 Java source code files, and the 10k projects contain 317,032 source files.

Keyword Filtering. Downloading the dependencies and inferring the type of all method calls in our initial set of projects is too costly to carryout. Instead, we perform a *keyword filtering* on the projects that consists in reviewing each method call of all the Java projects. The Java stream library provides a number of ways to directly create Stream objects, the most common are: `of`, `stream` and `parallelStream`. This keyword filtering step consists in detecting projects that have at least one method call with these keywords. As a result, we found 2,189 projects that meet this criteria.

Download Dependencies. We automatically download all project dependencies that use *Gradle* and *Maven*. Our automation uses two standard commands to download the dependencies[3]. From the 2,189 projects, 1,193 use *Maven* for dependency management, 908 use *Gradle*, and 88 use another project management tool. Using our process, we successfully download the dependency of 851 projects, 682 in Maven, and 169 in Gradle. Since our analysis highly depends on being able to determine if a method call is related to a stream object, we use these 851 project as a base of our study.

Type Inference Filtering. We use the JavaSymbolSolver type inferencer to determine the type of each method call in the 851 projects. From total method calls, 17% of them cannot be inferred. The reason is because the current type inference libraries have also a number of limitations in particular cases (*c.g.*, high polymorphic operations and reflection). After the type inference, we found that 241 projects do not contain any method call related to stream. Therefore these are considered false positives and were discarded from our study. Finally, we consider the remaining **610 projects** as the target projects for our stream usage study. You will find the information about the projects under study online[4].

3.4   Detecting Stream API Usage

We use the Java Parser library to analyze the projects under study. We parse all the files of each project, build an Abstract Syntax Tree and look for all method calls nodes in the tree that are performed on a stream object.

Stream Usage Detection. We categorize the method calls as follows: 1) *Stream factory*, a method call that returns a stream but the receiver object is not a stream; 2) *Stream intermediate operation*, a method call that returns a stream and the receiver is a stream, 3) *Stream terminal operation*, a method call that does not return a stream but the receiver is a stream.

Pipeline Detection. We define a pipeline a sequence of method calls that follow the pattern: stream factory, followed by a sequence of intermediate operations, and ended by a terminal operation.

---

[3] `mvn dependency: copy-dependencies` and `gradle dependencies`.
[4] https://bit.ly/2UPiGIO.

3.5   Categorization

To answer our research questions, we categorize the 610 projects and the stream usage as follows:

Projects Categorization. Two authors carefully read the project title, description and project page to categorize the projects into one of the two categories:

- *Frameworks-Libraries-&-Tools*: programs that developers use to create, debug, maintain, or otherwise support other programs, and programs esigned to be reused by other programs, often for software development.
- *Applications:* conventional applications, which do not fit in any of the other categories; this is the overwhelming majority

First, authors categorize projects separately. Then, they compare their categories and when to a consensus about which categories assign to each project.

Pipeline Categorization. We consider a pipeline as a method call chain on a stream object. For this categorization, we consider the set of consecutive operations done over a stream. This categorization was done automatically using a java parser and a type inference. We consider only operations performed over a stream object as receiver.

4   Results

4.1   What Is the Stream Usage Trend?

We present in Fig. 1 a stacked bar plot showing (i) the number of projects created by year and (ii) the portion of these projects resulting from the keyword filtering and type filtering. Our approach **estimate that the portion of the projects that use at least once the stream API is about 21%** $(2,189/10,000)$. Note the real proportion of stream adoption is likely to be smaller since we cannot efficiently avoid false positives without downloading dependencies. The figure also indicates that the share is in constant increase over the year, reflecting **an incremental and steady adoption of the stream library by practitioners**.

Regarding the type of projects that use streams, we present in Table 1 the distribution of the 610 projects that use streams across the two categories. Our results indicate that the **majority of projects (90%) that use streams are Frameworks, Libraries and Tools, rather than Java applications.** Note that the proportion may differ in the 2,189 projects.

4.2   What Are the Most Used Pipelines?

We present in Fig. 2 and Fig. 3 the most used stream pipelines from the 610 projects in our dataset. We found that only 113 (18%) of them create at least one parallel stream object, while the remaining 497 (82%) use solely non-parallel

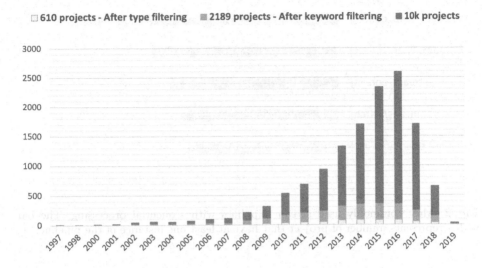

Fig. 1. Projects by creation year

Table 1. Number of projects by category that have at least one stream pipeline.

Category	# Projects	%
Frameworks, Libraries and Tools	549	90%
Applications	61	10%

streams. Furthermore, from all the stream factories in these 113 projects, only 20% of them create a parallel stream. This finding suggests that even in projects that use parallel streams, its usage is very infrequent. We conclude that **developers rarely rely on parallel processing** despite the large number of features for parallel computing provided by the Java Stream API. Figure 2 lists the five most popular sequential pipelines and Fig. 3 lists the five most popular parallel pipelines. The figure also indicates that **most of the parallel streams are used on simple `forEach` operations**, thus avoiding a large number of expressive features for parallelism.

On the other hand, Fig. 2 also shows that **the most common used non-parallel pipelines involve `map`, `filter` and `collect` operations**. These are arguably the most straightforward stream operations in the API, showing that developers prefer simple pipelines that are easy to understand and maintain. The most frequently used pipeline `stream-map-collect` indicates that developers frequently use streams to process data from one collection to the other. For instance, consider the following example:

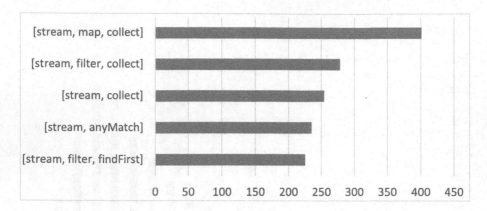

Fig. 2. Most commonly used stream pipelines with sequential processing. The bar width represents number of project that have at least one instance of the pipeline.

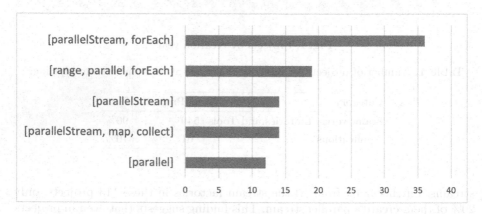

Fig. 3. Most commonly used stream pipelines with parallel processing. The bar width represents number of project that have at least one instance of the pipeline.

```
private boolean checkRole(User user, Set<Role> expectedRoles) {
    Set<String> roleNames = expectedRoles.
    stream().map(Role::getRoleName).collect(Collectors.toSet());
    return authorityRepository.checkRole(user.getUsername(), roleNames);
}
```

The example shows a snippet containing a stream pipeline that creates a stream from a set of role objects and return it as a set. Therefore, the stream is used as an intermediate step, and the rest of the execution use a collection as a main data structure.

Figure 3 also shows that **the most commonly used parallel pipelines involve forEach, map and collect operations**. Once again, parallelism is used in its most simple form, the most frequent pipeline `parallelStream-forEach` is used to process elements using a single behavioral function. For instance, consider the following example:

```
private void stopAllBrowsers() {
    if (allSessions == null) {
        return;
    }
    allSessions.getAllSessions().parallelStream()
        .forEach(session -> {
            try {
                session.stop();
            } catch (Exception ignored) {
                // Ignored
            }
        });
}
```

The example depicts a snippet where developers create a parallel stream from a set of session objects and stops each of them.

Stream Collectors. The Java Collector class provides a number of expressive reduction operations. These operations are commonly used together with the `collect` operations. The most used Collector operators are `toList` (9079), `toSet` (2000), `joining` (1326), `toMap` (981) and `groupingBy` (319). Although the library offers an efficient `mapping` function, developers use a `map` followed by a `collect`, thus representing a missed opportunity for using a dedicated optimization.

Partial Stream Pipelines. There are a number of partial pipelines. We consider partial stream pipelines to a method call chain that do not end with a terminal operation. For instance, `of` and `stream`, these represent program statements where a stream was instantiated, but none terminal operation was performed on them. Normally, these streams are used in different methods. We plan to consider inter-procedural stream operations as future work.

5   Conclusion and Future Work

As far as we are aware of, this paper describes the largest effort in mining Java stream usage. We initially analyzed 10,000 popular Java projects and considered 610 projects for a deeper analysis. Results of such a large scale analysis can be used to complement recent effort in studying Java streams [12]. For example, recent works [10] have proposed a sophisticated refactoring tooling of the pipelines `sort-collect`, `parallel-map-collect`, and `unordered-distinct`. Our empirical study shows that these pipelines are extremely rare, thus mitigating the possible impact of such a refactoring. As future work, we plan to pursue our effort in considering partial stream pipelines.

Acknowledgments. Bergel thanks ANID Fondecyt 1200067 for partially sponsoring this work.

References

1. Abelson, H., Sussman, G.J.: Structure and Interpretation of Computer Programs, 2nd edn. MIT Press, Cambridge (1996)
2. Basios, M., Li, L., Wu, F., Kanthan, L., Barr, E.T.: Darwinian data structure selection. In: Proceedings of the 2018 26th ACM Joint Meeting on European Software Engineering Conference and Symposium on the Foundations of Software Engineering, pp. 118–128. ESEC/FSE 2018, Association for Computing Machinery, New York (2018)
3. Bergel, A., Infante, A., Maass, S., Sandoval Alcocer, J.P.: Reducing resource consumption of expandable collections: The pharo case. Sci. Comput. Program. **161**, 34–56 (2018), advances in Dynamic Languages
4. Blog, I.I.: Intellij idea inspection settings for refactoring to java 8. Accessed 14 Jan 2020
5. Costa, D., Andrzejak, A.: Collectionswitch: a framework for efficient and dynamic collection selection. In: Proceedings of the 2018 International Symposium on Code Generation and Optimization, CGO 2018, pp. 16–26. Association for Computing Machinery, New York (2018)
6. Costa, D., Andrzejak, A., Seboek, J., Lo, D.: Empirical study of usage and performance of java collections. In: Proceedings of the 8th ACM/SPEC on International Conference on Performance Engineering, ICPE 2017, pp. 389–400. Association for Computing Machinery, New York (2017)
7. Costa, D., Mujahid, S., Abdalkareem, R., Shihab, E.: Breaking type-safety in go: an empirical study on the usage of the unsafe package. IEEE Trans. Softw. Eng. (01), 1 (2021)
8. Crasso, M., Mateos, C., Zunino, A., Misra, S., Polvorin, P.: Assessing cognitive complexity in java-based object-oriented systems: metrics and tool support. Comput. Inf. **35**, 497–527 (2014)
9. Evans, A.N., Campbell, B., Soffa, M.L.: Is rust used safely by software developers? In: Proceedings of the ACM/IEEE 42nd International Conference on Software Engineering, ICSE 2020, pp. 246–257. Association for Computing Machinery, New York (2020)
10. Khatchadourian, R., Tang, Y., Bagherzadeh, M., Ahmed, S.: [engineering paper] a tool for optimizing java 8 stream software via automated refactoring. In: 2018 IEEE 18th International Working Conference on Source Code Analysis and Manipulation (SCAM), pp. 34–39 (September 2018)
11. Khatchadourian, R., Tang, Y., Bagherzadeh, M., Ahmed, S.: Safe automated refactoring for intelligent parallelization of java 8 streams. In: Proceedings of the 41st International Conference on Software Engineering, pp. 619–630. IEEE Press (2019)
12. Khatchadourian, R., Tang, Y., Bagherzadeh, M., Ray, B.: An empirical study on the use and misuse of java 8 streams. In: FASE 2020. LNCS, vol. 12076, pp. 97–118. Springer, Cham (2020). https://doi.org/10.1007/978-3-030-45234-6_5
13. Martins, P., Achar, R., V. Lopes, C.: 50k-c: a dataset of compilable, and compiled, java projects. In: 2018 IEEE/ACM 15th International Conference on Mining Software Repositories (MSR), pp. 1–5 (May 2018)
14. Mastrangelo, L., Hauswirth, M., Nystrom, N.: Casting about in the dark: an empirical study of cast operations in java programs. In: Proceedings of the ACM on Programming Languages 3 (OOPSLA) (October 2019)
15. Mastrangelo, L., Ponzanelli, L., Mocci, A., Lanza, M., Hauswirth, M., Nystrom, N.: Use at your own risk: the java unsafe api in the wild. SIGPLAN Not. **50**(10), 695–710 (2015)

16. Mazinanian, D., Ketkar, A., Tsantalis, N., Dig, D.: Understanding the use of lambda expressions in java. Proc. ACM Program. Lang. **1**(OOPSLA), 1–31 (2017)
17. Misra, S., Cafer, F., Akman, I., Fernandez-Sanz, L.: Multi-paradigm metric and its applicability on java projects. Acta Polytechnica Hungarica **10**, 203–220 (2013)
18. Nagappan, M., et al.: An empirical study of goto in c code from github repositories. In: Proceedings of the 2015 10th Joint Meeting on Foundations of Software Engineering, pp. 404–414. ESEC/FSE 2015, Association for Computing Machinery, New York (2015)
19. Oliveira, W., Oliveira, R., Castor, F., Fernandes, B., Pinto, G.: Recommending energy-efficient java collections. In: 2019 IEEE/ACM 16th International Conference on Mining Software Repositories (MSR), pp. 160–170 (2019)
20. Sandoval Alcocer, J.P., Bergel, A.: Tracking down performance variation against source code evolution. In: Proceedings of the 11th Symposium on Dynamic Languages, pp. 129–139. DLS 2015, Association for Computing Machinery, New York (2015)
21. Sandoval Alcocer, J.P., Bergel, A., Valente, M.T.: Learning from source code history to identify performance failures. In: Proceedings of the 7th ACM/SPEC on International Conference on Performance Engineering, ICPE 2016, pp. 37–48. Association for Computing Machinery, New York (2016)
22. Sandoval Alcocer, J.P., Bergel, A., Valente, M.T.: Prioritizing versions for performance regression testing: the pharo case. Sci. Comput. Program. **191**, 102415 (2020)

Quality Histories of Past Extract Method Refactorings

Abel Mamani Taqui[1] , Juan Pablo Sandoval Alcocer[1](✉) ,
Geoffrey Hecht[2] , and Alexandre Bergel[2]

[1] Departamento de Ciencias Exactas e Ingenierías, Universidad Catolica Boliviana
"San Pablo", Cochabamba, Bolivia
jsandoval@ucb.edu.bo
[2] Department of Computer Science (DCC), University of Chile, Santiago, Chile

Abstract. Modern programming environments offer the Extract Method refactoring as a way to improve software quality by moving a source code fragment into a new method. This refactoring comes with an immediate positive feedback by shortening the refactored method. It can also increase code re-usage and encourage developers to remove code clones.

The impact of refactorings on the software quality has been the topic of many research efforts. However, these refactorings are usually studied in groups. Therefore the metrics evaluated and the observation are not tailored to a specific refactoring, thus hiding a valuable insight on how practitioners use a refactoring in particular.

In this paper, we conduct an assessment of the quality impact resulting from the Extract Method refactoring. Our results statistically confirm the tendency of the Extract Method to improve complexity and slightly worsen cohesion, respectively in 46% and 70% of the refactoring. In addition, we observe that the Extract Method favors re-use and reduces occurrences of code clones in 56% of the extracted methods. However, our results also show that some specific cases are contrary to the previously mentioned trends and that it is therefore necessary to study refactorings at a low granularity.

Keywords: Refactoring · Software quality · Software maintenance

1 Introduction

Refactoring is now an essential practice for improving the quality of a source code without changing its external behaviors [16,18,19]. Refactoring has multiple expected benefits, such as easing maintenance, reducing code complexity, improving code readability and removing potential code smells. But recent studies have shown that refactorings do not always improve the quality of the source code, and could even worsen it in some scenarios [3,4,6].

O. Gervasi et al. (Eds.): ICCSA 2021, LNCS 12955, pp. 336–352, 2021.
https://doi.org/10.1007/978-3-030-87007-2_24

This paper contributes to this line of research by building on a partial replication of existing efforts on characterizing the impact of the refactoring on software quality. Our paper contributes to the field of code quality and refactoring by focusing on one refactoring, and therefore lowering the granularity of our research. Most of the work on software quality and refactoring consider various refactorings, thus, missing opportunities to go in depth of the Extract Method refactoring.

The Extract Method is one of the most common refactorings [5,16,21]; it allows the developer to take a fragment of code, move it into a new method, and replace the refactored code with a call to the new method. It it supposed to improve readability, reduce code duplication and remove long method code smells.

Modern programming environments make the Extract Method refactoring a central feature. Consider this informal search on Google video: searching for "Extract Method refactoring" lists more than 69K different videos that illustrate how to perform the refactoring using many different programming environment end IDEs. This informal measurement highlights the relevance of this feature for practitioners. Understanding the implication of using this refactoring on software quality is important because it has been shown that a refactoring, when improperly employed, may degrade the quality of refactored software [3].

This paper presents new insights from a quantitative analysis of a large corpus of 2,712 Extract Method refactorings gathered from 200 Java projects hosted on GitHub. Our objective is to explore the usage of the Extract Method refactoring in Java in order to gain insight on how this refactoring helps developers improve the quality of their code. In particular, our study provides a detailed analysis of the impact of the Extract Method refactoring on cohesion, complexity, code clones, code re-usability and method visibility.

Findings. Our study reveals a number of facts on the Extract Method refactoring:

- 46% of the Extract Method refactorings help to reduce at least 4 complexity metrics of the refactored method and therefore of the class;
- 70% of the extracted methods reduce the class cohesion, but overall statistically this effect is very small. In addition, we found that 10% of these methods are not static and do not depend on any attribute/method of their class;
- 56% of the Extract Method refactorings favor code re-usability and help reduce code clones;
- 54% of the extracted methods are private, while 22% of the public extracted methods are overexposed and may reduce their scope to private.

As in previous works [3,4,6], our results confirm that the refactoring may have unexpected effects on code quality metrics in some cases. In addition, our results also show that Extract Method is often exploited partially and that the extracted method could be improved in terms of visibility, code clones and static modifiers. You will find the information of extract methods and commits under study online[1].

Outline. The paper is structured as follows: Sect. 2 reviews the studies related to refactoring and software quality; Sect. 3 highlights the need for conducting a focused study and highlights the opportunity exploited in this paper; Sect. 4 outlines our empirical setup, the collection process, and metrics we used; Sect. 5 discusses our findings; Sect. 6 captures any threats to the validity of our work; Sect. 7 concludes and presents our future work.

2   Related Work

Numerous studies have exploited mining tools to produce empirical studies on the relationship between code quality and refactorings [4,6–9,11,20].

Elish and Alshayeb [8] propose a classification of 12 refactorings based on their effect on nine internal and six external quality attributes. Evaluating three open source projects and three course projects, they determined if the refactoring tends to decrease or increase the quality attributes. They observed that Extract Method tends to increase Response For a Class, Number Of Methods, Numbers of Lines of Code and Lack of Cohesion in Methods, however the impact is not quantified.

Concerning the relation between Extract Method and code clones, Choi *et al.* [7] investigated how code clones are merged during the software evolution of three Java open-source projects. They observed that Replace Method with Method Object and Extract Method were the most commonly used refactorings to remove clones. They suggest improvements for refactoring tools allowing the detection of clones with different sequences of tokens. They did not study if clones could be introduced by the refactorings.

Bavota *et al.* [4] investigated the relations between metrics or code smells and refactoring activities on 63 releases of three open source applications. They observed that there is no clear relationship between the part of code which developers chose to refactor and quality metrics, moreover about 40% of the refactorings were performed on classes affected by code smells but only 7% of them removed the smell.

Kádár *et al.* [11] evaluated the impact of more than 40 types of refactorings on 50 metrics in seven open-source projects. They observed that the classes with the worst maintainability metrics are subject to more refactorings. Overall, they observed a positive effect of the refactorings on most of their metrics, including code clones occurrences. However, the results of the refactoring are grouped and therefore it is not possible to distinguish the influence of each refactoring on the results.

Based on 25 metrics related to five internal quality attributes: cohesion, coupling, complexity, inheritance, and size. Chávez *et al.* [6] observed that more than 94% of the applied refactorings in 23 open-source projects are performed

---

[1] http://bit.ly/RefactoringDataset.

on program elements with at least one quality metrics considered as critical. In 65% of the cases, these critical quality metrics were improved and the remaining 35% refactorings had no effect. Overall on all metrics, 55% of the observed refactorings improved internal quality attributes, and 10% were associated with a quality decline.

Al Dallal et al. [1] performed a systematic literature review on the impact of object-oriented refactoring on quality attributes. They found numerous studies on the impact of refactoring on quality, and confirmed that refactoring does not always improve all quality attributes. However 85.5% of the studies they considered did not apply any statistical techniques and most of the studies concerned multiple refactoring scenarios, which could not be distinguished from each other. These undesirable practices prevented them from precisely analyzing the individual impact of refactoring on quality.

Pantiuchina et al. [17] empirically investigated the correlation between seven commonly used metrics and the declared intentions of developers to improve some quality attributes (i.e. cohesion, coupling, complexity and readability) in 1,282 commits. The study shows that the quality improvements expected by developers is not always reflected in the associated metrics. In addition to pointing out inconsistencies between how code quality attributes are perceived by developers and commonly used metrics, the authors recommend that the combination of many quality metrics should be preferred over one.

AlOmar et al. [2] also investigated commits where developers showed intentions to perform refactorings. They discovered that developers use a variety of patterns to perform refactorings, and that they often directly mention quality attributes or removing code smells in the associated commit messages.

In another study, AlOmar et al. [3] investigated the correlations between refactorings and 27 quality metrics associated to 8 quality attributes such as cohesion, coupling or complexity in 3,795 open source Java projects. They observed that in most cases metrics can reflect the developer intentions of improving quality reported in the commit messages. However, they did not find any metrics which correlated with the developer's intentions to improve encapsulation, abstraction or design size.

In summary, we observe in most publications that refactoring does not always improve the quality of source code as one might expect. However, it is difficult to derive a more detailed consensus from these previous works. For some publications, the quality metrics are observed to be very relevant and the effect of refactorings on them correspond well to the intentions of the developers [2,3,6]. But for other publications, the usual metrics seem less relevant for analyzing the impact of refactorings [4,17]. However, it is important to note that the refactorings used and the metrics used vary between all these publications. In this paper, we focus on the Extract Method refactoring. In this way we can ensure that the chosen metrics, associated results and observations are relevant to this particular refactoring and that the effects observed are not due to another refactoring.

3 A Focused Study

The previous section shows that there are numerous high-quality works on the impact of refactoring on code quality. They provide valuable results, however the analyzed refactorings are studied together on many different metrics allowing only aggregated observations. As observed by Al Dallal et al. [1], it is hard to distinguish between the effects of individual refactoring when multiple refactorings are applied. Especially since the effects of refactorings on metrics can be conflicting. For example, the impact of dozens of refactorings on dozens of metrics are reported by AlOmar et al. [3] and Kádár et al. [11], but the results of all the refactorings are grouped together. The impact of a particular refactoring is therefore not explicit. Overall refactorings do improve cohesion but is it the case for the Extract Method (or any other particular refactoring)?

Publications like the one from Elish and Alshayeb [8] do report an evaluated impact for each refactoring on different metrics, for example that Extract Method does increase LCOM. However, it is reported as a tendency, which is not quantified and the possible exceptions to this tendency are not considered.

Chavez et al. [6] provide more detailed results, by reporting if the effects of each refactoring is positive, neutral or negative on most metrics (or at least one metric) of a group (cohesion, coupling, complexity, inheritance, size). However, the results are not detailed for each metric. Our paper contributes to the field by focusing on only Extract Method, in order to provide an in-depth analysis. It is complemented by statistical tests to allow precise comparisons with future works.

Our goal is to provide a detailed and quantified analysis on each of our metrics. In addition to cohesion and complexity, our research incorporates metrics which are not considered in previous works (e.g. visibility and code reuse) which we found relevant to report for Extract Method. We also consider a large dataset of open-source applications.

The results we obtained match some of the previous results, in particular:

- 46% of the extracted methods improves most of our complexity metrics, similar to the 45% observed by Chavez et al. [6] for their complexity group;
- 70% of the refactored methods increase LCOM, whereas Chavez et al. [6] observed a worsened cohesion in 59% of cases for their cohesion group.

However, as detailed in the subsequent sections, our effort lead us to new findings:

- 56% of the Extract Method helps reduce code clones;
- 10% of the extracted methods could be static;
- 51% of the extracted methods are called more than once;
- 22% of the public extracted methods are overexposed, and could be privatized.

The following sections details the methodology we adopted, and our results.

4   Empirical Study Setup

Our methodology has four-steps, which are described in the following subsections.

4.1   Collecting Open Source Projects

To build our dataset, we collect the two hundred most popular Java GitHub projects. For this, we use the GitHub API to collect the Java projects that have more stars. The stars in GitHub represents the number of GitHub accounts that follow this projects, which makes it a reliable proxy for popularity. The number of stars of these two hundred projects ranges from 2,199 to 2,786. These projects contain a total of 8,793 software versions and 7,885 files.

4.2   Detecting Extracted Methods

We use the tool Refactoring Miner to detect commits where developers perform an Extract Method refactoring [22]. We analyze all the commit history for each project. In total, refactoring miner reports 80,842 refactorings along the whole commit history of the two hundred projects under analysis. From these, 3,059 correspond to a unique Extract Method refactoring.

4.3   Computing Metrics

As the main difference from previous works [13–15], we focused only on the Extract Method refactoring, therefore we selected metrics relevant to that refactoring. The metrics were computed in the refactored class, refactored method and extracted method; depending on the metric. We categorize these metrics in four groups: complexity, cohesion, reuse, and visibility.

Complexity. We use seven complexity metrics to measure the complexity of the refactored method before and after the method extraction. Table 1 briefly describes each of these metrics.

Table 1. Complexity metrics computed in the refactored method

Name	Description
McCabe cyclomatic complexity	# Unique possible paths through the method
McClure's complexity	# Comparisons plus # control referenced variables
Nested block depth (NBD)	The maximum depth of nesting within a method
Number of control Variables	# Control variables reference within the method
Number of comparisons	# Comparisons in a method
Number of parameters	# Parameters a method takes as input
Input/Output variables	# Parameters plus 1 (assuming 1 as a return value)

Cohesion. We use the metric Lack Of Cohesion (LCOM) to measure the cohesion of a class before and after the extraction. For this, we use the Herdenson-Sellers method: $(< r > -|M|)/(1 - |M|)$. Where M is the set of methods defined by the refactored class, and F the defined fields. Let be $r(f)$ the number of methods that access a field f, where $f \in F$, and $< r >$ is the mean of $r(f)$ over F [10]. LCOM is greater when the class methods depend less on the attributes. However, LCOM could be controversial because a class may have methods that depend only on one class field (*i.e.,* an accessor), and accessors increase the lack of cohesion metric. For this reason, we use three additional metrics:

- *Number of used attributes* – It is the number of attributes that the extracted method used.
- *Number of internal method calls* – It is the number of calls performed by the extracted method to other methods within its class.
- *Static methods* – We count how many extracted methods are static. A static method does not depend on the instance variables of the class and therefore we consider this fact as a metric to better characterize the cohesion.

Re-Use & Code Clones. We measure the degree of which an extracted method helps reduce the number of code clones and favor code reuse. In particular, we measure the following metrics:

- *Number of Internal Callers* – We statically count the number of times that an extracted method is called within the class. For this, we only consider method calls that are performed over the `this` keyword, and have the same signature as the extracted method.
- *Code Clones* – We count the number of code clones that exist in the refactored class before and after the Extract Method refactoring. For this, we use the *Open Static Analyzer* tool[2], which detects syntax based code clones, also called Type-2 clones. Although, there are other tools that are useful to detect different kind of code clones, these tools need the compiled version of each program. Compiling GitHub projects is challenging, mainly because not all projects of provide their dependencies or build mechanisms [12].

Visibility. We count the number of extracted methods that are public, private, protected and static. We contrast this information with how many times these methods are called inside and outside the class. Since there may be several methods with the same signature as the extracted method in the system, to rigorously compute this metric we need to determine the type of receiver. However, inferring types is challenging and sometimes even impossible without a compilation process (which is extremely difficult to run over a high number of projects, as we do). One of the major reasons of the difficulties to infer types is that to do the inference accurately one also needs to analyze all the dependencies of the GitHub projects, and such dependencies are not always available or explicit. Since, our

---

[2] https://github.com/sed-inf-u-szeged/OpenStaticAnalyzer.

goal is to detect over-exposed extracted methods, which are methods that are public, but they are only used inside their class [24]. We compute the following metrics:

- *Internal Calls* – the number of method calls inside the refactored class that calls to a method with the same signature that the extracted method and the receiver the `this` keyword.
- *External Calls* – the number of method calls outside the refactored class that have the same signature as the refactored method. Here, we do not consider the receiver, if there is a potential call to the extracted method outside the refactored class then we consider that the extracted method is not overexposed.

4.4 Comparing Metrics

We compute the previously mentioned metrics in the refactored method and class before and after the refactoring. For this, we search each class and refactored method in the software version after the refactoring. This search was done by looking at the file corresponding to the refactored class, the class name and the method signature of the refactored method. However, in 347 cases, we could not identify the class or the refactored method in the new version after the refactoring. Since, some classes or methods were also renamed in the next version. For this reason, we focus on measuring the impact of Extract Method refactoring, and only keep the 2,712 remaining instances in which we were able to compare the metrics before and after the refactoring.

In particular, we contrast the metric values and then we detect if the metric: increases, decreases or remains the same after the refactoring. We then manually review the refactoring where the metrics reports a contradictory result. For instance, the Extract Method refactoring helps reduce the code complexity of the extracted method, therefore, if we detect the result is contrary to what one would expect, we manually contrast the change to understand these situations.

4.5 Statistical Analysis

We complete our results with a statistical analysis of the metrics that can be measured before and after the refactoring. A Shapiro-Wilk normality test confirms that the distribution of our metrics does not follow a normal distribution. In all cases the p-value is <0.01, so we can conclude that distributions are not normal. Therefore, for the remaining of this paper, we rely on non-parametric tests which do not make assumptions on the distribution of the data.

To observe the statistical significance of the effects of Extract Method on the metrics, we calculate a p-value using a Wilcoxon signed ranks test. It is a non-parametric statistical test suitable to compare paired data (before and after refactoring) and in summary the test aims to determine how different the two sets of paired data are from one another by focusing on the median. We perform the test with a 99% confidence level, therefore a p-value <0.01 means that the sets are significantly different.

We also compute Cliff's δ effect size to quantify the importance of the effect of the refactoring on the metrics. It is a non-parametric effect sizes measure, which represents the degree of overlap between two distributions. It ranges from -1 (if all the selected values in the first set are larger than the ones of the second set) to $+1$ (if all the selected values in the first set are smaller than the second set). It evaluates to zero when the two distributions are identical.

Cohen's d is more commonly used to calculate effect size and the effect are usually categorized as small, medium or large, however the accuracy relies of Cohen's d relies on normality. Fortunately, Cohen's d interpretation of results can be mapped to Cliff's δ : $0 \leqslant$ negligible < 0.147, $0.147 \leqslant$ small < 0.33, $0.33 \leqslant$ medium < 0.474 or $0.474 \leqslant$ large. This labeling is useful for comparisons, however it should be noted that this labeling was tuned for social science, and that for some fields of research most effects observed are likely to be small [23]. We also perform this test with a 99% confidence level.

5   Results

All the results of our statistical tests are presented in Table 2. For all the metrics, except Number of Parameters and Input/Output Variables, the Wilcoxon signed-rank test shows a statistically significant difference. The effect size confirms these results for the complexity metrics, however it is more marginal for LCOM. We describe the results in more detail in the rest of this section.

Table 2. Results of Wilcoxon signed-rank test and Cliff's δ on all metrics, a p-value <0.01 is statistically significant while an effect size>0.147 is a visible effect

	McClure	McCabe	Number of comparisons	Number of control vars	NBD	IO variables	Number of parameters	LCOM
p-value	<0.01	<0.01	<0.01	<0.01	<0.01	0.052	0.035	<0.01
Cliff's δ	0.300	0.262	0.290	0.269	0.274	−0.002	−0.002	−0.054

5.1   Complexity

Figure 1 details how many times the complexity metrics of the refactored methods increase, decrease, or remain the same. Raw values and percentages are reported in Table 3. Figure 1 shows that the complexity of most of the methods decrease or remain the same. The Extract Method refactoring mostly benefit metrics McCabe, McClure's complexity, number of comparisons, number of control variables, and nested block depth as we could observe in Table 2. In particular, 1,391 methods reduce their McCabe complexity (51%). However, 194 (7%) of them increase their complexity. We can also see that there is a considerable portion (42%) where the complexity of the refactored method remains the same. This means that the extracted code portion has no control-flow structures, and therefore the extracted methods have a low complexity. Number of Parameters and Input/Output Variable remain the same in most of the cases, therefore explaining the results of Table 2 where no significant difference is observed.

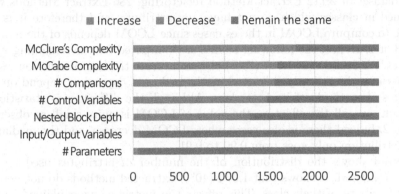

Fig. 1. Method complexity before and after a extract method refactoring

Table 3. Detailed results of complexity metrics

	McClure	McCabe	Number of comparisons	Number of control vars	NBD	I/O Variables	Number of parameters
Increase	220 (8%)	194 (7%)	179 (7%)	173 (6%)	125 (5%)	46 (2%)	36 (1%)
Decrease	1566 (58%)	1391 (51%)	1377 (51%)	1294 (48%)	1154 (43%)	27 (1%)	19 (1%)
Remain	926 (34%)	1127 (42%)	1156 (43%)	1245 (46%)	1433(53%)	2639 (97%)	2657 (98%)

We carefully performed a manual revision of the refactored methods that increase the complexity, and conclude that these methods increase their complexity because of additional changes besides the Extract Method refactoring. For instance, consider the method modification shown in Fig. 2 where the addStepPanel method was extracted from initTitleAndContent method. The extracted method is called twice after the extraction, one of these method calls was done inside an if control structure, which was added in the same commit as the extraction. For 61% of the methods that increase their complexity, these additional changes were related with the recently extracted method, for instance, conditionally calling to the extracted method. The remaining 39% of the methods represent additional changes which are not related to the Extract Method.

For comparison, we also used the "most metrics improved" proposed by Chavez et al. [6]. We found that 1249 of the 2712 (46%) Extract Method improve at least 4 complexity metrics, close to the 45% they observed.

> **Observation 1.** Our results confirm that most of the Extract Method refactorings help reduce the complexity of the refactored method and therefore of the class. Also, 42% of the extracted methods have a low complexity.

5.2   Cohesion

In our dataset of 2,712 Extract Method refactoring, 286 Extract Methods were performed in classes which do not have any attribute, and therefore it is not possible to compute LCOM in theses cases since LCOM depends of the number of attributes. Hence, the following results are computed for the remaining 2,426 instances. We found that 1,707 (70%) classes increase the lack of cohesion, essentially because the recently extracted methods do not depend or depend on few attributes of methods of its host class. Although the difference is statistically significant, overall the effect on the value of LCOM is quite small as observed in Table 2. Indeed there is also cases where LCOM decrease, and the median of both distribution only goes from 0.90 to 0.91.

Figure 3 shows the distribution of the number of attributes used by the extracted method. It shows that 1,074 (40%) extracted methods do not depend on any attribute of their class. This affects the metric as we explained earlier. Figure 4 gives the distribution of the number of internal method calls performed by the extracted method. Where zero means that the extracted method does

```
61  +       private void addStepPanel(Step step) {
62  +           StepPanel stepPanel = new StepPanel(session, step, previousStep);
63  +           content.getChildren().add(stepPanel);
64  +           stepPanels.add(stepPanel);
65  +           previousStep = Optional.of(stepPanel);
66  +       }
67  +
68          private void initTitleAndContent() {
    -           setText(scenario.getName());
    -           Optional<StepPanel> previousStep = Optional.empty();
69  +           setText(scenario.getName());
70  +           if (!scenario.isBackgroundDone()) {
71  +               for (Step step : scenario.getBackgroundSteps()) {
72  +                   addStepPanel(step);
73  +               }
74  +           }
75              for (Step step : scenario.getSteps()) {
    -               StepPanel stepPanel = new StepPanel(session, step, previousStep);
    -               content.getChildren().add(stepPanel);
    -               stepPanels.add(stepPanel);
    -               previousStep = Optional.of(stepPanel);
    -           }
76  +               addStepPanel(step);
77  +           }
78          }
```

Fig. 2. Extract method refactoring in the karate GitHub project

not have any single call to a method of its class. In total, 49% of the extracted methods do not depend on the other methods of the class. In addition, we have 506 (19%) methods that do not depend on any attributes and/or methods of the class. These methods normally are declared static, however, we found that 10% of these methods does not depend on the host class and may be easily converted to static or move to another class where they may be more cohesive.

> **Observation 2.** 70% of the extracted method slightly reduce the class cohesion, confirming the trend observed in previous studies. In addition, we found that 10% of these methods are not static and do not depend on any attribute/method of their class.

5.3   Re-Use and Code Clones

Code Clones. We analyze the number of code clones in the refactored class before and after each refactoring. Since, the code clone metric vary depending on a threshold, the minimum number of code lines in the clone, we compute the number of code clones using five thresholds (1 to 5). The idea is to assess whether this threshold may have an impact on the evolution of code clone. Figure 6 shows the proportion of increased, decreased and equal number of code clones remains.

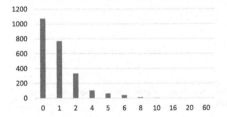
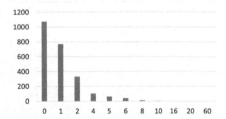

Fig. 3. Extracted method - Number of used attributes

Fig. 4. Extracted method - Number of internal method calls

As one would expect, the number of code clone decreases as the value of the threshold increases. However, the proportion of increase, decrease and remain is similar for all thresholds. For increase, the proportion varies between 23% and 24%, while it is between 55% and 58% for decrease and between 19% and 21% remain the same. For example, using the a threshold of four, we found that from the 2,712 refactorings 818 (30%) of the classes have code clones. In these classes, 473 (58%) of the Extract Method refactorings help reduce the code clones in the refactored class. However, 19% of the code clones remains in the class and there are 23% of the refactored classes that increase the number of code clones in the same commit.

The results of Wilcoxon signed-rank test and Cliff's δ for all the thresholds are presented in Table 4. There is statistical significance in all the cases, however

Table 4. Wilcoxon signed-rank test and Cliff's δ for the thresholds of code clone

Threshold	1	2	3	4	5
p-value	<0.01	<0.01	<0.01	<0.01	<0.01
Cliff's δ	0.132	0.131	0.125	0.114	0.087

the effect size is arguably small, although close to 0.137 for the firsts thresholds. It decreases with every thresholds since less code clones are found.

Figure 5 illustrate how Extract Method can affect code clones. Consider the method modification done where the method `action` was extracted from the method `actionPrimary`. The recently extracted method was called in two different places, in the source method at line 63 and 69. The method call in line 63 was done as a result of the Extract Method refactoring, where a set of line were replaced by this new method call. However, an additional method call was inserted in line 69, this additional change is not related to the Extract Method refactoring. Furthermore, a method call to `setPrimary` was added before both method calls and duplicate code.

Observation 3. Around 56% of the extracted methods reduce the code clones in the refactored class, and around 20% of the classes remain with code clones after the Extract Method.

```
60      @Override
61      public void actionPrimary(Vector3f point, int textureIndex, AbstractSceneExplorerNode ro
  -         if (radius == 0 || weight == 0)
  -             return;
  -         RaiseTerrainToolAction action = new RaiseTerrainToolAction(point, radius, weight, ge
  -         action.doActionPerformed(rootNode, dataObject);
62 +         setPrimary(true);
63 +         action(point, textureIndex, rootNode, dataObject);
64      }
65
66      @Override
67      public void actionSecondary(Vector3f point, int textureIndex, AbstractSceneExplorerNode
  -         // no secondary option
68 +         setPrimary(false);
69 +         action(point, textureIndex, rootNode, dataObject);
70      }
71
72 +    private void action(Vector3f point, int textureIndex, AbstractSceneExplorerNode rootNode
73 +        if (radius == 0 || weight == 0)
74 +            return;
75 +
76 +        if (!modifying)
77 +            modifying = true;
78 +
```

Fig. 5. Code clones before and after a extract method refactoring

Re-use. When a piece of code is extracted to a new method, this method may be re-used in the system. We count how many times the extracted method is called inside the refactored class. Figure 7 gives the distribution of the numbers of times that an extracted method is called inside their class. 51% of the extracted methods are called more than once, meaning that these extracted methods are reused at least once. However, 49% of the extracted methods are called only once and therefore were not reused.

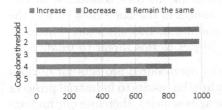

Fig. 6. Number of code clones

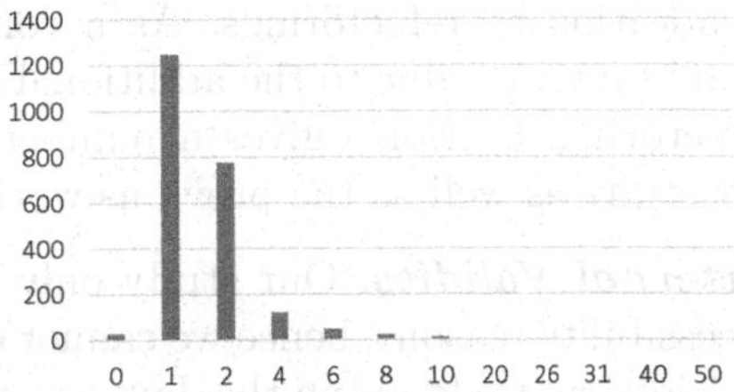

Fig. 7. Number of internal calls to the recently extracted method

---

Observation 5. 51% of the extracted methods are called more than once, thus favoring code reuse.

5.4 Visibility

One could expect a large majority of extracted methods to be private. However, We found that only 54% of the extracted methods are private, and 33% are public, the remaining are protected and package. We automatically review how many of the public extracted methods are reused from other classes besides the host class. We found that 22% of the public methods are only used inside their class, therefore we consider these methods as overexposed [24], since it is not necessary for them to be public.

Observation 6. 54% of the extracted methods are private, and 22% of the public extracted methods are overexposed and may reduce their visibility scope.

---

6 Threats to Validity

Construct Validity. We use refactoring miner to detect extract method refactoring instances along software versions. Although refactoring miner has a high precision and recall, it may still report false negatives and positives. In particular, for the Extract Method refactorings, Tsantalis *et al.* reported a precision of 98.63% [22]. We were able to manually analyze and confirm all the extracted methods we considered in our study. However, there is still a chance that we miss a number of extract method refactorings since studies on the Refactoring Miner report a recall of 84.72%. In addition, we measure the complexity metrics using *Jasome*, an open source project[3]. Therefore, the precision of our analysis is related to the precision of this tool. To verify the precision of this tool, we manually review a random sample of 200 extracted methods and all indicate that this tool computes the metrics accurately.

Internal Validity. A software version may contain different software changes in addition to refactorings. As a consequence, the metrics considered in this study may vary due to the additional code changes in the same class besides the refactoring. Section 5 gives a number of examples of this situation. Therefore, our study as well as the previous work are subject to this threat to validity.

External Validity. Our study only includes open-source projects for obvious accessibility reasons, hence we cannot generalize the results to industrial projects. In addition, we focus on the Java programming languages, therefore our findings are valid for Java.

Conclusion Validity. We believe that our sample considers a great variety of projects. However, our findings might be different for other dataset. We were careful not to violate the assumptions of the performed statistical tests. After observing that the distributions of our metrics were not normal, we only used nonparametric tests that do not require making assumptions about the distribution of the metrics. Concerning effect size, we relied as much as possible on the standard labeling of small, medium and large. However, our interpretations are not strictly limited to this labeling, as long as the Wilcoxon signed-rank test was significant. As mentioned earlier, this labeling was tuned for social science [23] and it is quite possible that it may not be fully adapted to our needs.

7   Conclusion

In this paper, we investigate the refactoring effects of Extract Method on quality. At the difference of previous studies that consider a great variety of refactoring, we focus on the Extract Method refactoring in order to provide a more tailored analysis and detailed results. We conducted an in-depth analysis by considering additional metrics which are related to this particular refactoring, such as, code clones, code re-usability and method visibility. Furthermore, we consider a large set of projects and analyze 2,713 Extract Method refactorings.

Our results are comparable to previous works in term of complexity and cohesion. We found that most of the Extract Method refactorings help reduce the complexity, however, they also tend to slightly reduce the class cohesion. This fact is mainly because the extracted method depends on a few (or none) attributes and methods of its class. In terms of reuse and code clones, we found that 56% of Extract Method refactoring helps reduce the number of code clones,

---

[3] https://github.com/rodhilton/jasome.

and 51% of the extracted methods are called more than once, favoring code reuse. Although, previous studies analyze the impact of refactorings on code smells, they do not consider code clones. Finally, we found that 22% of the extracted methods are overexposed, therefore, they may easily reduce its scope to private. Thus this study completes and nuances the results of previous research in this topic. As future work, we plan to replicate our experiment in other programming languages and focus on other refactorings, allowing us to adapt the metrics and interpret the results on a case-by-case basis.

Acknowledgments. Bergel thanks ANID Fondecyt 1200067 for partially sponsoring this work. Hecht is sponsored by ANID/FONDECYT Postdoctorado N°318056.

References

1. Al Dallal, J., Abdin, A.: Empirical evaluation of the impact of object-oriented code refactoring on quality attributes: a systematic literature review. IEEE Trans. Softw. Eng. **44**(1), 44–69 (2017)
2. AlOmar, E., Mkaouer, M.W., Ouni, A.: Can refactoring be self-affirmed? an exploratory study on how developers document their refactoring activities in commit messages. In: International Workshop on Refactoring, pp. 51–58. IEEE (2019)
3. AlOmar, E.A., Mkaouer, M.W., Ouni, A., Kessentini, M.: On the impact of refactoring on the relationship between quality attributes and design metrics. In: Proceedings of the ACM/IEEE International Symposium on Empirical Software Engineering and Measurement (ESEM), pp. 1–11. IEEE (2019)
4. Bavota, G., De Lucia, A., Di Penta, M., Oliveto, R., Palomba, F.: An experimental investigation on the innate relationship between quality and refactoring. J. Syst. Softw. **107**, 1–14 (2015)
5. Charalampidou, S., Ampatzoglou, A., Chatzigeorgiou, A., Gkortzis, A., Avgeriou, P.: Identifying extract method refactoring opportunities based on functional relevance. IEEE Trans. Software Eng. **43**(10), 954–974 (2016)
6. Chávez, A., Ferreira, I., Fernandes, E., Cedrim, D., Garcia, A.: How does refactoring affect internal quality attributes? a multi-project study. In: Proceedings of the 31st Brazilian Symposium on Software Engineering, pp. 74–83 (2017)
7. Choi, E., Yoshida, N., Inoue, K.: An investigation into the characteristics of merged code clones during software evolution. IEICE Trans. Inf. Syst. **97**(5), 1244–1253 (2014)
8. Elish, K.O., Alshayeb, M.: A classification of refactoring methods based on software quality attributes. Arab J. Sci. Eng. **36**, 1253–1267 (2011)
9. Fernandez-Sanz, L., Medina Merodio, J.A., Gómez Pérez, J., Misra, S.: Analysis of expectations of students and their initial concepts on software quality, pp. 284–288 (2016)
10. Henderson-Sellers, B.: Object-Oriented Metrics: Measures of Complexity. Prentice-Hall Inc, USA (1995)
11. Kádár, I., Hegedus, P., Ferenc, R., Gyimóthy, T.: A code refactoring dataset and its assessment regarding software maintainability. In: International Conference on Software Analysis, Evolution, and Reengineering (SANER), IEEE (2016)
12. Martins, P., Achar, R., V. Lopes, C.: 50k-c: A dataset of compilable, and compiled, java projects. In: 2018 IEEE/ACM 15th International Conference on Mining Software Repositories (MSR), pp. 1–5 (2018)

13. Misra, S., Akman, I., Palacios, R.: Framework for evaluation and validation of software complexity measures. IET Softw. **6**, 323–334 (2012)
14. Misra, S., Adewumi, A., Fernandez-Sanz, L., Damasevicius, R.: A suite of object oriented cognitive complexity metrics. IEEE Access **6**, 8782–8796 (2018)
15. Misra, S., Adewumi, A., Omoregbe, N., Crawford, B.: A systematic literature review of open source software quality assessment models. SpringerPlus 1936 (2016)
16. Murphy-Hill, E., Parnin, C., Black, A.P.: How we refactor, and how we know it. IEEE Trans. Softw. Eng. **38**(1), 5–18 (2011)
17. Pantiuchina, J., Lanza, M., Bavota, G.: Improving code: The (mis) perception of quality metrics. In: Proceedings of the IEEE International Conference on Software Maintenance and Evolution (ICSME), pp. 80–91. IEEE (2018)
18. Rodríguez, G., Esteberena, L., Mateos, C., Misra, S.: Reducing efforts in web services refactoring. In: International Conference on Computational Science and Its Applications, pp. 544–559 (2019)
19. Rodríguez, G., Mateos, C., Listorti, L., Hammer, B., Misra, S.: A novel unsupervised learning approach for assessing web services refactoring. Communications in Computer and Information Science ICCSA 2019, pp. 273–284 (10 2019)
20. Rodríguez, G., Mateos, C., Misra, S.: Exploring web service QoS estimation for web service composition. In: Lopata, A., Butkienė, R., Gudonienė, D., Sukackė, V. (eds.) ICIST 2020. CCIS, vol. 1283, pp. 171–184. Springer, Cham (2020). https://doi.org/10.1007/978-3-030-59506-7_15
21. Sandoval Alcocer, J.P., Siles Antezana, A., Santos, G., Bergel, A.: Improving the success rate of applying the extract method refactoring. Sci. Comput. Program. **195**, 102475 (2020)
22. Tsantalis, N., Mansouri, M., Eshkevari, L.M., Mazinanian, D., Dig, D.: Accurate and efficient refactoring detection in commit history. In: Proceedings of the 40th International Conference on Software Engineering, pp. 483–494. ICSE, ACM (2018)
23. Valentine, J.C., Cooper, H.: Effect size substantive interpretation guidelines: issues in the interpretation of effect sizes. What Works Clearinghouse 1–7 (2003)
24. Vidal, S.A., Bergel, A., Marcos, C., Díaz-Pace, J.A.: Understanding and addressing exhibitionism in java empirical research about method accessibility. Empirical Softw. Eng. **21**(2), 483–516 (2016)

Time Series for Forecasting Stock Market Prices Based on Sentiment Analysis of Social Media

Dakshinamoorthy Karthikeyan$^{(\boxtimes)}$ (iD), Babu Aravind Sivamani (iD),
Pavan Kalyan Tummala (iD), and Chamundeswari Arumugam (iD)

Sri Sivasubramaniya Nadar College of Engineering, Chennai, Tamil Nadu, India
dakshinamoorthy17030@cse.ssn.edu.in
https://ssn.edu.in

Abstract. This paper attempts to find a relation between the public perception of a company and its stock value price. Since social media is a very powerful tool used by a lot of people to voice their opinions on the performance of a company, it is a good source of information about its public sentiment. Previous studies have shown that the overall public sentiment collected from websites like twitter do have a relation to the market price of a company over a period of time. The goal is to build on their research to improve the accuracy of predictions and determine if the public perception surrounding a company is a driving factor of its stock growth.

Keywords: Stock market · Natural Language Processing · Sentiment analysis · Social media · Time series analysis · Stock growth prediction · LSTM · Random forest

1 Introduction

Previous studies [1] on the effect of social media on the stock market have shown that the aggregate public mood towards a company over a short time span has a relation to the closing price of that company at the end of the time span. Studies have been able to utilize data collected from any one reputed social media site (Ex: Twitter, Stocktwits, Weibo, etc.) to produce a model that predicts stock market prices with 70% accuracy [2]. This paper attempts to more accurately gauge the public sentiment of a company from social media websites such as Twitter by implementing time series analysis at minute intervals to find correlations that will likely produce a better stock estimate.

Stock price of a company is determined by a large number of independent traders all over the world. Previous studies have not taken into account the reasons why an individual trader makes the decision to buy or sell. As social media has been shown to offer an insight into the mindset of people, it was realized that the posts online may be an indication of how the market at large is

© Springer Nature Switzerland AG 2021
O. Gervasi et al. (Eds.): ICCSA 2021, LNCS 12955, pp. 353–367, 2021.
https://doi.org/10.1007/978-3-030-87007-2_25

inclined towards a company. The main objective of this paper is to find whether the public sentiment surrounding a company is able to determine the growth of its stock price. Here in this paper, the company Apple (NASDAQ: AAPL) was selected because it is prominent in the public spotlight and hence ideally suited for an analysis of this kind.

First the selected social media platform is queried for posts in the time period containing any of the keywords in our search term. The search term must be carefully selected to ensure that the number of off-topic posts is limited, while not missing out on any messages with important content. Then any irrelevant posts which passed through the search query are found and filtered out. Data pre-processing procedures such as the removal of non-english characters, stop words, hashtags and user mentions is carried out. Sentiment analysis is performed on the pre-processed text data and each post is classified as positive, negative or neutral corresponding to whether the market for Apple is bullish, bearish or not having any effect. Finally, the aggregate sentiment values from all collected websites will be fed into the model which would use a machine learning algorithm to produce a correlation between the media posts and the stock market price that can then be used to predict the closing market value, given the opening price and overall public sentiment.

The organization of this paper proceeds as follows. Section 2 discusses the literature survey, while Sect. 3 elaborates on the proposed methodology. Section 4 details the result and discussion, and Sect. 5 details the conclusion and future work.

2 Literature Survey

Venkata et al. [3] used Word2vec and N-gram representation of text to train a classifier model to predict the stock market movements and picked Word2vec representation due to its high accuracy in large datasets. Rakhi et al. [4] collected the sentiment data, and the stock price data to predict stock market price using a Support Vector Machine (SVM) classifier and observed that if the data size increases the accuracy obtained will also increase. Scott et al. [5] used smart user classification to filter the tweets by computing scoring weights based on number of likes, number of followers count and how often the user is correct. Further, they used Tf-Idf vectorizer for textual representation and linear regression classifier for the sentiment prediction. Zhaoxia et al. [6] used the sentiments of the news data to predict the stock market price using neural networks.

Sreelekshmy et al. [7] applied Recurrent Neural Networks(RNN), Long short-term memory (LSTM) and Convolutional Neural Networks (CNN) - sliding window architecture for stock price prediction of Infosys, TCS and Cipla and concluded that CNN outperforms the other two models in the stock market analysis due to the irregular changes that happen in the stock market. Few works have used the previous stock market data to predict the movements of the stock market while another few used the sentiments from social media to predict the same using SVM, random forest and other machine learning algorithms. Also it is clear that Word2Vec representation of text will be ideal for data that is fed into the neural network layers for building the classifier that predicts the trends of the stock market.

Behera R.K., et al. [16] describe a convolutional model for sentiment analysis of messages on social media that strives to be independent of the domain to which analysis of messages is applied. However, the limitation here is that words which are not available in the dictionary generated from training dataset are replaced with a generic identifier. This could have an adverse effect on sentiment prediction as there are many relevant words in the tweets that don't have counterparts in the dictionary, for example the names of Apple's devices, URLs of websites that post news about the company, etc.

Stock market predictions have become an interesting research area, correlation of social sentiment data about a company and its stock values there exists research papers that provide solid efficacy to perform a time series analysis on prediction of stock prices and ensemble models that increases the accuracy of the prediction by performing a sentiment analysis on the co-related socio-economic data of that particular company, though its limitation was performed on a 24-hour interval [18–20]. This research paper extends this notion by performing minute-wise stock price sentiment analysis that gives you a more through window for predicting stock rise and stock fall.

Bharathi et al. [13] used a combination of both sensex points and Really Simple Syndication(RSS) feeds for prediction. They extracted headlines from RSS feeds of major news websites and performed sentiment analysis on the text to establish a correlation between stock market values and the sentiments in the headlines. They produced an improvement of 14.43% as compared to standard algorithms like ID3. The proposed system aims to improve on their research by expanding on the methodology in two ways - 1) reduce the gap between consecutive predictions from 5-day averages to per-minute values and 2) improve the scope and quality of the text used for sentiment analysis by considering tweets from people all over the world instead of the news articles published by a few reporters working for media organizations.

3   Proposed Methodology

Twitter was considered to be the source for the dataset because many companies practice public relations via tweets and also as it provides a concrete API with filtering that would prove imperative to the selection criteria for a specified category of text data. Twitter's limitation of 280 characters per tweet also reduces the possibility of verbose text which would prove difficult to classify. The collected twitter dataset will be pre-processed for any missing inconsistencies, and cleaned using our custom data-cleaning libraries. After preprocessing, a subset of that dataset is manually labeled with a sentiment-value. A Random Forest Classifier is used to classify the rest of the sentiment based on the labeled dataset. For stock price prediction, the stock market data was downloaded from Finam and after it undergoes pre-processing, the processed prices dataset along with the labeled sentiment dataset is run through a LSTM model. A graphical overview of the system structure is shown in Fig. 1.

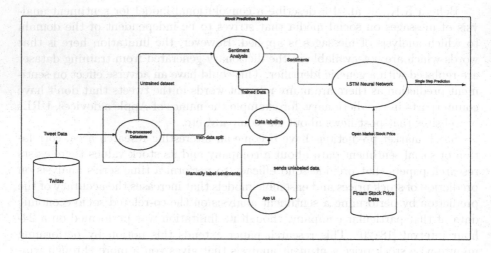

Fig. 1. Proposed system structure

3.1 Data Collection

Data collection is defined as "the process of acquiring raw, unprocessed data and storing in a mutable format". The data collection period was a little over three months, and approximately two million tweets were scraped for the last quarter of 2018. For collection of tweets from Twitter, a python module: 'Twitter-Scraper' was used. It supports querying of the Twitter database with advanced search parameters and operators (Available parameters include followers_count, friends_count, and also the logical operators AND, OR and NOT) [8] that limits its results to tweets that match our query, as well as additional metadata such as ensuring that the time of the tweet fits inside our selected time period. The exact search query given to the module is 'apple OR ((bullish OR bearish) AND (AAPL OR apple))'. This query has proven effective in filtering out the majority of completely unrelated tweets from the result set.

The result object returned by this module is a JSON array of tweet objects, where each tweet is a JSON Object with the following fields: username, user id, html, text, likes, retweets, comments, timestamp, profile-picture, profile display-name, etc. An Example of the raw tweet data is represented in Fig. 2.

The fields user_id, text, and timestamp are extracted from the tweets and other unwanted fields are deleted.

There are several services that provide access to historical intraday stock prices for NASDAQ listed companies like Apple [9]. Finam [10] is a Russian website that provides data for the stock, futures, ETF and Forex markets for

```
{
    "fullname": "BofM_Jeremy",
    "html": "<p class=\"TweetTextSize js-tweet-text tweet-text\" data-aria-label-part=\"0\"
lang=\"en\">Considering moving from non-smart watch to an <strong>Apple</strong> Watch - Series 3
with no cellular in order to save a few bucks. Am I forgoing anything critical by not getting
4+cellular?</p>",
    "is_retweet": 0,
    "likes": 1,
    "replies": 9,
    "retweet_id": "",
    "retweeter_userid": "",
    "retweeter_username": "",
    "retweets": 0,
    "text": "Considering moving from non-smart watch to an Apple Watch - Series 3 with no
cellular in order to save a few bucks. Am I forgoing anything critical by not getting
4+cellular?",
    "timestamp": "2018-11-18T23:59:35",
    "timestamp_epochs": 1542585575,
    "tweet_id": "1064307161742934017",
    "tweet_url": "/BofM_Jeremy/status/1064307161742934017",
    "user_id": "4645206635",
    "username": "BofM_Jeremy"
},
```

Fig. 2. Raw tweet data

Table 1. Raw finam stock datatset

DATE	TIME	OPEN	HIGH	LOW	CLOSE	VOL
20180926	100100	161.26	161.3	160.74	160.88	267350
20180926	100200	160.91	160.98	160.52	160.76	163520
20180926	100300	160.67	160.86	160.65	160.84	40670
20180926	100400	160.75	160.88	160.72	160.87	34280
20180926	100500	160.84	160.86	160.64	160.7	61070
20180926	100600	160.65	160.78	160.64	160.67	51490
20180926	100700	160.65	160.68	160.49	160.49	69370
20180926	100800	160.53	160.54	160.37	160.37	48950
20180926	100900	160.48	160.48	160.15	160.15	113360
20180926	101000	160.15	160.45	160.15	160.45	103510

research and analysis purposes. Finam provides data only for certain popular capitalized securities, however for these one can avail several months worth of tick data. A representation of the finam stock dataset is shown in Table 1.

3.2 Data Pre-processing

Data preprocessing is a technique which is used to transform the raw data in a useful and efficient format. In this section unnecessary data or noise is removed from the raw text twitter data. Firstly, the raw text data is converted to lower-case. Secondly, text data which contain words that begin with #(hashtags),

@(user mentions) are simply replaced with the actual word content of the hashtag and username. Thirdly, long URLs are replaced with just the domain name of the URL. For example, https://techcrunch.com/2019/10/19/the-new-iphone-is-ugly/ is replaced with techcrunch. The identification of these words is implemented through regex matching. Then the special symbols like non-english characters are removed.

The final step in pre-processing of text is stop-word removal, which is the removal of words in the text that do not contribute to the overall meaning of the post. Examples of such words include a, an, the, I, for, etc. The text of each post is tokenized and compared with any publicly available curated list of stop words [11]. The above preprocessing steps were repeated for the remaining two million raw text data. The data preprocessing outcome of an instance is displayed in Table 2.

Table 2. An instance of data pre-processing outcome.

Before data pre-processing	#Apple could have made all their productsćurrent design years ago, now their products are now left behind by @Samsung and others http://gizmo.do/Twg8I8i
After data pre-processing	Apple could made products current design years ago products left behind samsung others gizmodo

3.3   Sentiment Analysis Module

After collecting a large twitter dataset, sentiment analysis is performed on the text. For this purpose, the library Word2vec [12] is used, which is an advanced Natural Language Processing (NLP) technique for mapping words to a vector representation of any dimension. A 200-dimension vector is used for generation in this case. When run on the dataset of text, Word2vec will generate a unique vector for every word in the dataset which will exactly preserve the context of the words and the relation between similar meaning words in vector space. Then the Word2vec representations along with around 15000 messages manually labelled as positive (1), neutral (0) or negative (2). An android app was developed with google's firebase backend systems. The app was distributed to a group of trained people for labeling the tweets. The app contains three buttons for inputting the sentiments below the text data. An instance of the tweet in the app is shown in Fig. 3.

Fig. 3. An instance of app tweet data with sentiment labels.

The output of the app tweet data is then stored within a firebase datastore along with the labeled sentiment. This is highlighted in Fig. 4.

The final labelled dataset had a collection of 7500 neutral tweets, 4201 positive tweets and 3322 negative tweets.

The manually labeled tweets are first split into a training and validation set (by an 80-20% split) to train the random forest classifier. The XGBoost library [14] was used to automatically produce a good set of training parameters for the model. The algorithm was allowed to use 1200 estimators and to reach a maximum depth of 8. On the validation set, the random forest reached a precision score of 90%, Recall of 88% and F1 score 90%. Additionally, K-Fold cross validation was performed on the random forest classifier to ensure the validity of the results. The dataset was split into 10 partitions and each partition was used for validation one at a time, while the other 9 partitions were used to train the classifier. Across the 10 partitions, the classifier reached a mean accuracy of 85.46%.

The trained model is used to predict the sentiments for all the two million tweets in the datastore. To determine the stock price at a future point of time, the random forest classifier predicts social sentiments, and calculates the total sentiment for each one-minute interval as the number of positive minus negative sentiments. Some sample outputs from the random forest classifier are shown in Table 3.

Table 3. Five samples of random forest classifier output.

Text	Timestamp	Sentiment
Liveblog news apple making brooklyn event bit technology news tech	2018-10-27 14:55:00	1
spotify apple music	2018-11-16 19:56:08	0
Ready upgrade tv room ultimate home theater enter usa home entertainment sweepstakes chance win top line samsung 4k uhd tv apple tv 4k bose sound system swee ps	2018-11-08 21:22:05	0
Tech news trending apple launches portal users download data bloomberg uuid 11e8 url	2018-10-17 18:14:20	1
Depends type apple watch want come different sizes different bands cost	2018-12-25 20:40:32	1

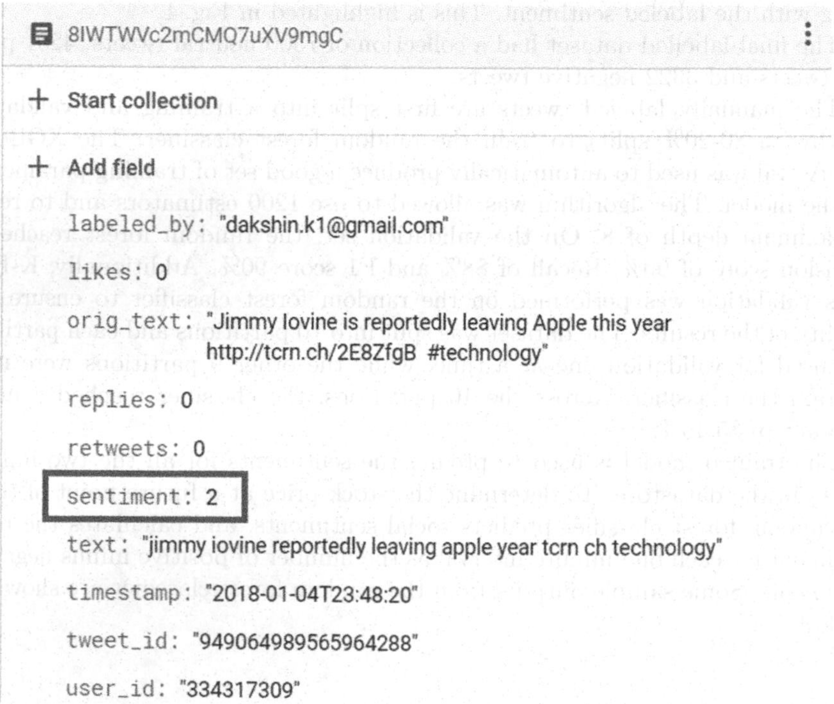

📄 8IWTWVc2mCMQ7uXV9mgC   ⋮

+ **Start collection**

+ **Add field**

  labeled_by: "dakshin.k1@gmail.com"

  likes: 0

  orig_text: "Jimmy Iovine is reportedly leaving Apple this year
              http://tcrn.ch/2E8ZfgB #technology"

  replies: 0

  retweets: 0

  sentiment: 2

  text: "jimmy iovine reportedly leaving apple year tcrn ch technology"

  timestamp: "2018-01-04T23:48:20"

  tweet_id: "949064989565964288"

  user_id: "334317309"

Fig. 4. An instance of labeled tweet data.

4   Results and Discussion

A time series forecasting method using LSTM is used here as both the social media posts as well as the financial stock price dataset has a time component. LSTM was trained using Google's open source TensorFlow libraries which comes with an implementation of LSTM. The model contained one LSTM layer with 32 units, densely connected to a second layer with one neuron that used the sigmoid activation function. The RMSProp algorithm [15] was used to speed up the training process.

As the dataset contains two distinct features namely the sentiment and the stock price, a multivariate version of the dataset was created for training. In this process, overlapping sliding windows of length 720 min (12 h) are applied on the dataset. Within the window the value is sampled every 10 min in order to smooth out the smaller variations every minute while still retaining the rises and falls of higher magnitude. Hence each window contains 72 points of data. To get a single step dataset, the starting point of the window is set to the point immediately after the start of the previous window, i.e. a new window begins every 10 min. Some samples of the data in each window are shown in Figs. 6, 7 and 8.

Finally the dataset contains 35634 entries of data, which is divided into a testing and validation set (80-20 % ratio). The LSTM was trained on the dataset for a total of 50 epochs. The training and validation loss for a dataset consisting of windows of history size 720 min, and step size 10 min is visualised in Fig. 5.

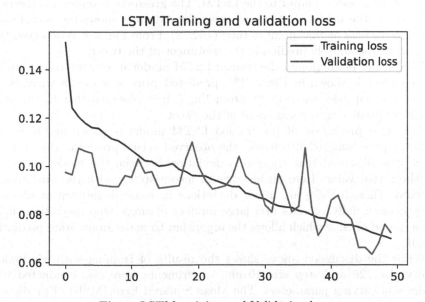

Fig. 5. LSTM training and Validation loss

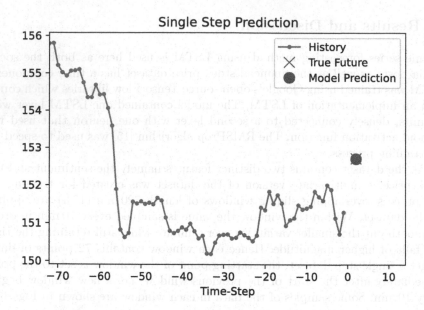

Fig. 6. First sample prediction of LSTM (Color figure online)

The first prediction of the trained LSTM model at a future time from the validation set is shown in Fig. 6. The blue line shows a subset of the stock price history passed as input to the LSTM. The green circle represents the price predicted by the model (152.71), whereas the red cross shows the actual value that came to pass at that point of time (152.72). From Fig. 6, it is observed that the model is accurately predicting the sentiment of the tweet.

The second prediction of the trained LSTM model at a future time from the validation set is shown in Fig. 7. The predicted price was 148.28 whereas the observed actual price was 148.49. From Fig. 7, it is observed that the model is accurately predicting the sentiment of the tweet.

The third prediction of the trained LSTM model is shown in Fig. 8. The predicted price was 152.42 whereas the observed actual price was 151.64. From Fig. 8, it is observed that there is a deviation between the model prediction and the actual value. Here an instance of inconsistency with the prediction is observed. Though there are minor deviations in some single step predictions, this process usually consists of a large number of single step predictions made over a period of time which allows the algorithm to make an accurate prediction overall.

While the discussion above shows the results of training with windows of history size 720 and step size 10 min, experiments were also conducted with windows of varying parameters. The Mean Squared Error(MSE) of predictions on the validation set using these parameters was calculated.

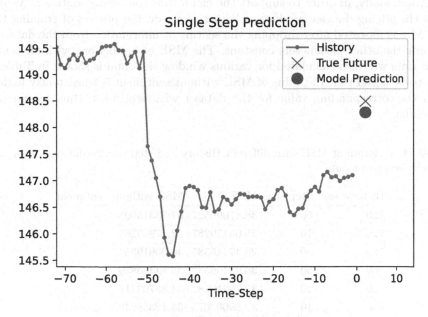

Fig. 7. Second sample prediction of LSTM (Color figure online)

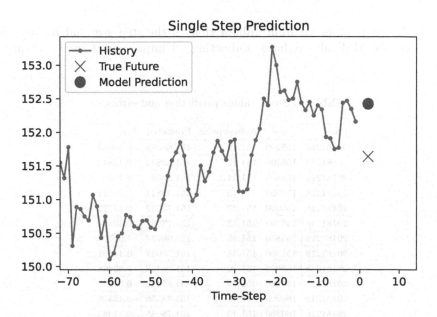

Fig. 8. Third sample prediction of LSTM (Color figure online)

Additionally, in order to support the claim that combining sentiment values with the pricing dataset produces a better accuracy, the process of training the LSTM was repeated after dropping the sentiment information from the dataset, keeping the other parameters constant. The MSE of predictions without sentiment data was also calculated for various window sizes and is shown in Table 4. It is to be noted that the value of MSE without sentiment is consistently higher than the corresponding value for the dataset with sentiment, thus supporting the claim.

Table 4. Variation of MSE with different History and step size for datasets with and without sentiment data.

History size	Step size	MSE	MSE without sentiment
720	50	38.47090527	67.73315905
720	10	35.05139267	52.17865264
720	80	28.47415585	36.00919354
360	50	36.9319954	35.84480859
60	20	35.79312783	34.83763717
30	10	32.89082675	33.12358949
15	5	5.930060326	34.24569216
15	10	5.187107316	14.64130006

Further, it is observed from Table 4 that as the step size and history size decreases, the MSE also reduces, indicating an improvement in the accuracy rate.

Table 5. Stock values prediction and errors.

Date	Time	Actual price	Predicted	Error
20181218	155200	151.42	151.68074	−0.26074
20181218	155300	151.27	151.69843	−0.42843
20181218	155400	151.44	151.9058	−0.4658
20181218	155500	151.49	151.82811	−0.33811
20181218	155600	151.27	151.72792	−0.45792
20181218	155700	151.33	151.73984	−0.40894
20181218	155800	151.35	151.96754	−0.61754
20181218	155900	151.34	151.75021	−0.41021
20181218	160000	151.36	151.98468	−0.62468
20181218	160100	151.35	151.85138	−0.50138
20181218	160200	151.35	151.78558	−0.43558
20181218	160300	151.46	151.78085	−0.32085
20181218	160400	151.55	151.88606	−0.33606
20181218	160500	151.61	151.85497	−0.24497

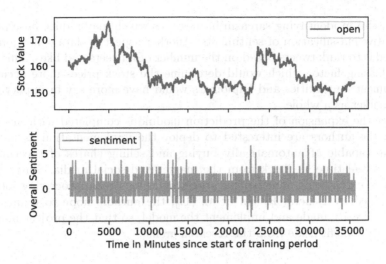

Fig. 9. Visualization of processed training dataset (Color figure online)

Table 5 displays the ground truth and the predicted price for a portion of the validation set. It is observed that the LSTM is able to learn and accurately predict with errors less than 1 in the vast majority of cases at each minute interval. The system is well trained over various curves, rises, falls over the last quarter of 2018.

Though there are a multitude of factors which could determine the exact values of stock prices, based on the outcome of the system. The public image of the company seems to be one of the driving forces. The LSTM Neural Network was accurate enough to forecast the stock values, which indicates the existence of a correlation between the sentiments and stock prices. This suggests that the public image of a company has a bearing on the market performance of a company. The visualisation found between the stock prices and sentiments are shown in the Fig. 9. The y-axis for the blue line shows the market price and the total sentiment is shown in the orange graph. The x-axis represents the time component, i.e. the number of minutes since the start of Q4 2018.

5   Conclusion and Future Work

In this paper, the rise and fall of stock prices were predicted at every minute interval. Intraday (1 min intervals) stock market data on Apple Inc. (NASDAQ: AAPL) was collected for Q4, 2018. Twitter was scraped to find all tweets related to Apple over the same time period. Total sentiment in each one-minute interval was calculated and combined with market price histories to forecast the future prices. Confirming the hypothesis there exists a correlation between a company's stock price and its public perception.

Posts on social media usually include one or more emoticons. These are more capable of conveying what people are feeling than plain text data. They are especially useful in identifying sarcasm in messages which may reduce false positive or negative classification of sentiments. Another aspect of data collection to be explored is to rank tweets based on the number of retweets and likes. This would add a biasing factor which would determine the stock prices more accurately. Government Authorities and Diplomats would have more say in impacting the stock market as a whole.

Once the expansion of the prediction module is completed with favourable results, the authors are interested to deploy the implementation as part of a program capable of automatically buying and selling shares of the company, based on real time feedback from the market and social media. Since there is already research being done on this aspect by using stream processing softwares as described by Behera, R. K., et al. [17], the authors hope to build on the progress already made and implement the model, so that the project may have a practical benefit aside from the research arena.

References

1. Mankar, T., Hotchandani, T., Madhwani, M., Chidrawar, A., Lifna, C.S.: Stock market prediction based on social sentiments using machine learning, pp. 1–3 (2018) https://doi.org/10.1109/ICSCET.2018.8537242
2. Acosta, J., Lamaute, N., Luo, M., Finkelstein, E., Andreea, C.: Sentiment analysis of twitter messages using Word2Vec. In: Proceedings of Student-Faculty Research Day, CSIS, Pace University (May 5th 2017)
3. Venkata, S.P., Kamal, N.C., Ganapati, P., Babita, M.: Sentiment analysis of twitter data for predicting stock market movements. In: International conference on Signal Processing, Communication, Power and Embedded System, pp. 1345–1350 (2016)
4. Rakhi, B., Sher, M.D.: Integrating StockTwits with sentiment analysis for better prediction of stock price movement. In: IEEE International Conference on Computing, Mathematics and Engineering Technologies – iCoMET (2018)
5. Coyne, S., Madiraju, P., Coelho, J.: Forecasting stock prices using social media analysis. In: IEEE 15th International Conference on Dependable, Autonomic and Secure Computing, 15th International Conference on Pervasive Intelligence and Computing, 3rd International Conference on Big Data Intelligence and Computing and Cyber Science and Technology Congress, pp. 1031–1038 (2017)
6. Wang, Z., Ho, S.B., Lin, Z.: Stock market prediction by incorporating social media news as sentiment https://ieeexplore.ieee.org/document/8637365
7. Selvin, S., Vinayakumar, R., Gopalakrishnan, E.A., Menon, V.K., Soman, K.P.: Stock price prediction using LSTM. RNN and CNN-sliding window model, pp. 1643–1647 (2017). https://doi.org/10.1109/ICACCI.2017.8126078
8. Standard search operators available in the Twitter search query field: https://developer.twitter.com/en/docs/tweets/rules-and-filtering/overview/standard-operators
9. Publicly Available sources o Intra-day stock market data for listed companies https://www.quantshare.com/sa-636-6-new-ways-to-download-free-intraday-data-for-the-us-stock-market
10. Finam.ru - A website that provides several months of tick data for highly capitalized securities https://www.finam.ru/profile/moex-akcii/gazprom/export/

11. Curated list of English stop-words extracted from Python's NLTK library: https://gist.github.com/sebleier/554280
12. Mikolov, T., Chen, K., Corrado, G., Dean, J.: Efficient Estimation of Word Representations in Vector Space, pp. 1–12 (2013)
13. Bharathi, S., Geetha, A.: Sentiment analysis for effective stock market prediction. Int. J. Intell. Eng. Syst. **10**, 146–154 (2017) https://doi.org/10.22266/ijies2017.0630.16
14. Chen, T., Guestrin, C.: XGBoost: a scalable tree boosting system. In: Proceedings of the 22nd ACM SIGKDD International Conference on Knowledge Discovery and Data Mining, pp. 785–794. New York, ACM (2016) https://doi.org/10.1145/2939672.2939785
15. Tieleman, T., Hinton, G.: Lecture 6.5-rmsprop: divide the gradient by a running average of its recent magnitude. COURSERA: Neural Netw. Mach. Learn. **4**(2), 26–31 (2012)
16. Behera R.K., et al.: Co-LSTM: convolutional LSTM model for sentiment analysis in social big data. Inf. Proc. Manage. **58**(1), 102435 (2021)
17. Behera, R.K., et al.: Comparative study of real time machine learning models for stock prediction through streaming data. J. Univ. Comput. Sci. **26**(9), 1128–1147 (2020)
18. Valle-Cruz, D., Fernandez-Cortez, V., López-Chau, A., Sandoval-Almazán, R.: Does Twitter affect stock market decisions? financial sentiment analysis during pandemics: a comparative study of the H1N1 and the COVID-19 periods. Cogn. Comput. 1–16 (2021). https://doi.org/10.1007/s12559-021-09819-8
19. Nti, I.K., Adekoya, A.F., Weyori, B.A.: Predicting stock market price movement using sentiment analysis: evidence from ghana. Appl. Comput. Syst. **25**(1), 33–42 (2020). https://doi.org/10.2478/acss-2020-0004
20. Carosia, A.E.O., Coelho, G.P., Silva, A.E.A.: Analyzing the Brazilian financial market through Portuguese sentiment analysis in social media. Appl. Artif. Intell. **34**(1), 1–19 (2020)

Assessing Ensemble Learning Techniques in Bug Prediction

Zsolt János Szamosvölgyi[1], Endre Tamás Váradi[1], Zoltán Tóth[1(✉)],
Judit Jász[1,2], and Rudolf Ferenc[1]

[1] University of Szeged, Szeged, Hungary
{szamos,idarav,zizo,jasy,ferenc}@inf.u-szeged.hu
[2] FrontEndART Ltd., Szeged, Hungary

Abstract. The application of ensemble learning techniques is continuously increasing, since they have proven to be superior over traditional machine learning techniques in various domains. These algorithms
could be employed for bug prediction purposes as well. Existing studies
investigated the performance of ensemble learning techniques only for
PROMISE and the NASA MDP public datasets; however, it is important to evaluate the ensemble learning techniques on additional public
datasets in order to test the generalizability of the techniques. We investigated the performance of the two most widely-used ensemble learning
techniques AdaBoost and Bagging on the Unified Bug Dataset, which
encapsulates 3 class level public bug datasets in a uniformed format with
a common set of software product metrics used as predictors. Additionally, we investigated the effect of using 3 different resampling techniques
on the dataset. Finally, we studied the performance of using Decision
Tree and Naïve Bayes as the weak learners in the ensemble learning. We
also fine tuned the parameters of the weak learners to have the best possible end results.

We experienced that AdaBoost with Decision Tree weak learner outperformed other configurations. We could achieve 54.61% F-measure
value (81.96% Accuracy, 50.92% Precision, 58.90% Recall) with the configuration of 300 estimators and 0.05 learning rate. Based on the needs,
one can apply RUS resampling to get a recall value up to 75.14% (of
course losing precision at the same time).

Keywords: AdaBoost · Bug prediction · Resampling · Unified bug
dataset

1 Introduction

As bugs having a high cost, especially in later stages of the development of a
software, it is crucial to reveal and eliminate as many of them as we can early in
order to keep the maintenance costs low [4]. Evidently, this fact implies defect
prediction being one of the most active research area [16,25].

O. Gervasi et al. (Eds.): ICCSA 2021, LNCS 12955, pp. 368–381, 2021.
https://doi.org/10.1007/978-3-030-87007-2_26

Recently, ensemble learning techniques have gained attention as they have performed better than traditional machine learning approaches in various domains covering a broad-spectrum [20]. Not surprisingly, ensemble learning techniques have been applied for defect prediction as well [12]. AdaBoost [23] is one of the most widely adopted ensemble learning method for bug prediction [12,21,27], where different base learning algorithms were investigated, such as Naïve Bayes, Logistic Regression, Multi-Layer Perceptron, Support Vector Machine, Decision Tree and more [18,28].

Machine learning algorithms take the input as a series of feature vectors, which means that one has to produce these numerical values for each entry (usually files, classes or methods). Hence, researchers tend to reuse existing datasets in order to reduce the amount of work to be done and increase the reproducibility of their approaches. One common form of input data is where entries are described with software product metrics such as in the PROMISE [22] or the NASA MDP bug datasets [19]. These datasets were used by numerous studies [12,27,28]. In our approach, we used a different dataset, namely the Unified Bug Dataset [10], to investigate whether the achieved results hold in general. The Unified Bug Dataset contains bug related information for class level entries, amongst others. The dataset brings different software product metric-based datasets together, such as the PROMISE dataset [22], Bug Prediction dataset [7], and the GitHub Bug Dataset [26].

In this study, we investigate whether AdaBoost is superior over Bagging, both applying decision tree and Naïve Bayes algorithms as their weak learners. Related papers investigated parameter tuning only in a limited fashion or not experimented with at all. We ran a fine-grained search for finding the best parameter setup which includes tuning *n estimators*, *learning rate*, *max depth*, *min samples leaf*, and the *criterion* (gini or entropy). Note that the latter 3 are parameters for decision trees only.

Since bug datasets usually suffer from imbalance in their data, we also investigated the effect of using various resampling methods. We employed *SMOTE* [5], *RUS* [13], and a custom one used in the Deep Water Framework [11].

Based on the above mentioned aspects and deficiencies, we composed the following research question to be answered in this paper:

RQ 1: Does AdaBoost performs better than other classifier methods for bug prediction?

RQ 2: Is there any resample technique which performs consistently better than others?

RQ 3: Which is the best weak learning algorithm and which parameter configuration is the most powerful?

The rest of the paper is organized as follows. In Sect. 2, we enumerate the related papers, then we show the tools and techniques in details of which our approach consists in Sect. 3. Next, we evaluate our approach and answer our research questions in Sect. 4. The threats to validity are listed in Sect. 5. Finally, Sect. 6 concludes the paper and gives future work directions.

2   Related Work

In this section, we present the most related works to our study.

As Catal et al. showed [3], the most widely used machine learning algorithms for bug prediction are Logistic Regression, Naïve Bayes, Decision Tree, and Random Forest. Recently, ensemble learning techniques have started to be adopted in the context of bug prediction. Nevendra and Singh showed that AdaBoost with Extra Tree base learner could improve the performance of bug prediction [17], but this technique focuses on the bug count (regression) instead of binary classification.

AdaBoost was also used to predict defects in an imbalanced dataset [12,21, 27]. Gao and Yang tried to use Back Propagation Neural Network to fight the imbalance in the data. We rather applied Decision Tree and Naïve Bayes base learners and investigated whether a resampling technique can help achieving better performance in the end. The work of Wang and Yao [27] is more close to ours as they investigated the usability of various resampling techniques. Beside AdaBoost, Bagging is also used as an ensemble learning technique [14], but these were not studied together in these papers. This missing comparison was provided by Peng et al. [18] by using Analytic Hierarchy Process (AHP) to rank the quality of ensemble methods. They found that AdaBoost is the best method, with the base learners of KNN, C4.5 decision tree and Naïve Bayes. Later, Khan concluded similar results [15] when used a hybrid ensemble approach to predict bugs. However, in their studies, they did not report any method to be applied in order to decrease imbalance in their data. We evaluated both AdaBoost and Bagging as an ensemble learner, with an additional resampling technique.

In a recent study, Yucalar et al. provided an exhaustive comparison of machine learning methods that are included in the popular WEKA machine learning framework [28]. They used numerous algorithms to form a baseline to which they compared the ensemble learning techniques. They found Rotation Forest (ROF), Random Forest, Logic Boost, Adaboost and Voting as the best fault predictors in terms of F-Measure and Area Under Curve (AUC). However, they did not consider the parameters of the base learners, only the number of learners used by the ensemble learners. In this study, we have tried to fine tune the parameters of the algorithms as well.

Ensemble learning techniques were also trialed in a narrowed domain of bug prediction, namely, in Aging Related Bugs prediction [24]. The study focuses on bagging, boosting, and stacking ensemble techniques which were justified to be effective in this narrowed domain as well. We stick with the general approach and evaluate ensemble learning methods on a wider range of datasets.

Most of the studies related to bug prediction; especially the ones using ensemble learning, are evaluated their approach on the PROMISE [22] and the NASA MDP dataset. However, it was shown that one should use these datasets with precautions [19]. Using only one dataset, which was constructed with one selected method, also makes the bug prediction techniques built on top of it more sensible. This generalizability threat should be eliminated by involving additional public bug datasets. The Unified Bug Dataset was previously used successfully in bug prediction [8,10], which gives an extra opportunity to test the ensemble learning techniques on.

3   Approach

3.1   Dataset

In order to test the AdaBoost and Bagging classifiers in fault prediction, a large and representative dataset is necessary. Our choice to measure the viability of ensemble learning classifiers is the class-level part of the Unified Bug Dataset [10], which contains 60 different metrics for every 47,618 classes. The Unified Bug Dataset is an integration of 3 well-known and widely-used datasets (namely, PROMISE [22], the Bug Prediction Dataset [7] and the GitHub Bug Dataset [26]). An entry in the dataset contains 60 different numeric metrics similar to the experiments of [8] (from the simplest LOC metrics to the more complex complexity metrics) and the number of bugs that were determined for the actual class. The features which is used by the classification process is calculated by the OpenStaticAnalyzer toolset [1]. The number of bug occurrences are transferred from the original datasets, which basically means that the bug proneness of the entries come from three different approaches.

There are projects that occur multiple times in different versions in the unified dataset. Using these kinds of datasets arises the question of whether it is a problem in our approach of using machine learning techniques for fault prediction? We did not treat this as a problem, because the whole approach relies on the calculated metrics and our goal is to prove that using this kind of information is enough to successfully detect possible faults in source codes.

3.2   Preprocessing

The preprocessing of training data starts with the deletion of unnecessary class- and file-related information for every entry such as filename, parent, path, etc. Furthermore, we binarized the target labels i.e., converting the number of bugs found in a class to 0 or 1. In other words, we separated the classes into "buggy" and "not buggy" sets in order to perform binary classification on it. On the other hand, we applied one-hot encoding on the "Type" feature (class, interface or enum) in pursuit of getting better results and drop one of the newly created features to avoid the Dummy Variable trap. The Dummy Variable trap is a scenario in which the independent variables are multicollinear, or in simple terms one variable can be predicted from the others. If we want to use categorical data such as "Interface", "Class", etc., encoding to numerical data is necessary. If there is no natural ordering over our variables one-hot encoding can be applied to encode our features. One-hot encoding create a new variable for all categorical value, which is highly correlated with each other.

Other preprocessing possibilities for the features are the normalization – where metrics are linearly transformed into the [0,1] interval and standardization

– where features are transformed in order to get zero mean and one standard deviation. Standardized data is essential for accurate data analysis, it is easier to draw clearer conclusions about the current data when one has other data to measure it against.

3.3   Resample Techniques

In our dataset the distribution of examples across the classes is biased. From the 47,618 samples there are 38,838 labelled as "not buggy" which makes up 82% of the overall data. Performing binary classification on an unbalanced dataset is a challenging task. In order to solve this problem, we used different resample techniques, such as SMOTE [5], RUS [13] and random upsampling method which was also used in the Deep Water Framework (DWF) [11]. In the following, let us dedicate a few sentences to these algorithms.

SMOTE (Synthetic Minority Oversampling Technique) selects a random sample from the minority class, then selects its k nearest neighbors from the feature space. It chooses a random point from the k neighbors then connects to the originally selected sample with a line, and creates new samples along the line in feature space. So the new samples will be convex combinations of the original samples of the minority class.

RUS (Random Under-Sampling) uses all the samples from the minority class and random points from the majority class in order to achieve a balanced dataset.

The random upsampling strategy works by duplicating randomly selected samples from the minority class until the size of the two classes reach the size of the majority class multiplied by the given factor. In our study we applied a 50% upsampling rate, as it was shown to be the best upsampling parameter on the same dataset [11].

3.4   Learners

During our experiments we applied several learning techniques, including different ensemble learners combined with various base learner techniques. Several experiments show that the use of ensemble models can improve the performance of base learning techniques [18,24]. Ensemble models combine the results of multiple base learner instances in order to provide a prediction for the class of the given sample. Different learner methods can be used as base learning methods as long as they provide a slightly better prediction than a random choice would. As base learners, we tried the Gaussian Naïve Bayes, along with the Decision Tree classifier, which considered to be a good choice for ensemble learning approaches [28]. We applied both Bagging and AdaBoost as ensemble learners for these base learners. The latter has shown to be one of the best choices as an ensemble learner [18].

During our experiments, we used the implementation of the learning techniques provided in the scikit learn python package[1].

---

[1] https://scikit-learn.org/.

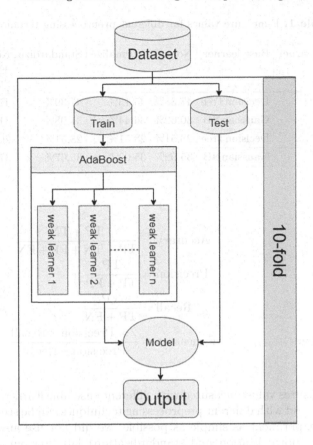

Fig. 1. Workflow of the approach

4   Evaluation

In our study, we used *10-Fold* strategy to evaluate our models. It means that we had 10 different splits of our data, which all contained separate sets for both the train and test data. Then, the given model has been evaluated on the 10 train-test datasets and the given results has been averaged. This workflow can be seen in Fig. 1.

During the evaluation to measure our models' performance, we mainly focused on F-measure, although we calculated Accuracy, Precision, and Recall as well. All of these metrics are calculated from the True Positive, False Positive, True Negative, and False Negative values of the confusion matrix with the following formulas.

True Positive: The number of correctly labeled "bugged" samples.
False Positive: The number of incorrectly labeled "not bugged" samples.
True Negative: The number of correctly labeled "not bugged" samples.
False Negative: The number of incorrectly labeled "bugged" samples.

Table 1. F-measure values for different preprocessing techniques

Ensemble learner	Base learner	None	Normalize	Standardize	Normalize + Standardize
AdaBoost	DecisionTree	47.38%	45.13%	47.39%	47.39%
AdaBoost	GaussianNB	30.62%	36.44%	31.08%	31.08%
Bagging	DecisionTree	28.51%	28.51%	28.51%	26.05%
Bagging	GaussianNB	35.02%	35.02%	35.67%	37.17%

Accuracy:

$$\text{Accuracy} = \frac{TP + TN}{TP + TN + FP + FN}$$

Precision:

$$\text{Precision} = \frac{TP}{TP + FP}$$

Recall:

$$\text{Recall} = \frac{TP}{TP + FN}$$

F-measure:

$$\text{F-measure} = \frac{2 \times \text{Precision} \times \text{Recall}}{\text{Precision} + \text{Recall}}$$

The F-measures values measured with different ensemble learner, base learner combinations, and with different preprocessing techniques can be seen on Table 1. To keep the experiment as simple as possible, we did not use any preprocessing technique (normalization and standardization) later on our dataset (the achieved results were similar when no normalization and/or standardization was involved).

4.1   RQ1: Does AdaBoost Performs Better Than Other Classifier Methods for Bug Prediction?

As previous studies also showed that AdaBoost can be a superior choice of ensemble learning techniques, we mainly focus on this algorithm. In order to measure the performance of AdaBoost, we compared AdaBoost with another widely-used classifier, namely the Bagging classifier. We selected Bagging instead of other classifiers, because Bagging is an ensemble learner as well, which gives us a good comparison base against the AdaBoost classifier. As mentioned in Sect. 3.4, we tried two different weak learners i.e. the Decision Tree and Naïve Bayes classifiers. Our measurements are shown in Table 2.

The table shows the ensemble learners in the first column before specifying the base learner in the second column. We have grouped the entries based on these two and separated the groups with a horizontal line. In each group, we highlighted the best configuration with bold typeface. Best algorithms were marked based on the F-Measure scores.

As the table shows, the configuration for the best result was AdaBoost with Decision Tree after some hyperparameter tuning. We could achieve an F-Measure of 54.61% with a high accuracy (81.96%) with the configuration of 300 estimators and a learning rate of 0.05. High accuracy in itself is not enough since the dataset is biased, however the precision is above 50% which means that half of entries marked as buggy were in fact buggy. Finally, we could identify 58.9% of the total buggy entries as the recall value suggests.

Answering RQ1: As we can see the AdaBoost performs better with the Decision Tree base learner than the Bagging. On the other hand, Bagging seems to provide slightly better results when used with Naïve Bayes and not with Decision Tree. Our measurements prove that with the best hyperparameters AdaBoost classifier with Decision Tree can outperform other classifiers on the Unified Bug Dataset [11].

4.2   RQ2: Is There Any Resample Technique Which Performs Consistently Better Than Others?

Since our dataset was imbalanced as mentioned in Sect. 3.3, some kind of resampling is necessary. SMOTE, RUS, and random upsampling techniques, which were briefly explained, can enhance the reliability and efficiency of the learning algorithms. Table 3 shows the F-Measure results of the ensemble learning algorithms with respect of the resampling methods. As it can be depicted, random

Table 2. Evaluation of ensemble learners

Ensemble learner	Base learner	Number of estimators	Learning rate	F-measure	Accuracy	Precision	Recall
AdaBoost	DecisionTree	100	0.05	54.13%	81.06%	48.91%	60.64%
AdaBoost	DecisionTree	200	0.05	54.61%	81.56%	50.00%	60.17%
AdaBoost	**DecisionTree**	**300**	**0.05**	**54.61%**	**81.96%**	**50.92%**	**58.90%**
AdaBoost	DecisionTree	400	0.05	54.12%	81.89%	50.75%	57.98%
AdaBoost	DecisionTree	500	0.04	53.93%	81.83%	50.62%	57.72%
AdaBoost	**GaussianNB**	**100**	**0.04**	**37.23%**	**77.41%**	**38.38%**	**36.52%**
AdaBoost	GaussianNB	200	0.04	36.10%	75.78%	35.32%	37.23%
AdaBoost	GaussianNB	300	0.04	35.34%	74.36%	33.18%	38.09%
AdaBoost	GaussianNB	400	0.04	34.94%	73.45%	32.04%	38.76%
AdaBoost	GaussianNB	500	0.04	34.58%	72.78%	31.21%	39.09%
Bagging	**DecisionTree**	**100**		**50.54%**	**79.21%**	**45.00%**	**57.67%**
Bagging	DecisionTree	200		50.48%	79.20%	44.98%	57.53%
Bagging	DecisionTree	300		50.48%	79.21%	45.00%	57.49%
Bagging	DecisionTree	400		50.48%	79.22%	45.01%	57.49%
Bagging	DecisionTree	500		50.51%	79.22%	45.02%	57.55%
Bagging	GaussianNB	100		35.14%	80.50%	45.39%	28.69%
Bagging	**GaussianNB**	**200**		**35.16%**	**80.49%**	**45.38%**	**28.71%**
Bagging	GaussianNB	300		35.09%	80.48%	45.33%	28.64%
Bagging	GaussianNB	400		35.12%	80.49%	45.34%	28.68%
Bagging	GaussianNB	500		35.10%	80.48%	45.32%	28.67%

upsampling (*RandUp.*) achieved the best results regarding the F-measure values in all cases (marked as bold in the table).

Besides the results of F-Measure, Table 4, 5 and 6 show the Accuracy, Precision, and Recall results, respectively. In case of Accuracy and Precision, none of the resampling techniques could improve upon the original results. However, in case of recall, RUS could improve a vast amount when used with Decision Tree as a base learner.

During our experiments, we primarily focus on the F-Measure metric, so we used random upsampling as our resampler in our workflow later on. These values are acquired with fixed hyperparameters because of consistency. The hyperparameters for AdaBoost were *300* for *Number of estimators*, *0.05* for the *Learning rate*, and the hyperparameters for Bagging were *100* for *Number of estimators*, *1.00* for *Max features*, *1.00* for *Max samples* as well. The Decision Tree's fixed hyperparameters were *6* for *Max depth*, *22* for *Min sample leaf* along with *gini* as *Criterion*. The rest of the parameters for learning was the default values provided by the implementation of scikit learn.

Answering RQ2: Our experiments show the three resampling techniques can get better scores regarding specific metrics. The question itself can depend on the context, but in our case, where F-measure was the primary evaluation metric, we can clearly state that the random upsampling is the best choice.

4.3 RQ3: Which Is the Best Weak Learning Algorithm and Which Parameter Configuration Is the Most Powerful?

As previously mentioned, Table 2 shows AdaBoost and Bagging classifiers work better with Decision Tree than the Gaussian Naïve Bayes classifier. The best

Table 3. F-measure values of different resampling techniques

Ensemble learner	Base learner	None	RandUp.	RUS	SMOTE
AdaBoost	DecisionTree	47.38%	**53.91%**	52.83%	48.01%
AdaBoost	GaussianNB	30.62%	**32.39%**	32.31%	33.21%
Bagging	DecisionTree	28.51%	**50.51%**	49.16%	47.49%
Bagging	GaussianNB	35.02%	**35.10%**	35.53%	36.14%

Table 4. Accuracy values of different resampling techniques

Ensemble learner	Base learner	None	RandUp.	RUS	SMOTE
AdaBoost	DecisionTree	**84.76%**	81.93%	75.27%	84.59%
AdaBoost	GaussianNB	**73.69%**	68.57%	69.15%	63.89%
Bagging	DecisionTree	**83.29%**	79.22%	71.32%	75.72%
Bagging	GaussianNB	80.47%	**80.48%**	80.34%	80.34%

Table 5. Precision values of different resampling techniques

Ensemble learner	Base learner	None	RandUp.	RUS	SMOTE
AdaBoost	DecisionTree	**65.12%**	50.86%	40.75%	63.55%
AdaBoost	GaussianNB	**29.83%**	26.97%	27.23%	25.26%
Bagging	DecisionTree	**67.57%**	45.02%	36.55%	39.50%
Bagging	GaussianNB	45.25%	**45.32%**	44.90%	44.99%

Table 6. Recall values of different resampling techniques

Ensemble learner	Base learner	None	RandUp.	RUS	SMOTE
AdaBoost	DecisionTree	37.26%	57.36%	**75.14%**	38.61%
AdaBoost	GaussianNB	31.49%	40.79%	40.00%	**48.68%**
Bagging	DecisionTree	18.08%	57.55%	**75.18%**	59.56%
Bagging	GaussianNB	28.58%	28.67%	29.41%	**30.21%**

parameters for Decision Tree classifier depends on the ensembler learner too. The best hyperparameters for the AdaBoost Classifier with different ensemblers shown in Table 7 and Table 8.

Only 100 estimators works best for Bagging which is positive, however, the achieved results were also lower. Optimal estimator number is 300 in case of Decision Tree which could be argued whether causes a slower runtime or not. Although we did not have the exact measurements for runtimes, we can state that runtime was never an issue.

In case of the other common parameters, Adaboost and Bagging are on consensus. Both ensemble learners performed the best with a decision tree having the max depth of 6 and min sample leaf as 22. Gini is superior over entropy in both cases for the Criterion parameter.

Answering RQ3: Based on our measurements, the best hyperparameters for the AdaBoost classifier and the Decision Tree were *300* for *Number of estimators*, *0.05* for the *Learning rate*, *6* for *Max depth*, *22* for *Min sample leaf* along with *gini* as *Criterion*, and the best hyperparameters for Bagging and Decision Tree were *100* for *Number of estimators*, *1.00* for *Max features*, *1.00* for *Max samples*, *6* for *Max depth*, *22* for *Min sample leaf* along with *gini* again as *Criterion*.

5 Threats to Validity

In our work we tried to be as objective as possible. However, there could be some factors that could make us produce invalid results. One factor could be the quality of the dataset we used. Since we used an already published dataset, we had no influence over the quality of it. The Unified Bug Dataset has numerous

Table 7. Best hyperparameters for AdaBoost and Decision Tree

Number of estimators	Learning rate	Max depth	Min sample leaf	Criterion
300	0.05	6	22	gini

Table 8. Best hyperparameters for Bagging and Decision Tree

Number of estimators	Max features	Max samples	Max depth	Min sample leaf	Criterion
100	1	1	6	22	gini

reviews [2,6,9,11], so it makes us believe that the dataset is a reliable source for software fault detection studies.

Another factor could be that we choose to fix the parameters of the preprocessing techniques, resample techniques and we had a limited search space for our experiments due to our limited resources. During our study we used 1,337 as a fixed seed for every execution in order to make our results reproducible. To measure how changes of these values would have made an impact on our results was out of the scope of this study, since it would have blown the search space.

6   Conclusion and Future Work

In this paper, we presented a detailed approach on how to apply AdaBoost classifier with different base learners in order to predict software faults from static source code metrics alone. We focused our study on revealing the capabilities of AdaBoost classifier in bug detection. We investigated the optimal parameter setup both for the ensemble learner and the base learner. We also tested whether different preprocessing steps would enhance the effectiveness of the ensemble learning method regarding F-Measure, Accuracy, Precision, and Recall metrics as well. Our study used a more recent public bug dataset, the Unified Bug Dataset as its input in order to check the generalizability of the ensemble learners.

We concluded that AdaBoost with a proper resampling technique can be an appropriate method for software fault prediction based on static source code metrics, especially combined with Decision Tree classifier. We could achieve 54.61% F-Measure, 81.96% Accuracy, 50.92% Precision, and 58.90% Recall with a proper parameterization.

Applying different resampling technique is highly context-sensitive. When F-Measure is the main focus of ours, we should employ random upsampling, while Recall is the most important metric, one should apply RUS with a decision tree.

The advantage of applying Decision Trees over Naïve Bayesian methods as base learners is clearly visible. We got the best end results by setting the number of estimators to 300, the learning rate to 0.05, max depth to 6, min sample leaf to 22 and the criterion to gini in case of AdaBoost with Decision Tree. In case of Bagging, 100 estimators gave the optimal results with max features and max samples both set to 1. Additional decision tree parameters (max depth, min sample leaf, criterion) should be unchanged in case of Bagging.

Out future plans include trying different ensemble learner methods combined with other base learner techniques. We would also like to try other preprocessing techniques as well in our future work. We also need to test the effectiveness of ensemble learning techniques on file and especially on method level to see if the conclusions hold.

Overall, we consider our findings a successful step towards understanding the AdaBoost classifier and the role it can play in software fault prediction.

Acknowledgement. This research was supported by the project "Integrated program for training new generation of scientists in the fields of computer science", no EFOP-3.6.3-VEKOP-16-2017-00002. The project has been supported by the European Union and co-funded by the European Social Fund.

The research was partly supported by the Ministry of Innovation and Technology NRDI Office within the framework of the Artificial Intelligence National Laboratory Program (MILAB), and by grant NKFIH-1279-2/2020 of the Ministry for Innovation and Technology, Hungary, and by grant 2018-1.2.1-NKP-2018-00004 "Security Enhancing Technologies for the IoT" funded by the Hungarian National Research, Development and Innovation Office.

References

1. OpenStaticAnalyzer static code analyzer (2021). https://github.com/sed-inf-u-szeged/OpenStaticAnalyzer
2. Bejjanki, K.K., Gyani, J., Gugulothu, N.: Class imbalance reduction (CIR): a novel approach to software defect prediction in the presence of class imbalance. Symmetry **12**(3) (2020). https://doi.org/10.3390/sym12030407. https://www.mdpi.com/2073-8994/12/3/407
3. Catal, C.: Software fault prediction: a literature review and current trends. Expert Syst. Appl. **38**(4), 4626–4636 (2011)
4. Chaturvedi, K., Bedi, P., Misra, S., Singh, V.: An empirical validation of the complexity of code changes and bugs in predicting the release time of open source software. In: 2013 IEEE 16th International Conference on Computational Science and Engineering, pp. 1201–1206 (2013). https://doi.org/10.1109/CSE.2013.201
5. Chawla, N.V., Bowyer, K.W., Hall, L.O., Kegelmeyer, W.P.: SMOTE: synthetic minority over-sampling technique. J. Artif. Intell. Res. **16**, 321–357 (2002)
6. Compton, R., Frank, E., Patros, P., Koay, A.: Embedding java classes with code2vec: improvements from variable obfuscation. In: Proceedings of the 17th International Conference on Mining Software Repositories. MSR 2020. pp. 243–253. Association for Computing Machinery, New York (2020). https://doi.org/10.1145/3379597.3387445
7. D'Ambros, M., Lanza, M., Robbes, R.: An extensive comparison of bug prediction approaches. In: 2010 7th IEEE Working Conference on Mining Software Repositories (MSR 2010), pp. 31–41 (2010). https://doi.org/10.1109/MSR.2010.5463279
8. Ferenc, R., Bán, D., Grósz, T., Gyimóthy, T.: Deep learning in static, metric-based bug prediction. Array **6**, 100021 (2020). https://doi.org/10.1016/j.array.2020.100021, http://www.sciencedirect.com/science/article/pii/S2590005620300060

9. Ferenc, R., Siket, I., Hegedűs, P., Rajkó, R.: Employing partial least squares regression with discriminant analysis for bug prediction. arXiv e-prints arXiv:2011.01214 (2020)
10. Ferenc, R., Tóth, Z., Ladányi, G., Siket, I., Gyimóthy, T.: A public unified bug dataset for java and its assessment regarding metrics and bug prediction. Softw. Qual. J. **28**, 1447–1506 (2020). https://doi.org/10.1007/s11219-020-09515-0
11. Ferenc, R., Viszkok, T., Aladics, T., Jász, J., Hegedűs, P.: Deep-water framework: the swiss army knife of humans working with machine learning models. SoftwareX **12**, 100551 (2020). https://doi.org/10.1016/j.softx.2020.100551. https://www.sciencedirect.com/science/article/pii/S2352711019303772
12. Gao, Y., Yang, C.: Software defect prediction based on adaboost algorithm under imbalance distribution. In: 2016 4th International Conference on Sensors, Mechatronics and Automation (ICSMA 2016). Atlantis Press (2016)
13. Hasanin, T., Khoshgoftaar, T.: The effects of random undersampling with simulated class imbalance for big data. In: 2018 IEEE International Conference on Information Reuse and Integration (IRI), pp. 70–79. IEEE (2018)
14. Jiang, Y., Cukic, B., Ma, Y.: Techniques for evaluating fault prediction models. Empirical Softw. Eng. **13**(5), 561–595 (2008)
15. Khan, M.Z.: Hybrid ensemble learning technique for software defect prediction. Int. J. Mod. Educ. Comput. Sci. **12**(1), 10 (2020)
16. Kumari, M., Misra, A., Misra, S., Fernandez Sanz, L., Damasevicius, R., Singh, V.: Quantitative quality evaluation of software products by considering summary and comments entropy of a reported bug. Entropy **21**(1) (2019). https://doi.org/10.3390/e21010091. https://www.mdpi.com/1099-4300/21/1/91
17. Nevendra, M., Singh, P.: Software bug count prediction via AdaBoost.R-ET. In: 2019 IEEE 9th International Conference on Advanced Computing (IACC), pp. 7–12 (2019). https://doi.org/10.1109/IACC48062.2019.8971588
18. Peng, Y., Kou, G., Wang, G., Wu, W., Shi, Y.: Ensemble of software defect predictors: an AHP-based evaluation method. Int. J. Inf. Technol. Decis. Making **10**(01), 187–206 (2011)
19. Petrić, J., Bowes, D., Hall, T., Christianson, B., Baddoo, N.: The jinx on the NASA software defect data sets. In: Proceedings of the 20th International Conference on Evaluation and Assessment in Software Engineering, pp. 1–5 (2016)
20. Polikar, R.: Ensemble learning. In: Zhang, C., Ma, Y. (eds) Ensemble machine learning, pp. 1–34. Springer, Boston (2012). https://doi.org/10.1007/978-1-4419-9326-7_1
21. Ren, J., Qin, K., Ma, Y., Luo, G.: On software defect prediction using machine learning. J. Appl. Math. **2014**, 8 (2014)
22. Sayyad Shirabad, J., Menzies, T.: The PROMISE repository of software engineering databases. school of information technology and engineering, University of Ottawa, Canada (2005). http://promise.site.uottawa.ca/SERepository
23. Schapire, R.E.: Explaining adaboost. In: Empirical inference, pp. 37–52. Springer, Heidelberg (2013). https://doi.org/10.1007/978-3-642-41136-6_5
24. Sharma, S., Kumar, S.: Analysis of ensemble models for aging related bug prediction in software systems. In: ICSOFT, pp. 290–297 (2018)
25. Singh, V.B., Misra, S., Sharma, M.: Bug severity assessment in cross project context and identifying training candidates. J. Inf. Knowl. Manage. **16**(01), 1750005 (2017). https://doi.org/10.1142/S0219649217500058

26. Tóth, Z., Gyimesi, P., Ferenc, R.: A public bug database of GitHub projects and its application in bug prediction. In: Gervasi, O., et al. (eds.) ICCSA 2016. LNCS, vol. 9789, pp. 625–638. Springer, Cham (2016). https://doi.org/10.1007/978-3-319-42089-9_44

27. Wang, S., Yao, X.: Using class imbalance learning for software defect prediction. IEEE Trans. Reliab. **62**(2), 434–443 (2013)

28. Yucalar, F., Ozcift, A., Borandag, E., Kilinc, D.: Multiple-classifiers in software quality engineering: combining predictors to improve software fault prediction ability. Eng. Sci. Technol. Int. J. **23**(4), 938–950 (2020)

Bug Prediction Using Source Code Embedding Based on Doc2Vec

Tamás Aladics[1]([✉])[iD], Judit Jász[1,2][iD], and Rudolf Ferenc[1][iD]

[1] University of Szeged, Szeged, Hungary
{aladics,jasy,ferenc}@inf.u-szeged.hu
[2] FrontEndART Ltd., Szeged, Hungary

Abstract. Bug prediction is a resource demanding task that is hard to automate using static source code analysis. In many fields of computer science, machine learning has proven to be extremely useful in tasks like this, however, for it to work we need a way to use source code as input. We propose a simple, but meaningful representation for source code based on its abstract syntax tree and the Doc2Vec embedding algorithm. This representation maps the source code to a fixed length vector which can be used for various upstream tasks – one of which is bug prediction. We measured this approach's validity by itself and its effectiveness compared to bug prediction based solely on code metrics. We also experimented on numerous machine learning approaches to check the connection between different embedding parameters with different machine learning models. Our results show that this representation provides meaningful information as it improves the bug prediction accuracy in most cases, and is always at least as good as only using code metrics as features.

Keywords: Source code embedding · Code metrics · Bug prediction · Java · Doc2Vec

1 Introduction

Detecting bugs is one of the most important steps in software development to ensure the quality of the product. It is a challenging task that varies greatly in difficulty based on the code, and it is very resource demanding. Numerous tools are used in the field of static code analysis to leverage this problem, but most of these lack robustness as they are mostly used to find manually defined patterns. Machine learning algorithms can help in improving the robustness of bug prediction by learning patterns from big quantities of examples.

One of the fundamental aspects of any machine learning method is the way the input features are generated. In the case of software related tasks, these features are mostly derived from the source code: code metrics, token sequences of functions, classes, or whole programs. There are numerous ways of source code representation, which we briefly introduce in the next section. These approaches vary in the structure chosen for the representation (token, statement, function, class, etc.), and in the form the code is used (as text, abstract syntax tree, etc.).

© Springer Nature Switzerland AG 2021
O. Gervasi et al. (Eds.): ICCSA 2021, LNCS 12955, pp. 382–397, 2021.
https://doi.org/10.1007/978-3-030-87007-2_27

However, most of the related code representation methods are not used in bug prediction tasks. As shown in the related literature, it is apparent that code metrics can be used for bug prediction tasks and achieve relatively good results [Ferenc et al. 2020a, Hammouri et al. 2018, Puranik et al. 2016]. In this work we are looking for the answer to how different results we can get during bug prediction by replacing traditional software metrics with feature vectors extracted from the abstract syntax tree (AST) in the learning process.

More precisely, we represent source code by traversing the AST in depth-first manner, and thus generate a sequence of tokens, on which we train numerous Doc2Vec models with different parameters. We then use these trained models to generate fixed length vectors for each Java class's source code. This vector can be used as a standalone feature vector or it can be supplemented with metrics. We discuss the details of our methodology in Sect. 3.

Finally, we validated the effectiveness of this source code representation to predict bugs on the Unified Bug Dataset [Ferenc et al. 2020b], which is a dataset of buggy and non-buggy classes implemented in Java. We report our results in Sect. 5, where we also sought answers to our research questions regarding this representation:

RQ1 Is there a Doc2Vec parametrization that would produce similar or better results than learning based on code metrics?

RQ2 Can we improve performance by combining source code embedding and code metrics?

RQ3 Do the features provided by source code embedding give valid information or was it only random noise learned?

Our main contributions are the following:

– A simple and scalable method to embed source code into a fixed length vector.
– An empirical evaluation of source code embedding with various machine learning models.
– A detailed discussion on the effects of using source code embedding with and without code metrics.

2   Related Work

In the field of source code analysis, different methods have been proposed to find ways to represent source code. One way to categorize these approaches is granularity, namely, what is the basic structure that is chosen to generate this representation - typically tokens, functions or classes. This categorization is applied by [Chen and Monperrus 2019] which we present in a brief overview of representation methods, focusing on the function and token embeddings, as our approach is a mix of the two.

The most fundamental structures that can be used as a basis for representation are tokens. [Harer et al. 2018] uses tokens as inputs for different kinds of models, one of which is Word2Vec, to generate word embedding for C/C++

tokens for software vulnerability prediction. Stepping one step up in granularity, [Devlin et al. 2017] use function embedding as input to repair variable misuse in Python. They encode the function AST by doing a depth first traversal of its nodes and create an embedding by concatenating the absolute position of the node, the type of node, the relationship between the node and its parent, and the string label of the node. In another work, [DeFreez et al. 2018] generate function embeddings for C code using control-flow graphs. They perform a random walk on interprocedural paths in the program, and use the paths to generate function embeddings. [Pan et al. 2019] used a specific CNN (Convolutional Neural Network) architecture to extract features from the AST, and then predicted bugs with logistic regression. There are works that use structures of wider scope like compilation units, but since our representation does not use these, we do not discuss them here.

Extracting features based on the source code directly is a good way to gather local information about the chosen piece of code. However, using code metrics can provide an additional, more global description of the code and its environment. Significant research has happened in this direction as well, where typically a number of metrics are derived from source code or based on results generated by test suites.

Concretely, [Ferenc et al. 2020a] use metrics such as LOC (Lines of Code), TCD (Total Comment Density), and NL (Nesting Level) etc. as input to a set of machine learning models, and they also provided comparisons for them based on the results. [Hammouri et al. 2018] used Naive Bayes, Neural Networks, and Decision Trees on datasets generated by testing processes. [Puranik et al. 2016] predicted bugs on the Eclipse JDT, using a set of 4 metrics.

Researchers also demonstrated the usefulness of using AST in software engineering tasks such as code completion. [Wang et al. 2016] leveraged Deep Belief Network (DBN) to automatically learn semantic features from token vectors extracted from programs' ASTs. [Shippey et al. 2019] use AST n-grams to identify features of defective Java code that improve defect prediction performance.

As already mentioned, related research shows that using natural language processing (NLP) methods, such as Word2Vec on source code can be promising. The now widespread Word2Vec method is a way to generate meaningful vector representations for words in text proposed by [Mikolov et al. 2013a]. Doc2Vec is a natural extension to Word2Vec published by [Mikolov et al. 2013b], which introduces distributed representation for documents, that is, sets of words.

Our proposed method is using a mix of the previously introduced ideas, which we explain more thoroughly in the next section.

3 Methodology

Our main objective in this paper is to create a code embedding based bug prediction model, and compare it with existing bug prediction methods based on code metrics. The brief overview of our method is as follows: we use class-like elements of Java codes (which means classes, enumerations, and interfaces, to which we refer to as classes in the future) as a basic structure to generate sequences. Then, we treat each of these sequences (corresponding to classes) as documents in a Doc2Vec model, and the tokens making up the classes as words making up the documents. Doc2vec assigns to each class a fixed size vector as output, which are thus suitable for inputs of the learning task. In our experiments we generate document vectors with different parametrizations, on which we perform bug prediction, using them as standalone features, or supplement them with code metrics.

3.1   AST Embedding

When considering source code representations, the first question is the form of the source code we work with. We decided to take an intermediate representation used by compilers, the abstract syntax tree (AST), because it captures structural information, which is an important aspect of programs. However, an AST is a tree structure, and we need a numeric representation for it.

```
public class Debug {
    public static boolean isDebugOn=true;
    public static void debug(String s) {
        if (isDebugOn) {
            System.out.println(s);
        }
    }
}
```

Fig. 1. Example Java code

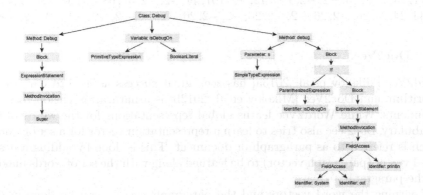

Fig. 2. The AST representation of the example Java code

One simple way to do this is to traverse the tree in a depth-first manner, and add each node to the sequence. Another question is how to map the nodes, since they contain specific data regarding the corresponding code part. For example, a node can be an element with the name "x", integer variable etc. In our representation – to remain general, and to limit the vocabulary size – we mapped each node to its kind (e.g. class definition, variable usage, assignment operator).

A problem with simple depth-first traversal is that it does not reflect scope changes. That is, for example, if we take an if statement with an expression following:

```
if (cond){
    expr1;
}
expr2;
```

and if we take an if statement with two expressions in its body:

```
if (cond){
    expr1;
    expr2;
}
```

they would map to the same sequences. To take this into account, we added a constant value to the sequence each time a step back occurs in the tree, which is approximately equivalent to scope changes. This way we can generate variable length vectors from functions while keeping structural information.

Figures 1 and 2 introduce a very simple Java class and its AST representation. The nodes in the AST are the source code elements of the example program.

In our implementation each node kind is represented by a positive number, while the constant value that denotes scope change in the AST could be any non-positive number (to avoid conflicts with node kinds), so we chose -2. So the example class is represented as a sequence of numbers: $85, 112, 42, -2, 15, -2, -2, 100, 42, -2, 107, 44, -2, -2, 57, 68, 39, 26, -2, -2, 57,$ $65, 33, 24, 24, 26, -2, 26, -2, -2, 26, -2, -2, 26, -2, -2, -2, -2, -2, -2, -2, -2.$

3.2 Doc2Vec

Word2Vec [Mikolov et al. 2013a] has seen great success as a word embedding algorithm, and Doc2Vec [Mikolov et al. 2013b] is a natural extension to it for documents. While Word2Vec learns global representations for the words of the vocabulary, Doc2Vec also tries to learn a representation vector for a set of words, which is referred to as paragraph or document. This is done by adding a designated vector (paragraph vector) to be learned along with the set of words making up the paragraph.

Learning the word vectors and the paragraph vectors can be done in two ways: by using the Distributed Memory version of Paragraph Vector (PV-DM) or the Distributed Bag of Words version of Paragraph Vector (DBOW).

PV-DM is built upon Word2Vec's continuous bag-of-words (CBOW) implementation with the extension of using document vectors. It learns by trying to
predict the missing word (target) based on a set of words (context) and the
paragraph vector, which represents the document that the context was sampled
from. To phrase it differently, word vectors represent the concept of a word while
the document vector represents the concept of a document.

The DV-DBOW algorithm is the Doc2Vec extension of the other approach
to train Word2Vec embedding: Skip-Gram. It uses only the paragraph vector as
input, and learns to predict a randomly sampled set of words from the paragraph,
so it does not learn global representations for the words, only for the paragraphs.
In DV-DBOW the word vectors are not learned nor stored and according to the
authors' findings in [Mikolov et al. 2013b], DV-DBOW is computationally better
and faster than PV-DM, at the same time it tends to perform a little worse in
general than PV-DM, even though for some tasks PV-DBOW can be better.

We chose to use Doc2Vec because we found that it is very reasonable to
think of classes as "paragraphs" and source code elements as "words" that make
up the source code itself. By learning to represent classes based on the code
elements making it up, we hoped to get a representation that preserves some of
the semantic connection between those elements. Another consideration, which
is more technical, is that Doc2Vec outputs fixed length vectors, which prevents
the need of taking care of the complications when dealing with variable length
inputs for machine learning models.

As most NLP models, Doc2Vec is trained on a corpus too. In our case, we
chose to use all of the source code that we had for the bug prediction task coming
from the Unified Bug Dataset.

4   Experiments

Our experiments are based on the work of [Ferenc et al. 2020a]. We partially rely
on their findings, in terms of which learning parameters yield the best results for
a given code metric. At the same time, we supplement their results by comparing
and combining them with the approach we present. So we used the database they
had used for our experiments. These experiments were evaluated by the Deep
Water Framework (DWF) [Ferenc et al. 2020c], which includes the Deep Bug
Hunter framework developed by them.

For reproducibility of the results presented in the following subsections, we
summarize the most important features of the datasets used and how we used
DWF for the evaluation.

4.1   Datasets

In order to be able to predict errors in software with different ML techniques,
we need a dataset of the right size and quality. The Unified Bug Dataset [Ferenc
et al. 2020b] is suitable for this purpose. This dataset merges several datasets,
which are the GitHub Bug Dataset [Tóth et al. 2016], the Promise [Jureczko

and Madeyski 2010] dataset, and the Bug Prediction Dataset [D'Ambros et al. 2010]. In this unified dataset, bugs found in Java code are assigned to source code elements at different levels, such as file, class, and method levels.

In our experiment, we examine all errors assigned to classes, interfaces, and enumerations, however, we do not treat nested classes as separate entities. As a result, not all of our results will be exactly what [Ferenc et al. 2020a] got, as they worked differently at these points. In our case, 48719 classes (including interfaces and enumerations) were analyzed, of which 8242 were faulty.

4.2   Code Metrics

In our experiments, we did not want to analyze which software metrics are most suitable for bug prediction, so we used the same metrics what were used by [Ferenc et al. 2020a] in their experiments. Even though the Unified Bug Dataset contains the metrics for it's entries, we wanted to have the most up to date versions of them. For this reason we incorporated OpenStaticAnalyzer toolset [Analyzer 2021], as they did. The used metrics are listed in Table 1.

Table 1. Metrics calculated by the OpenStaticAnalyzer

Abbr.	Name	Abbr.	Name
AD	API documentation	NOA	Number of ancestors
CBO	Coupling between object classes	NOC	Number of children
CBOI	Coupling between object classes inverse	NOD	Number of descendants
CC	Clone coverage	NOI	Number of outgoing invocations
CCL	Clone classes	NOP	Number of parents
CCO	Clone complexity	NOS	Number of statements
CD	Comment density	NPA	Number of public attributes
CI	Clone instances	NPM	Number of public methods
CLC	Clone line coverage	NS	Number of setters
CLLC	Clone logical line coverage	PDA	Public documented API
CLOC	Comment lines of code	PUA	Public undocumented API
DIT	Depth of inheritance tree	RFC	Response set for class
DLOC	Documentation lines of code	TCD	Total comment density
LCOM5	Lack of cohesion in methods 5	TCLOC	Total comment lines of code
LDC	Lines of duplicated code	TLLOC	Total logical lines of code
LLDC	Logical lines of duplicated code	TLOC	Total lines of code
LLOC	Logical lines of code	TNA	Total Number of attributes
LOC	Lines of code	TNG	Total number of getters
NA	Number of attributes	TNLA	Total number of local attributes
NG	Number of getters	TNLG	Total number of local getters
NII	Number of incoming invocations	TNLM	Total number of local methods
NL	Nesting level	TNLPA	Total number of local public attributes
NLA	Number of local attributes	TNLPM	Total number of local public methods
NLE	Nesting level else-if	TNLS	Total number of local setters
NLG	Number of local getters	TNM	Total number of methods
NLM	Number of local methods	TNOS	Total number of statements
NLPA	Number of local public attributes	TNPA	Total number of public attributes
NLPM	Number of local public methods	TNPM	Total number of public methods
NLS	Number of local setters	TNS	Total number of setters
NM	Number of methods	WMC	Weighted methods per class

4.3   Deep Water Framework

To speed up the extensive hyper parameter searching process in our experiments, we used the Deep Water Framework by [Ferenc et al. 2020c], which supports defining arbitrary feature extraction and learning methods for an input dataset, and helps in executing all the training tasks in a distributed manner. It also provides a simple overview of results, which can be used to compare the different feature extraction and learning model combinations. In our exact case, the feature extraction part was generating the input by using Doc2Vec on the sequences from the AST (to which process we refer as AST flattening) and/or metrics, while the learning part consists of the numerous ML models described in the following part of this section.

In the Deep Water Framework the F-score is calculated by using the already implemented metric scoring methods in Sklearn and Tensorflow (in case of the neural network based approaches). The performance evaluation was done by using 10 fold cross validation, where the folds were generated by Sklearn's StratifiedKFold in the model_selection module.

To achieve different embeddings, we tried a number of Doc2Vec parametrizations beforehand to have an idea about the general setup we should use in our experiments. We have also taken into account the experiences reported by the NLP community using Doc2Vec regarding vector and window sizes. Based on these, the Doc2Vec models were parametrized the following ways:

- **method**: DBOW or DV-DM
- **vector size**: 25, 50, 75, 150
- **window size**: 4, 8, 12
- **epoch**: 6, 10, 20, 40, 60, 80, 100.

We produced different vector representations of the flattened source codes with each combination of these parameters, and we looked at how each learning algorithm works on these.

In the case of the learning algorithms, we did not deal with their different parametrizations, as our goal was to find the most appropriate code embedding, so in the case of the learners we used the settings provided by [Ferenc et al. 2020a]. We experimented with some traditional machine learning methods. Their brief description and their parameters are follows:

Random Forest Random forest is an ensemble method that has seen big success in the realm of traditional (i.e. non deep learner) machine learning algorithms. We performed our tests with the following parameters: max depth for each tree: 10, splitting criterion: entropy, number of trees: 100

Decision Tree Decision tree is a machine learning approach with tremendous research background behind it. It is a simpler model, and is typically used in ensembles. For our tests we used decision trees with a max depth of 10 with the gini splitting criterion.

KNN K-Nearest Neighbour is a method that classifies entries based on the classes of their K closest neighbors. It is a method that typically scales badly, however, our dataset is rather small, and we can choose the embedding dimension. We classified points with a K value of 18, and uniform distance weights.

SVM A support vector machine is a supervised machine learning model that uses classification algorithms for two-group classification problems. We chose the Radial Basis Function as kernel function, the gamma value was 0.02, while C was 2.6 as penalty value.

Naive Bayes A simple method based on the Bayes theorem. It is rather simple without any hyper parameters, and can be viewed as a baseline for our experiments.

Linear Linear Classifier, another baseline method that fits a linear model with coefficients to minimize the residual sum of squares between the observed targets in the dataset, and the targets predicted by the linear approximation. Usually it is used for regression, here it is binned as above or below 0.5 to make a classifier.

Logistic The well studied logistic regression method, which is widely used for classification. We used it with L2 penalty, liblinear solver, regularization weight (C) of 2.0, and with 0.0001 tolerance value for stopping criteria.

And we also investigated two simple neural network architectures:

SDNNC Standard Deep Neural Network. A feed forward network with 5 layers, 200 neurons per layer, and an initial learning rate of 0.05. For all of the intermediate layers ReLu activation, for the output layer sigmoid function was used because the task is binary classification. The loss is accordingly binary crossentropy, the optimizer is AdaGrad. The training was done in 10 epochs with a batch size of 100.

CDNNC Custom Deep Neural Network. A feed forward net with similar configuration as the SDNNC - 5 layers, 250 neurons per layer, and L2 regularization is applied with 0.0005 beta value. During training F-score based early stopping is used.

Tests with both groups of machine learning approaches were performed using DWF, which uses *scikit-learn* [Pedregosa et al. 2011] as backbone for the traditional, and *Tensorflow* [Abadi et al. 2016] for the neural network based approaches.

Due to the peculiarities of the data set, we also applied the preprocessing strategy of [Ferenc et al. 2020a] in all cases. Thus, in addition to binarization and standardization of the data, 50% upsampling was also utilized on the training data, using Sklearn's resample class.

With the DWF we could easily define these tasks while continuously checking the progression. We could set the preprocessing we discussed to all of the experiments, then we defined a set of feature extraction methods and another set of machine learning models. DWF then executed all of them combined pairwise. The actual input of the DWF tool is three files extracted from the Unified Bug Dataset; one contains the bug information, the other the metrics, and the third the corresponding flattened abstract syntax trees. In order for anyone to check our results, or to compare the solutions we present with their own, we also make these files directly available at the following link: http://doi.org/10.5281/zenodo.4724941.

5 Results

We present the results of our experiments by giving detailed answers to the three research questions presented in Sect. 1. Using these, we hope to provide insight about this representation and the use cases it might prove useful for.

5.1 RQ1: Is There a Doc2Vec Parametrization that Would Produce Similar or Better Results Than Learning Based on Code Metrics?

The first topic we investigated is the existence of a Doc2Vec parametrization for bug prediction that would generate features which are similarly expressive as using code metrics. This was very likely, since code metrics are derived from source code and thus, an adequate representation of the AST is expected to perform comparably well. To find such a representation, we tried several Doc2Vec model parametrizations and also numerous machine learning models, because so far no clearly best algorithm or direction has emerged in the literature for bug prediction.

The models we tried are usually very simple with few hyperparameter tuning possibilities, since the Doc2Vec embedding part also introduces a challenge in finding the best parameters. Combining the parameter search on the Doc2Vec embedding and on simpler machine learning models already generates a huge search space. The set of parameters for both of these tasks and the concrete setup were discussed in Sect. 4.

The comparative results of these algorithms can be seen in Fig. 3. As in every subfield of anomaly detection, accuracy as measurement would not suffice, since the dataset is highly imbalanced. Better performance metrics for such problems are recall (what proportion of the relevant class was found) and precision (what proportion of the found instances are relevant). Typically there is a trade off between the two, as was observed in this case too: some models produce precision values as high as 0.58, but for them the recall value was around 0.34. On the other hand, some models performed with the recall value of 0.7, however the precision in these cases was only 0.3. To take into account both precision and recall, we used F-score. F-score is calculated as the harmonic mean of recall and precision, therefore it produces a value between 0 and 1. Since it's value is based on both recall and precision, and harmonic mean punishes extreme values, it gives a good intuition about a model's predictive power in imbalanced environments.

One could argue that the best value for F-score is around 0.5, which is still low, however firstly, the available datasets are much more limited for vulnerability and bug prediction than for other fields in deep learning, which constraints

Table 2. Comparison of learning based on source code embedding and metrics (values are F-scores)

Model name	Embedding	Code metrics	Parameters (vector size, window size, algorithm)
Bayes	**0.414**	0.325	75, 4, PV-DBOW
Linear	**0.424**	0.401	150, 8, PV-DBOW
Logistic	**0.425**	0.412	150, 8, PV-DBOW
Tree	0.403	**0.475**	150, 12, PV-DBOW
Random Forest	0.441	**0.515**	150, 4, PV-DBOW
CDNNC	**0.487**	0.474	150, 8, PV-DBOW
SDNNC	0.485	**0.520**	75, 8, PV-DM
KNN	0.491	**0.502**	75, 8, PV-DBOW

the models' performance. Secondly, our main goal was to investigate the effectiveness using ast flattenings compared to metrics. Our findings regarding this question can be found on Table 2. It can be seen that Doc2Vec vectors could indeed perform similarly, but code metrics in general still have an edge over them as their F-scores are usually higher.

Another observation regarding Doc2Vec parametrization is what can be found on Fig. 3: there is no universal best set of parameters for all of the learning models, as the distributions vary a lot in their variance and in their median value, yet they are executed on the same set of Doc2Vec models. This leads us to the conclusion that each machine learning algorithm works best with a custom Doc2Vec embedding. To put it another way, different models can understand relationships based on different source code representations.

When discussing the following research questions, we build upon these conclusions.

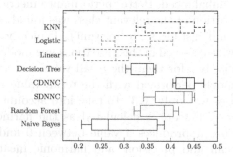

Fig. 3. Comparison of using AST embedding with various models (by F-score)

5.2   RQ2: Can We Improve Performance by Combining Source Code Embedding and Code Metrics?

The next topic we discussed was the way of applying this approach. In the previous RQ we tested how source code embedding would work as a standalone method. The question that remains is how would it perform as a supplementary tool to code metric based bug prediction. Since there is no best parametrization for the source code embedding, we chose one arbitrarily from those that performed well in most of the experiments: vector size of 25, windows size of 12, learned on 80 epochs using the PV-DM algorithm. We executed all of the learning algorithms with this embedding in the following ways:

- **Embedding:** Using only the chosen Doc2Vec embedding to predict bugs.
- **Metrics:** Using only code metrics to predict bugs.
- **Combined:** Combining the embedding and metrics vectors.

The results can be seen in Table 3. The best values are denoted with bold font. As discussed earlier, even though it can be seen that in most cases the embedding by itself is close in effectiveness, code metrics still gave relatively better results, even comparable to the values found in the work of [Ferenc et al. 2020a].

Table 3. Comparison of different machine learning methods with the same embedding (values are F-scores)

Model name	Embedding	Code metrics	Combined
Bayes	0.301	**0.325**	**0.325**
Linear	0.298	0.401	**0.418**
Logistic	0.311	0.412	**0.430**
Tree	0.374	**0.475**	0.461
Random Forest	0.423	0.515	**0.522**
CDNNC	0.451	0.474	**0.502**
SDNNC	0.467	0.520	**0.533**
KNN	0.463	0.502	**0.524**

However, the general pattern is that combining the two approaches, which is basically concatenating the metrics and embedding vectors is the best solution. And in cases where it is not the best (sometimes overshadowed by learning on metrics) it happens by a small margin which could probably be eliminated with a little more parameter tuning.

Also, regarding Table 3, it must be noted that the "Combined" and "Embedding" columns contain the values of a specific embedding (plus metrics in the case of "Combined"), which is defined earlier in this section. As discussed in RQ1, there is no best embedding for all the machine learning models, so it is possible that for some machine learning models the Embedding (and more importantly the Combined) values could be improved with further parameter search.

Based on this information we concluded that in this setup, our AST representation works best as a supplement to code metrics. Since combining the two almost always produces better or comparable results to code metrics, it is very likely that this representation provides some semantic information that the code metrics could not capture on their own, so it is indeed a useful addition for the bug prediction task.

5.3   RQ3: Do the Features Provided by Source Code Embedding Give Valid Information or Was It only Random Noise Learned?

The last research question that we evaluated during our experiments is the validity of our representation. On such imbalanced datasets with limited sample sizes, like in the case of bug prediction, it is always a question whether or not a given approach learns valid information. Concretely, does it capture patterns in the source that correspond to bugs, or does it only learn random noise that coincidentally works well in this case?

We tried to answer this question by choosing a specific embedding, and supplementing it with code metrics (based on the reasoning in RQ2), then in the database we did a number of permutations on the label column. This basically randomly generates a new distribution of the classes with no semantic relation to bug prediction. Each machine learning model is then trained on these permutated datasets to see if they provide comparable results to the ones with valid bug labels. This way, each machine learning model is "challenged" to learn random noise from the data.

Experimental Setup: We created 20 new databases by randomly permutating the bug label over the dataset entries. We chose to use the same embedding as we used in RQ2: Doc2Vec parameters of vector size 25, windows size of 12 on 80 epochs using DW-DM model. Our results can be seen in Fig. 4.

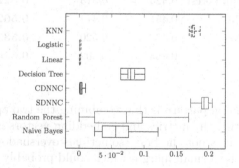

Fig. 4. The performance of learners on datasets with permutated labels (by F-score)

This diagram can be compared to the one in Fig. 3, keeping in mind that in accordance with the conclusions of RQ2, the results in Fig. 3 are nearly always worse than the combined performance with code metrics, so the difference between the distributions in Fig. 4 and the distribution of the best performing methods (which are learning on combinations of embedding methods and code metrics) is even greater. Based on these data, it can be clearly seen that the models did not learn well on the permutations. Even though some models could perform with minimal success, most of the results were not acceptable at all, with F-scores below 5. This leads us to the conclusion that the machine learning models generate valid results.

Also, it reinforced our reasoning about how this representation combined with code metrics indeed captures some inherent semantic information on which the downstream learning models could learn bug detection, since they could not learn random, probably non-existent relations between source codes.

6 Conclusions and Future Work

In our work we presented a simple but meaningful representation of the source code based on the AST and Doc2Vec embedding that captures semantic information. We presented some background information about the literature and the efforts that have already been made in this direction, and the works that served as the backbone for our investigations. We also answered three research questions in detail, which we hope helped to understand the use of this representation and the potential in it. Based on these results we concluded that in this specific setup, using metrics and the embedding together works best when predicting bugs, and we also provided experiments on the validity of our results.

However, we also made some observations that could provide a good direction for further research:

- No extensive parameter searching was done, so our results are very likely to be sub-optimal. Trying more Doc2Vec embedding and learning model parameters would probably improve the performance.
- Simple machine learning models were used, no real deep-learning techniques were employed on the word embedding. Considering the recent success of deep learning in NLP, using advanced architectures, for example those based on convolutional, recurrent, or attention-based neural networks could help a lot.
- The dataset we used is relatively small and the classes that are labeled as buggy can contain many different kinds of bugs, making effective learning very hard. Using a dataset with a bigger sample size and less variety in bug types would improve the chances of machine learning models already discussed and would facilitate the usage of deep learning models as they are typically trained on large amounts of data.
- Our mapping from AST to a fixed length vector using Doc2Vec relies heavily on NLP methods used on natural language texts, and thus, information could be lost by not taking more advantage of the AST's strict graph structure. A good research direction would be to use a representation method better suited for graphs, for example Graph2Vec [Narayanan et al. 2017].

Acknowledgments. This research was partly supported by EU-funded project AssureMOSS (Grant no. 952647) and by grant 2018-1.2.1-NKP-2018-00004 "Security Enhancing Technologies for the IoT" funded by the Hungarian National Research, Development and Innovation Office.

The research was also supported by the Ministry of Innovation and Technology NRDI Office within the framework of the Artificial Intelligence National Laboratory Program (MILAB) and by grant NKFIH-1279-2/2020 of the Ministry for Innovation and Technology, Hungary.

References

Abadi, M., et al.: TensorFlow: a system for large-scale machine learning. In: 12th USENIX Symposium on Operating Systems Design and Implementation, OSDI 2016, pp. 265–283 (2016)

OpenStaticAnalyzer (2021). https://github.com/sed-inf-u-szeged/OpenStaticAnalyzer

Chen, Z., Monperrus, M.: A literature study of embeddings on source code (2019)

D'Ambros, M., Lanza, M., Robbes, R.: An extensive comparison of bug prediction approaches. In: 2010 7th IEEE Working Conference on Mining Software Repositories. MSR 2010, pp. 31–41 (2010)

DeFreez, D., Thakur, A.V., Rubio-González, C.: Path-based function embedding and its application to specification mining. CoRR, abs/1802.07779 (2018)

Devlin, J., Uesato, J., Singh, R., Kohli, P.: Semantic code repair using neuro-symbolic transformation networks. CoRR, abs/1710.11054 (2017)

Ferenc, R., Bán, D., Grósz, T., Gyimóthy, T.: Deep learning in static, metric-based bug prediction. Array, 6:100021. Open Access (2020a)

Ferenc, R., Tóth, Z., Ladányi, G., Siket, I., Gyimóthy, T.: A public unified bug dataset for java and its assessment regarding metrics and bug prediction. Softw. Qual. J. **28**, 1447–1506 (2020b). Open Access

Ferenc, R., Viszkok, T., Aladics, T., Jász, J., Hegedűs, P.: Deep-water framework: the Swiss army knife of humans working with machine learning models. SoftwareX **12**, 100551 (2020c). Open Access

Hammouri, A., Hammad, M., Alnabhan, M., Alsarayrah, F.: Software bug prediction using machine learning approach. Int. J. Adv. Comput. Sci. Appl. **9**(2), 78–83 (2018)

Harer, J., et al.: Automated software vulnerability detection with machine learning (2018)

Jureczko, M., Madeyski, L.: Towards identifying software project clusters with regard to defect prediction. In: Proceedings of the 6th International Conference on Predictive Models in Software Engineering, PROMISE 2010. Association for Computing Machinery, New York, NY, USA (2010)

Mikolov, T., Chen, K., Corrado, G., Dean, J.: Efficient estimation of word representations in vector space (2013a)

Mikolov, T., Sutskever, I., Chen, K., Corrado, G., Dean, J.: Distributed representations of words and phrases and their compositionality (2013b)

Narayanan, A., Chandramohan, M., Venkatesan, R., Chen, L., Liu, Y., Jaiswal, S.: graph2vec: learning distributed representations of graphs (2017)

Pan, C., Lu, M., Xu, B., Gao, H.: An improved CNN model for within-project software defect prediction. Appl. Sci. **9**(10), 2138 (2019)

Pedregosa, F., et al.: Scikit-learn: machine learning in Python. J. Mach. Learn. Res. **12**, 2825–2830 (2011)

Puranik, S., Deshpande, P., Chandrasekaran, K.: A novel machine learning approach for bug prediction. Procedia Comput. Sci. **93**, 924–930 (2016). Proceedings of the 6th International Conference on Advances in Computing and Communications

Shippey, T., Bowes, D., Hall, T.: Automatically identifying code features for software defect prediction: using AST N-grams. Inf. Softw. Technol. **106**, 142–160 (2019)

Tóth, Z., Gyimesi, P., Ferenc, R.: A public bug database of GitHub projects and its application in bug prediction. In: Gervasi, O., et al. (eds.) ICCSA 2016. LNCS, vol. 9789, pp. 625–638. Springer, Cham (2016). https://doi.org/10.1007/978-3-319-42089-9_44

Wang, S., Liu, T., Tan, L.: Automatically learning semantic features for defect prediction. In: 2016 IEEE/ACM 38th International Conference on Software Engineering (ICSE), pp. 297–308 (2016)

Deep-Learning Approach with DeepXplore for Software Defect Severity Level Prediction

Lov Kumar[1][(✉)], Triyasha Ghosh Dastidar[1], Lalitha Bhanu Murthy Neti[1],
Shashank Mouli Satapathy[2], Sanjay Misra[3], Vipul Kocher[4],
and Srinivas Padmanabhuni[4]

[1] BITS -Pilani Hyderabad, Hyderabad, India
{lovkumar,f20170829,bhanu}@hyderabad.bits-pilani.ac.in
[2] VIT Vellore, Vellor, India
[3] Covenant University, Ota, Nigeria
sanjay.misra@covenantuniversity.edu.ng
[4] Testaing.Com, Bengaluru, India
{vipulkocher,srinivas}@testAing.com

Abstract. Fixing the defects of earlier releases and working on fast and efficient fixing of those software defects is detrimental for the release of further versions. Bug tracking systems like Bugzilla get thousands of software defect reports every day. Manually handling those report to assign severity to the defects is not feasible. Earlier traditional Machine Learning methods have been used to predict the severity level from the defect description. This paper presents different deep learning models to predict defect severity level. Furthermore, the deep neural network was tested using a framework developed similar to that DeepXplore. Different word-embedding techniques, feature-selection techniques, sampling techniques and deep learning models are analyzed and compared for this study. In this paper, we have considered Descriptive statistics, Box-plot, and Significant tests to compare the developed models for defect severity level prediction. The three performance metrics used for testing the models are AUC, Accuracy and Neuron Coverage. This is a preliminary study on DNN testing on this dataset. Thus, the paper focuses on DeepXplore DNN testing technique. However further studies would be undertaken on comparative analysis of different DNN testing techniques on this dataset.

Keywords: Severity prediction · Imbalance handling · Feature selection · Deep learning · Word embedding

1 Introduction

Software defect resolution is one of the core activities of software maintenance. A huge number of software bugs are reported every day by different bug tracking systems used by various developers. In the present era, it is extremely difficult

© Springer Nature Switzerland AG 2021
O. Gervasi et al. (Eds.): ICCSA 2021, LNCS 12955, pp. 398–410, 2021.
https://doi.org/10.1007/978-3-030-87007-2_28

to develop defect-free software considering its immense complexity, expending size and fluctuating customer requirements. Manual handling of defects is not a feasible task. Software defect severity level prediction is one of those areas of research, which has emerged very rapidly in the recent past. However, past studies have revealed that it is a time-consuming as well as expensive activity [1,2]. Also this process largely depends on the experience of the person handling the activity.

The Deep Learning (DL) approach helps the machines to process complex tasks with higher precision. With the growing use of DL systems, more uncertainty is prevailing towards the use of unaccounted test cases, which may lead to disastrous results. To solve this issue, DeepXplore was developed as a white-box testing framework for systematically testing real-world DL systems. In this paper, different DL techniques are being used to predict the software defect severity level. These deep neural networks were tested with DeepXplorer in order to check their neuron coverage using multiple DL systems with similar functionality for cross referencing. Three different performance metrics are also being used to test the DL models in order to assess their performance.

2   Related Work

When new software releases are created, it is necessary to fix errors in the older version with the inclusion of new features. Bug tracking systems are essential for any creation of software. The vulnerabilities and the definition of the bug are recorded on the bug monitoring systems. More bugs fixed help to create enhanced applications. Thousands of bugs are identified every day in certain well-known error monitoring software's like Bugzilla. This bug monitoring systems delete duplicate errors, assigns of bug severity and predicts bug severity level.

In the year 2006, **A. Sheta and D. Rine**, [3] in order to predict faulty modules, suggested using Linear Auto-regression models. To foresee possible errors, historical records on software defects have been used. The model was contrasted with the known Power Model (POWM) and the Root-Middle Square Error (RMSE) calculated efficiency, showing positive results.

In 2010, **Lamkanfi** [4] used text mining techniques to estimate the fault severity levels from the fault summaries. It was tested on three data sets, Mozilla, Eclipse and GNOME, open source. For both Mozilla and Eclipse it was between 0.65 and 0.75 based on the recall and precision values, while it was between 0.70 and 0.85 for GNOME. In 2011 [5], Lamkanfi continued the research to use the Naive Bayes, Naive Bayes Multinomial, KNN and SVM to compare different mined algorithms to estimate grade levels. Their success was compared using accuracy, recall and AUC. The operation of NB on both of these was also used in three selection techniques. For Naive Bayes Multinomial, the models' efficiency was better with a maximum range of 0.93 AUC. But regular NB also performed well when at least 250 bug reports were in the dataset package.

All the works in this field, to the best of our knowledge, have used only traditional machine learning methods for detecting software defect severity level. Through our work, deep learning methods have been used to detect fault severity levels.

3 Study Design

This section presents the details regarding various design settings used for this research.

3.1 Experimental Dataset

In this study, six different software datasets have been used, which are referred to as CDT, JDT, PDE, Platform, Bugzilla, and Thunderbird to validate our proposed models. These datasets have been collected from msr2013-bug_dataset-master [1]. Mining Software Repositories (MSR) conducted Challenge every year by provides software-related data and motivate participate to apply data mining techniques for finding important patterns. The datasets are the collection of defect reports wherein each defect report contains the defect ID, defect description, and severity level of the defects. Table 1 shows the details of the dataset used for this study. As shown in Table 1, the CDT software defect report consists of 2220 normal defects, 146 minor defects, 288 major defects, 42 trivial defects, 58 blocker defects, 106 critical defects.

Table 1. Experimental data set description

	Normal	% Normal	Minor	% Minor	Major	% Major	Trivial	% Trivial	Blocker	% Blocker	Critical	% Critical
CDT	2220	77.62	146	5.10	288	10.07	42	1.47	58	2.03	106	3.71
JDT	1906	66.71	261	9.14	430	15.05	104	3.64	50	1.75	106	3.71
PDE	2380	81.65	91	3.12	295	10.12	52	1.78	27	0.93	70	2.40
Platform	1485	52.07	215	7.54	715	25.07	145	5.08	77	2.70	215	7.54
Bugzilla	1342	46.68	598	20.80	352	12.24	302	10.50	167	5.81	114	3.97
Thunderbird	1100	37.72	387	13.27	655	22.46	91	3.12	25	0.86	658	22.57

3.2 Word Embedding:

The objective of this study is to develop defect severity level prediction models using defect reports. So, the performance of severity level prediction models is heavily dependent on the choice of features extracted from the defect reports. In this work, we utilized 7-word embedding techniques such as Continuous Bag of Words Model (CBOW), Skip-gram (SKG), Global Vectors for Word Representation (GLOVE), Google news word to vector (w2v), fasttext (FST), Bidirectional Encoder Representations from Transformers (BERT), and generative

---

[1] http://2013.msrconf.org/.

pre-training model (GPT) to convert the description text to an n-dimensional vector. These extracted vectors have been used an input to develop the models for predicting appropriate level of severity for defects. The performance of the models developed using these word-embedding are also compared with most frequently used technique i.e., term frequency-inverse document frequency (TF-IDF) to extract feature from text.

3.3 Feature Selection Techniques

The defect severity level prediction models are developed by taking extracted vector using word-embedding techniques for defect report as an input. So, the predictive ability of the models also depends upon the selection of important features vectors. In this paper, three different features selection techniques have been used to remove irrelevant sets of features and select sets of un-correlated sets of relevant features. Initially, the rank-sum test is applied on individual feature to find significant sets of features that have the ability to predict the level of severity for defects [6]. Next, we have used the cross-correlation analysis to compute uncorrelated sets of features. Finally, principal component analysis (PCA) [7] has been used to find new sets of values for features that have un-correlated with others.

3.4 Deep Learning Architecture

With the increase in the amount of data, traditional machine learning models seem to fail after a certain amount of time. Deep learning means the machine can grasp complex perception tasks with great precision. Deep learning is also known as deep structured learning with multiple layers composed of non-linear processing units for conversion and extraction of features. The findings from the previous layer are used as the input in any subsequent layer. The learning process is performed by means of distinctive stages of abstraction and various layers of representation, whether supervised or unsupervised. The basic computing device is a deep learning system or a deep neural network is neuron which takes several data as an input. It combines these signals linearly and transforms the combined signals into the non-linear tasks in order to generate outputs. In this study, three different architecture of deep learning models have been used to train the models for predicting defect levels of severity.

3.5 SMOTE

The information present in experimental data sets description of Table 1 suggests that the considered data does not have an equal number of the severity level of the defects; as for example, only 1.46 % of trivial defects present in the case of CDT. So, the models trained using these data without applying any sampling techniques may lead to an adverse effect on the actual performance. In this work, the Synthetic Minority Oversampling Technique (SMOTE) has been used to balance the data. SMOTE technique is identified as a very popular technique by different researches that helps to improve the predictive ability of the models.

3.6   DeepXplore

Deep Learning has come a long way in recent years. It is being used in all domains. There has been a growing use of DL systems in security-driven systems like self-driving cars, malware detection. In all those cases, there is a case importance of making sure we take into account all the test cases. Any sort of test case that has not been accounted for can lead to disastrous results in DL systems where security is of utmost importance. Earlier mostly manually labeled data was used for testing but that often led to the negligence of effects of rare test cases.

To solve this issue, DeepXplore was developed in 2019 as a white-box testing framework for systematically testing real-world DL systems. The main features taken into consideration are neuron coverage, using multiple DL systems with similar functionality for cross-referencing. These techniques reduce manual checking. This white-box testing method was tested on five very famous real-world datasets like Udacity, ImageNet, MNIST, Drebin and PDF.

To understand DL testing, it is necessary to understand DNN architecture first. DNN architecture is inspired by the human brain. It is used for extracting high-level features from raw inputs without any human intervention. The neuron is the smallest computing unit in the DNN. Each neuron has an activation function working on the raw input coming into it, after which the result is passed on to the neighbouring connected neurons. A typical DNN is made up of multiple layers where each layer consists of multiple neurons. There are three types of layers in the network: input, output and one or more hidden layers. Each neuron is directed towards the neurons in the next layer. Each connected neuron has an attached weight parameter which elaborates the strength with which they are connected. The weights of the network are learned during training to minimise the cost function using gradient descent. In each layer of this architecture, the DNN learns high-level representations of the raw-input which gradually gives us the highly meaningful outputs.

The first aim of the algorithm is to generate test inputs that can induce different behaviours in the tested DNNs, i.e. different DNNs will classify the same input into different classes. Next comes the objective to generate inputs which will increase the neuron coverage significantly. This is achieved through the selection of inactivated neurons in the process and modification of the input so that the neuron output exceeds the neuron activation threshold.

4   Results and Analysis

This section presents the results and analysis of the prediction models developed using word-embedding techniques, feature-selection techniques, sampling techniques, and deep learning techniques. In this work, seven word embedding techniques and Tf-IDF is applied on defect report of 6 data sets along 3 deep learning models with 5-fold cross-validations, 4 sets of features. Thus, in this research, we assessed the performance of 2880 (8*6*3*5*4) defect severity level prediction models with the help of Box-plot, and Significant tests. In this study, we have also considered Neuron Coverage to evaluate the feasibility of the developed models.

4.1 Word Embedding

This work makes the use of different word-embedding techniques to convert the text into a vector of numbers which could be fed in as input of the prediction models. In this work, we have used Accuracy, AUC and Neuron Coverage as performance parameters to compare the ability to predict the level of severity using models developed by considering word-embedding extracted vectors as an input.

Box-Plot: Word-Embedding Techniques. We have used seven different word embedding techniques such as Continuous Bag of Words Model(CBOW), Skip-gram(SKG), Global Vectors for Word Representation (GLOVE), Google news word to vector(w2v), fastText (FST), BERT, and generative pre-training model (GPT) to convert the defect descriptions into numerical vector representations. The performance of the models developed using above techniques are also compared using term frequency-inverse document frequency(TFIDF). Figures 1 and 2 show the box-plot diagram for Accuracy, AUC and Neuron Coverage of the models developed using different word-embedding techniques. While checking the box-plots for different word embedding in terms of AUC, we see that both w2v and GLOVE has average AUC value of 0.78, maximum value of 0.99 AUC for GLOVE and 0.98 AUC for w2v and the Q3 values for GLOVE and w2v are also comparable at 0.91 and 0.92 AUC respectively. So it can be summarized that GLOVE and w2v both are the contenders for the best fit for word embedding for predicting defect severity levels in terms of performance. Figure 2 compares the models using neuron coverage. The value of neuron coverage helps to predict the amount of logic explored by a set of test inputs. The high value of neuron coverage represents that the neurons of deep learning models are successfully tested using test inputs. It can be seen that the median value of neuron coverage for the models trained on TF-IDF relatively higher and also closely by the GLOVE word embedding.

Comparison Using Significant Test. We have also used significant test with the help of rank-sum test to find out whether the models that are developed using 7 different word embedding provide a significant improvement or not. The test is used to validate the considered null hypothesis like "The models developed on extracted vectors using different word-embedding have not significant improvement in ability to predict level of severity". The above null-hypothesis is accepted if the p-value is more than 0.05. The results obtained after applying rank-sum test are listed in Table 2. While checking the results of the significant tests in terms of AUC for different word embedding, we observed the above considered hypothesis is rejected for most of the pairs i.e., the performance of the

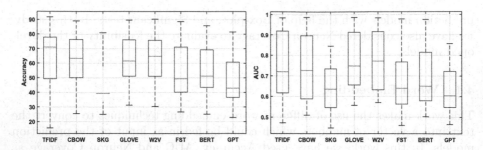

Fig. 1. Performance Box-Plot diagram: performance of different word embedding

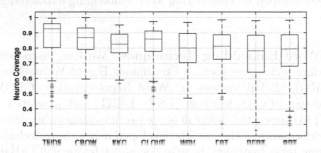

Fig. 2. Neuron coverage : different word embedding

models depended on the word-embedding techniques that used to extract features from defect reports. Similar, significant improvement in Neuron Coverage for models trained on different word-embedding techniques.

Table 2. Significant tests: different word embedding

	AUC								Neuron coverage							
	TFIDF	CBOW	SKG	GLOVE	W2V	FST	BERT	GPT	TFIDF	CBOW	SKG	GLOVE	W2V	FST	BERT	GPT
TFIDF	1.00	0.03	0.00	0.16	0.31	0.00	0.00	0.00	1.00	0.00	0.00	0.00	0.00	0.00	0.00	0.00
CBOW	0.03	1.00	0.00	0.00	0.00	0.00	0.01	0.00	0.00	1.00	0.00	0.10	0.00	0.00	0.00	0.00
SKG	0.00	0.00	1.00	0.00	0.00	0.04	0.00	0.49	0.00	0.00	1.00	0.04	0.14	0.27	0.00	0.06
GLOVE	0.16	0.00	0.00	1.00	0.73	0.00	0.00	0.00	0.00	0.10	0.04	1.00	0.01	0.01	0.00	0.00
W2V	0.31	0.00	0.00	0.73	1.00	0.00	0.00	0.00	0.00	0.00	0.14	0.01	1.00	0.65	0.12	0.60
FST	0.00	0.00	0.04	0.00	0.00	1.00	0.12	0.01	0.00	0.00	0.27	0.01	0.65	1.00	0.05	0.33
BERT	0.00	0.01	0.00	0.00	0.00	0.12	1.00	0.00	0.00	0.00	0.00	0.00	0.12	0.05	1.00	0.34
GPT	0.00	0.00	0.49	0.00	0.00	0.01	0.00	1.00	0.00	0.00	0.06	0.00	0.60	0.33	0.34	1.00

4.2 Sampling

The considered dataset has highly imbalanced that may give very poor performance in predicting the minority class. Thus the performance of the models can be improved by oversampling the minority class. This work makes the use of SMOTE technique to handle class imbalance. The work also make the box-plot and significant test analysis to compare the performance of the models trained on SMOTE data with original data.

Box-Plot: SMOTE. Figure 3 compares the performance of the trained models on SMOTE and original data with respect to Accuracy and AUC. The accuracy value data in Fig. 3 shows that the models trained on SMOTE data have similar ability to assign level of severity based on defect report with models train on original data. However, AUC is considered to be a better metric in case of class imbalance problem. So, based on AUC values, we observed that models trained on SMOTE data have better ability to assign level of severity based on defect report. Figure 4 compares the models using neuron coverage. It can be seen that the median value of neuron coverage for the models trained on SMOTE data relatively higher with models trained on original data.

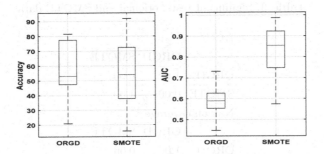

Fig. 3. Performance Box-Plot diagram: performance of original data and SMOTE

Comparison Using Significant Test. The main idea behind this test is to find out whether the models that are developed using SMOTE and original data provide a significant improvement or not. The result present in Table 3 confirmed that the models trained on SMOTE data have significant improvement in both AUC and Neuron Coverage.

4.3   Feature Selection

Feature Selection is the technique for selecting related features from the provided set of data and thus removing the other unrelated, irrelevant features that does not affect our target variable. This technique helps in improving the performance of the model. Irrelevant and lowly related features sometimes hinder the performance of the model. In this study, different varieties of feature selection techniques such as significant sets of features using the rank-sum test (SIGF), uncorrelated sets of features using cross-correlation analysis(UCRF), and principal component analysis(PCA) have been applied on datasets to find right combination of relevant features. The performance of these techniques is derived in terms of AUC and accuracy, and compared with box-plot and significant test.

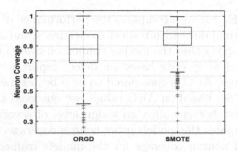

Fig. 4. Neuron coverage : original data and SMOTE

Table 3. Significant tests: original and SMOTE data

AUC		
	ORGD	SMOTE
ORGD	1.00	0.00
SMOTE	0.00	1.00
Neuron coverage		
	ORGD	SMOTE
ORGD	1.00	0.00
SMOTE	0.00	1.00

Box-Plot: Feature Selection Techniques. Figure 5 compares the performance of the different feature selection techniques using box-plot with respect to Accuracy and AUC. The box-plot of the different feature selection techniques in terms of accuracy shows the highest average value for the model using all the features but the interquartile ranges for ALLF, SIGF and UCRF are almost similar. However, AUC is considered to be a better metric in case of class imbalance problem. So, based on AUC values, we observed that the performance of models remain same after removing features using rank-sum test and cross-correlation analysis(UCRF) i.e., it is possible to develop good models with less numbers of features. Figure 6 compares the models using neuron coverage. It can be seen that the median value of neuron coverage for the models by taking all feature or significant features is almost similar.

Comparison Using Significant Test. The main idea behind this test is to find out whether the models that are developed using 3 different feature selection techniques provide a significant improvement or not. The result present in Table 4 confirmed that the models trained on all features, SIGF, and UCRF are significantly similar performance i.e., there exists small number of features that have better ability to predict level of severity. However, the models trained on different sets of features are significantly different in terms of Neuron Coverage.

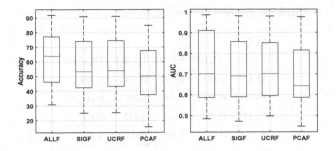

Fig. 5. Performance Box-Plot diagram: performance of different sets of features

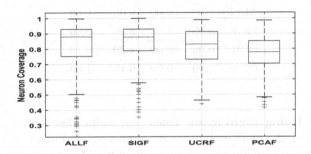

Fig. 6. Neuron coverage : different sets of features

4.4 Deep Learning Models

This study makes the use of three different variants of deep learning models by changing the numbers of hidden layers to train the models for predicting level of severity based on defect report. The activation function used for the hidden layers were ReLU (Rectified Linear Activation Function) and for the output layer softmax activation function was used. The optimization algorithm used for all the models were Adam which is used to update the network weights during training. Finally, the models ability to predict severity level trained using above deep learning techniques are compared with the help of AUC and accuracy and compared in terms of box-plot and significant test.

Box-Plot: Deep Learning Models. Fig. 7 compares the performance of the different models using box-plot with respect to Accuracy and AUC. The box-plot of the different deep learning models (DLM1, DLM2 and DLM3) in terms of accuracy shows the average value for all the models to be same and the interquartile ranges for DLM1, DLM2 and DLM3 are almost similar. However, AUC is considered to be a better metric in case of class imbalance problem. So, based on AUC values, we observed that the average AUC values for DLM2 and DLM3 are similar and is lesser than DLM1 by a very minuscule margin. Figure 8 compares the models using neuron coverage. It can be seen that the median value of neuron coverage for the all three models is almost similar.

Table 4. Significant tests: different sets of features

AUC

	ALLF	SIGF	UCRF	PCAF
ALLF	1.00	0.16	0.23	0.00
SIGF	0.16	1.00	0.81	0.01
UCRF	0.23	0.81	1.00	0.01
PCAF	0.00	0.01	0.01	1.00

Neuron coverage

	ALLF	SIGF	UCRF	PCAF
ALLF	1.00	0.00	0.00	0.00
SIGF	0.00	1.00	0.00	0.00
UCRF	0.00	0.00	1.00	0.10
PCAF	0.00	0.00	0.10	1.00

Comparison Using Significant Test. The main idea behind this test is to find out whether the models that are developed using 3 different deep learning techniques provide a significant improvement or not. The result present in Table 5 confirmed that the models trained using different techniques are significantly similar performance as well as similar Neuron Coverage.

Table 5. Significant tests: classification techniques

AUC

	DLM1	DLM2	DLM3
DLM1	1.00	0.94	0.67
DLM2	0.94	1.00	0.74
DLM3	0.67	0.74	1.00

Neuron coverage

	DLM1	DLM2	DLM3
DLM1	1.00	0.02	0.35
DLM2	0.02	1.00	0.11
DLM3	0.35	0.11	1.00

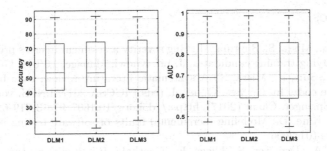

Fig. 7. Performance Box-Plot diagram: performance of different classification techniques

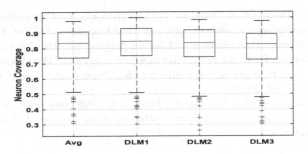

Fig. 8. Neuron coverage : different deep learning models

5   Conclusion

This research proposed models using word embedding, data sampling technique, deep learning, and feature selection to predict level of defect severity using defect reports. The proposed models have been validated with the help of six open source datasets and compared using AUC and Accuracy. This work also make use of DeepXplore to test the developed models. The quality of the models developed using the above techniques are compared with the help of neuron coverage. The value of neuron coverage helps to predict the amount of logic explored by a set of test inputs. The high value of neuron coverage represents that the neurons of deep learning models are successfully tested using test inputs. The experimental results suggested that the models trained on extracted vectors using word-embedding techniques have better ability to predict defect severity level. Similarly, the models trained on sampled data with relevant sets of features using deep learning technique have ability to assign right level of severity to the defects based on defect reports. More importantly, the high value of neuron coverage (Average 89%) confirms the better quality of defect severity level prediction models.

Acknowledgment. This research is funded by TestAIng Solutions Pvt. Ltd.

References

1. Singh, V.B., Misra, S., Sharma, M.: Bug severity assessment in cross project context and identifying training candidates. J. Inf. Knowl. Manage. **16**(01), 1750005 (2017)
2. Gupta, A., Suri, B., Misra, S.: A systematic literature review: code bad smells in java source code. In: Gervasi, O., et al. (eds.) ICCSA 2017. LNCS, vol. 10408, pp. 665–682. Springer, Cham (2017). https://doi.org/10.1007/978-3-319-62404-4_49
3. Sheta, A., Rine, D.: Modeling incremental faults of software testing process using AR models (01 2006)
4. Lamkanfi, A., Demeyer, S., Giger, E., Goethals, B.: Predicting the severity of a reported bug. In: 2010 7th IEEE Working Conference on Mining Software Repositories (MSR 2010), pp. 1–10, Los Alamitos, CA, USA, IEEE Computer Society (May 2010)
5. Lamkanfi, A., Demeyer, S., Soetens, Q.D., Verdonck, T.: Comparing mining algorithms for predicting the severity of a reported bug. In: 2011 15th European Conference on Software Maintenance and Reengineering, pp. 249–258 (2011)
6. Kumar, L., Misra, S., Rath, S.K.: An empirical analysis of the effectiveness of software metrics and fault prediction model for identifying faulty classes. Comput. Stan. Interfaces **53**, 1–32 (2017)
7. Kumar, L., Sripada, S.K., Sureka, A., Rath, S.K.: Effective fault prediction model developed using least square support vector machine (lssvm). J. Syst. Softw. **137**, 080–112 (2018)

10th International Workshop on Collective, Massive and Evolutionary Systems (IWCES 2021)

Distributed Framework for Task Execution with Quantitative Skills

Amar Nath[1] and Rajdeep Niyogi[2(✉)]

[1] SLIET Deemed University, Longowal 148106, India
amarnath@sliet.ac.in
[2] Indian Institute of Technology Roorkee, Roorkee 247667, India
rajdpfec@iitr.ac.in

Abstract. Collaborative task execution is an important area of research in multi-agent systems. In some situations, the agents are spatially distributed, have limited information about the environment, and update their knowledge via exchanging messages. Distributed approaches for task execution in such situations have been suggested in the literature. In these approaches, skills of robots and skills required for task execution are represented as p-dimensional binary skill vectors. However, in real-world applications, it would be more desirable to consider real-valued skills. In this paper, we develop a distributed framework that consider quantitative representation of skills. We have performed extensive experiments on a RoboCupRescue simulation environment. The experimental results show the efficacy of the approach.

Keywords: Task execution · Distributed framework · Quantitative skills

1 Introduction

Autonomous robots can be deployed for task execution in some applications (e.g., search and rescue [1], space exploration [10], demining [12]) where direct human intervention is impossible or impractical. In some situations a coalition (or team) is formed based on a complete information of the world. In such a setting, the coalition formation problem can be viewed as a combinatorial optimization problem that selects a subset (coalition) from a given set of members. A coalition is guaranteed to be formed although the computational time is exponential. Coalition formation algorithms for this setting have been suggested in [13,14].

In this paper, task execution is done in a partially observable environment where the agents are spatially distributed and no agent has a global view of the environment. Thus complete knowledge of the world is not known in advance and it can be determined partially when the need for a coalition formation arises (i.e., at run-time). In such situations no guarantee can be given that any previously found coalition will execute the task successfully. Moreover, unlike the centralized setting, there is also no guarantee that a coalition would be formed;

© Springer Nature Switzerland AG 2021
O. Gervasi et al. (Eds.): ICCSA 2021, LNCS 12955, pp. 413–426, 2021.
https://doi.org/10.1007/978-3-030-87007-2_29

414   A. Nath and R. Niyogi

the coalition formation process may be unsuccessful due to, say, suitable agents are unavailable for the task and/or some potential members are not reachable. So the information about the world should be acquired autonomously at run-time by an agent, who has detected a task that is indivisible, i.e., cannot be divided into subtasks, by exchanging messages (explicit communication) with other agents. This is quite challenging due to the following dynamic aspects of the environment.

The state of an agent changes depending on whether it is navigating, trying to form a coalition, participating in a coalition formation, or executing a task. The locations of the agents change, agents may enter or exit the environment, and task arrival is not known in advance. Task execution requires that all members of a coalition should be present at the location of the task. Distributed approaches for team formation in such settings have been suggested in [2–5].

In [4,5], skills of robots and skills required for task execution are represented as p-dimensional binary skill vectors. Such a specification merely states whether or not a robot has a particular capability. Likewise for task execution, the required set of capabilities is given. If a team is selected for task execution, it means that the combined capabilities of the team members is a superset of the capabilities required for task execution. In real world situations, a task should be specified not just by what capabilities are required for its execution but also by some measure of the capabilities. Similarly, a capability vector of a robot should also specify the quantitative value of the particular capabilities. In this paper, we extend these approaches [4,5] by considering quantitative representation of capability.

The remaining part of the paper is organized as follows. Related work is given in Sect. 2. A generic formal framework is given in Sect. 3. A distributed approach for task execution is described in Sect. 4. The experimental results are given in Sect. 5. Conclusions are given in Sect. 6.

2 Related Work

The works [2–5] consider collaborative task execution in a dynamic environment where all the agents associated with the execution should be present at the location of the task. In [2–5] distributed approaches for collaborative task execution are suggested based on different assumptions. In [2,3] team size is known in advance, and each agent in a team should have a set of skills that is a superset of the set of skills of the task. This means that the team is homogeneous with respect to the skills of the task. A formal framework of a dynamic environment is given in [2] and the behavior of an agent is modeled using communicating automata. A distributed approach for task execution based on this model is suggested in [2]. A distributed approach for road clearance with multiple robots in urban search and rescue environment is considered in [3], where the behavior of a robot is modeled using communicating automata.

Unlike [2,3], a generic situation is considered in [4,5], where the combined set of skills of the agents of a team should be a superset of the skills of a task.

Thus the team size is not known in advance; rather determined at run-time in [4,5]. This means that the team is heterogeneous with respect to the skills of the task. The primary difference between the types of tasks considered in [2,3] and [4,5] is as follows. In order to execute a task in [2,3], all the agents of the team should perform a same action (e.g., when a team is pushing a heavy box, all the agents of the team need to perform the action 'push'). In order to execute a task in [4,5], different agents of the team need to perform a different action (e.g., when a team is transporting an object, one agent may be involved in pushing, another involved in grabbing, and some other involved in obstacle avoidance). In this paper the type of tasks considered is the same as that in [4,5].

Whereas, [4,5] consider p-dimensional binary skill vectors, this paper considers a more general p-dimensional skill vectors where each element can be a non-negative real number. Such a representation of skills of robots and tasks has been considered in [6]. In [6] a coalition problem is considered such that there is no coalition imbalance, which informally refers to the degree of dependence on some members of a coalition. The notion of imbalance is beyond the scope of this paper.

Team formation in a networked multi-agent system is considered in [11], where each agent has a single fixed skill. Each task is associated a size and a corresponding sized skill vector is formed. In [11] a team formation algorithm is suggested where an agent joins a team using any one of the two strategies based on preferential attachment and performance and referrals. However, quantitative representation of skills is not considered in [11].

Distributed approaches for team formation have been suggested in [15–20]. However, representation of skills of agents and tasks are not quite relevant in these works. Unlike some works [15,18–20] where the roles of the robots are fixed in advance, the role of a robot is determined at run-time in this paper as well as in [2–5].

The centralized approaches for team formation [13,14] represent skills of agents and tasks by sets. The objective is to select some agents such that the combined skills of the agents cover all the skills of the task.

3   A Formal Framework for Task Execution

The intention behind the following definition is to capture (i) dynamic nature of robots: number of robots present in the environment and the locations of the robots change with time and (ii) dynamic nature of tasks: number of tasks in the environment and the locations of the tasks change with time. Moreover, this dynamic nature of the robots and tasks is not known in advance.

Definition 1 (Dynamic Environment) [2]. *A global view (snapshot) of an environment E, with a nonempty finite set of locations L, taken at time t, is given by a 4-tuple $E^t = \langle \mathcal{R}, \mathcal{T}, loc, loc' \rangle$ where $\mathcal{R}$ is a nonempty finite set of robots present in the environment at time t, and $\mathcal{T}$ is a nonempty finite set of tasks in the environment at time t, $loc : \mathcal{R} \times \mathrm{N} \to L$, is a function that gives the location* *of a robot at a discrete instant of time represented by the set of timestamps* $\mathbb{N}$, $loc' : T \times \mathbb{N} \rightarrow L$, *is a function that gives the location of a task at a discrete instant of time.*

Definition 2. *(Robot)* *A robot is defined as a 10-tuple* $r = \langle id, s, \psi, \mu, m_{snd}, m_{rcv}, bool, c, \theta, \theta' \rangle$ *where id is a unique identifier,* $s \in S$ *is a state from among a possible nonempty finite set of states* S, ψ *is a capability vector representing the capabilities,* $\mu : L \mapsto L$ *is a mapping from one location to another to represent mobility,* m_{snd}, $m_{rcv} \in M$ *is the message sent (received) from among a possible nonempty finite set of messages* M, *bool is a Boolean variable that is true/false depending on whether or not the robot is inside/outside an environment (if bool is true, location of robot is* $l_r \in L$), c *is a minimum cost that the robot charges for a task,* $\theta, \theta' \in (0, 1]$ *denote remaining battery backup and battery consumption rate respectively of the robot.*

A robot with higher θ ensures that it will not fail due to more remaining battery backup. A robot with lower θ' ensures that it will last for a longer period of time.

Definition 3 *(Capability vector). A p-dimensional capability vector v is denoted as* $v = [\alpha_1, \ldots, \alpha_p]$, *where* α_i *is a non-negative real number to give a quantitative representation of a particular capability.*

In an environment, we can assume that for the execution of a task, one or more capabilities may be required from a set of capabilities, e.g., holding, pushing, obstacle detection, and vision.

Example: Let the robots r_1, r_2, r_3, and r_4 have the following capabilities; r_1: navigation, r_2: holding, r_3: holding and pushing, r_4: pushing. The capability vectors are represented as $\psi_{r_1} = [30.5, 0, 0]$, $\psi_{r_2} = [0, 20, 0]$, $\psi_{r_3} = [0, 10.6, 10]$, and $\psi_{r_4} = [0, 0, 20.9]$ where the first component of the vector denotes navigation, the second holding, and the third pushing. This is shown in Table 1.

Table 1. Capability vector of the robots

Capability vector	Capability		
	navigation	holding	pushing
ψ_{r_1}	30.5	0	0
ψ_{r_2}	0	20	0
ψ_{r_3}	0	10.6	10
ψ_{r_4}	0	0	20.9

Definition 4 *(Capability vector operators). Let* v_1, v_2 *be two p-dimensional capability vectors,* $v_1 = [\alpha_1, \ldots, \alpha_p]$, $v_2 = [\beta_1, \ldots, \beta_p]$, *where* α_i, β_i *are capabilities represented by non-negative real numbers. Let* $v_j[i]$ *denote the* i^{th} *component of* v_j, *i.e.,* α_i *or* β_i. *We define the following operators on the capability vectors as:*

- $v_1 = v_2$ *equals true iff* $\forall i \in \{1, \ldots, p\}$, $v_1[i] = v_2[i]$.
- $v_1 \oplus v_2$ *equals true iff* $\exists i \in \{1, \ldots, p\}$, $(v_2[i] > 0) \wedge (v_1[i] > 0)$.
- $v_1 \odot v_2$ *equals true iff* $\forall i \in \{1, \ldots, p\}$, $v_2[i] > 0 \rightarrow (v_1[i] \geqslant v_2[i])$.

Two vectors are equal if all the corresponding components of the vectors are equal. $v_1 \oplus v_2$ equals true denotes that there is at least one component for which the values of the capabilities in both the vectors are greater than zero. $v_1 \odot v_2$ equals true denotes that for all components where the value of capability of v_2 is greater than zero, the value of capability of v_1 should be at least the value of v_2.

Let $v_1 = [20, 0, 12]$, $v_2 = [5, 2, 8]$. It is easy to see that v_1 and v_2 are not equal. $v_1 \oplus v_2$ is true since for the first component the values are 20 and 5 respectively which exceed 0. $v_1 \odot v_2$ is not true. The first component of v_2 is 5 which is greater than 0, and the first component of v_1 is 20 which is greater than 5. The same is true for the third component. However, for the second component, the value of v_2 is 2 which is greater than 0 but the value of v_1 is less than 2.

Definition 5 *(Necessary and sufficient conditions for task execution). Let v_1, v_2 be the p-dimensional capability vectors of a robot (a coalition) and a task τ respectively. If $v_1 \oplus v_2$ is true, it means that the robot (the coalition) can participate in the task execution. $v_1 \oplus v_2$ is true is a necessary but not a sufficient condition for task execution. $v_1 \odot v_2$ is true is a sufficient condition for the robot (the coalition) to execute the task.*

Definition 6 *(Task) [4]. A task τ is specified by a 4-tuple $\tau = \langle \nu, l, t, \Psi \rangle$ where, ν is the name of a task (e.g., move (carry) box B to location l', lift desk D), $l = loc'(\tau, t)$ is the location where the task arrived, t is the time at which the task arrived, and Ψ is a p-dimensional capability vector required to execute the task. The task is indivisible i.e., it cannot be divided into subtasks.*

When a robot detects a task τ, it acquires the information about τ, i.e., the p-dimensional capability vector $\Psi = [\beta_1, \ldots, \beta_p]$ required to execute the task. For instance, $\Psi = [\beta_1, \beta_2, \beta_3, \beta_4] = [0, 20, 0, 30]$ means that 20 units of capability β_2 and 30 units of capability β_4 are required.

Definition 7 (Capability vector of a coalition). *Let $\Gamma = \{r_1, \ldots, r_k\}$ be a coalition of k robots and the p-dimensional capability vector of the robots are $\psi_{r_1}, \ldots, \psi_{r_k}$. The ith component of the p-dimensional capability vector of the coalition Γ is defined as, $\Upsilon_\Gamma[i] = \psi_{r_1}[i] + \ldots + \psi_{r_k}[i]$, $i = 1, \ldots, p$.*

Example: Consider three robots r_1, r_2, and r_3 with 4-dimensional capability vectors $\psi_{r_1} = [10, 20, 0, 0]$, $\psi_{r_2} = [0, 0, 0, 20]$, and $\psi_{r_3} = [5, 15, 0, 5]$. The capability vector of a coalition $\Gamma = \{r_1, r_2, r_3\}$ is obtained by the point-wise addition of the corresponding capabilities of the members of the coalition. This is shown in Table 2.

Definition 8 (Task execution by a coalition). *A coalition Γ, of size at least 2, can execute a task $\tau = \langle \nu, l, t, \Psi \rangle$, if $\Upsilon_\Gamma \odot \Psi$ is true.*

Table 2. Capability vector of a coalition Γ

Capability vector	Capability			
	α_1	α_2	α_3	α_4
ψ_{r_1}	10	20	0	0
ψ_{r_2}	0	0	0	20
ψ_{r_3}	5	15	0	5
$\Upsilon_\Gamma[i] = \psi_{r_1}[i] + \psi_{r_1}[i] + \psi_{r_3}[i]$	15	35	0	25

Definition 9 *(Cost of a task execution). Let $\Gamma = \{r_1, \ldots, r_k\}$, $k \geqslant 2$, be a coalition that can execute a task $\tau = \langle v, l, t, \Psi \rangle$ where each member of the coalition was located at $l_{r_i} = loc(r_i, t')$, for some $t' > t$. The cost of coalition Γ for executing τ is $C_{\langle \Gamma, \tau \rangle} = \sum_{r_i \in \Gamma} (c_{\langle r_i, \tau \rangle} \times \frac{1}{\theta_{r_i}} + d(l_{r_i}, l) \times \theta'_{r_i})$, where d denotes Euclidean distance.*

Definition 10 *(Dominant Coalition). Let $\Gamma_1, \ldots, \Gamma_n$ be the possible coalitions for executing a task τ. We call Γ_i a dominant coalition if $C_{\langle \Gamma_i, \tau \rangle} \leqslant C_{\langle \Gamma_j, \tau \rangle}$ $\forall j \in \{1, \ldots, n\} \setminus \{i\}$.*

4   Distributed Approach for Task Execution

We present a distributed approach for collaborative task execution by extending [4,5] by considering quantitative representation of capabilities. We consider a wireless network that is lossless, message delay is finite, data is not corrupted during transmission. Messages are delivered in a FIFO (first-in-first-out) manner. No assumption is made on the network topology. A robot can enter the environment at any point in time, but can exit only if it is in IDLE state. No message is delivered to a robot who is outside the environment.

Let a robot i, in IDLE state, detect a task $\tau = \langle v, l, t, \Psi \rangle$ such that $\psi_i \oplus \Psi$ is true whereas $\psi_i \odot \Psi$ is not true. So the robot starts the coalition formation process and changes it's state from IDLE to ANALYZE. In order to form a coalition, i communicates with other robots. We refer to i as an initiator, and the other robots as non-initiators.

Team Formation: Initiator: To form a coalition, i broadcasts a Request message within its range (a local broadcast), starts its timer and waits for some time, say Δ. A Request message contains a field Ψ' that indicates the remaining capability required for executing the task; $\Psi' = \Psi - \psi_i$. For instance, if $\Psi = [10, 5, 4, 0]$ and $\psi_i = [6, 3, 0, 5]$, then $\Psi' = [4, 2, 4, 0]$ which is obtained by subtracting the corresponding components. Note that the last component of Ψ is 0, which means that this component is not required. So in Ψ' this component is kept as it is, i.e., 0. Now consider another situation where $\Psi = [10, 5, 4, 2]$ and ψ_i is same as above. Consider the fourth component. The capability value of i

for this component exceeds that of the task. No other robot is thus required to fulfill this component. So for this situation, $\Psi' = [4, 2, 4, 0]$ which is same as in the previous situation.

During the period when the timer is ON, if a Willing message is received, the counter c is incremented by one and the capabilities are recorded in a matrix. If a Willing message is received when the timer is OFF, a Not-required message is sent. If a coalition cannot be formed for the task, Not-required message is sent and the state of the initiator becomes IDLE. This situation manifests failure to form a team. If a coalition can be formed, a dominant coalition is found. Then Confirm and Not-required messages are sent to the respective non-initiators, and the state of the initiator becomes WAITING.

In the WAITING state the initiator waits for the non-initiators to arrive at the location of the task. When all the members arrive, the state becomes BUSY. Now the task is executed. Upon completion of the task, state becomes IDLE.

Team Formation: Non-initiator: A non-initiator j, who is in IDLE state and has some capability to execute the task responds to the Request message by sending a Willing message to the initiator. In other cases, the non-initiator just ignores the message. The following cases may arise. A non-initiator receives a Request message from another initiator in PROMISE state. Since a non-initiator engages itself with one initiator at a time, so this message is ignored. The non-initiator does not have any one of the capability of the task. So it ignores the message.

Now if a Confirm message is received when its state is PROMISE, j changes its state to APPROACH and starts moving towards the location l of the task. On the other hand, if a Not-required message is received when its state is PROMISE, j changes its state to IDLE and disengages itself from the coalition formation process. When j has come very close to l, it sends an Arrived message to the initiator i, and changes its state to BUSY. Thereafter the task would be executed and after its completion the state changes to IDLE. After completion of the task τ, the coalition is dissolved and the robots (initiator and non-initiators) change their states to IDLE.

5   Experiments and Results

5.1   Experimental Setup

To evaluate the distributed approach given in the previous Section, we used ARGoS [7], a realistic multi-robot simulator. The experiments were carried out by running the 3.0.0-beta50 version of ARGoS on Intel® Core™ i5-2600 CPU@3.40 GHz×8, 8 GB RAM and 64-bit Ubuntu operating system. Each experiment has been run multiple times.

The algorithm can also be simulated using other multi-robot simulators, for example, V-REP [8], ROS-Gazebo [9]. V-REP has a very feature-rich simulation environment that includes a scene and a model editor, large library of models, real-time mesh manipulation. ROS-Gazebo can utilize complex 3D meshes and physics engines. ARGoS, on the other hand, is a lightweight alternative that is open-source, and suitable for multi-robot applications. ARGoS is a multi-physics robot simulator. The code run in ARGoS can be directly deployed on a real robot system. We can customize ARGoS easily by adding new plug-ins. Based on these features we chose the ARGoS multi-robot simulator for the implementation.

Implementation of the distributed approach requires addressing some challenging issues, that are: (i) to control the movement of a robot to avoid obstacle or another robot based on proximity sensor data, where the sensor detects an obstacle or another robot, (ii) control speed and velocity of a robot, (iii) synchronizing the robots for task execution, (iv) to control the movement of a robot when boundaries are detected using motor-ground sensors, and (v) communication among robots using range_and_bearing sensor. We were able to suitably customize the functionalities of ARGoS to address these issues. We have implemented the distributed framework on a real-world environment.

5.2   Road Clearance Environment

A RoboCupRescue simulation is taken as a case study that mimic a disaster scenario of a city [1]. In the RoboCupRescue simulation environment, heterogeneous field agents (ambulance agent, police force agent, and fire-brigade agent) work collaboratively for rescue operations. Here, the role of police force agents is crucial, as they clear blocked roads to allow the other agents to access disaster sites.

A road clearance scenario is constructed (see Fig. 1) where the arena size is $(10\,\mathrm{m} \times 10\,\mathrm{m} \times 2\,\mathrm{m})$ and the borders are denoted by green light. The obstacles are represented by circular disk (colored green) and rectangular box (colored red) while the robots are shown in blue. The goal is to shift all the obstacles from road (gray) to the sides of the road (white).

A *LED* light is kept on top of each object for detection. When a foot-bot robot comes within a range of an object, the colored_blob_omnidirectional camera detects the *LED* light. Based on the color of the *LED* light, the robot can determine the type of the object. We took 5 robots and 4 different types of obstacles in the environment that were placed randomly for each experiment. The 6-dimensional capability vectors required for executing the tasks are given in Table 3.

Table 3. Capability vectors of the tasks

Tasks	Capability vector of the task
#1 (large disk)	$[20, 10, 0, 30, 0, 0]$
#2 (large box)	$[10, 0, 0, 0, 0, 10]$
#3 (small disk)	$[10, 20, 0, 0, 0, 0]$
#4 (small box)	$[0, 0, 0, 0, 20, 10]$

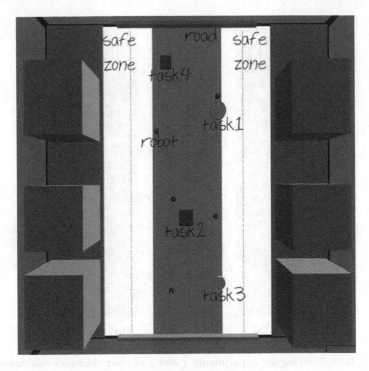

Fig. 1. A snapshot of the environmental setup of dimension $(10\,\text{m} \times 10\,\text{m} \times 2\,\text{m})$ (Color figure online)

Table 4. Capability vector and other detail of the robots

Robot	Capability vector of the robot	c	θ'
r_1	$[20, 0, 0, 0, 10, 0]$	60	0.6
r_2	$[0, 20, 0, 0, 0, 10]$	40	0.4
r_3	$[10, 20, 0, 10, 0, 0]$	80	0.5
r_4	$[10, 0, 0, 0, 10, 10]$	60	0.8
r_5	$[0, 0, 10, 20, 0, 0]$	80	0.7

The tasks $task1$, $task2$, $task3$, and $task4$ are represented with large disk, large box, small disk, and small box respectively. The capability vector and other details of each robot are given in Table 4; θ is taken as 1.0 for each robot.

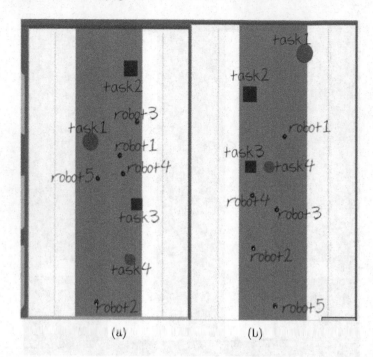

Fig. 2. Initial setting for experiments 1 and 2 of road clearance environment

In the environment, the robots start exploring the road to search for obstacles. The initial positions of the robots and tasks are shown in Figs. 2-a. and 2-b for two different experiments. If a robot finds an obstacle (see Fig. 3) and it cannot execute it alone, it starts the coalition formation process. The robots who are selected in the coalition reach the location of the obstacle (see Fig. 3). Then they grab the obstacle and make the final orientation for moving. They synchronize themselves and finally move with obstacle toward the white space and place the obstacle there (see Fig. 4). Then the coalition is dissolved. This process continues until all the obstacles are removed from the road.

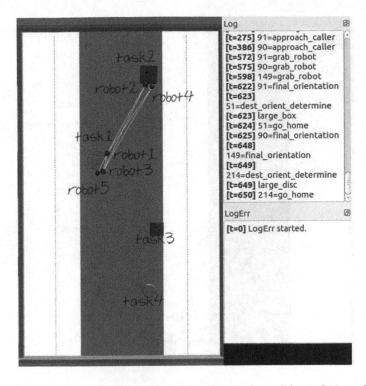

Fig. 3. r_3 and r_2 detect $task1$ and $task2$ respectively and form their coalitions

The experimental results are given in Tables 5, 6. The results indicate that an optimal coalition size cannot be decided in advance in a dynamic environment. For example, when the $task1$ is initialized with different robots, different coalitions are formed. The time to execute a task is the sum of the time taken for task detection, coalition formation, and placing an obstacle to a side of the road. The total time taken to execute all the tasks in experiments 1 and 2 are 1078.2 s and 1120.4 s respectively. The difference in time is due to the initial settings of the experiments—Fig. 2.

The $task1$ is initialized by robot r_3 in experiment 1; by r_1 in experiment 2 (see Tables 5 and 6). It can be seen that the same task, say ($task1$), is executed by different coalitions $[r_1, r_3, r_5]$ and $[r_1, r_2, r_3, r_5]$, in experiments 1 and 2 respectively. It is clear from these results that the initiator as well as the members of a coalition are decided at run-time.

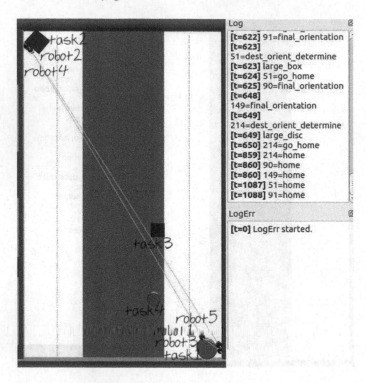

Fig. 4. Robots drop the obstacles on a side of the road

Table 5. Results of experiment 1 (road clearance environment)

Tasks	Task's initiator	Coalition	Cost
#1	r_3	$\{r_1, r_3, r_5\}$	230.00
#2	r_4	$\{r_2, r_4\}$	140.00
#3	r_2	$\{r_2, r_3\}$	125.00
#4	r_1	$\{r_1, r_2, r_4\}$	171.60

Table 6. Results of experiment 2 (road clearance environment)

Tasks	Task's initiator	Coalition	Cost
#1	r_1	$\{r_1, r_2, r_3, r_5\}$	275.00
#2	r_4	$\{r_1, r_4\}$	130.00
#3	r_2	$\{r_2, r_3\}$	121.00
#4	r_1	$\{r_1, r_4\}$	145.60

6   Conclusion

In this paper, we considered collaborative task execution in a dynamic environment, where the location and time of task arrival, the number of robots and location of the robots are not known in advance. A formal framework for cooperative task execution is provided. The distributed approach suggested in this paper considered quantitative representation of capability, and so it generalizes previous works that considered binary representation of capabilities.

A RoboCupRescue simulation environment is taken for implementing the distributed approach using ARGoS–a multi-robot simulation environment. Several experiments were carried out. The results are quite encouraging and it demonstrates how robots are executing the tasks and that different coalitions are formed in different simulation runs for the same task. Implementation of the distributed framework is quite challenging, and that is part of our future work.

Acknowledgments. The authors thank the anonymous reviewers of ICCSA 2021 for their valuable suggestions. The second author was in part supported by a research grant from Google.

References

1. Tadokoro, S., et al.: The robocup-rescue project: a robotic approach to the disaster mitigation problem. In: ICRA 2000, pp. 4089–4094 (2000)
2. Nath, A., Arun, A.R., Niyogi, R.: An approach for task execution in dynamic multirobot environment. In: Mitrovic, T., Xue, B., Li, X. (eds.) AI 2018. LNCS (LNAI), vol. 11320, pp. 71–76. Springer, Cham (2018). https://doi.org/10.1007/978-3-030-03991-2_7
3. Nath, A., Arun, A.R., Niyogi, R.: A distributed approach for road clearance with multi-robot in urban search and rescue environment. Int. J. Intell. Robot. Appl. **3**(4), 392–406 (2019). https://doi.org/10.1007/s41315-019-00111-5
4. Nath, A., Arun, A.R., Niyogi, R.: DMTF: a distributed algorithm for multi-team formation. In: ICAART 2020, vol. 1, pp. 152–160 (2020)
5. Nath, A., Arun, A.R., Niyogi, R.: A distributed approach for autonomous cooperative transportation in a dynamic multi-robot environment. In: SAC 2020, pp. 792–799 (2020)
6. Vig, L., Adams, J.A.: Multi-robot coalition formation. IEEE Trans. Rob. **22**(4), 637–649 (2006)
7. Pinciroli, C., et al.: ARGoS: a modular, parallel, multi-engine simulator for multi-robot systems. Swarm Intell. **6**(4), 271–295 (2012)
8. Rohmer, E., Singh, S.P., Freese, M.: V-REP: a versatile and scalable robot simulation framework. In: IROS 2013, pp. 1321–1326 (2013)
9. Sokolov, M., Lavrenov, R., Gabdullin, A., Afanasyev, I., Magid, E.: 3D modelling and simulation of a crawler robot in ROS/Gazebo. In: Proceedings of the 4th International Conference on Control, Mechatronics and Automation, pp. 61–65 (2016)
10. Agmon, N., Stone, P.: Leading ad hoc agents in joint action settings with multiple teammates. In: AAMAS 2012, pp. 341–348 (2012)

11. Gaston, M.E., DesJardins, M.: Agent-organized networks for dynamic team formation. In: AAMAS 2005, pp. 230–237 (2005)
12. Hemapala, M., Belotti, V., Michelini, R., Razzoli, R.: Humanitarian demining: path planning and remote robotic sweeping. Ind. Robot Int. J. **36**(2), 146–156 (2009)
13. Okimoto, T., Ribeiro, T., Bouchabou, D., Inoue, K.: Mission oriented robust multi-team formation and its application to robot rescue simulation. In: IJCAI 2016, pp. 454–460 (2016)
14. Lappas, T., Liu, K., Terzi, E.: Finding a team of experts in social networks. In: SIGKDD 2009, pp. 467–476 (2009)
15. Abdallah, S., Lesser, V.: Organization-based cooperative coalition formation. In: International Conference on Intelligent Agent Technology, pp. 162–168 (2004)
16. Coviello, L., Franceschetti, M.: Distributed team formation in multi-agent systems: stability and approximation. In: CDC 2012, pp. 2755–2760 (2012)
17. Tošić, P.T., Agha, G.A.: Maximal clique based distributed coalition formation for task allocation in large-scale multi-agent systems. In: International Workshop on Massively Multiagent Systems, pp. 104–120 (2004)
18. Gunn, T., Anderson, J.: Dynamic heterogeneous team formation for robotic urban search and rescue. J. Comput. Syst. Sci. **81**(3), 553–567 (2015)
19. Gerkey, B.P., Mataric, M.J.: Sold!: auction methods for multirobot coordination. IEEE Trans. Robot. Autom. **18**(5), 758–768 (2002)
20. Kong, Y., Zhang, M., Ye, D.: An auction-based approach for group task allocation in an open network environment. Comput. J. **59**(3), 403–422 (2010)

Parsing Tools for Italian
Phraseological Units

Alfredo Milani[1] ⓘ, Valentina Franzoni[1](✉) ⓘ, and Giulio Biondi[2](✉) ⓘ

[1] University of Perugia, Department of Mathematics and Computer Science,
06123 Perugia, Italy
alfredo.milani@ieee.org, valentina.franzoni@dmi.unipg.it
[2] University of Florence, Department of Mathematics and Computer Science,
50134 Florence, Italy
giulio.biondi@unifi.it

Abstract. Phraseological complexity plays a critical role in assessing the language competence level necessary to understand or produce text by a language learner and automated tools supporting international certifications for second languages. Appropriate syntactic-based parsing tools for pos/tagging texts are required to efficiently and correctly identify the components of phraseological units to apply computational and corpus-based measures. In this paper, we consider some of the main syntactic parsing tools publicly available for the Italian language and compare them in the framework of a project aiming at characterizing the phraseological complexity of a corpus produced by learners of Italian as a second language.

Keywords: Phraseological complexity · Corpus-based measures · PoS tagging · Parsing tools

1 Introduction

A single, widely accepted definition of phraseological complexity for second language learning research is not yet available in the literature. Attempts [2,15] to define the theoretical aspects of complexity and its measurement draw on the definition given by Rescher in [20]: *a matter of the number and variety of an item's constituent elements and of the elaborateness of their interrelational structure'* and share the view that it can be evaluated across various language domains (including syntax, lexis, and morphology). Subsequent studies [17,18] emphasized the importance of phraseological complexity in assessing the level of language proficiency required to understand or produce a text by a second language learner, particularly at the intermediate/advanced level. The same issue applies to automated text analysis systems for international second language (L2) certifications. There is therefore a call for a definition of appropriate measures of phraseological complexity because existing measures for the quantification of the linguistic complexity of a text are mostly based on lexical diversity

© Springer Nature Switzerland AG 2021
O. Gervasi et al. (Eds.): ICCSA 2021, LNCS 12955, pp. 427–435, 2021.
https://doi.org/10.1007/978-3-030-87007-2_30

[8], e.g., Advanced Guiraud [5] and MTLD [11], and syntactic complexity, e.g., Mean Length of Utterance (MLU) [1] and the amount of subordination per multiclausal unit [19]. Such measures, however, are not capable of recognizing the complex relations between words that frequently co-occur in combinations [6,7], often modifying their meaning and specialization. In [18], the use of Pointwise Mutual Information (PMI) [3] is proposed. The availability of appropriate Natural Language Processing (NLP) parsing software to efficiently and correctly identify components of phraseological units, e.g., by performing part-of-speech tagging, is paramount for any subsequent analysis such as the application of computational and corpus-based measures. Because of the peculiarities of each language, tools for Natural Language Processing must be trained on specific text corpora to identify common patterns, word relationships, and, in general, features that define a language. Most of the NLP research has been conducted on the English language, and the same happens in particular for L2 complexity. Thus, there is much wider availability of resources for English than for other languages; however, the increasing amount of digitalized corpora in other languages is driving the development of language-specific tools. In this paper, we consider some of the main syntactic parsing tools publicly available for the Italian language and proceed to a systematic comparison, in the framework of a project aiming at characterizing the phraseological complexity of a corpus produced by learners of Italian as a second language.

Section 2 explores tools for Natural Language Processing for the Italian language; Sect. 3 proceeds to their comparison; in Sect. 4 conclusions are drawn.

2   NLP Tools for Italian Language

2.1   UDPipe

UDPipe (Universal Dependencies Pipe) [25] is an open-source trainable pipeline for tokenization, tagging, lemmatization, and dependency parsing of CoNLL-U files, developed by Milan Straka at the Institute of Formal and Applied Linguistics, Faculty of Mathematics and Physics of Charles University, Czech Republic. UDPipe is language-agnostic and can be trained given annotated data in CoNLL-U format, a standard format used to annotate data at word/token and sentence level. CoNLL-U is the standard format of the Universal Dependencies project [14], which aims at providing annotated treebanks for several languages to facilitate the development of multilingual tools and cross-language learning. To date, over 200 treebanks in more than 100 languages have been published; for the Italian language, 7 treebanks are available, i.e. *ISDT, PUD, ParTUT, PostWITA, TWITTIRO, VIT, Valico.* Italian-ISDT is the most extensive, featuring 14167 sentences and nearly 280k tokens; comprehensive statistics on the text corpora used to create the different treebanks are available at [9]. UDPipe is available in three versions, at different development stages and using different techniques:

UDPipe 1 [23] includes modules to perform tokenization, tagging, lemmatization, and dependency parsing of CoNLL-U files. It is available in different languages, i.e. C++, Python, Perl, Java, C#, R, and as a web service.

UDPipe 2 [22] is a Python-only prototype, which retains the functionalities of UDPipe 1, except for tokenization. UDPipe 2, unlike the previous version, makes use of Deep Learning techniques; on the one hand, this led to an increase in the computational power requirements, balanced by a great improvement (40%–50%) in morphosyntactic analysis performance. Models are available for various languages, including Italian. UDPipe 2 achieved some remarkable results in competitions, including achieving first place in the *CoNLL 2018 Shared Task: Multilingual Parsing from Raw Text to Universal Dependencies* [24] and the EvaLatin 2020 Evaluation Campaign [21], with a specific model trained for the task.

UDPipe 3 is still under early development and will feature C++, Python, and other languages bindings. TensorFlow is chosen as the Deep Learning backend; along with morphosyntactic analysis tools, which were already available in the previous versions, additional modules, e.g. *Entity Linking* and *Named Entity Resolution*, are planned.

2.2 TINT

The Italian NLP Tool (TINT) [16] is an open-source Java-Based NLP pipeline focused on the Italian language, developed at Fondazione Bruno Kessler (FBK), Trento, Italy. It is based on the popular CoreNLP tool developed by the University of Stanford [10], which itself supports six languages, i.e. Arabic, Chinese, English, French, German, and Spanish. Tint has been used as a pre-processing tool for several NLP tasks, e.g. Hate Speech Detection [4], automatic text difficulty rating [12,13].

2.3 SpaCy

SpaCy is an open-source library for advanced NLP, written in Python, currently in its 3.0 version. It features multi-language support, pre-trained models, and word embeddings, and allows the usage of custom models in PyTorch, Tensorflow, and other Deep Learning frameworks. At the time of writing, three pipelines are provided for Italian language, i.e. *it_core_news_sm*, *it_core_news_md*, and *it_core_news_lg*.

3   Experimental Comparison

In this section, we perform a comparison among the three analyzed tools for Natural Language Processing of Italian as a second language.

3.1 Code and License

All the compared tools for Natural Language Processing are open source and currently actively maintained. The copyright license varies as follows:

- UDPipe is available under the Mozilla Public License (MPL) 2.0
- TINT is available under the GNU General Public License (GPL) 3.0
- SpaCy is available under the MIT License.

3.2 Comparison of General Functionalities

In Table 1 a comparison of the general functionalities available in the considered tools for Natural Language Processing is presented. We can see that TINT and SpaCy offer all the complete set of considered functionalities, while for UDPipe functionalities are distributed in different versions of the software and some tasks are under development for futures release.

Table 1. Functionalities Available in UDPipe, TINT, SpaCy

Functionalities	UDPipe	TINT	SpaCy
tokenisation	YES (v1)	YES	YES
sentence segmentation	YES(v1, v2)	YES	YES
morphological analysis	YES(v1, v2)	YES	YES
lemmatisation	YES (v2)	YES	YES
named entity recognition	NO (in development, v3)	YES	YES
part-of-speech tagging	YES (v2)	YES	YES
entity linking	NO (in development, v3)	YES	YES

3.3 Reference Text for Experiments

We consider, as a sample to compare the tool capabilities and quality of the following text which is taken by a corpus of subjects for exams on Italian as L2. Original text: *Se guardiamo la TV, se leggiamo un giornale o navighiamo in internet, ci vengono continuamente proposte pubblicità di vari prodotti. (sentence 1) La pubblicità è sempre più invadente, ci dà indicazioni su cosa mangiare e bere, su cosa fare quando siamo con gli amici, su quali vacanze preferire, su come vestirci. (sentence 2) Ognuno di noi dovrebbe essere in grado di non farsi condizionare da tutti questi messaggi che cercano di convincerci a comprare e scegliere prodotti commerciali. (sentence 3) Riferisca la Sua opinione a riguardo, spiegando quale influenza ha su di Lei la pubblicità e quale importanza le attribuisce. (sentence 4)*

For the sake of clarity in the figures and the tables, we will focus on sentence 1.

3.4 Dependency Threes and Parsing Information

All the considered tools have rendering functions that visualize the returned syntactic dependency tree associate with sentence processing. Figure 1 shows UDPipe tree while in Fig. 2 SpaCy's and TINT's trees are shown.

UDPipe trees are more user friendly than others because they use a layout which tries giving a visual global picture of the dependency structure. In the

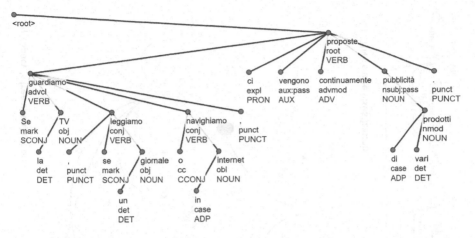

Fig. 1. Dependency tree of sentence 1 by UDPipe2 with *ISDT* treebank

case of TINT and SpaCy, the single line distribution of tokens is more difficult to understand the whole structure. On the other hand, the elements of the other trees are more informative. For instance, UDPipe shows dependency types in the dependant nodes, while both TINT and SpaCy show dependency types as labels overlapping the oriented arcs toward the depending node. TINT also uses colors to provide a glimpse of the POS role of the tokens. Usability of tree visalization is not relevant for automated tasks, where the three is not used by a human but automatically navigated.

The default output of the tools is textual, both for UDPipe and SpaCy, while in the case of TINT the output is provided in JSON format. In the tables in Fig. 3 the different outputs are shown. It is worth noting that UDPipe uses the number of text lines as pointers to define the dependencies, and is rich in information in the nodes (lemma, pos, tags, and elaborate description of mood and verbal form), while SpaCy defaults are very cheap in this regard. The structure of JSON, on the other hand, allows self-describing and easy navigation of the parsing tree, and additional JSON structures for additional information, where the dependency tree description is separated from the node description.

Regarding the quality of parsing, SpaCy fails to correctly analyze Italian sentences in many cases, even in the richer configuration for the Italian language, i.e. using the language package *it_core_news_lg*. For example, the dependency trees and the generated outputs (see Fig. 1, Fig. 2, and Fig. 3) show that even in the case of the sample text, SpaCy is not able to resolve the ambiguity of part of sentence 1. In the expression "vengono continuamente proposte", the word "proposte" is correctly interpreted by UDPipe and TINT as a part of the verbal form where is a verb (VERB V) in past tense form, in English *proposed*, associated with the auxiliary verb "vengono" (AUX V), while SpaCy recognizes "proposte" as nominal subject, in English *proposals*, composed with another noun "pubblicità", i.e. *advertising*. Similar problems of inaccurate parsing of

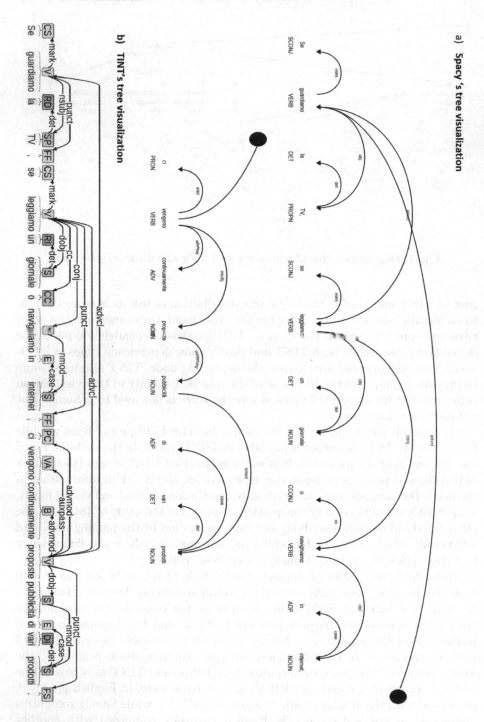

Fig. 2. Dependency tree of sentence 1 by (a) SpaCy *it_core_news_lg* trained pipeline, and (b) TINT

TINT JSON		

{ "dep": "auxpass",
  "governor": 18,
  "governorGloss": "proposte",
  "dependent": 16,
  "dependentGloss": **"vengono"**
},
{"index": 16,
  "word": "vengono",
  "originalText": "vengono",
  "lemma": "venire",
  "characterOffsetBegin": 73,
  "characterOffsetEnd": 80,
  "pos": **"VA"**,
"full_morpho": "vengono
venire+v+indic+pres+nil+3+plur"...}
	{ "dep": "advmod",
	  "governor": 18,
	  "governorGloss": "proposte",
	  "dependent": 17,
	  "dependentGloss":**"continuamente"**
	},
	{"index": 17,
	  "word": "continuamente",
	  "originalText":"continuamente"
	  "lemma": "continuamente",
	  "characterOffsetBegin": 81,
	  "characterOffsetEnd": 94,
	  "pos": **"B"**,
	"full_morpho": "continuamente
	continuamente+adv"...}
		{ "index": 18,
		  "word": **"proposte"**,
		  "originalText": "proposte",
		  "lemma": "proporre",
		  "characterOffsetBegin": 95,
		  "characterOffsetEnd": 103,
		  "pos": **"V"**,
		  "full_morpho": "proposte
		proporre+v+part+pass+f+nil+p
		lur proposta+n+f+plur"
		
		...}

UDPipe 2								
16	**vengono**	venire	**AUX**	**VA**				
	Mood=Ind|Number=Plur|Person=3|Tense=Pres|VerbForm=Fin				18	aux:pass		_
	TokenRange=73:80							
17	**continuamente**	continuamente	**ADV**	**B**	_		18	advmod	_
	TokenRange=81:94							
18	**proposte**	proporre	**VERB**	**V**				
	Gender=Fem|Number=Plur|Tense=Past|VerbForm=Part				0	root		_
	TokenRange=95:103							

Spacy				
text	*lemma*	*pos*	*tag*	*dep*
vengono	venire	VERB	V	ROOT
continuamente	continuamente	ADV	B	advmod
proposte	proposta	NOUN	S	nsubj

Fig. 3. Parsing output of TINT, UDPipe and SpaCy

SpaCy have been observed in several tests with texts from the mentioned corpus, while the accuracy of UDPipe and TINT is confirmed.

4   Conclusions

In this work, we analyzed the main available tools for NLP available for the Italian language, i.e. UDPipe, TINT, and SpaCy. Such tools are considered to be used for automatically performing the pre-processing tasks needed to further analyze texts Italian language, e.g. to assess the phraseological complexity of L2 language learner texts through the use of appropriate complexity measures. All three toolkits offer the basic NLP functions, e.g. tokenization, segmentation, morphological analysis, and lemmatization, while advanced features are currently offered by TINT and SpaCy only, and will be integrated into future releases of UDPipe. Concerning expressivity and usability, in automated tasks,

UDPipe and TINT default outputs are both usable. While the JSON format of TINT seems more portable and usable with other external software tools, UDPipe e SpaCy needs the explicit implementation of a portable format. Regarding quality and reliability, empirical tests done with a corpus of texts for assessing Italian L2 proficiency shows that TINT and UDPipe offer a better level for correctly accomplishing the NLP tasks.

Acknowledgements. This work is partially supported by the Italian Ministry of Research under PRIN Project "PHRAME" Grant n.20178XXKFY.

References

1. Brown, R.: A First Language: The Early Stages. Harvard U. Press, Oxford, England (1973)
2. Bulté, B., Housen, A.: Dimensions of L2 performance and proficiency: complexity, accuracy and fluency in SLA, chapter: defining and operationalising L2 complexity, pp. 21–46. JB (2012)
3. Church, K.W., Hanks, P.: Word association noms, Mutual information, and lexicography. In: Proceedings of the 27th Annual Conference of the Association for Computational Linguistics, vol. 16 no. 1, pp. 22–29 (1989). https://doi.org/10.3115/981623.981633
4. Corazza, M., Menini, S., Cabrio, E., Tonelli, S., Villata, S.: A multilingual evaluation for online hate speech detection. ACM Trans. Internet Technol. **20**(2) (2020). https://doi.org/10.1145/3377323
5. Daller, H., Van Hout, R., Treffers-D Aller, J.: Lexical richness in the spontaneous speech of bilinguals. Appl. Linguist. **24**, 197–222+267 (2003). https://doi.org/10.1093/applin/24.2.197
6. Franzoni, V., Li, Y., Milani, A.: Set semantic similarity for image prosthetic knowledge exchange. In: Misra, S., et al. (eds.) ICCSA 2019. LNCS, vol. 11624, pp. 513–525. Springer, Cham (2019). https://doi.org/10.1007/978-3-030-24311-1_37
7. Franzoni, V., Milani, A.: Semantic context extraction from collaborative networks. In: 19th IEEE International Conference on Computer Supported Cooperative Work in Design, CSCWD 2015, Calabria, Italy, May 6–8, 2015, pp. 131–136. IEEE (2015). https://doi.org/10.1109/CSCWD.2015.7230946
8. Franzoni, V., Milani, A.: Structural and semantic proximity in information networks. In: Gervasi, O., et al. (eds.) ICCSA 2017. LNCS, vol. 10404, pp. 651–666. Springer, Cham (2017). https://doi.org/10.1007/978-3-319-62392-4_47
9. https://universaldependencies.org/ : Universal dependencies: comparative statistics of italian treebanks (2021). https://universaldependencies.org/treebanks/it-comparison.html
10. Manning, C.D., Surdeanu, M., Bauer, J., Finkel, J., Bethard, S.J., McClosky, D.: The Stanford CoreNLP natural language processing toolkit. In: Association for Computational Linguistics (ACL) System Demonstrations, pp. 55–60 (2014)
11. McCarthy, P.M., Jarvis, S.: MTLD, vocd-D, and HD-D: a validation study of sophisticated approaches to lexical diversity assessment. Behav. Res. Methods **42**(2), 381–392 (2010). https://doi.org/10.3758/BRM.42.2.381
12. Menini, S., Tonelli, S., Gasperis, G.D., Vittorini, P.: Automated short answer grading: a simple solution for a difficult task. In: CLiC-it (2019)

13. Milani, A., Spina, S., Santucci, V., Piersanti, L., Simonetti, M., Biondi, G.: Text classification for Italian proficiency evaluation. In: Misra, S., et al. (eds.) ICCSA 2019. LNCS, vol. 11619, pp. 830–841. Springer, Cham (2019). https://doi.org/10.1007/978-3-030-24289-3_61

14. Nivre, J., et al.: Universal Dependencies v1: a multilingual treebank collection. In: Proceedings of the Tenth International Conference on Language Resources and Evaluation (LREC 2016), pp. 1659–1666. European Language Resources Association (ELRA), Portorož, Slovenia (May 2016)

15. Pallotti, G.: A simple view of linguistic complexity. Second Lang. Res. **31**(1), 117–134 (2015). https://doi.org/10.1177/0267658314536435

16. Palmero Aprosio, A., Moretti, G.: Italy goes to Stanford: a collection of CoreNLP modules for Italian. ArXiv e-prints (September 2016)

17. Paquot, M.: Phraseological competence: a missing component in university entrance language tests? insights from a study of efl learners' use of statistical collocations. Lang. Assess. Q. **15**(1), 29–43 (2018). https://doi.org/10.1080/15434303.2017.1405421

18. Paquot, M.: The phraseological dimension in interlanguage complexity research. Second Lang. Res. **35**(1), 121–145 (2019). https://doi.org/10.1177/0267658317694221

19. Polio, C.G.: Second language development in writing: measures of fluency, accuracy, and complexity. kate wolfe-quintero, shunji inagaki, and hae-young kim. honolulu: University of hawai'i press, 1998. pp. viii + 187. Stud. Second Lang. Acquisition **23**(3), 423–425 (2001). https://doi.org/10.1017/S0272263101263050

20. Rescher, N.: Complexity : a philosophical overview / Nicholas Rescher. Transaction Publishers New Brunswick, NJ (1998)

21. Sprugnoli, R., Passarotti, M., Cecchini, F.M., Pellegrini, M.: Overview of the EvaLatin 2020 evaluation campaign. In: Proceedings of LT4HALA 2020-1st Workshop on Language Technologies for Historical and Ancient Languages, pp. 105–110. European Language Resources Association (ELRA), Marseille, France (May 2020)

22. Straka, M.: UDPipe 2.0 prototype at CoNLL 2018 UD shared task. In: Proceedings of the CoNLL 2018 Shared Task: Multilingual Parsing from Raw Text to Universal Dependencies, pp. 197–207. Association for Computational Linguistics, Brussels, Belgium (October 2018). https://doi.org/10.18653/v1/K18-2020

23. Straka, M., Straková, J.: Tokenizing, pos tagging, lemmatizing and parsing ud 2.0 with udpipe. In: Proceedings of the CoNLL 2017 Shared Task: Multilingual Parsing from Raw Text to Universal Dependencies, pp. 88–99. Association for Computational Linguistics, Vancouver, Canada (August 2017)

24. Zeman, D., et al.: CoNLL 2018 shared task: multilingual parsing from raw text to universal dependencies. In: Proceedings of the CoNLL 2018 Shared Task: Multilingual Parsing from Raw Text to Universal Dependencies, pp. 1–21. Association for Computational Linguistics, Brussels, Belgium (October 2018). https://doi.org/10.18653/v1/K18-2001

25. About UDPipe. https://ufal.mff.cuni.cz/udpipe (July 2021)

Yeasts Automated Classification
with Extremely Randomized Forests

Valentina Franzoni[✉] ⓘ and Yana Kozak

Department of Mathematics and Computer Science, University of Perugia,
Perugia, Italy
valentina.franzoni@dmi.unipg.it, yana.kozak@studenti.unipg.it

Abstract. Several pathogenic yeast species are resistant to pharmaceutical agents and have evolved so quickly over time that often they cannot be stopped with antifungal treatments. In particular, Candida species can cause yeast infections in patients' blood or organs, and Candida outbreaks are particularly troublesome, often found in hospitals and healthcare facilities where people are most susceptible because of their weakened immune systems. Candida can live for weeks on walls and other surfaces, such as walls or furniture, becoming a major hidden danger. New, rapid, and reliable methods of classification and spread prevention are needed. In this preliminary work, we have considered off-the-shelf standard classifiers for yeast classification and applied them to Candida classification. Since performances of classifiers based on logistic regression, SVM, and Extremely Randomized Forests were not particularly remarkable, the possibility to improve their precision has been explored, applying different techniques of feature extraction and feature selection. Eight different Candida strains have been analyzed and systematically tested for classification. The experimental results show that classification with Extremely Random Forests and feature extraction can achieve promising results with the best precision in the automatic classification of candida yeasts, thus being a powerful tool for the prevention and treatment of candida yeasts outbreaks.

Keywords: Candida · Machine learning · Bioinformatics · Medical informatics · Yeast classification · Supervised classification

1 Introduction

The study of the classification of life forms is systematic in biology and pharmacology and is generally equivalent to the development of a taxonomy. For centuries, taxonomy referred to the description of various life forms and their components. Despite the usefulness of such a structure, the interrelation of life

Conceptualization and methodology, V.F., Y.K.; software planning and programming, Y.K.; results validation, V.F.; formal analysis, V.F.; original draft preparation, review and editing, V.F.; data visualization, Y.K.; supervision and funding acquisition, V.F.

O. Gervasi et al. (Eds.): ICCSA 2021, LNCS 12955, pp. 436–447, 2021.
https://doi.org/10.1007/978-3-030-87007-2_31

forms was poorly understood. Following the rise of Darwinism, systematic biology began to develop and replace what was simply a matter of nomenclature born out of Aristotle's understanding of the significance of animate life forms. Today, however, many biologists have entered the molecular realm seeking to understand biochemical changes at the molecular level, and this approach led to the evolution of the classification of life forms toward an elucidation of the mechanism of evolution, and the function of such organisms. Today, by feeding algorithms with input from classification features, this process can be automated with greater accuracy and speed. In this study, we focus on the *Candida* yeast.

Saccharomyces yeasts of the genus Candida comprise over 150 species. Many of the Candida species are found on the skin and mucous membranes of animals and are the most common cause of fungal infections worldwide. Many species are harmless commensals or endosymbionts of hosts, including humans; however, when mucosal barriers are disrupted or the immune system is compromised, they can invade and cause diseases, known as opportunistic infections. The worst situation is when such infection outbreaks happen in hospitals and healthcare facilities, where patients with an already compromised immune system can have dangerous side effects including mortality [9], even from easily tractable infections [14,15].

Candida classification [3]has been refined and diversified over the years, culminating in the current basic classification into eight main strains: *Candida Albicans* (CA), *Candida dubliniensis* (CD), *Candida glabrata* (CG), *Candida krusei* (CK), *Candida lusitaniae* (CL), *Candida Orthopsilosis* (CO), *Candida parapsilosis* (CP), and *Candida tropicalis* (CT). Candida exhibits such mutability and adaptability that makes it truly dangerous and highly pathogenic; an invasive capability that applies even to synthetic materials, e.g., used in prosthetics, replacement of internal organs, catheters.

Candida Albicans (CA) spreads ubiquitously. *Blastospores* and *mycelia* are found in tissues. To this day there is debate as to which form is invasive, depending on the type of acetosis and fluid pollution of colonized tissues. A further criterion of differentiation is the division into serotypes A, B and C. In Europe, serotype A is the most diffuse and, in general, CA causes the vast majority of candida mycoses, with a recent further shift of the pathogen spectrum. CA has the greatest adherence to the mucosa compared to other candida types, the fungus can actively penetrate the epithelium with the help of exoenzymes, where the host cell undergoes lysis by plasma membrane enzymes, in particular proteolytic and lipolytic enzymes. The oral variation of CA is particularly well known as a temporary side effect of chemotherapy for the treatment of cancer and lymphomas.

Candida Glabrata (CG) (former name: Torulopsis glabrata) rarely occurs in culture with other fungi and after CA is the most frequent pathogen of fungal infections of the urinary tract. It does not form pseudomycelia and has antigenic commonality with CA. The germ is often found as a cause of vaginal mycoses.

Candida Krusei (CK) is a weedy yeast involved in chocolate production. CK is a nosocomial emerging fungal pathogen found primarily in the immune-compromised patients and those with hematologic cancers. It has natural resistance to standard antifungal agents, e.g., fluconazole. CK is isolated from saliva, nails, bronchi, feces, and vagina. It is present in endocarditis and causes diarrhea in children. Infections with this fungus have increased in recent years.

Candida Tropicalis (CT) is less pathogenic than CA, forms hyphae and pseudophae, and requires more oxygen. The pathogen can proliferate on mucous membranes without any particular signs of disease being observed. However, it also appears as a pathogen of endocarditis and fungal sepsis. CT is also found in mixed cultures with CA, where is extremely resistant to treatment.

Candida Parapsilosis (CP) (synonymous with C. parakrusei) is found in onychomycosis and dermatomycosis, rarely on mucous membranes, identified as a pathogen of fungal endocarditis.

Candida Orthopsilosis (CO) is a human fungal pathogen belonging to the CP. Species complex. CO annotated genome harbors three putative agglutinin-like sequence (ALS) genes.

Similar or same-appearing strains of Candida can give rise to wide variation depending on the geographic area, organic environment, and conditions. Various types of Candida derived from a single ancestor are capable of genetically mutating to become different strains depending on the need for parasitism occurring in a particular condition, and the intoxicants and acidosis conditions of the intracellular and extracellular medium or fluid.

This study aims at an automated classification of candida strains as they might be identified by a human professional based on specific characteristics. The utility is evident in the areas of diagnosis, pharmacology, both for prevention and for treatment. Rapid and accurate identification of pathogenic yeast species is thus critical for clinical diagnosis because of the high level of induced mortality and morbidity, even after antifungal therapy. To this end, new rapid, high-throughput, and reliable identification methods are needed.

In the broad scenario of classification algorithms, we proceeded in two phases. In the first phase, we exploited several preliminary tests with different algorithms, evaluating and comparing the advantages and disadvantages of each algorithm. The advantages can include also interpretability characteristics, thus it is not trivial that the algorithm with the apparent best performance would be the best for the specialized application in health sciences. In the second phase, we chose to test random trees and extremely random forests in-depth, having the advantage to provide readable classification processes which can be analyzed for evaluation. The experimental results show that classification with Extremely Random Forests can achieve promising results in the automatic classification of candida yeasts, thus being a powerful tool for the prevention and treatment of candida yeasts outbreaks.

In Sect. 2, the original data set preprocessing and preliminary evaluation of basic classifiers is presented. In Sects. 3 and 4, the setup and choice of data, features, and evaluation metrics are explained. In Sects. 6 and 7, results are discussed and conclusions are proposed, including limits of the preliminary work to be outperformed in future studies.

2   Original Yeast Data Set

We analyze a collection of eight different strains, belonging to opportunistic species of the genus Candida isolated from two Italian hospitals (i.e., Pisa and Udine city hospitals) and included in the *Cemin Microbial Collection* of the Microbial Genetics and Phylogenesis Laboratory of Cemin, a center of excellence on nanostructured innovative materials for chemical, physical and biomedical applications based in the Italian University of Perugia.

Genomic DNA was extracted as indicated by Cardinali et al. [1,2] using *Fourier-transform infrared spectroscopy* (FTIR) [8,12]. FTIR is a technique based on the vibration of molecular forms (e.g., fatty acids, nucleic acids, proteins) that make up a microorganism in response to the stress received by infrared (IR) light at specific wavelengths. The data set includes approximately 1600 descriptors of Candida strains, with the related class label obtained by manual analysis of FTIR data on Candida samples. In FTIR, IR radiations strike the microorganism sample under study and its molecular components (e.g., fatty acids, nucleic acids, proteins). Depending on the wavelength of radiation from which samples are hit, the sample may respond by vibrating and thus originating visible spectra (i.e., our descriptors) [5]. Not all wavelengths are effective with all macromolecules, so we will not have detectable signals for all wavelengths used. The values recorded for the descriptors are related to absorbances, expressed in pure numbers (i.e., without units of measurement, see Table). The range of wavelengths between which the descriptors vary is 4000–400 cm^{-1}. Computerized classification allows studying in a rapid, high-throughput way the features obtained by the FTIR technique, and classify samples in an automated way. The researcher can then supervise the classification and proceed directly to further analysis, e.g. the yeasts phylogenetics, the process of branching lineages in the evolution of life, which reconstruction is fundamental to systematics and involved with reconstructing evolutionary kinship relationships of taxonomic groups of organisms at a methodical level.

3   Data Preprocessing and Preliminary Experiments

3.1   Data Preprocessing

The Candida Albicans (CA) class has been reduced for balancing aims from the starting data set, and the randomly removed samples have been used to test each of the classifiers in the preliminary experimental phase, to understand and evaluate the performance of basic classifiers.

A few other samples have been excluded because belonging to additional underrepresented strains, i.e. MG, CL, and CU. In the original data set three identical samplings have been also found (i.e. numbers 204, 205, and 206 of the original data set), and removed. After the preprocessing phase, the data set consists of strains CA, CG, CO, CP, and CT for a total of 201 samples. The cleaned and balanced data set is fed as input to the preliminary experimental phase to evaluate the performance of basic classifiers.

3.2   Preliminary Experiments

Three state-of-the-art classifiers have been considered for our preliminary experiments: *Logistic Regression, Support Vector Machines (SVM)* and *Extremely Randomized Trees*. In the version available in the *skearn* package, the classifiers have been run on the data set with all the 1660 features, and operating on an 80%-20% random split between the training set and test set, uniformly balancing the split over the classes.

3.3   Logistic Regression

Logistic Regression (LR) [10] is a machine learning technique allowing to find optimal data points in classification problems. The model, used when the value to be classified is categorical, takes the input features and attempts to predict a numerical value. The regression model touts the specifications that best fit the information in the experimented data set.

3.4   Support Vector Machines (SVM)

Support Vector Machines [13] are a particular machine learning model used in classification and regression, it builds a series of hyperplanes in n-dimensional space which aim to reach a suitable separation between classes, i.e. maximizing the functional margin, the distance from data of other classes, and minimize the classification error. A basic concept in SVM is the kernel, linear separation of classes can be obtained directly or with the so-called 'kernel trick' where non-separable data are mapped, by a problem specific kernel function, in a higher-dimensional space, and hyperplanes in that space can discriminate classes not separable in the original data space.

3.5   Extremely Randomized Forests

Random Forest classification models [11] are characterized by a training phase in which many decision trees are built and splitting features are selected with criteria of bagging and a random component [4]. The classification task is operated by all the forest trees and the output class is decided by votes the majority of the trees. In the extremely randomized forests [7]b the process of randomization is strongly enhanced in splitting a tree node, at attribute and cut-point level, as randomization grows the generated tree structure tends to be independent of the output of the training samples. One of the main advantages of extreme randomization is computational efficiency, while accuracy needs to be kept under control by appropriate tuning of randomization parameters.

3.6 Classifiers Parameters Settings

The setting of parameters for each classifier has been tuned after preliminary trials and maintained unchanged throughout further phases of the experiments.

Logistics Regression Parameters. The parameters chosen for the logistic regression classifier are characterized by the *OvR* multiclass specifier, which uses the One-vs-All (OvA, i.e. One-vs-Rest) scheme. Class weight has been set to *balanced*, where values of y are used to automatically adjust weights inversely proportional to class frequencies in the input data; *lbgfs* is the solver to be used in the optimization problem; and *max_iter* is the maximum number of iterations for the solver to converge, set for our case to 8000.

SVM Parameters. For Support Vector Machines, a linear kernel is in our case the best performant, with a random state set to 0 to ensure reproducibility.

Extremely Random Forests Parameters. In the case of Extremely Random Forests the *estimators* parameter, i.e. the number of trees inside the forest, has been set to 200 (which was the best performing size, after trying the increasing sequence 50, 100, 150, 200, 250), as criterion measuring the quality of the split the *gini impurity* has been chosen, finally, *random state* has been set to an integer, to obtain a deterministic behavior during fitting and to assure the reproducibility of the classifier.

3.7 Preliminary Results

The results of the preliminary experiments of basic classifiers, with the described settings and tested on an 80%–20% split are shown in Table 1, where best results are highlighted in **bold** case and worst in *italic* case.

Preliminary results with basic classifiers and preprocessed data are not particularly satisfactory. While the average precision is moderately acceptable, for both SVM and LR is greater than 0.92, on the other hand, the performance is not distributed uniformly among the Candida classes. CO and CP are, in fact, still misclassified in about 15% of the cases.

4 Features and Data Set Performances

To improve the performances of classifiers, we explore the application of techniques that change the characteristics of the data set by *feature selection* i.e., reducing the number of features and the noise of the data by focusing on the most significant ones, or by *feature extraction* i.e., improving the effectiveness of features in classification, by generating new features which are a function of existing ones.

4.1   Feature Selection Using Randomized Trees

A successful technique for assessing the importance of features for selection is based on Extremely Random Trees. Since in our preliminary experiments we obtained an 80% accuracy on the data set, the use of this technique is, therefore, a good and promising starting point in terms of reusing the information that our classifier returns on features that proved to be important, thus improving the results for this specialized classification task. This technique is built on the idea of estimating the relative relevance of features for each strain, observing how they are used in nodes of a decision tree. More specifically, if the feature is used in a low-depth node, it is considered more important because it contributes to decisions on a larger fraction of samples, i.e. on their branches.

The estimation of the predictive ability of each feature is averaged over several randomized trees. To reduce the variance of this estimate, the technique of *Min Decrease in Impurity* (MDI) is used, which consists of averaging the estimate over several random trees.

To exclude a major bias in the experiments, we need to avoid using the test set to evaluate the importance of the features. Therefore, for each split data set, the Extremely Randomized Forest feature selection technique is first applied to the training set only; the projection of the training data on the selected features is then finally used to train the different classifiers.

4.2   Feature Extraction Using Principal Component Analysis

Feature extraction has been implemented with the Principal Component Analysis (PCA) algorithm. PCA is a dimensional reduction technique grouping and combining features to create new relevant ones. After several experiments, the PCA technique generated 25 features out of the original 1660. This choice is an accommodation amidst a likely smaller number of features, yet powerful enough to guarantee better performance. With 25 features, the models performed better than with 20, 15, 10, while the performance remained identical for 30 and 35 features.

Table 1. Results of preliminary experiments: basic classifiers, complete set of 1600 features

Classifier	Avg Precision	Avg Accuracy	Avg Recall	Best (Class)	Worst (Class)
LR	0.924	0.925	**0.913**	**0.976 (CG)**	0.857 (CO)
SVM	**0.928**	**0.930**	0.913	0.970 (CG)	0.855 (CP)
ERF	*0.853*	*0.835*	*0.818*	*0.931 (CT)*	*0.763 (CA)*

LR = Logistic Regression, SVM = Support Vector Machine, ERF = Extremely Randomized Forests, Best/Worst Precision Class.

5   Evaluation Metrics

Because the division into training and testing sets is randomized, we should avoid performance metrics that may be biased by a random factor: this objective can be achieved using different techniques. The *Stratification* technique has been implemented: although randomized, the division is accomplished by a stratification, which ensures that the distribution is always proportional, i.e., it maintains the percentage of samples for each class, which is the same for both the training and testing sets. In each subdivision, 80% of the originally random samples are assigned to the training set and the remaining 20% to the test set.

One hundred random subdivisions were generated for each combination of *[algorithm/data set/feature selection/feature extraction]*. Classifiers were trained and tested, and their performances were averaged over the validation scores [6]. The overall average *recall, precision, accuracy, F1* scores were calculated both globally and for each class individually, to allow a more detailed performance analysis.

6   Experiments and Results

As previously described, systematic experiments have been conducted on each combination of classifier, feature extraction, or feature selection technique, with the classifiers parameter settings ascertained in the preliminary experiment. A total of six classifiers, including the basic versions, have been run:

- Logistic Regression basic
- Logistic Regression with Feature Selection
- Logistic Regression with Feature Extraction
- Support Vector Machine basic
- Support Vector Machine with Feature Selection
- Support Vector Machine with Feature Extraction
- Extremely Randomized Forests basic
- Extremely Randomized Forests with Feature Selection
- Extremely Randomized Forests with Feature Extraction.

A 100 folds random data splits have been created for each classifier and performance metrics described in Sect. 5 have been collected and averaged.

6.1   Results

The performance metrics obtained in experiments are shown in Tables 2, 3 and 4 where the best results are highlighted.

Table 2 illustrates the recall of each algorithm for each class, we notice that recall of CP is generally not very satisfactory for each algorithm, even in the feature selection or feature selection version. CA and CT recall are also problems with the basic version of Extremely Randomized Forests where the feature

Table 2. Average recall per class

Classifier	Average recall				
	CA	CG	CO	CP	CT
LR	0.913	0.972	0.905	0.792	0.981
LR_FS	0.935	0.974	0.926	0.820	**0.992**
LR_FE	0.893	0.954	0.851	0.688	0.981
SVM	0.946	0.967	0.909	0.756	0.990
SVM_FS	0.968	**0.993**	0.917	**0.826**	0.982
SVM_FE	0.951	0.957	0.877	0.700	0.987
ERF	0.777	0.952	0.914	0.612	0.836
ERF_FS	0.815	0.968	0.897	0.618	0.846
ERF_FE	**0.969**	0.944	**0.948**	0.806	0.967

LR = Logistic Regression, SVM = Support Vector Machine, ERF = Extremely Randomized Forests, _FS = plus feature selection, _FE = plus feature extraction.

extraction version dramatically improves the recall over 0.967. The average precision per class is shown in Table 0, all classifiers have some difficulty with CO and CP, the precision of basic classifiers starting below 0.868 and improving with *SVM plus feature selection* and *ERF plus feature extraction*, where the best improvement is reached by the latter with a remarkable 0.996 precision of CO compared to a 0.868 of its basic version. A feature-powered version seems not to have a uniform increasing effect in the per-class performance of logistic regression, in some cases worse, e.g., CO and CP, while in others, CA and CG, reach the best performances.

Table 3. Average precision per class

Classifier	Avg Precision			Avg Recall	Avg Precision
	CA	CG	CO	CP	CT
LR	0.951	0.976	0.867	0.857	0.971
LR_FS	**0.969**	**0.980**	0.891	0.884	0.982
LR_FE	0.911	0.948	0.835	0.793	0.962
SVM	0.953	0.970	0.874	0.855	**0.988**
SVM_FS	0.966	0.977	0.900	0.927	0.985
SVM_FE	0.937	0.972	0.854	0.810	0.987
ERF	0.763	0.875	0.828	0.868	0.931
ERF_FS	0.788	0.888	0.836	0.896	0.931
ERF_FE	0.935	0.952	**0.904**	**0.996**	0.97

LR = Logistic Regression, SVM = Support Vector Machine, ERF = Extremely Randomized Forests, _FS = plus feature selection, _FE = plus feature extraction.

Table 4. Average f1-score per class

Classifier	Avg f1-score				
	CA	CG	CO	CP	CT
LR	0.928	0.972	0.878	0.807	0.974
LR_FS	0.949	0.976	0.901	0.834	−0.986
LR_FE	0.896	0.949	0.834	0.719	0.869
SVM	0.947	0.967	0.886	0.782	**0.988**
SVM_FS	**0.965**	**0.985**	0.904	0.859	0.982
SVM_FE	0.941	0.962	0.856	0.728	0.985
ERF	0.762	0.908	0.861	0.685	0.873
ERF_FS	0.793	0.923	0.858	0.706	0.879
ERF_FE	0.949	0.945	**0.920**	**0.875**	0.966

LR = Logistic Regression, SVM = Support Vector Machine, ERF = Extremely Randomized Forests, _FS = plus feature selection, _FE = plus feature extraction.

Best per-class F1-score, see Tables 2, 3 and 4 is again obtained by *SVM plus feature selection* and *ERF plus feature extraction*, this latter shows the greatest increment and best values for CO and CP, while maintaining good performances, from 0.945 and more, for all other classes CA, CG, CP. Since F1-score takes into account both precision and recall, the performance of *ERF plus feature extraction* seems to prevail on the other classifiers.

The comparison of all classifier average performances compared to avg-precision, avg- recall, and avg-f1-score, without regard of any particular class, is shown in Table 5.

SVM in all the three versions (*basic, SVM plus feature extraction, SVM plus feature selection*) provide an average general performance greater of 90% in all

Table 5. Comparisons of average metrics per classifier

Classifier	Average accuracy	Average recall	Average precision	Average f1-score
LR	0.925	0.913	0.923	0.912
LR_FS	0.940	0.930	0.941	0.929
LR_FE	0.893	0.874	0.890	0.873
SVM	0.930	0.913	0.928	0.914
SVM_FS	**0.950**	**0.937**	0.951	**0.939**
SVM_FE	0.915	0.894	0.912	0.894
ERF	0.835	0.818	0.853	0.820
ERF_FS	0.847	0.829	0.868	0.832
ERF_FE	0.939	0.927	**0.952**	0.931

LR = Logistic Regression, SVM = Support Vector Machine, ERF = Extremely Randomized Forests, _FS = plus feature selection, _FE = plus feature extraction.

the three metrics, but as noticed above, this is misleading since precision and recall are not distributed uniformly over the classes, e.g., in the *almost perfect* recall of 0.993 for class CG which introduce a bias in its average performance. The general average performance of *ERT plus feature extraction* is also scoring over 90% in all three metrics, but considering the detailed per-class performance, this version of ERT obtains the best absolute f1-score (0.920 and 0.875) and the best absolute precision (0.904 and 0.996) for classes CP and CP, which showed to be problematic by the other classifiers.

7 Conclusions

In this work, we have presented a comparative study aimed at automatic Candida strains classification. Candida is responsible for yeast infections and the availability of fast, reliable, and automatic methods of detection and classification are of great interest and impact in healthcare. Techniques of feature selection and feature extraction have been applied to standard basic classifiers and experimented on a FITR (Fourier-transform infrared spectroscopy) based dataset of Candida strains.

The experimental results show that these techniques dramatically improve the original basic classifier. The overall best performant classifier the Extreme Randomized Forests improved with PCA-based feature extraction, while very close performance is reached by Support Vector Machine with a technique of feature selection based on Extreme Randomized Forests.

As pointed out in Sect. 3, describing the dataset preprocessing phase, some Candida strain samples, (i.e. MG, CL, and CU) have been excluded because underrepresented, these exclusions represent a clear limit, but extending classification experiments to these strains will be the object of future work. A topic worthy of further investigation is certainly the potential of Extremely Randomised Forests, which plays a decisive role in both best performant approaches.

Acknowledgments. Authors thank Prof. Gianluigi Cardinali for providing the data set, and Luca Roscini for explaining the basics of the FTIR technique. This work is partially supported by the Italian Ministry of Research under PRIN Project "PHRAME" Grant n. 20178XXKFY.

References

1. Colabella, C., Corte, L., Roscini, L., Shapaval, V., Kohler, A., et al.: Merging FT-IR and NGS for simultaneous phenotypic and genotypic identification of pathogenic *Candida* species. PLOS ONE *12*(12), e0188104 (2017). https://doi.org/10.1371/journal.pone.0188104
2. Cardinali, G., Bolano, A., Martini, A.: A DNA extraction and purification method for several yeast genera. Ann. Microbiol. **51**(1), 121–130 (2001). http://europepmc.org/abstract/AGR/IND23244635
3. Colabella, C., et al.: Merging FT-IR and NGS for simultaneous phenotypic and genotypic identification of pathogenic Candida species. PLOS ONE **12**(12), e0188104 (2017). https://doi.org/10.1371/journal.pone.0188104

4. Dietterich, T.: An experimental comparison of three methods for constructing ensembles of decision trees: bagging, boosting, and randomization. Mach. Learn. **40**, 139–157 (2000). https://doi.org/10.1023/A:100760751394
5. Essendoubi, M., Toubas, D., Bouzaggou, M., Pinon, J.M., Manfait, M., Sockalingum, G.D.: Rapid identification of Candida species by FT-IR microspectroscopy. Biochimica et biophysica acta **1724**(3), 239–247 (2005). https://doi.org/10.1016/j.bbagen.2005.04.019
6. Franzoni, V., Milani, A.: A semantic comparison of clustering algorithms for the evaluation of web-based similarity measures. In: Gervasi, O., et al. (eds.) ICCSA 2016. LNCS, vol. 9790, pp. 438–452. Springer, Cham (2016). https://doi.org/10.1007/978-3-319-42092-9_34
7. Geurts, P., Ernst, D., Wehenkel, L.: Extremely randomized trees. Mach. Learn. **63**, 3–42 (2006). https://doi.org/10.1007/s10994-006-6226-1
8. Helm, D., Labischinski, H., Schallehn, G., Naumann, D.: Classification and identification of bacteria by Fourier-transform infrared spectroscopy. J. Gen. Microbiol. **137**(1), 69–79 (1991). https://doi.org/10.1099/00221287-137-1-69
9. Hökenek, U.D., Özcan, F.G., Sevdi, M.S., Erkalp, K., Selcan, A.: Mortality predictors in sepsis: a retrospective study. Turk. J. Intensive Care **19**, 82–89 (2021)
10. Hosmer, D.W., Jr., Lemeshow, S., Sturdivant, R.X.: Applied Logistic Regression, vol. 398. Wiley, Hoboken (2013)
11. Kam, T.: Random decision forests. In: Proceedings of the 3rd International Conference on Document Analysis and Recognition, Montreal, QC, 14–16 August 1995, pp. 278–282 (1995)
12. Naumann, D., Helm, D., Labischinski, H.: Microbiological characterizations by FT-IR spectroscopy. Nature **351**(6321), 81–82 (1991)
13. Poggioni, V., Franzoni, V., Zollo, F.: Can we infer book classification by blurbs? In: Basili, R., Crestani, F., Pennacchiotti, M. (eds.) Proceedings of the 5th Italian Information Retrieval Workshop, CEUR Workshop Proceedings, Roma, Italy, 20–21 January 2014, vol. 1127, pp. 16–19. CEUR-WS.org (2014). http://ceur-ws.org/Vol-1127/paper3.pdf
14. Pramodhini, S., Srirangaraj, S., Easow, J.M.: Candiduria-study of virulence factors and its antifungal susceptibility pattern in tertiary care hospital. J. Lab. Phys., 1–7 (2021). https://www.thieme-connect.com/products/ejournals/html/10.1055/s-0041-1730880#info
15. Supatharawanich, S., et al.: Invasive fungal infection in children with acute leukemia and severe aplastic anemia: IFI in children with acute leukemia and saa. Mediterr. J. Hematol. Infect. Dis. **13**(1), e2021039 (2021)

Spatial Assignment Optimization of Vaccine Units in the Covid-19 Pandemics

Alfredo Milani[1]([✉])[iD] and Giulio Biondi[2][iD]

[1] Department of Mathematics and Computer Science, University of Perugia,
06123 Perugia, Italy
alfredo.milani@ieee.org
[2] Department of Mathematics and Computer Science, University of Florence,
50134 Florence, Italy
giulio.biondi@unifi.it

Abstract. In this work we present the application of evolutionary algorithms to the problem of spatial assignment optimization of vaccine units. In the framework of urban planning of health facilities, the problem consists into optimizing the overall cost of building and running vaccine units with respect to costs and benefit for the public by deciding their size and location. The complex non linear objective function, depends on populations distributions, transportation infrastructure costs, travel times and distances and vaccination units capacities. The problem domain is described by a model based on a layered approach, where the layers embed knowledge of different types at a scalable resolution. Although many purposely designed algorithms for spatial locations assignment of health facilities, have been proposed in the literature, in a pandemics situation, for vaccination units, faster optimization tools are needed not necessarily designed for a specific problem model, which can quickly change dynamically. We have investigated and compared the application of several evolutionary optimization algorithms from PSO to Differential Evolution. Results show that evolutionary algorithms allow an high degree of flexibility in objective function without compromising in optimisation performance.

Keywords: Spatial planning · Urban planning · Evolutionary algorithms · Particle swarm optimization · Differential evolution · Health management.

1 Introduction

Optimising the spatial allocation of health facilities is a very relevant problem in urban planning which is carefully considered by government organizations since

This work is partially supported by the Italian Ministry of Research under PRIN Project "PHRAME" Grant n.20178XXKFY.

O. Gervasi et al. (Eds.): ICCSA 2021, LNCS 12955, pp. 448–459, 2021.
https://doi.org/10.1007/978-3-030-87007-2_32

it heavily affect quality of life and financial budget. During major pandemics, like the current COVID-19 emergency, optimal spatial allocation of vaccination units is influenced by the typical factors of healthcare models, but in addition it is also complicated by the fact that there is the lack of precise model of people's behaviour, and there is not a long time available, the decision of unit allocation is usually a matter of weeks or days instead of years, like in normal situations. Therefore, there is the need of tools which allow to quickly model and optimize at different level of scale, depending on the actual current context.

In [18] five classes of factors that hamper access to healthcare for patients are listed, i.e. availability, accessibility, affordability, acceptability and accommodation. The latter three deal with the social organization and wealth of a population, reflecting cultural factors and political decisions, while the former two are solely related to the territorial distribution of facilities and people. In particular, availability refers to the number of healthcare facilities which can be chosen by a patient, while accessibility analyzes the travel distance or time between a patient and service points; the two factors are often merged in one concept, *Spatial Accessibility*, applicable to dense urban contexts. The allocation of healthcare facilities can be modeled as a location-allocation problem [17], where the demand is sustained by potential patients and the offer consists of medical centers, e.g., Covid-19 hospitals or vaccine centers during a pandemic needing special measures [5]. Spatial accessibility measures have been presented in literature and applied to different components of the healthcare system, which in turn may present specific requirements, e.g. primary health structures [12], mental health facilities [16], qualified work personnel [4], and hospitals [11]; notable classes of measures include *Provider-to-population ratios, travel impedance measures* and *gravity models* [22]. Because of the differences in terrain conformation of different areas, combined with usually un-even urban development spanning through decades or centuries and different economic history, each area presents specific challenges and impediments for patients; several case-studies are reported in literature for specific locations and at different data resolutions, e.g. the Chinese towns of Kaifeng [25] and Wuhan [24], the Sichuan Chinese province [23] and the Chicago region [15]. Globally, the Covid-19 pandemic highlighted the structural weaknesses of different healthcare systems. To limit the diffusion of the virus, disease spread control strategies were enforced; at the same time, sectors of existing facilities were dedicated to covid-19 patients and separated from the rest of the resources, to protect the rest of the patients, or completely built from the ground to cope with the needs of a rapidly growing portion of infected population. When vaccines became available, accurately planning the distribution on the territory of vaccination centers was of paramount importance, considering the population distribution and the availability of infrastructures, i.e. transportation routes, and specialized equipment to store, distribute and inoculate the vaccine doses. For this purpose, the design of planning tools to devise resources distribution plans became a crucial task. Planning the distribution of healthcare facilities is a process which usually spans several years, requiring major public works and considerable financial investments, in a slowly developing scenario, e.g. the construction of a new city district. A pandemic situation, instead, induces sudden changes which follow the contagion situation, which strongly influence both the logistics and the emotional response of the population [7], which can lead to management issues; therefore, tools need to provide users with the ability of performing rapid what-if analys is to plan ahead the response to various likely future scenarios.

In this work we present a novel layer-based model to efficiently distribute Covid-19 vaccination units in a territory. Our model can incorporate in specific layers several factors defining the total cost of building and running units, classes of stakeholder their behavior and consequently social costs. We analyze the performance of different evolutionary algorithms in optimizing a custom fitness function which takes into account the role of each considered layer. Evolutionary algorithms can be applied to numerical problems of various sorts, providing general optimization strategies which are independent from specific fitness functions. For this reason, they prove useful in the scope of this work, where an epidemic scenario is considered. In such a context, the requirements can rapidly change, in unpredictable manners; resources, often in limited amount, have to be diverted or re-located on the basis of unforeseeable developments in the spread of diseases, driven by factors including the movement of people and goods, or climate [20]. Evolutionary algorithms are more resilient to changes in the fitness function, which reflects updated needs in the pandemic context, whereas ad-hoc strategies are tailored to more static, predictable scenarios.

In Sect. 2 we introduce the architecture of our framework and provide details on the layer-based model, the problem parameters, the relevant costs, and the designed objective function In Sect. 3 we introduce the characteristics of the evolutionary optimizers and the Nevergrad framework which has been used in the experiments and integrated with the objective function. In Sect. 4 we describe the experimental settings, datasets used and the experimental results obtained. We finally draw conclusions and discuss future work.

2   Covid Facilities Distribution Model

The purpose of the model is to describe the territory characteristics in order to assess both cost for installation and running, i.e. management, of Covid-19 vaccination units, and evaluating the effectiveness of the service provided to the population in term of amount and quality of services supplied and reachability of the assigned locations, which influences both the logistics and the emotional affordance [10]. The territory features are modelled by $M = \{L^k\}$ a set of k overlapping bi-dimensional layers of the same size $m \times n$, $i \in m$, $j \in m$. Each layer k represents a dimension of the relevant information by a 2-dimensional grid containing values in its elements $L^k_{i,j}$. The approach is scalable, since it allows to approximate solutions for the allocation optimisation problem by compromising between the desired resolution of details and the available computational resources. The grid size determines the different scale levels, while it impacts the computational performances.

In computing the quality of a given solution, the different layers are traversed depending on specific algorithmic rules, which embed the semantic of the model and health facilities user behavior in terms of logistics and emotional response [9].

2.1   Population Distribution Layers

Population distribution layers gives an estimate of the population living in each square of a certain grid element. Each different layer of population L_t^{Pop} refers to a different population type t, which has different income, socio-cultural background and ultimately behavior. The unit used is the thousand of people. The approximation given the *Population distribution layer* provides, in each entry, the amount of population of a certain type living in each element of the territorial grid expressed in thousands of people units, i.e. $L_u^{Pop}pper[2,3] = 23$ $L_l^{Pop}ower[2,3] = 4$ indicate that 23 thousands upper class and 4 thousands lower class people lives in territory grid area (2,3). The general assumption is that users of the same type behave according to shortest path cost to services, verifying their own cost criteria, i.e. we assume that the populations assigned to an element is attracted by the Covid vaccination unit closest to its residence, i.e. the one needed a minimal cost to reach. The shortest path [8] between a given location and a Covid-vaccination unit is computed by taking into account of distance, travel time, transportation cost and quality, as expressed in the transportation infrastructure layer for a given population type.

2.2   Transportation Infrastructure Layers

Each layer L_t^{Trans} of the Transportation Infrastructure refer to a specific transportation network type t,i.e. road, highway, train, underground, taxi, etc. Each grid element (i,j) contains a value, $L_{train}^{Trans}(i,j) = d$ which represents the distance d needed to cross it and to reach its center from an adjacent element laying on the same infrastructure, here *train*, for example from position $(4,2)$ of the transportation grid shown in Fig. 1 we can move to positions $(4,1)$, $(3,2)$, $(4,3)$ and $(5,2)$ respectively with a distance cost of 6, 1, 9 and 1. To compute the actual path cost this distance value needs to be weighted with population specific cost for that type of infrastructure, predicting the paths to be chosen by the population [6]. The path are represented directly in the grid by sequences of 2D grid elements. A special value Inf is used to codify an empty square, see positions $(2,5)$ and $(3,5)$ in Fig. 1, i.e. a square which is at infinite distance and cannot be reached from its neighbor cells. Moreover, in addition to distance from neighbors, every infrastructure cell contains a boolean value which denotes that an entry/exit to the cell is available from the road crossing it, for instance, an underground or a railway have no exits in every grid element they traverses. A path can be composed by sections belonging to different transportation layers provided that each starting/ending point of each section has a entry/exit for the transportation layer type to which it belong, for instance a path can be made of a *bus* subpath connected to a *underground* path and then to a *walking* path section. In Fig. 1 the shortest path between cell $(4, 1)$ and cell $(3, 4)$ within a single transportation layer is highlighted .

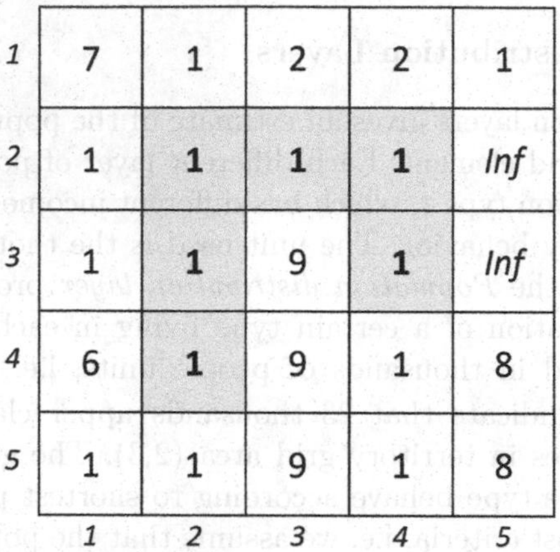

	1	2	3	4	5
1	7	1	2	2	1
2	1	1	1	1	Inf
3	1	1	9	1	Inf
4	6	1	9	1	8
5	1	1	9	1	8

Fig. 1. Path in a transportation layer grid

In the configuration settings, for each population type a *per km* cost is set. The *per km* cost summarizes for each population different elements: the actual monetary cost of the travel and the quality of life value in using the specific transportation network, it basically acts as a weight inducing a preferential choice behaviour in people from different classes. For example for "lower class" population the cost tend to directly reflect cost of tickets, i.e. bus is preferable than taxi, instead for "higher class" people, quality considerations will prevail and for example, for this people taking buses may have a higher cost than using own car, finally certain minority group, e.g. "environmental sensitive" people, may consider bicycles the most preferable transportation mean despite of their income level. The shortest cost paths will then depend both on the shortest distance weighted by the population depending cost.

2.3   Covid Facilities Layer

The Covid Facilities Layer represents the actual candidate solution for our optimization problem. Given a number k of Covid vaccination units to allocate in a territory grid, each grid element represents how many Covid units are allocated there, the values assigned have to be integer and the constraint $\sum_i^m \sum_j^n L_{units}^{Covid}(i, j) = k$ must hold. The entries of this layer are the inputs of the overall objective function described in Sect. 2.5.

2.4   Problem Parameters Setting

A set of parameters characterise a problem instance model, in addition to the population, transportation and Covid-19 facilities layers. The basic parameter is the pair $m \times n = r$ deciding the *layers dimensions*, they directly affect the resolution, how precisely the model approximate the reality, and determine the computational resource requirements. Since most algorithms used in computing fitness have a complexity $O(r^3)$, although it is not exponential, territory high resolution can easily become a bottleneck, because population based evolutionary algorithms strongly depend on a large number of fitness evaluations [2,3].

The number u of *Covid vaccination units* to allocate in the grid.

The *capacity* u_{cap} of a Covid vaccination unit in term of how much population can be vaccinated in a time period (usually a year).

The cost u_{est} of building a Covid unit from scratch,i.e. establishing the infrastructure, power lines, air conditioning systems, medical tools etc.

The u_{save} percentage of the *saving* obtained from establishing a Covid unit where already exist one. Building a vaccination center with a double capacity does not have a doubled cost, the saving mostly decreased cost in infrastructures, parkings, power lines, bureaucracy and organization.

The cost u_{mng} for managing a vaccination center in a time period.

The *time horizon* $t_1 - hor$ denotes the number of time periods over which optimization is held. A lower management cost u_{mng} with respect to u_{est} could favour different choice on a longer horizon.

Other important parameters are represented by the cost value assigned to each pair $(pop_{type}, trans_{type})$ in order to map preferences of different classes of people with respect to the use of different transportation infrastructures, and the population pop_{type}^{wait} waiting time cost, an percentage increment to be applied when a give vaccination unit attract more people of its capacity.

2.5   Overall Objective Function

Given a candidate solution, a spatial assignment of vaccination units to the Covid facilities layer, the *overall objective function* represents the costs to be optimized in a given time period. The general cost includes building the vaccination units, once, running them for a given time horizon, the cost of moving the population on a shortest path according to distances and their preferential behaviour, and finally adding the social cost due to bad quality services, i.e. time to wait in case of exceeding the units capacity. In order to formally define the overall objective function, we will use a function $[u_{pos}, s_{path_cost}] = fsp((i,j), pop_{type})$ which returns the position u_{pos} of the vaccination unit closest to position (i,j) and the cost $s_{path_{cost}}$ of the shortest path from (i,j) to u_{pos} according to the transportation cost mapping, inducing the preferential behavior of population type pop_{type}.

$$o(L_{units}) =$$
$$(\sum_{\forall u \in L_{units} \wedge L_{units}(u)=1}(u_{est}))$$
$$+(\sum_{\forall u \in L_{units} \wedge L_{units}(u)>1}(u_{est}*u*u_{save}))$$
$$+(\sum_{\forall u \in L_{units}}(u_{mng}*t_{hor}))$$
$$+(\sum_{\forall t \in Pop_{type}} \sum_{i \in m, j \in n}(L_t^{Pop}[i,j]*fsp((i,j),pop_t)*t_{hor}))$$
$$+\sum_{\forall u \in L_{units}} \begin{cases} \sum_{\forall t \in Pop_{type}}(assigned(u,t)*pop_t^{wait}*t_{hor}), & \text{if } (over\_capacity(u)) \\ 0, & \text{otherwise} \end{cases}$$

3   The Evolutionary Algorithms

The evolutionary algorithms, that we have considered, all share the characteristics of being population based. Despite of the different details of each algorithm, they all share the concepts of:

- *population* of candidate solutions,
- *fitness*, a function aimed at evaluating the performance of a single solution, i.e.the cost to be minimized;
- an *evolution mechanism*, which, is able to generate a new population of solution with an improved fitness.

The core difference between algorithms consists in how they create a new generation using fitness and current solution population. Variations range from applying mutation and crossover operators to solution representation, as in Differential Evolution [21], to applying the concept of inertial movement and attraction among individual solutions in the search space, as in PSO [14]. The mechanism is iterated thru generations, effectively exploring the solution search space, until a *termination condition*: typically when a given number of iterations or fitness threshold is reached.

3.1   The Nevergrad Environment

Nevergrad [19] is a Python library, developed by Facebook and released under the MIT license, which implements a set of popular gradient-free and evolutionary optimisers, to perform single-objective or multi-objective optimisation. The optimisers considered in this work are Particle Swarm Optimization (PSO) [14], Differential Evolution (DE) [21], Differential Evolution with Two Points Crossover (TwoPointsDE), ScrHammersleySearch, and Covariance Matrix Adaptation Evolution Strategy (CMA-ES) [13]. An additional pure RandomSearch optimiser is used as a baseline for comparison purposes only.

The structure of *Nevergrad* allows to easily integrate in the evolutionary algorithm loop an external fitness evaluator [1]. In our experiments the fitness evaluator consists in a implementation of the *overall objective function* taking as input the layers of the Covid facilities distribution model and the parameters and cost settings. Nevergrad solutions are returned as a vector of length u, containing the coordinates of Covid units locations.

4   Experiments

4.1   Data Set and Settings

The data sets consist of ten 10×10 grids with 600 randomly distributed inhabitants. People are distributed on the grids by randomly picking a location and placing from 10 to 25 inhabitants there; when the chosen budget of 600 is over, the remaining locations are filled with 0. The length of road segments for each location is set to 1 or 2km. Due to the randomness in the population distribution process, collisions are possible, i.e. some locations can have more than 25 inhabitants. In Fig. 2a, Fig. 2b, Fig. 2c and Fig. 2d four population distribution layers from different data sets are shown. In the figures, a darker shade means a higher density of population in the corresponding grid sector.

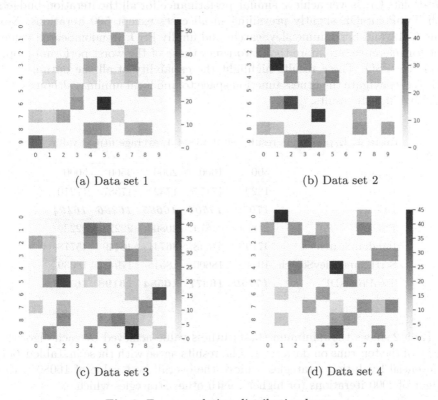

(a) Data set 1   (b) Data set 2

(c) Data set 3   (d) Data set 4

Fig. 2. Four population distribution layers

The Differential Evolution CR, F1 and F2 parameters are set, respectively, to 0.5, 0.8 and 0.8, and the adopted mutation strategy is current-to-best. The population consists of 30 randomly initialised individuals; such settings apply both to the DE and TwoPointsDE strategies. The PSO transformation function is set to "arctan", and the population size to 40. The "omega", "phip" and "phig" parameters are set, respectively, to $0.5/(\log(2))$, $0.5+\log(2)$ and $0.5+\log(2)$. The CMA scale is set to 1.0, and the population size to 7. The considered fitness evaluation budgets for Nevergrad are: $[500, 1000, 2000, 3500, 5000]$; each algorithm has been run for ten times on the same data set/budget pair to level possible differences due to the random initialisation.

4.2 Results

In this section we present the results of our experiments.

In Table 1 the results of the experiments are reported for data set 1. The best average results and the second best average are respectively shown in **bold** and ***bold-italic*** case. Differential Evolution (DE) and Differential Evolution with Two-Points Crossover achieve similar performance for all the iteration budgets, with TwoPointsDE slightly prevailing in all cases except 500 iterations. Next come CMA and ScrHammersleySearch, and finally PSO. RandomSearch values, kept for reference, are more than two times those of the worst performing optimiser, i.e. PSO. These results highlight the capability of all the optimisers to effectively navigate the fitness function space to find local minima, although with sensibly different results.

Table 1. Experiments results on data set 1, average fitness value

Algorithm	500	1000	2000	3500	5000
CMA	18202	17177	17425	17387	17210
DE	**17612**	*17501*	*16685*	*16286*	*16494*
PSO	21854	21874	20800	22223	22239
RandomSearch	47796	47848	46741	46449	45778
ScrHammersleySearch	19415	18600	18515	17941	18039
TwoPointsDE	*17750*	**16877**	**16584**	**16198**	**16192**

Table 2 shows the minimum (best) fitness value achieved by each algorithm in any of the ten runs on data set 1. The results agree with those in Table 1 both Differential Evolution strategies achieve the overall best value of 16080 with a budget of 2000 iterations (or higher), with other strategies which

Table 2. Experiments results on data set 1, minimum fitness value

Algorithm	500	1000	2000	3500	5000
CMA	17530	16830	16890	16330	16830
DE	**16450**	*16990*	**16080**	**16080**	**16080**
PSO	19230	18890	17880	18730	19800
RandomSearch	43430	45510	42190	40640	40640
ScrHammersleySearch	18120	17380	17390	17150	16990
TwoPointsDE	*16750*	**16140**	**16080**	**16080**	**16080**

5 Conclusions

This work presents a model for the optimal spatial assignment of vaccination units in a territory affected by a Covid-19 pandemics. The model is based on layers embedding knowledge about population types distribution and transportation infrastructures types. Different behaviors of different population types can be modeled. The model is scalable with a trade-off between accuracy and computational resources, obtaining rapid modeling and optimization for response units allocation, as required by a pandemics situation.

The model has been implemented and experimented with different evolutionary optimization metaheuristics on randomly generated datasets. Results comparisons show generally good performances of the evolutionary approach with a clear prevalence of differential evolution algorithms.

The grid based layers approach is a very flexible representation which allows to augment the expressivity of the model, by introducing new kind of layers connected to the territory, i.e. green area, climate info, crime rate etc., this knowledge can be incorporated in people behaviour and quality of solution evaluation algorithm.

Future Works. The scalability characteristics of the grid based layers approach suggest to explore the use of grids with different resolutions in order to better articulate the precision/computational resources balance. An extension toward a more accuracy model is also represented by differentiating the cost of developing units with respect to their position in the territory, this is not relevant for health facilities which usually enjoy the strong exemptions for public interest, while it would reflects more accurately the real situation, where private developing cost strongly depends on town areas.

References

1. Agresta, A., Baioletti, M., Biscarini, C., Milani, A., Santucci, V.: Evolutionary algorithms for roughness coefficient estimation in river flow analyses. In: Castillo, P.A., Jiménez Laredo, J.L. (eds.) EvoApplications 2021. LNCS, vol. 12694, pp. 795–811. Springer, Cham (2021). https://doi.org/10.1007/978-3-030-72699-7_50

2. Biondi, G., Franzoni, V.: Discovering correlation indices for link prediction using differential evolution. Mathematics **8**(11), 2097 (2020)
3. Biondi, G., Milani, A., Baia, A.E.: Differential evolution of correlation indexes for link prediction. In: 2018 International Conference on Computational Science and Computational Intelligence (CSCI), pp. 1483–1486 (2018). https://doi.org/10.1109/CSCI46756.2018.00296
4. Dussault, G., Franceschini, M.C.: Not enough there, too many here: understanding geographical imbalances in the distribution of the health workforce. Hum. Resour. Health **4**, 12 (2006). https://doi.org/10.1186/1478-4491-4-12
5. Franzoni, V., Biondi, G., Milani, A.: Exploring negative emotions to preserve social distance in a pandemic emergency. In: Gervasi, O., et al. (eds.) ICCSA 2020. LNCS, vol. 12250, pp. 562–573. Springer, Cham (2020). https://doi.org/10.1007/978-3-030-58802-1_40
6. Franzoni, V., Chiancone, A., Milani, A.: A multistrain bacterial diffusion model for link prediction. Int. J. Pattern Recognit. Artif. Intell. **31**(11), 1759024:1–1759024:16 (2017). https://doi.org/10.1142/S0218001417590248
7. Franzoni, V., Li, Y., Mengoni, P.: A path-based model for emotion abstraction on facebook using sentiment analysis and taxonomy knowledge. In: Proceedings of the International Conference on Web Intelligence, WI 2017, pp. 947–952. Association for Computing Machinery, New York (2017). https://doi.org/10.1145/3106426.3109420
8. Franzoni, V., Milani, A.: Heuristic semantic walk for concept chaining in collaborative networks. Int. J. Web Inf. Syst. **10**(1), 85–103 (2014)
9. Franzoni, V., Milani, A.: Emotion recognition for self-aid in addiction treatment, psychotherapy, and nonviolent communication. In: Misra, S., et al. (eds.) ICCSA 2019. LNCS, vol. 11620, pp. 391–404. Springer, Cham (2019). https://doi.org/10.1007/978-3-030-24296-1_32
10. Franzoni, V., Milani, A., Vallverdú, J.: Emotional affordances in human-machine interactive planning and negotiation. In: Sheth, A.P., et al. (eds.) Proceedings of the International Conference on Web Intelligence, Leipzig, Germany, August 23–26, 2017, pp. 924–930. ACM (2017). https://doi.org/10.1145/3106426.3109421
11. Goodman, D.C., Fisher, E., Stukel, T.A., Chang, C.: The distance to community medical care and the likelihood of hospitalization: is closer always better? Am. J. Public Health **87**(7), 1144–1150 (1997). https://doi.org/10.2105/ajph.87.7.1144
12. Guagliardo, M.F.: Spatial accessibility of primary care: concepts, methods and challenges. Int. J. Health Geographics **3**(1), 3 (2004). https://doi.org/10.1186/1476-072X-3-3
13. Hansen, N., Ostermeier, A.: Completely derandomized self-adaptation in evolution strategies. Evol. Comput. **9**(2), 159–195 (2001). https://doi.org/10.1162/106365601750190398
14. Kennedy, J., Eberhart, R.: Particle swarm optimization. In: Proceedings of ICNN 1995 - International Conference on Neural Networks. vol. 4, pp. 1942–1948 (1995). https://doi.org/10.1109/ICNN.1995.488968
15. Luo, W., Wang, F.: Measures of spatial accessibility to health care in a gis environment: Synthesis and a case study in the chicago region. Environ. Planning B: Planning Des. **30**(6), 865–884 (2003). https://doi.org/10.1068/b29120
16. Ngamini Ngui, A., Vanasse, A.: Assessing spatial accessibility to mental health facilities in an urban environment. Spatial spatio-temporal Epidemiol. **3**(3), 195–203 (2012). https://doi.org/10.1016/j.sste.2011.11.001
17. Peeters, D., Thomas, I.: Distance predicting functions and applied location-allocation models. J. Geogr. Syst. **2**(2), 167–184 (2000)

18. Penchansky, R., Thomas, J.W.: The concept of access: definition and relationship to consumer satisfaction. Med. Care **19**(2), 127–140 (1981). https://doi.org/10.1097/00005650-198102000-00001
19. Rapin, J., Teytaud, O.: Nevergrad - A gradient-free optimization platform. https://GitHub.com/FacebookResearch/Nevergrad (2018)
20. Scafetta, N.: Distribution of the SARS-CoV-2 Pandemic and Its Monthly Forecast Based on Seasonal Climate Patterns. Int. J. Environ. Res. Public Health **17**(10) 2020). https://doi.org/10.3390/ijerph17103493
21. Storn, R., Price, K.: Differential evolution - a simple and efficient heuristic for global optimization over continuous spaces. J. Global Optim. (1997). https://doi.org/10.1023/A:1008202821328
22. Wan, N., Zou, B., Sternberg, T.: A three-step floating catchment area method for analyzing spatial access to health services. Int. J. Geogr. Inf. Sci. **26**(6), 1073–1089 (2012). https://doi.org/10.1080/13658816.2011.624987
23. Wang, X., Yang, H., Duan, Z., Pan, J.: Spatial accessibility of primary health care in china: a case study in sichuan province. Soc. Sci. Med. **209**, 14–24 (2018). https://doi.org/10.1016/j.socscimed.2018.05.023
24. Yang, N., Chen, S., Hu, W., Wu, Z., Chao, Y.: Spatial distribution balance analysis of hospitals in wuhan. Int. J. Environ. Res. Public Health **13**(10) (2016). https://doi.org/10.3390/ijerph13100971
25. Zheng, Z., et al.: Spatial accessibility to hospitals based on web mapping api: an empirical study in kaifeng, china. Sustainability **11**(4) (2019). https://doi.org/10.3390/su11041160

Computational Wrist-Print Biometric Identification System Using Discrete Cosine Transform

Kennedy Chinedu Okafor[1,2]([✉]) and Omowunmi Mary Longe[2]

[1] Mechatronics Engineering, Federal University of Technology, Owerri, Nigeria
kennedy.okafor@futo.edu.ng
[2] Electrical and Electronic Engineering Science, University of Johannesburg, Johannesburg,
South Africa
omowunmil@uj.ac.za

Abstract. Biometric Wrist Authentication (BWA) is one of the best-known authentication schemes in many access control systems. The use of fingerprint biometrics as humans attempt to communicate with robots/machines, and their physical environments have inherent setbacks. However, various efforts have been proposed to fix the limitations. Most biometric efforts suffer from lack of computational derivatives and do not support optimal image compression. Motivated by these concerns, the goal of this paper is fivefold. First, we proposed BWA using Discrete Cosine Transform (DCT) to compress palm print images and develop Wrist-Print Biometric Identification System (WPBIS). Second, we developed a process model for DCT and characterized it for wrist templates considering both original and decoded images. Third, Bits per pixel (Bpp) and Compression ratio (Cr) for a wrist template/bioscript are used as metrics for evaluation. Fourth, after adopting various timestamps, we observed that the image template Bpp yielded 1.256 Bpp and compression of 63.26% based on DCT. Fifth, we showed a typical experimental scenario with a digital signal processor feeding images with DCT. Identification and verification of various wrist-prints (test-point samples) are equally carried out. From the results, WPBIS DCT offered higher image intensity compared with Wavelet transform.

Keywords: Computational science · Biometric access control · Digital signal processor · Human-Computer Interface (HCI)

1 Introduction

1.1 Background

Wearable technology has come a long way in the last two decades, thanks to significant advances in bio-physical signal processing and applications. In recent years, bioelectrical signals like the electrocardiogram (ECG), electromyogram (EMG), and electroencephalogram (EEG) have grown in popularity for Wrist-Human-Computer Interfacing (HCI) [1]. EMG devices, in particular, can detect electrical currents produced

© Springer Nature Switzerland AG 2021
O. Gervasi et al. (Eds.): ICCSA 2021, LNCS 12955, pp. 460–475, 2021.
https://doi.org/10.1007/978-3-030-87007-2_33

in muscles during movement [2] and use this data to control actuation systems. This is critical for engaging with wrist-powered devices such as Optitrack gloves [3], physical exercise equipment such as datalite [4], and controlling robotic devices or "bionic" praxes.

Wrists are being used in personal identification and authentication to provide accurate and reliable recognition. Wrist print authentication is a safe, effective, and private method of authentication. The rise of terrorism and other forms of illegal activities such as e-commerce fraud has piqued interest in more efficient and effective methods of determining a person's identity.

In mission-critical access control systems, biometric initiatives that will improve security ideology are always sought. Various integrations and algorithms have been proposed in the past works with a little contribution to wrist print-based biometric identification systems [5]. With rising demands for automatic personal identification, biometric authentication has gotten a lot of attention in the last decade [5]. Palmprint identification/recognition is among the most reliable biometric schemes available today [6].

To date, biometric is very useful in areas of forensic and commercial applications such as the banking sector, voting systems, and other image recognition systems. These leverage schemes like biometric encryption [7], bio-cryptography [8], fuzzy vaults [9]. Yet no work in the literature has dealt with Biometric Wrist Authentication (BWA) based on Discrete Cosine Transform (DCT) for image compression.

In general, a biometric is data about a person that can be used to establish that person's identity. DNA, ear form, ears, fingerprints, hand geometry, irises, keystroke pattern on a keyboard, signature, and voice are some of the biometrics currently being researched [10]. While each biometric has established merits and demerits, all biometrics must have the following four characteristics including accuracy, universality, uniqueness-, and invariance [11]. Some biometrics (faces, speech, signature, keystrokes, and ears) can be obtained without a person's knowledge, while others (fingerprints and hand geometry) require a person's cooperation, and others (irises and DNA) have yet to be determined [12]. This distinction is critical for a variety of applications. Remote surveillance and monitoring (border crossings and airport security) are potential applications for non-intrusive biometrics, while access control and checking electronic commerce transactions are potential applications for cooperative biometrics [13]. Faces, fingerprints, irises, and ears are all image-based, and implementing them necessitates image processing, pattern recognition, and computer vision techniques [12]. Hand geometry, keystrokes, signatures, and expression are all part of the signal processing and pattern matching/recognition domains. Multiple biometrics have been combinedly used in recent efforts [14, 15]. The essence of this work is to exploit cooperative biometrics with a shift to wrist prints.

1.2 Motivation

There are several identified constraints regarding the operability of the fingerprint method of identification. First, the inability for people with some forms of physiological defects, (as regards the fingers), to effectively use such systems. Some of these physiological defects could be congenital deformation of the fingers, loss of all fingers due to an accident, and severe damage to the fingers' skin due to leprosy. Second, the fingertips are used for virtually all daily activities and therefore are exposed to a greater number of risks, unlike the wrists.

Third, another serious drawback is the secretion of excess oil and/or sweat on the hand surface which inhibits adequate fingerprint capture by the sensor devices. Fourth, medical experts have raised serious concerns on the possibility of contracting a wide range of infections through the use of public fingerprint identification systems. Also, investigations have shown that a typical public fingerprint identification system is as dirty as a typical public toilet.

In this paper, we built WPBIS which leverages DCT for image compression. This can serve a wider category of people irrespective of the condition of their fingers. This eliminates the problems associated with oily/sweaty hands. In addition, due to the physiology of the wrists which makes it more hygienic than the fingers; it would tackle the numerous health concerns people have with using a public-deployed fingerprint-based biometric identification system. The sensor array captures an analog image of the wrist placed on the wrist-print module and sends this image to an ADC that converts this analog image into a digital equivalent code. This then represents the numerical characterization of the wrist-print features. Sample-data code from the wrist-print module is transmitted to the DSP controller for matching against several of such codes previously enrolled and stored in the memory. When there is a mismatch detected by the software agent in the DSP controller, an indication signal notification is generated while denying access and vice versa. Hence, the art of computational science is very apt for DCT.

1.3 Contribution and Article Organization

This paper develops WPBIS using the DCT algorithms while deploying it in an access control system. The specific sub-objectives of this research include:

1. To develop a DCT model that satisfies the requirement of image compression for the identification and verification contexts
2. To develop a WPBIS process model using Bit per pixel and Compression ratio as key evaluation metrics for the data acquisition system.
3. To develop conceptual models while formulating representative lock diagrams for the enrollment and identification procedures in WPBIS
4. To implement the WPBIS DCT algorithm using a software agent in a DSP controller for access control.

2   Literature Review

This section focused on biometric systems, approaches, and modes of operations while presenting gaps. Recall that [1] discussed two general approaches to verify or identify individuals:

- Once-and-for-all: the person is confirmed once and for all time. Until access to the system is granted, specific requirements may be defined to ensure correct and reliable access. However, since access is never re-verified, unauthorized use by someone other than the approved user is a possibility.
- On-going: verification/identification is repeated regularly. This eliminates the possibility of unauthorized use, but it may reduce verification accuracy by necessitating repeated repetition of verification exercises. In Sect. 2.1, related works are discussed.

2.1 Biometric Systems

This is referred to as an image-pattern identification/recognition model that extracts information from biophysical signals to identify individuals or groups [15]. Biometric systems such as Fingerprint [16], facial imaging [17], speech-notes [18], iris-identity [19], ECG [20, 21], EMG [22], and EEG) [23] are very common in most deployments. Each has a unique mix of weakness, ease of use, obtrusiveness, and complexity. There are two modes of operation in such biometric systems include verification: and identification [24]. In terms of authentication or image verification, different schemes have been explored to date. User scanning with complex image-data processing was required for biometric entities in [17, 18], and [19]. These, on the other hand, are not bio-signals in the traditional sense. Two two-factor authentication and multi-channel EMG signals for hand-trajectory are still popular schemes for verifying a person's identity. In some cases, keystroke dynamics when typing a password, as well as related EMG signaling are explored. Face, fingerprints, hand gestures, and speech are widely used for identification in literature. ECG analysis is widely used in bio-signals, but there has been little research on Wrist-Print Biometric Identification System for individual recognition [2]. Existing efforts appear to focus on one-time biometric identification/ verification with constrained controlled signals for image extraction. However, the use of biometric wrist authentication/identification schemes in a continuous image capturing system with optimal compression ratio is novel in access control systems.

2.2 Why Discrete Cosine Transform (DCT) for Image Compression

Existing works have not fully explored the potential of image compression using the DCT, especially in the context of a wrist print-based biometric identification system. DCT is a signal-to-elementary-frequency-component conversion technique that is commonly used in image compression. The major benefits include:

1. The existence of a well-defined pattern of data points summation at various frequencies, which is ideal for image compression.
2. High efficiency for image compression since fewer functions are required to estimate wrist signals.
3. Approximately twice as long as DFTs logic operation on real-datasets with even symmetry only.

3 System Formulation and Design Architecture

In this section, the computational perspectives on WPBIS are briefly established. Given an access control scenario case K, it is expected that writs samples $\{f_0{}^1 (x), f_0{}^2 (x)..., f_0{}^T (x)\}$ extracted from a base Client BC during enrollment, and verification. Assuming DCT $c_0{}^1 (x)$ is derived by getting the Fourier to transform of $f_0{}^T (x)$ i.e. $f_0{}^T (u)$ and the complex conjugate of $H(u)$ which is the output pattern. $c_0{}^T (x)$ should be bound with an N-bit randomly generated key with a linking algorithm and stored in a lookup table K. The authentication scheme can combine the wrist biometric images viz: $\{f_1{}^1 (x), f_1{}^2 (x)..., f_1{}^T (x)\}$ with $H_{stored(u)}$ to produce an output pattern $c_1{}^T (x)$ with the aid of the lookup table L to retrieve N-bits as shown in Fig. 1. Figure 2 shows the wrist palm biometric key retrieval process. The major difficulty in designing this model lies in the process of fusing wrist biometrics with a transparent sensor. In Wrist palm biometrics, no two wrist samples collected from the same base client are the same. In this study, the steps involved in the enrollment and verification are explained in Sect. 3.1.

3.1 System Enrollment and Verification Algorithms

Figure 1 briefly describes the sequence of steps in the enrollment and verification which the WPBIS explores. The enrollment algorithm is broken into three stages; the processing of images, key linking, and identification code creation. The verification algorithm also has three stages namely; image processing, key retrieval, and key validation. The enrollment procedure's goal is to build the user's Wrist Bioscrypt by linking an arbitrary N-bit key to the user's wrist print. A collection of valid Action Client wrist images, a randomly generated phase-only array, $R(u)$, and an N-bit cryptographic key, k_0, are needed for the enrollment process, as shown in Fig. 1. A random number generator is used to generate R(u) (RNG). The key, k_0, could be a previously produced key that is fed into the Biometric Encryption algorithm, or it could be generated by the RNG. The random phase array, $R(u)$, and the key, k_0, are fully independent of the wrist palm biometric images. This enrollment stage aims to create an output pattern, $c_0(x)$, that will be passed on to stage **En-2**, as well as the stored filter feature, Restored (u). T wrist palm photos, $T = n, n > 3$, are obtained from the base using a certain number of times. The images are then subjected to DCT Fourier transforms to convolve their 2D images. After that, the output pattern, $c_0(x)$, is evaluated.

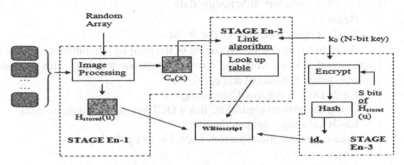

Fig. 1. Wrist palm biometric encryption enrollment process.

The relation algorithm is in charge of connecting the output pattern $c_0(x)$ to an N-bit key k_0. A lookup table will be generated and stored in the wrist Bioscrypt during the linking process for use in key retrieval during verification. The fact that the output pattern obtained during the registration, $c_0(x)$, and the pattern obtained during verification, $c_1(x)$, would differ to some degree is a significant consideration for this method. These variations are attributable to changes in the physical content of the base user's wrist and its location at the image capture device's point of capture, among other things. To account for these variations, some redundancy in the enrollment process is needed. The algorithm I describes the enrollment process.

Algorithm I. DCT Enrollment Process

Inputs: Image templates_Control-CallSchedule for image to $N+1$
                     History of WPBIS resources, Provisioning and transactional
                     workflow
                     $\prod \beta 1$ & $\prod \beta 2$// initialValue constant & trendPosteriorValue
                     pastValueForSubsytems, pastValueForSubsytems

Output: DCT Optimal Scale+ _DES

int i←0;

While i <DCT_monitorCallSchedule d **do**

    Begin ( )
    En-1: Image Processing on the Wrist
    Build two output arrays (product of the two) by combining a set of input
    wrist print images from the base client (wrist training) with a random
    (phase) array: Hstored(u) and $c_0\ (x)$.
    En-2: DCT Wrist Key Connecting
    Using the connect algorithm, link a DCT key, k_0, to a pattern, $c_0(x)$.
    En-3: Creating a unique identifier
    Create a unique identification code, id_0, using the key, k_0.
    i ++;

end while
    Return

Figure 2 shows the identification process for Wrist Biometric Encryption based on DCT. The idea in Algorithm II is to create a new identification code, id_1, and compare it to id_0 to validate k_1. The verification procedure aims to retrieve the N-bit key writ picture for a legitimate user successfully.

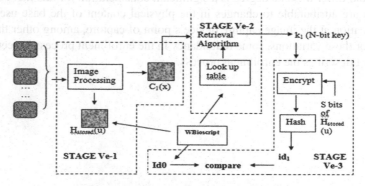

Fig. 2. Identification process for wrist biometric encryption

To retrieve and verify the validity of an N-bit key, a collection of wrist biometric images is obtained from the Action Client and combined with Hstored(u), the lookup table, and id_0., from Bioscrypt. This key will be passed on to the final output stage if it is found to be right. Wrist print images T are obtained from the base client, just as they were during registration. The images are subjected to DCT Fourier transformations, and the results are saved. The output pattern, $c_1(x)$, is evaluated using Hstored(u) retrieved from the wrist Bioscrypt. The cryptographic key will be retrieved using the $c_1(x)$ authentication pattern. In this case, the similarity of $c_1(x)$ and $c_0(x)$ performance patterns have an important impact on t. Algorithm II simplifies the procedure.

Algorithm II. DCT Key retrival and Validation Process

Inputs:	Image Bioscrypt _Control-featureSchedule for image to $N+1$; id_1, id_0
	History of WPBIS resources, Provisioning and transactional workflow
	$\prod \beta 1$ & $\prod \beta 2$// initialValue constant & trendPosteriorValue
	pastValueForSubsytems, pastValueForSubsytems
Output:	DCT Optimal Scale+ _DES

int $i \leftarrow 0$;

While $i <$ DCT_monitorCallScheduled **do**

> **Ve-1:** Image Processing,
>
> To create an output pattern, c_1, combine Hstored(u) from the Wrist Bioscrypt with a new set of input wrist images from the base client (also trained) (x).
>
> **Ve-2:** Key Retrieval
>
> Using the retrieval algorithm, extract a key, k_1, from $c_1(x)$.
>
> **Ve-3:** Key Validation
>
> The retrieval algorithm is in charge of extracting a key from the c_0 verification output pattern (x).
>
> To retrieve an N-bit key that was connected with $c_0(x)$ using the connection algorithm, the steps outlined below are valid.
>
> **Start now ( )**
>
> 1. Take the central part of $c_1(x)$ and extract it (a $N*N$ matrix).
> 2. To construct a verification prototype, concatenate the actual and imaginary bits, as in **En-2** enrollment level. Binarize each value to construct a binarized verification template, as in **En-2** (the equivalent of the binarized enrollment template).
> 3. Using the lookup table, extract the key's necessary constituent bits from the binarized verification template. Define k_1 as a vector with N elements. Sum the L bits of the binarized verification template whose indices are defined by the nth column of the lookup table for the nth element of k_1. If the number of these bits is greater than $L/2$, the nth element of k_1 is set to 1, otherwise, it is set to 0.
> 4. Check the validity of the key you just got. The verification stage **Ve-3** process is defined in the following section.
> 5. Release k_1 into the device if it is discovered to be the correct key.
> 6. Return to $c_1(x)$ and remove the center portion of $c_1(x)$ t if k_1 is found to be wrong.
> 7. Repeat steps 2 to 5 of the retrieval algorithm for all portions of $c_1(x)$ that are one pixel offset from the center, then two-pixel offsets, and so on, up to approximately sixteen-pixel offsets.
> 8. Stop the algorithm and release k_1 if the key retrieved is found to be correct at any point.
> 9. Release an "identification failed" message if the key is found to be incorrect for all pixel offsets.
>
> i ++;

end while

Return

The key retrieval construct in step 5 is needed to account for relative translations of the Action Client's input fingerprints at both biometric enrollment and its controlled verification. The legitimate user is granted access to the door security after the identification stage, which involves the key retrieval algorithm is completed. After the base client writs are captured for verification, this wrist Bioscript is automatically erased from the DSP controller memory, so even if the base client presents for the second time, this will not be recognized as a legitimate base client. The WPBIS ensures that only one person has access to information and that vulnerabilities are kept to a bare minimum. Wrist palm biometric key binding and Wrist palm biometric key retrieval are the core of the WPBIS design.

3.2 DCT Transform and Compression

DCT algorithm is applied in palmprint image compression to develop WPBIS. To maximize the benefits, this was optimized for door access control in a security-sensitive domain. A process model for DCT is characterized as a wrist template for both the original image and decoded image. Figure 3 shows the WPBIS principles behind image compression:

i.   Redundancy elimination, which helps to eliminate repetition from the signal source.
ii. Irrelevancy reduction—this omits portions of the signal that the signal receiver would not hear.
iii. Layered pattern recognition and good protection.

As shown in Fig. 3, there are three major sub-routines introduced when considering WPBIS namely Intelligent (i.e. identification analysis), serial communication, and control sub-routines. A DSP-based agent was used to create interrupt capability for the entire BWAS. Hence, it can suspend whatever action is executing whenever events of higher priority occur and attend to that event after which it goes back to what it was doing. It runs at the external clock speed of 24 MHz. With this, any identification can be analyzed within milliseconds. The structure of WPBIS is fully powered by intelligent computational algorithms controlling the wrist biometric end-to-end processes. The inputs to the system are captured with wrist prints from the sensors. Similarly, feedback is obtained from output actuators. The output devices include the buzzer alarm; dashboard display, drive mechanism, and electric motor. The software implementation is divided into three levels: the intelligent identification analysis sub-routine, serial communication sub-routine, and access control sub-routine in the WPBIS-DSP running DCT.

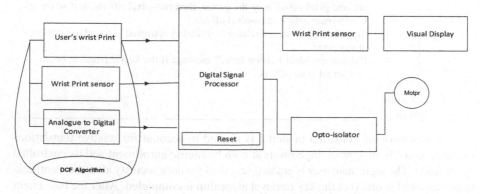

Fig. 3. Wrist-print biometric identification system (WPBIS)

3.3 WPBIS Model Integration

Figure 4 depicts that the Palm print WPBIS is made up of four subsystems, which are scanner, pre-processing, feature extraction, and matcher. The palm print scanner in the device collects photographs. Pre-processing involves setting up a coordinate scheme to align the palm print images and segmenting a portion of the image for feature extraction. Feature extraction is the method of extracting useful features from a palmprint that has already been processed. The authentic imagery is evaluated by the Matcher software. Image acquisition, pre-processing, feature extraction, and matching are the four stages in the palm print recognition scheme.

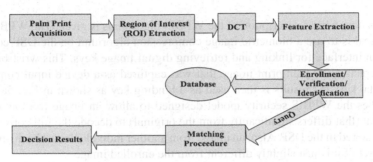

Fig. 4. General block diagram of WPBIS

Figure 4 depicts the system diagram of the palm-print identification device. The major elements of the WPBIS are divided into four sub-sections:

i.   Image capturing
     During this process, various types of digital cameras are used to capture images of palm prints. The accuracy of the acquired image can be blurred or noisy, which reduces the image's quality and directly affects the output rate of the palm print recognition system.

ii. Pre-processing
     Pre-processing is applied to the image after the data or image of the palm print has been captured. When noise is present in a captured image, it can be removed using filters during the processing step.

iii. Extraction of Characteristics
     Pre-processing follows feature extraction. Principal lines, orientation area, minutiae, density map, texture, singular points, and other palm features are extracted during the feature extraction process.

iv. Compatibility
     The feature extraction process is followed by the matching phase. The degree of similarity between the recognition template and the master template is determined by feature matching. This is done in a variety of ways. As shown in Fig. 4, individual input is matched with templates stored in the database. The system is optimized for efficient access control application integration addresses interface scalability, efficient control behavior, and in-depth security.

For efficiency in image compression in the access control template storage, an efficient interconnection of WPBIS must provide higher scalability and flexibility at large. The key goals considered in the WPBIS model, viz: maintain high throughput, low latency, rapid convergence, and scalable networks with low administrative overhead. If the input image is captured by a low-cost sensor, the DCT device performs a preprocessing procedure to reduce the blur effect that is common in the input image. Let's discuss the system characterization regarding the linking and digital key retrieval in Fig. 5a and 5b.

4   System Characterization

In this section, a brief description of the WPBIS algorithms is given. The WPBIS algorithm's goal is to use a biometric image compression algorithm on the DSP controller to give an interface for linking and retrieving digital image keys. This wrist-biometric image depicts a 2D palmprint image that was captured as a device input component. The digital key that results is then used as a binding key as shown in Fig. 5a and 5b. It describes the WPBIS security model designed to allow an image from an enrolled base client (that differs significantly from the original) to decode the full correct image template stored in the DSP. Also, an image from another individual must be distinct from others, even if it is just slightly different from the enrolled image.

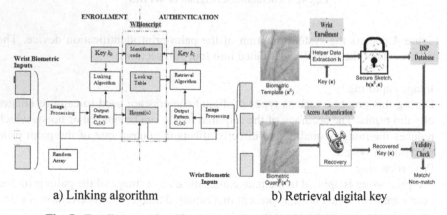

a) Linking algorithm   b) Retrieval digital key

Fig. 5. Enrollment and verification in wrist biometrically encrypted system

4.1   Modeling Assumptions

The WPBIS was presumed to fit into use case door access control systems (security sense only) for this study, as shown in Fig. 5. During the enrollment exercise, we conclude that several wrist samples F_0 are obtained and encrypted. The wrist samples obtained from base clients during the enrollment or registration process are processed and then bound with randomly generated strings of number N_k is a Biometric Key Binding (BKB) algorithm in DCT so that the randomly generated string N_k can be retrieved on the representation of the same wrist sample F_1 of which F_1F_0'. The interface connection used between the various door access point modules $pm1, pm2,...., pmn$ in this protection and privacy dependent algorithm for the WPBIS is mapped to the DSP-based controller where encrypted writs templates E_n is processed. During and after the access control processes, this DCT connection model provides a stable mapping mechanism between the various endpoints in the model.

For wrist biometric input signals in matrix form, an image compression model using the discrete cosine transform (DCT) was developed and implemented. The DCT is a technique for translating signals into elementary frequency components. This is required for biometric image footprint data to have enough storage space, a wide transmission bandwidth, and a longer transmission time. By spinning the frequencies of the different images before capturing them, a high level of encryption against any hacking attempt is ensured. This is to ensure that anyone who does not have the necessary knowledge of the number of spectra and their distributions in the spectral plane will be unable to decrypt this data. The shape of the spectra obtained with the DCT is very distinctive and easily observable even when the image spectrum is not rotated. This is very vital at the feature extraction and verification stages.

Following the application of the DCT method and the transmission of compressed and encrypted data, the images are extracted after reception by following the key steps of the transmission method, but in the opposite direction. To obtain the original images, the obtained image is multiplied by the inverse of random mask or the inverse wrist print spectrum considering the legitimate individual. Afterwards, numerous rotations is then activated in the opposite direction. Finally, the DCT is inversed as appropriate. These processes are used to drive the input sensor capture of the WPBIS in Fig. 5a and 5b. WPBIS Biosensor Integration.

In this Section, HyperTerminal implementation for Algorithm III and IV is presented. Algorithm III is used to connect the Biosensor to the terminal process for system setup and initialization.

Algorithm III. Biometric Sensor Connect to HyperTerminal Process

    Inputs: Biometric sensor module
                      History of biometric sensor module and transactional workflow
                      $\prod \beta 1$ & $\prod \beta 2$// initial parameters
    Output: DCT Optimal Scale+ _DES
    int i←0;
    While i <DCT_monitorCallSchedule d **do**
        Begin ( )
      1.   Connect the biometric sensor module to smart agent.
      2.   Call hyper terminal in windows ( );
      3.   Call project name ( );
      4.   Select modem from pop-up ( )
      5.   Select the com port to which the biometric sensor is attached from the "connect using" drop-down menu.
      6.   Set the Baud rate to 9600.
           None = parity
           Flow control = Hardware Data bits = 8 Stop bits = 1
        Activate ( );
      8. Set the module's serial speed to automatic.
      9. Call display dashboard ()
         End procedure ( )
         i ++;
    end while
    Return

Now, from Algorithm IV, the DSP controller was optimized based on the following desirable features: multi-level programming, fast response time, 32 input/output ports availability, serial communication capability, substantial memory space (4k), and low power consumption.

Algorithm IV. Biometric Sensor Port Connection with AT Command

    Inputs: Biometric sensor module

                       History of biometric sensor module and transactional workflow

                       $\prod \beta 1$ & $\prod \beta 2$// initial parameters

    Output: DCT Optimal Scale+ _DES

    int i←0;

    While i <DCT_monitorCallSchedule d **do**

           Begin ( )

           Begin ( )

        1.   Connect the serial port of the controller to that of the biometric sensor module.

        2.   Send the command "AT' to the sensor module.

        3.   Receive 'AT OK' from the sensor module.

        4.   Send 'AT+CMGF=1' to the sensor module.

        5.   Receive "AT+CMGF=1' OK' from the sensor module.

        6.   Send 'AT+CMGF=" digital code of a user"

        7.   Receive 'AT+CMGF=" digital code of a user",>

        8.   Send the message

        9.   Send the ASCII value of control z

      10. Receive + CMGS: memory storage of the user message sent

      11. Set up controller emulator

      12. Write the equivalent PDL to send/receive to and from the sensor module

      13. Display the result on the display dashboard.

          i ++;

    end while

    Return

---

5 Experimental Study

In this section, MATLAB Simulink [25] image vision was used to realize the validation of the WPBIS process model (image compression). Three main components are introduced. First, functional scanner module is used to carry out enrollment and verification in the system. It has a visual display unit (VDU), which enables users to interact with the door mechanism. This is similar to a Wrist-reader/module used in the acquisition of wrist palm images from end-users for authentication to access control systems. Second, the VDU dashboard provides the end-user with a simple image status of enrollment or verification transactions. Appropriate identity mapping is communicated by the VDU dashboard for listing invalid user/accessor legitimate access. Third, the stable DSP emulator processor is used for processing the DCT and is protected from scores manipulations. By applying Algorithms I to IV, the outcome is the biometric sensor module and the DSP. The experimental system with DCT algorithms sequentially sends messages to the biometric sensor module using a low latency DSP Microcontroller. The biometric sensor interface to the DSP was achieved in the WPBIS. Its output interface comprises: interface display dashboard to the controller, interface of the buzzer alarm to the controller, and interface of the motor to the controller.

In the process model for less complex writs template, a DSP block sends 8-by-8 submatrices of a wrist image frame to the subsystem for processing. Within this subsystem, the model quantizes each 8-by-8 sub-matrix after applying the DCT. To retrieve the original data, the model uses inverse quantization and inverse DCT in the decoder subsystem. The signal preprocessing module, an optical filter module, and a pattern recognition module are all integrated into the DSP. For the discrimination of eight hand movements, the online DSP controller can provide an 87.5% correct score. For the wrist bloc processing DSP model in WPBIS, this is validated using the Bpp test and compression ratio index for the sampled inputs. Both the original wrist image display and the optimized image display were obtained. As shown in Fig. 6a, the DCT Throughput/Compression ratio for the Wrist Image display is estimated at 93.55% which is very significant. Also, with the application of various timestamps, the sample image template Bpp yielded 1.256 Bpp (minimum) and compression of 63.26% based on the DCT as shown in Fig. 6b. The Wrist DSP model yielded 66.70% and 33.30% wrist image intensities respectively for the proposed DCT and wavelet scheme. DCT uses high throughput compression hits for massive data extraction from bioscript multispectral images efficiently. The main trade-off is observed in the computational system resources needed for DCT processing especially for complex image pixels.

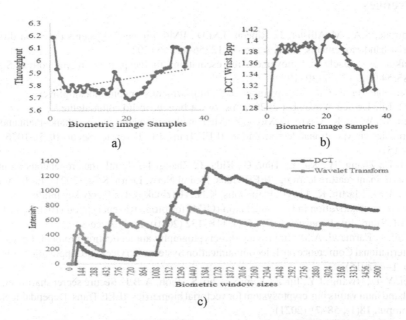

Fig. 6. a) DCT Throughput CR b) DCT Wrist_Bpp test extract c) DCT vs Wavelet intensities.

6 Conclusion

In this paper, Biometric Wrist Authentication (BWA) based on DCT for palmprint image compression is presented as an optimal scheme for image compression. The WPBIS-DCT is an efficient biometric technique considering two main areas: wrist-image extraction and line features from a 2/3D palmprint binary image. The system extracts orientation features and performs two distinct operations. Firstly, the encryption process changes the compressed data in such a way that it is unreadable to an unauthorized agent. Secondly, image compression is achieved involving the reduction of data sizes to be transmitted by removing redundant data. These two procedures are computed using DCT. This non-destructive spectral fusion allows for image compression and encryption concurrently. In summary, the proposed BWA leveraging DCT is useful in biometric access control systems and this has been applied in a DSP block for palmprint image compression. Results of the process model show that the sample (image template) Bpp yield 1.256 Bpp (minimum) and a Cr of 63.26% based on the DCT. Also, the DCT offered more acceptable palmprint image security and can carry more pixels than the wavelet scheme in typical deployment scenarios. Future work would deliver the optimal hardware prototype and machine interfacing with Field programmable gate arrays (FPGAs).

References

1. Raurale, S.A., McAllister, J., Rincón, J.M.D.: EMG biometric systems based on different wrist-hand movements. IEEE Access **9**, 12256–12266 (2021)
2. Kakei, S.: Muscle and movement representations in the primary motor cortex. Science **285**(5436), 2136–2139 (1999)
3. Wearable Manus Gloves, November 2020. https://manus-vr.com/mocap-gloves
4. DataLite Device, November 2020. https://www.biometricsltd.com/datalite
5. Fan, W., Wang, K., Cayre, F., Xiong, Z.: Median filtered image quality enhancement and anti-forensics via variational deconvolution. IEEE Trans. Inf. Forensics Secur. **10**(5), 1076–1091 (2015)
6. Fei, L., Zhang, B., Xu, Y., Tian, C., Rida, I., Zhang, D.: Jointly heterogeneous palmprint discriminant feature learning. IEEE Trans. Neural Netw. Learn. Syst. (2021). Early Access.
7. Bui, F.M., Martin, K., Lu, H., Plataniotis, K.N., Hatzinakos, D.: Fuzzy key binding strategies based on quantization index modulation (QIM) for biometric encryption (BE) applications. IEEE Trans. Inf. Forensics Secur. **5**(1), 118–132 (2010). Early Access
8. Fadil, I., Barmawi, A.M.: Improving bio-cryptography authentication protocol. In: 2015 9th International Conference on Telecommunication Systems Services and Applications (TSSA), pp. 1–6 (2015)
9. Lai, Y.-L., Hwang, J.Y., Jin, Z., Kim, S., Cho, S., Teoh, A.B.J.: Secure secret sharing enabled b-band mini vaults bio-cryptosystem for vectorial biometrics. IEEE Trans. Dependable Secure Comput. **18**(1), 58–71 (2021)
10. Drozdowski, P., Rathgeb, C., Dantcheva, A., Damer, N., Busch, C.: Demographic bias in biometrics: a survey on an emerging challenge. IEEE Transactions on Technology and Society **1**(2), 89–103 (2020)
11. Drozdowski, P., Rathgeb, C., Dantcheva, A., Damer, N., Busch, C.: Demographic bias in biometrics: a survey on an emerging challenge. IEEE Trans. Technol. Soc. **1**(2), 89–103 (2020)

12. Weaver, A.C.: Biometric authentication. Computer **39**(2), 96–97 (2006)
13. Pawar, N., Ingole, D.T., Ingole, M.D.: Normalization method for misaligned face samples in non-cooperative biometrics. In: 2017 International Conference On Smart Technologies For Smart Nation (SmartTechCon), pp. 330–333 (2017)
14. Luo, Z., Li, J., Zhu, Y.: A deep feature fusion network based on multiple attention mechanisms for joint iris-periocular biometric recognition. IEEE Signal Process. Lett. **28**, 1060–1064 (2021)
15. Edwards, T., Hossain, M.S.: Effectiveness of deep learning on serial fusion based biometric systems. IEEE Trans. Artif. Intell. **2**(1), 28–41 (2021)
16. Zhou, C., Liu, J., Sheng, M., Zheng, Y., Li, J.: Exploiting fingerprint correlation for fingerprint-based indoor localization: a deep learning based approach. IEEE Trans. Vehicul. Technol. (2021). Early Access
17. Yuan, C., Jiao, S., Sun, X., Wu, Q.J.: MFFFLD: a multi-modal feature fusion based fingerprint liveness detection. IEEE Trans. Cogn. Dev. Syst. (2021). Early Access
18. Hsu, J.H., Su, M.H., Wu, C.H., Chen, Y.H.: Speech emotion recognition considering nonverbal vocalization in affective conversations. In: IEEE/ACM Transactions on Audio, Speech, and Language Processing (2021). Early Access
19. Wang, C., Muhammad, J., Wang, Y., He, Z., Sun, Z.: Towards complete and accurate iris segmentation using deep multi-task attention network for non-cooperative iris recognition. IEEE Trans. Info. Forensics Sec. **15**, 2944–2959 (2020)
20. Shi, H., Liu, R., Chen, C., Shu, M., Wang, Y.: ECG baseline estimation and denoising with group sparse regularization. IEEE Access **9** 23595–23607 (2021)
21. Zhang, J., et al.: MLBF-Net: a multi-lead-branch fusion network for multi-class arrhythmia classification using 12-Lead ECG. IEEE J. Trans. Eng. Health Med. **9**, 1–11 (2021). Art no. 1900211
22. Stanley, P.K., et al.: Electromyogram based bot-assistive device for paralyzed people. In: Proceedings IEEE ESCI, pp. 623–626 (2021)
23. Ahmed, M.A., Deyu, Q., Alshemmary, E.N.: Electroencephalogram signal eye blink rejection improvement based on the hybrid stone blind origin separation and particle swarm optimization technique. IEEE Access **8**, 105671–105680 (2020)
24. Shahreza, H.O., Marcel, S.: Towards protecting and enhancing vascular biometric recognition methods via biohashing and deep neural networks. IEEE Trans. Biometr. Behav. Identity Sci. (2021). Early Access
25. Behrens, A., et al.: MATLAB Meets LEGO mindstorms—a freshman introduction course into practical engineering. IEEE Trans. Educ. **53**(2), 306–317 (2010)

International Workshop on Land Use Monitoring for Sustainability (LUMS 2021)

From Cost Benefit Analysis to Spatial Indicators: The Use of CO2 Segregation and Carbon Footprint for the Evaluation of Sustainable Land Use Transitions

Carmelo Maria Torre[✉], Pasquale Balena, Alessandro Bonifazi, and Ludovica Vitale

Department of Civil, Environmental, Land, Building Engineering and Chemistry, Polytechnic University of Bari, 70126 Bari, Italy
carmelomaria.torre@poliba.it

Abstract. The paper shows the first result of a research project, aiming at considering new useful environmental indicators that will be useful to describe, such as a unique parameter, the environmental impact of spatial artificialization of land. The well known concept of "soil take" can support the evolution towards new concepts, related to global environmental phenomena, such as the increase of "Global Warming" and of "Carbon Dioxide". Land transition from an existing natural category of soil coverage to a new artificial one is one of the main negative contribution to the increase of the temperature in the earth's atmosphere. Some recent studies developed by scholars in environmental economics, put on evidence the function of "cost of carbon dioxide segregation" as a relevant indicator of Heart's Global Warming. The paper highlights a double function of such kind of measures: "synthetic environmental indicators" on one hand represent the measure of a continuous check of global change in the atmosphere, and on the other hand consider the economic value of carbon segregation as an "easy" alternative to cost benefit assessment, able to describe in a unique dimension the trend of global phenomena.

Keywords: Environmental synthetic indicators · Cost-benefit · CO2 footprint · Soil take · Transition matrix · Multidimensional spatial assessment

1 Introduction

In the history of city and regional development, environmental issues due to soil take represent the most common example of a never-ending conflict among urban growth and nature preservation.

The need of using environmental resources and – in the same - of saving ecosystem services, always in order to increase human welfare, drive nowadays to the seek for new needful evaluative approaches regarding the impact due the increase of urban settlement on the natural environment [1, 2].

O. Gervasi et al. (Eds.): ICCSA 2021, LNCS 12955, pp. 479–489, 2021.
https://doi.org/10.1007/978-3-030-87007-2_34

In this continuously evolving context, since the past to nowadays Cost-benefit analysis (CBA) represent the "business as usual" approach for assessing advantages/disadvantages, in many social and private disciplinary activity. CBA (at the same time) is looking at balancing the reduction of natural capital due to the urban and economic growth, accompanied by the aim at understanding if the issues of an increase of welfare can balance the loss of some environmental resources.

Starting from the milestones of the Serageldin Triangle (Economy, Environment and Society) authors analyzed possible evaluative paths towards a more effective assessment of the sustainability of plans and programs.

This assessment has been often based on multiple indicators of performance, valuation criteria, multifunction formulas etc.

The debate "Cost Benefit Assessment (CBA) versus Sustainability Multidimensional Evaluation (SME) started in the Eighties, and still exists in the nowadays: the two approaches have been overtaken by several synthetic indicators of sustainability (SIS) having some peculiar issues [3–5].

Just to be more understandable the shift from a complex communicative result to a simplest, SIS have an educational scope, and invite people to understand more easily the limit of urban World Growth.

The task is based on making people more concerning about the ratio at the World scale, between the economic growth vs the reduction of environmental resources. Resources are usually measured by the "Ecological Footprint", "Ozone Hole", "Global Warming", "atmosphere CO2" etc.

In the most recent and contemporary era, the evolution of environmental economics coupled with the increased relevance of social communication, favored as consequence the idea to communicate with understandable indicators the state of the environment [6–8].

The relevance of such "universal indicators" [9] is due to the understandability that a unique estimate of global environmental changes, make people easily concerning about the importance to adopt a more sustainable lifestyle. The newest indicator of sustainability is related with the "Carbon Segregation" [10–12].

2   Aim of the Research

Starting from the idea that data about pollution, artificialization of soil, consumption of not-renewable resources, in the light of "environmental democracy" (aside the traditional technical approach based on the practice of environmental impact assessment) should communicate effective information to non-expert arenas, environmental planners and economists propose readable measures, such as the ecological footprint, the percentage of artificialization of Hearth surface, the global climate warming, and so on, as a fast communicative measure of environmental changes.

In the recent years, further scholars have been posed a new attention on the increase of CO2 in the atmosphere, just to support the environmental information to "non-expert" contexts by a simple parameter (represented by the increase of carbon dioxide and global temperature).

The need to stock "also but not only" Carbon dioxide, becomes therefore the new horizon for assessing global sustainable actions in the field of Urban and Spatial Planning (USP), Environmental Impact Assessment (EIA) and Strategic Environmental Assessment (SEA).

The diffusion and segregation of CO2, therefore, represent now a joint/global indicator of global warming and surface pollution.

Many scholars just in the recent time started studying effect of soil take, in official institutional researches, looking at artificial coverage and imperviousness, as one of the causes of global environmental issues as hearth climate changes.

3 Synthetic Indicators vs Cost Benefit Analyses for Environmental Impact Assessments

The aim of this paper is to test a new way of mapping the transition of soils from the previous coverages to new ones, and of calculating the effect of change the carbon stock as a complement of the most famous measures of soil take. The paper illustrates an example of a research about the potential absorption of CO2 emission, based on geographic mapping and GIS-supported multidimensional assessment at the local scale, that can demonstrate the possible usefulness of measure deriving form carbon segregation as measure of environmental issues.

The research started with the seek for a "measure" about effects of the transition from the existing natural/artificial soil towards new ones [13, 14]. The measure starts from the spatial analysis of Carbon segregation (CS) and Carbon Bi-oxide diffusion of soil (CO2), related to the peculiar characters of all land surfaces. Finally, the effect of CO2 segregation in land-use has been represented in the spatial and monetary dimension, as a result of the loss and revenue deriving from the measure of CO2 segregation cost and savings. The authors think that this study, looking at the evolution of land uses [15] [16], will contribute to a deeper research on the use a spatial indicator of the effectiveness man-driven CO2 segregation.

Different methods can be used to evaluate externalities: it is possible to approach by qualitative evaluation, weighting and ranking, cost-benefit, damage estimation and monetization of issues, multiple criteria analysis (sometime combined with cost-benefits) and so on.

The most frequently applied is still the Cost Benefit Analysis (CBA), especially in the ruling system.

CBA takes place by the identification of a cash-flow of costs and benefits (benefits, for instance are considerable as public/social revenues) brought to the community as consequence of land-use changes. A territorial transformation therefore is assessed by the use of a time-actualization of all (positive and negative) money quantities at the initial instant of flow, in order to make them comparable, and to obtain by a difference between benefits and costs, the overall net benefit. A wider application of the method has been considered preferable, from the past until nowadays, thanks to the apparent simplicity of the economic indicators that measure advantages and disadvantages of a given choice. Among these, the most known is the net present value (NPV).

NPV is characterized by its communicative power, that is based on the definition of a judgment through a single monetary measure: such measure can result positive or negative, and can refer to a farer or nearer future horizon.

The so-called "Extended CBA", refines the results of the "traditional" CBA (that refers on financial Cost and benefit in a social arena) by adding the evaluation of those overall social/environmental costs and benefits that will be generated by transformations [14].

CBA therefore, can base its judgment of appropriateness not only on the assessment of a financial cash flow, but also on a wider evaluation that collect both financial accounts and socio-environmental accounts, looking towards a wider cost-effectiveness balance.

As regards the monetary equivalence of social and environmental issue due to a land transformation (a project or a plan):

– on one hand, it can express positively the increase of the financial dimension of resources/revenues, and on the other hand the consequent expected advantage enjoyable for the community.
– on the other hand, it can express negatively the financial dimension of the disadvantage due to an unlucky or fallacious implementation, with a consequent difficulty for community, due to the deprivation of lost resources.

Last but not least, CBA also represented, in the recent past times, a complementary tool to Environmental Impact Studies.

Cost Benefit Analysis has often been criticized by the scientific community of environmental economists for decades, due to some well-known limits: the remoteness of time horizons of environmental issues, that makes ineffective the measure of costs and benefits. The balance between cost and benefit becomes "smaller" after the discounting from remote futures to nowadays. The cost-benefit analysis, however, has a very broad scope and is frequently indicated as relevant methodology in the law system, due to some technical approaches related with the evaluation of impacts/transformation inside the development and implementation of plans and projects.

A further limitation of CBA is due to the difficulty to manage several and multidimensional information, in the light of an accounting related with: land use changes, cost and revenues, social effects, environmental resources, enhancement/reduction: all are always measured with homogeneous money units that sometimes make a non-sense final determination of values. The balance, when based on the expression by money units, describing a multiple dimension of effects, implies several financial calculations with a high character of uncertainty.

Last but not least, the support of Cost-Benefit studies in decision-making processes, and many further complex evaluative approaches (e.g. Multicriterial or Environmental Impact Assessment) is politically useful, but in the same time it is not so easy to be explained to the community.

For these reasons, indicators and descriptors of impacts generated by the transformations and the evolution of a given environment, have been combined with the steady technique of cost-benefit analysis. The description of the effects of the environment generated by a "unique global indicator" is represented, for instance by the "ecological footprint" (EF). Ecological Footprint means "the measure of the resources needed to ensure the usual lifestyle of a community".

Claiming that the Ecological footprint is the measure of a consumption of environmental resources so that "three times bigger of the earth", for instance, represents easily that the level of consumption of resources has to be considered three times the sustainable one.

The use of the so-called "synthetic indicators', therefore, favors the application of the concept of "environmental democracy" based on the principles of the Aharus Convention, which establish the obligation to inform the community of the environmental impacts generated by territorial transformations.

The advantage of synthetic indicators lies in the ease of understanding the relevance of the environmental risk generated by human activities. The difficulty, instead is represented by upstream procedure that identifies the value of the indicator.

The aim of the experimentation is to verify the communicability of indicators that are represented with a monetary measure, which is very easy to communicate. In the case in question, we are talking about the cost of "Carbon segregation", measured with respect to changes in land use.

The cost of "Carbon Segregation" (CSC) is not only an easy communicative mono-dimensional measure: it represents also a synthetic money estimate of compensation of environmental issues, due to the evolution of settlements and activities on the Hearth surface. According with these premises, the paper will show a possible method of assessment that can be extended from a small piece of land to an entire regional or sub-regional context.

Last but not least, the assumption by the European Commission, concerning about the relevance of climate changes, amended the Regulation (EU) 2018/842 on "binding" annual greenhouse gas emission reductions from 2021 to 2030 in order to give a further contribution to action for climate regulation, according with the commitments coming from the "Paris Agreement".

The European Commission already from 2020 as part of the so-called "European Green Deal, had proposed to increase the minimum acceptable threshold for 2030, relating to the reduction of greenhouse gas emissions, to at least 55% compared to 1990".

Paris Agreement - COP 21, as well, produced the first universal agreement to reduce the atmospheric temperature by 2 degrees, below the levels of the first industrial revolution (1861–1880) from 2015 to 2100. Such reduction is equivalent in terms of Carbon Footprint, to the elimination of 2,900 billion tons of Co2, by 2050: the reduction is equal to a cut of emissions between 40% and 70%.

More in detail, the existing ambition for 2030 climate and energy framework are represented by the following Key targets: at least 40% of cuts in greenhouse gas emissions (from 1990 levels), 32% to share for renewable energy, 32.5% improvement in energy efficiency.

The minimum target for the 2030 is anyway represented by the reduction of greenhouse gas emission at the 55% respect to 1990, according with the forecast and the actions of the "European Green Deal".

In the light of these international agreements, it should be interesting to consider as a new approach the "economic measure" of "carbon footprint" as the base of a new "exercise of evaluation" aiming at translate in money dimension, the effect of carbon segregation changes, in the territorial structure.

4   The Case of Study

As already explained the story starts from an experimental approach aiming to find, test and propose a synthetic (one-dimensional) indicator of environmental impacts that can be implemented within an EIA procedure applied to a set of projects, and which acts for a new offer of rural leisure in the countryside of the Puglia Region. Rural contexts in Puglia are, - sometimes and partially - included inside "Sites of Interest for the Community" (SIC) by decree of the European Union (EU).

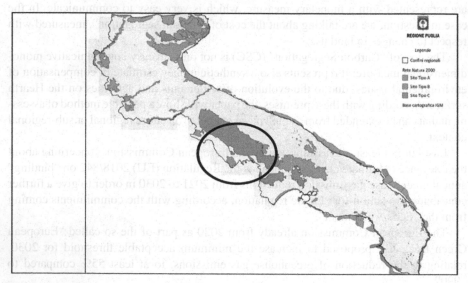

Fig. 1. Map of European "Sites of Interest for the European Community" in Apulian Region. The case study refers to the undersigned area inside the ellipse (Source: Apulian Region Geographic Information System)

The classification of SIC starts from the recognition of the environmental context, in those areas that guest listed species according with criteria of "EU Habitat Catalogue". This constrain requires maintaining a good conservation status of "habitat types" and "species" within the "Nature 2000" program (see Fig. 1).

Italian natural terrestrial sites included in the "Nature 2000" Repository (the so-called SIC-Sites of interest for the EU Community) cover 5.843.817 Hectares (more-less the 20% of the whole national surface).

In Apulian Region "SIC areas" cover an extension of 402.512 Hectares. In detail, the SIC area named "Murgia dei Trulli" is one of the biggest in the regional and national context.

All EU Member States, according with the Habitats Directive, must periodically monitor the status of "habitat types" and "listed species", just to confirm or to modify the perimeters of such special environmentally protected areas. Finally, the assessment of the state of conservation is mandatory, and all real modification or transformation project regarding Habitat Sites are subjected to a peculiar impact assessment procedure.

5   The Approach to Evaluation

The first test has been experimented in the core area of Apulia Region (put on evidence in Fig. 1), that contains a main "Site of Community Interest". Such environmental context is well identified by the presence of hilly and oak wooded highlands (see Fig. 2) and avian species, both listed in the Natura 2000 repository, also hosting the presence of the famous and peculiar rural houses named "Trulli" having the typical circular plant and the conic stone roof.

Fig. 2. Overall view of the countryside interested by projects of new rural settlements. In the far horizon the Adriatic Coast is visible (source: 3D vision - Google maps)

The area of study was analyzed, in order to discover the possibility of transition from the current land use to new ones. It takes necessary the assessment of environmental effects, just by simple indicators, according with norms. Just to experiment an innovative approach, a new set of indicators was provided. The peculiarity of new measures is based on the assessment of effects of transition from old land uses to the new ones. The impact of transition was measured in terms of variation of CO2 segregation connected with to the change of land uses. All typologies of surface can be classified in terms of CO2 segregation: as a consequence, the measure of CO2 segregation of a soil, looking at land use changes, changes as well. In the observed contexts the transition regarded mainly the shift from agricultural land-uses to the touristic ones, accompanied with new leisures and new complementary activities.

According to the EU legislation, the environmental issues due to the forecasts of new settlements provided by plans should be submitted to "Strategic environmental assessment" (SEA); in the same time the more detailed project should be submitted to "Environmental incidence assessment" (EIA).

In order to justify the usefulness of the new activities, when discovering environmental issues related to the implementation of plans/projects, it becomes necessary to make a balance between costs and benefits.

According to such approaches, the valuation of costs should consider environmental issues, and in the same time, the valuation of benefits should include "added values", due to the creation of new activities and jobs, and furthermore, to the increase of gross profit. The positive economic issues should be represented (as already underlined) by the net present value deriving from previous balances.

As regards economic literature, many researches put continuously on evidence the weakness points of Cost Benefit Studies.

Fig. 3. A possible project of new settlements inserted in the countryside.

Social costs, generally are referable to long-term time horizons, unlike the financial costs of intervention referring to the short term, consequently have a minimal impact on the cost-benefit balance, because they are greatly reduced by the high uncertainty they undergo in discounting.

Starting from the assumption of some weakness point in applying a traditional cost-benefit balance, the more recent thoughts about the study of environmental impacts due to the human activities suggest to use universal indicators, that have a technical and a social characterization. The most relevant technical aspect of an universal indicator is represented by its synthetic character: for instance, global warming can be measured by the increase of temperature or by the sea level rise; soil take can be measured by hectares of artificial soil, or by imperviousness; the loss of natural resources is measured by the reduction of biomass, and so on [16, 17].

As previously announced, the experiment related with the case-study consists in substituting the traditional cost-benefit analysis with the assessment of derived values from CO_2 segregation due to the variation of surfaces, in the transition from the early land use to the new one, with consequent coupled transition from an initial money value to the final one, expressing the economic dimension of carbon segregation [18, 19]. Among basic systems of carbon recapture and segregation, the Carbon Dioxide Removal (CDR) is mainly relevant. CDR is accompanied by several strategies [20]:

- reforestation, aiming at the creation of "carbon sink", useful for biofuel production,
- bio-energy with carbon capture and storage (BECCS),
- direct air capture (DAC) by air scrubbing,
- use of dedicated solvents ready to be used for solution.
- sequestration for soils increase, to be obtained by suitable techniques based on the content of organic compounds in rhizosphere.

When looking at the monetary dimension, furthermore, the value of CO2 segregation has been increasing during the time (Fig. 4). Such trends show a progressive increase of performance testified by cost-benefit balance of carbon segregation (Fig. 4). The table in Fig. 5, instead, shows the variation of of land coverage before and after the implementation of the project.

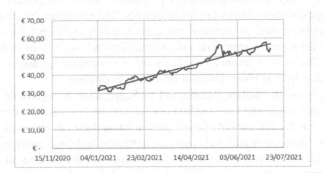

Fig. 4. Trend of value of CO2 segregation (euros per square meters)

SAMPLE n.3	m²	m²	m²	m²	m²	m²	m²
Uncultivated land	201.720						-42.770
Rare widespread wooded soil	20.250					-6.560	
Oaks	53.030				0		
Ornamental saplings	0			+51.280			
Wooded Soil	47.100		-27.080				
Built Environment	1.350	+25.130					+
New Surfaces		26.480	20.020	51.280	53.030	13.690	158.950
	Past Surfaces	Built Environment	Wooded Soil	Ornamental saplings	Oaks	Rare widespread wooded soil	Uncultivated land

Fig. 5. Transition among different typology of land use (before and after land use change)

Balance of CO₂ segregation	m²	m²	m²	Kg$_{CO2}$/m²	Unit Price of CO₂ kg	Total Kg$_{CO2}$	Cost of CO₂ Segregation
Uncultivated land	201.720	158.950	-42.770	0,35		-14.970	
Rare widespread wooded soil	20.250	13.690	-6.560	0,5		-3.280	
Oaks	53.030	53.030	0	1,99	€ 23,38		
Ornamental saplings	0	51.280	+51.280	4,33		222.042	
Wooded Soil	47.100	20.020	-27.080	0,98		- 26.538	
Built Environment	1.350	26.480	+25.130	1,1		27.643	
						204.897	€ 4.790.492

Fig. 6. Final money accounting of CO2 segregation

6   Last Remarks

The paper shows an experimental/pioneer proposal to assess the impact of composite land-use change due to the birth of new settlements. The economic dimension of carbon segregation has been used as "dummy" measure of a benefits/costs balance, associated to progressive urban and countryside evolutions. Similarly to various experiments, the case of study shows the relevance of innovation in environmental assessment, joint as well a new philosophy in environmental economic evaluation.

The reader can notice that the Balance of Co2 Segregation, as regards the dimensional aspect of the amount (about four million euros), can be comparable, from the formal point of view with the assessment of a net present value due to an economic recreational activity, as considered as traditional approach to benefit and costs analysis.

Just to foster this assumption, the amount is similar to the net present value that an ordinary construction company can estimate in a cash flow of more-less ten years.

Last but not least, a further reasoning can be connected with the double dimension of cost of carbon segregation. On one side, the monetary dimension of carbon segregation can be considered a measure of the capability of an economic activity (related with the transition from a natural environment to a built environment), of maintaining a low impact in terms of contribution to global warming. On the other side, monetization of carbon footprint can also represent a way of measuring the dimension of the interaction between the residential activity and the environmental context.

References

1. Attardi, R., Cerreta, M., Sannicandro, V., Torre, C.M.: Non-compensatory composite indicators for the evaluation of urban planning policy: the land-use policy efficiency index (LUPEI). Eur. J. Oper. Res. **264**(2), 491–507 (2018)
2. Berto, R., Stival, C.A., Rosato, P.: Enhancing the environmental performance of industrial settlements: an economic evaluation of extensive green roof competitiveness. Build. Environ. **127**, 58–68 (2018)

3. Morano, P., Guarini, M.R., Tajani, F., Anelli, D.: Sustainable redevelopment: the cost-revenue analysis to support the urban planning decisions. In: Gervasi, O., et al. (eds.) ICCSA 2020. LNCS, vol. 12251, pp. 968–980. Springer, Cham (2020). https://doi.org/10.1007/978-3-030-58808-3_69
4. Morano, P., Tajani, F.: Break Even Analysis for the financial verification of urban regeneration projects. Appl. Mech. Mater. **438**, 1830–1835 (2013)
5. Morano, P., Tajani, F.: Saving soil and financial feasibility. a model to support public-private partnerships in the regeneration of abandoned areas. Land Use Policy **73**, 40–48 (2018)
6. Sullivan, E., Ward, P.: Sustainable housing applications and policies for low-income self-build and housing rehabilitation. Habitat Int. **36**(2), 312–323 (2012)
7. Torre, C., Morano, P., Tajani, F.: Saving soil for sustainable land use. Sustainability. **9**(3), 350 (2017). https://doi.org/10.3390/su9030350
8. Foster L.S., Gruntfest I.J.: Demonstration experiments using universal indicators. J. Chem. Educ. 274–276 (1937)
9. Greenwood-Smith, S.L.: The use of rapid environmental assessment techniques to monitor the health of Australian rivers. Water Sci. Technol. **45**, 155–160 (2002)
10. VV.AA.: Interpretation Manual of European Union Habitats. European Commission - DG Environment Nature Env B3 (2013)
11. Solarin, S.A.: Convergence in CO 2 emissions, carbon footprint and ecological footprint: evidence from OECD countries. Environ. Sci. Pollut. Res. **26**, 6167–6181 (2019)
12. Pilogallo, A., Saganeiti, L., Scorza, F.M., B. : Ecosystem services' based impact assessment for low carbon transition processes. TeMA-J. Land Use Mobil. Environ. **12**(2), 127–138 (2019)
13. Mazzariello, A., Pilogallo, A., Scorza, F., Murgante, B., Las Casas, G.: Carbon stock as an indicator for the estimation of anthropic pressure on territorial components. In: Gervasi, O., et al. (eds.) ICCSA 2018. LNCS, vol. 10964, pp. 697–711. Springer, Cham (2018). https://doi.org/10.1007/978-3-319-95174-4_53
14. Perchinunno, P., Rotondo, F., Torre, C.M.: The evidence of links between landscape and economy in rural park. Int. J. Agricult. Environ. Inf. Syst. **3**(2), 72–85 (2012)
15. Attardi, R., Cerreta, M., Sannicandro, S., Torre, C.M.: The multidimensional assessment of land take and soil sealing. Lect. Notes Comput. Sci. **9157**, 301–316 (2015)
16. Castella, J.C., et al.: Effects of landscape segregation on livelihood vulnerability: moving from extensive shifting cultivation to rotational agriculture and natural forests in northern laos. Hum. Ecol. **41**, 63–76 (2013)
17. Feld, C.K., Sousa, J.P., Martins da Silva, P., Dawson, T.P.: Indicators for biodiversity and ecosystem services: towards an improved framework for ecosystems assessment. Biodiversity Conserv. **19**(10), 2895–2919 (2010)
18. Motavalli, P., Nelson, K., Udawatta, R., Shibu, J., Sougata, B.: Global achievements in sustainable land management. Int. Soil Water Conserv. Res.h **1**, 1–10 (2013)
19. Pontius, R.G.J., Shusas, E., McEachern, M.: Detecting important categorical land changes while accounting for persistence. Agr. Ecosyst. Environ. **101**, 251–268 (2004)
20. Vauhkonen, J., Packalen, T.: Shifting from even-aged management to less intensive forestry in varying proportions of forest land in Finland: impacts on carbon storage, harvest removals, and harvesting costs. Eur. J. Forest Res. **138**(2), 219–238 (2019). https://doi.org/10.1007/s10342-019-01163-9

A Multidimensional Approach for Cultural Ecosystem Services (CES) Assessment: The Cilento Coast Case Study (Italy)

Maria Cerreta[1,2]([✉]), Massimo Clemente[2], Benedetta Ettorre[1], and Giuliano Poli[1]

[1] Department of Architecture, University of Naples Federico II, via Toledo 402, 80134 Naples, Italy
{maria.cerreta,giuliano.poli}@unina.it
[2] Institute for Research On Innovation and Services for Development (IRISS), National Research Council Italy (CNR), via Guglielmo Sanfelice, 8, Naples, Italy
m.clemente@iriss.cnr.it

Abstract. The evaluation of the Cultural Ecosystem Services represents an evolving research field that analyses the processes of enhancing the landscape and its components. The contribution presents a multidimensional approach for identifying and evaluating the Cultural Ecosystem Services that characterize the coastal strip of Cilento and, specifically, within the Municipality of Camerota, in the South of Italy, and developing a culture-led enhancement strategy.

The methodological framework consists of three main phases: the first, knowledge and interpretation, the second evaluation, and the third elaboration of a situated strategy for the Baia degli Infreschi, a natural inlet of great interest in landscape and tourism in the Municipality of Camerota. A Decision Support System has been structured by developing a hybrid evaluative process that combines the SODA approach, the GeoTOPSIS spatial multi-criteria analysis and the ANP multi-criteria method by integrating the principles of Maritime Spatial Planning and the Cultural Ecosystem Services (CES) framework.

Keywords: Coastal landscape · Landscape assessment · Cultural Ecosystem Services · SODA approach · GeoTOPSIS method · ANP method

1 Introduction

Coastal areas appear as complex entities in continuous evolution, osmotic interfaces [1] natural seats of conflict between the two meanings of the word "border": limit and frontier. The transformations that occur along this line of demarcation are dictated simultaneously by the impulses of the hinterland and by what happens on the land-sea interface, both in physical-morphological and socio-cultural terms. The coastal strip of Campania, in southern Italy, is a landscape of great social, economic and cultural importance. With its 430 km of extension, it is configured as a place of continuous exchanges and flows that, on the one hand, contribute to feeding the metabolism of the territory; on the other hand, highlight its fragility.

© Springer Nature Switzerland AG 2021
O. Gervasi et al. (Eds.): ICCSA 2021, LNCS 12955, pp. 490–503, 2021.
https://doi.org/10.1007/978-3-030-87007-2_35

The coastal cities, on a semantic level, express the fusion of urban and maritime culture [2], defined by Konvitz as "Urban maritime culture" [3]. The natural headlands, coves and beaches are counterbalanced by urban infrastructure links such as roads, highways and railways, those purely coastal as ports and lighthouses and finally, the great maritime cities and ancient fishing villages.

In this perspective, the coastal landscape can be considered a "cultural ecosystem" [4, 5], characterized by the naturalistic and environmental components and cultural features, expression of local identity, and the system of material and immaterial relationships.

The ecosystem, in ecological terms, is defined as a fundamental unit formed by a community of living organisms in a specific area and the specific physical environment to which complex relationships link organisms. Usually, they are open and therefore have exchanges of materials and energy with other ecosystems. This definition, translated from ecology to the urban context, allows to include, in addition to the system itself, the inflows and outflows that pass through it, the "ecosystem services" [6, 7] and the "landscape services" which pay special attention to the multiple functions that the landscape can develop [8–10]. Several classification systems for Ecosystem Services have been proposed internationally, including the MEA (Millennium Ecosystem Assessment) [7], TEEB (The Economics of Ecosystems and Biodiversity) [11], and CICES (Common International Classification of Ecosystem Services) [12]. Four main categories of ES can be deduced from the text of the MEA, which have subsequently been taken up and enriched by the other classifications:

- Provisioning, that includes products obtained from natural and semi-natural ecosystems such as food, pure water, fibre, fuel, medicine;
- Regulating, that contains many services with direct and indirect human benefits such as climate stabilization, waste recycling, usually not recognized until they are lost or degraded;
- Supporting, that collects all those services necessary for the production of all other ES and contribute to the conservation (in situ) of biological and genetic diversity and evolutionary processes;
- Cultural, which is conceived as the set of non-material benefits obtained from ecosystems, such as spiritual, ethical, recreational, aesthetic sense, and social relations.

According to the above perspective, the primary purpose is to investigate the cultural ecosystem potential of the Cilento coastal strip, a sub-region of Campania (Fig. 1), and propose its reactivation and enhancement. Integrating the principles of Maritime Spatial Planning (Directive 2014/89/EU) [13] the Cultural Ecosystem Services (CES) framework, the different components of this environment have been analyzed with specific methods and tools. First, thematic maps have been elaborated through the software Q-Gis, whose aggregation has allowed to explore the spatial distribution of the phenomena and then return density maps related to the presence of CES along the entire coastal strip of Cilento. Subsequently, applying the multi-criteria method GeoTOPSIS, it was possible to create a map of the ecosystem potentials of the Municipality of Camerota. Finally, the attention has been turned to the Baia degli Infreschi, a natural inlet of the Municipality of Camerota. To address this step and obtain proposals for the enhancement of the area, a survey was conducted on social networks among the inhabitants of the municipality and neighbouring ones, members of associations operating in the area and tourists. The data obtained by the survey were first processed through the Decision Explorer software with the Strategic Options Development and Analysis (SODA) approach to obtain cognitive maps related to the categories of stakeholders interviewed, and then analyzed with the Analytic Network Process (ANP) method to get the preferred alternative of enhancement for the bay.

2   Cultural Ecosystem Services: An Open Debate

The debate about Cultural Ecosystem Services (CES) has developed recently. Although research on this topic offers many insights, there is still a struggle to give it an unambiguous definition. The benefits that this category of services provided to people are generally intangible, generated by natural or semi-natural physical environments, and can affect people's emotional state. In the 1997 publication by Costanza and Folke [6], CES are defined as the aesthetic, artistic, educational, spiritual, and/or scientific values offered by a given environment. Cultural services are covered in the three main classifications of ES and allow for the identification of several value categories [14]:

1. Spiritual and religious value, cultural diversity, aesthetic value, knowledge and education systems, recreation, and ecotourism values (MEA classification) [7];
2. Culture and arts, information for cognitive development, spiritual experience, aesthetic information, recreation, and tourism (TEEB classification) [11];
3. Spiritual, aesthetic, informational, community activity, and recreational value (CICES classification) [12].

The main characteristics of CES are intangibility, subjectivity and the difficulty of quantification in biophysical and primarily monetary terms [15]. Their value, linked to the emotional sphere of the individual, depends on individual and cultural assessments [16, 17].

3   The Case Study

Located in the southern end of the Campania region, Cilento is the second largest national park by extension and a UNESCO World Heritage Site since 1998. During Prehistory and the Middle Ages, the Cilento region was used as the central passage for cultural, political and commercial communications between peoples. These communications took place through the mountain ranges running from east to west, which created a very diversified cultural landscape made of contaminations and flows that have fertilized the whole territory.

Moreover, in some critical moments of the development of the Mediterranean human society, the Cilento area has been the only communication corridor between the Adriatic and the Tyrrhenian Sea in the central Mediterranean region. This is evident if we analyze what remains today of the cultural landscape. Thus, the environment is configured as a "cultural landscape", understood as a natural landscape forged by the work of a cultural group.

The culture represents the agent, the natural elements the means, the cultural landscape is the result [18]. The area selected for the study and evaluation of CES is the coastal strip of this sub-region, administratively divided into fifteen municipalities occupying 462 sq. km and hosting 76,540 resident inhabitants.

The ancient rural economy characterized by rather productive agriculture is flanked by thriving seaside tourist activity, the main economic driver of the coast and the entire Cilento territory.

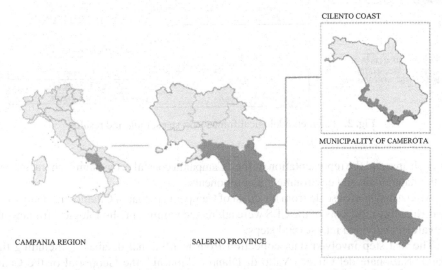

Fig. 1. The localization of the case study and the scales of the analysis

In a second phase of the work, the study focused on the municipality of Camerota and the Infreschi Bay, a natural harbour of great cultural, tourist and identity interest for the area. The bay falls within the Marine Protected Area "Costa degli Infreschi e della Masseta". It extends between the villages of Marina di Camerota to the north and Scario to the south. Salient features of this stretch of coast are the low population density and the total absence of major industrial settlements: the anthropic pressure is closely linked to seasonal tourism. In contrast, the "industrial" activities are concentrated around the stores of local artisans, engaged for centuries in the production of ceramics and woodworking.

4 Materials and Methods

The process followed for elaborating the proposal consists in a multidimensional approach divided in three main phases: the first one of knowledge and interpretation, the second one of evaluation, and the third one aimed at identifying a valorization strategy [19] for the Baia degli Infreschi (Fig. 2).

The first phase consists of the elaboration of interpretative maps at regional and sub-regional scales. Among the results of this phase are the definition of the driving polarities

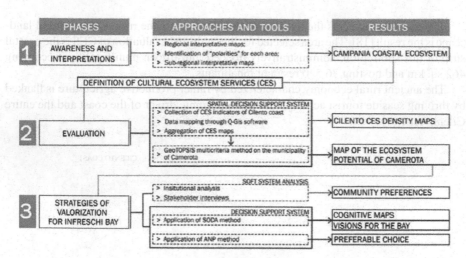

Fig. 2. The methodological framework: steps, tools and results

for each area and the representation of the "Campania coastal ecosystem", characterized by the naturalistic and environmental components.

After a first step of scale from the coast of Campania to that of Cilento, the analysis of the different components of the CES were addressed within a methodological framework of evaluation divided into several steps.

The first step involved data collection from institutional databases, including the "Parco Nazionale del Cilento Vallo di Diano e Alburni", the Geoportal of the Campania region and ISTAT databases and from informal sources such as social networks and Google pages. The selected data were aggregated into six classes of CES: Scientific/Educational, Historical/Cultural, Tourist/Recreational, Spiritual/Religious, Identitarian and Aesthetic.

The second step consisted of structuring a Spatial Decision Support System [20].

Through the software Q-Gis the data have been geo-referenced individually and then aggregated. This process made it possible to analyze the spatial distribution of the phenomena and, therefore, to return density maps of the presence of CES along the entire coastal strip of Cilento. The analysis was then reported on the municipality of Camerota and specifically on the single census sections that compose it. Finally, with the use of the multi-criteria method GeoTOPSIS, it was possible to draw up a map of the ecosystem potential of the Municipality of Camerota.

In the third and final step, the investigation moved to a "bridge" area of the municipality, i.e. a specific section on the map is located halfway between the sections with the highest and lowest ecosystemic potential: the Infreschi area.

To arrive at the definition of a valorization strategy capable of using culture as a natural lever, a Soft Decision Support System articulated in three steps has been structured. First, this system, proper primarily to address broad and unstructured decision-making problems, has allowed to include within the whole process different categories of citizens [21].

The first step involved elaborating an Institutional Analysis [22] on the territory. It was possible to define a map of the stakeholders, i.e. the actors potentially interested in an enhancement project for the Bay of Infreschi. Three groups of actors have been defined: promoters, operators and users, which differ according to their possible degree of involvement within the project. To these people, including inhabitants of the municipality and neighboring municipalities, members of associations active in the area, tourists and experts were administered a survey that allowed the respondents to explore the CES of the area and express their opinions about the hypothesis of enhancement for the bay. From this first step, it was possible to extract the preferences and perceptions of the community.

The second step involved applying the Strategic Options Development Analysis (SODA) approach [23] within the Decision Explorer software to the results obtained from the survey. In particular, the data processing for each category was carried out thanks to elaborating a cognitive map for each group to which a Central Analysis and a Domain Analysis were applied.

The first analysis aims to bring out the complexity of the links around each concept, of the second one to show the influence of the concept in the model context. The results of the two analyses were compared with each other and with the results obtained from the other maps and this allowed to arrive at the definition of the visions of future for the bay for each group.

Finally, the application of the Analytic Network Process (ANP) method [24, 25] [26] has allowed defining the absolute preferable alternative for the bay. This method articulates that the decision problem is decomposed into nodes (or elementary parts), and then the same nodes are aggregated into homogeneous series and connected. After having constructed this model inside the software Super Decision, it has been applied to compare the single elements of the net. In particular, the judgments have been expressed through the "scale of Saaty" [24]. From the definition of the priority, it has emerged the preferable alternative for the bay, able to satisfy the maximum needs and necessities of every class of stakeholders [27, 28].

4.1 The Spatial Decision Support System

In this phase, each set of CES elements were first geo-referenced individually and then classified according to natural intervals through the software Q-Gis. From this first analysis, density maps were obtained, one for each class of CES (Fig. 3).

The aggregation of all the maps showed that the area with the highest number of CES is the municipality of Camerota, followed by Agropoli and Castellabate.

The result obtained led the analysis to move to the municipality of Camerota and, in particular, to the census sections of which the locality is composed. To obtain a map of the ecosystem potentials that take into account not only the CES classes but also their value, a multi-criteria Geo-TOPSIS (Technique for Order of Preference by Similarity to Ideal Solution) analysis was carried out [29, 30] through the Vector MCDA plug-in of Q-Gis (Fig. 4).

The method is based on the concept that the chosen alternative should have, in Euclidean space, the shortest distance to the positive ideal solution and the longest geometric distance to the negative ideal solution. Thus, every geographic object, in our

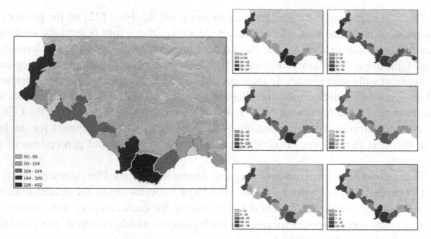

Fig. 3. Cultural ecosystem services density maps

case, every single CES described by an alphanumeric value in the table of attributes of Q-Gis, is a geo-alternative. In the plug-in's table, the columns are constituted by CES classes that become criteria to each of which weight must be assigned. Subsequently, the descriptive attributes of each geo-alternative are treated as evaluation criteria and processed through implemented algorithms of the plug-in.

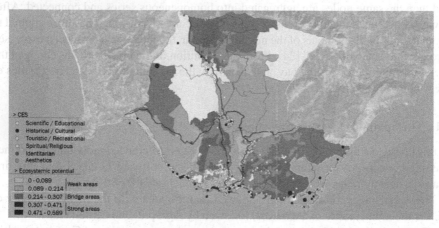

Fig. 4. Ecosystem potential of Camerota: The results of Geo-TOPSIS method application.

The last phase of this application provides the return of synthetic indices of preference for each element that translated into gradations of colour on the GIS map allows to identify, within the municipality, three different types of areas depending on their ecosystem potential. There are, specifically, areas with low potential, bridge areas and areas with high ecosystem potential. For the following analysis, we chose to study a location falling in a bridge area, precisely the Bay of Infreschi, inlet and first natural harbour of the municipality.

4.2 The Soft Decision Support System

The third and final phase of the work made use of different tools to reach the appropriate conclusions. The survey administered to the stakeholders allowed, first of all, to obtain information about the preferences of the community on the process to be implemented in the area. Members of local communities were asked to respond to 20 open-ended and multiple-choice questions regarding the bay.

The data obtained from the survey have been elaborated by the Strategic Options Development and Analysis (SODA) approach. Four cognitive maps have been structured, one for each interviewed group (Fig. 5):

- Map 1 for the citizens of Camerota;
- Map 2 for the associations active on the territory;
- Map 3 for the inhabitants of the neighbouring municipalities;
- Map 4 for the tourists.

The questions were divided into concepts, each of which was assigned a colour. At the end of the analysis, based on the preferences expressed, each group was associated with a vision of the future for the bay. In particular, for the group of citizens of Camerota, the vision was "Infreschi as a Cilento landing place for ecotourism"; for the members of the associations "Infreschi: a safe harbour for culture"; for the citizens of the neighbouring municipalities "Infreschi: slow natural park"; and for the tourists "Infreschi: a lonely oasis of the tourist".

The Analytic Network Process (ANP) method [24, 25] has been applied to define the preferable alternative among the four listed above (Fig. 6). After setting up the decision problem and establishing the appropriate connections between the elements of the nodes (criteria, stakeholders and visions of the future) and the clusters (objectives and actions for each objective), a pairwise comparison was made between all the elements present [31].

The preferred vision of the future for the bay turns out to be, according to the results of ANP analysis, the number 2, which sees Infreschi as "Cilento landing place of ecotourism". From the definition of priorities, moreover, it emerges that the actions/projects that achieve higher scores are: workshop activities linked to tradition (52.8%), environmental education activities (48.6%), outdoor food and wine itineraries (47.1%), accessible and safe trekking trails (38%), guided tours (36.7%), docking points for boats outside the bay (36.1%), shift entry in summer (35%), viewpoints and belvedere (35%), info points and services for tourists (34.2%).

5 Discussions

This paper has tried to investigate a new approach for evaluating Cultural Ecosystem Services, based not on their possible quantification in monetary terms but on their importance for the communities that conserve them.

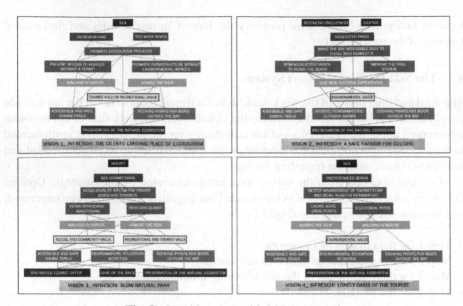

Fig. 5. Cognitive maps with SODA approach

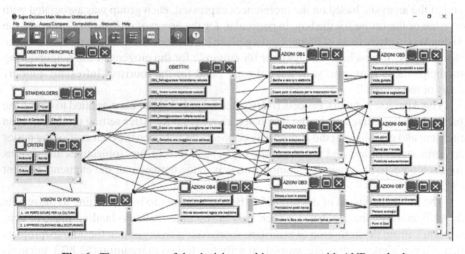

Fig. 6. The structure of the decision-making process with ANP method

The non-monetary methods referred to in this study are used when it is intended to assess the impact of hypothetical changes in the ecosystem and the provision of its services, producing an ex-ante helpful estimation to understand the possible scenarios and where it is necessary to act. These methods are usually applied to identify the socio-cultural values of a resource without a market [14, 32]. Especially in cultural landscapes, and therefore also in the study area of lower Cilento, socio-cultural assessment has offered a better understanding of the perception that people have of ecosystem services, which could lead to the activation of less conflictual, more supportive and cooperative behaviours.

The methodological hypothesis follows a process of planning-evaluation that takes into account, on the one hand, the assessment of the main cultural ecosystem services of the Cilento coast and, on the other hand, the planning of the coastal ecosystem itself through the activation of a model of collaborative governance on the area under study [33].

The potentials of such an approach find themselves to fill, at the same time, the role of significant criticalities. For example, suppose the identification of groups of local stakeholders favours the participation of communities in a bottom-up model that allows the project not to remain detached from the context, on the other hand. In that case, it requires a great communicative capacity by those who propose it.

For the discussion to be positive, it is essential to build a pact of trust between the parties. The main difficulty lies in making the community members understand that activating an enhancement project for an area of great value does not mean distorting it or exploiting it to make money. It means, on the contrary, transforming the material and immaterial resources to enhance the specificity and regenerate the existing capital [34, 35]. In this sense, culture can become a driving force for the sustainable regeneration of territory, being able, among other things, to give a new face to the landscape, to strengthen the feeling of belonging to the place by those who live there, to shape the flows and types of tourism that are sometimes harmful to fragile areas like ours.

The analyses of the first phase of the work have allowed a complete knowledge of the territory from the environmental and infrastructural perspective. The results obtained have constituted a solid base on which it has been possible to build and model the following phases.

The second phase, structured according to a spatial decision support system, has allowed instead to analyze the corpus of CES that connotes the Cilento coast. Starting from a decision tree, a set of indicators was structured, populated both by data already present in shapefiles in institutional databases and by raw data subsequently geo-referenced in Q-Gis. It was evident the almost total absence within the institutional sites of municipal authorities of sections dedicated to the cultural heritage of the places. The criticality just highlighted is the symbol of a failure to adapt to the times and the new challenges of digitization by a part of the country that is still experiencing significant difficulties in economy and inclusion.

The subsequent application of the Geo-TOPSIS multi-criteria method on the municipality of Camerota has allowed dividing the municipal area according to the "ecosystem potential" of each census section. This kind of evaluation permits understanding which areas to implement policies and projects of valorization and which are; instead, the services to improve and implement in the different sections.

The tested approach could be further enriched by the direct participation of citizens in the collection of data, made impossible by the current pandemic situation. Based on the knowledge and experience of each, the CES set could be significantly implemented. The third phase involved, as a first step, the distribution of interviews to stakeholders from which community preferences emerged. Also, in this case, the restrictions imposed by the pandemic wave have prevented the organization of working tables and co-planning.

Therefore, it was necessary to use a Google Form, which made it possible to reach people from different Italian provinces but prevented a direct relationship between the parts. The interviewees provided valid answers to the questions, but a direct discussion would have allowed them to touch on more issues and link them with greater ease. An attempt in this direction was made in the immediately following phase, during which, using the SODA approach, cognitive maps were constructed. While not proper to evaluate, this method offered the first set of solutions to the problem faced. The cognitive maps reproduce in graphic form the conceptualization of the nodal questions and the links between them. Through this approach, it was possible to understand which were the most critical issues for the respondents. It was interesting to note how the answers of the groups of stakeholders, who did not have the opportunity to confront themselves on the subject, converged towards the same points, allowing the elaboration of four different strategic maps to explain as many visions of the future for the bay. Finally, step four, during which the ANP method was applied, allowed for an understanding of which of the four proposals was preferable for the bay. Again, especially for the pairwise comparison step, direct group participation in the discussion would have been more effective (Fig. 7).

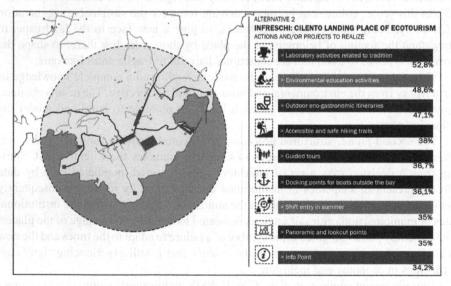

Fig. 7. Preferable choice, actions and projects for Infreschi

6   Conclusions

The study of the literature and applying the procedure described above have shown that the evaluation of CES can still be subject to experimentation and development. The fact that there is still no conventional methodological framework to refer to makes it possible to examine the issues on a case-by-case basis and with the most appropriate tools.

At the end of the study, what becomes evident is the importance of citizen participation and collaboration in decision-making processes if we want to implement choices capable of satisfying the needs and requirements of each individual and, therefore, of being accepted and absorbed by the population. To date, what seems to be missing for this hybrid approach to be standardized and become common practice is awareness on the part of institutions and trust on the part of citizens [36].

The proposed approach could be applied to other contexts to guide and support processes of enhancement that have as their purpose the activation of the cultural ecosystem potential of coastal areas and beyond.

The following steps of this research could be applying the methodology studied at different points of the coastal strip of Cilento to identify a network of coastal ecosystem nodes that can give rise to a virtuous process of revitalization of the territory that has culture and sustainability as its foundations.

Author Contributions. Conceptualization, M.Cerreta, M. Clemente, B.E., G.P.; methodology, M.Cerreta, M. Clemente, B.E., G.P.; validation, M.Cerreta, M. Clemente; formal analysis, B.E., G.P.; investigation, B.E.; writing-original draft preparation, B.E.; writing-review and editing, M.Cerreta, M. Clemente, B.E., G.P.; visualization, B.E.; supervision, M.Cerreta, M. Clemente. All authors have read and agreed to the published version of the manuscript.

References

1. Carta, M.: Dal waterfront alla città liquida. Patologie relazionali e nuovi orizzonti del progetto. In: De Luca, G., Lingua, V. (eds.) Arcipelago Mediterraneo. Strategie di riqualificazione e sviluppo nelle città-porto delle isole, Alinea, pp. 27–40 (2012)
2. Clemente, M.: Sea and the city: maritime identity for urban sustainable regeneration. TRIA Territorio Della Ricerca Su Insediamenti e Ambiente **11**(2), 19–34 (2013)
3. Konvitz, J.: Cities and the sea: port city planning in early modern Europe. Urban History **7**, 113 (1978). https://doi.org/10.1017/S0963926800004582
4. Ostrom, E.: A general framework for analyzing sustainability of social-ecological systems. Science **325**(5939), 419–422 (2009)
5. Antrop, M.: The language of landscape ecologists and planners: a comparative content analysis of concepts used in landscape ecology. Landsc. Urban Plan. **55**(3), 163–173 (2001)
6. Costanza, R., Folke, C.: Valuing ecosystem services with efficiency, fairness and sustainability as goals. Nature's Services: Societal Dependence on Natural Ecosystems, pp. 49–68 (1997)
7. Millennium Ecosystem Assessment (MEA): Ecosystems and Human Well-Being: Synthesis. Island, Washington (2005)
8. Wu, J.: Landscape sustainability science: ecosystem services and human well-being in changing landscapes. Landscape Ecol. **28**(6), 999–1023 (2013)
9. Bastian, O., Grunewald, K., Syrbe, R.-U., Walz, U., Wende, W.: Landscape services: the concept and its practical relevance. Landscape Ecol. **29**(9), 1463–1479 (2014). https://doi.org/10.1007/s10980-014-0064-5
10. Cerreta, M., Poli, G.: Landscape services assessment: a hybrid multi-criteria spatial decision support system (MC-SDSS). Sustainability **9**(8), 1311 (2017)
11. The Economics of Ecosystems and Biodiversity (TEEB): The Economics of Ecosystems and Biodiversity Ecological and Economic Foundations. Pushpam Kumar. Earthscan: London and Washington (2010)
12. European Environment Agency (EEA): Common International Classification of Ecosystem Services (CICES): 2011 Update. EEA/BSS/07/007, November 2011, pp. 1–14 (2011)

13. European Union: Maritime Spatial Planning 2014/89/UE (2014). https://eur-lex.europa.eu/legal-content/IT/TXT/PDF/?uri=CELEX:32014L0089&from=EN
14. Haines-Young, R., Potschin, M., Fish, R.: Classifying ecosystem services: an ecosystems knowledge network briefing paper. ecosystems knowledge network (2012). https://ecosystemsknowledge.net/sites/default/files/wpcontent/uploads/2012/10/
15. Arias-Arévalo, P., Gómez-Baggethun, E., Martín-López, B., Pérez-Rincón, M.: Widening the Evaluative Space for Ecosystem Services: A Taxonomy of Plural Values and Valuation Methods. The White Horse Press, Cambridge (2015)
16. Cerreta, M., Daldanise, G., Regalbuto, S.: Collaboriamo per Crapolla: una strategia di governance innovativa per una gestione integrata e adattiva. In: AA.VV. Supporto tecnico-scientifico a programmi di conservazione, miglioramento della fruizione e valorizzazione dell'Abbazia di San Pietro a Crapolla (2017)
17. Coccossis H., Nijkamp P.: Planning for our cultural heritage. Aldershot, Avebury (1995)
18. Sauer, C.O.: The morphology of landscape. Univ. Calif. Publ. Geogr. **2**, 19–54 (1925)
19. Selicato, M., Torre, C.M., La Trofa, G.: Prospect of integrate monitoring: A multidimensional approach, Lecture Notes in Computer Science (including subseries Lecture Notes in Artificial Intelligence and Lecture Notes in Bioinformatics), 7334 LNCS (PART 2), pp. 144–156 (2012)
20. Cerreta, M., Panaro, S., Poli, G.: A spatial decision support system for multifunctional landscape assessment: a transformative resilience perspective for vulnerable inland areas. Sustainability **13**(5), 2748, 1–23 (2021)
21. Cerreta, M., di Girasole, E.G., Poli, G., Regalbuto, S.: Operationalizing the circular city model for naples' city-port: a hybrid development strategy. Sustainability **12**(7), 2927 (2020)
22. Funtowicz S. O., Martinez-Alier J., Munda G., Ravetz J.: Multicriteria-based environmental policy. In: Abaza H., Baranzini A. (ed.), Implementing sustainable development. UNEP/Edward Elgar, Cheltenham, UK, pp. 53–77 (2002)
23. Eden, C., Simpson, P.: SODA and cognitive mapping in practice. In: Rosenhead, J. (ed.) Rational analysis for a problematic world, pp. 43–70. John Wiley and Sons, Chichester, UK (1989)
24. Saaty T.L.: The Analytic Hierarchy Process, Planning, Priority Setting, Resource Allocation. McGraw-Hill, New York (1980)
25. Saaty T.L., Vargas L. G.: Decision making with the Analytic Network Process. Springer Science, New York (2006). https://doi.org/10.1007/978-1-4614-7279-7
26. Saaty, T.L., Vargas, L.G.: The analytic network process. in: decision making with the analytic network process. International Series in Operations Research & Management Science, vol 195. Springer, Boston (2013)
27. Cerreta, M., Panaro, S.: Deliberative spatial multi-criteria evaluation (DSM-CE): forming shared cultural values. Lecture Notes in Computer Science (including subseries Lecture Notes in Artificial Intelligence and Lecture Notes in Bioinformatics), 10406 LNCS, pp. 77–90 (2017). https://doi.org/10.1007/978-3-319-62398-6_53
28. Torre, C.M., Morano, P., Tajani, F.: Social balance and economic effectiveness in historic centers rehabilitation. Lecture Notes in Computer Science (including subseries Lecture Notes in Artificial Intelligence and Lecture Notes in Bioinformatics) **9157**, 317–329 (2015). https://doi.org/10.1007/978-3-319-21470-2_22
29. Hwang CL., Yoon K.: Methods for multiple attribute decision making. in: multiple attribute decision making. Lecture Notes in Economics and Mathematical Systems, 186. Springer, Heidelberg (1981). https://doi.org/10.1007/978-3-642-48318-9_3
30. Olson, D.L.: Comparison of weights in TOPSIS models. Math. Comput. Model **40**, 721–727 (2004)
31. Cerreta, M., Malangone, V.: Valutazioni multi-metodologiche per il paesaggio storico urbano: la valle dei mulini di Amalfi. BDC Bollettino del Centro Calza Bini **14**, 39–61 (2014)

32. Chan, K.M.A., Satterfield, T., Goldstein, J.: Rethinking ecosystem services to better address and navigate cultural values. Ecol. Econ. **74**, 8–18 (2012)
33. Cerreta, M., De Toro, P.: Integrated spatial assessment (ISA): a multi-methodological approach for planning choices. In: Advances in Spatial Planning, Burian, J. Ed, IntechOpen: Rijeka, Croatia, pp. 77–108 (2012)
34. Daily, G.C., et al.: Ecosystem services in decision making: time to deliver. Ecol. Environ. **7**(1), 21–28 (2009)
35. Daldanise, G.: From place-branding to community-branding: a collaborative decision-making process for cultural heritage enhancement. Sustainability **12**, 10399 (2020)
36. Cerreta, M., Poli, G., Regalbuto, S., Mazzarella, C.: A multi-dimensional decision-making process for regenerative landscapes: a new harbour for Naples (Italy). In: Misra, S., et al. (eds.) ICCSA 2019. LNCS, vol. 11622, pp. 156–170. Springer, Cham (2019). https://doi.org/10.1007/978-3-030-24305-0_13

Assessing Infrastructures Alternatives: The Implementation of a Fuzzy Analytic Hierarchy Process (F-AHP)

Maria Cerreta(✉), Giuliano Poli, and Maria Somma

Department of Architecture, University of Naples Federico II, via Toledo 402, Naples, Italy
{cerreta,giuliano.poli,maria.somma}@unina.it

Abstract. The conventional approach that often dominated spatial planning has prioritized urban expansion and new urban transport infrastructure without fully considering environmental aspects. While this has generated new urban models and economies, it has also significantly impacted the territory and landscape negatively. The construction of road infrastructure can improve the sustainability of a city from the point of view of connectivity between places. However, it also generates a disruption of the landscape with a consequent loss of ecosystem services. The case study concerns the evaluation of the preferable alternative, between two proposals, for the construction of a new road called the Teramo-Mare, connecting the Abruzzo hinterland with the Adriatic coast. The methodological approach investigates the scientific background in landscape assessment related to the construction of road infrastructures. By modelling the Multi-Criteria Decision Analysis (MCDA) with Fuzzy set theory and the Fuzzy Analytic Hierarchy Process (F-AHP) an evaluation method is tested to face the choice of the preferable alternative. The study provides an initial review of the scientific reference landscape and identifying criteria to help evaluate the option that has the least impact on the landscape and ecological system.

Keywords: Spatial indicators · Sustainability indicators · GIS-based evaluation method · Spatial road analysis · Landscape impacts

1 Introduction

The Council of Europe Landscape Convention - as amended by the 2016 Protocol - provided a landscape's definition referred to as: "an area, as perceived by people, whose character is the result of the action and interaction of natural and/or human factors". Furthermore, it emphasized that the planning activities must include forward-looking strategies to restore or create new landscapes in a sustainability pathway [1].

The Convention has highlighted the landscape's character as a whole of material and immaterial factors which are strictly interrelated, dynamic, and variable, and whose understanding hybrid and integrated assessment methods are needed [2].

In this perspective, the Landscape Character Assessment (LCA) [3] (https://www.nature.scot/) attempted to provide stakeholders, practitioners, and academics with guidelines and tools to cope with the complexity, recognizing that each landscape is unique,

© Springer Nature Switzerland AG 2021
O. Gervasi et al. (Eds.): ICCSA 2021, LNCS 12955, pp. 504–516, 2021.
https://doi.org/10.1007/978-3-030-87007-2_36

and the landscape pattern variation can be detected and spatially represented and assessed [4].

The conventional approach dominating spatial planning has focused on the urban sprawl and the construction of new urban transport infrastructures for a long time, without fully including environmental aspects [5].

Geographical criteria generally considered in road alignment problems exclude the broadest landscape components prioritizing technical factors to the detriment of ecological, social, and aesthetic dimensions [6]. While this has generated new urban patterns and economies, it has also significantly impacted the territory and landscape [6]. On the one hand, new road infrastructures boost cities' sustainability regarding connectivity between places. On the other hand, roads generate a landscape break with a consequent loss of ecosystem services [7].

In England, the LCA methodology and its procedures have been matching up for several years with local authority plans and strategies, land use planning and land management, or other assessment tools, e.g., Strategic Environmental Assessment (SEA) and Environmental Impact Assessment (EIA) [3].

The primary LCA potential is inherent in providing evidence at an in-depth scale to inform decisions better using georeferenced data and mapping with a holistic approach. Moreover, its integration with GIS-based analysis is overwhelming when decisional agents examine maps before eliciting their preferences [8].

Visual maps or spatial indicators enhance the knowledge of complex phenomena linked to the landscape's characters. Indeed, the decision-making benefits from the spatial representation making geomorphological criteria, physical landscape characters, immaterial components, and constraints more explicit.

Significant limitations can refer to data availability and detection, which are time-consuming, expensive, and hard-to-build. In addition, including the broad scale in the evaluation - by modelling choice problems in a GIS environment - can incur extreme generalization of the landscape's features. Furthermore, site-specific surveys and epistemic knowledge can balance this problem [9].

The twofold research's purpose addressed to:

- Test a valuation procedure that includes uncertainty related to multiple experts' judgement into a spatial decision-making framework through Multi-Criteria Decision Analysis (MCDA).
- Experiment with an easy consulting questionnaire [10] to gather experts' relative preferences and derive a consistent judgment matrix with F-AHP.

The ambition is to expand the obtained valuation model from a discrete problem (MADM) to an ongoing problem (MODM) in a GIS environment.

The case study to test the proposed methodology is related to four Municipalities in Abruzzo (Italy) to construct new road alignments boosting connectivity among inner areas and the coastal zones.

2 The Scientific Landscape

For the last thirty years, the authors have aimed to find relationships between road infrastructure planning and landscape in the scientific literature. Connecting terms were searched in the scientific database SCOPUS using logical operators AND/OR with the following string: ("landscape" OR "landscapes") AND ("roads" OR "road" OR "highway" OR "road alignment" OR "highway alignment") AND ("valuation" OR "evaluation" OR "assessment") AND ("urban planning").

Four clusters made by the most recurring terms emerged within the thematic literature through the scientific landscape method [11].

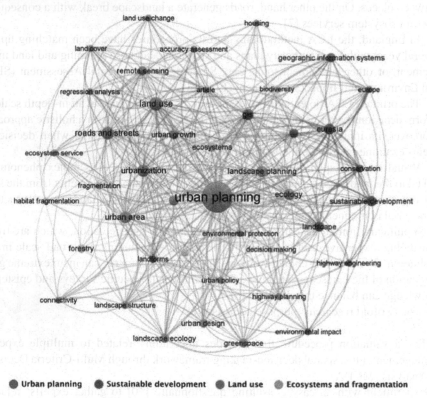

Fig. 1. The scientific landscape. Source: Authors' elaboration

These clusters refer to:

1) Urban planning;
2) Sustainable development;
3) Land use;
4) Ecosystem and fragmentation.

It has noticed the centrality of urban planning studies fostering cross-cutting issues and the multidisciplinary (Fig. 1).

Indeed, some authors remarked that the leading cause of land use and land cover change is urbanization [12, 13]. However, it is unrealistic to monitor and analyze urbanization's ecological and socio-economic effects [14], without a comprehensive understanding of how the city is changing.

A road has other lesser-known consequences on ecosystems, and more crucially, on the countryside dynamics of those places that it crosses, not just the acknowledged effects of transport like pollution, noise. In a relatively short period, these disturbances might lead to significant changes [15].

Numerous studies have addressed to understand the relationship between transportation and land use. The building of new transportation infrastructure would inevitably affect land development. Highways have essential social and economic purposes, but they facilitate ecosystem disruption through fragmentation, noise pollution, habitat loss, and species extinction through landscape segmentation and edge effects [16–21]. Because of the vast current and proposed road networks [22–24], it is more important than ever to consider the spatial and temporal distribution of these environmental impacts generated by highways [25].

About any expenditure on the road has benefited the national economy. However, this economic viewpoint is insufficient for examining all a transportation infrastructure's spatial impact, especially those linked to the transition it has wrought on the landscape over time. There is an inherent interplay between urban space and human-made development, such as unregulated urban sprawl and the proliferation of infrastructure. These elements must be understood from an environmental, economic, and social standpoint [26]. Several surveys have been addressed to determine the effects of highway building on the atmosphere and landscape, and social life. About any expenditure on the road has benefited the national economy. However, this economic viewpoint is insufficient for examining all a transportation infrastructure's spatial impact, especially those linked to the transition it has wrought on the landscape over time. The issues related to the "Ecosystem and fragmentation" cluster highlighted that the highway building has a much-varied landscape and ecological consequences [16, 20, 27] inadequately quantified and recognized [28]. For example, the influence distance or path-effect zone - the distance outward from a road where significant ecological effects occur [16] - is commonly used to measure road building and usage [27, 29, 30].

3 Materials and Methods

The research's purpose was to test a methodology for solving a choice problem linked to new road alignments in the Abruzzo region (Italy). Two alternatives were assessed concerning six geographical criteria: Naturality, Fragmentation, Urban density, Historicity, Proximity to urban areas, and Accessibility.

The goal concerns a discrete problem to be solved with Multi-Attribute Decision Making since environmental, socio-cultural, and technical performances related to two proposed road alignments have to be assessed by an experts group. Therefore, a three-step methodology has been structured to achieve a ranking for supporting the best-fit alternative choice (Fig. 2).

The first step is inherent to the knowledge and criteria related to the alternatives' features were set. The second step concerns the MCDA modelling with the Fuzzy set

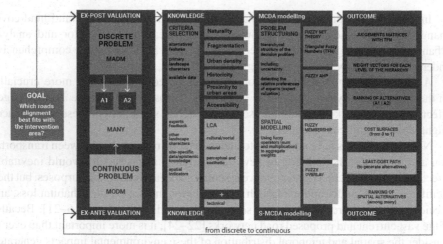

Fig. 2. A methodological workflow for managing a choice problem linked to new road alignments. Source: Authors' elaboration.

theory and the Fuzzy Analytic Hierarchy Process (F-AHP). Finally, the last step is related to the outcome that has determined the weight vectors for each hierarchy level and the final ranking of the alternatives.

3.1 The Case Study

The study area is in the northern of Abruzzo (Italy), east of the Teramo city, connecting the S.S. 80 with the S.S.16. The municipalities of Notaresco, Roseto degli Abruzzi, Mosciano Sant'Angelo, and Giulianova are involved in the building of the new highway, which aims to enhance connectivity between the Giulianova coast served by S.S. 16 "Adriatica", the Teramo region served by S.S. 80 "Raccordo di Teramo" and the major established infrastructures (A14 highway - Mosciano Sant'Angelo junction, Teramo-Giulianova railway line, Mosciano station) (Fig. 3).

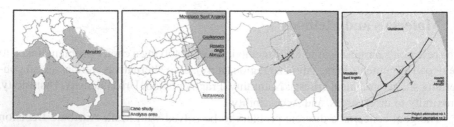

Fig. 3. The case study's geographical frame. In order: Italy; Abruzzo Region, the municipalies of Giulianova, Mosciano Sant'Angelo, Roseto degli Abruzzi, Notaresco; the case study: two hightways alternatives. Source: Authors' Elaboration

In the area of interest are located the main strategic roads:

- The SS. 80 "del Gran Sasso di Italia" that connects Teramo to Giulianova;
- The S.S. 80 Raccordo di Teramo connects the A24 and the A14 near the junction of Mosciano Sant'Angelo.
- The railway line Teramo-Giulianova connects to the Adriatic railway ridge.

These conditions have favoured the development of productive settlements. In this area, the Apennine chain reaches its maximum proximity to the Adriatic Sea.

The narrow alluvial plain characterizes the area at the bottom of the "Tordino" River valley, one of the five watercourses of piedmont origin that flow entirely within the administrative boundaries of Teramo's province. The project explicitly concerns the valley's final stretch from Mosciano S. Angelo (about 7 km from the mouth) to Cologna Marina (about 800 m from the mouth).

The fundamental data needed to frame and describe the intervention area's environmental, socio-cultural, and technical aspects were assumed from the most widely used urban and territorial planning tools, the ISTAT censuses, open regional and satellite data series (Copernicus).

The new road represents an alternative to the historical S.S. 80 of "Gran Sasso d'Italia", which has taken on the characteristics of a "local" road system serving the production and residential areas. The latter has led to a decline in the level of service typical of a secondary suburban road system due to the widespread presence of accesses, junctions, and traffic lights, which significantly reduce the level of service to users in terms of journey times and road safety.

The construction of the new Teramo - Mare section aimed to decongest the area of interest, linking them to the flourishing settlements in the "Colleranesco" area and the neighbouring regions, which are already putting a strain on the well-established S.S. 80 infrastructure, which no longer meets the efficiency criteria for current vehicle flows. Furthermore, there is a need to connect the inland areas with the areas along the coast. The inland areas are widespread economic obsolescence due to their location (poor accessibility that makes them marginal) and the prevalence of backward economic sectors compared to modern ones. In these terms, the economy is not self-propelling but in need of exogenous support [31–33].

3.2 Knowledge Phase

The knowledge phase has allowed the study area knowledge to be performed by defining natural, cultural, and technical criteria. Thus, the elaboration of spatial criteria maps has favoured consulting with stakeholders. The LCA [3] defined these criteria were implemented by technical criteria selected through interviews with ten experts and linked mainly to transport engineering. The interviewed experts are a project manager, a safety engineer, three construction engineers, two architects, an urban planner, a system engineer, and a professor of environmental appraisal. The spatial representation of the natural, cultural, and technical dimensions follow. As shown in Fig. 4, spatial and non-spatial data used to analyze the natural dimension come from the geoportal of the Abruzzo

Region (http://geoportale.regione.abruzzo.it) and the Fiume Sangro Regional and Inter-
regional Basin Authority (http://autoritabacini.regione.abruzzo.it). These maps merged
with the database provided by the Copernicus Land Monitoring Service portal (http://
land.copernicus.eu). For this dimension, the naturalness (C1) and fragmentation (C2)
criteria were analyzed.

3.2.1 Natural Dimension

The naturalness criterion was defined by reprocessing raw data from the Corine Land
Cover, the Abruzzo Region Landscape Plan and visual analysis through virtual navigation in Google Earth. This criterion defines a mapping where forest land, cultivated land,
grasslands, wetlands, dunes, beaches and riparian areas can be distinguished.

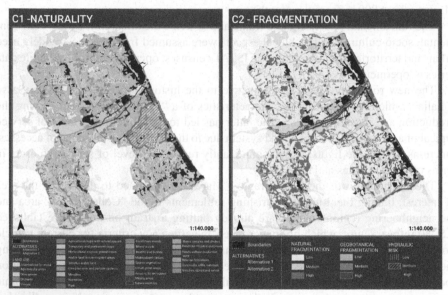

Fig. 4. Natural dimension maps with the analysis of Naturality (C1) and Fragmentation (C2)
criteria. Source: Authors' Elaboration

Both proposed alternatives fall within predominantly agricultural areas, simple alternating crops, and in non-irrigated areas with permanent crops with another predominance
of vineyards north of the Tordino's river.

The analysis related to fragmentation represents one of the main components of land
research [34]. For the fragmentation criterion, the degree of naturalistic, geobotanical
and hydraulic risk fragmentation was analyzed. In the initial stretch, which is common
to the two project routes, the areas crossed partly present a low level of naturalistic
fragmentation (in these areas, there are arable crops in non-irrigated areas and/or temporary crops associated with permanent crops). There is a medium level of fragmentation
(simple arable crops, forest formations with prevalent fruit production, other tree crops,
permanent meadows, complex crop and plot systems and agroforestry areas alternate)

in the other part. The final stretch, which is common to both solutions, is characterized by areas of high naturalistic fragmentation. In this section, portions of urbanized land are also intercepted.

In the area covered by alternative no. 1, there is medium. In the stretch of the Tordino's river, there is high naturalistic fragmentation about geobotanical aspects.

For the area south of the Tordino, where alternative No 2 locates, there is a medium level of naturalistic fragmentation, which tends to become low as it proceeds towards the coast, except for the stretch where the Tordino's river crosses. The alternative also does not intercept areas of geobotanical value.

In addition, both alternatives were designed outside the boundary of areas protected by law from hydrogeological constraint, except where they cross the River Tordino or some of its tributaries (Fosso Mustaccio, Fosso Cavone and Fosso Corno).

3.2.2 Socio-Cultural Dimension

The authors compared the database for the socio-cultural dimension provided by the Abruzzo Region was with Open Street Map (OSM).

The four municipalities involved in the intervention have a high concentration of settlements of high historical interest (C3 – Historicity). The buffer zone where the two alternatives fall does not intercept any works of historical value (Fig. 5, C3). The design of the junction would connect the historical heritage in the area, which is currently challenging to access. The infrastructure with its various exits and entrances will connect to local roads directly from the Adriatic and Teramo motorways.

The population data were fundamental in defining the population density criterion.

The data came from the latest population census provided by ISTAT and dating from 2011considering that the work's design process was started before 2011.

In 2011, a very high percentage of urban density (Fig. 5, C4) was recorded in the coastal municipalities, while inland municipalities recorded a lower population density.

In the buffer zone comprising the two project alternatives, there is a minimum population density due to industrial areas along the Tordino riverside and active and disused quarries, which have limited the appearance of new urbanization over time, especially housing (Fig. 5).

Alternative No. 1 will have an exit at Colleranesco and the industrial area. The population density here is medium. It is also foreseen rejoining with the present SS.16 Adriatica. For alternative No. 2, an exit is foreseen at Coste Lanciano (Roseto Degli Abruzzi) and a second one at the industrial area of Colleranesco (Giulianova).

3.2.3 Technical Dimension

The provided technical criteria maps help to standardize the landscape characteristics with the transport engineering factors. In addition, criteria related to proximity to urban areas (C5) and accessibility (C6) have been designed to evaluate the best-fit alternative. The road infrastructure database was provided by OSM, Copernicus and the Abruzzo Region territorial database.

Both alternatives, within a radius of 2 km, are close to the main urban settlements. In particular, Alternative No. 1 is well connected to all the main commercial and tertiary

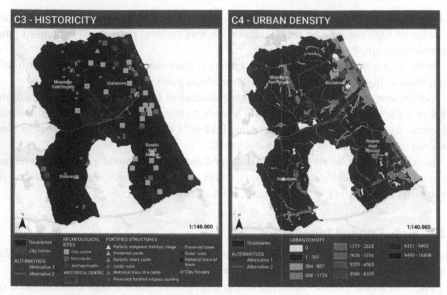

Fig. 5. Cultural dimension maps with the analysis of Historicity (C3) and Urban density (C4) criteria. Source: Authors' Elaboration

services and connects to the residential settlements along the coast. On the other hand, alternative No. 2 is detached from the leading manufacturers and residential areas (Fig. 6, Image C5). The accessibility criterion (Fig. 6, Image C6) involved the analysis of rails and roads. The central railway stops falling within the study area were identified. In particular, the two alternatives are much closer to the Mosciano Sant'Angelo stop, located to the north and parallel to the initial section of the two proposed alternatives. In addition, the study area in which the two project alternatives fall is crossed by infrastructures that are mainly local, alternating small roads and pedestrian roads). The only motorway (Autostrada Adriatica) intercepts the two alternatives in the initial section of the project. In the final section, from the hinterland to the coast, the two alternatives intercept the highway 16 Adriatica.

3.3 The MCDA Modelling

The operational steps of MCDA allowed data mapping to be used as explicitly spatial criteria. Indeed, the spatial criteria maps were provided to the experts to support them in answering an objective questionnaire. When the problem's hierarchical structure has been defined, the authors asked experts to attribute a score on a 1–9 scale at each level. Three levels of the AHP method are the following:

- The first level, which is related to natural, cultural and technical dimensions;
- The second level, which includes the six criteria (Naturality, Fragmentation, Urban density, Historicity, Proximity to urban areas, and Accessibility),
- The third level is related to the two alternatives.

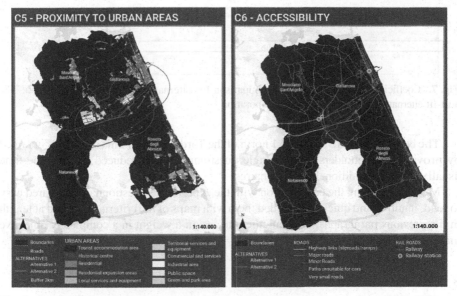

Fig. 6. Technical dimension maps with the analysis of Proximity to urban areas (C5) and Accessibility (C6) criteria. Source: Authors' Elaboration

F-AHP has allowed to include uncertainty in the evaluation, and it has been performed through the following steps, which are presented briefly:

- A range number with the lower and the highest score by the survey has been determined;
- A pairwise comparison matrix with the ratio of two-interval numbers has been shaped;
- A consistency check of the most likely crisp number representing this ratio has been calculated;
- A fuzzy judgment matrix for each hierarchy level has been obtained;
- The Fuzzy Synthetic Extent by Chang 2008 [18] has been calculated to produce the triangular fuzzy memberships;
- A likely value within the fuzzy membership was excerpted;
- The normalized weight vector for each hierarchy level has produced the ranking of the alternatives.

For more details on the operational steps, see Lyu et al. 2020 [10].

4   Outcomes

The operational steps briefly mentioned in Sect. 3.3 were fundamental in defining the preferred alternative. Figure 7 clarifies which of the two alternatives is preferable.

The results were obtained by comparing the different matrices obtained through the questionnaire provided to the experts. In this case, the coefficient matrix was defined by comparing the alternatives to the individual criteria (C1 to C6).

COEFFICIENT MATRIX OF PAIRWISE COMPARISON FOR ALTERNATIVES (Ai) TO C1-C6 CRITERIA								
	C1	C2	C3	C4	C5	C6	Normal weights	
Normal weight	0,125	0,181	0,192	0,185	0,160	0,155		
A1	0,7000224997	0,667896679	0,6363413237	0,332103321	0,6363413237	0,332103321	0,5451943748	THE BEST FIT ALTERNATIVE
A2	0,2999775003	0,332103321	0,3636586763	0,667896679	0,3636586763	0,667896679	0,4528056252	
	1	1	1	1	1	1	1	

Fig. 7. Coefficient matrix of pairwise comparison for alternatives (Aj) to C1-C6 criteria: The best-fit alternatives. Source: Authors' Elaboration

The best-fit alternative is the A1 north of the Tordino River. This result was obtained by providing stakeholders with a single questionnaire that reduced by 50% the time usually spent on traditional questionnaires.

Moreover, during the consultation with the experts, the questionnaire appeared easy to read, intuitive and quick. It provided them with maps of the criteria described at length in the previous paragraphs, allowing them to assign a weight in a completely objective manner.

5 Discussion and Conclusions

The proposed MCDA has allowed a best-fit alternative of road alignment to be chosen by including six criteria (Naturality, Fragmentation, Urban density, Historicity, Proximity to urban areas, and Accessibility) within natural, socio-cultural, and technical dimensions.

The Landscape Character Assessment (LCA) was chosen as an inclusive framework to expand evaluation criteria beyond technical factors generally included in infrastructure planning.

The adopted questionnaire (from Lyu et al. 2019 [10]) aided to simplify AHP judgements attribution by avoiding pairwise comparison, which is generally time-consuming and complex for Stakeholders. In addition, F-AHP allows uncertainty to be included in the weighting procedure by grasping global weights as the most likely values which experts can converge.

The computational procedures are time-consuming, complex, and error-prone, especially when the number of criteria and alternatives grows.

The feedback loop of the integrated valuations will provide decision-makers with further road alignments by shifting from a discrete problem (with a finite set of alternatives) to a multiobjective decision-making problem.

The proposed methodology will allow gathering no-spatial explicitly weights and shifting them into spatial explicitly tiers through F-AHP in a GIS environment.

The multi-group valuation within the spatial decision support systems constitutes a valuable tool for checking the transparency of preferences, which can be appropriately assimilated to objective procedures to structure more inclusive multi-stakeholder decision-making processes.

Author Contributions. Conceptualization, M.C., G.P., M.S.; methodology, G.P., M.S.; validation, M.Cerreta, G.P.; formal analysis, G.P., M.S.; investigation, M.S.; writing-original draft preparation, G.P., M.S.; writing-review and editing, M.C., G.P., M.S.; visualization, M.S.; supervision, M.C., G.P. All authors have read and agreed to the published version of the manuscript.

References

1. Council of Europe: Council of Europe Landscape Convention. Contribution to human rights, democracy and sustainable development, Strasbourg (2018)
2. Selicato, M., Torre, C.M., Trofa, G.L.: Prospect of integrate monitoring: a multidimensional approach. In: Murgante, B., et al. (eds.) ICCSA 2012. LNCS, vol. 7334, pp. 144–156. Springer, Heidelberg (2012). https://doi.org/10.1007/978-3-642-31075-1_11
3. Tudor, C.: An Approach to Landscape Character Assessment. Nature England, York (2014)
4. Attardi, R., Cerreta, M., Poli, G.: A collaborative multi-criteria spatial decision support system for multifunctional landscape evaluation. In: Gervasi, O., et al. (eds.) ICCSA 2015. LNCS, vol. 9157, pp. 782–797. Springer, Cham (2015). https://doi.org/10.1007/978-3-319-21470-2_57
5. Saganeiti, L., Favale, A., Pilogallo, A., Scorza, F., Murgante, B.: Assessing urban fragmentation at regional scale using sprinkling indexes. Sustain. **10**, 3274 (2018). https://doi.org/10.3390/SU10093274
6. Torre, C.M., Selicato, M.: The support of multidimensional approaches in integrate monitoring for SEA: a case of study. Earth Syst. Dyn. **4**, 51–61 (2013). https://doi.org/10.5194/ESD-4-51-2013
7. Millennium Ecosystem Assessment: Ecosystems and Human Well-being: Synthesis Island Press Washington, DC (2005)
8. Malczewski, J., Rinner, C.: Multicriteria Decision Analysis in Geographic Information Science
9. SDSN: United Nation: Indicators and a Monitoring Framework for the Sustainable Development Goals Launching a data revolution for the SDGs. A report to the Secretary-General of the United Nations by the Leadership Council of the Sustainable Development Solutions (2015)
10. Lyu, H.-M., Sun, W.-J., Shen, S.-L., Zhou, A.-N.: Risk assessment using a new consulting process in fuzzy AHP. J. Constr. Eng. Manag. **146**, 04019112 (2020). https://doi.org/10.1061/(asce)co.1943-7862.0001757
11. van Eck, N.J., Waltman, L.: Software survey: VOSviewer, a computer program for bibliometric mapping. Scientometrics **84**, 523–538 (2010). https://doi.org/10.1007/S11192-009-0146-3
12. Patra, S., Sahoo, S., Mishra, P., Mahapatra, S.C.: Impacts of urbanization on land use/cover changes and its probable implications on local climate and groundwater level. J. Urban Manag. **7**, 70–84 (2018). https://doi.org/10.1016/J.JUM.2018.04.006
13. Lambin, E.F., et al.: The causes of land-use and land-cover change: moving beyond the myths. Glob. Environ. Chang. **11**, 261–269 (2001). https://doi.org/10.1016/S0959-3780(01)00007-3
14. Zhu, M., Xu, J., Jiang, N., Li, J., Fan, Y.: Impacts of road corridors on urban landscape pattern: a gradient analysis with changing grain size in Shanghai. China. Landsc. Ecol. **21**, 723–734 (2006). https://doi.org/10.1007/s10980-005-5323-z
15. Ispra: L'inserimento paesaggistico delle infrastrutture stradali: Strumenti metodologici e buone pratiche di progetto (2010)
16. Klarenberg, G., MuñozCarpena, R., CampoBescós, M.A., Perz, S.G.: Highway paving in the southwestern Amazon alters long-term trends and drivers of regional vegetation dynamics. Heliyon **4**, e00721 (2018). https://doi.org/10.1016/j.heliyon.2018.e00721
17. Müller, K., Steinmeier, C., Küchler, M.: Urban growth along motorways in Switzerland. Landsc. Urban Plan. **98**, 3–12 (2010). https://doi.org/10.1016/j.landurbplan.2010.07.004
18. Wu, C.F., Lin, Y.P., Chiang, L.C., Huang, T.: Assessing highway's impacts on landscape patterns and ecosystem services: a case study in Puli Township. Taiwan. Landsc. Urban Plan. **128**, 60–71 (2014). https://doi.org/10.1016/j.landurbplan.2014.04.020

19. Creutzig, F., et al.: Transport: a roadblock to climate change mitigation? Science **350**(6263), 911–912 (2015). https://doi.org/10.1126/science.aac8033

20. Torres, A., Jaeger, J.A.G., Alonso, J.C.: Assessing large-scale wildlife responses to human infrastructure development. Proc. Natl. Acad. Sci. U. S. A. **113**, 8472–8477 (2016). https://doi.org/10.1073/pnas.1522488113

21. Shannon, G., Angeloni, L.M., Wittemyer, G., Fristrup, K.M., Crooks, K.R.: Road traffic noise modifies behaviour of a keystone species. Anim. Behav. **94**, 135–141 (2014). https://doi.org/10.1016/j.anbehav.2014.06.004

22. Ibisch, P.L.: A global map of roadless areas and their conservation status. Science **80**(354), 1423–1427 (2016). https://doi.org/10.1126/science.aaf7166

23. Southworth, J., et al.: Roads as drivers of change: trajectories across the tri-national frontier in MAP, the southwestern Amazon. Remote Sens. **3**, 1047–1066 (2011). https://doi.org/10.3390/rs3051047

24. Meijer, J.R., Huijbregts, M.A.J., Schotten, K.C.G.J., Schipper, A.M.: Global patterns of current and future road infrastructure. Environ. Res. Lett. **13**, 064006 (2018). https://doi.org/10.1088/1748-9326/aabd42

25. Brady, S.P., Richardson, J.L.: Road ecology: shifting gears toward evolutionary perspectives. Front. Ecol. Environ. **15**, 91–98 (2017). https://doi.org/10.1002/fee.1458

26. Elburz, Z., Cubukcu, K.M.: Spatial effects of transport infrastructure on regional growth: the case of Turkey. Spat. Inf. Res. **29**(1), 19–30 (2020). https://doi.org/10.1007/s41324-020-00332-y

27. Forman, R.T.T., Deblinger, R.: The ecological road-effect zone of a Massachusetts (U.S.A.) suburban highway. Conserv. Biol. **14**(1), 36–46 (2000). https://doi.org/10.1046/j.1523-1739.2000.99088.x

28. Feng, S., et al.: Quantification of the environmental impacts of highway construction using remote sensing approach. Remote Sens. **13**, 1340 (2021). https://doi.org/10.3390/rs13071340

29. Song, Y., Jin, L., Wang, H.: Vegetation changes along the Qinghai-Tibet plateau engineering corridor since 2000 induced by climate change and human activities. Remote Sens. **10**, 95 (2018). https://doi.org/10.3390/rs10010095

30. Forman, R.T.T.: Estimate of the area affected ecologically by the road system in the United States. Conserv. Biol. **14**, 31–35 (2000). https://doi.org/10.1046/j.1523-1739.2000.99299.x

31. Fusco Girard, L.: Sviluppo sostenibile ed aree interne: quali strategie e quali valutazioni. Aestimum (2009). https://doi.org/10.13128/Aestimum-7317

32. Morano, P., Tajani, F., Anelli, D.: A decision support model for investment through the Social Impact Bonds. The case of the city of Bari (Italy). Valori e Valutazioni, 163–178 (2020)

33. Anelli, D., Sica, F.: The financial feasibility analysis of urban transformation projects: an application of a quick assessment model. In: Bevilacqua, C., Calabrò, F., Spina, L.D. (eds.) NMP 2020. SIST, vol. 178, pp. 462–474. Springer, Cham (2021). https://doi.org/10.1007/978-3-030-48279-4_44

34. Serrano, M., Sanz, L., Puig, J., Pons, J.: Landscape fragmentation caused by the transport network in Navarra (Spain). Two-scale analysis and landscape integration assessment. Landsc. Urban Plan. **58**, 113–123 (2002). https://doi.org/10.1016/S0169-2046(01)00214-6

International Workshop on Machine Learning for Space and Earth Observation Data (MALSEOD 2021)

Deep Convolutional Neural Network for Classifying Satellite Images with Heterogeneous Spatial Resolutions

Mateus de Souza Miranda[1](✉)(iD), Valdivino Alexandre de Santiago Jr[1](✉)(iD),
Thales Sehn Körting[1](✉)(iD), Rodrigo Leonardi[2](✉)(iD),
and Moisés Laurence de Freitas Jr[3](✉)(iD)

[1] Instituto Nacional de Pesquisas Espaciais (INPE), Avenida Dos Astronautas, 1758,
São José Dos Campos, SP da Granja - 12227-010, Brazil
{mateus.miranda,valdivino.santiago,thales.korting}@inpe.br
[2] Agência Espacial Brasileira, Brasília, DF 70610-200, Brazil
rodrigo.leonardi@aeb.gov.br
[3] Instituto Federal de Educação, Ciência e Tecnologia do Tocantins, Povoado Santa
Tereza, Countryside, Araguatins, TO 77950-000, Brazil
moises.junior@ifto.edu.br

Abstract. Deep Learning, and most notable Deep Neural Networks, have largely driven Artificial Intelligence in the area of remote sensing, mainly image classification tasks. In this paper, we present an approach based on Convolutional Neural Networks to classify Earth Observation satellite images as environmental preserved or non-preserved areas. One interesting feature of our approach is the fact that we used sensors with different spatial resolutions to assess the performance of a traditional network. We relied on images from the Tocantins Cerrado obtained by the Wide-Scan Multispectral and Panchromatic Camera of the CBERS-4A satellite, with a spatial resolution of 8m to create the training dataset. For testing, we set up a set of images of the Sentinel satellite, with a spatial resolution of 10m from Goiás Cerrado. Results imply that Convolutional Neural Networks are feasible and are a good alternative for classifying remote sensing areas even when dealing with images from various sensors, and also with different spatial resolutions, where the model used in this study obtained an accuracy of 0.87. This study demonstrates the flexibility of Convolutional Neural Networks concerning the ability to generalize knowledge for classifying remote sensing images.

Keywords: Deep convolutional neural network · Satellite image classification · Remote sensing

1 Introduction

The Brazilian Cerrado has a rich biodiversity, being the second largest biogeographic region in South America. This biome can be found in the States of

© Springer Nature Switzerland AG 2021
O. Gervasi et al. (Eds.): ICCSA 2021, LNCS 12955, pp. 519–530, 2021.
https://doi.org/10.1007/978-3-030-87007-2_37

Maranhão, Piauí, Bahia, Goiás, Distrito Federal, Mato Grosso, Minas Gerais, São Paulo, Paraná, Rondônia, and Tocantins, corresponding to 23% of the Brazilian territory [4]. This biome has great floristic diversity, with flora characteristics that since the formation of forests, associated with watercourses; savannas, and fields, both characteristics congruent to climatic and geological conditions [21]. This biome presents large agricultural industries that, despite boosting Brazil in food production, collaborate for annual deforestation increments, as well as illegal exploitation activities in preserved areas [3].

The activities in the Brazilian Cerrado are monitored by space research institutions, such as Brazil's National Institute for Space Research (INPE), which observe the Earth through satellite images or aerial vehicles that carry sensors for imaging and mapping and perform tasks such as classification images. From this, deforestation measures can be monitored annually, checking agricultural and urban areas expansion. For example, in 2020 there was an increase of $7.3\,km^2$ on the Cerrado, as illustrated in Fig. 1. Compared to the last year, approximately $0.8\,km^2$ more kilometres were registered, the one with the lowest rate of deforestation since 2004, where more than $29.000\,km^2$ of original vegetation was deforested [2]. This may mean returning to the intense extraction of raw material or transforming this environmental area into pasture or for planting crops, for example, soy.

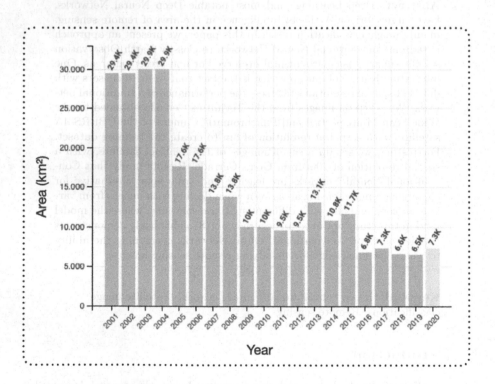

Fig. 1. Annual deforestation in the cerrado. Adapted from TerraBrasilis.

Image classification is a traditional Machine Learning/Pattern Recognition task that has been so long explored by the Remote Sensing community [19]. Classifying Land Use and Land Cover (LULC) using Remote Sensing imagery is not a trivial task, due to several factors, including that Remote Sensing is a source of big data [16], since every day new images are obtained (increasing *data volume*), and previously captured images are also combined as time series (*data velocity*). Moreover, the available imagery is expanding the number of spectral channels (i.e. Landsat 5 and 7 satellites contain 8 bands, and Landsat 8 has 11 bands), which means different ways to observe the interaction between targets and electromagnetic radiation (*data variety*).

Several authors have published in the areas of LULC classification, using different strategies, ranging from pixel-based techniques to state-of-the-art methodologies, including object-based approaches and more recently Deep Learning techniques [18]. Methods based on pixels and objects often rely on the use of data enhancements, which in accordance to [15] include feature extraction, statistical measures, texture, ancillary data, spectral indices, and others. However, the spotlight is now on Deep Learning techniques, which provide a pattern recognition system based more on automatic learning and less on hand-designed heuristics [17], or data enhancements.

Among all Deep Learning techniques, Convolutional Neural Networks (CNNs) [9] have attracted the attention of both academia and industry to solve problems related to computational vision. Despite this great interest and several studies that have already been published, we believe that it is interesting to realize whether CNNs are suitable to correctly classify satellite images considering heterogeneous sets of images, acquired by different sensors and with different spatial resolutions.

In this paper, we present an approach which relies on CNN to classify images as preserved and non-preserved areas. One interesting feature of our solution is the fact that we used sensors with different spatial resolutions to assess the performance of a traditional CNN. We relied on images from the Tocantins Cerrado obtained by the Wide-Scan Multispectral and Pancromatic Camera (WPM) of the CBERS-4A satellite, with a spatial resolution of 8m to create the training dataset. For testing, we set up a set of images of the Sentinel satellite, with spatial resolution of 10 m from Goiás Cerrado.

This paper is organized as follows. Section 2 introduce related works. Section 3 presents Material and Methods. Results and discussion are presented in Sect. 4. Section 5 presents conclusions and future directions.

2   Related Work

Convolutional neural networks (CNNs) are efficient not only because of the dynamics in extracting image characteristics but above all because of the ability to learn to recognize patterns. This artificial neural network provides several tools, including the creation of feature maps, encoder and decoder, for the improvement or development of new architectures with specific tasks, for example, classification of scenes from satellite images.

Given this, several studies in the field of remote sensing point to CNNs as indispensable tools for satellite image processing. Since these images are complex, both due to the variety of elements and information, as well as the type of sensor and spatial resolution. Thus, the research conducted by [1], describes how they implemented the late fusion technique using different deep CNN architectures and data sets, applied to recognize binary patterns, textures and classify remote sensing scenes, and presents relevant results precision in classification regarding the use of the architecture proposed by the authors.

Otherwise, [6] use CNN's techniques of the encoder and decoder for onboard cloud screening, selecting images with less cloud cover. For this, the authors made some changes in six CNNS encoder and decoder architectures, reducing the number of spectral bands, the input size, number of network filters and also making use of shallower networks. Another interesting factor regards the use of images with the same spatial resolution and imaging sensor for training, validation and testing. With that, the results indicate the possibility of employ a CNN in satellite with the mission of classifying images with great cloud cover.

Toward [24], one of the main challenges in the image classification performance is the addition of full layers at the end of models CNN, where in some cases can not be efficient in the assimilation of spatial information present in images, for example. Hence, presents suggestions for the best manager of the information contained in images, the first has a group of neurons as a capsule or a vector that replace the neuron in the traditional neural network and can encode the properties and spatial information of features in an image to achieve equivalence.

Another very important aspect is the use of the real size of the satellite image, although it requires high processing due quite rich in details and has a high spatial resolution [1]. Therefore, many studies use the technique of transfer of learning or pre-trained networks [6], in order to speed up processing and make the model more efficient. In addition, another technique used for pre-processing of data set, mainly when there are little data per class for training step, is Data Augmentation, where transformations are applied to images, such as rotate and flip, for example [23].

3   Materials and Methods

3.1   Study Sites

The regions of interest (ROI) are located in Tocantins (ROI1) and Goiás (ROI2), Brazilian states where the Cerrado is the predominant biome. These states stand out with their landscapes reminiscent of savanna and several species of animals, in addition to two large rivers flow between the Araguaia and Tocantins, from south to north.

In the Tocantins, there are not only large grain producers, but also traditional communities, such as quilombolas, indigenous and riverside ethnic groups, and associations of babaçu coconut breakers and others, which use natural resources for their own subsistence [5]. While Goiás stands out for its mineral extraction. This activity is essential for the state's economy, as well as collaborating for national and international production and consumption. As a result, Goiás not only stands out for these raw material exports but also for environmental problems that put the fauna and flora of the Cerrado biome at risk [7].

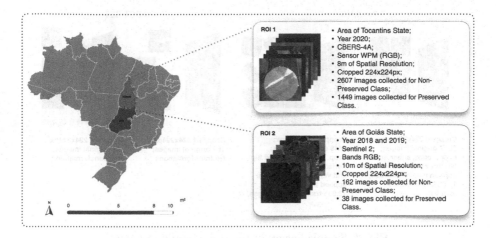

Fig. 2. ROI1 is represented in green and ROI2 in pink.

In Fig. 2, we identify on a map the regions of interest targeted in this study. Within ROI1, we selected images of the RGB bands obtained by the WPM camera of the CBERS-4A satellite, with 8-meter spatial resolution, in the period of 2020. Within ROI2, we also handled images on RGB channels, with a spatial resolution of 10 m, by the Sentinel 2 satellite from 2018 to 2019.

3.2 Datasets

The training dataset is formed by images of the ROI1. Hence, 21 images were considered, with 14.115 × 14.494px. The respective spectral bands of each image were composed and soon after the areas of interest were cut, in the TerraView software[1]. Hence, we got 1,449 images for the preserved and 2,607 images for the non-preserved classes. Given the significant difference in the amount of data between the two classes, we implemented a static data augmentation method using the tools from the imgaug library[2]. In addition, it helps the model to avoid overfitting or specializing the model on training data.

The static data augmentation was organized so that the quantity was the same for both classes, as illustrated in Fig. 3. In this way, 4 transformations were applied to the images of the non-preserved class, with center crop of

---

[1] http://www.dpi.inpe.br/terralib5/wiki/doku.php.

[2] https://imgaug.readthedocs.io/en/latest/.

224 × 224px: rotate (–50°, 30°); shear (0°, 40°), horizontal and vertical flips. For the preserved class, in addition to the other 4 transformations, rotate and shear was applied for each flip. Consequently, each class has 13,035 images, and hence the training set contains 26,070 images.

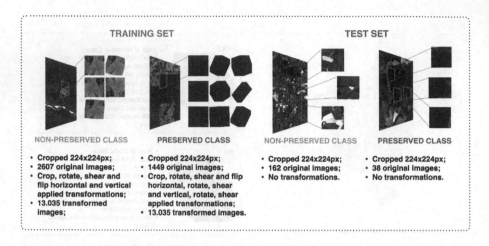

Fig. 3. Sample images of the training and test sets.

Regarding the test dataset (see Fig. 3), we selected 5 images from ROI2, with 16806 × 10986px. The respective spectral bands of each image were composed, using the TerraView software. The areas of interest were clipped, totalling 200 rasters, and standardized for the proportion of 224 × 224px. The clippings were exported to the QGIS software to make adjustments to the colour channels. We arranged them in two preserved and non-preserved sets, each containing 38 and 162 images, respectively.

In general, the preserved class has scenarios with the formation of forests, rivers, grasslands, and some savanna regions; the non-preserved class includes views of pastures, plantations, reforested areas, urban areas, and ore sites. However, we tried to standardize the types of data for each class in order to avoid ambiguities.

3.3   The Model

We designed a traditional CNN that works with satellite images to classify environmental areas as non-preserved or preserved area. This model was based on general recommendations to build a CNN for binary classification by Jones Granatyr [8], but we changed the number of convolutions and fully-connected (dense) layers, as well as we adjusted dropout, kernels in convolutions and neurons in hidden layers, number of epochs, calculation of loss as illustrated in Fig. 4.

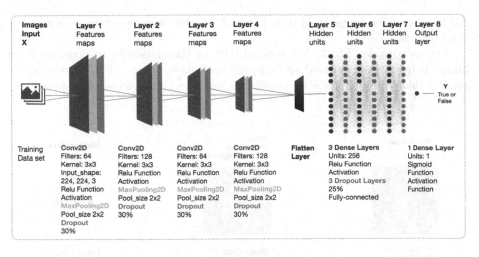

Fig. 4. Architecture of the proposed CNN.

The training images are inserted in the convolutional layers, with input-shape of 224 × 224, 3 × 3 kernel, activated by the ReLU function [12], after each convolution a MaxPooling2D layer [13], pooling 2 was added, 2, and a Dropout layer, with a probability of 30% [11]. After the convolution layers, we have 3 fully-connected layers each one with 256 neurons, activated by the ReLU function, and 3 Dropout layers with a probability of 25%. The output layer has only one neuron, activated by the Sigmoid Function in order to produce probabilistic results on a scale from 0 to 1 [12].

We use Adam's optimizer, adjusted for learning_rate = 0.001, beta_1 = 0.9, beta_2 = 0.999, epsilon = 1e−07, which consists of a descending stochastic gradient method that is based on adaptive estimation of first and second-order moments [10], and the loss function was binary-crossentropy [14]. For training, we defined 80 epochs, saving the models at the end of each epoch.

3.4 Accuracy Assessment

In order to evaluate the performance of our model, we used the following metrics:

1. Accuracy. The number of correct predictions per the total number of predictions;
2. F1-Score. This metric is defined as $F1 = 2 \times \frac{Precision \times Recall}{Precision + Recall}$. Precision is the ratio $\frac{TP}{TP+FP}$, where TP is the number of true positives and FP is the number of false positives. Recall is the ratio $\frac{TP}{TP+FN}$, where FN is the number of false negatives.

Accuracy and F1-Score metrics were used with each CNN's model saved after each epoch, separately, to label the test set images as preserved or non-preserved.

All these metrics range from 0 to 1, where 0 is the worst performance and 1 is the best one.

Let us consider Fig. 5. We defined 0.98 as the threshold to consider if an image is from the preserved or non-preserved class. Hence, if the prediction is greater than 0.98 the image is classified as preserved, otherwise is non-preserved.

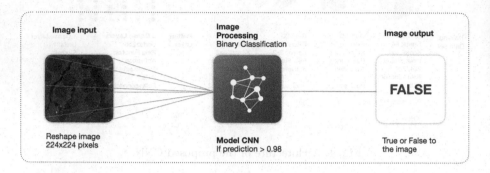

Fig. 5. Decision about the class of an image.

4   Results and Discussion

The first aspect observed in this research is the use of static data augmentation since few images were collected for the training stage. In this way, the number of images per class increased significantly, so that both sets of images had the same amount of data (balanced classes).

In Fig. 6, we can notice the values of the metrics obtained during the testing phase. Note that we assessed the CNN model obtained after each epoch during training. Moreover, we decided to provide metrics per class, i.e. Accuracy and F1-Score for classes preserved and non-preserved. With this, we can see that the non-preserved class started to be correctly labelled from model 1 onwards, while the preserved class achieved more accurate results from model 15. However, we noticed better performance between models 47 to 56, where there are low oscillation hits and misses.

Model 49 got the best scores in metrics, which as it correctly measured 137 images for the non-preserved class and 37 for preserved. This represents an Accuracy of 0.8456 and 0.9736 considering the non-preserved and preserved classes, respectively. F1-Scores are 0.9163 and 0.9866 considering the non-preserved and preserved classes, respectively. Hence, the overall Accuracy (acc) of the CNN is:

$$acc = \frac{137 + 37}{162 + 38} = 0.87 \tag{1}$$

Although the results were quite expressive, the model incorrectly labelled some images, as shown in Fig. 7. This happened more frequently with these

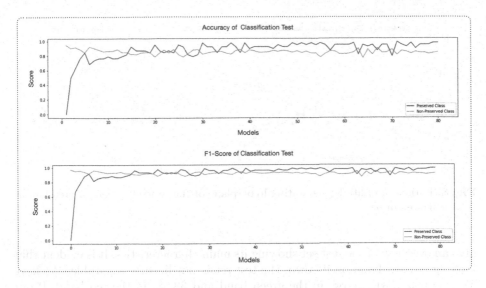

Fig. 6. F1-Score and accuracy metrics of classification test.

images non-preserved being classified as preserved. We explain this fact because of a higher concentration of dark green tones in certain regions of some non-preserved images confusing the CNN.

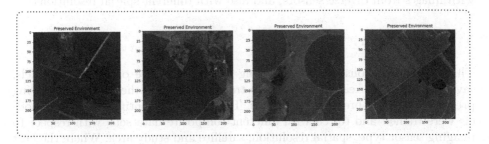

Fig. 7. Image classification errors that occurred in the tests, where reading preserved would actually be non-preserved.

To give an idea of the characteristics of the images in the test set, Figs. 8 show Ratio Band × Amplitude Band graphs, two spectral features, considering the green and red bands, respectively. These graphs show the separating hyper-plane (solid line) and margins (dashed lines) obtained via the Support Vector Machines (SVM) algorithm [20, 22] with a linear kernel. The support vectors are highlighted with a black circle around them. Moreover, the images of the preserved class are in pale blue and of the non-preserved one are in pale red.

Note that our idea here is not to use SVM as a classifier, even if we were to do that, we would use the training set to train the algorithm. Our goal is just to

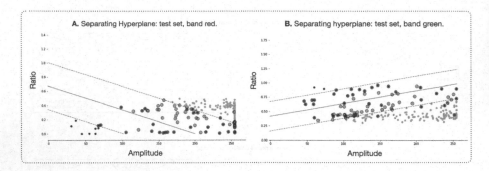

Fig. 8. Ratio × amplitude: separating hyperplane of the test set, green and red bands. (Color figure online)

give an overview of the test set showing its main characteristics. It is evident that looking at each band on its own, the test set is not linearly separable. We have 38.5% of support vectors in the green band and 33.5% in the red band. If our idea was to use this test set as, indeed, a training set for classification via SVM, we must remark that a large number of support vectors is often an indication of overfitting. Although the percentage of support vectors is not very high, we may say that it is not very low either. The whole point is to emphasize that we have used a non-trivial test set and the performance of our traditional CNN was very satisfactory, showing its feasibility for remote sensing classification when dealing with images from diverse sensors, and also with different spatial resolutions.

5   Conclusion

This experiment consisted of analyzing the performance of 80 CNN models, saved at the end of each epoch in the training stage, in the task of classifying preserved and non-preserved scenarios. The results are optimistic, as the models were trained and tested with different composite data sets, with respect to imaging sensor type, spatial resolution, satellite and study area. Where the best model achieved an Accuracy of 0.87 of image classification.

In this perspective, it is intended to improve this model, adding more classes, such as urban, agricultural, preserved, mining and deforestation, to the training and validation data sets, and tests, in order to increase the model's capacity in the task of classifying different scenarios. As well as studying more sophisticated methods to pre-process data; organization and arrangement of the number of filters by convolutional layers; the number of neurons per dense layers, so that you avoid overfitting the weights.

In addition, other evaluation methods will be researched and conducted, either by comparison with other architectures traditionally used for image classification obtained from satellite, either by testing performance in a supervised environment. As well as, using images with different spatial resolutions and sensors both in the training and testing stages, in order to analyze how well the model can do with low, medium or high-resolution images.

Certainly, use the Convolutional Neural Network and other techniques of Deep Learning for Earth observation means investing in a more sustainable and ecological society, since these digital tools boost other research on urban, industrial and environmental growth. With this, it is possible to anticipate possible climatic events, monitor land use and cover, and countless other applications and contributions to our society.

References

1. Anwer, R.M., Khan, F.S., de Weijer, J., Molinier, M., Laaksonen, J.: Binary patterns encoded convolutional neural networks for texture recognition and remote sensing scene classification. ISPRS J. Photogrammetry Remote Sens. **138**, 74–85 (2018). https://doi.org/10.1016/j.isprsjprs.2018.01.023
2. Assis, L., et al.: Terrabrasilis: a spatial data analytics infrastructure for large-scale thematic mapping. ISPRS Int. J. Geo-Information **8**, 513 (2019). https://doi.org/10.3390/ijgi8110513, http://terrabrasilis.dpi.inpe.br
3. Assis, T., Amaral, S.: Landscape and population in deforestation areas of the brazilian cerrado: The case of cerrado baiano. In: Proceedings of the XIX Brazilian Symposium on Remote Sensing (2019). https://bityli.com/3TdqJ
4. Brazil: An area of native vegetation suppressed in the cerrado biome in 2019 was 6,484 km^2. National Institute for Space Research (2019). https://bityli.com/d1Jtd
5. Corrêa, R.: Cerrado: the wealth of tocantins. Portal Tocantins (2020). https://portal.to.gov.br/noticia/2020/9/11/cerrado-a-riqueza-do-tocantins/
6. Ghassemi, S., Magli, E.: Convolutional neural networks for on-board cloud screening. Remote Sens. 11 (2019). https://doi.org/10.3390/rs11121417
7. Gonçalves, R.J.: Mining and territorial fracture of the cerrado in goiás. Élisée - Revista De Geografia Da UEG 9 (2020). https://www.revista.ueg.br/index.php/elisee/article/view/10852
8. Granatyr, J.: Deep learning com python de a a z - o curso completo. Udemy (2019). https://www.udemy.com/share/101uu0AEETcFpXRX8B/
9. Guo, Y., Liu, Y., Oerlemans, A., Lao, S., Wu, S., Lew, M.S.: Deep learning for visual understanding: a review. Neurocomputing **187**, 27–48 (2016)
10. Keras: Adam. Keras (2021). https://keras.io/api/optimizers/adam/
11. Keras: Dropout layer. Keras (2021). encurtador.com.br/drxLT
12. Keras: Layer activation functions. Keras (2021). https://keras.io/api/layers/activations/
13. Keras: Maxpooling2d layer. Keras (2021). encurtador.com.br/hszCH
14. Keras: Probabilistic losses. Keras (2021). encurtador.com.br/rCJ23
15. Khatami, R., et al.: A meta-analysis of remote sensing research on supervised pixel-based land-cover image classification processes: general guidelines for practitioners and future research. Remote Sens. Environ. **177**, 89–100 (2016)
16. Körting, T.S., Namikawa, L., et al.: How to effectively obtain metadata from remote sensing big data? In: GEOBIA 2016: Solutions and Synergies (2016)
17. LeCun, Y., Bottou, L., Bengio, Y., Haffner, P.: Gradient-based learning applied to document recognition. IEEE **86**(11), 2278–2324 (1998)
18. Ma, L., Liu, Y., Zhang, X., Ye, Y., Yin, G., Johnson, B.A.: Deep learning in remote sensing applications: a meta-analysis and review. ISPRS J. Photogrammetry Remote Sens. **152**, 166–177 (2019)

19. Ma, L., Li, M., Ma, X., Cheng, L., Du, P., Liu, Y.: A review of supervised object-based land-cover image classification. ISPRS J. Photogrammetry Remote Sens. **130**, 277–293 (2017)
20. Mohammadi, M., et al.: A comprehensive survey and taxonomy of the svm-based intrusion detection systems. J. Netw. Comput. Appl. **178**, 102983 (2021)
21. Ribeiro, J. F.; Walter, B.M.T.: Fitofisionomias do bioma cerrado. Cerrado: Ecologia e Flora, EMBRAPA, pp. 152–212 (2008)
22. Santiago Júnior, V.A., Silva, L.A.R., Andrade Neto, P.R.: Testing environmental models supported by machine learning. In: Proceedings of the III Brazilian Symposium on Systematic and Automated Software Testing, SAST 2018, pp. 3–12. Association for Computing Machinery, New York (2018). https://doi.org/10.1145/3266003.3266004
23. Shawky, O.A., Hagag, A., El-Dahshan, E.S.A., Ismail, M.A.: Remote sensing image scene classification using cnn-mlp with data augmentation. Elsevier **221**, 165356 (2020). https://doi.org/10.1016/j.ijleo.2020.165356
24. Zhang, W., Tang, P., Zhao, L.: Remote sensing image scene classification using cnn-capsnet. Remote Sens. **11**, 494 (2019). https://doi.org/10.3390/rs11050494

International Workshop on Building Multi-dimensional Models for Assessing Complex Environmental Systems (MES 2021)

The Regeneration of a Shopping Center Starts from Consumers' Preferences: A Best-Worst Scaling Application

Mauro Berta[1] (iD), Marta Bottero[2] (iD), Marina Bravi[2] (iD), Federico Dell'Anna[2](✉) (iD), and Andrea Rapari[3]

[1] Department of Architecture and Design, Politecnico di Torino,
Viale Mattioli 39, 10125 Turin, Italy
[2] Interuniversity Department of Regional and Urban Studies and Planning,
Politecnico di Torino, Viale Mattioli 39, 10125 Turin, Italy
federico.dellanna@polito.it
[3] Politecnico di Torino, Corso Duca degli Abruzzi 24, 10129 Turin, Italy

Abstract. Malling in the United States was characterized by the construction of large shopping centers in the suburbs of the city, in close connection with urban sprawl. These retail spaces have undergone a severe crisis resulting in their closure since the 1990s. In response to this phenomenon, the so-called "demalling" practice has spread intending to redevelop them with new functions. Although more incipient, in Europe this process is only evolving in the last few. This study illustrates a Best-Worst Scaling (BWS) experiment to rank consumer preferences to identify new functions to be installed in the existing shopping centers. Different items were considered in this study, including both commercial characteristics, such as type and size, and architectural-design aspects, such as internal organization, external areas feature, and services. An online survey was conducted and a total of 600 respondents was collected and analyzed through the Analytical Best-Worst Score (ABWS) algorithm. Starting from a real case related to a shopping mall in Turin (Northern Italy), the experiment results were used for definition of specific guidelines for regeneration projects.

Keywords: Demalling · Max Difference Analysis (MaxDiff) · Analytical Best-Worst Scoring (ABWS) · Survey experiment · Consumer preferences

1 Introduction

Originally born in the United States, shopping centers occupied the suburbs in the 1960s and 1970s, facilitated by the urban sprawl phenomenon. For some decades this growth has defined new aggregation centers in the immense American steppes. But in the 1990s, an unexpected crisis phenomenon favored numerous dead mall cases [1]. Although the social, economic and urban conditions of the context were radically different, this

O. Gervasi et al. (Eds.): ICCSA 2021, LNCS 12955, pp. 533–543, 2021.
https://doi.org/10.1007/978-3-030-87007-2_38

phenomenon followed a similar trend in Europe; the trial took place with a certain delay but with a frequency that has never reached that of the American cases. The reasons are different; in Europe the diffusion of urban sprawl, which is one of the favorable conditions for the success of the mall model, never touched the American levels and the new department stores, despite their widespread success, always had to compete with the attractiveness of the traditional shopping areas located in the city centers. On the other side - notwithstanding the frequent oppositions, especially by some categories of stakeholders, like merchants' associations, environmentalism activists etc. - the authorization of new malls has been for long time in the Old Continent an effective way to activate urban renovation projects, and to guarantee essential revenues for the local administrations. Anyway, the crisis of this commercial model that first appeared in the US. has not been circumscribed to the American cities, but it reached Europe in a generalized way in the last decades, also because of the widespread of the e-commerce. Italy is not exempt from this phenomenon [2] and in the outskirts of the Italian cities, many cases of abandoned or underused commercial structures can be counted nowadays, constituting a huge amount of real estate assets, stuck in a standoff of their lifecycles.

The urban, economic, and social effects of the decommissioning of shopping centers push policy makers to take preventive actions, aimed at reducing the impact of the new structures on the context. Furthermore, post-recovery interventions are envisaged with the development of so-called demalling projects. The term demalling refers to the process that aims to transform the disused shopping center into something new. Interventions of this type have already spread in the US since the 1990s; some disused structures have been reused with more or less invasive interventions (such as offices, libraries, or sports centers), others have maintained their commercial function, but have been integrated with complementary activities (such as residences, offices and public services), others are been converted into new retail formats closer to consumer preferences. From this point of view, the regeneration and enhancement processes of abandoned areas can represent a great opportunity for the local system, both from the point of view of a new use as an engine of economic development and as a driver to accelerate the transformations of cities and towns [3–8].

The demalling interventions tested at the international level represent a solid basis for the definition of project proposals for the transformation of commercial buildings also in other territorial contexts. Based on the dead mall phenomenon and good demalling practices, this study proposed a regeneration scenario for the Venaria Shopping Center located in Turin (Northern Italy), starting from consumers' preferences. Since in the context of an architectural and urban design it is useful to understand the users' preferences based on the variant utility attributed to the different project proposals [9–12], the Best-Worst Scaling (BWS) method was applied to support the design phase for the regeneration project [13]. The BWS method made it possible to identify a ranking of design elements in line with the needs and preferences of consumers and allowed to create a future vision as much realistic as possible.

After the Introduction, Sect. 2 presents the BWS methodology, the survey structure, and the Analytical Best-Worst Score (ABWS) algorithm used to analyze the responses. Section 3 describes the case study and lists the items selected to develop the BWS experiment. Section 4 presents a descriptive analysis of the sample (Sect. 4.1), the priority of the items according to the respondents' opinion (Sect. 4.2), and the regeneration project of the shopping center under study (Sect. 4.3). The conclusions and future perspectives follow.

2 Methods

2.1 Best-Worst Scaling

The preferences evaluation by means of market analysis and sample surveys has a long tradition in the field of marketing, as well as econometrics. In particular, the latter assumes that, within the framework governed by the principle of the rationality of consumer choice, the preferences of each individual are represented by a Random Utility Maximization (RUM) model. The choice modeling within the RUM theory has undergone a slow evolution that led them towards a gradual improvement, in an attempt to overcome some rigidities inherent in McFadden's original formulation [14]. In recent years, the experimentation of the BWS approach in the field of preference assessment perfected the conventional Choice Experiments and Conjoint Analysis.

BWS technique [15], also known as Max Difference Analysis (MaxDiff), is a method of detecting preferences requiring the respondent to select the best and worst alternative from the list of proposed items. BWS exploits the idea that when individuals evaluate a series of objects, the extreme choices (best and worst) should be more reliable than intermediate ones. This latter aspect is consistent with Helson's theory of adaptation level, according to which a certain judgment, in a given situation, is also the result of previous experiences and their relevance in terms of more intense positive/negative sensations [16].

2.2 Questionnaire

The BWS experiment was included in a questionnaire administered online. The software used to create the questionnaire was Sawtooth Software Discover®. After a brief presentation of the research goal, the questionnaire was organized into three main parts.

In the first part, the interviewee was asked about the activities that he/she usually attended in a shopping center, how he/she reached them or why he/she went there. The second part included the BWS method, evaluating the various features and services offered by a generic shopping center. Each respondent had to answered eight choice sets consisting of five items each. The elements of each choice set were randomly extracted by the software.

The final part of the survey investigated the respondent's personal data. The questions concerned gender, age, educational qualification, profession and family income. These responses were useful in validating the consistency and heterogeneity of the sample.

2.3 Analytical Best-Worst Scoring

For calculating the BWS score, the Analytical Best-Worst Scoring (ABW) proposed by Lipovetsky & Conklin [17] was chosen. ABW is part of simple methods for calculating MaxDiff scores. ABW is calculated as following Eq. (1):

$$ABW = ln\left(\frac{1 + NBW}{1 - NBW}\right) \tag{1}$$

where NBW is the best-worst score normalized by the unit calculated according to Eq. (2):

$$NBW = \frac{\#Bests - \#Worsts}{Total\ times\ shown} \tag{2}$$

where the difference between $\#Bests$ and $\#Worsts$ (the number of times an item is selected as best and worst respectively) is divided by the number of times the item is shown. ABW has a lower error than the Best Minus Worst Scoring for the estimation of elements latent values proposed by Finn and Louviere [15, 18], and can be compared to multinomial logit (MNL) models while being less computationally efficient [19].

3 Application

3.1 Case Study

The Venaria Shopping Center is in the north-western part of the city of Turin (Northern Italy) which borders the municipalities of Venaria and Collegno (Fig. 1). The area is well connected and accessible through numerous connecting roads, as well as the railway infrastructure. The area has a purely productive-industrial vocation. The extensive vegetation that characterized the area in the past is no longer present today, replaced over time with a building density consisting mainly of production structures. Over the years, numerous mass-selling commercial structures have sprung up.

The Venaria shopping center understudy was one of the first with typical characteristics of the American mall in the Turin area. It was built in the early 1980s under the name of "Città Mercato". The structure of the Venaria shopping center emulates the American and French malls, common to those that have spread throughout Italy. The distribution is based on an internal gallery that houses small shops and two anchor stores. The outdoor areas are mainly used for parking, resulting in underutilization of many hours of the day. The sales activities present are mainly personal services (pharmacy, laundry, tailoring, hairdresser), cosmetic, tobacco, telephone and internet shops, and catering (bar and restaurant). The hypermarket is the shop that most induces the regular customer to visit the site, even several times a week. However, the small shops guarantee a certain frequency of visitors during the week.

Although the Venaria Shopping Center is still an important hub for residents of the area and beyond, it has faced competition in recent years. The Allianz Stadium, also known as Juventus Stadium, was built in the immediate vicinity. Thanks to the different functions present inside, including the Area12 shopping area, it has become a reference place for the residents of the area. The differences between the Venaria shopping center and the Area12 are evident both from an architectural and functional point of view. Area12 shopping center is in a strategic position given the adjacency to the new Allianz Stadium, becoming a reference point for fans and regulars in the area. The Area12 center integrates various traditional functions (such as hypermarket, personal services, and services in general) with new destinations in line with new retail trends (such as exhibition spaces, medical centers, etc.).

The dead mall phenomenon inevitably impacted the Venaria Shopping Center due to the trend of change in commercial demand and considering the multiplicity of the commercial offer of the new Area12 settlement. In this perspective, a new redevelopment project of the Venaria Shopping Center should focus on a different business logic, which follows the changing tastes of consumers, and which points to new types of activities, such as lifestyle centers. New and complementary functions must be added to the traditional ones by defining a restyling that starts from the small intervention up to the total transformation of the site.

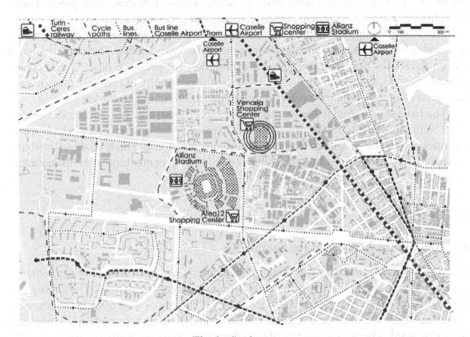

Fig. 1. Study area.

3.2   Items Selection

The regeneration of the shopping center was guided by a study based on the comparison of the architectural and functional characteristics present in today's and most innovative shopping centers in Italy and around the world. The study aimed primarily at defining a list of items that users could indicate as the most needed within a generic shopping mall.

Subsequently, the survey aimed to identify among the multitude of services those strategic for the regeneration of the shopping center starting from the preferences declared by consumers.

The items involved different spaces and dimensions of the shopping center, investigating the usefulness of the consumer for the different parts that make up the structure. The items can be classified into five dimensions.

The first group referred to the type, size, and sales offer (SO); small and single-brand stores, based on specialize retail, and the presence of the hypermarket, a larger selling space focused on quantity over quality.

The second group referred to the architectural design of the interior spaces (IS). The items investigated the internal distribution by covered or open-air galleries and defined two commercial typologies: classic shopping malls or lifestyle centers respectively. Other items referred to a multi-story center or open-air market structure.

The architectural design aspects for the external spaces (ES) constituted the third group of attributes. These items represented functions dedicated to socializing, such as the presence of open spaces dedicated to events, outdoor cinemas, open green spaces, greenhouses and winter gardens, urban gardens, and pedestrian squares.

The fourth group included the most innovative functions present in shopping centers and referred to complementary services and activities (CS). The items included the availability of play areas, spaces for exhibitions, the presence of a cultural center, coworking areas, restaurants, self-service areas, the possibility of charging electric cars, the presence of accommodation facilities, sports facilities, and multiplex cinemas.

The last issue referred to the type of parking space (PS), whether outdoor or covered.

The twenty-four items identified built an exhaustive list of characters, within which the interviewed the consumer had the opportunity to choose which of these attributes he/she considered the most important to get the shopping center closest to his/her needs and requests.

4 Results

4.1 Descriptive Analysis of the Sample

The link to the questionnaire was disseminated via email and social networks to obtain a heterogeneous sample for different age groups and geographical areas. The survey was carried out between September and December 2020. About 600 questionnaires were collected. After the verification phases, questionnaires that were not fully completed were discarded. The actual number of questionnaires considered reliable was 473. 43% of the interviewees were male, while 57% were female. The respondents were distributed according to age groups: 39.32% of the interviewees were between 18 and 24 years, 19.03% between 25 and 34 years, 13.32% between 35 and 44 years, 8% between 45 and 54 years old, 13.53% are over 55 years old. The limited number of adult respondents was mainly related to the type of compilation medium chosen, far from the daily uses of those age groups. The impossibility of carrying out face-to-face questionnaires in the period of the COVID-19 pandemic did not allow to obtain a large number of questionnaires filled out by individuals in the adult age group. Most of the interviewees belonged to families with at least 3 individuals (80.91%).

Regarding shopping habits, 28.54% of respondents visited a shopping mall at least once a week. The reasons for visiting the usual shopping center were the use of both the hypermarket and the shopping arcade for 52.01%. 26% visit the center only for the hypermarket, while about 22% only for the shops in the gallery. The usual shopping center was located for most of the sample within 10 km (88.37%). 56.45% said shopping habits have changed quite or a lot in the last year (56.45%), with more online shopping. This could be due to lifestyle changes or government restrictions in Italy adopted during the period of the COVID-19 pandemic.

4.2 Individuals' Priorities

Once the descriptive analysis of the sample was developed, a statistical model was constructed to determine the order of the 24 characteristics considered (Table 1).

The data from the survey experiment were analyzed using the ABWS. The ABWS defined an overall picture of individual preferences, stating that the most chosen items referred to the ES dimension; outdoor green spaces (2.46) and pedestrian squares (1.74). The results went towards configurations of open and usable public spaces, according to the "commercial square" common in many cases of redevelopment today. This was followed by the presence of some specialized shops inside the shopping center (1.67). The results confirmed that consumers tend to give importance to the type, size and sales offer, focusing on the quality of the products. This preference was also confirmed by the central position in the ranking of hypermarket presences (−0.16), underlining the indifference towards this type of retail sale.

Other interesting results referred to the open structure of the shopping center galleries (1.07) and the spaces intended for meeting, aggregation, and leisure places; open spaces dedicated to events (0.79), open markets (0.73). Consumers did not only visit shopping centers for shopping only but also to frequent meeting and entertainment spaces, dining places and spaces for events, especially in outdoor spaces (ES).

Among the elements considered less useful were the spaces of services and complementary activities (CS) for co-working (−1.07), multiplex cinema (−1.46) and the presence of hotels and accommodation facilities (−1.92). The multiplex cinema, often designed in the immediate vicinity of shopping centres, now seems to be a solution that is no longer in line with consumer needs. This result could be caused by the change in habits brought about by the restrictions set by the Italian government which included the closure of cinemas, theaters, and live entertainment venues from the earliest days of the global emergency COVID-19 [20]. There was also little interest in the use of shared workspaces for smart working, despite being defined as a practice in pandemic period.

The results were useful in defining the design characteristics of the Venaria shopping center based on the best and worst choices for the twenty-four items identified.

4.3 New Project of Venaria Shopping Center

The results deriving from the questionnaire defined the configuration of a commercial center profile more in line with the preferences and utilities of today's users. The results obtained were also in line with the various cases of current commercial redevelopment

Table 1. Attributes in order of importance.

Items	Dimension	Scoring
Presence of green open spaces	ES	2.46
Presence of pedestrian squares	ES	1.74
Specialized shops (single brand)	SO	1.67
Open air gallery	IS	1.07
Bar/café and self service	CS	0.81
Open space dedicated to events	ES	0.79
Open market	SO	0.73
Presence of a cultural center	CS	0.53
Space dedicated to exhibitions and shows	CS	0.35
Uncovered parking	PS	0.22
Restaurant and/or pizzeria	CS	0.11
Presence of the hypermarket	SO	− 0.16
Outdoor play area	ES	− 0.22
Urban gardens/Green roof	ES	− 0.27
Covered parking	PS	− 0.37
Outdoor cinema	ES	− 0.41
Multi-story shopping mall	IS	− 0.61
Covered gallery	IS	− 0.80
Charging stations for electric cars	CS	− 0.97
Greenhouses/Winter Garden	ES	− 1.00
Sports activities	CS	− 1.05
Presence of an area for coworking or conferences	CS	− 1.07
Cinema multiplex	CS	− 1.46
Presence of an accommodation facility	CS	− 1.92

[21]. Following the results of the evaluation model, the project defines solutions for the redesign of commercial spaces based on green spaces, mixed use (and not just mass sales), experience and leisure with an ever-stronger link between the architectural object and the urban context in which it is inserted. In this way, the new trade will have to open up to the context, even physically, supporting itself with some spaces and events that characterize urban everyday life. The existing centre will have to change by offering a new aggregation site that fills the gaps in the peripheral site of the urban context.

The design proposal of the building is intrinsically based on its structural aspect (Fig. 2). The structure of the centre consists of steel and reinforced concrete pillars supporting a repeatedly pitched roof, which have been specially designed to reconfigure the building. This peculiarity has made it possible to reconfigure the shopping center by regenerating it through an open distribution that changes the existing covered gallery. The plan of the center is completely modified favouring an open gallery by eliminating some original parts. In this way, open connections are defined that link a building that is more fragmented than today. The new organization of the structure offers the possibility to define, not only new functions, but to propose a new character to the open space. This space is created by slightly reducing the sales area and transforming part of the parking lot into new open and covered public spaces. The public space is not only an open distribution area, but also a place for temporary activities such as open-air cinema or other leisure activities.

A more detailed and sophisticated commercial offer is proposed, which gives room for possible hybridisation by looking at an alternative trade to the classic shopping centre model. The sale of the centre will not focus on the mass trade typical of a hypermarket, but on a multitude of sales structures of various sizes. The offer will be defined by different types of products and by experiential and specialised selling. Some of the added structures will be set up as cultural, hospitality and service centres.

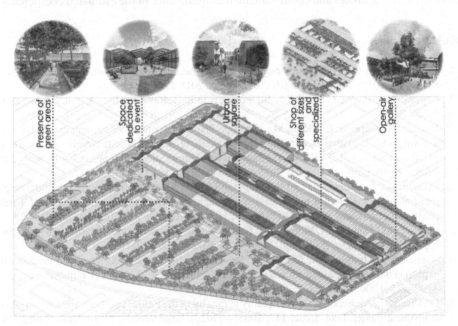

Fig. 2. Axonometry of the restyling project of the shopping center in Venaria.

5 Conclusions and Future Perspectives

The dead mall phenomenon has hit the United States and Europe, favouring numerous cases of closure and abandonment of shopping centers. These cases lead to significant negative consequences considering the impact not only on the shopping center but also on the territory and society of the surrounding areas, especially in peripheral contexts.

In this context, the study aimed to define new functionalities for innovative shopping centers in line with the new needs of consumers.

A survey based on the BWS method was structured with the objective of obtaining a ranking of 24 items defining different characteristics and functions within recent shopping centres. The items focused on the new role offered by public green spaces, the architectural features, the relationship with the context and the different functions and leisure facilities. The results showed a preference for the adoption of outdoor green spaces and pedestrian plazas, and an open structure for the shopping mall. Traditional features often combined with shopping centres did not seem more attractive, such as multiplex cinemas. The results were useful to define the restyling project of a shopping center located in Turin which in recent years has suffered from strong competition.

As future perspectives, the collected data could be segmented to define preferences for subsamples such as age group or geographic area. It would be appropriate to repeat the survey, to verify whether consumer preferences will change after the COVID-19 pandemic. Furthermore, models based on the multinomial model (MNL) could provide more effective estimates and could validate the significance of the estimated coefficients.

References

1. Coutinho Guimarães, P.P.: Shopping centres in decline: analysis of demalling in Lisbon. Cities **87**, 21–29 (2019). https://doi.org/10.1016/j.cities.2018.12.021
2. Cavoto, G., Limonta, G.: The demalling process in Italy. Rev. Lusófona Arquit. e Educ. **8–9**, 65–84 (2013)
3. Bottero, M., Caprioli, C., Berta, M.: Urban problems and patterns of change: the analysis of a downgraded industrial area in Turin. In: Mondini, G., Oppio, A., Stanghellini, S., Bottero, M., Abastante, F. (eds.) Values and Functions for Future Cities. GET, pp. 385–401. Springer, Cham (2020). https://doi.org/10.1007/978-3-030-23786-8_22
4. Bottero, M., Assumma, V., Caprioli, C., Dell'Ovo, M.: Decision making in urban development: the application of a hybrid evaluation method for a critical area in the city of Turin (Italy). Sustain. Cities Soc. **72**, 103028 (2021). https://doi.org/10.1016/j.scs.2021.103028
5. Bottero, M.C., Datola, G., Monaco, R.: Fuzzy cognitive maps: A dynamic approach for urban regeneration processes evaluation. Valori e Valutazioni **23**, 77–90 (2019)
6. Assumma, V., Bottero, M., Datola, G., De Angelis, E., Monaco, R.: Dynamic models for exploring the resilience in territorial scenarios. Sustainability **12**, 3 (2019). https://doi.org/10.3390/su12010003
7. D'Alpaos, C., Andreolli, F.: Urban quality in the city of the future: a bibliometric multicriteria assessment model. Ecol. Indic. **117**, 106575 (2020). https://doi.org/10.1016/j.ecolind.2020.106575
8. Mangialardo, A., Micelli, E.: Reconstruction or reuse? How real estate values and planning choices impact urban redevelopment. Sustainability **12**(10), 4060 (2020). https://doi.org/10.3390/su12104060
9. Antonini, A., Blečić, I., Canu, D., Cecchini, A., Fancello, G., Trunfio, G.A.: Using citizen-provided information to build purposeful knowledge for planning: principles, requirements, and three examples. In: Papa, R., Fistola, R. (eds.) Smart Energy in the Smart City. GET, pp. 329–342. Springer, Cham (2016). https://doi.org/10.1007/978-3-319-31157-9_17
10. Awang, M., Soltani, S.H.K., Hajabbasi, H.S.: Design preferences and consumer's selection principles. Procedia-Soc. Behav. Sci. **35**, 539–545 (2012). https://doi.org/10.1016/j.sbspro.2012.02.120

11. Forte, F.: "From Bata to Prada": Appraisal approach in new retail design. In: IOP Conference Series: Materials Science and Engineering. Institute of Physics Publishing, vol. 603, pp. 032018 (2019)
12. Giannelli, A.L., Giuffrida, S., Trovato, M.R.: Madrid Rio Park symbolic values and contingent valuation. Valori e Valutazioni 21, 75–86 (2018)
13. Louviere, J.J., Flynn, T.N., Marley, A.A.J.: Best-worst Scaling: Theory, Methods and Applications. Cambridge University Press, Cambridge (2015)
14. McFadden, D.: Econometric models of probabilistic choice. In: Manski, C.F., McFadden, D.L. (eds.) Structural Analysis of Discrete Data, pp. 198–272. The MIT Press, Cambridge (1981)
15. Finn, A., Louviere, J.J.: Determining the appropriate response to evidence of public concern: the case of food safety. J. Public Policy Mark. 11, 12–25 (1992). https://doi.org/10.1177/074 391569201100202
16. Helson, H.: Adaptation-level Theory: An Experimental and Systematic Approach to Behavior. Harper and Row, New York (1964)
17. Lipovetsky, S., Conklin, M.: Best-Worst Scaling in analytical closed-form solution. J. Choice Model. 10, 60–68 (2014). https://doi.org/10.1016/j.jocm.2014.02.001
18. Chrzan, K., Orme, B.K.: Applied MaxDiff. A Practitioner's Guide to Best-Worst Scaling. Sawtooth Software Inc., Provo, UT (2019)
19. Marley, A.A.J., Islam, T., Hawkins, G.E.: A formal and empirical comparison of two score measures for best–worst scaling. J. Choice Model. 21, 15–24 (2016). https://doi.org/10.1016/j.jocm.2016.03.002
20. Dell'Ovo, M., Dell'Anna, F., Simonelli, R., Sdino, L.: Enhancing the cultural heritage through adaptive reuse. A multicriteria approach to evaluate the Castello Visconteo in Cusago (Italy). Sustainability. 13, 4440 (2021). https://doi.org/10.3390/su13084440
21. Cavoto, G.: Demalling A Response to the Demise of Retail Buildings. Maggioli Editore, Milan (2014)

Nature-based Simulation to Address Climate Change-Related Flooding. Preliminary Insights on a Small-Sized Italian City

Carlotta Quagliolo[1]($\boxtimes$) (iD), Elena Comino[2] (iD), and Alessandro Pezzoli[1] (iD)

[1] DIST - Interuniversity Department of Regional and Urban Studies and Planning, Politecnico di Torino and Università Degli Studi di Torino, 10125 Torino, Italy
{carlotta.quagliolo,alessandro.pezzoli}@polito.it
[2] DIATI - Department of Environment, Land and Infrastructure Engineering, Politecnico di Torino, 10129 Torino, Italy
elena.comino@polito.it

Abstract. Climate change impacts on cities are likely to require changes in urban adaptation planning. Despite the low degree of climate change manageability, the Nature-Based Solutions (NBS) are considered resilient measures that integrate the ecological dimension into spatial planning while playing a crucial role in addressing societal challenges and multiple benefits.

In urban planning, ecosystem models can be used to develop flood management strategies even if the limited experience with models and model output is a challenge for planners in thinking about addressing potential climate change impacts effectively. Consequently, this new challenge is based on the need for spatially explicit biophysical assessment related to NBS scenarios' implementation.

This study considers the urban flood vulnerability assessment and how these vulnerabilities can be reduced through NBS simulation scenarios in a small-sized Italian coastal city of the Liguria Region. To quantify the amount of runoff during extreme rainfall events while identifying the greatest critical areas, the Urban Flood Risk Mitigation model (InVEST) integrated into a GIS environment have been employed. Furthermore, the biophysical assessment of NBS implementation has been supported by highlighting the crucial role of biodiversity type.

Keywords: Climate change adaptation · Pluvial flood · Spatial modelling

1 Introduction

Cities are becoming increasingly vulnerable to weather extremes, especially by considering flash flooding events resulting from short-duration intensive rainfall [1, 2]. In the context of climate change, this scenario is exacerbated mainly in coastal urban areas, where compound flooding due to simultaneous storm surge, sea-level rise and increased runoff during extreme rains requires deepening local knowledge of the flood-prone regions [3, 4]. The supply of urban ecosystem services (ES) can help mitigate

O. Gervasi et al. (Eds.): ICCSA 2021, LNCS 12955, pp. 544–553, 2021.
https://doi.org/10.1007/978-3-030-87007-2_39

these climate change effects while improving human health and well-being in cities [5, 6]. The concept of Nature-Based Solutions (NBS) is considered as the new planning tool for ecologically sensitive urban development. Indeed, NBS include the main ideas of green and blue infrastructures and ecosystem services overcoming the boundaries of traditional approaches "predict and prevent" [7]. These innovative solutions comprise natural features characterized by multifunctionality and connectivity, thus providing multiple co-benefits (environmental, social and economic) [8].

According to DG Environment of the European Commission (2011) in "Towards Better Environmental Options in Flood Risk Management" such measures *"can be effective in protecting against flooding, as well as provide other benefits deriving from ecosystem services, such as for leisure activities and nature protection"*[1]. In this view, the NBS implementation and the simulation of biophysical impacts of NBS to reduce runoff volume can be considered good practice to quantify the benefits of these measures, mainly in terms of water regulation and flood control. Only evaluating simulation scenarios helps to adopt site-specific performance-based solutions, also differentiating more suitable vegetation type. This kind of approach has the potential for future urban strategies in the face of climate change.

For these reasons, this study aims to show the important role of ecosystem services implementation to support climate change adaptation planning. Adopting an integrated evaluation method is used to explore alternative nature-based scenarios on the study case of a small Ligurian city (Italy). The application of InVEST modelling combined with Geographic Information System (GIS) enhances estimating the spatial distribution of urban flood-related vulnerabilities while identifying where and how NBS can contribute to adapting the city. The novelty of this research is related to the application of integrated ES spatial modelling to provide results regarding flood risk mitigation through the NBS implementation. This paper is structured as follow: methodology presenting firstly, the functioning and data input of the Urban Flood Risk Mitigation model (InVEST) and the combination with GIS environment; secondly, describing the NBS scenarios and lastly, presenting the catchment area for the analysis; the results and discussions sections describe the output of implemented scenarios; conclusions shortly explaining the limit of this research and setting possible applications for future research.

2 Methodology

Such spatial integrated approach combines Geographic Information Systems (GIS) tools with InVEST modelling. Furthermore, this method is scenario-based since it is characterized by simulating three scenarios through adopting the Urban Food Risk Mitigation model. This enables us to examine simulation results to finally quantify and evaluate the NBS benefits regarding flooding regulation.

2.1 InVEST Model and GIS Integration

The Urban Flood Risk Mitigation (UFRM) model is a recent product (2019) of the software InVEST - 3.9.0 (Integrated Valuation of Ecosystem Services and Tradeoffs) part of

---

[1] https://ec.europa.eu/environment/water/flood_risk/better_options.html.

the Natural Capital Project[2]. This spatial model focuses on urban areas' ability to reduce runoff due to extreme rainfall and flash flooding events [9]. The UFRM model considers the potentiality of permeable green places to mainly reduce runoff while slowing surface flows and creating space for water (as in floodplains or basins). The model output represents the amount of retained runoff per pixels assuming mainly the flood-prone areas due to the interaction between the permeable-impermeable surface layers (related to the land use type) and the soil drainage (depending on the soil characteristics). This urban flood model uses the USDA (United States Department of Agriculture) Soil Conservation Service – "SCS runoff curve number" (SCS-CN) method to estimate runoff, which is based on the water balance equation of the rainfall. The SCS-CN method has been developed for runoff volume estimation and it knew widespread use by public agency, local governments, and professionals [9, 10]. The runoff retention index estimated per pixel (R_i) represent the ratio between the quantity of precipitation retained (P-Q) and the total precipitation (see Eq. 1)) over the study area:

$$R_i = 1 - \frac{Q_{p,i}}{P} \tag{1}$$

Required model inputs, a short description and the source are synthesized in Table 1.

Since the InVEST software works with spatial models, the elaboration of model inputs and outputs is conducted through the employment of GIS tools. The UFRM model solves the empirical representation of the hydrological aspects for estimating runoff production and retention ability in the study area [12]. By applying GIS-based approaches to elaborate model's output, the potential localization of the implementation areas (opportunity spaces) for selected NBS is identified [13]. Overall, the resulting spatial index from GIS provides a picture of the vulnerability pattern and the biophysical assessment [14]. Figure 1 shows the flow diagram of the integration among various methodological steps.

2.2 NBS Scenarios

Although quantitative reduction targets of flood risk or proposed methodologies for NBS implementation are missing in the Flood Directive, an estimation of the possible contribution of NBS to manage flood risk is provided by simulating the biophysical impact derived by the diffuse implementation of these measures. This method provides a quantitative reduction target while setting the NBS scenarios by selecting the vegetation necessary to reach it.

The NBS biophysical benefits assessment has been developed by simulating changes on the curve number values for hydrological soil groups in the sensitivity table of model input to increase the city's retention capacity. This assumption keeps constant all the other data input. The base scenario represents the present state, while NBS-1 and NBS-2 concern the future adaptation scenarios after NBSs implementation (see Fig. 2). The prioritization of the suitable areas for implementing NBS follows the vulnerability analysis provided by the base scenario. Particularly, the scenario NBS-1 is characterized by

---

[2] Available at https://naturalcapitalproject.stanford.edu/software/invest.

Table 1. UFRM model inputs

Data type	Description	Source (year)
Watershed vector	Hydrographic basins delineating the studied area	- Geoportal Liguria (2019)
Depth of rainfall	Total rain for a given single storm event typical of the region. Value of 70 mm for 3 h of rainfall duration	- ARPA Liguria - [2]
Land Cover raster	Integration of two data, respectively Land cover and Imperviousness maps, to obtain this raster categorized following USDA (United States Department of Agriculture) classes	- Geoportal Liguria (2019) - SINANET (2015)
Soil Hydrological Group (HSG) raster	HSG represents the saturated hydraulic conductivity of soils (Ksat mm/h). Employment of 'Landscape Units' and 'Profili and Trivellate' to build the final map	- Geoportal Liguria (2000)
Sensitivity table	This table represents the land use classes associated with each HSG	- [11]

implementing 'Green parking' in areas classified as 'urban district' following the Land cover map. Only those areas with 72% of impervious surfaces that highlighted low-level runoff retention capacity below 60% in the base scenario set scenes of NBS-1 measures. Li et al. (2018) demonstrated that permeable pavements could absorb stormwater improving overland flow regulation by approximately 67% [15]. The scenario NBS-2 concerns the implementation of 'Rain gardens' along the streets. This measure has the function to collect and store stormwater attenuating runoff while having esthetical functions (amenity value). The classes categorized as 'street, roads and railways' for the Land cover map, which have shown low retention capacity around 50–60% from the base scenario, have been chosen for the implementation.

The definition of these two NBS-scenarios has been developed under the 'Piano Nazionale di Adattamento al Cambiamento Climatico' (PNACC - 2017), which identifies 21 key actions among various sectors synthesized in four main fields: hydrogeological instability, coastal area management, biodiversity, and urban settlement [17]. Particularly, both NBS-scenarios definition follows the Cloud Burst action plan of the Local Resilience Strategy - Genova Lighthouse. Indeed, through the Urban Agenda Genova 2050, this action foresees the implementation of adaptation measures based on nature (as NBS) integrated with grey approaches to reduce runoff volume due to extreme rainfall events by mainly integrating greenways and converting impervious surfaces [18].

GIS
Land use land cover
HSG
InVEST modelling
SCS-CN METHOD
Curve Number
Satured Hydraulic conductivity
Rainfall
Runoff retention
Runoff generation
GIS
NBS scenarios
Pluvial flood risk mitigation service
Biophysical assessment of NBS

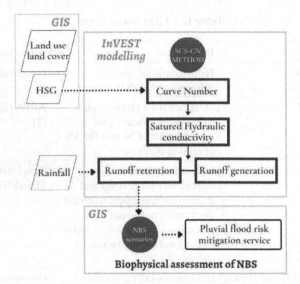

Fig. 1. Flow diagram of the integrated approach

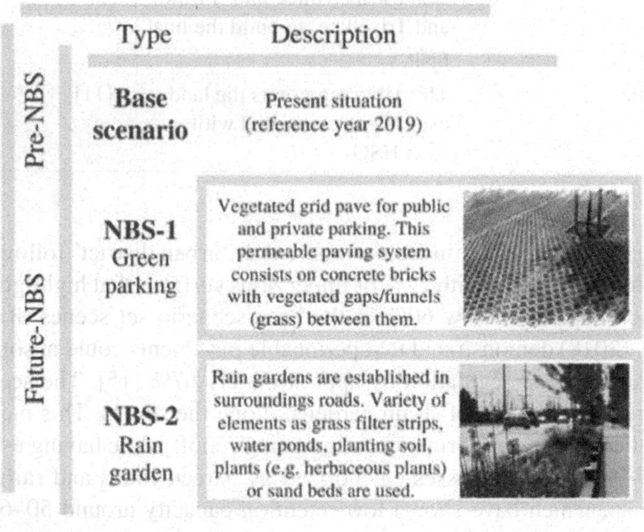

Type
Description
Pre-NBS
Base scenario
Present situation (reference year 2019)
Future-NBS
NBS-1 Green parking
Vegetated grid pave for public and private parking. This permeable paving system consists on concrete bricks with vegetated gaps/funnels (grass) between them.
NBS-2 Rain garden
Rain gardens are established in surroundings roads. Variety of elements as grass filter strips, water ponds, planting soil, plants (e.g. herbaceous plants) or sand beds are used.

Fig. 2. NBS scenarios overview (authors' elaboration from [16]).

2.3 Study Area: City of Rapallo

The area of analysis is the city of Rapallo. Rapallo is a coastal city in the Metropolitan area of Genoa in the Liguria Region (Italy) (see Fig. 3). The municipality, located 25 square kilometres southeast of Genoa, is part of the Tigullio Gulf. With an extension area of about 34 square kilometres, the city of Rapallo covers one major natural watershed linked to the Boate torrent and other seven smaller basins. The watershed boundaries have been used as a delimiting area to run the InVEST model. The town lies 3 m above sea level, mainly extending through a lowland between Boate and San Francesco torrents.

The Mediterranean climate characterizes this area through essentially rainier months during the winter season. However, from recent studies, extreme rainfall events frequently occurred in this Mediterranean region, causing intense flooding, especially in the eastern part (Levante) of Liguria[3].

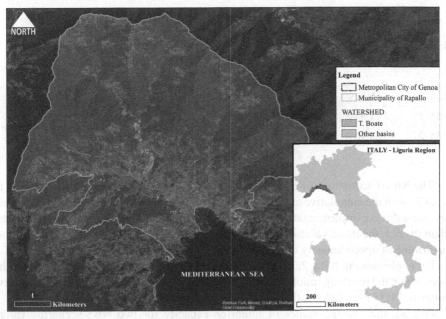

Fig. 3. The study area (authors' elaboration)

3 Results and Discussion

This section provides a critical analysis of the InVEST model's output for the study area by discussing the two NBS-scenarios implementations.

The hydrological curve number values in this study area vary between 30 to 98 across various pixels (excluding water bodies with curve numbers equal to 0). The dimension of pixels used for this analysis is of 5 m. The average values for the watersheds considered are between 61.26 and 86.79. This means that the studied catchment area presents a moderate degree of runoff production. As the urban landscape is more based on concrete surfaces, the runoff generation increases reflected through higher curve number values. Flood mitigation capacity by NBSs-scenarios is provided in terms of runoff retention index and quantified in runoff retention and runoff generated volume (see Table 2).

---

[3] https://www.arpal.liguria.it/homepage/meteo/analisi-climatologiche/atlante-climatico-della-lig uria.html.

The total cumulative runoff volume calculated by the InVEST model in the study area for a design storm of 3 h duration having 70 mm of intensity is around 21.33 m^3. This amount corresponds to the runoff estimated for the base scenario, which showed a runoff retention index equal to 69.52%. The runoff retention index represents the relative measure of runoff volume retained in respect to the precipitation volume and ranges from 0 (low retention) to 1 (high retention).

Table 2. Summary of biophysical impacts' simulation

Scenarios	Runoff retention index %	Cumulative runoff retention volume m^3	Cumulative runoff volume m^3
Base	69.52%	1.22 m^3	21.33 m3
NBS-1	71.44%	1.25 m^3	19.99 m^3
NBS-2	69.76%	1.22 m^3	21.15 m^3

The NBS-1 scenario showed an average value of runoff retention index equivalent to 71.44%, with the cumulative amount of runoff volume approximately 20 m^3. Therefore, through a diffuse implementation of 'green parking' for a portion equal to 10% of the urban district, the mean value of the retention capacity for Rapallo municipality is most performing of approximately close to 3%.

By implementing NBS-2, which is characterized by 'rain gardens' for 8.8% of the street zones, the resulting runoff volume is very little lower (21.15 m^3) regarding the base scenario (21.33 m^3). Indeed, the runoff retention capacity increased only by 0.035%.

Overall, the average values of retention capacity for two NBS-scenarios varied between 0.6976 and 0.7144, indicating that 69–71% of the precipitation amount is retained in the catchment area of Rapallo (3348.16 ha as total surface area calculated on all census areas for Rapallo municipality).

Figure 4 illustrates the runoff retention index spatially distributed using the mean retention value for each pixel for base scenario (a), NBS-1 (b) and NBS-2 (c) simulations. This way helps to visualize the entity of waterflow event by identifying where and how should be increased the mitigation capacity from higher values of retention represented by a blue colour on the map to a lower value of retention, red in the map. NBS intervention areas' frames show the location of the NBS-scenarios implementation in Fig. 4(b) and (c).

4   Conclusion and Future Perspectives

This study represents the preliminary results of an ongoing research for that study area. The analysis is a first attempt to test and estimate the biophysical effects of NBS implementation on pluvial-related floods mitigation. The employment of the recent InVEST model, Urban Flood Risk Mitigation, and spatially mapping of elaborated outputs

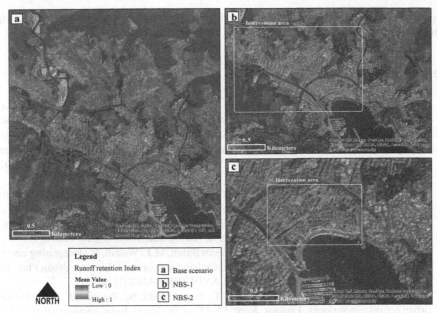

Fig. 4. Runoff retention capacity per pixel for the Base scenario, NBS-1 and NBS-2 (authors' elaboration)

through GIS environment in a small Italian coastal city highlights how performance-based adaptation planning could aid the decision-making process. The ES modelling output has been used to evaluate the biophysical values of runoff through measurable impacts at the urban level. This InVEST model for estimating urban flood risk is designed to suit hydrological aspects for easy implementation in adaptation policy research. Indeed, the SCS-CN method used by the model is a widely accepted empirical approach with limited data requirement. In addition, the GIS-based modelling enables to obtain detailed maps on pluvial flood vulnerability distribution while understanding where NBS can better contribute to adaptation. Nevertheless, the spatial variability and duration of the rainfall event are not integrated in the model. Further improvement by including this information into the analysis should be developed.

The results show that a diffuse implementation of NBS can improve the city's retention capacity. Still, the typology of measure and the chosen vegetation plays a crucial role for best performing. Indeed, changes in soil, climate and hydrological conditions call for defining how different ecosystems' restoration methods, including various landscapes, planning procedures and vegetation types, best fitted to local environments [10].

To manage the simulation NBS-scenarios implementation consistently, a deepening on threshold values to be employed by modifying curve numbers for hydrological soil groups will be conducted. This paper results could represent a starting point for future developments refining, for example, the NBS-scenarios building by selecting specific vegetation types for high-performance rate under changing climate conditions [19]. Indeed, this study is a contribution to assessing NBS effectiveness to reduce pluvial flood for Rapallo Municipality. Results could be improved by integrating a cost-benefit analysis of NBS implementation, considering the economic savings from flood damage reduction and other non-monetary benefits.

References

1. Aerts, J.C.J.H., Botzen, W.J.W., Emanuel, K., Lin, N., de Moel, H., Michel-Kerjan, E.O.: Evaluating flood resilience strategies for coastal megacities. Science **344**(6183), 473–475 (2014). https://doi.org/10.1126/science.1248222
2. Rosenzweig, B., et al.: Developing knowledge systems for urban resilience to cloudburst rain events. Environ. Sci. Policy **99**, 150–159 (2019). https://doi.org/10.1016/j.envsci.2019.05.020
3. Berndtsson, R., et al.: Drivers of changing urban flood risk: a framework for action. J. Environ. Manage. **240**, 47–56 (2019). https://doi.org/10.1016/j.jenvman.2019.03.094
4. IPCC Summary for policymakers. In: IPCC Special Report on the Ocean and Cryosphere in a Changing Climate. Pörtner, H.-O., Eds., et al. (2019). ISBN 978–0–521–88010–7.
5. Grêt-Regamey, A., Altwegg, J., Sirén, E.A., van Strien, M.J., Weibel, B.: Integrating ecosystem services into spatial planning—a spatial decision support tool. Landsc. Urban Plan. **165**, 206–219 (2017). https://doi.org/10.1016/J.LANDURBPLAN.2016.05.003
6. McPhearson, T., Andersson, E., Elmqvist, T., Frantzeskaki, N.: Resilience of and through urban ecosystem services. Ecosyst. Serv. **12**, 152–156 (2015). https://doi.org/10.1016/j.ecoser.2014.07.012
7. Brunetta, G., et al.: Territorial resilience: toward a proactive meaning for spatial planning. Sustain. **11**, 1–17 (2019). https://doi.org/10.3390/su11082286
8. Dushkova, D., Haase, D.: Not simply green: nature-based solutions as a concept and practical approach for sustainability studies and planning agendas in cities. Land **9**(1), 19 (2020). https://doi.org/10.3390/land9010019
9. Quagliolo, C., Comino, E., Pezzoli, A.: Experimental flash floods assessment through urban flood risk mitigation (UFRM) model: the case study of Ligurian coastal cities. Front. Water **3**, 1–16 (2021). https://doi.org/10.3389/frwa.2021.663378
10. Eli, R.N., Lamont, S.J.: Curve numbers and urban runoff modeling - application limitations. In: Proceedings of the Low Impact Development 2010: Redefining Water in the City - Proceedings of the 2010 International Low Impact Development Conference; San Francisco, CA, USA, vol. 41099, pp. 405–418 (2010)
11. USDA - United States Department of Agriculture Hydrologic Soil-Cover Complexes. In: National Engineering Handbook: Part 630 - Hydrology (2004)
12. Sharp, R., et al.: InVEST 3.9.0. User's Guide. The Natural Capital Project. https://storage.googleapis.com/releases.naturalcapitalproject.org/invest-userguide/latest/index.html. Accessed 12 Apr 2021
13. Albert, C., et al.: Planning nature-based solutions: principles, steps, and insights. Ambio **50**(8), 1446–1461 (2020). https://doi.org/10.1007/s13280-020-01365-1
14. Davies, C., Lafortezza, R.: Transitional path to the adoption of nature-based solutions. Land Use Policy **80**, 406–409 (2019). https://doi.org/10.1016/j.landusepol.2018.09.020
15. Li, Y., Huang, Y., Ye, Q., Zhang, W., Meng, F., Zhang, S.: Multi-objective optimization integrated with life cycle assessment for rainwater harvesting systems. J. Hydrol. **558**, 659–666 (2018). https://doi.org/10.1016/j.jhydrol.2018.02.007
16. UNaLab: Nature Based Solutions – Technical Handbook, Part II (2019)
17. Ministero dell'ambiente e della tutela del territorio e del mare - Direzione Generale per il Clima, l'Energia e l'Aria Piano Nazionale di Adattamento ai Cambiamenti Climatici (PNACC 2017) - Contribution (2017)

18. Colombari, L.: Funzionalità Dei Sistemi Informativi Geografici (Gis) Nella Risoluzione Del Conflitto Tra Uso Del Suolo. In: Area Urbana E Gli Effetti Del Cambiamento Climatico - Il Caso Di Genova E Del Quartiere Certosa - CAMPASSO, Università degli Studi di Torino (2020)
19. Kabisch, N., Korn, H., Stadler, J., Bonn, A.: Nature-based solutions to climate change adaptation in urban areas—linkages between science, policy and practice. In: Kabisch, N., Korn, H., Stadler, J., Bonn, A. (eds.) Nature-based Solutions to Climate change Adaptation in Urban Areas. TPUST, pp. 1–11. Springer, Cham (2017). https://doi.org/10.1007/978-3-319-56091-5_1

A Model of Analysis and Assessment to Support the Valorisation and Management of Green Areas: The Royal Gardens of Turin (Italy)

Vanessa Assumma(✉) ⬩, Daniele Druetto, Gabriele Garnero⬩, and Giulio Mondini⬩

Interuniversity Department of Regional and Urban Studies and Planning,
Politecnico di Torino, 10125 Turin, Italy
{vanessa.assumma,giulio.mondini}@polito.it,
daniele.druetto@studenti.polito.it, gabriele.garnero@unito.it

Abstract. This contribution aims to develop an integrated model of analysis and assessment for the valorisation and management of green spaces, with particular regard to historic gardens. The model is based on the combination of two main tools: on the one hand, the Geographic Information Systems (GIS), employed for the classification and geolocation of green areas, following the Italian legislation in force on Minimum Environmental Criteria (CAM), and on the other hand, an extended version of the SWOT Analysis, that aims at identifying the strengths, weaknesses, opportunities and threats both at the state of the art and a potential future scenario. The combination of the two tools is applied to a real case study in Northern Italy: the Royal Gardens of the City of Turin (Italy), known for their historical, social, economic and ecosystem-urban values. GIS systems and SWOT analysis can be used in parallel and provide distinct results, or be combined, in the *ex-ante*, *in-itinere* and *ex-post* phases of the assessment process, thus providing valid support to planners and Decision Makers, in the definition of strategic guidelines of valorisation and management of historical green heritage in the medium and long term, as well as professionals and specialized bodies to optimize the care and management of this heritage.

Keywords: Geographic information systems · SWOT analysis · Historic gardens and green management

1 Introduction

Green heritage requires careful valorisation and management especially when it represents the connective tissue between the architectural and urban context. The care and maintenance must regard the individual plants and tree species as well as the whole system. A purely economic intervention is not enough to ensure its valorisation and management. It requires more than ever a sustainability approach careful to the environmental quality, economic development and social equity, for a better quality of life of both present and next generations. Multiscale analysis and assessment approaches on the current and past conditions may support the building of a strategy of medium-long term and the citizens satisfaction through a new demand of services. In the context of the Habitats Directive [1], the growing role of Ecosystem Services (ES) in urban areas [2, 3], the achievement of 2030 Sustainability Development Goals (SDGs) and related targets [4], with particular reference to SGDs 11, 13 and 15, the Italian Ministerial Decree no. 63 of 10th March 2020 on the "Minimum Environmental Criteria for the service and management of public parks and the supply of products for the care of the green" [5] has recently been updated by introducing an innovative methodology for a proper classification, organization and management of the elements of green areas. Geographic Information Systems (GIS) provide useful tools to support the employment of the Minimum Environmental Criteria (MEC), through spatial analyses and/or project materials, thus obtaining a Topographic Database (TDB). The knowledge analysis of the green urban areas, thanks to GIS methods, along with the experience of professionals and specialized bodies, favour the creation of database that may effectively support the valorisation and management. To support this analysis, the evaluation methods can further enrich the knowledge of urban green areas and therefore aid the definition of strategic guidelines and actions. Among the various evaluation tools, SWOT Analysis is the most used in various and different fields, to identify strengths, weaknesses, opportunities and threats of a given decision problem. The paper intends to report the functioning of both GIS and SWOT tools and their integration to support the decision-making process in the valorisation and management of green areas. In particular, the paper employs this model in a real case study: the Royal Gardens of the City of Turin (Italy), which belongs to the Crown of Delights of the Savoy's dynasty. The Royal Gardens represent a suitable case study because is at the same time a green space, an urban garden, an historical garden, a prestigious reality, so that it cannot be crystalized like historical monuments. Since its extraordinary value, the constituting elements and the overall system need to be constantly analysed and compared. This model of analysis and assessment is finalized to support planners, Decision Makers in the definition of strategic guidelines and recommendation of medium-long term, as well as professionals and specialized bodies in the employment of specific interventions for the urban green and cultural heritage.

2 Methodology

The proposed model of analysis and assessment aims to valorise and manage green areas, with particular regard to historical gardens. It employs two main tools. On the one hand, it applies GIS methods according to the MEC regulation to build a knowledge analysis on the individual elements of the Royal Gardens and as a whole. On the other hand, the model employs an extended SWOT Analysis to identify strengths, weaknesses, opportunities and threats, by providing a photograph at the state of the art (t_0) and subsequently a potential trend scenario (t_1). The outputs deriving from the integration between the two methods are intended to support the decision-making process in defining strategic guidelines and recommendations for the enhancement and management of green areas, with reference to their historical value. Geographic Information Systems (GIS) are much more than a "tool" that associates alphanumeric data to a cartographic base. Indeed, they can process more complex information concerning the different city dimensions, from socio-economic to historical-cultural features, from naturalistic-environmental to infrastructural ones, through a multisce approach and replicable in different contexts [6]. GIS methods may contribute in solving complex problems of the decision-making process, especially when combined with evaluation models [7], thus providing a comprehensive knowledge and monitoring. In relation to the valorisation and management of green areas, the relevant literature counts many applications, for example dealing with the arboreal heritage, their history and evolution [8], or the ecological network between the different areas of the city according to an ecosystem perspective [9–11], among others.

Traditional SWOT Analysis was introduced in the 1960s-1970s in marketing sector as a tool for helping the decision-making strategy. It is able to provide information about endogenous factors of the investigation problem (Strengths, Weakness), and exogenous factors characterized by uncertainty (Opportunities, Threats).

SWOT Analysis has been used in many disciplinary fields, in particular this has proved to be particularly useful to solve complex spatial problems [12–15]. SWOT Analysis has recently been interested by modifications to be able to return both a general and specific vision of the problem, for example by integrating the STEEP Analysis [16, 17], or combining other methods and obtaining hybrid models, such as with the Multicriteria Decision Analysis (MCDA)(e.g. A'WOT, SWOT Spatial Multicriteria, or PROMETHEE Method) [18–20].

The GIS and SWOT Analysis tools can be used separately and combined once the respective outputs are obtained. In this application, an attempt was made to assist the two methodologies from the earliest stages of the analysis and assessment process. Thanks to the involvement of real stakeholders and specialists, constant feedbacks have been provided on the knowledge of the case study, during the development of this model. In this sense, the developed model followed a multi-phase process (Fig. 1):

1. *Knowledge analysis:* A multiscale territorial framework is finalized to provide a localization of the case study, in order to know where the Royal Gardens are located with respect to the City of Turin and the rest of the territory, and also to know on its elements. Subsequently, an analysis of the historical evolution of the Royal Gardens was considered essential to know the historical stratifications (XVI–XVIII centuries), as well as the most recent restoration processes, to reach the current state of the art;
2. *Data collection and elaboration:* Several data have been collected and processed in GIS, CAD and Excel environment: for example, spatial data (e.g. shapefiles, or as-built CAD drawings), considering the main statistical and cartographic sources (e.g. Geoportal of Piedmont Region and of City of Turin, high resolution orthoimages, or Treepedia MIT platform), tabular data (e.g. taxonomy and tree species classification, Visual Tree Assignment - VTA) and further materials made available by the Royal Museums of Turin;
3. *GIS application:* Specific tools of the software ArcGIS by Esri favoured the geolocation of the Royal Gardens elements (e.g. flower beds, trees or pots) based on the as-built project. The GIS software made it possible to unify all the information in a Topographic Database (DBT). Each element has been classified following the MECs criteria;
4. *SWOT Analysis application:* An extended version of the SWOT Analysis explores the strengths, weaknesses, opportunities and threats of the Royal Gardens through a qualitative-quantitative approach and at different times. Given the complexity of the

case study, and therefore the amounts of information regarding both different fields and several actors, a conventional SWOT matrix was considered as limited for this application. Therefore, it has been decided to develop a dedicated configuration;

5. *Models integration and final output:* the combination between GIS and SWOT Analysis provides as output a model applicable in the *ex-ante*, *in-itinere* and *ex-post* phases of the evaluation process, thus favouring the identification of strategic guidelines and actions of medium and long-term of valorisation and management of the Royal Gardens.

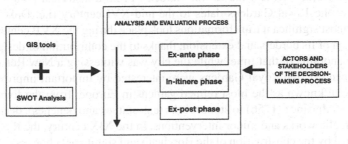

Fig. 1. Model structure [21]

2.1 The Minimum Environmental Criteria (MEC)

The Ministerial Decree no. 63/2020 has recently updated the "Minimum environmental criteria for the public green management service and the supply of green care products", introduced for the first time with art. 18 L.221/2015[1][5], specifies the methodology for a proper classification and organization of the elements of the green areas. Technical specifications are provided as a natural reference for the application of MECs to public green areas, according to the size of the municipality and following the principles of the INSPIRE European Directive on the management and sharing of geographical and territorial data [22].

3 Application

The integration between GIS and SWOT to analyse and assess historic gardens may provide a reliable support for building strategies of green valorisation and management of medium-long term. The subsequent paragraphs are devoted to the illustration of the case study and the application.

---

[1] https://www.minambiente.it/pagina/i-criteri-ambientali-minimi (Last access June 2021).

3.1   Case Study: Royal Gardens of Turin

The Royal Gardens represent one of the six main green spots in the core of the City of Turin (Piedmont, Italy). They represent a blend of art, nature and history between the heritage buildings, namely the Royal Palace and the Royal Armory Palace, belonging to the Crown of Delights of the Savoy's dynasty and recognized as UNESCO site for their Outstanding Universal Value (OUV) [23]. The Royal Gardens are publicly accessible so that it is possible to appreciate their heritage value and the relationships with the architectural and urban context. They consist of i) the Duke's Garden, ii) the Boschetto, iii) the Garden of Arts, iv) the Green Bastion (with the "Garittone"), v) the East Garden or Levante's Garden vi) and the Lower Gardens. From a historical point of view, the first plant of the Royal Gardens dates to the mid-XVI century (i.e. Duke's Garden), even if the most significant transformations took place during the XVII century, with the consolidation of its borders and extension, thanks to the contribution of designers of the European panorama of that time, while the city was witnessing a New Renaissance. In the XVIII century, the Royal Gardens were interested by important improvements, so that they were known as the most refined gardens in Europe: from the fountain of the Tritons by S. Martinez (1756) to stone works (e.g. statues and benches), decorative lead vases, hydraulic works and minor interventions. In the XIX century, the Royal Gardens were affected by the construction of the Boschetto and significant changes to the Garden of Arts and the Eastern Garden, whose original shape was restored at the beginning of the XX century. Following the tragic fire of the Shroud Chapel by G. Guarini in 1997, the Royal Gardens were closed to the public for a long time.

The restoration work, which began in 2008 and continued for a decade, led to a partial reopening in 2016 and a complete reopening only in 2018. Some interventions are still ongoing and benefit from some initiatives undertaken by the Royal Museums. The application of the analysis and evaluation model focuses on a part of the Royal Gardens, excluding the Eastern Garden and the Lower Gardens because they are closed for restoration work and property of the City of Turin [23] (see Fig. 2).

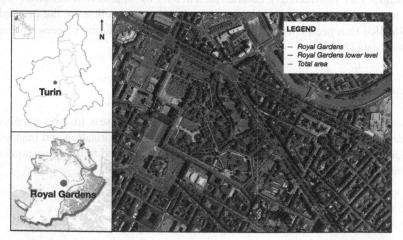

Fig. 2. Territorial localization of the Royal Gardens (Elaboration from Google Earth, 2019)

3.2 GIS Tools for the Creation of a Topographic Database

The GIS tools are retained as suitable for analysing the material provided by the Royal Museums of Turin, in particular the documents that certify their state of execution (or as-built drawings). The operational phase in the GIS environment was therefore anticipated by a process of data wiping and importing through the ArcGis tools (Fig. 3). Subsequently, a Topographical Database (TDB) was developed by classifying and organizing the elements acquired during the data importing. The TDB contains fields adequately filled to make each element as unique with respect to the others (Fig. 4):

1. The first step concerns the distinction of the type of geometry of the elements into points, lines and surfaces;
2. The second step identifies the Main Type of each element (TP), according to four macro-categories, such as i) vegetation, ii) street furniture, iii) use and management, iv) environmental factors (the latter item indicates those elements that impact on green areas and that are independent from them);
3. The third step indicates the Secondary Type of the elements (TS) and allows to differentiate for example in the TS "vegetation", a lawn from a flower bed rather than from a plant;
4. The last step is aimed at the Attribute Assignment (ATT). Considering the same example, assuming a TS code = "plant" as further classification, it allows to distinguish, for example, a tree from a bush.

The result of this operation finds the opportunity of using and processing new information acquired through ArcGIS tools and therefore of carrying out targeted analyses and/or representations where necessary (Fig. 5).

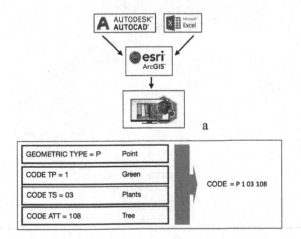

Fig. 3. Tools integration in GIS environment in data importing process

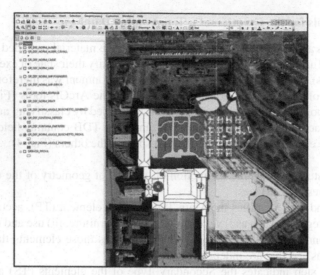

Fig. 4. Outcome in GIS environment, geometries superimposed on georeferenced orthophotos [21]

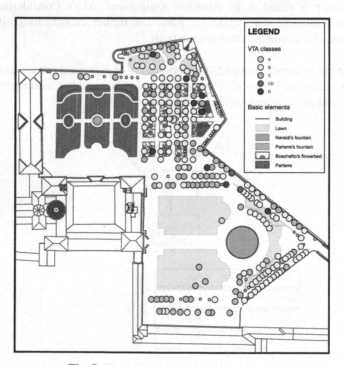

Fig. 5. Example of VTA classification [21]

3.3 SWOT Analysis to Explore the State of the Art

SWOT Analysis has explored the case study in the years 2019–2020 as the state of the art. In particular, the high uncertainty and negative impacts by Covid-19 of that period, especially in social and economic terms, have also negatively influenced on the Royal Gardens and their role for the city. The conventional SWOT analysis has been extended in a version that aims to integrate the information obtained from the GIS model and with respect to the specificity of the case study. The 4 quadrants of the SWOT have been related to the following elements:

- *Macro-ambits:* they are location and context, society, cultural heritage, traffic, tourism, health and well-being and environmental components;
- *Sub-ambits:* they are tourism origin, psycho-physical benefits, meaning the benefits provided by the greenery present throughout the Royal Gardens of Turin towards the end-users (i.e. residents and tourists).

Each macro-ambits and related sub-ambits related to the Royal Gardens are evaluated through a qualitative-quantitative approach with respect to the 4 components of the SWOT Analysis. The SWOT Analysis was compiled within a survey with real stakeholders, such as the Royal Museums of Turin, the City of Turin, residents and tourists. Scores were assigned according to the degree of incidence of each element, positive or negative, which can vary from 1 to 3 for strengths and opportunities, and from −1 to −3 for weaknesses and threats. The score attribution is also supported by both qualitative scale (i.e. 1 = low; 2 = medium; 3 = high) and semaphoric scale. This is considered useful to facilitate the user in the consultation of the SWOT matrix. An overall view of the results is reported as partial and total summations in support of the main matrix. This configuration was used to explore the state of the art and a potential future scenario (Fig. 6) that is deepened in the next paragraph.

In Fig. 7, for example, a score of 3 was assigned for the "international tourism" sub-ambit of the "tourism" macro-ambit, from the point of view of the Royal Museums and City of Turin, since the statistical data provided by the Royal Museums on the number of visitors differentiated by quantity and period, shows that a considerable part of the entrances to the Palace is represented by foreign tourists. Or for the "significant green spot" sub-ambit of the "health and well-being" macro-ambit, a score of 2 was assigned, from the point of view of the City of Turin since the Royal Gardens represent a green fulcrum in the city centre, even if it is not the only one. Indeed, Turin is recognized as one of the greenest cities in Europe and boasts other important parks (e.g. Valentine's Park, or Pellerina Park). Or again, for the sub-ambit "presence of fine dust deposited on the foliage" of the macro-ambit "health and well-being", a negative score of −3 was assigned, from the point of view of citizens as it appears to be a highly incisive factor regarding the physical health of an individual, especially in a city such as Turin which, according to Arpa Piemonte monitoring, records medium-low levels of air quality in winter season.

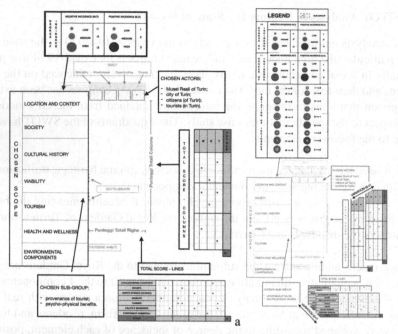

Fig. 6. Structure of the SWOT Analysis t_0 (a) and its extension $t_0 - t_1$ (b) [21]

3.4 SWOT Analysis to Explore a Different Temporal Dimension

The SWOT analysis was applied by considering different times that analyses the same information evolving towards a potential future scenario (t_1).

The SWOT evaluation scale is always of qualitative-quantitative type, even if the chromatic symbology is different: i) degree of incidence at t_0, the full coloured symbols proposed in the previous SWOT matrix remain unchanged because they are considered suitable; ii) degree of incidence at t_1, the symbols keep their shape, size and colour gradient unchanged and are differentiated with a black border to label a new assignment. In fact, solid-coloured symbols label a variation. The maintenance of the style of the chromatic symbology between the two SWOT Analyses is finalized to underline that the same type of evaluation is taken in different times. The two SWOT Analysis have been systematically developed. When both SWOT Analyses are reported in the same matrix, it is necessary to apply a distinctive sign $t_0 - t_1$; iii) variations in incidence, considering that there are two scales of scores, from 1 to 3 and from −1 to −3, 18 variations are expected to cover the entire range of possibilities, and 9 for each scale. Such variations may predict an increase or decrease of the degree of incidence.

In Fig. 8, for example, the "foreign tourism", sub-ambit of the "tourism" macro-ambit, has a dedicated symbol, which is a green background pattern with a blue centre, as it identifies a two-point decrease in the assigned degree of incidence and compared to the state of the art. The Covid-19 pandemic has significantly reduced the influx of foreign tourism which, however, was not absent. When the full coloured symbol is present, this

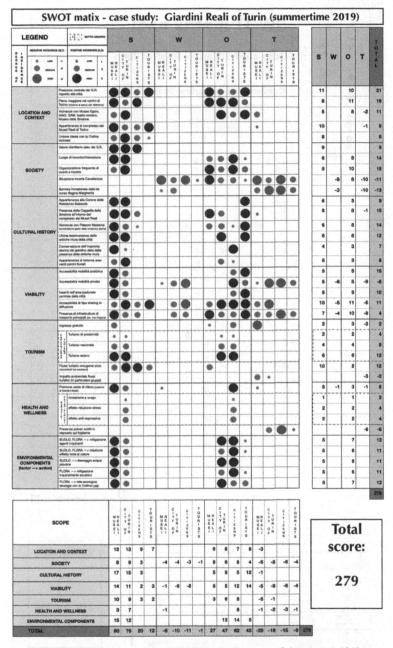

Fig. 7. Elaboration of the SWOT analysis: state of the art (t_0) [21]

means that no variation has been occurred: this value was already present in t_0. By contrast, when the same symbol is surrounded by a black, border it means a new t_1 assignment and the value is null at t_0.

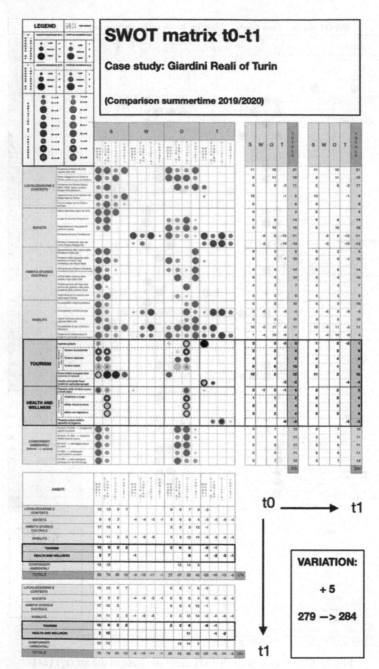

Fig. 8. Elaboration of the SWOT Analysis: $t_0 - t_1$ [21]

4 Discussion of Results

The combination of GIS and SWOT Analysis has provided a comprehensive knowledge analysis and assessment to build a strategy of valorisation and management for the Royal Gardens of Turin. Specifically, in a scope like the valorization and management of green areas, with particular regard to the historical gardens, it is required constant attention and maintenance, therefore management is the key. This application highlighted that, on the one hand, the GIS software with MEC classification, is a powerful tool that may strengthen its role if integrated by SWOT Analysis in envisioning medium to long term strategies. On the other hand, SWOT Analysis requires a comprehensive knowledge of the case study under investigation to support final users in the definition of priority interventions, so that GIS may provide it. In addition, the TDB Database, developed in GIS environment, according to the MEC legislation and the TSE classification, received during the survey highly positive feedback from the Royal Museum staff, in particular with regard to the managerial-organizational potential deriving from this application (Fig. 9). In fact, the research work reveals aligned to the pillars of the current cohesion policies and regional programming, such as the progressive digitalization of public bodies that could be supported by a very promising evaluation model for the management and valorization of the green heritage[2].

The extended configuration of SWOT Analysis has allowed a simultaneous reading between the different macro-ambits and sub-ambits. By focusing on the SWOT matrix $t_0 - t_1$, it has allowed the exploration of the individual elements and the degree of incidence at two different times. With this novel extension it is possible to analyse the new values and at the same time report the variations of the scores in the matrix, without losing information. In this sense, this version can effectively support the prioritization of strategic guidelines and actions for historic gardens, also considering both economic and political features, as well as supporting different procedures of strategic and spatial planning analysis and assessment.

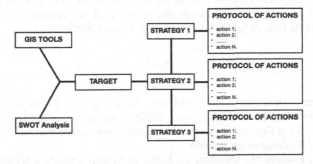

Fig. 9. Output derived by the GIS and SWOT integration [21]

---

[2] National Plan of Recovery and Resilience (PNRR- Piano Nazionale di Ripresa e Resilienza, Piemonte Cuore d'Europa) https://piemonte2021-2027.eu/pnrr-recovery-plan-italia/ (Last access June 2021).

5   Conclusions

The combination of GIS tools and SWOT Analysis has proved a suitable model in restoring a broader and multiscale vision, thus favouring a twofold support: on the one hand, helping both planners and Decision Makers in facilitating the dialogue between different analysis and assessment tools for an area extraordinary value, and on the other hand supporting public bodies to design strategies and actions for the valorisation and management of green areas in the medium and long term. Looking at the internal consistency of the model, some refinements have been identified regarding the MECs classification. If this is particularly suitable for the maintenance of green areas, compared to the specificity of the case study of the Royal Gardens, it would require further implementation. It should be noticed that a historical garden such as the Royal Gardens, given the value of its elements, many of which belong to a broader group, requires a site-specific classification. The SWOT analysis was applied at time t_0 and t_1 trying to investigate the potential variation $t_0 - t_1$ in the degree of incidence of the investigated elements. From a dynamic analysis and evaluation perspective, the SWOT analysis could be supported by the application of a dynamic approach and identify the different interdependencies between the investigated elements [24] and reproduce it in the *ex-ante*, *in-itinere* and *ex-post* phases of the process. The SWOT analysis could also be integrated as a component of a multi-phase evaluation process to define alternative scenarios of valorisation and management [25]. With regard to the replicability of the model, similar cases study will be investigated, such as other residences of the Crown of Delights, with the aim to work on the site-specific classification and other features to integrate tools with green realities. Looking at the external consistency of the model, we intend in the future to realize a software based on this model to be addressed to specialized users actively involved in the management of green areas and in particular of the green cultural heritage.

Acknowledgements. The authors would like to acknowledge the Royal Museums of Turin for their availability in providing materials and support to develop this research work. The research work has been developed in the context of the Bachelor Degree thesis by Daniele Druetto entitled "Modello di analisi e valutazione per la valorizzazione e gestione degli spazi verdi. Caso studio: i Giardini Reali della Città di Torino", Politecnico di Torino (2020).

References

1. EC (European Commission): Habitat Directive 92/43/CEE (1992). https://ec.europa.eu/env ironment/nature/legislation/habitatsdirective/index_en.htm. Accessed May 2021
2. MEA (Millennium Ecosystem Assessment): Ecosystems and human wellbeing: Synthesis. Island Press, Washington, DC (2005)
3. Caprioli, C., Bottero, M., Mondini, G.: Urban ecosystem services: a review of definitions and classifications for the identification of future research perspectives. In: Gervasi, O., et al. (eds.) Computational Science and Its Applications – ICCSA 2020. Lecture Notes in Computer Science, vol. 12253, pp. 332–344. Springer, Cham (2020). https://doi.org/10.1007/978-3-030-58814-4_23
4. UN (United Nations): Transforming our world: the 2030 Agenda for Sustainable Development, 21 October 2015, A/RES/70/1. https://www.refworld.org/docid/57b6e3e44.htmlUnite dNationsNazioniUnite2015GlobalAgenda. Accessed May 2021

5. MATTM (Ministero dell'Ambiente e della tutela del territorio e del mare): Ministerial Decree no. 63 10/03/2020 "Minimum environmental criteria for the public green management service and the supply of green care products". Gazzetta Ufficiale della Repubblica Italiana, 90 (2021). https://www.minambiente.it/sites/default/files/archivio/allegati/GPP/2020/guri_dm_63_del_2020_verde_002.pdf. Accessed May 2021
6. Worboys, M., Duckham, M.: GIS: a computing perspective. CRC Press, Boca Raton (2004)
7. Malcevski, J.: GIS-based multicriteria decision analysis: a survey of the literature. Int. J. Geogr. Inf. Sci. 20(7), 703–726 (2006). https://doi.org/10.1080/13658810600661508
8. Nagendra, H., Gopal, D.: Street trees in Bangalore: density, diversity, composition and distribution. Urban Forest. Urban Greening 9(2), 129–137 (2010). https://doi.org/10.1016/j.ufug.2009.12.005
9. Bolund, P., Hunhammar, S.: Ecosystem services in urban areas. Ecol. Econ. 29, 293–301 (1999). https://doi.org/10.1016/S0921-8009(99)00013-0
10. Chiesura, A.: The role of urban parks for the sustainable city. Landsc. Urban Plan. 68(1), 129–138 (2004). https://doi.org/10.1016/j.landurbplan.2003.08.003
11. Elmqvist, T., et al.: Urbanization, Biodiversity and Ecosystem Services: Challenges and Opportunities A Global Assessment. Springer, Dordrecht (2013). https://doi.org/10.1007/978-94-007-7088-1
12. Bottero, M., Mondini, G.: Valutazione e sostenibilità. Piani, programmi, progetti. Celid, Torino (2009)
13. Terrados, J., Almonacid, G., Hontoria, L.: Regional energy planning through SWOT analysis and strategic planning tools: impact on renewables development. Renew. Sustain. Energy Rev. 11(6), 1275–1287 (2007). https://doi.org/10.1016/j.rser.2005.08.003
14. Reihanian, A., Zalina, N., Mahmood, B., Kahrom, E., Hin, T.W.: Sustainable tourism development strategy by SWOT analysis: Boujagh National Park, Iran. Tour. Manage. Perspect. 4, 223–228 (2012). https://doi.org/10.1016/j.tmp.2012.08.005
15. Berte, E., Panagopoulos, T.: Enhancing city resilience to climate change by means of ecosystem services improvement: a SWOT analysis for the city of Faro, Portugal. Int. J. Urban Sustain. Develop. 6(2), 241–253 (2014). https://doi.org/10.1080/19463138.2014.953536
16. Szigeti, H., Messaadia, M., Majumdar, A., Eynard, B.: STEEP analysis as a tool for building technology roadmaps. In: EChallenges Conference Proceedings, pp. 1–12. Florence (2011).
17. Ighravwe, D.E., Babatunde, M.O., Denwigwe, I.H., Aikhuele, D.O.: A STEEP-cum-SWOT approach for maintenance strategy evaluation for an off-grid PV-powered street lighting system. Afr. J. Sci. Technol. Innov. Dev. 12(6), 703–714 (2020). https://doi.org/10.1080/20421338.2019.1701775
18. Bottero, M., D'Alpaos, C., Marello, A.: An Application of the A'WOT analysis for the management of cultural heritage assets: the case of the historical farmhouses in the Aglié Castle (Turin). Sustainability 12(3), 1–17 (2020). https://doi.org/10.3390/su12031071
19. Treves, A., Bottero, M., Caprioli, C., Comino, E.: The reintroduction of Castor fiber in Piedmont (Italy): An integrated SWOT-spatial multicriteria based approach for the analysis of suitability scenarios. Ecol. Indicators 118, 106748 (2020). https://doi.org/10.1016/j.ecolind.2020.106748
20. Bottero, M., Dell'Anna, F., Nappo, M.: Evaluating tangible and intangible aspects of cultural heritage: an application of the PROMETHEE method for the reuse project of the Ceva–Ormea Railway. In: Mondini, G., Fattinnanzi, E., Oppio, A., Bottero, M., Stanghellini, S. (eds.) SIEV 2016. GET, pp. 285–295. Springer, Cham (2018). https://doi.org/10.1007/978-3-319-78271-3_23
21. Druetto, D.: Modello di analisi e valutazione per la valorizzazione e gestione degli spazi verdi. Caso studio: i Giardini Reali della Città di Torino. Bachelor Degree thesis, Politecnico di Torino (2020)

22. Guzzetti, F., et al.: Modello dati per il censimento del verde urbano. Version 2.1 (2018). https://www.minambiente.it/sites/default/files/archivio/allegati/GPP/2020/mod ello_dati_per_il_censimento_del_verde_urbano_2_1_con_allegati.pdf. Accessed May 2021
23. WHC (World Heritage Committee): Residences of the Royal House of Savoy (1997). http:// whc.unesco.org/uploads/nominations/823bis.pdf. Accessed May 2021
24. Bezzi, C.: Teoria e metodi. Rendiamo dinamica la SWOT. Rassegna Italiana Di Valutazione, 1–8 (2005).https://doi.org/10.1400/66625
25. Bottero, M., Assumma, V., Caprioli, C., Dell'Ovo, M.: Decision making in urban development: the application of a hybrid evaluation method for a critical area in the city of Turin (Italy). J. Sustain. Cities Soc. **72**, 103028 (2021). https://doi.org/10.1016/j.scs.2021.103028

A Multidimensional Assessment of Ecosystem Services: From Grey to Green Infrastructure

Caterina Caprioli[1] [iD], Alessandra Oppio[2] [iD], Roberta Baldassarre[3], Riccardo Grassi[3], and Marta Dell'Ovo[2]([⊠]) [iD]

[1] Interuniversity Department of Regional and Urban Studies and Planning (DIST), Politecnico di Torino, Castello del Valentino: Viale Pier Andrea Mattioli, 39 - 10125 Torino, TO, Italy
caterina.caprioli@polito.it

[2] Department of Architecture and Urban Studies (DAStU), Politecnico di Milano, via E. Bonardi 3, 20133 Milano, MI, Italy
{alessandra.oppio,marta.dellovo}@polimi.it

[3] Politecnico di Milano, Piazza Leonardo da Vinci 32, 20133 Milano, MI, Italy

Abstract. The notion of Ecosystem Services (ESs) is constantly increasing in interest given their provision of multidimensional values (environmental, social, economic, etc.). Nowadays ESs are at the center of green cities policies tackling the challenges of sustainability. More than 55% of the population is already living in urban areas, and this number is still rising. Within this context, challenges for sustainable development considering a circular economy perspective will be more concentrated in cities and in particular urban green spaces where strategies could be more effective for achieving sustainable urban development goals, such as improving public health, preserving biodiversity, reinforcing social cohesion, supporting the economy, providing opportunities for recreation, and helping in adapting to climate change. More specifically, the role of urban green spaces is testified by many green infrastructures policies proposed by different cities around the world. Rooftops, abandoned infrastructures and downgraded areas are some of the places that can be reused for creating new natural and green spaces within cities. Given these premises, the present paper aims to investigate the role of green areas in urban context in improving the overall quality of the space and in providing multidimensional benefits. The innovation of the present paper regards the integration of cost-based and value-based methods for the assessment of ESs. Starting from a real case study located in the city of Milan, the article illustrates the potential of combining the valuation of biophysical and economic values.

Keywords: Integrated assessment · Multidimensional values · Urban regeneration

© Springer Nature Switzerland AG 2021
O. Gervasi et al. (Eds.): ICCSA 2021, LNCS 12955, pp. 569–581, 2021.
https://doi.org/10.1007/978-3-030-87007-2_41

1 Introduction

Climate change is severely challenging cities and urban areas. Instead of safe place from disasters, cities become the cause of possible risks [1, 2]. According to the definition provided by [3] the term disaster risk is both related to climatic (e.g. flood, sea level rise, etc.) and non-climatic hazard (e.g. earthquake, volcanic eruption, etc.) and the concept of risk reduction. This requires a systemic view and efforts to face and manage factors which cause the before mentioned issues. Within this context the urbanization has tightened many of these hazards and accelerated others. Nowadays 55% of the population lives in an urban area, and the percentage is expected to increase to 68% by 2050 [4, 5]. Moreover, considering the definition of risk reduction provided by [6], it is clear how it directly involves the population and affect communities. Several factors and characteristics of cities themselves strongly influence the climate change, starting from the urban fabrics morphology, the high population density, the high emissions and the constant processes of changes [1]. Adaptation to the existing hazards and the possible future ones could be the answer to address all the several risk factors. Among the different strategies, cities Authorities are increasing the attention on planning sustainable and resilient environments and the 17 Sustainable Development Goal (SDGs) adopted by all United Nations Members States in 2015 underlines this trend [7]. A potential role in this context can be engaged by green measures, nature-based solutions (NBS) and green infrastructures (GUI) which gained more attention in recent years given their effectiveness in impacts mitigation of climate change and the sustainability promotion [8]. In fact, compared to the monofunctional grey infrastructures, GUI are multifunctional ecological systems which create multi-purposes spaces and generate multiple benefits and values [9].

These strategies and their relative benefits can be better understood with the introduction of the concept of Ecosystem Services (ESs) which have been defined as benefits humans gain from ecosystem action [10–12]. The study of ESs has grown in importance over the years, especially thanks to the contribution provided by the Millennium Ecosystem Assessment (MA) [11], which clustered them in four main categories (i.e. provisioning services, supporting services, cultural services, regulating services) and given their provision of multidimensional values (environmental, social, economic, etc.). Within a circular economy perspective, challenges for sustainable development will be more concentrated in cities and in particular in urban green spaces where strategies could be more effective for achieving SDGs and obtaining both direct benefits and indirect co-benefits. In fact, evidence of positive externalities provided by the application of green strategies and the presence of GUI have been deeply discussed by several scholars and classified by [13] in *i)* Physical benefits, e.g. CO_2 reduction, thermal comfort and energy use reduction, and *ii)* Psychological and social benefits, e.g. health and restorative benefits, social and individual coping capacities and education. This classification underlines the need of a holistic approach aimed to plan new urban development projects and evaluate their impacts considering the contribution of systemic solutions [14–16].

Given these premises, the purpose of the present paper is to propose a multidimensional and multi-methodological approach aimed to assess the ecosystem values provided by the transformation of a grey infrastructure into a green infrastructure. Both cost-based and value-based approaches will be applied in order to have an overall scenario of costs and benefits generated by the urban intervention. The case study considers the regeneration of an existing overpass located in the southeast area of the city of Milan (Italy). The methodology proposes the comparative assessment of the state of the art scenario (T0) and the regeneration scenario (T1). The study wants to underline the role of the evaluation within design process and its support in understanding positive and negative externalities produced by the projects. This is in line with the concept of Complex Social Value provided by [17] proposing a more comprehensive perspective of the Total Economic Value [18] by including the intrinsic value.

The paper is divided into five sections. After a brief introduction of the topic the methodological approach is described (Sect. 2) and applied (Sect. 4) to the case study (Sect. 3). Discussion of the results, conclusions and future perspectives are presented in the last section (Sect. 5).

2 Methodological Approach

Given the complexity of the decision-making process for supporting the regeneration of an underused grey infrastructure and the multiple values involved, the methodology has been structured by considering both cost-based and value-based approaches. Figure 1 presents a flowchart aimed at explaining how the approaches proposed have been developed and which are the results.

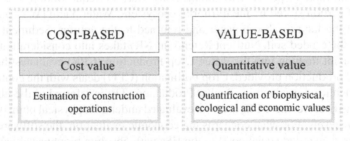

Fig. 1. Methodological approach flowchart

A detailed cost estimation has been performed in order to support the first phase of the analysis detecting all the construction costs of the project. In particular, the cost value has been developed by classifying the intervention according to the Work Breakdown Structure (WBS) which makes possible to divide it namely in: 1. Group of technological units, 2. Technological units, 3. Group of technical elements, 4. Technical elements and 5. Cost items. Following this classification, each work part of the project is described and detailed to assess the Cost items (the last element of the hierarchical frame). For this step, it was used the Regional Price List, which represent the reference tool for the preliminary quantification of planning and public works. Within this source it is also possible to find information about the percentage influence of materials, manpower, leasing and equipment. For all working activities, it was consulted the section related to the completed works to estimate the finished work.

For what concerns the value-based approach, and in detail the quantitative evaluation, the existing tool Simulsoil has been applied. Simulsoil is a free software able to support the planning process through the analysis and evaluation of eight ESs [19]. In detail, the provision of ESs is evaluated by considering changes in land-use of at least two alternatives in order to estimate the differences among the two. Usually, the state-of-art is compared with a new project to understand if and how much the changes proposed and designed provide benefits. Simulsoil allows to assess the values of the following ESs: Habitat Quality (HQ), Carbon Sequestration (CS), Water Yield (WY), Sediment Retention (SR), Nutrient Retention (NR), Crop Production (CPR), Crop Pollination (CPO) and Timber Production (TP)[1]. According to this analysis, it is possible to highlight the sensitivity of a territory in relation to ESs variation as well as to quantify the overall cost of a transformation on the existing Natural Capital. Even if the economic valuation cannot be used as an exact measure of gains or losses of Natural Capital and as a direct value for the determination of compensation measures, it provides for an additional and easy way to show the effects of plans and projects. Moreover, it is able to support the *ex-ante* phase assessment of a transformation by involving different stakeholders, helping their comprehension and participation to the entire decision-making process, as well as the enrichment of a more comprehensive view of the relevant aspects in land-use planning and promotion of sustainable and resilient actions [20]. The results obtained from Simulsoil are given graphically by spatial maps for each ES and schematically by a final comparative table that quantitatively reports the biophysical and economic values of all scenarios [20]. Among the ESs analyzed: Habitat Quality (HQ) considers if the land-use proposed minimize or preserve the biodiversity, Carbon Sequestration (CS) quantifies the level of carbon stored by the territorial ecosystem, Water Yield (WY) analyzes the property of the land to absorb water and returned to the aquifer, Sediment Retention (SR) maps the eroded soil, Nutrient Retention (NR) takes into consideration the quantity of pollutant flowing into the water, Crop Production (CPR) evaluates the effective agricultural production provided, Crop Pollination (CPO) deals with the contribution of bees to agricultural production, Timber Production (TP) is referred to the fiber supply. As mentioned before, these ESs are both evaluated under a biophysical point of view and in economic terms. For what concerns the economic evaluation, the software assigns a unit price (e.g. avoided social cost) to the ESs with absolute biophysical values, while for the ESs expressed by an index, the economic estimation is developed by simulating a market and asking for the willingness to pay for the use of the good.

Since the unit of measure is specific for each ES the biophysical results cannot be aggregated while the economic ones can be combined in order to have an overall evaluation of the value provided by the projects. This consideration is strategic since the methodological approach proposed aims at integrating both cost and benefits of the same project providing an additional information about the sustainability of the project under a multidimensional point of view.

3   Case Study

The case study under analysis is located in the southeast area of the city of Milan (Italy), in the neighborhood called Corvetto (Fig. 2). Here, in 2018, the municipality established the

---

[1] http://www.sam4cp.eu/Simulsoil/.

demolish of the viale Lucania overpass due to its underused. In contrast, a regeneration project has been proposed with the aim to maintain the artifact and give the community an open public space, characterized by cycle and pedestrian paths, equipped services and green spaces. The project objective is mainly to realize a new "green landscape" for the city able to increase the environmental quality of the area, but also to produce other benefits both for the community, such as well-being and health, and for the image of the area. The project is the result of an in-depth investigation of the main pros and cons of the context, supported by the development of a SWOT analysis which has been structured considering the following steps:

1. Definition of the objective of the analysis;
2. Analysis of the context by considering infrastructural, environmental, settlement and socio-economic aspects;
3. Development of the SWOT matrix for each aspect analyzed;
4. Definition of a set of strategies considering the results of the previous analysis and the objective to be achieved.

In particular, the project strategies derive from the main opportunities highlighted in the SWOT analysis as well as the reduction of the weaknesses and the control of the threats.

The main strategies developed consider: 1. the implementation of cycle-pedestrian paths by reducing the road size and the amount of car traffic; 2. new trees planting to reduce no-permeable surfaces, 3. the heat-island effect, the presence of pollutants in the air and the summer shade; 4. new public spaces for recreation and commercial activities; 5. people engagement in the regeneration project by increasing the safety perception; 6. the involvement of different age groups and 7. the organization of evening events.

This study wants to highlight the opportunity of the regeneration project in contrast to the demolition by the assessment of the two alternative proposals both in terms of economic benefits and ecosystem ones. On one hand, scenario T0 considers the state-of-art of the area with the presence of the overpass that is planned to be demolished. According to this demolition, the costs connected to this activity are estimated. On the other hand, scenario T1 refers to the regeneration project and the costs of intervention for this transformation (Fig. 3).

1. Italy   2. Lombardy Region   3. Municipality of Milan

Fig. 2. Location of the project area

Fig. 3. T0 (image on the top) and T1 (image above)

4   Application

Following the methodological approach proposed, the first step regards the quantification of the costs of the overpass demolition and the ones connected with the regeneration interventions (T1).

Firstly, the costs connected with the overpass demolition has been estimated, including the 17 vertical concrete supports, and aggregates disposal. After the calculation of the volume (6326 cm + 1189 cm) and aggregates weight (2400 kg/cm), it was considered a parametric cost of 151.78 €/cm for the demolition, and 1.9 €/ton for the disposal activity, as reported in the Lombardy Regional Price List of public works 2020 (Volume 1.1, respectively 1C.01.030.0040 and 1C.27.050.0100.d). The overall cost for this intervention is equal to 1,483,350 €, i.e. about 299 €/sqm.

Secondly, for T1, it has been estimated the construction costs of the linear park project section through a WBS in order to clearly state the costs for this intervention.

It is important to highlight that some costs, strictly related to the construction sites activities (e.g. security), are not listed in the table of costs but considered as a percentage of the overall intervention. Considering the hierarchical classification explained in Sect. 2, the project has been further described and the total cost for the realization of the linear park amounts to € 981,873.05 with a unit cost of the work equal to 178.83 €/sqm.

Once the first phase of the methodological approach has been assessed, the two scenarios (T0 and T1) are compared by considering the amount of ESs provided. For this stage, the existing tool, Simulsoil, was applied for assessing the eight ESs.

The two alternatives (T0 and T1) were designed in a georeferenced CAD environment, then imported in QGIS 2.18.28. The CAD and QGIS procedures were useful for the following analysis with Simulsoil. Both for the T0 and T1 scenarios, the polygons had specific layers corresponding to the different land-uses. The land-uses must be associated with the Corine Land Cover classification used by Simulsoil to calculate the biophysical values. Based on a set of algorithms associated with the land-uses, Simulsoil provides output data in raster maps with a resolution level of 20 × 20 meters per pixel.

As it is possible to see in Fig. 4, scenario T0 represents the business-as-usual scenario (BAU), i.e. the current state of the art of the area, while T1 shows the regeneration proposal. In particular, T0 is essentially characterized by a road network land cover, with only a small piece of green areas and some trees and bushes. Conversely, in T1, the road network land cover is strongly reduced due to the realization of recreational green areas on the overpass and in the north portion of the area. Moreover, additional trees are planted in the entire project area.

The output data provided by Simulsoil on the two scenarios analyzed are reported in Table 1 and showed in Fig. 5. It is important to underline that in Fig. 5, only the ESs with values higher than 0 are reported in maps. The reason why many ESs have obtained a zero value is connected with the specific land-use in the area. However, the output data of the other ESs provide interesting considerations on the difference between the two scenarios. The increase of CS, HQ and TP in T1 can be explained by the great amount of new green spaces and vegetation considered in the regeneration project. Moreover, T1 strongly reduces the fragmentation of (non-agricultural) green areas compared to T0. According to a consolidated rule in ecology, the concentration of green spaces, in fact, provides better environmental performances, as well as more interaction between habitat sources, the creation of corridors and the reduction of threats [21]. The new land uses provided by the intervention project certainly helps in the increase of these ESs values compared to the current state of the area, even if more potentialities are faced with social and cultural values generated by the regeneration scenario.

Moreover, since the economic results represent only an indication of the overall ESs performance, they are converted in a final incremental percentage of the increase of T1 over T0, as it is possible to see in the last row of Table 1.

According to the results of this research, the regeneration project is beneficial in terms of ESs provision, but it is also preferable from a merely financial perspective since the overall costs of the overpass demolition activities are higher than the ones of the project proposed. The comparative Table 2 shows how the differences in the performance of both alternatives in terms of economic values of ESs and of the financial ones. Even if the monetary savings are limited - as shown in the last row of Table 2 -, there are a lot of biophysical and environmental benefits provided by T1 (about 50% more than T0).

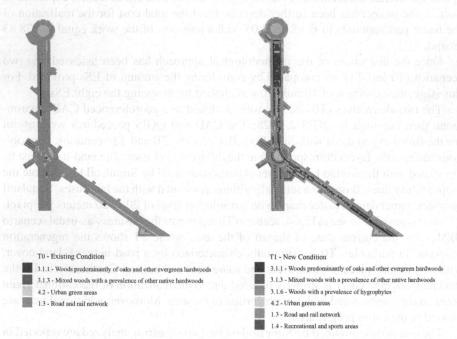

T0 - Existing Condition
- 3.1.1 - Woods predominantly of oaks and other evergreen hardwoods
- 3.1.3 - Mixed woods with a prevalence of other native hardwoods
- 4.2 - Urban green areas
- 1.3 - Road and rail network

T1 - New Condition
- 3.1.1 - Woods predominantly of oaks and other evergreen hardwoods
- 3.1.3 - Mixed woods with a prevalence of other native hardwoods
- 3.1.6 - Woods with a prevalence of hygrophytes
- 4.2 - Urban green areas
- 1.3 - Road and rail network
- 1.4 - Recreational and sports areas

Fig. 4. Land-uses assignment for T0 and T1 according to the Corine Land Cover classification

Table 1. Comparison of the ES values of the two transformation scenarios (T0 and T1) in biophysical (bio) and economic (econ) terms

Code	ES Name	u.m	T0 (bio)	T1 (bio)	u.m	T0 (econ)	T1 (econ)
CS	Carbon sequestration	ton	356.38	496.42	€	35,637.89	49,641.81
CPO	Crop pollination	0–1	0	0	€	0	0
HQ	Habitat quality	0–1	0.30	0.41	€	2,690.20	3,632.04
NR	Nutrient retention	ton	0	0	€	0	0
SDR	Sediment retention	ton	0	0	€	0	0
WY	Water supply	0–1	0	0	€	0	0
CPR	Crop production	€	0	0	€	0	0
TP	Timber production	€	10,570.64	19,355.08	€	10,570.64	19,355.08
Total						48,898.73	72,628.93
Incremental %						**48.53**	

Table 2. Differences between T0 and T1 according to the integrated framework in biophysical (bio) and economic (econ) terms

ES Name	u.m	T0 (bio)	T1 (bio)	u.m	T0 (econ)	T1 (econ)	Delta (T1- T0)
Carbon sequestration	ton	356.38	496.42	€	35,637.89	49,641.81	**14,003.92**
Habitat quality	0–1	0.30	0.41	€	2,690.20	3,632.04	**941.84**
Timber production	€	10,570.64	19,355.08	€	10,570.64	19,355.08	**8,784.44**
Total (econ)				€	**48,898.73**	**72,628.93**	**23,730.20**
Incremental %				%			**+48.53%**
Costs				€	−1,483,350	−981,873	**501.48**
Incremental %				%			**+0.034%**

5   Discussion and Conclusions

The paper presents the application of an integrated framework for the multidimensional assessment of a strategic project, that considers both financial and extra-economic aspects. This analysis has underlined the advantages of combining cost-based and value-based approaches in order to highlight both tangible and intangible benefits produced by the regeneration project of viale Lucania overpass in Milan (Italy).

On one hand, the application has shown how Simulsoil is a simple but very effective tool that clearly shows the relationship between urban morphology and land-use. More specifically, it helps to design and define projects capable of maximizing the provision of the benefits for man and its related environment by assessing ESs in different scenarios. This tool can be used by various professionals to rapidly assess, in an *ex-ante* phase, the ES generated in land-use scenarios and support the Strategic Environmental Assessment (SEA) that is a mandatory activity in urban planning. The integration of ES assessment, management tools and SEA makes possible to improve the sustainability of land use planning process [22, 23]. The spatial output data given by Simulsoil make the output very intuitive by all the stakeholders involved in the decision-making process, also with the conversion of biophysical performances in an economic dimension.

Then, the estimation of intervention and demolition costs can support a direct interaction with the Public Administration and its bodies in order to guide them in an efficient allocation of their resources, which are often limited and scarce. In fact, according to the results of this research, the regeneration project is not only beneficial in terms of ESs provision, but it is also preferable in a merely financial perspective since the overall costs of the overpass demolition activities are higher than the ones of the project proposed.

These results are in line with the concept of adaptation to which cities should aim to mitigate the effects of climate change and meet sustainable goals.

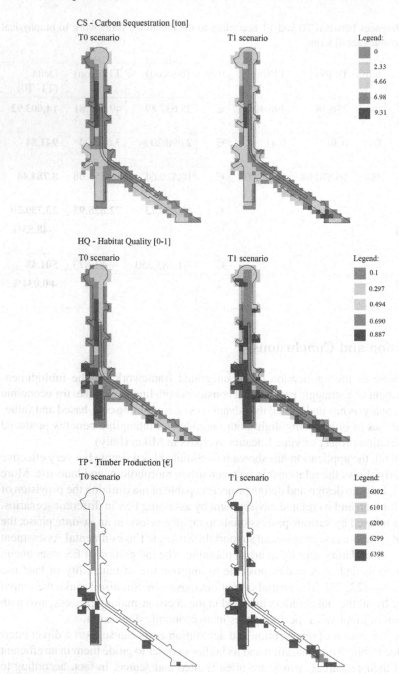

Fig. 5. ES quantification and spatial representation for the two transformation scenarios (T0 and T1)

Some limits, instead, can be highlighted, in particular concerning the Simulsoil tool. Future implementations of the present work will regard the adoption of more sophisticated tools for the ESs assessment, such as InVest or iTree, in order to consider all the different benefits of T1over T0. Moreover, the economic values obtained from Simulsoil can be connected with the estimated costs in an integrated approach, for example by using the Cost-Benefits Analysis. Another perspective that should be explored is related to the consideration of more intangible values [24], in particular socio-cultural ones, that are strongly relevant for the specific recreational use of the area and to have an overall view of the positive externalities produced by the regeneration project. In this perspective, multicriteria decision analysis (MCDA) can be a powerful method to assess all the different ESs values and give a comprehensive evaluation of the strategies under analysis and the multiple dimensions involved (i.e. well-being, ecological, tangin and economic aspect). Moreover, MCDA makes possible to include the distribution of gains and losses across beneficiaries of ESs [25]. This perspective is also in line with the recent trends of the ESs assessed literature, as testified by [26].

Finally, it can be of particular interest to propose the combination of the results of the previous analysis (costs estimation and Simulsoil quantifications) with the MCDA performances in order to have an overall index. For example the composite model for assessment approach (COSIMA) proposed by [27] could be tested. This proposal can be highly effective for a discussion with public bodies, and in particular the city of Milan, for supporting the project. In fact, the combined approach is able to clearly show how the project, in contrast to the overpass demolition, is an opportunity for the neighborhood to improve the community well-being, the environmental quality of the area and the economic externalities generated by the regeneration.

References

1. Wamsler, C., Brink, E., Rivera, C.: Planning for climate change in urban areas: from theory to practice. J. Clean. Prod. **50**, 68–81 (2013). https://doi.org/10.1016/j.jclepro.2012.12.008
2. UNDRR: Living with risk: a global review of disaster reduction initiatives, Geneva, New York (2004)
3. UNISDR: Terminology: disaster Risk Reduction, Geneva (2009)
4. Oppio, A., Bottero, M., Dell'Anna, F., Dell'Ovo, M., Gabrielli, L.: Evaluating the urban quality through a hybrid approach: application in the Milan (Italy) city area. In: Gervasi, O., et al. (eds.) ICCSA 2020. LNCS, vol. 12253, pp. 300–315. Springer, Cham (2020). https://doi.org/10.1007/978-3-030-58814-4_21
5. United Nations Department of Economic and Social Affairs: 68% of the world population projected to live in urban areas by 2050, says UN (2018)
6. Appiotti, F., et al.: Definition of a risk assessment model within a European interoperable database platform (EID) for cultural heritage. J. Cult. Herit. **46**, 268–277 (2020). https://doi.org/10.1016/j.culher.2020.08.001
7. Assumma, B.: Monaco: landscape economic attractiveness: an integrated methodology for exploring the rural landscapes in piedmont (Italy). Land. **8**, 105 (2019). https://doi.org/10.3390/land8070105
8. Dong, X., Guo, H., Zeng, S.: Enhancing future resilience in urban drainage system: green versus grey infrastructure. Water Res. **124**, 280–289 (2017). https://doi.org/10.1016/j.watres.2017.07.038

9. Pamukcu-Albers, P., Ugolini, F., La Rosa, D., Grǎdinaru, S.R., Azevedo, J.C., Wu, J.: Building green infrastructure to enhance urban resilience to climate change and pandemics. Landscape Ecol. **36**(3), 665–673 (2021). https://doi.org/10.1007/s10980-021-01212-y

10. Fisher, B., Turner, R.K., Morling, P.: Defining and classifying ecosystem services for decision making. Ecol. Econ. **68**, 643–653 (2009). https://doi.org/10.1016/j.ecolecon.2008.09.014

11. Assessment, M.E.: Living beyond our means: natural assets and human well-being statement from the board (2005)

12. Costanza, R., et al.: The value of the world's ecosystem services and natural capital. Ecol. Econ. **25**, 3–15 (1998). https://doi.org/10.1016/S0921-8009(98)00020-2

13. Demuzere, M., et al.: Mitigating and adapting to climate change: multi-functional and multi-scale assessment of green urban infrastructure. J. Environ. Manage. **146**, 107–115 (2014). https://doi.org/10.1016/j.jenvman.2014.07.025

14. Kabisch, N., et al.: Nature-based solutions to climate change mitigation and adaptation in urban areas: perspectives on indicators, knowledge gaps, barriers, and opportunities for action. Ecol. Soc. **21**, art39 (2016). https://doi.org/10.5751/ES-08373-210239

15. Faroldi, E., Fabi, V., Vettori, M.P., Gola, M., Brambilla, A., Capolongo, S.: Health tourism and thermal heritage: assessing Italian spas with innovative multidisciplinary tools. Tour. Anal. **24**, 405–419 (2019). https://doi.org/10.3727/108354219X15511865533121

16. Capolongo, S., Buffoli, M., Mosca, E.I., Galeone, D., D'Elia, R., Rebecchi, A.: Public health aspects' assessment tool for urban projects, according to the urban health approach. In: Della Torre, S., Cattaneo, S., Lenzi, C., Zanelli, A. (eds.) Regeneration of the Built Environment from a Circular Economy Perspective. RD, pp. 325–335. Springer, Cham (2020). https://doi.org/10.1007/978-3-030-33256-3_30

17. Fusco Girard, L., Nijkamp, P.: Le valutazioni per lo sviluppo sostenibile della città e del territorio. Franco Angeli (2003)

18. Pearce, D. W. , Turner, R.K.: Economics of Natural Resources and the Environment. Johns Hopkins University Press (1989)

19. Dell'Ovo, M., Oppio, A.: The role of the evaluation in designing ecosystem services. a literature review. In: New Metropolitan Perspectives Knowledge Dynamics and Innovation-driven Policies Towards Urban and Regional Transition, vol. 2, pp. 1359–1368 (2021)

20. Caprioli, C., Bottero, M., Zanetta, E., Mondini, G.: Ecosystem services in land-use planning: an application for assessing transformation scenarios at the local scale. In: Bevilacqua, C., Calabrò, F., Della Spina, L. (eds.) NMP 2020. SIST, vol. 178, pp. 1332–1341. Springer, Cham (2021). https://doi.org/10.1007/978-3-030-48279-4_124

21. Giaimo, C., Salata, S.: Ecosystem services assessment methods for integrated processes of urban planning. the experience of LIFE SAM4CP towards sustainable and smart communities. IOP Conf. Ser. Earth Environ. Sci. **290**, 012116 (2019). https://doi.org/10.1088/1755-1315/290/1/012116

22. Oppio, A., Dell'Ovo, M.: Strategic environmental assessment (SEA) and multi-criteria analysis: an integrated approach. In: Campeol, G. (ed.) Strategic Environmental Assessment and Urban Planning. GET, pp. 47–63. Springer, Cham (2020). https://doi.org/10.1007/978-3-030-46180-5_4

23. Stanganelli, M., Torrieri, F., Gerundo, C., Rossitti, M.: An integrated strategic-performative planning methodology towards enhancing the sustainable decisional regeneration of fragile territories. Sustain. Cities Soc. **53**, 101920 (2020). https://doi.org/10.1016/j.scs.2019.101920

24. Bottero, M., Dell'Anna, F., Nappo, M.: Evaluating tangible and intangible aspects of cultural heritage: an application of the PROMETHEE method for the reuse project of the Ceva-Ormea railway. In: Mondini, G., Fattinnanzi, E., Oppio, A., Bottero, M., Stanghellini, S. (eds.) Integrated Evaluation for the Management of Contemporary Cities, pp. 285–295. Springer, Cham (2018)

25. Caprioli, C., Bottero, M., Mondini, G.: Urban ecosystem services: a review of definitions and classifications for the identification of future research perspectives. In: Gervasi, O., et al. (eds.) ICCSA 2020. LNCS, vol. 12253, pp. 332–344. Springer, Cham (2020). https://doi.org/10.1007/978-3-030-58814-4_23
26. Saarikoski, H., et al.: Multi-criteria decision analysis and cost-benefit analysis: comparing alternative frameworks for integrated valuation of ecosystem services. Ecosyst. Serv. 22, 238–249 (2016). https://doi.org/10.1016/j.ecoser.2016.10.014
27. Barfod, M.B., Salling, K.B., Leleur, S.: Composite decision support by combining cost-benefit and multi-criteria decision analysis. Decis. Support Syst. 51, 167–175 (2011). https://doi.org/10.1016/j.dss.2010.12.005

How to Manage Conflicting Values in Minor Islands: A MCDA Methodology Towards Alternative Energy Solutions Assessment

Marco Rossitti[1]([envelope]) [iD] and Francesca Torrieri[2] [iD]

[1] DAStU, Politecnico di Milano, Via E. Bonardi 3, 20133 Milano, Italy
marco.rossitti@polimi.it
[2] DII, Università Degli Studi di Napoli Federico II, Piazzale V. Tecchio 80, 80125 Napoli, Italy

Abstract. The growing awareness towards the energy issue has led to a dramatic change in structuring decisional problems related to energy supplies by giving greater importance to the environmental impacts of projects and their effects on life quality. This kind of matter is enriched in complexity when Decision Makers (DMs) have to deal with cultural heritage in fragile areas. Indeed, this fact leads to consider an array of cultural values related to the area's peculiarities and deal with all the difficulties associated with marginalized territorial contexts. In this perspective, the paper aims to provide an analytic framework to support DMs in defining the favorable energy supply solution for a historical rural landscape. The methodological framework is based on a Multicriteria Decision Aiding Methodology (MCDA), which considers the conflicting values of such a decisional issue. This support tool is applied to a project in Pantelleria island, which has recently been the focus of different policies for energy efficiency. Indeed, Pantelleria richness in natural energy sources makes it possible to shift to sustainable energy supply models different from the current one. Furthermore, the island is an extraordinary example of a historical rural landscape but, at the same time, is undergoing a marginalization process. The evaluation process considers the multiple dimensions of sustainability through a MCDA methodology for assessing three different context-aware energy scenarios: a wind-based scenario, a solar-based scenario, and a traditional scenario. In conclusion, the main results from the evaluation process and the future research perspectives are discussed.

Keywords: Energy supply · Sustainability · Multi-criteria evaluation · Conflicting values · Minor islands

1 Introduction

The increasing attention to environmental issues has led to experimenting with innovative and economically sustainable solutions on energy and water in a circular economy perspective. Indeed, the *European Green Deal* foresees, among the actions necessary to achieve a more sustainable future, rethinking policies for "clean" energy supply in all sectors of the economy, including industry, infrastructures, transports, and constructions [1].

© Springer Nature Switzerland AG 2021
O. Gervasi et al. (Eds.): ICCSA 2021, LNCS 12955, pp. 582–598, 2021.
https://doi.org/10.1007/978-3-030-87007-2_42

In this context, the European project for minor islands [2] represents an experiment of great interest for the transition to a sustainable energy model because of their particular vulnerabilities, together with the rich availability of natural resources and landscape significance. Indeed, most of the minor islands' energy systems grounds on a traditional model based on fossil fuels, with inefficient and costly energy production. However, in most cases, renewable resources (such as sun, wind, tides, biomass, waste, and other renewable sources) are locally available, offering a solid potential to be exploited by promoting sustainable and innovative energy models.

The ongoing experiences display many current issues in complex territories, such as minor islands not interconnected to the *National Transmission Network* (NTG). The most significant challenges deal with the choice of technological, organizational, and financial solutions that can enhance the use of environmental resources locally available and improve the attractiveness of marginal areas, but not neglecting the protection of the landscape. So, the transition to a sustainable energy strategy is a technical, cultural, and landscape challenge [3].

The sustainability of renewable energy sources is valuable not only in terms of avoiding carbon emissions but also in terms of changes that occur in the landscape structure. Only through a strategic and culturally integrated approach, it will be possible to achieve the objectives of energy transition in the Minor Islands compatibly with the protection and enhancement of the landscape and the environment. In such sensitive areas, the energy transition intervention proposals must be conceived as "Landscape Projects". This concept hints that such interventions cannot merely focus on the energetic aspect of the decision issue but must necessarily consider all the impacts produced on the reference territorial context, considered in its landscape dimension [4].

The challenge is to define technical solutions that are efficient from an energy point of view and respectful of the complex values of the historical and rural territories that characterize the smaller islands. In particular, Sijmons et al. described five dimensions of energy transition: economic, political, technical, infrastructural, and emotional [3]. According to Kemp and Loorbach: "Energy Transition management consists of a deliberate attempt to work towards a transition offering sustainability benefits, not just environmental benefits but also economic and social benefits" [5].

In this context, the paper aims to provide an analytic framework to support DMs in defining the favorable energy supply solution for minor islands resting on a Multicriteria Decision Aiding Methodology (MCDA), which considers the conflicting values of such a decisional issue. This support tool is applied to a real case study: a project in Pantelleria island, which has recently been the focus of different policies for energy efficiency.

More in detail, after outlining the legislative reference framework at the European and national level for the energy transition in minor Italian islands, Sect. 2 focuses on the Pantelleria by explaining its suitability as a case study for testing the defined framework. Then, in Sect. 3, the methodological framework towards alternative energy solution assessment is described, and, in Sect. 4, its application to a project in Pantelleria island is illustrated. Section 5 discusses the results of applying the methodological framework to the case study. Finally, in Sect. 6, some conclusions on the novelty of the proposed approach, its replicability, and room for improvement are drawn.

2 The Case Study: Pantelleria Island

2.1 The Regulative Process Towards Energy Transition in Italian Island Contexts

Since the late 1970s, when the leading development model based on the intensive use of natural resources was rocked by the energy crisis [6], the regulative system, both at the national and international scale, has been forced to deal with the energy consumption issue and to promote sustainable development.

At the European level, the regulative process of tackling energy consumption has dramatically intensified in the last twenty years. Indeed, the European lawmaker has defined different measures, tackling energy consumption from several perspectives.

In this light, it is worth mentioning the Directive 2009/29/EC to promote reducing greenhouse emissions [7], and the Directive 2012/27/UE, geared towards promoting energy efficiency to reduce energy consumption and decrease energy imports [8]. More recently, the body of measures towards energy consumption reduction and energy transition enriches itself of the Communication 2016/860 *Clean Energy For All Europeans*, the Communication 2017/283 *Europe on the Move, an agenda for a socially fair transition towards clean, competitive, and connected mobility for all* [9, 10], and the Communication 2019/640 *The European Green Deal,* placing at its core the transition towards a clean and circular economy [1].

In the Italian context, this great concern about energy consumption and the need to move towards alternative and renewable energy sources is reflected in several legislative measures. Among them, the measures addressing the energy issue in Italian marginal areas, as the M.D. 14/02/2017 *Minor Islands* and the Directorial Decree n.340 14/07/2017 from the Ministry of the Environment, are of particular interest.

More in detail, the former, the D.M. 14/02/2017 *Minor Islands,* sets ambitious objectives towards renewable energy sources promotion in minor Italian islands, not connected to the national power grid, to reduce their energy dependence and environmental impact [11]. The latter, the Directorial Decree n. 340 14/07/2017, instead introduces and regulates the incentive towards energy efficiency, sustainable mobility, and climate change adaptation interventions in minor islands [12].

Both these legislative measures, in addressing the energy transition issue in minor islands, well recognize their potentials towards green and sustainable development and, at the same time, calls for proper tools to support decisions about alternative energy supply solutions [13].

2.2 Pantelleria: Between Natural Sources and Cultural Values

The pre-mentioned M.D. 14/02/2017 *Minor Islands* defines a list of minor Italian islands for its application, including Pantelleria island in the Sicily Region.

This island, located between Sicily and Africa (Fig. 1), owns a strong potential for renewable energy sources, like sun, wind, and geothermal energy. Thus, it stands as a perfect field for sustainable energy supply models' implementation [14]. However, at the moment, the island has no independence in terms of energy supply, and electricity comes from an oil-powered plant [15].

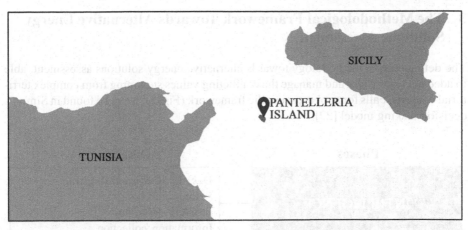

Fig. 1. Location of Pantelleria Island in the Mediterranean sea

Once acknowledged its potentials in terms of local renewable sources and the limits from the current energy supply model, the island in 2013 joined the European Covenant of Mayors for Climate & Energy [16]. Then, in 2015 it adopted the *Action Plan for Sustainable Energy.* This plan provides an integrated local strategy towards energy transition based on different fields of intervention. Its long-term vision is to create a 'zero-emission island' by promoting renewables for electricity production in place of diesel fuel and energy efficiency in water treatment, public lighting, and the building sector [17].

Furthermore, within the European initiative *Clean Energy for EU Islands* [1], in 2020, Pantelleria defined a *Clean Energy Transition Agenda,* aiming at its complete decarbonization and energy independence to high penetration of renewable energy sources and technological innovation. More in detail, this *Agenda* sets electricity production from renewable sources (wind, solar, and wave motion) and buildings' independence as pillars for energy transition [18].

The widespread and constant commitment of Pantelleria public administration in energy transition makes it appropriate to choose this island to apply a methodology towards alternative energy solution assessment.

However, in its application, the methodology cannot prescind from the values system the island is endowed with [19]. Indeed, the aesthetic and cultural significance of the Pantelleria landscape is such to make it worth the inscription in the *National Register for Historical Rural Landscapes* [20]. Nevertheless, the need to protect such a unique example of a historical rural landscape can be menaced by its alteration in favor of energy transition [21]. For this reason, an effective methodology towards alternative energy solution assessment, properly managing the conflicting values stemming from complex territorial contexts, finds in Pantelleria a perfect case study to be tested.

3 The Methodological Framework Towards Alternative Energy Solutions Assessment

The definition of a methodology towards alternative energy solutions assessment, able to adequately consider and manage the conflicting values stemming from complex territorial contexts, calls for a robust scientific framework (Fig. 2): it can be found in Simon's decision-making model [22].

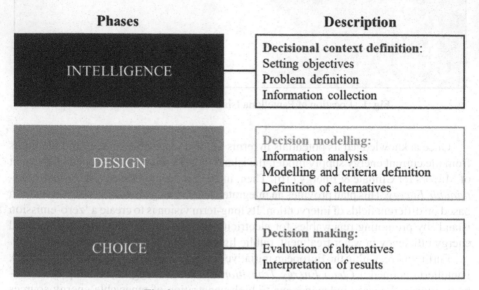

Fig. 2. Simon's decision-making model

Thus, according to the pre-mentioned model, the definition of the methodological framework for this work's purposes follows three main phases, as described below.

3.1 The Intelligence Phase

After setting the research's objective, supporting decision-makers in deciding among alternatives scenarios for the transition to green and circular energy supply models, this phase is geared towards the decisional context definition. In this light, in-depth knowledge of the energy issue from a sustainable perspective [23] and of the territorial context under study is fundamental. More in detail, the already set experiences or the existing regulative tools or plans stand as a crucial reference point for developing the decision-making process through a context-aware and feasible approach.

3.2 The Design Phase

Based on the analysis of the information collected through the *Intelligence phase,* this second step aims to model the methodological framework and define the energy supply alternatives to be assessed.

This phase moves from selecting the reference methodological approach for the evaluation of alternatives. It is identified in the MCDA. Indeed, applying a multi-criteria model makes it possible to consider the different and conflicting perspectives related to various energy scenarios' implementation and measure the alternatives' performance according to heterogeneous criteria set. For this reason, multi-criteria has found wide application in supporting decisions towards energy transition [24–27].

Once defined the model to be used, this phase delves into defining the criteria for the assessment and the related indicators for measuring alternatives' performances. More in detail, the criteria definition stems from a literature review process about the application of MCDA to alternative energy scenarios' assessment [28–31]. This process, indeed, allows recognizing the most relevant criteria used for similar decisional issues. Then, the criteria so defined are implemented to consider the conflicting values stemming

Table 1. Definition of criteria, indicators, scale, and units of measurement

Criteria	Sub-criteria	Indicators	Scale	U.M	min/max
Technical-Economic	Construction cost	Construction cost	*Ratio*	€	min
	Management and maintenance cost	Management and maintenance cost	*Ratio*	€/year	min
	Construction time	Natural and consecutive days	*Ratio*	days	min
	Service life	Number of years	*Ratio*	years	max
	Continuity of energy supply	Numbers of working hours per year	*Ordinal*	(0, +++)	max
	Access to funding	Presence of funding	*Binary*	Yes/No	max
Cultural-Environmental	Sustainability in facing climate change	CO_2 emissions reduction	Ratio	Kg/year	max
	Noise impact	Qualitative	*Ordinal*	(---,0)	min
	Ecosystem impact	Qualitative	*Ordinal*	(---,0)	min
	Visual impact	Qualitative	*Ordinal*	(---,0)	min
	Sustainability from production and disposal	Amount of pollutants emitted in the atmosphere	*Ordinal*	(0, +++)	max

from the application to complex contexts characterized by marginalization dynamics and high cultural and aesthetic significance [32]. The result from this intermediate step in the design process is displayed in the table below (Table 1).

Finally, the design phase is devoted to the definition of the energy supply alternatives to be evaluated. With this purpose, comprehensive knowledge of the territorial potentialities and the existing plans about energy transition is an essential requirement.

3.3 The Choice Phase

Based on the outputs from the design phase, this last step in the decision-making process aims at evaluating the different designed alternatives according to the criteria set. In this light, a specific MCDA method is selected for the calculation phase [33]: the *Electre method*. This method is based on a pairwise comparison of the alternatives to be assessed. Indeed, its grounding idea is to measure the degree to which scores and their associated weights confirm or contradict the dominant pairwise relationship among alternatives. More in detail, a dominance relationship for each couple of alternatives is derived using both a net *concordance index*, representative of how much an alternative is better than the others, and a net *discordance index*, expressing to what degree an alternative is worse than others. From their combination thus, a final ranking of the alternatives is obtained [34]. *Electre method* choice lies in the fact that it enables handling both quantitative and qualitative criteria and in its flexibility [35]. In addition, this MCDA methodology has been widely used in literature for supporting similar decisional issues [36–38].

Concerning one of the fundamental steps in the MCDA process, the weighting phase, aimed at considering the relative importance of the different criteria, the defined methodological framework rests on the SRF procedure. Indeed, by using a set of cards and indirectly determining numerical weights through a visual comparison, this procedure enables the involvement of different stakeholders in the decision process [39].

4   The Methodological Framework Application: A Project for Pantelleria Island

The previously defined methodological framework was tested on a case study to test its effectiveness, represented by a landscape regeneration project in Pantelleria island, focusing on the energy supply issue.

Thus, after collected and processed the preliminary and necessary information about the island and processed through a SWOT Analysis, different alternative energy supply scenarios were defined. More in details, the island's potentialities in terms of natural sources, clearly stated in the official documents towards Pantelleria energy transition and verified through a direct survey on the island, led to the definition of the following scenarios:

1. A *solar-based scenario*, based on installing PV modules on shelters and the ground, in proximity to the existing masonry retaining walls for the terraces (Fig. 3). According to the energy demand required by the project's functions, the number of PV modules

Fig. 3. Example of PV modules integration on shelters (Authors' elaboration)

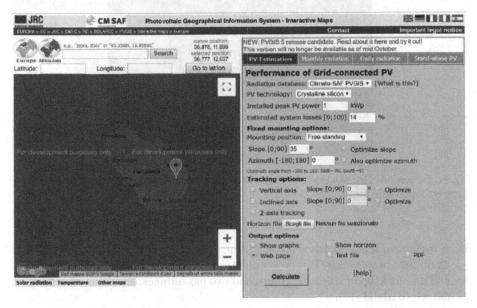

Fig. 4. *PVGIS* calculation tool for estimating the amount of PV modules to be installed

to be installed was calculated through the calculation tool *Photovoltaic Geographical Information System (PVGIS)* [40].

This tool, indeed, allows determining the number of PV modules necessary to answer a given energy demand based on the geographic location, the technology used, and the typology of installation (Fig. 4).

2. A *wind-based scenario* resting on the installation of three wind micro-turbines with a rated power of 5.5 kW. Indeed, by considering Pantelleria's average wind speed of 6 m/s [20], the three micro-turbines can cover the estimated energy demand (Fig. 5).

Furthermore, they will be placed on the non-cultivated terraces in the upper part of the project area, thus benefitting from good wind exposure.

Fig. 5. Integration of the wind micro-turbines in the project area (Authors' elaboration on a picture taken by Marco Rossitti)

3. A *traditional scenario*, based on the current system of electricity production through an oil-fired power plant. This power plant is located in Pantelleria industrial district, and it is made up of six diesel groups and two gas turbines, providing electricity for the whole island [17].

According to the defined methodological framework, after defined the assessment procedures (Table 2), the performances of the three alternative energy scenarios related to each sub-criterion were calculated, as shown in Table 3 and Fig. 6. More in detail, if for some sub-criteria, an accurate estimation in quantitative terms was possible, for others, the uncertainty related to their quantitative assessment led to the definition of qualitative scales as reference.

The criteria's weights were defined by interacting with two Pantelleria municipality officials by resorting to the SRF procedure [39].

This procedure, indeed, by grounding on the use of the set of cards, makes it easier understanding the weighting procedure and, thus, the involvement of different stakeholders [41]. Concerning the case study, the SRF method was used with two officials,

Table 2. Description of the assessment procedure for each sub-criteria

Sub-criteria	U.m	Description
Construction cost	€	Sum of all the costs to be borne for materials purchase, building activities, and connection to the island's energy grid. The related indicator is represented by the construction cost itself, expressed in euros. The performances are determined by referring to the cost items included in the *Prezzario Unico dei Lavori Pubblici* from Sicily Region (2019)
Management and maintenance cost	€/year	The sub-criteria, coincident with the indicator for its measurement, is expressed in €/year. The performances are calculated by referring to similar realized interventions for the *Solar-based* and *Wind-based* scenarios. The performance calculation grounds on the energy cost item shown in Pantelleria PAES for the *Traditional scenario*
Construction time	Days	The performances are calculated thanks to the *Man-days* method, starting from the data provided by the *Prezzario Unico dei Lavori Pubblici* from Sicily Region (2019)
Service life	Years	The performances are estimated in years by referring to service life values for the different installations provided by the scientific literature in the field
Continuity of energy supply	(0, +++)	This sub-criteria considers possible breaks in the energy supply that can affect the electric grid's functioning. The three performances are assessed through qualitative scores, based on a rough estimation of the *yearly activity hours*
Access to funding	Yes/No	The performances are measured through a *binary scale*, expressing if, for each designed scenario, funding opportunities are available or not

(*continued*)

Table 2. (*continued*)

Sub-criteria	U.m	Description
Sustainability in facing climate change	Kg/year	The performances are measured by resorting to the indicator *Reduction of CO_2 emissions*, measured in Kg/years. More in detail, the performance assessment moves from the calculation of electric power generated through renewable sources. Then, this value is turned into the *Reduction of CO_2 emissions* through the relationship of $0.267t = 1kWh$, which is valid for diesel-based electricity production
Noise impact	(---,0)	The performances are assessed through qualitative scores based on a rough estimation of each scenario's average noise level
Ecosystem impact	(---,0)	The performances are assessed through a qualitative scale, where scores are related to the different degrees of disturbance caused to bird flights by the different scenarios
Visual impact	(---,0)	The performances are assessed through a qualitative scale, where scores are related to different degrees of integration with the landscape and architecture of the designed installations
Sustainability from production and disposal	(0, +++)	The three performances are expressed in qualitative scores, based on a rough estimation of the percentage of components, for each facility that can be recycled

representative of the technical section and the political section of Pantelleria municipality's office. Indeed, such an approach enabled to bring in the analyses different perspectives towards the same decision issue.

Indeed, while the *technical official* showed a more significant concern towards the technical and economic aspects of the issue through the definition of the weight, the *political official* gave greater importance to the cultural-environmental dimension.

Table 3. Performance matrix

Sub-criteria	U.m	Solar-based	Wind-based	Traditional
Construction cost	€	35000	145000	0
Management and maintenance cost	€/year	450	200	5600
Construction time	days	16	42	0
Service life	years	20	30	20
Continuity of energy supply	(0, +++)	+	++	+++
Access to funding	Yes/No	Yes	Yes	No
Sustainability in facing climate change	Kg/year	8570	7930	0
Noise impact	(---,0)	0	--	--
Ecosystem impact	(---,0)	0	--	---
Visual impact	(---,0)	-	---	--
Sustainability from production and disposal	(0, +++)	+	++	+

5   Results and Discussion

The application of the Electre method, starting from each alternative's performances and considering the two different systems of weights defined by the two stakeholders, returned the solar-based scenario as the favorable one for the transition towards alternative energy supply solutions (Fig. 7).

This scenario performs as the best alternative when dealing with *Cultural-Environmental* sub-criteria. Indeed, it stands as the most environmental-friendly scenario concerning the multi-dimensional impacts defined in the decision problem (Fig. 6).

Concerning the *Technical-Economic* performances, instead, the solar-based scenario stands as the *middle-of-the-road* alternative among the ones considered.

However, when considering the energy transition issue in its whole complexity, thus including both cultural-environmental and technical-economic aspects, the solar-based scenario stands out as the favorable one.

Furthermore, this result is quite robust, as shown by the stakeholders' involvement in the weighting procedure. Indeed, even if the two different stakeholders had different views and goals, resulting in two diverging systems of weights, they both come to the same result in terms of alternatives ranking.

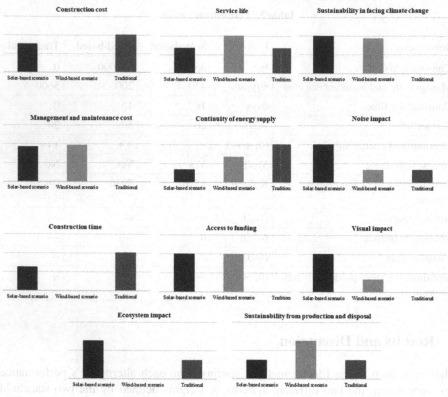

Fig. 6. Graphic visualization of the performances of the three alternatives for each criterion

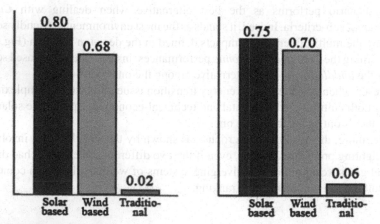

Fig. 7. Alternatives' ranking according to a 'political' (ranking on the left) and a 'technical' stakeholder (ranking on the right)

6 Conclusions

The paper proposes a methodological framework towards alternative energy solution assessment, based on MCDA, properly managing the conflicting values stemming from complex territorial contexts and test it on a project area in one of minor Italian islands: Pantelleria.

In the light of the growing attention towards green energy transition in minor islands, both in the European and national policymaking, such a framework can represent a useful and practical tool for supporting these peculiar policies in the energy field. Indeed, even if there are many applications of MCDA to support decisions among alternative energy solutions in the scientific literature, they often merely focus on a specific dimension of these solutions' impact. Instead, this methodology's novelty lies in considering the conflicting values stemming from the energy issue applied to complex territorial contexts, as Pantelleria is. Furthermore, its strength also lies in its replicability to similar contexts at the national and international levels. Indeed, the general framework can be easily exported to other contexts by carefully adapting the reference criteria to the specificities of the context under study in light of a *place-based* approach [42].

Besides these advantages, this methodology still shows room for improvement, especially when dealing with the cultural and environmental dimensions of the decisional issue. More in detail, from the environmental point of view, the results from the MCDA can be integrated with the ones from a Life Cycle Assessment, thus analytically considering the environmental impacts from different energy supply alternatives [43–45]. Instead, concerning the cultural dimension, more significant efforts can be made to include the impact of the different energy alternatives on the landscape in aesthetical terms and potential effects on its tangible and intangible value. Finally, a deepening could be devoted to the social impacts of such solutions at the territorial scale on the local community [46].

References

1. European Commission: Communication from the Commission. The European Green Deal (2019). https://eur-lex.europa.eu/legal-content/EN/TXT/HTML/?uri=CELEX:52019D C0640&from=IT. Accessed 13 May 2021
2. Clean Energy for EU Islands Homepage. https://euislands.eu/. Accessed 13 May 2021
3. Sijmons, D., Hugtenburg, J., van Hoorn, A., Feddes, F.: Landscape and Energy: Designing Transition. Nai Uitgevers Pub, Rotterdam (2014)
4. Treu, M.C.: Energy: territory and new landscapes scenarios. City Territory Arch. 5(1), 1–6 (2018). https://doi.org/10.1186/s40410-018-0092-6
5. Kemp, R., Loorbach, D.: Dutch policies to manage the transition to sustainable energy (2006). http://hdl.handle.net/1765/7629
6. Esseghir, A., Haouaoui Khouni, L.: Economic growth, energy consumption and sustainable development: the case of the union for the mediterranean countries. Energy 71, 218–225 (2014). https://doi.org/10.1016/j.energy.2014.04.050
7. European Parliament and the Council of the European Union: Directive 2009/29/EC of the European Parliament and of the Council of 23 April 2009 amending Directive 2003/87/EC so as to improve and extend the greenhouse gas emission allowance trading scheme of the Community. Off. J. Eur. Union 52, 63–87 (2009). https://eur-lex.europa.eu/legal-content/EN/ TXT/PDF/?uri=CELEX:32009L0029&from=EN. Accessed 13 May 2021

8. European Parliament and the Council of the European Union: Directive 2012/27/EU of the European Parliament and of the Council of 25 October 2012 on energy efficiency, amending Directives 2009/125/EC and 2010/30/EU and repealing Directives 2004/8/EC and 2006/32/EC. Off. J. Eur. Union 55, 1–56 (2012). https://eur-lex.europa.eu/legal-content/EN/TXT/PDF/?uri=CELEX:32012L0027&from=EN. Accessed 13 May 2021

9. European Commission: Communication from the Commission. Clean Energy For All Europeans (2016). https://ec.europa.eu/energy/sites/ener/files/documents/com_860_final.pdf. Accessed 13 May 2021

10. European Commission: Communication from the Commission. Europe on the Move, An agenda for a socially fair transition towards clean, competitive and connected mobility for all (2017). https://ec.europa.eu/transport/sites/transport/files/com20170283-europe-on-the-move.pdf. Accessed 13 May 2021

11. Ministero dello Sviluppo Economico: D.M. 14 febbraio 2017. Copertura del fabbisogno delle isole minori non interconnesse attraverso energia da fonti rinnovabili (2017). https://www.mise.gov.it/images/stories/normativa/decreto_ministeriale_14_febbraio_2017_energia_isole_minori.pdf. Accessed 13 May 2021

12. Ministero dell'Ambiente, della Tutela del Territorio e del Mare: Decreto Direttoriale n. 340 14/07/2017, Interventi di efficienza energetica, mobilità sostenibile e adattamento agli impatti ai cambiamenti climatici nelle isole minori (2017). https://www.minambiente.it/sites/default/files/archivio/allegati/isole_minori/d.d._20170714_prot_340.pdf. Accessed 13 May 2021

13. Rogna, M.: A first-phase screening method for site selection of large-scale solar plants with an application to Italy. Land Use Policy 99, 104839 (2020). https://doi.org/10.1016/j.landusepol.2020.104839

14. Riva Sanseverino, E., Riva Sanseverino, R., Favuzza, S., Vaccaro, V.: Near zero energy islands in the mediterranean: supporting policies and local obstacles. Energy Policy 66, 592–602 (2014). https://doi.org/10.1016/j.enpol.2013.11.007

15. D'Alberti, V., Governanti, A., Inglese, G., Rizzo, G., Rodonò, G.: Scenari sostenibili per il sistema energetico dell'isola di Pantelleria. In: 5° Congresso Nazionale CIRIAF Proceedings, 145–152. Università degli Studi di Perugia, Perugia, 8–9 aprile 2005

16. Covenant of Mayors Homepage. https://www.covenantofmayors.eu/en/. Accessed 13 May 2021

17. Comune di Pantelleria: Piano d'Azione per l'Energia Sostenibile (2015). http://www.smartisland.eu/images/documenti_report/Pantelleria_Paes.pdf. Accessed 13 May 2021

18. AA.VV.: Agenda per la transizione energetica. Isola di Pantelleria. Bozza – Aggiornamento luglio 2020 (2020). https://euislands.eu/sites/default/files/PR111040_CETA_Pantelleria_102020.pdf. Accessed 13 May 2021

19. Stanganelli, M., Torrieri, F., Gerundo, C., Rossitti, M.: An integrated strategic-performative planning methodology towards enhancing the sustainable decisional regeneration of fragile territories. Sustain. Cities Soc. 53, 101920 (2020). https://doi.org/10.1016/j.scs.2019.101920

20. Lotta, F., Savelli, S., De Pasquale, G.: Il paesaggio della pietra a secco dell'isola di Pantelleria. Dossier di candidatura al Registro Nazionale dei Paesaggi Rurali Storici (2018)

21. Lobosco, G.: The paradox of landscapes disturbed by the energy transition. The island of Pantelleria towards new ecosystems. Ri-Vista 18(2), 176–191 (2019). https://doi.org/10.13128/rv-8324

22. Simon, H.: The Sciences of Artificial, 1st edn. MIT Press, Cambridge (1969)

23. Hoekestra, A.Y., Wiedmann, T.O.: Humanity's unsustainable environmental footprint. Science 344(6188), 1114–1117 (2014). https://doi.org/10.1126/science.1248365

24. San Cristobal, J.R.: Multi-criteria decision-making in the selection of a renewable energy project in Spain: the Vikor method. Renew. Energy 36(2), 498–502 (2011). https://doi.org/10.1016/j.renene.2010.07.031

25. Bakhtiari, H., Naghizadeh, R.A.: Multi-criteria optimal sizing of hybrid renewable energy systems including wind, photovoltaic, battery, and hydrogen storage with ϵ-constraint method. IET Renew. Power Gener. **12**(8), 883–892 (2018). https://doi.org/10.1049/iet-rpg.2017.0706

26. Zambrano-Asanza, S., Qurios-Tortos, J., Franco, J.F.: Optimal site selection for photovoltaic power plants using a GIS-based multi-criteria decision making and spatial overlay with electric load. Renew. Sustain. Energy Rev. **143**, 110853 (2021). https://doi.org/10.1016/j.rser.2021.110853

27. Estevez, R.A., Espinoza, V., Ponce Oliva, R.D., Vasquez-Lavin, F., Gelcich, S.: Multi-criteria decision analysis for renewable energies: research trends, gaps and the challenge of improving participation. Sustainability **13**(6), 3515 (2021). https://doi.org/10.3390/su13063515

28. Afgan, N.H., Carvalho, M.G.: Multi-criteria assessment of new and renewable energy power plants. Energy **27**(8), 739–755 (2002). https://doi.org/10.1016/S0360-5442(02)00019-1

29. Cavallaro, F.: A multicriteria approach to assess sustainable energy options: an application of the Promethee Method. SSRN Electron. J. (2005)https://doi.org/10.2139/ssrn.666741

30. Fito, J., Dimri, N., Ramousse, J.: Competitiveness of renewable energies for heat production in individual housing: a multi-criteria assessment in a low-carbon energy market. Energy Build. **242**, 110971 (2021). https://doi.org/10.1016/j.enbuild.2021.110971

31. Bortoluzzi, M., Correia de Souza, C., Furlan, M.: Bibliometric analysis of renewable energy types using key performance indicators and multi-criteria decision models. Renew. Sustain. Energy Rev. **143**, 110958 (2021). https://doi.org/10.1016/j.rser.2021.110958

32. Torres Sibille, A.D.C., Cloquell-Ballester, V.A., Darton, R.: Development and validation of a multi-criteria indicator for the assessment of objective aesthetic impact of wind farms. Renew. Sustain. Energy Rev. **13**, 40–66 (2009). https://doi.org/10.1016/j.rser.2007.05.002

33. Kaya, I., Colak, M., Terzi, F.: Use of MCDM techniques for energy policy and decision-making problems: a review. Int. J. Energy Res. **42**(7), 2344–2372 (2018). https://doi.org/10.1002/er.4016

34. Figueira, J.R., Greco, S., Roy, B., Slowinski, R.: An Overview of ELECTRE methods and their recent extensions. J. Multi-Criteria Decis. Anal. **20**(1–2), 61–85 (2013). https://doi.org/10.1002/mcda.1482

35. Beccali, M., Cellura, M., Ardente, D.: Decision making in energy planning: the electre multi-criteria analysis approach compared to a fuzzy-sets methodology. Energy Convers. Manage. **39**(16–18), 1869–1881 (1998). https://doi.org/10.1016/s0196-8904(98)00053-3

36. Georgopoulou, E., Lalas, D., Papagiannakis, L.: A multicriteria decision aid approach for energy planning problems: the case of renewable energy option. Eur. J. Oper. Res. **103**(1), 38–54 (1997). https://doi.org/10.1016/S0377-2217(96)00263-9

37. Beccali, M., Cellura, M., Mistretta, M.: Decision-making in energy planning. application of the electre method at regional level for the diffusion of renewable energy technology. Renew. Energy **28**(13), 2063–2087 (2003). https://doi.org/10.1016/S0960-1481(03)00102-2

38. Papadopoulos, A., Karagiannidis, A.: Application of the multi-criteria analysis method Electre III for the optimisation of decentralised energy systems. Omega **36**(5), 766–776 (2008). https://doi.org/10.1016/j.omega.2006.01.004

39. Figueira, J.R., Roy, B.: Determining the weights of criteria in the ELECTRE type methods with a revised Simos' procedure. Eur. J. Oper. Res. **139**(2), 317–326 (2002). https://doi.org/10.1016/S0377-2217(01)00370-8

40. Photovoltaic Geographical Information System (PVGIS). https://ec.europa.eu/jrc/en/pvgis. Accessed 14 May 2021

41. Dell'Ovo, M., Bassani, S., Stefanina G., Oppio, A.: Memories at risk. How to support decisions about abandoned industrial heritage regeneration. Valori e Valutazioni, **24**, 107–115 (2020)

42. Bisello, A., Vettorato, D., Stephens, R., Elisei, P. (eds.): SSPCR 2015. GET, Springer, Cham (2017). https://doi.org/10.1007/978-3-319-44899-2

43. Pehnt, M.: Dynamic life cycle assessment (LCA) of renewable energy technologies. Renew. Energy **31**(1), 55–71 (2006). https://doi.org/10.1016/j.renene.2005.03.002
44. Paula Teixeira, W.: Life cycle assessment (LCA) photovoltaic solar energy: a bibliometric literature review. In: Thomé, A.M.T., Barbastefano, R.G., Scavarda, L.F., dos Reis, J.C.G., Amorim, M.P.C. (eds.) IJCIEOM 2020. SPMS, vol. 337, pp. 67–76. Springer, Cham (2020). https://doi.org/10.1007/978-3-030-56920-4_6
45. Uddin, M.S., Kumar, S.: Energy, emissions and environmental impact analysis of wind turbine using life cycle assessment technique. J. Clean. Prod. **69**, 153–164 (2014). https://doi.org/10.1016/j.jclepro.2014.01.073
46. Estevez, R.A., Espinoza, V., Ponce Oliva, R.D., Vasquez-Lavin, F.: Multi-criteria decision analysis for renewable energies: research trends, gaps and the challenge of improving participation. Sustainability **13**(6), 3515 (2021). https://doi.org/10.3390/su13063515

Geographically Weighted Regression Models to Investigate Urban Infrastructures Impacts

Federico Dell'Anna⊙, Marta Bottero(✉)⊙, and Marina Bravi⊙

Interuniversity Department of Regional and Urban Studies and Planning, Politecnico di Torino,
Viale Mattioli 39, 10125 Turin, Italy
{federico.dellanna,marta.bottero,marina.bravi}@polito.it

Abstract. Land transformation, producing effects on the physical and functional system, can generate externalities, modifying the individuals' perception of a given place. These effects, and in particular the changes in terms of urban quality, influence the success and effectiveness of an intervention in social, economic, environmental terms. To understand the perception of urban quality and define the elements that can contribute to its definition, urban infrastructures are increasingly subject to evaluation and quantitative measures and estimation. In the literature, it is possible to identify different types of approaches for assessing the quality of urban environments, both monetary and non-monetary. This study identified the impacts of urban infrastructure on residential property prices in Singapore. Through the application of the Hedonic Prices Method. Once the significance of the model variables was verified through an Ordinary Least Square (OLS) estimator, Geographically Weighted Regression (GWR) and Multi-scale Weighted Regression (MGWR) models were applied to take under control the spatial heterogeneity of the real estate market. Results show how MGWR model explained better the relationship between the selling price and structural and accessibility variables. This application built a bridge between economic valuation and local planning, supporting policy makers to map and identify weak areas in Singapore.

Keywords: Hedonic Prices Method (HPM) · Housing market · Spatial regression models

1 Introduction

The transformations of the territory that arise from the demand for services, connections, the usability of nature, and free time imply the use of monetary resources. Such investments inevitably induce and produce both positive and negative economic impacts on society. Often the results are not at all obvious and require a cost-benefit balance [1, 2]. In this perspective, the quantification of these effects appears to be an increasingly important operation to guide decision-making processes with a view to social equity [3]. The need to estimate and measure the effects of a transformation, and of changes in terms

© Springer Nature Switzerland AG 2021
O. Gervasi et al. (Eds.): ICCSA 2021, LNCS 12955, pp. 599–613, 2021.
https://doi.org/10.1007/978-3-030-87007-2_43

of urban quality, seems to have grown more and more over the years [4–6]. In the urban area, estimation methods have been applied over the years which made it possible to quantify the monetary value of the benefits/costs produced by the transformation of the territory. Mainly, these methodologies use the changes induced on the market value of private properties [7–9]. One of the most used techniques is the Hedonic Prices Method (HPM). The basic hypothesis lies in the assumption that the value of a property is linked to the utility attributed to the structural and external characteristics. Starting from this assumption, it is possible to break down the total price of the property into the marginal prices of the characteristics capable of determining its overall value.

Since 1974 when Rosen's first scientific article was published [10], a large literature has been produced on the subject from which the predictive capacity of this method emerges. HPM has been used extensively with real estate market data, primarily to obtain an estimate of the market value of the structural characteristics of real estate, but not only. Some studies have focused their attention on the value of environmental and public externalities. Others have used HPM to assess the effects of neighborhood characteristics on property values. Another branch of econometric research has instead focused on the valuation of the negative impact linked to environmental or noise pollution, considering, for example, the proximity to a certain source of pollution, which can be like an industrial site or a busy road. More recently, the literature has investigated how the construction of urban infrastructures, such as a new train station, a new park or public space, or even a new urban regulation of land use has affected property prices [11].

This research is part of the latter branch and develops ex-post valuations of the impacts of urban planning policies on the multi-family residential market in Singapore (Southeast Asia). In detail, the Geographically Weighted Regression (GWR) and Multi-scale Geographically Weighted Regression (MGWR) models were applied to study the spatial heterogeneity of property characteristics, in terms of structure and accessibility.

The document is structured as follows; after the Introduction, Sect. 2 offers a review of the literature on Spatial Hedonic Prices Methods (SHPM) applied in the study of the effects of urban infrastructures on property prices. Section 3 presents the methodology adopted in this study. The application to the Singapore case study is presented in Sect. 4. The results are presented in Sect. 5. Discussions and conclusions follow in Sect. 6.

2   Research Background

To investigate the determinants of properties prices, many studies have adopted the HPM [12–14]. Despite the many applications, the traditional model based on Ordinary Least Square (OLS) is limited because it cannot explicitly consider geographic location relationships, such as spatial connections. This limit has led scholars to propose new models that consider the dependence and spatial heterogeneity between transactions. To overcome the limitations of OLS-based models, the studies proposed to investigate the real estate market using local regression models such as GWR. Kopczewska and Ćwiakowski [15] filled the gap in the econometric literature by testing the space-time stability of real estate submarkets through the standard GWR estimate of the hedonic model. Massimo et al. [16] applied a GWR model in the analysis of the real estate market to identify homogeneous areas and to define the marginal contribution that the geographical location gives to the market value of the properties. In detail, the authors focused on identifying possible potential market rewards in the exchange and rental markets for green buildings in Reggio Calabria (Italy). Manganelli et al. [17] applied the GWR model to investigate residential real estate units in the city of Potenza (Italy). The results of the zoning of the territory in homogeneous market areas have provided useful information in terms of taxation, planning of territorial transformations and control of ongoing and ex-post planning.

GWR model has seen a limited application in the estimation of the externalities associated with urban infrastructures. Some researchers have recognized the importance of analyzing the housing market at local level rather than considering global impacts applying GWR calibration. The construction of spatial maps is a useful tool to represent additional information on phenomena occurring in the real estate market, providing more detailed local information. In this perspective, Cellmer and Trojanek [18] used a hedonic regression model in the form of OLS, Quantile Regression (QR) and GWR to analyze 12,219 apartment transactions in Poznan in the years 2013–2017. The maps created allowed to define and visualize the dynamics of the real estate market, demonstrating the increasing or decreasing attractiveness of the areas.

Despite the potential of the GWR method to represent the dynamics of the market in space, the literature has highlighted a non-negligible limit [19–22]. The GWR method uses a single bandwidth to calibrate the model and define the rate at which the location weights decline based on the distance for each observation to neighboring ones. The model, therefore, assumes that the bandwidth is constant for all covariates implying that the relationships vary at the same geographical scale. In GWR models, the presence of outliers, multicollinearity and spatial autocorrelation cause instability in its estimates [23–26]. The lack of diagnostic tools to measure multicollinearity could be a strong weakness for the model. To overcome this limitation, Fotheringham et al. [27] proposed a more generalized MGWR model than GWR, which assumes that each covariate varies differently in space.

3 Geographically Weighted Regression Models

The presence of spatial dependence of the characteristics of the neighborhood and accessibility on the location implies the inefficiency of the models based on the OLS estimator, as they can determine an incorrect determination of the coefficients. The implication of this spatial dependence is closely linked to spatial heterogeneity and autocorrelation issues. Many researchers have investigated these effects by proposing spatial regression models. GWR is a spatial statistical technique that recognizes that traditional "global" regression models can be limited when the elements that affect the dependent variable vary by context [28–30]. In the real estate sector, the GWR model can capture the spatial heterogeneity of the housing market, inevitably influenced by urban elements that are not uniformly distributed in the space. The GWR model is based on a set of local linear models which is calibrated considering the data of a number of nearby observations. The result is an estimate of the position characteristics for each observation in the model, as well as a single bandwidth parameter that provides insights into the geographic scale of the effects. A GWR model is specified as Eq. 1;

$$y_i = \beta_{i0} + \sum_{k=1}^{p} \beta_{ik} x_{ik} + \varepsilon_i \ i = 1, \ldots, n, \quad (1)$$

where y_i is the dependent variable at location i, β_{i0} is the intercept coefficient at location i, x_{ik} is the k-th explanatory variable at location i, β_{ik} is the k-th local regression coefficient for the k-th explanatory variable at location i, and ε_i represents the random error term associated with location i. Location i indicates the regression point, indexed by geographic coordinates (u_i, v_i). GWR estimator for local parameter estimates become in matrix form as Eq. 2;

$$\hat{\beta}(i) = [X'W(i)X]^{-1} X'W(i)y \quad (2)$$

where X is a n by k matrix of explanatory variables, $W(i)$ is the n by n diagonal weights matrix that weights each observation according to its distance from the position i, $\hat{\beta}(i)$ is a k by 1 vector of coefficients, and y is a k by 1 vector of observations of the dependent variable.

To calculate the weight matrix W, a kernel function is applied to the distances between the observations and the calibration points. This kernel places more emphasis on observations that are closer than those farther away. The three most used kernel functions are the Gaussian, exponential, and bi-square functions. Generally, the function is chosen based on the distribution of the dependent variable. In the real estate sector, the Continuous (Gaussian) Model Type since the dependent variable (sales price or rent) can take on a wide range of values is mainly selected. Bandwidth selection is done by optimizing a model fit criterion or by specifying it manually. Optimal selection (golden search) is preferable when there is no theoretical guide to manually specify bandwidth. The optimal bandwidth is that which minimizes the Akaike information criterion (AICc).

If GWR limits the relationships within each model to vary at the same local spatial scale, MGWR allows it to vary at different spatial scales [31], according to the Eq. 3;

$$y_i = \beta_{i0} + \sum_{k=1}^{p} \beta_{iwk} x_{ik} + \varepsilon_i \quad (3)$$

where β_{iwk} is the k-th local regression coefficient for the k-th explanatory variable at location i according to the bandwidth used for calibration of the j-th conditional relationship.

4 Singapore Case Application

4.1 Dataset Reference

As public housing in Singapore accounts for about 80% of total residential housing, the private sector was chosen to develop the study. This ensured that the coefficient estimates were not biased due to the different nature of transaction prices. In addition, dwellings in multi-storey buildings (condominium and apartment) were selected as they represent the largest portion of the housing stock. Moreover, the multi-family stock is efficient for the analysis of the urban context and infrastructure as it is uniformly distributed over the urban territory. The real estate transaction data was obtained from the Real Estate Information System (REALIS) database of the Urban Redevelopment Authority in Singapore [32]. The period covered was from January 2015 to December 2017. The initial dataset included approximately 45,000 georeferenced transactions of dwellings. To avoid having more than one observation per geographical point, it was decided to reduce the sample by eliminating duplicates. In detail, it was decided to order the observations in ascending temporal order and to eliminate the observations in the same geographical position. After eliminating the transactions with the same geographic coordinates, the final dataset had 3,444 transactions.

4.2 Variables Description

The literature in the real estate valuation industry has identified characteristics that affect the value of buildings. The characteristics can be classified into two different types: intrinsic characteristics, such as the surface, the presence of a lift, apartment level, quality of the property in which the apartment is located; extrinsic characteristics that characterize the urban area in which it is located, the quality of the neighborhood, including the quality of the environment and accessibility.

Table 1 presents the variables considered in the OLS, GWR, and MGWR models. The dependent variable considered refers to the total log-transformed amount of the transaction in local currency (Singapore dollars - SGD). The intrinsic characteristics included the surface area of the property in square meters, the floor on which the apartment is located within the multi-story building (Floor level), and the age of the property at time of sale (Age). As previously mentioned, the study will focus mainly on estimating the impacts of urban infrastructures, precisely because the positional characteristics group those properties that represent how the property relates to the external environment. The extrinsic characteristics investigated refer to the presence of urban green infrastructures (UGIs), understood both as an equipped public green area and as proximity to urban parks, accessibility to public transport (Mass Rapid Transit – MRT, bus stops), expressway network. Moreover, the proximity to the Central Business District (CBD) is investigated. As suggested by previous studies, distance from Orchard Road could be an effective proxy variable for distance from CBD [33, 34]. To consider accessibility to urban infrastructure, the QGIS tool was used to calculate the Euclidean distance in meters. In particular, the distance to each nearest urban infrastructure was considered for each flat.

Table 1. Variable included in the models.

Variable	Description
Market price	Natural logarithm of the price, SGD, Singapore dollars
Surface	Gross dwelling area expressed in square meters
Floor level	Floor level where the apartment is in the block
Age	Age of the property at the time of sale, calculating the difference between the year the apartment was sold and the year the building was constructed
Orchard Road	Euclidian distance expressed in meters from the apartment unit to the Orchard Road (where the CBD is located)
MRT	Euclidian distance expressed in meters from the apartment unit to the nearest MRT station
Bus stop	Euclidian distance expressed in meters from the apartment unit to the nearest bus stop
Expressway	Euclidian distance expressed in meters from the apartment unit to the nearest expressway
Natural Park	Euclidian distance expressed in meters from the apartment unit to the nearest natural park
Regional Park	Euclidian distance expressed in meters from the apartment unit to the nearest regional park

The functional form chosen for the regression analysis is the semi-logarithmic one, where only the dependent variable is log-transformed. In this case, the coefficient can be interpreted as the percentage change in the property price following an extra-unity of the independent characteristic.

5   Results

5.1   Global Regression Model

Global regression analysis was obtained through the OLS estimator. All variables achieved a significant influence of the dependent variable of 5%, as shown in Table 2. The value of R^2 and adjusted R^2 are 0.823 and 0.822 respectively. The examination of multicollinearity was performed by considering the Variance Inflation Factor (VIF) value. The results show that variables had no strong correlation (VIF < 2).

Table 2. OLS model results

Variable	Estimates	SE	t-value	p-value	VIF
Intercept	13.742781	0.016	834.962	0.000	n/a
Surface	0.006206	0.000	90.308	0.000	1.264
Level floor	0.006826	0.001	11.001	0.000	1.106
Age	−0.007087	0.000	−17.435	0.000	1.199
Orchard Road	−0.000039	0.000	−36.669	0.000	1.620
Expressway	0.000053	0.000	10.476	0.000	1.199
MRT	−0.000040	0.000	−3.765	0.000	1.166
Bus stop	0.000251	0.000	7.003	0.000	1.072
Natural Area	−0.000024	0.000	−16.360	0.000	1.217
Regional Park	−0.000021	0.000	−6.924	0.000	1.467
RSS	159.134	Log-likelihood	407.713	AICc	−793.349
R^2	0.823	Adj. R^2	0.822	DW	1.962

Number of observations: 3,444	Mean dependent variable: 14.10
VIF = Variance inflation factor SE = Standard Error	RSS = Residual Sum of Square DW = Durbin-Watson statistic

Focusing on accessibility variables, all coefficients obtained the expected sign. Having considered the distance between dwelling and the urban infrastructures as accessibility variables, the coefficients assume positive value for urban infrastructures that negatively impact property price; as the effect of the impact (distance) increases, the value increases. While the coefficients are negative if the urban infrastructures' proximity impact positively prices. As shown by the coefficient estimates, the distance from Orchard Road (−0.000039), nearest MRT station (−0.00004), Natural Area (−0.00024) and Regional Park (−0.00021) negatively affected property prices. Conversely, bus stops' distance had an unexpected positive effect (0.000251).

The study area is large and urban infrastructures are heterogeneously distributed over the territory. In the same way, the housing market is also heterogeneous. The results would be problematic if homebuyers' preferences for different urban infrastructures are heterogeneous. Starting from this, the local approach was needed to model and overcome the local variation of homebuyers' preferences.

5.2 Local Regression Models

The first step of GWR determined the value of optimum bandwidth with iterations to get minimum AICc. The weighted matrix was formed using the adaptive bisquare function since the observations were not spatially uniformly distributed. To calculate parameter estimates of local regressions, MGWR® software was used [31]. Table 3 summarizes the variation of the coefficient estimates from the GWR. The result of iteration yielded AICc was −2879 with a bandwidth value of 69. This bandwidth value described the number of neighbors giving the greatest influence. GWR improved the fit as expected (GWR adjusted R^2 = 0.931) compared to OLS (adjusted R^2 = 0.822).

Table 3. GWR model results

Variable	1Q	Med	3Q	IQR
Intercept	11.10075	14.33742	18.30478	7.20403
Surface	0.00577	0.00643	0.00727	0.00150
Level floor	−0.00241	0.00395	0.00863	0.01105
Age	−0.01400	−0.01048	−0.00579	0.00820
Orchard Road	−0.00064	−0.00010	0.00036	0.00100
Expressway	−0.00035	0.00008	0.00053	0.00088
MRT	−0.00047	−0.00013	0.00022	0.00068
Bus stop	−0.00027	0.00010	0.00047	0.00074
Natural Area	−0.00063	0.00003	0.00064	0.00127
Regional Park	−0.00054	0.00001	0.00067	0.00121
RSS	47.735	AICc	−2879.544	
R^2	0.947	Adj. R^2	0.931	
Number of observations: 3,444		Mean Dependent variable: 14.10		
1Q = 1st quartile, Med = median, 3Q = 3rd quartile, IQR = interquartile range				

Subsequently, the MGWR model was implemented, and an individual bandwidth was determined for each predictor variable. MGWR model defined a non-stationarity relationship for each predictor. The AICc was equal to −2,804. Both local regression models improved (decreased) the AICc than that found using OLS (AICc = −793). As the GWR model, MGWR one improved the fit between observed and predicted values (adjusted $R^2 = 0.91$) compared to the OLS model (Table 4).

Table 4. MGWR model results

Variable	1Q	Med	3Q	IQR	Bandwidth
Intercept	13.69379	13.79743	13.89224	0.19845	44
Surface	0.00569	0.00638	0.00702	0.00133	44
Level floor	0.00296	0.00498	0.00638	0.00342	334
Age	−0.00857	−0.00770	−0.00702	0.00155	1241
Orchard Road	−0.00004	−0.00004	−0.00004	0.00000	2499
Expressway	0.00006	0.00007	0.00008	0.00002	1943
MRT	−0.00004	−0.00004	−0.00004	0.00000	3442
Bus stop	0.00015	0.00015	0.00016	0.00001	3442
Natural Area	−0.00003	−0.00003	−0.00003	0.00000	3442
Regional Park	−0.00003	−0.00003	−0.00003	0.00000	3442
RSS	73.076	AICc	−2804.461		
R^2	0.919	Adj R^2	0.910		
Number of observations: 3,444		Mean Dependent variable: 14.10			
1Q = 1st quartile, Med = median, 3Q = 3rd quartile, IQR = interquartile range					

As indicated by the interquartile range (IQR), the GWR coefficient estimated show a higher variation than the MGWR ones. Comparing coefficients, some marked differences between the standard GWR and MGWR models can be summarized. First and foremost, all the covariate coefficient estimated in the GWR model inflect from negative to positive, indicating both negative and positive associations with Level floor and all accessibility variables. All the coefficients maintain the same sign in MGWR. The identification of specific bandwidth for each of the variables considered highlighted the limitations of the GWR model. The MGWR bandwidths for structural characteristics considered apartments very close; 44 for Surface, 334 for Level floor. Otherwise, the accessibility variables extended the analysis to more distant observations, sometimes referring to almost the entire sample; 2,499 for Orchard Road, 1,943 for Expressway, 3,442 for MRT, bus stop, Nature Area, and Regional Park. The MGWR outputs for Orchard Road, MRT, Natural Area, and Regional Park showed limited variation, indicating largely stationary processes. This stationary quality was reflected by their wide bandwidths.

The MGWR bandwidths for the intercept and other covariates indicated the relationship with real estate prices at different spatial scales. Structural variables in the model had impacts on prices that vary over relatively short distances. The intercept was distributed on a highly localized scale of 44 neighbors, with a spatial pattern similar to that observed in the OLS residual map (Fig. 1). This suggested that much of the residual autocorrelation could be captured by interceptions of variables via spatial models.

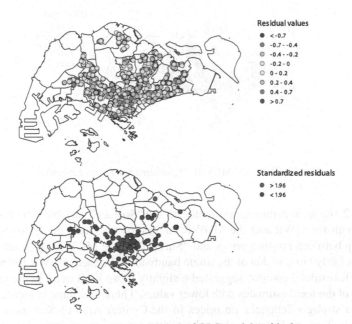

Fig. 1. Spatial distribution of OLS model residuals.

The MGWR coefficient estimates for Surface were like the GWR ones because the bandwidths of both models were similar. The difference between the GWR and MGWR was in the significance of those relationships; however, a greater number of apartments have significant coefficient estimates obtained from the MGWR calibration. The MGWR demonstrated that the building Age had a relatively strong relationship with transaction price (a median coefficient estimates of −0.00857). However, this relationship was some-what localized following the urbanization phase of the city (bandwidth equal to 1,241). On the other hand, the parameter estimated associated with the accessibility variables were global. To see more clearly the variations in the spatial scales at which different processes operated, in Figs. 2–3 we present the local parameter estimates both from GWR and MGWR associated with the variables "Floor level" (district area variation), "Regional Park" and "MRT".

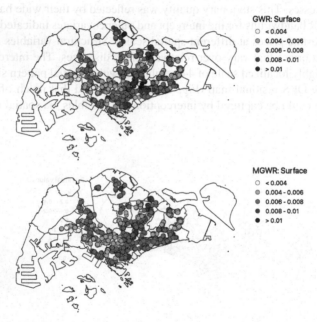

Fig. 2. GWR and MGWR coefficients for Surface covariate

In Fig. 2, the local parameter estimates for the "Surface" variable were broadly sim-ilar from both the GWR and the MGWR calibrations because the bandwidth for the relationship between housing prices and "Surface" in the MGWR (44 neighbors) cali-bration was fairly close to that of the single bandwidth obtained in GWR (69 neighbors). The MGWR results, however, suggested a slightly more local trend in the relationship with many of the local estimates with lower values. There was some evidence that "Sur-face" had a stronger influence on prices in the Central Area of Singapore (Orchard, Potong Pasir, Tanjong Katong), along the southwest coast, and west of the Catchment Central Area.

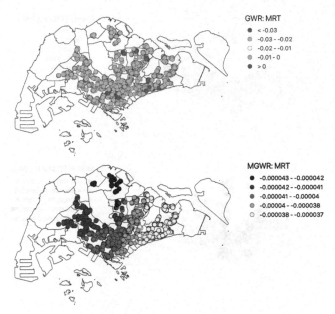

Fig. 3. GWR and MGWR coefficients for MRT covariate

Figure 3 shows that the local parameter estimates for the variable "MRT" derived from the MGWR model were uniformly negative across the country, varying from − 0.00004313 to −0.00003793, indicating that proximity to the MRT had little spatial variation. However, some interesting conclusions were drawn. From the map, it appeared that the properties most affected by the distance from the MRT were in the north and west of the city, where the network was not widely developed, and the stations were limited [19]. GWR calibration suggested a local effect and a weaker trend with many of the local estimates being close to zero.

As for MRT, parameter estimates associated with Regional Park were global with the optimal bandwidth as larger as it could be. Considering the MWGR model, estimates of local parameters varied very little over the territory of the city (−0.000026185 to − 0.000025408). However, the MGWR calibration allowed to highlight the spatial variation of regional park influence. As shown in Fig. 4, regional parks had a great influence on the North and Northeast regions, where these green infrastructures are limited or absent [35, 36]. However, in this part of the city, there is an abundance of green spaces, pristine forests, and even agricultural land, which are now a rarity in Singapore, perhaps constituting important drivers in the choice of real estate. Furthermore, given the industrial vocation of the area, proximity to the workplace can be a determining factor in choosing the location of the home.

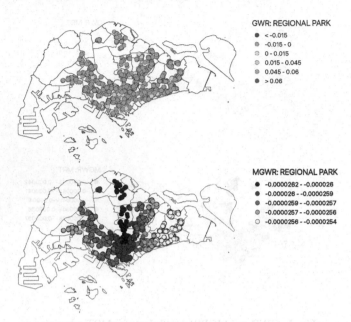

Fig. 4. GWR and MGWR coefficients for Regional Park covariate

6 Discussion and Conclusions

This study estimated the local effects of structural and accessibility characteristics on the real property prices of multi-family homes in Singapore. To estimate the economic effects of these infrastructures, the HPM was employed on a georeferenced dataset of 3,444 transactions of apartments sold between 2015 and 2017. To estimate the local coefficients, two local regression models were applied: GWR and MGWR.

Calibration by GWR allowed to investigate of the spatial variation of the variables introduced in the model by relaxing the assumption that the parameters are constant in space. Furthermore, the GWR model foreseen to calculate an optimal bandwidth that describes the spatial scale of the investigated phenomenon. The bandwidth is unique and is used to calibrate relationships between dependent variable and predictors. When several independent variables come into play, the GWR model appeared unable to represent the relationships, as they are not uniformly distributed in space. Therefore, an extension of the GWR model, called MGWR, was proposed which provides for relaxing the assumption that all relations operate at the same scale by calculating optimal bandwidth for each investigated variable. The model thus set up allowed to generate intuitive interpretations in terms of geographical scale; local, regional, or global.

The MGWR calibration highlighted the local spatial distribution (local variation) of the structural characteristics, such as Surface, Level floor, and Age. This makes sense because real estate developments often follow urbanization processes, resulting in buildings with the same structural and temporal characteristics. Compared to the GWR model, the MGWR one offered the possibility to improve the understanding of the local relationships between the selling prices of multi-family residential properties in Singapore and the structural and quality characteristics of the neighborhood.

The outcomes of the local models can help policy makers to map and identify vulnerable areas in Singapore that are affected negatively by urban infrastructures not planned correctly. By focusing on the variables of accessibility to important urban infrastructures, it is however possible to confirm that the results show that the distance from MRTs, urban parks, had a significant and positive effect on housing values, with the effect of decaying prices in relation to the increase in distance. On the other hand, heavily trafficked road infrastructure, such as the expressway, negatively impact property prices. These results demonstrated the ability of these SHPMs to consider the spatial heterogeneity of the real estate market, identifying the various positive and negative impacts provided by urban infrastructures.

As future perspectives, the walking distance could be tested as a better indicator when compared with Euclidian distance to investigate urban infrastructure heterogeneity through local regression models.

References

1. Bravi, M.: Processi di trasformazioni urbana e mercato abitativo: il caso della città di Torino (Italia). ACE Archit. City Environ. **2**, 6–19 (2006). https://doi.org/10.5821/ace.v1i2.2341
2. Oppio, A., Dell'Ovo, M.: Cultural heritage preservation and territorial attractiveness: a spatial multidimensional evaluation approach. In: Pileri, P., Moscarelli, R. (eds.) Cycling & Walking for Regional Development. Research for Development, pp. 105–125. Springer, Cham (2021). https://doi.org/10.1007/978-3-030-44003-9_9
3. Caprioli, C., Bottero, M.: Addressing complex challenges in transformations and planning: a fuzzy spatial multicriteria analysis for identifying suitable locations for urban infrastructures. Land Use Policy **102**, 105147 (2021). https://doi.org/10.1016/j.landusepol.2020.105147
4. Bottero, M., Datola, G., De Angelis, E.: A system dynamics model and analytic network process: an integrated approach to investigate urban resilience. Land **9**, 242 (2020). https://doi.org/10.3390/land9080242
5. Blecic, I., Cecchini, A., Plaisant, A.: Constructing strategies in strategic urban planning: a case study of a decision support and evaluation model. In: Murgante, B., Gervasi, O., Iglesias, A., Taniar, D., Apduhan, B.O. (eds.) Computational Science and Its Applications - ICCSA 2011. ICCSA 2011, LNCS, vol. 6783, pp. 277–292. Springer, Berlin, Heidelberg (2011). https://doi.org/10.1007/978-3-642-21887-3_22
6. Assumma, V., Bottero, M., Monaco, R.: Landscape economic attractiveness: an integrated methodology for exploring the rural landscapes in Piedmont (Italy). Land. **8**, 105 (2019). https://doi.org/10.3390/land8070105
7. Gabrielli, L., Giuffrida, S., Trovato, M.R.: Real estate landscapes and the historic city: on how looking inside the market. In: Calabrò, F., Della Spina, L., Bevilacqua, C. (eds.) ISHT 2018. SIST, vol. 101, pp. 269–276. Springer, Cham (2019). https://doi.org/10.1007/978-3-319-92102-0_29
8. Mangialardo, A., Micelli, E.: Reconstruction or reuse? How real estate values and planning choices impact urban redevelopment. Sustainability **12**, 4060 (2020). https://doi.org/10.3390/su12104060
9. Canesi, R., D'Alpaos, C., Marella, G.: Foreclosed homes market in Italy: bases of value. Int. J. Hous. Sci. Its Appl. **40**, 201–209 (2016)

10. Rosen, S.: Hedonic prices and implicit markets: product differentiation in pure competition. J. Polit. Econ. **82**, 34–55 (1974). https://doi.org/10.1086/260169

11. Boscacci, F., Camagni, R., Caragliu, A., Maltese, I., Mariotti, I.: Collective benefits of an urban transformation: restoring the Navigli in Milan. Cities **71**, 11–18 (2017). https://doi.org/10.1016/j.cities.2017.06.018

12. Morancho, A.B.: A hedonic valuation of urban green areas. Landsc. Urban Plan. **66**, 35–41 (2003). https://doi.org/10.1016/S0169-2046(03)00093-8

13. Bonifaci, P., Copiello, S.: Price premium for buildings energy efficiency: empirical findings from a hedonic model. Valori e Valutazioni. **14**, 5–15 (2015)

14. Berawi, M.A., Miraj, P., Saroji, G., Sari, M.: Impact of rail transit station proximity to commercial property prices: utilizing big data in urban real estate. J. Big Data **7**(1), 1–17 (2020). https://doi.org/10.1186/s40537-020-00348-z

15. Kopczewska, K., Lewandowska, A.: The price for subway access: spatial econometric modelling of office rental rates in London. Urban Geogr. **39**, 1528–1554 (2018). https://doi.org/10.1080/02723638.2018.1481601

16. Del Giudice, V., Massimo, D.E., De Paola, P., Forte, F., Musolino, M., Malerba, A.: Post carbon city and real estate market: testing the dataset of reggio calabria market using spline smoothing semiparametric method. In: Bevilacqua, C., Calabro, F., Della Spina, L. (eds.) New Metropolitan Perspectives, pp. 206–214. Springer, Cham (2018). https://doi.org/10.1007/978-3-319-92099-3_25

17. De Ruggiero, M., Forestiero, G., Manganelli, B., Salvo, F.: Buildings energy performance in a market comparison approach. Buildings **7**, 16 (2017). https://doi.org/10.3390/buildings7010016

18. Cellmer, R., Trojanek, R.: Towards increasing residential market transparency: mapping local housing prices and dynamics. ISPRS Int. J. Geo-Inf. **9**, 2 (2019). https://doi.org/10.3390/ijgi9010002

19. Franco, S.F., Macdonald, J.L.: Measurement and valuation of urban greenness: remote sensing and hedonic applications to Lisbon. Portugal. Reg. Sci. Urban Econ. **72**, 156–180 (2018). https://doi.org/10.1016/j.regsciurbeco.2017.03.002

20. Chang Chien, Y.-M., Carver, S., Comber, A.: Using geographically weighted models to explore how crowdsourced landscape perceptions relate to landscape physical characteristics. Landsc. Urban Plan. **203**, 103904 (2020). https://doi.org/10.1016/j.landurbplan.2020.103904

21. Mansour, S., Al Kindi, A., Al-Said, A., Al-Said, A., Atkinson, P.: Sociodemographic determinants of COVID-19 incidence rates in Oman: geospatial modelling using multiscale geographically weighted regression (MGWR). Sustain. Cities Soc. **65**, 102627 (2021). https://doi.org/10.1016/j.scs.2020.102627

22. Yu, H., Fotheringham, A.S., Li, Z., Oshan, T., Kang, W., Wolf, L.J.: Inference in multiscale geographically weighted regression. Geogr. Anal. **52**, 8C7-106 (2020). https://doi.org/10.1111/gean.12189

23. Páez, A., Farber, S., Wheeler, D.: A Simulation-based study of geographically weighted regression as a method for investigating spatially varying relationships. Environ. Plan. A Econ. Sp. **43**, 2992–3010 (2011). https://doi.org/10.1068/a44111

24. Griffith, D.A.: Spatial-filtering-based contributions to a critique of geographically weighted regression (GWR). Environ. Plan. A Econ. Sp. **40**, 2751–2769 (2008). https://doi.org/10.1068/a38218

25. Wheeler, D., Tiefelsdorf, M.: Multicollinearity and correlation among local regression coefficients in geographically weighted regression. J. Geogr. Syst. **7**, 161–187 (2005). https://doi.org/10.1007/s10109-005-0155-6

26. Bisello, A., Antoniucci, V., Marella, G.: Measuring the price premium of energy efficiency: a two-step analysis in the Italian housing market. Energy Build. **208**, 109670 (2020). https://doi.org/10.1016/j.enbuild.2019.109670

27. Fotheringham, A.S., Yang, W., Kang, W.: Multiscale geographically weighted regression (MGWR). Ann. Am. Assoc. Geogr. **107**, 1247–1265 (2017). https://doi.org/10.1080/24694452.2017.1352480

28. Manganelli, B., Pontrandolfi, P., Azzato, A., Murgante, B.: Using geographically weighted regression for housing market segmentation. Int. J. Bus. Intell. Data Min. **9**, 161–177 (2014). https://doi.org/10.1504/IJBIDM.2014.065100

29. Wang, C.-H., Chen, N.: A geographically weighted regression approach to investigating local built-environment effects on home prices in the housing downturn, recovery, and subsequent increases. J. Housing Built Environ. **35**(4), 1283–1302 (2020). https://doi.org/10.1007/s10901-020-09742-8

30. Zou, Y.: Air pollution and housing prices across Chinese cities. J. Urban Plan. Dev. **145**, 04019012 (2019). https://doi.org/10.1061/(asce)up.1943-5444.0000517

31. Oshan, T., Li, Z., Kang, W., Wolf, L., Fotheringham, A.: MGWR: a Python implementation of multiscale geographically weighted regression for investigating process spatial heterogeneity and scale. ISPRS Int. J. Geo-Inf. **8**, 269 (2019). https://doi.org/10.3390/ijgi8060269

32. URA: Welcome to REALIS. https://spring.ura.gov.sg/lad/ore/login/index.cfm

33. Dell'Anna, F., Bottero, M.: Green premium in buildings: evidence from the real estate market of Singapore. J. Clean. Prod. **286**, 125327 (2021). https://doi.org/10.1016/j.jclepro.2020.125327

34. Deng, Y., Wu, J.: Economic returns to residential green building investment: the developers' perspective. Reg. Sci. Urban Econ. **47**, 35–44 (2014). https://doi.org/10.1016/j.regsciurbeco.2013.09.015

35. Ibrahim, M.F.: Improvements and integration of a public transport system: the case of Singapore. Cities **20**, 205–216 (2003). https://doi.org/10.1016/S0264-2751(03)00014-3

36. Nghiem, L.T.P., et al.: Equity in green and blue spaces availability in Singapore. Landsc. Urban Plan. **210**, 104083 (2021). https://doi.org/10.1016/j.landurbplan.2021.104083

New Cohesion Policy 2021–2027: The Role of Indicators in the Assessment of the SDGs Targets Performance

Vanessa Assumma⬤, Giulia Datola(✉) ⬤, and Giulio Mondini⬤

Interuniversity Department of Regional and Urban Studies and Planning, Politecnico di Torino, 10125 Turin, Italy
{vanessa.assumma,giulia.datola,giulio.mondini}@polito.it

Abstract. The paper deals with the usefulness of indicators and indices in assessing the performance of a city or territory with respect to the Sustainable Development Goals (SDGs) and their targets, in the context of the new European cohesion policy 2021–2027. An impact matrix has been developed in order to measure the performance of each indicator in achieving the SDGs and their targets in a real case study: the municipality of Rivoli, located in Piedmont region, which is currently involved in the programming of European and National recovery funds. The proposed model on the one hand can support the decision-making process in the assessment and monitoring procedures and on the other hand it can be of interest of technicians and freelances to simplify and optimize the conventional planning procedures to present project proposals of territorial transformation and with respect to the building of strategies with medium and long perspective. In this sense, this first application can determine the usefulness of the method to assess in a simple way the wide range of potential impacts, considering both the quantitative and the qualitative scale.

Keywords: Indicators · Indices · Impact matrix · Cohesion policy · Sustainable development

1 Introduction

Governments are only recently approaching to the envisioning of future transformations according to a transformative perspective, related to both resilience and sustainability paradigms [1]. They progressively revolutionized the traditional planning, top-down based, to the strategic planning characterized by a place-based approach and learning by doing vision. In the meanwhile, International and European organizations solicited European country members to intervene on the environment health, to prevent and mitigate natural hazards, to avoid catastrophic implications of the ongoing climate change [2–6]. In 2020, this awareness has been emphasized by COVID-19 pandemic, that revealed new needs and services (or known needs but put aside for the fast city lifestyle). With regard to the Italian context, if the urban standards revealed unable to satisfy the citizens

demand, especially in big and medium-sized cities, COVID-19 pandemic has accentu-
ated this aspect, from the need of diffuse green areas to sustainable infrastructures that
connect cities and territories both inside and outside. Mismatches between governance
and environmental outcomes must be solved more than ever [7]. Environment must
become the engine of urban and territorial transformations of the next years. Considering the different pressures to which urban systems are exposed, different policies aim
at providing strategies and solutions, supporting the municipalities in giving the instrument and guidelines to achieve sustainability and resilience [8–10]. In this context, it is
inserted the New Cohesion Policy 2021–2027 [11]. It is grounded on four main pillars,
(1) the quality of work, (2) the environment and the natural resources for the future
generations, (3) homogeneity and the quality for citizens services and (4) the culture
for economic and social cohesion. Moreover, these pillars represent concrete challenges
for the future development of cities, that are strictly related and coherent with the SDGs
and their targets. As an example, the pillar related to the environment and the natural
resources specifically concerns the evaluation of the impacts that natural hazards (i.e.
floods, earthquake, landslide and climate risk) should have on citizens. As well as, the
pillar of the economic and social cohesion is coherent with the SDG 11 that aims at creating more sustainable cities and communities [12]. Within this context and targets, the
evaluation process becomes fundamental since the definition of the suitable actions to
achieve both the sustainability and resilience. Thus, assessment frameworks able both to
examine the impacts of actions in the ex-ante phase and to monitoring their effects over
time are required. The main task is providing tools that can support the decision-making
process, according to its main objectives [13]. The present research develops an impact
matrix, able to analyse the performance of different urban components related to the
risk (R) in achieving the SDGs and their targets. Moreover, this paper illustrates the first
application of this matrix to the real case study of the municipality of Rivoli, Italy.

2 Methodology

Evaluation frameworks can provide reliable support for the decision-making process in
solving complex problems that affect cities and territories [13], and identifying strategic
guidelines and recommendations for the planning and programming of medium and
long-term strategies. Evaluation methods employ suitable tools that may be developed
individually or in synergy with others, thanks to their versatility, from energy retrofit
assessment [14] to smart eco-districts [15], or even healthcare facilities [16], among
others. The paper provides an evaluation model that combines a set of indicators in
order to measure climate risk features and their impact with respect to the achievement
of the SDGs and their targets through an impact matrix. The combination between the
two tools can support the design of strategic guidelines for projects to be presented in
the 2021–2027 EU cohesion policy programming.

2.1 Components of Risk

The concept of risk (R), that refers to the of the probability of hazards, is generally described as the function of three fundamental elements, which are the hazard (H), that describes the potential occurrence of both natural and human-induced physical events that should imply damages, the vulnerability (V) that is conceived as the sensitivity of a given area to shocks or disturbances that interact with the area under investigation and the exposure (E) of all those elements that detains a social, economic and cultural value [3, 17, 18]. In this sense, the understanding and the assessment of risk, especially when climate features are included, require a comprehensive knowledge on social, economic and cultural values, as well as interactions between different actors and stakeholders [19].

2.2 Indicators and Indices

Indicators and indices play a fundamental role when they are employed within evaluation models. They can provide a measure of certain aspects of a phenomenon as well as an overall interpretation of the phenomenon recorded at a given time, by aggregating them through weighting and aggregation formulas [20–22]. Their wide application ranges from social inequality of distribution (i.e. Gini index) to environmental and climate change performance (i.e. EPI and CCPI), until to indices that are integrated as parameters of mathematical models to predict future scenarios [23] or to be integrated within tools such as System Dynamic Models [24].

The employment of indicators and indices within assessment and planning procedures are ever more retained fundamental for the monitoring of the environmental impacts derived by the actions of plans, programs and projects of urban and territorial transformations.

2.3 Impact Matrix

Tools like impact matrix usually support environmental assessment procedures of plans, programs and projects because they can help the understanding and the visualization of the impacts that anthropogenic activities generate on the individual environmental components and on the whole environmental system. Impact matrix can use qualitative scale (such as low, medium, high), quantitative scale (such as from 1 to 3), or symbols (e.g. – and + to label positive or negative impacts) and it can combine qualitative-quantitative evaluation to support properly the assessment. It can be applied by considering the state of the art of the territory under investigation and can refer to the potential planning scenarios that will inspire the design and/or the revision of plans, programs and projects, following both sustainable and resilient development principles. In fact, procedures like the strategic environmental assessment (SEA) [25] usually employ the impact matrix to investigate the internal and external consistency. In the application provided in this paper, the impact matrix recalls the external consistency of the SEA procedure because evaluates the set of indicators with respect to the SDGs.

3 Application

3.1 Case Study: The City of Rivoli

This paper illustrates the application of the proposed method to the municipality of Rivoli, that it is located in Piedmont region (Italy). In details, it belongs to the metropolitan city of Turin and it is far 14 km from Turin. Figure 1 illustrates the territorial framework of the municipality of Rivoli. Thus, the municipality of Rivoli can be considered as a natural conglomerate of the city of Turin. In fact, most of the settlements are allocated along the main streets that connect Rivoli to the city of Turin. Thus, the case study has been selected for this application in accordance to its level of accessibility to the city of Turin that is the main municipality of the analyzed metropolitan area. Moreover, this interest is also justified by the recent transfer of the people into the cities of the first belt of the metropolitan city of Turin, after the COVID-19 pandemic. This transfer is mainly due to the necessity of a better quality of life, always referred to the pressures to which the urban areas are mainly exposed.

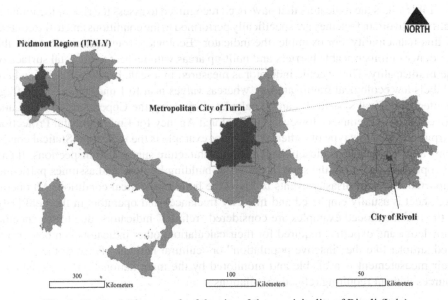

Fig. 1. Territorial framework of the city of the municipality of Rivoli (Italy)

3.2 List of Indicators

As above mentioned, this paper proposes an impact matrix to assess the performance of different urban components in enhancing the SDGs goals and their targets. For this purpose, a list of multidimensional indicators concerning the risk and specifically related to hazard, vulnerability and exposure has been developed.

As mentioned in Sect. 2, the risk (R) can be described as a combination of three different components. In details, risk can be evaluated through this formula:

$$Risk(R) = f(H, V, E) \qquad (1)$$

Where:

- H represents the potential occurrence of a natural or man-made event, that should cause loss of life, health impacts, as well as damages and losses to infrastructures, service supply and environmental resources. In details, these hazards strictly depend on the localization of the analyzed urban system. Thus, for each cities the specific hazards have to be identified;
- V concerns the vulnerability of the urban system, or rather the predisposition of the city to be adversely affected;
- E stands for the level of the exposure to the risk of infrastructural assets of the urban system. For instance, it includes the presence of people, environmental services and resources, as well as economic and social services.

Table 1 lists the indicators that have been recognized to assess the risk of the municipality of Rivoli. In fact, they are specifically performed to the conditions and to the context of this municipality. For example, the indicator "Ecological fragmentation" means the incidence of impermeable barriers and built-up areas with respect to the total surface of the municipality. This specific indicator is measured in a scale between 0 and 1, where 0 labels low ecological fragmentation, whereas values near to 1 underlines a high fragmented ecological system. It can be calculated by using the Copernicus Corine Land Cover and GIS methods. However, the Regional Agency for Environmental Protection (Arpa) provides this type of indicator. Another example is the indicator "Statical condition" and its calculation closely depends on architecture survey and inspections. It can be applied to figure out the state of the art of building heritage and assumes particular importance in post-disaster events to know the buildings statical condition. An operative sheet is usually employed and filled by freelances and operators in the field [19]. If the two mentioned examples are considered "refined" indicators, due to the specific knowledge and expertise required for their calculation, other indicators can be considered simpler like the "inactive population" or "cultural heritage" because the data for their measurement is available and monitored by the main national and regional data sources without requiring refined calculations.

3.3 Impact Matrix

This paper proposes an impact matrix to assess the performance of the defined set of indicators (Table 1) on the SDGs and their targets. Impact is conceived as any modification to the environment, negative and/or positive. This concept has been adapted to the aim of the paper to investigate the impact of the indicators performance in terms of facilitation or impairment of the SDGs achievement. Positive impacts can facilitate this achievement, whereas negative impacts may limit or undo it. The direct impacts, positive or negative, label direct correlation between the i-th indicator and the SDG target, whereas the indirect impact, refers to an indirect link between them.

Table 1. List of indicators related to hazard, vulnerability and exposure

Components	Indicators	Description	Unit	Source
Hazard (H)	H.1. Increase of hot days/frost days	The indicator measures the number of hot and frost days that overcome the annual average threshold	No. days/year	Arpa Piemonte
	H.2. Annual precipitation variation	It considers the precipitation variation detected in a year	%	Arpa Piemonte
Vulnerability (V)	V.1. Inactive population	It considers the number of inhabitants with less than 14 y.o. and with more than 65 y.o	No	ISTAT
	V.2. Fragile inhabitants	It counts the inhabitants who require medical and/or social/health assistance	No	ISTAT
	V.3. Production activities of I and II sectors	It refers to the number of activities related to the 1st and 2nd economic sectors (i.e. agriculture and industry)	No	ISTAT
	V.4. Ecological fragmentation	It measures the incidence of impermeable barriers and built-up areas with respect to the total surface of the considered territory	0; 1	Arpa Piemonte, Copernicus CLC
	V.5. Age of building	It refers to the age of buildings as an indirect measure of the percentage of buildings that may be affected by serious damages after a disaster	Year	Geoportale Piemonte

(*continued*)

Table 1. (*continued*)

Components	Indicators	Description	Unit	Source
	V.6. Statical conditions	It measures the statical conditions of building heritage through architectural surveys and inspections	0; 1	Computed after Appiotti et al., 2020
Exposure (*E*)	*E.1*. Total population	It measures the total number of inhabitants in the considered territory	No	ISTAT Census
	E.2. Strategic buildings	It counts the number of public buildings retained as of strategic importance in case of disasters (e.g. hospitals, schools)	No	Open Street Map
	E.3. Economic activities	It counts the number of economic activities that contribute to the building of the Gross Domestic Product (GDP)	No	ISTAT
	E.4. Infrastructures	It records the linear kilometers of infrastructures in the territory under investigation	Kml	Geoportale Piemonte
	E.5. Environmental components	It considers the state of environmental components and standardize them into an average value between 0 (bad) and 1 (good)	Average state 0;1	Arpa Piemonte
	E.6. Cultural heritage	It records the number of protected cultural assets in the considered territory	No	Geoportale Piemonte

In detail, this impact matrix allows to assess both the positivity or negativity of the impact and if it is direct or indirect.

Table 2. General structure of the Impact matrix to assess SDGs' target performance

SDGs	Target	Hazard		Vulnerability						Exposure					
		H.1	*H.2*	*V.1*	*V.2*	*V.3*	*V.4*	*V.5*	*V.6*	*E.1*	*E.2*	*E.3*	*E.4*	*E.5*	*E.6*
SDG 1	1.1														
	1.2														
	1.3														
	1.*n*														
SDG *n*	n.1														
	n.2														
	n.3														
	n.n														

Table 2 illustrates the general structure of the proposed matrix. As it is possible to see, the matrix puts in relation the different SDGs and their targets to the different indicators related to hazard, vulnerability and risk. Thus, it is possible to determine which typology of impacts the indicators can have on the achievement of the SDGs and their targets.

Table 3. Focus of the Impact Matrix related to the SDG 11

SDGs	Target	Hazard		Vulnerability						Exposure					
		H.1	*H.2*	*V.1*	*V.2*	*V.3*	*V.4*	*V.5*	*V.6*	*E.1*	*E.2*	*E.3*	*E.4*	*E.5*	*E.6*
	11.1				−					−			+		
	11.2			+	+					−	+		+	+	
	11.3						−		+	−	+		+	+	+
	11.4			+	+		+	+	+	+	+		+	+	+
SDG	11.5			+	+	+	+			+		+			
11	11.6	+	+				+			+	+	+	+	+	
	11.7			+	+		+			+	+	+	+	+	+
	11.A				+	+				+			+	+	
	11.B	+	+	+	+		+	+	+	+	+	+	+	+	+
	11.C			+	+					+					

Moreover, Table 3 reports a part of the compiled impact matrix. This illustrates the part that concerns the SDG 11 "make cities and human settlements inclusive, safe, resilient and sustainable". In details, the evaluation matrix assesses the positivity or negativity of the i-th impact on the SDG, and if their effects are direct or indirect.

Specifically, the color blue represents the direct impacts, while the color grey labels the indirect impact. Thus, in order to better understand how read this matrix, the symbol " + " in blue color represents a direct and positive impact, while the " +" in grey color stands for positive and indirect impacts. This reasoning is valid also for the negative impacts. While the white cells stand for no interaction between the indicator and the considered targets.

Moreover, some specific comments can be addressed in order to better explain the functioning of the matrix. As an example, the indicator *H.2* "Fragile Inhabitants" should have a negative direct impact on the target 11.1 that is referred to ensure to all the adequate access to safe and affordable housing and basic services. As well as, the indicator E.1 that is referred to the total of population. In fact, the number of the total population is too high, it can be very difficult to ensure the adequate quality of life to all.

Instead, the indicators *E.2* and *E.4* that are respectively referred to strategic buildings and infrastructures have a direct positive impact on the target 11.3 that concerns the inclusive and sustainable urbanization. The indicator *E.6* that involves the cultural heritage has a positive and direct impact on the target 11.4 that addresses the problem of the safeguard of the world's cultural and natural heritage.

4   Discussion of Results

The impact matrix has been applied to the municipality of Rivoli and the considered indicators have been selected according to the peculiarities of this urban system. Developing the assessment through this matrix, it was possible to address that the main significative SDGs and targets for the city of Rivoli are the following:

- the SDG 3 that concerns the ensure healthy lives and promote well-being for all at all ages. This interest is mainly due to the COVID-19 pandemic, that underlines the necessity and the urgency in intervening in this perspective;
- the SDG 4 that aims at ensuring inclusive and equitable quality education and promoting lifelong learning opportunities for all. This goals is fundamental, according to the transfer of a great number of people to municipalities of the first belt of the city of Turin. In fact, these municipalities should adapt their offer in educational field, according to the increasing of the demand;
- the SDGs 6 and 7 that are referred to the sustainable management of water and sustainable energy respectively are important in order to align the management of the municipality of Rivoli in reference to the pillar of the new cohesion policy 2021–2027 referred to the environment and the natural resources for the future generations. As well as for the SDG 8 that aims to promote inclusive and sustainable economic growth, that is coherent with the pillar of the new policy related to the quality of work;
- the SDG 11 that has been described in-depth in the previous sections, in order to contribute in creating an inclusive and sustainable city and community;
- the SDG 13 that concerns the urgency in taking appropriate actions for climate change. This goal within its targets can have an important role for the city of Rivoli, in which different stations to study the dynamic behavior and changes of the climate are located [26].

5 Conclusion

The presented evaluation model has revealed useful to assess the performance of the city of Rivoli in achieving the SDGs and their targets, thanks to the integration between the set of indicators and the impact matrix. Looking at the internal consistency of this model, the set of indicators allowed to focus on specific features of the city of Rivoli and may aid Decision-Makers in better interpreting complex dynamics such as climate risk factors. The impact matrix can identify the typology of impacts, directed or indirect, positive or negative, with respect to the achievement of the 17 SDGs and their specific targets. In this sense, it may be considered a useful support for the planning and programming of urban and territorial transformations, according to a medium and long term perspective. In fact, the structure of the proposed matrix is flexible, and the considered indicators should be chosen and performed according to the peculiarities of the analyzed urban system. In this sense, the proposed matrix may support Decision-Makers in designing projects proposals and prioritize the so-called "flag projects" that will lead the future transformation of the city. Considering the external consistency of the model, it may effectively support real procedures of environmental impact assessments, especially in the consistency assessment the process and in the monitoring phase, thus identifying the impacts and their entity over time. In fact, this kind of evaluation should highlight the performance of the different actions in improving the condition of the urban system. In this sense, it can support the definition of the preferable actions (ex-ante, in -itinere phases) and monitoring their impacts within their realization (ex-post phase) [27].

The limits of this evaluation model may be related to the degree of knowledge required of analysis and assessment of the case study, in order to identify general and site-specific characteristics to be measured through sets of indicators [23]. It is should be noticed that the desktop modality is not the proper one to support the planning and programming, rather than the participatory modality that allows to be constantly supported with materials, observations and site-specific needs and expectations deriving from the participatory process. The limits defined before are related to some future perspectives on the refinement of this evaluation model. First of all, it is very important to support the preliminary territorial analysis with the context definition, to know the real actors and stakeholders of the territory [28] and to identify the key players of the process.

The future perspective of this research concerns the integration of this impact matrix with the Multi-Criteria Decision Analysis (MCDA). In fact, it should be useful to evaluate the results, giving to the different SDGs within their targets a different importance that will be specifically related to the context and to the evaluation objective. As an example, this evaluation framework can support the definition and the evaluation of alternative scenarios for the plan development, within the context of Strategic Territorial Plans as well as the revision of the Regional Territorial Plan (PTR). Moreover, this matrix will be considered to structure an Analytic Network Process (ANP) based approach to assess the prioritization of these objectives and targets according to specific alternative planning scenarios. A panel of actors and stakeholders will be involved in the identification of meaningful and smart indicators, according to structural, qualifying factors and criticalities of the territories, but also indicators that may reveal useful to measure the performance of the adopted strategic guidelines and recommendation over time. The participatory modality of this evaluation model will be also supported by the scenario building and planning approach to identify alternative evaluation scenarios. The development of MCDA approaches will include both political and economic criteria to reach the best alternative scenario and then transferred it to the final users to support the receiving of economic financing and the begin of preliminary and executive design of projects.

References

1. Elmqvist, T., Andersson, E., Frantzeskaki, N., et al.: Sustainability and resilience for transformation in the urban century. Nat. Sustain. **2**, 267–273 (2019). https://doi.org/10.1038/s41893-019-0250-1
2. United Nation: Transforming Our World Agenda Sustainable Development 2030 EngFreSpa AEL 151004 (2015)
3. UNISDR: The Sendai Framework for Disaster Risk Reduction 2015–2030: the challenge for science. R Soc Meet Note. A/CONF.224/CRP.1 (2015)
4. United Nations General Assembly: Seventy-First Session Agenda Item 20 Implementation of the Outcomes of the United Nations Conferences on Human Settlements And on Housing and Sustainable Urban Development and Strengthening of The United Nations Human Settlements Programme (UN-Habitat) Dr. 20637:32 (2016)
5. IPCC: IPCC Special Report on the Impacts of Global Warming of 1.5°C (2018)
6. European Commission: Strategic Foresight Report 2020 (2020)
7. Pillay, Y.P., Buschke, F.T.: Misaligned environmental governance indicators and the mismatch between government actions and positive environmental outcomes. Environ. Sci. Policy **112**, 374–380 (2020). https://doi.org/10.1016/j.envsci.2020.07.010
8. Gencer, E.A.: A Handbook for Local Government Leaders (2017)
9. UNISDR: Making Cities Resilient Report 2012 (2012)
10. United Nations International Strategy for Disaster Risk Reduction: Hyogo Framework for Action 2005–2015: Building the Resilience of Nations and Communities to Disasters (2005)
11. DIPCOE: La programmazione della politica di coesione 2021–2027 - Documento preparatorio per il confronto partenariale (2019)
12. Utting, P.: Achieving the sustainable development goals through social and solidarity economy: incremental versus transformative change. In: Social Dimension of Sustainable development. UNRISD (2018)
13. Bottero, M., Mondini, G.: Valutazione e sostenibilità. Piani, programmi, progetti. CELID (2009)
14. Dell'Anna, F., Vergerio, G., Corgnati, S., Mondini, G.: A new price list for retrofit intervention evaluation on some archetypical buildings. Valori e Valutazioni **22**, 3–17 (2019)
15. Bottero, M., Caprioli, C., Cotella, G., Santangelo, M.: Sustainable cities: a reflection on potentialities and limits based on existing eco-districts in Europe. Sustainability (2019). https://doi.org/10.3390/su11205794
16. Brambilla, A., Lindahl, G., Dell'Ovo, M., Capolongo, S.: Validation of a multiple criteria tool for healthcare facilities quality evaluation. Facilities **39**, 434–447 (2021). https://doi.org/10.1108/F-06-2020-0070
17. UNISDR: Hyogo framework for action 2005–2015. In: United Nations International Strategy for Disaster Reduction (2005)
18. Lal, P.N., Mitchell, T., Aldunce, P., et al.: National Systems for Managing the Risks from Climate Extremes and Disasters (2012)

19. Appiotti, F., Assumma, V., Bottero, M., et al.: Definition of a risk assessment model within a European interoperable database platform (EID) for cultural heritage. J. Cult. Herit. **46**, 268–277 (2020). https://doi.org/10.1016/j.culher.2020.08.001

20. Saaty, R.W.: The analytic hierarchy process-what it is and how it is used. Math. Model. (1987). https://doi.org/10.1016/0270-0255(87)90473-8

21. Barron, F.H., Barrett, B.E.: The efficacy of SMARTER—simple multi-attribute rating technique extended to ranking. Acta Psychol. (Amst) **93**, 23–36 (1996). https://doi.org/10.1016/0001-6918(96)00010-8

22. Jesinghaus, J.: On the art of aggregating "apples & oranges". Fondazione Eni Enrico Mattei (FEEM), Milano (2000)

23. Assumma, V., Bottero, M., De Angelis, E., et al.: A decision support system for territorial resilience assessment and planning: an application to the Douro Valley (Portugal). Sci. Total Environ. **756**, 143806 (2021). https://doi.org/10.1016/j.scitotenv.2020.143806

24. Bottero, M., Datola, G., De Angelis, E.: A system dynamics model and analytic network process: an integrated approach to investigate urban resilience. Land **9**, 242 (2020). https://doi.org/10.3390/land9080242

25. Parliament THEE, Council THE, The OF, Union E: Directive 2001/42/EC of the European Parliament and of the Council of 27 June 2001 on the Assessment of the Effects of Certain Plans and Programmes on the Environment (OJ L 197 21.07.2001 p. 30). Doc Eur Community Environ Law 295–307 (2010). https://doi.org/10.1017/cbo9780511610851.021

26. Assumma, V., Bottero, M., Datola, G., Pezzoli, A.: Climate Change and Urban Resilience. Preliminary Insights from an Integrated Evaluation Framework, pp 1–10. Springer, Cham (2021). https://doi.org/10.1007/978-3-030-48279-4_63

27. Bottero, M., Dell'Anna, F., Nappo, M.: Evaluating tangible and intangible aspects of cultural heritage: an application of the PROMETHEE method for the reuse project of the Ceva–Ormea railway. In: Green Energy and Technology, pp. 285–295 (2018)

28. Yang, R.J.: An investigation of stakeholder analysis in urban development projects: empirical or rationalistic perspectives. Int. J. Proj. Manage. **32**, 838–849 (2014). https://doi.org/10.1016/j.ijproman.2013.10.011

Supporting the Transition from Linear to Circular Economy Through the Sustainability Protocols

Isabella M. Lami⬡, Francesca Abastante⬡, and Marika Gaballo⁽✉⁾⬡

Interuniversity Department of Regional and Urban Studies and Planning (DIST), Politecnico di Torino, Viale Mattioli 39, 20125 Turin, Italy
{isabella.lami,francesca.abastante,marika.gaballo}@polito.it

Abstract. The significant paradigm shift that contemporary cities are experiencing in terms of economic, social and environmental issues frames the particular urgency of a transition towards more sustainable urban systems.

In this context, the Ellen MacArthur Foundation (EMF) has begun to explore the possible applications of the circular economy (CE) principles and objectives within cities, promoting their relevance among city policy makers in order to address sustainable urban planning and design issues. In particular, the EMF emphasizing the importance of a sustainable design of the urban environment on people's quality of life, promoting the sustainability protocols such as useful tools to spread the design of a sustainable built environment through effective strategies.

In this perspective, this paper aims to investigate if and to what extent the sustainability protocols at the neighborhood scale are evolving towards the transition to the CE paradigm within cities. First, the two most internationally used sustainability protocols at the neighborhood scale, respectively the LEED-ND and the BREEAM Communities, are analyzed in terms of assessment structure and contents. Second, a comparative analysis is provided, stating how many criteria of these two tools can be traced back to the principles and key elements of CE in cities, and providing their relative importance. Furthermore, on the basis of this analysis, the paper highlights within the conclusions if and in what terms the sustainability protocols at the neighborhood scale analyzed support the paradigm shift toward circularity that is taking place within cities.

Keywords: Circular Economy · Sustainability protocols · Decision criteria · Sustainable cities

1 Introduction

The economic, social and environmental paradigm within cities is changing, underscoring the urgency of a transition to more sustainable systems able to address the challenges faced within cities [1, 2].

Accordingly, the concept of Circular Economy (CE) is gaining more and more importance among city policy makers and is becoming increasingly relevant in order to address

© Springer Nature Switzerland AG 2021
O. Gervasi et al. (Eds.): ICCSA 2021, LNCS 12955, pp. 626–641, 2021.
https://doi.org/10.1007/978-3-030-87007-2_45

sustainability issues [3] as emphasized by the European Commission. In the field of academic research, the CE has also gained strong attention especially during the last decade, with an increase in the number of articles and journals dealing with this topic [1].

Specifically, the concept of CE appears in the 1970s [4], emphasizing that the economy and the environment should coexist in balance, as natural resources influence the economy while providing inputs for production and consumption and serving as a container for outputs in the form of waste.

During the last decade, in order to incorporate concepts and elements that relate to the idea of closed loops, the concept of CE and its applications have evolved to include issues related to regenerative planning and design [5]. More recently, the Ellen MacArthur Foundation (EMF) has begun to explore possible applications of the CE concept within cities, considering them as the main places where the transformation processes take place and therefore where it is possible to drive the change towards the circular transition in terms of resource use [6, 7].

Hence, the land can be considered as a key resource not to be wasted within cities, thinking also about the relationship between the people's need to use the space and its limitation [7]. In view of this, the EMF highlights the importance of a sustainable design of the urban environment [8, 9], in particular identifying within its 10 urban policy levers, as useful orientation for city governments to enable the transition to an CE, the sustainability protocols as useful tools in order to implement effective strategies for spreading the culture and the design of a sustainable built environment [8]. Actually, the sustainability protocols as evaluative tools aim to ensure a low environmental impact in relation to the construction sector, incentivizing sustainable construction through the application of a rating system [7].

In this perspective, this paper aims to investigate how the neighbourhood-scale sustainability protocols can be useful tools in supporting the transition towards a CE within cities, thus highlighting whether they are evolving considering the paradigm shift that is taking place.

In particular, the paper is structured as follows: Sect. 2 analyses the links between the sustainability protocols at neighborhood scale and the CE principles and goals regarding cities. Moreover, Sect. 3 provides a comparative analysis between the two most widely used sustainability protocols at the international level, respectively the neighborhood scale protocols Leadership in Energy and Environment Design - Neighborhood Development (LEED-ND) [10] and the Building Research Establishment Environmental Assessment Methodology (BREEAM) Communities [11]. Specifically, trying to understand how the principles and the key elements of the CE in cities relate to the criteria of the sustainability protocols examined. Finally, Sect. 4 relates to the conclusions, in which an attempt is made to understand if and how the sustainability protocols are evolving within the paradigm shift towards a CE within cities.

2   Sustainability Protocols and Circular Economy: Interlinkages

2.1   The Evolution of the Sustainability Protocols at the Neighborhood Scale

Since the end of the twentieth century, a progressive attention has been emphasized towards sustainable issues, developing at the same time a growing need to measure the sustainability of the built environment, considering both the single building and the urban scale [12]. This need has found answers within the development of the sustainability protocols, developed as multi-criteria tools [13] aimed at assessing the sustainability of buildings, focusing mainly on the energy and environmental efficiency issues [14].

The first sustainability protocols were developed at the single building scale on a voluntary basis between the end of the twentieth century and the early 2000s [7]. In particular, in 1990, the BREEAM was the first sustainability protocol developed in the United Kingdom [14, 15], which provided the basis for the development of the other sustainability protocols that have progressively been developed within the international context. The purpose of the BREEAM protocol was to support the design and certification of the degree of environmental sustainability of the building's project, allowing comparability between different buildings and projects thanks to a rating system based on criteria and indicators. In particular, the criteria consist of thematic characteristics considered relevant in order to evaluate the sustainability of the project, while the indicators are both quantitative and qualitative descriptive measures, useful for expressing a measurable evaluation considering each criterion [15, 16].

On the wave of the success of the BREEAM protocol, between the late 90s and early 2000s, there has been a proliferation of sustainability protocols at the building scale, and to date each developed Country has one nationwide [17].

It is important to note that the sustainability protocols have evolved since their development [18] shifting the attention from the exploitation of resources in purely energy-environmental terms towards a broader perspective, increasingly considering the impact of the built environment on people's quality of life [7]. This paradigm shift has thus brought about the need to progressively bring the social and the economic issues on the same level as the environmental ones into the assessment framework [19, 20].

Moreover, this needs to consider in a comprehensive manner the different issues of the multidimensionality of the sustainability within the urban environment [14], has progressively led to the desire to include a wider portion of the territory within the assessment [7]. Therefore, since the early 2000s in the international contexts the single building scale progressively began to be considered too limited to fully guarantee the sustainability of the built environment, which instead refers to broader concepts that can only be implemented on a larger scale [14].

Consequently, the sustainability protocols have progressively shifted from the single building scale to the neighborhood and the city scale to fully assess the sustainability of the built environment also considering the processes of strain and resource use that characterize cities [15, 16].

This need for a broadening of scale is also confirmed within the EMF early explorations of the application of CE principles within cities [21]. In particular, the neighborhood scale provides ideal conditions for the proximity of resources, materials and products, within which this scale is in fact shared and reused several times by different users. Therefore, with a view to transformation processes and use of resources, special attention should be paid to planning and designing cities from this scale, assessing physical, social and environmental factors and determining the development and use of urban structures [21].

2.2 The Circular Economy Within Cities

The fundamental role that cities have in the transition toward more sustainable societies it is clearly highlighted by the European Union (EU) [6]. Cities represent the greatest challenges of the linear economy, since they host most of the world's population increasing the pressures on urban infrastructure and resource consumption [22]. In addition, a holistic approach to urban management still does not exist, inevitably leading to economic losses due to wasted resources and negative environmental impacts [21]. So, the potential of cities in becoming both centers of changes is recognized, considering that within the global economy cities play a key role being the main site of transformation processes [7].

The CE has been often described as "a concept that mimics living systems" made up of many dynamic, active and interdependent subsystems. In cities the process is analogous: the different urban systems must work together to make thriving, livable and resilient cities [23].

The CE could therefore constitute a tangible path to a prosperous recovery by giving urban systems a key role in achieving a paradigm shift to look beyond the current economic model of "take-make-waste" by focusing on the benefits for society [4].

Accordingly, the EMF defined the following 5 universal CE policy goals [24] applicable to local contexts: Goal 1 "Stimulate the design of circular economy", Goal 2 "Manage resources to preserve value", Goal 3 "Make the economics work", Goal 4 "Invest in innovation, infrastructure, and skills" and Goal 5 "Collaborate for system change". These goals consider several application areas, including the urban context, providing a useful reference for aligning the common goals of governments to facilitate the transition from a linear economy to a CE [24].

In fact, the goals and the principles expressed within the concept of the CE can offer concrete solutions for city governments, which in this sense play a key role by establishing and encouraging a framework for incorporating those elements into urban policy levers [24].

In order to facilitate city governments in putting into practice the transition towards a CE, the EMF in coherence with the 5 universal Goals [24] has identified 10 political levers based on 5 interconnected categories [8]. Among those levers, the sustainability protocols are identified as a potential economic incentive lever to design and evaluate the sustainability of the built environment [7]. In fact, the implementation of fiscal measures to encourage the diffusion of these tools can be particularly effective also to encourage positive behaviors regarding resource use processes within urban planning policies [22].

The adoption of the sustainability protocols entails many advantages, including the control in the application of sustainable approaches during the design process, the reduction of the environmental impacts by increasing the construction quality and the access to common economic, social and environmental benefits, considering both the construction and the management of the building stock [17].

Therefore, the sustainability protocols could play a potential role in creating new values towards livable and circular cities [22], contributing to the achievement of the CE policy Goals identified by the EMF with reference to local contexts. However, despite having their potential [7] in many Countries the sustainability protocols are voluntary tools and incentives to encourage their use is still missing.

3 Research Methodology

In order to understand how the neighbourhood-scale sustainability protocols can be effective tools in supporting the transition from a linear economy to a CE within cities, this paper first investigates the principles and the key elements highlighted by the EMF. Then, starting from the two widely used international sustainability protocols [25] at the neighborhood scale (LEED-ND [10] and BREEAM Communities [11]), the paper provides a comparative analysis to highlight whether the principles and the key elements of the CE within cities are effectively considered in the assessment frameworks of the sustainability protocols.

In particular, the comparative analysis is based on two consecutive steps:

- Framing the LEED-ND and the BREEAM Communities protocols in terms of both structure and content, highlighting which categories are considered and the weight given to each of them within the whole protocol;
- Analyzing the criteria contained within each category of the LEED-ND and the BREEAM Communities protocols, both in terms of descriptions and credits assigned, stating how many criteria can be traced back to the principles and key elements of CE in cities, and providing their relative importance.

3.1 The Principles and the Key Elements of Circular Cities

In 2017 the EMF began exploring possible applications of the general concepts and principles of the CE within cities, outlining them as the main driver towards the transition to circular economy and cities [6]. Particularly, the EMF outlines 3 principles to be pursued on which 5 key elements are based (Fig. 1).

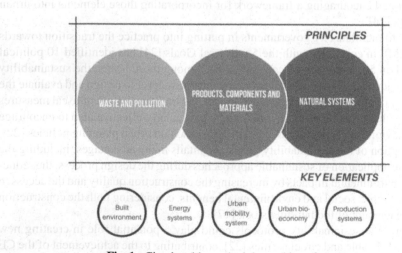

Fig. 1. Circular cities: principles and key elements.

The 3 principles to be considered (Fig. 1) are mainly related to:

1. Waste and pollution: considering the negative externalities within the urban context, such as the release of toxic substances, greenhouse gas emissions, air, soil and water pollution and traffic congestion;
2. Products, components and materials: maintaining them at maximum value and in use, especially in reference to design for reuse and remanufacturing to keep components and materials circulating and contributing to the economy;
3. Natural systems: considering the enhancement of natural capital, creating the conditions for its regeneration.

In a circular city the 3 principles are applied in all its functions considering 5 key elements [21] to create a regenerative, livable urban system, that keeps resources at their highest value (Fig. 1). The 5 key elements include:

1. A built environment which is widely used, thanks to flexible and modular spaces and includes materials which should be renewed and not harmful to the quality of life of the residents;
2. Efficient and renewable energy systems to reduce costs and having a positive impact on the urban environment;
3. A multimodal urban mobility system, aiming at reducing air pollution and congestion, also considering a conversion of excess road infrastructure;
4. An urban bioeconomy to generate value and minimize food waste, using the organic component of municipal solid waste and wastewater flows in local circuits, in order to produce food and provide a more resilient and diversified energy system;
5. Production systems that encourage local economic circuits, also through digital applications.

Therefore, considering the principles and the key elements outlined (Fig. 1) within the urban policies, city administrations could encourage and set up a regulatory framework to establish favorable conditions for cities to become more circular. In particular, paying attention to spreading the importance of creating responsible production and consumption and to adopt a responsible approach towards materials, stimulating new values.

3.2 Comparative Analysis: The Assessment Framework of LEED-ND and BREEAM Communities Protocols

Once the principles and the key elements to be considered in order to develop circular cities have been considered, the following phase consists of deepening the LEED-ND and the BREEAM Communities protocols [10, 11].

Accordingly, the aim of this analysis is both trying to highlight the assessment framework of the LEED-ND and BREEAM Communities protocols and frame the categories mainly considered within them in terms of the concepts analyzed, providing the first step of the comparative analysis.

In particular, the LEED-ND protocol develops its application at neighborhood scale first compared to the BREEAM Communities protocol and will therefore be presented first.

Leadership in Energy and Environmental Design - Neighborhood Development (LEED-ND)

The LEED protocol was developed as a voluntary tool at single building scale by the US Green Building Council (USGBC) in 1998, but over time has seen widespread implementation also in Europe.

In 2009, the LEED protocol was implemented by expanding its scale of application with reference to the neighborhood context, introducing the LEED Neighborhood Development (LEED-ND) [10]. The aim of this tool is mainly to promote the cycle of sustainable resources and materials, to improve the global climate, environmental justice and the quality of life, with particular attention to individual well-being and to build a green economy protecting the natural ecosystems.

The LEED-ND protocol within its assessment framework highlights 5 categories with a different percentage weight within the overall system (Fig. 2). Each of the 5 categories within the LEED-ND protocol is divided into mandatory prerequisites, which are not given a score but are mandatory elements to have in order to proceed with the evaluation, and credits, aiming at better structure the contents for evaluation purposes.

In particular the LEED-ND protocol stresses 12 total prerequisites, relating to 3 categories out of 5, respectively "Neighborhood pattern and design (NPD)", "Green infrastructures and buildings (GIB)" and "Site location and linkages (SLL)". Furthermore, the total criteria considered are 44, to which credits are assigned in order to differentiate their importance within the final assessment. Accordingly, the evaluation model of the LEED-ND protocol assigns a predetermined number of credits to each criterion, that can reach a maximum value of 10 [26].

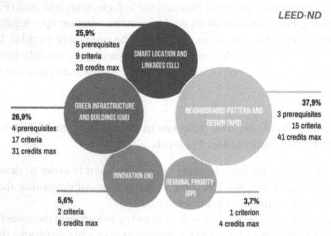

Fig. 2. Composition of the categories considered within the LEED-ND protocol evaluation framework: weight and related prerequisites, criteria and credits.

Figure 2 underlines that the "Neighborhood pattern and design (NPD)" category provide the highest weight (37.9%), immediately followed by the categories "Green infrastructures and buildings (GIB)" (26.9%) and "Site location and linkages (SLL)" (25.9%). In fact, the choice of the intervention site and the design choices adopted are both considered fundamental from a sustainable point of view. Finally, the categories "Innovation (IN)" and "Regional priority (RP)" show the lower percentage weights (respectively 5,6% and 3,7%), as they are considered specific categories of contexts [27].

Within the final evaluation of the LEED-ND protocol it is possible to reach a maximum of 110 credits obtained based on the sum of the credits within each category.

Consequently, a different level of certification can be obtained, respectively: not certified, certified, silver, gold and platinum.

Building Research Establishment Environmental Assessment Methodology Communities (BREEAM Communities)

The BREEAM has been the first voluntary protocol. It has been developed in 1990 in the UK and applied for new construction projects at the building scale.

The BREEAM protocol has a flexible structure, with the aim of being implemented in multiple international contexts, presenting criteria that can be modified according to how to achieve the necessary performance for a sustainable project in reference to the context of application [11].

The BREEAM protocol, as well as the LEED protocol, has developed over the years, extending its scale of application to the neighborhood context with the aim of also considering economic and social aspects, as well as environmental ones.

BREEAM Communities was thus developed in 2012 as a voluntary and independent assessment and certification tool for new development projects on the urban scale of the neighborhood [11]. This protocol aims to ensure quality through a holistic and balanced quantified measurement of impacts on sustainability, to also integrate construction professionals into operational processes and, where possible, to adopt existing industry tools to support developments and minimize costs.

The BREEAM Communities protocol considers a set of 40 criteria (over 44 of the LEED-ND), useful for measuring the actual degree of sustainability of each project under consideration [11].

Similar to the LEED-ND protocol, the criteria of the BREEAM Communities protocol are divided into 5 categories with a different percentage weight (Fig. 3).

Figure 3 shows that the category "Social and economic well-being (SEW)" has the highest weight (42,7%), also underlining a significant difference with the other 4 categories considered. This highlights the predominance of social and economic elements within the BREEAM protocol.

Furthermore the "Resources and energy (RE)" category is the second in terms of weight (21,6%), while the "Transport and movement (TM)", "Soil use and ecology (SE)" and "Governance (G)" categories have similar weights (respectively 13,8%, 12,6% and 9,3% respectively). In this sense, the BREEAM community protocol recognizes that site selection and subsequent management are almost as important as sustainable mobility policies and strategies [11]. Furthermore, aspects related to governance are less significant in defining the degree of sustainability of a neighborhood (Fig. 3).

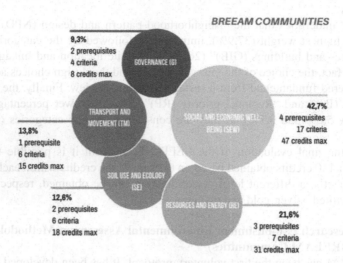

Fig. 3. Composition of the categories considered within the BREEAM Communities protocol evaluation framework: weight and related prerequisites, criteria and credits.

It is significant to underline that similar to the LEED-ND protocol, a further category, called "Innovation (IN)" recognizes the importance of developing innovative sustainable practices, capable of adapting to changes related to the climate issues. However, unlike the LEED-ND protocol (Fig. 2), within the BREEAM protocol no weight is assigned to this category, considered optional and specific for those projects capable of obtaining innovative results to which further credits can be assigned as part of the final evaluation [14, 16].

Similarly, to the LEED-ND protocol, each of the categories are divided into prerequisites, criteria and credits. However, the BREEAM Communities protocol assigns credits to the prerequisites in addition to the criteria, thus assessing not only their compliance but the degree of response quantifying their value. In particular, the highest number of credits can be reach though one prerequisite within the "Resources and energy (RE)" category, which ranges from 1 to a maximum of 11 credits. Accordingly, it is emphasized that in the BREEAM Communities protocol the maximum value of credits that can be obtained is equal to 11, unlike the LEED-ND in which it is possible to reach up to 10 [11, 26].

Moreover, the number of criteria differs between the categories considered and the subdivision of credits reflects the weight of each category within the protocol. In fact (Fig. 3), the "Social and economic well-being (SEW)" category having the highest weight, also shows the highest number of criteria and credits (respectively 17 criteria and 47 credits), while the "Governance (G)" category having the lowest weight, also shows the lowest number of both criteria and credits (4 and 8 respectively).

Moreover, in the BREEAM Communities protocol the sum of the credits of all the categories does not correspond to the final assessment of the degree of sustainability [11, 14, 26]. In fact, all credits are normalized and translated into percentage weight, subordinated to the total weight of the reference category.

In particular, the final score is obtained through a few consecutive steps. The first step is the attribution of credits for each criterion on the basis of the scale of reference values. Subsequently, a percentage ratio is created for each criterion, between the credits obtained and the total available credits, which is consequently multiplied by the corresponding percentage weight of each criterion. After this, any credits are added, up to a maximum of 4, if the project responds to innovative applications in the field of sustainability. Finally, the sum of the final percentages is provided, determining the placement of the project in one of the final certifications of the protocol, which are one more than the LEED-ND protocol, including: not certified, certified, good, very good, excellent and exceptional.

4 Results and Discussion

In order to understand if the principles and key elements emphasized by the EMF are captured within the LEED-ND and BREEAM Communities protocols, the criteria of both protocols were analyzed in depth.

Specifically, starting with each category contained within the sustainability protocols, an analysis of the description of each criterion was conducted to optimally capture its content [27]. Consequently, it was possible to list how many criteria for each category considered within the LEED-ND and the BREEAM Communities protocols meet the principles and key elements of the CE in cities (Fig. 4).

In particular, the acronyms of the categories (Fig. 2 and Fig. 3) included within the examined protocols were used in Fig. 4.

Figure 4 shows that the LEED-ND protocol categories contain a total of 36 criteria out of 44 that meet the principles and key elements of the CE in cities.

Specifically, the majority of criteria are contained within the "Green infrastructures and buildings GIB" category (17 out of 36), which is the second highest weighted category within the LEED-ND protocol (Fig. 2). Moreover, the "Neighborhood pattern and design NPD" category, which is the first most weighted category within the protocol, contains 9 out of 36 criteria, equally to the " Site location and linkages SLL" category. While it is interesting to note that the categories with less weight within the protocol, respectively "Innovation (IN)" and "Regional priority (RP)", do not contain any criteria meeting the CE principles.

From this first analysis, Fig. 4 underlines that despite the efforts made to include aspects related to social issues and mobility in terms of transition towards circular cities, the LEED-ND protocol still provides a focus on energy-environmental aspects.

Figure 4 also points out that the categories of the BREEAM Communities protocol contain a total of 32 criteria out of 40 that meet the principles and key elements of the CE in cities. This first element leads to the preliminary consideration that in comparison with the LEED-ND (which reports 36 out of 44) the two sustainability protocols are therefore balanced.

In the BREEAM Communities protocol, the "Social and economic well-being SEW" category has the highest weight (Fig. 3) also containing the highest number of criteria (14 out of 32). While the other categories contain 6 out of 32 criteria, with the exception of the " Governance G" category which contains none. Accordingly, within this protocol,

		LEED-ND					BREEAM Communities				
		SLL	NPD	RP	IN	GIB	G	SEW	RE	SE	TM
CE Principles	Waste and pollution					3	2	1	1		
	Products, components and materials	1				5		4			
	Natural systems	4	2			1		4		5	
CE Key elements	Built environment	1	2			2	4				
	Energy systems				4			1			
	Urban mobility systems	3	4					1			6
	Urban bio-economy				2						
	Production systems					1		3			

Fig. 4. Number of criteria from the LEED-ND and BREEAM Communities protocols that meet the principles and key elements of the CE in cities

as opposed to the LEED-ND protocol, there is a clear willingness to move beyond the energy-environmental aspects including also the social ones. This is emphasized both by the number of criteria of the "SEW" category and by the protocol's ability to include evaluation criteria useful for supporting a CE. In fact, although the CE principle "Natural systems" is the one related to the highest number of criteria (9 out of 32) highlighting a similar environmental focus as within the LEED-ND protocol (Fig. 4), however within the BREEAM Communities protocol there is an attempt to include also other aspects in terms of CE, related to the social and economic well-being.

Since to each criterion within the assessment framework of both the LEED-ND and the BREEAM Communities protocols is given a different weight in term of credits assigned (Fig. 2 and Fig. 3), after analyzing the criteria of the two protocols in terms of content, a comparative analysis was also conducted in order to highlight the importance of the criteria identified.

Therefore, both in terms of principles and key elements of the CE (Fig. 1), each criterion identified in Fig. 4 was analyzed by highlighting how many credits were assigned to each. Subsequently, in order to understand its importance within the protocol, the credits assigned to each criterion were compared to the overall credits considered in the protocol. Finally, the values obtained were normalized to bring them into percentage terms (Fig. 5 and Fig. 6).

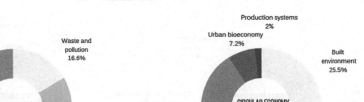

Fig. 5. The LEED-ND protocol: importance of the principles and key elements of the CE in cities

Figure 5 shows how within the LEED-ND protocol the principle of the CE considered having more weight is the "Natural systems" principle (49,7%), which is also the principle containing the highest number of criteria (Fig. 4). The "Product, components and materials" principle has the second highest weight (33,7%), followed by the "Waste and pollution " principle (16.6%). This analysis confirms the energy-environmental footprint of the LEED-ND protocol outlined in the previous analysis of the criteria (Fig. 4).

Furthermore, Fig. 5 underlines that the key element "Urban mobility system", which is also the one containing the highest number of criteria (Fig. 4), significantly differs from the others, reporting the highest weight of 50,9%. This may be due to the fact that the LEED-ND protocol has endeavored to evolve to include aspects of mobility in terms of CE, paying attention to promoting a multimodal system and therefore incorporating public transport with other forms of sustainable mobility [10]. This is particularly in line with the CE key element on mobility, which considers the private car only as a last-mile solution [21], favoring more sustainable alternatives and encouraging a mobility system that is accessible and efficient, but also cost-effective and environmentally friendly [21].

Moreover, the key elements "Built environment" and "Energy system" stress respectively a weight of 25,5% and 14,6%, while the "Urban bio-economy" key element shows a weight of 7.2%. Finally, the "Production system" weights only for 2%, which is also the one containing only 1 criterion (Fig. 4).

Figure 6 shows how the principle of the CE with more weight within the BREEAM Communities protocol is "Natural systems" (48.1%), which is also the principle containing the majority of criteria (Fig. 4). In fact, although the BREEAM Communities protocol highlights an effort to also include social and economic aspects in terms of CE within its assessment framework, the CE principle "Natural systems" is the one related to more criteria (Fig. 4).

Moreover, the following principles with more weight are respectively the "Product, components and materials" (33.3%) and the "Waste and pollution" (18.5%). Looking at the CE principles, the two protocols analyzed are similar showing a propensity for assessing the regeneration of natural systems. This could be due to the fact that "natural systems", "product, components and materials" and "waste and pollution" can be seen as consequential principles. It seems that a rational control of waste and pollution and a

BREEAM COMMUNITIES

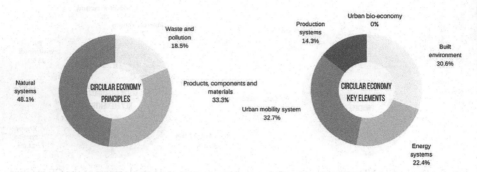

Fig. 6. The BREEAM Communities protocol: importance of the principles and key elements of the CE in cities.

"green" management of the products components and materials contribute equally to the regeneration of natural systems. In this sense, those two principles are not seen as less important, but rather as instrumental in achieving the goal of protection and regeneration of natural systems.

Looking at the BREEAM protocol, the key elements "Urban mobility system" and "Built environment" are the ones with the greatest weight, presenting a low percentage difference (respectively 32.7% and 30.6%). The key elements "Energy system" and "Production system" instead show a weight of respectively 22.4% and 14.3%, while the key element "Urban bio-economy" reports a weight of 0%, in line with the fact that this key element does not refer to any criteria inside the protocol (Fig. 4).

It is interesting to note how the key element "Energy systems" within the BREEAM Communities protocol weighs more (22,4%) than the LEED-ND protocol (14,6%) even though it has only one criterion, compared to the 4 criteria considered in the LEED-ND (Fig. 4). Accordingly, this difference is due to the fact that the only criterion considered within the BREEAM Communities protocol has a significantly greater weight than the 4 criteria considered within the LEED-ND protocol.

In the perspective of translating the CE principles into the key elements, the "urban mobility" and the "built environment" seem to be fundamental for both LEED and BREEAM protocols, although with very different importance among the two.

This is may be attributable to the fact that those are largely investigated phenomena and therefore their measurement is more reliable. One can therefore assume that the greater reliability may result in a greater capacity of intervention on these two elements in a view of the sustainability.

5   Conclusion and Future Developments

The comparative analysis developed in this paper allowed to understand how the neighbourhood-scale sustainability protocols can be useful tools considering the transition to a CE which are characterizing cities. Through the methodology carried out it was possible not only to identify how many criteria of the two analysed sustainability protocols can be traced back to the principles and the key elements of the CE, but also to understand their relative importance within the protocols' assessment framework. In this sense, the analysis made it possible to highlight whether the sustainability protocols are evolving considering the paradigm shift that is taking place.

In particular, it can be noted that the neighbourhood-scale sustainability protocol LEED-ND and BREEAM Communities already give a significant contribution towards the CE transition. In fact, from the analysis emerges that the three CE principles are strongly represented in the descriptive modalities since they can be considered as inter-related and consequential. Moreover, it should be considered that some progress has been made in consideration of an assessment framework within the protocols that also considers issues that pursue long-term sustainability in a "closed loop system" view [1], for example giving more importance to aspects such as the reduction of externalities caused by mobility or the value of materials and components used (Fig. 5 and Fig. 6).

In spite progress, some principles and key elements of a transition to CE within cities are still not considered within the sustainability protocols analysed. In fact, the comparative analysis shows that issues related to the production systems that improve the local economy and to the urban bioeconomy are hardly considered. In particular, the key element of the urban bioeconomy is only considered within the LEED-ND protocol, meeting no criteria within the BREEAM Communities protocol (Fig. 4).

The sustainability protocols aim to improve the quality of urban design, so despite their scale considering the broader vision of the neighbourhood, the focus is still on considering design-related issues [14, 16].

Finally, regarding the limits of the research, it should be emphasized that only neighborhood-scale protocols were considered in this comparative analysis and if this methodology were applied to sustainability protocols at different scales (e.g. single building scale) the results might change.

Furthermore, the analysis developed in this paper does not capture how and in what terms the neighborhood-scale sustainability protocols analyzed can help towards the transition of more circular cities. This research lays the foundations for further developments of the work, which will include a more in-depth analysis that will seek to understand in what terms the sustainability protocols can really help in achieving the CE paradigm and towards transition within cities. In particular, the purpose will be to analyse in depth the criteria and indicators used within the assessment framework of the LEED-ND and BREEAM Communities neighbourhood-scale sustainability protocols to understand their contents and functions, and eventually implement them within a new neighbourhood-scale sustainability protocol that intercepts the principles and the key elements of the CE.

References

1. Geissdoerfer, M., Savaget, P., Bocken, N.M., Hultink, E.J.: The CE–A new sustainability paradigm? J. Clean. Prod. **143**, 757–768 (2016)
2. Abastante, F., Lami, I.M., Mecca, B.: How to revitalise a historic district: a stakeholders-oriented assessment framework of adaptive reuse. In: Mondini, G., Oppio, A., Stanghellini, S., Bottero, M., Abastante, F. (eds.) Values and Functions for Future Cities. GET, pp. 3–20. Springer, Cham (2020). https://doi.org/10.1007/978-3-030-23786-8_1

3. European Commission: Closing the Loop - an EU Action Plan for the CE, Com (2015) 614 Communication from the Commission to the European Parliament, the Council, the European Economic and Social Committee and the Committee of the Regions. European Commission, Brussels (2015)
4. Ellen MacArthur Foundation: Towards the CE. J. Ind. Ecol. **2**, 23–44 (2013)
5. Lyle, J.T.: Regenerative Design for Sustainable Development. John Wiley & Sons, New York (1994)
6. Paiho, S., et al.: Towards circular cities—conceptualizing core aspects. Sustain. Cities Soc. **59**, 102143 (2020)
7. Abastante, F., Lami, I.M., Gaballo, M.: Pursuing the SDG11 targets: the role of the sustainability protocols. Sustainability **13**(7), 3858 (2021)
8. Ellen MacArthur Foundation: Towards the circular economy. Economic and business rationale for an accelerated transition (2013). https://www.ellenmacarthurfoundation.org/ass ets/downloads/publications/Ellen-MacArthur-Foundation-Towards-the-Circular-Economy-vol.1.pdf. Accessed 15 Apr 2021
9. Ellen MacArthur Foundation and ARUP: Circular economy in cities: project guide. (2019a). https://www.ellenmacarthurfoundation.org/publications/circular-economy-in-cities-project-guide. Accessed on 16 Apr 2021
10. USGBC: LEED v4 for neigborhood ddevelopment, Washington DC: U.S. Green Building council (2018)
11. BREEAM: BREEAM Communities Technical manual. BRE Global, Watford (2012)
12. Attaianese, E., Acierno, A.: La progettazione ambientale per l'inclusione sociale: il ruolo dei protocolli di certificazione ambientale. Techne, 76–87 (2017)
13. Abastante, F.: Multicriteria decision methodologies supporting decision processes: empirical examples. Geam-Geoingegneria Ambientale E Mineraria-Geam-Geoengineering Environment and Mining 149, 5–18 (2016)
14. Berardi, U.: Beyond sustainability assessment systems: upgrading topics by enlarging the scale of assessment. Int. J. Sustain. Build. Technol. Urban Dev. **2**(4), 276–282 (2012)
15. Castanheira, G., Bragança, L.: The evolution of the sustainability assessment tool SBToolPT: from buildings to the built environment. Sci. World J. **2014**, 1–10 (2014)
16. Haapio, A.: Towards sustainable urban communities. Environ. Impact Assess. **32**(1), 165–169 (2012)
17. Dall'O', G., Zichi, A.: Green protocols for neighbourhoods and cities. In: Dall'O', G. (ed.) Green Planning for Cities and Communities. RD, pp. 301–328. Springer, Cham (2020). https://doi.org/10.1007/978-3-030-41072-8_13
18. Díaz-López, C., Carpio, M., Martín-Morales, M., Zamorano, M.: Analysis of the scientific evolution of sustainable building assessment methods. Sustain. Cities Soc. **49**, 101610 (2019)
19. Shan, M., Hwang, B.-G.: Green building rating systems: global reviews of practices and research efforts. Sustain. Cities Soc **39**, 172–180 (2018)
20. Illankoon, I.M.C.S., Tam, V.W.Y., Le, K.N.: Environmental, economic, and social parameters in international green building rating tools. J. Prof. Issues Eng. Educ. Pract. **143**, 05016010 (2017)
21. Ellen MacArthur Foundation: Cities in the CE: An initial exploration (2017). ellenmacarthur-foundation.org. Accessed 20 Apr 2021
22. Levers, U.P.: City governments and their role in enabling a CE transition (2019)
23. Scheurer, J., Newman, P.: Vauban: A European Model Bridging the Green and Brown Agendas (2009)
24. Ellen MacArthur Foundation: Universal CE Policy Goals (2021). ellenmacarthurfounda-tion.org. Accessed 20 Apr 2021

25. Roderick, Y., McEwan, D., Wheatley, C., Alonso, C.: Comparison of energy performance assessment between LEED, BREEAM and Green Star. In: Eleventh International IBPSA Conference, pp. 27–30 (2009)
26. Borges, L.A., Hammami, F., Wangel, J.: reviewing neighborhood sustainability assessment tools through critical heritage studies. Sustainability 12(4), 1605–1620 (2020)
27. Yoon, J., Park, J.: Comparative analysis of material criteria in green certification rating systems and urban design guidelines. In: Proceedings of 8th Conference of the International Forum on Urbanism (IFoU), pp. 1–19 (2015)

Evaluating the Health-Related Social Costs Associated with the Thermal Uses of the Residential Sector: The Case of Turin

Giulia Crespi[1](✉) , Federico Dell'Anna[2] , Tiziana Binda[3], Cristina Becchio[1] , and Marta Bottero[2]

[1] TEBE-IEEM Research Group, Energy Department, Politecnico di Torino, Corso Duca degli Abruzzi 24, 10129 Torino, Italy
giulia.crespi@polito.it
[2] Interuniversity Department of Regional and Urban Studies and Planning, Politecnico di Torino, Viale Mattioli 39, 10125 Torino, Italy
[3] Politecnico di Torino, Corso Duca degli Abruzzi 24, 10129 Torino, Italy

Abstract. Nowadays, due to the constant increase of outdoor air pollution, the impact on people's health is alarming. Moreover, in the current vulnerable and crucial historical period during which society is experiencing and dealing with the COVID-19 pandemic consequences, this issue is becoming even more important. In line with this, there is an urgent need to provide scientific input to decision-makers to include the assessment of the health-related benefits and costs into urban planning processes. Special attention is devoted to the building sector since the heating service is considered among the main sources of air pollution in the urban environment. In the light of this, the paper aims to estimate the social costs associated with the thermal uses of the residential buildings in Turin (Northern Italy), integrating the energy assessment of the residential building stock, taking advantage of the Reference Building approach for the stock characterization, and the economic quantification and monetization of the air pollution health impacts, using the Cost of Illness (COI) method. Starting from the current situation, different retrofit scenarios for the residential buildings of Turin are hypothesized, to evaluate their capability in reducing the environmental impact of the sector, as well as to increase the social benefits they can guarantee.

Keywords: Outdoor air quality · Health effects · Human capital approach · Retrofit scenarios · Reference building approach

1 Introduction

Today, due to the significant impact that outdoor air pollution has on people's health, the concept of outdoor air quality is becoming increasingly important [1, 2]. In this context, the COVID-19 pandemic has highlighted the importance of adopting resilient spaces to ensure high air quality. However, as early as 2015 the issue was raised by the introduction of health and welfare insurance as a goal for all countries within the

© Springer Nature Switzerland AG 2021
O. Gervasi et al. (Eds.): ICCSA 2021, LNCS 12955, pp. 642–654, 2021.
https://doi.org/10.1007/978-3-030-87007-2_46

Sustainable Development Goals defined by the United Nations [1]. In particular, Goal 3 aims to ensure a healthy life and to promote well-being at all ages for sustainable development [1].

The literature has identified air pollutants involved in urban processes and their effects on different categories of damage, including impacts on human health, damage to buildings and materials, crop and biodiversity losses, and loss of ecosystem services in general [3–6]. Among these damage categories, the health impacts caused by air pollution contribute to most of the estimates of external costs [7, 8]. Public health experts linked air pollution inevitably to worsening morbidity (especially respiratory and cardiovascular diseases) and premature mortality (e.g., Years of Life Lost) [9, 10].

Due to the current high levels of pollutants concentration in cities, the problem of outdoor air quality is becoming particularly relevant in the urban context. Indeed, anthropogenic activities, which are the main sources of pollutants, are more concentrated in urban areas, rather than rural ones. Moreover, according to future projections, almost two-thirds of the world population will live in cities by 2050 [1]. The significant weight of the consequences of atmospheric pollution on people's health, combined with increasing urbanization, requires the identification and development of suitable tools to quantify and estimate the social costs associated with the pollutants emissions on health [11]. In particular, among the anthropogenic causes of outdoor air pollution, the building sector is recognized as one of the main ones, especially considering the heating sector [12]. Indeed, at European level, heating systems alone represent about 30% of total PM10 emissions [13]. This is because space heating and domestic hot water production end-uses cover almost 80% of total final consumption, and a significant portion of this energy is still met by using fossil fuels [14].

In line with this, the study intends to provide scientific outcomes for decision-makers, to support and guide a new form of urban planning, capable of putting people at the center, giving relevance to health and well-being aspects. In detail, the study aims to investigate the relationship between buildings, air pollutants, and people in urban environments, examining the health impacts caused by the PM10 emissions associated with thermal uses of residential buildings. PM10 was selected for the analysis, as it was found to be among the most dangerous pollutants, being responsible for severe respiratory and cardiovascular diseases [15]. In addition, attention was also devoted to the quantification of the CO_2 emissions caused by the residential sector, in line with the global attention on reducing greenhouse gas emissions and with the ambitious targets defined for the building sector at local, national, and international scales. These considerations are also in line with the EU Green Deal, which aims to move the European Union towards a climate-neutral society by 2050, giving importance to satisfy the quality of life for current and future generations [16]. Moreover, the EU Green Deal recognizes the building sector as promising for energy and economic savings [17].

Given the complexity in the design and implementation of energy re-development strategies for buildings and the rigid constraints of financial resources, multiple objectives related to energy saving and environmental compatibility must be pursued. In this perspective, a comprehensive view of costs and benefits is necessary [18–20]. To this end, a multi-step methodological approach was proposed and applied to the case study of the residential sector of the city of Turin, in the North-West of Italy. Its urban residential stock was classified and characterized using the Reference Building (RB) approach [21]. The identified RBs allowed estimating the impact of the sector in terms of PM10 and CO_2 emissions. Then, to investigate and quantify the relationship between air pollutants and health effects, the social costs associated with emissions from the residential sector in its current state were estimated using the Cost of Illness (COI) method to translate the health impacts related to PM10 emissions from buildings in monetary terms [22]. By associating the energy analysis with the socio-economic one, a multi-domain Key Performance Indicator (KPI) was identified, named Social Cost Index, able to estimate the total social cost generated by each unit of emitted PM10. To investigate the effects of different retrofit strategies on the overall social health costs for the case study, a scenario analysis was proposed, to study possible renovation pathways for the residential sector, able to guarantee a reduction of its energy and environmental impact, as well as an increase of the associated social benefits, guaranteed by a lowering of air pollution.

The paper is structured as follows: after the conceptualization of the methodological framework in Sect. 2, Sect. 3 is dedicated to the description of the case study and the main assumptions; Sect. 4 shows the main results of the application, while Sect. 5 draws the main conclusions, illustrating the possible future perspectives.

2   Methods

This section aims to describe the multi-step methodological approach exploited to investigate the impact of the residential building stock in terms of health-related social costs, as well as to explore possible renovation pathways for it, to both reduce its air pollutant emissions and increase the social benefits for the community. The methodological approach couples the energy and environmental assessment of the residential building stock in its current state (developed using the archetype modeling approach) with the socio-economic quantification and estimation of the health-related social costs associated with PM10 pollution. Going into detail, based on the current state analysis, a multi-domain KPI, named Social Cost Index (SCI), was defined to couple the energy and the socio-economic dimensions, allowing to develop an analytical tool able to identify the total social costs associated to the PM10 emissions generated by the building sector. Then, by developing a scenario analysis, diverse renovation pathways are compared and assessed using the developed KPI, to investigate the strategies able to reduce the environmental impact of the sector (in terms of air pollutants emissions reduction) and to increase the social benefits for the community (in terms of social cost reduction) with respect to the current state.

2.1   Energy and Environmental Assessment of the Current State

This section focuses on the estimation of the energy and environmental impact of the residential sector in its current state. Due to the difficulty in individually modeling all the buildings within the stock, the RB approach was used. This term is used to indicate a real or statistically determined typical building, which can be considered representative of a portion of the building stock [21]. The archetype modeling allows estimating the energy consumption of a specific RB, which can be then scaled up to estimate the energy consumption of the whole portion of building stock the RB is representative of, by means of appropriate multiplicative factors (e.g., the total floor area of the portion of building stock represented by the RB or the number of buildings represented by the RB) [21].

In line with this, once the RBs were fully characterized in energy terms, it was possible to estimate the Total Energy Consumption (TEC) of the building stock, as in Eq. (1):

$$TEC(j)\left[\frac{kWh}{y}\right] = \sum_{i=1}^{N} EC(i,j) \cdot SF(i) \tag{1}$$

where j represents the j-th energy vector (e.g. natural gas, oil, biomass, electricity) used to provide the energy service, $EC(i,j)$ represents the annual specific energy consumption of the j-th energy vector of the i-th RB (expressed in kWh/(m²·y)), N is the total number of RBs used to represent the whole residential stock, and $SF(i)$ represents the total stock floor area represented by the i-th RB (expressed in m²).

Then, using appropriate emission factors for each j-th energy vector, it was possible to estimate the Total Pollutants Emissions (TPE) generated by the building stock, according to Eq. (2):

$$TPE(z)\left[\frac{kg}{y}\right] = \sum_{j} TEC(j) \cdot EF(j,z) \tag{2}$$

where z represents the pollutant under investigation (e.g., CO_2, PM10, etc.), $TEC(j)$ represents the total energy consumption of the j-th energy vector (expressed in kWh/y), as resulting from Eq. (1), and $EF(j,z)$ represents the emission factor of the z-th pollutant under investigation for the j-th energy vector (typically expressed in kg/kWh or g/kWh).

2.2 Socio-economic Evaluation of Health-Related Social Costs

To estimate the health-related social impacts caused by the air pollutants emissions from the residential sector, it is necessary to correlate the emissions with the social costs [23]. The estimation of the social costs was developed using the COI method, which allows estimating the economic burden that an illness imposes on the entire society, according to Eq. (3):

$$COI = DC + IC + INC \tag{3}$$

where DC represents the direct costs, IC the indirect costs and INC the intangible costs. The former represents all the healthcare and non-healthcare costs due to treatment and care, which are usually estimated based on market values. Indirect costs, instead, are those associated with productivity losses, as a consequence of workers' absence from workplaces due to the occurrence of the disease. Finally, intangible costs, which are the most difficult to estimate, represent all the costs associated with more subjective factors (e.g., quality of life, pain, and suffering perceptions, etc.) [22].

In order to estimate the total costs associated with air pollution effects, two methods were exploited: the Human Capital Approach (HCA), which was used to estimate the tangible costs (both DC and IC) and the Willingness to Pay (WTP), which was deployed to quantify the intangible costs (*INC*). On the one side, the HCA approach is based on the loss of productivity, which is estimated as the total amount of time from the moment of the pathological event occurrence for the worker and his/her return to work [24]. According to this approach, direct costs are computed by taking into account all the hospitalization and healthcare costs (e.g. ticket visits, exams, medications, etc.) potentially associated with air pollution diseases (e.g. respiratory diseases, cancers, cardiac diseases, etc.). Instead, indirect costs were assumed based on the Work Lost Days (WLD) metric, which is defined as the total number of days during which a worker is unavailable for working [25].

On the other side, the WTP method allows the estimation of non-marketed goods and the measurement of the amount of money that an individual is willing to pay to reduce his/her probability of illness or premature death [24]. This approach estimates the intangible costs, quantified in terms of the Years of Lost Life (YLL) metric, which represents the total years of potential life lost due to premature deaths correlated to PM10 emissions [26].

2.3 Definition of the Multi-domain KPI

Based on the results coming from Sects. 2.1 and 2.2, the environmental impact of the building stock and the associated health-related social costs were calculated. To couple the energy-environmental analysis with the socio-economic assessment, a multi-domain KPI was developed, named Social Cost Index (SCI), aiming to estimate the total social costs associated with each PM10 unit emitted by the building stock under investigation. The indicator was calculated according to Eq. (4):

$$SCI \left[\frac{\text{€}}{t \cdot person} \right] = \frac{COI \left[\frac{\text{€}}{person \cdot y} \right]}{TPE_{PM10} \left[\frac{t}{y} \right]} \tag{4}$$

where *COI* represents the total annual health-related social costs per person (expressed in €/(person·y)), computed using the COI approach, while TPE_{PM10} corresponds to the total annual PM10 emissions caused by the building stock (expressed in t/y).

2.4 Definition and Assessment of Retrofit Scenarios

With the scope of exploring the potential for reducing the environmental and socio-economic impacts of the residential building stock, different retrofit scenarios were hypothesized, all assuming to intervene on the sole HVAC system, by substituting the existing thermal generators. The scenarios allowed to investigate the capability of the renovation strategies to reduce the environmental impact of the analyzed buildings, in terms of reductions of CO_2 and PM10 emissions. Moreover, by keeping fixed the SCI metric calculated in Sect. 2.3 (Eq. (4)), and, thus, keeping fixed the ratio between the socio-economic and the environmental impact in the different scenarios, depending on the changes in PM10 emissions, it was possible to estimate the potentiality of the diverse retrofit scenarios in reducing the total social costs.

3   Application

The methodological framework was applied to the residential sector of the city of Turin (886837 inhabitants [27]), located in the Piedmont Region, in the North-West of Italy. According to the last national census [28], Turin has 63764 buildings, 98% of which are occupied. The analysis described in this paper focused on the residential sector, which represents approximately 57% of the total occupied buildings. In particular, the study was devoted to the assessment of the impact of the thermal uses (space heating and domestic hot water) on urban emissions, since these end-uses represent the most relevant voice of energy consumption in residential buildings and are still mostly based on combustible fuels. Indeed, in Turin, almost 80% of residential buildings use natural gas for thermal uses and less than 1% of the residential stock is equipped with renewable energy systems (e.g., solar thermal collectors, photovoltaic systems, etc.) [28].

3.1   Energy and Environmental Assessment of the Current State

As previously mentioned, to estimate the energy and environmental impact of the residential building stock, the RB approach was used [21]. RBs were derived from the outcomes of the European project "Typology Approach for Building stock energy Assessment (TABULA)", conducted between 2009 and 2012 [21]. The project aimed to create a well-defined database of residential building typologies in Europe, including Italy [21]. According to the TABULA project, 32 typologies of buildings were identified for Italy (and mainly for the Piedmont Region), sub-divided in terms of building typology (apartment block (AB), multi-family house (MFH), terraced house (TH) and single-family house (SFH)) and period of construction (before 1900, 1901–1920, 1921–1945, 1946–1960, 1961–1975, 1976–1990, 1991–2005 and after 2005) [29]. Within the project, each RB was fully characterized in terms of geometry, envelope thermal properties, and space heating (SH) and domestic hot water (DHW) systems characteristics (i.e., type of generator, type of distribution system, type of emission system, and associated efficiencies). Per each RB, SH and DHW energy needs and primary energy consumptions were computed.

In this paper, the whole set of TABULA RBs was considered as representative for the residential stock of Turin, and information on the total stock floor area of Turin households in each construction period identified by TABULA was gathered. Per each RB under investigation, starting from the energy needs for SH and DHW and knowing the efficiencies of the installed sub-systems (generation, distribution, emission, storage), the specific energy consumption associated with each RB ($EC(i,j)$ of Eq. (1)) was computed. Moreover, according to the distribution of the total stock floor area, the total energy consumption per each j-th energy vector was calculated (see Eq. (1)). Finally, using appropriate emission factors for the energy vectors used to satisfy SH and DHW needs [30, 31], CO_2 and PM10 emissions were assessed for the entire residential stock (Eq. (2)).

3.2   Socio-economic Evaluation of Health-Related Social Costs

To estimate the health-related social costs due to PM10 emissions, the COI approach was considered and the HCA and WTP methods were used to compute the different cost voices. Specifically, HCA was used to compute the tangible costs (both direct and indirect). Direct costs were calculated as the sum of hospitalization and medication costs for cardiovascular and respiratory system diseases, using statistical values from [32–34]. Regarding the indirect costs, which are typically computed based on the WLD metric, the value of a single working day (equal to 130.73 €) was estimated as the ratio between the average value of an employee's annual salary [27] and the number of annual productivity days [35]. Total indirect costs were then calculated by multiplying the daily cost by WLD [36]. Finally, WTP was used to estimate the intangible costs. The method is usually exploited by submitting surveys to the concerned population, in order to estimate the value they give to a year of life; due to time constraints, a reference value equal to 145320 €/y was derived from [26] and used as an estimation of the YLL metric.

Based on the results of Sect. 3.1 (in terms of total PM10 emissions generated by the residential sector) and on the obtained COI estimations, SCI was computed for the current state, allowing to quantify the total social costs associated with each PM10 unit emitted by the building stock under analysis.

3.3 Definition and Assessment of Retrofit Scenarios

To explore the potential social benefits associated with the renovation of the residential building stock of Turin, different retrofit scenarios were hypothesized. Specifically, two scenarios were defined for the residential buildings under investigation, assuming to retrofit only SH and DHW generation systems, by substituting the original RB energy systems, without intervening on the envelope. Assuming not to retrofit the most recent buildings (built after 2005) and the oldest category (built before 1945) due to retrofit restrictions for historical or artistical reasons, retrofit scenarios were applied only to buildings built between 1946 and 2005, which represent approximately 75% of the urban residential stock.

The developed System Retrofit (SR) scenarios differ in the alternative technological options considered eligible for retrofit. Specifically, the first SR scenario (SR1) considered the substitution of the original generation system of the RBs with either a condensing gas boiler, a biomass boiler, or an electric heat pump. The distribution of the technologies among the RBs to retrofit was done based on the available information of the total number of incentive requests in Italy in 2018 for the three considered technologies [37]. Moreover, in order to highlight the impact of the biomass source in terms of local air pollution, the second SR scenario (SR2) assumed to have at disposal for the substitution of the original RB system only condensing gas boilers and electric heat pumps.

For both SR1 and SR2 scenarios, four diverse renovation rates were considered, assuming to intervene on the 25%, 50%, 75%, and 100% of the portion of building stock to be potentially retrofitted (i.e. 75% of the residential building stock, as previously mentioned).

4   Results and Discussion

From the energy-environmental standpoint, according to the RB-based modeling of Turin residential building stock in its current state, a total of approximately 1735 kt/y of CO_2 emissions and 12 t/y of PM10 emissions was obtained. Moving to the socio-economic analysis and focusing solely on PM10 emissions (due to their well-known impact on people's health), an overall social cost of 1192 €/(person·y) was obtained, in accordance with the COI approach. In particular, based on the HCA method, a social cost of 492 €/(person·y) was attained, regarding the sole direct and indirect costs, while, according to the WTP method, a value of 700 €/(person·y) was correlated to the intangible costs. Based on these results, the multi-domain KPI was calculated to show the link between the PM10 emissions generated by the residential buildings and the associated social costs estimated according to the COI method. A SCI value of approximately 98 €/(t·person) was obtained, meaning that ton of PM10 emissions caused a total social cost of almost 100 € per person.

The scenario analysis allowed, on the one side, to estimate the potential environmental benefits of the assumed renovation strategies, assessing both global (CO_2) and local (PM10) emissions reductions. On the other side, socio-economic benefits (or costs) associated with the retrofit scenarios can be estimated, based on the developed SCI multi-domain metric.

According to the first topic, Fig. 1 and Fig. 2 summarize the results obtained for SR1 and SR2 scenarios, in terms of CO_2 and PM10 emissions for the four considered renovation rates. Both scenarios guarantee improvements in terms of CO_2 emissions, obtaining approximately 27% and 24% reductions with respect to the current state for SR1 and SR2 scenarios, respectively, considering the 100% renovation rate. In particular, the presence of the biomass source in SR1 (see Fig. 1a) guarantees a higher reduction of CO_2 emissions, due to the lower emissions generated by biomass boilers with respect to the other alternative solutions (due to lower emission factors for biomass). Conversely, when moving to PM10 emissions trends, an opposite result is visible; indeed, the SR1 scenario provokes an increase of PM10 emissions (see Fig. 2a), being the biomass option the highest PM10 emitter among the considered alternatives; moreover, biomass generators efficiencies are lower with respect to the other technological options, for both SH and DHW. For this reason, when moving to the biomass-free SR2 scenario, indeed, a decrement of PM10 emissions is visible (see Fig. 2b), reaching a 30% reduction with respect to the current state, for the 100% renovation rate. Clearly, the renovation rate influences the results; as mentioned, both scenarios were built assuming different renovation rates, varying from 25% to 100%, to simulate strong retrofit uptakes. As expected, the higher the renovation rate, the higher the associated emissions reductions are.

Furthermore, the scenario analysis allowed to estimate the social benefits (or costs) induced by the variations of PM10 emissions per each scenario and renovation rate. Figure 3 shows the obtained environmental benefits, in terms of avoided PM10 emissions (expressed in t/y) and the health-related social benefits (expressed in €/(person·y)) for SR1, while Fig. 4 summarizes the same results for SR2. In both figures, a negative value for the emissions corresponds to an increment of buildings-related emissions with

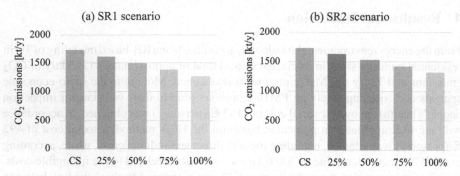

Fig. 1. CO$_2$ emissions trends for the current state (CS) and the four renovation rates (25%, 50%, 75%, 100%), for SR1 (a) and SR2 (b).

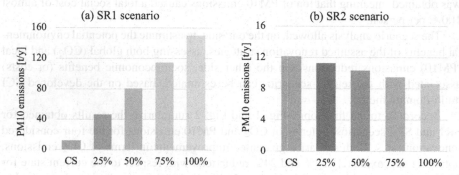

Fig. 2. PM10 emissions trends for the current state (CS) and the four renovation rates (25%, 50%, 75%, 100%), for SR1 (a) and SR2 (b).

respect to the current state, while a negative value for the net social benefits represents a cost (i.e., increment of social costs compared to the current state).

As expected, the SR1 scenario provokes an increase in social costs with respect to the current state, due to the increment of PM10 emissions. As reported in Fig. 3, an economic

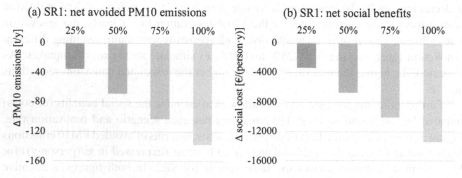

Fig. 3. Net avoided PM10 emissions (a) and net social costs/benefits (b) for SR1 scenario.

loss of 3351 €/(person·y) is visible for the lowest renovation rate (25%), which increases up to approximately 13406 €/(person·y) for the 100% renovation rate case. Conversely, when considering the SR2 scenario (Fig. 4), a socio-economic benefit is highlighted; in particular, the highest renovation rate of 100% allows achieving a social benefit of 351 €/(person·y).

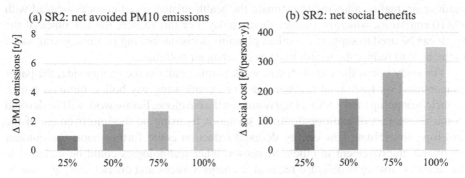

Fig. 4. Net avoided PM10 emissions (a) and net social costs/benefits (b) for SR2 scenario.

5   Conclusions and Future Perspectives

Nowadays, outdoor air quality is a challenge for the urban environment, especially considering the impact that air pollutants have on people's health. This topic needs to be carefully addressed and introduced in new urban energy planning, aiming to put people's well-being, health, and satisfaction at the center, and to transform cities into safer and healthier environments. In the future energy transition of cities, the role of the building sector is crucial, due to its still high environmental impact, mainly associated with the use of heating systems, which are still mostly based on fossil fuels.

The paper fits with this background, aiming to explore the relationship between the air pollution caused by the residential building sector (and mainly by thermal uses) and the health-related social costs for the community, using the city of Turin as case study. Moreover, thanks to the definition of a multi-domain KPI, named Social Cost Index, the work allowed to estimate the social cost due to the PM10 emissions generated by the building stock under investigation. The social cost estimation was developed using the Cost of Illness approach, coupling two evaluation methods (Human Capital Approach and Willingness to Pay).

Starting from the energy and socio-economic assessment of the current state, the work developed a scenario analysis, evaluating the capability of diverse retrofit strategies for the heating systems substitution to reduce the environmental impact of the sector, and, thus, to obtain benefits for the entire society. The results brought out that the use of biomass can produce a negative local environmental effect, increasing PM10 emissions with respect to the current state; on the other side, when biomass is excluded from the renovation strategies, a 30% PM10 emission reduction can be achieved. Based on the SCI metric, the social costs related to the developed retrofit scenarios were estimated, allowing to compute the possible benefits achievable thanks to the renovation of the building stock. As a consequence of the environmental considerations, only SR2 scenario (which does not consider the possible exploitation of biomass boilers in urban environments) permits to obtain some benefits for the society, clearly increasing with the increment of the renovation rate.

In conclusion, the obtained results have shown the impact of residential heating on outdoor air quality, allowing to estimate the health-related social costs associated with PM10 emissions, which is a major theme today. For this reason, the outcomes of the work can be used to support the urban planning decision-making process, giving value to the need to reduce the health impacts of urban air pollution.

The study opens the way to future work in this field. On the energy side, the paper concentrated on traditional technologies (i.e., condensing gas boiler, biomass boiler, electric heat pump) and without intervening on the envelope. Future work will be devoted to the assessment of additional retrofit scenarios focusing on the improvement of the envelope, to evaluate how energy demand reduction could further boost the outdoor air quality improvement in cities. Moreover, other technologies could be included in the analysis, among which also renewable energy sources and district heating. Finally, concerning the socio-economic assessment, future work can be deployed to estimate the local WTP, by submitting ad-hoc surveys to the population of Turin.

References

1. United Nations: Department of economic and social affairs, sustainable development. https://sdgs.un.org. Accessed 10 May 2021
2. Becchio, C., Crespi, G., Binda, T., Corgnati, S.P.: Air pollution and health effects: review of indicators and evaluation methods. In: Proceedings of the 15th ROOMVENT Conference - Energy efficient ventilation for healthy future buildings (2021)
3. Assumma, V., Bottero, M., Datola, G., Pezzoli, A., Quagliolo, C.: Climate change and urban resilience. preliminary insights from an integrated evaluation framework. In: Bevilacqua, C., Calabrò, F., Della Spina, L. (eds.) NMP 2020. SIST, vol. 178, pp. 676–685. Springer, Cham (2021). https://doi.org/10.1007/978-3-030-48279-4_63
4. Mutahi, A.W., Borgese, L., Marchesi, C., Gatari, M.J., Depero, L.E.: Indoor and outdoor air quality for sustainable life: a case study of rural and urban settlements in poor neighbourhoods in Kenya. Sustainability 13(4), 2417 (2021). https://doi.org/10.3390/su13042417
5. D'Alessandro, D., et al.: COVID-19 and living space challenge. Well-being and public health recommendations for a healthy, safe, and sustainable housing. Acta Biomed. 91, 61–75 (2020). https://doi.org/10.23750/abm.v91i9-S.10115
6. Underhill, L.J., Milando, C.W., Levy, J.I., Dols, W.S., Lee, S.K., Fabian, M.P.: Simulation of indoor and outdoor air quality and health impacts following installation of energy-efficient retrofits in a multifamily housing unit. Build. Environ. 170, 106507 (2020). https://doi.org/10.1016/j.buildenv.2019.106507
7. Becchio, C., Bottero, M.C., Corgnati, S.P., Dell'Anna, F.: Evaluating health benefits of urban energy retrofitting: an application for the city of Turin. In: Bisello, A., Vettorato, D., Laconte, P., Costa, S. (eds.) SSPCR 2017. GET, pp. 281–304. Springer, Cham (2018). https://doi.org/10.1007/978-3-319-75774-2_20
8. Silveira, C., et al.: Assessment of health benefits related to air quality improvement strategies in urban areas: an impact pathway approach. J. Environ. Manage. 183, 694–702 (2016). https://doi.org/10.1016/j.jenvman.2016.08.079

9. Boesch, H.-J., Kahlmeier, S., Sommer, H., van Kempen, E., Staatsen, B., Racioppi, F.: Economic valuation of transport-related health effects: review of methods and development of practical approaches with a specific focus on children. WHO Reg. Off. Eur. (2008). https://doi.org/10.5167/uzh-152023

10. Pervin, T., Gerdtham, U.G., Lyttkens, C.H.: Societal costs of air pollution-related health hazards: a review of methods and results (2008). http://www.resource-allocation.com/content/6/1/19

11. Saptutyningsih, E., Ma'ruf, A.: Measuring the impact of urban air pollution: hedonic price analysis and health production function. J. Ekon. Pembang. Kaji. Masal. Ekon. dan Pembang. **16**, 146 (2015). https://doi.org/10.23917/jep.v16i2.1459

12. Caprioli, C., Bottero, M., De Angelis, E.: Supporting policy design for the diffusion of cleaner technologies: a spatial empirical agent-based model. ISPRS Int. J. Geo-Inf. **9**, 581 (2020). https://doi.org/10.3390/ijgi9100581

13. European Environmental Agency (EEA): Air quality in Europe – 2018 Report (2018)

14. European Commission. https://ec.europa.eu/energy/topics/energy-efficiency/heating-and-cooling_en. Accessed 18 April 2020

15. Silvera, C., et al.: Economic evaluation of air pollution impacts on human health: an overview of applied methodologies. WIT Trans. Ecol. Environ. **198**, 181–192 (2015)

16. European Commission: Communication from the commission to the European parliament, the council, the European economic and social committee and the committee of regions, The European Green Deal, COM/2019/640 final (2019)

17. Napoli, G., Barbaro, S., Giuffrida, S., Trovato, M.R.: The European green deal: new challenges for the economic feasibility of energy retrofit at district scale. In: Bevilacqua, C., Calabrò, F., Della Spina, L. (eds.) NMP 2020. SIST, vol. 178, pp. 1248–1258. Springer, Cham (2021). https://doi.org/10.1007/978-3-030-48279-4_116

18. D'Alpaos, C., Bragolusi, P.: Prioritization of energy retrofit strategies in public housing: an AHP model. In: Calabrò, F., Della Spina, L., Bevilacqua, C. (eds.) ISHT 2018. SIST, vol. 101, pp. 534–541. Springer, Cham (2019). https://doi.org/10.1007/978-3-319-92102-0_56

19. Gabrielli, L., Ruggeri, A.G.: Developing a model for energy retrofit in large building portfolios: energy assessment, optimization and uncertainty. Energy Build. **202**, 109356 (2019). https://doi.org/10.1016/j.enbuild.2019.109356

20. Dell'Ovo, M., Frej, E.A., Oppio, A., Capolongo, S., Morais, D.C., de Almeida, A.T.: FITradeoff method for the location of healthcare facilities based on multiple stakeholders' preferences. In: Lecture Notes in Business Information Processing, pp. 97–112. Springer Verlag (2018). https://doi.org/10.1007/978-3-319-92874-6_8

21. Ballarini, I., Corgnati, S.P., Corrado, V.: Use of reference building to assess the energy saving potentials of the residential building stock: the experience of TABULA project. Energy Policy **68**, 273–284 (2014). https://doi.org/10.1016/j.enpol.2014.01.027

22. Marisha, S., Sunarya, S., Yustiana, Y.: Economic valuation on carbon sequestration and carbon stocks at green open space based on cost of illness. In: IOP Conference Series: Earth and Environmental. Science, vol. 528, pp. 012035 (2020). https://doi.org/10.1088/1755-1315/528/1/012035

23. Jo, C.: Cost-of-illness studies: concepts, scopes and methods. Clin. Mol. Hepatol. **20**(4), 327–337 (2014)

24. Grattini, L., Ghislandi, S., Tediosi, F.: L'inclusione dei costi indiretti nella valutazione economiche: la situazione italiana. Centro di economia sanitaria (2000)

25. Martuzzi, M., Mitis, F., Iavarone, I., Serinelli, M.: Health impact of PM10 and Ozone in 13 Italian cities. World Health Organization Regional Office for Europe (2007)

26. Hurley, F., et al.: Service contract for carrying out cost-benefit analysis of air quality related issues, in particular air for European (CAFÉ) program. Methodology for the cost-benefit analysis for CAFÉ, Volume 2: health impact assessment, AEA Technology Enviroment (2005).

27. ISTAT Statistics. http://dati.istat.it/Index.aspx?DataSetCode=DCCV_REDNETFAMFONT ERED. Accessed 25 March 2021

28. ISTAT   Statistics.   http://dati-censimentopopolazione.istat.it/Index.aspx?DataSetCode= DICA_EDIFICI1_COM. Accessed 25 March 2021

29. Corrado, V., Ballarini, I., Corgnati, S.P.: Building Typology Brouchure - Italy, Fascicolo sulla tipologia Edilizia Italiana (2014)

30. European Energy Agency: EMEP/EEA air pollutant emission inventory guidebook 2019 (2019)

31. Istituto Superiore per la Protezione e la Ricerca Ambientale (ISPRA). http://www.sinanet. isprambiente.it/it/sia-ispra/serie-storiche-emissioni/fattori-di-emissione-per-le-sorgenti-di-combustione-stazionarie-in-italia/at_download/file. Accessed 25 March 2020

32. Prezzario Regione Piemonte. https://www.regione.piemonte.it/web/sites/default/files/media/ documenti/2018-10/tariffario_prestazioni_ricoveri_rp.pdf. Accessed 31 March 2020

33. Prezzario Regione Piemonte. https://www.regione.piemonte.it/web/sites/default/files/media/ documenti/2018-10/tariffario_prestazioni_specialistiche_rp.pdf. Accessed 31 March 2020

34. Agenzia Italiana del Farmaco (AIFA). https://www.aifa.gov.it/storico-liste-di-trasparenza. Accessed 31 March 2020

35. Agenzie delle Entrate. https://www.agenziaentrate.gov.it/. Accessed 20 April 2020

36. Ostro, B., Feng, W.Y., Broadwin, R., Green, S., Lipsett, M.: The effect of components of fine particulate air pollution on mortality in California: results from CALFINE. Environ. Health Perspect. 115(1), 13–19 (2007)

37. Bertini, I., Federici, A.: Analisi e risultati delle policy di efficienza energetica del nostro paese. Rapporto Annuale Efficienza energetica (2019)

International Workshop on Ecosystem Services: Nature's Contribution to People in Practice. Assessment Frameworks, Models, Mapping, and Implications (NC2P 2021)

Can Planning Policies to Counter Hydro-Geological Hazard be Grounded on Ecosystem Service Assessment? Suggestions from a Sardinian Case Study

Federica Isola⬵, Sabrina Lai(✉)⬵, Federica Leone⬵, and Corrado Zoppi⬵

Department of Civil and Environmental Engineering and Architecture, University of Cagliari, via Marengo, 2, 09123 Cagliari, Italy

`{federica.isola,sabrinalai,federicaleone,zoppi}@unica.it`

Abstract. This study focuses on the relations between the definition and implementation of regional green infrastructure (RGI or GI, in the general case) and environmental hazard, identified by flooding and landslide phenomena. The implementation of GI within planning policies could improve the effectiveness of policies aimed at promoting landscape and environmental protection. GIs are spatial structures supplying a wide range of ecosystem services, which entail interactions with areas characterized by different levels of environmental hazard. GI is considered in this study as a provider of ecosystem services related to the following aspects: nature, natural resources and conservation and enhancement of biodiversity; landscape, culture and recreation; agricultural and forestry production; local climate regulation; and, climate change impact mitigation through capture and storage of carbon dioxide. A methodological framework is defined and implemented into a subregional spatial context located in the coastal zone of Eastern Sardinia. The methodology is aimed at assessing the relations between GI and environmental hazard through inferential analysis based on dichotomous-choice Logit models in order to increase the understanding and interpretation of the role that could be played by GI as regards control of environmental risk, and to identify policy recommendations thereof.

Keywords: Environmental hazard · Green infrastructure · Ecosystem services

1 Introduction

Climate change negatively impacts on the hydrological cycle of the Earth and on phenomena connected with water management. Hydrogeological instability is conceptualized as a change of the natural flow of water on, above and below the surface of the Earth due to its interaction with the anthropized spatial system [1]. Therefore, hydrogeological instability represents a hazard to local population, infrastructures, and the economic and productive system [2]. For instance, in 2018 in Italy 7,275 municipalities (91% of the Italian ones) were found to be exposed to landslide and/or flooding hazards. Moreover,

© Springer Nature Switzerland AG 2021
O. Gervasi et al. (Eds.): ICCSA 2021, LNCS 12955, pp. 657–674, 2021.
https://doi.org/10.1007/978-3-030-87007-2_47

16% of the national territory is classified as high-hazard area, and 1.28 million of residents live in areas featured by landslide hazard and more than 6 million in flooding hazard areas [2].

Typical consequences of hydrological phenomena are landslides, flooding, coastal erosion, subsidence, and avalanche. Although for a long time gray infrastructure has represented the only operational tool to address landslide and flooding hazard and related environmental damages [3], the implementation of nature-based solutions has more recently advocated to be very effective in mitigating the impacts of such disasters [4]. Therefore, the use of green infrastructure (GI) has gained increasing importance within the international debate. Although the technical functions of GI are connected to the management of the integrated water cycle, GI should be mainly identified in relation to three issues [4]: smart growth, climate change adaptation, and social health and wellbeing [5]. The relation between GI and hydrological instability is a matter of study in the current literature. Chen et al. [6] assess the effectiveness of the implementation of practices based on GI on water supply and quality. Papathoma-Koehle and Glade [7] analyze how changes in vegetation land cover influence landslide events in terms of occurrences, consequences, and implications. However, although the implementation of GI based on natural and semi-natural areas is quite effective to mitigate the negative impacts of landslides and floods, its use is still limited due to the difficulty to project and forecast economic impacts and feasibility [4, 8]. Indeed, the assessment of GI-related planning policies is often based on counterfactual methodologies which imply the availability of huge databases and complex economic approaches, often too costly in terms of financial resources and time needed to obtain reliable outcomes [9].

The article is structured into four sections as follows. The second section describes the study area, shows how the dataset is built, and discusses the methodological approach, which combines a GIS-based spatial analysis with a regression model. The third section presents the results derived from the implementation of the methodological approach in relation to the study area. The results are discussed in the fourth section which also identifies some implications of the study in terms of planning policy recommendations.

2   Materials and Methods

This section is organized as follows. In the first subsection the study area is described. In the second, the discrete-choice Logit model estimated to detect the relations between RGI and environmental hazard is defined and discussed. In the last subsection, the data which operationalize the model are presented.

2.1   Study Area

The area chosen for this study lies on the eastern side of Sardinia, one of the main islands in the Mediterranean Sea (Fig. 1). Bordering the Tyrrhenian Sea to the East, the study area stretches over 1306.12 km², roughly amounting to one twentieth of the whole island. As shown in Fig. 1 (panel "C"), fourteen coastal municipalities are fully comprised within the study area, with a fifteenth one (Gairo) only included as far as its coastal area is concerned; the latter is an enclave completely separated from the rest of the inland municipal territory to which it belongs, and enclosed between the sea and the two municipalities of Cardedu and Tertenia.

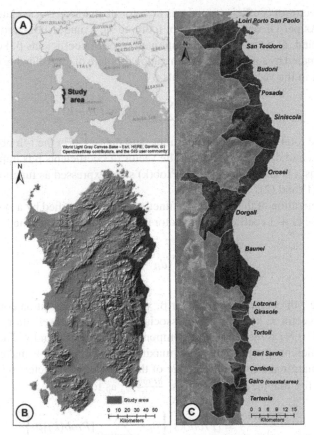

Fig. 1. Location of the study area within Italy (A) and Sardinia (B), and municipalities included therein (C).

2.2 Methodological Framework

Building on Nerlove and Press' [10], Greene's [11], and Zoppi and Lai's [12] research, this study implements a Logit dichotomous choice model. Logit models (LMs) associate a logistic probability distribution to the two events that characterize the phenomenon at stake. The model considers a set of two events {0,1}, with probability of event "1" and "0" given by, respectively:

$$\text{Prob}(1) = \frac{e^{\beta_1' x_1}}{1 + \sum_{k=0}^{1} e^{\beta_k' x_k}} \tag{1}$$

$$\text{Prob}(0) = \frac{1}{1 + \sum_{k=0}^{1} e^{\beta'_k x_k}} \tag{2}$$

where β is a vector of coefficients and x is a vector of characteristics related to the event k, k $\in \{0,1\}$. As per Greene ([11], p. 666, footnote 3), a unique non-zero vector β_1 can be identified, and, as a consequence, a unique vector of coefficients β, i.e. vector β_1 in Eq. (1), is estimated by solving the maximization problem of the following log-likelihood function, ln L, in the vector of coefficients β^1:

$$\ln L = \sum_{i=1}^{M} \sum_{k=0}^{1} d_{ik} \ln Prob(k) \tag{3}$$

where M is the total number of observations, and $d_{ik} = 1$ if in the i-th observations the event k occurs, and $d_{ik} = 0$ otherwise. The vector of coefficients β is implemented into (3) through Eqs. (1) and (2), where the Prob(k)'s are expressed as functions of vector β through Eqs. (1) and (2).

The maximization of the likelihood function ln L is identified by a system of $N + 1$ equations in the $N + 1$ coefficients of vector β. Each equation takes the following form:

$$\frac{\partial \ln L}{\partial \beta_j} = \sum_{i=1}^{M} [d_{ik} - Prob(k_i)] x_{ij} \tag{4}$$

where β_j is the j-th coefficients of vector β, x_{ij} is the i-th observation concerning characteristic j of vector x, k_i is the event associated to the i-th observation, such that k $\in$ i$\{0,1\}$, and j $\in \{0,N\}$ is the number of components of vectors β and x. The values of the vector of coefficients β which solve the maximization problem (4) make it possible to calculate the marginal effects of a change of the value of a characteristic x_i of vector x on the probability that the event k occurs, $\frac{\partial Prob(k)}{\partial x_i}$, as follows:

$$\frac{\partial Prob(k)}{\partial x_i} = [Prob(k)] \left\{ \beta_i - \sum_{j=0}^{N} [Prob(k)] \beta_j \right\} \tag{5}$$

The model's estimates make it possible to derive the marginal effects of Eq. (5), for instance as regards the x_i's mean values, and the probabilities of the events k's. Furthermore, the model makes it possible to derive the standard errors of the components of vector β and of the marginal effects of Eq. (5).

Model (1) through (5) operationalizes as follows.

Two models are estimated, where the dependent dichotomous variables are, respectively, flood hazard and landslide hazard. These variables correspond to the k's events in model (1) through (5), k $\in \{0,1\}$.

The characteristics which are the components of vector x $= (1, x_1, ..., x_N)$ and their descriptive statistics are reported in Table 1. The occurrences of the k's events are conditional upon the X_i's characteristics, according to a logistic distribution estimated

---

[1] If $\beta_j^* = \beta_j + q$ for any nonzero vector q, the identical set of probabilities result, as the terms involving q all drop out. A convenient normalization that solves the problem is to assume vector $\beta_0 = 0$. The probability for Y $= 0$ is therefore given by Eq. (2) ([11], p. 666).

through the identification of the coefficients which are the components of vector β, by implementing model (1) through (5). The characteristics are the following: natural value, conservation value, landscape value, recreational value, agroforestry value, land surface temperature and carbon dioxide capture and storage capacity. Moreover, altitude and slope are used as control variables. These characteristics are described and discussed in the following subsection.

2.3 Data

Because the island of Sardinia is identified as a single macro-basin, a single watershed management plan and its PAI (an acronym for "Piano di Assetto Idrogeologico", verbatim

Table 1. Definition of variables and descriptive statistics.

Variable	Definition	Mean	St.dev.
FH	Flood hazard - dichotomous variable: - 1 if any level of flood hazard but no hazard is detected; - 0 if no hazard is detected	0.090	0.286
LH	Landslide hazard - dichotomous variable: - 1 if the level of flood hazard is "very high," "high" or "medium"; - 0 if either the level of landslide hazard is moderate or no hazard is detected	0.448	0.497
Natval	Natural value. Continuous variable in the interval [0,1]. Potential capability of biodiversity to supply final ecosystem services in face of threats and pressures it is subject to The value was calculated using the software "InVEST"[a], tool "Habitat quality". Data inputs for the model were: - land cover types as per the 2008 Regional land cover map (rasterized); - raster maps of ten spatial threats listed in the standard data forms for Natura 2000 sites. The ten selected threats are as follows: cultivation; grazing; removal of forest undergrowth; salt works; paths, tracks, and cycling tracks; roads and motorways; airports; urbanized areas; discharges; fire and fire suppression; - weights and decay distance for each threat from expert judgments; - sensitivity of each land cover to each threat from expert judgments; - accessibility to sources of degradation, in terms of relative protection to habitats provided by legal institutions. The three categories we used are as follows: natural parks, areas protected and managed by the regional Forestry Agency, Natura 2000 sites	0.844	0.269

(*continued*)

Table 1. (*continued*)

Variable	Definition	Mean	St.dev.
Consval	Conservation value. Continuous variable in the interval [0,1]. Presence of natural habitat types of Community interest (as listed in Annex I of the Habitats Directive) and conservation importance thereof *Consval* = 0 for areas where no habitats of Community interest have been identified; else *Consval* = P*(R + T + K) (normalized in the interval [0,1]) where: - priority habitats P = 1.5 in case of priority habitat, else P = 1; - rarity R = [1, 5] depending on the number of Natura 2000 standard data forms in which the habitat is listed within the regional Natura 2000 network; the higher the occurrences, the lower the value of R; - threats T = [1, 5] depending on the number of threats recorded in the standard data forms for the Natura 2000 sites in our study area; the higher the number of threats, the higher the value of T; - knowledge K = [1, 4] depending on the level of current knowledge (e.g. number of onsite surveys, existence of up-to-date and reliable monitoring data) of a given habitat within the regional Natura 2000 network; the lower the knowledge, the higher the value of K	0.148	0.195
Landsval	Landscape value. Discrete variable in the interval [0,1] accounting for whether, and to what extent, a given parcel of land is protected under the 2006 Regional Landscape Plan either as "Environmental landscape asset" or as "Cultural-historic landscape asset". For each protection level defined in the Regional Landscape Plan, a score was assigned in the [0,1] interval depending on the level of restriction. In case of overlapping protection levels, the maximum score was assigned to the parcel	0.521	0.497
Recrval	Recreation value. Continuous variable in the interval [0,1]. Recreational attractiveness of landscapes and natural habitats. The average photo-user-days per year between 2010 and 2014 was calculated using the software "InVEST" (tool "Recreation") and a 3-km grid, and subsequently normalized in the interval [0,1]	0.006	0.027
Agrofor	Agroforestry value. In the absence of comprehensive spatial data on agricultural and forestry productivity, estimated value of rural plots (k€/ha) as of 2017 was used as a proxy	3.601	4.029
LST	Land surface temperature detected in August 2019 (K)	311.174	3.554
CO2Stor	Carbon dioxide storage per unit of area ($Mg/(100\ m^2)$)	1.098	0.350
Altitud	Elevation (m)	234.084	226.531

(continued)

Table 1. (*continued*)

Variable	Definition	Mean	St.dev.
Slope	Slope. The inclination of slope is provided as percent rise, also referred to as percent slope. The values range from 0 to essentially infinity. A flat surface is 0% and a 45-degree surface is 100%, and as the surface becomes more vertical, the percent rise becomes increasingly larger[b]	23.009	21.501

[a]InVEST (Integrated Valuation of Ecosystem Services and Tradeoffs) is a free software program developed by the Natural Capital Project and available from http://data.naturalcapitalproject.org/nightly-build/invest-users-guide/html/index.html.
[b]https://desktop.arcgis.com/en/arcmap/10.7/tools/spatial-analyst-toolbox/slope.htm.

"Hydrogeological Setting Plan") concern the whole region. The Sardinian PAI, first approved in 2004, in its initial version mapped hydrogeological risk and hazard only within specific parts of the island, such as, for instance, those in which severe landslides were known to have taken place in history, or those in which so-called "critic river segments" were identified through hydraulic models [13].

Since 2004, both flood and landslide hazard and risk maps in the Sardinian PAI have continuously been updated through two main mechanisms: first, studies commissioned by the regional administration; second, studies commissioned by municipal administrations, usually as part of their land-use making processes, because updated flood and landslide assessments concerning the whole municipal territory are prerequisite for the approval of land-use plans. Municipal assessments make use of the same hazard levels as the PAI, i.e. those listed in Table 2, and of the same methodologies as the River Basin Authority, which means that the outcomes of the regional and municipal assessments are comparable.

Despite being thoroughly examined and approved by the River Basin Authority, not all the assessments and maps commissioned by the municipalities call for a revision of the PAI; in other words, it is up to the River Basin Authority to decide when the maps commissioned and produced at the municipal level are to be integrated within a new version of the regional PAI. Therefore, when looking for data on landslide and flood hazard in Sardinia, one must necessarily take account of four datasets, two for each type of hazard, freely available from the Regional geoportal[2]: first, the most updated versions of the PAI maps; second, the maps commissioned by the municipalities and approved by the River Basin Authority.

In the study area, for each hazard type the two spatial datasets partly overlap in twelve of the fifteen municipalities, while for three of them (Bari Sardo, Dorgali, and Baunei) a study at the municipal level has not been produced and approved so far. However, the area of interest for this research was analyzed within a study commissioned by the regional administration and approved in 2011[3] that led to an early revision of the Sardinian PAI, which means that both landslide and flood hazard data for the three

---

[2] http://www.sardegnageoportale.it/webgis2/sardegnamappe/?map=pai.
[3] http://www.regione.sardegna.it/index.php?xsl=509&s=1&v=9&c=9305&tb=8374&st=13.

Table 2. Flood and landslide hazard classes as per the Sardinian PAI ([14], pp. 23–25).

Hazard level	*FH* level definition	*LH* level definition
0	Absent (not even mapped)	Absent
1	Low (return period: 500 years)	Moderate
2	Moderate (return period: 200 years)	Medium
3	High (return period: 100 years)	High
4	Very high (return period: 50 years)	Very high

aforementioned municipalities can be retrieved from the regional PAI, although in some parts of Dorgali's territory the landslide hazard map is void. For each municipality in the study area, Table 3 provides details on the most updated landside and flood hazard maps (bearing in mind that the PAI *LH* and *FH* maps concern all of the 15 municipal territories).

The rest of this section looks briefly at the nine independent variables (defined in Table 1) and data used to map them.

For a full methodological account about the production of *Natval, Consval, Landsval*, and *Recrval* maps, the reader can refer to [15] and [16].

With regards to *Agrofor*, the value of rural plots in 2017 was estimated using the 2018 CORINE land cover map[4] as spatial reference and two main datasets for agriculture and forestry areas, both providing monetary values of the land per unit of area. As for agricultural areas, a spreadsheet[5] produced by the National Research Council of Agriculture and Agricultural Economics was used, which provides the value of land parcels based on the type of crop, on elevation area, and on location (by taking provinces, i.e. Italian NUTS3 statistical regions, as the basic spatial units). As for forestry areas, data are available from the National Revenue Agency[6] and the values are here differentiated according to type of production, provinces, and rural regions (i.e., smaller spatial units contained within provinces).

The *LST* map was developed based only on Landsat 8 satellite imagery acquired in 2019, on August 11 and 20, and available by the USGS's Earth Resources Observation and Science[7]. A full methodological account is provided in [17].

The carbon dioxide capture and storage capacity (*CO2Stor*) map was produced using the InVEST "Carbon Storage and Sequestration" model[8] fed with the regional 2008 land-cover map coupled with look-up tables associating land covers to three carbon pools as follows: i. above-ground biomass, ii. soil organic content, iii. dead organic matter; a fourth carbon pool (concerning below-ground biomass) can actually be fed into the

---

[4] https://land.copernicus.eu/pan-european/corine-land-cover/clc2018.

[5] https://crea-qa.cube.extrasys.it/-/banca-dati-valori-fondiari-bdvf.

[6] https://www.agenziaentrate.gov.it/portale/web/guest/schede/fabbricatiterreni/omi/banche-dati/valori-agricoli-medi/valori-agricoli-medi-sardegna.

[7] USGS. Science for a Changing World—EarthExplorer: https://earthexplorer.usgs.gov.

[8] https://storage.googleapis.com/releases.naturalcapitalproject.org/invest-userguide/latest/carbonstorage.html.

Table 3. Municipalities included in the study area: size and approval date of the most recent hazard maps.

Municipality	Area [km²]	Approval of the hazard maps [year]	Study commissioned by
Bari Sardo	37.43	2011	Sardinian regional administration
Baunei	212.08	2011	Sardinian regional administration
Budoni	56.17	2012	Municipal administration
Cardedu	32.35	2013	Municipal administration
Dorgali	224.82	2011	Sardinian regional administration
Gairo (coastal area only)	8.62	2014	Municipal administration
Girasole	13.23	2012	Municipal administration
Loiri Porto San Paolo	118.43	2012	Municipal administration
Lotzorai	16.51	2015	Municipal administration
Orosei	90.55	2013	Municipal administration
Posada	33.07	2010	Municipal administration
San Teodoro	104.76	2015	Municipal administration
Siniscola	199.87	2013	Municipal administration
Tertenia	117.76	2015	Municipal administration
Tortolì	40.47	2011	Municipal administration

model, but no information was available. Data for the three remaining carbon pools was gathered from the 2005 National Inventory of Italian Forests[9] and from a regional pilot

---

[9] https://www.sian.it/inventarioforestale.

project concerning land units and soil capacity in Sardinia[10]. For a full methodological account, the reader can refer to [18].

Finally, elevation (*Altitud*) and slope (*Slope*) were retrieved from the 10-m resolution digital terrain model available from the Regional geoportal[11].

For each variable, Table 4 summarizes data inputs and their sources, tool employed (when available; otherwise, ordinary GIS tools were used), and references.

Finally, through rasterization of vector maps and resampling of raster maps, a 30-m resolution raster map was developed for each variable; by overlaying such maps, an attribute table providing for each cell the corresponding value of each variable was produced to feed the regression model presented in Sect. 2.2.

3   Findings

This section contains two subsections. In the first, the spatial features of the hazard-related dichotomous variables and of the covariates of the Logit models are presented. In the following subsection, the estimates of the models are described and discussed.

3.1   Flood and Landslide Hazards and Their Drivers

Figure 2 provides the spatial distribution of both dependent (left-hand side panel) and independent (right-hand side panel) variables.

Very high landslide hazard values concern less than 5% of the study area; as Fig. 2 shows, they form elongated clusters along the southwest-northeast direction due to geo-logical and geomorphological reasons, along deep canyons in Baunei, Dorgali, and coincident with the northern side of the Monte Albo karst mountain chain in Siniscola. Nearly 15% of the study area is classed as high hazard, while most of the study area is classed as either medium (about 25.5%) or moderate hazard (circa 40%).

Only about 6% of the study area is classed as having no landslide hazard, while in the remaining part (approximately 8.5%), included in the municipality of Dorgali, landslide hazard was not assessed and mapped. As for flood hazard, 90.5% of the study area shows null values; in the remaining parts, its level is mostly (6%) very high. The remaining 3.5% concerns high, moderate, and low values. This is because flood hazard usually takes the maximum value in correspondence to riverbeds, river estuaries, coastal wetlands and their closest surroundings, while its level decreases (more or less quickly depending on factors such as morphology or soil type) as the distance increases. As shown in Fig. 2, flood hazard is mostly found to the south and the north of the study area, and almost absent in the central part.

Concerning the independent variables, *Natval* takes extremely high values in most of the study area (around 72.8%) and medium values in around 23.5%, while the null value only concerns the remaining 3.7% circa of the study area, corresponding to artificial surfaces such as villages and towns' footprints. *Consval*, which in principle can range in

---

[10] http://www.sardegnageoportale.it/index.php?xsl=2420&s=40&v=9&c=14481&es=6603&na=
1&n=100&esp=1&tb=14401.

[11] http://www.sardegnageoportale.it/areetematiche/modellidigitalidielevazione/.

the 0–1 interval, in the study area takes 0.76 as maximum value and it is null in around 61% of the territory. This is because habitats of Community interest are identified and mapped mostly within Natura 2000 sites, while comprehensive assessments outside the network are missing. It is therefore not surprising that non-zero values are mostly found in the central part of the study area, hosting one of the largest Sardinian Special Conservation Area (ITB020014 "Golfo di Orosei").

Landsval is null in approximately 47.5% of the study area and, as clearly visible in Fig. 2, it takes the highest values along the coastline, because the Regional Landscape

Table 4. Spatial datasets developed for this study: input data, sources, tools, and references.

Variable	Input data	Input data source(s)	Tool	References
FH	PAI *FH* maps Municipal *FH* maps	Regional geoportal		
LH	PAI *LH* maps Municipal *LH* maps	Regional geoportal		
Natval	Regional land cover map Protected areas map Threats to biodiversity	Regional geoportal	InVEST - Habitat quality model	[15, 16]
	Expert judgments	Questionnaires		
Consval	Habitats of Community interest	Regional administration		
	Regional monitoring report			
	Natura 2000 standard data forms	Environmental ministry's website		
Landsval	Regional landscape plan dataset	Regional geoportal		
Recrval	Study area	Regional geoportal	InVEST - Visitation: recreation and tourism model	
Agrofor	2018 Corine land cover map	Copernicus Land monitoring service		
	Land value (Agricultural areas)	National Research Council of Agriculture and Agricultural Economics' website		
	Land value (Forestry areas)	National Revenue Agency's website		

(continued)

Table 4. (*continued*)

Variable	Input data	Input data source(s)	Tool	References
LST	Landsat 8 TIRS and OLI satellite imagery	USGS's Earth Resources Observation and Science's website	LST QGIS plugin [19]	[17, 20]
CO2Stor	Regional land cover raster map	Regional geoportal	InVEST - Carbon storage and sequestration model	[18]
	Carbon pool data	2005 National Inventory of Italian Forests		
		Regional pilot project on land units and soil capacity in Sardinia		
Altitud	10-m resolution Digital terrain model	Regional geoportal		
Slope	10-m resolution Digital terrain model	Regional geoportal		

Plan strictly protects coastal landscapes, and along some the main rivers and creeks, also protected under the national landscape law.

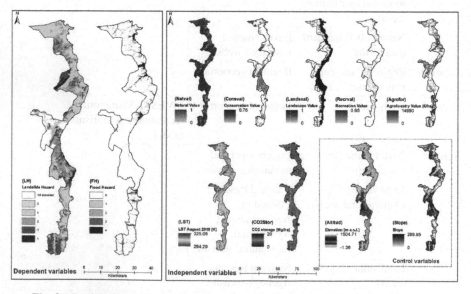

Fig. 2. Spatial distribution of dependent and independent variables in the study area.

Recrval takes the null value in most of the study area (around 78.3%), meaning that no geotagged pictures were uploaded onto Flickr in these areas. Non-zero values can be found mostly along the coastline and usually peak close to the towns and to coastal facilities, although in Dorgali and Baunei, well-renowned hikers' and climbers' destinations due to their outstanding natural characters, lighter shades of blue in Fig. 2 are visible also in inner areas across their territories.

Agrofor is null in nearly a half (49.4%) of the study area. The highest values are observed in the southern and northern parts of the study area, especially in river valleys and coastal plains, as far as agricultural activities are concerned.

LST high and low values are rather clustered, and the clusters mostly correspond to those having high elevation or high slope values, as the maps in Fig. 2 show.

Finally, *CO2Stor* ranges between zero and two Mg per hectare, with more than 61% of the study area above 1 Mg/ha, while low values are clustered mainly along the coastline to the north and along rivers and wetlands to the south.

3.2 Estimates of the Logit Models

Table 5 and Table 6 show the results of the estimates of the Logit models related to the dichotomous variables *FH* and *LH*, and their correlations with the seven environmental features that characterize the RGI. The outcomes partly differ for the two variables, and the differences can be explained through the environmental profiles of the two types of hazards. In the case of *FH*, *Natval* and *Consval* reveal opposite impacts on the probability of a parcel to be associated either to a relevant or to a weak hazard condition. *Natval* shows a positive correlation to hazard decrease, i.e. a negative marginal effect, whereas *Consval* reveals a negative correlation, or a positive marginal effect. The estimates of the Logit model concerning *LH* show the opposite correlations.

Secondly, *Recrval* and *Landsval* reveal impacts on the probability of weak flood and landslide hazards consistent with each other and positive in case of *Recrval* and negative as regards *Landsval*, which indicates that these two features of the RGI should be targeted in opposite ways with reference to prevention and control of flood and landslide hazards. This implies that environmental and cultural attractiveness, and identification and protection of landscape and cultural resources, should be targeted as points of reference to fight environmental hazard.

Thirdly, the impacts of *Agrofor* on *FH* and *LH* are opposite as well. Agricultural and forestry productive land shows a positive impact on decrease of landslide hazard and a negative effect on flood hazard. Therefore, effective control on environmental hazard implies that the most productive agricultural and forestry activities should not be located close to floodplains and their surroundings, where agricultural and forestry land should be used just to counter flooding. Productive agriculture and forestry should be implemented elsewhere, and especially near areas characterized by a relevant landslide hazard.

The sixth characteristic of the RGI is *LST*, which is an indicator of how, and to what extent, land covers help to mitigate negative phenomena such as heat islands and waves, and to improve the quality of rural and urban environments [17]. As in the cases of *Recrval* and *Landsval*, the estimates of the two Logit models reveal impacts on the probability of weak flood and landslide hazards consistent with each other and positive,

Table 5. Marginal effects on the probabilities of $FH = 1$ of variables described in Sect. 2, whose definitions and descriptive statistics are reported in Table 1.

Variable	Marginal effect	z-statistic	p-value
Marginal impact on $FH = 1$ probability, ∂Prob $(FH = 1)/dx_j$, Prob $(FH = 1) = 9.00\%$			
Natval	−0.0043	−13.042	0.0000
Consval	0.0132	22.859	0.0000
Landsval	0.0113	30.012	0.0000
Recrval	−0.0042	−1.867	0.0619
Agrofor	0.0014	36.580	0.0000
LST	−0.0020	−35.729	0.0000
CO2Stor	−0.0055	−21.299	0.0000
Altitud	−0.0001	−72.983	0.0000
Slope	−0.0003	−22.713	0.0000
Log-likelihood goodness-of-fit test			
Log-likelihood ratio = 72946.20 – Prob. > chi-square = 0.00000 (9 degrees of freedom)			

which indicates that this feature of the RGI does not need particular attention in terms of landslide and flood hazard control. Indeed, the estimates of the Logit models imply that the higher the *LST*, the lower the two hazards. Therefore, as climate-change mitigation and adaptation focus on policies to decrease *LST*, it can be concluded that the issue of *LST* is not relevant to address landslide and flood hazard.

Furthermore, *CO2Stor* shows opposite impacts on the probability of a parcel to be associated to either a relevant or a weak hazard level. This is entirely consistent with expectations: in the case of flood hazard, areas vegetated and rich in soil are likely to increase the probability of weak hazard, since they work as drainage areas to absorb excess flooding and filter sediment, whereas, in the case of landslide hazard, the positive impact on the probability of hazard increase is likely to be connected to the fact that areas rich in soil are comparatively more suitable to debris flow, especially in zones characterized by steep slopes. That being so, adequate monitoring of environmental hazard implies that the RGI should encourage the conservation of vegetated and rich-in-soil areas in the surroundings of floodplains, even though not used as croplands, as already mentioned with reference to *Agrofor*, while the most productive agricultural and forestry activities should be located not close to floodplains and their surroundings, and likewise not close to zones featured by steep slopes.

Finally, the estimated marginal effects of the two control variables, *Altitud* and *Slope*, reveal the expected signs in both cases, since, on the one hand, it is expected that the lower the altitude and the lower the slope, the higher the probability of severe flooding to take place, whereas the higher the altitude and the higher the slope, the higher the probability of serious landslide events. Moreover, all the estimated marginal effects are

Table 6. Marginal effects on the probabilities of $LH = 1$ of variables described in Sect. 2, whose definitions and descriptive statistics are reported in Table 1.

Variable	Marginal effect	z-statistic	p-value
Marginal impact on $LH = 1$ probability, ∂Prob $(LH = 1)$/dxi, Prob $(LH = 1) = 44.80\%$			
Natval	0.3351	64.191	0.0000
Consval	−0.2787	−46.522	0.0000
Landsval	0.0155	7.137	0.0000
Recrval	−0.6352	−12.970	0.0000
Agrofor	−0.0170	−56.433	0.0000
LST	−0.0274	−72.544	0.0000
CO2Stor	0.0533	17.930	0.0000
Altitud	0.0002	44.439	0.0000
Slope	0.0087	128.132	0.0000
Log-likelihood goodness-of-fit test			
Log-likelihood ratio = 122653.10 – Prob. > chi-square = 0.00000 (9 degrees of freedom)			

significant in terms of p-values, and, in general, the marginal effects on the probability of relevant flood hazard are much lower than the impacts on the probability of relevant landslide hazard since the cumulative probability of relevant flood hazard (lower than 10%) is much lower than the cumulative probability of relevant landslide hazard (about 50%). The goodness of fit of the estimates of the two models are excellent, as shown by the two log-likelihood ratios measures.

4   Conclusions

Some policy implications and recommendations can be derived from the outcomes of the study, as follows. The results concerning the influence of *Natval* and *Consval* on the probability of comparatively higher flood and landslide hazards imply that, in case of landslide hazard, prevention and control should target areas with relevant natural value, that is, areas endowed with a significant potential supply of ecosystem services, while, in case of flood hazard, they should focus on areas featured by the presence of natural habitats types of Community interest, as identified under the Habitats Directive. Since areas showing high values of *FH* are mostly concentrated in the floodplains and their surroundings, while areas having high values of *LH* are widespread over the study area, and, in more general terms, over the whole Sardinian island, these findings entail different implications concerning prevention and control hazards when defining spatial planning policies to implement the RGI. Therefore, the definition and implementation of the RGI should carefully study and develop spatial policies related to waterways and their surroundings, which should entail strict regulations related to anthropic access and visits in floodplains areas characterized by significant values of *Consval*, i.e. by a relevant concentration of habitats of Community interest. Moreover, the RGI-related spatial policies should carefully balance the relationship between *Natval* and landslide hazard, that is, they should address the issue of the exploitation of natural ecosystem services located in areas endowed with high supply potentials, and likewise characterized by a relevant landslide hazard. This is entirely consistent with the position of the Commission of the European Communities, which recommends that "working with nature's capacity to absorb or control impacts in urban and rural areas can be a more efficient way of adapting than simply focusing on physical infrastructure" [21]. Since Natura 2000 sites within Sardinia include most coastal wetlands, estuaries, waterways, and large stretches of coastal areas, it is straightforward that parcels located in these areas should show a relevant impact on flood hazard. Spatial planning policies should therefore include strict regulations related to new settlement development in floodplains, oriented to protect nature and natural resources belonging to riparian areas and their surroundings, which are characterized by high figures of *Consval*. Consistently with these observations, the Lower Danube Green Corridor Agreement focuses on the restoration of around 2,000 square kilometers of floodplains, side channels and associated habitats along the Danube as a control measure to mitigate the destructive impacts of floods in the region. The estimated cost (about 50 million euros) is lower than the cost related to the environmental damages caused by floods in 2010 [22]. To sum up, the methodological approach proposed in this study may represent a tool in support of spatial decision-making processes that can be exported to other European contexts, due to its adaptability to the national planning and normative framework, on the basis of the European legislation concerning protection and improvement of nature and natural resources. A promising direction for future research should focus on building a new normative framework to implement the RGI conceptual and technical category, conceived as a provider of ecosystem services, into the theoretical and technical approaches of the European and national spatial planning practices.

Acknowledgments. Author Contributions: Sabrina Lai (S.L), Federica Isola (F.I.), Federica Leone (F.L.), and Corrado Zoppi (C.Z.) collaboratively designed this study. Individual contributions are as follows: F.I. wrote Sect. 1; S.L. wrote Sects. 2.1, 2.3, and 3.1; C.Z. wrote Sects. 2.2 and 3.2; F.L. wrote Sect. 4.

The study was implemented within the research project "Paesaggi rurali della Sardegna: pianificazione di infrastrutture verdi e blu e di reti territoriali complesse" [Rural landscapes of Sardinia: Planning policies for green and blue infrastructure and spatial complex networks], funded by the Autonomous Region of Sardinia under the 2017 call for "Projects related to fundamental or basic research". This article was excerpted from Lai S., Isola F., Leone F. & Zoppi C. (2021). Assessing the potential of green infrastructure to mitigate hydrogeological hazard. Tema - Journal of Land Use, Mobility and Environment, s.i. 1/2021: 109–133. http://doi.org/10.6092/1970-9870/7411.

References

1. Margottini, C., Un contributo per gli Stati Generali dei cambiamenti climatici e l'arte della difesa del territorio [A contribution to General States of climate change and soil

defense] (2015). https://www.minambiente.it/sites/default/files/archivio/allegati/italiasicura/114Contributodisses.pdf. Accessed 25 March 2021

2. Trigila, A., Iadanza, C., Bussettini, M., Lastoria, B.: Dissesto idrogeologico in Italia: pericolosità e indicatori di rischio [Hydrogeological instability in Italy: hazard and risk indicators]. ISPRA, Rome, Italy (2018)

3. Badiu, D., Nita, A., Ioja, C., Nita, M.: Disentangling the connections: a network analysis of approaches to urban green infrastructure. Urban Forestry & Urban Greening 41, 211–220 (2019)

4. Caparrós-Martínez, J.L., Milán-García, J., Rueda-López, N., de Pablo-Valenciano, J.: Green infrastructure and water: an analysis of global research. Water 12(6), 1760 (2020)

5. United States Environment Protection Agency: What is green infrastructure?. https://www.epa.gov/green-infrastructure/what-green-infrastructure. Accessed 25 March 2021

6. Chen, J., Liu, Y., Gitau, M.W., Engel, B.A., Flanagan, D.C., Harbor, J.M.: Evaluation of the effectiveness of green infrastructure on hydrology and water quality in a combined sewer overflow community. Sci. Total Environ. 665, 69–79 (2019)

7. Papathoma-Köhle, M., Glade, T.: The role of vegetation cover change for landslide hazard and risk. In: Renaud, G., Sudmeier-Rieux, K., Marisol, E. (eds.) The Role of Ecosystems in Disaster Risk Reduction, pp. 293–320. UNU-Press, Tokyo (2013)

8. European Commission Green infrastructure (GI)—Enhancing Europe's natural capital: communication from the commission to the European Parliament, the council, the European economic and social committee and the committee of the regions (2013). https://eur-lex.europa.eu/resource.html?uri=cellar:d41348f2-01d5-4abe-b817-4c73e6f1b2df.0014.03/DOC_1&format=PDF. Accessed 25 March 2021

9. Palmer, M., Liu, J., Matthews, J., Mumba, M., D'Odorico, P.: Water security: gray or green? Science 349(6248), 584–585 (2015)

10. Nerlove, M., Press, S.: Univariate and multivariate log-linear and logistic models. Report no. R1306-EDA/NIH. RAND Corporation Santa Monica, CA, United States (1973)

11. Greene, W.H.: Econometric Analysis. Macmillan, New York, NY, United States (1993)

12. Zoppi, C., Lai, S.: Differentials in the regional operational program expenditure for public services and infrastructure in the coastal cities of Sardinia (Italy) analyzed in the ruling context of the regional landscape plan. Land Use Policy 30, 286–304 (2013)

13. Regione Autonoma della Sardegna: Attività di individuazione e di perimetrazione delle aree a rischio idraulico e geomorfologico e delle relative misure di salvaguardia. Linee guida. [Identifying and mapping areas subject to flood risk and landslide risk, and delineation of safeguard measures. Guidelines] (2000). http://www.regione.sardegna.it/documenti/1_26_20060913170604.pdf. Accessed 25 March 2021

14. Regione Autonoma della Sardegna: Piano Stralcio per l'Assetto Idrogeologico (PAI). Relazione generale. [Hydrogeological Setting Plan. Comprehensive Report] (2004). http://www.regione.sardegna.it/documenti/1_26_20060913170906.pdf. Accessed 25 March 2021

15. Lai, S., Leone, F.: Bridging biodiversity conservation objectives with landscape planning through green infrastructures: a case study from Sardinia, Italy. In: Gervasi, O., et al. (eds.) ICCSA 2017. LNCS, vol. 10409, pp. 456–472. Springer, Cham (2017). https://doi.org/10.1007/978-3-319-62407-5_32

16. Cannas, I., Lai, S., Leone, F., Zoppi, C.: Green infrastructure and ecological corridors: a regional study concerning Sardinia. Sustainability 10(4), 1265 (2018)

17. Lai, S., Leone, F., Zoppi, C.: Spatial distribution of surface temperature and land cover: a study concerning Sardinia, Italy. Sustainability 12(8), 3186 (2020)

18. Floris, M.: I servizi ecosistemici nella pianificazione spaziale come strumenti interpretativi per la definizione di tassonomie territoriali innovative [Ecosystem services within spatial planning as knowledge-interpreting tools for the definition of innovative spatial taxonomies], unpublished doctoral thesis discussed at the University of Cagliari on March 6 (2020)

19. Ndossi, M.I., Avdan, U.: Application of open source coding technologies in the production of Land Surface Temperature (LST) maps from Landsat: a PyQGIS Plugin. Remote Sens. **8**(5), 413 (2016)
20. Lai, S., Leone, F., Zoppi, C.: Policies to decrease land surface temperature based on land cover change: an assessment related to Sardinia, Italy. TEMA – J. Mobility Land Use Environ. **13**(3), 329–351 (2020)
21. Commission of the European Communities: White paper. Adapting to climate change: towards a European framework for action (2009). https://eur-lex.europa.eu/legal-content/EN/TXT/PDF/?uri=CELEX:52009DC0147. Accessed 25 March 2021
22. European Commission: Promoting the socio-economic benefits of Natura 2000. Natura 2000 (2010). https://ec.europa.eu/environment/nature/info/pubs/docs/nat2000newsl/nat29_en.pdf. Accessed 25 March 2021

One Place, Different Communities' Perceptions. Mapping Cultural Ecosystem Services in the Asinara National Park (Italy)

Sabrina Lai[1] (ID), Andrea Motroni[2], Laura Santona[3], and Matilde Schirru[4]([⊠]) (ID)

[1] Department of Civil and Environmental Engineering and Architecture, University of Cagliari, via Marengo 2, Cagliari, Italy
sabrinalai@unica.it
[2] Environmental Protection Agency of Sardinia (ARPAS), Sassari, Italy
amotroni@arpa.sardegna.it
[3] Regional Administration of Sardinia, Department for the Protection of the Environment, via Roma 80, Cagliari, Italy
lsantona@regione.sardegna.it
[4] National Research Council – Institute of BioEconomy (CNR-IBE), Trav. La Crucca 3, Sassari, Italy
matilde.schirru@ibe.cnr.it

Abstract. As innovative approaches emerge, the concept of Cultural Ecosystem Services (CES) is periodically revised and enhanced, presenting new value nuances. Due to their intrinsic site-specific character, CES usually call for subjective, rather than objective, perspectives. Therefore, assessing CES through alternative, non-monetary approaches, is fundamental. This issue becomes even more urgent when attempting to assess and map CES within natural protected areas, and even more so when such areas are non-inhabited, as the absence of any local communities poses additional challenges. In this study, initiated within the GIREPAM (Integrated Management and Ecological Network of Marine Protected Areas) Interreg project and developed within the NEPTUNE Interreg project, the way stakeholders perceive CES supplied by the Asinara National Park in Northern Sardinia (Italy) was investigated. Interviews and questionnaires were delivered in December 2019: more than 600 observations related to CES were mapped and recorded through a participatory GIS in order to investigate whether the different perception of CES supplied by a given natural protected area varies depending on the community. Differences were recorded among three local communities. Results show that significant differences exist in the choice of places, rather than in the perceived values of a natural protected area, and that such differences depend on the local community engaged in recognizing the various types of cultural values.

Keywords: Cultural ecosystem services · Natural protected areas · Participatory mapping · Toponyms

O. Gervasi et al. (Eds.): ICCSA 2021, LNCS 12955, pp. 675–691, 2021.
https://doi.org/10.1007/978-3-030-87007-2_48

1 Introduction

Ecosystem services (ES) are understood as those benefits (be they good or services) that nature provides to human beings through well-functioning ecosystems, and that contribute to human well-being either directly or indirectly. So far, various taxonomies and classification schemes have been proposed in the literature. For instance, the Millennium Ecosystem Assessment [1] categorizes ES into four groups as follows: provisioning (including, for instance, food and timber provision), regulating (among which coastal protection or carbon storage and sequestration), cultural (such as nature-based recreation, or sense of place and belonging), and supporting services (as, for instance, soil formation). A more sophisticated and hierarchical taxonomy is the one proposed by the Common International Classification of Ecosystem Services (CICES) [2], which only focuses on three groups (provisioning, regulating, and cultural): in this framework, supporting services are regarded as processes and functions that are indeed necessary prerequisites for the supply of the first three types of ES, but are not demanded and consumed by humans *per se*. Due to debates arisen on the very concept of ES, which focused on a supposedly anthropocentric perspective leading to "commodification" of nature [3, 4], in recent years the Intergovernmental Science-Policy Platform on Biodiversity and Ecosystem Services (IPBES) has introduced the concept of "nature's contributions to people" [5] as complementary to that of ES, in an attempt to remark that the link between nature and human beings is heavily dependent on context, place, time, and culture.

Such dependency is of outmost importance as far as cultural ecosystem services (CES) are concerned. Defined by the Millennium Ecosystem Assessment [1, p. 58] as the "non material benefits obtained [by humans] from ecosystems", they are delivered through each person's or group's relationship with nature, be it physical, experiential, intellectual, spiritual, or emotional. Therefore, CES are intrinsically affected by individual perceptions and subjective values, which makes them the outcome of the socio-ecological system of interest. The very subjective character of CES, the emphasis on their immaterial and intangible nature [6, 7], as well as their inadequate definition leading to unclear operationalization [8], make it difficult to assess CES based on quantitative or monetary approaches, except for cultural heritage and recreation ES, for which travel cost and contingent valuation methods are widely applied (among many: [9–11]). It is therefore not surprising that a number of socio-cultural approaches to assessing CES have been proposed in academic research, including document analysis, expert-based approaches, observation approaches, in-depth interviews, focus groups, questionnaires [12]. The latter approaches are advocated as the ones that can provide a better picture of the relationship between CES and their users [7]; moreover, they can be integrated into spatially-explicit assessments of CES that often take the form of participatory mapping techniques.

Ryfield et al. [6], for instance, combined observation approaches, focus groups, and cartographical modes of knowledge to analyze a specific CES (i.e., sense of place). Cabana et al. [13] integrated qualitative research (questionnaires, stakeholder meetings, storytelling) and ecosystem mapping to develop a participatory map investigating sense of places, perceptions, and meanings that people attach to the Dublin Bay area. Plieninger et al. [14] implemented a participatory map of various CES as perceived by residents of five villages in Eastern Germany, building upon in-depth interviews and questionnaires.

Sherrouse et al. [15] developed a GIS-based application to map social values of a national forest in the United States as perceived by various groups of CES beneficiaries. Such studies highlight the absence of a one-fits-all approach to CES appraisal; to the contrary, methods and approaches must be tailored to contexts, communities, and CES that are being investigated. Building upon such approaches, we therefore aim to investigate how social values attached to ES can be elicited in a very specific context, i.e. that of a non-inhabited (yet open to the scientific community, tourists, and some economic activities) natural protected area, where the current absence of any local community poses an additional challenge to understanding how people perceive a place.

This study is organized as follows: Sect. 2 provides some background information on the chosen study area, the Asinara National Park in Sardinia (Italy) and describes the methodological approach. The results are provided in Sect. 3, and next discussed in Sect. 4, which also highlights limitations and future directions of this research.

2 Materials and Methods

In order to assess how local communities perceive CES supplied by the Asinara National Park through a qualitative approach, a social survey was implemented, by targeting the main communities that have interests in the island, for historical, geographical and institutional reasons. Such communities belong to three municipalities as follows: Stintino, Porto Torres, and Sassari (Fig. 1).

We developed two ways to involve locals in a public participatory GIS. A geographically based survey was elaborated and next delivered both in presence, during two dedicated living labs, and online. In both cases, we asked people to identify both recognized and perceived values of the Asinara Park's environment, by mapping or indicating/naming places that would come up to their minds when thinking about their experience or knowledge of the island.

During in-person activities, hosted at the National Archaeological Museum of Porto Torres and at the Tuna Factory Museum of Stintino, participants were asked to choose "their" places by pinning colored flags in a 2.5 × 1.5 m floor map. Each flag color corresponded to a specific CES; the full set of CES among which participants could choose corresponded to a set of values representing ecosystem services, following the simplified landscape values proposed by García-Martín et al. [16]. In order to enhance the composite pattern of the cultural, recreational, and emotional sphere, among the nine flag colors only one corresponded to the wilderness value as "natural" and only one concerned a specific provisioning service, identified as agricultural value, while the remaining seven are related to CES and are as follows: Historical and archaeological value; Recreational value; Existence value, understood as the psychological benefits stemming from the knowledge that a good exists and will continue to exist; Iconographic value, which accounts for landscapes and ecosystems being used as source of inspiration for arts; Scientific interest, in terms of characteristics of ecosystems that enable scientific investigation; Landscape and aesthetic value; Holiness and sacred value, resulting from people's spiritual interaction with nature. Examples of the values were provided through both facilitation and a legend to build a common understanding of the values. In this way 790 points were collected, as selected by the 100 participants involved in the activities and coming from the three above mentioned municipalities (Table 1), here selected as the communities of interest. Next, points selected by participants who had identified themselves as tourists or as residents in municipalities other than Stintino, Sassari or Porto Torres were excluded, which resulted in a reduction of the number of valid places/values from 790 to 606.

Table 1. Communities involved in activities.

Communities	No. of participants	%
Other communities	7	8.54
Porto Torres	27	32.93
Sassari	27	32.93
Stintino	21	25.61
Total	82	100

As far as participants in the online survey are concerned, they were asked to associate values to places by using place names (toponyms). Online respondents were asked to describe values (related to ecosystem services) through a multiple-choice questionnaire; a built-in legend in the online version helped them pick their choices. Moreover, they could select as many values as they liked for each single place they chose.

In order to spur voluntary participation from the three selected local communities, both in-presence activities and online survey were promoted through articles in local newspapers, networking activities carried out by the three local authorities of Porto Torres, Sassari, and Stintino, as well as by the staff of the Asinara National Park. Advertisements in the social media pages of the GIREPAM project were also constantly posted. Finally, it is worth mentioning that this study carries over the work by Schirru et al. [17], who mapped the ecosystem types in the Asinara island, therefore establishing the ground for the assessment of CES.

2.1 Study Area

Stretching from South-West to North-East to the North of Sardinia (Italy), Asinara is an island of approximately 52 km^2 in size. The geology of the island is characterized by granitic rocks in the southern part and metamorphic ones in the northern one, with high cliffs on the western coast and smoother sandy profiles in the eastern one facing Italy's mainland. Mean annual rainfall amounts to about 480 mm, while the annual average temperature is approximately 18 °C [18]. According to Canu et al. [19], who described six isobioclimates of the island, the dominant one is the Upper thermomediterranean, upper dry, euoceanic strong, affecting more than 50% of the island; second in order of importance is the Lower mesomediterranean, upper dry, euoceanic strong isobioclimate (31%), while only 6,5% of the island is characterized by the Lower mesomediterranean, lower subhumid, euoceanic strong isobioclimate. The vegetation is characterized by

Mediterranean maquis with some degraded areas. Endemic flora has been described by Bocchieri and Filigheddu [20], by Pisanu et al. [21], and by Drissen et al. [22]. The island was inhabited by shepherds' and fishermen's families until 1885,when they were forcefully removed to build first a *lazzaretto* (i.e. a sanatorium to isolate people with contagious diseases) and next an agricultural penal colony (i.e., an open-air prison where inmates were forced to work in the fields); during this period, the environment of the island was largely affected by the presence of farming activities carried out by convicts [23, 24]. Later, in the early 70s', abandonment of farming activities carried out by prisoners led to land degradation due to the overgrazing by cattle and other rewilded animals, together with frequent forest fires across the island, as summarized also by Mantilla-Contreras et al. [25]. In 1997 the Asinara National Park was established, and this marked the beginning of a new era for the island, which turned into a great important biodiversity hotspot, due to the presence of several rare, threatened, endemic marine and terrestrial habitat and species.

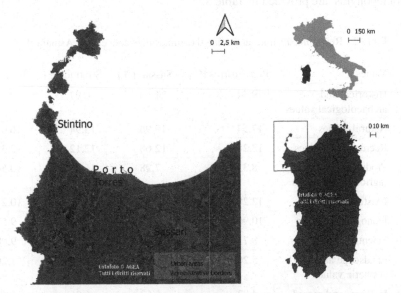

Fig. 1. To the left: Asinara and its gulf, with the municipalities of Stintino, Porto Torres and Sassari in a satellite image; to the right: its location within Sardinia.

2.2 Methodology

More than a hundred people participated in a two-day event, held on the 7th and the 14th of December 2019. A total of one hundred answers were collected either during these in-presence meetings or through an online survey, and through such replies a total of 770 geolocated dots related to Asinara's valued places were collected. Next, 164 dots were filtered out because they had been identified by tourists, hence people who do not belong to the communities of interest in our study (i.e., residents of Porto Torres, Sassari and

Stintino), which left us with 606 valid geolocated dots (each corresponding to a value) distributed across the island. Geolocated dots were next converted into a shapefile and analyzed in a GIS environment, in order to investigate the spatial distribution of values across the island. The dots are represented in Fig. 2, Fig. 3, and Fig. 4.

3   Results

Table 2 provides an overview of each community's recognized value in terms of percentage of total dots placed by members of that community. Interestingly, historical and archaeological values dominate across the three communities, while holiness and sacred values consistently get the lowest number of recognitions. In between, some distinctive aspects appear. For instance, productive values are quite significant for Stintino residents, but not so much for the other two communities, where natural and recreation values prevail. Detailed figures of recognized values, grouped by communities and associated to Asinara toponyms, are provided in Table 3.

Table 2. Recognized values and related communities concerning Asinara (%).

	Values	Porto Torres [%]	Sassari [%]	Stintino [%]	Total [%]
HAV	Historical and archaeological values	19.74	21.13	16.97	19.47
NV	Natural values	17.54	15.96	13.94	16.01
RV	Recreational values	12.28	12.68	12.12	12.38
PV	Productive (agricultural) values	8.33	7.98	16.97	10.56
EV	Existence values	12.28	6.57	12.12	10.23
IV	Iconographic value	10.96	9.39	7.88	9.57
SI	Scientific interest	8.77	10.80	7.27	9.08
LV	Landscape and aesthetic values	5.26	9.86	6.67	7.26
HV	Holiness and sacred values	4.82	5.63	6.06	5.45
	Total	100.00	100.00	100.00	100.00

Following García-Martín et al.'s methodology [16], a chi-squared (χ^2) test was next performed, to understand whether any significative difference in value recognition across the involved communities could be detected (Table 4). This test allows for comparisons among groups and detects statistically significant differences between the observed and the expected frequencies; in other words, it detects "unexpected" values, as well as the distance between unexpected and expected values. Finally, we also calculated a global χ^2 for Asinara toponyms chosen by each community's respondents as vector of the sum of values, as shown in Table 5 and Table 6 (ordered by rank).

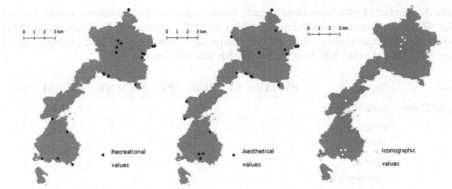

Fig. 2. Asinara maps for Recreational, Landscape-aesthetic, and Iconographic values.

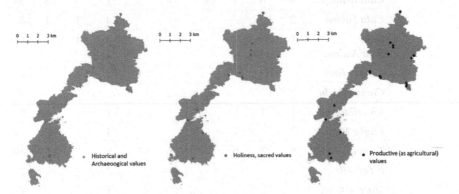

Fig. 3. Asinara maps for Historical and archaeological, Holiness and sacred, and Productive (agricultural) values

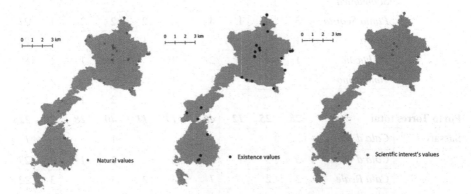

Fig. 4. Asinara maps for Natural, Existence, and Scientific interest values.

Table 3. Number of spots associated to each Asinara toponym, per community (**Com**) and per value (**RV**: Recreational value; **IV**: Iconographic value; **LV**: Landscape and aesthetic value; **HAV**: Historical and archaeological value; **PV**: Productive (agricultural) value; **HV**: Holiness, sacred value; **NV**: Natural value; **EV**: Existence value; **SI**: Scientific interest.

Com	Toponym	RV	IV	LV	HAV	PV	HV	NV	EV	SI	Tot
Porto Torres	Cala d'Arena			1					1		2
	Cala dei Detenuti	1						1			2
	Cala di Sgombro di Dentro								1		1
	Cala d'Oliva	3	4	2	9	3	1	1	4	3	30
	Cala Reale	7	6	1	9	4	2	1	5	3	38
	Cala Sabina	2						4	1	1	8
	Cala Sant'Andrea	1		1				5	1		8
	Campo Faro						1				1
	Campo Perdu				2	2					4
	Castellaccio	1	2		3			1	1	1	9
	Elighe Mannu	2		1				7	2	2	14
	Fornelli	5	7	6	12	6	2	8	7	6	59
	Il Pecorile							2			2
	Mare di fuori							1			1
	Ossario				1		2				3
	Punta Scomunica		1					1	1		3
	Punta Scorno	3	4	1	4	2	2	2	2	1	21
	Stretti	1					1				2
	Trabucato	1	1		2	1		1	1	1	8
	Tumbarino				1	1		3		2	7
	-	1			1			2	1		5
Porto Torres total		**28**	**25**	**12**	**45**	**19**	**11**	**40**	**28**	**20**	**228**
Sassari	Cala d'Arena							1			1
	Cala d'Oliva	3	3	1	5	3	2	2	1	3	23
	Cala Reale	2	2		7	3	2	3		3	22
	Cala Sabina	1	1	1				2	1	1	7

(continued)

Table 3. (*continued*)

Com	Toponym	RV	IV	LV	HAV	PV	HV	NV	EV	SI	*Tot*
	Cala Sant'Andrea		1		1		1	1		1	*5*
	Campo Perdu	1	1		2	1	1	2			*8*
	Case Bianche	1		1		1		1	1	1	*6*
	Castellaccio	1	1		1			1			*4*
	Elighe Mannu	1		1				1	1	1	*5*
	Fornelli		3	5	11	2	3	4	1	2	*31*
	Punta Barbarossa	1		1				1		1	*4*
	Punta Maestra Serre	1		1		1		1	1	1	*6*
	Punta Scomunica	1	2	1	1		1	2	1	1	*10*
	Punta Scorno	11	6	8	15	6	1	8	6	5	*66*
	Trabucato	1		1	1	1		1	1	1	*7*
	Tumbarino	1		1				2		1	*5*
	n.d	1						1		1	*3*
Sassari total		**27**	**20**	**21**	**45**	**17**	**12**	**34**	**14**	**23**	**213**
Stintino	*Baddiggiu di lu diauru o Badde Lunga*							1			*1*
	Cala d'Arena					1		1			*2*
	Cala di Luzzu/ Lutzu (Saline)			1							*1*
	Cala di Sgombro di Dentro	1	1			1					*3*
	Cala di Sgombro di Fuori					1		1			*2*
	Cala d'Oliva	4	1	1	4	4	3	1	3		*21*
	Cala Reale	3		2	5	2		2	1	3	*18*
	Cala Sant'Andrea			1		2	1	5	1	1	*11*

(*continued*)

684   S. Lai et al.

Table 3. (*continued*)

Com	Toponym	RV	IV	LV	HAV	PV	HV	NV	EV	SI	*Tot*
	Campo faro						1				1
	Campo Perdu			1		1					2
	Cannapilo								1		1
	Case Bianche					1					1
	Castellaccio		1		3			1	1		6
	Elighe Mannu	1		1	1	1		1	1	1	7
	Fornelli	5		2	4	5		4	5	2	27
	Il pecorile				1						1
	Lu Lioni		1								1
	Monsignore		1								1
	Monte Tumbarino				1				1		2
	Ossario		1	1	2		3				7
	Ovili Punta Ruia								1		1
	Punta Barbarossa				1						1
	Punta Crabara							1			1
	Punta Scomunica	2	2	1	1	2	1	2	2	2	15
	Punta Scorno		2	1	1	2	1	3	1	2	13
	Secca del Cavallo /dei Cavalli	1									1
	Spalmatore	1									1
	Strada Pagliaccetto		1								1
	Stretti	1			1	1		1			4
	Tamburi di Mizioni		1								1
	Trabucato	1		1	1	4					7
	n.d		1						1	1	3
Stintino total		*20*	*13*	*11*	*28*	*28*	*10*	*23*	*20*	*12*	*165*
Grand total		*75*	*58*	*44*	*118*	*64*	*33*	*97*	*62*	*55*	*606*

Table 4. Perceived values as summarized by the communities involved in the survey, through the χ^2 value. Freedom degrees = 16; critical limit = 26.30.

Values	Porto Torres	Sassari	Stintino	Total
Historical and archaeological values	0	0.3	0.52	0.82
Wilderness/natural values	0.34	0	0.44	0.78
Recreational values	0	0	0	0
Productive (agricultural) values	1.1	1.34	6.5	8.94
Existence values	0.95	2.8	0.57	4.32
Iconographic value	0.47	0	0.5	0.97
Scientific interest	0.02	0.71	0.6	1.33
Landscape and aesthetic values	1.23	1.95	0.08	3.26
Holiness and sacred values	0.16	0	0.11	0.27
Total	*4.27*	*7.1*	*9.32*	*20.69*

Table 5. χ^2 test values for the main locations emerging from the survey. "Other places" represent aggregations of locations (toponyms) cited fewer than five times, in order to better perform the χ^2 test (freedom degrees = 22; critical limit: 33.92).

Toponym	Porto Torres	Sassari	Stintino	Total
Cala d'Oliva	0.17	0.35	0.04	0.56
Cala Reale	2.6	1.06	0.5	4.16
Cala Sabina	1.03	0.55	4.1	5.68
Cala Sant'Andrea	0.11	1.38	3.12	4.61
Campo Perdu	0.32	1.96	0.85	3.13
Castellaccio	0.51	1.09	0.12	1.72
EligheMannu	1.8	1.85	0	3.65
Fornelli	5.11	2.63	0.75	8.49
Punta Scomunica	5.36	0	7.21	12.57
Punta Scorno	7.33	27.2	7.41	41.94
Trabucato	0.01	0.06	0.17	0.24
Other (less frequent) places	1.68	1.27	7.87	10.82
Total	26.03	39.4	32.14	97.57

Results of the χ^2 test show that no statistically significant differences among recognized values can be detected across the three communities, as shown in Table 4. In Table 5 some interesting findings are shown and, in order to make the significant difference clearer, for p-value < 0.05 and degrees of freedom = 22 (critical limit = 33.92), in

Table 6 toponyms are ranked, per each interested community, according to the χ^2 value from the lowest to the highest value. Moreover, for a better understanding of preferences concerning places, the number of choices per places was standardized, as shown in Fig. 5.

Table 6. Asinara toponyms ranking according to communities' choices, ordered according to the χ^2 value.

Ranking	Porto Torres		Sassari		Stintino	
1)	Trabucato	0.01	Punta Scomunica	0.00	Elighe Mannu	0.00
2)	Cala Sant'Andrea	0.11	Trabucato	0.06	Cala d'Oliva	0.04
3)	Cala d'Oliva	0.17	Cala d'Oliva	0.35	Castellaccio	0.12
4)	Campo Perdu	0.32	Cala Sabina	0.55	Trabucato	0.17
5)	Castellaccio	0.51	Cala Reale	1.06	Cala Reale	0.50
6)	Cala Sabina	1.03	Castellaccio	1.09	Fornelli	0.75
7)	Other places	1.68	Other places	1.27	Campo Perdu	0.85
8)	Elighe Mannu	1.80	Cala Sant'Andrea	1.38	Cala Sant'Andrea	3.12
9)	Cala Reale	2.60	Elighe Mannu	1.85	Cala Sabina	4.1
10)	Fornelli	5.11	Campo Perdu	1.96	Punta Scomunica	7.21
11)	Punta Scomunica	5.36	Fornelli	2.63	Punta Scorno	7.41
12)	Punta Scorno	7.33	Punta Scorno	27.20	Other places	7.87

4   Discussions and Conclusions

If the number of participants in the public participatory GIS activities is considered, respondent sample groups were balanced across the three communities, and well balanced were also the values recognized by respondents and associated to places across the Asinara National Park (Table 2). No significative differences emerge through the chi-squared test; however, an in-depth reading concerning percentage of expressed values can help build a narrative about possible differences across the concerned local communities in perceiving Asinara's CES.

A first consistent narrative concerns Historical and archaeological values, which dominate in all of the three involved communities (Sassari 21.13%, Porto Torres 19.74%, and Stintino 16.97%). This fact can be explained by the presence of the remains of various human settlements spanning across time from prehistory up to the XX century, which marked the landscape with a rich heritage comprising ruins of a castle, a monastery, towers, houses, a main village and scattered rural infrastructures. More recent historic remains, such as the sanatorium, the prisoners camp built during World War I, the war cemeteries, and the most iconic ones, that is the buildings that hosted the inmates when the whole island was an agricultural penal colony, are also of interest.

The second place consistently concerns Natural value (Porto Torres 17.54%, Sassari 15.96%, and Stintino 13.94%). Natural characteristics and assets of the Asinara island are directly related to the National Park environmental protection status due to its richness in biodiversity [21, 22]. This is further confirmed by the fact that Natural values are more recognized in Porto Torres, where the headquarter of the managing institution and administration offices of the National Park are located.

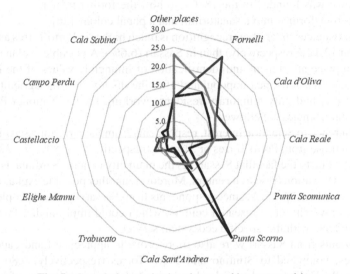

Fig. 5. Cumulative choice by places and by communities.

Recreational values come consistently third across the three communities (Sassari 12.68%, Porto Torres 12.28%, Stintino 12.12%): nature-based recreation is the most common way to explore and enjoy the island, and, even more important for the three communities, it provides a significant opportunity for the economic development of their territories, since tourism-related economic activities (accommodation, boat services, diving, etc.) are not located within the island but in the surrounding areas.

A special remark concerns Productive (agricultural) values, which are very significant in the Stintino case, where the score (16.97%) matches that of Historical and archaeological values, while Porto Torres and Sassari only score 8.33% and 7.98%, respectively. Under this category, both farming and fishing are comprised, and, unlike the previous value, they are only partly connected to the experience of the island and the way its landscape is perceived. Currently, the only agricultural activity in the island is a cosmetic farm and laboratory that produces niche cosmetics from the island spontaneous vegetation (such as *Helichrysum italicum, Pistacia lentiscus, Rosmarinus officinalis*, or *Lavandula stoechas*), while the former olive grove in Trabucato has recently been restored with a view to bringing back the production of olive oil. Notwithstanding the current marginality of agriculture in the island, respondents could still mention signs of rural activities from the past or from memories, sometimes even memories passed by older relatives. Vineyards and vine-making activities, and olive and oil productions, both in Trabucato area, animal farming activities in Campo Perdu or in Santa Maria and Fornelli, are productive "*geni loci*" imprinted in the landscape, and date back to the times when the island was an agricultural penal colony. Even though the χ^2 test did not show statistical significance, among Stintino's respondents the Productive (agricultural) value returned a very high score. Personal and family memories play here a strong role, since the town was founded in the 1880s, to host the former inhabitants of the island when it was transformed into a sanatorium and a penal colony [26].

As for Existence values, their recognition is much higher in Porto Torres and Stintino (12.28% and 12.12% respectively) than in Sassari (6.6%). A possible explanation could be linked to place attachment and identification of intangible values of the landscape, since the island has remained unpopulated after the dismissal of the agricultural penal colony in 1997, and only temporary residents working for the National Park or for environmental agencies are allowed.

With reference to Scientific interest, respondents from Sassari expressed higher preferences than those from Porto Torres or Stintino (respectively, 10.80%, 8.77%, 7.27%). This might be due to the fact that Sassari, as the main city in north Sardinia, is home to a university and to various research centers. Moreover, another possible explanation could lie in the respondents' profiles, since respondents from Sassari included people affiliated to the local university or to research centers, which could imply higher familiarity of these respondents with this specific ecosystem service.

Respondents from Sassari were also more prone to appreciate Landscape and aesthetic values, compared to Stintino and Porto Torres (respectively: 9.86%, 6.67%, 5.26%). Finally, Holiness and sacred values scored the lowest percentage of preferences among the three communities (Stintino 6.06%, Sassari 5.63%, Porto Torres 4.8%).

As for toponyms, respondents from Stintino named 31 places, many more than those from Porto Torres (20) or from Sassari (16), which reveals how the three communities developed different geographic maps for the island, Stintino being the more accurate possibly again due to family memories carried on from ancestors from the XIX century who had actually lived within the island. Not only is the town of Stintino the closest human settlement to the Asinara island (approximately nine miles from Stintino to Fornelli), but also many residents are descendants of fishermen and shepherds that once lived on the island, in the former Cala d'Oliva village. Still today roads and streets in Stintino are named after places in Asinara, hence carrying on the memory of the ancestors' land.

Results from the chi-squared test shown in Table 5 highlight that the higher statistically different values are those concerning Punta Scorno, for which Sassari peaks at 27.00, against Stintino and Porto Torres that sit around 7 (respectively, 7.41 and 7.33). While it is hard to provide a firm explanation for this difference, we could speculate that it has to do with the peculiar character of this place: Punta Scorno is located to the northern part of the Asinara island (i.e., the farther apart from Sardinia) and hosts an ancient lighthouse (built in 1854), suspended among the rocks towards the sea and owned by the Italian Marine Army, which until 2006 hosted a meteorological station. For the Stintino community only the cumulative value associated to "Other places" (7.87) is higher than that of Punta Scorno, which highlights the fragmented values of the many toponyms enlisted by its respondents.

The second position in ranking order for significant χ^2 values is that of Punta Scomunica (scoring 7.21 for Stintino and 5.36 for Porto Torres), the highest peak of the island with its 408 m above the sea level. From this place, the whole Asinara island can be viewed, together with the namesake gulf in north Sardinia and the French island of Corsica.

Fornelli lands the third place, but only for the Porto Torres community, which is surprising since it is the main boat mooring place for those who leave Sardinia from Stintino. It might have something to do with the fact that in the recent past (i.e., at the end of XX century) Fornelli hosted a high security prison, infamous because of its many important convicts, comprising high-profile mafiosi, kidnappers and terrorists. Another possible explanation could lie in the past uses of the Fornelli area, as the biggest farm was located there during the times of the penal colony, as well as a shepherd scattered settlement in the pre-sanatorium and pre-penal colony times.

Fourth in ranking is Cala Sabina, but for the Stintino community only. Since the two main beaches in Asinara (i.e., Cala d'Arena and Cala Sant'Andrea) are nature reserves, where access is forbidden, Cala Sabina is currently the first beach of the island in terms of tourist attendance. Its ancient name is Cala dei Ponzesi, an homage to people coming from the Ponza island (which lies in front of the Italian peninsula, at a latitude approximately in between Rome and Naples), expert fishermen who settled in Cala d'Oliva prior to the 1884 eviction and the subsequent establishment of the village of Stintino.

The fifth χ^2 value is associated to Cala Reale, for Porto Torres locals only. This place hosts the headquarter of the National Park of Asinara on the island and is the main mooring place for ferries departing from Porto Torres, which could explain why it is more important for this community than for the other two. Cala Reale is also the place where the main buildings of the sanatorium (quarantine stations) were built, and it has always been the main harbor and institutional center of the island.

Lower values concerning places are lower not merely due to a lesser importance of those places; in all likelihood, lower values are associated to their lesser "familiarity" and "normality" compared to other places. Moreover, Stintino and Porto Torres response patterns differ from Sassari ones, with Stintino expressing the most complex relationship with the environment of the island; such relationship reflects the complexity of a biocultural object such as this little island, currently a National Park that has inherited (and has also got rid of) a dense past of nature and human interactions.

The analysis of places through toponyms made it the exploration of community values and relationships between places and communities possible in a way that no quantitative analysis of cultural ecosystem services would have allowed. By reflecting on their experience and feelings about Asinara, respondents let their inner values emerge, together with their personal way of "living" the island, be it through the lens of their communities' memories, or by applying, even subconsciously, the conservation schemes of the Asinara National Park, with its biodiversity hotspots, functional areas, or no-entry no-take areas. Hence, the analysis of the evidence collected from the responses has helped not only in building a multifaceted perspective of CES supplied by the island, but also in identifying multiple, and overlapping, identities of the island, which could further be expanded in future research by investigating tourists' perceptions.

A limitation of this study can be related to the limited sample of respondents; notwithstanding, because the approach is simple and easily replicable, as well as effective in identifying connections between value-ridden ecosystem services, as the CES are, and local communities, we regard it as a pilot study that we hope to reproduce in the future with a larger dataset.

Acknowledgment. While all the authors contributed to this study, credit goes to Matilde Schirru for data collection and analysis, as well as for the design of the research. This study has been carried out in the framework of the projects NEPTUNE (PatrimoNio naturalE e culTUrale sommerso e gestione sosteNibile della subacquEa ricreativa), and GIREPAM (Gestione Integrata delle Reti Ecologiche attraverso i Parchi e le Aree Marine), both funded by INTERREG Maritime Programme Italy-France 2014–2020, Axis 2.

References

1. Millennium Ecosystem Assessment: Ecosystems and Human Well-being: A Framework for Assessment. Island Press, Washington, DC, United States (2003)
2. Haines-Young, R., Potschin, M.: Common International Classification of Ecosystem Services (CICES) V5.1. Guidance on the application of the revised structure (2018), https://cices.eu/content/uploads/sites/8/2018/01/Guidance-V51-01012018.pdf. Accessed 10 May 2021
3. Peterson, M.J., Hall, D.M., Feldpausch-Parker, A.M., Peterson, T.R.: Obscuring ecosystem function with application of the ecosystem services concept. Conserv. Biol. **24**, 113–119 (2010)
4. Gómez-Baggethun, E., de Groot, R., Lomas, P.L., Montes, C.: The history of ecosystem services in economic theory and practice: from early notions to markets and payment schemes. Ecol. Econ. **69**, 1209–1218 (2010)
5. Díaz, S., et al.: Assessing nature's contributions to people. Science **359**(6373), 270–272 (2018)
6. Ryfield, F., Cabana, D., Brannigan, J., Crowe, T.: Conceptualizing 'sense of place' in cultural ecosystem services: a framework for interdisciplinary research. Ecosyst. Serv. **36**, 100907 (2019)
7. Milcu, A., Hanspach, J., Abson, D., Fischer, J.: Cultural ecosystem services: a literature review and prospects for future research. Ecol. Soc. **18**(3), 44 (2013)
8. Blicharska, M., et al.: Shades of grey challenge practical application of the cultural ecosystem services concept. Ecosyst. Serv. **23**, 55–70 (2017)
9. Nielsen, A.B., Olsen, S.B., Lundhede, T.: An economic valuation of the recreational benefits associated with nature-based forest management practices. Landscape Urban Plann. **80**(1–2), 63–71 (2007)
10. Rosenberger, R.S., Needham, M.D., Morzillo, A.T., Moehrke, C.: Attitudes, willingness to pay, and stated values for recreation use fees at an urban proximate forest. J. For. Econ. **18**(4), 271–281 (2012)
11. Fleming, C.M., Cook, A.: The recreational value of Lake McKenzie, Fraser Island: an application of the travel cost method. Tour. Manage. **29**(6), 1197–1205 (2008)

12. Scholte, S.S.K., van Teeffelen, A.J.A., Verburg, P.H.: Integrating socio-cultural perspectives into ecosystem service valuation: a review of concepts and methods. Ecol. Econ. **114**, 67–78 (2015)
13. Cabana, D., Ryfield, F., Crowe, T.P., Brannigan, J.: Evaluating and communicating cultural ecosystem services. Ecosyst. Serv. **42**, 101085 (2020)
14. Plieninger, T., Dijks, S., Oteros-Rozas, E., Bieling, C.: Assessing, mapping, and quantifying cultural ecosystem services at community level. Land Use Policy **33**, 118–129 (2013)
15. Sherrouse, B.C., Clement, J.M., Semmens, D.J.: A GIS application for assessing, mapping, and quantifying the social values of ecosystem services. Appl. Geogr. **31**(2), 748–760 (2011)
16. García-Martín, M., Bieling, C., Hart, A., Plieninger, T.: Integrated landscape initiatives in Europe: multi-sector collaboration in multi-functional landscapes. Land Use Policy **58**, 43–53 (2016)
17. Schirru, M., Canu, S., Santona, L., Lai, S., Motroni, A.: From ecosystems to ecosystem services: a spatial methodology applied to a case study in Sardinia. In: Gargiulo, C., Zoppi, C. (eds.) Planning, Nature and Ecosystem Services. InputaCAdemy 2019 Conference Proceedings, pp. 130–141. FEDOA Press, Napoli, Italy (2019)
18. Carboni, D., Congiatu, P., De Vincenzi, M.: Asinara National Park. An example of growth and sustainability in tourism. J. Environ. Tourism Anal. **3**, 44–60 (2015)
19. Canu, S., Rosati, L., Fiori, M., Motroni, A., Filigheddu, R., Farris, E.: Bioclimate map of Sardinia (Italy). J. Maps **11**, 711–718 (2015)
20. Bocchieri, E., Filigheddu, R.: Aspetti floristici e vegetazionali. In: Forteleoni, C., Gazale, V. (eds.) Asinara. Parco Nazionale Area Marina Protetta. Carlo Delfino Editore, Sassari, Italy (2008)
21. Pisanu, S., Farris, E., Caria, M.C., Filigheddu, R., Urbani, M., Bagella, S.: Vegetation and plant landscape of Asinara National Park (Italy). Plant Sociol. **51**, 31–57 (2014)
22. Drissen, T., Faust, C., Stadtmann, R., Treitler, J.T., Zerbe, S., Mantilla-Contreras, J.: Plant composition and diversity in a semi-natural Mediterranean island landscape: the importance of environmental factors. Plant Biosyst. Int. J. Dealing Aspects Plant Biol. **153**, 756–766 (2019)
23. Gutierrez, M., Mattone A., Valsecchi F.: L'Isola dell'Asinara. La storia, l'ambiente, il Parco. Poliedro, Nuoro, Italy (1998)
24. Forteleoni, C., Gazale, V.: Asinara. Parco Nazionale Area Marina Protetta. Carlo Delfino Editore, Sassari, Italy (2008)
25. Mantilla-Contreras, J., Drissen, T., Wätzold, M., Stadmann, R., Zerbe, S.: What we can learn from the current vegetation for forest restoration in the Mediterranean region – a case study from the island of Asinara. J. Mediterr. Ecol. **16**, 51–66 (2018)
26. Gallent, N.: Bridging social capital and the resource potential of second homes: the case of Stintino, Sardinia. J. Rural Stud. **38**, 99–108 (2015)

An Ecosystem Services-Based Territorial Ranking for Italian Provinces

Angela Pilogallo[✉] [iD], Francesco Scorza, and Beniamino Murgante

University of Basilicata, Viale dell'Ateneo Lucano 10, 85100 Potenza, Italy
angela.pilogallo@unibas.it

Abstract. Cities' Rankings are increasingly used to compare territorial performances related to different dimensions of well-being or territorial development. In the context of urban and territorial planning, they often contribute to legitimizing governance processes and have a marked influence on the evaluation of the policies' success. Therefore, even if those analytical practices cannot be considered as robust tools, they express a great potential in terms of communication capacity and as an awareness raising tool.

The aim of this work is to combine the concept of ranking with the methodological framework of Ecosystem Services (ES), considered a reference in the evaluation of urban and territorial development components towards sustainability. Based on a spatially explicit assessment of a relevant set of ES, the Multiple Ecosystem Services Landscape Index (MESLI) was assessed for the Italian national territory. The resulting spatial distributed layer was subsequently aggregated in order to obtain a ranking of Italian territories based on the concept of ecosystem multifunctionality. The results show an unexpected representation of the environmental performance of the territorial units, which are markedly affected by the reciprocal relationships between environmental and anthropic components of the territorial system. The conclusions highlight the potential of this synthetic indicator that provides valid arguments for the public debate about sustainability and ecosystem multifunctionality driving the attention of decision makers and citizens on the role of ESs' value in strategic planning and development. The aims are to stimulate a debate concerning environmental performances and to contribute in increasing the non-experts demand for sustainability in the territorial governance processes.

Keywords: Ecosystem services · Cities ranking · Transdisciplinary · Ecosystem multifunctionality · MESLI · Sustainable governance processes

1 Introduction

In the last years decision making processes are heavily driven by unstructured knowledge frameworks often based on informal surveys. Rapid consensus building often deadens the role of science and research as conduits for robust and reliable advice. This attitude gives rise to lists that are hierarchically organized from 'best' to 'worst', but which prove

© Springer Nature Switzerland AG 2021
O. Gervasi et al. (Eds.): ICCSA 2021, LNCS 12955, pp. 692–702, 2021.
https://doi.org/10.1007/978-3-030-87007-2_49

to be an effective support in urban decision-making and in the definition of operational priorities.

This drift in rational decision making [1–3] is also found in urban and land use planning as a decision support discipline in the field of people-centered management of land resources oriented towards sustainable land transformations.

In the framework of this kind of unstructured knowledge, we consider the "Cities Ranking" as a heterogeneous system of indicators to which we recognize a strong potential of communication towards different target groups and able to influence urban and territorial policies as well as investments.

The potential of the "Cities Ranking" lies in contributing to the awareness of citizens on issues such as sustainable development, resilience, well-being, quality of life, environmental quality, etc.

Assessing sustainability in land use policies and management becomes a benchmarking exercise in which ranking cities is a way to legitimize a government decision or the success of a specific choice. According to Mc Manus [4] this trend encourages the ranking of cities through extensive use of sustainability indices in comparative studies of urban sustainability.

While it continues to fall short of the promise of prosperity for all [5], it still grounds current policies that link the "smart city" approach with the "post-pandemic recovery" claim.

In this global process, tools such as "city rankings" become more important in management and strategic planning. Indeed, best practices are those that allow a city to climb the rankings. These topics are often the focus within the discourses of decision-makers and support the debate of ordinary people by influencing the behaviors and choices of individual citizens.

In addition, the presence for long periods of time in the upper reaches of the rankings translated for some cities into being identified as examples, inspiring urban models and incentivizing researchers to identify laws and structures that contribute to city effectiveness. The scholarly debate concerns those who deplore the effort in developing large-scale urban models [6] and opposed those who invested in modeling cities [7–11] by the rank-size rule.

On the one hand, there are those who oppose the simplification of reality through the use of indicators to unpack complex phenomena and communicate them more easily [12]. On the other hand there is a domain for professionals and politicians but also for scholars who place their complex urban and territorial modeling in an applied perspective.

Within this debate, it is our intention to assume transdisciplinarity as part of a "science-policy interface" capable of pursuing goals of integrating ecosystem value into governance processes by resorting to the synergy of different perspectives and contributions (researcher, policy makers, practitioners, stakeholders). Interactive communication" thus assumes a more relevant role than discipline-specific knowledge, and synthetic indicators can be more effective than detailed descriptions based on a structured technical background.

If Ecosystem Services (ES) represent an innovative approach to guide territorial development towards sustainability, an ES City Ranking can be a more effective way to better position this thesis in the public debate by gaining priority on the political agenda and building public trust.

These topics are included in the challenges regarding the inclusion of (ES) in integrative landscape planning and decision making under the concept of "interactive communication tools" [13]. Indeed, we recognize that the ES approach is gaining an increasingly important role in policy and legislative frameworks but agree with those who argue [14–17] that there is a lack of fully explicit use of ES assessments.

Stimulating public debate is indeed the first step to pave the way for a bottom-up definition of territorial governance policies and strategies in which ES assessment is fully integrated.

The aim of this work is a proposal for a new Cities Ranking developed on the basis of ES perspectives and analytics and based on a multifunctionality ES index: the MESLI. The result is a new territorial rank that finds applications from short to long term: in the short term it can stimulate public debate on prioritizing ES' fully integration in policies; in the medium term, it can improve the green deal transition by integrating ES values into governance processes; in the long term to pursue sustainability goals described in terms of performance of natural and semi-natural systems.

2 Materials and Methods

In the ES perspective, "multifunctionality" constitutes a broad concept that refers to the joint supply of multiple services, functions and benefits. From the planning perspective, assessing ES multifunctionality is an integrated approach to investigate the efficiency [18] of land uses patterns and to express the interaction between ecosystems and the anthropic components in terms of multiple benefits derived from nature [19].

In this work we refer to multifunctionality as a synthetic index expressing the capacity to *simultaneously* provide several ES that, following a social-ecological perspective [20], supports the comparison between different territorial units and produces a strong communicative representation allowing citizens to perceive ES multifunctionality as a proxy of the quality of environment where they live. With this aim, we selected a meaningful indicator for ES multifunctionality considered fairly consistent on various spatial scales [21]: the Multiple ES Landscape Index (MESLI).

It is a synthetic index based on the sum of the standardized ES indicators [22] that consider several ES relevant of the environmental performances from different ecosystems [23]. It is thus both representative of the number of ES provided and their intensity [24].

Because ES biophysical assessment implies the comparison among non-comparable quantities, synthetic indices require normalization of the dataset for each ES considered.

The MESLI index was calculated according to the formula (1):

$$\sum_{i=1}^{n} \frac{Observed\ value_i - Low\ performance\ benchmark_i}{Target - Low\ performance\ benchmark_i} \tag{1}$$

for n ES providing a positive contribution to the territorial performance.

All the ES layer were normalized in a 0–1 scale where 0 values correspond to the lowest performance benchmark and the value 1 is significant of the ES target fulfillment.

According to its original formulation, if the ES are not characterized by well-defined target and low-performance benchmark, the minimum (equal to 0) and the maximum (equal to 1) values are assigned to the minimum and the maximum biophysical assets considering a time series.

In our case, we considered seven ES belonging to several class according to the CICES v5.1 classification [25]. The following table summarizes the values used as target and low performance benchmark, the methodologies used to assess each ES. For details on the methodologies and datasets used, we refer to previous work [26–30] (Table 1).

Table 1. List of selected ES with their indicators and low and high performance benchmarks (Min. t. s., Max. t. s.: minimum and maximum value in entire time series data).

Class	Indicators	Methodology	Unit	Low Perf. benchmarks	Target
Regulation of chemical composition of atmosphere	Carbon stock	InVEST model	Shades/Ha	0	Max t.s
	CO_2 uptake	Equation by Clark et al. 2001 [25, 26]	$g/m^2/yr$	Min t.s	Max t.s
Pollination	Pollination abundance	InVEST model	Index (dimensionless)	0	1
	Pollination supply	InVEST model	Index (dimensionless)	0	1
Maintaining nursery populations and habitats	Habitat quality	InVEST model	Index (dimensionless)	0	1
	Habitat degradation	InVEST model	Index (dimensionless)	0	Max t.s
Control of erosion rates	Erosion rates	InVEST model	Shades/Ha	0	Max t.s
Regulation of the chemical condition of freshwaters	Effective nutrients retention	InVEST model	Index (dimensionless)	0	1
Cultivated terrestrial plants grown for nutritional purposes	Crop production	InVEST model	q/Ha	0	Max t.s
Ground (and subsurface) water for drinking	Water yield	Equation by Budyko [31]	mm/yr/Ha	0	Max t.s

The MESLI index calculated for n ES, ranges between 0 and n: the higher the value, the more the system performs well in terms of ES multifunctionality.

The methodology provides a spatially continuous distribution of the MESLI index, resulting in a raster that keeps the resolution of the Corine Land Cover (100 m).

3   Results and Discussion

From the MESLI raster, we performed a spatial aggregation of MESLI values considering the administrative boundaries of the Italian provinces as the reference territorial unit. In particular, with the aim of assess the territorial performance as a unique value, we run in a GIS environment a zonal statistics analysis where the mean value of the data distribution was assigned to each Province.

The next chart show how MESLI value varies among Italian Provinces. It is an heterogeneous distribution that we aggregates in three classes in order to consider such values as a comprehensive measure of ES multifunctionality more than a responsive analytical tool to describe in details each territorial unit (Fig. 1).

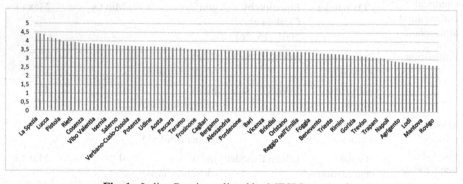

Fig. 1. Italian Provinces listed by MESLI mean value

The result is the Fig. 2, a representation of the Italian territory classified in 3 classes based on the MESLI mean value. First considerations emerge from this representation: low values characterize the Provinces of the Northern part of the Country: of the Po Valley, and in most of the Provinces of the Sicily Region; on the other hand, the Apennine areas emerge, with mean values of ecosystem multifunctionality that vary from medium to high. The coastal areas assume quite variable values while generally the provinces that correspond to the metropolitan areas assume average values lower than the surrounding territory.

Provinces that are nationally recognized as major poles for agricultural productivity (part of the Apulia Region and Matera Province) take MESLI low values.

The role of Parks, Reserves, and protected areas also emerges: in facts, natural areas contribute significantly to MESLI as characterized by a marked multiple ecosystem services delivery capacity. This is the case of the Province of Trento and Belluno in Northern Italy, the Province of L'Aquila in Central Italy, and the Provinces between Cilento Park and Pollino National Park in the Southern part of the Peninsula.

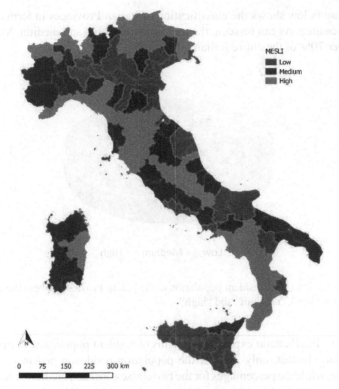

Fig. 2. Classification of the Italian Provinces according to the MESLI index

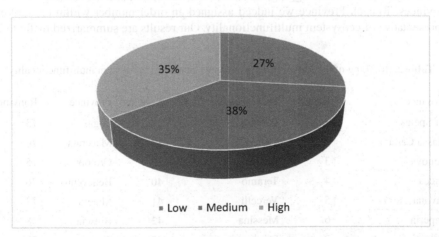

Fig. 3. Classification of the administrative area of the Italian Provinces where the average value of the MESLI is "low", "medium" and "high"

The figure below shows the classification of Italian Provinces in terms of administrative surface area. As can be seen, the provinces with high and medium MESLI values make up over 70% of the entire Italian territory (Fig. 3).

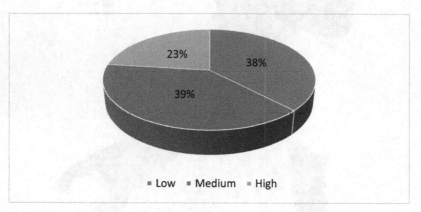

Fig. 4. Classification of the resident population in the Italian Provinces where the average value of the MESLI is "low", "medium" and "high"

The same classification expressed in terms of resident population shows a different picture of Italy. In fact, only 23% of the population resides in provinces with a high MESLI value, while the percentages for the two classes, low and medium, are comparable (Fig. 4).

Finally, MESLI spatial aggregated values allowed us to build the ranking of Italian Provinces. To each Province we indeed assigned an order number within the ranking representative of ecosystem multifunctionality. Our results are summarized in Table 2.

Table 2. Ranking of the Italian Provinces representative of ecosystem multifunctionality

Province	Ranking	Province	Ranking	Province	Ranking
La Spezia	1	Pescara	37	Foggia	73
Massa Carrara	2	Cuneo	38	Macerata	74
Genova	3	Perugia	39	Crotone	75
Lucca	4	Teramo	40	Benevento	76
Savona	5	Vercelli	41	Matera	77
Imperia	6	Messina	42	Brescia	78
Pistoia	7	Frosinone	43	Trieste	79
Belluno	8	Torino	44	Latina	80
Arezzo	9	Piacenza	45	Ravenna	81
Rieti	10	Cagliari	46	Rimini	82

(*continued*)

Table 2. (*continued*)

Province	Ranking	Province	Ranking	Province	Ranking
Catanzaro	11	Sud Sardegna	47	Campobasso	83
Prato	12	Sassari	48	Pavia	84
Cosenza	13	Bergamo	49	Gorizia	85
Trento	14	Sondrio	50	Siracusa	86
L'Aquila	15	Caserta	51	Catania	87
Vibo Valentia	16	Alessandria	52	Treviso	88
Firenze	17	Novara	53	Ancona	89
Reggio di Calabria	18	Livorno	54	Ferrara	90
Isernia	19	Pordenone	55	Trapani	91
Lecco	20	Chieti	56	Verona	92
Biella	21	Avellino	57	Fermo	93
Salerno	22	Bari	58	Napoli	94
Como	23	Asti	59	Ragusa	95
Forlì'-Cesena	24	Barletta-Andria-Trani	60	Palermo	96
Verbano-Cusio-Ossola	25	Vicenza	61	Agrigento	97
Parma	26	Lecce	62	Enna	98
Bolzano	27	Pisa	63	Monza e della Brianza	99
Potenza	28	Brindisi	64	Lodi	100
Nuoro	29	Bologna	65	Cremona	101
Varese	30	Taranto	66	Milano	102
Udine	31	Oristano	67	Mantova	103
Terni	32	Pesaro e Urbino	68	Caltanissetta	104
Ascoli Piceno	33	Viterbo	69	Padova	105
Aosta	34	Reggio nell'Emilia	70	Rovigo	106
Grosseto	35	Roma	71	Venezia	107
Siena	36	Modena	72		

The ranking returns a singular image of Italy in which it is difficult to find correspondence in terms of territorial displacement. As can be seen, in fact, the first positions are occupied by provinces in Northern Italy, immediately followed by southern provinces (Catanzaro and Cosenza). Similarly, in the last positions are found Provinces of Northern and Southern Italy. This confirms that the MESLI-based ranking represents an alternative way to classify the territorial performances in terms of ecosystem services multifunctionality as a function of land use and spatial distribution of anthropogenic activities that pose a threat to biodiversity and beneficial habitat conservation.

4 Conclusions

The aim of this work was to propose an alternative territorial ranking based on the concept of ecosystem multifunctionality derived on the basis of a spatially explicit assessment of a relevant set of ESs. This spatial analytic may contribute to the public debate on territorial sustainability assessment providing a valid argument for comparing spatial units in terms of multi-ecosystem performance [32–36].

"Cities Ranking" indeed constitute increasing used tools in urban and regional planning debate because of their potential in influencing policies and investments as well as their communication toward beneficiaries and the general public.

The MESLI-based ranking, based on ecosystem services multifunctionality, represents an influencing tool to argue the relation between natural and semi-natural territorial endowment and the perceived level of well-being that citizens perceive as the result of local development policies.

This represents a step to integrate ES thinking into decision-making, urban governance processes and in policy design [37]. However, its operationalization [38] requires an effort by the scientific community and greater public support in legitimizing protection and conservation policies and GI development [39, 40]. In this regard we explored the ranking tool as an approach for paving the way for the definition of ES-integrated governance processes stimulating the awareness about ES from a non-expert public [41] and increasing the citizens' demand for sustainable territorial management more than make place to informal and ghost planning [42].

References

1. Faludi, A.: A Decision Centered View of Environmental Planning. Pergamon Press, Oxford (1987)
2. McLoughlin, J.B.: Urban and Regional Planning. Faber and Faber, London (1969)
3. Faludi, A.: Critical rationalism and planning methodology. Urban Stud. **20**, 265–278 (1983). https://doi.org/10.1080/00420988320080521
4. McManus, P.: Measuring Urban Sustainability: the potential and pitfalls of city rankings. Aust. Geogr. **43**, 411–424 (2012). https://doi.org/10.1080/00049182.2012.731301
5. Sheppard, E., Leitner, H., Maringanti, A.: Provincializing global urbanism: a manifesto. Urban Geogr. **34**, 893–900 (2013). https://doi.org/10.1080/02723638.2013.807977
6. Lee, D.B.: Requiem for large-scale models. J. Am. Plan. Assoc. **39**, 163–178 (1973)
7. Batty, M.: Rank clocks. Nature **444**, 592–596 (2006). https://doi.org/10.1038/nature05302
8. Batty, M.: The New Science of Cities. MIT Press, Cambridge (2013)
9. Batty, M.: The computable city. Int. Plan. Stud. **2**, 155–173 (1997). https://doi.org/10.1080/13563479708721676
10. Klosterman, R.E.: Large-scale urban models retrospect and prospect. J. Am. Plan. Assoc. **60**, 3–6 (1994). https://doi.org/10.1080/01944369408975545
11. Harris, B.: The real issues concerning Lee's "Requiem." J. Am. Plan. Assoc. **60**, 31–34 (1994). https://doi.org/10.1080/01944369408975548
12. Parker, P.: From sustainable development objectives to indicators of progress. N. Z. Geogr. **51**, 50–57 (1995). https://doi.org/10.1111/j.1745-7939.1995.tb02051.x

13. de Groot, R.S., Alkemade, R., Braat, L., Hein, L., Willemen, L.: Challenges in integrating the concept of ecosystem services and values in landscape planning, management and decision making. Ecol. Complex. **7**, 260–272 (2010). https://doi.org/10.1016/J.ECOCOM.2009. 10.006
14. Kistenkas, F.H., Bouwma, I.M.: Barriers for the ecosystem services concept in European water and nature conservation law. Ecosyst. Serv. **29**, 223–227 (2018). https://doi.org/10. 1016/j.ecoser.2017.02.013
15. Bouwma, I., et al.: Adoption of the ecosystem services concept in EU policies. Ecosyst. Serv. **29**, 213–222 (2018). https://doi.org/10.1016/j.ecoser.2017.02.014
16. McKinley, E., Ballinger, R.C., Beaumont, N.J.: Saltmarshes, ecosystem services, and an evolving policy landscape: a case study of Wales. UK. Mar. Policy. **91**, 1 (2018). https://doi. org/10.1016/j.marpol.2018.01.021
17. Grizzetti, B., et al.: Ecosystem services for water policy: insights across Europe. Environ. Sci. Policy. **66**, 179–190 (2016). https://doi.org/10.1016/j.envsci.2016.09.006
18. Galler, C., von Haaren, C., Albert, C.: Optimizing environmental measures for landscape multifunctionality: effectiveness, efficiency and recommendations for agri-environmental programs. J. Environ. Manage. **151**, 243–257 (2015). https://doi.org/10.1016/j.jenvman.2014. 12.011
19. Queiroz, C., et al.: Mapping bundles of ecosystem services reveals distinct types of multifunctionality within a Swedish landscape. Ambio **44**(1), 89–101 (2015). https://doi.org/10. 1007/s13280-014-0601-0
20. Hansen, R., Pauleit, S.: From multifunctionality to multiple ecosystem services? A conceptual framework for multifunctionality in green infrastructure planning for urban areas. Ambio **43**(4), 516–529 (2014). https://doi.org/10.1007/s13280-014-0510-2
21. Stürck, J., Verburg, P.H.: Multifunctionality at what scale? A landscape multifunctionality assessment for the European Union under conditions of land use change. Landscape Ecol. **32**(3), 481–500 (2016). https://doi.org/10.1007/s10980-016-0459-6
22. Shen, J., Li, S., Liang, Z., Liu, L., Li, D., Wu, S.: Exploring the heterogeneity and nonlinearity of trade-offs and synergies among ecosystem services bundles in the Beijing-Tianjin-Hebei urban agglomeration. Ecosyst. Serv. **43**, 101103 (2020). https://doi.org/10.1016/j.ecoser.2020. 101103
23. Manning, P., et al.: Redefining ecosystem multifunctionality. https://www.nature.com/art icles/s41559-017-0461-7 (2018). https://doi.org/10.1038/s41559-017-0461-7
24. Rodríguez-Loinaz, G., Alday, J.G., Onaindia, M.: Multiple ecosystem services landscape index: a tool for multifunctional landscapes conservation. J. Environ. Manage. **147**, 152–163 (2015). https://doi.org/10.1016/j.jenvman.2014.09.001
25. Haines-Young, R., Potschin, M.: Common International Classification of Ecosystem Services (CICES) V5.1 Guidance on the Application of the Revised Structure (2018)
26. Scorza, F., Pilogallo, A., Saganeiti, L., Murgante, B.: Natura 2000 areas and sites of national interest (SNI): measuring (un)integration between naturalness preservation and environmental remediation policies. Sustainability **12**, 2928 (2020). https://doi.org/10.3390/su12072928
27. Scorza, F., Pilogallo, A., Saganeiti, L., Murgante, B., Pontrandolfi, P.: Comparing the territorial performances of renewable energy sources' plants with an integrated ecosystem services loss assessment: a case study from the Basilicata region (Italy). Sustain. Cities Soc. **56**, 102082 (2020). https://doi.org/10.1016/J.SCS.2020.102082
28. Pilogallo, A., Saganeiti, L., Scorza, F., Murgante, B.: Ecosystem services' based impact assessment for low carbon transition processes. TeMA - J. L. Use Mobil. Environ. **12**, 127–138 (2019). https://doi.org/10.6092/1970-9870/6117

29. Pilogallo, A., Saganeiti, L., Scorza, F., Murgante, B.: Soil ecosystem services and sediment production: the Basilicata region case study. In: Gervasi, O., et al. (eds.) ICCSA 2020. LNCS, vol. 12253, pp. 421–435. Springer, Cham (2020). https://doi.org/10.1007/978-3-030-58814-4_30

30. Pilogallo, A., Scorza, F.: Mapping regulation ecosystem services (ReMES) specialization in Italy. J. Urban Plan. Dev. (2021)

31. Marlatt, W.E., Budyko, M.I., Miller, D.H.: Climate and life. J. Range Manag. 28, 160 (1975). https://doi.org/10.2307/3897455

32. Las Casas, G., Scorza, F., Murgante, B.: Razionalità a-priori: una proposta verso una pianificazione antifragile. Ital. J. Reg. Sci. 2, 329–338 (2019). https://doi.org/10.14650/93656

33. Pilogallo, A., Saganeiti, L., Scorza, F., Las Casas, G.: Tourism attractiveness: main components for a spacial appraisal of major destinations according with ecosystem services approach. In: Gervasi, O., et al. (eds.) ICCSA 2018. LNCS, vol. 10964, pp. 712–724. Springer, Cham (2018). https://doi.org/10.1007/978-3-319-95174-4_54

34. Scorza, F., Pilogallo, A., Las Casas, G.: Investigating tourism attractiveness in inland areas: ecosystem services, open data and smart specializations. In: Calabrò, F., Della Spina, L., Bevilacqua, C. (eds.) ISHT 2018. SIST, vol. 100, pp. 30–38. Springer, Cham (2019). https://doi.org/10.1007/978-3-319-92099-3_4

35. Scorza, F., Fortunato, G., Carbone, R., Murgante, B., Pontrandolfi, P.: Increasing urban walkability through citizens' participation processes. Sustainability 13, 5835 (2021). https://doi.org/10.3390/su13115835

36. Las Casas, G., Scorza, F., Murgante, B.: New urban agenda and open challenges for urban and regional planning. In: Calabrò, F., Della Spina, L., Bevilacqua, C. (eds.) ISHT 2018. SIST, vol. 100, pp. 282–288. Springer, Cham (2019). https://doi.org/10.1007/978-3-319-92099-3_33

37. Braat, L.C., de Groot, R.: The ecosystem services agenda: bridging the worlds of natural science and economics, conservation and development, and public and private policy (2012). https://doi.org/10.1016/j.ecoser.2012.07.011

38. Stępniewska, M.: Ecosystem service mapping and assessment as a support for policy and decision making. CLEAN - Soil, Air, Water. 44, 1414–1422 (2016). https://doi.org/10.1002/clen.201500777

39. Lai, S., Leone, F., Zoppi, C.: Implementing green infrastructures beyond protected areas. Sustainability 10, 3544 (2018). https://doi.org/10.3390/su10103544

40. Lai, S., Leone, F., Zoppi, C.: Assessment of municipal masterplans aimed at identifying and fostering green infrastructure: a study concerning three towns of the metropolitan area of Cagliari. Italy. Sustain. 11, 1470 (2019). https://doi.org/10.3390/su11051470

41. Ehrlich, P.R., Pringle, R.M.: Where does biodiversity go from here? A grim business-as-usual forecast and a hopeful portfolio of partial solutions. Proc. Natl. Acad. Sci. U.S.A. 105, 11579–11586 (2008). https://doi.org/10.1073/pnas.0801911105

42. Scorza, F., Saganeiti, L., Pilogallo, A., Murgante, B.: Ghost planning: the inefficiency of energy sector policies in a low population density region. Arch. di Stud. Urbani e Reg. 34–55 (2020). https://doi.org/10.3280/ASUR2020-127-S1003

Regulation and Maintenance Ecosystem Services (ReMES): A Spatial Assessment in the Basilicata Region (Southern Italy)

Angela Pilogallo(✉) [ID] and Francesco Scorza

University of Basilicata, Viale dell'Ateneo Lucano 10, 85100 Potenza, Italy
angela.pilogallo@unibas.it

Abstract. The current spatial planning system in Italy demonstrates its lack of a data infrastructure so robust, flexible and adaptive to provide adequate performance in the capacity to support the decision-making process. This weakness is manifested even more in the management of the territorial transformations under the pressure of rapid changes involving social, environmental and economic dimensions. The ecosystem services (ES) approach constitutes a robust framework to contribute to the renewal of the planning system by making explicit complex dynamics until now considered only marginally and by introducing spatially explicit knowledge as an effective decision support system (DSS). This work focuses on the class of Regulating and Maintaining Ecosystem Services (ReMES) as it is considered particularly relevant with respect to the ecosystems' potential of expressing environmental performance and contributing to human well-being. A further characteristic of this class is the often significant mismatch between the spatial scale of the territorial transformations and the (larger) scale at which changes in ES supply are measured.

The aim of this work is therefore to represent the spatial distribution of a relevant set of ES in the Basilicata Region (Southern Italy) thus contributing to the development of a cross-sectoral spatial knowledge infrastructure with respect to components still managed within the planning processes in a sectoral and fragmented way. The results highlight the usefulness of such a tool for the comparison between different planning scenarios including both environmental conservation issues and socio-economic development strategies.

Keywords: Ecosystem services · Regulation and Maintenance Ecosystem Services (ReMES) · Territorial specialization · Territorial transformations

1 Introduction

The rapid changes occurred in recent decades from the environmental, social, and economic perspectives revealed some limits of traditional approaches of the planning discipline and in the management of territorial transformations and land use changes.

The planning system showed structural weaknesses from both a regulatory and informative perspective. The first concerns the un-adaptive nature of traditional zoning and of

© Springer Nature Switzerland AG 2021
O. Gervasi et al. (Eds.): ICCSA 2021, LNCS 12955, pp. 703–716, 2021.
https://doi.org/10.1007/978-3-030-87007-2_50

the regulatory models applied in urban and regional planning; the second relates to the provision of spatial data infrastructures capable to support decision making accounting the three components of sustainability (environmental, social and economic) [1] and the human well-being [2, 3].

We need to make the planning processes more comprehensive and integrated [4] since they still do not fully meet the demand for tools to support policy making and the development of alternative transformation scenarios [5, 6].

In this regard we refer to the *"ultimate goal of spatial planning"* [7] that should be improving the decision-makers' territorial knowledge about current and future issues of the contexts where the plan will be implemented.

The Ecosystem Services (ES) Approach proved to be a robust framework for territorial analysis [8] and for spatially explaining the trade-offs associated to different land use patterns [9] and transformations [10], improving the communication and the debate among the stakeholders [8] involved in the different levels of governance.

The aim of this work is to contribute to building territorial knowledge by mapping a relevant set of Regulation and Maintenance Ecosystem Services (ReMES) at the regional scale of the Basilicata Region (Southern Italy) referred to the year 2018.

According to the CICES classification [11], they have a strong influence on the ability of the environment to contribute to the quality of human life even if they are not directly consumed. Furthermore, belonging to the Division of "Regulation of physical, chemical, biological conditions", they are relevant for express a measure of the ecosystems quality [12].

For the purposes of this work, we selected the following 5 classes [13]: i) Regulation of chemical composition of atmosphere; ii) Pollination; iii) Maintaining nursery populations and habitats; iv) Control of erosion rates; v) Regulation of the chemical condition of freshwaters.

We developed this data infrastructure as a baseline of reference to encourage the comparison between alternative development scenarios in an ex-ante evaluation of the planning process. Our results are also useful to monitor the transformation and the relative environmental performances following the implementation of territorial policies [14].

The conclusions highlight the contribution that a data infrastructure based on ReMES mapping as a crosscutting informative layer useful in different planning processes, from the urban to the regional scale.

2 Materials and Methods

According to the CICES classification, five ES classes were selected in relation to their significance for the assessment of the current status of ecosystems in the Basilicata Region.

Most of them were assessed by the means of the InVEST models, a set of spatial-explicit software widely used to map not belonging to traditional markets [15].

The basic spatial information layer necessary for all of the ES assessed, was the "land use map", i.e. the CORINE Land Cover (year 2018) made available as part of the Copernicus program.

The results are maps representing the spatial distribution of the ES supply to be intended as a baseline of reference to compare alternative development scenarios. This data layers constitute the basis for future territorial analysis oriented to explicate the relations between multiple ES and to support the development of win-win solutions in both land use management and territorial planning [16–18].

A methodology is finally applied in order to define "areas of specialization" and identify part of the regional territory actually performing better in terms of ES multifunctionality.

2.1 Carbon Storage

The assessment of Carbon storage constitutes an increasingly relevant layer for the design of policies defined into strategies for climate change adaptation and mitigation.

The recent classification of the CICES v.5.1 [11] consider Carbon stock an ecosystem function [19] but allows its assessment as a proxy of the regulatory effect that the ecosystem provides with respect to all atmospheric components [20].

For the purposes of this work, we considered the Carbon stock strictly related to the land use pattern [21] so we employed the InVEST Carbon Storage and Sequestration Model to map the spatial distribution of carbon stock extending previous case studies [22] and referring to biophysical tables depending on the Land Use/Land Cover class [23].

The processing results (Fig. 1) still have the resolution of the CORINE land-use map. According to the nature of the implemented model, the values are distributed among discrete ranges varying from 0 t/ha for "urbanized areas" to 168 t/ha for "forests" that corresponds to the maximum pixel value.

Fig. 1. Carbon stock

The carbon stock map shows that the most significant reservoirs in the Region are located along the Apennine chain in the western part of the regional territory.

2.2 Crop Pollination

The pollination is recognized as a fundamental ReMES since its importance is linked to both the protection of biodiversity and to agricultural productivity related to the food security.

At the European level, there is an explicit policy demand for the protection of the pollinators habitats: the EU Biodiversity strategy [24] for example explicitly requires the Member States to map spatial distribution of pollination services and to evaluate their economic value.

In this work we used the InVEST Crop pollination tool based on the territorial availability of suitable nesting grounds and food considered as necessary conditions to provide pollinators' habitat.

Input data required are: the potential availability of nesting sites and floral resources, the flight range of pollination species and their seasonality [25].

Basing on land use classes [26], the model uses expert estimations about nesting and floral resources to give as results two maps: the "pollinator supply" describing the availability of pollinators; the "pollinator abundance" representing the potential presence of pollinators, i.e. the area where pollination services are delivered.

The results thus depend not only on the land cover class but also on the pattern of land uses.

Literature dataset for each Land Use Class [27] were used to derive information about floral availability and nesting suitability as well as data concerning the flight range and seasonality of pollinators [28].

The results' resolution is the same of the Corine Land Use Map (Fig. 2).

Fig. 2. Pollination abundance

Being significant of an observation probability, both maps vary between 0 and 1.

As can be seen, the areas where the pollination service is provided with a greater intensity correspond to "forestlands" and vegetated areas in which the herbaceous and shrub cover is intermixed. The pollinator supply distribution assumes its maximum value in correspondence of "transitional woodland shrub", "forests" and "sparsely vegetated areas".

The pollination abundance is relevant in those areas where the regulating services are delivered and its intensity reaches the maximum where extensive "natural grasslands" are present (Fig. 3).

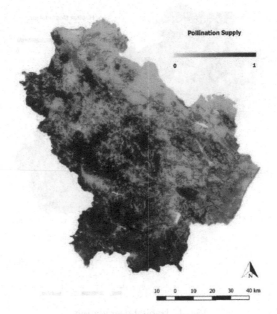

Fig. 3. Pollination supply

2.3 Habitat Quality and Degradation

Habitat quality and degradation was assessed as a proxy of the CICES class "Maintaining nursery populations and habitats". We used InVEST 'Habitat Quality and Degradation' [25] module that combines information on habitat suitability, depending from the land use, and different threats deriving from anthropic activities.

The model is sensitive to the spatial distribution of habitat and pressures and it can support the monitoring of the interactions between natural and anthropic components.

The results are two maps: "habitat degradation" resulting from the cumulative effects of anthropic pressure that contribute to degradation; "habitat quality", ranging from 0 (low habitat quality) to 1 (high habitat quality) and derived from the combination of the overall impact and the habitat suitability.

Data needed are: (1) land use map (2) a table describing the weight (in a range between 0 and 1) and the radius of influence where the threat generates an impact (expressed in km) of each threats; (3) a binary raster map for each threats; (4) the sensitivity matrix for each land use class.

In our case, dataset were derived from the literature for both the threats [61–63] and the sensitivity matrix [64–66].

For the Basilicata Region, the degradation map (Fig. 4) varies between 0 and 0.24, with the lowest values corresponding to the higher zones of the Apennines Chain.

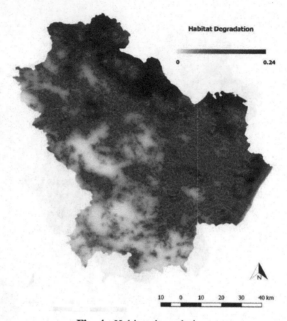

Fig. 4. Habitat degradation

As can be seen from Fig. 4, the highest values of habitat degradation occur in correspondence of the main agricultural areas. The north-eastern part of the Region is in fact characterized by intensive cereals production and very homogeneous land cover.

Habitat Quality (Fig. 5) ranges between 0 and 1, with the null values corresponding to the major urban and industrial centers. Apart from artificial surfaces, the lowest value can be observed in the eastern part of the Region, where an intensive agriculture is practiced. The values closest to one are observed in correspondence of wetlands along the coast strip which have been assigned a very high naturalness value, and in the more remote wooded areas where the distance from the sources of threat is higher.

Fig. 5. Habitat quality

2.4 Control of Erosion Rates

There's a general agree about the need to conserve the soil since it is one of the main provider of ES [29] being essential for agricultural productivity, for the carbon cycle regulation [30] and the biodiversity preservation [31] and a key component to pursue sustainable development objectives [32].

In this work we used Sediment Delivery Ratio (SDR) InVEST module [33], a spatially-explicit software able to model erosive phenomena and to represent the spatial variability of soil loss [34]. It is based on the Revised Universal Soil Loss Equation (RUSLE) [35] that allows to map the distribution of the annual average soil loss (tons/ha/yr).

Data required are: (1) the Land Use Map; (2) a table of the values of the crop management (C) and support practice (P) parameters assigned to each Land Use Class; (3) the Digital Elevation Model (DEM); (4–5) two raster dataset for the rainfall erosivity (R) and the soil erodibility (K).

The "crop management factor" (C) represents the capability of land use cover to limit the rainfall impact [36]; we used the dataset developed by Panagos et al. [37].

The support practice (P) accounts for agricultural management practices that contrast erosive phenomena; for these values, we referred to datasets available in the literature [38].

The "rainfall erosivity" (R) is a measure of the rainfall energy [39] expressed in [MJ $\cdot$ mm $\cdot$ ha^{-1} $\cdot$ hr^{-1}] and it depends from the total kinetic energy, the duration and the intensity of a rainfall [40]. We used available dataset with 1 km resolution and based on the Rainfall Erosivity Database on the European Scale (REDES) [39].

The "soil erodibility factor" (K) (Mg$\cdot$h$\cdot$MJ^{-1}$\cdot$mm^{-1}) represents the susceptibility of soil particles to be detached and transported by rainfalls and runoff [40]. In this work, we used the dataset derived from the JRC's European Soil Data Centre (ESDAC) [41] with 1 km resolution.

Fig. 6. Erosion rates

The result of this elaboration is a map (Fig. 6) representing the phenomenon of soil loss: the highest value thus characterize the area where the provisioning of the ES is minimum. As can be seen, in the Basilicata Region the most intensive erosive phenomena occur in the central part of the territory, in particular along the western slope of the Apennine Chain where morphological characteristics significantly influence hydrogeological processes.

2.5 Regulation of Freshwaters' Quality

Mapping the Regulation of freshwaters' quality as ReMES constitute a useful data layer because it supports the interpretation of the interactions occurring between: land uses representing a source of pollution (e.g. agricultural uses); land use representing a potential filter to mitigate contamination (e.g. areas covered by riparian vegetation); water bodies. The results are thus support the design for action aimed at improving the surface water quality [42].

The model applied, the InVEST Nutrient Delivery Ratio, simulates the movement of pollutants (Nitrogen and Phosphorus) by computing a mass balance combined with the territorial morphology. It can model both the components transported through surface and subsurface flows. Input data required are: (1) The land use map; (2) the Digital elevation model (DEM); (3) the nutrient runoff proxy representing the capacity to transport pollutants downstream; (4) the watersheds vector layer; (5) a biophysical table summarizing the nutrient loading (kg/Ha/yr).

Fig. 7. Nutrients effective retention

For the biophysical table the data used in this work were collected by Salata et al. [42].

Among the outputs of the model, we considered the layer called "effective nutrients retention" (Fig. 7) as the most relevant output for the purposes of this work since it represents the filtering potential of each territorial unit. This layer is indeed a function of land use and the runoff pattern depending on territorial morphology.

The value of Effective Retention varies between 0 and 1, in our application it is 0, in correspondence with watercourses, and goes up to the maximum values where vegetated areas are located in proximity to watercourses.

3   Results and Discussion

Basing on the results obtained following the software implementation, we identified for each of the ReMES considered an "area of specialization" that is the area of the Regional territory were the supply of each ES reach its maximum values. The criteria used for this identification was a simple classification, based on the third quantile of the overall raster values distribution.

The ultimate goal is defining some area of the Region that are specialized in the ES multifunctionality provision. For this reason, the results (Fig. 8) allow to highlight the areas that play a relevant role in the provision of ReMES, that doesn't mean that only a single ES is supplied in a specific area, but several ES show a relevant magnitude in that area following to different site characteristics.

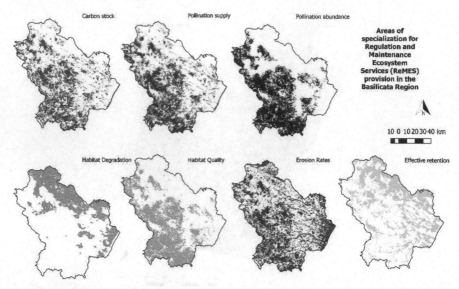

Fig. 8. Areas of specialization for ReMES in the Basilicata Region

Some comprehensive consideration arise: for example the relevance of woods and forests in eastern part of the Region, along the Apennines Chain, emerges. The value of carbon stored ranges from 168 tons/ha for forests, to 125 tons/ha for shrubland and sclerophyllous vegetation. These areas occupy a relevant extension and are characterized by a significant spatial continuity along the entire regional territory. This is a necessary precondition to reinforce biodiversity conservation objectives.

The habitat degradation map highlights the areas where the anthropic pressure is more intense due to the wide presence of anthropic areas and industrial centers, a branched network of transport infrastructures and, above all, the prevalence of intensive agricultural activities. This consideration supports the need to prioritize in territorial governance policies actions and measures that encourage the differentiation of agricultural production and greater ecosystem multifunctionality.

The issue of habitat degradation linked to the intensive agriculture can be furtherly investigated including in the evaluation of the environmental quality, the component related to the freshwaters' quality. As can be seen, in fact, the water component of the environmental matrix is not so affected by the pollution generated by agricultural activities because the advantagious morphological conditions aloow a good degree of natural filtration by soil.

Finally, the pollination abundance and supply are useful if compared with other specialization areas since pollinators' demand and supply can be compared and assessed in function of a comprehensive and systemic environmental quality evaluation. Pollination is in fact essential for agricultural productivity, and the individuation of new ecotonal areas that ensure the sufficient presence of suitable sites for nesting and foraging pollinators and an higher sustainability of current agricultural practices may reinforce the ES multifunctionality supply.

4 Conclusions

The traditional planning system showed to be weak in governing territorial transformations and land use changes according to sustainable principles, especially in view of the growing pressures due to ongoing climate change [43–48].

To tackle these structural challenges, we need to overcome the contraposition between the protection of the natural capital and the sicio-economic development [49, 50].

The main assumption by the authors is that the ES approach can support decision making and the planning processes by enhancing the comparison among different scenarios and thus allowing the formulation of win-win governance solutions.

This work was aimed at propose a methodology oriented to reinforce the knowledge building process, making explicit complex dynamics between ES and anthropic land-uses currently not fully integrated within the plan evaluation process.

Our results highlight the potential of mapping ES multifunctionality in terms of areas of specialization for the supply of multiple ES. Assessing and representing the spatial distribution of this areas are useful to define territorial complementarity among areas of provisioning and areas of major demand. Furthermore, such methodology could support the definition of supplementary measures for example for designing green infrastructures [51, 52].

References

1. Pacione, M.: Urban environmental quality and human wellbeing - a social geographical perspective. In: Landscape and Urban Planning, pp. 19–30. Elsevier (2003). https://doi.org/10.1016/S0169-2046(02)00234-7.
2. Groenewegen, P.P., Van Den Berg, A.E., De Vries, S., Verheij, R.A.: Vitamin G: effects of green space on health, well-being, and social safety. BMC Public Health **6**, 149 (2006). https://doi.org/10.1186/1471-2458-6-149
3. Martín-López, B., et al.: Delineating boundaries of social-ecological systems for landscape planning: a comprehensive spatial approach. Land Use Policy **66**, 90–104 (2017). https://doi.org/10.1016/j.landusepol.2017.04.040
4. Kopperoinen, L., Itkonen, P., Niemelä, J.: Using expert knowledge in combining green infrastructure and ecosystem services in land use planning: an insight into a new place-based methodology. Landscape Ecol. **29**(8), 1361–1375 (2014). https://doi.org/10.1007/s10980-014-0014-2
5. Grêt-Regamey, A., Altwegg, J., Sirén, E.A., van Strien, M.J., Weibel, B.: Integrating ecosystem services into spatial planning—a spatial decision support tool. Landsc. Urban Plan. **165**, 206–219 (2017). https://doi.org/10.1016/j.landurbplan.2016.05.003
6. Cerreta, M., Mele, R., Poli, G.: Urban ecosystem services (UES) assessment within a 3D virtual environment: a methodological approach for the larger urban zones (LUZ) of Naples Italy. Appl. Sci. **10**, 6205 (2020). https://doi.org/10.3390/app10186205
7. Faludi, A.: The performance of spatial planning. Plan. Pract. Res. **15**, 299–318 (2000). https://doi.org/10.1080/713691907
8. Albert, C., Galler, C., Hermes, J., Neuendorf, F., Von Haaren, C., Lovett, A.: Applying ecosystem services indicators in landscape planning and management: the ES-in-planning framework. Ecol. Indic. **61**, 100–113 (2016). https://doi.org/10.1016/j.ecolind.2015.03.029

9. Haase, D., Schwarz, N., Strohbach, M., Kroll, F., Seppelt, R.: Synergies, trade-offs, and losses of ecosystem services in urban regions: an integrated multiscale framework applied to the leipzig-halle region, Germany. Ecol. Soc. **17** (2012). https://doi.org/10.5751/ES-04853-170322

10. Bagstad, K.J., Johnson, G.W., Voigt, B., Villa, F.: Spatial dynamics of ecosystem service flows: a comprehensive approach to quantifying actual services. Ecosyst. Serv. **4**, 117–125 (2013). https://doi.org/10.1016/j.ecoser.2012.07.012

11. Haines-Young, R., Potschin, M.: Common International Classification of Ecosystem Services (CICES) V5.1 guidance on the application of the revised structure. (2018)

12. Maes, J., Barbosa, A.L.: Mapping and assessment of ecosystems and their services: trends in ecosystems and ecosystem services in the European accounting for ecosystem services view project critical raw materials view project (2015). https://doi.org/10.2788/341839

13. Haines-Young, R., Potschin-Young, M.B.: Revision of the common international classification for ecosystem services (CICES V5.1): a policy brief. One Ecosyst. **3**, e27108 (2018). https://doi.org/10.3897/oneeco.3.e27108

14. Scorza, F., Pilogallo, A., Saganeiti, L., Murgante, B.: Natura 2000 areas and sites of national interest (SNI): measuring (un)Integration between naturalness preservation and environmental remediation policies. Sustainability **12**, 2928 (2020). https://doi.org/10.3390/su12072928

15. Isely, E.S., Isely, P., Seedang, S., Mulder, K., Thompson, K., Steinman, A.D.: Addressing the information gaps associated with valuing green infrastructure in west Michigan: Integrated Valuation of Ecosystem Services Tool (INVEST). J. Great Lakes Res. **36**, 448–457 (2010). https://doi.org/10.1016/j.jglr.2010.04.003

16. Yang, Y., Zheng, H., Kong, L., Huang, B., Xu, W., Ouyang, Z.: Mapping ecosystem services bundles to detect high- and low-value ecosystem services areas for land use management. J. Clean. Prod. **225**, 11–17 (2019). https://doi.org/10.1016/j.jclepro.2019.03.242

17. Paulin, M.J., et al.: Towards nationally harmonized mapping and quantification of ecosystem services. Sci. Total Environ. **703**, 134973 (2020). https://doi.org/10.1016/j.scitotenv.2019.134973

18. Burkhard, B., Santos-Martin, F., Nedkov, S., Maes, J.: An operational framework for integrated mapping and assessment of ecosystems and their services (MAES). One Ecosyst. **3**, e22831 (2018). https://doi.org/10.3897/oneeco.3.e22831

19. Maes, J., et al.: Mapping ecosystem services for policy support and decision making in the European Union. Ecosyst. Serv. **1**, 31–39 (2012). https://doi.org/10.1016/j.ecoser.2012.06.004

20. Chaabouni, S., Saidi, K.: The dynamic links between carbon dioxide (CO_2) emissions, health spending and GDP growth: a case study for 51 countries. Environ. Res. **158**, 137–144 (2017). https://doi.org/10.1016/j.envres.2017.05.041

21. Paquit, J.: Modeling the spatial pattern of carbon stock in central Mindanao university using invest tool. J. Biodivers. Environ. Sci. **10**, 103–113 (2017)

22. Mazzariello, A., Pilogallo, A., Scorza, F., Murgante, B., Las Casas, G.: Carbon stock as an indicator for the estimation of anthropic pressure on territorial components. In: Gervasi, O., et al. (eds.) ICCSA 2018. LNCS, vol. 10964, pp. 697–711. Springer, Cham (2018). https://doi.org/10.1007/978-3-319-95174-4_53

23. Sallustio, L., Quatrini, V., Geneletti, D., Corona, P., Marchetti, M.: Assessing land take by urban development and its impact on carbon storage: findings from two case studies in Italy. Environ. Impact Assess. Rev. **54**, 80–90 (2015). https://doi.org/10.1016/j.eiar.2015.05.006

24. European commission: our life insurance, our natural capital: an EU biodiversity strategy. Brussels (2011)

25. Nelson, E., et al.: InVEST 3.5.0 User's Guide. The Natural Capital Project. (2018)

26. Davis, A.Y., et al.: Enhancing pollination supply in an urban ecosystem through landscape modifications. Landsc. Urban Plan. **162**, 157–166 (2017). https://doi.org/10.1016/j.landur bplan.2017.02.011

27. Zulian, G., Paracchini, M.L., Maes, J., Liquete, C.: ESTIMAP: Ecosystem services mapping at European scale. https://doi.org/10.2788/64369

28. Lonsdorf, E., Kremen, C., Ricketts, T., Winfree, R., Williams, N., Greenleaf, S.: Modelling pollination services across agricultural landscapes. Ann. Bot. **103**, 1589–1600 (2009). https://doi.org/10.1093/aob/mcp069

29. Kibblewhite, M.G., Ritz, K., Swift, M.J.: Soil health in agricultural systems (2008). https://doi.org/10.1098/rstb.2007.2178

30. Stringer, L.: Can the UN convention to combat desertification guide sustainable use of the world's soils? Front. Ecol. Environ. **6**, 138–144 (2008). https://doi.org/10.1890/070060

31. Udawatta, R.P., Gantzer, C.J., Jose, S.: Agroforestry practices and soil ecosystem services. In: Soil Health and Intensification of Agroecosystems, pp. 305–333. Elsevier Inc. (2017). https://doi.org/10.1016/B978-0-12-805317-1.00014-2

32. Muzzillo, V., Pilogallo, A., Saganeiti, L., Santarsiero, V., Scorza, F., Murgante, B.: Impact of renewable energy installations on habitat quality. In: Gervasi, O., et al. (eds.) ICCSA 2020. LNCS, vol. 12253, pp. 636–644. Springer, Cham (2020). https://doi.org/10.1007/978-3-030-58814-4_50

33. Sediment Delivery Ratio — InVEST 3.6.0 documentation. http://data.naturalcapitalproj ect.org/nightly-build/invest-users-guide/html/sdr.html#quantitative-valuation. Accessed 27 March 2020

34. Hamel, P., Chaplin-Kramer, R., Sim, S., Mueller, C.: A new approach to modeling the sediment retention service (InVEST 3.0): case study of the cape fear catchment, North Carolina, USA. Sci. Total Environ. **524–525**, 166–177 (2015). https://doi.org/10.1016/j.scitotenv.2015.04.027

35. Renard, K.G., Foster, G.R., Weesies, G.A., Porter, J.P.: RUSLE: revised universal soil loss equation. J. Soil Water Conserv. **46**, 30–33 (1991)

36. Lee, S.: Soil erosion assessment and its verification using the universal soil loss equation and geographic information system: a case study at boun Korea. Environ. Geol. **45**, 457–465 (2004). https://doi.org/10.1007/s00254-003-0897-8

37. Panagos, P., Borrelli, P., Meusburger, K., Alewell, C., Lugato, E., Montanarella, L.: Estimating the soil erosion cover-management factor at the European scale. Land Use Policy **48**, 38–50 (2015). https://doi.org/10.1016/j.landusepol.2015.05.021

38. Panagos, P., Borrelli, P., Meusburger, K., van der Zanden, E.H., Poesen, J., Alewell, C.: Modelling the effect of support practices (P-factor) on the reduction of soil erosion by water at European scale. Environ. Sci. Policy. **51**, 23–34 (2015). https://doi.org/10.1016/j.envsci.2015.03.012

39. Panagos, P., et al.: Rainfall erosivity in Europe. Sci. Total Environ. **511**, 801–814 (2015). https://doi.org/10.1016/j.scitotenv.2015.01.008

40. Wischmeier, W.H., Smith, D.D.: Predicting rainfall erosion losses - a guide to conservation planning. (1978).

41. Panagos, P., Meusburger, K., Ballabio, C., Borrelli, P., Alewell, C.: Soil erodibility in Europe: a high-resolution dataset based on LUCAS. Sci. Total Environ. **479–480**, 189–200 (2014). https://doi.org/10.1016/j.scitotenv.2014.02.010

42. Salata, S., Garnero, G., Barbieri, C., Giaimo, C.: the integration of ecosystem services in planning: an evaluation of the nutrient retention model using InVEST software. Land. **6**, 48 (2017). https://doi.org/10.3390/land6030048

43. Scorza, F., Saganeiti, L., Pilogallo, A., Murgante, B.: Ghost planning: the inefficiency of energy sector policies in a low population density region. Arch. di Stud. Urbani e Reg. 34–55 (2020). https://doi.org/10.3280/ASUR2020-127-S1003

44. Scorza, F.: Towards self energy-management and sustainable citizens' engagement in local energy efficiency agenda. Int. J. Agric. Environ. Inf. Syst. **7**, 44–53 (2016). https://doi.org/10.4018/IJAEIS.2016010103
45. Dvarioniene, J., Grecu, V., Lai, S., Scorza, F.: Four perspectives of applied sustainability: research implications and possible integrations. In: Gervasi, O., et al. (eds.) ICCSA 2017. LNCS, vol. 10409, pp. 554–563. Springer, Cham (2017). https://doi.org/10.1007/978-3-319-62407-5_39
46. Scorza, F., Casas, G.B.L., Murgante, B.: That's ReDO: ontologies and regional development planning. In: Murgante, B., et al. (eds.) ICCSA 2012. LNCS, vol. 7334, pp. 640–652. Springer, Heidelberg (2012). https://doi.org/10.1007/978-3-642-31075-1_48
47. Scorza, F., Fortunato, G.: Cyclable cities: building feasible scenario through urban space-morphology assessment. J. Urban Plan. Dev. **147**, 05021039 (2021)
48. Scorza, F., Santopietro, L.: A systemic perspective for the Sustainable Energy and Climate Action Plan (SECAP). Eur. Plan. Stud. (2021)
49. Scorza, F., Murgante, B., Las Casas, G., Fortino, Y., Pilogallo, A.: Investigating territorial specialization in tourism sector by ecosystem services approach. In: Stratigea, A., Kavroudakis, D. (eds.) Mediterranean Cities and Island Communities. PI, pp. 161–179. Springer, Cham (2019). https://doi.org/10.1007/978-3-319-99444-4_7
50. Scorza, F., Pilogallo, A., Las Casas, G.: Investigating tourism attractiveness in inland areas: ecosystem services, open data and smart specializations. In: Calabrò, F., Della Spina, L., Bevilacqua, C. (eds.) ISHT 2018. SIST, vol. 100, pp. 30–38. Springer, Cham (2019). https://doi.org/10.1007/978-3-319-92099-3_4
51. Lai, S., Leone, F., Zoppi, C.: Implementing green infrastructures beyond protected areas. Sustainability. **10**, 3544 (2018). https://doi.org/10.3390/su10103544
52. Zoppi, C.: Ecosystem services green infrastructure and spatial planning. Sustainability. **12**, 4396 (2020). https://doi.org/10.3390/su12114396

Author Index

Printed in the United States
by Baker & Taylor Publisher Services